Geographica

Geographica

The Complete Illustrated Atlas of the World

KÖNEMANN

Publisher:	Gordon Cheers
Associate publisher:	Margaret Olds
Managing editors:	Philippa Sandall (text)
	Valerie Marlborough (maps)
Editors:	Scott Forbes
	Sue Grose-Hodge
	Gillian Hewitt
	Siobhan O'Connor
	Sarah Shrubb
	Carolyn Beaumont
	Anna Cheifetz
	Clare Double
	Kate Etherington
	Denise Imwold
	Heather Jackson
Map editors:	Janet Parker
	Fran Church
	Heather Martin
	Marlene Meynert
	Jan Watson
Chief designer:	Clare Forte
Senior designer:	Robert Taylor
Cover design:	Bob Mitchell
Production designers:	Deborah Clarke
	Max Peatman
	James Young
Cartographic manager:	Graham Keane
Senior cartographer:	Andrew Dunlop
Cartographers:	Weimin Gu
	Paul McDonald
	David Morris
	Melissa O'Brien
	Clare Varney
Consultant for water areas:	Tony Davidson
Thematic maps:	John Frith
Contour shading:	John Gittoes
	Oliver Rennert
	Ray Sims
Cartographic coordinator:	James Mills-Hicks
Researchers:	Derek Barton
	Claudia Zipfel
Gazetteer:	Valerie Marlborough
	Heather Jackson
	Janet Parker
	Dee Rogers
	Clare Double
Typesetting:	Dee Rogers
Photo research:	Gordon Cheers
Photo library:	Susan Page
Production manager:	Linda Watchorn
Publishing coordinator:	Sarah Sherlock
Publishing assistant:	Olivia Kleindienst

Published by Random House Australia Pty Ltd
20 Alfred Street, Milsons Point, NSW Australia 2061

First published in 1999

Photos © Random House Australia Pty Ltd 1999
from the Random House Photo Library apart from the following:
pages 6 and 7 top left and bottom right, page 8 center and top right © Anglo-Australian Observatory (photograph by David Malin);
page 7 top right © Anglo-Australian Observatory/Royal Observatory Edinburgh (photograph from UK Schmidt plates by David Malin);
page 13 © 1999 by Fred Espenak;
pages 4, 5, 6 (bottom), page 8 (left), pages 9, 10, 12, 15, 17, courtesy of NASA.

Text © Random House Australia Pty Ltd 1999

Copyright © 1999 for this edition
Könemann Verlagsgesellschaft mbH
Bonner Str. 126, D-50968 Cologne

Production: Ursula Schümer
Film separation: Pica Colour Separation, Singapore
Printing and Binding: Mohn Media – Mohndruck GmbH, Gütersloh
Printed in Germany

ISBN 3-8290-3000-2
10 9 8 7 6 5

Page i: Part of the Swiss Alps, showing strata folds.

Pages ii–iii: The European Parliament building in Brussels, Belgium.

Page v: A Parisian sidewalk café, France.

Page xii: Overlooking the principality of Monaco.

Pages xiv–xv: View from Plaka toward the hill of Lykavittos in Athens, Greece.

Pages 52–53: An Aboriginal man fishing with spears in wetlands in the Northern Territory, Australia.

Pages 98–99: The countryside near Yangshuo in Guangxi Zhuangzu Zizhiqu Province, China.

Pages 106–07: A village on the Sepik River, Papua New Guinea.

Pages 142–43: Terraced hills looking toward the Himalayas, Nepal.

Pages 226–27: The village Trebarwith Strand at the north coast of Great Britain.

Pages 310–11: Rhinoceroses and calves in the waters of the Luangwa River in Zambia, Africa.

Pages 374–75: Grand Canyon, Arizona, USA.

Pages 432–33: Autumn colors in Tierra del Fuego, Argentina.

Pages 462–63: Polar bears in Arctic Siberia.

Pages 472–73: A whale shark in Californian waters.

Consultants and Contributors

GENERAL EDITOR

Professor Ray Hudson BA, PhD, DSc
(University of Bristol), DSc (Honoris Causa, University
of Roskilde); Department of Geography, University of
Durham

CONSULTANTS

Professor Tom McKnight BA, MA, PhD (University
of Wisconsin); Professor Emeritus of Geography,
University of California, Los Angeles

Professor Joan Clemons PhD (University of
Minnesota); Visiting Professor, Graduate School
of Education and Information Studies, University
of California, Los Angeles

Professor John Overton MA, PhD (Cambridge);
Professor, Institute of Development Studies, School
of Global Studies, Massey University

Professor Toru Taniuchi BA, MSc, DSc, (University
of Tokyo); Professor of Human Geography,
University of Tokyo, Japan

Professor Bruce Thom BA, PhD (Louisiana State
University), FIAG; Emeritus Professor of Geography,
University of Sydney, Visiting Professor of Geography,
University of New South Wales,

Professor William Wonders BA (Hons), MA, PhD
(University of Toronto), Fil.Dr.h.c. (Uppsala);
University Professor and Professor Emeritus of
Geography, University of Alberta

CONTRIBUTORS
Part 1 Planet Earth

Professor Bruce Thom BA, PhD (Louisiana State
University), F.I.A.G.

Dr John O'Byrne BSc, PhD (University of Sydney)
Dr Noel de Souza BSc (Hons), MSc., Doctorat de
Specialité (University of Paris)

Dr Ron Horvath BA, MA, PhD (University of
California, Los Angeles)

Dr Scott Mooney BSc (Hons), PhD (University of
New South Wales

Part 2 People and Society

Dr Ron Brunton BA, MA, PhD (La Trobe
University)

Associate Professor Sybil Jack MA, BLitt (Oxon),
DipEd (University of New England)

Dr Ron Horvath BA, MA, PhD (University of
California, Los Angeles)

Tess Rod BA (Hons), MA, BComm

Roger Sandall BA, MA (Columbia University)

Part 3 Regions of the World

Professor Bruce Thom BA, PhD (Louisiana State
University), F.I.A.G.

Roger Sandall BA, MA (Columbia University)

Dr Noel de Souza BSc (Hons), MSc, Doctorat de
Specialité (University of Paris)

Robert Coupe MA, DipEd

CARTOGRAPHIC CONSULTANTS

Henk Brolsma, Associateship in Land Surveying;
Australian Antarctic Division, Tasmania,
Australia
> *Antarctica*

Dr John Cornell BA, PhD (University of London)
> *Papua New Guinea, Pacific Islands, Island
> Nations and Dependencies*

Tony Davidson
> *Europe, Russian Federation, former Soviet Republics*

Dr Noel de Souza BSc (Hons), MSc, Doctorat de
Specialité (University of Paris)
> *India, Sri Lanka, Nepal, Bangladesh, Bhutan,
> Pakistan*

Dr Joan Hardjono BA, LittB, PhD (University of New
England); Padjadjaran State University, Bandung,
Indonesia
> *Indonesia, Malaysia, Singapore*

Dr Philip Hirsch BA, PhD
> *Thailand, Laos, Myanmar, Cambodia, Vietnam,
> Philippines*

Professor Naftali Kadmon BA, MSc, PhD (University
of Wales); Professor Emeritus, The Hebrew University
of Jerusalem, Israel
> *Israel, Turkey, Iran, Cyprus, Afghanistan*

Gerry Leitner
> *South America, Central America*

Dr Zhilin Li BEng, PhD (University of Glasgow)
Assistant Professor, The Hong Kong Polytechnic
University, Hong Kong
> *China*

Professor Tanga Munkhtsetseg; International Relations
Institute, Ulan Bator, Mongolia
> *Mongolia*

Chonghyon Paku MA BSc; Baito-Bunka University,
Tokyo, Japan
> *Korea*

Karen Puklowski NZCD/Survey; Massey University,
New Zealand
> *New Zealand*

Professor Chris Rogerson BSc (Hons), MSc, PhD
(Queens), FSAGS; University of Witwatersrand,
Johannesburg, South Africa
> *SubSaharan Africa*

Dr Nasser Salma PhD (University of Washington,
Seattle); Associate Professor, King Saud University,
Riyadh, Saudi Arabia
> *Arabic speaking countries of the Middle East
> and Saharan Africa*

Brian Stokes BBus (Tourism), AssDipCart
> *Australia*

Professor Toru Taniuchi BA, MSc, DSc (University
of Tokyo); Professor of Human Geography,
University of Tokyo, Japan
> *Japan*

Glenn Toldi BSc, DipCart&GIS
> *United States of America, Canada*

Lillian Wonders BA, MA
> *Canada*

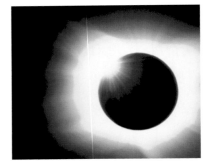

Contents

Contents

ASIA AND THE MIDDLE EAST   142

EUROPE AND THE RUSSIAN FEDERATION   226

Contents

Contents

How This Book Works

Geographica is an authoritative, comprehensive and fully illustrated reference guide to the world. With maps, photographs, illustrations and text, *Geographica* will carry readers on a journey from outer space and Earth's place in the universe to the nations and cities, towns and even villages on the furthermost parts of the globe. An expert team of geographers, historians, anthropologists, astronomers, writers, editors and cartographers have worked together to create this reference.

The early part of the book is organized in topics which are each presented on a double-page spread for easy access to information. The text has been written by leading experts in the field. The very best photographs have been chosen, and illustrations and thematic maps have been specially commissioned to complement the text. Many of the double-page spreads contain a feature box which looks in detail at one aspect of the topic on the spreads.

Geographica then moves on to the core of the book; this contains maps and detailed text on the world's 192 nations which are members of the United Nations and 65 dependencies and overseas territories. The world has been divided into major continents or regions (Oceania, Asia and the Middle East, Europe and the Russian Federation, Africa, North America and Central America, South America, Polar Regions, and Oceans). Each region starts with an introductory essay on the region in general and then moves on to entries for every country, territory or dependency. The country entries feature informative descriptions of the nation and its people, physical features and land use, culture, and economy and resources. Each country entry includes a locator map, the national flag, a locator globe, and a Fact File. Entries for the major nations also include a historical time-line. The entries for the dependencies and territories follow the country entries.

The Fact Files contain a wealth of carefully researched information for quick access to each nation's key indicators, such as form of government, infant mortality, literacy, ethnic diversity, religions, and economy, as well as basic data

| MAP TITLE | ALPHA NUMERIC GRID | COUNTRY NAME | MAJOR CITY | LOCATOR GLOBE |

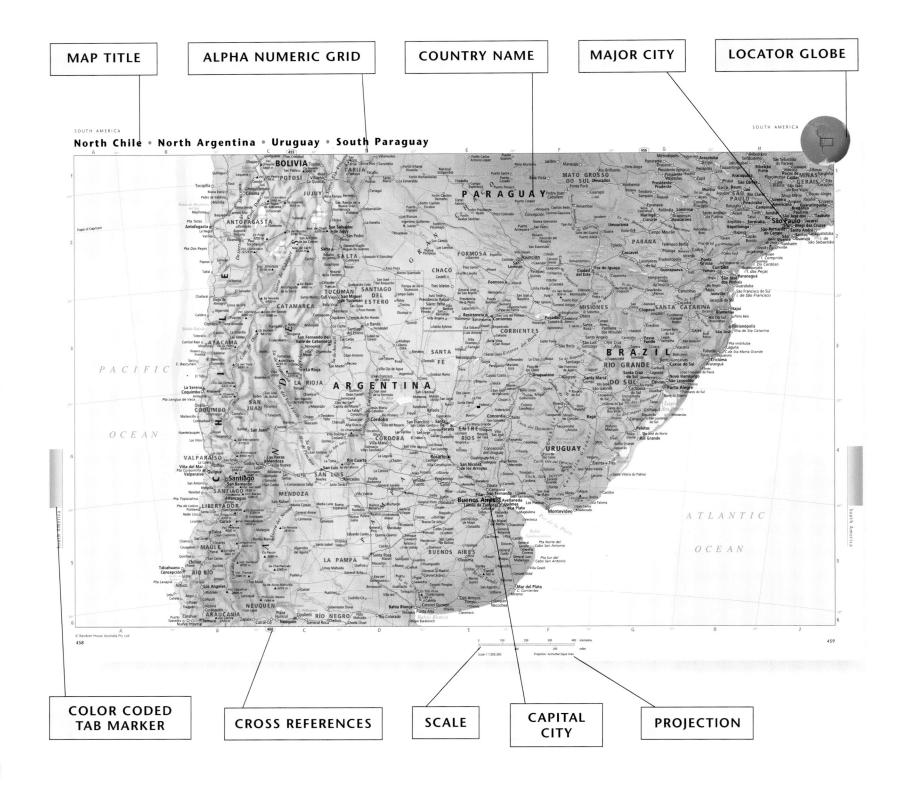

| COLOR CODED TAB MARKER | CROSS REFERENCES | SCALE | CAPITAL CITY | PROJECTION |

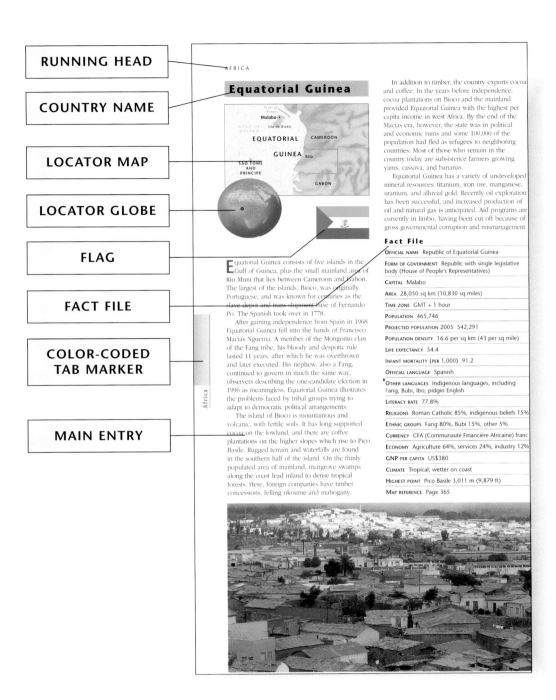

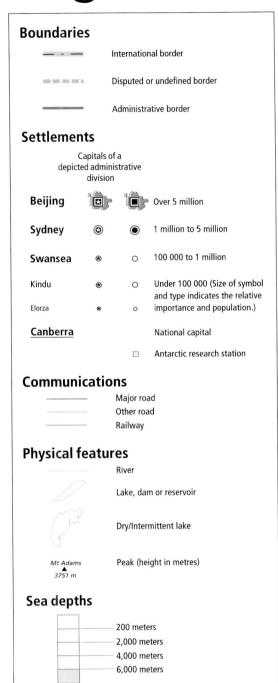

including offical name, population, language, currency, and climate. All figures are the latest available and have been drawn from internationally recognized sources such as the US Bureau of the Census International Database, CIA World Factboook, United Nations Human Development Report, The Statesman's Yearbook, The SBS World Guide (fifth edition), and World Bank Data Tables.

Regional maps fall at the end of each section for ease of reference. Physical and political maps for each region are followed by more detailed mapping. Editorial policy on the spelling of place names was decided after researching a wide number of sources. The cartographic and editorial team used the US Board of Geographic Names database as a guide, and a team of international cartographic experts consulted on maps for every region. Our editorial policy has been to use English for the names of countries (e.g., France), international bodies of water (e.g., Pacific Ocean, Black Sea), and regional features that cross international borders (e.g., Carpathian Mountains). Local name forms have been used for all other names, but for capital cities and for some major cities and features, the English name is also provided in brackets. These English names are cross-referenced in the gazetteer, which includes all names on the physical and political maps, and the regional maps.

Recent name changes and boundary changes are shown on the maps including, for example, the new territory of Nunavut in Canada. The contour shading used on the maps is based on a combination of altitude and vegetation and provides an idea of how the area would appear from space.

Foreword

Geographica should be seen as a pathway for a journey of each reader's discovery of the world. Our journey commences with the origin of the universe and the birth of Earth, the planet of life. Land, water and the atmosphere provide sustenance for complex evolving life forms, culminating in the arrival of those dominant creatures, humans. Geological history, influenced by ever-changing natural forces, gradually turns into documented human history. Then our journey leads us into an understanding of how Earth has been transformed by the actions of countless millions of humans and their immediate ancestors over the past million years or so.

Geographica is about a world that has, and will continue to be, changed. It is designed to be a substantial reference of world information. Original maps convey a vast amount of place-names and boundaries, many of which have changed with the course of history. Timelines describe events that have influenced how humans relate to their environment and to each other. Fact Files for each country offer readers comprehensive descriptions of national identities as they have emerged in recent times, many of which are still undergoing change. (The breakup of Yugoslavia and the Kosovo conflict is just one illustration of the savagery of change.) A number of essays are used to highlight key characteristics of the way landscapes have evolved and how humans relate to each other. These features are documented by new maps on a world scale and also at national scales.

The journey Geographica offers readers is the exploration of a world often ravaged by war, pestilence, human suffering, and the degradation of the environment. But it is also a world where we can conquer great challenges, discover the unknown, and improve the quality of life of many people through the better use of natural and human resources. The future always holds great uncertainty; yet knowledge of the past and present geographical and historical conditions of our planet can only strengthen our ability to plan for a peaceful and ecologically sustainable world in which we and the generations to come can lead fulfilling lives.

This volume represents the combined efforts of many people. As geographers, cartographers, historians, illustrators and editors we seek to offer our readers a substantial educational experience— a journey into the past and an appreciation of the present as it has evolved.

PROFESSOR BRUCE G. THOM
BA, PhD (Louisiana State University), FIAG

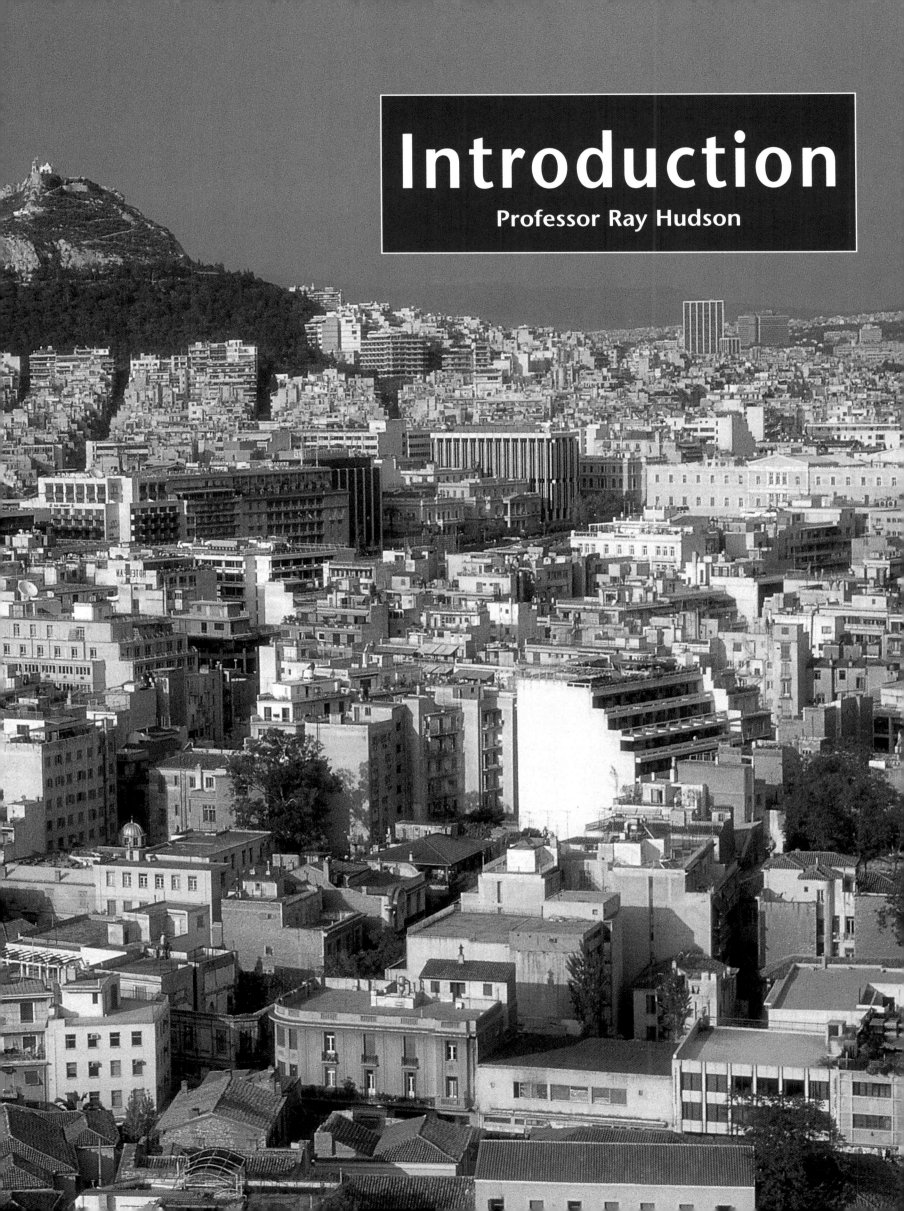

Introduction
Professor Ray Hudson

Europe and the Russian Federation: The Changing Scene

The Mediterranean area is the birthplace of the ancient Greek and Roman civilizations. The Acropolis in Athens (above) shows the ruins of buildings from around 400 BC. Carcassone Castle, France (opposite), is an excellent example of medieval fortification.

If you look at Earth on a globe, the extent of the roughly triangular landmass covered by Europe and the Russian Federation is staggering—an enormous swathe of land extending almost around the world and from around 35° north of the equator to well into the Arctic Circle.

On two and a half sides, this large triangle is bounded by seas and oceans. This gives an initial indication of one of the many problems of defining precisely where the boundaries of Europe and the Russian Federation lie—many of the islands (of which arguably the most significant are those that make up the United Kingdom and the Republic of Ireland) lie off the coasts of Europe and the Federation. Furthermore, some European countries continue to have overseas territories that are colonies or dependencies, legacies of former Empires, and a few have offshore islands that are an integral part of the national state—the Azores and Canary Islands in the Atlantic Ocean, parts of the territories of Portugal and Spain respectively, for example.

There are fairly clear physical boundaries to continental mainland Europe to the west (the Atlantic Ocean), to the north (the Arctic Ocean) and to the south (the Mediterranean Sea), although the southern boundary is less clear-cut around the eastern extremities of the Mediterranean Sea. Turkey, for example, is a member of NATO (the North Atlantic Treaty Organization) but is not generally regarded as a member of Europe.

In the same way, the Russian Federation has clear physical boundaries to the north, east and south, but at its western edge the European landmass slides into the Asian landmass without a precise border. Often the range of the Ural Mountains is taken as the boundary between European Russia to the west and the vast Siberian Plain and Asia to the east. In other respects, however, the boundary between Europe and Asia is more of a political and cultural divide than one that can be defined unambiguously by topography and physical geography.

THE NATURAL ENVIRONMENT

The natural environment of Europe and the Russian Federation is extremely diverse, as variations in latitude, longitude, and altitude combine to produce a great range of climatic and physical conditions and corres-ponding flora and fauna. Some of these environments have offered attractive possibilities for human settlement, influencing early patterns of habitation and also migration; others are harsh and unwelcoming, and have proved difficult to colonize even with the help of developments in contemporary technology.

The legacies of geology offer great opportunities in some parts of Europe and the Russian Federation, which have rich deposits of carboniferous and metallic minerals. Historically, these resources have been critical in influencing the pattern of economic development within these areas.

CLIMATE

Europe and the Russian Federation exhibit a vast latitudinal and longitudinal spread that is reflected in great climatic variation. The landmass extends almost round the globe, from a little more than 20°W at the westernmost tip of Ireland (though the western tip of Greenland is more than 70°W) all the way east (to around 170°E at the tip of the Bering Strait, which separates Asia from Alaska).

From its southernmost point, just below 35°N on the Greek island of Crete (although the Canary Islands lie not far north of the Tropic of Cancer in the Atlantic Ocean, just off the west African coast) Europe stretches northwards, above the Arctic Circle, to North Cape in Norway. Much of Russia also lies well north of the Arctic Circle, extending almost to Alaska. Land in these latitudes is typically tundra, with the soil frozen for much of the year (permafrost) and a very short growing season.

The mean January temperature is below 0°C (32°F) over much of central, eastern and northern Europe and much of the Russian Federation; in inland Siberia it even falls below −50°C (−58°F). Few people live in these harsh environments.

In contrast, much of western and southern Europe has a more temperate climate and support larger populations, though heavy urbanization means that distributions are uneven. The moderation of climatic extremes is especially noticeable in the west of the continent. Here, the effects of the Atlantic Ocean and the Gulf Stream soften the climatic extremes found in the continental interior in areas of eastern Europe and the Russian Federation. Mean July temperatures rarely exceed 30°C (86°F) even in the southernmost parts of Europe, but often exceed 20°C (68°F) over much of the inland continental areas of the Russian Federation. Given the longitudinal extent of Europe and the Russian Federation, the climatic contrast between maritime and inland continental areas is extremely marked.

The climate in the southern areas of Europe, around the Mediterranean Sea is warm temperate, with mild, wet winters and hot, dry summers—the classic Mediterranean climate in which much of European civilization and culture first took root during the classical Greek and Roman periods of history.

This broad climatic pattern generated by latitudinal and longitudinal variation is further complicated by altitudinal variation which adds to the pattern of climatic variation.

LANDFORMS

The landscape of much of the area, and of Europe in particular, is the product of past (but in geological time, fairly recent) periods of orogenesis—when upward movements of the Earth's crust formed mountain ranges—especially during the Alpine period. Major mountain ranges stretch from the Iberian Peninsula through the Massif Central of France, to the French, Swiss, Italian, and Austrian Alps, to the Dynaric Alps and Apennines on either side of the Adriatic Sea in Italy and the former Yugoslavia respectively, and as far east as the Carpathian Alps, mainly in the eastern part of Romania. Most of Europe's major rivers, including the Danube, Rhine, Rhone, Loire and Po, rise in these upland areas and drain to the various seas surrounding the continent.

To the southeast, the Caucasus form a land boundary—on the bridge of land separating the Black Sea and the Caspian Sea, between Armenia and Azerbaijan and Turkey and Iran to their southeast. In the northwest, much of Scandinavia is also mountainous. A large part of these mountainous areas have been glaciated and processes of glaciation are still continuing.

To the north of the main mountain regions, most of Europe and the Russian Federation comprise the north European and Siberian plains. While some major rivers, such as the Ob and Yenisei, drain from the Siberian Plain to the Arctic Ocean, much of the drainage of the plain is to inland seas and lakes. The Volga River, for example, drains into the Caspian Sea, and other rivers drain into the Aral and Black seas. The plains are periodically interrupted by ranges of mountain (such as the Urals) and by lower lying hills, bounded to the south by the hill and mountain ranges of Iran, Afghanistan, China and Mongolia.

In the far east, the Siberian Plain gradually rises in height and eventually gives way to the Verkoyhansk and then the Kolyma Mountains before the Russian Federation finally reaches its eastern boundaries in the Bering Sea and the Sea of Okhotsk.

Much of these plains have been formed by various types of glacial deposits. In the north, much of Finland and southern Scandinavia also exhibit considerable evidence of glacial erosion, as in the numerous lakes of Finland.

VEGETATION

Much of Europe is forested, especially in the higher regions. The natural vegetation of the vast majority of Europe and a fair part of the Russian Federation is a mixture of broad-leafed deciduous and coniferous forest. Deciduous trees are generally more prevalent in the milder and wetter temperate areas with conifers found further north in the colder regions; where the climate becomes too harsh for trees, tundra is dominant.

Around the Mediterranean region, evergreen trees and shrubs are the most common form of vegetation. As rainfall decreases with increasing distance eastwards, however, forested areas give way to steppe grassland. Within the milder temperate and Mediterranean areas, increasing altitude produces the same changes in vegetation as increasing latitude.

ENVIRONMENTAL TRANSFORMATION

While forest is the natural vegetation of much of Europe and Russia, the majority of this, especially in Europe, has been cleared for agriculture and other uses. Manufacturing industry, mining, and the expansion of cities and towns have all dramatically changed the landscape and advances in technology have also allowed us to exploit the resources that offered by the natural environment. Indeed, much of what is often thought of as the natural landscape is in fact a social product—the result of extended interactions between people and the environment. This process of environmental transformation has a very long history—it started when people first began to make the transition from peripatetic hunter-gatherers to become sedentary agriculturalists and farmers, establishing communities and settlements.

It is only in the last two or three hundred years, however, that dramatic technological advances in agriculture, combined with the developments of the Industrial Revolution, have allowed people to radically alter the natural environment in Europe. Irrigation and artificial fertilizers have permitted agriculture to flourish in formerly uncultivable regions, and the gradual process of removing natural vegetation and adding chemicals to the soil has altered the natural balance which had evolved over thousands of years.

While large-scale environmental processes remain beyond human control, the capacity to alter environmental conditions on a local or regional scale and to overcome environmental constraints has increased greatly in moder time, especially in the more wealthy countries. Such transformations have become integral to the development of industrial capitalism in Europe. One spectacular example of this is the reclamation of the Dutch polders and the subsequent development of intensive commercial glasshouse agriculture on this land which used to be part of the sea. Conquering nature was also an important preoccupation, in the communist former USSR (Union of Soviet Socialist Republics), where it was seen as proof of the capacity of state socialism to triumph over a hostile environment for the collective good.

Thus in a whole variety of ways, and for a variety of motives, people have learned to modify their local environments so that they can live more comfortably, so that plants can be cultivated and animals reared.

It is also worth remembering, however, that human efforts to transform the natural environment and improve material living standards in turn have their own impact on the environment. One of the most spectacular—and unwanted—examples of this is the dramatic shrinkage of the inland Aral Sea in Kazakhstan in the Russian Federation. Another is the extensive soil erosion induced by large-scale agriculture in formerly fertile natural grassland transformed to cereal and cotton-growing areas. Manmade disasters can also have a devastating environmental impact—radioactive waste and smoke from the fire at the Chernobyl nuclear reactor, in Ukraine, in 1986,

spread widely over much of Russia and Europe as a result of westerly winds.

In addition, other human activities in the countries of Europe and the Russian Federation are a major contributing force to processes such as global warming which threatens possible climatic change and rising sea levels. Low-lying, coastal areas and those that have been reclaimed from the sea (like the polders of the Netherlands) are particularly vulnerable to such changes.

A CHANGING POLITICAL–ECONOMIC MAP

For much of their history, the lands of Europe and the Russian Federation have been the arena for a succession of migrations and movements of people. As they gradually became settled, people sought to establish the boundaries of their own territories and armed conflict and wars became almost endemic as different groups sought to expand their territory, or to protect it from others seeking to take it from them. Empires were built, then declined within Europe—from the Roman to the Austro-Hungarian.

For several hundred years, this ebb and flow of political fortunes, as an assortment of emperors, kings, queens and princes fought to consolidate and increase their territory, was accompanied by economic stagnation as European economies were predominantly organized around various forms of subsistence agriculture.

THE GROWTH OF EMPIRES

Towards the end of the fifteenth century, a number of European states began to explore the

The Church of Sveti Jovan Bogoslov Kaneo, on the shores of Ohrid Lake, Macedonia (right). Blaenau Ffestiniog in Wales, where the houses are dwarfed by the slate mine workings (above).

possibilities of creating empires outside Europe. This added a new dimension to the political struggle between states, and a new source of economic dynamism, as new subtropical and tropical crops and products began to arrive in Europe.

A number of European states sought to establish new empires in the "New World", and there was much competition between the British, Dutch, French, Portuguese, and Spanish. By the nineteenth century, however, Britain had emerged as the dominant power (despite the loss of its colonies in North America). Trade began to allow the accumulation of capital and, in due course, that capital was channelled into economic development within Europe.

The agricultural and industrial revolutions gave considerable impetus to the economies of the leading European states, as industrial capitalism

became established first in Britain and then in Belgium, Germany, France and other continental European countries. This diffusion was an uneven process, however, and many areas of Europe and Russia were virtually untouched by these new developments, remaining locked in a pre-industrial and pre-capitalist world until well into the twentieth century.

The rise of industrial powers within Europe increased the pressure among them to create empires. New colonies would provide European countries with cheap food and raw materials while also creating a new market, beyond the national markets, for the sale of industrial goods made in Europe. In the latter part of the nineteenth century European countries such as Belgium and Germany joined in the race to establish their own foreign empires. At the same time the struggle for supremacy within Europe intensified, as larger modern national states became established. This process of state building often led to people of different nations becoming citizens of the same state. People and places moved between states as national boundaries shifted (for example, Alsace and Lorraine moved between France and Germany on an almost regular basis). This process of economic and territorial competition finally culminated in the appalling destruction of the First World War, and the postwar settlement led to the creation of completely new states in the Baltic and the Balkans as the old Austro-Hungarian Empire was broken up.

There followed a period of deep economic recession and dislocation, part of a wider global slump. This helped produce a resurgence of nationalist sentiment, most infamously in Germany, with the rise of fascism and its concepts of racial supremacy and *lebensraum* (living space), which were used to justify ethnic cleansing and territorial aggrandizement. Other parts of Europe followed a different path—most notably Russia. Here the October 1917 Revolution established a communist government and presaged the emergence of the USSR, dominated by Russia, in 1922. In 1939, the growing ambitions of fascist Germany culminated in the outbreak of the Second World War, leading to further devastation and carnage in Europe.

AFTER THE SECOND WORLD WAR

The immediate postwar period was to reshape the map of Europe for the next fifty or so years—in ways that had global implications—until the de facto collapse of socialism in Europe in 1989 and the formal break-up of the USSR in 1991. At the end of the Second World War, the USSR occupied most of eastern Europe. The partitioning of Berlin between East and West in 1948 and the creation of two Germanies (the Federal Republic of Germany and the German Democratic Republic) confirmed that postwar Europe would be divided into two ideologically opposed blocs, a capitalist west and communist east. The "Cold War" had descended on Europe.

In 1949 NATO was established as a common defense organization in the west. The USSR developed a series of buffer satellite states between itself and western Europe, and became the center of both economic (COMECON) and defense (the Warsaw Pact) alliances. In these ways, the USSR sought to prevent the spread of capitalism into the east and to limit the ambitions of the USA, with which it vied to become the dominant global power.

There were also significant moves to redraw the political map within western Europe—in large part stimulated by a wish to avoid future European wars—by creating new supranational institutions. Thus in 1951 the European Coal and Steel Community (the ECSC) was established with the signing of the Treaty of Paris by Belgium, France, Germany, Italy, Luxembourg, and the Netherlands. This sought to guarantee the future peace of Europe by inextricably binding together the coal and steel industries of France and Germany, then seen as the key to the capacity to wage war. Plans for a greater degree of political unification and the creation of a common European Defense Force foundered.

In response, the six signatories of the Treaty of Paris then signed the Treaty of Rome (in 1957) creating the European Economic Community (EEC). The aim of the EEC was to promote democratic political systems and economic growth and the free movement of capital and labor within the territory of the member countries. This posed problems for those western European states that had not signed the Treaty of Rome. In 1960 Austria, Denmark, Portugal, Norway, Sweden, Switzerland and the United Kingdom signed the Stockholm Convention, which established the European Free Trade Area (EFTA). This effectively divided western Europe into two free trade areas, EFTA and the EEC. Much of the next thirty or so years witnessed a redefinition of the boundaries between these two groupings.

In the late 1950s and 1960s the countries of the EEC enjoyed sustained high rates of economic growth—so much so that they drew in migrant workers from Mediterranean Europe and north Africa as a way of avoiding labor shortages. Other western European countries began to gaze with envious eyes at the economic growth rates of the six signatories to the Treaty of Rome, and to consider whether their interests would not be better served by joining the EEC. In 1973 Denmark, Ireland, and the UK became members of the EEC, significantly shifting the balance between it and EFTA.

In the 1960s and 1970s, the EEC concluded a series of trade treaties with a number of southern European, Mediterranean and north African states and former colonies in other regions of the developing world. These trade and aid agreements tied these countries closely into the EEC's economy in various ways—as markets for their agricultural produce and migrant workers and as suppliers of technology, especially that needed for industrial development.

Several of the southern European states actively sought full membership of the EEC but failed to meet a key condition for entry to the club—Greece, Portugal and Spain had dictatorial rather than democratic political systems. With a return to democracy in the mid-1970s in these countries, however, the way was clear for full membership—Greece joined the EEC in 1981, Portugal and Spain in 1986. The reunification of the two Germanies in 1990 further enlarged the European Community, while in 1995, Austria, Finland and Sweden also joined. The EEC now had 15 members.

There are strong pressures for further expansion, predominantly south and east, with Cyprus, the Czech Republic, Estonia, Hungary, Poland and Slovenia next in line for entry. Thus former members of COMECON will become members of the European Union following the break-up of the USSR and the emergence of the looser federation of the Commonwealth of Independent States (CIS) in 1991.

This is seen as a way of underwriting capitalism and democracy throughout eastern Europe in the twenty-first century, much as the Mediterranean enlargement of the 1980s was seen as a way of underpinning democracy and ensuring the end of dictatorships in Greece, Portugal and Spain.

At the same time as extending territorially, there have also been processes of deepening integration, leading to a transition from the EEC to the European Union following the 1992 Maastricht Treaty. There have been significant moves to complete the Single European Market and towards Economic and Monetary Union, with eleven of the member states signing up to a common currency (the Euro) from 1 January 1999 (the non-participants are Denmark, Greece, Sweden and the UK).

There has been a complex process of political change throughout Europe since the 1950s, with tendencies towards the creation and collapse of supranational organizations. Of particular significance has been the collapse of the former USSR and, related to this, of the federal Yugoslav Republic. Here, ethnic and religious tensions which had been kept in check for many decades were suddenly released with devastating and tragic consequences. Much of the Balkans and many of the republics in the southeastern European part of the Commonwealth of Independent States erupted into violence as a range of national groups sought to secure their own territorial states. They often pursued this goal using savage military force and ethnic cleansing on a scale not seen in Europe since the horrors of the Holocaust in the 1930s.

At the the beginning of the twenty-first century, as at the start of the twentieth century, much of Europe has again been engulfed in war, centered on the Balkans. Unlike the early years of the last century, however, developments in the global media now ensure that individuals worldwide are kept informed of events in the European arena as televisions broadcast pictures (transmitted iin real time) of the damage wrought by missile attacks and "smart" bombs, and of refugees forced to flee their homes under threat of death.

ECONOMIC DIVERSITY: VARIETIES OF CAPITALISM

With the formal dissolution of the USSR in 1991, the economic landscape was no longer one of competition between capitalism and socialism but rather one of competition between varieties of capitalism found over Europe and the Russian Federation.

One immediate consequence of the collapse of socialism was to increase poverty and inequality within this new shared space. Attempts to establish thriving capitalist economies over much of eastern Europe and Russia and its republics failed initially, as the cultural and institutional requirements for such a change were simply not present. Moreover, the social welfare supports of the former socialist system were swept away.

Economic transition was reasonably smooth in the more economically advanced countries of the former COMECON in which forms of private property ownership had survived in the socialist period or emerged well before 1989 (in the Czech Republic, Hungary and Poland).

Elsewhere, however, economies simply collapsed, while in Russia and several of the other member states of the Commonwealth of Independent States, black markets, gangsterism and criminal capitalism of a sort associated with

the Mafia became the norm. Where economic collapse went hand-in-hand with the devastation of war and forced population movements, problems of poverty, ill-health and death became even more acute.

In contrast, over much of the European Union, economic fortunes have become more assured and lifestyles correspondingly more comfortable. There are differences in the forms of capitalism (for example, Germany, and Sweden remain much more committed to corporatist approaches, the UK to a neo-liberal market approach), but even these differences have been reduced by the need to conform to the criteria for entry to the European Monetary Union. This is not to deny that considerable inequalities remain within the European Union—both at national, regional and local scales and between people—but these are insignificant compared with the situation in much of eastern Europe, Russia and the rest of the CIS.

There are marked variations in population densities within the European Union, with people heavily clustered in urban areas, which typically rely on service-based economies. There are similar variations in output and income per capita and also in the sectoral structure of economies, with the more developed and affluent regions generally relying less upon agriculture and more upon advanced services. National economies vary greatly in size and structure, but the pattern and variation at subnational scales is more complex still.

The scope of welfare state provision has certainly been reduced over much of western Europe, often as a direct response to the need to meet the fiscal and macroeconomic requirements for entry to the European Monetary Union. Nevertheless, the welfare net still remains in place to an extent no longer found over much of the

remainder of Russia and the CIS and parts of southern and eastern Europe.

This provision, along with the perception of more and better job opportunities in the West, has encouraged fears of floods of economic migrants (as opposed to political refugees) from eastern Europe and the Russian Federation (as well as possibly from north Africa). One consequence of this has been concern about both immigration polices into the European Union and

the status of individuals of varied ethnic origins who have lived in Europe for decades, after arriving as temporary migrant workers, but who still lack citizenship rights.

We began with a question—where is Europe? However, more important questions to consider for the future are perhaps who are Europeans now, what does it mean to be European, and what are the rights and responsibilities of each putative European citizen?

The mild climate of Madeira makes these Portuguese islands a popular resort all year round (left). An aerial view of the old city of Salzburg (top) on the south bank of the Salzach River, in Austria. Dubrovnik (above), in Croatia, is another city that retains its Old Town charm; here the Franciscan belltower is featured.

Part 1

Planet Earth

PLANET EARTH

Earth in Space

Humans have always been fascinated by Earth's place in the universe. Earth (above) is just one of many planets, moons, and stars that form our solar system. We still have much to learn about how the solar system formed, and to predict about how it will end. An artist's impression of the surface of Earth (right) shows the land and water that cover its crust.

Ideas on the origin of Earth, other planets, the Sun and stars can be traced to the time of classical Greece. They range from an Earth-centered universe to one where the position of this tiny, life-generating planet is placed in a context of an expanding universe populated by billions of stars, with an unknown number of planets similar in composition and structure to ours.

It was late in the eighteenth century that the great early geologist James Hutton (1726–97), a Scot, captured in a few poignant words the vastness and the immensity of time over which Earth, the Sun, the solar system, the galaxies, and the universe have evolved. He noted that there is "no vestige of a beginning, no prospect of an end." This phrase challenged the established thinking of a very limited time for the creation of the natural world and opened up a new era of geological and cosmological thought.

We live on a planet that is circling a single star of apparently limitless energy. Yet we now know that the engine of nuclear heat driving the Sun has a birth and a stable phase, and, as it runs short of hydrogen fuel, will go through enormous cataclysms. This process will absorb the Sun's dependent planets, and eventually lead to its own slow "death".

Our views of Earth as part of the universe have varied over time. New concepts and theories, such as Einstein's general theory of relativity, have offered scientists different perspectives on the origin of the universe and all matter. New technologies ranging from telescopes to satellites have opened up vast vistas within and beyond our solar system. Now available to scientists are tools to measure the composition and structure of matter racing through space. We understand much better the characteristics of various forces at work, such as those driving the expansion of the universe, the clustering of stars, the condensation of gases, the orbits of planets, and the movement of meteorites.

The big-bang model for the universe is based on a number of observations. It is not speculation. Yet, as a model of how the universe evolved, it has been modified by cosmologists and scientists over time. New observations should lead to further changes as we continue to explore whether there is enough matter and energy in the universe to slow and stop the expansion started 10 billion or 15 billion years ago.

As gases condensed to form stars, there was a distinct tendency for these stars to cluster. The Milky Way Galaxy is an example of a large spiral galaxy or cluster of stars composed of a thin, circular disk surrounding a central bulge. Interestingly, new technologies show that many galaxies, including the Milky Way, have more mass than can readily be seen. There also appears to exist at the core of some galaxies a central powerhouse generating narrow jets of high-energy particles streaming outwards. Only more observations and theorizing will help us understand the significance of these phenomena.

Yet it is the stars themselves which offer so many clues to the origin of the universe and, ultimately, ourselves. They vary widely in size, color, and temperature. Stars are powered by nuclear reactions whereby hydrogen is fused to helium. We now possess knowledge of sequences through which stars may change from one state to another. Our Sun is no exception and can be seen as representative of an average star in the Milky Way Galaxy. It generates light and heat, which are transmitted through space to help transform life on the surface of one of its planets, Earth.

Radiometric dating of ancient rocks on Earth and its moon give some clue as to the age of the solar system— about 5 billion years. Cooling and consolidation under gravity of interstellar gases and dust created the Sun and progressively hardened objects accreted and condensed to form the nine planets and their moons. Early in the period of planet formation, the sweeping up of solar system debris led to bombardment of planet and moon surfaces, a phenomenon dramatically depicted today by photographs of the cratered surface of Earth's moon.

The Sun is the ultimate source of energy for life processes on planet Earth. As the Sun formed, it captured most matter in the Solar system, leaving only 0.1% to form the planets, their moons, asteroids, comets and dust. The Sun possessed sufficient mass needed to generate electromagnetic or radiant energy at various wavelengths. The hot Sun mostly radiates shorter wavelength energy especially at visible wavelengths. There are also large sunspots caused by magnetic storms on the Sun's surface. They can be observed as visible dark patches and as areas of X-ray activity ejecting electrically charged particles, the solar wind. Sunspot activity is not constant but is cyclic in behavior. When these particles meet the Earth's atmosphere dramatic visual displays occur, especially in polar latitudes. Whether sunspots influence the weather is uncertain.

The spinning Earth orbits the Sun, traveling a distance of approximately 150 million km (93 million miles). Energy is received at a more or less constant rate, but is distributed unevenly because of the tilt of Earth's axis, yielding seasonal changes in temperature away from the equator. Yet Earth processes its own heat engine: radioactive processes within its core help generate gases into the atmosphere and drive movements of its crustal plates. The presence of different gases, including water vapor, has provided that vital mixture of substances from which life has evolved, as well as the thin protective envelope high in oxygen and nitrogen which forms the atmosphere.

Thus spaceship Earth, spinning systematically around the Sun, receiving heat, generating gases and driving its crust into mountains, offers various life forms an environment for evolution. Over time these environments change. Ultimately the future of the planet itself is tied to that of its solar system and its Sun.

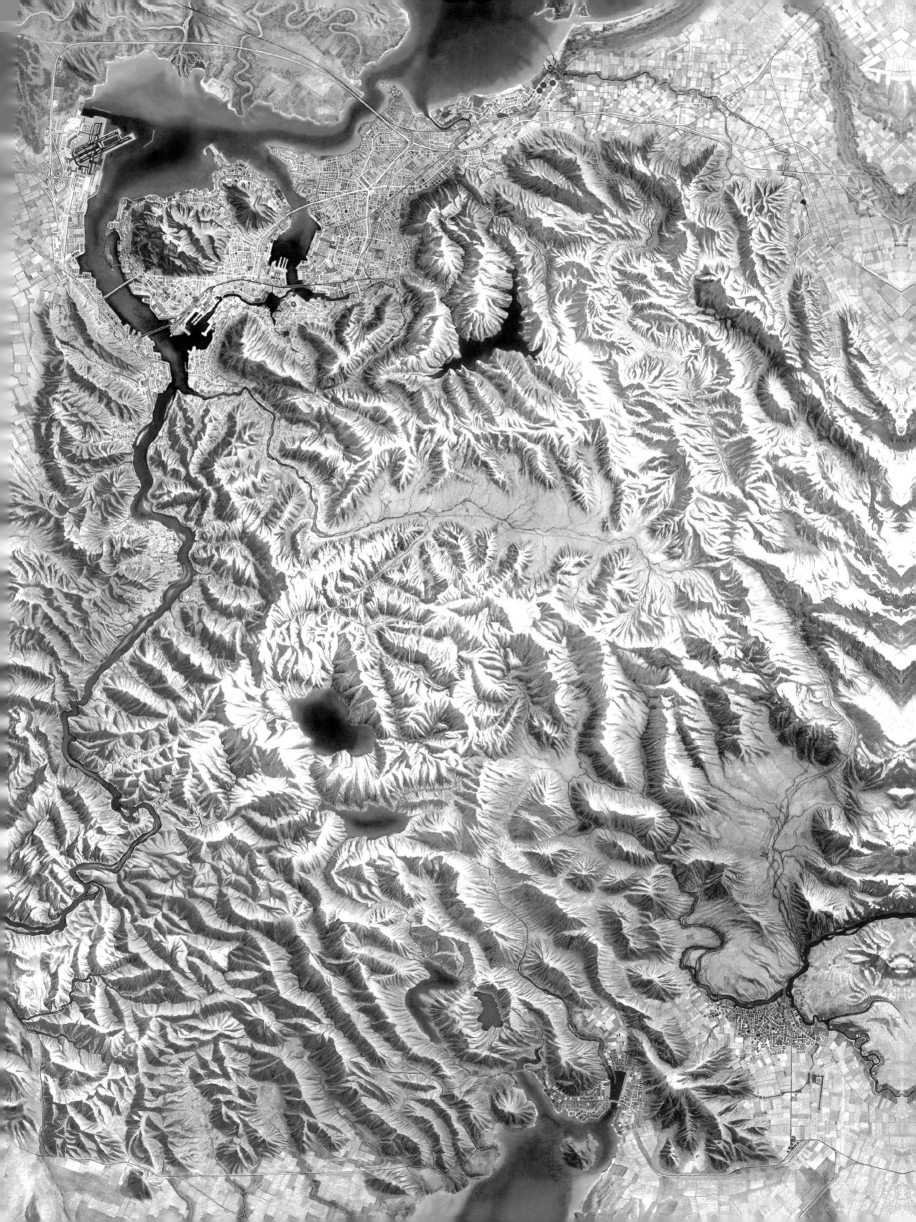

ORIGINS OF THE UNIVERSE

When we look out across the universe, we look back in time. Light traveling from distant galaxies, speeding across 300,000 km (186,000 miles) every second, has taken billions of years to reach Earth. We see the most distant galaxies across billions of light years, as those galaxies were when the universe was younger.

What is the universe really like? The modern view of the origins and future of the universe is based on the idea of a Big Bang that marked the beginning of the ongoing expansion of the universe. The popular view of the Big Bang, however, imagines galaxies flying away from one another out into empty space after a massive explosion. This naturally leads to questions about what happened before the Big Bang, and where it occurred. However, these questions arise from a misunderstanding of the Big Bang concept. Galaxies do not fly away from each other through space; rather, space itself expands, carrying the galaxies with it. The Big Bang was not an explosion *in* space, but an explosion *of* space and time. All of space and time arose in the Big Bang. There was no time before the Big Bang, and all of space was involved.

A brief history of the universe

Ten to fifteen billion years ago, the universe of space and time began, as a hugely hot cauldron of energy governed by physical laws that we do not yet understand. Within a tiny fraction of a second the expansion after the Big Bang had moderated the conditions to a point from which (we believe) our current understanding of physical laws can begin to describe what happened. The universe was expanding and cooling, but there may also have been a brief spurt of dramatic inflation in size—this is critical to understanding today's universe. If this sudden growth spurt *did* occur, then the part of the universe that telescopes can survey today was merely a tiny fraction of the total.

After no more than 10 millionths of a second, the universe had become a sea of high energy radiation—gamma ray photons characteristic of a temperature well over 1 trillion degrees. At such energy, photons can produce a pair of particles, a matter particle and its anti-matter partner, which exist fleetingly before annihilating each other in a flash of gamma ray radiation.

As the universe continued to expand, the photons dropped in energy as the temperature fell. Particle production ended, first for the heavy particles and then for the light ones. Most of the particle and anti-particle pairs were annihilated, leaving only a small residue—the protons, neutrons, and electrons that we see today.

As the temperature dropped further, some of these particles combined to build simple atomic nuclei. Within half an hour this phase was over, and, for the next few hundred thousand years, the universe was an expanding gas of light nuclei and electrons in a sea of photons. It was an opaque fog until continued cooling allowed the atomic nuclei to capture electrons and form atoms of simple elements, mostly hydrogen and helium. Without the free electrons to scatter them, the photons streamed freely through space and the fog cleared.

Matter was then free to respond to the influence of gravity alone. The first generations of individual stars formed from small knots in larger gas clouds that became whole galaxies of stars. The galaxies formed into clusters and superclusters that are still scattered through the universe today.

Are we sure of this picture?

This view of the universe is rather different from earlier versions. Ancient Egyptian cosmology featured the sky goddess Nut arched over Earth, with the Sun god Ra traveling across the sky every day. Greek thinkers removed gods from their cosmology, and constructed their world view largely on philosophical grounds. A more scientific approach to cosmology began to

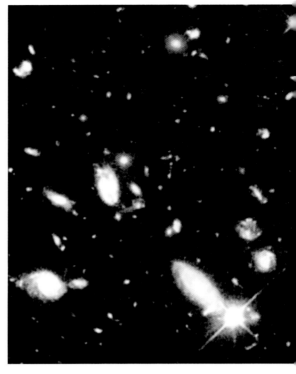

emerge after Copernicus, in the sixteenth century, discovered that it was the Earth that traveled around the Sun. The current view is the latest step in scientific cosmology, but can we be sure that the modern picture will not also be superseded?

Three important observations form the basis of the Big Bang model. The first emerged early in the twentieth century, when observations revealed the expansion of the universe. This fits into Einstein's theory of General Relativity, which describes the nature of space and time. The second key observation is recent measurements of the abundance of light elements, especially helium, in the universe. These observations agree with the amount that the Big Bang model predicts to have been formed in its first few minutes.

Perhaps the most compelling plank supporting the Big Bang concept was the discovery in 1965 of the cosmic background radiation—an all-pervasive glow coming from all parts of the sky. It is our view of radiation from the era when the universe became transparent. It is the glow of the Big Bang itself, cooled by the universe's expansion.

Recent years have been exciting in cosmology, because new observations have begun to allow us to choose between variations of the basic Big Bang cosmology and some alternative concepts to the Big Bang itself. In particular, the Cosmic Background Explorer (COBE) satellite

After about two minutes the temperature had dropped below 1 billion degrees—low enough for nuclear reactions to build some of the light elements, especially helium.

In its first seconds, the universe was a dynamic soup of gamma ray photons and particles such as protons and electrons, which are the building blocks of atoms.

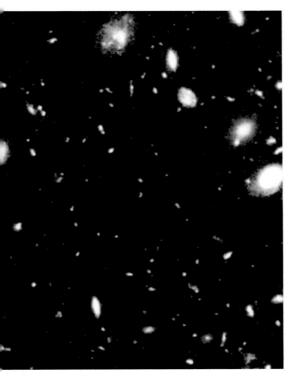

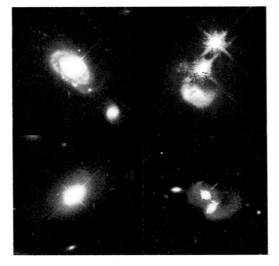

This cluster of yellow, elliptical and spiral galaxies, far left, has a gravitational force so strong that it can bend light—the blue arcs are actually images of one more distant galaxy, not scattered objects at all. Each object in this Hubble Deep Field picture, center, is a distant galaxy. Above: Although rather different in appearance, each of these galaxies harbors an intensely bright quasar.

Gravitational lenses

In recent years astronomers have discovered a new way in which to probe further into the universe and at the same time seek out dark matter nearer home. Einstein's theory of General Relativity predicted that the straight line path of light across the universe is affected by gravity. This was first observed in 1919, when light from stars was observed to be minutely deflected as it passed the Sun.

Recent observations have revealed the gravitational effect of whole galaxies and even clusters of galaxies, which can act as a lens to bend and focus light coming from more distant galaxies. Although the images produced by these gravitational lenses are distorted, they do enable us to study light from galaxies that would otherwise be far beyond the reach of our telescopes.

This gravitational lensing has also been seen—on a smaller scale—when the light of distant stars brightens briefly; this is because of gravitational lensing caused by an intervening object. Knowing this allows us to study the lensing objects that are part of the halo of dark matter believed to encircle our galaxy. What is this dark matter? It seems that gravitational lensing may be able to tell us.

revealed the incredible smoothness of the cosmic background radiation, in all directions, challenging us to explain how the clumpy distribution of galaxies we see today could have had time to develop. Exactly how much time has passed in building this pattern remains uncertain, since astronomers are only now beginning to agree on just how fast the universe is expanding. This is a time of dramatic developments for cosmology.

Will the expansion continue?
Will the universe go on expanding until all the stars have died? The force of gravity governs the fate of the universe, so the question becomes: is there enough matter and energy in the universe to slow and stop the expansion?

In mapping the distribution of matter, it is now clear that there is more matter out there than is apparent. This "dark matter" must surround many galaxies, including the Milky Way, to explain the motions of stars within them. There is more in clusters of galaxies, helping to hold them

together. Studies are seeking further evidence of this matter, trying to determine what it is: small dark planets, star-sized bodies, or something less familiar.

Adding all this together, normal forms of matter appear to account for less than 10 percent of the matter needed to halt universal expansion. But many cosmologists think that less than 10 percent is quite close to 100 percent in this instance. Moreover, there are theoretical reasons for thinking the universe may in fact be on that balance point between eternal expansion and ultimate halt and collapse. It may be that most of the matter in the universe is in forms as yet unseen.

The history of the Sun and Earth play only a small part in this picture. Born long after the Big Bang, both will die long before the universe changes much from the way it looks today.

Tiny bumps in the density of matter in the early universe grew, under the influence of gravity, to form the galaxies and clusters of galaxies that we see today.

After several hundred thousand years, at a temperature of around 3000°C (5450°F), the electrons were captured by atoms and the universe suddenly became transparent.

One of the galaxies that formed over 10 billion years ago was the Milky Way. A mere 4.6 billion years ago the Sun was born within it.

GALAXIES

Many people today are city dwellers whose view of the night sky is hindered by the bright lights of the modern world. When we are fortunate enough to look at the night sky from a dark place, we see thousands of stars and the faint starry band of the Milky Way meandering across the sky. We now know that this is an insider's view of the vast collection of more than 100 billion stars we call the Milky Way Galaxy.

A dark sky will also reveal the Andromeda Galaxy, an even larger star system lying beyond the boundaries of the Milky Way. Both are members of the small cluster of galaxies called the Local Group, which lies on the edge of a super-cluster of galaxies. Beyond lies the vast expanse of the universe—countless more distant galaxies.

The Milky Way

In 1785, William Herschel, the astronomer who discovered Uranus, counted stars in various directions across the sky and decided that the Sun lay near the center of a flattened disk of stars. In 1917, Harlow Shapley studied the distribution of globular clusters—clusters of hundreds of thousands of stars—and concluded that they clustered around the center of the galaxy in the direction of the constellation of Sagittarius. Herschel had been deceived by the clouds of dust which are scattered through the Milky Way and which obscure our view of more distant stars.

The modern view reveals the Milky Way to be a large spiral galaxy composed of a thin circular disk surrounding a central bulge, with a halo of stars

and globular clusters. Light would take about 100,000 years to speed across the disk: a distance of 100,000 light years. Traveling as fast as the fastest spacecraft, a trip across the galaxy would take well over a billion years! The Sun lies in the disk, some 28,000 light years from the center, completing an orbit around the central bulge every 240 million years.

Around 95 percent of the visible mass of the galaxy is composed of stars, in particular the vast mass of faint Sun-like stars that contribute the yellowish background glow of the disk and bulge. Despite their vast numbers, the distances between the stars are immense, compared with their sizes. The nearest stars to the Sun are 4.3 light years away (40 trillion km; 25 trillion miles). Traveling on the fastest spacecraft, this trip would take some 60,000 years.

The heart of the galaxy is a mystery being slowly unveiled by observations using radio and infrared telescopes which can pierce the veil of dust which hides it from our eyes. Astronomers suspect that it harbors a black hole with the mass of more than a million suns.

The remaining mass we see in the galaxy is the thin interstellar medium of gas and dust lying between the stars. Most of this is compacted into dense, cold clouds of gas laced with traces of dust.

This spiral galaxy, above, has two prominent arms, showing red patches of ionized hydrogen where stars have formed. A barred spiral galaxy, right, showing the yellow color of old stars at its nucleus, with blue, young stars in its arms.

The Milky Way system originated in a vast condensation of gas, which began to form stars within a billion years of the Big Bang. Early generations of stars in this cloud included those that form the halo of stars and globular clusters surrounding the galaxy. Successive generations of stars had orbits much closer to the thin disk we see today. When the Sun was formed 4.6 billion years ago, the galaxy was already middle aged, and would have looked much as it does today.

New stars are still being born from clouds of gas. While they live, these beacons and their gaseous birthplaces trace out the spiral arms within the background glow of the disk.

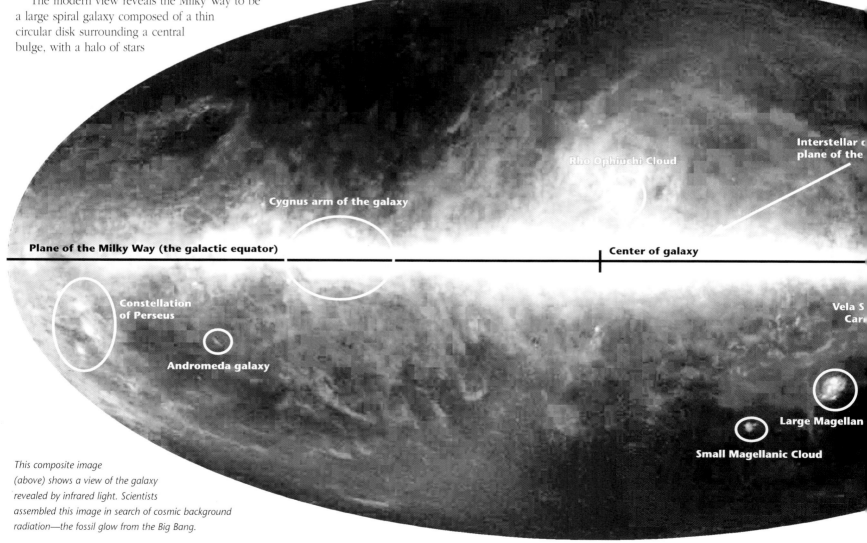

Rho Ophiuchi Cloud

Interstellar c plane of the

Cygnus arm of the galaxy

Plane of the Milky Way (the galactic equator)

Center of galaxy

Constellation of Perseus

Vela S Car

Andromeda galaxy

Large Magellan

Small Magellanic Cloud

This composite image (above) shows a view of the galaxy revealed by infrared light. Scientists assembled this image in search of cosmic background radiation—the fossil glow from the Big Bang.

Some of the bright galaxies of the Virgo cluster, top. Above: This galaxy, Centaurus A, features an unusual obscuring dust cloud and is a powerful source of radio, X- and gamma rays.

Individual stars will live and die, but the Milky Way will probably continue to look much as it does today for billions of years, until stars such as the Sun are long dead.

Other galaxies

The existence of galaxies other than the Milky Way was long suspected, but only became accepted in the 1920s, when Edwin Hubble measured the distance to some nearby galaxies. We classify galaxies according to their overall appearance, since only in the nearest ones can even the brightest stars be discerned individually.

Most familiar are the spiral galaxies like the Milky Way. Photos of these galaxies reveal that they are in beautiful spiral patterns, traced out by bright stars and gas, hiding the fainter background glow of the disk in which they lie. The spiral patterns range from loosely wound S-shapes to arms so tightly wound that the spiral cannot be discerned. The Milky Way falls midway in this range. Some spirals have a distinct bar across the nucleus from which the spiral arms trail.

Other galaxies show no apparent structure beyond a smooth spherical or elliptical shape. Unlike the spirals, these elliptical galaxies usually lack any significant signs of recent star formation or the gas to promote it. Giants of this class are rare, but are the most massive galaxies known. On the other end of the scale, faint dwarf ellipticals, little larger than a globular star cluster, are probably the most common type of galaxy.

Perhaps a quarter of all galaxies are classified as irregular because they do not fit neatly into either of these categories. They are typically faint, but with a mix of old and young stars, gas, and dust.

Many galaxies, including the Milky Way, show signs of more mass than can readily be seen. Some galaxies hide another enigma—a central powerhouse at their core that generates narrow jets of high-energy particles streaming outward. These active galaxies are believed to be powered by matter swirling around a massive black hole. It may be that many large galaxies have a central black hole with a mass equal to millions of suns, but in most of them, as in the Milky Way, this lies dormant unless brought to life by an inflow of gas.

Clusters of galaxies

Galaxies, like stars within galaxies, tend to exist in clusters. The Milky Way's Local Group is a small cluster, with 30 or so members, most of them small elliptical or irregular galaxies. The nearest large cluster of galaxies is the Virgo cluster, with some 2,500 members, lying about 60 million light years away. The Virgo cluster is a major component of the Local Supercluster.

Compared with the amount of space between the stars, galaxies in these clusters are relatively close together. As a result of this proximity, they sometimes run into one another, causing cosmic fireworks. The stars within the galaxies almost never collide, but the tenuous interstellar clouds crash together and form new stars, changing the appearance of the galaxy and possibly triggering the nuclear powerhouse into activity.

Exploring space

Before the telescope, astronomy consisted largely of measuring and predicting the positions of stars and planets observed by eye. In 1609 a revolution began, when Galileo Galilei used a telescope to reveal mountains on the Moon, Jupiter's moons, and countless stars in the Milky Way. Despite these amazing discoveries, however, for the next 250 years astronomy was predominantly devoted to measuring positions and cataloging.

Almost 150 years ago, the first identification of a chemical element in the Sun was made using a spectrograph, which separates sunlight into its component colors. This marked the start of our ability to deduce the composition of the stars. The science of astrophysics was born.

Today, spectrographs are used on optical telescopes hundreds of times the size of Galileo's first instruments. One of these, the Hubble Space Telescope, views the sky from above the distorting effect of Earth's atmosphere. Optical telescopes joined by radio telescopes on the ground and in space can be used to form large radio arrays. Other observatories in space search for sources of infrared and ultraviolet light, X-rays, and gamma rays.

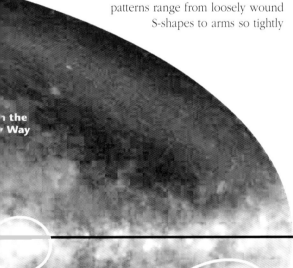

n the Way

nova Remnant and rm of the galaxy

Orion Nebula

Constellation of Orion

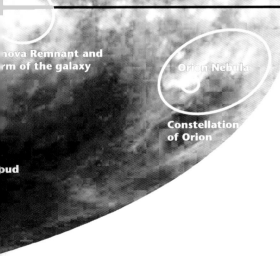

oud

STARS

When we look at the stars in the night sky, it is easy to understand how people in ancient times imagined them to be flickering lights attached to the dark vault of the sky. It was not until 1838 that the first stellar distance was measured and the enormous distances of the stars from Earth and from each other were confirmed.

The first half of the twentieth century saw the development of the physics necessary to understand the composition and structure of the stars and the sources of nuclear energy that power them. As a result, astronomers today have an extensive understanding of the stars and the way they have evolved.

Types of star

While stars vary widely in size, color, and temperature, they are all essentially vast balls of hot gas powered by nuclear reactions deep in their cores. For most of the life of a star, these reactions fuse hydrogen into helium. Late in its life, a star leaves behind this main sequence phase and develops into a giant, converting helium into carbon and heavier elements. In both processes, a small fraction of the matter is converted into energy. The temperatures that are required in a star's core in order to achieve this are measured in tens of millions of degrees.

The main factor determining the characteristics of a main sequence star is its mass—how much matter it contains. Stars range in mass from less than one-tenth of the Sun's mass to perhaps more than 50 times its mass. At the top end of the range are the rare massive stars, which are a few times the size of the Sun but radiate hundreds of thousands of times more energy from their blue–white surfaces. The Sun itself has a slightly yellow color to its 6,000°C (10,800°F) surface. A less massive main sequence star will be somewhat smaller than the Sun, perhaps less than 1 percent as bright, with a cooler, red hue. Red dwarfs of this sort can only be seen from relatively nearby, but are the most common stars in the galaxy.

At the end of their main sequence lifetimes, stars swell to become giants and supergiants. The largest of these are cool red stars, which are more than a thousand times larger and a million times brighter than the Sun. Many of the giants will end their days as white dwarfs only as big as Earth— the faint glowing embers of old stars.

The nearest star

The Sun, which is the only star that we can readily see as anything other than a point of light, is representative of an average star in the Milky Way. Its surface displays a cycle of activity that

This globular cluster—47 Tucanae, above—is an enormous group of stars formed early in the life of the Milky Way galaxy; it contains some of the oldest known stars. One hundred and eighty years ago, the massive star Eta Carinae experienced an outburst which created the lobes of gas now surrounding it, right.

is roughly 11 years long. The most obvious manifestations of the cycle are sunspots, the numbers of which rise and fall during the course of the cycle. Sunspots are often larger than Earth, and are relatively dark in appearance because magnetic effects make them slightly cooler than their surroundings. They are also centers of other activity—powerful solar flares, for instance, which last for a few minutes, glowing brightly and pouring hot gas into space. This gas is channeled by the solar magnetic field and sometimes strikes Earth, causing intense auroral displays near the poles and disrupting radio communication and, sometimes, electrical power systems.

The sudden outburst of a flare punctuates a more general outflow from the Sun's hot outer atmosphere, known as the corona. This solar wind is relatively mild when compared with the massive outflows from certain other stars. While the Sun will lose little mass through the solar wind during the course of its life, larger stars can blow away a sizeable proportion of their mass in this way.

Observations reveal that some other stars have cycles of activity that resemble those of the Sun. Although we are unable to see sunspots on their surfaces, we can detect the slight changes in brightness that accompany changes in activity.

The Sun's magnetism arises from the flow of electrical currents within its outer layers, but most of its material is packed closer to the core, where the energy is generated. In recent

This pillar of gas, left, contains cool hydrogen gas and dust and can incubate new stars. It is a part of the Eagle Nebula, a star-forming region 7,000 light years away. The Trifid Nebula, above, contains hot young stars which cause the gas to emit red light, and cooler gas and dust reflecting blue light.

A star like the Sun takes millions of years to form. It then embarks on the main part of its existence, living for 10 billion years as a stable main sequence star.

As the gas falls in under the force of gravity, it heats up, becoming a protostar, glowing warmly with infrared light through an obscuring cocoon of gas and dust.

Star birth begins deep in a tenuous cloud of interstellar gas and dust. Perhaps triggered by the birth or death of stars nearby, the cloud begins to collapse.

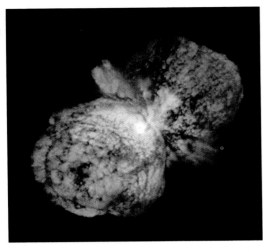

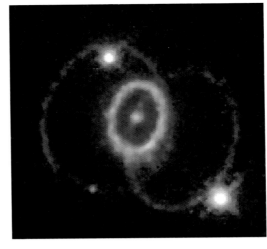

Left: These rings of glowing gas surround an exploded star which was first observed in 1987—a supernova. It is 169,000 light years away in the Large Magellanic Cloud, a nearby galaxy visible from the southern hemisphere.

After a supernova

Massive stars die spectacularly in a supernova explosion. If the remnant after the explosion is less than about three times the mass of the Sun, a neutron star will result. Despite the intense force of gravity, the neutrons making up much of the star refuse to collapse any further than a dense ball 20 km (12 miles) across. Neutron stars are sometimes seen as pulsing sources of radiation—they are then called pulsars.

If the remnant of the star contains more than three solar masses of material, the strength of the gravitational force cannot be resisted, and the collapse produces a black hole. Not even light can escape from within a black hole. Any matter that falls within the boundary of a black hole is lost from view.

The importance of black holes and neutron stars to astronomy lies more in what happens in the intense gravitational field around them than in what is inside them. Gas falls onto black holes or neutron stars with tremendous energy, producing intense radiation. The largest black holes are believed to be millions of times the mass of the Sun, and reside in the nuclei of active galaxies. They are the powerhouses of these beacons that shine across the universe.

years, astronomers have begun to probe beneath the surface of the Sun using a technique called helioseismology. This is helping to clarify our picture of the Sun's structure.

The life of a star

A constant battle takes place between gravity, which is attempting to pull a star inward, and the pressure of hot gas pushing outward. The battle starts when gravity begins to collapse a small part of an interstellar gas cloud. As the cloud falls in, the temperature at its core increases, and eventually hydrogen begins to fuse together to form helium. The collapse slows as the growing pressure of the hot gas resists the gravitational force. Finally the collapse comes to a halt; the protostar has become a stable main sequence star.

A star such as the Sun will remain balanced in this state for around 10 billion years, constantly converting hydrogen to helium at its core and by degrees growing a little bigger and a little brighter. The Sun is currently about halfway through its main sequence phase.

In approximately 5 billion years, after it has circled the center of the galaxy some 20 more times, the Sun will begin to grow quite rapidly. By the time it has doubled in size, the oceans on Earth will have completely boiled away. Eventually, the Sun will become a red giant, perhaps 100 times larger and 1,000 times

brighter than it is at the moment. It will envelop Mercury, Venus, and Earth, evaporating Earth's atmosphere and eventually causing the planet to spiral inward to oblivion.

Cooler, lower-mass stars will follow much the same path, but over spans of time so long that not even the oldest of them has yet had time to complete its sedate main sequence life. In contrast, massive stars consume their nuclear fuel at a prodigious rate and become red giants in a matter of only a few million years.

Once it has become a red giant, the Sun will begin to fuse helium to carbon in its core. However, this new energy source will only delay the inevitable victory of gravity. Within about a billion years the Sun will peel off its outer layers to reveal a white dwarf remnant that will cool slowly, over billions more years.

Stars that begin life larger than about eight times the mass of the Sun will blow away much of their mass during the course of their lives, but will still end up too large to survive as white dwarfs. Instead, they blow up in brilliant supernova explosions, leaving neutron stars or black holes to mark their passing.

About 10 billion years after it formed, the Sun will run short of hydrogen fuel in its core, but it will actually increase its energy output and swell to become a red giant.

After perhaps 1 billion years as a giant, the Sun will eject its outer layers to form a short-lived planetary nebula surrounding the cooling core.

The Sun will live on as a white dwarf for billions of years, slowly fading from view, with little or no nuclear fusion to slow the cooling.

THE SOLAR SYSTEM

Among more than 100 billion stars in the Milky Way Galaxy, one is unique. It is the Sun—the only star that we know has a planetary system, including at least one planet which can support life as we know it. That planet is Earth, of course, although Mars may also be a candidate.

Until recently, the Sun's family was the only planetary system we knew of, but evidence that large planets circle several Sun-like stars is now accumulating. In time, observations may reveal that they also have Earth-sized planets.

The solar system's formation

A little less than 5 billion years ago, the Sun was formed in a cloud of interstellar gas. The infant Sun was surrounded by a cooling disk of gas and dust—the solar nebula—where knots of material were forming, colliding, breaking, and merging. The larger objects, called planetesimals, grew by accreting smaller particles, until a few protoplanets dominated. The protoplanets from the warm inner parts of the disk became the small rocky planets. Further out, in a cooler region where ices of water, ammonia, and methane could condense, the giant planets formed. These planets grew in mass more rapidly, forming deep atmospheres around rocky cores. The giant planets copied the Sun's accretion disk in miniature to create their moons.

As the Sun settled into its present stable state, the pressure of radiation and the gas of the solar wind streaming outward blew away the remains of

the solar nebula. The newborn planets swept up the larger debris. In the process they were subjected to an intense bombardment, evidence of which we see in the craters on the rocky surfaces of the inner solar system and the icy surfaces of the moons of the outer solar system.

The solar system today has been largely swept clean of the debris of its formation. It is dominated by the Sun, at its center, which constitutes almost 99.9 percent of the solar system's mass. Most of the remainder is contained in the two giant planets Jupiter and Saturn, while Earth represents less than 0.0003 percent of the Sun's mass.

The region of space inhabited by the planets is a flat plane centered on the Sun and about 15 billion km (just under 10 billion miles) across. This is almost 50 times the span of Earth's orbit. Vast as this sounds, it is only 0.02 percent of the distance to the nearest star! The great void of interplanetary space is sparsely populated by debris orbiting the distant Sun, ranging in size from particles of dust to rocky asteroids and icy comets—these may be tens or even hundreds of kilometers across.

The family of planets

The inner rocky planets and asteroids and Earth's Moon share a common heritage, yet visits by spacecraft have revealed their histories to be quite different. The smaller ones, Mercury and the Moon, are geologically dead worlds retaining little or no atmosphere. Mars has had more geological activity and features Olympus Mons, the solar system's largest volcano. The larger inner planets, Venus and Earth, are similar in size but differ geologically. Both show evidence of volcanic activity, but Earth's activity includes moving plates of rock causing active mountain building; this has not occurred on Venus.

The common thread in the surface histories of the rocky planets is the heavy bombardment they underwent early in their existence. Occasional impacts still occur, as was dramatically illustrated in 1994 when Comet Shoemaker-Levy 9 broke into fragments and crashed into Jupiter.

Above: An image of the Sun taken using the red light of hydrogen, showing a loop of gas, called a prominence, erupting from the solar surface.

Of the inner planets, Venus, Earth, and Mars have significant atmospheres, although these are only thin veneers over their rocky surfaces. The atmospheres of Venus and Mars today are mostly carbon dioxide. Earth's atmosphere is unique in having only traces of carbon dioxide in an atmosphere consisting mainly of nitrogen and oxygen. A combination of oceans of liquid water, an active geological history and abundant plant life has stripped the atmosphere of much of its carbon dioxide, and released oxygen.

In stark contrast, the faces presented by the giant outer planets, Jupiter and Saturn, are clouds of ammonia compounds and water in layers riding high in deep atmospheres. These gaseous envelopes are believed to surround a mantle of liquid metallic hydrogen overlying a rocky core. The clouds are split into bands by high-speed winds circulating in regular patterns within the atmosphere. They are punctuated now and then by cyclonic storms, the best known being Jupiter's Great Red Spot, which has survived for at least 300 years.

The asteroid Ida, top, seen by the Galileo spacecraft; a tiny moon can be seen to the right. Comet West displays its tails across the sky, above. Above right: Jupiter, showing the short-lived scars of the impact of Comet Shoemaker-Levy 9. Right: The planets' relative distances from the Sun (see box opposite).

Above: The Sun's family
is comprised of nine major planets and
many smaller moons and asteroids (not to scale).

The smaller, colder giants, Uranus and Neptune, have few atmospheric features, and their blue–green coloring results from methane in the atmosphere. Their atmospheres overlie an icy core of water, methane, ammonia, and rock.

The giant planets all have large moons in orbit around them which were formed in their surrounding nebulae, plus smaller objects that are probably captured asteroids. The largest moons, Jupiter's Ganymede and Saturn's Titan, are larger than the planet Mercury. Most of the moons have thick, icy crusts pitted with craters that date from the heavy bombardment which scarred the inner planets. Distant Pluto and its moon Chiron are much like them, but Pluto's elongated orbit grants it status as a planet. The one exception is Jupiter's large inner moon Io, which has a surface covered in sulfur-rich rock. Io is locked in a gravitational embrace with Jupiter and its neighboring moons, Europa and Ganymede, which causes heating and results in it being the most volcanically active place in the solar system.

All four giant planets have systems of thin rings orbiting over their equators. Saturn's famous rings are by far the most substantial, but none of the rings is solid. They are composed of icy particles that range in size from tiny specks to blocks as large as houses, and their orbits are shepherded by the gravitational influences of nearby moons.

What the future holds

As in the past, the future of the solar system will be dominated by the evolution of the Sun. About 5 billion years from now, the Sun will suddenly increase in size and brightness, ultimately encompassing most of the inner planets, causing their orbits to decay and the planets to spiral into the Sun. The outer planets and their moons will be subjected to 1,000 times the current energy output from the Sun; this will melt icy surfaces and alter their atmospheres. Within a few hundred million years the Sun will decrease in size to become a white dwarf, only feebly illuminating the remains of its family.

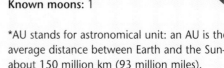

Planetary facts

Mercury
Diameter: 4,878 km (3,031 miles)
Average distance from Sun: 0.4 AU*
Known moons: None

Venus
Diameter: 12,104 km (7,521 miles)
Average distance from Sun: 0.7 AU*
Known moons: None

Earth
Diameter: 12,756 km (7,925 miles)
Average distance from Sun: 1.0 AU*
Known moons: 1

Mars
Diameter: 6,787 km (4,217 miles)
Average distance from Sun: 1.5 AU*
Known moons: 2

Jupiter
Diameter: 143,800 km (89,400 miles)
Average distance from Sun: 5.2 AU*
Known moons: 16

Saturn
Diameter: 120,660 km (75,000 miles)
Average distance from Sun: 9.5 AU*
Known moons: 18

Uranus
Diameter: 51,120 km (31,765 miles)
Average distance from Sun: 19.2 AU*
Known moons: 17

Neptune
Diameter: 49,500 km (30,760 miles)
Average distance from Sun: 30.1 AU*
Known moons: 8

Pluto
Diameter: 2,360 km (1,466 miles)
Average distance from Sun: 39.4 AU*
Known moons: 1

*AU stands for astronomical unit: an AU is the average distance between Earth and the Sun— about 150 million km (93 million miles).

PLANET EARTH

With the exception of Pluto, all the planets in the solar system lie in almost the same plane. This reflects their common origin in the disk surrounding the infant Sun. Pluto wanders far from this disk, indicating a history we can only suspect, but clearly one that differs considerably from those of the other planets. Earth is a better-behaved member of the Sun's family but, like the rest of the planets, it has its own particular characteristics and history.

Earth's motion

The orbits of all the planets around the Sun are elliptical, but, like those of most of the planets, Earth's orbit is quite close to circular. The distance between Earth and the Sun varies between 147 and 152 million km (92 and 95 million miles), known as 1.0 AU (astronomical unit). The point of closest approach occurs on 2 January each year, during the southern hemisphere's summer. It is a common misconception that the small change in distance produces the Earth's seasons.

Apart from its revolution around the Sun, Earth also spins around a rotation axis which passes through the north and south geographic poles. Seen from above the north pole, Earth spins on its axis in a counterclockwise direction, and it circles the Sun in the same counterclockwise

direction. Most of the other planets and major moons behave in the same way, which again points to their having common origins.

Earth travels around its orbit at 30 km per second (18 miles per second). At this speed, it takes 365.25 days to complete one circuit—that period defines our calendar year. The period of a day is defined by the rotation of Earth on its axis relative to the stars—once every 23 hours and 56 minutes. In that time, however, Earth has also advanced 2.6 million km (1.6 million miles) along its curving orbit, so it has to turn a little further to rotate once relative to the Sun. This takes about 4 extra minutes, and makes the time from midday one day to midday the next exactly 24 hours.

Changing seasons

The Earth's axis is tilted relative to the plane of its orbit by 23.5°. This axis remains pointed in the same orientation relative to the stars as Earth circles the Sun. As a result, Earth's northern hemisphere is tilted more directly toward the Sun in the middle of the calendar year.

From the ground, the Sun then appears higher in the sky and the direct sunlight leads to warmer weather—the northern summer. At the same time, the southern hemisphere has a more oblique view of the Sun, resulting in cooler winter weather. The situation is reversed six months later when Earth is on the opposite side of its orbit.

The direction of Earth's axis is not strictly fixed, but swings around in a circuit lasting 26,000 years. As a result of this precession, our seasons today would seem out of step to the ancient Egyptians, who lived some 5,000 years ago. Their seasons would have differed by around two months from ours, Earth's rotation axis having changed its direction somewhat since that time.

Other effects also operate over periods of tens of thousands of years to slightly change Earth's tilt and how close Earth gets to the Sun. Acting together, these effects produce changes in the amount of heat Earth receives from the Sun, and these changes may significantly affect Earth's

Earth's orbit, right: The Earth orbits the Sun in 365.25 days, or one calendar year. It also rotates in slightly less than 24 hours on an axis which is tilted relative to the orbit. This tilt leads to the progression of the seasons each year.

climate. There is some evidence that these changes result in periodic ice ages, but the concept remains controversial. Links between the Sun's 11-year sunspot numbers cycle and the Earth's climate also remain speculative.

The largest rocky planet

The Earth is a ball of rock 12,756 km (7,925 miles) in diameter at the equator, but its rotation causes it to be slightly flattened at the poles. It is the largest of the rocky planets in the solar system and, as a result of its bulk, it retains a hot interior; the temperature may reach 6,000°C (10,830°F) at the core—as hot as the surface of the Sun.

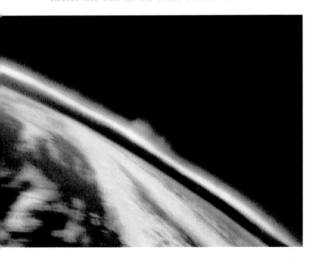

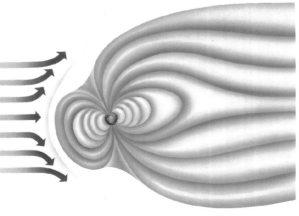

The Earth is surrounded by a protective magnetic envelope called the magnetosphere (in blue and brown, above). Some charged particles from the Sun (red arrows) tend to be channeled down onto the Earth's poles where they cause the air to glow as an aurora, as seen from a space shuttle (top).

Magnetic reversals

When molten lava from a volcano cools and solidifies, it captures the orientation and strength of the Earth's magnetic field at that time and place. This built-in compass needle has proved a powerful tool for studying the gradual drift of Earth's continents. It has also revealed periods, usually spaced by a few hundred thousand years, when Earth's magnetic field has briefly disappeared. Within a geological instant of only about 5,000 years, the field shrinks to zero and then reappears with magnetic north and south swapped. The magnetic imprint of this swapping is found in alternating bands of rocks along mid-oceanic ridges. Each band is made of rocks formed around the same time, and with the same magnetic signature. This provides dramatic confirmation of the picture of

continents drifting apart with new crust forming between them. The origin of this change in magnetic directions lies in the electrical dynamo working in Earth's outer core to create the field. How it happens so quickly and why the interval is so irregular remain unknown.

How this change would affect those migratory animals that seem to use the direction of the magnetic field to navigate on their journeys, we do not know. And what if we lost the protective cloak of the Earth's magnetosphere? Cosmic ray particles from the Sun and interstellar space that are normally deflected or trapped by the magnetosphere would reach the surface of Earth. This would cause dramatically higher rates of genetic damage to animals and plants and lead to mutations and perhaps extinctions.

The core is a mix of metallic nickel and iron split into a solid inner core and an outer fluid zone which reaches halfway to the surface. Enclosing the outer core is Earth's mantle. The dense rocks in this zone flow, over geologic time, under the intense heat and pressure. Overlying the mantle, Earth's crust is a skin of lightweight rocks: a mere 60 km (36 miles) deep at its thickest.

Its inner heat makes Earth one of the most seismically active objects within the solar system. On the surface, it causes volcanic activity, and at depth, it drives the separate plates of the crust into motion. This motion—folding the rocks of the crust—creates mountain ranges. At the perimeters of the plates, new crust is created or old crust destroyed. Atmospheric forces such as wind and water flow also act to reshape Earth's surface, by eroding rock and depositing weathered material to form new sedimentary rock strata.

All these processes together act to renew the planet's surface over hundreds of millions of years, removing or altering the ancient impact scarring that can be seen on the surfaces of so many other objects in the solar system. Only a few recent impact craters are visible, providing hints of Earth's turbulent early history.

Earth's atmosphere

Earth is surrounded by a thin atmospheric envelope which tapers off into space and is all but gone 100 km (62 miles) above the surface. This envelope maintains the surface at a higher

Right, top: A total solar eclipse occurs when the Moon passes in front of the Sun and obscures it. As the Sun is finally eclipsed, rays of sunlight filtering through the hills and valleys on the Moon's edge create an effect known as Baily's beads, center. Right, bottom: A lunar eclipse—the Moon darkens as it passes through the Earth's shadow.

temperature than it would otherwise be, permitting oceans of liquid water on the surface. The atmosphere is a unique mixture of nitrogen and oxygen, with only traces of carbon dioxide and other gases, and is certainly not Earth's primeval atmosphere. Oxygen only began to build up when primitive forms of life developed photosynthesis. Oxygen reacts to form ozone, which protects the surface of the planet from intense ultraviolet radiation. Life has crafted the environment of the blue planet to suit itself.

Above the atmosphere lies the protective cocoon of the magnetosphere—the domain of Earth's magnetic field. While most of the particles flowing from the Sun are deflected by the magnetosphere, some become ensnared and are channeled onto the north and south poles, forming the glowing aurorae.

The magnetic field originates in electrical currents within Earth's outer fluid core, and its axis is at a slightly different angle from the planet's rotation axis. As a result, Earth's magnetic and rotation poles are not quite the same, creating a difference between magnetic north, as measured by a compass, and "true" north.

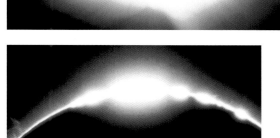

13

THE MOON

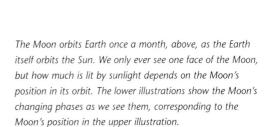

A light in the darkness of night, the Moon was considered a deity in many ancient cultures and has provided humans with their calendar. The 29¹/₂ days it takes to go through its cycle of phases is close to the length of a month, the word "month" coming from the word "moon."

Galileo's telescopic observations in 1609 of mountains on the Moon played an important part in showing people that the Moon and planets were worlds something like Earth. But the greatest step in this process was the series of six Apollo landings on the Moon between 1969 and 1972. So far, the Moon is the only other world that humans have visited.

Phases of the Moon

The Moon orbits Earth in just under 27¹/₂ days relative to the stars. Earth moves appreciably along its curving path around the Sun in that time, however, so the Moon needs to travel for two more days to get back to the same position relative to the Sun and Earth and complete its cycle of phases. At the same time, the Moon is rotating on its own axis, but the strong gravitational pull of Earth has locked these two

motions together. As a result, the Moon always presents the same familiar face to us on Earth: apart from a little around the edges, we never see the "far side" of the Moon. It also means that a "day" on the Moon is two weeks long!

Half of the Moon is always lit by the Sun, and the amount of that sunny half we can see from Earth depends on where the Moon is in its orbit. If it lies directly sunward of the Earth, the Moon's night side (not the far side) is presented to our view. It appears dark and invisible when it is near the Sun in the sky. This is New Moon. Over the following days the sunlight begins to illuminate one edge of the visible face and the Moon appears as a crescent shape in the twilight sky. The crescent expands through First Quarter and on to Full Moon, when the fully illuminated disk is opposite the Sun in the sky. Over the following two weeks the sunlit portion of the disk shrinks back through Third Quarter towards New Moon.

Solar and lunar eclipses

The Moon's orbit is tilted by just over 5° to the plane of Earth's orbit. As a result, the New Moon usually passes close to the Sun in the sky, but does not cross it.

About twice a year, however, the orbital angles converge—the Sun and Moon line up and the Moon's shadow is cast towards Earth. Sometimes the shadow only just reaches Earth, as a dark spot no more than 270 km (170 miles) across. As Earth turns underneath it, the spot draws a thin line of darkness across the globe.

The Earth-bound observer sited somewhere along the total eclipse track sees the Moon as just big enough to cover the disk of the much larger but more distant Sun. Day turns to night for a few minutes as the solar disk is covered, revealing the faint glow of the surrounding corona. Observers usually find the few minutes of a total solar eclipse a remarkable

The Moon orbits Earth once a month, above, as the Earth itself orbits the Sun. We only ever see one face of the Moon, but how much is lit by sunlight depends on the Moon's position in its orbit. The lower illustrations show the Moon's changing phases as we see them, corresponding to the Moon's position in the upper illustration.

experience, and some have felt compelled to travel around the world, chasing further opportunities to see one.

A wider swath of Earth's surface lies off the track of totality, and sees the Sun only partly eclipsed. Also, about half the time, the shadow falls short of Earth, causing the Moon to appear too small to cover the Sun in the sky; this is called an annular eclipse, and it lacks the darkness and magic of a total eclipse.

When the situation of Earth and the Moon are reversed, the Full Moon can be eclipsed by Earth's shadow. Sky watchers on the whole night side of Earth will see the Moon darken for several hours as it traverses Earth's wide shadow. The effect is somewhat less dramatic than a solar eclipse, but more commonly seen.

The motions of the tides

The most obvious effect of the Moon on Earth is the tides. These alterations in sea level twice a day are caused by the gravitational pull of the Moon on water and on Earth itself.

The water on the side of Earth nearest the Moon feels a stronger force from the Moon than does the center of Earth, which is itself more

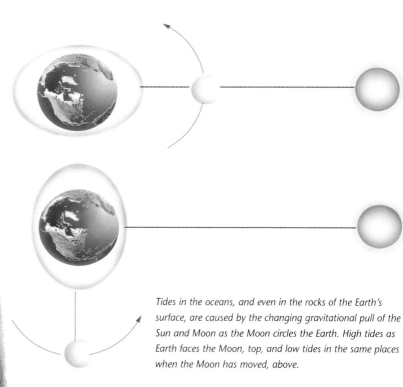

Tides in the oceans, and even in the rocks of the Earth's surface, are caused by the changing gravitational pull of the Sun and Moon as the Moon circles the Earth. High tides as Earth faces the Moon, top, and low tides in the same places when the Moon has moved, above.

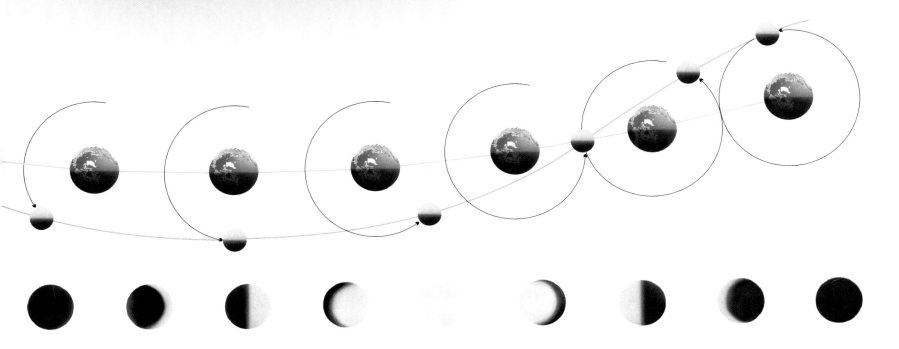

strongly attracted than water on the side away from the Moon. This results in water accumulating in two high tides: one on the side of Earth facing the Moon, and one on the far side. In between these regions of high tide are regions of low tide, where the water level is at its lowest. Tide heights vary greatly because of local effects, but they can range as high as 10 m (33 ft) in some locations. Tides of a few centimeters are also raised in the rocky crust of Earth itself.

But tidal forces have even more profound consequences. The Earth's rotation slows by 0.0023 seconds per century. This makes a day now four hours longer than a day was when the first complex life forms arose in Earth's oceans. The same effect on the smaller Moon has already slowed its rotation to make its "day" equal its orbital period. Tidal forces are also causing the Moon to recede from Earth by about 4 cm (1^{1}/$_{2}$ in) a year. As a result, solar eclipses will eventually all be annular, because the Moon will be too far away to ever fully cover the Sun's disk.

Lunar history

The origin of the Moon has long been a subject of debate, but current theory imagines a collision over 4 billion years ago between the infant Earth and another planetesimal as large as Mars. Some of the lighter debris then collected in orbit around Earth to become the Moon.

Both Earth and the Moon were subjected to intense bombardment early in their histories, as the solar system was swept clear of most of the debris of its formation. On the Moon, the last stages of this cosmic storm are still recorded in the bright highland areas of the surface, which are covered with impact craters. Other areas suffered large impacts late in the bombardment; these gouged enormous basins in the surface. Many of the basins on the side nearest Earth were soon flooded by dark lava flows from within the Moon. Rocks brought back to Earth by Apollo astronauts reveal that the youngest of these maria (singular mare, Latin for "sea") is over 3 billion years old, despite being marked by relatively few craters.

Since that time, the Moon has cooled to inactivity, with only occasional impacts changing the scene. The last large impact occurred perhaps 100 million years ago, creating the crater Tycho and splashing debris across the surface.

A new generation of spacecraft has recently begun to build on the legacy of the Apollo missions, by studying the Moon again. The most exciting finding from these recent studies has been the apparent discovery of water ice on the Moon's cold crater floors. These crater floors are shielded from the glare of radiation from the Sun, which bombards the rest of the surface unhindered by any atmosphere.

Man on the Moon

Man's first step on the Moon was taken on July 20, 1969, during the US Apollo XI mission, and was watched by millions around the world as it was broadcast live on television.

The excitement this event generated may seem extraordinary now, but man seems to have always dreamt of walking on the Moon.

Since that first landing, when Buzz Aldrin and Neil Armstrong both stepped onto the Moon, there have been six other Apollo Moon missions, all between 1969 and 1972. One was aborted, but on each of the others, two more astronauts walked on the surface of the Moon.

Below: Buzz Aldrin taking a historic step on the Moon, watched by millions of television viewers on July 20 1969. Bottom: Earthrise—taken from Apollo 11, this picture shows the Earth coming up over the Moon's horizon.

SPACE EXPLORATION

Our view of the solar system and the wider universe has improved dramatically in recent years. The exploration of the solar system by robot probes has revolutionized our perspective on the planets and their moons. Closer to home, telescopes in Earth orbit have studied the universe using ultraviolet, X-ray and gamma-ray radiation which is invisible from the ground. Arrays of radio telescopes, including one in space, probe the radio universe at finer resolution than any single optical telescope can achieve. On the ground, optical astronomers are building a new generation of larger telescopes which will probe the visible universe more deeply than ever before, and scan the infrared radiation coming from the sky to study regions hidden from visible light.

Exploring the solar system

The space age began with the beeping voice of Sputnik 1 circling Earth in 1957. In retrospect, it seems a small step, but Sputnik led to a series of Soviet Luna and American Pioneer and Ranger spacecraft over the next few years; they sped past the Moon or deliberately crashed into it.

The exploration of the planets began with attempts to reach Venus and Mars in the early 1960s. In 1973, the US Mariner 10 spacecraft successfully flew past Venus and then continued to Mercury, where it captured what are still the only close-up images we have of the surface of that planet. The surface of Venus is hidden by perpetual clouds, but in 1975 the Soviet Venera 9 and 10 landers returned images of a rocky, desolate surface. More recently, radar maps of the

The first spacecraft to orbit Earth was Sputnik 1 in 1957. Since then, Skylab and Mir have paved the way for a larger space station to orbit the Earth.

surface have been produced by the Pioneer Venus and Magellan spacecraft.

While the Soviets explored Venus, the Americans were visiting Mars. In 1976, the Viking 1 and 2 orbiters arrived to map the surface from space for several years, while their accompanying landers studied two sites on the surface and tested, unsuccessfully, for evidence of life. This exploration of the surface was not resumed for another 21 years until, in 1997, the Mars Pathfinder landed, with its rover Sojourner. The exploration of Mars continues today with renewed vigor.

The exploration of the giant outer planets began in 1972 with the launch of Pioneer 10, followed soon after by Pioneer 11. They returned the first stunning images of Jupiter's colorful clouds and the surfaces of its major moons. Pioneer 11 continued on to a repeat performance at Saturn in 1979. By that time a new generation of explorers, Voyager 1 and 2, had already reached Jupiter. Both journeyed on to Saturn, and Voyager 2 then made a foray to the realms of Uranus and Neptune. All four of these interplanetary explorers are still journeying outward, reaching in different directions towards the edge of the Sun's domain. Meanwhile, the exploration of the giant planets continues, with the Galileo spacecraft surveying Jupiter and Cassini on its way to a rendezvous with Saturn.

While the outer reaches of the solar system were being explored, objects closer to home were also under investigation. Comets, asteroids and the Moon have all recently been explored.

Humans in space

The exploration of the solar system by robot spacecraft has been paralleled by a program of human spaceflight closer to Earth. It began in 1961, four years after Sputnik 1, with the flight of Yuri Gagarin in a Vostok spacecraft. The Soviets continued with the Voskhod and Soyuz programs. After being beaten into orbit, the US rapidly developed the techniques of working in space in the Mercury and Gemini programs, with the ultimate goal of satisfying President Kennedy's challenge of landing a man on the moon before the end of the 1960s.

A lunar landing was the objective of the

Planetary science spacecraft

PAST MISSIONS

Mariner 9 (1971, NASA)
The first spacecraft to orbit Mars. Carried out detailed photography of the surface and of Phobos and Deimos, Mars' two moons.

Apollo 11, 12, 14, 15, 16, 17 (1969–72, NASA)
Manned landings on the Moon and sample returns.

Pioneer 10 (1973, NASA)
First spacecraft to flyby Jupiter. Now about 10.6 billion km (6.6 billion miles) from the Sun.

Pioneer 11 (1974–79, NASA)
Followed Pioneer 10 in 1974; first probe to study Saturn (1979). Now about 7.6 billion km (4.7 billion miles) from the Sun.

Mariner 10 (1974–75)
Used Venus as a gravity assist to Mercury; returned the first close-up images of the atmosphere of Venus in ultraviolet; made three flybys of Mercury.

Venera 9 (1975, USSR)
Landed on Venus, returned pictures of the surface.

Pioneer Venus (1978, NASA)
An orbiter and four atmospheric probes; made the first high-quality map of the surface of Venus.

Viking 1 (1976, NASA)
Probe in Martian orbit and lander set down on the western slopes of Chryse Planitia; returned images and searched for Martian microorganisms.

Viking 2 (1976, NASA)
Arrived in Martian orbit a month after Viking 1:

Apollo program. It began disastrously with a fire in early 1967 which killed three astronauts. The first piloted mission was Apollo 7 in 1968, followed in rapid succession by Apollo 8, 9, and 10, which tested the equipment needed for the landing. On July 20, 1969, the program reached its culmination, with the landing of the Apollo 11 lunar module Eagle on the dusty floor of the Moon's Sea of Tranquillity. Soon afterward, Neil Armstrong became the first human to set foot on the Moon.

The Apollo program continued through five more successful landings, returning 382 kg (844 lb) of lunar rock and soil, plus photographs and other data which have shaped our current understanding of the history of the Moon.

The 1970s were the in-between years of US manned space activities: between the Apollo program and the advent of the reusable space shuttle. In 1981 the much-delayed space shuttle Columbia was launched for the first time, and a schedule of regular launches has continued since then, but with a break of more than two years after the loss of all seven crew members in the Challenger accident in 1986.

The Soviet human spaceflight program concentrated on learning how to cope with long periods in space aboard the Salyut and Mir space stations. The US program featured

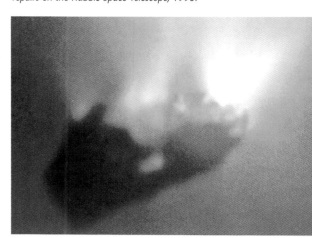

lander touched down in Utopia Planitia; same tasks as Viking 1, plus seismometer.

Magellan (1989, NASA)
Mapped 98 percent of the surface of Venus at better than 300 m (1,000 ft), and obtained comprehensive gravity-field map for 95 percent of the planet.

ONGOING MISSIONS

Voyager 1 (1977– , NASA)
Flew past Jupiter (1979) and Saturn (1980). At mid-1998, the craft was 10.7 billion km (6.6 billion miles) from Earth.

Voyager 2 (1977– , NASA)
Launched just before Voyager 1, Voyager 2 flew by Jupiter (1979), Saturn (1981), Uranus (1986), and Neptune (1989). At mid-1998, the craft was 8.3 billion km (5 billion miles) from Earth.

Galileo (1989– , NASA)
While in transit to Jupiter, returned the first resolved images of two asteroids (951 Gaspra and 243 Ida), plus pictures of the impact of Comet SL9 on Jupiter (1994). Now in Jupiter orbit. Atmospheric probe has studied Jupiter's upper atmosphere. Mission hampered by antenna problems.

Ulysses (1990– , ESA/NASA)
Launched to investigate the Sun's polar regions. Gravity boost from Jupiter in 1992 took it out of the plane in which the planets orbit and over the Sun's south, then north, poles.

SOHO (1996– , ESA/NASA)
Solar Heliospheric Observatory (for studying the Sun and its structure), in solar orbit 1.5 million km (1 million miles) from Earth.

Pathfinder (1996–7, NASA)
A low-cost planetary discovery mission, consisting of a stationary lander and a surface rover. Operated on Mars for 3 months in 1997 measuring wind and weather, photographing the surface and chemically analyzing rocks.

Mars Surveyor Program (1996– , NASA)
Mars Global Surveyor is the first mission of a 10-year program of robotic exploration of Mars. It entered polar orbit in September 1997 and is mapping surface topography and distribution of minerals, and monitoring global weather.

Cassini (1997– , ESA/NASA)
Consists of an orbiter to study Saturn's clouds and a probe to land on Titan, Saturn's largest moon. Will use gravity to assist flybys of Venus, Earth, and Jupiter before arriving at Saturn in 2004.

NEW MISSION

Stardust (1999– , NASA)
Launched on February 7 1999, Stardust is scheduled to flyby Comet Wild 2 in 2004, collect particles from the comet's tail and return to Earth in 2006.

Skylab in the early 1970s and then lapsed until US astronauts began to visit Mir during the 1990s. The future of long-term human presence in space lies with the international space station.

Exploring the universe

One function of an orbiting space station is to serve as an astronomical observing platform. However, most astronomical observations from within Earth's orbit are performed by unmanned telescope observatories controlled from the ground. The best known is the Hubble Space Telescope (HST), a 2.4 m (95 in) aperture telescope which offers views of unprecedented sharpness in infrared, visible, and ultraviolet light. It orbits at a height of about 600 km (375 miles) above the Earth's surface—well above the blurring effects of Earth's atmosphere.

Equally important is the range of astronomical satellites studying other radiation from space. Satellites such as the International Ultraviolet Explorer (IUE) and the InfraRed Astronomical Satellite (IRAS) have made major contributions in the past. More recently, the Cosmic Background Explorer (COBE) has probed the glow of the Big Bang, while satellites such as BeppoSAX have hunted down elusive sources of energetic gamma-ray bursts. The Japanese Halca satellite is a radio telescope which observes the sky in conjunction with Earth-bound telescopes to create a radio telescope thousands of kilometers across. The Solar Heliospheric Observer (SOHO) observes the Sun from a point 1.5 million km (1 million miles) closer to the Sun than Earth.

Search for life

One of the reasons for exploring the solar system is to search for life beyond Earth. The desolate surfaces of Mercury, Venus, and the Moon are not promising sites. Mars, historically the most popular source of alien neighbors, remains a far more likely candidate after the discoveries of the space age. Although the surface is cold and dry today, evidence indicates it was once warmer and water flowed on it. The Viking landers searched for life in 1976 without success. There is no evidence yet that life ever arose on Mars.

The Galileo mission to Jupiter has enlivened speculation that Europa (right) may have a warm ocean of water under its icy crust. Perhaps life could arise there. The Cassini spacecraft will soon examine Saturn's moon, Titan, and may show whether it has lakes or oceans of carbon compounds where some sort of life might have appeared.

Life elsewhere in the solar system is likely to be primitive, but its discovery may be within reach of interplanetary spacecraft from Earth. The search

for life among the stars is far more difficult. Current efforts are directed at listening with radio telescopes for signals from distant civilizations. This project is known as SETI—the Search for Extra-Terrestrial Intelligence.

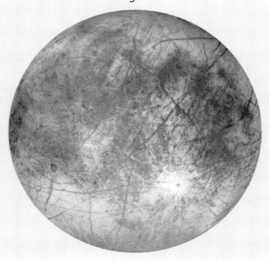

Earth as a biophysical system

The plants and animals we know today—such as this Chinstrap Penguin in Antarctica, above—have evolved over thousands of years to adapt to their surroundings. Opposite: Volcanoes, such as this one in New Zealand, can provide geologists with clues to the puzzle of Earth's history.

There are many factors that make Earth a unique planet. Its atmosphere, oceans, moving plates, escaping gases, diverse life forms, soils, and the presence of humans all contribute to a distinctive biophysical system. Above all else, it is the dynamic, ever-changing ways in which the air, land, and oceans interact that create particular landscapes available for human use and abuse. From the equator to the poles, from mountains to the depths of ocean basins, plants and animals go through their life cycles nurtured by the climates and the nutrients in soils and waters.

Yet what we observe today has not always been present. The world humans inhabit has been transformed not once, but many times since the hard, rocky crusts of continents and the watery masses of oceans first formed, around 4 billion years ago.

Charles Darwin was one of many scientists who conceptualized patterns of evolution. Organisms did not immediately find their place in the world, he proposed; rather, there were countless histories of evolving life for the different plants and animals that have occupied space on land or in the sea over geological time. These patterns of evolution were not uniform. Past life histories show punctuated successions of periods dominated by particular organisms, followed by extensive extinctions of various species. The cause and meaning of such changes are often a mystery and remain to be explained.

It is very difficult to unravel Earth's history. Geologists and paleontologists are like detectives. They are required to piece together fragmentary evidence using their imagination, and their sense of adventure and curiosity, exploring the world and discovering for themselves what has happened in the past. Some geologists, such as Charles Lyell, have had the ability to synthesize masses of information and develop generalized histories from field observations and interpretations. Increasingly, new technologies, including the capacity to calculate accurately the age of rocks using radiometric dating methods, have opened new vistas of thought, allowing the testing of theories such as that of continental drift.

Discoveries of magnetic reversals in rocks on the floor of oceans, the volcanic character of mid-oceanic ridges, and the age of oceanic basalts covered by a veneer of geologically young sediment, have contributed to our understanding of the processes of sea-floor spreading and hence to the development of plate tectonic theory. This was one of the most remarkable scientific advances of the twentieth century. It formalized the grand dreams of those who could see evidence for the validity of continental drift theory in the rock record and in the distribution of plants and animals. Yet, for decades, these geologists and biologists were not able to convince the skeptics, because they had no mechanism to explain the movement of the relatively light continental crust over vast distances.

New technologies in ocean research changed all that; with plate tectonics, it is possible to explain much more satisfactorily the formation of mountains, as well as the distribution of earthquakes, volcanoes and many life forms.

Plants and animals, or biota, occur in particular groups, reflecting their adaptation to each other and to the environment. Interaction of biota with climatic, soil, landform, and other conditions has been the subject of much ecological discovery. Competition and predation are just two of the ways in which species function—on a range of scales from microorganisms in the soil to whales at sea. On land and in the ocean, there are clear regional groupings of biota which contribute to the differences between places. But even these differences are not static— they too are subject to change.

Changes in climate, for instance, whether it be over millions of years or tens of years, require organisms to adjust. On a global scale, it is possible to document periods of Earth cooling and the consequent expansion of ice sheets and falls in sea level. Vast areas of Europe and North America were under 1 km ($5/8$ mile) of ice as little as 15,000 years ago. Yet Earth warmed, and the glaciers retreated. Today, these areas are home to millions of people.

Rising sea levels flooded continental shelves and river valleys, creating new habitats for plants and animals; in the fertile deltaic plains of many countries, for instance. Such changes have taken place many times over the past 2 million years, the so-called Quaternary period of Earth's history. Understanding why these and other, smaller-scale climatic fluctuations such as the El Niño phenomenon occur is still the subject of much scientific debate.

Against the background of natural variability in climate, another factor comes into play—the impact of humans disturbing the chemistry of the atmosphere and inducing global warming, or the greenhouse effect.

Plants, animals, and human productivity are highly dependent on the state of soils. Continental rocks are of varied chemical composition; on exposure to the atmosphere, they disintegrate or weather into different mixtures of mineral matter combined with decayed matter from plants and animals. The close inter-relationship between soils and climate, vegetation, landforms, and rock type is well known, and this knowledge has helped us develop crops which can be grown successfully in different soils. Again, however, we are confronted with lands that become transformed as soils are overused and exploited, losing their productive capacity and causing populations to decline and migrate.

Landscapes derived from the changing yet distinctive combinations of these biophysical factors constitute part of the human inheritance. Increasingly, we are recognizing our responsibility towards the management or stewardship of this heritage.

EVOLUTION OF THE EARTH

Earth is believed to have developed, along with the rest of the solar system, some 4,500 to 5,000 million years ago, when whirling dust aggregated to form the Sun and the planets. In the process, Earth may have attracted a primordial gaseous atmosphere around itself. The planet was then dominated by volcanic eruptions pouring out gases, including water vapor, onto its surface.

These gases gave rise to Earth's present atmosphere. As Earth's surface cooled, the water vapor condensed to form oceans. The oxygen content of the atmosphere was built up through photosynthesis by primitive life forms. Earth's plant life, through photosynthesis, gives off oxygen, which is then available to help sustain animals, including humans.

Earth's average density is about 5.5 g/cu cm (3.2 oz/cu in), but this is not uniformly distributed. Earth is formed of concentric layers, the innermost layers having the greatest densities. The density of Earth's crust is only about 2.7 g/cu cm (1.6 oz/cu in), about half its average density; the highest densities (around 12.5 g/cu cm—7.2 oz/cu in) lie at the planet's core, which is believed to consist of iron and nickel, both of which are dense materials.

The surface of Earth

When compared to its diameter, Earth's crust is very thin—only 5 to 40 km (3 to 25 miles). Much of Earth's surface is covered by water bodies, such as oceans, inland seas, lakes, and rivers, and these constitute the hydrosphere. The atmosphere and the hydrosphere together sustain plants and animals, which form the biosphere.

Earth's crust is cool on the surface, with temperatures in most cases not exceeding 30°C (86°F), but its deepest parts have temperatures as high as 1,100°C (2,010°F). The material of which the crust is composed can be divided into light continental material and heavier oceanic material. Light continental material has a density of 2.7 gm/cu cm (1.6 oz/cu in), and is often granitic. Heavier oceanic material has a density of 3.0 gm/cu cm (1.7 oz/cu in), and is mostly basaltic.

The thickness of Earth's crust is very variable; it is much thicker under the continents (an average of 40 km [25 miles]) and much thinner under the oceans (an average of 5 km [3 miles]). The crust is thickest below young, folded mountains such as the Alps and the Himalayas. In places such as these, it can be as thick as 64 km (40 miles).

Below Earth's crust

Below Earth's surface lie the mantle and the core. The mantle is a thick, mostly solid layer. It is about 2,895 km (1,800 miles) thick, with temperatures ranging from 1,100°–3,600°C (2,010°–6,510°F). The upper mantle is about 670 km (420 miles) thick and contains pockets of molten material. In some places, this molten material finds its way to Earth's surface through fractures, causing volcanic eruptions such as those along the mid-oceanic ridges or in isolated hot spots. A feature of the upper mantle is the low-velocity zone, as defined by the decrease in seismic waves penetrating through the Earth. The rock here is near or at its melting

The core of Earth is made of solid iron, and has a temperature of 4,000°C (7,230°F). This is surrounded by liquid iron, and it is this layer that generates Earth's magnetic field. Above this is the mantle, made of rocks. This is topped by Earth's crust, which is made of lighter rocks.

Crust

Mantle

Outer Core

Inner Core

point, and forms material known as "hot slush", which is capable of motion or flow. It is a mobile layer, over which crustal plates can move. In contrast to this, the much thicker lower mantle (2,230 km; 1,385 miles) is entirely solid.

Earth's core is divided into an outer liquid core (2,250 km; 1,400 miles thick) and an inner solid core (1,255 km; 780 miles thick). The outer core has temperatures ranging between 3,600°C (6,510°F) and 4,200°C (7,590°C). Its liquid nature has been deduced from earthquake information.

Earthquakes transmit seismic P- and S-waves. S-waves cannot pass through liquid layers and are therefore deflected from Earth's core. In contrast, P-waves, which can be transmitted through liquids, pass through the liquid outer layer and eventually emerge on the other side of Earth.

Above Earth's surface

Earth's present atmosphere and water make it unique amongst the other planets of the solar system. The atmosphere, however, has undergone many changes in its long history. If Earth still had an atmosphere of primordial gases, that atmosphere would resemble the gaseous mix which occurs elsewhere in the solar system. This mixture contains an abundance of hydrogen and helium, as well as of carbon.

These gases, however, occur in very small amounts in Earth's present atmosphere. It is very likely that those primordial gases were lost from Earth's atmosphere and that a secondary atmosphere developed around the planet from gases emitted by volcanoes and produced by chemical and biological processes.

It is significant that the elements which form Earth's atmosphere are also found in its crust and thus an exchange between the two can take place. For example, carbon occurs in carbon dioxide in the atmosphere and in the oceans, in calcium carbonate in limestones, and in organic compounds in plant and animal life. Both carbon dioxide and oxygen form part of the cyclic process that involves photosynthesis by plants and respiration by animals. Oxygen was actually absent or present only in very small amounts in

Active volcanoes, such as Volcan de Pacaya, in Guatemala (left) generally occur along fault lines between plates or along mid-oceanic ridges. Molten lava bursts through the Earth's crust and flows downwards, sometimes causing great loss of life and the destruction of entire towns.

Earth's early atmosphere, but became abundant much later. The abundance of plant life that had developed by about 400 million years ago must have boosted oxygen supplies to their current level in Earth's atmosphere. It now seems that oxygen levels which could sustain animal life may possibly have existed as early as some 700 million years ago.

The atmosphere, which rises above Earth's surface to 100 km (60 miles), is mainly made up of nitrogen (78 percent) and oxygen (21 percent), with the remaining 1 percent made up of small quantities of carbon dioxide (0.04 percent), hydrogen, water vapor, and various other gases such as argon. The atmosphere has a layered structure: the densest layers lie close to Earth's surface and the atmosphere becomes more and more rarefied as one moves upwards.

The layer of most concern to us is the troposphere. It is about 12 km (7.5 miles) thick, and contains 75 percent of all the atmospheric gases, including those essential for life. It is within this layer that all our weather occurs. The temperature falls as one rises in this layer.

The stratosphere lies above the troposphere and is about 40 km (25 miles) thick. It contains a narrow layer of ozone molecules. This ozone layer protects life on Earth by shielding it from harmful ultraviolet radiation from the Sun. This ozone layer is under threat from the emission of chemicals produced by human activities—especially chlorofluorocarbons (CFCs), which have been used in aerosol cans and refrigerators. When chlorine is released from CFCs, it rises to the ozone layer and destroys ozone molecules.

In 1985, a large hole (7.7 million square km; 3 million square miles) was discovered in the ozone layer over Antarctica. The depletion of ozone in the area where the hole is has been linked to the increase in skin cancers, especially in Australia. Damage to the ozone layer implies that human impact reaches out 15 to 55 km (9 to 35 miles) into the atmosphere. Worldwide concern about ozone depletion has led to government action; there are now international agreements relating to phasing out the use of CFCs.

Human contribution to Earth's evolution

The changes in the composition of Earth's atmosphere, and the damage to the ozone layer, vividly demonstrate that since the advent of industrialization, humans have had considerable impact on Earth's environment and, as a consequence, on its biosphere. Many of these adverse effects were not foreseen.

It is becoming increasingly clear that human behavior can have far-reaching consequences; not only on our own local environment, but on the entire evolution of Earth. Therefore, all proposed industrial, agricultural, and other developments need to be carefully evaluated in terms of their impact on the environment before they are approved and implemented.

The gaseous mix of the troposphere has also been inadvertently altered by humans, particularly since the acceleration of industrialization in the nineteenth century. The principal change is the increase of carbon dioxide due to emissions from the burning of fossil fuels (coal, natural gas, and petroleum) by factories, power plants, railway engines, and automobiles.

Although carbon dioxide forms only about 0.04 percent of Earth's atmosphere, it is a critical component because, along with the other greenhouse gases, it acts as a blanket, trapping some of the heat of the Earth that would otherwise escape into space.

The emission of carbon dioxide and other gases (methane, nitrous oxide, and ozone) is believed to have caused global warming—the greenhouse effect. Global temperatures have risen by 0.3°C to 0.6°C (32.5°F to 33.1°F) since the mid-nineteenth century and, at the current rate of increase of greenhouse gases, this figure could double by the middle of the twenty-first century. Some predictions place the increase at between 1.5°C (34.7°F) and 5.5°C (41.9°F).

The weather patterns in the world have shown great disturbance in recent decades, according to some observers. This also is being attributed to the greenhouse effect. If global warming continues, it could result in the melting of polar ice sheets and the consequent rising of sea levels, which in turn would seriously threaten low-lying areas, including quite a number of major coastal cities.

The troposphere is the layer of the atmosphere where life exists. The stratosphere is the next layer. The ozone layer, which absorbs most of the Sun's harmful ultraviolet rays, is in the stratosphere. The next layer is the mesosphere. The thermosphere is the outer layer of our atmosphere. Gases are very thin here, and this is where auroras and meteors are seen. The red line shows the decreases and increases in temperature through each layer of the atmosphere.

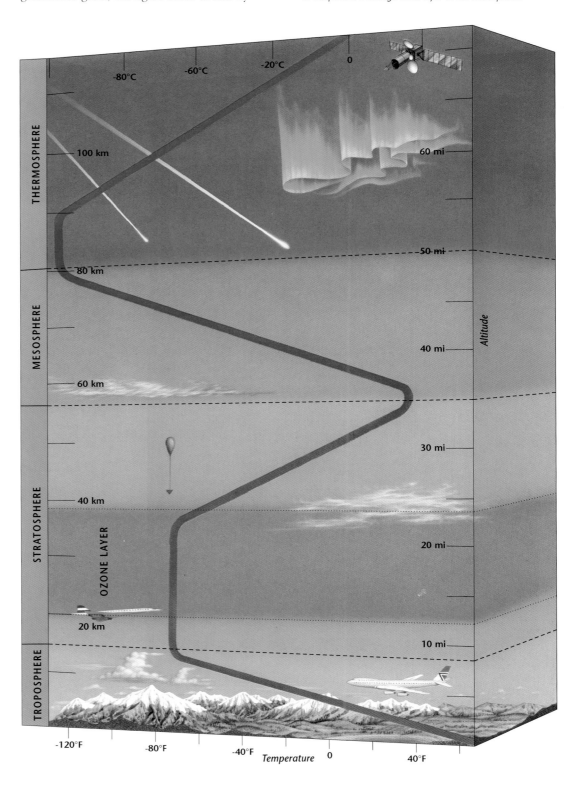

MOVEMENT OF PLATES

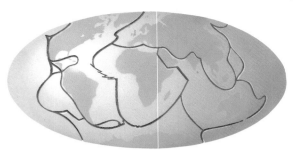

arth is a dynamic planet, and forces within it are continuously active. Continents and oceans have changed in position and shape over time. Earthquakes and other evidence prove that Earth's crust, which is a solid and rigid layer, is broken up into parts called lithospheric or tectonic plates. Plate boundaries coincide with major earthquake zones, many of which also have volcanic chains along them. Seven major plates (Pacific, North American, South American, Eurasian, African, Indo-Australian, and Antarctic), and perhaps twice as many minor plates, have been identified.

Over many millions of years, crustal plates have moved considerably. They have separated (divergent plates), giving rise to oceans, collided (convergent plates), forming the world's highest mountains and the deep oceanic trenches, and slid past each other along fault lines. Thus Earth's crust has spread at divergent plate boundaries and contracted at convergent plate boundaries.

Divergent plate boundaries
In the middle of the Atlantic and Indian oceans, and in the eastern part of the Pacific Ocean, long rifts exist where molten material has risen to form undersea chains of volcanoes. This molten material originates from magma pockets within Earth's upper mantle, and crystallizes as basalt on cooling. These oceanic volcanic chains, called mid-oceanic ridges, form an interlinked system about 60,000 km (37,300 miles) long. In some places, the volcanoes have erupted above the water level, forming islands such as Iceland and the Azores.

Mid-oceanic ridges are not continuous features, but are fractured at several places, with parts being offset by transform faults. Shallow-focus earthquakes, recorded by sensitive instruments, occur frequently along mid-oceanic ridges.

Each time a new series of volcanic eruptions takes place, the existing ridge is split in two and the parts are pushed apart, spreading the sea floor. The corresponding parts of the early ridges are now far apart, on opposite sides of the current mid-oceanic ridge. The separated bands can be identified on the basis of their recorded magnetic directions and age. When the basaltic bands crystallized, Earth's magnetic direction at the time of formation was imprinted in them. Such data proves that Earth's magnetic direction has reversed many times during geological history.

Sea-floor spreading is believed to have produced the Atlantic and Indian oceans, and to have enlarged the Pacific Ocean. Plates move very slowly—on average, only about 2–5 cm ($^3/_4$–2 inches) per year—with the spreading of the Atlantic Ocean having taken about 65 million years. Some plates are separating much more quickly—the Nazca and Pacific plates move at about 18 cm (7 inches) per year.

Compared with the continental crust, which is more than 1,000 million years old, most of the oceanic crust (at less than 65 million years old) is geologically very young, the youngest parts being those that lie along the mid-oceanic ridges.

The Red Sea is an example of new sea-floor spreading, whilst the elongated Great Rift Valley in Africa, which extends for more than 2,890 km (1,800 miles), possibly represents new continental rifting and splitting. There are several centers of volcanic eruptions along the Rift Valley; to the north and south of Lake Kivu, for example.

Convergent plate boundaries
Crustal plates may split and diverge on one side, and collide with other plates on the opposite side, giving rise to volcanic chains and oceanic ridges.

Earth's crust is made up of rigid tectonic plates. Their movement, over millions of years, has determined the structure of our continents and oceans, the formation of mountains and volcanoes, and the distribution of earthquakes.

When plates collide, one plate slides under the other one in a process called subduction, the subducted plate being pushed deep into Earth's mantle. As a result of subduction, collision zones are marked by deep focus earthquakes, such as have occurred in recent times in Japan, Iran and Afghanistan. Subducted plates are dragged deep into the Earth, where they melt. This molten material later rises to form volcanoes.

The deep oceanic trenches lying parallel to the volcanic island arcs, which formed as a result of oceanic-to-oceanic plate collisions, are the deepest features on Earth's surface, ranging from 7,000 to 11,000 m (23,000 to 36,000 ft) deep. The Marianas Trench in the West Pacific is nearly 11,000 m (more than 35,000 ft) deep. There are several trenches in the western Pacific, along the coasts of Japan and the Philippines.

Where continental and oceanic plates collide, the continental plate is crumpled and the oceanic plate buckles downward deep into Earth, where it melts and mixes with the molten material inside the Earth. Lavas from this mixed molten material are lighter in density and color than oceanic basalt. The rock formed is andesite and it is found along a long chain around the Pacific Ocean.

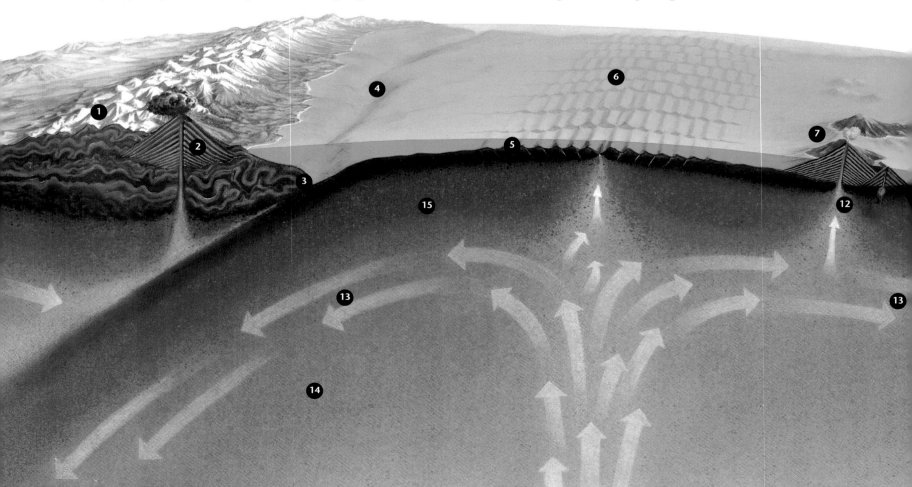

A panoramic view of the Himalayas, the world's highest mountain range (left). The Himalayas are actually made up of three ranges, formed at different times. The koala (below), unique to Australia, may be an animal that became isolated after the break-up of the supercontinent Gondwanaland.

Several plates have collided with the Pacific Plate, giving rise to folded mountain chains, including the Cascade Range in the western USA, and the Andes in South America. This circum-Pacific zone is often referred to as the "Ring of Fire" because of the presence of active volcanoes.

Continent-to-continent plate collisions result in the formation of mountain ranges such as the European Alps and the Himalayas, in Asia. The process gives rise to crustal thickening.

The stupendous Himalayan range arose when the Indo-Australian Plate collided with the Eurasian Plate. The Eurasian Plate rode over the Indian side, pushing up huge sedimentary strata from the then-existing sea into great mountain folds, some of which were thrust towards the south and almost overturned.

Three parallel ranges were formed in successive geological epochs. The southernmost chain is the lowest, ranging from 900 to 1,200 m (2,950 to 3,935 ft) in height, whilst the middle chain rises 2,000 to 4,500 m (6,560 to 14,765 ft).

The chain of highest elevation, lying in the north, has the world's highest peaks (topped by Mount Everest, at 8,848 m [29,028 ft]), which are about 8,500 m (27,885 ft) in height. Its average altitude is 6,000 m (19,685 ft). It adjoins the high Tibetan Plateau, which has an average altitude of 4,000 m (13,125 ft).

Transform fault boundaries

The third type of plate boundary involves two plates sliding past each other along a fault line. There is no collision or separation involved, but earthquakes result from the movement of these plates. The best-known example of this is the San Andreas Fault in California, which has been associated with major earthquakes in San Francisco and Los Angeles. Along that fault line, the Pacific Plate is sliding northwards in relation to the adjacent North American Plate.

Continental drift

It was in 1922 that Alfred Wegener first expounded his theory that the continents had drifted to their present positions. His hypothesis centered on the close jigsaw fit of Africa and South America. The English philosopher and essayist Francis Bacon had drawn attention to this much earlier and, in 1858, so did Snider-Pellegrini, who pointed to the similarities in the characteristics of plant fossils in coal deposits found in both continents.

Wegener marshalled evidence to show that the fit involved the juxtaposition of river valleys, mountain chains, and similar rock formations and mineral deposits. Those rock formations contained similar fossils. Wegener hypothesized that all the continents once formed a single landmass, which he named Pangaea, and which, he claimed, began breaking up in the Carboniferous Period (divided into the Pennsylvanian and Mississipian epochs in the United States) about 300 million years ago. That split first resulted in two continents: a northern one

called Laurasia and a southern one called Gondwanaland. The various supposed parts of the southern continent (South America, Africa, India, Australia, and Antarctica) showed a much better geological fit than did the supposed parts of the northern one.

Wegener's theory was based on the premise that the light continents floated on a denser underlying crust, and that these continents thus drifted to their present positions. The absence of an acceptable mechanism for drifting was used as an argument against Wegener's ideas—it was thought physically impossible that the solid continents could have moved through an underlying rigid, denser layer.

Nevertheless, many scientists were inclined to accept that the continents had moved to their present positions because there was mounting geological evidence, such as that marshalled by Alex du Toit of South Africa, which proved similarities in areas which had been said to have once been joined together.

During the past 50 years, modern technology has provided much new information about the sea floors. In particular, evidence has emerged leading to the acceptance of sea-floor spreading. This, in turn, has led to the development of plate tectonics, which may be considered an update of Wegener's ideas about continental movement. As a result, his main ideas about the original juxtaposition of the continents have now been largely vindicated.

The processes and results of plate movement:
1. Fold mountains 2. Active volcano 3. Subduction zone 4. Subduction trench 5. Spreading sea-floor 6. Mid-oceanic ridge 7. Hot spot island chain (volcanic) 8. Oceanic crust 9. Colliding plates form mountain chain 10. Fold mountains 11. Rift valley 12. Hot spot 13. Magma (convection currents) 14. Asthenosphere 15. Lithosphere

ROCKS

Earth's crust consists of rocks. These rocks combine a variety of minerals that may or may not be crystalline, and which can form in several ways. Igneous rocks are made of crystalline minerals which originate during the cooling of molten material called magma. In contrast, sedimentary rocks result from the compaction or consolidation of loosened minerals, rock fragments, and plant and animal matter. Metamorphic rocks are formed when existing rocks are altered through pressure and temperature—they result either from compaction under pressure or from partial remelting, when new minerals can be formed from crystallization.

Minerals

Minerals are inorganic substances with defined chemical and atomic structures. When magmas cool, minerals crystallize. Each mineral exhibits its own unique crystalline shape. Minerals can also originate in the breakdown of pre-existing

minerals, as in the case of clays, or from the reconstitution of existing materials, as in the case of metamorphic rocks.

A common mineral is quartz (an oxide of silica), which occurs as large crystals in some rocks and as sand on sea shores. It is a light-colored mineral. Other light-colored minerals include felspars, which are silicates combining silica, aluminum, potassium, sodium, and calcium. These light-colored minerals are commonly found in rocks of light density, such as granite. Dark-colored silicates, which are combinations of silica, magnesium, and iron (pyroxenes, amphiboles, olivine, and dark micas), predominate in dark-colored rocks such as basalt.

Igneous rocks

When molten material lying deep within Earth's crust cools, minerals form large crystals, because of slow cooling, producing plutonic igneous rocks. The most common plutonic rock is granite, which is also the rock that is most widespread in the continental crust. Granite is light colored and low in density because it contains silica and felspars.

When magma is extruded onto the Earth's surface as lava, faster cooling takes place, resulting in smaller crystals, even glass. The most common volcanic rock is basalt, which is dark colored and dense because of dark-colored minerals such as biotite, pyroxenes, amphiboles, and olivine. The ocean floors are largely made up of basalt.

Large pockets of magma inside the crust give rise to large rock bodies called batholiths, which are mostly made of granite and are often found in great mountain ranges. Smaller igneous intrusions may form in cracks and joints in other rocks. When these intrusions cut through sedimentary strata, they are called dikes; intrusions between the bedding planes of strata are known as sills.

The vapors emanating from igneous intrusions often crystallize in neighboring rocks as valuable minerals—gold, silver, copper, lead, and zinc. Such deposits are found in recent geological formations such as those around the Pacific "Ring of Fire," as well as in more ancient rocks such as those near the Kalgoorlie goldfields of Western Australia. A rare igneous rock called kimberlite, which occurs in pipe-like shapes, contains diamond deposits such as those found in South Africa.

Sedimentary rocks

Sedimentary rocks can be made up of either organic or inorganic particles. Organic sediments are the remains of plants and animals—one example of a sedimentary rock made up of plant

remains is coal. Large deposits of limestone are mostly the result of the precipitation of calcium carbonate, but can also be the result of the agglomeration, or clustering, of sea shell fragments and the building of coral reefs. Inorganic sedimentary rocks include those made up of sand (sandstone), clays (shale), or pebbles cemented together (conglomerate).

Sedimentary strata deposited in large basins like the sea sometimes become exposed through vertical uplift, in which case the strata may remain horizontal. When strata are folded in the process of mountain formation, however, they form complex structures such as anticlines (dome-shaped folds) and synclines (basin-shaped folds). Anticlines have often become reservoirs for petroleum, while basin-type structures can often contain artesian water.

Several valuable minerals are found in sedimentary rocks: iron ores; oxides of aluminum (bauxite); and manganese. Coal deposits are sedimentary accumulations of transformed ancient forests. Building materials such as sandstones and materials for producing cement and fertilizers also come from sedimentary rocks.

Metamorphic rocks

When sedimentary rocks are subjected to high pressure they alter to become metamorphic rocks. Thus shale is converted to the more solid slate, sandstone to the very hard rock called quartzite and limestone to the crystallized rock known as marble. The presence of chemical impurities in limestone can result in marbles of a variety of colors and patterns.

When sedimentary and igneous rocks are subjected to high pressure as well

Era	Major geological events	Period	Millions of years ago
CENOZOIC	• Ice age • First humans	Quaternary	
CENOZOIC			1.6
CENOZOIC	• Rockies, Alps and Himalayas begin to form • First hominids	Tertiary	
			65
MESOZOIC	• First flowering plants • Extinction of giant reptiles	Cretaceous	
			145
MESOZOIC	• Pangaea splits into Gondwanaland and Laurasia • First birds and mammals	Jurassic	
			208
MESOZOIC	• First dinosaurs • Supercontinent of Pangaea in existence	Triassic	
			245
PALEOZOIC	• First amphibians	Permian	
			288
PALEOZOIC	• Extensive forests which later formed coal deposits	Carboniferous	
			360
PALEOZOIC		Devonian	408
PALEOZOIC	• First land plants	Silurian	438
PALEOZOIC		Ordovician	
			508
PALEOZOIC	• Age of the trilobites, the first complex animals, which had hard shells and were marine	Cambrian	570
PRE-CAMBRIAN	• Oldest rocks on Earth's crust identified • First life forms: single cell forms like bacteria and algae • Continents and oceans formed • Extensive sedimentary rocks like iron ore deposits were laid down		4,560

The Grand Canyon, USA (right), with a color-coded strip added (see geological time scale, left) to illustrate the geological history of the area. The diagram shows geological eras from the origin of Earth (4,560 million years ago) until the Cenozoic Era, which began 65 million years ago.

An area of the East Sussex, United Kingdom, coast known as the Seven Sisters (far left) consists primarily of limestone, a sedimentary rock. The banded boulders (left) in the Canadian Rockies, and the Waitomo Caves in the North Island, New Zealand (below), are also limestone; its appearance depends on the depositional environment in which it formed.

as high temperature, partial melting can take place. This partially remelted material gives rise to crystalline metamorphic rocks called schist and gneiss. Gneiss resembles granite in appearance, but it generally has a layered structure. Schists are made of platy minerals, including micas.

Large igneous intrusions often change the rocks into which they intrude to metamorphic rocks through the effects of the heat and the gases that they carry. Batholiths, the largest igneous intrusions, have created metamorphic aureoles in contact zones such as are found in the Alps.

Two important building materials, slate and marble, are metamorphic rocks. Other commercially valuable metamorphic mineral deposits include talc (used for cosmetics) and graphite (used for making pencils).

The rock cycle

In recent years, the concept of the rock cycle has proven useful. It represents the continuous recycling of rock materials and their conversion into different rock types, and helps link the various kinds of rocks found on Earth's surface.

When igneous rocks are exposed on the surface of Earth, they become weathered. Solar radiation, running water, ice, wind, and waves all weather rocks mechanically. Water acidified through the absorption of carbon dioxide and organic acids weathers rocks chemically. Over a long period, mechanical and chemical weathering produces pebbles, sands, and clays, which often consolidate into sedimentary rocks.

When these rocks are then dragged deep into Earth's crust by the process of plate subduction, they enter zones of very high pressure and temperature, resulting in partial melting and producing crystalline metamorphic rocks. If the rocks are carried still deeper into the Earth, however, where the

temperatures are high enough to melt the rocks completely, a new magma is formed. This new magma may either crystallize deep inside Earth and form new plutonic igneous rocks, or be extruded as volcanic lavas.

Where volcanoes have erupted along zones of plate subduction, a rock named andesite has formed from lavas; this rock is a mixture of dark- and light-colored minerals, as it reflects the mixing of light continental and dark oceanic materials.

LANDFORMS

Earth's surface is constantly being transformed by falling rain, glaciers, rivers, underground water, wind, and waves. These constantly erode the land, transporting debris and depositing it elsewhere. The land is moulded into new forms through erosion, and new landforms are also created by the deposition of eroded debris.

Rainfall and water flow in creeks and rivers are the main agents of landform creation in humid areas; glaciers are the most important agents at high latitudes and in mountainous areas of heavy snowfall; and wind is important in arid areas.

Landforms of erosion

Glaciers, rivers, winds, and waves are powerful erosive agents. Glaciers pluck pieces of rock from valley sides, rivers carry rock fragments along in their current, and winds lift and transport particles of dust. Air and water velocities determine the erosive force of winds and rivers, and the rock fragments they carry with them make these agents additionally abrasive.

Rock fragments embedded in glaciers scour rock surfaces on the glacier's floor and sides; sand and gravel in fast-flowing rivers erode their floors and banks; and wind-borne sand blasts rock surfaces, creating intricate structures. Platforms, caves, and cliffs are formed by the action of waves carrying sand, pebbles and boulders and beating them against rocky coasts.

Rivers in mountainous areas flow rapidly because of steep slope gradients. Such streams may be highly erosive, and may cut their channels vertically, producing V-shaped valley profiles.

Glaciers are made of solid ice, and result from the compaction of snow. Some of the longest

The following features are those typically found in glacial areas, showing the close interconnection between current landforms and past glaciers: 1. Cirque basin 2. Hanging valley in a glacial trough 3. Outwash plain from glacial meltwater 4. Terminal moraine of a valley glacier 5. Lateral moraine 6. Medial moraine 7. Ground moraine 8. Arête or sharp-crested ridge 9. Horn or sharp peak

glaciers remaining, at 39 to 73 km (24 to 46 miles) in length, are found in the Karakoram ranges in the Himalayas. Although they generally move very slowly (2 to 3 cm [3/4 to 11/4 inches] per day), glaciers are powerful eroders, and can move 4 to 5 m (13 to 161/2 ft) a day.

Glaciers typically create U-shaped valleys called troughs. Glaciers at the head of sloping valleys give rise to basin-shaped features known as cirques. When cirques from two opposing sides meet through erosion, a pass, or col, is formed. Between glacial valleys, sharp ridges, known as arêtes, develop. At the top of glacial mountains, arêtes meet at sharp peaks called horns, such as those on the Matterhorn and Mt Everest.

Where glaciers have disappeared, troughs are exposed, along with tributary glacial valleys, and these form hanging valleys perched above scarps. They often have streams cascading over them as waterfalls, and are often used as sites for the generation of hydroelectric power.

Depending on their velocity, winds can lift loose rock particles or soils. Generally speaking, the wind transports particles which are dry and not protected by plant cover—so wind action is mostly restricted to arid and semiarid regions, and some coastal areas. Strong winds can scoop out hollows in loose, dry soil. This process is known as deflation, and the hollows formed are called blowouts. These can range in diameter from about a meter to a kilometer or more.

When waves approach a coastline made up of headlands and bays, they gather around the headlands and spread out in the bays. Wave energy becomes concentrated on the headlands, where the steady pounding carves platforms and cliffs. In bays, by contrast, wave energy is dissipated, and the waves deposit sand and other detritus. These may also be transported along the shore, depending on the angle of the coast in relation to the direction of the waves.

Rock debris—such as loose, unsupported material and waterlogged soil—tends to move down hill slopes through the action of gravity.

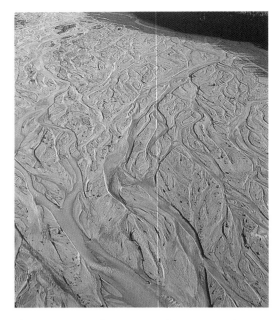

Slow movements known as soil creep are often imperceptible, and are indicated only by the changed position of fixed objects—trees, fences, and houses. The shaking of sloping ground by earthquakes can trigger a more rapid movement of loose materials. Fast movements such as landslides (or snow avalanches) tend to occur after heavy rains (or snowfalls) on steep slopes. In contrast to landslides, slumps are formed when slopes slip in a backward rotation, a phenomenon sometimes found in waterlogged soils.

Transportation and deposition of rock debris

The debris resulting from erosion is transported by glaciers, rivers, winds, and waves. A glacier carries assorted rock debris (boulders, pebbles, or finer materials) on or beneath its solid surface.

As a glacier moves, it plucks rocks from the valley walls, and the rock debris falls along the sides of the glacier to form what are known as lateral moraines. When two glaciers meet and coalesce, two lateral moraines join in the center of the new, larger glacier, forming a medial moraine.

As mountain glaciers reach lower, warmer levels, they melt and drop their debris, which forms terminal moraines. The resulting meltwater carries a fine glacial flour, which may be spread as a vast depositional plain. Rich soils have

An aerial view of a braided river channel showing the build up of sediment on the river bed (far left), and a coastline dramatically eroded by wave action (left). The cirque (below) shows typically steep walls—carved by the movement of glacial ice—and a flat floor.

developed in such plains in both northern Europe and the northern United States.

The amount of rock particle rivers and winds carry is determined by velocity; in general, larger particle sizes need greater velocities. At lower speeds, rivers deposit their sediment load, which then forms fertile alluvial flats and broad alluvial plains. These areas may be periodically inundated by floods. Much of the sediment carried by rivers in flood is deposited at the coast as deltas. Several major rivers carry high sediment loads—the Huang River in China carries more than one and a half million tonnes annually.

Wind

Other landforms result from wind. Strong winds can lift and carry sands, while lighter winds lift and carry silts and clays. High winds rework sand masses into dunes of various types, depending on sand availability and wind direction. Sand dunes in deserts include crescent-shaped barchans, which have gentle windward slopes and abrupt leeward slopes—the crescent's horns point downwind. Silt-sized particles are transported by the wind to form thick, fertile deposits known as loess. Extensive deposits of loess are found on the edges of some deserts and in areas once glaciated (northern China and the Mississippi Valley, for instance).

Waves

Waves tend to approach a beach perpendicularly. The movement of the wave as it runs onto the beach is known as swash; the water, or backwash, then returns to the sea. Swash and backwash move sand along beaches, which contributes to littoral or longshore drift (when waves approach the beach at an angle). Along coastal plains, waves tend to build sand barriers by the shore. Lagoons develop behind these barriers, which are connected to the sea by tidal inlets. These lagoons can later fill with sediment, a stage in the gradual seaward extension of the coastal plain. The sea-level rise, on the other hand, along with storm wave erosion, can drive the sand barriers landward.

During the next several decades, because of global warming, the sea level may rise at rates up to 100 mm (4 inches) per year. This would cause the loss of sand barriers and adjacent lagoons and wetlands, and the loss of some islands on coral reefs.

CLIMATE

Just as weather is the day-to-day condition of the atmosphere, climate consists of the long-term average of weather conditions, including seasonal and year-to-year variability, and extremes. Many distinctive climatic types can be identified. These vary with regard to incoming solar radiation, temperature, wind, precipitation (rainfall and snowfall), evaporation, storms (type, frequency and magnitude), and seasonal patterns.

Solar radiation

Solar radiation (insolation) is received unequally in different parts of Earth. The equatorial belt receives strong solar radiation uniformly throughout the year, whilst places close to the poles, in contrast, have great differences between summer and winter solar radiation; perpetual ice climates exist at the poles. Along the equator, the lands are warm throughout the year, but, in the latitudes further away from the equator, seasonal variations become more discernible, with marked differences in the temperate zone.

General atmospheric circulation

The large amount of heat received at the equator means that air becomes heated and expands, and this air rises and flows towards the poles. Some of this air flows back to the equator in the form of trade winds as part of the Hadley Cell circulation. Flowing from the east, these winds are called easterlies. The subtropical belt (up to about 30° latitude), is the zone of large high-pressure cells from which winds move through more temperate latitudes towards the poles. Cold, dense air from the poles flows, as polar fronts, back through these latitudes towards the equator. These fronts clash with tropical air masses in the temperate

zones, giving give rise to cyclones (low-pressure cells), which bring inclement weather and rainy days. Such weather conditions are more common in the northern hemisphere, where there are extensive landmasses. In the southern hemisphere, in contrast, there are more extensive oceans. In that belt, between 40° latitude and Antarctica, a westerly wind blows eastward along an almost unbroken stretch of seas throughout the year.

Climatic types

Of the several proposed climatic classifications, the best known is that devised by Köppen, who divided climates broadly into five classes: A, B, C, D, and E. The humid climates are A, C, and D, with A being the warmest and lying in the tropics, C being found in the warm temperate regions, and D covering cold climates with regular winter snowfall. Arid climates, both tropical and temperate, are classed as B climates. Ice sheets are represented by E climates.

Humid tropical climates (A)

Type A climates are found between 25°N and 25°S latitudes. These humid tropical climates receive abundant rainfall and have year-round high temperatures, with the areas further away from the equator having hot summers and mild winters.

These areas favor the abundant growth of vegetation, particularly rainforest. This climatic belt has extensive agriculture and often large populations. Heavy rainfall and high temperatures, however, leach soils of their valuable nutrients, which is detrimental for agriculture.

A typical A climate is the tropical monsoon climate that is found in Southeast Asia. It is characterized by a distinct season of heavy rainfall,

Monsoon flooding in Vietnam (above). Monsoons are usually annual events, and deliver 85% of East Asia's annual rainfall, but can also cause devastation to low-lying areas.

preceded and followed by dry months; for example, large parts of India and Southeast Asia receive most of their rain between June and September, while March to May are typically dry months. Along the west coast of India, annual rainfall can be as high as 25,400 to 28,800 mm (9,900 to 1,123 inches).

Desert climates (B)

Deserts are found in subtropical and temperate zones, and are classified by Köppen as B-type climates. Being areas of low rainfall, deserts have either few plants, or only small plants that are particularly well suited to dry environments.

Hot deserts lie in the subtropics—in the belt extending from North Africa (the Sahara Desert) and the Middle East to northwestern India (the Thar Desert)—and in the Central Australian Desert. These deserts have high daily temperature ranges; it can be very hot during the day and quite cool at night. The Gobi Desert, which lies in central Asia, is the best-known cold desert.

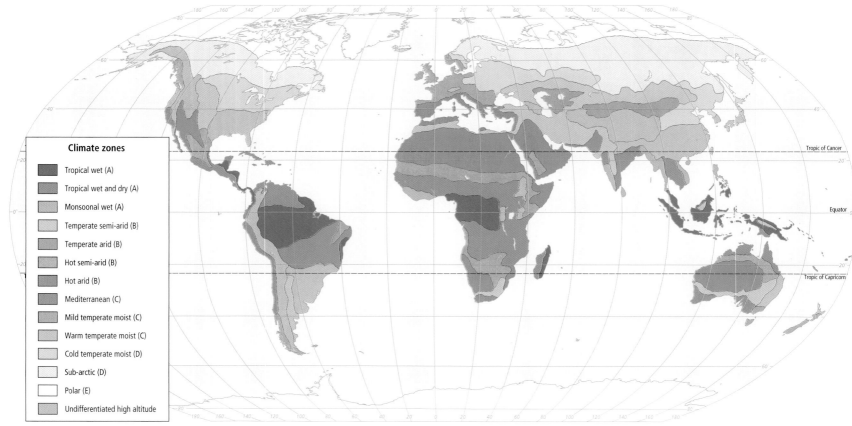

Climate zones

- Tropical wet (A)
- Tropical wet and dry (A)
- Monsoonal wet (A)
- Temperate semi-arid (B)
- Temperate arid (B)
- Hot semi-arid (B)
- Hot arid (B)
- Mediterranean (C)
- Mild temperate moist (C)
- Warm temperate moist (C)
- Cold temperate moist (D)
- Sub-arctic (D)
- Polar (E)
- Undifferentiated high altitude

Tropic of Cancer

Equator

Tropic of Capricorn

Projection: Robinson   Equatorial Scale approx 1:110 million

The Valley of the Moon, in the high-altitude Atacama Desert, Chile, said to be the driest desert on Earth (left). Lush mountainous terrain in Bolivia (below). An ice floe, with walrus, in Arctic Siberia (left, below). Productive agricultural land in a temperate zone—southern France (far left, below).

The Valley of the Moon, in the high-altitude Atacama Desert, Chile, said to be the driest desert on Earth (left). Lush mountainous terrain in Bolivia (below). An ice floe, with walrus, in Arctic Siberia (left, below). Productive agricultural land in a temperate zone—southern France (far left, below).

Humid temperate climates (C)

Type C climates lie between latitudes of 25° and 45°. They have marked seasonal variations, with temperature differences between summer and winter being quite large. The Mediterranean climate is a good example of a B climate; summer temperatures can on occasions soar to the mid-40s (110°F) in southern Greece and Italy, while winter temperatures can fall to 10°C (50°F). The Mediterranean climate is characterized by cold, wet winters and hot, dry summers.

The temperate zone close to the tropics (25° to 35° latitudes) is warm. It is now common to find that belt referred to as the subtropics. The subtropical areas lying along the eastern sides of the continents are particularly warm, as they receive the warm easterly tropical winds, and warm ocean currents flow along their coasts. This east coast climate is found in southeast China, eastern Australia and South America.

In contrast, the westerlies in the higher latitudes (35° to 60° latitudes) give rise to a cooler west coast climate. Year-round rainfall and adequate temperatures promote the growth of forests in both east and west coast climates.

Grasslands generally occur in the continental interiors of C climate areas, where annual rainfall is moderate (300 to 400 mm; 12 to 16 in), and water in the soil is not abundant. These areas lie in the rainshadows of major mountain ranges. Seasonal temperature ranges are usually sizeable.

Cold temperate climates (D)

Moving into the temperate zone close to the poles, temperatures fall because there is reduced solar radiation. This is exacerbated by cold polar winds.

Polar winds are easterlies, although their directions can be variable in temperate latitudes. Such type D climates lie between 45° and 65° latitudes, and are only significant in the northern hemisphere—the equivalent belt in the southern hemisphere is mostly covered by the oceans.

The taiga climate is a good example of this climate; lying close to the Arctic polar region, the area is characterized by abundant snowfall and unique woodlands. Temperatures in winter commonly fall to –30°C (–22°F), and in some places can go as low as –40°C (–40°F). During midsummer, however, temperatures can rise to around 15°C (60°F) or higher.

Ice climates (E)

E-type climates are found between 65° and 90° latitudes, the principal examples being Antarctica and Greenland. These ice sheets cover about 10 percent of Earth's surface, and form an essential part of the system which regulates the global atmospheric circulation. These areas are subject to long periods of darkness, and temperatures rise above freezing level for only 2 to 4 months a year.

If global warming reduces the extent of these ice sheets, climatic conditions in the world will alter: ice melting would contribute to rises in sea level, with adverse effects on low-lying areas.

The El Niño phenomenon

Deviations from normal temperature patterns of the waters in the southern Pacific Ocean, between Australia and South America, result in the phenomenon called El Niño. Under normal conditions, eastern trade winds blow across the Pacific. These drive the sun-warmed surface water from the central Pacific to the coast off northern Australia. When clouds form above this area of warm water and move over Indonesia, Papua New Guinea, and Australia, they bring rain with them.

Every two to seven years, however, this pattern is interrupted by the El Niño event. During El Niño, the Pacific Ocean off Australia does not warm as much as it normally does. Instead, it becomes warmer right up to the coast of Peru in South America. At the same time, the easterly trade winds that blow across the Pacific reverse their direction. This causes high-pressure systems to build up to the north of and across the Australian continent, preventing moist tropical air reaching the continent. These conditions in turn result in storms, and in rain falling in the eastern Pacific Ocean and in South America instead of in Australia, Papua New Guinea, and Indonesia, which then suffer drought conditions.

While the effects of El Niño are sometimes weak, at other times they are very strong. During a severe El Niño period, extreme drought conditions prevail, as in 1982–83 and 1997–98. In contrast, heavy rainfall and flooding occurred in parts of North and South America. In 1997, there were severe storms and floods in Mexico and further north along the west coast of the United States.

The converse of the El Niño effect is the La Niña effect, which is an exaggeration of normal conditions. This takes place when trade winds blow strongly and consistently across the Pacific towards Australia. This pushes the warm waters from the central Pacific, off the northern Australian coast, to build up into a mass that is bigger than normal. Thus, much more cloud develops than usual, and this brings considerably more rain to Australia and neighboring countries.

THE WATER CYCLE

The Arrigetch peaks and glacier, in Alaska (above). Water is released as steam into the atmosphere from electric power plants (right). A hot water artesian bore (far right).

Earth, in contrast to all the other planets in the solar system, has an abundant supply of water. Much of this, of course, lies in the oceans and seas (more than 97 percent), and is saline. The polar ice caps lock up slightly more than 2 percent of the remaining water, leaving less than 1 percent of fresh water to sustain life on Earth. Human needs are met by the water from rainfall, rivers, and underground supplies (plus a small amount from desalination plants).

Water falls as rain and snow, and flows as rivers and glaciers before ultimately reaching the sea. It also sinks into the ground to form underground water reservoirs, to emerge as springs or to seep into river water. Fresh supplies of water are continuously needed and nature provides this supply through the water cycle.

How the water cycle works

Solar energy evaporates exposed water from seas, lakes, rivers, and wet soils; the majority of this evaporation takes place over the seas. Water is also released into the atmosphere by plants through photosynthesis. During this process, known as evapotranspiration, water vapor rises into the atmosphere.

Clouds form when air becomes saturated with water vapor. The two major types of cloud formations are a stratified or layered gray cloud called stratus, and a billowing white or dark gray cloud called cumulus. Nimbostratus clouds and cumulonimbus clouds are the cloud types that are associated with rainy weather; nimbostratus clouds will bring steady rain, and cumulonimbus clouds will bring stormy weather.

Precipitation as rain, snow, or hail ensures that water returns to Earth's surface in a fresh form. Some of this rain, however, falls into the seas and is not accessible to humans. When rain falls, it either washes down hill slopes or seeps underground; when snow and hail melt, this water may also sink into the ground.

Rainfall also replenishes river water supplies, as does underground water. Snowfall may consolidate into glaciers and ice sheets which, when they melt, release their water into the ground, into streams, or into the seas.

Water in river courses

Rivers pass through several phases on their journey from hilly and mountainous areas to the seas and oceans. In their early phases—that is, close to their sources in the hills and mountains—they have steep slope gradients and, therefore, move with high velocities. They carry rock fragments and have high erosive force.

In these areas, the energy from these streams provides the potential for hydroelectric development. This potential has been harnessed in many places, such as in the foothills of the Himalayas in Nepal.

On flat plains, rivers tend to wind their way in meandering courses. Here, the water flow has now lost most of its erosive capacity. Massive clay deposits may also give rise to fertile alluvial plains. During times of heavy rainfall, flooding can take place, and this is a serious issue along some of the major rivers of the world, such as the Mississippi in the United States, the Yangtze in China and the Ganges in India.

Human interference in the water cycle

There has been considerable human interference in the water cycle throughout recorded history, but far more so since the beginning of the twentieth century. For centuries, humans have built dams across rivers to store water, which is then used for irrigation, or for domestic or industrial water supply. Dams have also been built to control river flooding, such as across the Huang River in China, and to produce electricity.

The Aswan Dam across the Nile provides arid Egypt with essential water. The two highest dams in the world, more than 300 m (985 ft) in height, have been built across the Vakhsh River in Tajikistan. The dam with by far the largest reservoir capacity—2,700 million cubic meters (3,530 million cubic yards)—is the Owen Falls Dam, across the Nile, in Uganda.

Hydroelectric power is generated in several parts of the world, such as at Itaipu, across the Parana River, in Brazil—this dam can generate

Artesian wells

When rain falls, some of it sinks into the ground and is held in the soil—this water is known as ground water. A layer under the ground becomes saturated with this seeped water; the surface of this layer is called the water table. Wells are mostly dug to tap water in the water table. There is another way, however, that water can seep under the ground to form water reservoirs. Some types of rock are porous, and this allows them to hold water; water can move through such permeable rock.

Sandstone is a permeable rock. If a sandstone bed is dipping at an angle, rainwater can penetrate the exposed part of the rock and travel along the stratum into the ground. The water will be retained by the sandstone layer if the rocks above and below it are impermeable. If this water reservoir lies well below the ground, it is held under pressure; if a well is bored to the reservoir, the water will gush out under this pressure. These reservoirs are called artesian wells. The permeable strata that carry the water are called aquifers; the

impermeable layers which lie above and below the aquifers are known as aquicludes.

Artesian waters are important where rainfall is low and water supplies uncertain. Overuse of artesian water can result in the ground sinking, and if the reservoir is close to the sea, excessive removal of water can allow saline water to penetrate the reservoir, reducing water quality.

12,600 megawatts of power. The building of dams in areas prone to earthquakes, such as Japan, however, causes great concern because of the potential for serious damage.

Water is necessary for agriculture, industry, and domestic use. Agriculture depends on rainfall, as well as on irrigation from stored water. The provision of water for domestic use—particularly the need for clean drinking water—has become very important with the spread of urbanization. Reservoirs are often built to ensure urban water supplies and water is purified before being channelled to consumers.

The discharge of industrial, agricultural, and domestic effluents into streams and lakes (especially in the twentieth century) has reduced water quality and damaged aquatic life. These effluents include metallic substances. One of the most dramatic examples has been the discharge of mercury into rivers in Japan. This mercury has now entered the food chain through fish, creating serious health problems. The discharge of

pesticides has also been detrimental to aquatic life, and excessive use of fertilizers, along with salts released into rivers and lakes by poor land use practices, have also altered the ecological balance.

Changes in air quality brought about by humans have also affected the water cycle. The use of fossil fuels to generate electricity and power transport has resulted in substantial sulfur dioxide and nitrogen oxide emissions. When these gases and water react, sulfuric and nitric acids are produced. These pollutants are present in clouds and fog, and fall with rain and snow as acid rain. A pH value of 5 in water is acidic enough to damage aquatic life.

This acid rain phenomenon is most likely to occur in dense industrial centers such as those in the United States, Canada, and Europe. The problem, however, is not confined to these areas, as winds blow polluting gases over long distances. Acids can become concentrated in still waters and threaten aquatic life. The entire ecology of affected lakes, including the natural food chains, can be very seriously harmed.

The water cycle (below): the sun heats water, which evaporates and rises into the atmosphere as water vapor, only to fall again later as rain and snow. The rain and snow then concentrate in rivers, or flow as ground water to the sea.

OCEANOGRAPHY

Earth is the only planet of the solar system with seas and oceans, and these cover more than 70 percent of its surface. The oceans lie in large and deep basins in Earth's crust. The seas, however, spread to the margins of the continents, drowning their shelves. The melting of the ice sheets following the end of the last ice age (about 15,000 years ago) resulted in a rise in sea levels and thus an increased area covered by seas.

Ocean currents

The waters of the oceans are in constant motion. This motion takes the form of ocean currents. These currents move at an average of 8 km (5 miles) per hour, and redistribute heat energy, thus influencing climate. Winds are the most important originators of ocean currents in the upper layers of the seas: they produce a frictional drag on the water which pushes it along.

As water is a fluid, it is subject to the Coriolis effect (caused by Earth's rotation)—that is, currents tend to move towards the right in the northern hemisphere and towards the left in the southern hemisphere. The resulting deflection is 45° to that of the direction of the wind. In the deeper parts of the oceans, it is water density that produces ocean

currents. Water density depends upon two factors: temperature and salinity. The colder the water is, the denser it is; and the higher the salinity, the higher the density. The circulation which results from temperature and salinity difference is referred to as thermo-haline circulation.

There are broadly two types of ocean current: warm currents, which originate in tropical areas; and cold currents, which originate in polar areas. Warm currents are mostly located in the upper 100 m (330 ft) of the seas. Cold currents, on the other hand, are often encountered at greater depths. They move more slowly because of the overlying pressure exerted by surface water. The exchange of heat energy occurs as equatorial currents move towards the poles and polar currents move towards the equator. This exchange moderates Earth's heat patterns, preventing the equatorial belt becoming unbearably hot and the waters in the temperate zone becoming much colder than they are today.

Ocean water temperatures are a major influence on climatic conditions; warm currents bring warmth to the coastlines along which they flow and, likewise, cold currents reduce temperatures in the lands along which they flow.

Warm tropical ocean currents

Winds blowing westward along the equatorial belt generate west-flowing ocean currents called equatorial currents. When water from the equatorial currents piles up against land, the current reverses its direction and flows eastward, resulting in equatorial counter currents.

Equatorial currents turn towards the right in the northern hemisphere and towards the left in the southern hemisphere as a result of the Coriolis

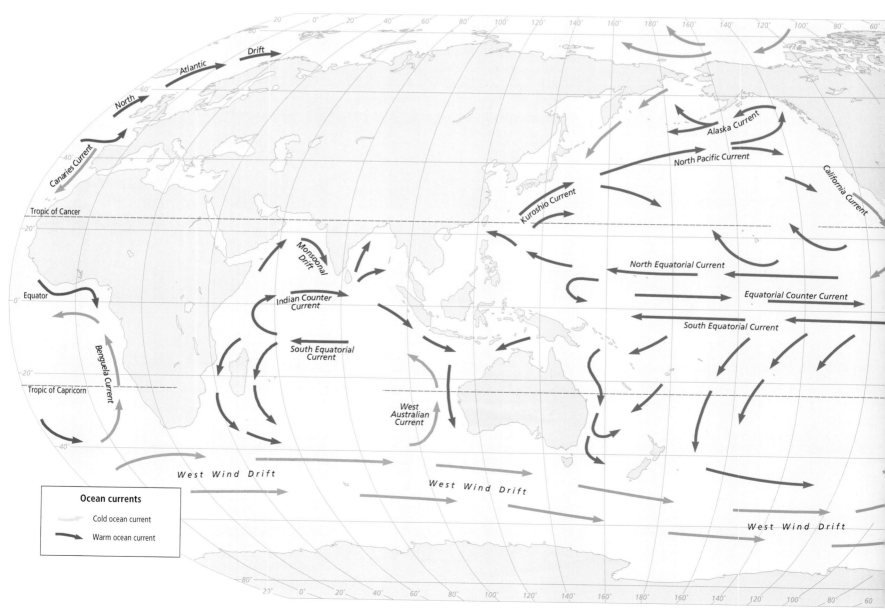

Ocean currents
- Cold ocean current
- Warm ocean current

Projection: Robinson   Equatorial Scale approx 1:110 million

A sea whip in the warm waters of the Indian Ocean (far left). Coral islands (left) are at risk if sea levels rise because of the greenhouse effect. Polar bears in Arctic Siberia (below) survive on the ice floes, which are broken off icebergs by strong currents and winds. The southern right whale (far below) feeds off aquatic life that thrives in the nutrient-rich Antarctic waters, which are now threatened by ozone depletion.

effect, and because of that motion, they develop into huge, circular, whorl-like rotating systems. These systems are known as gyres. Gyres rotate in a clockwise direction in the northern hemisphere and an anticlockwise direction in the southern hemisphere.

The distribution of the continental landmasses influences the size and shape of these gyres. There are major gyres in the northern and southern Atlantic and Pacific oceans, and in the southern Indian Ocean. There is also a gyre in the northern Indian Ocean, but it is restricted by the landmasses surrounding it, and so is much smaller.

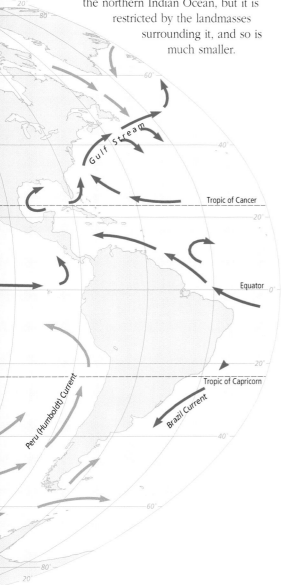

Gyres carry warm equatorial water into the temperate zone. These currents carry about 25 percent of all the heat that moves polewards from the equator. In the North Atlantic, the Gulf Stream or North Atlantic Drift, which flows from the Gulf of Mexico towards Western Europe, warms the seas around those countries, making their climates warmer. Thus London (51°32'N) is warmer than New York, even though New York lies at a much lower latitude (40°43'N), because of this warming effect.

The Japan Current, flowing from Southeast Asia, warms the eastern coasts of China and Japan. The west coast of Japan, on the other hand, is cooled by cold currents originating in northern areas. The magnitude of large ocean currents is demonstrated by the enormous amount of water they can carry—for example, the Gulf Stream carries more than 50 million cubic meters (65.5 million cubic yards) per second.

The build-up of warm waters can have significant effects on climate. For example, tropical cyclones or hurricanes or typhoons develop in the areas of warm water in Southeast Asia. These can have devastating effects on those areas.

Also, temperature changes in the waters of the South Pacific Ocean provide indications of the El Niño and La Niña weather disturbances. The onset of El Niño is heralded by unusually high water temperatures in the central Pacific, with the warm water spreading across to South America.

Cold polar currents

Cold ocean currents originate in polar regions. They flow deep in the oceans and only surface through upwelling—when winds blowing from the land drive warm surface water back out into the ocean. Cold water then rises to the surface.

Two well-known upwelling sites, both on the western sides of continents, are the Humboldt or Peru Current along the coast of South America and the Benguela Current in southern Africa. Their nutrient-laden waters are rich breeding grounds for fish.

Two important cold currents flowing on the eastern sides of continents are the Kamchatka Current, which flows alongside Siberia and Japan, and the Labrador Current, which flows along the east coasts of Canada and the United States.

Icebergs and ice floes

Seas in the polar zones can freeze, forming pack ice that covers the sea surface. If subjected to strong currents or winds, this pack ice can break into pieces, called floes. Ice broken from ice sheets can also be seen floating in the seas as icebergs. Ice floes are mostly less than 5 m (16½ ft) thick—much thinner than icebergs.

Icebergs can be very thick indeed—up to hundreds of meters in thickness—but only about one-sixth of an iceberg floats above water. The rest of it remains submerged or hidden below the water. This makes icebergs a major navigational hazard. There are always likely to be icebergs in the North Atlantic; they originate from the Greenland ice sheet and its glaciers.

The Antarctic zone

The waters around Antarctica flow in an unbroken band around the globe because there are no land areas to obstruct them. The West Wind Drift, as the winds blowing incessantly from the west to the east are called, results in some of the world's most turbulent seas. The seas in latitudes between 40°S and 60°S have been referred to as the "Roaring Forties," the "Furious Fifties," and the "Screaming Sixties."

In the Southern Ocean around Antarctica, between the latitudes 50°S and 60°S, cold currents interact with the warm currents coming from the tropics. The cold, nutrient-rich waters are driven upwards by this convergence, becoming the breeding ground for abundant oceanic life. These waters are thus a vital component of the food chain which depends upon that aquatic life.

PLANTS AND ANIMALS

Earth is about 4,500 million years old. After about 1,000 million years, most of the basic metabolic processes on which modern life depends were in place. The first eukaryote cells (cells that were capable of resisting oxidation) appeared about 1,500 million years ago. After about 4,000 million years, multicellular animals and plants appear in the fossil record. In the past 600 million years, life has exploded into a vast array of forms, but many of the animals and plants we are familiar with are relatively recent arrivals.

To deduce the history of Earth's life forms (collectively known as biota), and the prevailing environmental conditions, scientists primarily rely on physical evidence: the character of rocks or the fossils contained within them. Increasingly, however, biochemical evidence is also used.

The first life forms

Life is defined as a self-contained system of molecules that can duplicate itself from generation to generation. In Earth's early history, the elements that make up the vast majority of living tissues (hydrogen, carbon, oxygen, and nitrogen) were available in some form, and energy was abundant. Also, the concentration of

atmospheric oxygen was low, which probably allowed a period of chemical evolution before the development of life. The earliest life forms may have resembled the bacteria-like organisms that exist today in hot springs associated with volcanic activity.

The first bacteria-like microfossils are dated at 3,500 million years old. Stromatolites, fossilized mats of cyanobacteria (a bacteria secreted by blue–green algae), first appear in the fossil record at about this time. These are the dominant fossils found in rocks older than about 550 million years. Between about 3,500 and 1,500 million years ago, cyanobacteria and blue–green algae were probably the main forms of life. Importantly, they slowly contributed oxygen to the atmosphere.

The build-up of free oxygen, hazardous to most life forms, may have stimulated the development of organisms with more complex cellular organisation (the eukaryotes) about 1,500 million years ago. The eukaryotes could reproduce sexually, thus allowing

Stromatolites in Hamelin Pool, Shark Bay, Western Australia.

evolutionary change. They generated more oxygen and eventually (by about 1,300 million years ago) an ozone shield—this is probably what enabled further biotic evolution.

The earliest fossil record of protozoans, which are animals and so derive their energy from ingesting other organisms, is from about 800 million years ago. By about 680 million years ago, the protozoa were a highly diverse and complex range of multicellular animals—mostly coral- or worm-like life forms.

Invertebrates and vertebrates

During the late Proterozoic or early Paleozoic Era, the principal groups (or phyla) of invertebrates appeared. Trilobites were probably the dominant form of marine life during the Cambrian Period. The seas teemed with a huge diversity of animals, including a group with an elongated support structure, a central nerve cord, and a blood circulatory system—members of the phylum to which humans belong, the Chordata.

A major extinction event ended the Cambrian Period. The Ordovician Period (500 to 435 million years ago) is characterized by another increase in species diversity. The fossil record is dominated by marine invertebrates, but vertebrates also appear. The primitive jawless fish of 485 million years ago are the first ancestors of all advanced life forms: fish, amphibians, reptiles, birds, and mammals. Another major extinction event ended this period.

From ocean to land

The first land plants—probably similar to modern liverworts, hornworts, and mosses—seem to have arisen about 450 million years ago. The move onto land was a significant evolutionary step; life on land was very different, demanding innovation and evolutionary change.

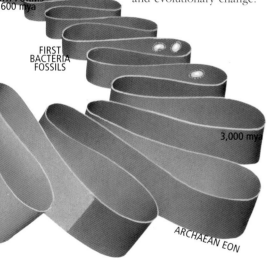

BIG BANG
11–14,000 mya

TH FORMS
,600 mya

FIRST
BACTERIA
FOSSILS

3,000 mya

ARCHAEAN EON

CENOZOIC ERA

65 mya

2 mya

The diagram (above) illustrates all the major stages in the evolution of plants and animals, from the first bacteria-like organisms, around 3,500 million years ago (mya), till humans, who first appeared in the late Quaternary Period.

During the Silurian Period (435 to 395 million years ago), algae diversified and all the major fish groups appear. Fossils of vascular plants (with specialized systems for moving nutrients, liquids, and so on) are found at about 430 million years ago. *Cooksonia*, a small moss-like plant common at this time, may have resulted in two distinct lines of evolution, one leading to all other higher plants. Floras of the late Silurian to early Devonian time are very similar worldwide, and may constitute evidence that the supercontinent Pangaea existed then.

During the mid-Devonian Period (395 to 345 million years ago), plants underwent a remarkable diversification, resulting in the development of Devonian "forests," which included giant clubmosses (lepidodendrons) and horsetails (calamites). The fossil record of the amphibians also begins here—animals were moving onto land—and the first fern-like foliage and gymnosperms appeared. The late Devonian was also marked by a mass extinction event.

Fossils from the Carboniferous Period (345 to 280 million years ago) suggest that the clubmoss forests teemed with spiders, scorpions, and centipedes. Amphibians gave rise to the first reptiles about 300 million years ago—vertebrates were no longer dependent on returning to water to reproduce. A trend towards an ice age occurred in the late Carboniferous Period, leading to low-diversity flora dominated by primitive seed ferns.

The Permian Period (280 to 245 million years ago) is dominated by the fossil remains of primitive members of the conifer line. By this period, reptiles with skeletal features characteristic of mammals were present.

The Age of Reptiles

The largest mass extinction event on record marks the end of the Permian Period. During the Mesozoic Era (245 to 65 million years ago), the "Age of Reptiles," flowering plants, dominated by cycads and gymnosperms early on, developed. Birds and mammals also appeared.

During the Triassic Period (245 to 200 million years ago), mammals, lizards, and dinosaurs appear in the fossil record. Some long-established reptiles were replaced by new groups, including the turtles, crocodilians, dinosaurs, and pterosaurs.

Dinosaurs date from early in the Triassic Period. From about 220 million years ago they dominated land habitats—for almost 160 million years. Mammals (initially small, perhaps nocturnal, shrew-like creatures) appear to have arisen from mammal-like reptiles. There was another mass extinction event (about 200 million years ago) in the late Triassic Period. Frogs and toads may have appeared around this time.

Pangaea began to break up during the Jurassic Period (200 to 145 million years ago). Ocean currents and the global climate were altered. The position of the continents and the break-up sequence determined the migration routes available and, therefore, the interrelation or common features of the plants and animals that we now see in the modern world.

Jurassic rocks include Earth's earliest fossils of flies, mosquitoes, wasps, bees, and ants; modern types of marine crustaceans were abundant. It was also a critical point in the evolution of birds, which evolved either from the dinosaurs or from an earlier group of reptiles. The *Archaeopteryx*, which existed about 150 million years ago, is perhaps the most famous early bird-like animal.

The early Cretaceous Period (145 to 65 million years ago) had a cosmopolitan flora. The first record of bats appears at this time. From about 80 million years ago, gymnosperms and angiosperms expanded at the expense of cycads and ferns. Mammals were also becoming dominant.

The Cretaceous Period also saw the apparent rise of the monotreme and marsupials and placentals, and the first predatory mammals. The diversification and spread of angiosperms provided the impetus for the co-evolution of animals.

The Age of Mammals

A great extinction event occurred at the end of the Cretaceous Period, causing the demise of the dinosaurs and the loss of about 25 percent of all known animal families. This change marks the beginning of the Cenozoic Era (65 million years ago to the present). This era saw the formation of the famous mountain systems of the world, the movement of the continents to their present positions and a cooling trend that culminated in the ice ages of the Quaternary Period.

After dinosaurs died out, mammals quickly expanded into newly vacated habitats and roles, adapting and diversifying. Eventually, the warm-blooded animals came to dominate, so the Cenozoic Era is often called the "Age of Mammals." Late in the era, humans finally appear.

The Tertiary Period (65 to 1.8 million years ago) saw major new groups developing within pre-established plant families. Grasses appeared (about 50 million years ago), expanding particularly in the Miocene Period.

The development of grasslands resulted eventually in a proliferation of grazing mammals. Hoofed, placental herbivores are first recorded as fossils 85 million years ago. The first horses appeared about 55 million years ago. A similar explosion in small rodents also occurred from about 40 million years ago.

Although birds have been essentially modern since the start of the Cenozoic Era, the first songbirds seem to appear at about 55 million years ago; all the major bird groups of the modern world had evolved by 50 million years ago. At about the same time (mid Eocene Period), the carnivorous mammals split into two major lines: the dogs and the cats, basically. The first toothed whales are from the Oligocene epoch and the first plankton-feeding whales are from the Miocene.

The first primates seem to date from the end of the Cretaceous Period, though it seems that both monkeys and apes did not separate from earlier groups until the Oligocene epoch. The oldest biped yet found—usually taken as the start of the hominids—is from about 4.4 million years ago.

Nearly 2.5 million years ago, stone tool users—the hallmark of our own genus, Homo—seem to have arisen. Homo erectus, dating from about 1.8 million years ago, migrated from Africa as far as China and Southeast Asia. Our species, Homo sapiens, seems to have evolved in Africa within the past 200,000 years and to have migrated out of that continent only during the past 100,000 years.

EARTH'S BIOSPHERE

The biosphere is the zone where all living organisms on Earth are found. It includes parts of the lithosphere (Earth's crust and mantle), the hydrosphere (all the waters on Earth), and the atmosphere. The term "biosphere" can also refer collectively to all Earth's living organisms.

Imagine a sort of biological spectrum, arranged from the simple to the complex; it would start with subatomic particles, then move through atoms, molecules, compounds, protoplasm, cells, tissues, organs, organ systems, organisms, populations, communities, and ecosystems, to, eventually, the biosphere. Each stage represents another level of organization, and each level implies new attributes and different properties.

"Population" refers to a group of organisms of a particular kind that form a breeding unit. Not all individuals of a kind (or species) can mix—for example, due to geographic isolation—so a population is the functional group that is capable of breeding. A "community" is all the populations of plants, animals, bacteria, and fungi that live in an environment and interact with one another. Populations within a community are linked by their interaction and effects on each other, and by their responses to the environment they share.

"Ecosystem" is a shortening of "ecological system," the concept that the living (biotic) community and the non-living (abiotic) environment are a functioning, integrated system. An ecosystem involves transfer and circulation of materials and energy between living and non-living systems. There is almost infinite variety in the magnitude of ecosystems, from a global ecosystem that encompasses the entire biosphere to the ecosystem of a fallen log or of the underside of a rock, or even of a drop of water.

Environmental conditions influence the distribution of individual organisms. Limiting factors may be physical (such as temperature and moisture availability) or biotic (such as competition, predation, and the presence of suitable food or other resources). A limiting factor is anything that tends to make it more difficult for an organism to grow, live, or reproduce—that makes some aspect of physiology or behavior less efficient and therefore less competitive.

The distribution of organisms is strongly influenced by the fact that each kind can tolerate only a certain set of conditions. For many organisms, distribution is critically associated with, or determined by, relationships with other organisms. A community of organisms is thus likely to include a loose collection of populations with similar environmental requirements, and possibly another, tighter, collection of organisms that are dependent in some way on each other.

Due to genetic variation, individuals within a population have a range of tolerances around their ecological optimum, but beyond a particular tolerance limit, the species is unable to live. Importantly, this spread means a group may be able to cope with environmental change. A species must be able to complete all phases of its life cycle in a given region if it is to persist for a prolonged period, and different species vary in their tolerance of environmental factors.

The major biomes

Communities are strongly linked to their physical environment or habitat; this habitat is also modified by its communities. Since climate, soils, and biotic factors vary around the world, communities are bound to change. Vegetation is often the most visible aspect of communities, so they are often classified on the basis of vegetation. Communities recognized by their vegetation structure are termed "associations" or "formations;" when the definition also implies the consideration of animal communities, the term "biome" is used.

A biome is a grouping of communities or ecosystems that have similar appearances or structures (physiognomy). As physiognomy generally reflects the environment, the environmental characteristics of a specific biome on one continent will be similar to that same biome on any other. Furthermore, widely separated biomes are likely to include unrelated animals with a similar role and possibly similar morphology (form and structure), due to convergent evolution (animals evolving separately, but having similar characteristics).

At the global level, a number of distinctive features are generally recognized. There are several forest biomes, ranging in diversity and ecological complexity from tropical rainforest to the coniferous high-latitude forests of the northern hemisphere. In regions with seasonal contrasts in rainfall, trees become more widely spaced, species less diverse, and savanna grasses more characteristic of grassland areas develop. Other grassland biomes occur in temperate climates. Shrublands are dominated by shortish, scraggly trees or tall bushes, and may have an understorey

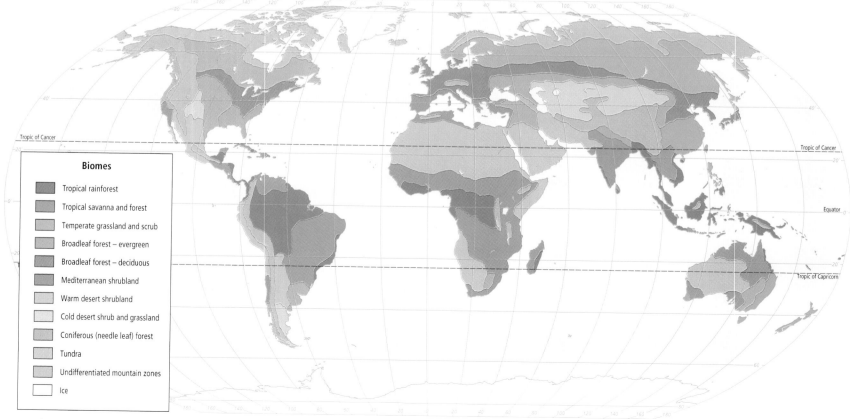

Biomes

- Tropical rainforest
- Tropical savanna and forest
- Temperate grassland and scrub
- Broadleaf forest – evergreen
- Broadleaf forest – deciduous
- Mediterranean shrubland
- Warm desert shrubland
- Cold desert shrub and grassland
- Coniferous (needle leaf) forest
- Tundra
- Undifferentiated mountain zones
- Ice

Projection: Robinson Equatorial Scale approx 1:110 million

These monkeys have adapted to life in the trees in Lombok, Indonesia (left). They find their food there, sleep there, and can move quickly through the branches at considerable heights from the ground. The Weddell seal in Antarctica (below) has few predators, and finds plenty of food in the nutrient-rich waters of the Ross Sea.

A frill-necked lizard from Australia (left) is well adapted to live in its dry environment, and giraffes in Tanzania (above) fill the large herbivore ecological niche of their environment.

of grasses. In drier climates, scrub vegetation may be quite scattered and small in size.

The boundaries of Earth's biomes are rather blurred and maps can only show approximate distributions. Human activity has greatly disturbed natural ecosystems, often leaving mere remnants of once-vast areas of forest or grassland.

Energy in the biosphere

Most life on Earth is supported by the continuous flow of energy from the Sun into the biosphere. A tiny proportion of this radiant energy is used by plants, which are then able to maintain the biomass and the vital processes of the entire biosphere. Energy is eventually converted to heat and lost from the system.

Plants are capable of capturing and storing energy from sunlight. In the process called photosynthesis, plants absorb the radiant energy of the Sun and transform it into the energy of chemical bonds. The energy left after that used for the vital processes of the plant may accumulate as organic matter, and is available for harvest by animals and decomposition by bacteria and fungi.

As only plants can trap solar energy, their productivity determines the energy limits of the entire biosphere, and the total size of all consumer populations, including humans. The amount of this leftover energy is highest in regions with optimum conditions for plant growth.

On land, productivity is controlled primarily by water availability; in aquatic environments, nutrient availability is crucial. The most productive regions are found at the interface between the land and the sea. Generally, terrestrial communities are much more productive than aquatic systems.

The energy stored by plants as organic matter sustains other organisms. This transfer of energy, as food, from plants to herbivores, and from herbivores to carnivores, is a food chain. At each level of a food chain, a large amount of energy is degraded into heat and other forms of non-recoverable energy, so there is a steep decrease in productivity for each step up the sequence of the food chain. Correlated with this is usually a decrease in the number of organisms, and thus a decrease in total biomass.

The ecological niche

An ecological niche is the role that an organism plays in the ecosystem. Whereas habitat is the physical position of the organism, the ecological niche represents its functional position. For example, within grasslands, the kangaroo in Australia occupies the same niche as the bison in North America. They have the same role—large herbivores. Natural selection has often resulted in organisms adapting to their role, which means that the morphology of an animal can often be a good indicator of its niche.

Species vary in the breadth of their niche—some are specialists, others are generalists. Specialists are usually more efficient in the use of resources, due to adaptation, but they are also more vulnerable to change.

Importantly, two species with similar ecological requirements cannot occupy the same niche within an environment. This principle, called competitive exclusion, means that cohabiting organisms either use different resources, behave in such a way that resources are shared, or exist in a variable environment that favors each species alternately. Species that do have similar niches must compete for resources.

Specialization reduces this competition and, given time, adaptation to this new role may result in an altered morphology. Competitive exclusion is thus an extremely important evolutionary force.

The diagram (below) illustrates the food chain in the tundra. At the top of the chain is the wolf, who has no predators. At the bottom is the vegetation. In between are insects, small mammals (such as lemmings, ground squirrels, and Arctic hares) and birds, followed by other larger mammals such as caribou and Arctic foxes.

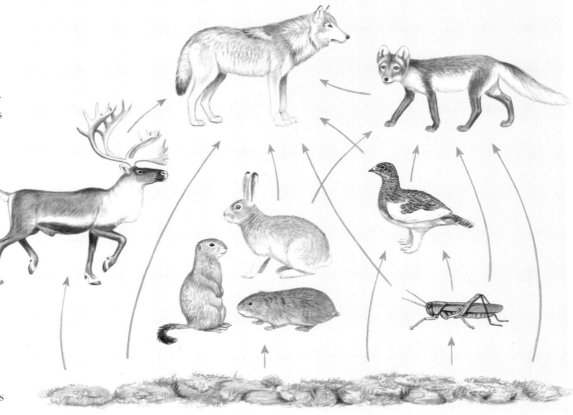

SOILS

Soil formation is a very complex process. It involves the interaction of climate, type of rock, topography and biota (the total plant and animal life of a region). These factors operate over time, and the amount of time required for soil formation varies substantially from place to place—some soils and their associated weathered products have been forming for millions of years. Soils are formed from weathered materials, usually with the addition of organic matter. The disintegration or weathering of rocks is the result of both physical and chemical processes. Physical weathering breaks rocks down into fragments, while chemical weathering leads to the transformation of rock minerals into products of different composition.

Climate and soils

Weathering products are largely determined by climatic conditions. Mechanical weathering is particularly powerful in drier environments; in hot deserts, the heating of rocks induces expansion and subsequent breakdown of exposed surfaces; freezing has a similar effect. Salt crystallization in crevices mechanically disintegrates rocks. Root growth also leads to mechanical dislodgment.

In wet climates, moisture helps remove particles from exposed rocks, and provides a means by which minerals in those rocks can be attacked chemically to form clay minerals. Pure water is not a significant chemical agent; but the presence of dissolved carbon dioxide and complex organic substances in soil waters generates a chemical environment able to decompose, remove and redeposit rock (clay-rich) materials and salts.

Hot wet climates, plus the opportunity for plants to grow on stable surfaces for long periods of time, leads to extensive decomposition of rocks.

In humid tropical climates, mineral decomposition results in the formation of oxides of aluminum and iron-producing red soils, sometimes cemented into a brick-like substance known as laterite. Such soils are much less fertile than those formed under somewhat drier grassland climates, where organic (or humic) matter and calcium-rich salts accumulate into a nutrient-rich soil capable of growing crops such as wheat and barley.

Rock type and soils

Within one climate area, soil type can vary as a result of the weathering of rocks of different mineral composition. Granites, basalts, quartz-rich sandstones and limestones are common rock types containing distinctive minerals. Chemical decomposition of these rocks over time will yield soils with different types and quantities of clays, varying amounts of precipitated salts, and different degrees of water retention and mobility (due to the existence of pore spaces and the capacity of minerals to absorb moisture).

Similar rock types in contrasting climate zones may also produce different soils. For instance, different rates and intensities of weathering can yield dark, organic-rich soils in grassland areas, underlain by basalt, whereas basalt soils in tropical areas are likely to be red and iron-rich.

Soil processes

The essence of soil formation is the breakdown and mobilization of mineral and organic matter in the presence of water. Living and dead organisms, both microscopic and larger (such as earthworms), assist in this process. The result is the formation of layers, or horizons. Each horizon has distinctive color, grain size (texture), chemical composition,

organic matter content and pore space size (porosity). In some soils, binding agents such as organic colloids or iron oxides harden the layers. Over time, these layers may thicken, depending on slope position and the rate of landscape removal or deposition. Ground water movements can lead to precipitation of salts in soil layers, or even on the surface, leading to reduced soil productivity, as in lands bordering the Aral Sea.

Well-structured soils generally display "A," "B" and "C" horizons; A and B horizons are the real soil layers, known as the solum, while the C horizon consists of the weathered parent rock. The A horizon—the exposed soil—is often dark at the top because of the accumulation of organic material. A horizons are subject to leaching (eluviation). Leached material is transported to the B horizon, where it is deposited (illuviation); some B horizons are poor in organic material. Eluviation is assisted by the organic acids produced by decaying vegetation.

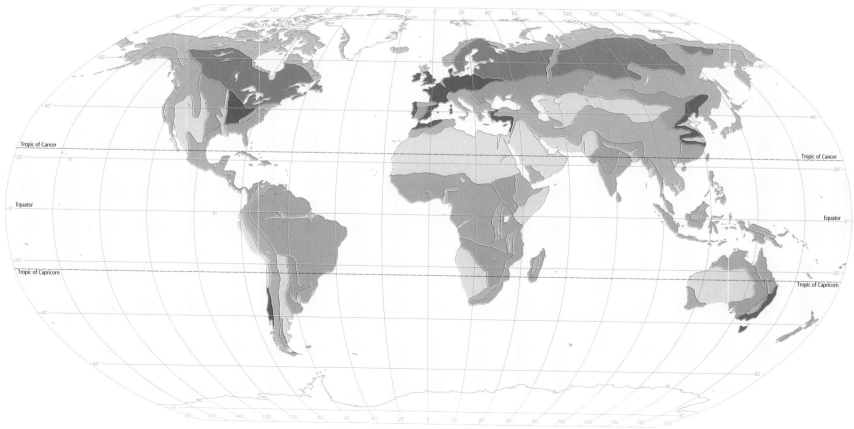

Projection: Robinson   Equatorial Scale approx 1:110 million

Layers of soil are exposed in this weathered escarpment, Australia (far left); parched, eroded ground leaves trees unable to tap into food and water in the soil, Papua New Guinea (left); this plant from the desert of Angola and Namibia has adapted to life in desert soil.

Soil nutrients

Soil texture and composition influence plant growth and therefore the suitability of a soil for agricultural use. Chemical and organic materials form colloids. Colloids are negatively charged, and attract plant nutrients such as calcium, magnesium, and potassium, which are positive ions (or cations). These nutrients are essential to the existence of all life on Earth.

Gray sandy soils of temperate regions are generally acidic; these soils are not rich in plant nutrients such as calcium and potassium, but this can be corrected by adding lime and fertilizers. On the other hand, some dry desert soils, which often contain mineral accumulations such as calcium carbonate and salts, are alkaline. Whilst many such soils have excessive salt levels, some are quite fertile and, irrigated, can be used for agriculture.

Soil types

Many attempts have been made to classify soils. Properties such as color, texture, composition, horizon thickness and porosity are used to define soil types. But even locally there can be considerable variation in soil type, given changes in elevation, slope angle, rock type and vegetation. In mountainous or hilly areas, for example, many different soil types may exist within short distances over a range of altitudes and slope positions.

At the global scale, soil types largely reflect climatic conditions. However, the history of a land surface may also be significant. The "fresh" deposits of recently deglaciated places in North America and Europe contain relatively poorly leached minerals, contrasting markedly with ancient unglaciated tropical plateaus, from which nutrient-rich minerals have long been removed.

Any world map of soil types must be a broad generalization. Iron-rich weathered soils can occur in areas where past climates have had a significant effect (for instance, southwest Western Australia). Alluvial soils, on the other hand, are constantly forming and reforming as new sediments are deposited in flood plains. Yet soils in both areas may be extremely rich in nutrients and thus of great agricultural significance. By way of contrast, the sparsity of moisture and biota in desert regions, or the presence of ice on the ground, will greatly inhibit soil development.

Soil zones

▨	Warm to cool temperate forest soils, moderately to highly leached, moderate to low in mineral bases and organic material, well developed horizons [Alfisols, Gray-brown podzolics].
▨	Cool temperate forest soils with highly leached upper profile, acidic accumulation of humus, iron and aluminum in illuvial horizon [Spodosols, Podzols].
▨	Grassland soils of subhumid and semiarid areas, often mixed with shrubs, organic rich in upper profile in more moist regions, also rich in mineral bases, fertile [Mollisols, Chernozems, Vertisols].
▨	Latosolic soils of tropical and subtropical climates with forest and/or savanna cover; highly to moderately leached profile, low in mineral bases but high in oxides [Ultisols, Oxisols, Red Podzolics, Laterites some relic of past climates].
▨	Desert soils of arid areas with little soil profile development and very low organic material but may contain abundant salts [Aridisols].
▨	Alluvial soils in all climates especially in deltas, subject to frequent flooding and new deposition of river silt, fertile (only major areas shown), [Entisols].
▨	Tundra soils in subpolar areas with permanently frozen subsoils; subject to mass movement on slopes (solifluction) [Inceptisols].
▨	Mountainous areas: soils are typically shallow and stony and highly variable in profile and thickness depending on climate and slope position; includes localized areas of fertile soils especially in mountain basins and near volcanoes.
☐	Ice sheets

A soil section, showing horizons enriched by organic matter (A1), and leached of humus and minerals (A2). A horizon of accumulation (B) contains mineral matter leached from above. The bedrock (D) is decomposed into a weathered horizon (C).

Earth as a home for humans

All humans live by exploiting Earth's natural resources, whether by small-scale fishing in Malawi (above) or employing modern farming techniques to farm cattle in Australia (opposite).

As humans, we dominate our planet. There are very few places where our impact is not felt. Even the atmosphere has now been altered by gases produced by humans, and some of these—such as chloroflurocarbons (CFCs)—are the result of chemical processes alien to natural systems. Many who travel or work at sea are aware of human debris in our waters. Lakes are drying up and are often heavily polluted, as are rivers. Much of the forests and grasslands of Earth have been disturbed. Over the past 200 to 300 years, in particular, we have transformed this planet in ways which at times enhance our welfare, but at others threaten the existence of societies.

As the human race evolved, so did its capacity to utilize natural resources. The mineral uranium was of little use to societies for much of human history, but, from the end of the Second World War, its value as a destructive force and as a source of power has grown immensely. In contrast, the fertile soils of river floodplains and deltas have long been utilized in some areas, and civilizations such as those of Egypt have depended upon their richness. But as a resource, soils need nourishment. Without appropriate care, their ability to maintain the levels of productivity necessary for agriculture will decline. History is full of accounts of battles waged to maintain social structures and population levels in the face of soil degradation. On the other hand, other societies, such as in China, Japan, and Western Europe, have carefully nurtured their soil resources.

For the early humans, the vast forests of Earth were largely avoided. There is some evidence that forests displaced human activities during the period of global warming immediately following the Ice Age in Europe. Progressively, however, forests in tropical, temperate and high latitude areas have been removed or exploited to create new land uses. Today, fires sweep across vast areas of Amazonian and Indonesian rainforests as more timber is removed and land is cleared for cattle grazing and crops.

Marine life has long provided food for humans. Fishing in shallow waters using primitive lines and spears has developed into sophisticated technologies enabling large ships to roam the oceans capturing fish over a vast range of depths. Fears of exploitation and the reduction of stocks to levels at which particular species will not survive have resulted in international agreements on resource use, although the effectiveness of these agreements is in question, with countries such as Japan and Norway still actively hunting whales, for example. Other forms of more sustainable fishing have been developed to feed societies which are heavily dependent upon food from the sea. This includes various forms of aquaculture at sea, in sheltered bays, and on reclaimed land.

Pressures placed on natural resources are closely linked to population growth. One of the most amazing and environmentally significant aspects of the twentieth century has been the rate of increase in population. With nearly 6 billion people alive at the moment and perhaps close to 10 billion by the year 2050, it is no wonder that environmental managers, planners, and scientists are deeply worried about the consequences. Also, population increases are not distributed evenly across the world; it is often in developing countries already suffering from depleted resources that the impacts of many new mouths to feed will be most harshly felt. The effective and equitable distribution of food to those in need will become increasingly important. Unfortunately, major health problems also arise in countries where food supplies are threatened. The impacts of poverty and disease, and the capacity of international aid and economic organizations to support developing countries, create further uncertainties in a world beset with environmental and other problems.

Higher standards of living using available natural resources have been made possible through human inventions, including those designed to increase food production and to resist the ravages of pests and diseases in plants and animals. Many areas of high population have benefited from the so-called "green" revolution, but the ability of pathogens and parasites to undergo genetic change and therefore develop resistance to controls reminds us of the need for constant vigilance and research. Undertaking this research and acting on knowledge gained from other countries remain issues of global concern.

What has changed dramatically in recent years is the ability of individuals and groups to communicate quickly across vast distances. In one sense, space has "shrunk." Geographical isolation—such as that imposed by mountain ranges—no longer impedes the information flow; in the past, such barriers meant that separate languages developed in Papua New Guinea (for instance) in regions which, although physically close, were separated by their inaccessibility. Today, satellite television communications, electronic mail facilitated by fiber optic networks, and 24-hours-a-day business transactions are part of a global economic system which enables information to flow within and between nations.

The ability of societies to respond to natural hazards is another issue of great concern to international aid agencies and governments. Natural hazards may be insidious (droughts) or virtually instantaneous (earthquakes). Great loss of life and property can ensue; the impacts do not respect national economic strength (for example, the number of deaths as a result of tornadoes in the United States). Yet some areas are subject to frequent disasters of a scale which disturbs the economy. Floods in Bangladesh are of this category. Greenhouse-effect-induced rises in the sea level are another more insidious hazard which potentially threatens the futures of coral island nations such as the Maldives in the Indian Ocean.

LAND RESOURCES

Humans meet their principal needs—for water, minerals, and plants—from the land. Inorganic resources include minerals, water, and various elements in soils, whilst organic or biotic resources include plant and animal life. Fossil fuels (coal, petroleum, and natural gas) are of biotic origin. Both mineral and biotic resources are unequally distributed throughout the world—while some countries have abundant plant and water resources, others do not.

The presence or absence of water is often reflected in population densities, with high rainfall areas generally attracting, and being able to support, greater concentrations of people. China, for example, lacks water in its western half, but has a water surplus in its eastern half, and this is reflected in its population distribution.

Mineral resources are also very unevenly distributed. Some countries possess abundant reserves of certain minerals (such as petroleum in the Middle East), and others have gold reserves (Russia and South Africa).

The fact that resources are unequally distributed means that countries must trade what they have for what they need. The highly industrialized countries of Western Europe and Japan, for instance, import raw materials to run their industries. Also, many countries depend upon fossil fuel imports for their energy supplies.

Climate

Climate can be considered a resource because agriculture is so highly dependent on climate. The world's industries and urban centers are mostly located where there is a favorable climate—in areas which have comfortable temperature ranges and adequate rainfall.

Agricultural products can, generally, only be grown economically in suitable climatic conditions. Since the middle of the nineteenth century, plantations in the tropics have produced sugar, tea, coffee, and rubber for international consumption—these areas have been exploited for the production of crops that do not grow elsewhere and are much in demand. Likewise, wheat and other cereals are produced in temperate climates and exported internationally.

Landforms

Human settlement concentrates along river plains and deltas because of fertile soils and available water. In Japan, flat land is prized because of its

A beef cattle feedlot in California, USA (above). This is a method of intensive agriculture; less land is needed per head of cattle, but cattle lead a more restricted existence.

scarcity. In some places, such as in Japan and on the island of Java in Indonesia, hillsides have been terraced for agriculture. In Europe and North America, deposits of sediment, encrusted with ice age glaciations, form fertile plains.

Agriculture

A long-established agricultural practice is "slash-and-burn." This involves clearing a forest patch, then burning to fertilize the soils; cultivation only

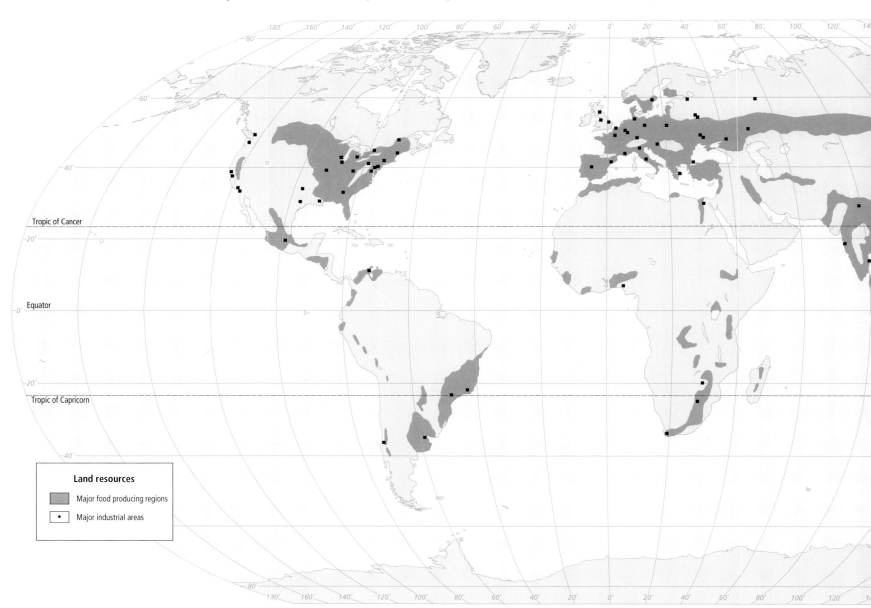

Land resources

Major food producing regions

Major industrial areas

Projection: Robinson Equatorial Scale approx 1:155 million

Vast wheatfields like these in Saskatchewan, Canada (left) and the "Super Pit" in Kalgoorlie, Australia (below) both show human interference with the environment, and depend on high levels of mechanization. Near Beijing, China (bottom), people still use donkeys to plow—a pre-industrial farming method still used in less developed countries.

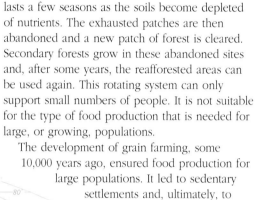

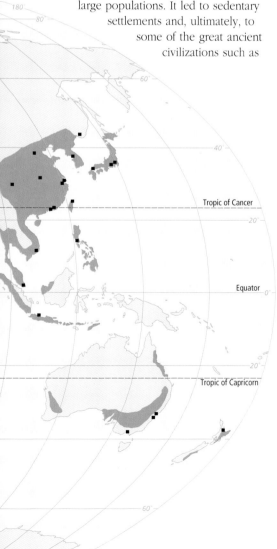

lasts a few seasons as the soils become depleted of nutrients. The exhausted patches are then abandoned and a new patch of forest is cleared. Secondary forests grow in these abandoned sites and, after some years, the reafforested areas can be used again. This rotating system can only support small numbers of people. It is not suitable for the type of food production that is needed for large, or growing, populations.

The development of grain farming, some 10,000 years ago, ensured food production for large populations. It led to sedentary settlements and, ultimately, to some of the great ancient civilizations such as Egypt, northern China, and the Indus Valley. Since the nineteenth century, agriculture has seen the development of mechanization, the use of fertilizers and pesticides, and improved varieties of both plant and animal species. These new developments paralleled the great milestones in industrialization, such as the invention of steam engines, the internal combustion engine, electric power and, more recently, the silicon chip.

The population explosion in several developing countries within the past 50 years greatly increased their demand for food, and it became necessary to increase crop yields per unit of land. This ushered in the so-called Green Revolution, which involved using high-yielding seeds, fertilizers, and pesticides. Although these products increased grain output, the increase has been at some environmental and social cost.

Brazil is a good example of changing uses of the land. Before becoming a colony, its agriculture was of the slash-and-burn type practiced by forest Indians. Colonialism brought in plantation agriculture. The development of coffee plantations boosted Brazil's economy. Great increases in population have placed pressure on its once largely untapped resource, the Amazon rainforest. Large tracts of the Amazon are being transformed by people wishing to establish farms; forests are being burnt down to clear land for agriculture. Large areas are also being cleared to raise beef cattle for export; this also, of course, results in the large-scale loss of forests.

Tropical rainforest clearance cannot easily be reversed. Currently, more than 10 million hectares (24.7 million acres) of forests are being lost each year. These large-scale clearances have adverse effects globally—they accelerate global warming and its effects on climate.

Minerals

Minerals supply the raw materials for several major industries: for the extraction of metals (primarily iron); for fuels such as uranium, coal, and petroleum; and for manufacturing fertilizers and cement. Minerals are valuable resources because they only occur in some places and are finite in nature: once extracted, they cannot be renewed. Minerals are very important for sustaining modern civilization and, as standards of living continue to rise on a global scale, so too does the demand for minerals. In fact, more minerals have been mined in the twentieth century than in all previous centuries. As demand for minerals increases and they become more scarce, their strategic importance to industry—including, especially, the defence industry—also increases, placing even greater strain on already vulnerable finite resources.

The principal metal in demand is iron for making steel; steel forms the basis of much of the world's manufacturing, and every major industrial country produces steel. Other important metals include aluminum, copper, lead, and zinc.

Coal, petroleum, and natural gas provide energy supplies, and, in recent decades, uranium has provided the basis for nuclear energy. Coal is used for electricity generation and in the manufacture of steel. The ever-growing use of automobiles ensures continuing demand for petroleum, while natural gas is being used extensively for heating. Nuclear energy is currently the subject of much controversy because of dangers associated with nuclear power generation, the problems of nuclear waste disposal, and the potential for using nuclear materials from such plants for nuclear weapons.

The greatly increased use of minerals by the developed countries, and the increasing use by newly industrializing countries, has led to concerns about there being adequate mineral supplies for the future. Substitution of new materials for metals and the search for new or renewable energy sources—such as solar power or wind generation—are amongst the developments aimed at conserving our mineral resources.

OCEAN RESOURCES

The oceans, covering more than 70 percent of Earth's surface, are the source of enormous amounts of valuable resources. These broadly fall into two main categories: marine life and minerals. Marine life can be divided into pelagic forms and benthic forms. Pelagic forms move about in the waters—these resources include fish and marine mammals. Benthic forms, which live on the sea floor, include corals, molluscs, and crustaceans. There are also marine plants such as kelp that are harvested and used by humans.

The oceans also contain mineral deposits, including petroleum and gas, and mineral nodules. These resources are more difficult and expensive to obtain, generally, than marine life, but they are of great economic importance.

Within the past 50 years, modern technology has meant that detailed mapping of the oceans has become possible. Recent studies of the oceans, using this technology, have revealed some well-defined physiographic patterns: close to the land lie continental shelves which often end in steep continental slopes; these are followed, further from the shore, by gently sloping features called continental rises, which end in deep ocean basins; and the latter are intersected by mid-oceanic ridges. There are different marine resources commonly found in the different zones where these physiographic features are found.

Many nations, realizing the potential riches of the oceans, have declared resource boundaries under the United Nations' Law of the Sea Convention. Territorial seas are normally set at 12 nautical miles (22 km), whilst exclusive economic zones extend to 200 nautical miles (370 km). These mostly include the resource-rich continental shelves.

Continental shelves, however, can vary in width from 110 to 170 nautical miles (200 to 320 km); the shelves in the Atlantic Ocean and the Gulf of Mexico are exceptional in being up to 260 nautical miles (480 km) wide. A nation can legitimately claim all its adjacent continental shelf, even if that shelf extends beyond 200 nautical miles (370 km), as is the case with the United States and Australia. As a result of this law, some small island nations, such as in those in the South Pacific, have maritime claims that far exceed their land areas.

Fishing

Fishing is the most important resource-gathering activity from the seas. In recent decades, however, overfishing of the seas has reached, in some places, crisis proportions. For example, the North Pacific haddock catch dwindled in 1974 to less than 10 percent of what it had been a decade earlier, and the once highly productive cod fishing industry in Canada, employing an estimated 40,000 people, collapsed in 1992.

Several nations grant licenses to foreign fishing fleets to fish in their waters, and this can exacerbate the situation, as has been the case with the southern bluefin tuna from the waters of Australia, New Zealand, and the Southern Ocean. Overfishing is threatening the very existence of this tuna species; the numbers of this species have fallen, it is estimated, to just 2 to 5 percent of its original population.

Until recently, whales were one of the most threatened species of marine life, but a huge international outcry against whale hunting has resulted in most whaling nations giving up whaling altogether and international agreements for whale protection being enacted. The outcry

Brightly colored fishing boats docked at Nha Trang, Vietnam (above). During the late twentieth century, fishing has been affected by changes in technology, and by ocean pollution.

was generated not only as a result of concern for preservation of whale species, but also because of the horrific nature of the hunting itself.

By the time that whale protection measures were agreed upon, however, several species—including the bowhead, gray and right whale species—had been hunted almost to extinction.

An extensive whale sanctuary in the Southern Ocean now covers the territory of more than 90 percent of the world's whale population. Japan and Norway, however, continue to hunt whales. Japan justifies its whaling operations on the grounds of scientific research, but this explanation is not generally accepted by conservation groups, many of which continue to campaign against all forms of whale hunting.

Coastal fishing

Seas close to shore are usually rich in a wide variety of marine organisms, and have traditionally been fishing grounds for coast-dwelling

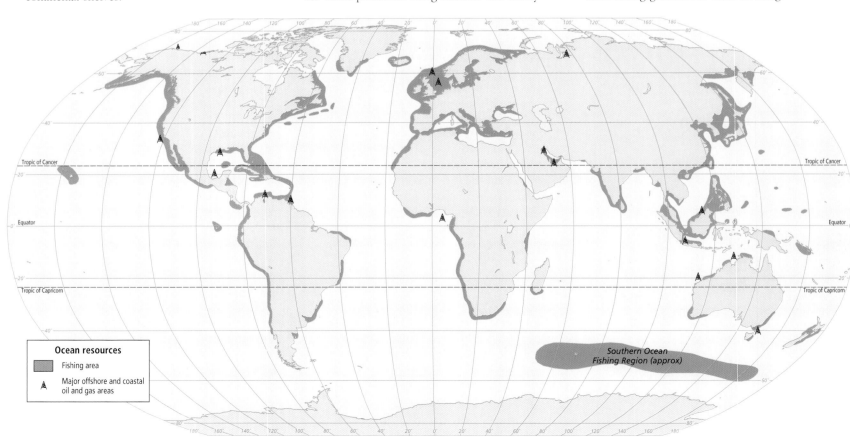

Ocean resources
- Fishing area
- ⚓ Major offshore and coastal oil and gas areas

Southern Ocean Fishing Region (approx)

Projection: Robinson   Equatorial Scale approx 1:155 million

This busy container port in Singapore (left), and fish farming (of Atlantic salmon in Australia, below), are relatively new commercial uses of ocean resources. Human predation has seriously affected creatures like the humpback whale (bottom), though international agreements aiming to reduce commercial hunting of whales may help to restore numbers.

communities. These are also the areas, not surprisingly, where shellfish farming, aquaculture (fish farming), and salt extraction have, more recently, been widely undertaken.

Kelp, which is rich in potash and iodine, is another product harvested from the seas in coastal areas. It is used for both food and fertilizer.

Fish breeding and shellfish farming, such as oyster breeding, are carried out close to the land. Aquaculture can provide reliable and convenient fish supplies, in contrast to fishing—it is no longer possible to depend upon the ever-dwindling supplies from the seas. Fish farming has been practiced for a long time—the breeding of fish in freshwater lakes in China, for instance, has been carried out for a great many years.

Modern aquaculture is a high-technology industry, as it requires meticulous monitoring of water conditions (such as salinity, oxygen levels, and water temperature) and nutrition. Only a limited number of species—salmon in the Outer Hebrides of Great Britain, for example—are being farmed at present.

In the Inland Sea of Japan, an arm of the sea has been completely cut off by metal nets, thus creating a confined space in which fish can be bred. In Japan particularly, seaweed is another important product of aquaculture.

Coastal countries that do not have sufficient supplies of fresh water can extract fresh water from sea water. However, the capital equipment required to establish these desalination plants is costly. There are several such plants for producing fresh water from salt water in the oil-rich countries bordering the Persian–Arabic Gulf—Kuwait, for instance, has desalination plants.

Continental shelves
These shallow, gently sloping features range in depth between 120 and 180 m (400 to 600 ft). When surface sea water is blown away from the land by offshore winds, colder nutrient-rich water rises to the surface. Where such waters are sunlit—these are known as epipelagic or euphotic zones—they make excellent breeding grounds for the minute marine organisms known as plankton. Plankton are tiny plant (phytoplankton) and animal (zooplankton) organisms that provide nutrition for other larger marine organisms.

Although sunlight can penetrate as far as 1,000 m (3,300 ft) below the ocean surface, photosynthesis can only take place in depths of up to 200 m (660 ft). As a result, phytoplankton can only survive within this shallow layer of ocean water. Small zooplankton feed on the phytoplankton in this layer and they, in turn, are preyed upon by larger organisms such as anchovies and squid. Larger fish such as tuna feed on the smaller marine life, only to be, in turn, consumed by still larger fish. This marine food chain extends even beyond the seas, to the seabirds which are the predators of fish.

The cold and extremely nutrient-rich waters in the continental shelves surrounding Antarctica are the breeding ground for small crustaceans known as krill. Species including seals and whales, as well as penguins, feed on krill.

In recent decades, rich petroleum and natural gas deposits have been discovered in the continental shelves. The petroleum deposits originated from the debris of marine organisms in oxygen-free shelf bottoms millions of years ago. Amongst the well-known deposits that are currently being exploited are those in the North Sea, the Gulf of Mexico, and off the city of Bombay on India's west coast.

Improvements in drilling technology have enabled exploration in ever-deeper seas; drilling for natural gas deposits is currently being carried out at depths of more than 1,700 m (5,600 ft) in the Marlim field, off Brazil.

Ocean basins
The ocean basins are made up of large, flat areas called abyssal plains. These abyssal plains lie at depths of about 4,000 m (15,000 ft). In these dark and cold areas, temperatures are low, perhaps only 4°C (40°F), compared with around 20°C (68°F) at the ocean surface.

These deep ocean basins lack plankton and are, therefore, not rich in marine life. Large parts of these plains, however, are covered with minerals, the most important of which are manganese nodules in the Pacific, Atlantic and southern Indian oceans. These nodules could be exploited at depths of up to 5,000 m (16,500 ft) using technology that has already been developed, but this is currently not economically viable.

The ocean basins are intersected by mid-oceanic ridges, which are formed by volcanic eruptions. The sea water and sediments around them often contain concentrations of zinc, lead, copper, silver, and gold. While these minerals are of considerable economic value and, therefore, importance, no method has yet been devised to extract them economically.

Ocean pollution
The seas have, unfortunately, long been considered convenient dumping grounds for waste—anything from urban sewage to nuclear materials. Chemicals from factories, fertilizers and pesticides from agricultural areas, and oil slicks from ships are also being released, often illegally, into the seas. Ballast water taken on by large ships on one side of the world is released on the other, with all its attendant marine organisms thus finding their way into other environments. The effects of such pollution are quite severe already in some areas, particularly in the semi-enclosed waters of the Mediterranean Sea.

Pollution threatens the existence of marine life, and thus, because marine ecological systems are entwined with land-based ecological systems, it will eventually affect life on land, including human life. There are more immediate effects, too, in some cases: dangerous oil spills such as that from the Exxon Valdez in Alaska threaten the livelihood of the nearby fishing communities who depend on the sea for their economic existence. Fishing communities in the Gulf of Mexico have also experienced this threat following oil spills from offshore petroleum wells.

COMMERCE

The movement of goods and services from place to place has long been a characteristic of human endeavour. The exchange of products, information and ideas within an economic system extends beyond subsistence societies, and into the "global village" of today. The scale of transactions has changed, though—it now ranges from village or tribal bartering to the almost instantaneous transfer of vast sums of money on the international foreign exchange market. The size and bulk of trade also varies with the commodity, and there are great contrasts—camel trains range across deserts and huge bulk carriers roam the oceans.

Trade is the transport and/or communication of commodities from place to place, and is generally measured in terms of the monetary value of the items moved. Until the advent of steam-driven trains and ships and the extensive use of iron and steel for the manufacture of such carriers, the time taken and capacity to move large volumes of materials was limited. These technological limitations helped determine what could be traded, and what could be traded economically.

The volume and scope of trade, the movement of people, and the flow of information increased enormously in the nineteenth century, and continue to do so. The effects of the increasing numbers of roads, cars, and trucks since the Second World War, for example, are so all-encompassing that it is difficult for many people to imagine life without these relatively recent transportation innovations. Add to these changes the enormous advances in electronic communication technology, and it is easy to see why today's modern suburbanites have become almost completely dependent upon their cars and their electronic communication devices.

The communication of information (ideas, images, audio signals, and written texts), especially as it converges with computer technology to produce information technology (IT), is undergoing another technological revolution. Information technology, combined with cable, satellite, optical fiber, and other technologies, can now transmit digitized information (including money) over cyberspace from one part of the globe to another instantaneously, and with potentially staggering effects. Entire national economic systems can suffer very quickly as a result of currency crises facilitated by the use of such technologies—this happened in parts of Asia during 1997 and 1998.

International trade imbalances

To appreciate the effects of recent changes in transportation and communication technology on trade, it is useful to compare trade between highly industrialized nations (such as the United Kingdom) and other parts of the world in the 1950s with that today.

An international division of labor existed then. Some countries produced manufactured goods in factories, using a highly skilled and well-paid labor force. These goods were traded for primary commodities (coffee and gold, for instance), which were produced by poorly paid and relatively unskilled labor. This unbalanced market system

generated an unequal exchange: wealth accumulated in the industrialized areas, leading to unprecedented levels of development, while the other regions remained underdeveloped, largely because of these trade imbalances. That is, the Western world became richer and the Third World remained underdeveloped and poor.

Recent developments

In the 1960s, manufacturing jobs began to move to selected sites in the so-called developing countries, resulting in deindustrialization in the center, and selective industrialization in the periphery, of the global economy. The textile industry was an early industrial sector to move to the periphery, so some "banana" republics became "pajama" republics. The term "newly industrialized nation" applied to former peripheral nations such as Singapore, South Korea, Taiwan, Mexico, and a dozen or so other countries that were undergoing sustained, rapid growth in manufacturing.

The term "economic tiger" also arose, to describe the performance of some countries in the Pacific Rim. Their economies grew faster than those of the USA or Europe during the 1980s and early 1990s, but as those economies were export-oriented, they suffered greatly as a result of the withdrawal of foreign funds after 1987.

International commerce is led by the wealthy economies; it increasingly involves service industries based on innovation and technology—finance, insurance, transport, marketing and information flow. Trade in raw materials, including those from countries heavily dependent on agriculture or mining, today accounts for little more than 20 percent of total world trade.

Satellite receiving dishes like this one (left) are more common now, as international trade becomes increasingly dependent on satellite communications.

Container ships like the Katie (left) transport all manner of goods worldwide today. Increased freeway traffic (in San Diego, California, US, below) and the pollution it causes are a result of increased technology use in many countries. Simpler forms of transport, such as those that are used in Agra, India (far below), are still used in developing countries.

Manufactured goods are now produced and supplied by a range of developed and developing countries with former closed economies—China, for instance, is becoming more market-oriented and is contributing significantly to world trade.

Multinationals and trade blocs

Another major trend is the spread of multinationals in an ever-widening global process. This is occurring in a number of fields that are engaged in world trade. This process is epitomized by the internationalization of stock markets—they operate around the clock and now even penetrate countries such as Russia.

A further feature of world commerce has been the emergence of powerful trade groups or blocs. These represent collections of countries which, as groups, have accepted rules and regulations that permit a freer exchange of goods and services between the countries in the group. Three main trade blocs are the European Union (EU), the signatories to the North American Free Trade Agreement (NAFTA), and the Association of South-East Asian Nations (ASEAN). The release of a single currency, the Euro, in parts of the EU in 1999 signalled another major development in the concept of trade between and within blocs.

Adverse effects of the global economy

Despite the benefits which have arisen from the growth and development of international trade, there are many areas where market liberalization and the availability of funds for investment and growth have created problems.

The replacement of subsistence agriculture by a limited range of "cash" crops is one. This change has placed many societies at the mercy of declines in commodity prices, or the failure of the crop itself, due to climatic or other factors.

The need for capital has raised debt levels in countries such as Thailand, Mexico, and Indonesia to amounts which, at times of crisis, may induce political and social instability. International funding agencies such as the International Monetary Fund (IMF) and the World Bank, as well as aid agencies operating through the United Nations (UN), have become critical in sustaining these economies in the face of changes in technology and the global marketplace, which they may not have survived or been able to exploit.

"E" stands for "electronic"

Email and e-commerce (electronic mail and electronic commerce) are still quite new to many, but they represent changes in the way business and communication are conducted, worldwide, that will soon affect everyone.

Email allows people to write messages on their computer screens and then, via a phone connection, and for the cost of only a local telephone call, send those messages instantaneously to any person (or group of people) who has the equipment to receive them. It is therefore cheaper (and of, course, faster!) than mailing a letter, cheaper than faxing written material overseas, and cheaper than telephoning overseas. And it is user-friendly—a genuine revolution in communication.

E-commerce means the buying and selling of goods and services via the Internet. It is even newer than email, and has not yet won the acceptance that email has. There are issues—credit card security (the majority of purchases made on the Internet are made by credit card), censorship and copyright, to mention just three—that are as yet unresolved. These issues are particularly difficult as the Internet does not reside in any country; it exists only in "cyberspace", and it is not clear who has jurisdiction to regulate behavior on it, nor how, in practical terms, such regulation could occur effectively. Despite these uncertainties, e-commerce is growing.

The attractions of e-commerce are many: the buyer can, from home, view and compare a range of alternative products; there are web sites that specialize in comparison shopping, so the purchaser can find very low prices for some products; and consumers can buy products that are not available locally at all. The sorts of things that are succeeding in this brave new market range from groceries to clothes, books and compact discs, computers, airplane tickets and shares.

While it is claimed that at present only 1% of commercial activities take place on the Internet, online consumer sales will soon reach $US20 billion, and online commerce between companies will reach $US175 billion. A 1998 US survey found that 46% of commerce-related web sites were currently profitable, and an additional 30% were expected to be within two years. Consumers will determine, as time passes, what sorts of products can be successfully sold this way.

POPULATION AND HEALTH

The growth of the human population in just the last 50 years has been staggering. In 1950, the global population was 2.5 billion, and it is currently 5.5 billion. It is projected that 8.5 billion people will live on the planet in 2025 and perhaps 10 billion people by 2050. If you are 30 years of age or less by the year 2000 and living in a developed country, according to current life expectancy figures, you will probably live through the final exponential surge in the human population—it is estimated that the total number of people may start to decline in the second half of the twenty-first century.

Exponential growth refers to the doubling of a population over a given time period. The growth of the human population is of deep concern, as 5.5 billion people at current levels of resource consumption and waste generation are already causing major environmental problems.

Factors causing population growth

How is the growth in population explained? Demographers and population geographers generally begin explaining world population growth by discussing its two immediate causes: increased fertility and changes in mortality. Fertility refers to the number of children born to women of childbearing age. Mortality refers to various aspects of death, including how long people tend to live (life expectancy) and the causes of death (viruses, cancers, accidents, etc.).

Other factors that play a part in any explanation of population growth include the level of economic development of a given place, the availability of birth control, and the way people in different societies think about children.

Before the Industrial Revolution, the world's population grew slowly or did not grow at all. Although fertility was high in pre-modern societies—women commonly gave birth to between 8 and 12 children—mortality was also high. One out of four children died before reaching its first birthday (infant mortality) and perhaps another one out of five died before reaching 5 years of age (child mortality). Infectious diseases and poor diet were the major causes of high mortality, including infant and child mortality.

Why was the fertility rate so high then? If a family wanted or needed six children, mortality rates alone would require them to have ten or more. Families required the children for agricultural and domestic labor, and as a source of support when a parent grew old—children were the only pension fund available.

The early exponential growth of population resulted from a substantial improvement in the health of populations, especially with respect to control of infectious diseases and the improvement of nutrition, both of which reduced the mortality rate without a corresponding decline in the fertility rate. Infant and child mortality plummeted, and population growth surged.

As economic and social development moved into a more advanced stage, the economic meaning of children also changed. As children began attending school, they were no longer available for labor, and children became an expense rather than an asset. Raising a child today in a developed country may now cost between $US250,000 and $US750,000. Thus, fertility rates have declined with advanced development because of the increased survival rates of children (increased health) and because parents become

economically poorer by having many children (though not necessarily socially poorer) today, as against the past, when children labored for their parents for a substantial portion of their lives.

The advent of modern birth control has also played an important role in the decline of fertility. Most, if not all, developed countries have fertility rates below that required for maintaining current levels of population; immigration is the major factor responsible for continued population growth within developed countries.

Life expectancy—the individual

Looking at changes in health in greater depth, the health of a population has three components: mortality, morbidity (sickness), and disability. Life

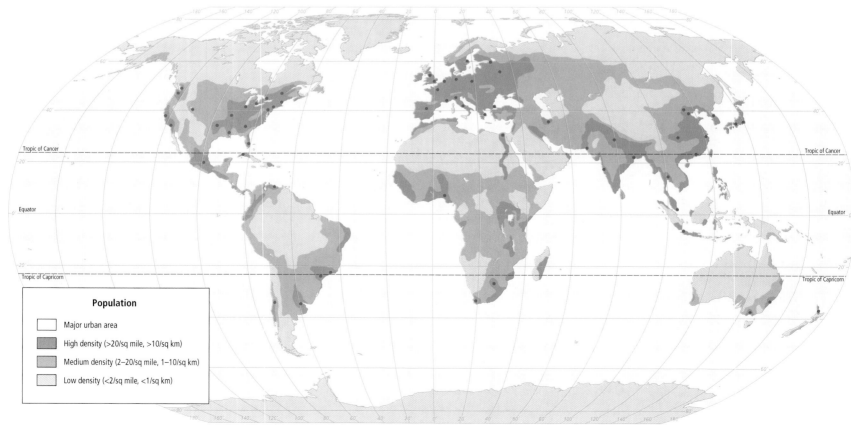

Population

- ☐ Major urban area
- High density (>20/sq mile, >10/sq km)
- Medium density (2–20/sq mile, 1–10/sq km)
- Low density (<2/sq mile, <1/sq km)

Tropic of Cancer

Equator

Tropic of Capricorn

Projection: Robinson   Equatorial Scale approx 1:110 million

Exponential population growth occurs when rising prosperity coincides with high fertility rates, as in Bangladesh (above). Communities in Zimbabwe (above right) work to improve their health, while some countries such as India (right) continue to suffer low life expectancy.

expectancy is commonly accepted in demography and development studies as a good general index of the health of a population. In fact, many see life expectancy as the single best index of the development of a nation or population, but it is important to remember that life expectancy specifically measures only the effects of mortality changes; it does not relate to the sickness and disability aspect of human health.

Life expectancy was generally low before the Industrial Revolution. If life expectancy is expressed in terms of years a population as a whole lives, then life expectancy was low (between 45 and 55 years), mainly because of the prevalence of infectious diseases (measles, pneumonia, polio, and malaria, for instance), poor nutrition, lack of family planning, and the like.

Substantial advances in the reduction of a range of infectious diseases, coupled with improvement in nutrition, represent what the United Nations Children's Fund describes in their annual publication *The Progress of Nations* as simply that—the progress of nations. Life expectancy increases by 10 to 15 years because of these improvements to health.

Further increases in life expectancy—when compared with, say, life expectancy in the late 1960s and into the 1970s—are the result of advances in the reduction of death due to degenerative diseases (strokes, cancers, and heart attacks, for example) and the greater emphasis on improving lifestyle—a healthy diet, regular exercise and a reduction in smoking.

For a few nations, life expectancy is slightly more than 81 years at present. At the global scale, life expectancy at birth was 46 years in 1950, 65 years in the late 1990s, and is projected to be 77 years in the year 2050.

Life expectancy—the global view

Considerable regional diversity in the causes of population growth and life expectancy is evident in the late 1990s. Generally speaking, North America, Australia and Europe have high life expectancy and have internal growth rates below population replacement; South America and East and Southeast Asia are not far behind; and Africa south of the Sahara has low life expectancy, but population growth remains explosively high.

Many of the countries in the former communist world are experiencing deterioration in health, and life expectancy is actually declining in some of those nations, including Russia. It is interesting to compare the two most populous nations, China and India. Changes to population growth and life expectancy in China resemble those in other East and Southeast Asian nations, whereas India continues to have a very high growth rate and a moderately low life expectancy.

The future for life expectancy

Is there a limit to life expectancy? This is a most controversial topic about which there is no agreement. Under natural conditions, all life forms have a limit, called senescence: the point where an organism simply wears out. For the human population, senescence was believed to be roughly 85 years; however, a few population

Famine

Famine can be defined as a high degree of lack of food within a population, and it often goes along with widespread mortality. Malnutrition, on the other hand, refers to levels of nourishment that are below those needed to maintain health, and can apply to a whole population or part of a population.

Both are thought to be results of population pressure —the pressure that builds, in developing countries particularly, between the size of the population and the economic resources (especially food) of the country. Falling living standards can be an early sign, in countries with rapidly growing populations, of this pressure. Many societies have suffered famines; in modern times, famine has most often affected societies in Africa.

The links between famine and malnutrition and mortality and fertility now seem not nearly as clear as may previously have been thought. Investigations into mortality in developing countries have found that it is the combination of malnourishment and infectious disease that is responsible for high mortality among infants and children, not simply lack of food.

It seems that populations are able to maintain their rates of fertility despite quite large reductions in nutritional levels—metabolic rates actually appear to readjust.

groups live into the low 90s. Genetic and other medical research, however, may well change the upper limit of life expectancy during the first half of the twenty-first century.

Of course, all of this optimistically assumes that improvements in health will continue. It remains to be seen whether or not the impact of diseases such as AIDS will retard or even reverse the historical improvement in human health, the resistance of some forms of bacteria to antibiotics, in particular, will give rise to deaths from diseases or infections previously thought to be under control, and whether the advances that come through medical research will be affordable to a sizeable proportion of the world's population.

NATURAL HAZARDS

Natural events which cause damage and loss of life are classified as natural hazards. These hazards are generally unpredictable—they strike suddenly and can therefore leave the affected populations traumatized. Natural hazards can result from movements taking place inside the Earth or on its surface, or in its atmosphere.

Movements within the Earth result in volcanic eruptions and earthquakes. Changing weather conditions generate wind storms, cyclones, tornadoes, heavy rainfall, and snowfall, as well as lightning strikes, which can trigger forest fires. River floods and tsunamis can cause loss of life and serious damage to property.

Earthquakes

Plate collision along the Japanese archipelago makes that area vulnerable to earthquakes and to tsunamis generated by earthquakes on the ocean floor. Plates sliding past each other can also cause earthquakes, such as along the San Andreas Fault in California, where earthquakes have occurred in San Francisco and in Los Angeles.

Earthquakes strike suddenly, and if they are of high intensity, buildings can be toppled and life and property lost. The famous San Francisco earthquake of 1906 was devastating to that city and its people—hundreds of buildings were destroyed and the resulting fires swept through the city center, leaving about 3,000 people dead and many thousands more homeless.

An intense earthquake in 1995 toppled and wrecked the tall buildings and infrastructure of Kobe, in Japan, killing more than 6,000 of its inhabitants and injuring more than 35,000 others. The worst scenarios involve earthquakes located close to inhabited areas, notably cities.

On the Richter scale, earthquakes are serious when they exceed a magnitude of 4, cause damage when they exceed 5 and are intensely destructive when they are between 7 and 8.6. Although more than a million earthquakes occur every year, most of these are of low magnitude, and cause no loss of life or damage to property. High-intensity earthquakes, on the other hand, are capable of causing great damage and therefore receive the most publicity, particularly when they are centered on densely populated areas.

Tsunamis

Earthquakes taking place on the sea bed can trigger tsunamis (tidal waves) which, on reaching land, can assume enormous proportions and result in great damage. Such waves may be less than 1 m (3 ft) in height where they begin, in the deep oceans, but they can reach the enormous heights of more than 30 m (100 ft) as they approach land, and they cause devastation to low-lying areas. Worse still, within seconds, more than one such giant tidal wave can strike.

In 1983, a tsunami resulted in the deaths of 30,000 people in Japan. On 17 July 1998, a tsunami struck the northern coast of Papua New Guinea, sweeping over the village of Arop and others nearby, which lay on a low-lying sandy spit; entire villages and their populations were swept away, and it is estimated that the death toll could be as many as 4,000 people.

Volcanoes

Volcanic eruptions are common along certain paths, which are also seismic zones. Here, crustal plates separate and collide. Volcanoes erupt where molten material (magma) accumulates just below

Earth's surface and then rises to the surface. A volcanic explosion ejects ash and superheated steam into the atmosphere and cascades very hot lava along the sides of the volcanic cones. Volcanic eruptions are another natural disaster that can be devastating to life and property.

In AD 79, lava and ash destroyed the ancient city of Pompeii in southern Italy when Mt Vesuvius erupted. Mt Pelée, in Martinique, erupted in 1902, destroying the city of St Pierre and killing most of its inhabitants. Mt Pinatubo, in the Philippines, erupted in 1991, ejecting steam, ash, and lava, and threatened hundreds of thousands of people just 27 km (17 miles) away in Angeles; its ash even blanketed parts of Manila. Volcanic eruptions are also common in Bali and Java (Indonesia).

Volcanic eruptions are rated on the Volcanic Explosivity Index. The Krakatoa eruption of 1883 in Indonesia, one of the most spectacular on record, is rated at 6. No recorded eruption has

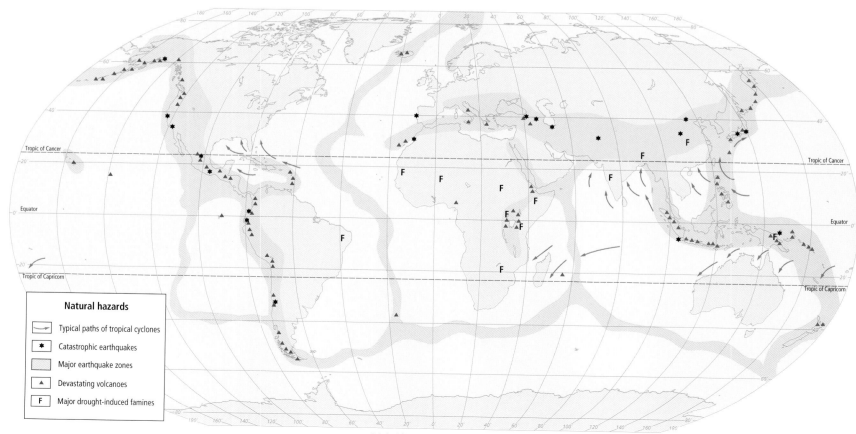

Natural hazards

- Typical paths of tropical cyclones
- * Catastrophic earthquakes
- Major earthquake zones
- ▲ Devastating volcanoes
- F Major drought-induced famines

Projection: Robinson   Equatorial Scale approx 1:155 million

Wildfires (bushfires, far left) consume large tracts of forest in many countries every year. Often lives are also lost, and millions of dollars worth of property is destroyed. Mt Pinatubo in the Philippines erupted in 1991 (left), causing widespread damage with devastating mud slides which swamped a large area including the town of Lahar (bottom). Drought (below) is a more predictable natural hazard.

reached 8, which is the highest possible rating. The Krakatoa eruption was heard more than 4,500 km (2,800 miles) away; it generated tsunamis, and more than 30,000 people are believed to have perished as a result.

Tropical cyclones and tornadoes

Tropical cyclones, known as typhoons in East Asia and hurricanes in the Caribbean, are also very destructive atmospheric hazards. Tropical cyclones are whirling, low-pressure vortices that can be up to 500 km (310 miles) in diameter and have wind speeds reaching more than 200 km (125 miles) per hour. They can pick up trees, rooftops, light boats, and planes and destroy them. This flying debris is enormously dangerous to people, too.

In coastal areas, large waves, or surges, which sweep the land may be generated, resulting in considerable damage. These cyclones have a calm center, called the "eye" of the cyclone; when the eye passes over an area there is a period of calm, after which the storm returns in all its fury, but with the winds now reversed in direction.

The coastal areas of Southeast and East Asia, the Bay of Bengal, the Pacific Ocean west of Mexico, the Caribbean and Florida, plus island groups of the Pacific Ocean such as Fiji, and northern Australia, are amongst the areas most prone to tropical cyclones.

Cyclones have struck with great fury along the coast of Bangladesh, a small country which mostly consists of the combined deltas of the Ganges and Brahmaputra rivers. That low-lying deltaic area is particularly vulnerable to the surges which cyclones can generate. This has resulted, on several occasions, in considerable loss of life and damage to property.

In contrast to tropical cyclones, tornadoes are small low-pressure cells, not more than 0.5 km (³/₁₀ mile) across. They are, however, very intense, and their wind speeds can exceed 400 km (250 miles) per hour. They thus have the potential to inflict sudden and serious damage. Their vortices become vividly visible as they whip up soil and other debris. The most damaging tornadoes occur in the central parts of the United States, although mini-versions are also found in parts of eastern Australia.

River floods

River floods are a common hazard in floodplains. Spectacular floods, covering thousands of square kilometers, often occur over the immense plains of the major rivers of China, India, and Bangladesh. These areas are often densely populated because of the fertile soils and abundant water supplies.

The Huang River in China flows along a course which is elevated over the surrounding plains; this is because levees have naturally built up on its sides. These levees have been further reinforced by human action. The bursting of the levees in 1887 inundated more than 130,000 sq km (50,000 sq miles) and resulted in a million deaths.

In the case of the Ganges River in India and Bangladesh, the deforestation in the Himalayas has resulted, at times, in water from heavy rainfall and snowmelt rushing onto the vast plains through which the Ganges runs and flooding them. In 1988, 90 percent of Bangladesh lay under water when the Ganges flooded.

Floods regularly bring human and economic disasters to many parts of the world—in 1998 alone, 250 million people were affected by the flooding of the Yangtze River in China—and dams and irrigation networks have been built across many flood-prone rivers in an attempt to mitigate and control flood damage.

Wildfires

Wildfires or bushfires strike when forests are dry. These fires can cause serious damage and result in significant air pollution. The 1997 wildfires in the tropical forests of Sumatra, Indonesia, for instance, released a dense pall of smoke over a large area, including parts of Malaysia and Singapore. These fires were lit by humans clearing land for agriculture or woodchipping. Normally, rains ensure that wildfires are temporary, and restricted to a small area. In Sumatra, however, the prolonged drought, blamed on the El Niño effect, resulted in the uncontrollable spread of the wildfires.

The naturally occurring eucalypt forests of Australia and the eucalypt forest plantations of California are also particularly prone to wildfires, as the volatile oil the eucalypts contain makes them highly flammable. Every year, wildfires wipe out large areas of these forests and damage human settlements or property in the process.

Remote sensing, using satellites and highly sophisticated monitoring techniques, is now being used to track possible natural disasters. It provides data to ground centers about the development of tropical cyclones, the spreading of flood waters from rivers, and the build-up of lava in volcanoes. Such advance warning systems have already helped save lives and limit damage.

Part 2

People and Society

The Changing Scene

Human societies have changed more during the 20th century than during any previous one, but mechanized facilities are not yet available to all—no running water for these Indian women in Varanasi, opposite. Conversely, highly sophisticated cultures developed thousands of years ago without modern conveniences, leaving treasures such as this floor mosaic, above, from Cyprus.

Today's global pattern of peoples and nations rests on a long process of social evolution, going back about 2 million years. It was then that humanity began to clearly distinguish itself as something special on the planet—and unlike the great apes—by physical and mental changes such as a fully upright way of walking, and much bigger brains than the apes possessed. Then, some time in the past 40,000 years, the great evolutionary breakthrough occurred—a fully developed capacity for language, an ability to create new tools for new purposes, and a talent for forward planning. Previously nomadic, hunting wild animals and foraging for seeds and fruits, humans now chose to live a more settled existence. People began to live in regular campsites and used shelters they made themselves. In some places they dug pits for food storage, and had well-built, regularly used fireplaces as far back as 20,000 years ago. Art and religion also appeared, with remarkable cave paintings and evidence of ritual associated with the burial of the dead.

It is thought that *Homo sapiens sapiens* (the technical name for modern humans) originated in Africa. From there waves of migration carried people to every corner of Earth: to distant Australia perhaps 50,000 years ago, to North America across a land bridge (where the Bering Strait is now) perhaps 20,000 years ago. As they moved, they took their languages with them, and when they settled, their languages continued to evolve, many soon becoming mutually unintelligible. Then, around 10,000 years ago came a major development—the rise of agriculture and of permanent settlements. In Turkey and Iraq, in China, and in Mexico, farmers began to grow wheat and barley, or rice, or maize. At around the same time, the first farm animals were domesticated: pigs and cattle, goats and sheep, and llamas in South America.

Permanent farming settlements transformed human life economically, and on this foundation civilizations arose in different parts of the world. In Egypt and Iraq, in China and India, in Mexico and Peru, some towns became cities, with centralized political systems, strong rulers, and monumental buildings. The buildings were often religious temples associated with a class of priests, and in Egypt they were tombs for divine kings, built to preserve their bodies and effects for the afterlife. These social and political developments were accompanied by equally significant developments in science and technology.

The Stone Age, which for millions of years had provided stone implements for hunters, and then stone adzes and reaping blades for the first farmers, came to an end. First bronze was invented, then people found out how to make iron—by 500 BC, iron tools and weapons were spread throughout Europe and Asia. Metals and metallurgical science gave those who had them a huge military advantage over those who did not, as did the wheel, when it appeared around 3,500 BC. Horses harnessed to chariots changed the nature of warfare in ancient times.

War and conquest were normal conditions of life. Other things being equal, victory went to those whose weapons were most advanced. Some dominant cities developed into empires, subjecting other cultures to their rule. The Roman Empire, at its height, included large areas of Europe, North Africa, and the Middle East. By 206 BC, China was united under the Qin Dynasty, while by 1,520 AD the Incas controlled some 2,000 miles (3,330 km) of territory west of the Andes in South America. The military advantages of steel weapons and guns were demonstrated by the easy victories of Cortez over the Aztecs (1521) and Pizarro over the Incas (1533) against vastly greater numbers of ill-equipped Amerindian forces. The consequences of empire were that the knowledge, ideas, religion, technology and language of the dominant civilization were spread far and wide. Trade, both private and state-sponsored, also played a major role in this. The Han Empire in China (206 BC to 220 AD), for instance, traded its silks with the Syrians of the Roman Empire far to the west. Arab trade spread round the Indian Ocean, and by 1200 AD had reached as far east as Java.

The spread of the main world religions has also been of major importance in the last two thousand years. These religions have been responsible for the most enduring examples of the art, literature, and architecture of civilization. A major distinction can be made between proselytizing religions, which actively seek to convert people to their beliefs (such as Chistianity, Islam, and Buddhism) and those which do not, such as Hinduism and Judaism. The world's three major religions are Christianity (33.0%), Islam (19.6%), and Hinduism (12.8%), the first two being derived from early Judaism (0.3%).

In the past 200 years, industrialization has been the biggest force for social change. Beginning in England with textile manufacturing in the 1780s, then progressing to manufacturing based on iron and steel in the nineteenth century, industrialization now combines science with technology in an unending cycle of invention and discovery. What began in Europe has now spread to every country in the world. Industry, which takes raw materials and then turns them into products to be traded, has provided millions of jobs for peasants who would otherwise be tied to the land. But in order to take those jobs they have moved into the cities. Urbanization has created huge concentrations of people in Asia and in South America, and while raising incomes, it has brought social problems too.

Political changes have come thick and fast. The nation-state arose as a political movement in Europe in the nineteenth century, where it superseded an earlier pattern of city-states such as Venice, Antwerp and Amsterdam. After the Second World War it spread through Asia and Africa during the process of decolonization, and since 1989 it has disrupted the domains of the former Soviet Union. Endemic conflicts born of nationalism continue to plague troublespots in Africa, Indo-China, the Balkans, and the Middle East. However, there has been at the same time a balancing move toward large, over-arching international organizations. The European Union steadily moves toward greater political and economic unity. Meanwhile, the United Nations, its resources and abilities increasingly overstretched, its goals more honored in the breach than in the observance, endeavors to keep international peace.

HUMAN EVOLUTION

The oldest primate fossils found in Africa and Asia date from between 45 and 50 million years ago. Around 15 million years ago, Asian and African hominoids (the earliest known ancestors of both humans and apes) diverged. The African hominoids adapted to woodland and savanna habitats and developed the ability to walk on two legs, while the Asian hominoids continued their tree-climbing existence. Although the fossil record is incomplete, a later divergence probably occurred among African hominoids between gorillas and the common ancestors of humans and chimpanzees.

Early hominids

The first hominids (the earliest ancestors of modern human beings not also related to modern great apes) developed about 5 to 6 million years ago. During the earliest phases of their evolution, hominids underwent anatomical changes that resulted in an erect posture, allowing them to walk habitually on two legs. Other changes included the reduction of canine teeth and the development of a comparatively vertical face. Features that are widely accepted as hominid hallmarks, such as a larger brain and the capacity for cultural life (indicated by stone or bone tools), appeared later.

The earliest hominid fossils have been found in southern and eastern Africa. The Olduvai Gorge in the Great Rift Valley of

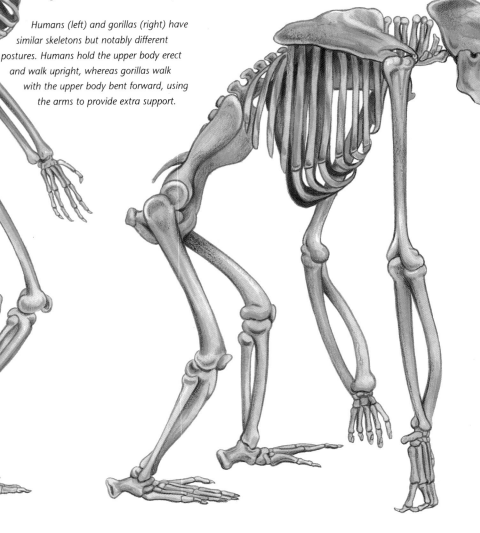

Humans (left) and gorillas (right) have similar skeletons but notably different postures. Humans hold the upper body erect and walk upright, whereas gorillas walk with the upper body bent forward, using the arms to provide extra support.

Tanzania has proved to be a rich source. In the 1930s, the anthropologist Louis Leakey began excavations there, and, in the ensuing years, he and others found a large number of hominid fossils and stone tools. The most famous find occurred in 1959 when his wife Mary uncovered a hominid fossil she called *Zinjanthropus*, believed to be 1,750,000 years old. Most scholars now believe that *Zinjanthropus* is an example of *Australopithecus* (specifically *Australopithecus boisei*), the earliest group of hominids yet found.

Handy man

Other hominid fossils found at Olduvai Gorge were more clearly identifiable as members of our own genus, *Homo*. These hominids were tool users and have been classified as *Homo habilis* ("handy man"). Tools similar to those found at Olduvai have been found at sites elsewhere in Africa and dated at between 1,800,000 and 2,340,000 years old.

Fossils of species that are more recognizably like ourselves have also been found in Africa and dated at about 1.9 million years ago. The best example is a nearly complete 1.6-million-year-old skeleton found in northern Kenya and known as Turkana Boy. The boy died in adolescence, but, had he lived to maturity, he would have been tall (about 1.8 m [6 ft]), with long, slender limbs, and well adapted to living on the open savanna.

Turkana Boy and other similar fossils found in Africa were originally thought to resemble specimens discovered in Java and China. All were classified as *Homo erectus* and it

was believed that *Homo erectus* had evolved in Africa and then migrated to Asia about 1 million years ago. Discoveries in China in the past decade, however, together with the application of more sophisticated dating methods to previously excavated Asian sites, have pushed back the date of the first appearance of early hominids in Asia to about 2 million years ago. Hominid fossils found in Longgupo Cave in Sichuan province in China, dated at around 1.9 million years old, more closely resemble the earlier hominid species *Homo habilis*. This suggests a much earlier migration out of Africa. As a result, some scholars now believe that *Homo erectus* evolved independently in Asia and was not an African species. African hominid fossils of a more modern appearance, such as Turkana Boy, are now classified as a separate species, *Homo ergaster*.

Although there are a number of early hominid sites in Europe, they have yielded few fossils. Sites containing tools have been dated at around 1 million years old, with the earliest being about 1.5 million years old. Until recently, some of these were classified as *Homo erectus* sites. Since this species is now considered to be an Asian evolutionary sideline, however, the fossil record is being reassessed. In 1994, excavations in northern Spain produced numerous simple stone tools and some hominid fossils subsequently classified as a separate species, *Homo heidelbergensis*. This find has been dated at more than 780,000 years old and may provide evidence for the European ancestors of the Neanderthals.

Archaic *Homo sapiens*

The earliest archaeological discoveries made in Europe were fossils of archaic *Homo sapiens*. The fossils were named Neanderthals, after the Neander Valley near Düsseldorf in Germany, where they were first discovered in 1865. This find caused widespread excitement as it was the first discovery of an extinct ancestor of modern humans. Since then, numerous Neanderthal sites have been found throughout Europe and the Middle East. The Neanderthals are generally considered to be a subspecies of *Homo sapiens*, known as *Homo sapiens neanderthalensis*. However, some scholars believe that the Neanderthals' less evolved physical characteristics and less sophisticated technology indicate that they were a separate species, *Homo neanderthalensis*.

The Neanderthals lived in Europe and Western Asia approximately 35,000 to 130,000 years ago, overlapping with the modern human species (*Homo sapiens sapiens*). They had larger brain cases and smaller back teeth than earlier populations, but differed from modern humans in their receding forehead and large, protruding face with front teeth and forward-projecting jaw. The Neanderthals had a relatively short, bulky stature and considerable strength, and showed evidence of complex cultural traits and social organization. For example, they used planning and cooperation to hunt large mammals. They also buried their dead and seem to have had some knowledge of art, demonstrating a capacity for symbolic behavior. Their vocal apparatus and neurological structure provide indirect evidence that they may also have developed speech.

Neanderthals disappear from the archaeological record around 40,000 years ago in the Middle East and about 35,000 years ago in Europe. It may be that they slowly evolved into modern humans, contributing to the gene pool of the present-day inhabitants of Europe and the Middle East. However, many scholars now think that they were gradually overwhelmed and replaced by incoming populations of a more advanced species classified as *Homo sapiens sapiens*, or modern humans.

Out of Africa

The early history of modern humans is still uncertain, as the fossil record is far from complete. Some scholars argue that *Homo sapiens sapiens* developed independently, in a number of different geographical locations. Others consider that what is popularly called the "out of Africa" theory better reflects what is now known about the process of evolution. This proposes that modern human populations are all descended from a single ancestral population that emerged at one location between 150,000 and 100,000 years ago. Increasing archaeological evidence suggests that the place of origin of modern humans was somewhere in Africa. From this homeland, *Homo sapiens sapiens* migrated northward into Europe some 40,000 to 100,000 years ago, and then spread throughout the world, gradually replacing more archaic populations wherever they encountered them.

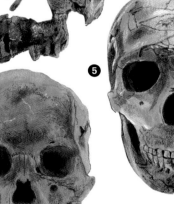
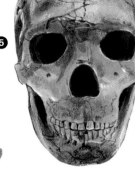

Human fossil skulls: 1. Australopithecus boisei. 2. Homo habilis. 3. Homo ergaster. 4. Homo erectus. 5. Homo sapiens neanderthalensis. 6. Homo sapiens sapiens. *Note the gradual disappearance of the thick brow ridges, and the growth of the cranium—indicative of increasing brain capacity and intelligence.*

The classification of primate fossils

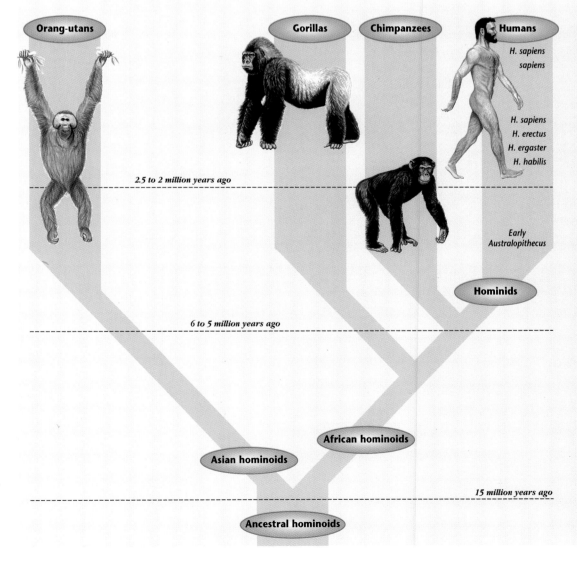

Orang-utans
Gorillas
Chimpanzees
Humans

H. sapiens sapiens

H. sapiens
H. erectus
H. ergaster
H. habilis

Early Australopithecus

Hominids

2.5 to 2 million years ago

6 to 5 million years ago

African hominoids

Asian hominoids

15 million years ago

Ancestral hominoids

In 1735, the Swedish naturalist Carl Linnaeus caused a public outcry when he classified human beings as part of the animal kingdom. Today, however, his taxonomy—which has been extensively revised and expanded—is the accepted way of classifying all forms of plant and animal life.

The human species, *Homo sapiens sapiens*, belongs to the genus *Homo* (which includes our hominid ancestors) in the family *Hominidae* (which includes the apes). This family is in turn part of the Primate order. The relationship between humans, apes, and early hominid fossils is problematic. Recent studies by molecular biologists have shown that there is a much closer genetic link between humans and the African great apes (especially chimpanzees) than might have been predicted from comparing their anatomies. This has led some taxonomists to place humans, gorillas, and chimpanzees in one family, *Hominidae*, and Asian apes such as the orang-utan in another, *Pongidae*.

The currently accepted classification of hominid fossils establishes a chronology for modern humans from the development of the first australopithecine species (appearing around 5 million years ago), to early *Homo* species such as *Homo habilis* and *Homo erectus* (from around 2 million years ago), through to later *Homo species* (around 1 million years ago) and archaic *Homo sapiens* such as the Neanderthals (about 130,000 years ago). Both the classification and the chronology are likely to be revised as new fossil discoveries are made.

THE FIRST MODERN HUMANS

The success of modern humans, *Homo sapiens sapiens*, in colonizing Earth's landmasses owes much to the evolutionary changes that occurred in the physical form and mental capacity of hominids. Although the basic hominid anatomy changed little, the features that distinguished hominids from other hominoids, such as their erect posture, ability to walk habitually on two legs, vertical face, smaller teeth and enlarged brain, were refined in each successive species and subspecies. By far the most significant change, and the one that signaled the emergence of *Homo sapiens sapiens*, was the progressive enlargement of the brain, which was out of all proportion to changes in body size. In absolute terms, the average brain capacity of modern humans is three times that of the great apes.

Increased brain capacity allowed *Homo sapiens sapiens* to develop greater intelligence and problem-solving capabilities. This led to the appearance of tools as well as speech and language (although full language capacity emerged less than 40,000 years ago). It also enabled modern humans to develop strategies for coping with harsh environments, such as camp fires, clothing, natural food storage facilities, and primitive cooking methods. Further intellectual development resulted in a flourishing cultural life and increased capacity for social organization, which in turn stimulated the growth of civilizations and led to the evolution of modern society.

Making and using tools

Many people believe that it is the presence of tools that distinguishes early humans (*Homo* spp.) from other hominids, but a number of other animals also make and use tools. Chimpanzees, for instance, have demonstrated an ability to make

and use tools for digging for food. More specifically, some scholars have argued that it is the power and complexity of human tool assemblages that distinguishes humans. However, the simplicity of the tool assemblages of archaic humans and certain hunter–gatherers of the recent past makes this explanation inadequate. What *is* unique about human tool making and tool use is that the tools were made for particular purposes. Moreover, they were constantly improved and adapted for new purposes, to the extent that tools eventually pervaded all aspects of human life. This is not the case among chimpanzees.

The first hominid fossils associated with hand-made tools were those of *Homo habilis*, found at Olduvai Gorge in Tanzania, and dated at about 2 million years old. Tools have been found in older East African sites, but without any fossil remains. Although earlier hominid species knew how to make and use tools, it was probably only with the emergence of the genus *Homo* that tools became part of daily life.

The early *Homo habilis* tools were crude, stone hand-axes. Unsurprisingly, stone and some bone tools dominate the archaeological record. Tools made of perishable materials such as wood are found occasionally at waterlogged, frozen, or arid sites, but such finds are rare. From about one million years ago, tool assemblages became more specialized, but it is only in the past 40,000 years that there has been a proliferation of designs.

The simplicity of early tools clearly indicates that hominids obtained their food by foraging and scavenging. The traditional view that the hunting of animals accompanied and influenced the evolutionary development of modern humans has been reassessed in the light of this evidence.

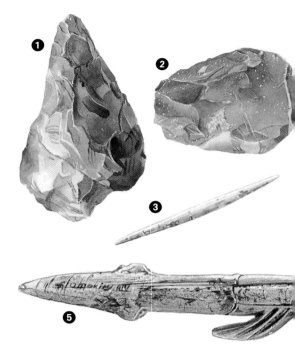

Regular hunting, particularly the killing of large mammals, probably began later. Far more important at this stage in the evolution of modern humans was the development of an ability to plan ahead. Although this would become essential for organizing hunts, it was also required at an earlier stage to enable humans to forage for food and store supplies for lean times.

Art and cooking skills

There seems to have been a watershed in the development of modern humans around 40,000 years ago. This is reflected in a dramatic worldwide

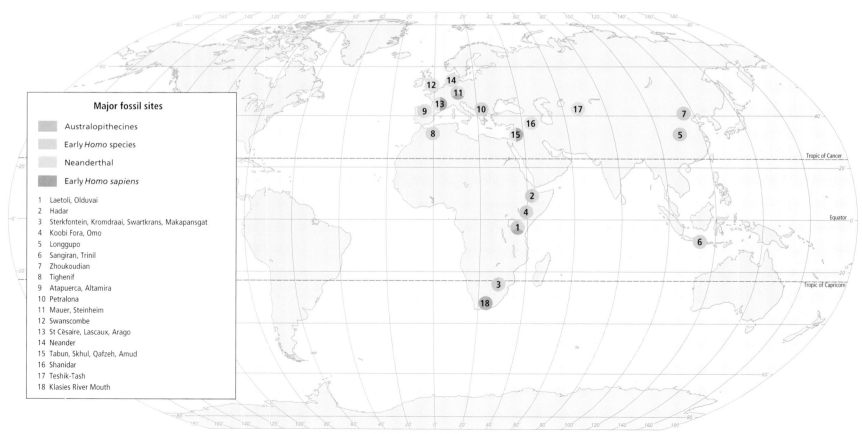

Major fossil sites

Australopithecines

Early *Homo* species

Neanderthal

Early *Homo sapiens*

1 Laetoli, Olduvai
2 Hadar
3 Sterkfontein, Kromdraai, Swartkrans, Makapansgat
4 Koobi Fora, Omo
5 Longgupo
6 Sangiran, Trinil
7 Zhoukoudian
8 Tighenif
9 Atapuerca, Altamira
10 Petralona
11 Mauer, Steinheim
12 Swanscombe
13 St Cèsaire, Lascaux, Arago
14 Neander
15 Tabun, Skhul, Qafzeh, Amud
16 Shanidar
17 Teshik-Tash
18 Klasies River Mouth

Projection: Robinson   Equatorial Scale approx 1:155 million

Many people believe that the invention and use of tools marked out the early humans from other hominids. The development of human technology is reflected in these tools (below):

1. *Scraper from Swanscombe, England; 300,000–200,000 BP*
2. *Sidescraper from Le Moustier, France; 70,000–35,000 BP*
3. *Bone point from Aurignac, France; 35,000–23,000 BP*
4. *Bifacial stone knife from Solutré, France; 20,000–17,000 BP*
5. *Bone harpoon from Le Morin, France; 16,000–8,000 BP*

❹

change in the archaeological evidence. Not only did tool assemblages become more sophisticated, but art, in the form of jewellery, figurines, paintings, and engravings (often depicting hunting scenes), also become prevalent. The widespread use of raw materials that could only have been obtained from distant sources suggests that trade networks had expanded. Camp sites show evidence of more settled living, including artificial shelters, food storage pits, and well-built, regularly used fireplaces. Burial sites become more elaborate, containing ornaments and other cultural objects. The disposal of the dead clearly involved some form of ritual, reflecting metaphysical concerns and symbolic behavior.

There also appears to have been a "culinary revolution," with stone knives being used to cut up food. This allowed for more thorough cooking, which may in turn have resulted in changes in the cranial structure of humans, as large teeth would no longer have been necessary for tearing raw or partially roasted meat.

These cultural and physical changes occurred during the last ice age, which culminated about 15,000 to 20,000 years ago, when glaciers covered large areas of the world. Successful strategies developed by modern humans to cope with the deteriorating climate gave them a clear advantage over more archaic forms of *Homo sapiens*. Despite the spread of hostile environments during the ice age, *Homo sapiens sapiens* succeeded in colonizing the world far more rapidly and extensively than earlier hominid migrants.

Colonization on the scale undertaken by *Homo sapiens sapiens* required all of the species' new-found technical and social skills. Its success depended not just on tools and an ability to plan ahead, but also on the existence of extensive social structures which could provide the support and cooperation necessary for the completion of long, hazardous journeys into unknown lands.

The art of early hunter–gatherers

Art is widely believed to have originated during the last ice age and appears to have flourished mainly in Europe and the southern hemisphere (southern Africa and Australia). Little has been found at ice-age sites in North Africa, China, or elsewhere in Asia. This does not mean, however, that art did not exist in these areas—it may simply be that the forms of artistic expression were more temporary or that the materials used did not survive.

Ice-age art is linked with major innovations in tool technology, including well-crafted and highly efficient blades, and hafted spears. With the rapid evolution of hunting techniques, obtaining food would no longer have been as difficult and, consequently, more effort could be expended on the development of art, language, and spiritual interests. No record remains of stories, songs, or dances of these pre-literate cultures, nor of artworks made out of perishable materials. The art that has survived can be divided into two main types: moveable objects and rock art.

Moveable objects comprise small figures or decorated weapons made of stone, bone, antler, ivory, or clay, which were sometimes placed in graves to accompany the deceased in the afterlife. Rock art, such as engravings and paintings, is often found in caves. While drawings of human figures have been found, most rock art depicts game animals such as bison, mammoths, deer, and bears, which were important sources of food, clothing, tools, weapons, and ornaments. Outstanding examples of cave art were discovered in the nineteenth century at Altamira in northern Spain and at Lascaux in southwestern France.

This ancient cave painting (above) was found in Rhodes-Matapos National Park in Zimbabwe, Africa. Fertility figures, such as the 20,000-year-old Willendorf Venus from Austria (left), are among the earliest indications of a human concern with rituals and symbols.

HUMAN MIGRATIONS

Recent research undertaken on fossil and genetic evidence suggests that hominids migrated "out of Africa" on many occasions, probably beginning with *Homo erectus, Homo habilis*, or the taller and more slender *Homo ergaster* more than 2 million years ago. Changes in the climate may have been a major factor in these early migrations. One theory suggests that between 2 million and 3 million years ago, a widespread drop in temperature led to the replacement of the tropical woodlands in eastern Africa by savanna grassland. This change in vegetation favored the *Homo* species over the australopithecines. With their larger brains, more generalized diets, and greater tool-using ability, the *Homo* species adapted more readily to the open terrain and soon began to roam widely. Initially, they probably followed the land mammals on which they scavenged, as the animals moved north and east following the expansion of the grasslands.

To date, early *Homo* sites have been discovered at several Asian sites in the Republic of Georgia, in China, and on the island of Java in Indonesia. Early humans did not make an appearance in Europe until some time later (around 1 to 1.5 million years ago), and this region remained sparsely populated until 500,000 years ago.

During their migrations, early *Homo* species would have crossed various land bridges that appeared during the recurring ice ages of the past 2 million years. However, to explain the presence of 800,000-year-old stone tools on the Indonesian island of Flores, which would have remained at least 20 km (12 miles) offshore even at the height of the ice ages, scientists have tentatively suggested that *Homo erectus* made use of simple vessels such as bamboo rafts to cross short stretches of sea.

Migrations by modern humans

Compared with the migrations made by archaic populations, the spread of modern humans during the last 100,000 years occurred remarkably rapidly. Furthermore, *Homo sapiens sapiens* ventured much farther than earlier hominids, eventually reaching the Americas and Australia. These more extensive migrations were made possible by this species' greater adaptability and by the exposure of numerous land bridges during the last ice age.

Scientists are still debating when and how the Americas were colonized, although it is generally accepted that hunting groups crossed into Alaska via a land bridge in the Bering Strait. This could have occurred either between 63,000 and 45,000 years ago or between 35,000 and 10,000 years ago. Although some argue that the earlier crossing is more likely because the Alaskan ice sheet would not have been as extensive as during the later period, the earliest reliable dates for archaeological sites in North America are no more than 20,000 years old. Consequently, the more widely held view is that the crossing occurred between 12,000 and 20,000 years ago, with people gradually drifting south down the continent. Recent evidence suggests that Monte Verde in southern Chile may have been settled as early as 12,500 years ago.

The question of whether there was one or more crossings is also unresolved. Some researchers believe that genetic variations among the indigenous peoples of the Americas are so great that they suggest three or four waves of migration. A more recent assessment cautiously suggests that there were no more than two waves—one arriving about 20,000 to 25,000 years ago and the other around 11,300 years ago.

These early settlers were probably of more diverse origins than previously thought, and some may even have arrived by sea rather than across the land bridge.

Debates of a similar nature surround the colonization of Australia. The earliest direct evidence of humans is about 40,000 years old (claims that various artefacts and sites in the Northern Territory date from around 60,000 years ago have not been confirmed). Since some of these sites are in the south of the continent, dates of up to 50–60,000 years ago for the initial arrival of humans from Southeast Asia have been proposed to allow for the settlement of large areas

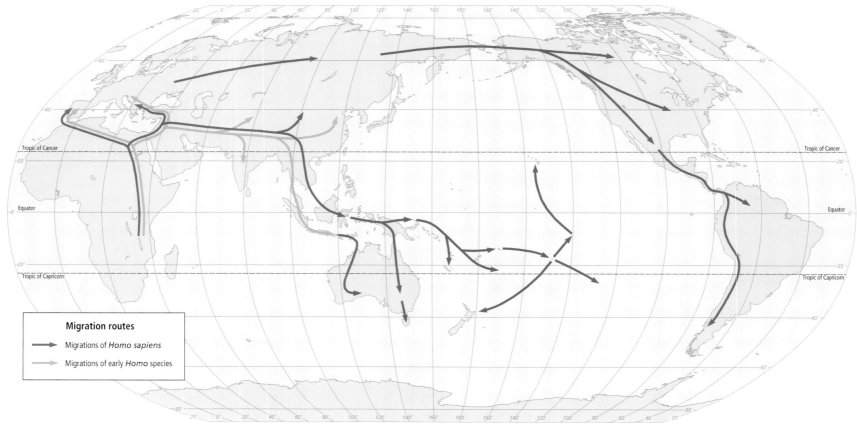

Migration routes

→ Migrations of *Homo sapiens*

→ Migrations of early *Homo* species

Tropic of Cancer
Equator
Tropic of Capricorn

Projection: Robinson   Equatorial Scale approx 1:155 million

The expansion of African grasslands (left) as a result of climatic changes assisted early migrations. The first people to settle in North America would have had a lifestyle similar to that of present-day Inuit (below). Early Polynesian watercraft may have resembled this canoe from the Solomon Islands (bottom).

of the continent by 40,000 years ago. The absence of Asian fauna in Australia indicates that there must have been a substantial stretch of sea between the two continents for millions of years.

Colonizing the Pacific

The islands along the western rim of the Pacific were probably colonized around the same time as Australia and New Guinea, when sea levels were sufficiently low for them to be linked to the Asian mainland. Of course, *Homo erectus* may also have occupied these islands while they were linked to the mainland during earlier periods of glaciation, but the earliest signs of human occupation in Japan have been dated at around 30,000 years ago. Based on the evidence currently available, it appears that other islands on the western Pacific rim, such as most of the Philippines, were probably occupied 10,000 to 15,000 years later.

By the time European explorers reached the Pacific region in the early sixteenth century, virtually every inhabitable island was populated. Exactly when and how all the islands of the Pacific were first settled, however, is not entirely clear. The archaeological evidence is still meager, and there is considerable speculation about early migrations.

Not long after the Second World War, in an attempt to prove that the population of the Polynesian islands originated in South America, the Norwegian ethnologist and adventurer Thor Heyerdahl and his small crew sailed from the Pacific coast of South America to Polynesia on a balsa raft named *Kon-Tiki*. Although Heyerdahl showed that such a voyage was possible, most scholars still believe that the great bulk of linguistic and botanical evidence suggests that the populations originally came from Southeast Asia rather than South America.

The Pacific Islands are customarily divided into three ethnogeographic areas: Melanesia, Micronesia, and Polynesia. Melanesia includes the

predominantly dark-skinned peoples of New Guinea, the Bismarck Archipelago, the Solomons, Vanuatu, New Caledonia, and Fiji. Micronesia comprises the very small islands and atolls in the northern Pacific, including the Marianas, Carolines, and Marshalls. Polynesia forms a large triangle in the eastern Pacific, from Hawaii in the north, to New Zealand in the south, and Easter Island in the east. Despite these classifications, however, archaeological evidence, linguistic studies, and blood group analyses all suggest similar origins for the people of the three areas. The physical and cultural differences between modern-day peoples may result from the fact that the islands were occupied by successive waves of migrants.

The Lapita people

The earliest dates for settlement of the Pacific Islands in Micronesia and Polynesia go back no further than the second millennium BC. As they moved eastward, these early settlers took with them a well-developed agricultural tradition based on taro, yams, and pigs. This agricultural tradition was associated with a coarse, finely decorated pottery known as Lapita ware. By studying the distribution of this pottery, archaeologists have been able to trace the movement of this people across the Pacific.

One theory suggests that the Lapita people began to make their way eastward from eastern Indonesia or the Philippines about 4,000 years ago and then spread farther eastward through New Guinea to the southwestern Pacific. It is thought that they may have been forced to keep moving as a result of pressure from incoming groups of rice-growers. As they moved, they gradually developed distinctive Polynesian characteristics, which included complex hierarchical social, political, and religious systems.

The last region of the Pacific to be settled by Polynesians was New Zealand. Colonists probably arrived there by canoe from the Hawaiian islands some time around AD 1,000, although many scholars now favor a date closer to AD 750.

LANGUAGES AND WRITING

As with many other questions about human evolution, there is still no consensus about the origin of speech and language. A number of scholars have suggested that art and language must be closely intertwined because they both require the ability to understand abstract ideas and symbolic concepts and to share these understandings with others as part of a cultural system. According to this theory, fully fledged languages would not have existed before the appearance of art—which first emerged about 40,000 years ago. If this argument is correct, archaic *Homo sapiens* such as the Neanderthals, who coexisted for some time with *Homo sapiens sapiens* and also created primitive art, would have possessed some form of language. Certainly, no one doubts that the Neanderthals were able to communicate with each other, although changes to the brain and facial structure would have meant the linguistic ability of *Homo sapiens sapiens* was markedly superior.

The complexity of human language and speech is dependent on a number of neural and anatomical mechanisms found only in *Homo sapiens sapiens*. These include a vocal tract that permits a wide range of speech sounds, areas of the brain that control and interpret these sounds, and an efficient memory that can use past experiences as a guide to the future. Although scientists believe that earlier hominid species were able to communicate both vocally and by gestures (just as animals do), their use of words, concepts, and sentence construction (syntax) would have been limited. Even chimpanzees can be taught to use words when placed in a human-like environment, yet they never progress beyond the vocabulary or grammatical ability of an average three-year-old child. Humans alone are able to talk to each other, rather than just transmit words.

Although fully fledged linguistic ability would have been found only among *Homo sapiens sapiens*, it is still possible that language of some sort existed among the first anatomically modern humans in East Africa as early as 130,000 years ago. Some scientists even argue that *Homo habilis* may have been able to communicate vocally, albeit in a much simpler fashion. In other words, early humans may have had speech, but not a complete language.

Further evidence that early hominids were able to communicate verbally has recently emerged from what may at first seem an unlikely source: scientific research into the evolution of dogs. Studies in molecular biology suggest that wolves evolved into domestic animals more than 130,000 years ago, and wolf bones have even been found with 400,000-year-old hominid bones. These facts suggest that the association between humans and canines goes back a very long time. Some scientists now think that the domestication of canines had a profound effect on human evolution. The close association with dogs would have made it less crucial for early hominids to have a keen sense of smell that would alert them to other hominids or animal predators. In turn, this would have allowed the development of the facial and cranial modifications necessary for speech.

Languages of the world

Thousands of languages are spoken in the world today. Populations that share similar cultures and live only a short distance apart may still speak languages that are quite distinct and not readily understood by neighboring populations.

For example, the inhabitants of New Guinea and adjacent islands speak approximately 1,000 different languages, or about one-fifth of the world's total.

At the same time, similarities exist between languages used in different parts of the world, which suggests that they developed from a common source. Scholars group such languages in families on the basis of similarities in vocabulary, sound systems, and grammar. English, for example, is part of the Indo-European family, which includes languages of antiquity, such as Sanskrit and classical Greek, as well as contemporary languages in both Asia and Europe, such as Hindi and Russian. Other geographically dispersed language families are Malayo-Polynesian (also known as

The world's major languages

Language	Speakers (millions)
Mandarin (Chinese)	885
English	322
Spanish	266
Bengali	189
Hindi	182
Portuguese	170
Russian	170
Japanese	125
German	98
Wu (Chinese)	77
Javanese	75.5
Korean	75

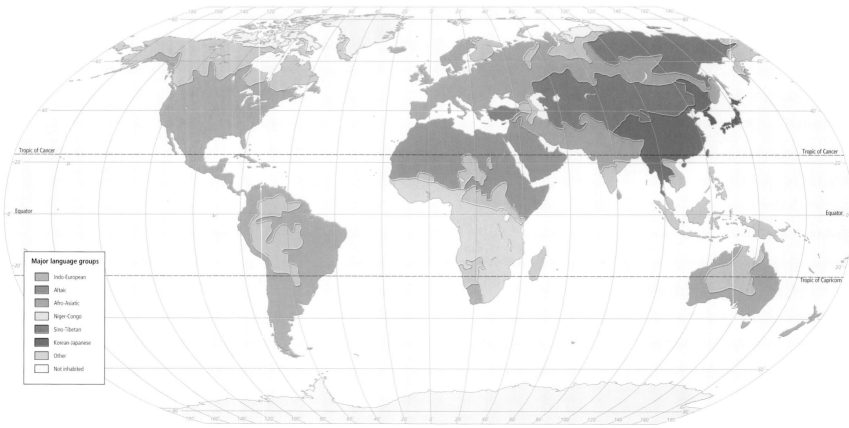

Major language groups
- Indo-European
- Altaic
- Afro-Asiatic
- Niger-Congo
- Sino-Tibetan
- Korean-Japanese
- Other
- Not inhabited

Projection: Robinson   Equatorial Scale approx 1:155 million

As a result of geographical isolation, the Papuan tribes that gather at traditional sing-sing ceremonies (left) may speak many different languages. Egyptian hieroglyphs (bottom) are a form of pictorial writing, whereas the Latin script on this tablet from the Coliseum (below) illustrates alphabetic writing.

Austronesian), which includes Hawaiian, Javanese, and the languages of Madagascar, and Uralic, which includes Finnish, Hungarian, and the Samoyed language of Northern Siberia.

The first languages were disseminated in a number of ways. The most obvious was migration. As they spread out across the globe, early peoples carried their languages into uninhabited territory. Languages would also have spread as a result of contact between different peoples. For example, the invention and adoption of food production would have encouraged agricultural peoples to migrate into territory occupied by hunter–gatherers, who may then have adopted both the cultivation techniques and language of the immigrants.

A third form of language dissemination involves the replacement of an existing language by one spoken by a dominant group. The development of complex societies allowed incoming minorities with some form of centralized organization to dominate larger populations, who, in many cases, subsequently adopted the language of the elite. For example, the adoption of the Chinese language family in southern China in historical times occurred as a result of the military expansion of the Chinese empire.

The origins of writing

Writing is thought to have arisen around 5,000 to 6,000 years ago in Sumeria (southern Mesopotamia), and to have appeared shortly afterward in widely separate parts of the world, including Egypt (3000 BC), the Indus Valley (2500 BC), and China (2000 BC). Writing may have spread from Sumeria to the Indus and probably also to Egypt, but it was almost certainly independently invented in both China and, later, Mesoamerica, where it first appeared in the third century AD. Writing was unknown elsewhere in the Americas, even in the highly developed Inca civilization of the central Andes which flourished in the fifteenth century.

Scholars usually distinguish three broad kinds of writing systems, although in practice

some systems combine elements of more than one kind. They are known as logographic, syllabic, and alphabetic writing.

In logographic writing, separate symbols are used to represent single words. This can complicate the representation of even simple statements. Because most of the symbols in logographic writing have, or originally had, a pictorial basis, it is believed that this is the earliest form of writing. Examples of logographic writing include early Sumerian cuneiform, Egyptian hieroglyphs, and modern Chinese characters.

In syllabic writing, symbols represent syllables. Examples of this type include later Sumerian cuneiform and the remarkable Cherokee syllabary developed by a Native American called Sequoyah in Arkansas in the early nineteenth century.

The third, and now most common, form of writing is alphabetic, in which symbols represent units of sound, or phonemes. Widespread alphabetic systems include Arabic, Roman (which is used for English and most other European languages), and Cyrillic (used for Russian and some other Slavic languages).

It has been suggested that these three types of writing reflect an evolutionary progression, from logographic to alphabetic; however, most scholars now regard this view as too simplistic. For instance, in a number of writing systems, logographic elements have been adopted, discarded, and then reintroduced.

The development of writing is closely associated with the rise of hierarchical societies. Literacy contributed to the formation of more complex state structures and bureaucratic institutions. In its early stages, it was often closely linked to religious activities and authorities. In Sumeria, for instance, the recording of economic transactions was controlled by religious officialdom. Writing also arose as a religious practice in Mesoamerica, remaining the preserve of the elite until the Spanish conquest in the sixteenth century.

THE RISE OF AGRICULTURE

Humanity's transition from a mobile life of hunting and gathering to a sedentary farming lifestyle in settled communities was not a sudden "revolution." It took place by degrees, with the dependence on cultivation increasing slowly as selective breeding modified wild plant species. Nevertheless, in terms of the prehistory of modern humans (100,000 years or so), the emergence of full-scale agriculture, which includes the development of both plant cultivation and animal husbandry, was relatively rapid.

It is probable that the cultivation of plants developed independently in a number of different regions, including the Fertile Crescent (a region stretching from present-day central Turkey southeastward through Iraq to the Persian Gulf), China, Mesoamerica (roughly

Foods and their origins

Most agricultural products were native to one part of the world and then spread gradually to other regions. The following list shows the origins of selected foods.

wheat	Fertile Crescent
potatoes	Central Andes
rice	China
corn	Mesoamerica
sugar	New Guinea
coffee	Ethiopia
tea	China
apples	Western Europe
oranges	Southeast Asia
sheep	Fertile Crescent
turkey	Mexico

present-day Mexico and Guatemala), and the Central Andes. Some scholars suggest that food production also originated in other centers such as New Guinea and West Africa.

Plant cultivation first occurred in the Fertile Crescent, where evidence for the domestication of grains such as wheat and barley, and other foods such as pulses and olives, begins to make an appearance in the archaeological record around 11,000 years ago. Flax was also cultivated as a source of fiber for making cloth. Although much of this area was then, as it is now, rocky and rather arid, the fertility of the river floodplains probably encouraged an increasing reliance on cultivation. In the region between the Tigris and Euphrates rivers in present-day Iraq, the development of canal-based irrigation allowed farming centers to flourish. From there, agricultural methods spread throughout the Mediterranean, across the Balkans, and along the Danube River into central Europe. By 7,000 years ago, farming was also firmly established in Egypt's Nile Valley.

Recent archaeological finds have indicated that plant cultivation may have begun in Asia not long after it began in the Fertile Crescent. For example, it is possible that rice was cultivated along the middle Yangtze of central China as early as 9,500 years ago. In northern China, there is evidence that millet and rapeseed were grown around the same time. Farming practices spread along the fertile floodplains of Chinese rivers, where many early sites have been found. At about the same time, local people also began to domesticate animals, including pigs, cattle, sheep, dogs, and chickens.

Food production may have arisen independently in at least two parts of the Americas. One of these

is the Peruvian Andes, where beans were cultivated perhaps as early as 7,000 years ago. At around the same time, people in Mesoamerica also started to grow beans, together with squash and pumpkins. Maize, which became the most important staple, may not have been cultivated until more than a thousand years later. The early archaeological record is sparse in South America, but it appears that plants such as manioc, amaranths, peanuts, potatoes, cotton, and chili peppers were slowly domesticated in different parts of the continent.

Agriculture may have begun earlier in New Guinea. In the island's central highlands, archaeologists have discovered evidence of irrigation ditches in areas of swamp which date from around 9,000 years ago. They remain uncertain about the types of crops grown there, although taro and other native noncereal plants are likely candidates.

The domestication of animals

Although the dog was domesticated somewhat earlier, the process of rearing animals for food—and later for clothing and as draft and pack animals—began at around the same time as plant cultivation. Many animals hunted by humans were unsuitable for breeding as a result of such factors as their diet, growth rate, ability to breed in captivity, or behavioral disposition. Domestication therefore had to proceed by trial and error, and gradually it modified many species.

Some animals, such as the wild pig and the auroch (a large, long-horned wild ox), were distributed over a wide area of Europe and Asia, and were probably domesticated independently in a number of places. Others, such as goats and sheep, were confined largely to the Middle East and western Asia, and were later introduced into Europe.

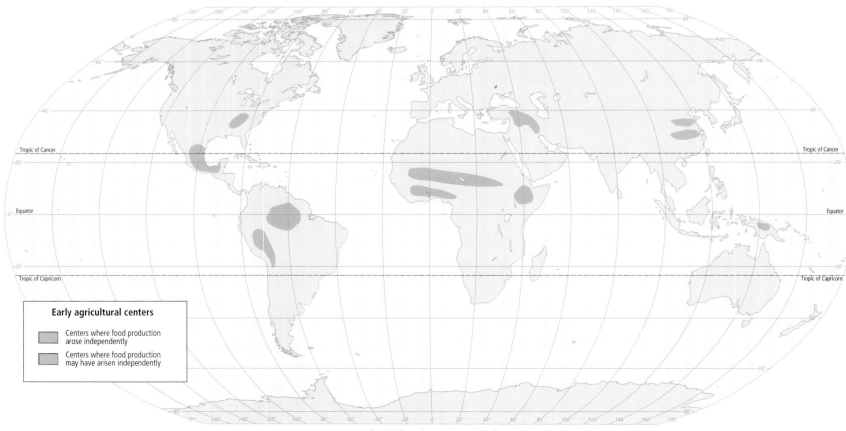

Early agricultural centers

Centers where food production arose independently

Centers where food production may have arisen independently

Projection: Robinson   Equatorial Scale approx 1:155 million

Food production began independently in China when rice was cultivated about 9,000 years ago in the valley of the Yangtze River. From there, rice cultivation spread throughout Southeast Asia, reaching Indonesia (left) about 4,000 years ago. The shift from hunting-gathering to agriculture resulted in the development of new technologies, including animal-driven pulley systems like the one on this well in Egypt (below).

The people of the Andes domesticated llamas for use as pack animals and guinea pigs for food. The earliest evidence for the domestication of cats has been found in Greece. Cats were subsequently domesticated in many areas, usually to protect grain stores from rodents.

Why choose agriculture?

Not all communities switched to agriculture as soon as they came into contact with it. Many early peoples remained dependent on food collecting and hunting, and hunter-gatherer societies continue to exist to this day. These communities may modify their environment—for example, by burning vegetation to encourage growth that attracts game—and some also undertake minimal husbanding of plant resources, such as replanting rootstock cuttings and protecting fruit-bearing trees. But despite this and the fact that they may have often come into contact with people practicing agriculture, they have chosen not to switch to a sedentary lifestyle based on farming.

The reason for this is that subsisting as a hunter-gatherer usually requires less work than subsisting as a farmer. As long as population densities remain low, a food-collecting lifestyle can be more attractive and efficient, and provide a more balanced and diverse diet. In fact, scientists find it hard to explain why certain populations ever became totally dependent on farming. However, once the switch had been made, the demographic and social consequences of an agricultural lifestyle would have made it difficult to reverse the trend.

The consequences of agriculture

Agriculture transformed both human societies and landscapes. The need to make cultivation more efficient encouraged rapid technological innovations. The use of clay, which was already known in pre-agricultural times, became

Despite the attractions of new technologies, many communities, including the San of the Kalahari desert in southwestern Africa, rejected agriculture and continue to follow a hunting-gathering lifestyle to this day (below right).

widespread and people began to make large receptacles for food and water. In turn, these receptacles transformed diets, as grains and pulses could be soaked and boiled, making them easier to eat and digest. Other innovations that emerged in agricultural societies were metalworking, the wheel (which improved the making of pots and stimulated progress in transport), and the use of sails on boats. Small copper objects have been found at early agricultural sites in the Middle East, but extensive metalworking and purification techniques were not developed until a few thousand years later.

Early agricultural societies were based on small village communities. As the range of domesticated plants and animals grew, the village economies became increasingly diverse and food production techniques improved. These developments enabled communities to create surpluses which could be used to support full-time craftspeople. Specialization led to internal barter and to trade with other communities. Items and commodities that were found or produced in only certain localities were traded over considerable distances. Social divisions also increased and, in many areas, complex hierarchies, headed by hereditary leaders, came into existence. In some societies, elite classes emerged who were able to devote their time to religious, cultural, and military pursuits while living off the surplus produced by subordinate groups.

Agriculture and demographics

Some scholars believe that population growth encouraged the adoption of agriculture, while others think that it was agriculture that triggered

an increase in population. Although there is no firm demographic evidence to decide the question, archaeological research suggests that the number and size of settlements usually increased following the appearance of food production in a region.

The rapid expansion of agriculture affected the environment, in some cases quite catastrophically. For example, archaeologists have found that the barren landscape of modern Greece is the result of more than 5,000 years of farming, during which deforestation and land clearance led to the loss of topsoil and severe soil erosion.

EMERGING CIVILIZATIONS

The first civilizations arose on the fertile alluvial basins of major rivers such as the Tigris-Euphrates in Iraq, the Nile in Egypt, the Indus in Pakistan, and the Yellow (Huang Ho) in China. These regions shared many common features, including arid environments that made agricultural communities dependent on irrigation, and readily available supplies of raw materials such as stone, metal, and wood. The Tigris-Euphrates, Nile, and Indus regions were probably linked by trade well before the appearance of the early cities, but Chinese civilization developed in relative isolation.

The first urban societies

Cities emerged in all four regions during the third millennium BC as villages and towns slowly grew into cities with large public buildings and developed specialized and well-organized production and trade, forms of writing, hierarchical social structures, and centralized political systems. This process of evolution varied, although the cultural attributes of emerging cities were similar.

In most cases, cities arose following the emergence of a social elite. As a class or family became dominant, it usually sought to create a power base in one region. This power base attracted immigrants and businesses, resulting in the rapid growth of the urban community. Scholars have suggested various reasons for the emergence of social elites. Some propose that the construction and maintenance

The pyramids at Giza in Egypt (below) were built during the Fourth Dynasty to house the remains of the rulers Khufu, Khafra, and Menkau-re.

of the large-scale irrigation works needed to support a growing population would have required considerable organization and encouraged the development of a managerial class. Others emphasize the role of specialized production and trade in creating a dominant commercial class. Another explanation is the growing influence of warfare: as settlements were overrun by invading peoples, their inhabitants were often forced to become the subjects of their conquerors. It was probably a combination of all these factors that led to the development of the first "upper classes" and the first sophisticated urban societies.

Cradles of civilization

In the region between the Tigris and Euphrates rivers known as Mesopotamia, farming gradually became more productive, canals were built, large temple platforms (called ziggurats) were erected, and the cuneiform script was simplified and standardized. Crafts, such as pottery and metalwork, became more specialized and production more organized, leading to greater social divisions in society. The city-states had their own monarchs, and were often heavily fortified. Their ascendancy came to an end, however, around 2350 BC, when Sargon, a military ruler from Agade in central Mesopotamia, forcibly amalgamated them into the Akkadian empire.

In Egypt, by contrast, it was the unification of the cities and towns of Upper and Lower Egypt at the beginning of the third millennium that caused civilization to flourish, giving rise to a well-developed political and administrative system, writing, and a complex religion. During this period, the massive stone

pyramids of Giza were constructed to preserve the bodies, knowledge, and wealth of the Egyptian kings in the afterlife. The pyramids also symbolized the structure of Egyptian society, with the god-king at the apex, officials in the middle levels, and the mass of the population at the bottom.

The emergence of the Indus civilization was marked by the appearance of distinctive artistic styles in pottery, copper, and bronze (a copper–tin alloy). These objects were traded with nomadic pastoral peoples who, in turn, transported the merchandise into central Asia and along the coast of the Arabian Sea. Around 2400 BC, the different cultural traditions of the Indus merged into one, called Harappa by archaeologists after the first city to be excavated in this region. Harappa culture had writing, a form of centralized control for administration and commerce, and large buildings made out of baked brick. In contrast to other early civilizations, however, Harappan society does not seem to have included a priest-king class, nor did its spread depend on military conquest.

In China, it is likely that villages merged to form states in several areas, but legend and archaeological evidence locate the first civilization, that of the Xia, in the middle and lower valleys of the Yellow River, from about the end of the third millennium BC. Texts written much later suggest that the Xia united a number of groups in a loose confederation. One of these was the Shang, who gained ascendancy in the second millennium BC. They developed an early form of Chinese script and expanded their territory through military campaigns. They were defeated by the Zhou, another Xia confederate, at the end of the second millennium BC.

Culture and trade

The expansion of civilizations was assisted by trade and migration as well as conquest. Trade routes in particular allowed knowledge and practices to be dispersed across sometimes vast distances. They were particularly significant in the expansion of

These bas-reliefs (left), which date from about 500 BC, decorate the walls of the ancient Mesopotamian city of Persepolis. Greek city-states such as Athens (bottom) emerged around 750 BC. At that time, Teotihuacán (below) in Mesoamerica was one of the largest cities in the world.

Chinese culture into Southeast Asia, and in the spread of Egyptian and Middle Eastern traditions as far as North Africa, southern Asia, and Europe.

The first major European civilization emerged in Crete at the end of the third millennium BC. The Minoans, whose powerful navy controlled the Aegean Sea for much of the second millennium BC, constructed large cities centered on elaborate palaces including those at Knossos, Malia, and Phaistos. Later, urban societies also sprang up on the Greek mainland, the most notable being the Mycenean civilization, which came to prominence during the late second millennium BC. Classical Greek civilization emerged during the first millennium BC in a number of self-governing cities such as Athens and Sparta. These urban societies were distinguished by the formal constitutions that directed their political life and by the increasing power held by the male citizenry at the expense of a centralized leadership.

Civilizations also developed independently, but much later, among the agricultural communities of Mesoamerica and the central Andes. Mesoamerican civilizations emerged during the first millennium BC. The most important was that of the Maya, who developed a form of writing around AD 300. The Maya maintained commercial ties to city-states developing elsewhere in the region. One of these, Teotihuacán, in central Mexico, was an important trade center with a population that peaked at more than 100,000 around AD 600. During the same period, several interrelated civilizations existed in the central Andes, with territories that are now in present-day Peru and Bolivia. These societies created monumental buildings and elaborate crafts, but left no evidence of any written languages.

The meaning of "civilization"

In eighteenth-century Europe, "civilization" meant cultural refinement—the opposite of barbarism. Nineteenth-century social philosophers found this meaning too restrictive, so they used the term in the plural sense to refer to large-scale societies. This usage is followed by present-day sociologists and anthropologists.

Human societies can be classified in terms of their size and complexity. Small-scale or tribal societies comprise small bands loosely coordinated by kinship relations. These groups often live together at permanent settlements, although some may be nomadic. Medium-sized communities are usually made up of clusters of villages or small towns united under some form of confederation or chiefdom. In large-scale societies, at least some of the inhabitants live in large urban societies which are linked by a network of social, economic, and cultural ties, and normally unified under a centralized political organization.

Early Mesopotamian artworks such as this ivory carving often include portraits of members of the ruling elite.

THE IMPACT OF CIVILIZATION

The main impetus for rapid progress over the past few thousand years was the development of large-scale urban societies. Their benefits in enriching human experience through technological innovation, scientific knowledge, and diversity in social life appear obvious. Certain consequences of civilization were less benign, however. These include the increasing destructiveness of warfare, the spread of disease, and the life-long bondage imposed on certain classes of people.

Innovation and adaptation

Many thousands of years elapsed between the development of specialized stone and bone tool assemblages and the beginnings of food production. After the adoption of agriculture and a sedentary lifestyle, however, the widespread diffusion of the latest innovations occurred remarkably rapidly. This was partly due to the obvious usefulness of the technology. Many inventions were developed in one location and then rapidly dispersed because of their immediate utility. The wheel, for example, appears to have been invented near the Black Sea around 3400 BC, and within a few hundred years, it was being used throughout Europe and Asia.

Another reason for the exponential growth of technology was that new inventions were rapidly adapted to diverse local needs. For example, shortly after the emergence of the wheel, innovations based on this technology—such as pulleys, water wheels, and windmills—appeared and then spread quickly along ever-expanding trade routes.

Some innovations, however, did not travel as extensively as may be expected. For example, the wheel was probably also invented independently in Mesoamerica, where it was used in children's toys, but it was never adopted for transportation in this region due to the lack of draft animals. Nor did the wheel spread from Mesoamerica to South America, even though the people of the Andes had the Americas' only beast of burden—the llama—and despite the fact that technologies such as metallurgy had already spread northward from the Andes to Mesoamerica.

Technology and warfare

New technologies led to the expansion of production and, consequently, an increase in the size of urban populations. As cities grew in size, conflict over land with neighboring agricultural and pastoral peoples often led to warfare. In turn, this stimulated the manufacture of weaponry.

Early weapons were made of bronze, but by the beginning of the first millennium BC, iron weapons were being widely produced in the Fertile Crescent, and smelting techniques, which produced an early form of steel, were already well understood there. By 500 BC, iron tools and weapons were widespread throughout Europe and Asia. However, ironworking did not appear in the Americas until after the Spanish conquests of the 16th century. The devastating effectiveness of steel weaponry was demonstrated by the Spanish conquest of the Incas. In 1532, the conquistador Pizzaro, with an army of only 168 soldiers, was able to defeat the Inca army of more than

Monuments to royalty, such as the massive temple of Abu Simbel in Egypt (above) built during the reign of Ramses II (1279–1213 BC), reflect both the development of technology and the emergence of complex social hierarchies.

80,000 soldiers and capture their emperor Atahualpa. The Spanish soldiers had chain mail, helmets, steel swords, lances, daggers, and horses, whereas the Inca army was protected by quilted padding, armed with blunt clubs, and traveled on foot.

Science and disease

Although many advances in the domestication of plants and animals and in technology were the result of accidental discoveries or trial and error, written records indicate that early civilizations were making careful observations of natural phenomena. For example, the Maya developed a calendar based on the solar year and lunar month, and could predict eclipses—a feat that required advanced mathematical skills. The Egyptians acquired considerable medical knowledge and surgical skills. Among the sophisticated techniques they developed was the practice of trepanation. This involved the cutting of bone in the skull to relieve pressure on the brain resulting from a skull fracture, or to treat headaches or epilepsy.

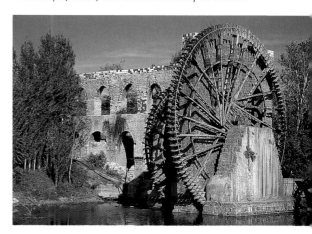

Invented in western Asia, the wheel was rapidly adapted to create devices such as the water wheel (below). As a result of their preference for cooler climates, llamas (left) never spread northward to Mesoamerica. Sophisticated soceieties such as that of the Maya (bottom) thus remained without pack animals.

A sedentary lifestyle enabled ailing individuals to receive better care than they would receive if they remained nomadic. However, large concentrations of people living in close proximity to domestic animals and (initially, at least) dependent on a relatively limited range of foods created the perfect environment for the spread of disease. When human populations are small and move frequently, the opportunities for parasitic infections to spread are limited. Urban lifestyles, in contrast, with their permanent housing and large refuse dumps, attract disease-carrying vermin and insects, and allow parasites to spread more quickly. Land clearance, irrigation, and the use of natural fertilizers would also have encouraged certain diseases in sedentary communities, particularly where diets were deficient and the population less resilient. Even more significant was the domestication of animals. Today, people associate animals with diseases such as rabies, anthrax, and parasitic worms, but domestic animals were also the original source of infections that are now commonly transmitted by humans, such as smallpox, measles, and influenza.

The spread of disease was encouraged by trade, migration, and conquest. For example, bubonic plague is thought to have been restricted to Asia until it was spread to other parts of the world by traders. When it reached Europe in the mid-fourteenth century, it wiped out one quarter of the population. Diseases carried by conquering armies were often more destructive than their military campaigns. For example, in 1520, the Spaniards under Cortés inadvertently brought smallpox to the Aztecs, causing a massive epidemic that killed more than half the population and led to the demise of the empire.

As civilizations grew and technology spread, warfare, as depicted in this bas-relief from Nineveh in Assyria, became more sophisticated and more commonplace.

Social hierarchies

The increasing division of labor and the steady enhancement of specialized skills in urban communities led to the development of ever-more sophisticated social hierarchies. People directly involved in food production—the commoners—were often obliged to provide tribute payments to a centralized authority. This did not necessarily mean that commoners were physically separated from the elite—in many early cities, they lived in close proximity to each other and even shared in decision-making. But as urban populations increased and relationships became more complex, so the social distinctions became more marked.

In China, for instance, the Shang, and later the Zhou, administered a feudal system of vassal states. Members of the royal clan, and others who assisted the king, were granted fiefdoms over parts of the kingdom. Below these nobles and loyal administrators were the farmers from whose ranks the soldiers were recruited. At the lowest end of the social scale were the slaves, who were usually nomadic pastoralists captured by the ruling elite. This pattern of enslaving captives was common in these evolving nation-states, probably because mass production and large-scale public works provided many uses for slaves in menial occupations.

Domestic horses

Today's domestic horses are descended from wild species native to southern Russia. Horses were first domesticated there around 4000 BC—much later than most other domestic animals—and before long had become the principal means of transportation throughout much of Asia and Europe. Horses transformed warfare, providing formidable military advantages when yoked to battle chariots or ridden. At the same time, however, they transmitted several diseases to humans, including tetanus and the common cold.

Mongolian horses are the only surviving relatives of the species from which all domestic horses are descended.

FROM CITY-STATES TO EMPIRES

There is no doubt that warfare was a part of human experience long before historical records were kept—even the small-scale societies of Melanesia that existed at the time of the first European contact were involved in frequent and violent tribal conflicts. However, the scale, range, and destructiveness of war increased significantly with the development of the first states. High population density, advances in transport and weapons technology, centralized decision-making, and a new fervor among troops willing to die for a powerful leader allowed extensive resources to be mobilized for warfare. This in turn meant that military engagements could take place much farther from home. Whereas war had previously involved only the annexation of adjacent territories from enemies who had either been chased away, killed, or enslaved, now they could lead to the amalgamation of entire societies into larger political units. Furthermore, the subjugated peoples could be forced to pay tribute, thereby increasing the ruler's resources for further campaigns. In this way, empires were born.

The rise of empires greatly enhanced the diffusion of knowledge, ideas, technology, languages, and cultural traditions. It also expanded trade links and imposed administrative and political unity on previously dispersed communities, laying the foundations for future nation-states.

There are three broad reasons why rulers of small city-states and medium-sized kingdoms ventured into empire-building. One was to create alliances that would provide protection against an external threat—the formation of the Chinese Empire is a good example of this. Another reason was to subdue a persistent enemy—this is why Alexander the Great began his conquests. The third was to acquire control over desired commodities, trade routes, and other resources—Roman expansion can be explained in this way. All three reasons influenced most expansionist ambitions, but one tended to be more dominant than the others in the building of individual empires.

The threat from the north

By the third century BC, the Zhou kingdom of northeastern China was breaking up, having been weakened by years of attacks perpetrated by warring tribal peoples to the north and northwest. Following the collapse of the kingdom, wars broke out between rival states and various alliances were formed and severed. Eventually, one of the Zhou vassal states, the Qin (221–206), gained ascendancy and brought the other states under their control. They then set about uniting the states into a single Chinese empire. The principle objective of this policy was to secure Qin territory against the foreign invaders that had plagued the Zhou. To ensure the protection of the empire, the Qin began to construct an enormous physical barrier to invasion by linking defensive structures originally built during the Zhou period. The Great Wall, as this barrier became known, would eventually stretch 3,000 km (1,860 miles) across northern China. The Qin also built an extensive network of highways and canals to improve communications throughout their empire.

Following the death of the First Emperor, the Qin Empire was taken over by the Han in 206 BC. The Han expanded their empire further south beyond the floodplains of the Yellow (Huang Ho) and Yangtze rivers, and also defeated tribes to the west. This helped silk merchants to create a new trade route through central Asia which eventually extended all the way to Europe.

Alexander the Great

The rise of the Persian Empire in the sixth century BC posed a significant threat to Greek city-states such as Athens and Sparta. They responded by forming strategic alliances, which they managed to maintain long enough to defeat the Persians during the following century. However, subsequent disputes between the cities allowed Philip II of Macedon to take advantage of their disunity and unite Greece with Macedonia in 338 BC. In the following year, Philip declared war on Persia to revenge the Persian devastation of Greece, but before the war could begin he was assassinated.

Philip was succeeded by his son, Alexander, who realized his father's plans to crush Greece's formidable enemy. He successfully engaged the Persian army in Turkey and the eastern Mediterranean, moved westward to Egypt where he founded the city of Alexandria, and finally crushed the Persians in a decisive battle at Gaugamela in Mesopotamia in 331 BC. His conquests continued to the Indus River before he turned back, only to die suddenly at the age of 33 in Mesopotamia in 323 BC. Alexander's vast empire was divided up between his generals, and, without a strong leader, it soon disintegrated, although the kingdoms of Egypt, Persia, and Macedonia persisted.

Despite his short reign, Alexander left a long-lasting legacy. His decision to take scholars and scientists on his campaigns ensured that Greek learning, language, and cultural traditions were disseminated widely. He founded a number of Hellenic cities with Greeks and Macedonians, the most notable being Alexandria, which became a renowned center of learning.

Although the Greek city-states had previously established trade centers throughout the northern Mediterranean, they had largely left the southern shore to the Phoenicians. Alexander's conquests extended Hellenistic influence into North Africa and the Middle East. In this way, Alexander imposed a cultural unity on the Mediterranean region which stimulated trade and learning and which later played a significant part in the advancement of the Roman Empire.

The Roman Empire

In the seventh century BC, Rome was one of several small towns in the Tiber Valley that were situated on a strategically important road leading to saltworks at the mouth of the River Tiber. During the following two centuries, Rome gained control of neighboring territories, including the valuable saltworks, and became a potent force in local politics and commerce. Like other Mediterranean cities in that era, Rome was strongly influenced by Greek culture, but it never came under Greek control.

In the fifth century BC, Rome became a republic ruled by a Senate formed by an aristocratic clique. From that time, Rome gradually expanded its territory to encompass the whole of the Italic peninsula—while Alexander was conquering Persia, Rome was winning decisive battles for the control of southern Italy.

Success in southern Italy encouraged the Romans to seize Sicily, which was then under the

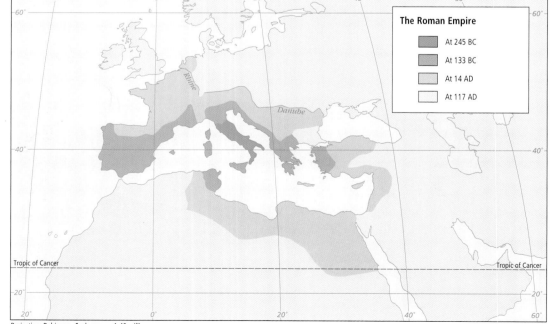

The Roman Empire

At 245 BC
At 133 BC
At 14 AD
At 117 AD

Projection: Robinson   Scale approx 1:40 million

This map (left) shows the gradual expansion of the Roman Empire, which reached its greatest extent during the reign of Trajan (AD 98–117). Construction of the Great Wall of China (right) began during the Qin Empire (221–206 BC). Extensive sections of the wall were rebuilt during the fifteenth and sixteenth centuries.

influence of the North African city of Carthage. Over the next 100 years, the Romans fought three major wars—known as the Punic Wars—against Carthage to gain control of the western Mediterranean. By the end of the Third Punic War (146 BC), Carthage had been completely destroyed and Rome had emerged as by far the strongest force in the region. The empire subsequently extended eastward to Greece and the Middle East, where it benefited greatly from Greek advances in art, learning, and technology. Later still, the empire expanded to include large areas of present-day France, Germany, and England, spreading Hellenic culture and Roman political and social institutions across most of Europe.

During the first century BC, the Roman Empire expanded rapidly. Under Pompey, Roman armies seized parts of the Middle East, including Syria (above) in 64 BC; in the west, Julius Caesar (above right) led the conquest of Gaul in 58–50 BC. Both generals subsequently laid claim to the title of emperor. Victory in a short civil war allowed Caesar to begin his reign in 48 BC.

RELIGIONS OF THE WORLD

Religions are a feature of almost all of the world's cultures. They have been the inspiration for much of the world's great art, music, architecture, and literature, but also the source of longstanding disputes and local, regional, and international conflicts.

The tenets and forms of religious belief vary widely. While most religions involve the worship of a deity or deities, supreme beings play only a minor role in some faiths such as Theravada Buddhism. Nor do all religions have practices, core doctrines, and moral codes that are common to every follower. For example, while Hinduism retains a self-identity developed historically through confrontation with other religious traditions such as Buddhism, Islam, and Christianity, it remains extremely diverse internally.

The great majority of the world's religions evolved among particular peoples who had no interest in attracting converts. Few tribal peoples, for instance, would attempt to persuade their neighbors to adopt their religious beliefs and practices. Similarly, some prominent religions such as Hinduism and Judaism make no effort to seek converts. However, religion is frequently the cause of great social conflict, particularly where two or more proselytizing religions are in competition. Even within religions that have a core doctrine, comparatively minor differences of faith or practice can cause bitter divisions—past tensions between Christian denominations are a good example of this. Frequently, religious conflicts are aggravated by historical factors and by the extent to which religious divisions are overlaid by other divisions, such as language, ethnicity, and class.

World religions

One-third of the world's population identify themselves as Christians, with about half belonging to the Roman Catholic Church. The next largest religious group is Islam, which includes nearly one-fifth of the world's population. These two major faiths are monotheistic—that is, they are based on the belief that there is only one God—and both developed out of Judaism. Hinduism, a non-proselytizing religion followed by almost 13 percent of the world's population, is the third largest faith. Buddhism, which is the third largest proselytizing religion, has approximately 325 million adherents.

Judaism was originally the tribal religion of a people who traced themselves back to Abraham. Abraham is said to have migrated with his clan from the city of Ur in Mesopotamia to Canaan in the eastern Mediterranean. His descendants moved to Egypt, where they were later enslaved, and were

then led back to Canaan by Moses around 1200 BC. Although Judaism has a comparatively small number of contemporary adherents (around 14 million), it is significant both for its role in the development of Christianity and Islam and for its continuing influence on cultural and historical events.

Christianity originated as a movement within Judaism. Fundamental to its doctrine is the belief that Jesus Christ was the Messiah prophesied in the Old Testament. After Christ's crucifixion, Christian doctrines were disseminated throughout the Mediterranean by the apostles and by missionaries, the most prominent of whom was Saint Paul (also known as Saul of Tarsus). Christianity then spread throughout the Roman Empire, first among Jewish communities and then into the general population.

Pie chart

Ethnic religions 4.0%
Sikhism 0.4%
Judaism 0.3%
Christianity 33.0%
Islam 19.6%
Other 4.7%
Buddhism 6.0%
Chinese folk religions 6.2%
Hinduism 12.8%
No religion 13.0%

This pie chart shows the percentages of the world's population belonging to the major religions. Despite their small number, the Jews (above right) have had a major influence on history, culture, and other religions.

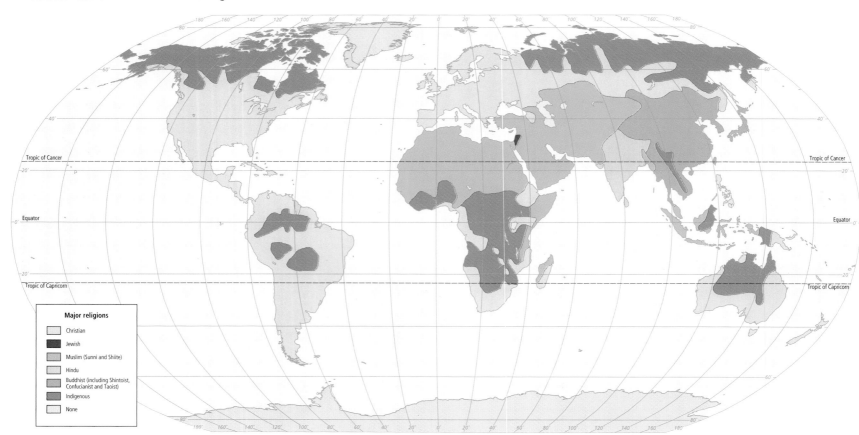

Major religions

Christian
Jewish
Muslim (Sunni and Shiite)
Hindu
Buddhist (including Shintoist, Confucianist and Taoist)
Indigenous
None

Projection: Robinson   Equatorial Scale approx 1:155 million

Early persecution of Christians by the Romans gave way to tolerance early in the fourth century AD when the Emperor Constantine converted and Christianity became the official state religion. Christianity continued to spread after the fall of the empire in the fifth century, reaching most of Europe by the end of the first millennium. Later, particularly during the era of European expansion in the fifteenth and sixteenth centuries, missionary activity disseminated Christianity to other parts of the world. Over the centuries, theological disputes have resulted in major schisms, out of which have grown the Orthodox, Catholic, Protestant, and other traditions.

Islam was founded early in the seventh century AD by Muhammad, a merchant from the prosperous Arabian city of Mecca. Muhammad had contact with both Jewish and Christian communities, and he came to regard the Judaeo-Christian prophets, including Christ, as forerunners of Islam. After receiving revelations about the worship of one God (Allah), Muhammad began to preach against the polytheistic practices of his home city. Persecution then forced him and his followers to flee to Medina. This migration (Hegira), which took place in AD 622, marks the beginning of the Muslim calendar. By the time of his death in AD 632, Muhammad had become the political and spiritual leader of much of Arabia. After his death, Muslims expanded their territory beyond the Arabian peninsula. At its peak, the Arabic empire stretched from Spain and Morocco in the west to Afghanistan and central Asia in the east, but the Islamic religion was carried even farther into Asia and Africa by Muslim traders.

Eastern deities

Hinduism has its roots in Vedism, the religion of the Indo-European peoples who inhabited northern India during the second millennium BC. The religion's sacred texts are the Vedas which explore humankind's place in the cosmos and describe the roles played by various gods in the functioning of the universe. During the first millennium AD, cults associated with two of these deities, Vishnu and Shiva, spread throughout the continent. Hinduism has a large and faithful following among the diverse peoples of the Indian subcontinent, but it has relatively few adherents elsewhere, except among the descendants of Indian emigrants. This is in part due to its non-proselytizing nature.

Like Christianity and Islam, Buddhism, the third major proselytizing religion, is also based on the religious enlightenment experienced by one man. However, it has much earlier origins. According to tradition, Siddhartha Gautama lived in northeastern India in the sixth century BC, and was reared in the royal household. In his adulthood, Siddhartha is said to have sought enlightenment, which he achieved through a night of meditation, thereby becoming the Buddha or Awakened One. For 45 years he traveled India as an itinerant teacher while formalizing his religious precepts. His teachings spread into southern Asia, where the first Buddhist tradition, the Theravada (meaning "doctrine of the elders"), still prevails in Sri Lanka, Myanmar, Cambodia, Laos, and Thailand. However, it retains few followers in India. Buddhism also spread to the east (Tibet, China, and Japan), where the second tradition, Mahayana (meaning "great vehicle") Buddhism, emerged in the second century BC. A more liberal tradition, Mahayana is said to express greater compassion and social concern than the more aloof Theravada Buddhism.

What is religion?

Scholars have found it extremely difficult to come up with a definition that will allow a clear-cut distinction between religious and non-religious phenomena. In broad terms, religion covers the beliefs and associated practices that focus on the relationship between humans and the supernatural, represented by a god or gods. These beliefs and practices address the ultimate questions of human existence, providing a sense of meaning and purpose to life. Frequently, they also create a feeling of fellowship and community with others who share the same beliefs and practices.

Approached in these terms, religions or religious activity can be found in all, or nearly all, eras and places, although the emphasis placed on religion by particular communities may vary greatly. Scholars have sometimes been surprised to discover that certain tribal or peasant peoples, who might have been assumed to be preoccupied with religion, are in fact relatively indifferent to it.

Religious practices may also have their origins in the need to regulate or control communities. Religion may enforce "taboo" or unacceptable behavior in order to preserve a peaceful and sustainable society.

TRADERS AND TRAVELERS

Humans moved from place to place either individually or in groups long before written records existed. The earliest records show they were impelled by a desire to occupy more fertile areas, by a desire for booty, by an urge to trade, by religious piety, which took them on pilgrimages, by a thirst for knowledge, and sometimes by the fear of invasion.

Before the Christian era, Buddhism led monks from the East to travel to India to visit sites where Gautama had been. Nearly 2,000 years later, Ibn Battúta, an Islamic qadi (religious judge), after setting out in AD 1325 to go to Mecca, as all good Mohammedans sought to do, found that he could not rest until he had visited every Muslim state in Asia, Africa, and Europe. Although on his return to Fez, the sultan's court was incredulous at Battúta's stories, they were written down, and in such ways knowledge of the world was spread.

The spread and decline of empires

The growth of empires fostered trade and treaties, both with neighbors and with more distant powers. The Han Empire in China, for example, traded with Phoenicians, Carthaginians, Syrians, and the Roman Empire in silks, iron, furs, glass, and other exotic goods. Merchants also brought back knowledge—in the first century AD, a Greek navigator wrote of the Indian Ocean, where Hindu traders competed with merchants from the Red Sea and Arabs dealing in wax and ivory, rhinoceros horns, tortoiseshell, and palm oil.

However, nomads were always pressing at the frontiers of such empires, seeking to loot and ransack. Loose confederations of "barbarians"—as the civilized empires considered them—hungry for plunder, breached the defences. The Roman

Empire bought their "barbarians" off for a time by settling some on the borders, as confederates, to keep out other tribes, but eventually the weight of empire saw the defences tumble. In AD 410, Rome itself was overrun.

The influx of mixed Germanic tribes was precipitated by the driving force of the Huns, who, according to the Goths, were the offspring of witches and evil spirits. No one knows where they originated. From the Carpathian mountains, however, they moved into the Mediterranean countries and, by AD 450, under Attila, were poised to crush and drive out the Goths. Then their alliances crumbled, and they disappeared as quickly as they had come.

Instead, Ostrogoths, Visigoths, Franks, and Saxons settled in England, France, Spain, Italy, and parts of North Africa, mixing with the local inhabitants, quarrelling amongst themselves and moving on to settle in new areas.

The Arab Empire

While Western Europe was fragmented and trade was declining, in the East, the Byzantine Empire remained the bulwark of Christianity against the rising Arab Empire. Mohammed's followers were spurred on by the idea of jihad, or Holy war, which combined religion with military exploits. After taking Syria and Egypt, they swept along the North African coast, took the Maghrib, and crossed into Spain. They attacked Byzantium by sea and blockaded Constantinople between AD 673 and 678. In the eighth century, the Caliphs of Damascus and Baghdad ruled an empire that stretched from Persia to Morocco.

The Arabs were also starting to dominate Africa. The peoples of the plateau between the

Niger and the Benin had mined and used gold and copper, and later iron, long before Christ. Exotic archaeological finds and the presence of Asian food plants clearly show that trade began early in these areas. Tribal organization became more sophisticated, in order to control and tax trade and the trade routes. By the eighth century, empires such as Ghana had emerged. The Arabs had been pushing their way down the east coast of Africa well before Mohammed. They visited trading posts such as Sofala and dealt with the inland kingdoms, exchanging exotic goods for gold. After AD 700, they began colonizing the coast, establishing settlements such as Mogadishu and Mombasa. They also moved south across the Sahara, and established Arabic kingdoms.

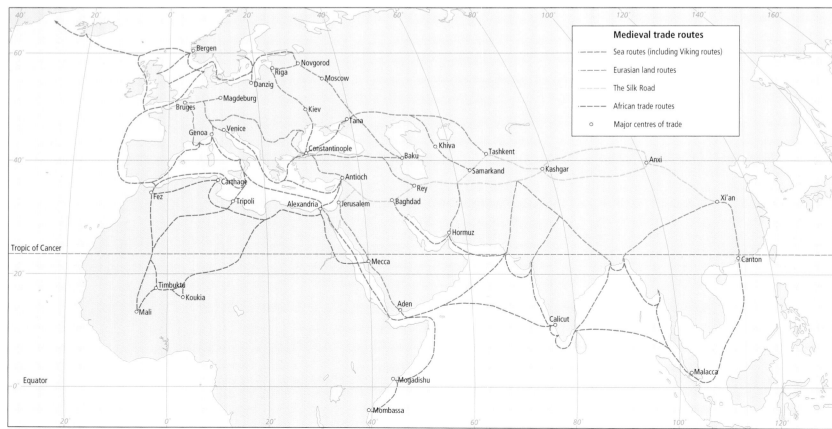

Medieval trade routes

- - - - Sea routes (including Viking routes)
- - - - Eurasian land routes
------- The Silk Road
- - - - African trade routes
○ Major centres of trade

Projecion: Robinson   Scale approx 1:70 million

Viking graves in Denmark (far left) are a reminder of the early European territorial wars. Khiva (left) was a trading post on the trade route between East and West. Zanzibar (below), an island south of Mombassa, was for many years the center of the slave trade in Africa. Venice today (far below) is a far cry from its days of trading power in the thirteenth century.

They then pushed east across the Indian Ocean, carrying Islam to India and overwhelming the Hindu trading colonies of Sumatra, Java, and Borneo, and eventually acquiring a firm footing in Canton and other major Chinese cities.

The Chinese Empire

In the period after the Han, successive empires had been established in China, some ruled by nomad invaders. The Tang had subdued their neighbors and ruled from Korea to the frontiers of Persia. They also had extensive links with the West. When Canton was sacked in 879, the slaughtered included large numbers of Nestorian Christians, Arabs, Jews, and Zoroastrians.

Western Europe

In the eighth century, driven by population pressure, those who had settled in Scandinavia set out along the inland rivers to Constantinople to fight for the Emperor, and by sea in longboats to prey upon the coasts of Northern Europe. Sturdy fighters and skilled sailors, the Vikings explored the western routes via Iceland and Greenland towards the American continent, perhaps even landing there. In time, they settled—in parts of Scotland, Ireland, northern England, and Normandy—and turned to trading.

After the spread of the Arab Empire had been halted in the West by the battle of Poitiers in 732, a new and fragile balance of power saw trade reviving in Western Europe. In 1095, the West felt strong enough to challenge Islam for possession of Jerusalem, and two centuries of Crusades began. The Crusades, however, did not hinder the growing trade in the Mediterranean.

Merchants sought protection behind city walls and, by the twelfth century, fought for the right to govern themselves as independent communities. In Italy, luxury goods brought overland from the mythic Eastern lands of India and Cathay could now be imported from the Near Eastern ports. Genoa, Florence, and Venice became the starting point for travelers and pilgrims going to Jerusalem.

In the north, cities along the great rivers and the Baltic coasts joined in a federation called the Hanse to strengthen their power and regulate trade in the fish and forest products they exported.

Even so, it was the Arabs who could move freely and upon whose knowledge the West relied—few Western merchants traveled to Asia.

The Mongols

Paradoxically, it was the Mongols who reopened the great land trade routes to the West and enabled Western merchants and missionaries to visit the East. The nomads who inhabited the great steppes were united by Genghis Khan in the first part of the thirteenth century into a powerful empire, with its capital at Korokaras. The Mongol hordes provided an extremely effective army, whose tactics left all who faced it outmatched—so much so that that it was seen as an instrument of divine will and punishment. They annexed Russia, ravaged Hungary, overwhelmed China, and set up the Mongol Empire. This empire was ruled in Marco Polo's time by Kublai Khan, whose ambitions stretched to conquering Java and Japan.

In 1258, the Mongols defeated the Turks and took Iraq and Persia. They controlled communications between these centers and enticed or forced skilled workers and traders to live with them.

It was only when the Mongols were eventually converted to Islam and became more sedentary that the Ottoman Turks were able to retake the Arabic Empire and once again cut off Western travelers from land routes to India and China.

Marco Polo

Marco Polo, a thirteenth-century Venetian, is possibly the most famous of early Western travelers. His journey to the Mongol Empire followed a long trading journey that his father and his uncle had made. He learnt Mongolian, and for many years served as an official for the emperor Kublai Khan. His account of his travels, which he dictated while in prison after having been captured by the Genoese, was the major source of Western knowledge of the Far East until the nineteenth century.

EXPLORERS AND SETTLERS

Carrying goods by water may have been cheap in the days of the great empires, but it was fraught with difficulties. Sailing out of sight of land required astronomical and mathematical skills, and sophisticated instruments. The combination of wind, tide, and current with a difficult and rocky shore could be a lethal one.

At the height of the era of world exploration, no one ruled the seas, and pirates were a constant threat. Many of the most honored explorers, such as Vasco da Gama, Alfonso de Albuquerque, and Francis Drake, were also pirates. Seaborne empires such as that of Sri Vijaya had existed before, but during this time, the European empires were unparalleled in their domination of the oceans.

Early explorers

The disruption of overland trade that occurred as a result of the Turks taking Constantinople in 1453 stimulated the search for sea routes to the east. Portugal had long been pushing down the western coast of Africa, albeit slowly, and had established a military hold on that coast which excluded traders from other countries. In 1488, Bartholomew Dias reached the Cape of Good Hope.

Many had sailed west from Europe by this time, and all had been lost. But in 1492, Christopher Columbus found a route and, upon his return, brought the unexpected news of "unknown lands" which were not part of Asia. However, the eastward passage was still of more immediate promise, and in 1497, Vasco da Gama, with the help of an Arab pilot, penetrated the Arab-dominated Indian Ocean.

In an epic voyage that took from 1519 to 1522, Ferdinand Magellan, sailing westward, showed that the world was indeed round. French, Dutch, and

English explorers and seafarers were soon blocking the Spanish and Portuguese attempts to monopolize these trading routes.

Southeast Asia

In Asia, trade was the primary objective of exploration. The existing highly developed, wealthy, sophisticated empires were largely invulnerable. However, Portuguese merchants, in well-armed ships, and protected by forts and royal fleets, did succeed in competing with the established Arab merchants.

In 1500, the Portuguese obtained trading rights on the west coast of India. In 1510, they settled in Malacca, the great emporium from which ships went to Borneo, Ternate, Tidore, and Amboina, and eventually to China and Japan. About 1565, the Spanish established an alternative route, with ships regularly crossing the Pacific to the Philippines. As the market for spices became saturated, trade in gold, ivory, silks, Indian cotton textiles, Chinese porcelain, tea, and coffee developed. By 1600, the Dutch and English East India companies had entered the competition, and eventually the Dutch controlled most of the spice trade from Batavia.

For more than two centuries, the costs of governing a distant state restricted colonization. In India, for instance, the British East India Company hesitated to assume direct rule until pushed by French competition. Only in the nineteenth century did direct rule become common.

South and Central America

The discovery of gold, silver, pearls, and industrial raw materials made the Americas attractive to the Europeans. The conquest of the Aztec and Inca

empires enabled Spain to establish its rule from the Caribbean to Mexico, Peru, and Chile, while the Portuguese colonized Brazil. A steady trickle of fortune hunters from Spanish dominions in Europe took over the land and its inhabitants, causing an economic and cultural transformation. Despite the humanitarian protests of missionaries, exploitation of local labor, plus epidemics and diseases brought by the Europeans resulted in up to 95 percent of the indigenous population dying.

African slaves were imported to work the mines whose silver had such profound effects on sixteenth-century Europe. Sugar, cotton, and tobacco production also required intensive labor, and so the slave trade grew. Hides, indigo, cochineal, forest products, dyes, and drugs also

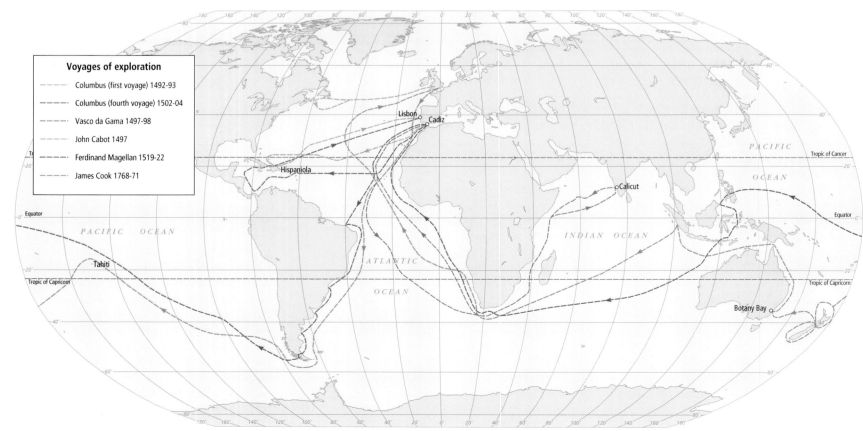

Voyages of exploration

- ------- Columbus (first voyage) 1492-93
- ------- Columbus (fourth voyage) 1502-04
- ------- Vasco da Gama 1497-98
- ------- John Cabot 1497
- ------- Ferdinand Magellan 1519-22
- ------- James Cook 1768-71

Projection: Robinson   Equatorial Scale approx 1:110 million

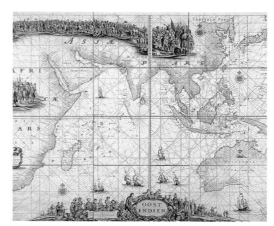

Workers in Cochin, India (left), still deal in spices—here, turmeric. This Dutch map of the East Indies (below) is from the early colonial days. A replica of Captain Cook's 'Endeavour' (bottom) reminds us of the vessels sailed during the age of exploration. Machu Picchu, in Peru (bottom left), is a moving record of a long-dead civilization.

went east in return for manufactured metals, guns, and textiles. By the seventeenth century, the Dutch, English and French were also involved.

North America

The temperate areas of North America, already inhabited by Native American Indians, were initially less interesting to the European states. Cod fishing off Newfoundland did not need shore settlements. The French, Dutch, and English, however, all eventually established east coast settlements, from the early seventeenth century. There was royal supervision, but no state financing of these colonies. Each of the colonies had its own government, constitution, and purpose. Many were established as a refuge from religious persecution, and sought self-sufficiency. Staple exports were hard to find, migrants hard to entice, and transportation of convicts was an unsatisfactory solution. So total populations remained low.

Southern colonies such as Virginia grew tobacco and, later, cotton, and increasingly used slave labor. The other colonies supplied basic foodstuffs to the Caribbean. In the eighteenth century, sugar, cotton, and tobacco still dominated as exports. Migration was becoming more attractive, though, as the economic revolution in Europe displaced laborers. The wars of independence opened the United States to migrants from all over Europe, and as the numbers of migrants grew, settlers moved west. In the nineteenth century, this trickle became a flood.

Growth of a world system

European exploration established a worldwide network—regular long-distance trading voyages took up to two years or more, so exploiting the new discoveries required some form of settlement. Europeans established trading posts wherever they went. They also soon required more capital, bigger ships, and new forms of organization. Shipyards alone required the kind of complex organization that was soon used in the factories of the Industrial Revolution. European merchants became

global carriers, meeting local requirements and introducing new commodities—horses and cotton to America; maize and turkeys to Europe.

Australasia was the last area to be drawn into this global network. In 1787, the British government chose Australia as a destination for convicts; the plan included the colonies being self-supporting. Initially, there was little but timber to offer world trade, and Europeans struggled to adapt the livestock and crops they brought with them to local conditions. Eventually, minerals were discovered as the interior of Australia was explored, wool became a staple, and convict transportation was replaced by free migration.

Ecologically, the world has been transformed by exploration and its consequences—and not always for the better. In many places, the indigenous population has been largely swept aside through disease, displacement, and massacre, and survives today only as a small minority.

As worldwide trading routes developed, so too did the movement of people attracted by the prospect of personal betterment. In the nineteenth and twentieth centuries, population pressure and sometimes persecution in the homeland pushed millions, mainly young males, to move to new countries. The Scots and Irish went to the United States and Australia; Jews left Eastern Europe for Israel, Britain, and America; Indian workers settled

in South Africa, the South Pacific islands, and East Africa; and Chinese laborers went to the goldfields in America, Australia, and elsewhere. Cultures have become mixed and modified as people intermarried and adapted to new conditions.

The world is round

On September 20, 1519, the *Trinidad, San Antonio, Victoria, Concepción,* and *Santiago,* under the command of Ferdinand Magellan, set out to travel west from Spain and return from the east. News of the terrors and dangers of the journey—the empty Pacific, the difficulties of finding water and victuals, the strange cultures of the natives—only served to increase Western fascination with new horizons.

Magellan himself died en route in 1521, and it was del Cano who brought the single surviving ship back to Spain in September 1522. The expedition members had suffered mutiny and desertion, disease and famine, attacks by natives, involvement in local wars, and the treachery of supposed allies. They had proven that the Spice Islands could be reached by sailing west, but concluded that the length of the voyage made it uneconomic.

THE INDUSTRIAL WORLD

Modern industrial societies were born in the eighteenth century, when an expanding workforce and rapid developments in technology resulted in the transformation of the social and economic structure of British society. Over the past 200 years, industrialization has spread to other parts of the globe, distributing the commercial benefits of technology and improving the lifestyles of many, but also creating social and political problems, particularly in urban areas.

Preindustrial Britain
The Industrial Revolution began in Great Britain in the second half of the eighteenth century. Several factors made Britain ripe for industrial development. Improvements in agricultural methods during the first half of the century had reduced the number of workers required to produce sufficient food for the population, making agricultural laborers available for industrial production. At the same time, wealth for investment had accumulated to a considerable degree, and much of it was concentrated in the hands of commercially minded individuals. A growing class of artisans and practical scientists possessed a high level of expertise in technologies, such as machinery, that could be readily applied to production processes. Continuing improvements in inland transportation, particularly river, canal, and road transport, allowed the rapid distribution of goods. Finally, Britain's growing empire provided it with access to vast overseas markets.

The Industrial Revolution
The first phase of the Industrial Revolution took place between the 1780s and 1830s, and was based on the early mechanization of production

processes. The new industrial system focused on textiles (especially cotton) and textile machinery, and employed waterpower as its principal source of energy. It centered on the city of Manchester, in northern England. Here, in 1780, Richard Arkwright, inventor of the water-powered spinning frame, opened the largest factory yet built, employing 600 workers. Britain's position as head of the world's largest empire gave it a massive advantage in the textile trade; it could ensure a plentiful and cheap supply of cotton from the slave-labor-based plantations in the American South, and its powerful navy could protect its trade.

This first phase of industrial development was limited in two senses: it was narrowly focused (upon the textile industry), and it applied existing knowledge and skills rather than transforming the country's technological base. It was, however, revolutionary in that new economic relationships were forged between people, a new system of production was created, and a new society and historical epoch emerged.

The evolution and spread of industry
The second phase of the Industrial Revolution occurred between the 1840s and 1880s, and was revolutionary in technological terms. Iron and steel manufacture in factories powered by steam engines represented a major innovation. When this technology was used to develop railroads and steamships, the country entered a new phase of production and transport. Britain became "the workshop of the world," supplying the materials for a remarkable burst of railroad-building activity in Europe and in former colonies of European nations. Factories now employed thousands of

workers, rather than hundreds. The effects of this iron-and-steel-based Industrial Revolution on Britain were much more pronounced than were those of its predecessor. The employment generated was considerably greater, wages and living standards increased significantly, and British exports, which included foreign investments in railroads, rose phenomenally.

The revolution soon spread, with Germany and the USA among the first nations to industrialize on a large scale. Railroads helped achieve the integration of nation-states in Europe and opened up the Americas, as well as new colonies elsewhere. In the USA, the expansion and settlement of the frontier beyond the Mississippi River is closely associated with the penetration of the new railroads, the "Iron Horse."

Industrial centers

- Major industrial center
- Country borders in 1914

A steam train (above) and a textile mill (below) are potent symbols of early industrializaion. The Firth of Forth bridge (left) is more recent—a marvel of Victorian engineering. In countries such as India (bottom), modern technologies are replacing those of earlier times.

Modern industrialization

The third phase of the Industrial Revolution began in the last decades of the nineteenth century up to the First World War. Advances in electrical and heavy engineering and industry, and the exploitation of steel alloys and heavy chemicals allowed warfare on an unprecedented scale. New factory systems combined electricity with power tools, overhead cranes, and more durable materials. Giant firms, cartels, and monopolies became the leading commercial organizations, and the ownership of capital rapidly became concentrated. The map on the left shows major European industrial centers at the time of the war. Germany and the USA had already began to rival the United Kingdom for industrial supremacy. At the same time, other nations, including Switzerland and The Netherlands, industrialized. Soon, Europeans introduced industrial practices to other parts of the world.

The Industrial Revolution continues to this day with the industrialization in the last few decades of nations like Taiwan, Korea, Singapore, Mexico, Brazil, and Thailand. This process has created a somewhat artificial but widely adopted distinction between "developed" countries—those which are industrialized—and "developing" countries, which still depend largely on agriculture.

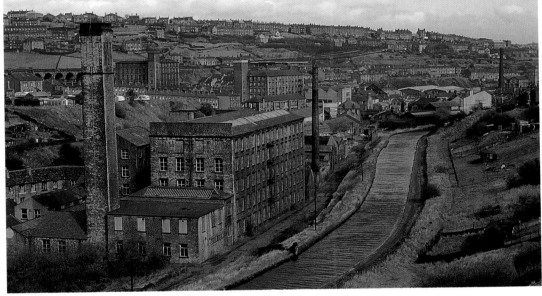

The consequences of industrialization

The application of industrial technology to an economy generally results in a population shift from rural to urban areas, as agricultural employment dwindles and people move to cities to work in industries and services. This process is known as urbanization. In the nineteenth century, the population of London, for example, rose from about 1 million in 1800 to almost 7 million in 1900.

While new industries raised living standards for many, the urban poor suffered overcrowding, poor sanitation, and pollution. There are many parallels between the social conditions in nineteenth-century United Kingdom cities and those in newly industrialized cities today. For example, the rapid expansion of an urban area such as Mexico City, which has grown from 3 million inhabitants in 1950 to about 10 million today, has resulted in acute social problems—water shortages, severe air pollution, and a chronic lack of adequate housing.

Recently, the industrialization of certain developing countries has had an interesting effect on the economies of the world's first industrial nations. Newly industrialized nations, particularly in Southeast Asia, have attracted manufacturing investment from the older developed countries; to such an extent that there has actually been a decline in manufacturing jobs—a deindustrialization process—in the countries where the first and second phases of the Industrial Revolution initially occurred. The United Kingdom, Germany, and the USA have all deindustrialized to some extent.

But today's era of industrialization differs significantly from its earlier phases. Owing to new forms of technology, particularly in transport and communications, the contemporary industrial system extends to all corners of the globe, and encompasses most commodities. The Industrial Revolution has now entered its worldwide phase, integrating selected localities as workshops of emerging global factories.

THE NATION-STATE

The world's nation-states, as represented today by the lines on a political map of the world, evolved over the past 500 years. Sixteenth-century Europe, for example, consisted of approximately 1,500 politically independent units. Yet by the start of the twentieth century, the continent was made up of only 20 nation-states. Since then, nation-states have flourished—today there are 191 nations and 58 territories on the political map of the world. New supranational groups emerging at the end of the twentieth century have led many commentators to question the ability of nation-states to solve problems within their own borders and deal with the powerful forces operating at a regional or worldwide level.

From city state to nation-state

Before the appearance of the nation-state in Europe, city states such as Venice, Antwerp, and Amsterdam occupied centre stage in politics and economics. For much of the seventeenth and eighteenth centuries, Amsterdam was the control

center for local, regional, and even worldwide affairs. The creation of the first nation-states, or more accurately, territorial nation-states, occurred during the 1770s and 1780s.

The catalyst was competitive rivalry between Amsterdam, England, and France. The incorporation of national territory was a new feature of the political landscape, and it gave nation-states major economic and military advantages over city states. In economic terms, for example, the nation-state could profit from its national market for goods. In military terms, it could more readily raise an army from its citizenry.

What do we mean by the term nation-state? It is useful to think of a nation-state as a combination of three elements: nation (ethnicity), state (the institutionalized regime of power), and territory (the spatially bounded area of state control).

A nation is a group of people who believe that they are an ethnic community with deep historical roots and the right to their own sovereign state. Nationalism is the cause through which such groups claim their right to be a sovereign power within a particular territory. Nationalism has its origins in the convergence of capitalism with print technology in the sixteenth century. The creation of separate vernacular print communities led to the decline of Latin as a lingua franca, and played a critical role in forming national identities.

Although ethnic identity was a significant factor in the formation of many nation-states, nations

The city-state of Venice (left) was an important trading center from the tenth century onward. Today it forms part of a modern nation-state, the republic of Italy. These Dutch-style buildings in Suriname (below), hint at the nation's past history when it was part of the Dutch colonial empire.

seldom consist of a single ethnic group. Indeed, such entities are extremely rare, Iceland being one of very few contemporary examples. A survey of 164 nations in 1984 counted 589 ethnic groups, an average of more than three ethnic groups per nation. A major role of mass education has been to integrate diverse ethnic groups and regional minorities into a single community, often called the "melting-pot approach" to nation-building.

The second element of a nation-state, the state, refers to the institutions of political power within a country. These include its legislature, judiciary, political parties, and security forces. State power is organized into a wide variety of regimes, including constitutional monarchies, republics, theocracies, and totalitarian dictatorships. In the 1990s, three out of five states in the world were democracies—this is a historic high.

The third element that is used to define a nation is its territory, the physical area over which it has control. This area is normally marked out by geographical boundaries. Nation-state territories have typically been viewed as economic, political, social, and cultural containers that are largely sovereign and entitled to be free from outside interference. However, disputes over boundaries and national sovereignty have led to a number of major conflicts, particularly during the years of the twentieth century.

The rise of the nation-state

The process of dividing the world outside Europe into nation-states occurred largely in the context of the empires that the major colonizers—Spain, Portugal, The Netherlands, France, and the United Kingdom—had built during the previous four centuries. Most of the border lines on the

Internal conflicts between groups who consider themselves to be of a separate nation can lead to a state fragmenting into smaller ones, as in the former Yugoslavia (right). Indian Sikhs on parade (below right): the world's largest democracy is home to a wide range of ethnic groups.

contemporary political map of the world have their origins in two major phases of decolonization.

The first phase unfolded over the half-century following the American War of Independence in 1776. About 100 colonies combined to form the current nation-states in the Americas. Little further decolonization occurred for more than a century, until around the time of the Second World War. Notable exceptions were the British settler colonies of Canada, Australia, and South Africa. The second major phase of decolonization began after the Second World War, when "the winds of change" blew through Africa, South and Southeast Asia, and islands in the Caribbean and the Pacific and Indian Oceans. This resulted in the formation of another approximately 110 nation-states.

Nation-states continued to be created in the 1990s—15 nations were created as a result of the break-up of the Soviet Union in 1991, for example. Eritrea, Slovenia, Croatia, and Macedonia became independent in 1991, as did the Czech Republic, Slovakia, and Namibia in 1994. The final outcome of the break-up of Yugoslavia is still uncertain. Internal ethnic tension in some areas has grown enormously, and ethnic-based nationalist movements continue to emerge. This kind of conflict is currently the most common—of the 89 armed conflicts that occurred between 1989 and 1992, only 3 were between nations.

At the same time, in Europe, where the nation-state first began, the European Union, a supra-

national regional state, continues to transform the European political landscape. Most of Western Europe has now been combined within the European Union, while a number of other European states have applied for admission and await entry. Some commentators see the European Union as the beginning of the end of the territorial nation-state as we have known it; it has undoubtedly changed long-held ideas on what makes a nation.

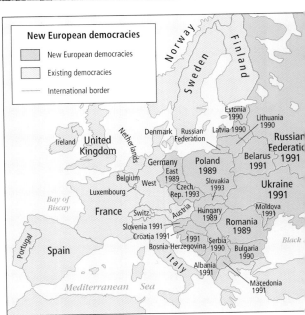

New European democracies

- New European democracies
- Existing democracies
- International border

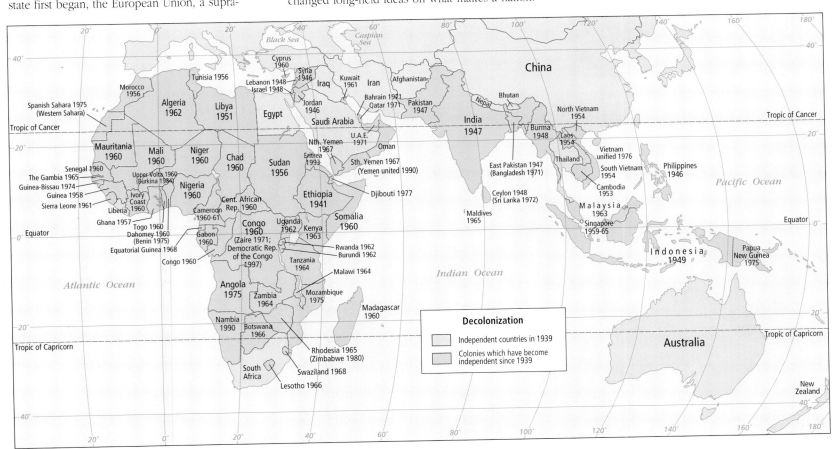

Decolonization

- Independent countries in 1939
- Colonies which have become independent since 1939

INTERNATIONAL ORGANIZATIONS

During the second half of the twentieth century, international organizations, including intergovernmental and nongovernmental bodies, have grown significantly in both number and stature. Today, there are about 500 inter-governmental organizations, such as the United Nations (UN) and the International Monetary Fund (IMF), and approximately 5,000 nongovernmental organizations (NGOs), including the Red Cross and Amnesty International. That represents roughly five times the number that were active at the end of the Second World War.

International organizations form an important part of the social glue that binds the nations and peoples of the world together. They create a set of rules, norms, and procedures—encapsulated in international law, particularly in the form of treaties and conventions signed by nation-states—that define the expected conduct of participants in the international community.

United Nations

The largest and most influential intergovernmental organization is the United Nations. Its predecessor was the League of Nations, which was founded at the end of the First World War, in an attempt to prevent further international conflict. Based in Geneva, the League gradually expanded its membership and became a focus for growing numbers of nongovernmental bodies. However, the refusal of the United States to ratify the League's covenant, and the League's inability to prevent expansion by Germany, Italy, and Japan in the 1930s led to its ceasing operations during the Second World War.

The United Nations (UN) was established in San Francisco in 1946, and now has its headquarters in New York. As with the League of Nations, the main motivation for the creation of the UN was collective security. Half a century later, the membership of the UN has grown to 185, and only a small number of nations (such as Switzerland and Taiwan) and territories (including French Polynesia and the Channel Islands) are not formal member states.

On the world stage, the UN is critically important, but relatively weak and often controversial. At times it has appeared to be an impotent and ineffective institution that more resembles a debating society for the superpowers, their client states, and major power blocs than anything remotely like a "world government."

It is, of course, important to remember that the UN is not a world government, in that its member-states remain independent and sovereign entities. Furthermore, most of the member states clearly have an ambivalent attitude towards the organization. For example, the Norwegians are strong supporters of the UN, but refuse to accept

Refugees in the Sudan (below) and the young Somali girl (left) are likely to receive assistance from international organizations—via UN peacekeeping forces.

UN directives on whaling. The USA frequently seeks UN support for military intervention abroad, but constantly defers payment of its UN dues. Resulting financial difficulties hamper UN operations. Even after the Cold War, when it seemed to have grown enormously in importance and stature, the UN operated on about the same budget as the Tokyo fire department.

During the half-century following the establishment of the UN, other collective issues, including environmental, economic, and legal issues, have been placed under the umbrella of the intergovernmental system. For example, the World Bank and the International Monetary Fund (IMF) have become responsible for managing a wide variety of international economic issues: the IMF coordinates international currency exchange and the balance of international payments, and the World Bank borrows the savings of rich nations and lends them to poor nations under conditions not available on the private capital markets.

Nongovernmental organizations

Nongovernmental organizations (NGOs) are private organizations that are today regarded as legitimate players on the world stage alongside nation-states and intergovernmental organizations. Generally, however, NGOs have significantly less power and far fewer financial resources.

Most NGOs are primarily concerned with the empowerment of marginal and impoverished sectors of the world's population through increasing those people's participation in resolving their own problems. NGOs tend to focus upon specific issues. For example, Greenpeace raises awareness of environmental issues, Planned Parenthood campaigns for reproductive rights and family planning, groups such as the International Federation of the Red Cross and the Red Crescent Societies provide disaster relief, and Médecins Sans Frontières provides medical care.

International organizations and human rights

Human rights is one highly significant area where international organizations have created the emerging rules, norms, and legal instruments that link nations and their citizens together in an embryonic worldwide system. Human rights are the laws, customs, and practices that have evolved to protect people, minorities, groups, and races from oppressive rulers and governments.

Before the Second World War, international human rights issues were restricted to matters such as slavery or armed conflict, and discussions about human rights (and recognition of them) took place mainly within the borders of particular nation-states. A turning point in the history of human rights occurred on December 10, 1948, when the Universal Declaration of Human Rights was adopted by the General Assembly of the UN without a dissenting vote.

Over the next half-century, major advances were made. Most significantly, a series of international covenants was drafted and adopted

A land rights protest in Australia (above). International human rights organizations are increasingly exerting pressure on governments to recognize indigenous peoples' rights.

by the UN and subsequently ratified by individual nation-states. Once ratified by a nation-state, the human rights legislation was usually incorporated within the state's own legal system.

Although the UN has been prominent in human rights legislation, private individuals and nongovernmental organizations such as Amnesty International have frequently provided the political pressure that has persuaded intergovernmental and national agencies to act. Often, though, such action has been taken only reluctantly and retrospectively. The fact that countless millions of people have suffered (and many still do) terrible violations of their rights as human beings, even since the Declaration of Human Rights, is something of an indictment of the Declaration and of the UN's ability and will to enforce it. Most observers still regard the Declaration of Human Rights as inadequate and in need of enforcement. Its emergence, and the opportunity it created to bring such issues to world attention, are one positive result of the growth in importance of international organizations. While this has certainly produced a world that is better than it was, it is still by no means all that it could be.

Again, the ambivalent attitudes of nation-states to international organizations is a significant factor, affecting their ability to function effectively. For example, when concerns about human rights in Afghanistan were raised by the UN and NGO representatives in 1998, the ruling Taliban militia asked the organizations to leave the country. Yet, when it appeared that Iran may be ready to invade Afghanistan to protect some of its own citizens, the Taliban sought support from the UN to keep Iran out. At the end of the twentieth century, the idea of setting up global governance is still on the world's agenda, but only just.

THE UNITED NATIONS SYSTEM

International Court of Justice

Secretariat

Trusteeship Council

General Assembly
Committees

Security Council
Peacekeeping Operations
International Tribunals
Military Staff Committees
Standing Committees

Economic and Social Council (ECOSOC)

UN Programs:

INSTRAW	UN International Research and Training Institute for the Advancement of Women
ITC	International Trade Center
UNCHS	UN Center for Human Habitats
UNCTAD	UN Conference on Trade and Development
UNDCP	UN Drug Control Program
UNDP	UN Development Program
UNEP	UN Environment Program
UNFPA	UN Fund for Population Activities
UNHCF	UN High Commission for Refugees
UNICEF	UN Children's Emergency Fund
UNIFEM	UN Development Fund for Women
UNITAR	UN Institute for Training and Research*
UNU	UN University
WFP	World Food Program
WFC	World Food Council

Functional Commissions

Regional Commissions

Standing Committees

Expert Bodies

Specialized Agencies:

FAO	Food and Agriculture Organization, Rome
ICAO	International Civil Aviation Organization, Montreal
IFAD	International Fund for Agricultural Development, Rome
ILO	International Labor Organization, Geneva
IMF	International Monetary Fund, Washington
IMO	International Maritime Organization, London
ITU	International Telecommunications Union, Geneva
UNESCO	UN Educational, Scientific, and Cultural Organization, Paris
UNIDO	UN Industrial Development Organization, Vienna
UPU	Universal Postal Union, Berne
WHO	World Health Organization, Geneva
WIPO	World Intellectual Property Organization, Geneva
WMO	World Meteorological Association, Geneva
WTO	World Trade Organization, Geneva*

World Bank Group, Washington

IBRD	International Bank for Reconstruction and Development
IDA	International Development Association
IFC	International Finance Corporation
MIGA	Multilateral Investment Guarantee Agency

* Does not report to ECOSOC

GLOBALIZATION

Globalization refers to a change of scale in human processes and activities which has occurred during the last quarter of a century—one in which the nation-state is giving way, in many fields, to global organizations. Until recently, it was generally felt that human and environmental affairs could and should be conducted at a national level. Nation-states were, in principle at least, sovereign or independent units. Of course, nation-states had relations with one another, and these were referred to as international, as in the terms "international trade" and "international relations." In the 1990s, however, "international" and "internationalization" have been increasingly replaced by "global" and "globalization," as national boundaries have begun to seem less significant in economic, political, cultural, and environmental terms.

The global economy

Transnational corporations—companies that operate in a large number of countries—are the movers and shakers of the modern global economy. Among the firms with operations that are nearly worldwide are Exxon and Royal Dutch Shell in petroleum; McDonalds, Seagrams, Sara Lee, Nabisco and Nestlé in food and beverages; BMW, Ford, Volkswagen, and General Motors in automobiles; and Mitsubishi and Mitsui in banking, manufacturing, and trade.

Although few (if any) companies can be described as truly global at this time—most still focus on certain markets and report to share-holders in their home country—the term "global" is commonly used in business circles to identify a level of operations that many companies hope to attain in the not-too-distant future. This would involve a truly international workforce, share-holders in a number of nation-states, and products that are sold in all markets.

The flow of money from country to country is also encouraging the surge in economic global-ization. National boundaries are no barrier to the movement of funds; thanks to modern telecom-munications and computer technology, funds can now be rapidly transferred to any part of the globe. Such transactions have, it now appears, created a much more volatile and less secure world. In a matter of weeks in the middle of 1997, the Asian economic miracle became the Asian economic meltdown as a result of the massive and rapid withdrawal of global funds.

The phenomenal growth of the Internet has created opportunities for even small companies to operate at a global level. By selling goods via the World Wide Web, a firm can now compete in markets where it could not previously have established a presence, whether for geographical, political, or financial reasons. Governments are struggling to cope with the implications of this for the regulation of trade within their countries. How, for example, do they impose sales taxes on goods or services that are purchased in the virtual market of cyberspace?

Many commentators assert that globalization will transform the world economy in the twenty-first century, leaving no national products, no national corporations, no national industries, and no national economies. To succeed in the global marketplace, countries will have to depend entirely on the skills of their inhabitants, and will have to deal with powerful external forces that could create an ever-widening gulf between skilled, globally aware citizens and a growing unskilled, out-of-touch underclass.

World politics

The globalization of politics has resulted in the decline of the nation-state and the growth of international organizations. Although they remain the principal players on the world political stage, nation-states now appear less independent and less sovereign than they used to. One response to this has been to look to international organizations such as the United Nations to assume some of the roles previously played by nation-states.

Perhaps the most significant political event in the 1990s was the end of the Cold War. During the Cold War (1946–91), most nation-states belonged to one of three geopolitical worlds: the First World, consisting of developed capitalist nations, and dominated by the USA; the Second World, consisting of developed communist nations, and dominated by the Soviet Union; and the Third World, consisting of developing nations that were in theory not aligned with either of the super-powers. The demise of the Cold War brought an end to these divisions, and created a geopolitical situation no longer driven by the rivalry of two opposing superpowers.

Some commentators believe that this has created a vacuum, where no effectively organized power system exists. In the past, when major geopolitical shifts occurred, one dominant power was typically replaced by another: Great Britain (as the United Kingdom then was) replaced Amsterdam, and the USA later replaced the United Kingdom. Globalization has produced a world so complex and integrated that it no longer seems possible for a single nation-state to play the dominant role that these nations once played. The growing emphasis on and allocation of power to international organizations can be seen as an attempt to fill this power vacuum.

The global village

Discussions of the globalization of culture often begin with the expression "global village," a term coined in the 1960s by Marshall McLuhan, an American commentator. He believed that television would replace the printed word as the primary medium of wider social integration, eventually uniting the people of the world through their collective participation in media events. In the 1990s, events such as the Gulf War, the annual Academy Awards, the death of an English princess, and certain sporting competitions were watched on television by people in almost all the world's countries—an audience of between 1 and 2 billion people.

Dealings on the Tokyo Stock Exchange (right) can affect the economy of many other countries; financial centers such as Chicago (below) are experiencing the globalization of trade.

The fact that a rapidly growing number of people are involved in maintaining the global village raises a number of questions. For instance, will globalization mean an inevitable cultural homogenization? Opinion is sharply divided on this question. A great deal of evidence supports the view that a global culture is developing. On the other hand, powerful movements which actively resist this cultural homogenization have also emerged—militant Islamic, Hindu, and Zionist organizations, for example.

One issue that has played a major role in raising awareness of the ways in which we truly are a global community is the environment. The first Earth Day in 1970 marked the beginning of mass awareness of the global significance of environmental issues. Over the next three decades, evidence of the extent of degradation of Earth's natural environment caused by human activity has mounted. This has forced governments and individuals to examine their impact on the natural world, and has encouraged political cooperation at a global level to effect change.

A series of international environmental forums have been held, including Stockholm (1972), the Earth Summit at Rio de Janeiro (1992), and the Population Conference at Cairo (1994). All stressed the worldwide and interconnected nature of the growing environmental crisis. The Earth Summit was attended by an unprecedented 130 heads of state, 1,500 nongovernmental organizations, and 7,000 accredited journalists. However, despite the willingness of many nations to discuss these issues globally, the desire or ability to act locally may be absent.

The slogan "Think globally, act locally" has been widely employed to express the scale shift involved in this transformation of economics, politics, culture, and nature—from what used to be thought local or national concepts to what are now recognized as (or have become) international, global concerns.

Globalization may prove to be the key change in the twenty-first century.

Advertising signs in this village in Peru (below) are an example of the penetration of multi-national corporations into a developing country.

Oceania and Antarctica

Asia and the Middle East

1.8 MILLION BP
Hominids of *Homo erectus* species living in Java, Indonesia

130,000 BP *Homo neanderthalensis* (Neanderthals) living in western Asia; they have social organization and hunt using strategy and cooperation

Skull of Homo erectus

1.9 MILLION BP Modern hominids resembling *Homo habilis* living in caves in Sichuan Province, China

800,000 BP *Homo erectus* using simple rafts on Indonesian island of Flores

460,000 BP Earliest known controlled use of fire at Zhoukoudian Cave, China

90,000 BP *Homo sapiens sapiens* present at several sites in Israel

Europe and the Russian Federation

780,000 BP Tool-using hominids living in northern Spain. Classified as *Homo heidelbergensis*, they may have been the ancestors of Neanderthals

130,000 BP Emergence of *Homo neanderthalensis* (Neanderthals); they have social organization and hunt using strategy and cooperation

1.5 MILLION BP Hominids arrive from Africa

500,000 BP Archaic *Homo sapiens* appears in Europe

100,000 BP Neanderthals burying their dead; possibly using burial rituals and decorating graves

Africa

4.0 MILLION BP Earliest recognizable hominid (form of human), *Australopithecus ramidus*, living in southern and eastern Africa

3.0 MILLION BP Hominids living in caves in southern Africa feeding on plants and animals

2.3 MILLION BP Emergence of *Homo habilis* in East Africa, a hominid associated with first use of crude stone tools

1.5 MILLION BP Hominids spread northward, crossing Sahara Desert region at time of abundant vegetation

150,000–100,000 BP Modern humans, *Homo sapiens sapiens*, appear in various parts of Africa and begin to migrate northward

5.0 MILLION BP The southern ape (Australopithecine) family splits into three branches, which will slowly evolve into gorillas, chimpanzees, and humans

3.5 MILLION BP Footprints left at Laetoli, Tanzania, by *Australopithecus afarensis*, a hominid that walks upright

1.9 MILLION BP Hominids of more modern appearance, *Homo ergaster*, appear in Africa, probably evolving from *Homo habilis*

Skull of Homo ergaster

800,000 BP Archaic *Homo sapiens* evolves in Africa

200,000 BP Anatomically modern humans, distinguished by larger brain and use of more sophisticated tools, inhabit a number of cave sites in southern Africa

North and Central America

South America

40,000 BP Rock art appears in Australia; many early works consist of simple patterned engravings etched in rock

30,000 BP Earliest evidence of cremation at Lake Mungo, southeastern Australia

Seafaring groups inhabit the islands east of New Guinea

18,000 BP Rock paintings appear in Arnhem Land, northwestern Australia

Obsidian is traded in the Bismarck Archipelago, Melanesia

8000 BP Land bridge between New Guinea and Australia is submerged

60,000–40,000 BP *Homo sapiens sapiens* enters Australia and New Guinea from Southeast Asia, possibly by raft or canoe—the earliest known seaworthy vessels

35,000 BP Humans hunting wallabies on grasslands of Tasmania, Australia

28,000 BP Buka Island in the Solomons group is colonized

25,000 BP Stone blades and hatchet tools in use in northern Australia and New Guinea

Sharpened kangaroo femur, 12,000 BP

9000 BP Crops including bananas, taro, and sugar-cane cultivated in New Guinea

---

68,000 BP *Homo sapiens sapiens* living in parts of China

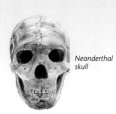

Neanderthal skull

40,000 BP Neanderthals disappear from the fossil record in western Asia

20,000 BP Modern humans (*Homo sapiens sapiens*) migrate across Eurasia as far as Siberia

11,000 BP Cultivation of domesticated grains such as wheat and barley in the Fertile Crescent

9500 BP Evidence of rice cultivation in central China

12,000 BP Dogs domesticated in southwestern Asia

12,500 BP Jomon people of Japan produce the world's first clay vessels

Jomon pot, 12,500–9,500 BP

10,000 BP Cattle domesticated in Anatolia, in present-day Turkey

9000 BP Crops including sesame and eggplant are cultivated in the Indus Valley

Pigs domesticated in Anatolia, Turkey

8500 BP Smelting of copper, gold, and lead in south-western Asia

7500 BP Pottery is produced in China

50,000 BP Simple engravings carved on cave walls in eastern Europe

35,000 BP Neanderthals disappear from the fossil record, perhaps displaced by *Homo sapiens sapiens*

Appearance of Cro-Magnon peoples, noted for their use of bone tools and sewn hides

15,000 BP First evidence of use of watercraft in the Mediterranean

14,000 BP Elaborate huts of interlocked mammoth bones built to provide shelter during winter at Mezhirich, Ukraine

8000 BP Permanent farming settlements established in southeastern Europe

Sidescraper tool from France, 70,000–35,000 BP

Austrian fertility figure, 20,000 BP

40,000 BP *Homo sapiens sapiens* arrives from Africa, bringing more sophisticated tools and skills

32,000 BP First cave art appears in southwestern France and northern Spain

15,000–12,000 BP Magdalenian phase, during which most of the best-known cave art is produced, including the galleries of Lascaux, France, and Altamira, Spain

10,500 BP Beginning of colonization of Mediterranean islands, which takes 4,000 years

---

23,000 BP Rock paintings on inland shelters show ceremonial dancers and herds of game animals, including antelope

9000 BP Pottery containers in use in settled areas of the Nile Valley, Egypt

Skull of Homo sapiens sapiens

25,000 BP Paintings on rock slabs made by Stone Age hunter-gatherers in Namibia show animals such as elephants and giraffes

12,000 BP Rock carvings in the Sahara Desert, in present-day Algeria, depict North African aurochs

8000 BP Crops including figs and chufa are cultivated in the Nile Valley, Egypt

---

12,000 BP Date of earliest reliable evidence of human habitation of North America, found at sites in Alaska

11 000 BP Numerous human settlements appear across present-day United States

Humans hunt mammoths at Clovis, New Mexico

Dogs domesticated

North American Clovis point tool, c.11,500 BP

35,000–12,000 BP *Homo sapiens sapiens* enters North America across Bering Strait land bridge between Asia and present-day Alaska, and spreads southward

14,500 BP Disputed date for evidence of human habitation at Meadowcroft Shelter in southwestern Pennsylvania; site includes firepits, stone tools, and plaited basketry

10,000 BP Hunters use trenches to trap and kill bison at Casper, Wyoming

9,000 BP Native peoples of Mesoamerica begin to collect plants more intensively, perhaps beginning domestication

---

12,500 BP Humans inhabiting Monte Verde in southern Chile; evidence includes stone tools, animal skins on poles, and plant remains

12,000 BP Well-organized hunter-gatherers living in the cold high-altitude puna grasslands of modern-day Peru, feeding on plants and vicuñas (a relative of the llama)

8,500 BP Beans and chili peppers cultivated in central Andes

Monte Verde hut, 12,500 BP

25,000 BP Disputed date for evidence of human habitation of eastern South America, including Pedra Furada in Brazil

11,000 BP Humans inhabit Cueva Fell, Tierra del Fuego, southern Chile

10,000 BP Potatoes cultivated in the Andes of present-day Bolivia

Oceania and Antarctica

4000 BC Pig husbandry and vegetable growing (mainly taro) in mainland New Guinea

Forest cleared on the Bismarck Archipelago to increase agricultural production

4500–4000 BC People living on High Cliffy Island off Western Australia build stone structures as dwellings or for ceremonial purposes

3600 BC Simple pottery is made on Vanimo coast of northern New Guinea

3500 BC Giant clam-shell adzes in use in Sepik-Ramu basin of New Guinea

Lapita pottery, c.1100 BC

2500 BC "Saltwater" people of the Kimberley Coast region of northwestern Australia use fire-hardened spears for fishing

1600 BC Austronesian colonization of New Guinea and the Bismarck Archipelago followed by emergence of Lapita culture, named for its distinctive pottery bearing complex geometric designs

1500 BC Fiji is settled by Lapita people

1200 BC Lapita people colonize New Caledonia, Tonga, Samoa

Asia and the Middle East

4200 BC Copper and bronze being worked in Mesopotamia

5000 BC First settlements appear in Mesopotamia, the fertile area between the Tigris and Euphrates rivers

3500 BC Small cities based on earlier farming communities appear in Sumer, the southern part of Mesopotamia

3000 BC Sumerians develop a writing system consisting of pictograms pressed in clay tablets; they also develop the first wheeled vehicles

People from southern Asia (Austronesians) begin expansion south and east into the Philippines, eastern Indonesia, and New Guinea

4000 BC Sailing ships in use in Mesopotamia

2400 BC Harappa civilization merges diverse cultures in the Indus Valley; Harappan building methods involve use of bricks and architectural planning

2500 BC Rice farming reaches southern China

1800 BC Indo-Europeans spread to the Middle East and eastern Mediterranean

2200 BC Semites migrate from Arabia to Mesopotamia and found Babylonian and Assyrian kingdoms

1500 BC The Aryans, an Indo-European people, migrate from central Asia to northern India

1595 BC The Hittites, a powerful Indo-European people from Hattusas in present-day Turkey, sack Babylon; by 1500 BC they control all of Asia Minor

1290 BC Traditional date for Moses leading the Hebrews from slavery in Egypt back to tribal lands in Canaan (Palestine)

1200 BC Writing system based on pictograms in use in China

Europe and the Russian Federation

4000 BC Farming reaches northern Europe

Horses domesticated in the Ukraine; they become the main means of transport throughout Europe and Asia and confer major advantages in battle

5000 BC Earliest evidence of burials in Scandinavia

Land bridge between Britain and Europe submerged by rising sea levels

Copper in use in southeastern Europe

Poulnabrone tomb, Ireland, 3000 BC

2500 BC Rise of Minoan civilization—Europe's first—on the island of Crete and in surrounding Aegean region

Dolmen, large standing stones usually topped by a horizontal stone, are erected in Scandinavia

1800 BC Stone circle at Stonehenge, Wiltshire, England, completed; work may have started as early as 3500 BC

1650 BC Writing systems known as Linear A and Linear B in use in Crete and mainland Greece; Linear A is a Minoan script, whereas Linear B constitutes an early form of Mycenaean Greek

1600–1500 BC Minoan centers destroyed by invaders or earthquakes

Rise of Mycenaean civilization on Greek mainland

1250–1200 BC Mycenean centers destroyed by conflict or earthquakes

Africa

4000 BC People living in central Sudan in loosely organized communities, tending cattle, sheep, and goats as well as continuing to hunt and fish

Copper smelting in Egypt

5000 BC Growth of Nubian settlement in the Nile Valley; agricultural methods begin to spread southward

3000 BC Donkeys used for farming in the Nile Valley

First scientific astronomy observations in Egypt and Babylonia

Yams and palm oil domesticated in tropical West Africa

Beginning of Bantu expansion from West Africa into Congo Basin

2650 BC Nile Valley civilization flourishes; pyramids constructed during this period are the most elaborate burial tomb structures to date

2200 BC Ducks and geese domesticated in Egypt

2000 BC Kingdom of Kush established in middle Nile Valley

Invention of the water wheel in Egypt

1500 BC Trade routes between North Africa and the rest of Africa are disrupted by the spread of the Sahara Desert

Egyptians conquer Kush

1333–1323 BC Tutankhamun reigns as Pharaoh of Egypt, coming to the throne at age nine and ruling from Memphis near Cairo with the help of regent, Ay

1290 BC Rock temples of Abu Simbel built in Egypt by Rameses II

North and Central America

3500 BC Bison hunted on the Great Plains

Beginning of classic period of Northwest Coast culture of Pacific Northwest, characterized by lavish ceremonies and ornate woodwork

Turkeys domesticated in Mesoamerica

5000 BC Caribbean islands colonized by people arriving in dugout canoes from the Yucatan Peninsula, present-day Mexico

Plants such as squash, amarinth, chili, and gourds cultivated in Tehuacán Valley, Mesoamerica

Gill-net fishing practiced in Pacific Northwest

2500 BC Squash cultivated in eastern North America, as well as sumpweed, goosefoot, and sunflowers, whose large seeds are stored as winter food

Simple pottery appears in North America

Olmec head

1200 BC Olmec civilization spreads throughout much of Mesoamerica; it lasts for 900 years

1300 BC People in southeastern North America, in the area known as the lower Mississippi, build major earthworks such as those found at Poverty Point in Louisiana

South America

3500 BC Valdivia culture begins to develop in the Andes (in present-day Ecuador); it is characterized by a complex social culture and village life

Manioc (cassava) and potato cultivated in many parts of the Andes and Amazonia

4000 BC Llamas, alpacas, and guinea pigs domesticated in Peru

3000 BC Cotton grown at Valdivia centers of Ancon and Huaca Prieta in coastal valleys of present-day Peru; mound architecture built at nearby sites such as El Paraiso

Valdivia culture produces incised ceramics at Puerto Horniga

Squash, capsicum, and peppers grown in Peruvian Andes

2500 BC Elaborate temples and mounds constructed in Peruvian highlands

1800 BC Huge ceremonial complexes built in coastal valleys of Peru at sites including Casma Valley

1200 BC Terracing used to increase agricultural output in Andes

1000 BC Settlement of southern Mariana islands of Micronesia

500 BC A distinctive Polynesian culture emerges in islands of southwestern Pacific

528 BC Buddhism begins under Siddhartha (Gautama Buddha) in Benares, India, and later spreads to Sri Lanka, Myanmar, Laos, Thailand, and other parts of southern Asia

331 BC Alexander the Great conquers the Persian Empire, winning a decisive battle at Gaugamela, Mesopotamia

112 BC Development of the Silk Road as a trading route between China and the West

Bronze vessel from China

221–211 BC Shih Huang orders construction of Great Wall of China to protect Qin Empire against nomadic tribes of northern steppes

1020 BC Israelites establish a kingdom in Palestine

400 BC Cast iron in use in China

c.5 BC Birth of Jesus Christ in Bethlehem

800 BC Etruscans settle in central-western Italy between the Arno and Tiber rivers

Phoenician colonies established in Spain, Sardinia, and Sicily

620 BC Roman alphabet, derived from Etruscan, in use

336 BC Alexander the Great succeeds father Philip II as ruler of Macedonia; he soon tightens control of Greek city-states and expands Macedonian Empire into Asia

218–201 BC Hannibal crosses the Alps to invade Italy from the north, beginning the Second Punic War

146 BC Rome emerges victorious from Third Punic War

776 BC The Olympic Games, a combination of religious festival and athletic contest, first held in Delphi and Olympia, Greece

750 BC Rise of Greek city-states including Athens, Corinth, Sparta, and Thebes

Etruscan alphabet in use

Work begins on the Acropolis, Athens

600–400 BC Growth of Celtic warrior societies; major centers include Hunsrück-Eifel region of Germany and Champagne district of France

c.350–322 BC Aristotle writes his major works, advancing the idea that Earth is the center of the universe around which other planets revolve

290 BC Romans take control of central Italy

264–241 BC First Punic War between Rome and Carthage initiates long battle for dominance of Mediterranean

51 BC Julius Caesar conquers Celtic tribes of Gaul as far as the Rhine; he reaches Britain in 55 BC, but Romans do not occupy the country until 43 AD

750 BC Kingdom of Kush-Meroë conquers Egypt and rules until 670 BC

Phoenicians colonize coast of North Africa

480 BC City of Carthage flourishes and holds sway over the western Mediterranean

275 BC The first lighthouse to use reflected light from a fire to warn sea traffic of danger is built at Alexandria in Eygpt

200 BC Paper made from papyrus in use in Egypt

Gold sheath from Kush-Meroë Kingdom

1000 BC Bantu expansion reaches Rift Valley

Kush becomes independent

300 BC African rice is grown in the Niger delta

146 BC Carthage destroyed by Roman army at end of Third Punic War

1000 BC Agriculture, in the form of the cultivation of maize, established in southwestern North America

650 BC Appearance of Zapotec hieroglyphs, the earliest form of Mesoamerican writing

500 BC Adena people of midwestern North America build mounds for ceremonial purposes

Monte Albán, in Mexico's southern highlands, becomes capital city of Zapotec culture; it thrives for about 1,250 years

300 BC Hohokam, Mogollon, and Anasazi peoples inhabit southern North America; the Anasazi occupy villages built beneath overhanging cliffs in and around Chaco Canyon, New Mexico

600 BC Team games played with a rubber ball on ball courts in San Lorenzo and La Venta in present-day Mexico; the games may have involved human sacrifices

200 BC In northeastern North America, Hopewell culture begins to take over from Adena; the Hopewell become the region's first farmers

900 BC Carving of Tello Obelisk, an ornate granite monolith from Chavín de Huántar, one of the most remarkable artefacts of Chavín culture

200 BC Rise of Nasca culture in Peru, noted for its immense geometric figures etched into the ground and only visible from the air; the patterns may mark the sun's passage at solstice

Tello Obelisk, 900 BC

1000 BC The Chavín culture begins to flourish in northern Andes

750 BC Gold mining taking place in central Andes

Oceania and Antarctica

AD 186 One of the world's most violent volcanic eruptions occurs at Mt Taupo, New Zealand, destroying surrounding forests over a radius of 75 km (47 miles)

Fishhook from Marquesas Islands

AD 0 Marquesas Islands colonized

AD 500 Polynesian settlers reach Hawaii and Easter Island

Asia and the Middle East

AD 220 Demise of Han Empire in China

AD 527–565 Byzantine Empire (359–1453) reaches its zenith under Justinian I

Stone sculpture, Gupta dynasty

C. AD 30 Crucifixion of Jesus Christ in Jerusalem

AD 319–450 Gupta dynasty flourishes in India

C. AD 500 Buddhism and Confucianism introduced to Japan from China

AD 622 Followers of Mohammed (570–632), founder of Islam, flee to Medina to escape persecution; this event denotes the start of the Muslim calendar

Europe and the Russian Federation

AD 117 Roman Empire reaches its greatest extent under Trajan; in Britain, the northern boundary is later marked by Hadrian's Wall (built AD 122)

AD 330 Roman Emperor Constantine I converts to Christianity, which subsequently becomes the Empire's official religion

AD 450 Germanic tribes from northern Europe, such as the Angles, Jutes, and Saxons, begin to settle in England

AD 476 Western Roman Empire comes to an end when Romulus Augustus is ousted by Goths

AD 79 The cities of Pompeii and Herculaneum, Italy, are destroyed by the eruption of Mt Vesuvius

AD 140 The Greek astronomer Ptolemy publishes his *Almagest*, an encyclopaedia of scientific information, including his theory that Earth is the center of the universe

AD 443 Attila leads Huns and other barbarian tribes into western Europe; he is turned back in 450 at Châlons by a coalition of Franks and Visigoths led by Aetius

AD 452 Venice founded by refugees from central Europe fleeing the attacks of Attila the Hun

Africa

C. AD 350 Aksum converts to Christianity; the empire extends inland

C. AD 570 Nubian kingdom converts to Christianity

Pillar at Aksum

AD 0–100 Kingdom of Aksum in present-day Ethiopia becomes a major trading center; elaborate temples and palaces are constructed

AD 400–500 Bantu people migrate to southern Africa seeking land for grazing sheep and cattle and planting crops; they soon displace Khoisan hunter-gatherers

AD 600 Arabs begin to colonize North Africa

North and Central America

C. AD 200 Pyramid of the Sun is built at Teotihuacán in eastern Mexico

AD 426 Mayan dynasty of 16 kings founded at Copán in present-day Honduras

AD 700 Start of the Pueblo period in southwestern North America; native peoples including Hopi and Zuni live in villages built mainly of adobe

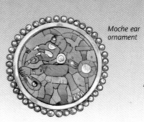

Jade ritual offering, Copán dynasty

AD 100 Mayan hieroglyphic writing comes into use

AD 250 Start of the Classic phase of Mayan civilization; growth of Mayan city-states on Yucatan Peninsula (Mexico) and in present-day Guatemala

AD 550–800 Mayan civilization reaches its zenith

South America

AD 200–600 Moche civilization of Peru produces highly decorated ceramic pots and murals for public buildings; the Pyramid of the Sun in Moche Valley is the region's largest adobe structure

Moche ear ornament

AD 700 Sicán culture flourishes in the Batán Grande area of Peru's northern coast; the capital city includes 12 adobe pyramids and tombs for leaders

AD 100 Tiwanaku and Wari develop as principal urban centers of southern-central Andes

AD 500 Wari becomes major Andean city with strong administrative structures, large buildings, and highly developed crafts, including ceramics

AD 800 Fishhooks in use along the southeast coast of Australia, similar to those found in New Guinea

AD 900–1000 Polynesians first reach New Zealand islands and settle

Gigantic stone statues are erected on Easter Island

Pitcairn Islands are colonized by Polynesians

1300 Chatham Islands, 800 km (500 miles) east of New Zealand, become the last Pacific islands to be colonized by Polynesian settlers

Easter Island statue

AD 868 The first woodblock-printed book, The Diamond Sutra, appears in China

1000 Chinese scientists invent gunpowder

1038 Seljuk Turks start Turkish Muslim dynasty; by 1071, it controls Asia Minor

1096–99 First Crusaders temporarily wrest Jerusalem from Arab control

1189 Third Crusade led by Richard I of England and Philippe II of France leads to truce with Arabs

1275–92 Italian merchant Marco Polo resident at court of Mongol emperor Kublai Khan in China

1369 Mongol leader Tamerlane assumes leadership of Samarkand; he later extends his empire into Persia and India

AD 960 Beginning of Song Dynasty in China, which will last until 1279; it adopts Neo-Confucianism as official philosophy

1048 First movable type in use in China, consisting of clay characters in an iron frame

1100 Chinese invent the magnetic compass

1147–49 Second Crusade ends in failure to recapture Holy Land

1192 Yoritomo becomes first Shogun (commander-in-chief) of Japan, initiating the so-called Kamakura period, which is dominated by Samurai and lasts until 1333

1368 After a century of Mongol rule, the Ming dynasty takes power in China, initiating a 300-year period of isolation during which art and culture flourish

AD 711 Moors invade Spain, bringing Islamic influence to Europe

AD 800 Charlemagne crowned Holy Roman Emperor in Rome by Pope Leo III

Viking people of Scandinavia begin to explore and plunder the European coastline; they eventually colonize Iceland and parts of Britain and set up trading posts in eastern Europe

1232 Pope Gregory IX establishes the Inquisition, a special court set up at Toulouse, France, to investigate heresies against the Catholic Church

1280 Windmills in use in western Europe

1300 The Renaissance begins in Italy and spreads throughout Europe

1337 Start of the Hundred Years War between England and France

1346 Black Death (bubonic plague) spreads from Asia Minor to Italy and from there to the rest of Europe; 25 percent of the European population die within five years

AD 771 Charlemagne becomes king of the Franks; he soon expands Frankish Empire in western Europe

1066 Norman king William I (Conqueror) invades England and commissions Domesday Book to assess the wealth of the country; population estimated at around 2 million

1326 Gunpowder being used in cannons

AD 800 Rise of the Kingdom of Ghana in West Africa, which lasts until 1050

c.1000 Growth of urban centers in southern Africa; craftworks are traded widely

Rise of kingdoms of Yoruba in present-day Nigeria

Rise of empire of Great Zimbabwe in East Africa, which flourishes until 1400

1100 Different language groups begin to emerge, including the Xhosa and the Zulu

1150 Emergence of Hausa city-states in present-day Nigeria

1300 Emergence of the Benin Empire of Nigeria, West Africa

Construction of royal court at Great Zimbabwe

1340 Empire of Songhai, a strong trading state in present-day Mali, founded on Niger River

AD 900 Trading routes established between East and West Africa as well as across the Sahara

1050 Tokolor people of Senegal, West Africa, become the first group south of the Sahara to follow Islam

1062 Almoravid Muslim sect takes control of Morocco, establishing its capital at Marrakesh

1130 Almohad Muslim sect rises up against corrupt Almoravids, taking control of North Africa and ruling until 1212

1200 Mali Empire, in present-day Ghana, establishes Muslim rule in West Africa; it lasts 200 years

1312–1337 Mali Empire reaches its zenith

1350 Complex irrigation methods in use in East African Rift Valley

AD 980 Viking outlaw Erik the Red establishes settlement in Greenland; population of settlement may have reached 5,000, but it is eventually abandoned in 15th century when climate becomes colder

1200 Several tribes, including the Mexica, migrate to the Valley of Mexico, leading to the foundation of Aztec civilization; they begin terracing mountain slopes for food cultivation

1250 Emerald Mound, a huge ceremonial site near Natchez Trace Parkway, Mississippi, in use

c.1300 Drought in southwestern USA forces Anasazi and other native peoples to abandon homelands

AD 800 Native Americans living in present-day Illinois start to abandon hunter-gatherer way of life in favor of agriculture; maize becomes a major crop

Mayan population of Copán Valley reaches 20,000

1000 Viking explorers land on various parts of American coast including Baffin Island, Labrador, and Newfoundland (possibly the place known as Vinland in Norse legends)

Toltecs of Tula (in present-day Hidalgo, Mexico) found an empire which flourishes for next 200 years

1150 Growth of communities in present-day Alabama, Georgia, and Oklahoma; they produce many decorated ceremonial objects

1325 Aztecs establish their capital of Tenochtitlán, which grows into a major city with 250,000 inhabitants; it later becomes Mexico City

AD 800 Machu Picchu, a site of religious and symbolic importance for the Inca people, is built in the mountains above the Urubamba Valley in Peru

1200 Cuzco becomes capital of Inca civilization; Inca cultivate mountainous areas with irrigation canals in order to feed a growing population

Inca ceramic plate

AD 725 Tiwanaku becomes a major Moche population center with up to 50,000 inhabitants

AD 850 Chimú people found Chimor Empire and build capital of Chan Chan in the Moche valley; by 1100 it has a population of 8,000

1250 Emergence of Killke style of ceramics in the Cuzco area; this will later become the distinctive style of the Inca civilization

Oceania and Antarctica

1400 Traders and fishing vessels from the islands of present-day Indonesia visit the north coast of Australia

Temple city of Nan Madol in use off the island of Temwen, Micronesia; built of stone on artificial islands, it is only accessible by boat

c.1500 Moas hunted to extinction in New Zealand

Moa

Asia and the Middle East

1453 Constantinople falls to the Ottoman Turks

1526 Mogul Empire founded when Babar invades Hindustan and conquers all of northern India; for 200 years the empire is well administered, centralized, and prosperous

1543 Shipwrecked Portuguese traders become the first Europeans to visit Japan; they introduce the first firearms to the country

Ottoman Constantinople

1405 Death of Tamerlane

1498 Portuguese sailor Vasco da Gama reaches the Malabar coast in India after sailing round the Cape of Good Hope

1502 Founding of Safavid dynasty in Persia by Ismail, who proclaims himself shah; the dynasty lasts until 1736

1534 Ottoman Turks invade Mesopotamia taking Tabriz and Baghdad

Europe and the Russian Federation

1450 Beginning of Little Ice Age which brings harsh winters, wet summers, and food shortages to Europe for next 400 years

Johannes Gutenberg builds the first printing press

1455 Gutenberg prints the Mazarin Bible at Mainz, Germany

1492 Spanish expel Moors from Granada, their last stronghold in Spain

1538 Flemish geographer Gerardus Mercator uses the name "America" on maps for the first time

1543 Nicholas Copernicus proposes that Earth revolves around the Sun, challenging the traditional Ptolemaic view that the opposite was true

1517 Reformation begins when German priest Martin Luther nails 95 theses challenging the power of the Catholic Church to a church door in Wittenberg; the movement soon spreads throughout Europe

1478 Queen Isabella of Spain sets up Spanish Inquisition to investigate heretical activities

1400 Leprosy eradicated in most parts of Europe due to improved diet and sanitation

1453 End of the Hundred Years War between England and France

1546 Mercator declares that Earth has a magnetic pole

Africa

1415 Portuguese explore North and West African coast in caravels, a new kind of sturdy sailing vessel, capturing Ceuta under Henry the Navigator

1464 Songhai secedes from Mali; in 1468, it captures Timbuktu

1486 Portuguese reach Angola on West African coast

1500 Rise of the Bornu Empire in northern Nigeria following Kanem Empire's demise; it reaches its zenith at end of century

1450 Rise of empires of Congo and Ndongo in central Africa (present-day Congo and Democratic Republic of the Congo)

State of Bono in West Africa becomes an important gold-mining center

1471 Portuguese establish forts on West African coast and begin trading in gold

1488 First Portuguese vessels arrive at the Cape of Good Hope

1517 Ottoman Turks take control of Egypt after defeating the Mamelukes (Muslim slave soldiers) and rule for the next 250 years

1400–1500 Rise of Nyoro kingdom in present-day Uganda

North and Central America

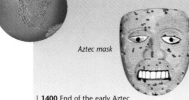

Aztec mask

c.1450 Pueblo farmers of southwestern North America trade with plains-hunters of the north, exchanging corn, cotton goods, and pottery for buffalo meat and hides

1492 Italian seafarer Christopher Columbus reaches the Caribbean and discovers Watling Island, Cuba, and Haiti

1497 John Cabot and son Sebastian explore the east coast of North America

1524 Italian navigator Giovanni da Verrazzano explores northeast coast of North America

1540–42 Spanish explorer Francisco Coronado explores southwestern North America

1500 Aztec Empire at its height

Spanish conquer Mayan lands

1400 End of the early Aztec phase sees widespread use of chinampas, swamplands reclaimed for agricultural plantations

c.1460 Mississippian Native American societies living along river valleys of eastern North America increasingly dependent on agriculture; they build large earthen mound structures for religious ceremonies

1494 Treaty of Tordesillas divides the New World between Spain and Portugal; the treaty is rejected by other European maritime powers

1519 Spanish conquistador Hernán Cortéz meets Aztec ruler Montezuma II at Tenochtitlán, Mexico; two years later, he seizes the city and Montezuma

1539 Spanish explorer Hernando de Soto reaches Florida and travels up the Mississippi River

South America

1438 Pachacuti becomes Inca leader and begins expanding empire

Gold Inca beaker, 1500s

1499 Amerigo Vespucci sails from Spain to South America

1516 Spanish explorer Juan Diaz de Solís becomes the first European to land in present-day Argentina; he is killed by Querandi indians

1525 Civil war breaks out in Inca Empire between north led by Atahualpa and south led by his brother Huáscar

1545 Spanish discover silver at Potosí in central Andes, starting a rush to exploit this valuable resource

1400 Rise of Inca Empire known as Tawantinsuyu; Incas develop building techniques of great precision and begin to construct an extensive road system

1450 Incas conquer Chimú state in Peru

1500 Pedro Alvarez Cabral discovers Brazil and claims it for Portugal

1521 Spanish explore northern coast of South America and start a colony in what becomes Venezuela

1532 Spanish conquistador Francisco Pizarro imprisons Inca emperor Atahualpa; despite an enormous ransom being paid, Atahualpa is executed

1568 Spanish sailors visit the Solomon Islands

1595 Spanish sailor Pedro Fernandez de Quiros discovers and names the Marquesas Islands; he has earlier visited the Santa Cruz group

1606 Dutchman Willem Jansz lands on north coast of Australia

Spanish navigator Luis Vaez de Torres sails through the strait that subsequently bears his name without realizing that a continent lies to the south

1616 Dutch sea captain Dirck Hartog lands on the west coast of Australia

Dutch navigators Willem Schouten and Jakob le Maire visit Tonga

1642–43 Dutch navigator Abel Tasman lands on Van Diemen's Land (now Tasmania), claiming possession for the Netherlands; he then discovers the west coast of New Zealand and sights the eastern island islands of Fiji and Tongatapu in the Tongan group

1644 Tasman charts part of the coastline of northern and western Australia

1688 English adventurer William Dampier spends two months on the west coast of Australia

1699 Dampier returns to explore the west coast of Australia; unimpressed, he sails north for New Guinea

---

1568 Akbar, greatest of the Moghuls and grandson of the empire's founder Babar, conquers Chitor in Rajasthan, quells the Rajput princes, and takes control of the region

1580 Unification of Japan under Oda Nobunaga

1600 British East India Company established to develop trade in Asia and challenge the trading empires of the Portuguese and Spanish; similar trading companies subsequently set up by Dutch (1602) and French (1604)

1597 Dutch establish trading post at Batavia (Jakarta) in Dutch East Indies

1603 Tokugawa Shogunate begins rule in Japan, continuing until 1867

1623 At trading center of Ambon, Dutch behead British traders accused of plotting to take over the Dutch fortress; incident creates friction between trading powers

1632–43 Taj Mahal, a white marble mausoleum, built at Agra, India, by Emperor Shah Jehan in memory of his wife Mumtaz Mahal

1639 English colonists settle at Madras in India

1643 First French missionaries arrive in Vietnam

1644 The Manchus, a people from Manchuria, invade China from northwest and establish Qing dynasty, bringing peace and prosperity

1674 Dutch traders help local Muslim leader, Amangkurat I, head of the kingdom of Maturam, Indonesia, to suppress rebellion; in return, Dutch gain possession of parts of central Java

1683 China seizes Formosa (Taiwan)

1569 Mercator produces *Cosmographia*, which includes the first navigational maps of the world

1571 Battle of Lepanto halts maritime expansion of Ottoman Empire

1572 In France, 10 years of religious conflict climax in St Bartholomew's Day Massacre of 2,000 Huguenots (Protestants) in Paris; many Huguenots seek refuge in England

1588 Spanish Armada, Philip II of Spain's invasion force against England, is defeated by Sir Francis Drake in the English Channel

1603 King James VI of Scotland becomes James I of England

1609 Mathematician–astronomer Galileo Galilei improves the recently invented telescope and describes Jupiter's satellites

Johannes Kepler announces his laws of planetary motion

1618 Start of Thirty Years War between Protestant powers—England, Holland, Scandinavia, and German states—and Spain and the Hapsburg Empire

1643 Barometer invented by Italian scientist Evangelista Torricelli

1642–48 English Civil War leads to execution of Charles I

1665 The Great Plague of London takes 70,000 lives between July and October; the following year much of the city is destroyed by a fire lasting from February 2 to 9

1661 Ottoman Turks invade Transylvania and Hungary

1682 Edmund Halley identifies a bright comet and correctly predicts that it will reappear in 1758 and approximately every 77 years thereafter

1675 Greenwich Observatory established by English astronomer Edmund Halley

1699 Under Treaty of Carlowitz, defeated Turks forced to cede most of Balkans to Austrian Hapsburgs

---

Yoruba sculpture

1591 Morocco defeats Songhai, bringing the empire to an end

1600 Oyo Empire becomes one of the most successful of the Yoruba states after the leader Orompoto uses proceeds of trade to build a large army

1613 Portuguese priest and explorer Pedro Paez discovers the source of the Blue Nile: Lake Tana in Tanzania

1619 First slaves from West Africa shipped to Virginia, North America, by Dutch traders

1626 French establish settlements on Madagascar but island does not become a colony until 1896

1637 French establish military base in Senegal, West Africa

1652 Dutch East India Company establishes garrison at site of modern-day Cape Town

1657 First Dutch settlers take up land grants at Liesbeeck River near Cape Town

First slaves brought to the Cape from India, Indonesia, and West Africa by Dutch

1660 Rise of Bambara kingdoms of Segu and Kaarta on the Niger River; by 1670 they have replaced the Mandingo Empire

1670 Rise of Ashanti Empire in West Africa in modern-day Ghana; by early eighteenth century its rulers are supplying slaves to Dutch and British traders

---

1583 The English found a colony at St Johns, Newfoundland

1584 Sir Walter Raleigh claims Virginia on east coast of North America for England; attempts to form a permanent settlement fail

1605 Port Royal in Nova Scotia becomes the first French settlement in North America

1607 Jamestown, Virginia, becomes first permanent English settlement in North America

1619 The first slaves from West Africa are sold in Virginia, North America, by Dutch traders

1620 The Pilgrim Fathers leave Plymouth, England, and cross the Atlantic to the New World in the *Mayflower*

1624 The Dutch establish a settlement at New Netherlands, North America

1642 The French establish site of Montréal on the St Lawrence seaway

1663 The North American French colonies form a Province by amalgamating as New France, with Québec as the capital

1670 Hudson's Bay Company founded in London by English and French merchants seeking to establish fur trade in the Hudson Bay region of northeastern Canada

1682 Renée La Salle explores the Mississippi River and claims Louisiana for France

---

1553 First settlements of Santiago del Estero and Tucumán in Argentina founded by Spanish arriving from Peru in search of gold and silver

1567 Two million of South American Indian population die from typhoid fever introduced by Spanish soldiers

1573 Córdoba and Mendoza grow as part of trade routes between Chile and Argentina

1580 Spanish colonists establish settlement at Buenos Aires on La Plata estuary

1616 Dutch navigator Willem Schouten sights Cape Horn, the tip of South America

1620 Expansion of silver mining at Potosí, Bolivia

1624 Dutch seize Brazilian territory of Bahia; they later take control of the rich sugar-producing area of Pernambuco (1630–54)

1630 Portuguese begin to import large numbers of slaves from Africa to work on sugar plantations of northeastern Brazil, displacing native populations

Ankle fetter used to secure slaves

1695 Large gold deposits discovered in central Brazil, in the area now known as Minas Gerais, triggering an influx of prospectors

93

Oceania and Antarctica

1765 British explorer John Byron sails through the Pacific while searching for the "Great South Land," and visits numerous islands including the Gilbert Islands

1788 First Fleet under Captain Arthur Phillip arrives at Botany Bay to found a British penal colony; disappointed with Botany Bay, Phillip establishes the colony at Port Jackson

Captain James Cook, 1728–79

1722 Dutch explorer Jacob Roggeveen explores the Pacific, visiting Samoa and Easter Island as well as Makatea, Bora-Bora, and Maupiti

1766–69 Comte Louis Antoine de Bougainville, scientist and navigator, travels widely throughout the Pacific, visiting Tahiti, the New Hebrides, New Britain, and New Guinea

1770 After visiting Tahiti and New Zealand, English navigator Captain James Cook charts the east coast of Australia and lands at Botany Bay

1793 First free settlers arrive in New South Wales, Australia, from Britain

Asia and the Middle East

1715 Chinese conquer Mongolia and Turkestan

1755 The Nawab of Bengal occupies Calcutta, taking many British prisoners, some of whom die in the "Black Hole," a small room used as a jail; British, led by Robert Clive, retake Calcutta

1761 British capture of Pondicherry marks the end of French colonial power in India

British East India Company coat of arms

1707 Mt Fuji, Japan's biggest volcano, erupts

1730 An earthquake on the island of Hokkaido, Japan, causes the deaths of 137,000 people

1740 British East India Company takes over Mogul land

Dutch and British armies oust Portuguese spice traders and establish ports at Madras, Bombay, and Calcutta

1769 Severe famines in Bengal lead to rural depopulation for more than 20 years

1771 Political crisis of the "Tay Son Rebellion" in Vietnam under which the old Confucian order is threatened by reforms inspired by Western ideas

Europe and the Russian Federation

1707 Act of Union unites Scotland and England as Great Britain

1725 John Harrison, English clockmaker, invents a device for measuring longitude at sea and on land

1755 Lisbon is destroyed by a major earthquake; it is the first earthquake to be studied by scientists

1769 After several years of development, Scotsman James Watt invents the double-acting rotary steam engine which is introduced to textile mills and other factories

1713 Peace of Unsikaupunki ends the Great Northern War between Sweden and Russia; after more than 350 years of allegiance to Sweden, Finland comes under Russian control (until 1721)

1701–14 War of Spanish Succession

1735 Swedish naturalist Carl Linnaeus publishes *Systema Naturae*, a system for classifying plants and animals; his basic hierarchy is still in use

1760 Rise of Amsterdam as world's major economic center

1781 German-born English astronomer Sir William Herschel discovers the planet Uranus; Herschel's studies form the basis of modern astronomy

1789 The French Revolution begins with the storming of the Bastille and lasts for 10 years

Africa

South African San or Bushman

1757 Sultan Muhammad ibn Abd Allah brings peace and stability to Morocco after a period of unrest and economic decline

1779 Sporadic warfare breaks out in south between Dutch and British colonists and indigenous Xhosa people; the conflict lasts for the next 100 years

1787 British set up a colony at Sierra Leone, West Africa

1790 In present-day northern Nigeria, the Islamic Fulani people from Senegal wage a holy war (jihad) against the Hausa kings

1713 Native Khoikhoi pastoralists of South Africa replaced by "trekboer" settler farmers in search of grazing land; huge numbers of native Khoisan people die in smallpox epidemic

1760 Slaves are traded in increasing numbers in what is now Gabon, West Africa, often in exchange for European goods such as guns, textiles, and rum

1795 British occupy Cape Town, a vital supply post on Britain's expanding trade routes prior to opening of the Suez canal; British settlers arrive in increasing numbers

Scottish explorer Mungo Park reaches the Niger River

North and Central America

1740–48 War between Britain and France over North America

1763 Peace of Paris treaty ending Seven Years War in Europe awards Canada to Britain

1775 Beginning of American War of Independence (to 1783); the following year the 13 American colonies adopt the Declaration of Independence, thereby founding the USA

1787 Delegates at a national constitutional convention—the "Founding Fathers"—create the US Constitution

1789–93 Alexander Mackenzie explores northwestern North America, crossing over the Rockies to reach the Pacific Ocean

1752 American scientist and diplomat Benjamin Franklin proves that lightning is an electrical discharge and invents the lightning conductor

1720 Spanish soldiers invade Texas

1770–72 British adventurer Samuel Hearne explores territories to the northwest of Hudson Bay in northern Canada

1791 Canada is divided into French- and English-speaking territories by the Constitutions Act

1793 Eli Whitney invents the cotton gin, a mechanical threshing machine

South America

1770–80 Improved navigational methods strengthen links between Europe and Latin America, creating opportunities for economic growth

1790 Native people and imported Africans used as slaves on plantations in Brazil; many die from European diseases

1700 Bourbon Spain establishes the Viceroyalty of New Grenada in central and South America; Peru is forced to release control of Guayaquil in modern-day Ecuador

1743 Charles-Marie de la Condamine, a French scientist given the task of measuring a degree of longitude on the equator, takes measurements in Ecuador and then explores the Amazon, bringing back samples of the rubber tree and platinum

1780 Tupac Amaru II leads an unsuccessful revolt by native people against Spanish rule in Peru

1799–1804 German scientist Alexander von Humboldt explores central and South America

1803 British penal settlements founded in Hobart and Port Arthur in Tasmania

1837 Frenchman Lieutenant Jules Dumont d'Urville discovers Joinville Island, off Antarctica

1840 The Treaty of Waitangi gives Britain sovereignty over New Zealand but also gives Maori people sovereignty over their lands (as well as British citizenship), creating conflicting expectations

1861 Thomas Mort builds the first refrigeration unit for the transportation of meat in Sydney, Australia

Gold Rush in New Zealand

1895 Norwegian whaler Henryk Johan Bull becomes the first person to land on the Antarctic continent at what is now Cape Adare

Beginning of severe droughts in Australia which last for the next seven years

1820 Russian naval officer Captain Fabian von Bellingshausen is possibly the first person to see Antarctica

1839–43 British explorers Ross and Crozier map the coast of Antarctica in the *Erebus* and the *Terror*; two volcanoes are later named after the ships

1851 Beginning of the Australian Gold Rush

1868 Transportation of convicted criminals from Britain to Australia ends with the arrival of the last convict ship in Western Australia

1893 New Zealand becomes the first country in the world to give the vote to women

1800 British East India Company trading in China; British smuggle opium into China to offset other exports and Opium War breaks out when Chinese object

1842 Treaty of Nanjing ends first Opium War; China cedes Hong Kong to Britain

1850 Failure of monsoon rains in northern India causes famine lasting more than 30 years

1883 Krakatau, Indonesia, erupts, killing 36,000 people; the explosion is heard up to 3,650 km (1,400 miles) away

1894–95 Sino-Japanese War breaks out over Korea—Japan emerges victorious and annexes Formosa (Taiwan)

1880s Indian Nationalist Movement, including Indian National Congress, campaigns for an end to British rule

1815 The largest volcanic eruption ever, at Tambora, Indonesia, kills at least 10,000 people; more than 80,000 later die of starvation and disease resulting from climatic effects of eruption

1857 The Indian Revolt against heavy taxes results in considerable loss of British and Indian lives; it is ruthlessly suppressed

1876 Queen Victoria becomes Empress of India

1887–88 Huang (Yellow) River in China floods, killing up to 2.5 million people

1891 A severe earthquake in Japan kills up to 10,000 people

1804 After conquering much of western Europe, including the Netherlands, Switzerland, and northern Italy, Napoleon crowns himself emperor of France

1834 British mathematician William Babbage invents the "analytical machine," forerunner of the computer

1848 Revolutions occur in various parts of Europe, including Germany, France, Austria, and Italy

1859 Publication of Charles Darwin's *The Origin of Species*, which expounds the theory of natural selection

1871 Unification of Germany under Emperor William I

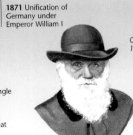

Charles Darwin, 1809–82

1835 French mathematician Gaspard de Coriolis describes how winds and ocean currents are deflected clockwise around high-pressure systems in northern hemisphere and anti-clockwise in southern hemisphere

Halley's comet reappears, as he had predicted

1850 Karl Marx, a German economist living in London, publishes *The Communist Manifesto*

French physician Louis Pasteur advances a theory that germs cause disease

1861 Italy becomes a single state under King Victor Emmanuel II of Sardinia after Giuseppe Garibaldi and his "red shirts" defeat Bourbon troops

1899 French meteorologist Teisserenc de Bort discovers that temperature stops decreasing at around 10 km (6 miles) above sea level; this leads to discovery of atmospheric layers

1815 Napoleon defeated by British army at Waterloo

c.1800 Zulu nation founded in what is now Kwazulu-Natal, South Africa, forcing Shoshangane clan into Swaziland and Mzilikazi clan into Zimbabwe

1853 Scottish explorer and missionary David Livingstone begins his exploration of central Africa

1860 Laborers from India are imported by Natal farmers to work on farms and plantations

1870 Gold and diamonds discovered in South Africa

1884–85 Conference held in Berlin divides up remaining African territories between Germany, France, and Britain

1899 Start of the Second Boer War between British and Afrikaners (Boers)

Gold-mining industry in South Africa employs 110,000 workers; almost 100,000 are African laborers

1861 British occupy Lagos in Nigeria

1871 US journalist Henry Morton Stanley locates Livingstone, who has mapped the river systems of central Africa and traced the source of the Zambeze

1836–38 10,000 Boer (Dutch) settlers unhappy with British rule in the Cape set out on Great Trek to seek new territories in Natal and Orange River region

1858 English explorers John Speke and Richard Burton discover Lake Victoria; Speke later discovers the source of the Nile

1869 The Suez Canal opens, allowing a much reduced voyage time between the Mediterranean Sea and the Indian Ocean

1880–81 British attempts to bring the Boer republics (of Orange Free State and Transvaal) into a federation fail when the Boers defeat the British in the First Boer War

1830–48 France conquers Algeria

1803 Napoleon sells almost 3 million sq km (900,000 sq miles) of southern central North America to the USA in a deal known as the Louisiana Purchase

1813 Mexico declares its independence

1837 Samuel Morse demonstrates the electric telegraph in New York

1861–65 American Civil War between the North and the South caused by disputes over political and economic issues, including the abolition of slavery

1876 Scots-born American Alexander Graham Bell invents the telephone

1886 The transcontinental Canadian Pacific Railway is completed

1804–05 US army officers Meriwether Lewis and William Clark explore the Missouri River, cross the Rocky Mountains, and reach the Pacific Ocean

1824 The Erie Canal opens, creating a navigational route between the Great Lakes and the Atlantic Ocean

1848 As a result of victory over Mexico, the USA gains vast areas of western and southern North America

Discovery of gold in California causes an influx of prospectors in the first Gold Rush

Gold nugget

1867 USA purchases Alaska from Russia

1879 Thomas Edison invents electric lighting

1898 Spanish-American War ends with Cuba becoming independent and the USA gaining Puerto Rico, Guam, and the Philippines

1808 Prince John, royal ruler of Portugal, is forced to flee from Portugal and declares Rio de Janiero capital of the worldwide Portuguese Empire; he returns to Portugal in 1821

1824 Simón Bolívar wins a victory over Spanish troops at Ayacucho, Peru, ending Spanish control in South America

1866 San Roque Dam built on the Primero River, Argentina, to supply hydroelectric power and water for irrigation

1879 Population of Gran Chaco region of Argentina grows rapidly as a result of the expansion of the beef industry, with large numbers of immigrants arriving from Europe

1880 Japanese immigrants begin to settle in southeastern Brazil to profit from rapid growth of coffee plantations

1889 Brazil becomes a republic

1822 Prince John's son Pedro declares Brazil's independence and is crowned Emperor

1830 Argentina lays claim to Islas Malvinas (the Falkland Islands); three years later, Britain occupies the islands

1870 Rubber production soars in the Amazon area of Brazil, attracting migrants from the eastern seaboard and from Europe

1879–83 Pacific War between Chile, Peru, and Bolivia over nitrate deposits results in Chile taking territory in southern Peru

1816 Argentina declares independence from Spain

1888 Brazil abolishes slavery: 750,000 people are freed

Oceania and Antarctica

1901–04 British navy captain Robert Scott undertakes the first inland exploration of Antarctica

1907 Englishman Ernest Shackleton, a member of Scott's earlier expedition, reaches the South Magnetic Pole in Antarctica

1914–18 330,000 Australians and 100,000 New Zealanders travel overseas to fight in the First World War

1928 Australian aviator Bert Hinkler arrives at Darwin, Australia, after a 15-day flight from Croydon, England, via Rome, Egypt, India, Malaya, and Java

1939 Australia and New Zealand send troops to support Britain in the Second World War; hundreds of thousands fight in Europe and the Pacific

1947 New Zealand's parliament adopts the Statute of Westminster (1931) which gives it formal independence from the UK

1901 Federation of the six Australian colonies results in the formation of the Commonwealth of Australia

1911 Norwegian explorer Roald Amundsen and his team become the first to reach the South Pole on December 11; just over one month later a British expedition under Captain Scott accomplishes the same feat, but the team perishes on the return journey

1919 Influenza pandemic leaves thousands of Australians dead

First World War digger's hat

1930 The Depression hits Australia and New Zealand

Amy Johnson arrives at Darwin, Australia, having flown solo from London, UK; she fails by only 4 days to beat Hinkler's record

1942 Japanese troops occupy New Guinea

Japanese submarines enter Sydney Harbour, Australia

Asia and the Middle East

1907 France seizes Lao territories east of the Mekong River; formerly under control of Thailand, they include much of present-day Cambodia, Laos, and Vietnam

1934 Mao Ze Dong leads the Long March of the Communist revolutionaries across China

1945 First atomic bombs dropped on Japanese cities of Hiroshima and Nagasaki by USA, bringing the war in the Pacific to an end

1946 Start of war in Indochina between French colonial power and Vietnamese nationalists led by Ho Chi Minh (to 1954)

1900 In Peking (Beijing), the Boxer Rebellion of Chinese nationalists against foreign interests is put down by British and Russian forces

1911 Rebels proclaim Chinese republic under Sun Yat-sen; last Chinese Emperor Pu Yi relinquishes throne during following year

1927–28 Civil War in China between the Communist party and the Kuomintang (Nationalist Party) under Chiang Kai-Shek; Nationalists take Beijing

Mao Ze Dong, 1893–1976

1948 State of Israel proclaimed following partition of Palestine

1947 India gains independence and is partitioned, with Pakistan becoming separate Muslim state

1949 Communist party takes control of China

Europe and the Russian Federation

1914 Assassination of Archduke Francis-Ferdinand at Sarajevo in Bosnia triggers the First World War between Germany, Austria-Hungary, and the Ottoman Empire on one side, and Britain, France, and Russia on the other; more than 8 million soldiers die

1917 The second Russian Revolution takes place in March and Russian royal family killed; in October, the Bolsheviks seize power

1928 The world's first antibiotic, penicillin, is discovered by Scottish scientist Alexander Fleming

1936–39 Spanish Civil War between Nationalists and Republicans results in General Franco becoming Nationalist head of state of the Falangist (Fascist) government

1945 Second World War ends in Europe (7 May) and the Pacific (2 September); the death toll includes more than 14 million soldiers and about 27 million civilians

1905 Bloody suppression of riots in St Petersburg leads to the first Russian Revolution

1916 German-born physicist Albert Einstein publishes his General Theory of Relativity, which suggests that the universe is expanding

1918–19 Influenza pandemic leaves millions of Europeans dead and kills up to 40 million worldwide

1933 Adolf Hitler becomes Chancellor of Germany; his National Socialist Party ends democratic rule

1939 Germany invades Poland, starting the Second World War

Africa

1907 Mahatma Gandhi campaigns in South Africa for civil rights of ethnic Indian population

1931 South Africa granted independence by Britain as a member of the Commonwealth

1949–50 Racial apartheid becomes the official policy of the National Party government of South Africa

African National Congress flag

1912 The African National Congress (ANC) founded in South Africa by a small group of educated black Africans seeking political rights

1935 Seeking to expand its African territories, Italy invades Ethiopia, capturing Addis Ababa in 1936; Haile Selassie flees until British troops restore him to office during Second World War

1902 Britain emerges victorious from Second Boer War

North and Central America

1903 First successful flights in heavier-than-air machines made by brothers Orville and Wilbur Wright at Kitty Hawk, North Carolina

1917 United States enters First World War

1927 Charles Lindbergh makes the first nonstop solo flight across the Atlantic Ocean from Roosevelt Field, New York, to Le Bourget near Paris

1941 Japanese attack on US naval base at Pearl Harbor, Oahu Island, Hawaii, brings USA into the Second World War; during the war, the USA loses 292,000 troops, Canada 43,000

1948 Universal Declaration of Human Rights adopted by General Assembly of UN in New York; it sets out minimum standards of civil and political rights to which all people are entitled

1902 Mt Pelée, Martinique, erupts, killing 20,000 and burying the town of St Pierre

1906 San Francisco is devastated by a major earthquake measuring 8.3 on the Richter scale

Wright brothers' Flyer III, 1905

1918 Influenza pandemic begins in North America; it eventually kills up to 40 million worldwide

1929 The Wall Street Crash of October 24 causes widespread financial instability; it is followed by the Great Depression which spreads worldwide

1945 Founding charter of United Nations (UN) signed by 51 nations in San Francisco

South America

1930s Huge population growth and urbanization occurs, particularly in Argentina and Uruguay, chiefly as a result of large-scale immigration

1942 Brazil supports Allies in Second World War and sends 25,000 troops to fight in Italy

1946 Juan Perón becomes President of Argentina with backing of both army and labor unions

1914 First World War initially disrupts Latin American trade, but for some countries this is followed by an export-led boom which lasts until the Depression

1932–35 Paraguay defeats Bolivia in war over Chaco region; final settlement negotiated in 1938 awards Chaco territory to Paraguay

1944 A massive earthquake kills 5,000 people in the Andean San Juan province of Argentina

1951 Australia, New Zealand, and the USA sign the ANZUS defence treaty; the signatories agree to offer mutual support in the event of an attack on any of the other parties

Antarctic penguin

1959 Antarctic Treaty bans military activity in Antarctica; signatories also agree to suspend territorial claims

1960 Swiss diver Jacques Piccard and the US navy's Donald Walsh explore the Mariana Trench in the Pacific Ocean to a depth of 11,000 m (36,089 feet)—the lowest known point on the ocean floor

1974 Cyclone Tracy destroys Darwin in northern Australia

1975 Papua New Guinea becomes independent

Thousands of refugees from Vietnam, Laos, and Cambodia, many of them ethnic Chinese, begin to flee to Australia by boat

1979 Scientists discover a hole in the ozone layer above Antarctica

1985 New Zealand's anti-nuclear policy sours relations with traditional allies France and the United States

1996–97 Despite worldwide protests, France concludes a series of nuclear weapon tests on Muraroa Atoll in the South Pacific before agreeing to sign the UN Test Ban Treaty

---

1950 Korean War begins when North Korean communist troops invade South Korea; the war lasts until 1953, with US troops fighting on the South Korean side

1953 Mt Everest is climbed for the first time by New Zealand explorer Edmund Hillary and Sherpa Tenzing Norgay

1957 Vietnam War starts when North Vietnamese (Viet Cong) attack South Vietnamese

1959 China suppresses revolt in Tibet; Tibet's spiritual leader, the Dalai Lama, flees to India

Potala Palace, Tibet

1965 US troops based in South Vietnam committed to aid South Vietnamese forces

1975 Vietnam War ends with the fall of Saigon after the withdrawal of US troops

1976 An earthquake in Tangshan near Beijing, China, kills more than 200,000 people and injures another 150,000

1991 Mt Pinatubo in the Philippines erupts killing 30 people and leaving 10,000 homeless

Following Iraq's occupation of the oil-rich state of Kuwait, US combines with the UK, France, and other allies to defeat Iraq in the Gulf War

1995 A massive earthquake lasting less than a minute kills 5,000 people in Kobe, Japan, and causes massive disruption to transport and industry

---

1957 The space age starts with the launching by Russia of Sputnik I, a satellite capable of orbiting Earth

1961 Russian cosmonaut Yuri Gagarin becomes the first man in space and the first to orbit Earth

Berlin Wall erected by the East German government to stop citizens escaping to the West

Sputnik 1, 1957

1973 A military junta of army colonels siezes power in Greece after overthrowing the elected Government of President Georgios Papadopoulos

1974 Turkish troops invade northern Cyprus following the overthrow of the island's president, Greek Archbishop Makarios; fighting between Greek and Turkish Cypriots results in the creation of a neutral corridor across the island

1984 HIV, the virus that causes AIDS and has already taken the lives of millions worldwide, is identified by Luc Montaigner at the Institut Pasteur, Paris

1989 Collapse of Communism in the Soviet Union and Eastern Europe: Russian leader Mikhail Gorbachev and US President George Bush declare the end of the Cold War, and the Berlin Wall is dismantled

1986 An accident at the Chernobyl nuclear power station in the Ukraine contaminates a huge area and spreads fallout across Europe

Russia launches Mir, an Earth-orbiting space station

1991 Civil War in former Yugoslavia between Croatia and Bosnia; UN sends peacekeeping forces

Collapse of the Soviet Union

1995 Talks at Dayton, Ohio, USA, aimed at ending conflict in Bosnia, lead to a peace agreement; hostilities are gradually halted

---

1953 Military coup in Egypt ends monarchy of King Farouk and imposes republic

1956 Egypt closes Suez Canal; British, French, and Israeli troops invade to reopen it but UN intervenes to halt fighting

Independence of Morocco, Tunisia, and Sudan recognized by France

1960 Massacre of 67 anti-apartheid demonstrators at Sharpeville, Johannesburg, South Africa

1961 South Africa becomes a republic; sanctions imposed by several countries in response to apartheid policies

1962 Nelson Mandela and other members of ANC imprisoned in South Africa

Algerian war of independence ends French rule

1964 Former British colony of Rhodesia (now Zimbabwe) declares independence

1967 Civil war in Nigeria; Biafra secedes until 1970

World's first heart transplant carried out in Cape Town by Dr Christiaan Barnard

1976 Young blacks protesting against compulsory Afrikaans language lessons are gunned down by police at Soweto, Johannesburg, South Africa

1977 Commencement of civil war and famine in Ethiopia, which lead to thousands of deaths

1990 ANC leader Nelson Mandela freed from prison in South Africa; the following year, apartheid is abolished

1993 Civil war in Rwanda between Hutu and Tutsi people results in the slaughter of hundreds of thousands of Tutsi

1994 Global population problems discussed at World Population Conference, Cairo, Egypt

Nelson Mandela elected President in first nonracial, democratic general election in South Africa

---

1961 US President John F. Kennedy backs an invasion of communist Cuba by exiled Cubans but fails to send US troops; Fidel Castro's forces easily repulse the attack at the Bay of Pigs

1963 Assassination of President John F. Kennedy

1968 Martin Luther King and Robert Kennedy assassinated

1969 US astronauts Neil Armstrong and Buzz Aldrin make first landing on the moon from the spaceship *Apollo 11*

1974 US Space probe Mariner 10 sends back the first close-up pictures of the rings surrounding the planets Mercury and Venus

1980 Eruption of Mt St Helens, Washington State, USA—one of the largest in modern times

1981 First flight of the space shuttle *Columbia*

First case of AIDS recognized

1982 A volcanic eruption at El Chichón, Mexico causes the deaths of 3,500 people and blackens the sky for almost two days

1989 US invades Panama

Space shuttle

1955 General strike in Argentina; Perón and wife Eva sent into exile

1960 In Santiago, Chile, 5,000 people are killed by an earthquake

1970 Salvador Allende of Chile becomes the world's first freely elected Marxist president

1973 Allende is deposed in a military coup led by General Augusto Pinochet

1973–76 Perón returns to Argentina and is re-elected, but dies in 1974; his third wife Isobel governs until Army chiefs arrest her; thousands subsequently killed by security forces

1982 Argentina invades Falkland Islands; Britain uses military force to retake the islands by 14 June

1982–83 The century's most severe episode of the El Niño effect: Chile experiences record rainfall

1988 General Pinochet's rule in Chile rejected by large majority in plebiscite

1992 Global environmental problems debated at first Earth Summit in Rio de Janiero, Brazil

Alberto Fujimori, President of Peru, suspends parliament claiming corruption among government officials; a new constitution is approved in 1993

Part 3
Regions of the World

The Changing Scene

Culture is one way of defining world regions: the Middle East and Central Asia, for example, have a broadly Islamic culture in common (above). North America stretches from Canada (opposite) to Mexico and can be defined by its geographical, as well as its cultural, boundaries.

Geographers, in their attempt to subdivide Earth's land surface into coherent areas, developed the concept of regions. Regions can be delineated within continents or within countries, depending at what scale study is being conducted.

Regions are parts of the world that have a degree of similarity in one or more characteristics, such as climate, physiography, culture, or economy. For example, a Himalayan region can be based on physiography, a Saharan region determined by its desert climate, a Confucian East Asia region determined by a dominant culture, and a European Community region defined by countries linked by economic cooperation. In this book, however, much larger regions have been identified.

Regions, under whatever criteria they are defined, must be geographically contiguous. Countries adjacent to each other often share a major characteristic. Thus, the countries of Southeast Asia have a tropical, humid climate which ensures the growing of tropical crops such as tropical fruits, tea, coffee, and rubber. In contrast, several Middle Eastern countries have arid climates which inhibit large scale agriculture. Southeast Asia and the Middle East can be considered as regions where climate is one of the distinguishing characteristics.

In other cases, culture may be an important criterion for defining a region. The Middle East, besides being climatically different from other parts of Asia, also differs culturally. North America and Central America have considerable cultural and economic differences that justify their being differentiated. This is also true for Africa, as North Africa differing in several aspects from the countries south of the Sahara.

Very often a number of small countries lying close to each other may share one or more characteristics. This is the case with the small island nations of the Pacific. They can then be said to lie within an identifiable region or sub-region. On the other hand, some large countries, such as the Russian Federation, are so large that they have sufficient climatic and cultural diversity within their borders for sub-regions to be usefully identified.

The naming and defining of continents was the first attempt to mark out large regions on the map of the world. Because the continents were named and defined by Europeans, the perspectives used were European. For example, some names came from ancient Greece where the lands lying to its east were named Asia and the lands to its west were called Europe. Because of the European perspective, it became customary to refer to the eastern lands close to Europe as the Near East, the lands lying far to the east as the Far East, and the lands in between these as the Middle East.

Europe and Asia are geographically contiguous, forming the Eurasian landmass, but there are sufficient differences between them for them to be identifiable as two separate continents. This traditional separation is largely based on cultural and historical factors, the lines dividing the two continents being accepted by convention.

Africa, the two American continents, Australia, and Antarctica are easily defined because of their separation from other landmasses. Australia, New Zealand, and several Pacific islands are customarily included in a large region known as Oceania that includes a variety of climates, economies, and cultures. The only factor that gives Oceania its coherence is that these lands form a large cluster in the Central and South Pacific Ocean.

Regions or sub-regions can be identified within most of the world's continents. For instance, the large continent of Asia contains areas with distinctive characteristics that allow them to be considered as regions. Asia can be sub-divided into East Asia, Southeast Asia, South Asia (the Indian subcontinent), West Asia (the Middle East), Central Asia, and North Asia (Siberia). Monsoon Asia (or Asia-Pacific), a larger region, defined on the basis of climate, stretches across East, Southeast, and South Asia. Monsoon Asia is humid, extremely populous, and has extensive agriculture. Central Asia and the Middle East, on the other hand, are more arid, less populated, and have limited scope for agriculture, except where water for irrigation is available.

Europe was within the last half century politically divided into Eastern and Western Europe. This ideological divide resulted in contrasting economic systems, the residual effects of which can still be seen. On economic grounds, Eastern and Western Europe can be considered as sub-regions. Climate can be used to differentiate Mediterranean Europe from lands north of the Alps.

In this book, the continents and regions have been treated in the following order: Oceania, Asia and the Middle East, Europe and the Russian Federation, Africa, North America and Central America, South America, Polar Regions, and Oceans.

Information is provided on each region in a systematic way, recognizing that for some areas and countries data is relatively sparse and incomplete. The descriptions of each country show the differences and similarities, as well as highlighting those factors responsible for natural, economic, and social conditions.

The World: Physical

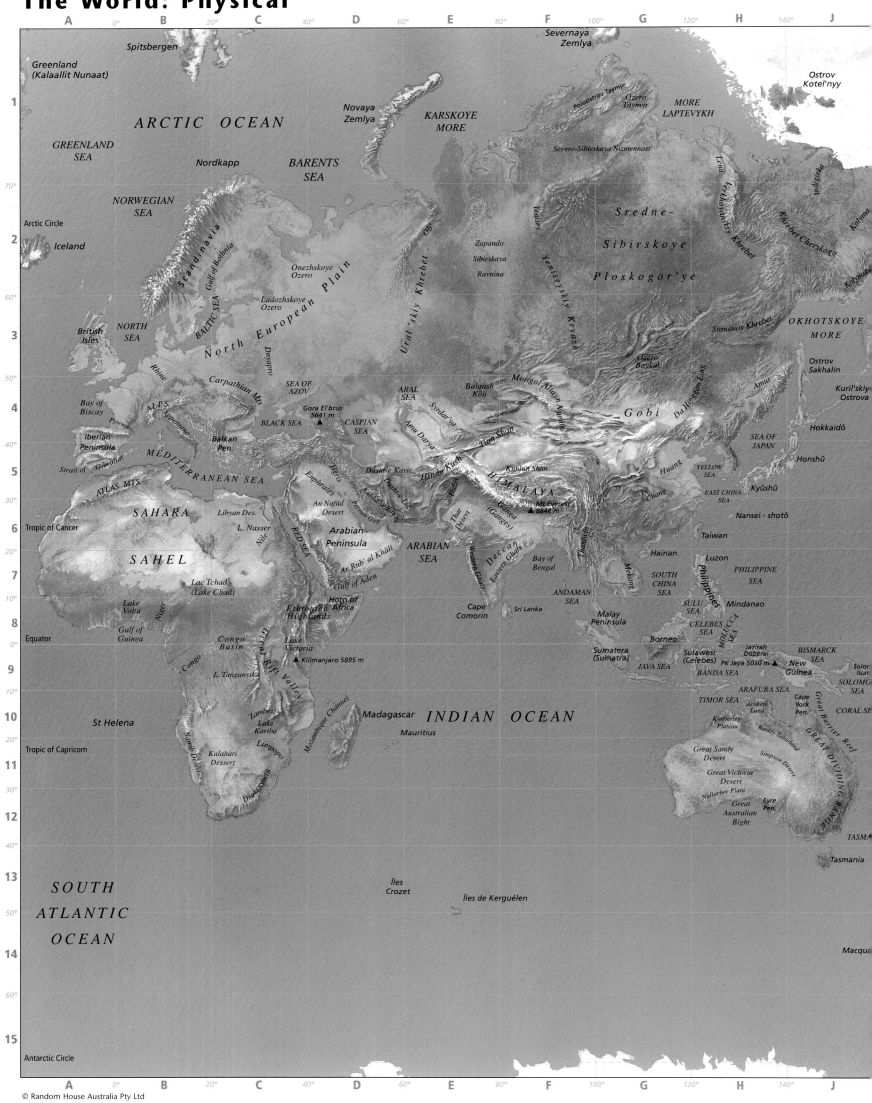

Spitsbergen

Greenland
(Kalaallit Nunaat)

Severnaya
Zemlya

Ostrov
Kotel'nyy

ARCTIC OCEAN

Novaya
Zemlya

KARSKOYE
MORE

Poluostrov Taymyr

Ozero
Taymyr

MORE
LAPTEVYKH

GREENLAND
SEA

Severo-Sibirskaya Nizmennost'

Nordkapp

BARENTS
SEA

NORWEGIAN
SEA

Arctic Circle

Iceland

Scandinavia

Gulf of Bothnia

Onezhskoye
Ozero

North European Plain

Ural'skiy Khrebet

Ob

Yenisey

Zapando
Sibirskaya
Ravnina

Sredne-

Sibirskoye

Ploskogor'ye

Lena

Verkhoyanskiy Khrebet

Khrebet Cherskogo

Indigirka

Kolyma

Kolyma

Ladozhskoye
Ozero

Yeniseyskiy Kryazh

Stanovoy Khrebet

OKHOTSKOYE
MORE

British
Isles

NORTH
SEA

BALTIC SEA

Dnyepro

Rhine

Ozero
Baykal

Ostrov
Sakhalin

Carpathian Mts.

SEA OF
AZOV

Mongol Altayn Nuruu

Da Hinggan Ling

Amur

Kuril'skiye
Ostrova

Bay of
Biscay

ALPS

Pyrenees

Apennines

BLACK SEA

Gora El'brus
5641 m

CASPIAN
SEA

ARAL
SEA

Syrdar'ya

Balqash
Köli

Tien Shan

Gobi

SEA OF
JAPAN

Hokkaidō

Iberian
Peninsula

Balkan
Pen.

Anu Darya

Kunlun Shan

Huang

Honshū

Strait of
Gibraltar

MEDITERRANEAN SEA

ATLAS MTS.

Dasht-e Kavir

Hindu Kush

Dasht-e Lut

Tigris

Kavir Salt Desert

HIMALAYA

Mt Everest
8848 m

Chang

YELLOW
SEA

EAST CHINA
SEA

Kyūshū

SAHARA

Libyan Des.

An Nafud
Desert

Persian Gulf

Thar
Desert

Ganga
(Ganges)

Nansei - shotō

Tropic of Cancer

L. Nasser

Euphrates

Arabian
Peninsula

Deccan

Western Ghats

Eastern Ghats

Taiwan

SAHEL

Nile

RED SEA

ARABIAN
SEA

Bay of
Bengal

Tianjin

Hainan

Luzon

PHILIPPINE
SEA

Lac Tchad
(Lake Chad)

Ar Rub' al Khali

Gulf of Aden

ANDAMAN
SEA

Mekong

SOUTH
CHINA
SEA

Philippines

Lake
Volta

Niger

Horn of
Africa

Cape
Comorin

Sri Lanka

Malay
Peninsula

SULU
SEA

Mindanao

Gulf of
Guinea

Ethiopian
Highlands

CELEBES
SEA

MOLUCCA SEA

Equator

Congo
Basin

Lake
Victoria

Kilimanjaro 5895 m

Sumatera
(Sumatra)

Borneo

Sulawesi
(Celebes)

Jazirah
Doberai

Pk Jaya 5030 m

New
Guinea

BISMARCK
SEA

Solor
Islar

Congo

L. Tanganyika

Great Rift Valley

JAVA SEA

BANDA SEA

SOLOMO
SEA

ARAFURA SEA

St Helena

Zambezi

Lake
Kariba

Mozambique Channel

Madagascar

INDIAN OCEAN

TIMOR SEA

Arnhem
Land

Cape
York
Pen.

CORAL SE

Namib Desert

Mauritius

Kimberley
Plateau

Barkly Tableland

GREAT DIVIDING RANGE

Tropic of Capricorn

Kalahari
Dessert

Linpopo

Drakensberg

Great Sandy
Desert

Great Victoria
Desert

Simpson Desert

Nullarbor Plain

Great
Australian
Bight

Eyre
Pen.

SOUTH

ATLANTIC

OCEAN

Îles
Crozet

Îles de Kerguélen

Tasmania

TASMA

Macqua

Antarctic Circle

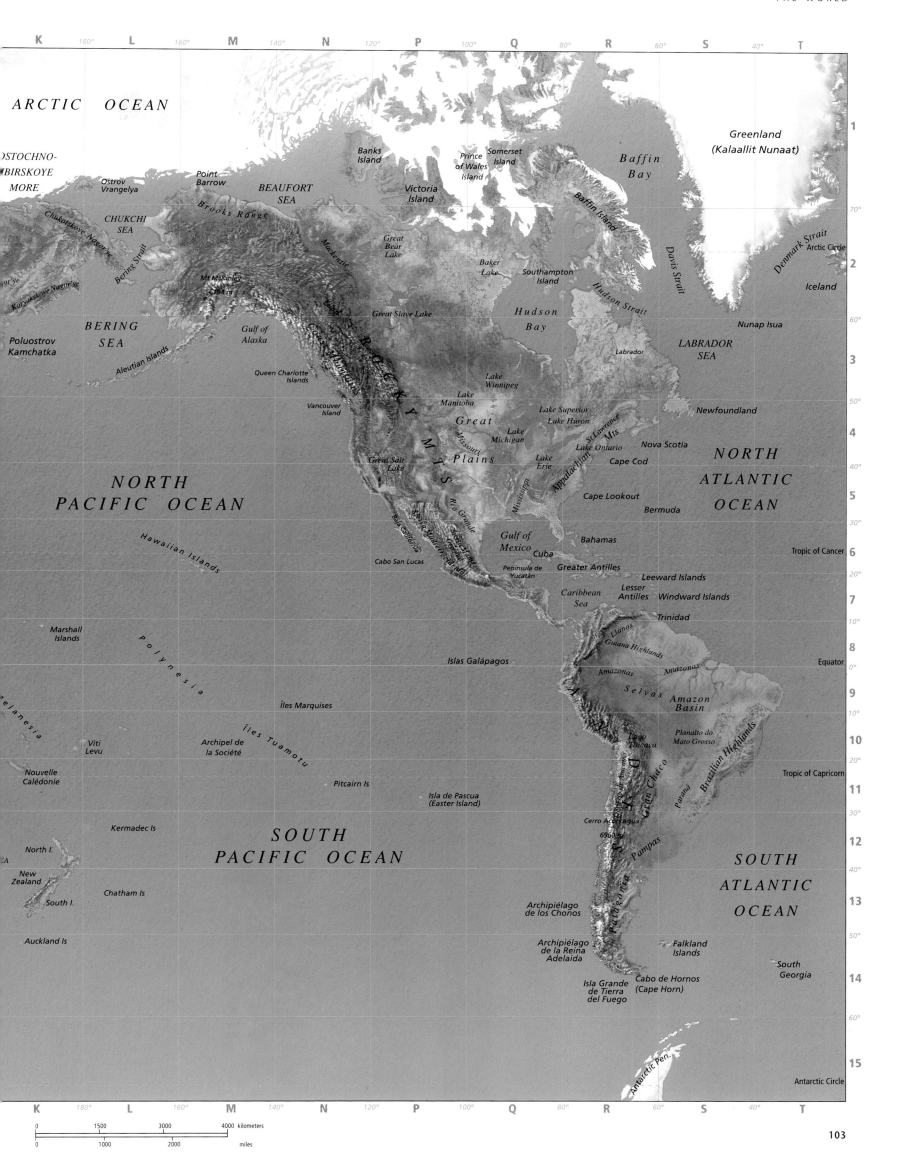

ARCTIC OCEAN

OSTOCHNO-
BIRSKOYE
MORE

Ostrov
Vrangelya

Point
Barrow

Banks
Island

Prince
of Wales
Island

Somerset
Island

Greenland
(Kalaallit Nunaat)

Baffin
Bay

CHUKCHI
SEA

BEAUFORT
SEA

Victoria
Island

Baffin Island

Denmark Strait

Arctic Circle

Chukotskoye Nagor'ye

Brooks Range

Great
Bear
Lake

Baker
Lake

Southampton
Island

Hudson Strait

Davis Strait

Iceland

Koryakskoye Nagor'ye

or'ye

Mt McKinley
6194 m

Mackenzie

Great Slave Lake

Hudson
Bay

Nunap Isua

Bering Strait

BERING
SEA

Gulf of
Alaska

Poluostrov
Kamchatka

Aleutian Islands

Labrador

LABRADOR
SEA

Queen Charlotte
Islands

Coast Mountains

ROCKY MTS

Lake
Winnipeg

Lake
Manitoba

Lake Superior
Lake Huron

St Lawrence

Newfoundland

Nova Scotia

Vancouver
Island

Great
Plains

Lake
Michigan

Lake Ontario

Cape Cod

NORTH
ATLANTIC
OCEAN

Great Salt
Lake

Missouri

Lake
Erie

Appalachian Mts

NORTH
PACIFIC OCEAN

Rio Grande

Sierra Madre Oriental

Mississippi

Cape Lookout

Bermuda

Hawaiian Islands

Baja California

Sierra Madre Occidental

Gulf of
Mexico

Bahamas

Tropic of Cancer

Cabo San Lucas

Cuba

Peninsula de
Yucatán

Greater Antilles

Leeward Islands

Marshall
Islands

Caribbean
Sea

Lesser
Antilles

Windward Islands

Polynesia

Islas Galápagos

Trinidad

Llanos

Guiana Highlands

Equator

Melanesia

Îles Marquises

Amazonas

Amazonas

Selvas

Amazon
Basin

Viti
Levu

Archipel de
la Société

Îles Tuamotu

A
N
D
E
S

Lago
Titicaca

Planalto do
Mato Grosso

Brazilian Highlands

Nouvelle
Calédonie

Pitcairn Is

Isla de Pascua
(Easter Island)

Gran Chaco

Paraná

Tropic of Capricorn

Kermadec Is

Cerro Aconcagua
6960 m

North I.

SOUTH
PACIFIC OCEAN

Pampas

SOUTH
ATLANTIC
OCEAN

New
Zealand

Chatham Is

Patagonia

South I.

Archipiélago
de los Chonos

Auckland Is

Archipiélago
de la Reina
Adelaida

Falkland
Islands

South
Georgia

Isla Grande
de Tierra
del Fuego

Cabo de Hornos
(Cape Horn)

Antarctic Pen.

Antarctic Circle

0   1500   3000   4000 kilometers

0   1000   2000   miles

103

The World: Political

A | 0° | **B** | 20° | **C** | 40° | **D** | 60° | **E** | 80° | **F** | 100° | **G** | 120° | **H** | 140° | **J**

SVALBARD (Nor.)

ARCTIC OCEAN

Novaya Zemlya

Novosibirskiye Ostrova

1

JAN MAYEN (Nor.)

BARENTS SEA

OKHOTSKOYE MORE

Arctic Circle

ICELAND

SWEDEN

FINLAND

R U S S I A N

2

FAEROE IS (Den.)

NORWAY

Oslo

Helsinki

Tallinn

Ostrov Sakhalin

Stockholm

Riga

ESTONIA

F E D E R A T I O N

UNITED KINGDOM

DENMARK

København

LITHUANIA

Vilnius

LATVIA

Minsk

Moskva

3

ISLE OF MAN (U.K.)

Dublin

Amsterdam

NETH.

Berlin

POLAND

BELARUS

Astana

Kuril'skiye Ostro

IRELAND

London

BELG.

GERMANY

Warszawa

Kyyiv

KAZAKHSTAN

Ulaanbaatar

Bruxelles

LUX.

Praha

SLOVAKIA

UKRAINE

Beijing

P'yŏngyang

CHANNEL ISLANDS (U.K.)

Luxembourg

Wien

Bratislava

MOLDOVA

Chişinău

MONGOLIA

NORTH KOREA

4

Paris

Bern

LIECH.

AUST. HUNG.

Budapest

ROMANIA

Bucureşti

GEORGIA

T'bilisi

Bishkek

Sŏul

FRANCE

SWITZ.

SLOV.

Ljubljana

CROAT.

Zagreb

YUG.

Beograd

Sofiya

BULGARIA

Ankara

Yerevan

ARM.

AZER.

Bakı

KYRGYZSTAN

SOUTH KOREA

Tōkyō

ANDORRA

Madrid

Roma

Tiranë

B.-H.

Sarajevo

MACE.

Skopje

ALBANIA

TURKEY

Bayrūt

Ashgabat

UZBEKISTAN

Toshkent

Dushanbe

TURKMENISTAN

TAJIKISTAN

C H I N A

JAPAN

5

PORTUGAL

SPAIN

ITALY

GREECE

Athina

Lefkosia

Dimashq

SYRIA

IRAQ

Tehrān

Kābol

Islāmābād

Lisboa

Madeira (Port.)

GIBRALTAR (U.K.)

Rabat

Alger

TUNISIA

Tūnis

MALTA

Valletta

CYPRUS

LEBANON

Yerushalayim

ISRAEL

JORDAN

Amman

Baghdād

I R A N

AFGHANISTAN

Islas Canarias (Sp.)

MOROCCO

W. SAHARA

Tarābulus

Al Qāhirah

Al Kuwayt

KUWAIT

BAHRAIN

Al Manāmah

Ad Dawḥah

QATAR

Abū Ẓaby

U.A.E.

PAKISTAN

Masqaṭ

New Delhi

Kathmandu

NEPAL

BHUTAN

Thimphu

T'ai-pei

6

Tropic of Cancer

MAURITANIA

Nouakchott

A L G E R I A

L I B Y A

E G Y P T

SAUDI ARABIA

Ar Riyāḍ

OMAN

ARABIAN SEA

Suquṭrá (Yemen)

I N D I A

MYANMAR

Dhaka

BANGLADESH

Bay of Bengal

Hà Nôi

TAIWAN

NORTHERN MARIANA IS (U.S.A.)

SENEGAL

M A L I

N I G E R

C H A D

S U D A N

Asmara

ERITREA

YEMEN

San'ā

Djibouti

DJIBOUTI

LAOS

Viangchan

VIETNAM

Manila

PHILIPPINES

GUAM (U.S.A.)

7

Dakar

GAMBIA

GUINEA-BISSAU

Bamako

BURKINA FASO

Niamey

NIGERIA

Ndjamena

Al Kharṭūm

C.A.R.

ETHIOPIA

Ādīs Ābeba

Yangon

THAILAND

Krung Thep

CAMBODIA

Koror

GUINEA

Conakry

CÔTE D'IVOIRE

GHANA

BENIN

TOGO

Ouagadougou

Abuja

Porto-Novo

CAMEROON

Bangui

SOMALIA

Muqdisho

Phnum Pénh

PALAU

MICRONES

SIERRA LEONE

Freetown

LIBERIA

Monrovia

Yamoussoukro

Accra

Lomé

Malabalo

EQ. GUINEA

Yaoundé

UGANDA

Kampala

KENYA

MALDIVES

Male

Chagos Archipelago

SRI LANKA

Colombo

M A L A Y S I A

Bandar Seri Begawan

BRUNEI

Palik

8

Equator

SÃO TOMÉ & PRÍNCIPE

GABON

Libreville

DEM. REP. OF THE CONGO

Kigali

RWANDA

BURUNDI

Bujumbura

Nairobi

TANZANIA

Victoria

SEYCHELLES

Kuala Lumpur

SINGAPORE

I N D O N E S I A

PAPUA NEW GUINEA

9

Brazzaville

CONGO

Kinshasa

Dodoma

Moroni

BRITISH INDIAN OCEAN TERRITORY (U.K.)

Jakarta

Port Moresby

ASCENSION ISLAND (ST HELENA)

Luanda

ANGOLA

ZAMBIA

MALAWI

Lilongwe

COMOROS

MAYOTTE (Fr.)

COCOS (KEELING) ISLANDS (Aust.)

ASHMORE & CARTIER ISLANDS (Aust.)

CHRISTMAS ISLAND (Aust.)

CORAL SEA ISLANDS (Aust.)

10

ST HELENA (U.K.)

Lusaka

Harare

ZIMBABWE

MOZAMBIQUE

Antananarivo

MADAGASCAR

MAURITIUS

Port Louis

RÉUNION (Fr.)

INDIAN OCEAN

Tropic of Capricorn

NAMIBIA

Windhoek

BOTSWANA

Gaborone

AUSTRALIA

11

Pretoria

Bloemfontein

Maputo

Mbabane

SWAZILAND

Maseru

LESOTHO

SOUTH AFRICA

12

Cape Town

Île Amsterdam (Fr.)

Canberra

SOUTH

FRENCH SOUTHERN & ANTARCTIC ISLANDS (Fr.)

Tasmania

TASMA SEA

TRISTAN DA CUNHA (U.K.)

Prince Edward Is (S. Africa)

Îles Crozet (Fr.)

Îles de Kerguélen (Fr.)

13

ATLANTIC OCEAN

HEARD & McDONALD ISLANDS (Aust.)

Macquarie (Aust.)

14

SOUTHERN OCEAN

BOUVET ISLAND (Nor.)

15

A N T A R C T I C A

Antarctic Circle

A | 0° | **B** | 20° | **C** | 40° | **D** | 60° | **E** | 80° | **F** | 100° | **G** | 120° | **H** | 140° | **J**

K 180° L 160° M 140° N 120° P 100° Q 80° R 60° S 40° T

*BEAUFORT
SEA*

*Banks
Island*

GREENLAND
(KALAALLIT NUNAAT)
(Den.)

1

*Ostrov
Vrangelya*

*CHUKCHI
SEA*

Victoria Island

*Baffin
Bay*

Baffin Island

70°

Davis Strait

Arctic Circle

U.S.A.

CANADA

ICELAND

2

Reykjavík ⊛

60°

Bering Strait

*BERING
SEA*

*Gulf of
Alaska*

*Hudson
Bay*

3

Aleutian Islands

50°

Newfoundland

*NORTH
ATLANTIC
OCEAN*

4

Ottawa ⊛

ST PIERRE
AND MIQUELON
(Fr.)

40°

UNITED STATES OF AMERICA

Washington D.C. ⊛

*Azores
(Port.)*

5

BERMUDA
(U.K.)

PACIFIC OCEAN

30°

*Isla Guadalupe
(Mex.)*

*Gulf of
Mexico*

BAHAMAS

Tropic of Cancer

MIDWAY ISLANDS
(U.S.A.)

MEXICO

La Habana ⊛

Nassau ⊛

CAPE VERDE

6

*Hawaiian Islands
(U.S.A.)*

México ⊛

CUBA

HAITI

DOMINICAN REPUBLIC

20°

WAKE ISLAND (U.S.A.)

*Islas Revillagigedo
(Mex.)*

Kingston ⊛

Santo Domingo ⊛

ANTIGUA & BARBUDA

Praia ⊛

7

JOHNSTON ATOLL
(U.S.A.)

Guatemala ⊛
GUATEMALA
EL SALVADOR
San Salvador ⊛

BELIZE
Belmopan ⊛
HONDURAS
⊛ Tegucigalpa
⊛ NICARAGUA
Managua ⊛

JAMAICA

DOMINICA
ST VINCENT
& THE GRENADINES

ST KITTS & NEVIS
ST LUCIA
BARBADOS
GRENADA

10°

MARSHALL ISLANDS

San José ⊛
COSTA RICA
Panamá ⊛
PANAMA

Caracas ⊛
VENEZUELA

Port of Spain ⊛
TRINIDAD & TOBAGO
Georgetown ⊛
Paramaribo ⊛

Dalap-Uliga-Darrit ⊛

KINGMAN REEF (U.S.A.)
PALMYRA ATOLL (U.S.A.)

Bogotá ⊛

GUYANA
SURINAME
FRENCH GUIANA (Fr.)

Equator

8

Bairiki ⊛

BAKER AND
HOWLAND ISLANDS
(U.S.A.)

JARVIS ISLAND (U.S.A.)

*Islas Galápagos
(Ecu.)*

COLOMBIA

Quito ⊛
ECUADOR

0°

NAURU

9

Honiara ⊛
SOLOMON ISLANDS

Funafuti ⊛
TUVALU

K I R I B A T I

TOKELAU
(N.Z.)

PERU

B R A Z I L

10°

Lima ⊛

VANUATU
Port-
Vila ⊛

WALLIS & SAMOA
FUTUNA
(Fr.)

AMERICAN
SAMOA
(U.S.A.)

Apia ⊛

Îles Marquises

La Paz ⊛
BOLIVIA

Brasília ⊛

10

NEW
CALEDONIA
(Fr.)

FIJI
Suva ⊛

TONGA
Nuku'alofa ⊛

NIUE
(N.Z.)

COOK
ISLANDS
(N.Z.)

*Archipel de
la Société*

Îles Tuamotu
Tahiti

Sucre ⊛

*Trindade
(Brazil)*

20°

Tropic of Capricorn

PARAGUAY

FRENCH
POLYNESIA
(Fr.)

PITCAIRN IS.
(U.K.)

Asunción ⊛

NORFOLK
ISLAND
(Aust.)

*Isla de Pascua
(Chile)*

*Sala y Gómez
(Chile)*

30°

11

*Kermadec Is
(N.Z.)*

ARGENTINA

URUGUAY

12

*Archipiélago Juan Fernández
(Chile)*

Santiago ⊛

Buenos Aires ⊛

Montevideo ⊛

40°

North I.

*SOUTH
ATLANTIC OCEAN*

13

Wellington ⊛

*Chatham Is
(N.Z.)*

South I.

NEW ZEALAND

*Bounty Is
(N.Z.)*

*Antipodes Is
(N.Z.)*

50°

*Auckland Is
(N.Z.)*

FALKLAND ISLANDS
(U.K.)

SOUTH GEORGIA &
SOUTH SANDWICH
ISLANDS (U.K.)

14

*Campbell I.
(N.Z.)*

Cabo de Hornos

60°

*South Shetland
Islands (U.K.)*

*South Orkney
Islands (U.K.)*

15

*Balleny Is
(N.Z.)*

*BELLINGSHAUSEN
SEA*

*Antarctic
Peninsula*

Antarctic Circle

60° K 180° L 160° M 140° N 120° P 100° Q 80° R 60° S 40° T

105

0   1500   3000   4000 kilometers

0   1000   2000   miles

Scale 1:87,500,000   Projection: Mercator

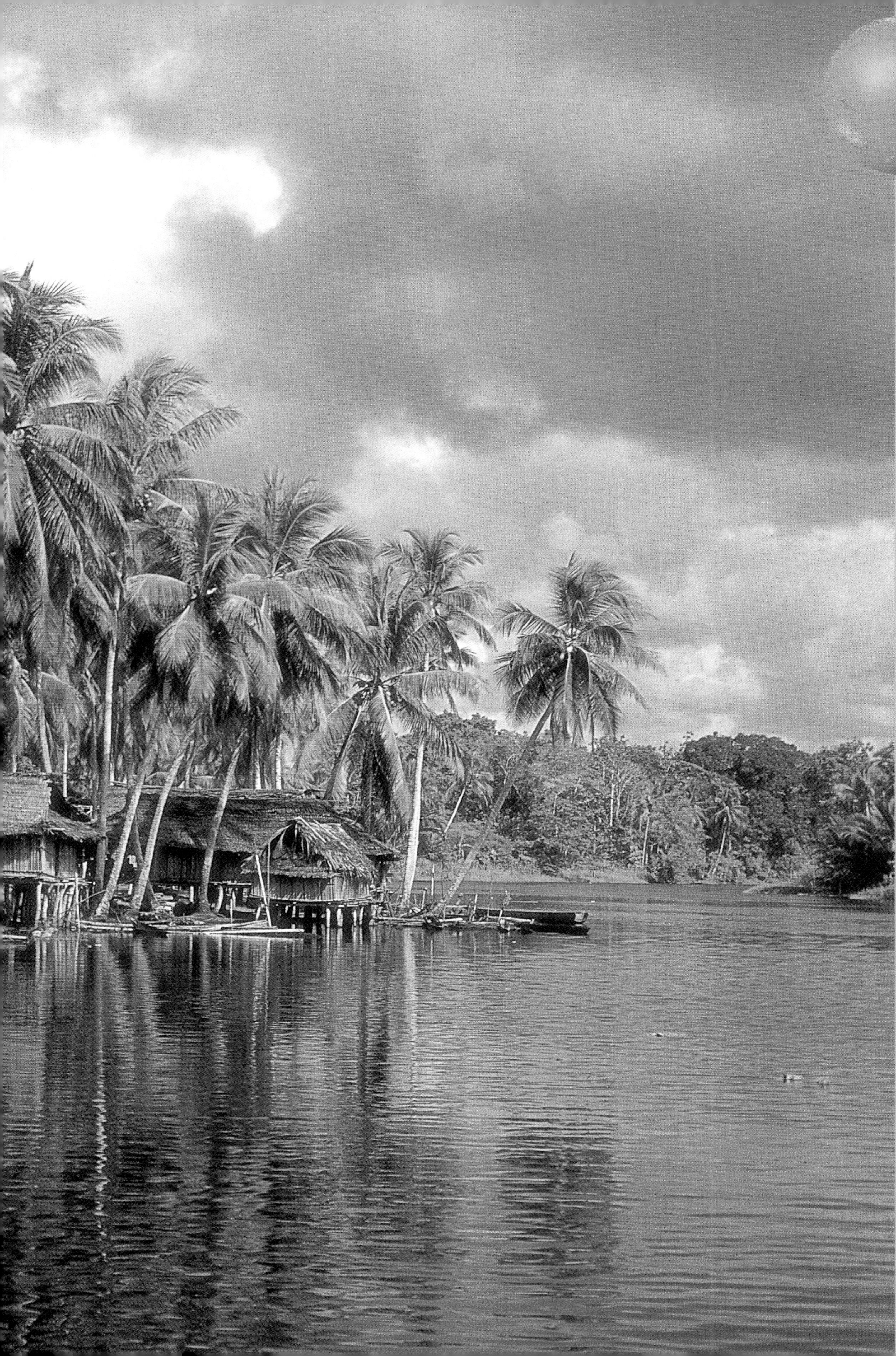

Oceania

Oceania

Oceania is the name given to a group of islands spread over 8.5 million sq km (3.3 million sq miles) in the Pacific Ocean, the majority of which lie in the southern hemisphere. The islands range in size from the large island continent of Australia, through medium-sized nations such as Papua New Guinea and New Zealand, to much smaller countries, such as Vanuatu and Tonga.

On cultural grounds, the islands can be divided into four groups. The first, Micronesia, lies east of the Philippines and includes the Federated States of Micronesia, Palau, the Marshall Islands, Nauru, and the USA dependencies of Guam and the Northern Mariana Islands. Melanesia, the second group, lies east of Indonesia and Australia, and includes Papua New Guinea, the Solomon Islands, Vanuatu, Fiji, Tonga, Tuvalu, and Samoa and the dependencies of New Caledonia (France) and American Samoa. Polynesia, the third, lies in the center of the Pacific Ocean, and includes Kiribati, French Polynesia, and the dependencies of Niue, the Cook Islands (NZ), the Pitcairn Islands (UK), and Hawaii (part of the USA). The fourth group comprises Australia and New Zealand. Unlike the other groups, these islands have indigenous populations, but the majority of the population are people who have migrated from Europe over the last two centuries. Australian dependencies include Norfolk Island in the Pacific Ocean and the Cocos (Keeling) and Christmas Islands in the Indian Ocean.

Physical features

Physiographically, the islands of Oceania can be classed into four categories. First there is Australia, situated in the middle of the Indo-Australian Plate, where there was no mountain building during the Tertiary geological era. Australia's eastern highlands, the eroded remnants of old mountains, are a series of elevated plateaus; the western half of the country is an ancient eroded plateau linked to the east by vast sedimentary basins.

In the second category are the islands lying along the collision boundaries between crustal plates. In the South Pacific, New Zealand, Papua New Guinea, the Solomon Islands, and Fiji are within the collision zone between the Indo-Australian and the Pacific plates. In the North Pacific, the Mariana Islands lie along the collision boundary of the Eurasian

and Pacific plates. These collisions have produced folded mountain ranges. New Zealand and Papua New Guinea have young mountain ranges, some peaks exceeding 3,000 m (10,000 ft).

The third category includes volcanic islands such as Fiji, which rise from the floor of the Pacific Ocean basin. Much smaller than the countries in the second category, they are mostly made up of high mountains, with some low-lying fringes along the coastlines, including coral reefs.

Finally, there are coral islands and atolls, such as Tuvalu. Atolls form low-lying circular coral reefs which enclose lagoons. The atolls typically develop around submerged volcanic cones. In some places, such as in Guam, coral islands have been raised by crustal movements.

Climate and vegetation

Oceania can be divided into two climatic zones: temperate and tropical. A large part of Australia and all of New Zealand lie in the temperate zone, while most of the island countries of the Pacific are tropical. Persistent trade winds dominate much of Oceania, and tropical cyclones often cause considerable damage.

Large parts of Australia are arid or semiarid. Humid zones are found along most of the east coast and Tasmania, and in part of the northern coast during summer. Most of New Zealand, Papua New Guinea and most of the islands in the Pacific are humid. However, droughts associated with the El Niño phenomenon have been frequent in recent decades in northern Australia and Papua New Guinea.

Rainforests, both tropical and temperate, occur in all the humid regions of Oceania—Australia and the larger and high (mostly volcanic) islands. However, deforestation has taken place in several places, such as parts of eastern Australia, Tasmania, New Zealand, and the Solomon Islands.

The kangaroo, probably Australia's most well known native animal. While some such animals are threatened with extinction, kangaroos are in fact regarded as pests by many.

Isolation has been a major factor in the development of unique species of animals, birds, and plants in the Pacific islands. The spread of human habitation and hunting has seriously affected native animals, especially in Australia—several species are extinct or endangered.

Population

In 1998 the population of Oceania totalled 29.5 million. Australia and New Zealand accounted for 22.1 million people and Papua New Guinea for 4.6 million people. The remaining 2.8 million inhabitants are scattered on many small islands over a large area. Life expectancy for the area as a whole is 71.5 years for males and 76.4 for females. The annual population growth rate averages 1.3 percent but this varies widely, with 1.1 percent for Australia and New Zealand, 4 percent for Papua New Guinea, and 3.6 percent for Melanesia. Rates of urbanization vary widely too, being 85 percent for Australia and New Zealand and 16 percent for Papua New Guinea.

Agriculture

Agriculture in Oceania can be divided into three kinds: labor-intensive subsistence agriculture, which occurs in most of the tropical islands of the Pacific; plantation crops, which are cultivated in the medium-sized tropical islands; and capital-intensive agriculture, which is found in Australia and New Zealand.

Subsistence agriculture in the Pacific islands consists of short-life items such as cassava, taro, yams, breadfruit, and sweet potatoes. Bananas and papayas are the most commonly grown fruits. Coconut palms grow on almost all the islands, and are a source of fresh food. Oil is extracted from the dried coconut meat (copra). Copra is exported from countries such as Vanuatu and Samoa. Cash crops, often a legacy of colonial times, are also important in some of the Pacific nations—sugar in Fiji and cocoa in Vanuatu.

Fishing is important for the majority of Pacific islands, as their economic zones extend to the 200 nautical mile limit—a large area compared to the size of many of the islands. Several islands have granted fishing licenses to Japanese, South Korean, and Taiwanese companies.

Palms in the Finke Valley, central Australia (left), and forests edging Lake Matheson in southern New Zealand (above). The New Ireland coast (right), and a young girl in traditional dress and face paint (above right), both in Papua New Guinea.

Industrialization

Australia and New Zealand both have modern diversified economies with well-established infrastructures. Australia is particularly well favored as it has rich mineral deposits and energy sources. Manufacturing, including food processing, makes an important contribution to the economy of these two Pacific nations.

In contrast, the other islands of the Pacific are not industrially developed. Papua New Guinea, is rich in minerals such as copper and gold, and has recently dis-covered natural gas fields. There are nickel deposits in New Caledonia and gold in Fiji, both of which are exported rather than used in local industries.

Many islands in the Pacific have few resources; some have insufficient land for their people and a number lack adequate supplies of drinking water. This shortage of natural resources, coupled with poor infrastructures, has impeded industrial development. Industry in most of the islands is limited to food processing.

Tourism has become an important source of revenue for much of Oceania. Australia and New Zealand offer tourists modern amenities and facilities, while the beautiful scenery of tropical Pacific Islands like Fiji, Tahiti, Vanuatu, and the Northern Mariana Islands attract visitors.

Languages

Culturally, Oceania can be divided into two major groups: the predominantly European settlements of Australia and New Zealand, and Melanesia, Polynesia, and Micronesia, which have been long settled by Oceanic peoples. New Caledonia is partially settled by Europeans.

During the colonial era, the entire region came under European influence. This resulted in English and French becoming important languages, depending on the colonial powers (Britain, America, and France). English is the official language of New Zealand, Australia, Papua New Guinea, the Solomon Islands, Vanuatu, and Fiji. French is

spoken in New Caledonia and French Polynesia. On several of the Pacific islands, particularly Papua New Guinea and Vanuatu, pidgin is a common lingua franca.

In Australia, only remnants of the numerous Aboriginal languages that were spoken in the continent before European settlement still exist. Several of these languages are found in the Northern Territory and the northern part of Western Australia (the Kimberleys), where Walmadjeri is becoming a common language among several Aboriginal tribes. In New Zealand, which has a significant Maori population, the Maori language is widely spoken.

Numerous languages are found in Melanesia, Polynesia, and Micronesia. In Papua New Guinea, hundreds of languages are spoken, Austronesian languages being spoken along the coastline and Papuan languages in the highlands. Austronesian languages such as Fijian in Fiji and Tahitian, Tongan, and Samoan in Polynesia are widespread.

Boundary disputes and wars

The whole region was affected by the Japanese invasion during the Second World War, and was the site of many important battles. No significant boundary disputes exist in the region. In recent decades, boundaries have been drawn up for Oceanic economic zones. However, there have been civil disturbances in both Fiji and New Caledonia—the former related to the struggle for a less racially biased government in the years after Fiji became a republic in 1970, the latter related to the wish of some of the people to become independent from France.

Australia

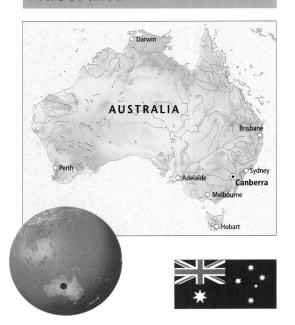

Fact File

OFFICIAL NAME Commonwealth of Australia

FORM OF GOVERNMENT Federal constitutional monarchy with two legislative bodies (Senate and House of Representatives)

CAPITAL Canberra

AREA 7,686,850 sq km (2,967,893 sq miles)

TIME ZONE GMT + 10 hours

POPULATION 18,783,551

PROJECTED POPULATION 2005 19,728,533

POPULATION DENSITY 2.44 per sq km (6.3 per sq mile)

LIFE EXPECTANCY 80.1

INFANT MORTALITY (PER 1,000) 5.1

OFFICIAL LANGUAGE English

OTHER LANGUAGES Indigenous languages, Italian, Greek

LITERACY RATE 99%

RELIGIONS Roman Catholic 27%, Anglican 22%, other Christian 22%, other 12.4%, none 16.6%

ETHNIC GROUPS European 95%, Asian 4%, other (including Aboriginals) 1%

CURRENCY Australian dollar

ECONOMY Services 78%, industry 16%, agriculture 6%

GNP PER CAPITA US$18,720

CLIMATE Hot and arid in center; tropical in north with one wet season (November to March); temperate in southeast and along southern coasts

HIGHEST POINT Mt Kosciuszko 2,229 m (7,313 ft)

MAP REFERENCE Pages 134–35

The Apostles, Port Campbell National Park, Victoria (right). Finke Gorge National Park in the Northern Territory (top right).

Australia is both the world's smallest continental landmass and the sixth-largest country. Most of it consists of low plateaus, and almost one-third is desert. First occupied about 40,000 to 50,000 years ago by peoples from Asia (the ancestors of today's Aboriginals), Australia was visited by Dutch explorers in the seventeenth century, including Abel Tasman in 1642 and 1644, and by the Englishman William Dampier in 1688 and 1699. After being claimed for Britain by Captain James Cook in 1770, a penal colony was established by the British in what is now Sydney in 1788. Some 160,000 convicts arrived before "transportation" from Britain was phased out in the nineteenth century. By then many free settlers had also arrived, and the gold rushes of the 1850s attracted still more people. With both wool and wheat exports providing economic security, the settler population sought greater independence from Britain, and a measure of self-government was granted in 1850. In 1901 the six states formed themselves into the Commonwealth of Australia, and in the 100 years since federation the country has become a successful, prosperous modern democracy. Current concerns include the consequences of economic dependence on Asian markets at a time of recession, demands for the frank acknowledgment of the history of Aboriginal displacement and dispossession, and whether there should be a republican government.

The Western Plateau constitutes the western half of the Australian continent. Made of ancient rocks, the plateau rises near the west coast—the iron-rich Hamersley Range representing its highest elevation in the northwest—and then falls eastward toward the center of the continent. The arid landscape alternates between worn-down ridges and plains, and depressions containing sandy deserts and salt lakes. There is little surface water. The flatness of the plateau is interrupted by the MacDonnell and Musgrave ranges in the center of the continent and the Kimberley and Arnhem Land plateaus in the north. Sheep and cattle are raised on large holdings in parts of this region.

The Central Lowlands forming the Great Artesian Basin, and river systems including the Carpentaria, Eyre, and Murray basins constitute a nearly continuous expanse of lowland that runs north to south. The river systems feed into Lake Eyre, the Bulloo system, or the Darling River. While the Murray Basin is the smallest of the three, its rivers—the Murray and its tributary the Darling—are Australia's longest and most important. Artesian bores make cattle and sheep raising possible through much of the semiarid Central Lowlands.

The Eastern Highlands (known as the Great Dividing Range) and the relatively narrow eastern coastal plain constitute Australia's third main geographic region. This has the greatest relief, the heaviest rainfall, the most abundant and varied

vegetation, and the densest human settlement. A notable feature of the eastern marine environment is the Great Barrier Reef. The world's biggest coral reef complex, it lies off the northeast coast, stretching some 2,500 km (1,550 miles) from the Tropic of Capricorn to Papua New Guinea. A major tourist attraction, with over 400 types of coral and 1,500 species of fish, it is now protected as the Great Barrier Reef Marine Park.

The island of Tasmania, to the southeast of mainland Australia, has spectacular mountain wilderness areas and more than 30 percent of the state is protected World Heritage areas, national parks, and reserves.

Australian plant and animal life is distinctive. The most common trees are the gums (*Eucalyptus*) and wattles (*Acacia*). Highly adaptable, *Eucalyptus* varieties range from the tall flooded gum, found on rainforest fringes, to the mallee which grows on dry plains. Most native mammals are marsupials, and include kangaroos, koalas, wombats, and possums. Australia's monotremes—the platypus and the echidna—which lay eggs and suckle their young, are unique. There are also about 400 species of reptile and some 700 species of bird. Australia's vulnerability to introduced plant and animal species was dramatically shown by the spread of prickly pear, which took over vast areas of rural New South Wales and Queensland in the 1920s, and the plagues of rabbits that devastated pastures for a century until the 1960s. Both scourges have been tamed by biological controls.

Once heavily dependent on the pastoral industry—nearly one-third of Australia is still used for grazing sheep—the nation's economy is now diversified, with an important manufacturing sector. Australia is rich in mineral resources, the leading export earners being iron ore from Western Australia and coking coal from Queensland and

Timeline	**c.15,000 BP** Rock art paintings created in shelters and caves of northwest Australia	**c.13,000 BP** People of robust appearance with thick skulls and large jaws living at Kow Swamp, Murray Valley, Victoria	**1606** Dutch navigator Willem Jansz, first European to set foot in Australia, lands on Cape York Peninsula	**1770** James Cook explores the east coast of Australia and the New Zealand islands, claiming both for Great Britain	**1813** First European crossing of the Blue Mountains, west of Sydney, opens up inland plains to pastoralists	**1851** Gold discoveries first in New South Wales and then Victoria; gold rushes generate wealth and population increase	**1868** Transportation of convicts abolished; last ship lands in Fremantle, WA	**1919** More than 6,000 people die in the worst 'flu epidemic in New South Wales history
	c.40,000 BP First Australians arrive in log canoes or sail boats from southeast Asia	**c.25,000 BP** Earliest evidence of cremation, Lake Mungo, New South Wales	**c.6–5000 BC** Dingoes brought to Australia, probably domesticated dogs belonging to people migrating from southeast Asia	**1642** Dutch navigator Abel Tasman lands in Van Diemen's Land (now Tasmania), taking possession for Holland	**1788** First Fleet under Captain Arthur Phillip arrives; penal colony set up in Port Jackson. Aboriginal population c. 750,000	**1829** Charles Sturt explores the Darling River system and later travels inland to disprove the myth of an inland sea	**1855–56** Augustus Charles Gregory makes first west-to-east land crossing of the continent	**1914–18** Australia sends 416,809 troops to fight in First World War; 53,993 killed in battle and 155,133 wounded	**1933** Aboriginal population reduced to 66,000 as a result of suppression and disease

New South Wales, while bauxite is mined in the Northern Territory and Queensland. In recent years Australia has produced more than one-third of the world's diamonds, 14 percent of its lead, and 11 percent of its uranium and zinc. Because commodities account for more than 80 percent of exports, falling commodity prices have severe economic effects: an apparently irreversible decline in world demand for wool has cast a shadow over the pastoral industry. The government has been encouraging increased exports of manufactured goods—cars are being exported to the Gulf States— but international competition is intense. The 1998 Asian economic downturn affected the tourist industry, which was the largest single foreign exchange earner, with 12.8 percent of the total.

STATES

New South Wales • Sydney
Queensland • Brisbane
South Australia • Adelaide
Tasmania • Hobart
Victoria • Melbourne
Western Australia • Perth

TERRITORIES

Australian Capital Territory • Canberra
Northern Territory • Darwin

OVERSEAS TERRITORIES

Ashmore and Cartier Islands
Christmas Island
Cocos (Keeling) Island
Coral Sea Islands
Heard and McDonald Islands
Norfolk Island

1939 Australia's involvement in Second World War dominated by entry of Japanese after Pearl Harbor

1967 Referendum accords citizenship to Aboriginal people for the first time by a vote of 90.8 percent of the population

1991–92 Severe drought associated with El Niño climate pattern affects eastern Australia

1949 Construction of Snowy Mountains hydroelectric scheme, Australia's largest (completed 1972)

1974 Cyclone Tracy destroys most of Darwin, Northern Territory

1993 High Court ruling (Mabo) that Australia was not "empty" when Europeans arrived allows native title claims to proceed

Fiji

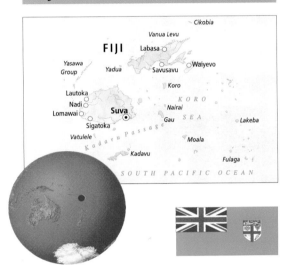

Fiji consists of an archipelago of more than 800 islands and islets, 110 of them inhabited, located about two-thirds of the way from Hawaii to New Zealand. Lying on the air route from Australia to the west coast of the USA, Fiji is well served by flights, and is attracting an increasing number of tourists. Originally inhabited by Melanesian islanders organized into a number of tribes, the islands were visited by Dutch explorers in 1643, and from 1800 attracted growing numbers of traders, along with missionaries who converted the people to Christianity. A period of intense tribal warfare was brought to an end when the paramount chief ceded sovereignty to the British in 1874. Five years later, in 1879, the British began bringing in Indian laborers for the purpose of sugar production; by the time Fiji obtained its independence in 1970 their descendants outnumbered the country's ethnic Fijians.

Racial divisions have been a source of major tension and instability, since for many years the Indian immigrants were treated as second-class citizens, despite their vital role in the sugar industry. A coup in 1987, led by a Fijian army officer against a democratically elected government in which Indians were the majority, led to a new constitution being introduced in

1990. This was racially weighted to ensure permanent indigenous Fijian rule. As a result, large numbers of Indian-Fijians chose to emigrate. The security of land tenure for Indian sugarcane farmers remains a contentious issue.

The main islands are of volcanic origin. About 70 percent of the population live on the two biggest—Viti Levu and Vanua Levu. These have a sharp and rugged relief, rising to Mt Tomanivi on Viti Levu. The islands lie in a cyclone path (Cyclone Kina caused much damage in 1993) and trade winds bring heavy rain to their eastern sides. Dense tropical forest covers the higher slopes. Sugarcane is grown on the fertile coastal plains, sugar exports and tourism being Fiji's main sources of foreign exchange. About 250,000 tourists, many bound for resorts on the smaller coral atolls, visit the islands each year. Fiji has a variety of forest, mineral, and marine resources, and is one of the most developed of the Pacific island economies, producing (as well as sugar) copra, gold, silver, clothing, and timber.

Fact File

OFFICIAL NAME Republic of Fiji

FORM OF GOVERNMENT Republic with two legislative bodies (Senate and House of Representatives)

CAPITAL Suva

AREA 18,270 sq km (7,054 sq miles)

TIME ZONE GMT + 12 hours

POPULATION 812,918

PROJECTED POPULATION 2005 877,594

POPULATION DENSITY 44.5 per sq km (115.2 per sq mile)

LIFE EXPECTANCY 66.6

INFANT MORTALITY (PER 1,000) 16.3

OFFICIAL LANGUAGE English

OTHER LANGUAGES Fijian, Hindustani

LITERACY RATE 91.3%

RELIGIONS Christian 52% (Methodist 37%, Roman Catholic 9%), Hindu 38%, Muslim 8%, other 2%

ETHNIC GROUPS Fijian 49%, Indian 46%, other (including European, other Pacific Islanders, Chinese) 5%

CURRENCY Fiji dollar

ECONOMY Agriculture 67%, services and industry 33%

GNP PER CAPITA US$2,440

CLIMATE Tropical, with wet season November to April

HIGHEST POINT Mt Tomanivi 1,323 m (4,341 ft)

MAP REFERENCE Pages 137, 141

The Parliament House buildings in Suva (below).

Kiribati

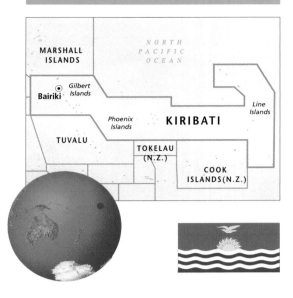

The Republic of Kiribati (pronounced Kiribass) consists of 33 scattered coral atolls in three separate groups in the mid-Pacific, plus the volcanic island, Banaba. The three groups are the 17 former Gilbert Islands in the west, the 8 Phoenix Islands, and the 8 Line Islands.

Banaba Island has provided the region with the most income. It is one of three great phosphate rock islands in the Pacific Ocean, the others being Nauru and Makatea. The people of Kiribati are Micronesian, though the Banabans pride themselves on being ethnically distinct.

Kiritimati Island (also known as Christmas Island), one of the Line Islands, was the site of the first British nuclear tests in the Pacific in 1957, but is now a favored location for tourist development. For Kiribati as a whole, it is difficult to see what else besides tourism can be developed as a national source of income—it is classified by the United Nations as a Least Developed Country. The phosphate deposits on Banaba had been exhausted by the time of independence in 1979. Copra (50 percent), seaweed (16 percent) and fish (15 percent) are now the main exports. A basic subsistence economy still flourishes, with small farms and gardens producing taro, breadfruit, and

sweet potatoes. Kiribati imports little food but it depends heavily on foreign aid, largely from the UK and Japan. Aid has been 25 to 50 percent of gross domestic product in recent years.

Though Kiribati is a democracy, the political parties continue to be strongly influenced by a traditional chief system and have little formal organization. A major difficulty for Kiribati today is the problem of environmental degradation from the overpopulation of Tarawa, the island capital to which many Kiribati have migrated because of the lack of job opportunities elsewhere.

Fact File

OFFICIAL NAME Republic of Kiribati

FORM OF GOVERNMENT Republic with single legislative body (National Assembly)

CAPITAL Bairiki

AREA 717 sq km (277 sq miles)

TIME ZONE GMT + 12/11 hours

POPULATION 85,501

PROJECTED POPULATION 2005 91,614

POPULATION DENSITY 119.2 per sq km (308.67 per sq mile)

LIFE EXPECTANCY 62.9

INFANT MORTALITY (PER 1,000) 48.2

OFFICIAL LANGUAGE English

OTHER LANGUAGE Gilbertese

LITERACY RATE 90%

RELIGIONS Roman Catholic 52.5%, Protestant (Congregational) 41%, other (including Seventh-Day Adventist, Baha'i, Church of God, Mormon) 6.5%

ETHNIC GROUPS Predominantly Micronesian with small Polynesian and non-Pacific minorities

CURRENCY Australian dollar

ECONOMY Agriculture, copra production, fishing

GNP PER CAPITA US$920

CLIMATE Tropical, moderated by trade winds

HIGHEST POINT Unnamed location on Banaba Island 81 m (266 ft)

MAP REFERENCE Page 139

Marshall Islands

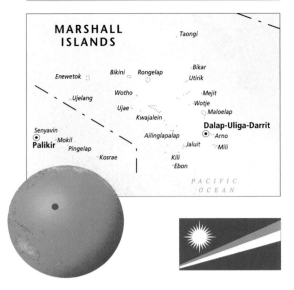

A group of 31 coral atolls, 5 islands, and 1,152 islets, the Republic of the Marshall Islands is situated in the northern Pacific about halfway between Hawaii and Papua New Guinea. Settled around 2000 BC, the islands were visited by Spanish seafarers in 1529, and since 1874 have been successively under Spanish, German, Japanese, and US control. In 1986 they entered into a Compact of Free Association with the US. During the years after the Second World War the Marshalls became known as the location where the USA carried out nucleur bomb tests (on Bikini and Enewetak Atolls between 1946 and 1958). Claims for compensation by those affected or displaced by the tests have been settled in recent years, an award of US$40 million to 1,150 Marshall Islanders being made by the Nuclear Claims Tribunal in 1995. Cleanup work to remove residual radiation from Bikini Lagoon continues.

The terrain consists of low coral limestone and sand islands. Two archipelagoes of islands run roughly parallel northeast to southwest, the easternmost chain being a continuation of the Gilbert Islands of western Kiribati. Originating as coral reefs formed upon the rims of submerged volcanoes, each of the main islands encloses a lagoon. Bordering the cyclone belt, and nowhere higher than 10 m (30 ft) above sea level, they are vulnerable to storms and tidal waves. In June 1994 a tidal wave swept over the capital on Majuro Atoll.

On the outlying atolls a typical Pacific island subsistence economy survives, centered on agriculture and fishing. Small farms produce commercial crops such as coconuts, tomatoes, melons, and breadfruit, and a handful of cattle ranches supplies the domestic meat market. Industry consists of handicrafts, fish processing, and copra production, and the main exports are tuna, copra, and coconut oil products. About 10 percent of the population is employed in the tourist industry (visitors come from Japan and the USA), now the main source of foreign exchange. Imports are 11 times export rates, all fuel must be imported, and the country as a whole is heavily dependent on aid from the US plus income from the US leasing of Kwajalein Atoll for missile testing. With US grants due to be scaled back after 2001, every economic activity that can help the country stand on its own feet is being explored.

Huts on a coconut plantation in Kiribati (bottom left). An aerial view of some of the Marshall Islands (left). Mangroves in Micronesia (below left).

the Pacific Ocean. Tourists now come to the island to scuba dive among the numerous wartime wrecks in the lagoon.

The 607 widely scattered islands of Micronesia vary geologically from high and mountainous terrain to low coral atolls. Most of the islands are volcanic in origin, and the hot, rainy climate produces lush vegetation and tropical rainforest. Volcanic outcrops occur on Pohnpei, Kosrae, and Chuuk. Some of the atolls lack any surface water. Droughts occur frequently on Chuuk, often leading to water rationing. In 1992 emergency supplies of water had to be brought from Guam to Chuuk by the US Navy.

Subsistence fishing and farming occupies the majority of the population, with farmers growing tropical fruits and vegetables, coconuts, cassava (tapioca), sweet potatoes, and black pepper, and raising pigs and chickens. Fish, bananas, and black pepper are exported, and as a result of attempts at economic diversification a clothing industry has been developed.

Aside from deposits of high-grade phosphate the islands have few mineral resources. Imports exceed exports by a ratio of more than four to one, and the country as a whole depends heavily on financial aid from the USA. There is some potential for tourism—with their rich marine life the islands are a prime destination for scuba divers—but poor infrastructure and the country's remoteness hinder further development.

Fact File

OFFICIAL NAME Republic of the Marshall Islands

FORM OF GOVERNMENT Republic in free association with the USA; two legislative bodies (Parliament and Council of Chiefs)

CAPITAL Dalap-Uliga-Darrit

AREA 181 sq km (70 sq miles)

TIME ZONE GMT + 12 hours

POPULATION 65,507

PROJECTED POPULATION 2005 82,686

POPULATION DENSITY 361.9 per sq km (937.3 per sq mile)

LIFE EXPECTANCY 64.8

INFANT MORTALITY (PER 1,000) 43.4

OFFICIAL LANGUAGE English

OTHER LANGUAGES Marshallese, Japanese

LITERACY RATE 93%

RELIGIONS Protestant 90%, Roman Catholic 9%, other 1%

ETHNIC GROUPS Micronesian 97%, other 3%

CURRENCY US dollar

ECONOMY Agriculture, fishing, tourism

GNP PER CAPITA Est. US$766–3,035

CLIMATE Tropical, with wet season May to November

HIGHEST POINT Unnamed location on Likiep 10 m (33 ft)

MAP REFERENCE Pages 138–39

Micronesia

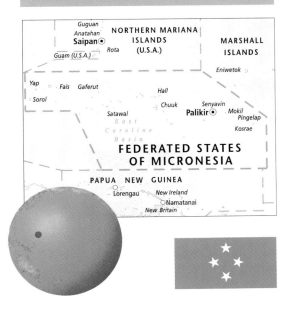

The Federated States of Micronesia consist of four states—Yap, Chuuk (Truk), Pohnpei, and Kosrae—made up of four island groups spread out across 3,200 km (2,000 miles) of ocean. Formerly known as the Caroline Islands, they are located in the northern Pacific about halfway between Australia and Japan. They are populated by Micronesian and Polynesian peoples divided into nine separate ethnic groups.

First settled around 1000 BC, the islands were visited by Spanish seafarers in 1565 and were annexed by Spain in 1874. In 1899 Spain sold them to Germany, and at the beginning of the First World War Japan took posession of them. After Japan's defeat in the Second World War, the USA took over the administration of the islands. US control ended in 1986 when the Federated States of Micronesia and the USA signed a 15-year Compact of Free Association. This granted internal self-government, the USA retaining responsibility for the country's defense.

During the course of the Second World War Chuuk was one of Japan's most important bases in

Fact File

OFFICIAL NAME Federated States of Micronesia

FORM OF GOVERNMENT Federal Republic in free association with the USA; single legislative body (Congress)

CAPITAL Palikir

AREA 702 sq km (271 sq miles)

TIME ZONE GMT + 10 hours

POPULATION 131,500

PROJECTED POPULATION 2005 138,739

POPULATION DENSITY 187.3 per sq km (485.1 per sq mile)

LIFE EXPECTANCY 68.5

INFANT MORTALITY (PER 1,000) 34.0

OFFICIAL LANGUAGE English

OTHER LANGUAGES Micronesian languages

LITERACY RATE 90%

RELIGIONS Roman Catholic 50%, Protestant 47%, other and none 3%

ETHNIC GROUPS Micronesian and Polynesian

CURRENCY US dollar

ECONOMY Agriculture, fishing, services, textiles

GNP PER CAPITA Est. US$766–3,035

CLIMATE Tropical. Heavy rainfall year-round and occasional typhoons

HIGHEST POINT Totolom 791 m (2,595 ft)

MAP REFERENCE Page 138

Oceania

Nauru

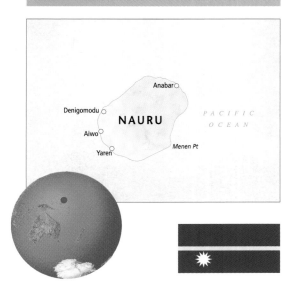

Fact File

OFFICIAL NAME	Republic of Nauru
FORM OF GOVERNMENT	Republic with single legislative body (Parliament)
CAPITAL	None; government offices in Yaren
AREA	21 sq km (8.1 sq miles)
TIME ZONE	GMT + 12 hours
POPULATION	10,605
PROJECTED POPULATION 2005	11,118
POPULATION DENSITY	505 per sq km (1,307.9 per sq mile)
LIFE EXPECTANCY	Not available
INFANT MORTALITY (PER 1,000)	Not available
OFFICIAL LANGUAGE	Nauruan
OTHER LANGUAGE	English
LITERACY RATE	99%
RELIGIONS	Protestant 66.7%, Roman Catholic 33.3%
ETHNIC GROUPS	Nauruan 58%, other Pacific Islander 26%, Chinese 8%, European 8%
CURRENCY	Australian dollar
ECONOMY	Phosphate mining, financial services, coconut production
GNP PER CAPITA	US$8,100
CLIMATE	Tropical, with wet season November to February
HIGHEST POINT	Unnamed location 61 m (200 ft)
MAP REFERENCE	Pages 138–39

Nauru is a tiny island in the Pacific 3,000 km (2,000 miles) northeast of Australia. It is the world's smallest republic and, because of the wealth of its phosphate deposits, Nauruans enjoy one of the highest per capita incomes in the Third World. This situation is coming to an end, however. By the year 2006 the phosphate is expected to run out, and it is not clear what the people will do then.

Although little is known of the original Polynesian inhabitants of the island, it was first visited by Europeans when a British ship stopped there in 1798. Clan warfare among the Polynesians became widespread in the 1870s, leading the Germans (who then controlled the Marshall

Islands, and whose traders were active on Nauru) to incorporate it into their administration in 1888. Phosphate mining by both a German and a British company began in 1906. After the First World War the administration of Nauru passed to Australia and independence was granted in 1968. In 1970 Australia, New Zealand, and Great Britain relinquished their joint control of the phosphate industry to a Nauruan governmental agency, the Nauru Phosphate Corporation.

The island is a 20 sq km (8 sq mile) raised coral reef with a central plateau. This plateau consists of phosphate beds created by seabird droppings over many centuries. It is encircled by a fertile belt of semicultivated land where most of the people live. A ring road forms a continuous strip settlement around the coastal perimeter, where houses and other buildings occupy the only habitable land. After more than 90 years of phosphate mining, much of the rest of the island—in effect a largely worked-out quarry—has an aspect of lunar desolation. The climate is hot and humid, but because clouds sometimes miss the island, years can pass without rainfall. What little vegetation there is consists of coconut palms, breadfruit trees, and scrub.

Phosphate is the country's only resource. About 80 percent of the island is now uninhabitable and uncultivable, and food, fuel, manufactured goods, building materials, and machinery are all imported. The diet of processed foods has led to widespread obesity, and one-third of the people suffer from non-insulin-dependent diabetes. Although many Nauruans live in traditional houses, they tend to spend their considerable incomes on luxury cars and electrical goods. Much phosphate income has been invested in trust funds to serve long-term needs, but not all the investments have been wise and since 1990 dividends have fallen sharply.

New Zealand

Mountainous, partly volcanic, and situated about 1,600 km (1,000 miles) southeast of Australia, New Zealand is the biggest of the island groups of Oceania. It consists of two main islands, separated by Cook Strait, several smaller islands, and three small territories in the Pacific. The country's temperate climate has wide regional variations, the northern part of the North Island

Timeline

c.1500–1600 Maori build many *pa*, earthwork forts, to protect communities, and settle Chatham Islands	1642–43 Abel Tasman explores coasts of the islands for Dutch East India Co. Does not land and recommends no action be taken	1835 Britain establishes a protectorate over New Zealand	1852 European population 28,000, including 15,000 colonists brought in by New Zealand Co (founded 1838)	1853 New Zealand granted self-government; first provincial superintendents and councils are elected
C.AD 900 Polynesians reach New Zealand islands and settle, founding *Aotearoa*— land of the long white cloud	**c.1500–1600** Moas, large flightless birds, hunted to extinction; Maori live off seals, fish, root fern, and cultivate kumera, taro	**1769** Captain James Cook sails around both islands and claims them for Britain; Maori population 100,000	**1791** Traders from Sydney begin sealing and whaling, some settling in Bay of Islands	**1840** Treaty of Waitangi gives Britain sovereignty over New Zealand and Maori sovereignty over their lands

A sheep farm on New Zealand's North Island (bottom left). Snowcapped Mt Taranaki on the North Island (left). The kea, the world's only alpine parrot, is widespread on the South Island of New Zealand (below left).

New Zealand has limited petroleum resources, though it produces natural gas—almost a third of which is used to make synthetic petrol. There are large reserves of coal. The most important source of domestic energy is hydroelectric power, easily generated because of the favorable rainfall and terrain. This has allowed the development of aluminum production using imported bauxite. In recent years, new products have been developed for new international markets. One of these is kiwifruit, the main fresh fruit export in 1996; new varieties of high-quality apples are currently a leading export. A minor feature of the rural scene only 20 years ago, vineyards are now widespread, Marlborough, Hawke Bay, and Gisborne being the main wine-producing regions. Forest products play a vital economic role. Radiata pine, the main commercial timber, is grown in vast state pine forests. Cutting rights to parts of these have been sold and the industry as a whole widely privatized. New Zealand's varied scenery, combining quiet harbors and sunlit beaches, with volcanoes, lakes, alpine snowfields, and fiords, draws more than 1.5 million visitors per year. As a dollar-earner tourism is second only to primary industry.

being subtropical while in the southern extremity of the South Island winter snow is common.

New Zealand has a liberal and progressive political history, pioneering votes for women in 1893, introducing a welfare state including a health service in 1938, and having a creditable record in ethnic relations.

The first people to arrive in the country were the Polynesian ancestors of the Maori around 1,000 years ago. In 1642 the Dutch explorer Abel Tasman was probably the first European to sight the islands, and in 1769 Captain James Cook was the first to land. A period of settlement by whalers and sealers, and of Maori tribal warfare using modern firearms, ended when the Maori chiefs ceded sovereignty to the British Crown and the Treaty of Waitangi was signed in 1840. After this date systematic and mostly peaceful colonization took place. By the 1860s, however, conflicts over land between settlers and Maori, especially in the North Island, gave rise to outright war. When hostilities ceased in 1872 the outcome in terms of landholding was in the settlers' favor. In recent years claims for compensation to Maori have become a major political issue. 'Aotearoa' is the Maori name for New Zealand.

Geologically, New Zealand is a young country. The Southern Alps in the South Island emerged from the sea in the past 10 to 15 million years, while the volcanic action that shaped much of North Island occurred between 1 and 4 million years ago. The comparatively low ranges in North Island are formed from folded sedimentary rocks with higher volcanic peaks. Overlaying these rocks in the center of the North Island is a plateau of lava, pumice, and volcanic tuff. Minor earthquakes are common, and there are many areas of volcanic and geothermal activity on the North Island. Three volcanoes dominate the central plateau (Ruapehu being the most active) while Lake Taupo, the

country's largest natural lake, occupies an ancient crater. In the South Island the Southern Alps form a northeast–southwest oriented ice-capped central massif with Mt Cook at its center. Glaciers descend the flanks of this massif and on the rainy western side forested slopes fall steeply to the sea. On the east, broad outwash fans lead to the much drier, treeless lowlands of the Canterbury Plains. The rugged, forested coastline of the South Island's far southwest, deeply indented with fiords, comprises Fiordland, the country's largest national park.

Few landscapes have been as transformed by humans as New Zealand's. From 1850 to 1950 vast areas of forest in the North Island were cleared, leaving steep, bare hills which were sown with grass for grazing sheep. Erosion is now a serious problem in many areas. Rich pastures produced by year-round rain made agriculture the original foundation of the economy. The export of frozen mutton to Britain began in 1882, and New Zealand is still one of the world's main exporters of wool, cheese, butter, and meat. This produce goes to Australia, the USA, Japan and other parts of Asia. Since 1984 successive governments have sought to reorient the largely agrarian economy toward a more industrialized, open economy that can compete globally. This was part of a wider attempt at economic reform which aimed to reduce the role of the state and increase that of private enterprise.

Fact File

OFFICIAL NAME	New Zealand
FORM OF GOVERNMENT	Monarchy with single legislative body (House of Representatives)
CAPITAL	Wellington
AREA	268,680 sq km (103,737 sq miles)
TIME ZONE	GMT + 12 hours
POPULATION	3,662,265
PROJECTED POPULATION 2005	3,868,442
POPULATION DENSITY	13.6 per sq km (35.3 per sq mile)
LIFE EXPECTANCY	77.8
INFANT MORTALITY (PER 1,000)	6.2
OFFICIAL LANGUAGE	English
OTHER LANGUAGE	Maori
LITERACY RATE	99%
RELIGIONS	Anglican 17.5%, Roman Catholic 13%, Presbyterian 13%, other Christian 17%, other 2.5%, unaffiliated 37%
ETHNIC GROUPS	European 71.7%, Maori 14.5%, other (including Samoan, Tongan, Cook Islander, Asian) 13.8%
CURRENCY	New Zealand dollar
ECONOMY	Services 70%, industry 20%, agriculture 10%
GNP PER CAPITA	US$14,340
CLIMATE	Temperate: warmer in north, colder in south and wetter in west
HIGHEST POINT	Mt Cook 3,764 m (12,349 ft)
MAP REFERENCE	Pages 132–33

OVERSEAS TERRITORIES

Cook Islands

Niue

Tokelau

1860 Maori Wars between Maori and British over land; Maori resistance worn down after defeat at Te Ranga	**1900** Maori population down to 40,000 due to disease and warfare; European population about 1 million	**1931** Country's worst earthquake hits Hawke Bay, killing more than 250 people and devastating cities of Napier and Hastings	**1950s** Postwar boom leads to migration from rural areas to the cities by Maori	**1985** David Lange's Labour Government bans nuclear-powered and nuclear-missile carrying ships from New Zealand ports
1860 Gold rush in Otago brings European and Asian immigrants; another rush occurs in Canterbury in 1864	**1881** Refrigeration allows export of dairy produce and meat to European markets, helping to overcome economic depression	**1914** New Zealand troops join Australians in support of Allies; in 1915 they help establish ANZAC legend in landings at Gallipoli	**1939–45** New Zealand supports Allies in Europe, also raising a Third Division to aid US forces in the Pacific and defend their own country	**1975** Maori protests culminate in a Land March from the far north to Wellington

Palau

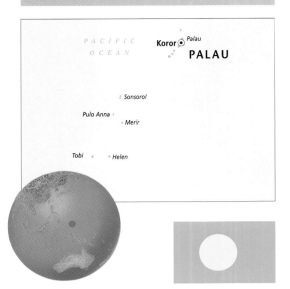

Palau consists of several groups of islands in the northwest Pacific, about 750 km (450 miles) east of the Philippine island of Mindanao. The westernmost of the Micronesian Caroline chain, and settled by Southeast Asian migrants from about 1000 BC, the islands have in the past 100 years been successively occupied and controlled by Spain, Germany, Japan, and the USA. After Spain's defeat in the 1898 Spanish–American War they were sold to Germany. Japan seized and held the islands from the outbreak of the First World War until the Second World War, when they were fought over by Japanese and US forces. In 1978 Palau rejected incorporation into the neighboring Federated States of Micronesia (a union of the rest of the Caroline Islands); in 1981 it adopted a constitution banning nuclear weapons and military bases in the area; and in 1982 it entered into a Compact of Free Association with the USA which contained military provisions in conflict with its constitution. After a lengthy political stalemate, in 1993 voters approved the Compact, which provides US$500 million in aid over 15 years in exchange for the right of the USA to maintain military facilities. In 1994 Palau became the 185th member of the UN, and in 1995 it joined the South Pacific Forum.

Palau, an archipelago of six separate groups of islands, consists of 26 islands and over 300 islets. The terrain varies from the mountainous main island of Babelthuap to low coral islands usually

fringed by reefs. Natural resources consist of forests, minerals (including gold), marine products, and deep-seabed minerals. The rural people live by subsistence agriculture, growing coconuts, cassava, and sweet potatoes (though the rugged terrain of the larger islands makes farming difficult), and by fishing. Industries include tourism, craft items made from shell, wood, and pearls, and some commercial fishing. Exports include trochus shell, tuna, copra, and handicrafts. The government is the main employer, and relies heavily on aid from the USA. As a result, the population has a per capita income twice that of the Philippines.

Fact File

OFFICIAL NAME	Republic of Palau
FORM OF GOVERNMENT	Republic in free association with the USA; two legislative bodies (Senate and House of Delegates)
CAPITAL	Koror
AREA	458 sq km (177 sq miles)
TIME ZONE	GMT + 9 hours
POPULATION	17,797
PROJECTED POPULATION 2005	19,075
POPULATION DENSITY	38.9 per sq km (100.7 per sq mile)
LIFE EXPECTANCY	71
INFANT MORTALITY (PER 1,000)	25.1
OFFICIAL LANGUAGES	Palauan, English
OTHER LANGUAGES	Sonsoral, Angaur, Japanese, Tobi
LITERACY RATE	99%
RELIGIONS	Roman Catholic 40%, indigenous Modekngei religion 27%, Protestant 25%, other 8%
ETHNIC GROUPS	Palauan (mixed Polynesian, Melanesian, Malayan) 83%, Filipino 10%, other 7%
CURRENCY	US dollar
ECONOMY	Government, agriculture, fishing, tourism
GNP PER CAPITA	US$5,000
CLIMATE	Tropical, with wet season May to November
HIGHEST POINT	Mt Ngerchelchauus 242 m (794 ft)
MAP REFERENCE	Page 138

Some of the islands of Palau, seen from the air (below). A Samoan church with a Mediterranean influence (top right). Mudmen at Mt Hagen, in the Papua New Guinea highlands (right).

Papua New Guinea

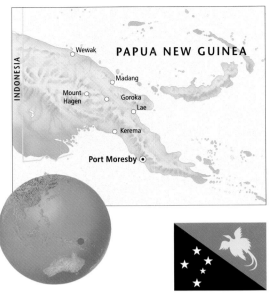

Papua New Guinea consists of the eastern half of the large island of New Guinea, the 600 or so smaller islands of the Bismarck Archipelago, and Bougainville. It lies north of northeastern Australia, just south of the equator. The largely rural population of "mainland" Papua New Guinea is made up of hundreds of distinct tribal groups, speaking more than 750 different languages. They can be broadly divided into the lowlanders of the coast and the more isolated highlanders of the mountainous interior. The main island was named New Guinea in 1545 by a Spanish explorer who thought its people resembled those of the African Guinea coast. During the last two centuries the Netherlands, Germany, Japan, and Australia have controlled parts of it at different times. The western half—West Irian (Irian Jaya)—is now part of Indonesia; the eastern half, most recently administered by Australia, became fully independent as Papua New Guinea in 1975. Australia's relationship remains close, and it contributes 20 percent of the state budget.

A cordillera of rugged mountains runs down the main island. Covered with tropical forest, these mountains have an average elevation of between 2,500 m and 4,600 m (8,000 ft and 15,000 ft). In high and isolated valleys there are settlements where people live by cultivating traditional garden crops such as sweet potato, sugar cane, bananas, maize, and cassava. Pigs are raised, but are eaten mainly at ceremonies for status and ritual purposes. Taro is a staple food of the villagers in the lowlands, where yams and sago are also grown. Soils are mostly heavily leached, and fertile only in lowland areas and upland basins. On the southwestern coast the Fly River forms a vast swampy delta plain, one of the world's biggest wetlands. The other major islands further east (New Ireland, New Britain, Manus, and Bougainville) are mainly of volcanic origin and are generally ringed by coral reefs. Nearly three-quarters of the land area of Papua New Guinea is covered with dense rainforest.

The country has a variety of natural resources but rugged terrain and high infrastructural costs make their extraction difficult. Much travel and transport is only possible by air. While most people live by subsistence agriculture, copper and gold

account for about 60 percent of export earnings. The main cash crops are coffee, cocoa, coconuts, palm kernels, tea, and rubber. Timber from the forests is also important. The government is looking to petroleum and mineral exports to drive its program of economic development, but there are social and political obstacles to be overcome. Corruption is endemic, tribal and criminal violence are high, and what was once the world's biggest copper mine—Panguna on Bougainville—has been closed for years. The Bougainville people are culturally kin to the people of the Solomons and strongly resent their domination by Papua New Guinea. Grievances over their share of the mine's earnings and compensation have become a demand for independence.

Fact File

OFFICIAL NAME Independent State of Papua New Guinea

FORM OF GOVERNMENT Constitutional monarchy with single legislative body (National Parliament or House of Assembly)

CAPITAL Port Moresby

AREA 461,690 sq km (178,258 sq miles)

TIME ZONE GMT + 10 hours

POPULATION 4,705,126

PROJECTED POPULATION 2005 5,363,582

POPULATION DENSITY 10.2 per sq km (26.4 per sq mile)

LIFE EXPECTANCY 58.5

INFANT MORTALITY (PER 1,000) 55.6

OFFICIAL LANGUAGES English, Pidgin, Motu

OTHER LANGUAGES About 750 indigenous languages

LITERACY RATE 71.2%

RELIGIONS Protestant 44% (including Lutheran 16%; Presbyterian, Methodist, London Missionary Society 8%; Anglican 5%; Evangelical Alliance 4%; other sects 11%), indigenous beliefs 34%, Roman Catholic 22%

ETHNIC GROUPS New Guinea Papuan 84%; Polynesian, Chinese, European and other 16%

CURRENCY Kina

ECONOMY Agriculture 64%, services and industry 36%

GNP PER CAPITA US$1,160

CLIMATE Tropical, with wet season December to March

HIGHEST POINT Mt Wilhelm 4,509 m (14,793 ft)

MAP REFERENCE Page 140

Samoa

The Samoan islands lie in the South Pacific about midway between Hawaii and New Zealand. Consisting of the two big islands of Savai'i and Upolu, plus seven small islands and a number of islets, Samoa is a larger island group with a much greater population than American Samoa, which lies further east, but has a more uncertain economic future.

Believed to have been originally settled by Tongans around 1000 BC, the islands of Samoa were first visited by Europeans when the French explorer Louis Antoine de Bougainville arrived in 1766. A mission was established in 1835 by the London Missionary Society. In the late nineteenth century control of the islands was contested by three colonial powers—Britain, Germany, and the USA—Germany taking control for a short period from 1899. After the First World War the islands were administered by New Zealand. In 1962 Samoa regained full independence and signed a friendship treaty with New Zealand.

Samoa is a society in which chiefly rank plays an important part, matai (men who head extended families) having a good deal more power, prestige, and authority than commoners. This system has delayed the introduction of full democracy. In 1991 the first direct elections under a universal franchise were held but only matai were allowed to be candidates.

The larger islands of Samoa are volcanic, Savai'i experiencing major eruptions in 1902 and 1911. The interiors of Savai'i and Upolu are broadly similar; their mountainous central regions are densely forested and cut by a number of fast-flowing rivers. Major streams include the Sili and Faleata on Savai'i, and the Vaisigano on Upolu. Narrow coastal plains lie between the highlands and the sea; coral reefs lie offshore. Other than arable land (19 percent), the only natural resources are hardwood forests and fish. Yams, breadfruit, banana, and papaya are grown for food, and cocoa, taro, and coconuts (for oil, copra, and cream) are cultivated for export.

Women at Maketti Fou Market in Samoa (above). A coastal village in the Solomon Islands, with some Second World War pontoons (right).

With assistance from the United Nations, fishing has also become a significant export industry. Reforestation programs have been introduced with the aim of keeping timber exports at a sustainable level. Power for industry—a Japanese automobile parts factory opened in 1991—is mainly provided by hydroelectricity.

The economy depends heavily on remittances from Samoans working overseas and on foreign aid to support a level of imports that significantly exceeds export earnings. Tourism has become the most important growth industry. Many of the more than 50,000 visitors per year come to see the house that was once lived in by the Scottish writer Robert Louis Stevenson. It is now the official residence of the Samoan Head of State.

Fact File

OFFICIAL NAME	Independent State of Samoa
FORM OF GOVERNMENT	Constitutional monarchy with single legislative body (Legislative Assembly)
CAPITAL	Apia
AREA	2,860 sq km (1,104 sq miles)
TIME ZONE	GMT – 11 hours
POPULATION	229,979
PROJECTED POPULATION 2005	261,857
POPULATION DENSITY	80.4 per sq km (208.2 per sq mile)
LIFE EXPECTANCY	69.8
INFANT MORTALITY (PER 1,000)	30.5
OFFICIAL LANGUAGES	Samoan, English
LITERACY RATE	98%
RELIGIONS	Christian 99.7% (50% associated with London Missionary Society), other 0.3%
ETHNIC GROUPS	Samoan 92.6%, mixed Polynesian–European 7%, European 0.4%
CURRENCY	Tala
ECONOMY	Agriculture 65%, services and tourism 30%, industry 5%
GNP PER CAPITA	US$1,120
CLIMATE	Tropical, wet season from December to April followed by a cooler dry season from May to November
HIGHEST POINT	Mauga Silisili 1,858 m (6,092 ft)
MAP REFERENCE	Pages 136, 141

Solomon Islands

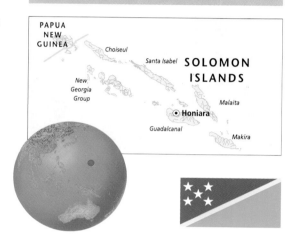

The Solomon Islands lie in the western Pacific, northeast of Australia. Inhabited by Melanesian people since about 1000 BC, they consist of two chains of islands running southeast of Bougainville. They were named by the Spanish navigator Alvaro de Mendana, who visited them in 1568 and thought he had found "the riches of Solomon." Twenty years later he returned and established a small, short-lived colony on the Santa Cruz Islands. Outside contacts were few in the ensuing centuries. In the 1870s and 1880s labor recruiters called "blackbirders" were busy inveigling islanders into working on Australian sugar plantations and their unsavory activities led Britain to establish a protectorate over the Southern Solomons in 1893.

In the Second World War the Solomons were occupied by the Japanese. The battle for Guadalcanal saw fierce fighting between Japanese and US forces, the islands overall being the scene of several major Allied naval and military victories. In recent years relations with Papua New Guinea have been strained because of the Solomon Islands' support for secessionists on Bougainville and the rebels of the Bougainville Revolutionary Army. Although Bougainville is geographically and ethnically a part of the Solomon Islands group, it has been treated politically as a part of Papua New Guinea for more than one hundred years.

Geologically, the islands represent a part of the submerged outermost crustal fold of the ancient Australian continent. Their interiors are rugged and mountainous. The six main islands—Guadalcanal, Malaita, New Georgia, Makira (formerly San

Cristobal), Santa Isabel, and Choiseul—are all of volcanic origin, and have densely forested ranges with steep-sided river valleys. Around the coasts are narrow plains where most of the population live as subsistence farmers growing beans, coconuts, palm kernels, rice, potatoes, and vegetables. Palm oil, cocoa and copra are leading agricultural exports, and tuna fish is the single biggest earner. Forestry is an important industry but the unsustainable level of timber extraction is an environmental concern. The islands are rich in undeveloped mineral resources such as lead, zinc, nickel, gold, bauxite, and phosphate—significant phosphate deposits are being mined on Bellona Island. The government is nearly insolvent and depends on foreign aid.

Fact File

OFFICIAL NAME	Solomon Islands
FORM OF GOVERNMENT	Constitutional monarchy with single legislative body (National Parliament)
CAPITAL	Honiara
AREA	28,450 sq km (10,985 sq miles)
TIME ZONE	GMT + 11 hours
POPULATION	455,429
PROJECTED POPULATION 2005	544,573
POPULATION DENSITY	16 per sq km (41.4 per sq mile)
LIFE EXPECTANCY	72.1
INFANT MORTALITY (PER 1,000)	23.0
OFFICIAL LANGUAGE	English
OTHER LANGUAGES	Pidgin, indigenous languages
LITERACY RATE	62%
RELIGIONS	Protestant 77% (including Anglican 34%, Baptist 17%, United 11%, Seventh-Day Adventist 10%), Roman Catholic 19%, indigenous beliefs 4%
ETHNIC GROUPS	Melanesian 93%, Polynesian 4%, Micronesian 1.5%, European 0.8%, other 0.7%
CURRENCY	Soloman Islands dollar
ECONOMY	Agriculture 85%, services 10%, industry 5%
GNP PER CAPITA	US$910
CLIMATE	Tropical, most rain falling November to April
HIGHEST POINT	Mt Makarakomburu 2,447 m (8,126 ft)
MAP REFERENCE	Pages 140, 141

Tonga

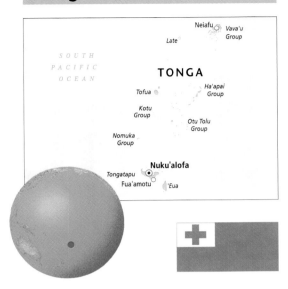

The Polynesian kingdom of Tonga consists of an archipelago of 170 islands (36 of them inhabited) northeast of New Zealand in the South Pacific. Samoa lies to the north and Fiji to the west. Inhabited since about 1000 BC, they were named the "Friendly Isles" by Captain James Cook when he visited them in the 1770s. When Wesleyan missionaries arrived in the 1820s the people quickly began to adopt Christianity. In 1900, after Germany made colonial moves toward the islands, the King of Tonga signed a Treaty of Friendship and Protection with Britain.

Tonga was never fully colonized, and its people see themselves and their royal family as unique in the Pacific. A monarchy in which the king and a small group of hereditary nobles have a permanent majority in the Legislative Assembly, Tonga is now experiencing growing demands for a more democratic form of government. Although politicians of the newly established Pro-Democracy Movement have been harrassed for sedition and defamation there are signs the king may be ready for change: in 1995 he announced that it would only be a matter of time before a fully elected government was created.

North to south Tonga's three main groups of islands are Vava'u, Ha'apai, and Tongatapu, the archipelago dividing into two parallel belts of islands. In the east there are low, fertile coralline-limestone formations. In the west the terrain is higher and volcanic, the island of Kao, north of Tofua, rising to 1,033 m (3,389 ft). Mountainous landscapes of volcanic rock are found on the Vava'u group and one island in the Ha'apai group. In 1995 a new volcanic island which had emerged from the sea was discovered in the Ha'apai group. About 25 percent of Tonga's land area is arable, but surface water is rare on the coral islands.

Most of the people of Tonga live by subsistence farming, the main food crops being yams, taro, and cassava. Two-thirds of exports come from coconuts, bananas, and vanilla beans, other cash crops being pumpkin, fruits and vegetables, cocoa, coffee, ginger, and black pepper. Despite the high level of agricultural activity a good deal of food has to be imported, most of it coming from New Zealand. In the early 1990s the economy continued to grow, largely because of a rise in pumpkin exports, increased foreign aid, and a number of construction projects. Tourism is now the main source of hard currency earnings, but Tonga remains dependent on sizeable aid funds, plus remittances from its many citizens who live and work in New Zealand, Australia, and the USA.

One of Tonga's many islands (bottom). An aerial view of Smi Island and its fringing reef, Tonga (below).

Fact File

OFFICIAL NAME Kingdom of Tonga

FORM OF GOVERNMENT Constitutional monarchy with single legislative body (Legislative Assembly)

CAPITAL Nuku'alofa

AREA 748 sq km (289 sq miles)

TIME ZONE GMT + 12 hours

POPULATION 109,082

PROJECTED POPULATION 2005 114,386

POPULATION DENSITY 145.8 per sq km (377.6 per sq mile)

LIFE EXPECTANCY 69.8

INFANT MORTALITY (PER 1,000) 37.9

OFFICIAL LANGUAGES Tongan, English

LITERACY RATE Not available

RELIGIONS Protestant 60% (including Free Wesleyan 43%, other 17%), Roman Catholic 16%, Mormon 12%, other 12%

ETHNIC GROUPS Polynesian 98%, European 2%

CURRENCY Pa'anga

ECONOMY Agriculture 70%, industry and services 30%

GNP PER CAPITA US$1,630

CLIMATE Tropical, moderated by trade winds; wettest period December to March

HIGHEST POINT Mt Kao 1,033 m (3,389 ft)

MAP REFERENCE Pages 136, 141

Tuvalu

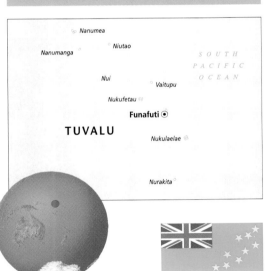

Tuvalu is a tiny Pacific island state with the world's smallest economy. It consists of five coral atolls and four reef islands, none more than 5 m (15 ft) above sea level, about midway between Hawaii and Australia. Formerly known as the Ellice Islands (and once part of the British colony of the Gilbert and Ellice Islands), they were first populated by Polynesian migrants from Samoa and Tonga some time in the fourteenth century—the language used today is a Polynesian–Samoan dialect. Though sighted by the Spanish in the sixteenth century, further European contact did not take place until the eighteenth century; it was not until 1826 that the whole group was finally discovered and mapped. In the 1860s labor recruiters known as "blackbirders" became active, either inveigling or abducting islanders for work on Fijian and Australian sugar plantations (the population fell from 20,000 in 1850 to 3,000 in 1880).

The abuses of the labor trade led the British government to annex the islands as a protectorate in 1892. Though brought together as a single administrative unit, the Micronesian Gilbertese and the Polynesian Tuvaluans were not comfortable with this arrangement, and in 1978 Tuvalu became an independent state closely linked with Britain.

Tuvalu's chain of coral islands is 579 km (360 miles) long, consisting north to south of the islands of Nanumea, Niutao, Nanumanga, Nui, Vaitupu, Nukufetau, Funafuti (the capital), Nukulaelae, and Niulakita. There are no streams or rivers, and groundwater is not drinkable. All water needs must be met by catchment systems with storage facilities. The soil is of poor quality, subsistence farming supporting 70 percent of the population. The limited range of food crops such as taro must be grown in special pits dug out of the coral. Although the islands support no export crop other than coconuts, the area of the maritime Exclusive Economic Zone is 1.2 million sq km (500,000 sq miles). The rich fishing grounds within this zone are a source of revenue from license fees paid by fishing fleets from Taiwan, Korea, and the USA. Too small, remote, and lacking in amenities to be able to establish a tourist industry, government revenues come mainly from the sale of stamps and coins and from remittances: large numbers of Tuvalu men live and work abroad, some as seamen and others mining phosphate on Nauru. The value of imports exceeds exports by 200 to 1. Substantial income is generated by an international trust fund established in 1987 by Australia, New Zealand, and the United Kingdom, which is also supported by Japan and South Korea.

Fact File

OFFICIAL NAME Tuvalu

FORM OF GOVERNMENT Constitutional monarchy with single legislative body (Parliament)

CAPITAL Funafuti

AREA 26 sq km (10 sq miles)

TIME ZONE GMT + 12 hours

POPULATION 10,588

PROJECTED POPULATION 2005 11,485

POPULATION DENSITY 407.2 per sq km (1,054.6 per sq mile)

LIFE EXPECTANCY 64.2

INFANT MORTALITY (PER 1,000) 25.5

OFFICIAL LANGUAGES Tuvaluan, English

LITERACY RATE 95%

RELIGIONS Church of Tuvalu (Congregationalist) 97%, Seventh-Day Adventist 1.4%, Baha'i 1%, other 0.6%

ETHNIC GROUPS Polynesian 97%, other 3%

CURRENCY Tuvaluan dollar, Australian dollar

ECONOMY Agriculture and fishing 70%, services 28%, industry 2%

GNP PER CAPITA US$400

CLIMATE Tropical, moderated by trade winds

HIGHEST POINT Unnamed location on Niulakita 4.6 m (15 ft)

MAP REFERENCE Page 139

Vanuatu

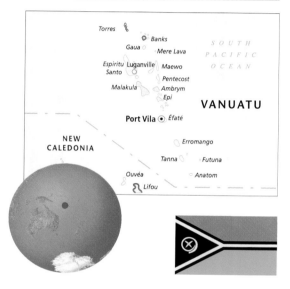

Fruit and vegetables for sale at Port Vila Market, Vanuatu (above). A wall-free house standing in a coconut grove in the Pacific islands (below right).

Vanuatu is an archipelago in the South Pacific consisting of 13 large islands and 70 islets. Part of Melanesia, it lies northeast of New Caledonia and west of Fiji. Inhabited since 5000 BC, it was first visited by Europeans when the Portuguese arrived in 1606. After Captain Cook explored the islands in 1774 he named them the New Hebrides, and they were jointly administered by France and Britain from 1887. In the late 1800s labor recruiters inveigled and sometimes kidnapped islanders for work on sugar plantations in Australia and Fiji. Aside from this, the islands remained isolated until the Second World War, when Espíritu Santo and Port Vila became major US military bases in the Pacific. In 1980 the archipelago became independent under the name Vanuatu. Since then, after surviving a secession attempt by a francophone movement on the island of Espíritu Santo, the country has had a volatile but democratic political life. Vanuatu is populated almost entirely by ethnic Melanesians speaking 105 distinct languages—the world's highest per capita density of language forms. The lingua franca is a form of pidgin known as Bislama.

Most of the islands are mountainous and volcanic in origin, with coral beaches and offshore reefs. The interior is forested, with limited land for coastal cultivation. Some 75 percent of the people live by subsistence farming, growing taro, yams, sweet potatoes, bananas, and cassava for food, as well as cash crops such as coconuts, cocoa, and coffee. Fishing is also important. Unlike most south Pacific islands, beef raising is of economic significance, livestock numbering some 130,000 head of cattle. Meat canning is an industry. Frozen beef and fish are exported. Other exports include copra, shells, coffee, and cocoa. Mineral deposits are negligible. Recently the government has emphasized tourist development (tourism is now the second largest earner of foreign exchange after copra), off-shore banking, and foreign investment, advertising Vanuatu's potential as a finance center and tax haven. There is a "flag of convenience" shipping registry of some 60 ships from 20 countries.

Fact File

OFFICIAL NAME Republic of Vanuatu

FORM OF GOVERNMENT Republic with single legislative body (Parliament)

CAPITAL Port Vila

AREA 14,760 sq km (5,699 sq miles)

TIME ZONE GMT + 11 hours

POPULATION 189,036

PROJECTED POPULATION 2005 211,781

POPULATION DENSITY 12.8 per sq km (33.1 per sq mile)

LIFE EXPECTANCY 61.4

INFANT MORTALITY (PER 1,000) 59.6

OFFICIAL LANGUAGES English, French

OTHER LANGUAGE Bislama, 105 indigenous languages

LITERACY RATE 64%

RELIGIONS Presbyterian 36.7%, Anglican 15%, Catholic 15%, indigenous beliefs 7.6%, Seventh-Day Adventist 6.2%, Church of Christ 3.8%, other 15.7%

ETHNIC GROUPS Melanesian 94%, French 4%, other (including Vietnamese, Chinese, Pacific Islanders) 2%

CURRENCY Vatu

ECONOMY Agriculture 75%, services 22%, industry 3%

GNP PER CAPITA US$1,200

CLIMATE Tropical, moderated by trade winds

HIGHEST POINT Mt Tabwemasana 1,879 m (6,158 ft)

MAP REFERENCE Pages 136, 141

Dependencies and Territories

American Samoa

A group of five volcanic islands and two atolls in the South Pacific, about midway between Hawaii and New Zealand, American Samoa has been settled by Polynesian peoples since about 800 BC. The first European contact was made by the Dutch in 1722. British missionaries were active in the region from 1830. In 1872 the USA won exclusive rights from the High Chief to use Pago Pago as a strategic base for the American fleet. Pago Pago has one of the best natural deepwater harbors in the region, sheltered by surrounding mountains from rough seas and high winds. About 90 percent of trade is with the USA, which heavily subsidizes the economy. Tuna fishing, processing, and export are the foundation of private sector economic activity.

Fact File

OFFICIAL NAME Territory of American Samoa

FORM OF GOVERNMENT Unincorporated and unorganized territory of the USA

CAPITAL Pago Pago

AREA 199 sq km (77 sq miles)

TIME ZONE GMT – 11 hours

POPULATION 66,475

LIFE EXPECTANCY 72.9

INFANT MORTALITY (PER 1,000) 18.8

LITERACY RATE 97.3%

CURRENCY US dollar

ECONOMY Fishing 34%, government 33%, other 33%

CLIMATE Tropical; wet season November to April

MAP REFERENCE Pages 136, 141

Ashmore and Cartier Islands

Uninhabited islands in the Indian Ocean northwest of Australia, Ashmore and Cartier Islands are at no point higher than 3 m (10 ft) above sea level. The terrain consists of sand and coral. The islands are surrounded by reefs and shoals that can pose a maritime hazard. The Australian government monitors the state of the Ashmore Reef National Nature Reserve. The Royal Australian Navy and Air Force make visits from time to time.

Fact File

OFFICIAL NAME Territory of Ashmore and Cartier Islands

FORM OF GOVERNMENT External territory of Australia

CAPITAL None; administered from Canberra

AREA 5 sq km (2 sq miles)

TIME ZONE GMT + 8 hours

POPULATION No permanent population

CLIMATE Tropical

MAP REFERENCE Page 134

Baker and Howland Islands

Baker Island is an uninhabited atoll in the North Pacific, midway between Hawaii and Australia.

The terrain consists of a low coral island surrounded by a narrow reef. Climate is equatorial with little rain, constant wind, and burning sun. Used by the US military during the Second World War, it is now mainly a nesting habitat for seabirds and marine wildlife. Howland Island is an uninhabited atoll nearby. Another low coral island surrounded by a narrow reef, it has no fresh water. Entry to Baker and Howland Islands is by special-use permit only.

Fact File

OFFICIAL NAME Baker and Howland Islands

FORM OF GOVERNMENT Unincorporated territory of the USA

CAPITAL None; administered from Washington DC

AREA 3 sq km (1.2 sq miles)

TIME ZONE GMT – 10 hours

POPULATION No permanent population

CLIMATE Hot, dry, and windy

MAP REFERENCE Page 139

Christmas Island

A small island in the Indian Ocean, Christmas Island is about 300 km (200 miles) south of Java. Coastal cliffs rise steeply to a central plateau. Formerly uninhabited, Chinese and Malayan labor was brought in to mine the island's rich phosphate deposits in the 1890s, and from 1900 the people enjoyed something of an economic boom. The mine now operates under strict environmental controls to preserve remaining rainforest. After heavy Australian government investment in infrastructure, a hotel and casino complex was opened in 1993, drawing visitors mainly from Southeast Asia.

Fact File

OFFICIAL NAME Territory of Christmas Island

FORM OF GOVERNMENT External territory of Australia

CAPITAL The Settlement

AREA 135 sq km (52 sq miles)

TIME ZONE GMT + 7 hours

POPULATION 1,906 (1996)

LIFE EXPECTANCY Not available

INFANT MORTALITY (PER 1,000) Not available

LITERACY RATE Not available

CURRENCY Australian dollar

ECONOMY Mining, tourism

CLIMATE Tropical, moderated by trade winds

MAP REFERENCE Page 134

Oceania

Cocos (Keeling) Islands

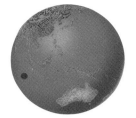

The Cocos (Keeling) Islands are a group of 27 coral atolls in the Indian Ocean midway between Australia and Sri Lanka. When discovered in 1609 by the East India Company's Captain William Keeling they were uninhabited. In 1827 the Scot John Clunies-Ross brought some Malays with him and established a settlement. The inhabited islands today are Home Island, where the Cocos Malays live, and West Island, with a small European community. The group has been administered directly by the Australian government since a referendum in 1984. Coconuts are the sole cash crop, copra and fresh coconuts the major export earners. Though local gardens and fishing make a contribution, additional food and other necessities must come from Australia.

Fact File

OFFICIAL NAME Territory of Cocos (Keeling) Islands

FORM OF GOVERNMENT External territory of Australia

CAPITAL West Island

AREA 14 sq km (5.4 sq miles)

TIME ZONE GMT + 7 hours

POPULATION 655 (1996)

LIFE EXPECTANCY Not available

INFANT MORTALITY (PER 1,000) Not available

LITERACY RATE Not available

CURRENCY Australian dollar

ECONOMY Coconut and copra production

CLIMATE Tropical, moderated by trade winds

MAP REFERENCE Page 134

Cook Islands

About 3,500 km (2,175 miles) northeast of New Zealand, the Cook Islands consist of 24 widely separated coral atolls in the north, and hilly, vol-canic islands in the south. The Polynesian inhabitants are believed to have settled the islands around AD 500 to 800. They were visited by the Spanish in 1595; explored by Captain James Cook in 1773 and 1777; Christianized by British missionaries

Pristine waters off the Cook Islands (right). Bora Bora resort and lagoon on the Society Islands (top right). The peaks of Anau and Nunue Bora Bora, French Polynesia (center right). Looking out over the city and bay, Guam (far right).

after 1821; and annexed to New Zealand in 1901. Since independence in 1965 the islands have been self-governing in free association with New Zealand. They have a fully responsible government, with elections every five years to a 25-member parliament, based on full adult suffrage. The climate is tropical with plentiful rainfall. Agriculture provides the economic base, and the main export earners are fruit, copra, and clothing. Marine culture has recently led to the production of black pearls and trochus shell. Financial services are available. New Zealand is both the main trading partner (taking 96 percent of exports) and the source of substantial aid. Tourism is expanding.

Fact File

OFFICIAL NAME Cook Islands

FORM OF GOVERNMENT Self-governing territory of New Zealand

CAPITAL Avarua

AREA 240 sq km (93 sq miles)

TIME ZONE GMT – 10 hours

POPULATION 20,200

LIFE EXPECTANCY 71.1

INFANT MORTALITY (PER 1,000) 24.7

LITERACY RATE Not available

CURRENCY New Zealand dollar

ECONOMY Agriculture, services, industry

CLIMATE Tropical, moderated by trade winds

MAP REFERENCE Pages 136–37, 139

Coral Sea Islands

These uninhabited sandy islands and coral reefs are located in the Coral Sea northeast of Australia's Great Barrier Reef. The numerous small islands and reefs are scattered over a sea area of about 1 million sq km (386,000 sq miles), with Willis Islets the most important. Nowhere more

than 6 m (20 ft) above sea level, the area is an important nesting area for seabirds and turtles. There are no permanent freshwater resources and the islands are occasionally subject to cyclones. Although there are no indigenous inhabitants, three meteorologists are stationed there. Defense is the responsibility of Australia, the islets being regularly visited by the Royal Australian Navy. Australia controls the activities of visitors.

Fact File

OFFICIAL NAME Coral Sea Islands Territory

FORM OF GOVERNMENT External territory of Australia

CAPITAL None; administered from Canberra

AREA 3 sq km (1.2 sq miles)

TIME ZONE GMT + 10 hours

POPULATION No permanent population

CLIMATE Tropical

MAP REFERENCE Page 135

with employment, high wages, and improved infrastructure, and resulted in 70 percent of the population moving to live on Tahiti. Tourism now accounts for 20 percent of the gross domestic product. Cultured pearls are the main export.

Uninhabited Clipperton Island, a coral atoll in the Pacific Ocean west of Mexico, is administered by France from French Polynesia.

Guam

Fact File

OFFICIAL NAME Territory of Guam

FORM OF GOVERNMENT Organized, unincorporated territory of the USA

CAPITAL Agana

AREA 541 sq km (209 sq miles)

TIME ZONE GMT + 10 hours

POPULATION 167,590

LIFE EXPECTANCY 74.3

INFANT MORTALITY (PER 1,000) 15.2

LITERACY RATE 99%

CURRENCY US dollar

ECONOMY Services and tourism 54%, government 40%, other 6%

CLIMATE Tropical, moderated by trade winds; wet season July to October

MAP REFERENCE Page 138

The largest and most southerly of the Mariana Islands in the northwest Pacific, Guam lies about 2,000 km (1,200 miles) due east of Manila in the Philippines. Originally settled by Malay-Filipino peoples around 1500 BC, Guam was mapped by Ferdinand Magellan in 1521, claimed by Spain from 1565, and administered by the USA from 1899 after Spain's defeat in the Spanish-American War. Of volcanic origin, Guam consists of a relatively flat coralline limestone plateau (the

source of most fresh water), with steep coastal cliffs and narrow coastal plains in the north, low-rising hills in the center, and mountains in the south. About half its population are Chamorro, of mixed Indonesian, Spanish, and Filipino descent. The island is of great strategic importance to the USA and about one-third of its land is occupied by American naval and airforce facilities. This has resulted in a high standard of living, and there are concerns about the unemployment that is likely to follow the planned closing of four naval installations. As a Pacific tourist destination Guam is second only to Hawaii.

Jarvis Island

Fact File

OFFICIAL NAME Jarvis Island

FORM OF GOVERNMENT Unincorporated territory of the USA

CAPITAL None; administered from Washington DC

AREA 4.5 sq km (1.7 sq miles)

TIME ZONE GMT – 10 hours

POPULATION No permanent population

CLIMATE Hot, dry, and windy

MAP REFERENCE Page 139

An uninhabited island in the South Pacific, Jarvis Island lies about midway between Hawaii and the Cook Islands. A sandy coral islet with a fringing reef, it has a tropical climate with little rain and no fresh water. Guano deposits were worked until late in the nineteenth century, and Millersville settlement on the west of the island was used as a weather station from 1935 until the Second World War. Ground cover consists of sparse bunch grass, prostrate vines, and low-growing shrubs. The island is mainly a nesting place for seabirds and marine wildlife. Entry is by special-use permit only.

French Polynesia

Fact File

OFFICIAL NAME Territory of French Polynesia

FORM OF GOVERNMENT Overseas territory of France

CAPITAL Papeete

AREA 4,167 sq km (1,609 sq miles)

TIME ZONE GMT – 10 hours

POPULATION 242,073

LIFE EXPECTANCY 72.3

INFANT MORTALITY (PER 1,000) 13.6

LITERACY RATE Not available

CURRENCY CFP (Comptoirs Français du Pacifique) franc

ECONOMY Services 68%, industry 19%, agriculture 13%

CLIMATE Tropical

MAP REFERENCE Page 137

French Polynesia comprises five archipelagoes in the South Pacific, midway between Australia and South America, scattered over an area of ocean as large as Europe. They include the Society Islands (Archipel de la Société), the Marquesas (Îles Marquises), the Tubuai Islands, and the Tuamotus (Archipel des Tuamotu). The Polynesian inhabitants first settled the islands about 2,000 years ago. European contact dates from 1767. The conversion of the islanders to Christianity began in 1797 and after three years of armed resistance the chiefs of Tahiti accepted French colonial control in 1843. The islands send two deputies and a senator to the French Assembly in Paris, and since 1984 have had a local territorial assembly as well. Famous for providing the artist Gauguin with his best-known subjects, French Polynesia has been in the news more recently as a site for French nuclear testing on the atoll of Mururoa. This ceased in 1995. Large military expenditures over the preceding 30 years have provided the islands

Johnston Atoll

Fact File

OFFICIAL NAME Johnston Atoll

FORM OF GOVERNMENT Unincorporated territory of
the USA

CAPITAL None; administered from Washington DC

AREA 2.8 sq km (1.1 sq miles)

TIME ZONE GMT – 10 hours

POPULATION No permanent population

ECONOMY US military base

CLIMATE Hot, dry, and windy

MAP REFERENCE Page 139

This remote coral atoll consisting of two islets, Johnston Island and Sand Island, lies in the North Pacific about one-third of the way between Hawaii and the Marshall Islands. The atoll is 5 m (16 ft) above sea level at its highest point and has a dry tropical climate, northeast trade winds ensuring little seasonal temperature variation. Mined during the nineteenth century for its extensive guano deposits, the atoll is now home to approximately 1,200 US military personnel. It was formerly used as a nuclear weapons testing site. The territory is administered by the US Defense Nuclear Agency and managed cooperatively by the DNA and the Fish and Wildlife Service of the US Department of the Interior as part of the National Wildlife Refuge system.

Kingman Reef

A barren triangular-shaped reef in the North Pacific, Kingman Reef is about halfway between Hawaii and American Samoa. No more than 1 m (3 ft) above sea level, and awash most of the time, the reef is a maritime hazard. Although no economic activity takes place and the reef is uninhabited, the deep interior lagoon was used as a halfway station between Hawaii and American Samoa when Pan American Airways used flying boats in the Pacific in 1937 and 1938. While there is no land flora, the reef is rich in marine life. It is administered by the US Navy.

An aerial view of Amadee Island, New Caledonia (right). Historic colonial buildings and ruins on Norfolk Island (top right). Clear blue waters form an inlet on the South Pacific island of Niue (bottom right).

Fact File

OFFICIAL NAME Kingman Reef

FORM OF GOVERNMENT Unincorporated territory of
the USA

CAPITAL None; administered from Washington DC

AREA 1 sq km (0.4 sq miles)

TIME ZONE GMT – 10 hours

POPULATION No permanent population

CLIMATE Tropical, moderated by sea breezes

MAP REFERENCE Page 139

Midway Islands

The two Midway Islands constitute part of an atoll in the northern Pacific at the extreme western end of the Hawaiian chain, 1,931 km (1,200 miles) northwest of Hawaii. Their name derives from their position midway along the old shipping route from California to Japan.

The atoll is almost completely flat, and none of the land is higher than 4 m (13 ft) above sea level. During the Second World War it was the scene of a major battle between Japan and the USA, and today it is used as a naval airbase. It is also a wildlife refuge. The islands have no indigenous inhabitants and the population is confined to about 450 US military personnel and civilian contractors. They are serviced by the port of Sand Island, Johnston Atoll.

Fact File

OFFICIAL NAME Midway Islands

FORM OF GOVERNMENT Unincorporated territory of
the USA

CAPITAL None; administered from Washington DC

AREA 5.2 sq km (1.9 sq miles)

TIME ZONE GMT – 10 hours

POPULATION No permanent population

ECONOMY US military base

CLIMATE Tropical, moderated by sea breezes

MAP REFERENCE Page 139

New Caledonia

Fact File

OFFICIAL NAME Territory of New Caledonia and Dependencies

FORM OF GOVERNMENT Overseas territory of France

CAPITAL Nouméa

AREA 19,060 sq km (7,359 sq miles)

TIME ZONE GMT + 11 hours

POPULATION 197,361

LIFE EXPECTANCY 75.4

INFANT MORTALITY (PER 1,000) 12.2

LITERACY RATE 93.1%

CURRENCY CFP (Comptoirs Français du Pacifique) franc

ECONOMY Services 40%, agriculture 32%, industry 28%

CLIMATE Tropical, moderated by trade winds

MAP REFERENCE Pages 136, 141

New Caledonia is a group of islands 1,500 km (900 miles) off the northeast coast of Australia. Rich in minerals, and with more than 40 percent of the world's known nickel resources, it is France's largest overseas territory. First populated by indigenous Kanaks (who call the land Kanaky) around 4000 BC, the islands were visited by the Spanish in the sixteenth and seventeenth centuries, were named by Captain James Cook in 1774, and were used as a penal settlement by France between 1853 and 1897. By the end of the nineteenth century French settlers owned more than 90 percent of the land. Dissatisfaction with their situation led to violent resistance from the Kanaks during the 1970s and 1980s, but more recently they have come to accept French rule. The Kanaks now represent only 43 percent of the population, while 37 percent are of European descent. The main island, Grand Terre, consists of coastal plains with a mountainous interior. Only a small amount of land is suitable for cultivation. New Caledonia's prosperity is almost entirely dependent on nickel production, so the economy is at the mercy of varying world demand. Tourism from France, Japan, and Australia is also important.

Niue

Niue is one of the world's biggest coral atolls, lying about 700 km (400 miles) east of Tonga in the South Pacific. The terrain consists of a central limestone plateau with steep cliffs around the coast; the highest point is 68 m (223 ft). The economy is heavily dependent on aid from the New Zealand government. Most of the inhabitants live by subsistence farming. Light industry consists of processing passionfruit, lime oil, honey, and coconut cream. The sale of postage stamps and tourism are also a source of foreign currency. Remittances from family members living overseas supplement domestic income: lack of employment opportunities on the island means that five out of six of the people of Niue live and work in New Zealand.

Fact File

OFFICIAL NAME Niue

FORM OF GOVERNMENT Self-governing territory in free association with New Zealand

CAPITAL Alofi

AREA 260 sq km (100 sq miles)

TIME ZONE GMT – 11 hours

POPULATION 2,321 (1994)

LIFE EXPECTANCY Not available

INFANT MORTALITY (PER 1,000) Not available

LITERACY RATE Not available

CURRENCY New Zealand dollar

ECONOMY Agriculture, industry (food processing, coconuts), services

CLIMATE Tropical, moderated by trade winds

MAP REFERENCE Pages 132, 136

Norfolk Island

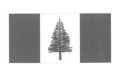

Some 1,400 km (850 miles) east of Australia, Norfolk Island is inhabited by descendants of the famous mutineers from HMS *Bounty*. Of volcanic origin, the island was uninhabited when discovered by Captain James Cook in 1774. After serving as a penal settlement in Australia's early history it became a refuge for the entire population of the Pitcairn Islands' *Bounty* mutiny survivors, who were resettled there in 1856. (Some later returned to live on Pitcairn Island.) The present inhabitants speak a mixture of nineteenth century English, Gaelic, and Old Tahitian. They enjoy a degree of autonomy and have rejected proposals to become a part of the Australian state. While there is no income tax, the government raises revenue from customs duty, liquor sales, a public works levy, financial institutions levy, and departure fees. Tourism is the main activity, the island receiving around 30,000 visitors each year.

Fact File

OFFICIAL NAME Territory of Norfolk Island

FORM OF GOVERNMENT External territory of Australia

CAPITAL Kingston

AREA 35 sq km (14 sq miles)

TIME ZONE GMT + 11.5 hours

POPULATION 2,756 (1995)

LIFE EXPECTANCY Not available

INFANT MORTALITY (PER 1,000) Not available

LITERACY RATE Not available

CURRENCY Australian dollar

ECONOMY Tourism, agriculture

CLIMATE Subtropical

MAP REFERENCE Pages 133, 136

Northern Mariana Islands

Spanish, and Filipino), Micronesians, Japanese, Chinese, and Koreans. The economy is substantially supported by the USA. Tourism is a fast-growing source of income, employing increasing numbers of the workforce and bringing in most revenue. Cattle ranches produce beef, and small farms produce coconuts, breadfruit, tomatoes, and melons. Industry consists of handicrafts, light manufacturing, and garment production.

A privately owned uninhabited atoll in the northern Pacific, Palmyra Atoll lies about halfway between Hawaii and Samoa. At no point more than 2 m (6 ft) above sea level, the atoll consists of about 50 islets covered with dense vegetation, coconut palms, and balsa-like trees that grow up to 30 m (100 ft) tall. A number of roads and causeways were built during the Second World War, but they are now overgrown and unserviceable, as is the airstrip. In 1990 a Hawaiian property developer took out a 75-year lease from its owners, the Fullard-Leo brothers. There are plans to turn the atoll into a "get away from it all" tourist complex.

Fact File

OFFICIAL NAME Commonwealth of the Northern Mariana Islands

FORM OF GOVERNMENT Territory of the USA; commonwealth in political union with the USA

CAPITAL Saipan

AREA 477 sq km (184 sq miles)

TIME ZONE GMT + 10 hours

POPULATION 69,343

LIFE EXPECTANCY 76

INFANT MORTALITY (PER 1,000) 6.5

LITERACY RATE Not available

CURRENCY US dollar

ECONOMY Tourism, industry, agriculture

CLIMATE Tropical, moderated by trade winds

MAP REFERENCE Page 138

These islands are located in the North Pacific about three-quarters of the way between Hawaii and the Philippines. Unlike the nearby Caroline Islands, the Northern Marianas chose not to seek independence in 1987, preferring to remain part of the USA. There are 14 main islands including Saipan, Rota, and Tinian. The southern islands are limestone with level terraces and fringing coral reefs; the northern islands are volcanic, with active volcanoes on Pagan and Agrihan. There is little seasonal variation in the tropical marine climate, as the temperature is moderated by northeast trade winds. The people of the islands belong to a variety of ethnic groups and include Chamorros (mixed Indonesian,

Palmyra Atoll

Fact File

OFFICIAL NAME Palmyra Atoll

FORM OF GOVERNMENT Incorporated territory of the USA

CAPITAL None; administered from Washington DC

AREA 12 sq km (4.6 sq miles)

TIME ZONE GMT – 10 hours

POPULATION No permanent population

CLIMATE Tropical

MAP REFERENCE Page 139

Pitcairn Islands

Fact File

OFFICIAL NAME Pitcairn, Henderson, Ducie, and Oeno Islands

FORM OF GOVERNMENT Dependent territory of the United Kingdom

CAPITAL Adamstown

AREA 47 sq km (18 sq miles)

TIME ZONE GMT – 8.5 hours

POPULATION 54 (1995)

LIFE EXPECTANCY Not available

INFANT MORTALITY (PER 1,000) Not available

LITERACY RATE Not available

CURRENCY New Zealand dollar

ECONOMY Fishing, agriculture, services

CLIMATE Tropical, with rainy season from November to March

MAP REFERENCE Page 137

The Pitcairn Islands are located in the southern Pacific about midway between Peru and New Zealand. They have a rugged volcanic formation, cliffs along a rocky coast, and a tropical, hot, and humid climate. The islands are the United Kingdom's most isolated dependency. Uninhabited when they were discovered by Europeans, they were used as a refuge by the mutineers from HMS *Bounty* in 1790, some of whose descendants still live there speaking a dialect that is part-Tahitian, part-English. They exist by fishing and subsistence farming. The fertile valley soils produce fruits and vegetables including citrus, sugarcane, watermelons, bananas, yams, and beans. Barter is an important economic activity. The main source of revenue is the sale of postage stamps and handicrafts to passing ships.

Newly harvested coconuts are piled on a beach in the Pacific Islands (left). Bananas are widely grown on Pacific Islands like Tokelau (above left).

Tokelau

Fact File

OFFICIAL NAME Tokelau

FORM OF GOVERNMENT Territory of New Zealand

CAPITAL None; administrative center on each atoll

AREA 10 sq km (3.9 sq miles)

TIME ZONE GMT – 11 hours

POPULATION 1,503 (1995)

LIFE EXPECTANCY Not available

INFANT MORTALITY (PER 1,000) Not available

LITERACY RATE Not available

CURRENCY New Zealand dollar

ECONOMY Agriculture, industry

CLIMATE Tropical, moderated by trade winds April to November

MAP REFERENCE Page 139

Tokelau is a small group of islands in the South Pacific about midway between Hawaii and New Zealand. The islands consist of low coral atolls, no higher than 5 m (16 ft) above sea level, enclosing large lagoons. Lying in the Pacific typhoon belt (a cyclone in 1990 wrecked much of Tokelau's infrastructure), they have a tropical climate moderated by trade winds. There are limited natural resources, subsistence farmers growing coconuts, breadfruit, papaya, and bananas. Small-scale industry produces copra, woodwork, plaited craft goods, stamps, and coins. A tuna cannery is expected to help the economy, and it is hoped that a catamaran link between the atolls will boost tourism. Aid from New Zealand is the main source of revenue and money remitted by relatives in New Zealand is a vital source of domestic income.

Wake Island

Wake Island is located in the North Pacific about two-thirds of the way between Hawaii and the Northern Mariana Islands. It consists of three tiny coral islets linked by causeways around a lagoon. The islets are built on fragments of the rim of an extinct underwater volcano, the lagoon being the former crater. With no indigenous inhabitants or economic activity, the 300 or so US military personnel stationed on Wake Island provide help in the case of emergency landings by aircraft on transpacific flights.

The problem of coral bleaching

Coral reefs constitute one of the Earth's great diverse ecosystems. They are made of limestone formed by millions of tiny marine animals and can only live in tropical seas within a narrow range of physical and chemical conditions. Coral reefs generally form only when winter water temperatures exceed 18°C (64°F) and when light levels are high. Coral is found in the rock record in the form of fossils dating back to the Paleozoic Era. However, although coral has survived this long, it is not immune to the impact of human activities.

In recent years scientists have become interested in the apparent link between the death of large tracts of coral in the Pacific and Caribbean regions and global warming. The greenhouse effect—a result of changes in the amounts of carbon dioxide and other gases in the atmosphere since the industrial revolution—is the cause of this global warming. Satellite data from the US National Oceanographic and Atmospheric Administration show a warming trend in sea-surface temperatures since 1982. In some areas, such as along the Great Barrier Reef in Australia, a combination of higher than usual summer temperatures and the run-off from floods (which reduces salinity) appears to be damaging the coral. As the essential conditions required for the maintenance of a healthy reef system are disrupted, the coral formations turn white.

What will happen to coral reefs in the future? Are the bleaching episodes observed in recent years in so many tropical areas really due to global warming or are there other causes? Predictions that ocean surface temperatures in the tropics may rise by up to 5°C (41°F) in the 21st century are no longer considered fantasy. If this happens, it could greatly disturb even resilient ecosystems, such as coral reefs, and reduce the Earth's biodiversity as well as the ability of societies to live and work in these areas.

Fact File

OFFICIAL NAME Wake Island

FORM OF GOVERNMENT Unincorporated territory of the USA

CAPITAL None; administered from Washington DC

AREA 6.5 sq km (2.5 sq miles)

TIME ZONE GMT – 10 hours

POPULATION No permanent population

ECONOMY US military base

CLIMATE Tropical

MAP REFERENCE Page 138

Wallis and Futuna Islands

This group comprises three main islands—Futuna, Alofi and Wallis (Uvea)—and 20 islets, located west of Samoa and northeast of Fiji. They are of volcanic origin, with low hills rising to 765 m (2,510 ft) at Mt Singavi. All the main islands have fringing reefs. In the hot wet season from November to April 2,500–3,000 mm (100–120 in) of rain may fall. This rain, combined with deforestation (timber is used locally for fuel), has eroded the terrain of Futuna. The people live by subsistence farming. Exports are negligible and French aid is essential to the islands. First settled perhaps 2,000 years ago, and visited by the Dutch in 1616, the islands became a French protectorate in 1886. In a referendum on independence in 1959 they chose to become a French Overseas Territory. There is no independence movement.

Fact File

OFFICIAL NAME Territory of the Wallis and Futuna Islands

FORM OF GOVERNMENT Overseas territory of France

CAPITAL Mata Utu

AREA 274 sq km (106 sq miles)

TIME ZONE GMT + 12 hours

POPULATION 15,129

LIFE EXPECTANCY Not available

INFANT MORTALITY (PER 1,000) Not available

LITERACY RATE Not available

CURRENCY CFP (Comptoirs Français du Pacifique) franc

ECONOMY Agriculture, fishing

CLIMATE Tropical, with wet season November to April

MAP REFERENCE Page 139

Oceania: Physical

Oceania

A · 120° · B · 130° · C · 140° · D · 150° · E · 160°

CELEBES SEA

Borneo

Sonsorol
Pulo Anna
Merir

Tobi
Helen

Namoluk
Mortlock Is Lukunor
Ngatik

Caroline Island

Nukuoro

Kep. Togian

MOLUCCA SEA

Halmahera

Waigeo

Biak

Yapen

Ninego Group Kaniet Is
Manus
Admiralty
Islands

St Matthias
Group

New Hanover

Kapingamarangi
Atoll

Melanesia

Solomon Islands

Nukum

Sulawesi
(Celebes)

CERAM SEA

Buru

Seram

Laut

JAVA
SEA

Buton

BANDA
SEA

Kai
Besar

Kep. Aru

New Guinea

Mt Wilhelm
4509 m

BISMARCK
SEA

New Ireland

New
Britain

Bougainville

Nuguria Is
Green Is

Buka Tauu Is

Ontong
Java

Choiseul

SOLOMON

Santa Isabel Mala

Kep. Kangean

Selayar

Jawa
(Java)

Bali Lombok
Sumbawa

Flores

Timor

Kep.
Babar

Kep. Tanimbar

Kep.
Sermata

Dolak

Mt Victoria
4038 m

Owen Stanley Range

Gulf of
Papua

Lake
Murra

Trobriand Is
Woodlark

Louisiade Arch.

New Georgia
Group

SEA

Guadalcanal

Maki

Bellona

Rennell

Sumba

Sawu Roti

ARAFURA SEA

Tagula Rossel

Melville I.

Wessel Is

Prince of
Wales I

Torres Strait

C. York

Cape
York
Peninsula

Cape
Melville

Coral Sea
Islands

CORAL

SEA

Cape Londonderry

Joseph
Bonaparte
Gulf

Daly

Arnhem
Land

Groote
Eylandt

Gulf
of
Carpentaria

Great Barrier Reef

Hinchinbrook
Island

Îles
Chesterfield

TIMOR
SEA

Kimberley
Plateau

Lake
Argyle

Victoria

Tanami

Barkly

Great Dividing Range

Whitsunday Group

Great Sandy

Desert

Desert

Tableland

Torilla Pen.

Barrow I.
North West
Cape

Pilbara

Hamersley Range

Ashburton

Tropic of Capricorn

Lake
Mackay

Lake
Disappointment

MacDonnell Ranges

Great Artesian

Diamantina

Hervey Bay

Sandy Cape
Fraser I.

Shark
Bay

Mt Augustus
1105 m

Murchison

Gibson Desert

Australia

863 m
Uluru (Ayers Rock)

Simpson

Basin

Cooper

Moreton I.
North Stradbroke I.

Lake
Carnegie

Desert

Strzelecki

Grey Range

Paroo

Lake Eyre
North

Lake Eyre
South

Desert

Great Victoria

Lake
Barlee

Lake
Frome

Darling

Lord Howe I.

Desert

Lake
Torrens

Lake
Macfarlane

Lachlan

Great Dividing Range

Lake
Moore

Darling
Range

Nullarbor Plain

Lake
Gairdner

Eyre
Pen.

Murrumbidgee

Cape Hawke

Botany Bay

Cape Leeuwin
Point
d'Entrecasteaux

Cape Pasley

Great

Australian Bight

Spencer Gulf

Murray

Jervis Bay

TASMAN

Kangaroo I.

Encounter Bay

Cape
Jaffa

Glenelg

Mt Kosciuszko
2229 m

Cape Howe

SEA

Cape Otway

Bass Strait

Furneaux

King I.

Cape Grim

Flinders I.
Group

Tasmania

Mt Ossa
1617 m

Macquarie
Harbour

Great
Oyster Bay

South Bruny I.

South East
Cape

SOUTHERN OCEAN

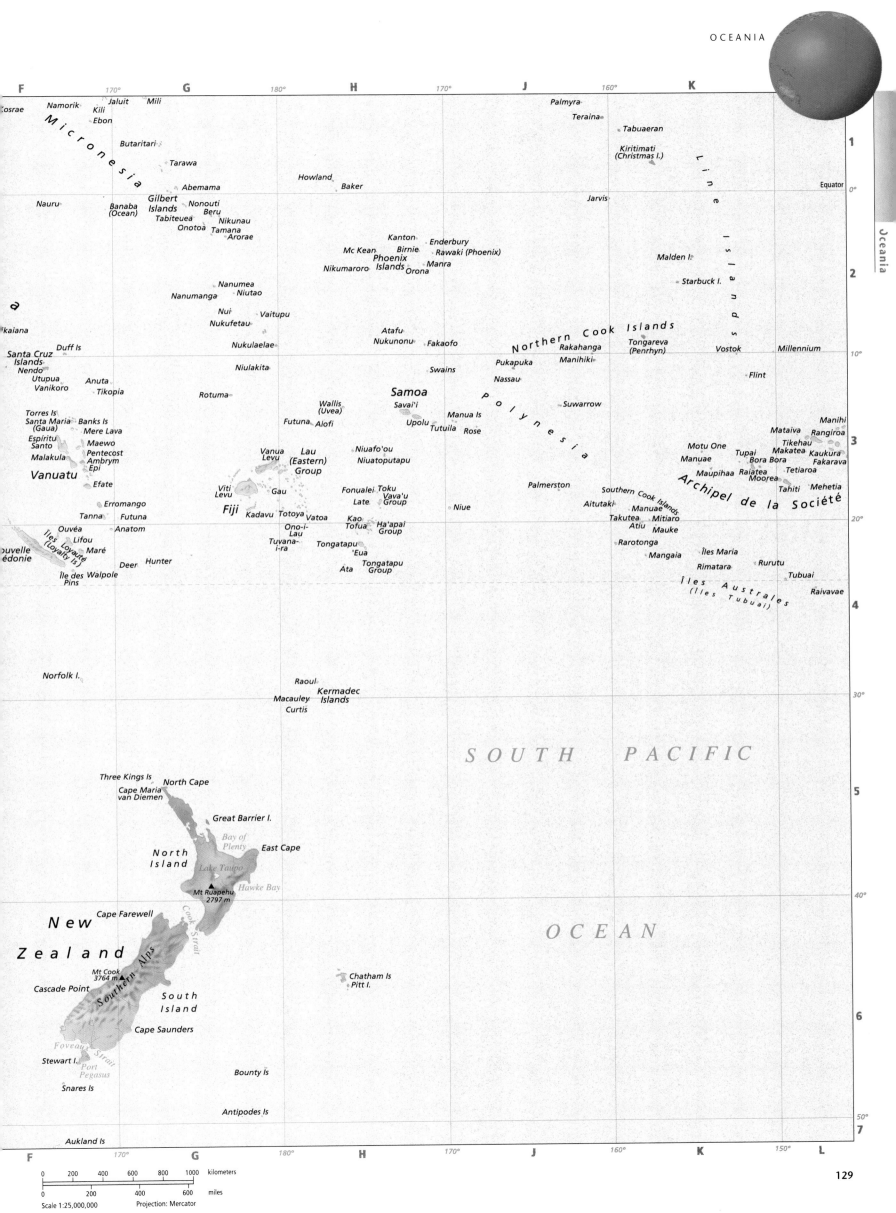

F | 170° | G | 180° | H | 170° | J | 160° | K

Kosrae Namorik Kili Jaluit Mili
Micronesia Ebon
Butaritari
Tarawa
Abemama Howland Baker Equator
Nauru Banaba Gilbert Nonouti Beru
(Ocean) Islands Tabiteuea Nikunau
Onotoa Tamana Arorae
Kanton Enderbury Palmyra Teraina
Mc Kean Birnie Rawaki (Phoenix) Tabuaeran
Nikumaroro Phoenix Manra Kiritimati
Islands Orona (Christmas I.)
Nanumea Jarvis
Nanumanga Niutao
Malden I.
Nui Vaitupu Starbuck I.
Nukufetau
Ikaiana Atafu
Duff Is Nukulaelae Nukunonu Fakaofo Northern Cook Islands
Santa Cruz Niulakita Rakahanga Vostok Millennium
Islands Pukapuka Manihiki Tongareva
Nendo Swains (Penrhyn)
Utupua Anuta Nassau Flint
Vanikoro Tikopia Rotuma Samoa
Torres Is Savai'i Suwarrow Manihi
Santa Maria Banks Is Wallis Mataiva Rangiroa
(Gaua) Mere Lava (Uvea) Upolu Manua Is Tikehau
Espíritu Maewo Futuna Alofi Tutuila Rose Motu One Tupai Makatea Kaukura
Santo Pentecost Polynesia Manuae Bora Bora Fakarava
Malakula Ambrym Vanua Lau Niuafo'ou Maupihaa Raiatea Tetiaroa
Epi Levu (Eastern) Niuatoputapu Moorea
Vanuatu Efate Group Tahiti Mehetia
Viti Fonualei Toku Palmerston Archipel de la Société
Erromango Levu Gau Late Vava'u Southern Cook Islands
Tanna Futuna Fiji Kadavu Totoya Vatoa Group Aitutaki Manuae
Ouvéa Anatom Kao Niue Takutea Mitiaro
Îles Loyauté Lifou Ono-i- Tofua Ha'apai Atiu Mauke
Nouvelle (Loyalty Is) Maré Tuvana- Lau Group Rarotonga Îles Maria
Calédonie i-ra Tongatapu Mangaia Rimatara Rurutu
Île des Deer Hunter 'Eua Tubuai
Pins Walpole Ata Tongatapu Îles Australes Raivavae
Group (Îles Tubuai)

Norfolk I.

Raoul Kermadec
Macauley Islands
Curtis

SOUTH PACIFIC

Three Kings Is North Cape
Cape Maria
van Diemen Great Barrier I.
Bay of
Plenty East Cape
North Lake Taupo
Island Hawke Bay
Mt Ruapehu
2797 m
Cape Farewell
New
Zealand Cook Strait OCEAN
Mt Cook Chatham Is
3764 m Pitt I.
Cascade Point Southern Alps South
Island
Cape Saunders

Stewart I. Foveaux Strait
Port
Pegasus Bounty Is
Snares Is

Antipodes Is

Aukland Is

F | 170° | G | 180° | H | 170° | J | 160° | K | 150° | L

0 200 400 600 800 1000 kilometers
0 200 400 600 miles
Scale 1:25,000,000 Projection: Mercator

Oceania: Political

BRUNEI
PHILIPPINES
Sonsorol
PALAU
Namoluk Ngatik
Mortlock Is Lukunor
MALAYSIA
Caroline Island
Nukuoro
MICRONESIA
CELEBES
SEA
Tobi
Helen
Kot
Kapingamarangi
Atoll
Borneo
Halmahera
Waigeo
MOLUCCA
SEA
Ninego Group
Sulawesi
(Celebes)
Yapen
New Hanover
Admiralty
Islands
PAPUA
New Ireland Nuguria Is
Buru
Wewak
BISMARCK
SEA
Green Is Tauu Is
Buka
Nukumanu
JAVA
SEA
INDONESIA
Madang
Goroka
NEW
New
Britain
Bougainville
Onton
Java
BANDA
Mount
Hagen
Lae
Choiseul
Jawa
(Java)
SEA
Kep. Aru
Santa Isabel Mala
Bali
Kep.
Babar
Kep. Tanimbar
Kerema
Trobriand Is
SOLOMON
New Guinea
GUINEA
Woodlark
New Georgia
Group
Honiara
FLORES SEA
Flores
Timor
Dolak
SEA
Guadalcanal
Maki
Sumba
ARAFURA SEA
Torres Strait
Louisiade Arch.
Bellona
Roti
Port Moresby
Tagula Rossel
Rennell
TIMOR
Melville I.
Wessel Is
CORAL
ASHMORE AND
CARTIER ISLANDS (Aust.)
SEA
Darwin
Gulf
of
Carpentaria
Joseph
Bonaparte
Gulf
Katherine
CORAL SEA
ISLANDS
(Aust.)
NEW
Wyndham
Cairns
SEA
Derby
Halls
Creek
NORTHERN
Broome
Townsville
Whitsunday Group
Îles
Chesterfield
CALED
(Fr.)
Port
Hedland
Karratha
Tennant
Creek
TERRITORY
Mount Isa
Mackay
Newman
Alice Springs
AUSTRALIA
QUEENSLAND
Rockhampton
Tropic of Capricorn
WESTERN
Barcaldine
Gladstone
Carnarvon
Maryborough
Fraser I.
Meekatharra
AUSTRALIA
Charleville
Noosa Heads
Toowoomba
Brisbane
Geraldton
Coober Pedy
SOUTH
Ballina
Grafton
Kalgoorlie-Boulder
AUSTRALIA
Bourke
Coffs Harbour
Broken Hill
Tamworth
Lord Howe I.
(Aust.)
Perth
Ceduna
Dubbo
Port Macquarie
Busselton
Bunbury
Whyalla
Port Augusta
NEW SOUTH
Orange
Newcastle
Port Pirie
Esperance
Great
Port
Lincoln
WALES
Bathurst
Sydney
Wollongong
Albany
Australian Bight
Gawler
Adelaide
Murray Bridge
Wagga Wagga
A.C.T.
Albury
Canberra
Queanbeyan
Kangaroo I.
VICTORIA
TASMAN
Mount Gambier
Ballarat
Geelong
Melbourne
Warrnambool
Bass Strait
Furneaux
King I.
Flinders I.
Group
SEA
Burnie
Devonport
Launceston
TASMANIA
Hobart
South Bruny I.

S O U T H E R N   O C E A N

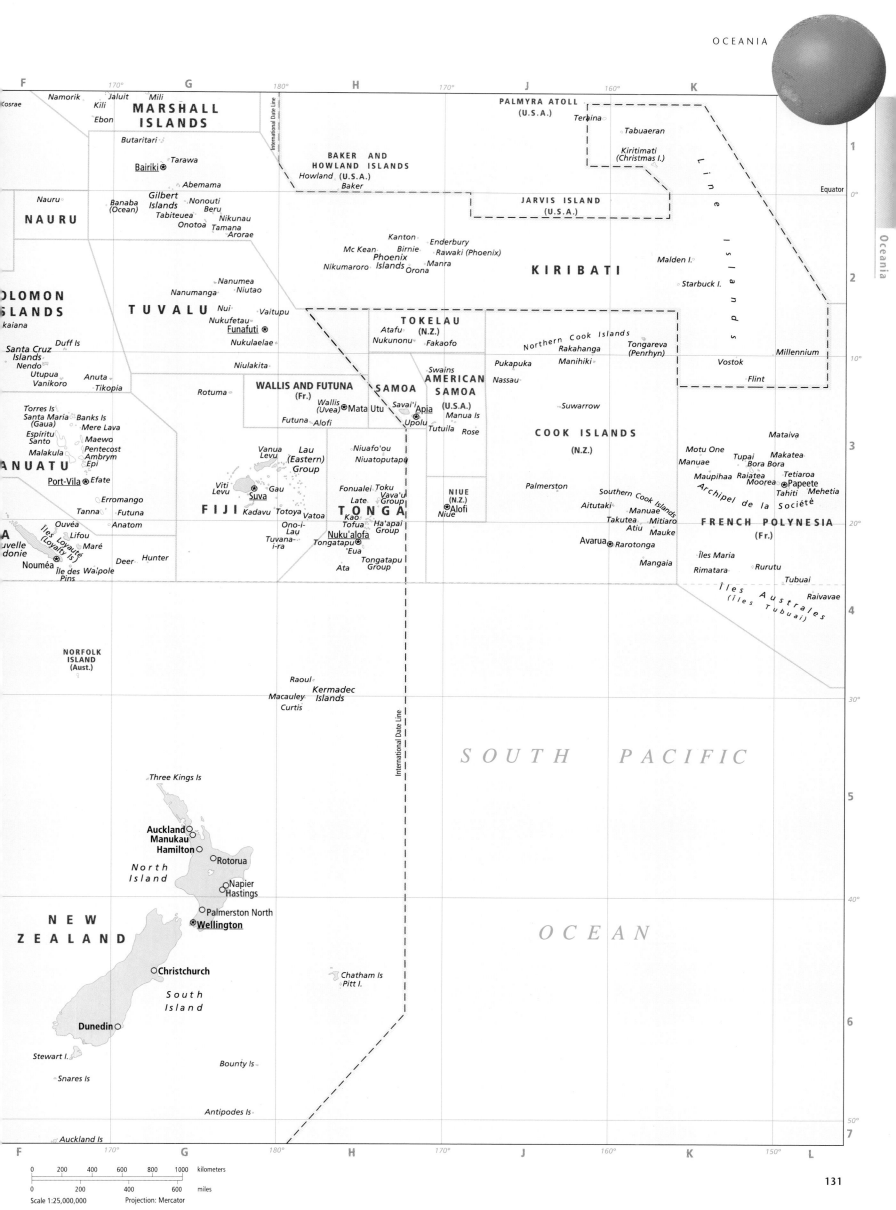

Oceania

F 170° **G** 180° **H** 170° **J** 160° **K**

Kosrae · Namorik · Jaluit · Mili

MARSHALL ISLANDS

Kili · Ebon

PALMYRA ATOLL (U.S.A.) · Teraina

Tabuaeran

1

Butaritari

Bairiki ⊛ · Tarawa

Kiritimati (Christmas I.)

BAKER AND HOWLAND ISLANDS

Howland (U.S.A.)
Baker

· Abemama

NAURU

Nauru · Banaba (Ocean) · Gilbert Islands · Nonouti · Beru · Nikunau · Onotoa · Tabiteuea · Tamana · Arorae

JARVIS ISLAND (U.S.A.)

Equator **0°**

Kanton · Enderbury

Mc Kean · Birnie · Rawaki (Phoenix)

Phoenix Islands

Nikumaroro · Orona · Manra

KIRIBATI

Malden I.

Starbuck I.

Line Islands

2

OLOMON SLANDS

kaiana

TUVALU

Nanumea · Niutao

Nanumanga

Nui · Vaitupu

Nukufetau

Funafuti ⊛

Nukulaelae

TOKELAU (N.Z.)

Atafu · Nukunonu · Fakaofo

Northern Cook Islands · Rakahanga · Tongareva (Penrhyn)

Vostok

Millennium **10°**

Duff Is

Santa Cruz Islands
Nendo

Utupua
Vanikoro

Niulakita

Anuta · Tikopia

Rotuma

WALLIS AND FUTUNA (Fr.)

Wallis (Uvea) ⊛ Mata Utu

Futuna · Alofi

SAMOA

Savai'i · Apia ⊛ Upolu

Swains

AMERICAN SAMOA (U.S.A.)

Manua Is

Tutuila · Rose

Pukapuka · Manihiki

Nassau

Suwarrow

COOK ISLANDS (N.Z.)

Flint

Mataiva

3

Torres Is
Santa Maria (Gaua)
Espíritu Santo
Malakula

Banks Is
Mere Lava
Maewo
Pentecost
Ambrym
Epi

Vanua Levu

Lau (Eastern) Group

Niuafo'ou
Niuatoputapu

Motu One · Tupai · Makatea
Manuae · Bora Bora
Maupihaa · Raiatea · Tetiaroa
Moorea ⊛ Papeete
Tahiti · Mehetia

ANUATU

Port-Vila ⊛ Efate

Viti Levu ⊛
Suva

Gau

Fonualei · Toku
Late · Vava'u Group

NIUE (N.Z.)

Palmerston

FRENCH POLYNESIA (Fr.)

Archipel de la Société

20°

Erromango

Tanna · Futuna

FIJI

Kadavu · Totoya

Vatoa

TONGA

Kao
Tofua

Ha'apai Group

Alofi
Niue

Southern Cook Islands
Aitutaki · Manuae
Takutea · Mitiaro
Atiu · Mauke

Avarua ⊛ Rarotonga

Îles Maria

Rimatara · Rurutu

Tubuai

A

Île des Pins

Ouvéa
Îles Loyauté (Loyalty Is)
Lifou
Maré

uvelle
donie
Nouméa

Anatom

Deer · Hunter

Ono-i-Lau
Tuvana-i-ra

Nuku'alofa ⊛ Tongatapu
'Eua
Ata · Tongatapu Group

Mangaia

Îles Australes (Îles Tubuai) · Raivavae

4

NORFOLK ISLAND (Aust.)

5

SOUTH PACIFIC

Raoul

Kermadec Islands

Macauley
Curtis

International Date Line

30°

Three Kings Is

Auckland ○
Manukau ○
Hamilton ○

○ Rotorua

North Island

Napier ○
Hastings ○

○ Palmerston North

OCEAN

40°

NEW ZEALAND

Wellington ⊛

Christchurch ○

South Island

Chatham Is
Pitt I.

Dunedin ○

6

Stewart I.

Snares Is

Bounty Is

7

Auckland Is

Antipodes Is

F 170° **G** 180° **H** 170° **J** 160° **K** 150° **L**

0 · 200 · 400 · 600 · 800 · 1000 kilometers

0 · 200 · 400 · 600 miles

Scale 1:25,000,000   Projection: Mercator

131

New Zealand

Niue (New Zealand) 1:500,000

Mutalau
Liha Point
Maketu
Lakepa
Hikutavake
Liku
Makapu Point
Alofi Bay
Alofi
Halagigie Pt
Fonuakula
Tamakautoga
Hakupu
Avatele
Tepa Point
Limufuafua Point

Snares Islands (New Zealand) 1:250,000

North Promontory
North East I.
130 m
South Promontory
Vancouver Rock
Broughton I.
Western Rock

Auckland Islands (New Zealand) 1:2,000,000

Enderby I.
North West Cape
Disappointment I.
Port Ross
Norman Inlet
Auckland Island
Cavern Peak 664 m
Bristow Pt
Mt Dick 668 m
Cape Bennett
South West Cape
Adams I.
Carnley Harbour

Kermadec Islands (New Zealand) 1:5,000,000

Herald Islets
Raoul I.
Macauley I.
Curtis I.
L Esperance Rock

Campbell Island (New Zealand) 1:1,100,000

Courrejolles Point
North East Harbour
Dent I.
Mt Lyall 413 m
Mt Honey 569 m
Perseverance Harbour
Jacquemart I.
South East Harbour

North Island

NEW ZEALAND

Three Kings Is
Great I.
Cape Reinga
Cape Maria van Diemen
North Cape
Te Paki 311 m
Te Kao
Spirits Bay
Great Exhibition Bay
Houhora
Kaitaia
Awanui
Waiharara
Ahipara Bay
Tauroa Peninsula
Herekino
Whinoki
Hokianga Harbour
Broadwood
Kohukohu
Rawene
Kaikohe
Okaihau
Kaeo
Kaitaia
Mangamuka
Kerikeri
Paihia
Russell
Cape Brett
Bay of Islands
Cavalli Is
Doubtless Bay
Karikari Pen.
Mangonui
Cape Karikari

Poor Knights Is
Cape Brett
Whangaruru
Whakapara
Hikurangi
Whangarei
Bream Bay
Ruakaka
Waipu
Maungaturoto
Dargaville
Kaipara Harbour

Hen and Chicken Is
Ocean Beach
Waipu
Mangawhai
Leigh
Warkworth
Wellsford
Kaiwaka
Helensville
Silverdale
Albany
Orewa
Waiwera
Kawau I.
Whangaparaoa
North Head
Waitakere
Takapuna
Auckland
Manukau
Papatoetoe
Papakura
Pukekohe
Waiuku
Tuakau
Pollok
Port Waikato
Raglan

Great Barrier I. (Aotea I.)
Cape Barrier
Great Mercury I.
Mercury Is
The Aldermen Is
Mayor I. (Tuhua)
Matakana I.
Motiti I.
White I. (Whakaari)
Bay of Plenty
Port Fitzroy
Moehau 892 m
C. Colville
Colville
Coromandel Rge
Coromandel
Thames
Paeroa
Waihi
Katikati
Tauranga
Mt Maunganui
Te Puke
Papamoa
Matata
Whakatane
Matata
Kawerau
Edgecumbe
Opotiki
Te Kaha
Cape Runaway
Matakaoa Point
East Cape
Tikitiki
Te Araroa
Hicks Bay
Tolaga Bay
Tokomaru Bay
Gisborne
Mahia Pen.
Mahia
Portland I.
Wairoa
Cape Kidnappers
Hawke Bay
Napier
Hastings
Waipawa
Waipukurau

Hamilton
Cambridge
Te Awamutu
Morrinsville
Matamata
Putaruru
Tokoroa
Tirau
Rotorua
Lake Rotorua
Kaingaroa
Murupara
Ruatahuna
Taupo
Lake Taupo
Mangakino
Te Kuiti
Otorohanga
Piopio
Mokau
Awakino
New Plymouth
Waitara
Inglewood
Stratford
Eltham
Mt Egmont (Mt Taranaki) 2518 m
Opunake
Hawera
Patea
Waverley
Wanganui
Bulls
Marton
Feilding
Palmerston North
Levin
Foxton
Shannon

Kahurangi
Ruapehu
Mt Ruapehu 2797 m
Mt Ngauruhoe 2291 m
Mt Tongariro 1968 m
Turangi
Waiouru
Taihape
Mangaweka
Ruahine Range
Dannevirke

TASMAN SEA

Cape Farewell
Farewell Spit
Whanganui Inlet
Port Puponga

South Island

SOUTH PACIFIC OCEAN

Bounty Islands (New Zealand) 1:400,000 **14**

Western Group
Eastern Group
Centre Group

N

Antipodes Islands (New Zealand) 1:1,000,000 **15**

Bollons I.
North Cape
Antipodes Island
Windward Is
Mt Galloway 366 m
Leeward I.
Albatross Point

P

Chatham Islands (New Zealand) 1:2,500,000 **16**

The Sisters
Cape Young
Point Munning
Okawa Point
Taupeka Point
The Forty Fours
C. Pattisson
Te Whanga Lagoon
Hanson Bay
Te One
Waitangi
Petre Bay
Point Durham
Owenga
Cape Fournier
Chatham I.
Cape L'Eveque
Mangere I.
Kahuitara Point
Pitt I.
Rangatira I.
Pyramid I.

Q

Pitt Strait

North region

Castlepoint
Wainuioru
Riversdale
Dreyers Rock
Mt Hector 1529 m
Masterton
Greytown
Martinborough
Mt Adams 663 m
Carterton
Mt Ross 983 m
Pakuratahi
Upper Hutt
Lower Hutt 938 m
Porirua
Tuturumuri
Broadmeadows
Wellington
Turakirae Head
Te Kaukau Point (Mungaroa)
Acton Point
Kapiti I.
Waikanae
Palliser Bay
Cape Palliser
Cook Strait
Chetwode Is
Cape Jackson
Cape Campbell
Stephens I.
Mt Stokes 1204 m
Picton
Blenheim
Havelock
Wairau Valley
D'Urville I.
Seddon
Tasman Bay
Nelson
Mt Richmond 1760 m
Tapuae-o-Uenuku 2885 m
Motueka
Takaka
Mapua
Hira
Mt Owera
Richmond
Belgrove
Murchison
Kekerengu
Clifford Bay
Clarence
Wekakura Point
Mt Dometa 1615 m
Devil River Peak 1775 m
729 m
Mt Kendall
Mt Franklin 2327 m
Pinnacle 2131 m
Saint Arnaud 2088 m
Mt Una 2301 m
Marakau 2610 m
Kaikoura
Kaikoura Peninsula
Karamea
Corbyvale
Ngakawau
Mt Owen 1875 m
Mt Victor 1540 m
Mt Uriah 1532 m
Tutaki
Mt Hutton 1400 m
Bumbrae 2081 m
Mt Harata 1379 m
Mt Alex 1832 m
Spyglass Point
Hawkswood
Hanmer Springs
Charleston
Punakaiki
Westport
Karamea Bight
Rotokohu
Reefton
Ikamatua
Springs Junction
Mt Birser 1859 m
Mt Enys 2195 m
Cheviot
Motunau Beach
Waiau
Cape Foulwind
Cape Providence
Mt Ryall 1065 m
Rapahoe
Stillwater
Ahaura
Rotomanu 1958 m
Arthur's Pass 2271 m
Mt Rolleston
Mt Whitcombe 2637 m
Mt Hutt 2199 m
Oxford
Waddington
Waipara
Amberley
Pegasus Bay
Greymouth
Kumara Junction
Hokitika
Ross
Kumara
Jacksons
Mt Arrowsmith 2795 m
Staveley
Methven
Rakaia
Eyreton
Rangiora
Kaiapoi
Woodend
Christchurch
Banks Peninsula
Spencerville
Mt Herbert 917 m
Sumner
Lyttelton
Akaroa
Akaroa Harbour
Canterbury Bight
SOUTHERN ALPS
Otira
Haritki
Okarito Lagoon
The Forks 2545 m
Ete de Beaumont 3117 m
Mt Cook 3764 m
Mt Stevenson 2366 m
Fox Peak 2332 m
1833 m
Mayfield
Mt Somers
Ashburton
Hinds
Rangitata
Franz Joseph Glacier
Fox Glacier
Mount Cook
Bruce Bay
Otorokua Point
Mt Hooker 2652 m
Mt St Mary 2332 m
1863 m
Twizel
Fairlie
Temuka
Timaru
Pareora
Makikihi
Waimate
Lake Moeraki
Haast
Mt Alba 2355 m
Lake Tekapo
Lake Pukaki
The Hunter's Hills
Cave
Otematata
Mt Orr 1021 m
Ikawai
Pukeuri
Oamaru
Jackson Bay
Cascade Point
Mt Aspiring 3027 m
Mt Tutoko 2746 m
Mt Earnslaw 2819 m
Mt Cardrona 1934 m
2502 m
Glenorchy
Lake Hawea
Wanaka
Mt Pisa 1961 m
Omarama
Kurow
Kohurau 2012 m
Idaburn
Ranfurly
Mt Pisgah 1643 m
Maheno
Hampden
Katiki Point
Shag Point
Waikouaiti
Milford Sound
Cleddau
Te Anau
Queenstown
Double Cone 2324 m
Obelisk 1695 m
Cromwell
Gorge Creek
Alexandra
Lawrence
Raes Junction
Tapanui
Clydevale
Maungatua 895 m
Outram
Mosgiel
Dunedin
Waitati
Port Chalmers
Otago Peninsula
Brighton
Waihola
George Sound
Cuswell Sound
Dusky Sound
1256 m
Secretary I.
1242 m
Mt Lyall 1853 m
Lake Manapouri
Mararoa
Mt Pisa
Jane Peak 2085 m
Mid Dome 1479 m
Kingston
Lumsden
Riversdale
Mokoreta 713 m
Balclutha
Kaka Point
Clarksville
Kaitangata
Maclennan
Breaksea I.
Resolution I.
Mt Solitary 1709 m
1454 m
Manapouri
Ohai
1654 m
Nightcaps
Winton
Hedgehope
Edendale
Gore
Mataura
Owaka
Treble Mtn 1067 m
1049 m
Pyseygur Point
Preservation Inlet
Cape Providence
The Hump
Orepuki
Otautau
Riverton
Colac Bay
Centre I.
Oreti
Invercargill
Waituna
Bluff
Toetoes Bay
Foveaux Strait
Solander I. (Hautere)
Black Rock Point
Codfish I.
Mt Anglem 980 m
Ruapuke I.
Owen Head
Muttonbird (Titi) Is
Big South Cape I. (Taukihepa)
Mt Allen 750 m
Halfmoon Bay
Stewart Island
Port Pegasus
South Cape
Te Waewae Bay
Paterson Inlet

Scale 1:3,500,000   Projection: Conic Equidistant

0 50 100 150 200 kilometers

0 50 100 miles

133

Australia

Inset Maps

Christmas Island
(Australia)
1:1,000,000

North West Pt
Flying Fish Cove
North East Pt
Murray Hill 359 m
Egeria Pt
Ross Hill 321 m
South Pt
Medwin Pt
Smithson Bight

Ashmore Reef and Cartier Islet
(Australia)
1:2,000,000

Hibernia Reef
West Islet
Ashmore Reef
Middle Islet
East Islet
Cartier Islet

Cocos (Keeling) Islands
(Australia)
1:1,000,000

Wreck Pt
North Keeling I.
INDIAN OCEAN
South Keeling Islands
Horsburgh I. (Luar)
Direction I.
Home I.
Ujong Tanjong
Pulo Pandang
West I. (Panjang)
South I. (Atas)

Macquarie Island
(Australia)
1:1,000,000

Hasselborough Bay
North Head
Anare Station
Buckles Bay
Langdon Pt
Mt Elder 371 m
Bauer Bay
Sandy Bay
Mt Waite 422 m
Prion Lake
Mt Eitel 341 m
Sandell Bay
Victoria Pt
Major Lake
Mt Hamilton 433 m
Mt Fletcher 428 m
Mt Jeffryes 399 m
Caroline Cove
Hurd Pt
South West Pt

Heard Island and McDonald Islands
(Australia)
1:2,500,000

Anzac Peak 715 m
Corinthian Head
Laurens Pen.
Morgan I.
McDonald Islands
West Bay
Spit Pt
Heard I.
Mawson Peak 2745 m
Lambeth Bluff

Main Map

INDONESIA
Sawu
Roti
TIMOR SEA
Melville I.
Croker I.
Goulb Is
Bathurst I.
Van Diemen Gulf
Cobourg Pen.
Ashmore Reef Cartier I.
ASHMORE AND CARTIER ISLANDS (Aust.)
Cape Londonderry
Cape Ford
Joseph Bonaparte Gulf
Darwin
Palmerston
Berry Springs
Jabiru
Adelaide River
Annabunoo
Pine Creek
Bigge I.
Bonaparte Archipelago
Kalumburu
Wyndham
Kununurra
Victoria River Wayside Inn
Katherine
Mataranka
Larrimah
KIMBERLEY
Kupingarri
Lake Argyle Village
Timber Creek
Top Springs
Daly Waters
Elliott
Cape Leveque
Lombadina
King Leopold Ranges
Derby
Mt Broome 935 m
Lake Argyle
Kalkarindji
NORTHERN
Broome
Fitzroy Crossing
Halls Creek
TERRITORY
Roebuck Bay
Lagrange
Sandy Lake
Tanami Desert
Tennant Creek
Eighty Mile Beach
Sandfire Roadhouse
Lake Gregory
AUSTR
Port Hedland
Pardoo Roadhouse
GREAT SANDY
Lake White
Dampier
Roebourne
Marble Bar
Percival Lakes
Karratha
PILBARA
Nullagine
DESERT
Lake Mackay
Ti-Tree
Barrow I.
Onslow
Pannawonica
Lake Dora
Lake Auld
Lake MacDonald
Yuendumu
North West Cape
Nanutarra Roadhouse
Hamersley Range
Wittenoom
Lake Disappointment
Alice Springs
Exmouth
Mt Tom Price 1073 m
Tom Price
Newman
MacDonnell
Coral Bay
Paraburdoo
Mt Meharry 1253 m
Gibson Desert
Lake Hopkins
Lake Neale
Erldunda
Minilya Roadhouse
Mt Augustus 1105 m
Lake Anadeus
Katatjuta (Mt Olga) 1066 m
Uluru (Ayers Rock) 863 m
Kulgera
Carnarvon
Lake Carnegie
Boyd Lagoon
Yulara
Bernier I.
Dorre I.
Ashburton
Gascoyne
Mt Woodroffe 1435 m
Tropic of Capricorn
Lake MacLeod
Musgrave Ranges
Shark Bay
Murchison
Marla
Dirk Hartog I.
Denham
Wiluna
GREAT VICTORIA
SOUTH
Steep Point
Overlander Roadhouse
Meekatharra
Lake Wells
DESERT
AUSTRALIA
WESTERN AUSTRALIA
Lake Maurice
Kalbarri
Mount Magnet
Lake Noondie
Jubilee Lake
Northampton
Lake Austin
Laverton
Lake Carey
Houtman Abrolhos
Mullewa
Leonora
Lake Minigwal
Geraldton
Lake Barlee
Menzies
Lake Rebecca
INDIAN
Dongara
Lake Ballard
Lake Marmion
Nullarbor Plain
OCEAN
Wubin
Lake Moore
Kalgoorlie-Boulder
Moora
Coolgardie
Kambalda
Madura
Eucla
Penong
Wongan Hills
Southern Cross
Lake Lefroy
Fowlers Bay
Cedu
Goomalling
Merredin
Lake Cowan
Great
Muchea
Northam
Australian Bight
Streaky Bay
Perth
York
Balladonia
Twilight Cove
Rockingham
Kwinana
Corrigin
Norseman
Anxious B
Mandurah
Pinjarra
Hyden
Lake Dundas
Narrogin
Lake King
Bunbury
Collie
Wagin
Ravensthorpe
Esperance
Busselton
Katanning
Kojonup
Jerramungup
Cape Arid
Margaret River
Bridgetown
Archipelago of the Recherche
Cape Leeuwin
Augusta
Manjimup
Mount Barker
Walpole
Albany
Denmark
Flinders Bay
SOUTHERN OCEAN

SOLOMON
SEA

Oceania

PAPUA NEW
GUINEA

Alotau Normanby I.
Samarai
Misima I.
The Calvados Bwagaoia
Chain Louisiade
Archipelago
Tagula I. Rossel I.

Rennell

CORAL SEA

CORAL SEA ISLANDS
(Aust.)
Willis Group
Magdaleine Cays
Chilcott I.
Diamond Is

°les Chesterfield
(New Caledonia)

Tropic of Capricorn

SOUTH

PACIFIC

OCEAN

Lord Howe I.
(Aust.)

TASMAN SEA

Australia (detail labels)

Gulf of Carpentaria region:
Cape Wessel, Wessel Is, Cape Arnhem, Nhulunbuy, Arnhem Land, Cape Shield, Blue Mud Bay, Groote Eylandt, Limmen Bight, Maria I., Sir Edward Pellew Group, Vanderlin I., Borroloola, Wellesley Is, Mornington I., Bentinck I., Wollogorang, Burketown, Karumba, Normanton, Croydon, Forsayth, Einasleigh, Georgetown

Badu I., Moa I., Prince of Wales I., Cape York, Bamaga, Cape Grenville, Weipa, Duyfken Point, Albatross Bay, Portland Roads, Cape Direction, Coen, Cape Melville, Cape Flattery, Cooktown, Lakeland, Mossman, Mareeba, Atherton, Cairns, Ravenshoe, Bartle Frere 1614 m, Innisfail, Tully, Hinchinbrook I., Ingham, Cardwell

Cape York Peninsula, Pormpuraaw

GREAT BARRIER REEF

Magnetic I., Townsville, Ayr, Bowen, Whitsunday Group, Proserpine, Long I., Torilla Peninsula

Barkly Tableland, Barkly Homestead Roadhouse, Camooweal, Mount Isa, Cloncurry, Kajabbi, Julia Creek, Richmond, Hughenden, Charters Towers, Lake Dalrymple

QUEENSLAND

Middleton, Winton, Boulia, Longreach, Barcaldine, Alpha, Clermont, Mackay, Sarina, Emerald, Blackwater

GREAT DIVIDING RANGE

Simpson Desert, Alberga, Bedourie, Birdsville, Betoota, Windorah, Bilpa Morea Claypan, Lake Yamma Yamma, Quilpie, Eromanga, Charleville, Mitchell, Roma, Springsure, Yeppoon, Rockhampton, Curtis I., Gladstone, Biloela, Miriam Vale, Moura, Monto, Bundaberg, Sandy Cape

Strzelecki Desert, Noccundra, Thargomindah, Cunnamulla, St George, Dirranbandi, Hebel, Barringun, Tibooburra, Goondiwindi, Maryborough, Hervey Bay, Fraser I., Childers, Mundubbera, Gympie, Murgon, Kingaroy, Nambour, Noosa Heads, Maroochydore, Caloundra, Caboolture, Moreton I., Ipswich, Brisbane, Toowoomba, Dalby, Chinchilla, Miles

NEW SOUTH WALES

Marree, Leigh Creek, Lake Frome, Lake Torrens, Roxby Downs, Glendambo, Woomera, St Mary Pk 1168 m, Flinders Ranges, Broken Hill, Wilcannia, Cobar, Nyngan, Coonamble, Walgett, Bourke, Moree, Wee Waa, Narrabri, Gunnedah, Coonabarabran, Gilgandra, Narromine, Dubbo, Muswellbrook, Singleton, Warialda, Inverell, Glen Innes, Tenterfield, Stanthorpe, Warwick, Texas, Mungindi, Casino, Lismore, Ballina, Murwillumbah, Coolangatta, Gold Coast, Nerang, North Stradbroke I., Grafton, Coffs Harbour, Sawtell, Nambucca Heads, Kempsey, Port Macquarie, Armidale, Round Mtn 1587 m, Tamworth, Mt Barrington 1556 m, Taree, Forster

Port Augusta, Quorn, Port Pirie, Peterborough, Gladstone, Snowtown, Burra, Whyalla, Cowell, Eyre Peninsula, Kimba, Iron Knob, Port Wakefield, Wallaroo, Moonta, Maitland, Yorketown, Yorke Pen., Port Lincoln, Tumby Bay, Menindee, Ivanhoe, Hillston, Lake Cargelligo, West Wyalong, Forbes, Parkes, Orange, Bathurst, Lithgow, Cessnock, Newcastle, Gosford, Katoomba, Camden, Sydney, Wollongong, Kiama, Nowra

Kangaroo I., Kingscote, Victor Harbor, Adelaide, Gawler, Murray Bridge, Tailem Bend, Renmark, Berri, Robinvale, Mildura, Balranald, Hay, Griffith, Narrandera, Temora, Young, Cowra, Goulburn, Bowral, Queanbeyan, JERVIS BAY TERRITORY, Batemans Bay

Kingston Southeast, Cape Jaffa, Naracoorte, Bordertown, Keith, Nhill, Hopetoun, Swan Hill, Kerang, Cobram, Jerilderie, Deniliquin, Echuca, Shepparton, Wangaratta, Wodonga, Albury, AUST. CAPITAL TERRITORY, Canberra, Cooma, Narooma, Bega, Eden, Cape Howe

VICTORIA, Millicent, Mount Gambier, Cape Duquesne, Discovery Bay, Casterton, Hamilton, Mt William 1167 m, Stawell, Horsham, Warracknabeal, Bendigo, Seymour, Sunbury, Melbourne, Geelong, Colac, Ballarat, Melton, Mt Hotham 1867 m, Mt Kosciusko 2229 m, Snowy Mtns, Bairnsdale, Orbost, Lakes Entrance, Sale, Moe, Morwell, Wonthaggi, Warrnambool, Portland, Port Phillip Bay, Torquay, Rye, Cape Otway, Wilsons Promontory

TASMANIA, King I., Currie, Hunter I., Flinders I., Robbins I., Lady Barron, Furneaux Group, Cape Barren I., Eddystone Point, Smithton, Burnie, Devonport, George Town, St Helens, Scottsdale, Mt Ossa 1617 m, Queenstown, Launceston, Strahan, Swansea, Freycinet Pen., Bridgewater, Macquarie Harbour, Lake Gordon, Lake Pedder, Hobart, Geeveston, Sorell, Port Arthur, Southport, South Bruny I., South East Cape

Bass Strait

Insets

Norfolk Island (Australia) 1:1,000,000
Norfolk I., Anson Pt, Burnt Pine, Point Ross, Kingston, Nepean I., Steels Pt, Cascade Bay, Philip I.

Lord Howe Island (Australia) 1:1,000,000
Admiralty Is, North Head, Mutton Bird I., Mt Malabar 212 m, East Pt, Lord Howe I., Mt Lidgbird 777 m, King Pt, Mt Gower 875 m, Ball's Pyramid

Scale 1:12,500,000   Projection: Azimuthal Equal Area

0 200 400 600 kilometers
0 100 200 300 miles

South Pacific

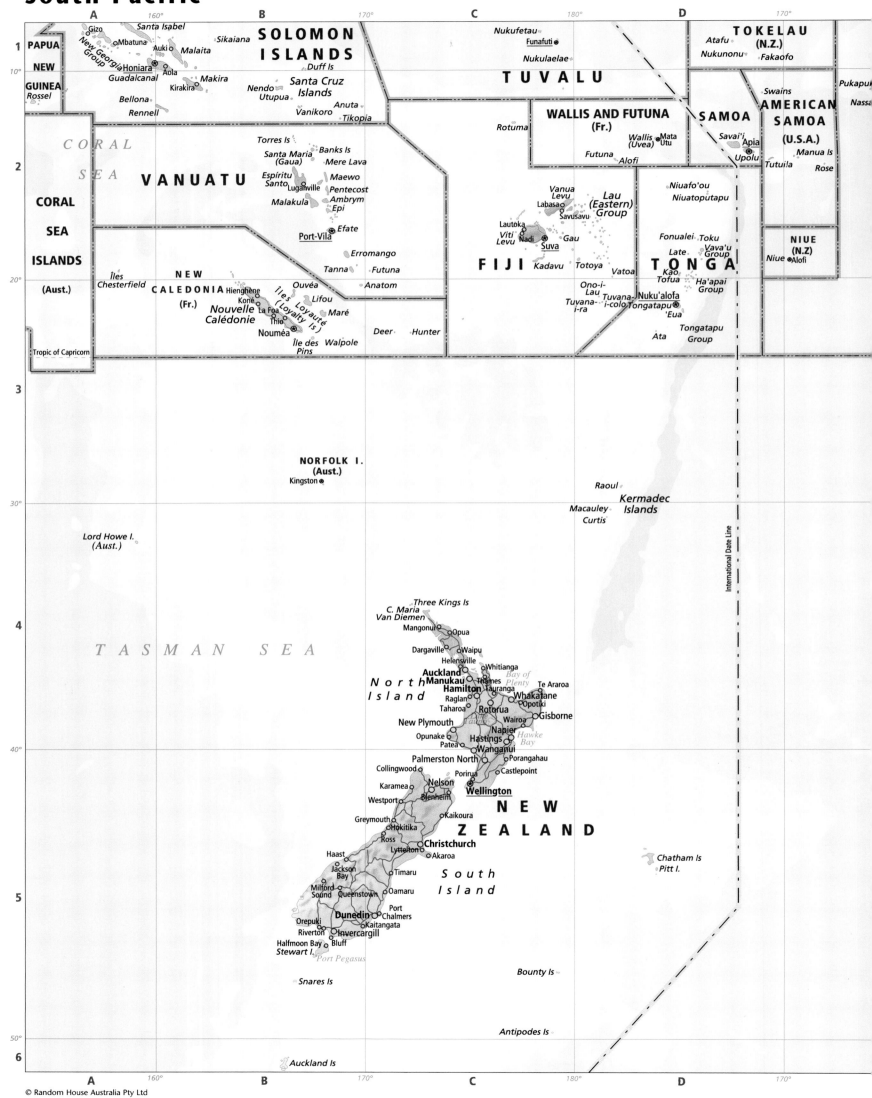

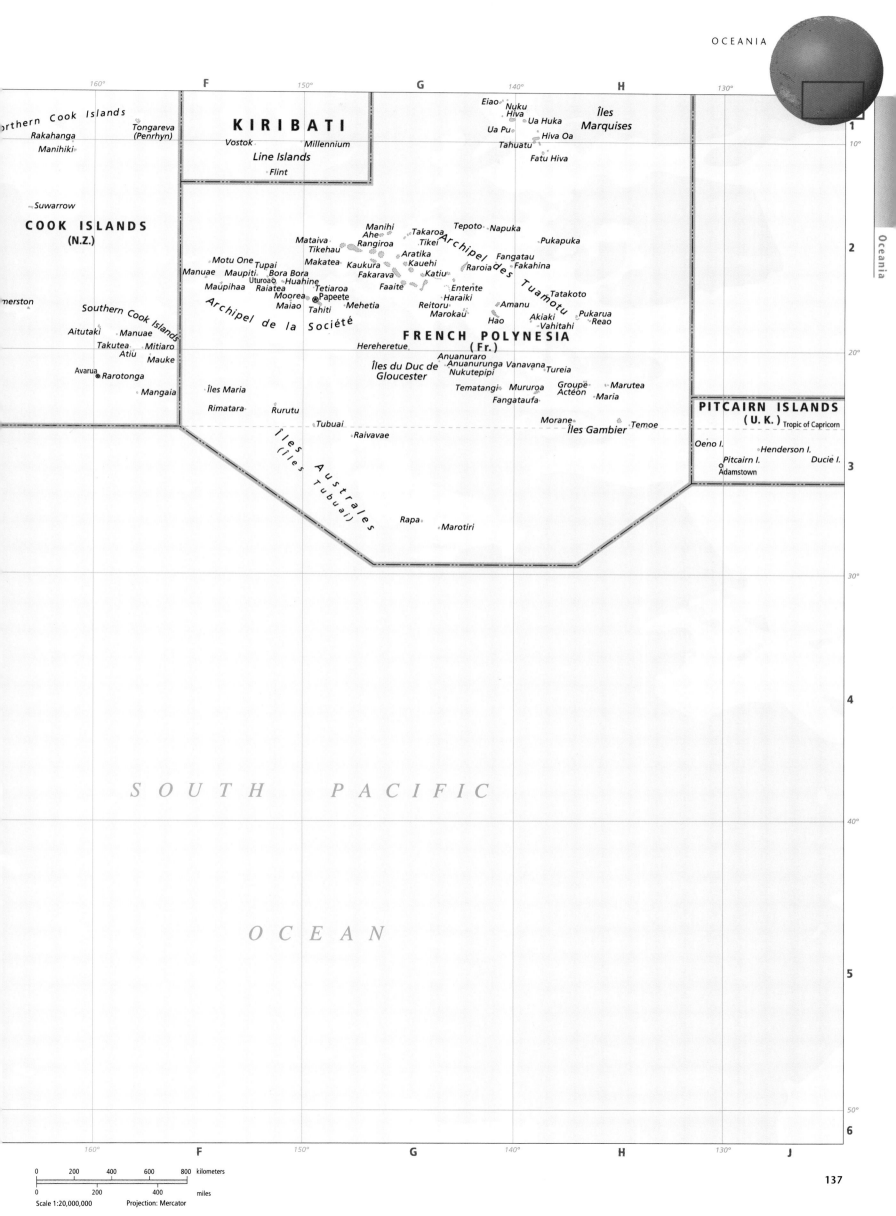

Oceania

160°   F   150°   G   140°   H   130°

Northern Cook Islands

Rakahanga

Manihiki

Tongareva
(Penrhyn)

KIRIBATI

Eiao   Nuku
         Hiva   Ua Huka   Îles
Ua Pu   Hiva Oa   Marquises
    Tahuatu
        Fatu Hiva

1

10°

Vostok   Millennium

Line Islands

Flint

Suwarrow

COOK ISLANDS
(N.Z.)

Manihi
Ahe   Takaroa   Tepoto   Napuka
Mataiva   Rangiroa   Tikei   Pukapuka
Tikehau   Aratika   Archipel
Motu One   Makatea   Kaukura   Kauehi   Fangatau
Manuae   Maupiti   Bora Bora   Raroia des   Fakahina
Maupihaa   Uturoa   Huahine   Fakarava   Katiu   Tuamotu
Raiatea   Faaite   Entente   Tatakoto
Moorea   Tetiaroa   Haraiki
Papeete   Reitoru   Amanu   Pukarua
Maiao   Tahiti   Mehetia   Marokau   Akiaki   Reao
Hao   Vahitahi

2

Commerston

Southern Cook Islands

Aitutaki   Manuae

Takutea   Mitiaro
Atiu
Mauke

Avarua   Rarotonga

Mangaia

FRENCH POLYNESIA
(Fr.)

Hereheretue

Îles du Duc de   Anuanuraro
Gloucester   Anuanurunga   Vanavana
Nukutepipi   Tureia

Tematangi   Mururoa   Groupe   Marutea
Actéon   Maria
Fangataufa

20°

Îles Maria

Rimatara   Rurutu

Archipel de la Société

Tubuai

Raivavae

Morane   Îles Gambier   Temoe

PITCAIRN ISLANDS
(U. K.)   Tropic of Capricorn

Oeno I.   Henderson I.

Pitcairn I.   Ducie I.
Adamstown

3

Îles Australes
(Îles Tubuai)

Rapa   Marotiri

30°

4

S O U T H   P A C I F I C

40°

O C E A N

5

50°

160°   F   150°   G   140°   H   130°   J   6

0   200   400   600   800 kilometers

0   200   400 miles

Scale 1:20,000,000   Projection: Mercator

North Pacific

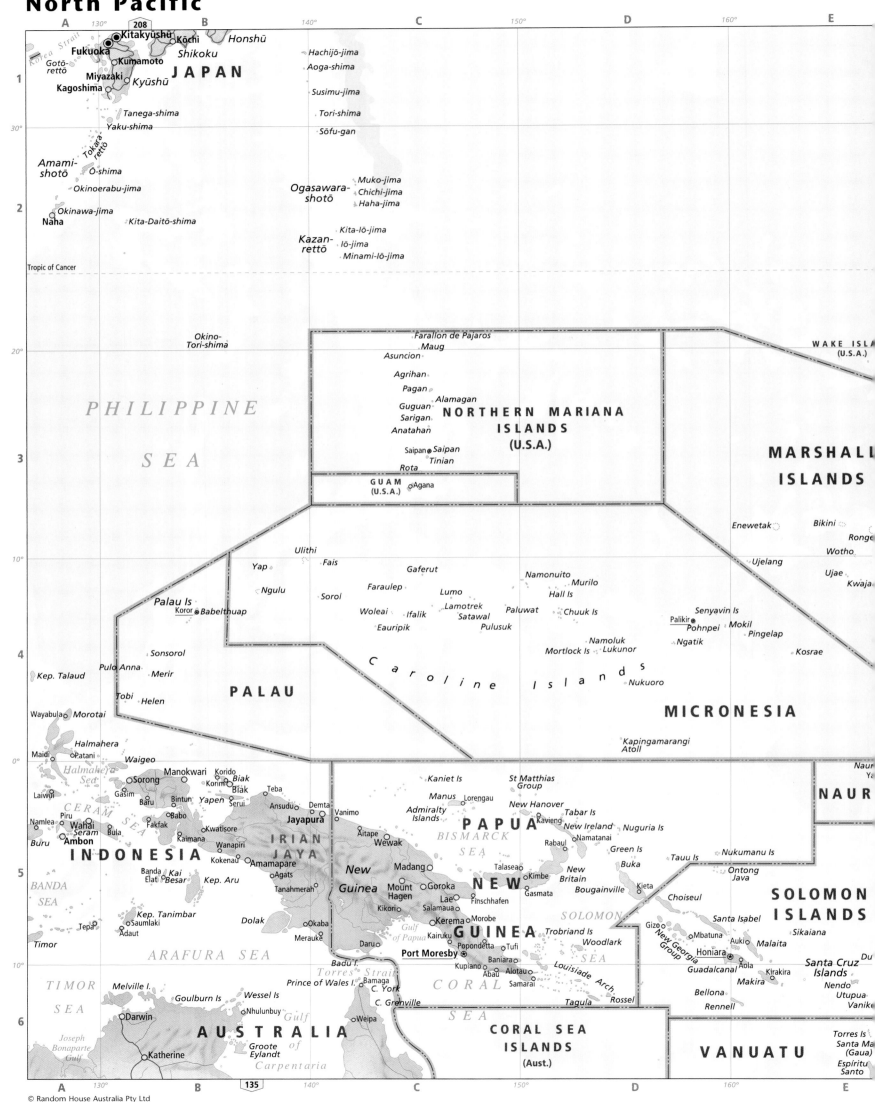

208

A   130°   B   140°   C   150°   D   160°   E

Kitakyūshū · Kōchi · Honshū
Fukuoka · Kumamoto · Shikoku
Gotō-rettō
Miyazaki · Kyūshū
Kagoshima

JAPAN

Hachijō-jima
Aoga-shima

Tanega-shima · Susimu-jima
Yaku-shima · Tori-shima

30°

Sōfu-gan

Amami-
shotō · O-shima
Okinoerabu-jima

Muko-jima
Ogasawara-
shotō · Chichi-jima
Haha-jima

Naha · Okinawa-jima · Kita-Daitō-shima

Kazan-
rettō · Kita-Iō-jima
Iō-jima
Minami-Iō-jima

Tropic of Cancer

Okino-
Tori-shima

Farallon de Pajaros · WAKE ISLA
20° · Maug · (U.S.A.)
Asuncion

PHILIPPINE · Agrihan
Pagan
Alamagan · **MARSHALL**
Guguan
Sarigan · **NORTHERN MARIANA** · **ISLANDS**
SEA · Anatahan · **ISLANDS**
(U.S.A.)
Saipan · Saipan
Tinian
Rota · Enewetak · Bikini
Ronge
GUAM · Agana · Wotho
(U.S.A.) · Ujelang · Ujae · Kwaja

10°
Ulithi · Fais
Yap · Gaferut · Namonuito · Murilo
Ngulu · Faraulep · Lumo · Hall Is
Palau Is · Sorol · Lamotrek · Senyavin Is
Koror · Babelthuap · Woleai · Ifalik · Satawal · Paluwat · Chuuk Is · Palikir · Pohnpei · Mokil
Eauripik · Pulusuk · Pingelap
Namoluk · Ngatik
Sonsorol · Mortlock Is · Lukunor · Kosrae
4° · **Caroline** · **Islands**
Kep. Talaud · Pulo Anna · Merir · Nukuoro
Wayabula · Morotai · Tobi · Helen · **MICRONESIA**
Maidi · **PALAU**
Patani · Kapingamarangi
Halmahera · Atoll
Laiwui · Halmahera · Waigeo
0° · Sea · Kaniet Is · St Matthias · Naur
Sorong · Manokwari · Korido · Biak · Group · Ya
Gasim · Korim · Biak · Manus · Lorengau · New Hanover
Baru · Bintun · Yapen · Serui · Admiralty · Tabar Is · **NAUR**
Piru · Babo · Teba · Islands · Kavieng · New Ireland · Nuguria Is
Namlea · Wahai · Fakfak · Ansudu · Demta · **PAPUA** · Namatanai
Buru · Seram · Bula · Jayapura · Vanimo · **BISMARCK** · Rabaul · Green Is · Nukumanu Is
Ambon · Kwatisore · Aitape · Wewak · **SEA** · Buka · Ontong
Kaimana · **IRIAN** · Talasea · New · Java
Banda · Kai · Wanapiri · **JAYA** · Madang · Kimbe · Britain · Bougainville · Kieta · **SOLOMON**
Elat · Besar · Kokenau · Amamapare · Goroka · **NEW** · Gasmata · Choiseul · **ISLANDS**
BANDA · Agats · New · Mount · Lae · Finschhafen · Mbatuna · Sikaiana
SEA · Tanahmerah · Guinea · Hagen · Salamaua · Gizo · Santa Isabel
Kep. Tanimbar · Kikori · Morobe · **SOLOMON** · New Georgia · Malaita
Saumlaki · Dolak · Kerema · **GUINEA** · Honiara · Aukio
Tepa · Adaut · Okaba · Kairuku · Trobriand Is · **SEA** · Guadalcanal · Aola · Kirakira
Merauke · Popondetta · Tufi · Woodlark · Makira · Santa Cruz
Timor · Badu I. · Port Moresby · Baniara · Louisiade · Bellona · **Islands**
Prince of Wales I. · Kupiano · Arch. · Nendo
Melville I. · Bamaga · Abau · Alotau · Tagula · Rennell · Utupua
TIMOR · Goulburn Is · C. York · Samarai · Rossel · Vanike
SEA · Darwin · Wessel Is · C. Grenville · **CORAL** · Torres Is
Nhulunbuy · Gulf · Santa Ma
Joseph · Katherine · Groote · of · **AUSTRALIA** · Weipa · **CORAL SEA** · **VANUATU** · (Gaua)
Bonaparte · Eylandt · Carpentaria · **ISLANDS** · Espíritu
Gulf · (Aust.) · Santo

A   130°   B   135°   140°   C   150°   D   160°   E

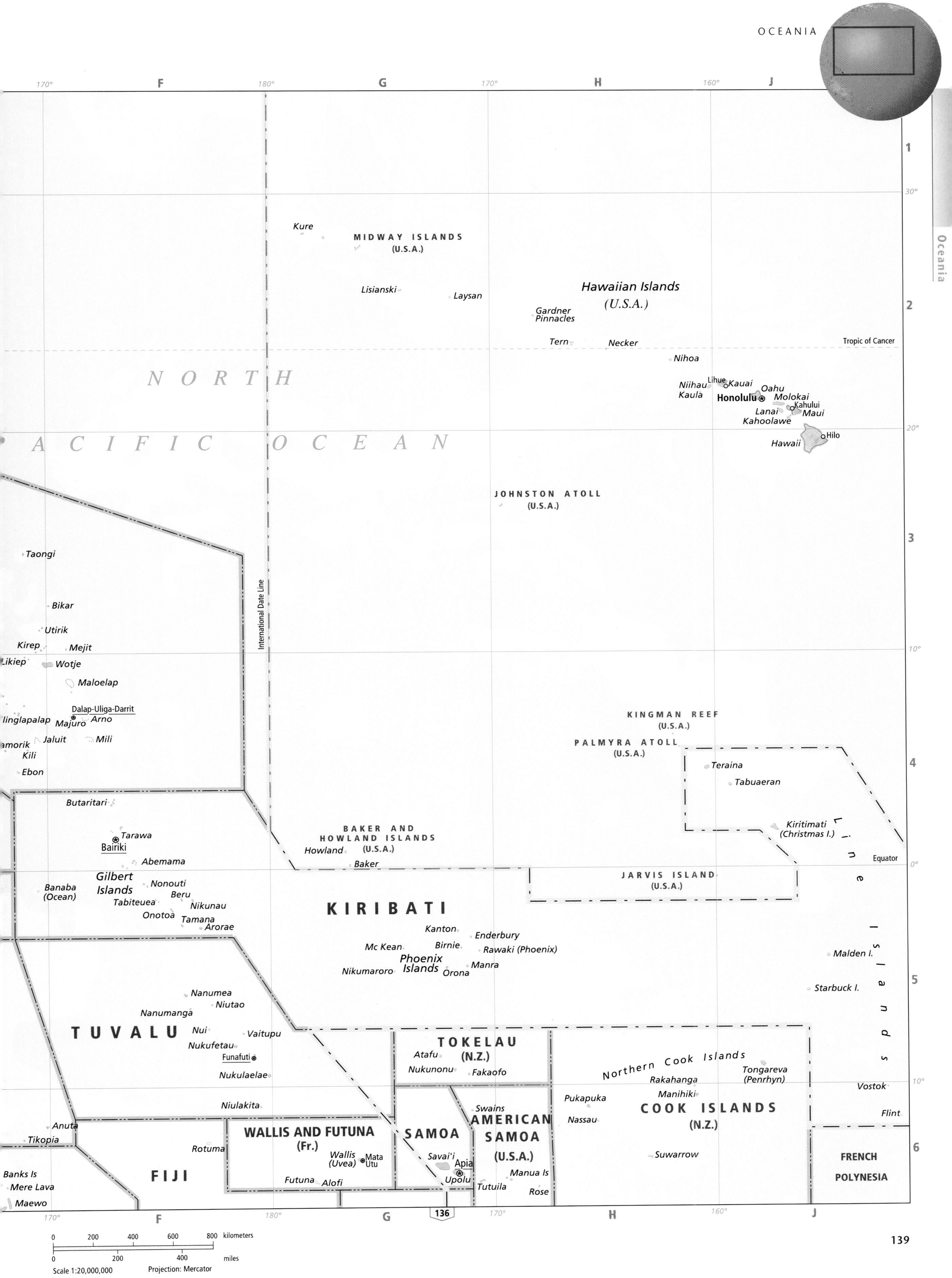

Oceania

1

30°

Kure

MIDWAY ISLANDS
(U.S.A.)

Lisianski • *Laysan*

Hawaiian Islands
(U.S.A.)

2

Gardner
Pinnacles

Tern • *Necker*

Tropic of Cancer

Nihoa

Niihau *Lihue* *Kauai*
Kaula **Honolulu** ⊛ *Oahu* *Molokai*
Lanai *Kahului*
Kahoolawe *Maui*

N O R T H

20°

P A C I F I C   O C E A N

Hawaii ○*Hilo*

JOHNSTON ATOLL
(U.S.A.)

3

Taongi

Bikar

Utirik

Kirep • *Mejit*

Likiep *Wotje*

Maloelap

Dalap-Uliga-Darrit
Jinglapalap *Majuro* *Arno*

KINGMAN REEF
(U.S.A.)

PALMYRA ATOLL
(U.S.A.)

4

Teraina

Tabuaeran

amorik *Jaluit* *Mili*
Kili

Ebon

Butaritari

⊛ *Tarawa*
Bairiki

Abemama

Banaba
(Ocean)

Gilbert
Islands

Nonouti
Beru

Tabiteuea

Nikunau
Onotoa *Tamana*
Arorae

BAKER AND
HOWLAND ISLANDS
(U.S.A.)

Howland

• *Baker*

Kiritimati
(Christmas I.)

Equator

JARVIS ISLAND
(U.S.A.)

0°

K I R I B A T I

Kanton

Enderbury

Mc Kean *Birnie*
Rawaki (Phoenix)

Phoenix
Islands *Manra*
Nikumaroro *Orona*

Malden I.

5

Starbuck I.

Nanumea
Niutao

Nanumanga

Nui *Vaitupu*

T U V A L U
Nukufetau

Funafuti •

Nukulaelae

TOKELAU
(N.Z.)

Atafu

Nukunonu

Fakaofo

Northern Cook Islands

Rakahanga
Manihiki

Tongareva
(Penrhyn)

Vostok

10°

Niulakita

Anuta

Tikopia

Rotuma

WALLIS AND FUTUNA
(Fr.)

SAMOA

AMERICAN
SAMOA
(U.S.A.)

Pukapuka

Nassau

COOK ISLANDS
(N.Z.)

Flint

FRENCH

Banks Is

Mere Lava

F I J I

Wallis *Mata*
(Uvea) •*Utu*

Futuna *Alofi*

Savai'i
Apia ⊛
Upolu

Swains

Manua Is

Tutuila

Rose

Suwarrow

POLYNESIA

Maewo

International Date Line

Line   Islands

Papua New Guinea

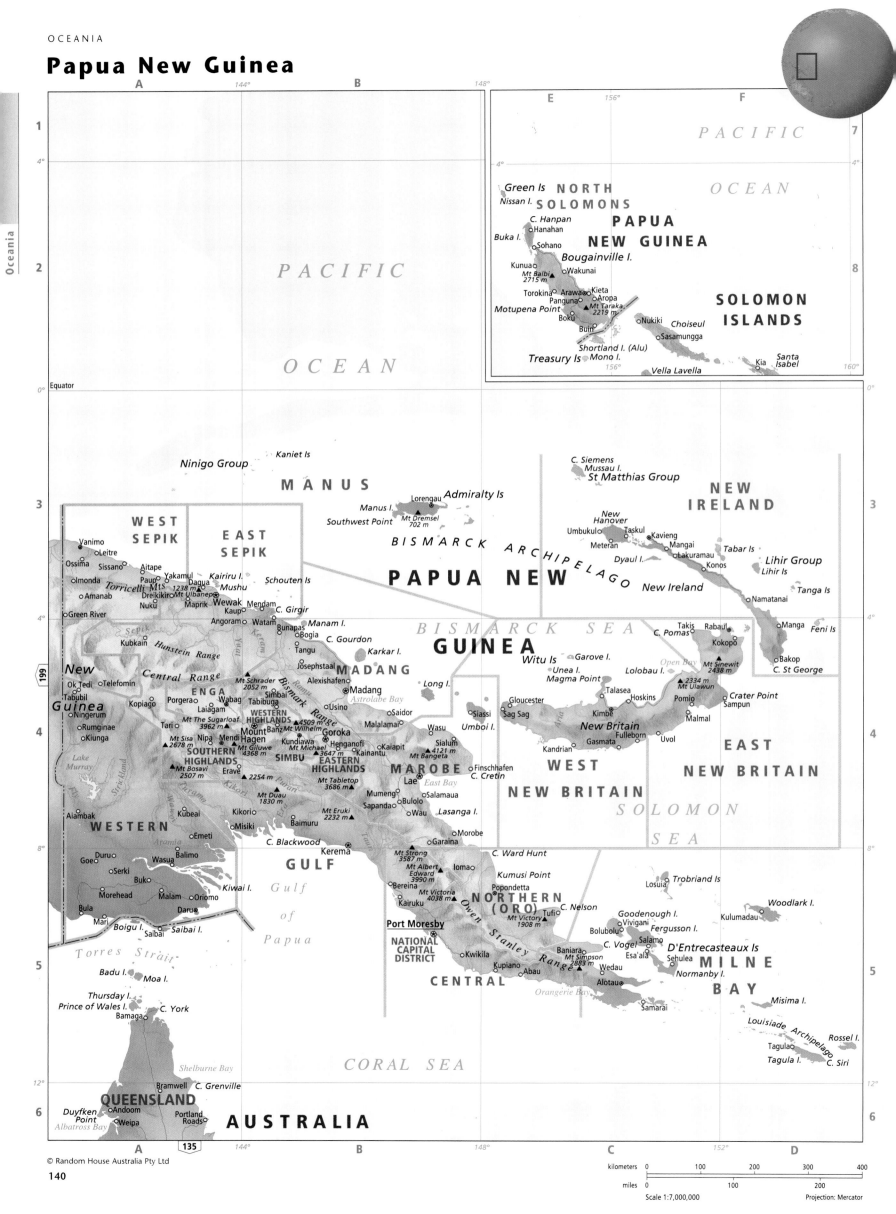

Scale 1:7,000,000   Projection: Mercator

Islands of the Pacific

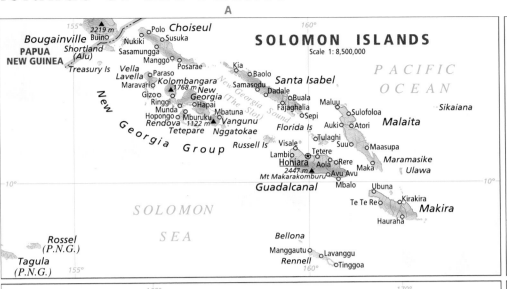

SOLOMON ISLANDS
Scale 1: 8,500,000

Bougainville
PAPUA NEW GUINEA
Shortland (Alu)
Treasury Is
Buino
2219 m
Polo
Nukiki
Susuka
Sasamungga
Manggo
Posarae
Vella Lavella
Paraso
Kolombangara
Maravari
Gizo
New Georgia
Ringgi
1768 m
Munda
Hapai
Hopongo
Mburuku
Rendova
1122 m
Vangunu
Tetepare
Nggatokae
New Georgia Group
Russell Is
Kia
Baolo
Santa Isabel
Samasodu
Dadale
Buala
Jaghalia
Maluu
Sulofoloa
Sepi
Malaita
Visale
Lambio
Florida Is
Aoki
Atori
Tulaghi
Maasupa
Honiara
Tetere
Rere
Maka
Maramasike
Aola
Avu Avu
Ulawa
2447 m
Mt Makarakomburu
Mbalo
Ubuna
Guadalcanal
Te Te Reo
Kirakira
Makira
Hauraha
Bellona
Manggautu
Lavanggu
Rennell
Tinggoa
Choiseul
Santa Isabel
Sikaiana
PACIFIC OCEAN
SOLOMON SEA
Rossel (P.N.G.)
Tagula (P.N.G.)

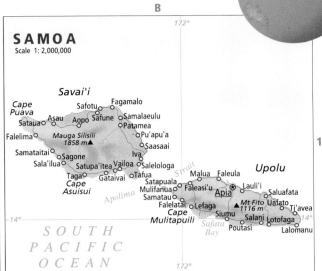

SAMOA
Scale 1: 2,000,000

Savai'i
Cape Puava
Sataua
Falelima
Asau
Agoo
Safotu
Fagamalo
Safune
Samalaeulu
Patamea
Pu'apu'a
Samataitai
Mauga Silisili 1858 m
Sagone
Sala'ilua
Satupa'itea
Vailoa
Iva
Saasaai
Salelologa
Sala'ilua
Taga
Gataivai
Tafua
Malua
Faleula
Upolu
Cape Asuisui
Mulifanua
Satapuala
Satamau
Falelatai
Lefaga
Apia
Mt Fito 1116 m
Ti'avea
Lauli'i
Uafato
Saluafata
Cape Mulitapuili
Siumu
Salani
Lotofaga
Poutasi
Lalomanu
SOUTH PACIFIC OCEAN
Apolima Strait
Safata Bay

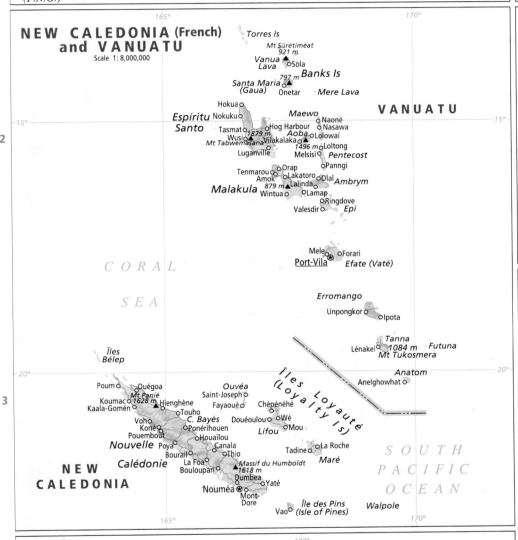

NEW CALEDONIA (French) and VANUATU
Scale 1: 8,000,000

Torres Is
Mt Sürétiméat 921 m
Vanua Lava
Sola
Banks Is
Santa Maria (Gaua)
797 m
Onetar
Mere Lava
Hokua
Maewo
VANUATU
Espíritu Santo
Nokuku
Naoné
Tasmat
Hog Harbour
Nasawa
Wusica
1879 m
Aoba
Lolowai
Vilakalaka
Luganville
1496 m
Loltong
Pentecost
Mt Tabwemasana
Melsisi
Tenmarou
Orap
Panngi
Amok
Lakatoro
Olal
Ambrym
879 m
Lalinda
Malakula
Wintua
Lamap
Valesdir
Ringdove
Epi
Mele
Forari
Port-Vila
Efate (Vaté)
Erromango
Unpongkor
Ipota
Tanna
Futuna
Lénakel
1084 m
Mt Tukosmera
Anatom
Anelghowhat
Îles Bélep
Poum
Quégoa
Ouvéa
Saint-Joseph
Koumac
Mt Panié 1628 m
Hienghène
Fayaoué
Kaala-Gomén
Touho
Chépénéhé
Voh
C. Bayès
Doueoulou
Wé
Koné
Ponérihouen
Mou
Pouembout
Houaïlou
Lifou
Poya
Canala
Bourail
La Foa
Thio
Tadine
La Roche
Nouvelle
Bouloupari
Maré
Calédonie
Massif du Humboldt 1618 m
NEW CALEDONIA
Dumbéa
Yaté
Nouméa
Mont-Dore
Vao
Île des Pins (Isle of Pines)
Walpole
Îles Loyauté (Loyalty Is)
CORAL SEA
SOUTH PACIFIC OCEAN

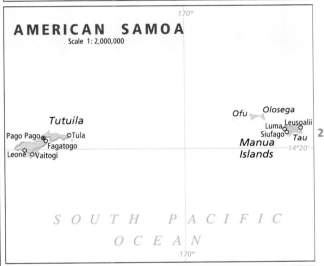

AMERICAN SAMOA
Scale 1: 2,000,000

Tutuila
Ofu
Olosega
Luma
Leusoalii
Pago Pago
Tula
Siufago
Tau
Leone
Fagatogo
Manua Islands
Vaitogi
SOUTH PACIFIC OCEAN

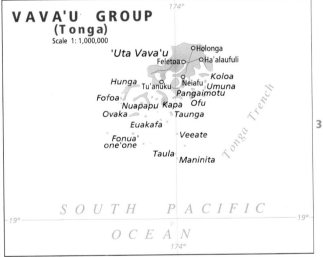

VAVA'U GROUP (Tonga)
Scale 1: 1,000,000

'Uta Vava'u
Holonga
Feletoa
Ha'alaufuli
Hunga
Koloa
Tu'anuku
Neiafu
Umuna
Fofoa
Pangaimotu
Ofu
Nuapapu Kapa
Ovaka
Taunga
Euakafa
Veeate
Fonua' one'one
Taula
Maninita
Tonga Trench
SOUTH PACIFIC OCEAN

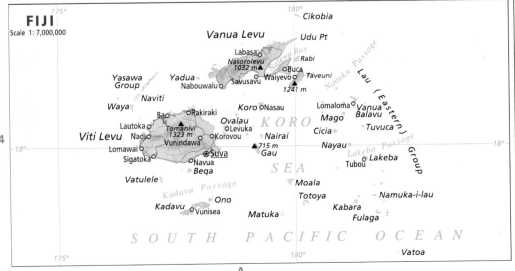

FIJI
Scale 1: 7,000,000

Cikobia
Vanua Levu
Udu Pt
Labasa
Rabi
Nasorolevu 1032 m
Buca
Yasawa Group
Yadua
Waiyevo
Taveuni
Lau (Eastern) Group
Nabouwalu
Savusavu
1241 m
Waya
Naviti
Koro
Nasau
Lomaloma
Rakiraki
Ovalau
Nairai
Vanua Balavu
Lautoka
Bao
Levuka
Mago
Tuvuca
Nadi
Tomanivi 1323 m
Korovou
Cicia
Viti Levu
Vunindawa
715 m
Nayau
Lomawai
Suva
Gau
Lakeba
Sigatoka
Navua
Tubou
Beqa
Moala
Vatulele
Totoya
Namuka-i-lau
Ono
Matuka
Kabara
Kadavu
Vunisea
Fulaga
KORO SEA
SOUTH PACIFIC OCEAN
Nakelo Bay
Namuku Passage
Lakeba Passage
Kadavu Passage
Vatoa

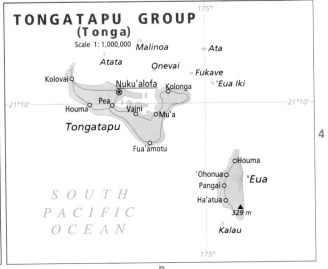

TONGATAPU GROUP (Tonga)
Scale 1: 1,000,000

Malinoa
Ata
Atata
Onevai
Fukave
Kolovai
Nuku'alofa
Kolonga
'Eua Iki
Pea
Houma
Vaini
Mu'a
Tongatapu
Fua'amotu
Houma
'Ohonua
Pangai
'Eua
Ha'atua
329 m
Kalau
SOUTH PACIFIC OCEAN

Asia and the Middle East

Asia

Asia, the largest continent, covers 43.6 million sq km (16.8 million sq miles), about one-third of the world's land surface. Its western boundaries are the Ural Mountains, the Ural River, the Caspian and Black seas and the Dardanelles Straits, which separate Europe from Asia. The Red Sea and the Suez Canal separate Asia from Africa. Indonesia is the southeasternmost country of Asia.

Asia is traditionally divided into East, Southeast, South, West (Middle East), Central, and North Asia (Siberia, which is part of the Russian Federation). The Middle East and the Russian Federation are discussed in separate sections.

East Asia includes China, Japan, North and South Korea, Taiwan, and Mongolia. Southeast Asia contains the three archipelagic nations of Indonesia, Malaysia and the Philippines; Singapore and Brunei; and the Indochinese nations of Laos, Vietnam, Cambodia, Thailand, and Myanmar (Burma). South Asia includes India, Pakistan, Bangladesh and Sri Lanka; Nepal and Bhutan in the Himalayas; mountainous Afghanistan; and the coral island archipelago of the Maldives. Central Asia includes the former Soviet republics of Kazakhstan, Uzbekistan, Kyrgyzistan, Tajikistan, Turkmenistan, Azerbaijan, and Armenia.

Physical features

Asia is a very geologically active continent. Large areas are covered by mountain and volcanic chains—the world's highest mountain range (the Himalayas), the Indonesian volcanic arc, and the volcanic chains of Japan and the Philippines. Asia also contains some parts of the world's most ancient (Pre-Cambrian) formations, in the Indian and Arabian peninsulas and in Siberia.

Mountain ranges, plateaus, and basins lie within Asia's heartland. The world's highest plateau is in Tibet, averaging 4,000 m (13,000 ft) in altitude, and is bounded to the south by the Himalayas, to

the north by the Kunlun Range, and to the west by the Karakoram Range. Further north, the Tarim and Dzungarian basins lie close to sea level, while the Turfan Depression is 142 m (470 ft) below it.

Numerous streams and 19 major rivers, ranging from 2,500 to 5,500 km (1,500 and 3,400 miles) in length, flow in Asia. These include the Yangtze and Huang rivers in China, the Indus and Ganges rivers of the Indian subcontinent and the Mekong River on the Indochinese Peninsula.

Climate and vegetation

Asia can be broadly divided into a humid monsoon belt, in South, Southeast, and East Asia, and an arid to semiarid zone, in Central Asia.

During summer, the monsoons blow north, toward the continental margins, while in winter they reverse direction and blow toward the south. Some East Asian areas receive rainfall from both monsoons. The Himalayan Range and adjacent mountain ranges concentrate summer rainfall in parts of South and Southeast Asia. Hot, humid climates prevail in South and Southeast Asia while cold climates, with snowfall during winter, are found in more northern parts (the Himalayas and the mountain ranges in Central Asia). The Plateau of Tibet has an extremely cold climate.

Tropical rainforests once covered large parts of South and Southeast Asia, but are now being cleared for agriculture and logging, especially of hardwoods. This threatens the plant and animal diversity of these forests, which is very high.

Broad-leaf evergreen forests cover parts of subtropical East Asia. There are deciduous forests further north in cool, temperate climates, and boreal forests where the winters are cold. The Plateau of Tibet is an almost treeless tundra, with mosses, grasses, lichens, and a few small shrubs.

Grasslands cover areas in the rainshadow belts where rainfall is limited: tropical grasslands in the Deccan Plateau in India and the Khorat Plateau in Thailand, and temperate grasslands (steppes) in the semiarid parts of Central Asia.

Central Asia is predominantly arid to semiarid, with warm summers and winters where the temperature can fall below freezing. The Gobi Desert, the coldest dry desert, lies in this region.

Terraced fields in India (left), a carved entrance in Bali (top), and a curious monkey in Indonesia (above) demonstrate the variety of landform zones and land uses in Asia.

Population

Asia's vast population (3,588.9 million inhabitants, as of 1998, representing some 60 percent of the world's people) is predominantly found in the monsoon belt. The population explosion within the last 50 years (some countries experienced a three-fold increase during this period) is the result of advances in agriculture and improved medical facilities. During this period, life expectancies improved throughout Asia. Life expectancy is currently highest in East Asia (69 years for males and 73 years for females) and lowest in South Asia (61.7 years for males and 62.8 years for females). The high population growth rate has subsided, being currently 1.4 percent overall (0.9 in East Asia to 1.8 in South Asia).

Population indicators for the most developed Asian countries are similar to those for many Western countries: low population growth rates and high life expectancies characterize the more industrialized nations such as Japan and Singapore. High growth rates and much lower life expectancies, however, are found in the least developed countries, such as Bangladesh and Nepal. These characteristics reflect the enormous differences in standards of living between the most and least developed countries in Asia. Urbanization is highest in the most developed areas, but despite having a number of large cities and growing urbanization, Asia still has a low urban population—35 percent.

Industrialization in most Asian countries has, as elsewhere, centered on major urban areas. Labor from rural areas has drifted to urban centers in search of employment. The ensuing urban population explosion has put pressure on infrastructure, and given rise to problems such as the growth of slum dwellings, traffic congestion, and air and water pollution.

Agriculture

A high proportion of Asia's population lives on the alluvial plains of rivers (and their deltas) of the monsoon belt, and is engaged in agriculture.

The monsoon belt is noted for its intensive rice and wheat farming. The population explosion created enormous demand for food. The area under cultivation was expanded through deforestation and by farming marginal areas, such as the borders of deserts, but the Green Revolution was more successful: high-yielding seeds, fertilizers and pesticides often tripled grain yields. However, environmental problems, caused by the chemicals used and by invasions of insects, have raised a number of concerns. In semiarid Central Asia, wheat farming and animal rearing are the main forms of agriculture. With irrigation, cotton is now successfully grown in several places.

Industrialization

By the 1980s, several East Asian countries had developed industrialized economies, largely dependent on imported raw materials, particularly minerals and energy supplies. Manufacturing in Asia ranges from labor-intensive industries such as clothing in the less developed economies to electronics, computers, and motor vehicles in the more developed ones. Japan, the world's second-largest economy, manufactures electronic goods, steel, motor vehicles and ships. Japan's approach has been imitated by South Korea, Taiwan, Hong Kong and Singapore, which have all rapidly industrialized. Thailand, Malaysia, the Philippines, and Indonesia have followed suit.

China and India initially aimed at agricultural and industrial self-sufficiency to support their enormous populations. They possess huge agricultural sectors, but their exports have shifted progressively to industrial products. They have considerable scientific expertise—in nuclear and space technology and satellite launching services (China), and computer programming (India).

The Central Asian nations, following the breakup of the former Soviet Union, are making a slow and painful transition from a state-controlled to a free market economy. There is, as yet, limited industrialization in the countries of Central Asia. Kazakhstan produces metals and chemicals and Azerbaijan, which is rich in petroleum deposits and may establish petroleum-based industries, currently manufactures mining equipment.

The Flaming Cliffs in Mongolia's arid Gobi Desert, Central Asia (above). This Vietnamese woman (below) is carrying wood from her home in the hills to sell.

Languages

Many languages, belonging to several language families, are spoken in Asia. Chinese Mandarin, Cantonese, and Wu are the most widely spoken in East Asia. Japanese is increasingly important. In Southeast Asia, Indonesian and Malaysian predominate, while languages of the Chinese-Tibetan family, such as Burmese and Thai, are spoken in the mainland belt. South Asia has two major language families: Indo-Aryan in the north, of which Hindi and Urdu are the most widespread, and Dravidian, which includes Tamil, in the southern areas. In Central Asia, Ural-Altaic languages, several of which are related to Turkish, are mainly used.

Russian is widely spoken in the former Soviet republics, and of the colonial languages, only English is still important, and continues to spread.

Boundary disputes and wars

Armed conflicts continued after the Second World War in Asia, especially during the decolonization phase. The communist revolution in China resulted in the separation of Taiwan, which China does not accept. Wars resulted in the division of both Korea and Vietnam into two nations: communist North and democratic South. The Vietnam war ended in 1975, when the country reunified. North and South Korea remain technically at war.

Following the division of British India into India and Pakistan in 1947, there was armed conflict over the divided Himalayan state of Jammu and Kashmir; this issue is still unresolved. War between India and Pakistan resulted in 1971 in the creation of the Bangladesh.

Armed conflicts along the disputed boundaries of China have taken place between China and India along the Himalayas, between China and Russia along the Amur River, and between China and Vietnam along their common border.

Indonesia's occupation and then incorporation of the former Portuguese colony of East Timor remains in dispute.

The ownership of the Spratly Islands in the South China Sea is causing tension between China, Malaysia, Philippines, Vietnam, and Taiwan.

The Middle East

The term "Middle East" applies to the belt of countries in Southwest Asia that lies between Afghanistan and Turkey. It stretches southward to include the Arabian Peninsula. The Middle East is characterized by its arid climate, its petroleum riches, and the prevalence of Islam as its predominant religion. The Middle East forms a strategic belt between the dynamic developing industrial countries of Asia and the long-developed countries of Europe.

The countries of Iran, Iraq, Syria, Turkey, and Cyprus form the northern belt, while toward their south lie Lebanon, Israel, Jordan and the states of the Arabian Peninsula. Saudi Arabia occupies a large part of the peninsula; Oman and Yemen share the southern part of the peninsula and the United Arab Emirates, Bahrain, Qatar, and Kuwait lie along the Arabian (also known as Persian) Gulf.

Afghanistan lies in the area where the Middle East, South Asia, and Central Asia meet. The North African nations of Egypt, Sudan, and Libya are also sometimes considered part of the Middle East, for linguistic and cultural reasons.

Physical features

The collision of the Iranian and Arabian tectonic plates with the Eurasian Plate resulted in the mountain ranges that run from Turkey to Iran. The belt between Turkey and Iran is characterized by elongated mountain ranges such as the Zagros and Alborz ranges in Iran and the Pontic and Taurus mountains in Turkey. These ranges form part of the extensive Alpine-Himalayan Mountain Range System that was formed during the Tertiary geological period. This area is prone to earthquakes, of which there have been several in recent decades. There are plateaus in both Turkey (Anatolian Plateau) and Iran.

In contrast to the geologically active Tertiary mountain belt, the Arabian Plateau is part of an ancient and geologically stable shield.

Jumeura Mosque, Dubai, in the United Arab Emirates (below). Shiraz-style grapevines with clay supports in Iran (right).

Climate and vegetation

The Middle East is predominantly arid to semiarid, except for the areas that adjoin the Mediterranean, Aegean, Black and Caspian seas. The region is characterized by high temperatures, especially in the Arabian, Syrian and Iranian deserts. In contrast, winter temperatures close to freezing point occur in the highlands and snow falls in some of the higher mountainous areas. There are great seasonal temperature differences on the plateaus, as shown by Tehrān and Ankara, which reach temperatures of about 30°C (85°F) in summer and fall as low as freezing point in winter.

The region receives little annual rainfall, except for winter rain in the areas bordering the Mediterranean, and there is a serious shortage of fresh water in the Gulf area. Vegetation in this region is dominated by thorny scrubland.

The Euphrates and Tigris are the largest rivers in the Middle East. Several short rivers flow into the Mediterranean, Black, and Caspian seas.

Population

The population of the region is about 297.4 million (1998). Life expectancies have improved in recent years and now stand at 65.9 years for males and 70.3 years for females. The population growth rate is moderate, at 2.2 percent. Urbanization has been increasing steadily during recent decades and now stands at 66 percent; this reflects the decreasing importance of agriculture and pastoralism in the economies of these countries. In several countries, particularly in the Gulf States, petroleum has indirectly assisted the growth of urbanization as oil-generated revenues have been invested in urban areas and projects.

Agriculture

Because of the arid climate, only a small part of the region can support agriculture. The Euphrates and Tigris Rivers, with their alluvial plains and extensive irrigation, are significant agricultural areas, but their rising salinity levels

constitute a major problem. The region has a great need for irrigation—Syria, for example, has built the Euphrates Dam to irrigate the northeastern part of the country. Israel has also developed areas of intensive irrigation-based agriculture.

Wheat, barley, and rice are the major cereals. Important cash crops include tobacco, sugarcane, cotton, fruits and tea. Dates are a common fruit and are cultivated in oasis areas. Livestock mostly consists of camels, sheep, and goats; herds of goats have been blamed for stripping the ground bare of vegetation, which has resulted in soil erosion and the acceleration of desertification in some areas.

Agriculture based on growing olives, grapes, citrus fruits and apples is found in the Mediterranean coastal areas.

Fishing is important in several places, including the Black and Caspian seas.

Industrialization

Petroleum reserves are the region's most abundant resource. Oil-rich Saudi Arabia, Iran, Iraq, Kuwait, and the United Arab Emirates have economies

The birthplace of Aphrodite in Cyprus (far left). Traditional trading dhows in Doha, Qatar (left), still have a place in this modern capital. Women in the Gaza Strip demonstrate for the release of Palestinian prisoners (below).

predominantly based on petroleum exports, which makes them vulnerable to fluctuations in the price of petroleum. Petroleum prices escalated during the mid to late 1970s, but since then prices have fallen considerably. Oil wealth has facilitated the import of foodstuffs, manufactured goods, and luxury items, and has been also used for military purchases and development.

The hot, arid areas of the region are largely unsuited to the establishment of industries. The lack of fresh water is so severe in the Gulf region that desalinization plants have been set up to produce potable water.

Oil-based electricity is generated in the oil-rich countries, and coal-based electricity is widely used in Turkey. Hydroelectric power is produced in Syria and Turkey.

Industries that use local materials, such as food processing, petroleum refining, and petrochemical industries, have been developed in some places. Some light consumer-based industries, including textiles, footwear, cigarettes, and paper, have also been established.

The countries of the eastern Mediterranean are comparatively more industrialized than the rest of the region, but frequent conflicts with neighboring countries in the area have hampered their ability to maintain production.

Languages
Three language families—the Indo-European, Turkic, and Semitic—are found in the Middle East. The Indo-European languages represented include Persian, Pashto, Kurdish, Armenian, and Baluchi. Turkish and Azerbaijani are Turkic languages, and Arabic and Hebrew are Semitic.

Boundary disputes and wars
The region has experienced several conflicts and wars within the last 50 years. The Israeli-Arab conflict has been the most prominent and is yet to be resolved. Lebanon was drawn into the conflict, which adversely affected its economy.

Iraq's attempt to conquer the Arab-speaking region of southwestern Iran lasted for years, and drained both Iraq and Iran of resources. Iraq's conquest of Kuwait, the subsequent Gulf War and

the blockade on Iraq has seriously affected the growth of Iraq's economy.

The Kurdish-speaking area, shared by Turkey, Iraq, and Iran, has also been involved in armed conflict, in its attempt to secure independence.

The Turkish conquest of the northern, Turkish-speaking part of Cyprus has strained relations between Greece and Turkey.

These ancient ruins at Buṣrá ash Shām, in Syria (below), remind us how long human civilization has existed in this area. International fast food in Dubai (above).

Nations

Bahrain	PAGE 150
Cyprus	PAGE 158
Iran	PAGE 163
Iraq	PAGE 164
Israel	PAGE 165
Jordan	PAGE 167
Kuwait	PAGE 168
Lebanon	PAGE 170
Oman	PAGE 177
Qatar	PAGE 180
Saudi Arabia	PAGE 180
Syria	PAGE 184
Turkey	PAGE 187
United Arab Emirates	PAGE 188
Yemen	PAGE 192

Autonomous regions

Gaza Strip	PAGE 193
West Bank	PAGE 193

Afghanistan

Afghanistan is a landlocked country in the central part of South Asia with nearly three-quarters of its territory mountainous. It shares a western frontier with Iran, while Pakistan is across the southeastern border. Once a part of the ancient Persian Empire, Afghanistan was conquered by Alexander the Great in 328 BC. In the seventh century AD it adopted Islam, today the country's dominant religious and cultural force. From 1953 it was closely allied with the former Soviet Union. In 1979 the Soviet government intervened to install a communist faction more to its liking, and though constantly beseiged by mujahideen guerrilla fighters, maintained its military occupation until 1989. After the overthrow of the communist government in 1992 the mujahideen began fighting among themselves along ethnic lines. Twenty years of internal war appeared to have ended in 1998 with the Sunni Muslim Taliban militia, associated with the majority Pashtun, in control of the country. The Taliban has imposed strict Islamic rule.

Geographically, the country's largest area is the thinly populated central highlands. This comprises most of the Hindu Kush, the second highest range in the world, with several peaks over 6,400 m (21,000 ft). The northeast is seismically active. Much of the rest is desert or semidesert, except for a few fertile and heavily populated valleys, among them Herāt in the northwest. Most agriculture

takes place on the northern plains, near the frontiers of Turkmenistan, Uzbekistan, and Tajikistan. The country's main river basins are those of the Amu Darya, Helmand, and Kābol.

Afghanistan is very poor: a list of 192 countries ranked for calorie intake in 1995 placed Afghanistan 191. It depends largely on wheat farming and the raising of sheep and goats. During the Soviet occupation and the subsequent internecine conflict, one-third of the population left the country, 6 million refugees fleeing to Pakistan and Iran. Many have now gone home to an economically devastated land. Millions of people lack food, clothing, housing, and medical care. Though data are shaky, it is likely that the country's most profitable crop is opium, Afghanistan reputedly being the world's second largest producer after Myanmar (Burma), and a major source of hashish.

Fact File

OFFICIAL NAME	Islamic State of Afghanistan
FORM OF GOVERNMENT	Transitional government
CAPITAL	Kābol (Kabul)
AREA	647,500 sq km (250,000 sq miles)
TIME ZONE	GMT + 4.5 hours
POPULATION	25,824,882
PROJECTED POPULATION 2005	30,189,273
POPULATION DENSITY	39.8 per sq km (103 per sq mile)
LIFE EXPECTANCY	47.3
INFANT MORTALITY (PER 1,000)	140.6
OFFICIAL LANGUAGES	Dari (Afghan Persian), Pashto
OTHER LANGUAGES	Uzbek, Turkmen, Indi and Pamiri languages, Dravidian
LITERACY RATE	31.5%
RELIGIONS	Sunni Muslim 84%, Shi'a Muslim 15%, other 1%
ETHNIC GROUPS	Pashtun 38%, Tajik 25%, Hazara 19%, Uzbek 6%, other 12%
CURRENCY	Afghani
ECONOMY	Agriculture 61%, services 25%, industry 14%
GNP PER CAPITA	Est. < US$765
CLIMATE	Mainly semiarid, but arid in southwest and cold in mountains; hot summers and cold winters
HIGHEST POINT	Nowshak 7,485 m (24,557 ft)
MAP REFERENCE	Page 221

Armenia

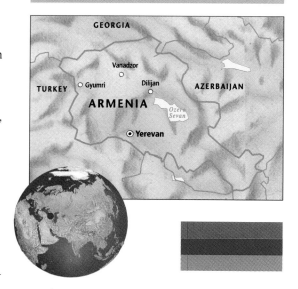

Armenia is a small, mountainous, Christian country, landlocked between hostile Muslim neighbors. To the east is Azerbaijan, and to the west is Turkey, which inflicted genocidal massacres on the Armenian people between 1894 and 1915. The legendary resting place of Noah's Ark after the Flood (its capital supposedly founded by Noah himself), Armenia had already existed as a distinct country for 1,000 years when in the fourth century AD it became the first in the world to make Christianity its state religion. The country has been fought over at various times by Romans, Persians, and Mongols. It became a Soviet Socialist Republic in 1922 and gained its independence from the Soviet Union in 1991. In 1988 there was a devastating earthquake which killed 25,000 people and destroyed power stations and other infrastructure and in the same year conflict began over Nagorno-Karabakh, an internal Azerbaijani area largely populated by Christian Armenians, which is claimed by Armenia.

The mountains of the Lesser Caucasus (Malyy Kavkaz) cover most of the country. The landscape is rugged, and includes extinct volcanoes and high lava plateaus cut with ravines. An active seismic area, the frequency of earthquakes in Armenia indicates that mountain-building is still taking place. Although the city of Ararat is in Armenia, Mt Ararat itself is across the border in Turkey. The centrally located Lake Sevan (Sevana Lich) lies nearly 2,000 m (6,000 ft) above sea level, but its use for hydropower has drained it to a point where drinking water supplies are threatened. Steppe vegetation is the main cover and drought-resistant grasses and sagebrush grow on the lower mountain slopes, where jackals, wildcats, and the occasional leopard are found.

As a Soviet Republic, Armenia developed an industrial sector, supplying machine building tools, textiles, and other manufactured goods to other republics in return for raw materials and energy. It has few natural resources, although formerly lead, copper, and zinc were mined, and there are deposits of gold and bauxite. Agriculture is an important source of income. In irrigated areas around Yerevan, crops include grapes, almonds, figs, and olives, while apples, pears, and cereals are grown on higher ground. Armenia is also known for its quality brandies and wines.

Asia and the Middle East

The city of Kābol in Afghanistan, devastated by years of warfare (below left). View over the city of Yerevan in Armenia, with Mt Ararat in the background (above).

Economic decline in the period 1991 to 1994 was a direct result of the ongoing conflict over Nagorno-Karabakh. In retaliation for Armenia's military activities in the region, Turkey and Azerbaijan blockaded pipeline and railroad traffic into the country, causing chronic energy shortages. There have been improvements, but full economic recovery is unlikely before Armenia's conflict with its neighbors is settled.

Fact File

OFFICIAL NAME Republic of Armenia

FORM OF GOVERNMENT Republic with single legislative body (National Assembly)

CAPITAL Yerevan

AREA 29,800 sq km (11,506 sq miles)

TIME ZONE GMT + 4 hours

POPULATION 3,409,234

PROJECTED POPULATION 2005 3,351,982

POPULATION DENSITY 114.4 per sq km (296.2 per sq mile)

LIFE EXPECTANCY 66.6

INFANT MORTALITY (PER 1,000) 41.1

OFFICIAL LANGUAGE Armenian

OTHER LANGUAGE Russian

LITERACY RATE 98.8%

RELIGIONS Armenian Orthodox 94%, other (Russian Orthodox, Muslim, Protestant) 6%

ETHNIC GROUPS Armenian 93%, Azeri 3%, Russian 2%, other (mainly Kurdish) 2%

CURRENCY Dram

ECONOMY Industry 28%, agriculture 27%, services 26%, other 19%

GNP PER CAPITA US$730

CLIMATE Mainly dry, with cold winters and warm summers; cooler in mountains

HIGHEST POINT Aragats Lerr 4,090 m (13,419 ft)

MAP REFERENCE Page 222

Azerbaijan

Oil was being collected from the Caspian Sea near Baku at least 1,000 years ago, when the area was known as "the land of eternal fire" because of burning natural gas flaming out of the ground. Today oil from Baku continues to be the mainstay of the Azerbaijani economy. The home of an independent Azeri state as early as the fourth century BC, the region later fell under the influence of Persia, then in the eleventh century Turkic-speaking people moved in and assumed control. A period of affiliation with the Soviets following the Russian Revolution led to Azerbaijan becoming a member of the Soviet Union in 1936. In 1991 it was one of the first Soviet Republics to declare independence.

Since 1988 there have been troubles with Armenia over the region of Nagorno-Karabakh in southwestern Azerbaijan. This territorial dispute (Armenia now holds 20 percent of the region, most of the people in Nagorno-Karabakh being Christian Armenians) remains a major political problem for the newly independent state.

A range of the Great Caucasus (Bol'shoy Kavkas) running at an angle toward the Caspian Sea separates Russia from Azerbaijan, and reaches almost as far as Baku. South of this range, draining out of the foothills of the Caucasus in Georgia, the

Kura (Kür) River reaches a broad floodplain, some of it lying below sea level. The mountains of the Lesser Caucasus (Malyy Kavkaz) form much of Nagorno-Karabakh in the southwest and also stand between Azerbaijan and its isolated enclave-territory Naxçivan. Although a Naxçivan independence movement exists, this territory, which is surrounded by Iran and Armenia, is regarded by the government as part of the Azerbaijan state.

Dry and subtropical, the lowlands experience mild winters and long, hot summers, and are frequently affected by drought. Plant cover consists of steppe grassland in the drier lowland regions, woods in the mountains, and swamps in the southeast.

Early this century Baku supplied as much as half the world's oil, but production declined steadily during the final years under Soviet control as plant became antiquated and maintenance was neglected. The 1994 ratification of a $7.5 billion deal with a consortium of Western oil companies marked a turning point, and should see a revival in this sector. Baku was the fifth biggest city in Soviet Russia and had a well diversified industrial sector. It is hoped the oil deal will stimulate new production of chemicals, textiles, and electrical goods.

Though Azerbaijan has only a small amount of arable land, it is a major producer of cotton, tobacco, grapes, and other fruit. Sturgeon from the Caspian was an important source of caviar but this industry is threatened by serious water pollution. One hundred years of intensive oil production, plus overuse of toxic defoliants in cotton growing, have taken a severe environmental toll. Azerbaijani scientists consider the Abseron Peninsula, where Baku stands, to be one of the most ecologically devastated areas in the world.

Fact File

OFFICIAL NAME Azerbaijani Republic

FORM OF GOVERNMENT Federal republic with single legislative body (National Assembly)

CAPITAL Baki (Baku)

AREA 86,600 sq km (33,436 sq miles)

TIME ZONE GMT + 4 hours

POPULATION 7,908,224

PROJECTED POPULATION 2005 8,171,979

POPULATION DENSITY 91.3 per sq km (236.5 per sq mile)

LIFE EXPECTANCY 63.1

INFANT MORTALITY (PER 1,000) 82.5

OFFICIAL LANGUAGE Azerbaijani

OTHER LANGUAGES Russian, Armenian

LITERACY RATE 96.3%

RELIGIONS Muslim 93.5%, Russian Orthodox 2.5%, Armenian Orthodox 2%, other 2%

ETHNIC GROUPS Azeri 90%, Dagestani peoples 3%, Russian 2.5%, Armenian 2.5%, other 2%

CURRENCY Manat

ECONOMY Services 42%, agriculture 32%, industry 26%

GNP PER CAPITA US$480

CLIMATE Mainly semiarid

HIGHEST POINT Bazardüzü Dağ 4,466 m (14,652 ft)

MAP REFERENCE Page 222

Bahrain

Fact File

OFFICIAL NAME State of Bahrain

FORM OF GOVERNMENT Traditional monarchy

CAPITAL Al Manāmah (Manama)

AREA 620 sq km (239 sq miles)

TIME ZONE GMT + 3 hours

POPULATION 629,090

PROJECTED POPULATION 2005 701,662

POPULATION DENSITY 1,014.6 per sq km
(2,627.8 per sq mile)

LIFE EXPECTANCY 75.3

INFANT MORTALITY (PER 1,000) 14.8

OFFICIAL LANGUAGE Arabic

OTHER LANGUAGES English, Farsi (Persian), Urdu

LITERACY RATE 84%

RELIGIONS Shi'a Muslim 75%, Sunni Muslim 25%

ETHNIC GROUPS Bahraini 63%, Asian 13%, other Arab
10%, Iranian 8%, other 6%

CURRENCY Bahraini dinar

ECONOMY Industry and commerce 85%, agriculture
5%, services 7%, government 3%

GNP PER CAPITA US$7,840

CLIMATE Mainly arid, with mild winters and hot,
humid summers

HIGHEST POINT Jabal ad Dukhān 122 m (400 ft)

MAP REFERENCE Page 220

A cluster of 35 small, low-lying islands in the
Persian Gulf, Bahrain is 28 km (17 miles)
from the west coast of the Qatar Peninsula.
The islands were once the heart of the ancient
Dilmun civilization and have been a trading center
for over 4,000 years. Bahrain was the first of the
Gulf states to export oil, soon after oil was
discovered in 1932. A 25 km (16 mile) causeway
links the main island to Saudi Arabia.

After the 1970s' collapse of Beirut in Lebanon,
previously the region's main commercial center,
Bahrain began to provide banking and financial
services, at the same time increasing its transport
and communication facilities. When the elected
assembly was dissolved in 1975 and the country
reverted to traditional authoritarian rule, there was

growing unrest among the fundamentalist Shi'ite
Muslim majority. Encouraged in their resistance
by Iran, the Shi'ites resent their low status under
Bahrain's Sunni Muslim ruling family. In the
opinion of Shi'ite fundamentalists this family is
unacceptable for a number of reasons—it belongs
to a branch of Islam they regard as oppressive, it
is liberal and modernizing in its economic policies,
and it is a supporter of US policy. US air bases
on Bahrain were vital military assets during the
1990–91 Gulf War.

Consisting of barren rock, sandy plains, and salt
marshes, the landscape of Bahrain is low-lying
desert for the most part, rising to a low central
escarpment. Winters are dry and mild, summers
hot and humid. There are no natural freshwater
resources. All the country's water needs must be
met by groundwater from springs and from
desalinated sea water. Imported soil has been used
to create several small fertile areas, and domestic
agricultural production is capable of meeting local
demand for fruit and vegetables. However, the
degradation of existing arable land is an
environmental concern, along with damage to
coastlines, coral reefs, and sea life resulting from
spills of oil and oil-tanker discharges.

Waning oil production since the 1970s has
forced Bahrain to diversify. Since the opening of
the causeway linking the country to Saudi Arabia
in 1986 there has been a boom in weekend
tourism, visitors pouring in from the Gulf states.
Bahrain is now the Arab world's major banking
center, and numerous multinational firms with
business in the Gulf have offices in the country.
Ship repairs are also undertaken in Bahrain.
Petroleum production and processing account for
80 percent of export receipts. Natural gas has
assumed greater importance, and is used to supply
local industries, including an aluminum smelting
plant. However, unemployment among the young,
especially among the Shi'ite majority, is a cause of
social unrest and continuing economic concern.

*A spice seller in a Bahrain market (below). Bangladeshi
women doing agricultural work (top right). Bus station in
Dhaka, Bangladesh (bottom right).*

Bangladesh

K nown for tropical cyclones and endemic
poverty, the small and densely populated
country of Bangladesh lies north of the Bay of
Bengal. Most of its frontier is with India and it has
a short border with Myanmar (Burma) in the
southeast. The name Bangladesh means "the land
of the Bengalis," a people who have contributed a
great deal to Indian history. Once a part of the
Mauryan Empire of the fourth century BC, Bengal
has been mainly Muslim since the thirteenth
century, and during its more recent history its
Muslim people have often been ruled by Hindu
overlords. At the time of the partition of India in
1947, this situation led to the founding of East
Pakistan, the oriental wing of the Muslim state that
was set up following independence. In 1971
resentment of the power and privileges of West
Pakistan resulted in East Pakistan breaking away
and forming the independent state of Bangladesh.
Since then its history has been one of political
coups, dissolved parliaments, and civil unrest,
compounded by natural disasters. In 1991 the worst
cyclone in memory killed over 140,000 people.

Bangladesh is low and flat, its physiography determined by three navigable rivers—the Ganges (Padma), Brahmaputra (Jamuna) and the smaller Meghna. At their confluence they form the biggest delta in the world. The western part of this delta, which is over the border in India, is somewhat higher, and is less subject to flooding. What is called the "active delta" lies in Bangladesh and this region is frequently flooded. During monsoons the water rises up to 6 m (18 ft) above sea level, submerging two-thirds of the country, and the delta's changing channels are hazardous to life, health, and property. However, the floods are also

Issues in Bangladesh

After 15 years of military rule multi-party politics returned to Bangladesh in 1990, and the country's first woman prime minister, Begum Khaleda Zia, leader of the Bangladesh Nationalist Party (BNP), was elected in 1991. However, factionalism divides the nation and Bangladesh remains politically unstable.

Despite the country's prominent female politicians (the opposition Awami League is also led by a woman), women in Bangladesh face discrimination in health care, education, and employment. In addition, dowry-related violence against women does occur.

Religious divides exist, as elsewhere in the region. Tension between Bangladesh's Hindus and the Muslim majority is a problem, and Buddhist tribes in the southeast are agitating for autonomous rule. Relations with neighboring India are also strained, although in 1996 the countries signed a treaty agreeing to share resources after an Indian dam on the Ganges River reduced irrigation water for Bangladesh.

An exodus of refugees from Myanmar (Burma)—as many as 200,000 by early 1992— also stretched Bangladesh's scarce resources.

International aid finances 90 percent of state capital spending and an economic liberalization program has been introduced.

beneficial in that they renew soil fertility with silt, some of it washed down from as far away as Tibet. Whole new islands are formed by alluvial deposition, and the highly fertile silt can yield as many as three rice crops a year. The far south-eastern region of Chittagong has the only high country in Bangladesh, with forested ridges and rubber plantations.

Bangladesh is a major recipient of international aid. Disbursements of aid are currently running at more than 1,000 times the annual value of foreign investment. Despite the efforts of the international community, however, it remains one of the world's poorest and least developed nations. Rice is the main crop in the country's basically agrarian economy, followed by jute, tea, and sugarcane. Bangladesh is the world's largest supplier of high quality jute. About half the crop is exported in its raw form and the rest is processed for export as hessian, sacking, and carpet-backing. A modern paper industry uses bamboo from the hills. Other industries include textiles, fertilizer, glass, iron and steel, sugar, cement, and aluminum. Fishing is also economically important. However, there are a number of serious impediments to progress. They include frequent cyclones and floods, inefficient state-owned enterprises, a labor force growing (as a consequence of a steady population growth) faster than it can be absorbed by agriculture alone, and delays in developing energy resources such as natural gas.

Fact File

OFFICIAL NAME People's Republic of Bangladesh

FORM OF GOVERNMENT Republic with single legislative body (National Parliament)

CAPITAL Dhaka (Dacca)

AREA 144,000 sq km (55,598 sq miles)

TIME ZONE GMT + 6 hours

POPULATION 129,859,779

PROJECTED POPULATION 2005 142,921,111

POPULATION DENSITY 901.8 per sq km (2,335.7 per sq mile)

LIFE EXPECTANCY 57.1

INFANT MORTALITY (PER 1,000) 95.3

OFFICIAL LANGUAGE Bangla

OTHER LANGUAGE English

LITERACY RATE 37.3%

RELIGIONS Muslim 83%, Hindu 16%, other (mainly Buddhist, Christian) 1%

ETHNIC GROUPS Bengali 98%, Biharis and tribal peoples 2%

CURRENCY Taka

ECONOMY Agriculture 57%, services 33%, industry 10%

GNP PER CAPITA US$240

CLIMATE Tropical, with three seasons: cool, dry winter (October to March); hot, humid summer (March to June); and cool, wet monsoon (June to October)

HIGHEST POINT Mt Keokradong 1,230 m (4,035 ft)

MAP REFERENCE Page 219

Bhutan

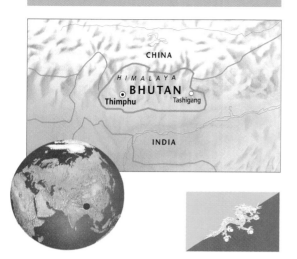

Fact File

OFFICIAL NAME Kingdom of Bhutan

FORM OF GOVERNMENT Monarchy with single legislative body (National Assembly)

CAPITAL Thimphu

AREA 47,000 sq km (18,147 sq miles)

TIME ZONE GMT + 5.5 hours

POPULATION 1,951,965

PROJECTED POPULATION 2005 2,226,481

POPULATION DENSITY 41.5 per sq km (107.5 per sq mile)

LIFE EXPECTANCY 52.8

INFANT MORTALITY (PER 1,000) 109.3

OFFICIAL LANGUAGE Dzongkha

OTHER LANGUAGES Tibetan, Nepalese

LITERACY RATE 41.1%

RELIGIONS Lamaistic Buddhism 75%, Hinduism 25%

ETHNIC GROUPS Bhote (Tibetan) 50%, ethnic Nepalese 35%, indigenous or migrant tribes 15%

CURRENCY Ngultrum

ECONOMY Agriculture 93%, services 5%, industry and commerce 2%

GNP PER CAPITA US$420

CLIMATE Tropical on southern plains; cool winters and hot summers in central valleys; cold winters and cool summers in mountains

HIGHEST POINT Kula Kangri 7,554 m (24,783 ft)

MAP REFERENCE Page 219

A tiny landlocked kingdom nestling in the Himalayas between India and Tibet, Bhutan is difficult to visit, and remains largely closed to the outside world. It is the world's most "rural" country, with less than 6 percent of its population living in towns and over 90 percent dependent on agriculture for a living. Despite its isolation and apparent tranquillity, the country is torn by fierce ethnic tensions which its absolute monarch does little to mitigate. Bhutan's longest-resident ethnic group consists of the Tibetans who probably migrated there 1,000 years ago. Early in the twentieth century, in order to end continual fighting between rival warlords in the area, the British administration in neighboring India established a hereditary monarch in Bhutan, the "Dragon King," in 1907.

The monarch is both head of state and government. Though a modernizer, intent on changing Bhutan's feudal ways, his emphasis on a sense of national identity founded on the language, laws, and dress of his own Drukpa group has stirred up bitter opposition among the resident Hindu Nepalese in southern Bhutan. Many have been deported, and others have fled to refugee camps in southeast Nepal. Dzongkha, which has been proclaimed the official language, is the natural language of only 16 percent of Bhutanese. In 1998 the king announced that in future Bhutan's rulers would have to step down if they received a no-confidence vote from the National Assembly.

There are three main regions distinguished largely by altitude—the Great Himalayas, crowned by huge peaks along the border with Tibet; the slopes and fertile valleys of the Lesser Himalayas, which are divided by the Wong, Sankosh, Tongsa and Manas rivers; and the Duars Plain which opens out toward India from the foothills of the mountains. The central uplands and foothills are cultivated, food staples including maize, wheat, barley, and potatoes. This area supports the bulk of the population. Below this the Duars Plain falls away into broad tracts of semitropical forest, savanna, and bamboo jungle. Forests still cover nearly 75 percent of Bhutan's land area, and timber is exported to India.

Almost all trade is with India. As an export, timber is outweighed in importance by cement. Other revenue-earning activities include a closely supervised and limited tourist industry (visitors are restricted to 4,000 per year), and the sale of stamps. Bhutan has huge hydropower potential but most manufacturing is of the cottage-industry type. Development projects such as road construction rely on Indian migrant labor. Though stabilized at a low level (the economy is one of the world's smallest and poorest) the country's balance of payments is strong, with comfortable reserves.

Brunei

O il was discovered in the sultanate of Brunei in 1929. By the time it became independent on 1 January 1984 this small country on the north coast of Borneo was already prosperous. Today its oil revenues have made Brunei's sultan perhaps the richest man in the world, and given its people one of the highest per capita incomes in Asia. There is no income tax, the government subsidizes food and housing, and provides free medical care. The downside is that all government employees (two-thirds of the workforce) are banned from political activity, and the Sultan of Brunei rules by decree. Some nongovernmental political groupings have been allowed but the sultan remains firmly in control. There is disquiet among Bruneians over the rising number of resident foreigners, as demand for both skilled and unskilled labor brings contract workers in from outside.

Brunei consists of two semi-enclaves on the northwest coast of Borneo which are bordered by the Malaysian state of Sarawak. They are separated by a few kilometers of coastline where the Limbang River enters Brunei Bay. The topography in both consists of hills bordering a

narrow, swampy coastal plain. More than two-thirds of the country is tropical forest.

Brunei is almost entirely supported by exports of oil and natural gas. Petroleum revenues account for more than 40 percent of gross domestic product. Production is carried out by Brunei Shell Petroleum in which the government holds a 50 percent stake. Most crude oil is exported to Japan, South Korea, Taiwan, and the USA. Liquefied natural gas is produced in one of the world's biggest plants, at Lumut in Malaysia, and is sold to power and gas companies in Tokyo and Osaka. About 80 percent of Brunei's food is imported, but there has been a push to achieve agricultural self-sufficiency. Small farms grow rice, fruit, and vegetables. The government Forestry Department, which controls all forest reserves, is expanding into value-added activities such as furniture production.

Fact File

OFFICIAL NAME	State of Brunei
FORM OF GOVERNMENT	Sultanate with advisory council of Cabinet Ministers
CAPITAL	Bandar Seri Begawan
AREA	5,770 sq km (2,228 sq miles)
TIME ZONE	GMT + 8 hours
POPULATION	322,982
PROJECTED POPULATION 2005	369,691
POPULATION DENSITY	56 per sq km (145 per sq mile)
LIFE EXPECTANCY	71.8
INFANT MORTALITY (PER 1,000)	22.8
OFFICIAL LANGUAGES	English, Malay
OTHER LANGUAGE	Chinese
LITERACY RATE	87.9%
RELIGIONS	Muslim 63%, Buddhism 14%, Christian 8%, indigenous beliefs and other 15%
ETHNIC GROUPS	Malay 64%, Chinese 20%, other 16%
CURRENCY	Bruneian dollar
ECONOMY	Services 87%, industry 9%, agriculture 4%
GNP PER CAPITA	Est. > US$9,386
CLIMATE	Tropical
HIGHEST POINT	Gunong Pagon 1,850 m (6,070 ft)
MAP REFERENCE	Page 201

Cambodia

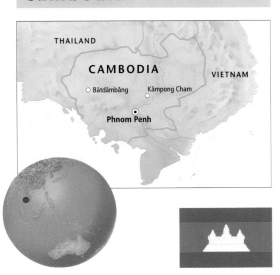

The Southeast Asian country of Cambodia is famous both culturally and politically. At Angkor Wat and Angkor Thom it has the world's largest group of religious buildings, a priceless relic of the Hindu Khmer Empire (AD 802 to 1432). It also, in the 1970s, saw an outbreak of communist fanaticism in which over 2 million people died. Under French rule from 1863, Cambodia won independence in 1954. In the late 1950s and during the 1960s there was a short period of relative stability in which the country developed its agricultural resources and rubber plantations and managed to achieve self-sufficiency in food.

Years of internal political struggles, plus its involvement in the Vietnam War, led to a takeover by the Khmer Rouge under Pol Pot in 1975. With the aim of creating a classless agrarian society, money and private property were abolished, the professional classes were murdered (anyone with glasses was at risk), and townspeople were brutally moved into the countryside and left to fend for themselves. Half a million refugees fled to Thailand, and between a quarter and one-eighth of the entire population died. The regime fell in 1978 and Pol Pot went into hiding but civil war continued for some years; Pol Pot died in 1998. A devastated and desperately poor nation, stripped of what little economic infrastructure and trained

personnel it once had, Cambodia is now trying to put itself together again.

The country's heartland consists of a wide basin drained by the Mekong River. In the center of this lies the Tonlé Sap (Great Lake), surrounded by a broad plain. When the rain is meager and the Mekong is low—from November to June—the lake drains south toward the sea. But during the rainy season when the Mekong is high—from July to October—the flow reverses, and the lake doubles its area to become the largest freshwater lake in Southeast Asia. The wealth of the fabled "gentle kingdom" of Cambodia consists of fish from the lake and rice from the flooded lowlands, a year-round water supply being provided by an extensive system of irrigation channels and reservoirs. Directly south of the lake the Cardamom (Chuŏr Phnum Kravan) and Elephant (Chuŏr Phnum Dâmrek) Mountains look out over a narrow coastal plain.

Reconstructing the Cambodian economy is bringing almost as many costs as benefits. Tropical rainforest timber, especially teak and rosewood, is Cambodia's most important resource. For 20 years it was sold in huge quantities by all factions to finance their war efforts. Now indiscriminate tree-felling is a major environmental problem, a 1992 moratorium on logging largely being ignored. Gems are another resource but strip mining is causing habitat loss, and the destruction of mangrove swamps threatening fisheries. Starting from a very low base, growth was strong in the early 1990s, but a lack of skills at all levels of administration and management is slowing progress.

Fact File

OFFICIAL NAME	Kingdom of Cambodia
FORM OF GOVERNMENT	Constitutional monarchy with single legislative body (National Assembly)
CAPITAL	Phnom Penh
AREA	181,040 sq km (69,900 sq miles)
TIME ZONE	GMT + 7 hours
POPULATION	11,780,285
PROJECTED POPULATION 2005	13,786,677
POPULATION DENSITY	65.1 per sq km (168.6 per sq mile)
LIFE EXPECTANCY	51.1
INFANT MORTALITY (PER 1,000)	102.4
OFFICIAL LANGUAGE	Khmer
OTHER LANGUAGE	French
LITERACY RATE	35%
RELIGIONS	Theravada Buddhism 95%, other 5%
ETHNIC GROUPS	Khmer 90%, Vietnamese 5%, Chinese 1%, other 4%
CURRENCY	Riel
ECONOMY	Agriculture 80%, services and industry 20%
GNP PER CAPITA	US$270
CLIMATE	Tropical, with wet season May to November
HIGHEST POINT	Phnum Aôral 1,771 m (5,810 ft)
MAP REFERENCE	Page 203

China

Fact File

OFFICIAL NAME People's Republic of China

FORM OF GOVERNMENT Communist republic with single legislative body (National People's Congress)

CAPITAL Beijing

AREA 9,596,960 sq km (3,705,386 sq miles)

TIME ZONE GMT + 8 hours

POPULATION 1,246,871,951

PROJECTED POPULATION 2005 1,296,199,683

POPULATION DENSITY 129.9 per sq km (336.4 per sq mile)

LIFE EXPECTANCY 69.9

INFANT MORTALITY (PER 1,000) 43.3

OFFICIAL LANGUAGE Mandarin Chinese

OTHER LANGUAGES Yue (Cantonese), Wu (Shanghaiese), Minbei (Fuzhou), Minnan (Hokkien-Taiwanese), other minority languages

LITERACY RATE 80.9%

RELIGIONS Officially atheist; traditionally Confucian, Taoist, Buddhist; small Muslim and Christian minorities

ETHNIC GROUPS Han Chinese 92%, other (including Zhuang, Uygur, Hui, Yi, Tibetan, Miao, Manchu, Mongol, Buyi, Korean) 8%

CURRENCY Yuan

ECONOMY Agriculture 74%, industry 14%, services 12%

GNP PER CAPITA US$620

CLIMATE Varies widely: subtropical in southeast; temperate in east; cold and arid on southwestern Tibetan plateau; arid in northern deserts; cold temperate in northeast

HIGHEST POINT Mt Everest 8,848 m (29,028 ft)

MAP REFERENCE Pages 205, 206, 210–11, 212–13, 214–15

The third largest country in the world, and the most populous, China is today something of an enigma: it has an increasingly capitalistic economy but with an old-style Communist Party leadership remaining in political control. Much depends on how successfully this "socialist market economy" works. With a civilization going back 5,000 years, China's history has combined long periods of dynastic stability with shorter periods of sudden change. In the last 100 years it has gone through a series of convulsive social, political, and economic transformations. Once isolated, agrarian, and indifferent to other societies and cultures, China's future is now that of a modern industrial nation trading with much of the world. Politically it remains a one-party state. The political reforms needed for greater democracy are widely discussed in western media, as are civil liberties and human rights issues, but they are not yet on the agenda of China itself.

Physical features and land use

China can be divided into three major regions: the mountains to the west, including the vast Plateau of Tibet; the series of deserts and desert basins starting in the northwest with the Tarim Basin and the Taklimakan Desert, reaching across the Nei Mongol Plateau (Nei Mongol Gaoyuan) to Manchuria (Taklimakan Shamo) in the northeast; and the largely low-lying eastern region consisting of the valleys and floodplains of the Chang Jiang (Yangtze) and Huang (Yellow) rivers, extending to the coastal plains including the Pearl River in the south.

The melting snows of the Plateau of Tibet feed several major rivers—the Brahmaputra, flowing south to India, the Salween (Nu) of Myanmar (Burma), and the Mekong which skirts Laos and Thailand before passing through Cambodia and reaching the sea in Vietnam. In addition it is the source of both the Huang (Yellow), and the mighty Chang Jiang (Yangtze), China's two main rivers which drain into the East China Sea. In some parts permanently covered in snow, the

Plateau of Tibet is the highest region in the world, averaging about 4,900 m (16,000 ft), with ranges rising from 6,100 to 7,300 m (20,000 to 24,000 ft). It is bounded to the north by the Kunlun Shan Range, and to the south along the borders of India, Nepal, and Bhutan by the mountain system of the Himalayas. A harsh environment, hostile to human settlement, most of the plateau's 2 million people live in the south. The Himalayan ranges also have a political significance. Forming a massive rampart along China's southwestern frontier, for centuries they have provided a natural defensive barrier against the west. This is one reason why China is unwilling to allow the pressure for Tibetan independence to take it beyond the status of an "autonomous region."

The second region, stretching from the Tarim Basin and Dzungarian Basin (Junggar Pendi) in the northwest, past the southern fringes of the Gobi Desert to Northern Manchuria, is mostly too arid and cold for agriculture. Here, pastoralists such as the Uighurs of Xinjiang keep sheep, goats, and herds of horses. Some oasis crops, however, are grown around the rim of the Taklimakan Desert, and there are small farming settlements in the Gansu corridor to the north of the Qilian Mountains. The Turfan Depression (Turpan Pendi) (both the lowest and the hottest place in China at –154 m [–505 ft]) lies northeast of the Tarim Basin. East of the Gobi Desert lies the agricultural area of the Manchurian Plain, where coarse grains and soya beans are cultivated. In Northern Manchuria the growing season is short: only 90 days a year are frost free.

The eastern region of central China is where two-thirds of the country's people live. This was the cradle of Chinese civilization. On the region's

fertile alluvial plains the most distinctive features of China's economic and social life developed—intensive irrigated agriculture and the Chinese peasant family. Known as "China's Sorrow," the Huang (Yellow) River makes its way across the North China Plain. For hundreds of years it caused frequent flooding, with serious loss of life, but today modern flood-control schemes have reduced this danger.

Further south, near the Chang Jiang (Yangtze) delta, the plain changes into a land of large lakes and intricate networks of canals, many of them centuries old. The Chang Jiang is China's largest and most important river, much of it navigable. When the river level is high, vessels of 10,000 tonnes may reach Wuhan; and 1,000-tonne barges can reach Chongqing in Sichuan. What is called the "Red Basin" of Sichuan is a fertile and highly productive area far up the Chang Jiang, separated from the lower valley by steep-sided gorges. It is intensively cultivated, the landscape dominated by rice fields arranged in terraces up the hillsides. Summer weather in the central valley of the Chang Jiang is hot and humid, temperatures at Nanjing reaching 44°C (111°F).

A distinctive landscape in southern China (famous for centuries as an inspiration for Chinese landscape painters) is found in northeastern Guizhou Province, where limestone spires and pinnacles rise above small, intensively cultivated plains. This heavily eroded area is marked by sinkholes, caverns, and underground streams. In the coastal lowlands of Guangdong Province, in the far south, the climate is tropical and farmers enjoy a year-round growing season. On Hainan Island, flanking the Gulf of Tongking, three crops of rice per year are possible, while other crops in

the south include sugar, bananas, and tropical fruits. During the summer, cyclones and typhoons often strike the southeast coast.

Early history

Civilization arose along the margins of the North China Plain. Here, about 1700 BC, the Shang Dynasty originated in the Huang Valley. Noted for craftsmanship in bronze, along with the use of the wheel, the calendar, and a form of writing, the Shang lasted until 1122 BC. During the next dynasty, the Zhou, the teachings of the philosopher-teacher Confucius (551–479 BC) provided a pattern for Chinese society for centuries to come. Iron casting, metal coinage, and silk were also introduced at

this time. During the short-lived Qin Dynasty (221–206 BC) a ruler arose named Qin Shihuang. He unified the nation, fortified China's northern boundary with the Great Wall, established the civil service, and was buried at Lintong with an army of 6,000 terracotta warriors which are today a major tourist attraction.

In 206 BC the Han Dynasty was begun. During the four centuries of the Han, paper and the seismograph were invented, steel was first made, Buddhism was introduced from India, and the boundaries of China were extended nearly to their present limits. Under the Sui (AD 581–618) a large part of the Grand Canal linking the north with the Chang Valley was built. During the 300 years of

The countryside near Yangshuo in Guangxi Zhuangzu Zizhiqu Province (left). Buddhist prayer flags in the Potala Palace, in Lhasa, Tibet (top). Threshing rice after harvesting (center). A shopkeeper outside her fruit and vegetable store (above).

Asia and the Middle East

the Tang Dynasty which followed, China became the world's biggest empire. Paper money was adopted, block printing invented, and priceless ceramic vases produced. In these centuries, and those of the Song Dynasty (AD 960–1269) China's population, threatened by incursions of nomads from the north, began to concentrate in the warmer, more productive south. By the thirteenth century most people lived in the south, including the Chang Valley. The Song Dynasty is sometimes regarded as China's Golden Age. Trade expanded, and Chinese shipping took porcelain and silk to the East Indies, India, and Africa.

Northern invaders ended the Song Dynasty. By 1223 Ghengis Khan's Mongols held much of the north and in 1260 Kublai Khan proclaimed himself emperor, with Beijing as his capital. Unified by the conquests of the Mongol tribes, the empire by 1300 reached from Kiev to the Persian Gulf, and from Burma to Korea. Muslims, Christians, and Armenians all came to China at this time—among them the Italian Marco Polo, who served under Kublai Khan. After the Mongols were overthrown, Chinese rule was re-established under the Ming Dynasty in 1368, and the Great Wall was restored and extended to its present length of 6,400 km (4,000 miles). In the three centuries of Ming rule many palaces were built, including the Imperial Palace at Beijing, and ships explored as far afield as the Red Sea. It was during this period that the first Christian missions began to appear in China, the Jesuits establishing themselves with the Portuguese at Macao in the sixteenth century.

Chinese civilization's main features, however, had been laid down in the time of the Han, Tang, and Song. During their rule Confucianism became the pervasive social ethic, the individual becoming

subordinated to both family and state; porcelain manufacture and silk production reached a rare perfection; and various inventions were made which found their way to the West, notably that of gunpowder. Despite the development of large cities, and the growth of an educated bureaucratic elite, Chinese society was largely agricultural, and its economic base depended on the productivity of the rural peasantry.

The Qing Dynasty (1683–1912) represented a return to power of northern people, the Manchus, descendants of the Mongols. Aggressive at first, seizing Taiwan and garrisoning Tibet, by the nineteenth century the Qing government had become weak and corrupt. Famine and unrest had made the country vulnerable to outside pressure and by the century's end China had been divided into spheres of influence among the major Western powers, a disintegration hastened by peasant uprisings (the Taiping Rebellion of 1850–64), and military defeats (the Sino-Japanese War of 1894–95). In 1912 the last of China's emperors abdicated and a republic was proclaimed.

Modern history

Political and military disorder prevailed during the next 40 years. At first the country was fought over by rival warlords. Two hostile competing political movements offered solutions to this chaos—the Kuomintang (or Chinese National Party), and the Communist Party (founded in 1921)—but neither gained overall control. Then in 1931 Japan seized Manchuria, and in 1937 war broke out between China and Japan. During this time the communists sharpened their military and political skills, Mao Zedong winning the support of the peasantry and showing it was possible to succeed at guerrilla warfare. Hostilities between the Kuomintang and the communists were suspended in order to defeat Japan. But once this was achieved, in 1945, civil war broke out, costing 12 million lives. Victory went to the communists, and the People's Republic of China was proclaimed in October 1949.

Mass starvation, malnutrition, and disease were all brought under control in the inital years of communist rule and land reform began. As part of a planned economy the rural population was organized into 50,000 communes—units which farmed the land collectively. Communes also ran rural industries, schools, and clinics. During these years morale and dedication were high. Many of the old middle classes suffered grave privations in "re-education camps" but living standards improved for most people, and corruption and bureaucratic sloth were not a major problem. But Mao Zedong was determined to push ahead with radical programs of industrialization and political change. In 1958 the "Great Leap Forward" movement tried to industrialize the country using the organization of the communes, and increase steel production by using backyard furnaces. It was a disaster.

Timeline

460,000 BP Earliest claimed evidence of controlled use of fire (Zhoukoudian Cave) by so-called *Homo erectus* Peking Man	**1200 BC** Writing system based on pictograms in use—many characters similar to those still used today	**5500 BC** First thick clay pottery used in fishing villages along southern coastline	**214 BC** First part of Great Wall of China completed under Qin Dynasty to protect against Turkish and Mongol invasions	**c.100 AD** Paper made from hemp and rags in use with solid inks in northwest China	**1213** Genghis Khan leads Mongolian invasion—up to 30 million Chinese are slaughtered

1.9 MYA Appearance of early hominids who closely resemble *Homo habilis* (Longgupo Cave, Sichuan Province)	**800,000 BP** Hominid *Homo erectus*, now considered to have evolved in Asia; present in China possibly 1.8 MYA	**68,000 BP** *Homo sapiens sapiens* present in China	**7500 BC** Farmers of central and southern China domesticate foxtail millet and rice	**800 BC** Population under the Chou Dynasty more than 13 million	**206 BC** Shi Huangdi (First Emperor) is buried with 6,000 life-size terracotta warriors at Chang-an near Xi'an	**618** Tang Dynasty sees great economic development; Grand Canal links Huang and Chang rivers (completed 1283)	**1279** The Mongols under Kublai Khan (grandson of Genghis) take control of all China; Beijing now the capital

Between 1959 and 1961 failed economic policies led to famine, disease, and attempted rebellion. As many as 20 million people died.

Mao increasingly suspected his associates of disloyalty, believing some wanted to take "the capitalist road." In 1966 he launched the Great Proletarian Cultural Revolution to extirpate "old thought, old culture, old customs and old habits." China's local authorities were, in effect, put on trial, many community members were abused and tormented, and the Red Guards rampaged through the many cities destroying property and wrecking ancient works of art. In 1967 the army was called in to restore order. Mao's death in 1976 brought change. There was even, in 1978, a brief flirtation with free speech. Deng Xiaoping, a new leader with a different vision of Chinese communism but no less determined to assert his power, began the process of economic liberalization which has led to today's state-managed capitalism and rigid political regime.

Taiwan and Tibet complicate China's relations with the West. China insists that Taiwan must rejoin the mainland as a province. Tibet has suffered under the regime, and thousands of its people have been killed, China's historic use of the region as a defensive bulwark in the west means that independence is unlikely. Civil rights do not exist in China. Law is arbitrary, the courts usually being conducted by army personnel without legal training. Students demonstrating in Beijing in 1989 for

A portrait of Mao Zedong in the Forbidden City (far left). Girl eating noodles (below left). Part of the Great Wall of China (top left). Downtown Hong Kong, seen from the air (right). A government building in Shanhaiguan (below).

greater democracy were met with tanks and hundreds were killed and injured. In 1998 an attempt to organize an independent political party was crushed and its leaders jailed.

The economy

Coal deposits exist in most provinces, and there are 70 production centers, of which Hebei, Shanxi, Shandong, Jilin, and Anhui are the most important. China also has deposits of iron ore, and is a major producer of tungsten. Industries produce iron, steel, coal, machinery, armaments, textiles, and petroleum, while the main exports are textiles, oil and oil products, chemicals, light industrial goods, and armaments. Questions about the economy are not centered on resources, skills or capacity. They concern the ideological clash between a market-oriented economy and the rigid controls of the Communist Party.

In 1978 the leadership began moving away from Soviet-style central planning. In agriculture, household responsibility replaced collectivization and brought an immediate rise in productivity. In

industry, the power of plant managers and local officials was increased, small-scale private enterprise was allowed, and foreign investment and trade encouraged. As a result, agricultural output doubled in the 1980s and industry made major gains. Gross domestic product has tripled since 1978.

The present system, however, combines some of the worst features of communism (bureaucracy, inertia, and corruption) and of capitalism (windfall gains and high inflation). Additional difficulties arise from revenue collection of every kind; from extortion and other economic malpractices; and from inefficient state enterprises. Up to 100 million rural workers are adrift between country and city. The amount of arable land continues to decline. Serious environmental problems exist—air pollution from the use of coal, and water pollution from industrial effluents; falling water tables and nation-wide water shortages; and the fact that less than 10 percent of sewage is treated.

PROVINCES AND CAPITALS

Anhui • Hefei
Fujian • Fuzhou
Gansu • Lanzhou
Guangdong • Guangzhou
Guizhou • Guiyang
Hainan • Haikou
Hebei • Shijiazhuang
Heilongjiang • Harbin
Henan • Zhengzhou
Hubei • Wuhan
Hunan • Changsha
Jiangsu • Nanjing
Jiangxi • Nanchang
Jilin • Changchun
Liaoning • Shenyang
Qinghai • Xining
Shaanxi • Xi'an
Shandong • Jinan
Shanxi • Taiyuan
Sichuan • Chengdu
Yunnan • Kunming
Zhejiang • Hangzhou

AUTONOMOUS REGIONS

Guangxi Zhuangzu • Nanning
Nei Monggol • Hohhot
Ningxia Huizu • Yinchuan
Tibet (Xizang) • Lhasa
Xinjiang Uygur • Ürümqi

SPECIAL ADMINISTRATIVE REGION

Xianggang (Hong Kong) • Xianggang (Hong Kong)

Macao • Macao

MUNICIPALITIES

Beijing, Shanghai, and Tianjin

1275 Marco Polo, a Venetian, visits China (until 1292) to establish trade links with the country he calls "Cathay"

1800 British smuggle in opium; war breaks out when Chinese object. Treaty in 1842 ends war; China cedes Hong Kong to Britain

1900 Chinese "Boxer" rebellion in Peking (Beijing) against foreign interests put down by British and Russian forces

1927–28 Civil War between Communist party and Kuomintang under Chiang Kai-Shek; Nationalists take Beijing

1949 Mao Zedong proclaims People's Republic of China after a four-year civil war costing 12 million lives

1958 "Great Leap Forward" to foster development damages economy and leads to severe food shortages; 20 million die by 1962

1989 Pro-democracy demonstrations crushed by the use of tanks in Tiananmen Square, Beijing, with hundreds killed

1997 China regains control of Hong Kong, imposes 'One China, two systems' policy

1644 The Manchus establish Qing Dynasty, bringing peace and prosperity; the population rises to 400 million by 1700

1887–88 Huang River floods killing as many as 2.5 million people. It has flooded 1,500 times in the last 3,500 years

1911 Rebels proclaim republic—Emperor Pu Yi leaves throne 1912. In 1913 Sun Yat-sen founds Kuomintang (Nationalist Party)

1934 Mao Zedong leads Long March of the Communists across China

1950 China invades Tibet; the Dalai Lama, Tibet's spiritual leader, flees to India

1979 "One-child families" policy introduced to curb population growth

1990 Census shows population of China exceeds 1.1 billion people

1998 Chang Jiang River floods kill 3,000 with 250,000 homeless

Cyprus

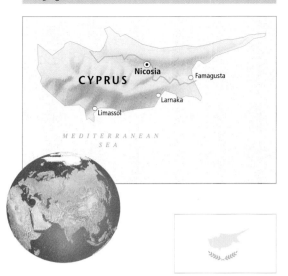

Cyprus takes its name from "kypros," the Greek word for copper. It was an important metal 3,000 years ago, in classical times, and is still exported today. Occupied by a succession of Phoenicians, Greeks, and Romans, held from 1571 by the Turks and by the British from 1878, Cyprus today is a deeply divided island. The southern part forms the Republic of Cyprus proper, where most of the population live. Since 1982 the northern part has consisted of an autonomous region calling itself the Turkish Republic of Northern Cyprus (see box).

Along the north coast runs the long limestone range of the Kyrenia Mountains. Just south of this range is the fertile Mesaoria Plain between Morphou and Ammochostos (Famagusta) where grapes, potatoes, citrus fruits, and cereals are grown, and the steeper land supports sheep, goats, and cattle. In the south is the broad, mineral-rich massif of Troödos from where the copper comes. This constitutes 50 percent of the country's total land area and is a good geological example of an ophiolite, a dome of mineral-rich sub-oceanic rocks. Both major rivers flow from this massif—the Pedieas to Ammochostos Bay (Famagusta Bay), the Karyoti to Morphou Bay. Nearly half the total area of Cyprus is arable and 20 percent of this is irrigated.

The gap between the economic fortunes of the two parts of Cyprus continues to grow wider. The agriculturally based Turkish north, severely disrupted by the events of 1974, has not recovered well, and has suffered considerably from inflation. It continues to produce some cereals, meat, fruits, and olives. The Greek Cypriot southern half of the island has prospered from a greater diversity of activities, including tourism, manufacturing, and the income from military installations, such as the British air base of Akrotiri near Limassol. Manufactured products include cigarettes, wine, clothing, footwear, and cement.

Fact File

OFFICIAL NAME	(Greek/Turkish) Republic of Cyprus
FORM OF GOVERNMENT	Two de facto republics each with single legislative body: House of Representatives in Greek area, Assembly of the Republic in Turkish area
CAPITAL	Lefkosia (Nicosia)
AREA	9,250 sq km (3,571 sq miles)
TIME ZONE	GMT + 2 hours
POPULATION	768,895
PROJECTED POPULATION 2005	816,812
POPULATION DENSITY	83.1 per sq km (215.2 per sq mile)
LIFE EXPECTANCY	77.1
INFANT MORTALITY (PER 1,000)	7.6
OFFICIAL LANGUAGES	Greek, Turkish
OTHER LANGUAGE	English
LITERACY RATE	94%
RELIGIONS	Greek Orthodox 78%, Muslim 18%, other 4%
ETHNIC GROUPS	Greek 78%, Turkish 18%, other 4%
CURRENCY	Cypriot pound, Turkish lira
ECONOMY	Services 67%, industry 19%, agriculture 14%
GNP PER CAPITA	Est. > US$9,386
CLIMATE	Temperate, with cool, wet winters and warm, dry summers
HIGHEST POINT	Olympos 1,951 m (6,404 ft)
MAP REFERENCE	Page 224

The Cyprus question

What seems to be a national dispute between Greece and Turkey has religious roots. The early Christians Paul, Barnabas, and Mark all visited Cyprus, and the Cypriots were among the first to adopt Christianity. Later, the rise of Islam saw the island subjected to repeated Arab invasions between 644 and 975. From 1195 it was ruled by the family of Guy de Lusignan, to whom it was given after the Third Crusade, and in 1487 it passed into the hands of the Venetian Republic.

In 1571 rule by Venice was replaced by Turkish rule—the Turks massacring many Greeks before settling a large number of their own people on the island. With the decline of the Ottoman Empire in the nineteenth century an agreement was made in 1878 giving Britain the administration of Cyprus (it became a crown colony in 1925). Greek Cypriots soon began agitating for union with Greece. This was also supported by Greek Orthodox Church leaders, who argued that four-fifths of the population (the

A flourishing olive tree in Cyprus that is about 1,000 years old (bottom left). Fortress-like walls surrounding a church in Georgia (far left). An aerial view of a village in the Caucasus Mountains in Georgia (left).

stands, and which divides the northern and southern ranges. Further east, the Kura (Kür) River and its tributaries drain through a number of upland valleys toward Azerbaijan and the Caspian Sea. The mountains contain extensive woodlands (nearly 40 percent of the country is forested) with broadleaf beech, oak, and chestnut at lower levels, and a sparse cover of birch on the higher slopes.

Georgia is an agricultural country, and the main industries are food processing and wine production. Collectivization had less impact on Georgia than elsewhere in the Soviet Union, so the recovery of its rural sector post-1991 has been fairly painless. Privately owned plots flourish, agriculture as a whole producing citrus fruits, tea (the main crop), grapes, tobacco, wheat, barley and vegetables, while perfumes are made from flowers and herbs. The Imeretia district has a flourishing silk industry. Other products from a small industrial sector include machinery, chemicals, and textiles. Manganese, copper, cobalt, and vanadium are mined. Tourism was once important, but has been damaged by civil strife. There are severe energy shortages. In the long term, hopes for Georgian economic progress hinge on re-establishing trade ties with Russia, and on international transportation (such as handling oil from Azerbaijan) through its Black Sea ports.

Fact File

OFFICIAL NAME	Republic of Georgia
FORM OF GOVERNMENT	Republic with single legislative body (Parliament)
CAPITAL	T'bilisi
AREA	69,700 sq km (26,911 sq miles)
TIME ZONE	GMT + 4 hours
POPULATION	5,066,499
PROJECTED POPULATION 2005	4,914,353
POPULATION DENSITY	72.7 per sq km (188.3 per sq mile)
LIFE EXPECTANCY	64.6
INFANT MORTALITY (PER 1,000)	52
OFFICIAL LANGUAGE	Georgian
OTHER LANGUAGES	Russian, Armenian, Azeri
LITERACY RATE	94.9%
RELIGIONS	Christian Orthodox 75% (Georgian Orthodox 65%, Russian Orthodox 10%), Muslim 11%, Armenian Apostolic 8%, unknown 6%
ETHNIC GROUPS	Georgian 70%, Armenian 8%, Russian 6.5%, Azeri 5.5%, Ossetian 3%, Abkhaz 2%, other 5%
CURRENCY	Lari
ECONOMY	Services 44%, industry 31%, agriculture 25%
GNP PER CAPITA	US$440
CLIMATE	Temperate, with cool winters and hot, dry summers; subtropical on Black Sea coast
HIGHEST POINT	Gora Kazbek 5,047 m (16,558 ft)
MAP REFERENCE	Page 222

Greek Cypriots) wanted union with the "Mother Country." Riots occurred in Nicosia in 1931. After the Second World War this campaign for Greek union was renewed, the political situation on the island being complicated by a left-wing Greek Cypriot push for full independence.

Independence from Britain came in 1960, but violence soon flared. For 10 years the Greek majority and the Turkish minority struggled for control. In 1974 Turkey invaded and occupied 40 percent of the land in the north, expropriating and expelling 200,000 Greek Cypriots to the south. Nine years later Turkish Cypriots declared the northern third of the island a "Turkish Republic of Northern Cyprus," and although this is recognized only by Turkey, the region is effectively controlled by its own government and president. Along a buffer zone that separates the two regions, and divides Nicosia itself, some 2,000 UN troops costing more than US$100,000,000 per year continue to supervise an uneasy peace.

Georgia

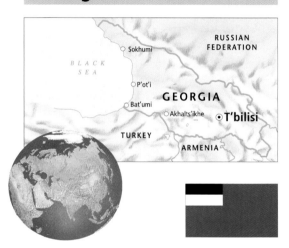

A mountainous country in the shadow of the Great Caucasus (Bol'shoy Kavkas), Georgia lies on the shore of the Black Sea between the Russian Federation and Turkey, and has borders with Armenia and Azerbaijan in the southeast. It has a long national history. The land of the Golden Fleece in Greek mythology (Colchis was today's Plain of Kolkhida) Georgia was conquered by Romans, Persians, Arabs, Tartars, and Turks, before falling to the Russians around 1800. Nevertheless, it has a strong culture, with a literary tradition based on a distinctive language and alphabet.

In 1991 Georgia rushed to proclaim its independence from the crumbling Soviet Union. Since then it has been chronically unstable, fighting off internal secessionist demands from both Abkhazia and South Ossetia. The town of Gori is the birthplace of Georgia's most famous son, Josef Stalin.

Georgia has four main areas: the Great Caucasus Range (Bol'shoy Kavkas) to the north which provides a natural boundary with Russia; the Black Sea plain in the west, including the subtropical Kholkida lowlands; the eastern end of the Lesser Caucasus (Malyy Kavkaz) to the south, whose peaks and plateaus extend into Turkey and Armenia; and a central plateau called the Kartalinian Plain, where the capital of T'bilisi

India

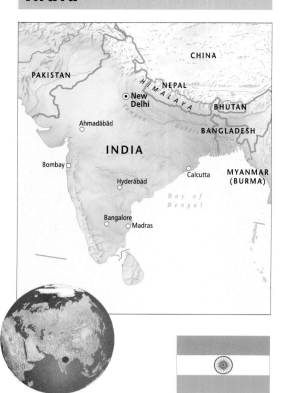

India is the world's largest democracy, and one of the oldest and most successful in Asia. It is also the world's second most populous country, with a great variety of peoples, several major religious groupings, and 700 languages. In the 50 years since independence, in 1947, it has on the whole managed humanely and responsibly where other countries in the region have become totalitarian, or succumbed to military rule. However, there are major conflicts—there have been three wars with Pakistan alone. The dispute with Pakistan over Kashmir remains unresolved. The caste system also produces endemic injustice. Millions live in desperate poverty. But Indians can change their government democratically by going to the polls, and the lot of most people has slowly but steadily improved. After a long period of state regulation of industry, barriers to outside investment, and a maze of protectionist controls, the country has begun to open its economy to the outside world. Population growth, however, with a figure of 2 percent on a base of almost a billion, tends to cancel out the nation's gains.

Physical features and land use

North to south, India can be divided into three regions: the Himalayas and their foothills; the Indo-Gangetic Plain; and the Deccan Plateau. From the northernmost border, the heavily glaciated terrain of the Himalayas—the world's highest mountains—cover 15 percent of the total surface area. The name Himalaya comes from the Nepalese *him*

("snows") and *alya* ("home of"), the mountains being revered as the home of the gods. The peaks rise to elevations of over 7,000 m (23,000 ft) in the Ladakh and Karakoram ranges. The western highlands towards the Karakoram mountains are harsh, dry, and inhabited only by small communities of herdspeople. At lower altitudes alpine meadows are grazed by the sheep of migratory pastoralists who arrive in the summer with their flocks. Lower still, rice terraces and orchards are found in the Vale of Kashmir.

The eastern highlands of northern Assam are markedly different. They are much wetter—this is where rhododendrons and magnolias grow wild and where terraced hills support rice, buckwheat, and barley. The climate of the high plateau of Meghalaya, separated from the Himalayas by the valley of the Brahmaputra, is damp and cool. On its southern flanks, Cherrapunji has one of the world's highest rainfalls, averaging 10,798 mm (421.1 in) per year.

South of the northern mountains lie the terai or foothill plains; still further south the main plains region of India stretches from the western coastal lowlands, in a northern arc past the Thar Desert and down the Gangetic Plain to the mouth of the Hooghly on the Bay of Bengal. In the northwest—the Punjab and Haryana—farmers grow winter wheat, summer rice, cotton, and sugarcane, with sorghum in the drier areas. On the lowlands of the central part of Uttar Pradesh millet and sorghum are preferred to wheat and rice. Jute is cultivated where the Ganges enters the distributary system of the delta, while mangrove swamps line the marine margins of the delta itself.

The Thar Desert in the northwest contains a broad area of dunes in Rajasthan; southwest of

this lie the cotton-growing lands of Gujarat, which includes the low peninsular plateau of Kathiawar between the Gulf of Khambhat and the Gulf of Khachchh, not far from the Pakistan border. The Vindya Range east of the Gulf of Khambhat separates the Indo-Gangetic Plain from peninsular India and the Deccan Plateau. This plateau contains some of the world's oldest rocks, large tracts being covered with later basalt flows. The western edge of the plateau is defined by the mountain chain of the Western Ghats. At the foot of these mountains lies a coastal plain with coconut groves, fishing villages, ricefields, and tapioca plantations. On the plateau itself the main crops are millet and pulses.

Timeline

530 BC First invasion by Persians (Iranians) who sieze Gandhara (now Afghanistan) and parts of Punjab	**326 BC** Alexander the Great invades India near the Indus River (now Pakistan) but is unable to sustain the colony when attacked	**300 AD** Gupta Dynasty begins. Separate kingdoms allowed to prosper within the Gupta Empire for 200 years	**1497** Vasco da Gama reaches trading port of Calicut; Portuguese later establish trading supremacy in Indian Ocean	**1526** Babar conquers northern India, establishing Mogul Empire. Empire prospers for 200 years	**1632** Taj Mahal built at Agra by Emperor Shah Jehan in memory of his wife Mumtaz Mahal (completed 1643)		

c.3500 BC First civilizations in Indus Valley (now Pakistan) —planting crops and domesticating sheep, cattle, and goats	**2600 BC** Dravidian peoples develop cities of Harappa and Mohenjo Daro in Indus Valley	**1500 BC** Aryan tribes from central Asia force Dravidians southward. Aryans plant wheat and barley, and introduce caste system	**c.500 BC** Buddhism becomes widely accepted over the next 300 years but Hinduism eventually predominates	**320 BC** Maurya Dynasty (until c.185 BC) rules an empire covering almost all India from a base at Patna	**1200** Delhi Sultanate brings Muslim rule to India, destroying many Hindu temples and instead building great mosques	**1555** Emperor Akbar the Great, regarded as the greatest of the Moguls, subdues Rajput princes to control India

History

Of India's various civilizations, the earliest developed in the Indus Valley (c.2600 BC) and in the Ganges Valley (c.1500 BC). At this time, the subcontinent was mainly peopled by ethnic Dravidians. It is thought that the Indus civilization succumbed to an invasion of Sanskrit-speaking Aryan peoples who introduced the caste system, a scheme of social division that is fundamental in Indian life. Another important early civilization was the Maurya, which under Ashoka, who reigned from 273 to 232 BC, came to dominate the subcontinent. Later, a succession of Arab, Turkish, and Mongol influences led to the founding in 1526 of the Mogul Empire, which under Akbar (1542–1605) was extended throughout most of northern India and part of the Deccan. It was during the time of Mogul rule that the Taj Mahal was built by Shah Jahan.

The British effectively controlled India from 1805, during the nineteenth century introducing a civil service and a code of law which have profoundly shaped the nation since that time. With the coming of independence in 1947, the division between Hindus and Muslims resulted in the violent and tumultuous partition of the country into India and Pakistan. This first major division to split the country indicates that the most serious rifts within Indian society tend to be religious. In recent years the Sikhs of the Punjab have also been agitating for independence.

Economy

Once essentially rural, India's economy is now a mix of village farming, modern agriculture, handicrafts, a variety of modern industries, and innumerable support services. During the 1980s economic growth allowed a marked increase in real per capita private consumption. Since 1991 production, trade, and investment reforms have provided new opportunities for Indian business and some 200 million middle-class consumers. Among the nation's strengths is a home market of some 900 million, along with a workforce that includes many who are highly skilled, including those trained in high-tech areas such as computer programming. The textile sector is highly efficient. There has been a massive rise in foreign investment as the country has opened up to foreign competition. The downside of this situation is a sizeable budget deficit along with high defense spending (including that for nuclear weapons) because of the longrunning and continuing conflict with Pakistan. Other negative features include an absence of even elementary social services, poor roads, inadequate port facilities, and an antiquated telecommunications system.

Women washing clothes beside the Ganges in Varanasi (left). Drying chilis in Rajasthan (top left). The Taj Mahal (top right).

Fact File

OFFICIAL NAME Republic of India

FORM OF GOVERNMENT Federal republic with two legislative bodies (Council of States and People's Assembly)

CAPITAL New Delhi

AREA 3,287,590 sq km (1,269,338 sq miles)

TIME ZONE GMT + 5.5 hours

POPULATION 999,826,804

PROJECTED POPULATION 2005 1,096,929,474

POPULATION DENSITY 304.1 per sq km (787.7 per sq mile)

LIFE EXPECTANCY 63.4

INFANT MORTALITY (PER 1,000) 60.8

OFFICIAL LANGUAGES Hindi, Bengali, Telugu, Marathi, Tamil, Urdu, Gujarati, Malayalam, Kannada, Oriya, Punjabi, Assamese, Kashmiri, Sindhi, Sanskrit, English

OTHER LANGUAGES Hindustani, about 700 indigenous languages

LITERACY RATE 51.2%

RELIGIONS Hindu 80%, Muslim 14%, Christian 2.4%, Sikh 2%, Buddhist 0.7%, Jain 0.5%, other 0.4%

ETHNIC GROUPS Indo-Aryan 72%, Dravidian 25%, Mongoloid and other 3%

CURRENCY Indian rupee

ECONOMY Agriculture 63%, services 26%, industry 11%

GNP PER CAPITA US$340

CLIMATE Tropical in south, temperate in north; monsoons June to September

HIGHEST POINT Kanchenjunga 8,598 m (28,208 ft)

MAP REFERENCE Pages 216–17, 218–19

STATES AND CAPITALS

Andhra Pradesh • Hyderabad
Arunachal Pradesh • Itanagar
Assam • Dispur
Bihar • Patna
Goa • Panaji
Gujarat • Gandhinagar
Haryana • Chandigarh
Himachal Pradesh • Simla
Jammu and Kashmir • Srinagar (summer)
Jammu (winter)
Karnataka • Bangalore
Kerala • Trivandrum
Madhya Pradesh • Bhopal
Maharashtra • Mumbai (Bombay)
Manipur • Imphal
Meghalaya • Shillong
Mizoram • Aizawi
Nagaland • Kohima
Orissa • Bhubaneswar
Punjab • Chandigarh
Rajastan • Jaipur
Sikkim • Gangtok
Tamil Nadu • Madras
Tripura • Agartala
Uttar Pradesh • Lucknow
West Bengal • Calcutta

UNION TERRITORIES

Andaman and Nicobar Islands • Port Blair
Chandigarh • Chandigarh
Dadra and Nagar Haveli • Silvassa
Daman and Diu • Daman
Delhi • Delhi
Lakshadweep • Kavaratti
Pondicherry • Pondicherry

1769 Severe famines in Bengal lead to rural depopulation for more than 20 years

1857 Indian Revolt against heavy taxes results in considerable loss of British and Indian lives. It is ruthlessly suppressed

1876 Queen Victoria becomes Empress of India

1883 Commision into famine recommends building irrigation canals to supply water from Himalayas to grain-producing areas

1943 Severe food shortages in Bengal made worse by the army using scarce supplies results in loss of many lives

1965 Border war with Pakistan over Kashmir

1998 India tests nuclear weapons, followed by Pakistan; tension over Kashmir issue continues

1740 East India Co (founded 1600) takes over Mogul land. Dutch, British establish ports at Madras, Bombay, Calcutta

1800 East India Co trades between Britain, Europe, China. India produces raw materials for British factories

1850 Failure of monsoon rains causes famines in northern India for more than 30 years

1880s Indian Nationalist Movement begins pressure for an end to British rule; violent attacks by extremists

1921 After more than 12 million deaths in 'flu epidemic of 1918–19 India's population surges; by 1921 it passes 250 million

1947 India gains independence. Pakistan becomes a separate Muslim state (East and West). India takes over Kashmir

1971 East Pakistan becomes independent country of Bangladesh; India's population reaches 500 million

1999 Population of India predicted to reach 1 billion

Indonesia

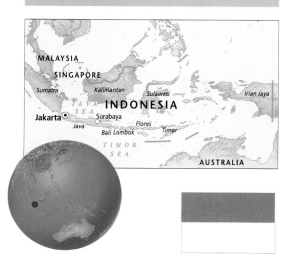

Fact File

OFFICIAL NAME Republic of Indonesia

FORM OF GOVERNMENT Republic with single legislative body (House of Representatives)

CAPITAL Jakarta

AREA 1,919,440 sq km (741,096 sq miles)

TIME ZONE GMT + 7/9 hours

POPULATION 216,108,345

PROJECTED POPULATION 2005 234,875,553

POPULATION DENSITY 112.6 per sq km (291.6 per sq mile)

LIFE EXPECTANCY 62.9

INFANT MORTALITY (PER 1,000) 57.3

OFFICIAL LANGUAGE Bahasa Indonesia

OTHER LANGUAGES English, Dutch, indigenous languages

LITERACY RATE 83.2%

RELIGIONS Muslim 87%, Protestant 6%, Roman Catholic 3%, Hindu 2%, Buddhist 1%, other 1%

ETHNIC GROUPS Javanese 45%, Sundanese 14%, Madurese 7.5%, coastal Malays 7.5%, other 26%

CURRENCY Rupiah

ECONOMY Agriculture 54%, services 38%, industry 8%

GNP PER CAPITA US$980

CLIMATE Tropical, with wet season December to March (except in Moluccas where wet season is June to September)

HIGHEST POINT Puncak Jaya 5,030 m (16,502 ft)

MAP REFERENCE Pages 198–99, 200–01

Geologically, Indonesia is an active volcanic zone, but it was a political volcano which blew up in 1998. After 30 years of solid economic progress, during which a variety of political and ethnic conflicts were militarily contained, the collapse of the economy in 1998 triggered an outbreak of violent protest against the government. A change of leadership followed, and promises of new and more open elections. Nevertheless, long-suppressed class, ethnic, and religious conflicts have been unleashed, and a climate of political instability prevails. The national unity imposed on the numerous Indonesian islands has always been somewhat artificial. Insurrectionary guerrilla groups such as Aceh Merdeka (Free Aceh) in

north Sumatra, for example, have long been at odds with the urban elite in Jakarta.

The 13,677 islands that make up the world's largest archipelago (6,000 of them inhabited) rest on the platform of two continental shelves. The southern chain of islands, from Sumatra in the west to Timor in the southeast, and including Borneo to the north, form part of the Sunda shelf. This is a largely submerged extension of the Asian continent. Eastward, the northern Moluccas and New Guinea rest on the Sahul shelf, which is a northern extension of the Australian continent. Between the Asian and Australian ocean shelves, Sulawesi and the southern Moluccas form the island summits of suboceanic mountain ranges which are flanked by sea trenches 4,500 m (14,800 ft) deep.

All Indonesia's main islands are mountainous: this is an area of great crustal activity. Sumatra, Java, and the Lesser Sunda Islands (Nusa Tengara) form an arc containing 200 volcanoes, many of which are active—Krakatoa (Pulau Rakata) among them.

In Sumatra the Barisan Mountains run the length of the southwest-facing coastline. Along with 10 active volcanoes there are a number of crater lakes, Lake Toba, at an altitude of 900 m (2,953 ft), being one of the more spectacular. Much of Sumatra was once forested but over-cutting of timber in the lowlands means that native forest is now virtually restricted to reserves and national parks. However, isolated mountain forests remain over wide areas. The heavily populated island of Java, next in the island chain, has a long range which contains 50 active volcanoes and 17 that are only recently dormant.

Throughout the archipelago many coasts are lined with mangrove swamps, notably in eastern Sumatra and southern Kalimantan. Several of the islands are of great beauty: tourism, not only to Bali, has been a major activity in recent years.

Indonesia's complex and varied population, and its four major religions—Islam, Hinduism, Christianity, and Buddhism—reflect the country's varied history. Hinduism was the first major religious influence 2,000 years ago, followed by Buddhism in the seventh century AD. Hindu-

Borobudur, the world's largest Buddhist monument, was built in the ninth century BC on the island of Java. Islam is the dominant religion in Indonesia today.

Buddhist religious authority began to decline with the collapse of the Majapahit Empire in the fourteenth century, and the arrival of Arab traders from the west gradually established Islam as the dominant religion.

Under Dutch colonial rule from 1608, the islands were from 1830 subject to a severe extractive regime known as the Culture System. This involved the forced cultivation of commercial crops for export and resulted in a distortion of the traditional economy. Indonesia fell to the Japanese in the Second World War. This additional colonial experience guaranteed that the Indonesians would expect independence after 1945 and not accept the return of the Dutch.

About one-tenth of Indonesia's land area is under permanent cultivation. The majority of the people live by agriculture, growing rice, maize, cassava, and sweet potato. There are also extensive plantations producing rubber, palm oil, sugarcane, coffee, and tea. The last 30 years, however, have seen an intensive state-directed drive toward industrialization, based on diverse and abundant natural resources: oil, natural gas, timber, metals, and coal.

Foreign investment has played in important role in increased industrialization. Prosperity was initially tied to oil exports, but now the economy's growth depends on the continuing expansion of non-oil exports.

East Timor

East Timor, mainly Catholic after 300 years of Portuguese rule, was forcibly incorporated into Indonesia in 1975. Since that time, the Revolutionary Front of Independent East Timor (Fretilin) has continued to fight for independence. Indonesian troops have bombed villages and carried out mass executions of suspected Fretilin sympathizers. The situation is still unresolved.

Iran

Fact File

OFFICIAL NAME Islamic Republic of Iran

FORM OF GOVERNMENT Theocratic republic with single legislative body (Islamic Consultative Assembly)

CAPITAL Tehrān

AREA 1,648,000 sq km (636,293 sq miles)

TIME ZONE GMT + 3.5 hours

POPULATION 70,351,549

PROJECTED POPULATION 2005 80,138,875

POPULATION DENSITY 42.7 per sq km (110.6 per sq mile)

LIFE EXPECTANCY 68.7

INFANT MORTALITY (PER 1,000) 47.0

OFFICIAL LANGUAGE Farsi (Persian)

OTHER LANGUAGES Turkic, Kurdish, Luri, Baloch, Arabic

LITERACY RATE 68.6%

RELIGIONS Shi'a Muslim 89%, Sunni Muslim 10%, other (including Zoroastrian, Jewish, Christian, and Baha'i) 1%

ETHNIC GROUPS Persian 51%, Azerbaijani 24%, Gilaki and Mazandarani 8%, Kurd 7%, Arab 3%, Lur 2%, Baloch 2%, Turkmen 2%, other 1%

CURRENCY Rial

ECONOMY Services 46%, agriculture 33%, industry 21%

GNP PER CAPITA Not available (c. US$766–3,035)

CLIMATE Mainly arid, temperate in far north; cold winters and hot summers

HIGHEST POINT Qolleh-ye Damāvand 5,671 m (18,605 ft)

MAP REFERENCE Pages 220–21, 222

Iran is one of the largest of the Persian Gulf states. It has borders with 10 other states in the region including Afghanistan, Pakistan, and Turkey. Now the home of the world's largest theocracy, and the main center for militant Shia Islam, Persia (as it was formerly known) has seen the rise and fall of a number of civilizations—Medes, Persians, Greeks, and Parthians. In the seventh century it was overrun by an invasion of Arabs who introduced Islam, a religion which under the Safavids in 1502 became the Shi'ite form of the faith which prevails today. Oil was discovered in 1908. From that time on Persia (retitled in the 1920s by a Shah who adopted the name Iran because it meant "Aryan") became of growing interest to the great powers, and the requirements of international oil companies began to figure in Iranian life.

After the Second World War the Iranians found the corrupt and despotic rule of Shah Reza Khan intolerable, and in 1979 he was overthrown in the first national revolution to be led by Islamic fundamentalists. This event has had profound effects and repercussions throughout the Muslim world. Iran's subsequent support for Islamic radicalism abroad soon produced strained relations with Central Asian, Middle Eastern, and North African nations, as well as the USA. More recently, Iran's economic difficulties and isolation have caused a general relaxation both in the domestic regime and in its external affairs.

The entire central region is dominated by a high, arid plateau (average elevation 1,200 m; 3,937 ft), most of it salt desert, containing the Dasht-e Lūt (Great Sand Desert) and the Dasht-e-Kavīr (Great Salt Desert). Mountain ranges surround the plateau: the volcanic Elburz Range (Reshteh-ye Kūhhā-ye Alborz) along the Caspian Sea; the Khorasan and Baluchestan Ranges in the east and southeast; and the Zagros Mountains (Kūhhā-ye Zāgros) inland from the Persian Gulf. The most productive parts of Iran, and the most heavily populated, lie on its periphery. In the north are the fisheries, tea gardens, and rice fields of the Caspian shore. In Khuzestan to the south there are sugar plantations and oilfields—a prime target of the Iraqis when they invaded in 1980 at the start of the eight-year Iran–Iraq War. Westward lie the wheatfields of Azarbaijan, while to the east are the fruit groves of the oases of Kavir in Kavir (Dasht-e Kavir) and Lut in Lut Desert (Dasht-e Lūt).

Some 8 percent of Iran's land is arable, and 11 percent of it is forested, mostly in the provinces of Gilan and Mazandaran which border the Caspian Sea. The province of Tehrān in the north is by far the most densely populated region supporting about 18 percent of the population.

In the years after 1945 Iran's economy became almost totally dependent on oil, and earnings from oil exports still provide 85 percent of its export revenue. But by the end of the war with Iraq (1980–88) production was half the level of 1979. This, combined with the general fall in oil prices, and a surge in imports that began in 1989, has left Iran in severe financial difficulties, and there has been a marked decline in general standards of living. Ideological considerations hamper effective reforms: there is a continuing struggle over how to run a modern economy between the powerful religious leadership on the one hand, and reformist politicians on the other. The mullahs (the Islamic clergy) object to the government using borrowed money and are against the importation of "corrupt" Western technology.

Overall, the Iranian economy is a mix of centrally planned large-scale state enterprise; village agriculture producing wheat, barley, rice, sugar beet, tobacco, and pistachio nuts; and small-scale private trading and service ventures.

Riding a donkey, an Iranian girl leads her cows out to pasture (below). A portion of the facade of the Imam Mosque in Eşfahan, Iran (bottom).

Iraq

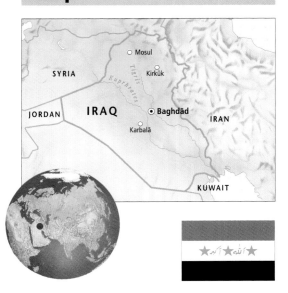

Fact File

OFFICIAL NAME Republic of Iraq

FORM OF GOVERNMENT Republic with single legislative body (National Assembly)

CAPITAL Baghdād

AREA 437,072 sq km (168,753 sq miles)

TIME ZONE GMT + 3 hours

POPULATION 23,871,623

PROJECTED POPULATION 2005 29,366,367

POPULATION DENSITY 54.6 per sq km (141.4 per sq mile)

LIFE EXPECTANCY 68.3

INFANT MORTALITY (PER 1,000) 52.5

OFFICIAL LANGUAGES Arabic, Kurdish

OTHER LANGUAGES Assyrian, Armenian

LITERACY RATE 56.8%

RELIGIONS Muslim 97% (Shi'a 60%–65%, Sunni 32%–37%), Christian or other 3%

ETHNIC GROUPS Arab 75%–80%, Kurdish 15%–20%, other (including Turkoman, Assyrian) 5%

CURRENCY Iraqi dinar

ECONOMY Services 48%, agriculture 30%, industry 22%

GNP PER CAPITA Est. US$766–3,035

CLIMATE Mainly arid, with cold winters and hot summers; winter snows in northern mountains

HIGHEST POINT Kūh-e Hājī Ebrāhīm 3,600 m (11,811 ft)

MAP REFERENCE Page 220

If any country has the right to call itself the cradle of Western civilization it is Iraq. The first city states in the region date from nearly 3500 BC. The land "between the waters" of the Tigris and the Euphrates rivers (the meaning of the old name Mesopotamia) has seen many empires come and go. Babylon defeated its old rival Assyria here in 612 BC, and in the seventh century BC the territory was seized by the Persians; Baghdad became the greatest commercial and cultural center of the Muslim world. The Persians held Iraq until they were conquered by Alexander the Great in 334 BC. Part of the Ottoman Empire from 1534 to 1918, Iraq became independent in 1932.

Modern Iraq has been involved in two major conflicts in the space of 20 years: the First Gulf War between Iraq and Iran, 1980–1988, and the Second Gulf War when it invaded Kuwait, 1990–91.

After the days of the early Mesopotamian empires, the Arab peoples brought Islam to Iraq in the seventh century AD. Like Iran, Iraq has a majority of Shi'ite Muslims. Unlike Iran, the ruling elite in Iraq are Sunni Muslims who fear their own Shi'ites are secretly loyal to Iran. This underlies the tension within Iraqi society. The situation of the Kurds relates to an ethnic rather than a religious division. Distrusted and persecuted in every land in which they live (Turkey, Iran, Iraq, Syria, and Armenia) Iraq's Kurds were assaulted by Baghdad with chemical weapons in the 1980s.

In the far northeast Iraq shares part of the Zagros Mountains (Kūhhā-ye Zāgròs) with Iran. In the west its territory includes a piece of the Syrian Desert. The rest of the country falls into two broad physiographic categories—the lowland desert to the west which makes up nearly 40 percent of the total land area; and the Tigris–Euphrates basin known formerly as Mesopotamia. Here the two rivers flow southeast roughly parallel, before meeting in a vast swamp on their way to the Gulf. In this swamp live communities of Marsh Arabs, Shi'ite Muslims targeted by the leadership in Baghdad after an attempted rebellion following the Second Gulf War. Most Iraqi agricultural activity takes place in the alluvial Tigris–Euphrates plain, where one-third of the farms are irrigated. Vegetables and cereals are the more important crops. In addition to the rice grown in warmer lowland areas, wheat and barley are cultivated in the temperate country near the Zagros Mountains. Exports have fallen sharply, but in better times Iraq's date crop met 80 percent of world demand.

Two wars, followed by international embargoes designed to force acceptance of UN inspection of weapons of mass destruction, have severely damaged the Iraqi economy. It was formerly dominated by the oil sector, but today oil exports are probably no more than 10 percent of their old level. Agricultural development has been hampered by labor shortages, salinization, and the dislocation caused by earlier land reform and collectivization programs. Living standards continue to deteriorate. Shortages are exacerbated by the government's spending of huge sums on both its army and internal security.

Middle East conflict

1964 Iran: Ayatollah Khomeini exiled for criticism of Shah's secular state.

1967 Israel: The Six Day War with Arab states. Israel seizes the Gaza Strip, Sinai, the Golan Heights, and the West Bank of the Jordan River.

1972 Iraq: Nationalization of Western-owned Iraq Petroleum Company.

1973 Egypt and Syria join in attack on Israel and fight 18-day war.

1978 Israel occupies southern Lebanon in response to Palestine Liberation Organization (PLO) attacks.

1979 Israel: Peace Treaty signed with Egypt. Iraq: Saddam Hussein takes over. Iran: Fall of the Shah. Ayatollah Khomeini returns from exile. Iran declared an Islamic Republic.

1980 Iraqi invasion starts Iran–Iraq War.

1981 Egypt: President Anwar Sadat, the first Arab leader to visit Israel, is assassinated.

1986 UN Security Council blames Iraq for war with Iran.

1987 Lebanon: Terry Waite, special envoy, arrives in Beirut to try to secure the release of western hostages and is himself captured.

1988 Iran: US naval ship shoots down Iranian airliner, 290 killed. Iran–Iraq War ends. Iraqi troops use chemical weapons on Kurds.

1990 Iran and Iraq resume diplomatic relations. Iraq invades and annexes Kuwait.

1991 Western allies liberate Kuwait. UN requires Iraq to accept weapons monitoring and to destroy weapons of mass destruction.

1993 Israel: PLO recognizes Israel in return for Palestinian autonomy in Gaza Strip and Jericho.

1994 Iraq recognizes Kuwaiti sovereignty.

1995 Israel: Palestinian autonomy extended to much of West Bank. Prime Minister Rabin assassinated.

1997 UN charges Iraqi officials with blocking weapons inspections. Iran: Mohammed Khatami, more liberal than his predecessors, becomes president.

1998 Iraq: Obstruction of UN weapons inspectors and fears of Iraq's biological weapons program leads to heavy bombing by US and UK.

Israel

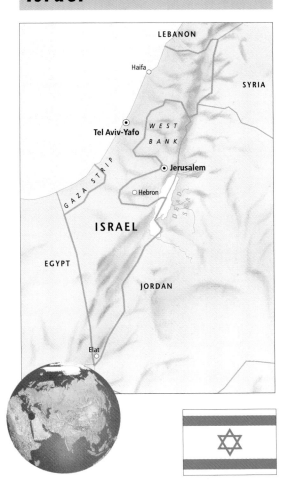

Fact File

OFFICIAL NAME State of Israel

FORM OF GOVERNMENT Republic with single legislative body (Knesset)

CAPITAL Jerusalem

AREA 20,770 sq km (8,019 sq miles)

TIME ZONE GMT + 2 hours

POPULATION 5,749,760

PROJECTED POPULATION 2005 6,303,057

POPULATION DENSITY 276.8 per sq km (717 per sq mile)

LIFE EXPECTANCY 78.6

INFANT MORTALITY (PER 1,000) 7.8

OFFICIAL LANGUAGES Hebrew, Arabic

OTHER LANGUAGES English, French, German, Hungarian, Romanian, Russian, Spanish

LITERACY RATE 95%

RELIGIONS Jewish 82%, Muslim 14%, Druze 2%, Christian 2%

ETHNIC GROUPS Jewish 82%, Arab 17%, other 1%

CURRENCY Shekel

ECONOMY Services 75%, industry 21%, agriculture 4%

GNP PER CAPITA US$15,920

CLIMATE Temperate along coast, hot and dry in south and east

HIGHEST POINT Har Meron 1,208 m (3,963 ft)

MAP REFERENCE Page 225

View across the rooftops of Sāmarrā', Iraq, to the River Tigris (top left). Pilgrims outside the Church of the Holy Sepulchre in Jerusalem, Israel (top right). The Old City of Jerusalem from the Mount of Olives (right).

Created as a Jewish homeland in 1948, Israel is a small country with an illustrious past that involves three of the world's great religions, and an uncertain future. For 50 years, through a succession of wars with hostile Arab neighbors, a secular, democratic political system has managed to constrain strong religious tendencies deeply rooted in the past. Key events in the Jewish history of the region are first, the occupation of the land by the 12 tribes of Israelites 4,000 years ago; second, the scattering (or "diaspora") of the one surviving tribe, the Jews, following a failed revolt against Rome in AD 138; third, the rise of Zionism in the nineteenth century advocating a Jewish homeland in Palestine as a solution to centuries of exile and persecution; fourth, the Holocaust, which reinforced arguments for territorial independence; and fifth, the proclamation of the State of Israel in May 1948, leading to the emigration of many Palestinian Arabs. Since then there has been continual strife between the new state and its neighbors. The subsequent seizure and occupation by Israel of additional territories (see entries for Gaza Strip and West Bank) has been bitterly resisted by their Arab inhabitants. This conflict has intensified as Jewish religious fundamentalists extend their settlements in contested areas.

Geographically, Israel consists of four main regions: the Mediterranean coastal plain of Sharon, irrigated by the Qishon, Soreq, and Sarida rivers; the rolling hills extending from Galilee in the north to Judea in the center; the Jordan–Red Sea section of the Rift Valley running north to south the full length of the eastern frontier from the Golan Heights to the Gulf of Aqaba; and the great southern wedge of desert plateau called the Negev (Ha Negev), which makes up about half of Israel's total land area. With irrigation, the Mediterranean coastal plain is fertile fruit-growing country. In the drier southern stretches its dunes have been stabilized with grass and tamarisk and reclaimed for pasture. The northern hill country around Galilee has good rainfall and a rich black soil weathered from basalt. Here and around Judea, pine, and eucalyptus trees have been planted to fix the soil and hold the water. The Valley of Jezreel ('Emeq Yizre'el), lying between Galilee and Samaria to the south, has deep alluvial soils which are intensively tilled for market gardening. The

Jordan–Western Negev Scheme—the most ambitious of Israel's various irrigation projects—diverts water from the upper Jordan and other sources through a series of culverts and canals south to the Negev. The desert is widely covered with blown sand and loess but tomatoes and grapes grow well when supplied with water.

Israel has the most industrialized economy in the region. Iron is smelted at Haifa and there are steel foundries at Acre. Chemical manufacturing takes place at Haifa and at plants by the Dead Sea. A national electricity grid provides power to widely dispersed towns where factories produce textiles, ceramics, and other products. In the Negev south of Beersheba new settlements mine oil, copper, and phosphates, the factories using potash and salt from the Dead Sea. Israel is largely self-sufficient in food production except for grains. Diamonds, high-technology equipment, and agricultural products are leading exports. About half the government's external debt is owed to the USA, its main source of aid. To earn foreign exchange the government has been targeting high-tech international market niches such as medical scanning equipment. Matters of continuing economic concern include the high level of unemployment following large-scale immigration from the former USSR, and the need to import strategically important raw materials.

Asia and the Middle East

Japan

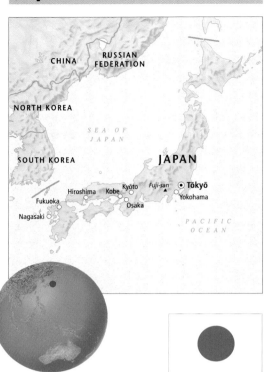

Fact File

OFFICIAL NAME Japan

FORM OF GOVERNMENT Constitutional monarchy with two legislative bodies (House of Councillors and House of Representatives)

CAPITAL Tokyo

AREA 377,835 sq km (145,882 sq miles)

TIME ZONE GMT + 9 hours

POPULATION 126,182,077

PROJECTED POPULATION 2005 127,337,581

POPULATION DENSITY 334 per sq km (865 per sq mile)

LIFE EXPECTANCY 80.1

INFANT MORTALITY (PER 1,000) 4.1

OFFICIAL LANGUAGE Japanese

LITERACY RATE 99%

RELIGIONS Shinto and Buddhist 84%, other (including Christian 0.7%) 16%

ETHNIC GROUPS Japanese 99.4%, other (mostly Korean) 0.6%

CURRENCY Yen

ECONOMY Services 69%, industry 24%, agriculture 7%

GNP PER CAPITA US$39,640

CLIMATE Ranges from cold temperate in north to subtropical in south; wet season June to July

HIGHEST POINT Fuji-san (Mt Fuji) 3,776 m (12,388 ft)

MAP REFERENCE Pages 208–09

Mainly mountainous, with intensively cultivated coastal plains, the archipelago of Japan lies off the east Asian coast close to Korea and China. By the early 1990s it had become an industrial and trading colossus second only to the USA. But cracks in the country's apparently impregnable economic facade began to appear in 1998 as the yen slid steadily against the dollar. The nation's vast scientific and technological resources, its highly educated personnel, and its substantial trade surpluses, mean that it is better placed than most countries to cope with this and other problems.

History

First populated by migrants from mainland Asia, by the fifth century AD Japan was controlled by a number of clans. During the next 300 years several features of Chinese civilization were introduced, including Buddhism, Chinese script, and methods of administration, while cities modeled on those of the Tang Dynasty were built at Nara (AD 710) and Kyoto (AD 794). Centralized government, however, failed to eventuate and the clan basis of society prevailed. From the twelfth century until the rise of the Tokugawas power was held by rival groups of feudal lords, or shoguns, the emperor becoming a largely symbolic figure. Lasting from 1192 to 1867, the shogun era fostered a ethical code known as *bushido* (the path of the warrior, or samurai) that stressed loyalty, frugality, and courage.

Until 1945 Japan remained unconquered. Two Mongol fleets sent to invade the country were destroyed by typhoons in 1274 and 1281, founding the legend of a *kamikaze* or "divine wind" sent to protect "the land of the Gods." From 1603 a form of semi-centralized feudal rule was imposed by the ruling shogunate, the Tokugawas. Under this family, some 250 *daimyo* (or "great names") ran their own estates watched by state inspectors and a network of spies. Western influence appeared

briefly in 1542, when missionaries arrived from Macao bringing clocks, carpets, guns, and Christianity. The reaction of the Tokugawas was to close the door: from 1639 Japan's citizens were not allowed to travel abroad, and trading contacts were limited to a single Dutch settlement at Nagasaki.

This ended in 1853 when Commodore Perry of the US Navy brought a squadron of warships into Yokohama Harbor, demanding that the country's ports be opened to Western trade. The now weak Tokugawa shogunate collapsed, imperial rule was resumed under the Meiji Restoration, and within 50 years Japan had become westernized and a rising industrial force. Victories in wars with China (1894–95) and Russia (1904–05) led to the seizure of Taiwan and Korea. Expanding imperial ambitions led later to the invasion of China, and eventually, in 1941, to an attack on Hawaii and Japan's entry into the Second World War. Allied victory in 1945 was followed by the introduction of a liberal, US-imposed democratic constitution which has since guided the nation's development.

Physical features and land use

Four large islands, so closely grouped that bridges and a tunnel now connect them, make up 98 percent of Japan's territory. They occupy a

Asia and the Middle East

Timeline

660 BC Legendary leader Jimmu Tenno is Japan's first emperor and founds imperial dynasty which still holds office today	**AD 200** In the Yayoi period (until c.AD 700) rice is grown in irrigated fields and people live in villages protected by moats and wooden palisades	**550** Buddhism introduced from China	**1281** Mongol conqueror Kublai Khan's invasion plans fail when his fleet is destroyed by a typhoon	**1600** Honshu, Shikoku, and Kyushu united under the Tokugawa shogunate which rules for more than 250 years	**1730** An earthquake on the island of Hokkaido causes the deaths of 137 000 people	**1883** Tsunami kills 30,000 people. Three years later a tsunami occurs off Honshu and kills 28,000 people
4500 BC Islands of Japan inhabited by peoples from Asia. They are later known as Jomon after their pottery	**c.1500 BC** Rice is introduced from China and cultivated in the islands for the first time	**400 BC** Wet rice-farming introduced from Korean Peninsula; intensive agriculture enables larger population to survive	**300** Large-scale immigration from the Asian continent until around 750 leads to a big increase in the population	**794** Japanese capital moves from Nara, the eastern end of the Tang Silk Road trade route, to Heian (called later Kyoto) until 1185	**1543** Portuguese sailors visit islands of southern Kyushu, making Europe aware of the wealth of the Japanese islands	**1707** Mt Fuji, Japan's biggest volcano, erupts	**1875** Population reaches more than 35 million; Tokyo 1 million by end of the century

highly unstable zone on the earth's crust, and earthquakes and volcanic eruptions are frequent: 140,000 died in the 1923 earthquake which hit Yokohama and part of Tokyo; 6,000 died in the Kobe earthquake of January 1995. Folding and faulting has produced a mosaic of landforms throughout Japan, mountains and hills alternating with small basins and coastal plains. Inland there are several calderas and volcanic cones, the most famous being Fuji-san (3,776 m; 12,388 ft), the highest mountain in Japan, which last erupted in 1707.

Hokkaido, the northernmost of the main islands, is the most rural and traditional. Japan's biggest and most productive farming region, it has a climate similar to the US midwest—which may be why American advisors established wheat farming there in the 1860s. Hokkaido now produces more than half of Japan's cereal needs. Southwest of Hokkaido lies the island of Honshu, where the Japanese Alps provide spectacular scenery. The Kanto Plain where Tokyo stands is the largest of various small alluvial plains, their soils enriched by centuries of careful cultivation. Today the conurbation this plain supports is Japan's most heavily industrialized and densely populated region. From southwestern Honshu across the two southern islands of Shikoku and Kyushu a complex of mountain peaks and undulating uplands stretches down to the Ryukyu Islands (Nansei-Shotō), which includes Okinawa, before extending south toward Taiwan.

Economy

Japan's economy is notable for government–industry cooperation, a motivated population with a strong work ethic, high educational levels and a mastery of high technology. These factors combined with a small defense allocation (1 percent of gross domestic product) have made it the second most powerful economy in the industrialized world. Japan is one of the world's largest and most advanced producers of steel and non-ferrous metallurgy, heavy electrical equipment, construction and mining equipment, motor vehicles and parts, communications and electronic equipment, machine tools, automated production systems, railroad rolling stock, ships, chemicals, textiles, and processed foods. Industry depends heavily on imported raw materials and fuel. The small agricultural sector is highly protected and subsidized; its crop yields are among the world's highest. Self-sufficient in rice, Japan imports about 50 percent of its other grain needs. After decades of spectacular growth, the late 1990s saw a marked contraction. The need for reconstruction remains evident, amid mounting fears of a banking crisis due to bad debts.

The Ginza district in Tokyo, Japan (left). A traditional house in rural Japan (top left). One of the many rock-cut facades in the ancient city of Petra in Jordan (right).

| 1945 USA drops atomic bombs, destroying Hiroshima and Nagasaki. Second World War ends | 1994 Population of Tokyo-Yokohama exceeds 8 million |

| 1923 The Great Kanto earthquake, fires, and tsunamis destroy much of Tokyo-Yokohama and kill more than 140,000 people | 1964 Shinkansen high-speed "bullet train" links Tokyo and Kyoto traveling at speeds of 210 km (130 miles) an hour | 1995 Earthquake destroys much of Kobe city and kills 6,000 people |

Jordan

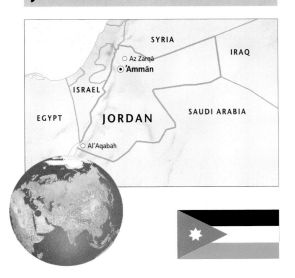

The small Arab kingdom of Jordan, rich in historic associations and sites, lies between Saudi Arabia, Israel, and Syria, and also shares a border with Iraq. It has to deal with Israel on the one hand and with Israel's various Arab antagonists on the other, while accommodating huge numbers of refugees. After the Ottoman Turks were driven out during the First World War the British installed the Hashemite monarchy in 1921. In 1946 Jordan became independent, and King Hussein reigned from 1952 until his death in 1999.

Governing Jordan has not been easy, many problems being connected with the West Bank. In 1967 this area, containing both Jerusalem and much of Jordan's best land, was lost to Israel. With emigré Palestinians using Jordan as a base for guerrilla activities (they were expelled in 1970–71), through two Gulf Wars in which Jordan was sympathetic to its oil supplier Iraq, and with the recent expansion of Israeli settlements in the area, the West Bank became impossible to regain or to administer. In 1988 Jordan ceded it to the PLO.

The Red Sea–Jordan section of the Rift Valley forms the country's western border. It contains the Jordan River valley, the Dead Sea (the lowest point on the earth's surface, at 400 m/1,312 ft below sea level), the Sea of Galilee, and Wadī al Arabah. Parts of the Jordan Valley and the highlands east of the Rift Valley are irrigated, making arable farming possible. Crops include vegetables, olives,

and fruit. Eighty percent of Jordan's land area is desert. In the north it merges with the Syrian Desert and in the south with the deserts of Saudi Arabia. Less than 0.5 percent of the country is forested, mainly in the east. Vegetation ranges from Mediterranean plants in the mountains to grass, sagebrush and shrubs in the steppe country.

Jordan has poor water, oil, and coal supplies. In the late 1970s and early 1980s it received Arab aid and the economy grew at more than 10 percent a year. In the late 1980s reductions in aid and in worker remittances slowed and imports outstripped exports. In 1991 the Second Gulf War overwhelmed the country. Worker remittances stopped, trade contracted, and further refugees arrived, straining resources. Recovery has been uneven. Poverty, debt, and unemployment are continuing problems.

Fact File

OFFICIAL NAME Hashemite Kingdom of Jordan

FORM OF GOVERNMENT Constitutional monarchy with two legislative bodies (House of Notables and House of Representatives)

CAPITAL 'Ammān

AREA 89,213 sq km (34,445 sq miles)

TIME ZONE GMT + 2 hours

POPULATION 4,561,147

PROJECTED POPULATION 2005 5,403,895

POPULATION DENSITY 51.1 per sq km (132.3 per sq mile)

LIFE EXPECTANCY 73.1

INFANT MORTALITY (PER 1,000) 32.7

OFFICIAL LANGUAGE Arabic

OTHER LANGUAGE English

LITERACY RATE 85.5%

RELIGIONS Sunni Muslim 92%, Christian 8%

ETHNIC GROUPS Arab 98%, Circassian 1%, Armenian 1%

CURRENCY Jordanian dinar

ECONOMY Services 64%, industry 26%, agriculture 10%

GNP PER CAPITA US$1,510

CLIMATE Mainly arid, but northwest temperate with cool, wet winters and hot, dry summers

HIGHEST POINT Jabal Ramm 1,754 m (5,755 ft)

MAP REFERENCE Page 225

Kazakhstan

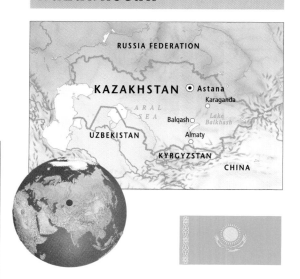

iron ore, bauxite, copper, nickel, tungsten, zinc, and silver. In addition, it holds 70 percent of CIS gold reserves. The government has been pursuing a moderate program of reform and privatization—investment incentives have been established, state controls have been lifted, and assets privatized. But government control of key industries remains extensive. Lack of pipeline transportation for oil export hinders a likely source of economic growth.

Environmental problems are extensive and severe. Radioactive or toxic chemical sites associated with weapons development are widespread. The drying up of the Aral Sea has left a crust of chemical pesticides which is periodically blown about in noxious dust storms.

Kuwait

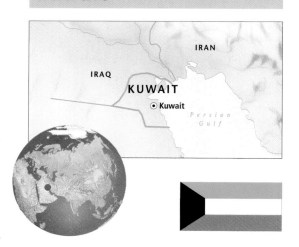

Whith a land area nearly as large as India, Kazakhstan is an important member of the newly formed Commonwealth of Independent States (CIS). In earlier times, when it was a Soviet Republic, authorities used the region for testing nuclear weapons and for exiling ethnic minorities.

In the 1950s and 1960s when the Soviet "virgin lands" project was underway, vast tracts of pasture were plowed up and sown with wheat or given over to livestock production, and waters from rivers running into the Aral Sea were used in irrigation schemes. As a result, the sea shrank by 70 percent.

During the years of Soviet domination, high levels of immigration from Russia resulted in the Kazakhs being outnumbered. Outmigration of Russians since 1991 and the return of many expatriates has resulted in a Kazak majority once more, but ethnic tensions remain high.

Much of the country is tablelands—the eroded tableland of the east featuring shallow uplands, depressions, and lakes—and there are also several mountains ranges in the east including the Altai Range (Mongol Altayn Nuruu). Running from north to south, steppe country gives way to desert or semidesert, though irrigation schemes have made large areas productive between the Aral Sea and Lake Balkhash (Balqash Köli).

With a climate marked by intense winter cold and extreme summer heat, rainfall is generally low. The lakes in the center of the country are saline, as are the marshes in the west, and in the central region there are few permanent rivers. The grassy steppes of the north are the most naturally fertile part of the country. Though the region has traditionally been associated with livestock rearing (Kazakhstan still supports up to 200,000 nomadic shepherds and herdsmen) the agricultural policies of the Soviet period converted much pasture to grain cultivation. By 1989 the country accounted for 20 percent of the entire cultivated area of the Soviet Union and 12 percent of its grain output.

Other crops grown include fruits, potatoes, vegetables, sugar beet, and cotton. High quality wool is produced, and Kazakhstan supplies meat to surrounding countries. Industry is based mainly on processing raw materials: fuel, metals, textiles, chemicals, and food. Products include rolled metals, agricultural machinery, plastics, clothing, footwear, paper, and cement. Well endowed with oil and gas reserves, the country also has deposits of coal,

Fact File

OFFICIAL NAME Republic of Kazakhstan

FORM OF GOVERNMENT Republic with two legislative bodies (Senate and Majilis)

CAPITAL Aqmola (Astana)

AREA 2,717,300 sq km (1,049,150 sq miles)

TIME ZONE GMT + 6 hours

POPULATION 16,824,825

PROJECTED POPULATION 2005 16,903,895

POPULATION DENSITY 6.2 per sq km (16 per sq mile)

LIFE EXPECTANCY 63.4

INFANT MORTALITY (PER 1,000) 58.8

OFFICIAL LANGUAGE Kazakh

OTHER LANGUAGE Russian

LITERACY RATE 97.5%

RELIGIONS Muslim 47%, Russian Orthodox 44%, Protestant 2%, other 7%

ETHNIC GROUPS Kazak 42%, Russian 37%, Ukrainian 5.3%, German 4.7%, Uzbek 2%, Tatar 2%, other 7%

CURRENCY Tenge

ECONOMY Services 43%, industry 31%, agriculture 26%

GNP PER CAPITA US$1,330

CLIMATE Mainly arid; cold winters and hot summers; cooler in north

HIGHEST POINT Khan Tängiri Shyngy 6,995 m (22,949 ft)

MAP REFERENCE Pages 222–23

The Arab emirate of Kuwait lies in the northwest corner of the Persian Gulf, dwarfed by its neighbors Iraq, Iran, and Saudi Arabia. Beneath its surface lie huge oil reserves. It was settled by wandering Arab peoples in the eighteenth century. When Germany and Turkey were eyeing Kuwait possessively in the nineteenth century it formed a defensive alliance with Great Britain, becoming a British protectorate in 1914. In 1961, when it gained independence, Kuwait was claimed by Iraq.

A constitution was inaugurated by the al-Sabah ruling family in 1962. Whenever the National Assembly has been critical, however, it has been suspended. In 1990, despite Kuwait having lent millions of dollars to Iraq during the Iran–Iraq War of 1980–88, Iraq invaded. The Kuwaitis endured six months of brutality and the destruction of the city of Kuwait before a US-led international coalition expelled the Iraqis in 1991. During the occupation 400,000 residents fled the country—200,000 Palestinian migrant workers not being allowed to return as the Palestinian Liberation Organization had supported Iraq. The destruction of Kuwaiti oil wells by Iraq and deliberate oil-spills in the Gulf have caused environmental costs still difficult to assess.

Kuwait consists of an undulating sandy plateau which rises westward to an elevation of about 300 m (1,000 ft) on the Iraq–Saudi Arabia border. Along the border the plateau is cut to a depth of 45 m (150 ft) by the Wādī al Bāṭin. In the northeast there are a few salt marshes and in the northwest is the Jal az-Zawr escarpment. Vegetation is mostly limited to salt-tolerant plants along the coast, though in modern urban areas green spaces have been produced by irrigating imported soil. The territory of Kuwait also includes nine islands, of which Bubiyan is the largest.

Kuwait owns 10 percent of the world's proven crude oil reserves. Its petroleum sector currently accounts for nearly half of gross domestic product, 90 percent of export revenues, and 70 percent of government income. With the exception of fish, Kuwait depends almost wholly on food imports, though hothouses and hydroponics produce some fruit and vegetables. About 75 percent of potable water must be distilled or imported. The shortage of water constrains industrial activities, which at present include petrochemical production, food processing, desalination, construction materials, and salt. The World Bank has urged the government to push ahead with privatization, including in the oil industry.

Fact File

OFFICIAL NAME State of Kuwait

FORM OF GOVERNMENT Constitutional monarchy with single legislative body (National Assembly)

CAPITAL Al Kuwayt (Kuwait)

AREA 17,820 sq km (6,880 sq miles)

TIME ZONE GMT + 3 hours

POPULATION 1,991,115

PROJECTED POPULATION 2005 2,436,509

POPULATION DENSITY 111.7 per sq km (289.3 per sq mile)

LIFE EXPECTANCY 77.2

INFANT MORTALITY (PER 1,000) 10.3

OFFICIAL LANGUAGE Arabic

OTHER LANGUAGE English

LITERACY RATE 77.8%

RELIGIONS Muslim 85% (Sunni 45%, Shi'a 30%, other 10%), other (including Christian, Hindu, Parsi) 15%

ETHNIC GROUPS Kuwaiti 45%, other Arab 35%, South Asian 9%, Iranian 4%, other 7%

CURRENCY Kuwaiti dinar

ECONOMY Services 90%, industry 9%, agriculture 1%

GNP PER CAPITA US$17,390

CLIMATE Arid, with cool winters and hot, humid summers

HIGHEST POINT Unnamed location 306 m (1,004 ft)

MAP REFERENCE Page 220

Kyrgyzstan

Kyrgyzstan is a small, mountainous, landlocked country in central Asia. China lies over the massive peaks of the Tian Shan Range along its southeast border, Kazakhstan is to the north, and Uzbekistan and Tajikistan are to the southwest. Not only is Kyrgyzstan the least urbanized of all the ex-Soviet republics, its population is growing faster in rural areas than in the towns. Native Kyrgyz are barely a majority and ethnic tension with Uzbeks and other nationals from nearby countries is a feature of everyday life. Fierce clashes between Kyrgyz and Uzbeks took place in the border city of Osh in 1990. Historically, the once nomadic Muslim Kyrgyz pastoralists are descended from refugees of Mongolian and Turkic origin who entered the region in the thirteenth century, escaping from Mongol invaders. For a while in the eighteenth century the region came under Manchu domination, then during the nineteenth century Russia began to colonize the country. Russian immigrants took the best land, settling in the low-lying, fertile areas. For years after the country's incorporation into the Soviet Union in the 1920s, resistance was carried out by local guerrilla groups called *basmachi*. Since independence in 1991, Kyrgyzstan has pursued liberal political and economic policies.

Geographically, Kyrgyzstan is dominated by the western end of the Tian Shan Range, which rises

to Pik Pobedy (7,439 m; 24,406 ft) on the Chinese border. A large part of this mountain range is permanently snow-capped. The rest of the country is made up of a series of mountainous parallel ridges, separated by deep valleys and basins. The deep waters of Lake Ysyk-Köl are surrounded by snowy mountains in the northeast. The Fergana Valley, which is the main lowland region, lies in the southwest.

Much of the lower land is pasture for sheep, pigs, cattle, goats, horses, and yaks. Irrigated land is used to produce crops ranging from sugar beet and vegetables to rice, cotton, tobacco, grapes, and mulberry trees (for feeding silkworms). There are major salination problems caused mainly by the excessive irrigation of cotton.

Cotton, wool, and meat are the main agricultural products and exports: one of Kyrgyzstan's strengths is agricultural self-sufficiency. It has small quantities of coal, oil, gas, and the extensive snow-covered ranges ensure great hydropower potential. Energy policy aims at developing these resources in order to make the country less dependent on Russia. After the introduction of market reforms, and a program to control inflation, attention has turned to stimulating growth. This will not be easy: the economy is still dominated by the state and by the mentality of collective farming. Foreign aid plays a major role in the country's budget.

Fact File

OFFICIAL NAME Kyrgyz Republic

FORM OF GOVERNMENT Republic with two legislative bodies (Assembly of People's Representatives and Legislative Assembly)

CAPITAL Bishkek

AREA 198,500 sq km (76,641 sq miles)

TIME ZONE GMT + 6 hours

POPULATION 4,546,055

PROJECTED POPULATION 2005 4,829,120

POPULATION DENSITY 22.9 per sq km (59.3 per sq mile)

LIFE EXPECTANCY 63.6

INFANT MORTALITY (PER 1,000) 75.9

OFFICIAL LANGUAGE Kyrghiz

OTHER LANGUAGE Russian

LITERACY RATE 97%

RELIGIONS Sunni Muslim 70%, Christian (predominantly Russian Orthodox) 30%

ETHNIC GROUPS Kyrghiz 52.5%, Russian 21.5%, Uzbek 13%, Ukrainian 2.5%, German 2.5%, other 8%

CURRENCY Som

ECONOMY Services 41%, agriculture 38%, industry 21%

GNP PER CAPITA US$700

CLIMATE Subtropical in southwest, temperate in valleys, cold and snowy in mountains

HIGHEST POINT Pik Pobedy 7,439 m (24,406 ft)

MAP REFERENCE Page 223

Dome of the Khodja Ahmed Yasavi Mausoleum in Turkestan, Kazakhstan (far left). Women at the market in the town of Osh, Kyrgyzstan (center left). Kuwait City (left).

Asia and the Middle East

Laos

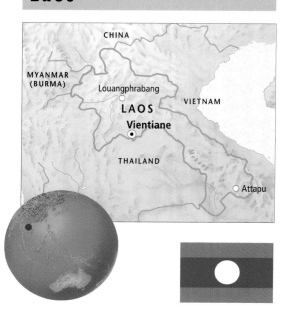

Fact File

OFFICIAL NAME Lao People's Democratic Republic

FORM OF GOVERNMENT Communist state with single legislative body (National Assembly)

CAPITAL Vientiane

AREA 236,800 sq km (91,428 sq miles)

TIME ZONE GMT + 7 hours

POPULATION 5,407,453

PROJECTED POPULATION 2005 6,337,670

POPULATION DENSITY 22.8 per sq km (59 per sq mile)

LIFE EXPECTANCY 54.2

INFANT MORTALITY (PER 1,000) 89.3

OFFICIAL LANGUAGE Lao

OTHER LANGUAGES French, English, indigenous languages

LITERACY RATE 55.8%

RELIGIONS Buddhist 60%, animist and other 40%

ETHNIC GROUPS Lao Loum (lowland) 68%, Lao Theung (upland) 22%, Lao Soung (highland) 9%, ethnic Vietnamese and Chinese 1%

CURRENCY Kip

ECONOMY Agriculture 80%, services and industry 20%

GNP PER CAPITA US$350

CLIMATE Tropical monsoonal, with wet season May to October

HIGHEST POINT Phou Bia 2,818 m (9,245 ft)

MAP REFERENCE Pages 202–03

Novice Buddhist monks in a Laotian monastery (above). A Laotian village (top). Byblos Harbor in Lebanon (right).

Laos is the only landlocked country in Southeast Asia. It also has one of the last official communist regimes, and is the poorest state in the region. Once the home of the fourteenth century kingdom of Lan Xang (the Million Elephant Kingdom), Laos became a French protectorate in 1893. Independent in 1953, it was fought over by royalists, communists, and conservatives from 1964 onward. It was used as a military supply route by the North Vietnamese during the Vietnam War and was heavily bombed with defoliants by the USA during the late 1960s. In 1975 it fell into the hands of the communist Pathet Lao who established a one-party state. Although the leadership has for economic reasons relaxed its doctrinal grip—the 1978 collectivization of agriculture was reversed in 1990—many hill-tribe people, such as the Hmong, remain alienated from the regime. Some continue guerrilla resistance, while others live in exile in Thailand. A new constitution in 1991 confirmed the monopoly of the communist Lao People's Revolutionary Party.

From the mountains in the northwest and the Plateau de Xiangkhoang, the country extends southeast, following the line of the Chaîne Anamitique Range. A number of rivers cross the country westward from this range to the Mekong River which forms the western border, among them the Banghiang, the Noi, and the Theun. The fertile Mekong floodplains in the west provide the only generally cultivable lowland. Despite deforestation and erosion, forest still covers 55 percent of the country.

Most of the Laotian people are engaged in subsistence agriculture. In addition to the staple, rice, other crops grown include maize, vegetables, tobacco, coffee, and cotton. Opium poppies and cannabis are grown illegally: Laos is the world's third-largest opium producer.

The policy of privatization and decentralization that was adopted in 1986 has produced growth averaging an annual 7.5 percent since 1988. Textile and garment manufacture was established, as well as motorcycle assembly. The country's primitive infrastructure is a major handicap to growth. Laos has no railroads, its roads are inadequate, and its telecommunications severely limited. For the foreseeable future the economy will depend heavily on overseas aid.

Lebanon

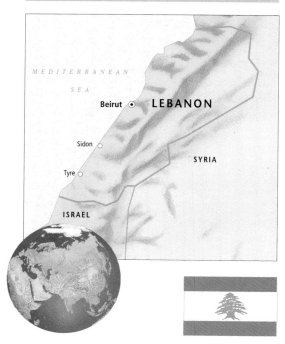

Fact File

OFFICIAL NAME	Republic of Lebanon
FORM OF GOVERNMENT	Republic with single legislative body (National Assembly)
CAPITAL	Beirut
AREA	10,400 sq km (4,015 sq miles)
TIME ZONE	GMT + 2 hours
POPULATION	3,562,699
PROJECTED POPULATION 2005	3,904,380
POPULATION DENSITY	342.5 per sq km (887 per sq mile)
LIFE EXPECTANCY	70.9
INFANT MORTALITY (PER 1,000)	30.5
OFFICIAL LANGUAGES	Arabic, French
OTHER LANGUAGES	Armenian, English
LITERACY RATE	92%
RELIGIONS	Muslim 70%, Christian 30%
ETHNIC GROUPS	Arab 95%, Armenian 4%, other 1%
CURRENCY	Lebanese pound
ECONOMY	Services 60%, industry 28%, agriculture 12%
GNP PER CAPITA	US$2,660
CLIMATE	Temperate, with short mild, wet winters and long, hot, dry summers. In winter rainfall in mountains often turns to snow
HIGHEST POINT	Qurnat as Sawdā' 3,088 m (10,131 ft)
MAP REFERENCE	Page 225

Lebanon, a small country on the eastern shore of the Mediterranean Sea, consists of the region that was once known as the Levant. It has a history that goes back at least 5,000 years. First settled by the Phoenicians around 3000 BC, it saw Alexander the Great (356–323 BC) conquer the Phoenician city of Tyre, and it later became part of the Roman Empire. Early in the seventh century AD Maronite Christians (named after Maro, a Syrian monk who was the sect's founder) settled in northern Lebanon; later, Druze Arabs, who are aligned with Shi'ite Islam, settled in the south of

the country, and Sunni Muslims came to the coastal towns. From the eleventh to the thirteenth century the region was a center of confrontation between Western Christians and Muslims during the Crusades. It then became part of the Muslim Mameluke Empire. In 1516 the Ottoman Turks took control of the country, their rule finally ending with conquest by the British and French during the First World War.

From 1920, following the withdrawal of Turkish forces, a French administration sought to balance the interests of the country's various religious groups. During this period Beirut, which already had a cosmopolitan air, took on a distinctly French flavor. The city became both a center of international commerce and a playground of the rich. The country gained independence in 1946. Deep and persistent tensions between Muslim and various non-Muslim sections of the population led to an outbreak of guerrilla war in 1975. For the next 15 years much of the country was devasted by civil war, and much of its urban infrastructure was destroyed.

From the narrow coastal plain along the Mediterranean, where crops are grown with the

aid of irrigation, the land rises eastward to form the Lebanon Mountains (Jabal Lubnān). Running from north to south, these cover about 30 percent of Lebanon's land area. Between the harsh slopes of this range and the Anti-Lebanon Chain (Jabal ash Sharqī) that borders Syria, lies the fertile el Beqaa Valley which is another agricultural area. This is traversed by the River Litani on its journey south, before emptying into the Mediterranean Sea above Ṣūr (the ancient city of Tyre).

Decades of fighting have left the Lebanese economy in ruins and there is a severe housing shortage. Tourism, which was once an important source of revenue, is beginning to revive with the rebuilding of the once-popular Corniche seafront area at Beirut. Since the decline of industry as a result of the war, agriculture has come to play a more important role: crops include apples, citrus fruits, bananas, carrots, grapes, tomatoes, and olives. Opium poppies and cannabis are illegally produced for export. Traditional areas of activity in the past were banking, food processing, textiles, cement, oil refining, and chemicals. The country now depends heavily on foreign aid.

Beirut

With a population of only 6,000, Beirut was little more than a village in the year 1800. But the nineteenth century saw continuous commercial growth, and by 1850 its population had swelled to 15,000. An ominous development in 1860 also increased Beirut's population: in the nearby mountains there was a massacre of Christians by Druzes (an Islamic sect originating in Syria), with the result that large numbers of Christian refugees entered the city. During the second half of the century a variety of Western missionaries, both Catholic and Protestant, were active, and several major educational institutions (one becoming the highly regarded American University of Beirut) were founded.

In 1926 the Lebanese Republic was established, under French control, and as the city grew rapidly so did its social tensions. Under the terms of a French-brokered unwritten understanding in 1943 the Christians were able to dominate the Muslim population through a fixed 6:5 ratio of parliamentary seats. The Muslims bitterly resented this arrangement. After they had tried for three decades to change the situation, with a serious outbreak of violence between Christians and Muslims in 1958, full-scale civil war erupted in 1975 between numerous armed militias. On the Christian side the major groups consisted of Maronite Christians and Greek Orthodox, along with smaller numbers of Armenians, Greek Catholics, Protestants, and Roman Catholics. On the non-Christian side were the dominant Sunni Muslims, the minority Shi'ites, and the Druzes. As the war extended Beirut became first a divided city, then a city destroying itself. Lebanon had already been destabilized by a deluge of Palestinian refugees following the 1967 Arab–Israeli War, and by a further influx when the Palestinians in Jordan were expelled in 1970. The Palestinians used southern Lebanon as a base for attacks on Israel, and their militias behaved like an

occupying army in the area. West Beirut was virtually destroyed in 1982 when Israel launched a full-scale assault on Palestinian Liberation Organization (PLO) bases in the city, action which led to the evacuation of PLO troops and leaders.

While some degree of order existed in East Beirut, West Beirut collapsed into endless anarchic battles between rival factions trying to settle scores. Hostage-taking became common, some captives being held for years on end. In 1986 West Beirut sought Syrian intervention to try to establish order; after a period of intensified fighting the major antagonists accepted the Ta'if Accord in 1989. Since then the level of internal conflict has declined. Syria remains a powerful influence in Lebanese affairs and its forces continue to occupy large areas. It is estimated that about 150,000 people died in the civil war.

Malaysia

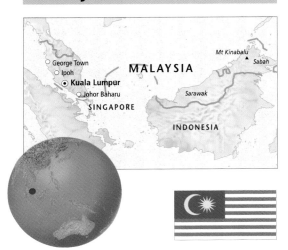

Fact File

OFFICIAL NAME Malaysia

FORM OF GOVERNMENT Federal constitutional monarchy with two legislative bodies (Senate and House of Representatives)

CAPITAL Kuala Lumpur

AREA 329,750 sq km (127,316 sq miles)

TIME ZONE GMT + 8 hours

POPULATION 21,376,066

PROJECTED POPULATION 2005 24,086,817

POPULATION DENSITY 64.8 per sq km (167.8 per sq mile)

LIFE EXPECTANCY 70.7

INFANT MORTALITY (PER 1,000) 21.7

OFFICIAL LANGUAGE Malay (Bahasa Malaysia)

OTHER LANGUAGES English, Chinese languages, Tamil

LITERACY RATE 83%

RELIGIONS Muslim 53%, Buddhist 17.5%, Confucian and Taoist 11.5%, Christian 8.5%, Hindu 7%, other 2.5%

ETHNIC GROUPS Malay 59%, Chinese 32%, Indian 9%

CURRENCY Ringgit (Malaysian dollar)

ECONOMY Agriculture 42%, services 39%, industry 19%

GNP PER CAPITA US$3,890

CLIMATE Tropical, with northeast monsoon October to February and southwest monsoon May to September

HIGHEST POINT Gunung Kinabalu 4,101 m (13,453 ft)

MAP REFERENCE Pages 200–01

Malaysia consists of the southern part of the Malay Peninsula, with Thailand to its north, plus Sarawak and Sabah in northern Borneo. Like Singapore, which lies at the southern tip of the Malay Peninsula, it has had an impressive record of economic growth in recent times.

In the fifteenth century a part of Malaysia was famous as the Kingdom of Malacca (now Melaka), a state that became powerful through its control of local sea routes and shipping. In 1414 the ruler of Malacca adopted Islam, which is the religion of Malaysia today. Seized by the Portuguese as a base for the spice trade in 1511, and held by the Dutch from 1641, Malacca was captured by the British in 1795. The British took control of Singapore in 1819 and in 1867 they established the Straits

Settlements, which consisted of Penang Island (Pinang) in the northeast, Malacca, and Singapore, as a crown colony. During the Second World War Malaysia was occupied by the Japanese. In 1948 it received its independence from the British. A guerrilla war then broke out, led by communists who were sympathetic to the Chinese Revolution. Following the defeat of this insurgency, after a four-year military campaign, the country evolved into the modern state it is today. Ethnic tensions exist, principally between the Malays, who are the most numerous, and the Chinese, who are considerably more prosperous. There were riots between the Malays and Chinese in 1969 with heavy loss of life. The many "affirmative action" provisions that are now in place to help Malays at the expense of Chinese and Indians are strongly resented by the latter groups. There are also a number of unresolved territorial disputes with neighboring states—Sabah in Borneo, for example, being claimed by the Philippines.

Fold mountains aligned on a north–south axis dominate the Malay Peninsula. There are seven or eight distinct chains of mountains, often with exposed granite cores. Climbing to 2,189 m (7,181 ft) at Gunung Tahan, the main range divides the narrow eastern coastal belt from the fertile alluvial plains in the west. To the south lies poorly drained lowland, marked by isolated hills, some of which rise to over 1,060 m (3,500 ft). Several smaller rivers have also contributed to the margin of lowland around the peninsular coasts.

About 2,000 km (1,250 miles) east of the Malay Peninsula, northern Borneo has a mangrove-fringed coastal plain about 65 km (40 miles) wide, rising behind to hill country averaging 300 m (1,000 ft) in height. This ascends through various secondary ranges to the mountainous main interior range. The granite peak of Gunung Kinabalu, the highest mountain in Southeast Asia, rises from the northern end of this range in Sabah, towering

above Kinabalu National Park. Dense rainforest in Sarawak and Sabah support a great diversity of plants and animals.

With a mixture of private enterprise and public management, the Malaysian economy averaged 9 percent annual growth from 1988 to 1995. Poverty is being substantially reduced and real wages are rising. New light industries including electronics are playing an important role in this development: Malaysia is the world's biggest producer of disk drives. Heavy industry has also grown: Malaysia's "national car", the Proton, is now being exported. The traditional mainstays of the economy, however, remain rice, rubber, palm oil, and tin—Malaysia being the world's biggest producer of palm oil and tin. Rice is a problem. Subsistence farming has regularly failed to ensure self-sufficiency in food, and rice production does

Maldives

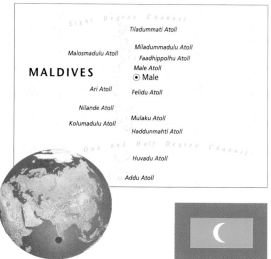

Eight Degree Channel

Tiladummati Atoll

Miladummadulu Atoll

Malosmadulu Atoll   Faadhippolhu Atoll

MALDIVES   Male Atoll

⊙ Male

Ari Atoll   Felidu Atoll

Nilande Atoll

Kolumadulu Atoll   Mulaku Atoll

Haddunmahti Atoll

One and Half Degree Channel

Huvadu Atoll

Addu Atoll

Fact File

OFFICIAL NAME Republic of the Maldives

FORM OF GOVERNMENT Republic with single legislative body (Citizens Council)

CAPITAL Male

AREA 300 sq km (116 sq miles)

TIME ZONE GMT + 5 hours

POPULATION 300,220

PROJECTED POPULATION 2005 364,147

POPULATION DENSITY 1,000.7 per sq km (2,591.8 per sq mile)

LIFE EXPECTANCY 68.3

INFANT MORTALITY (PER 1,000) 38.1

OFFICIAL LANGUAGE Divehi

OTHER LANGUAGES Arabic, English, Hindi

LITERACY RATE 93%

RELIGIONS Predominantly Sunni Muslim

ETHNIC GROUPS Sinhalese, Dravidian, Arab, African

CURRENCY Rufiyaa

ECONOMY Tourism, fishing, manufacturing

GNP PER CAPITA US$990

CLIMATE Tropical, with wet season May to August

HIGHEST POINT Unnamed location on Wilingili 24 m (79 ft)

MAP REFERENCE Page 216

The Maldive Archipelago consists of an 800 km (500 mile) string of nearly 2,000 islands and atolls (202 of them inhabited) southwest of India's southern tip, Cape Comorin. Made up of tiny islets ringed by white sands and clear blue lagoons, they have recently been developed as tourist resorts and receive up to 300,000 visitors each year. Long ago, their first visitors were probably Dravidians from southern India, in around 400 BC. Centuries later, the islands seem to have been taken over by people from Sri Lanka—Divehi, the national language, is a form of Sinhalese. In 1153 the king of the Maldives ordered his subjects to adopt Islam in place of Buddhism: today the people are mainly Sunni Muslims and there are 689 mosques. For the next 800 years the islands were ruled as a Muslim sultanate, though there was a brief period, between 1558 and 1573, of Portuguese control from Goa. The British established a protectorate in 1887, the islands achieved independence in 1965, and the sultan was deposed in 1968. Since then government has been in the hands of a small group of influential families, and by 1995 the president then in office, a wealthy businessman, had survived three attempted coups. Younger political contenders who have tasted democracy abroad are pressing for a more open regime.

The atolls of the Maldives are coral reefs which have grown up around the peaks of a submerged volcanic mountain range. None of them rise more than 1.8 m (6 ft) above sea level. There is concern that if the Greenhouse Effect causes a rise in sea levels, some may be submerged. Adequate rainfall supports a variety of tropical vegetation, and palm and breadfruit trees occur naturally.

Food crops include coconuts, bananas, mangoes, sweet potatoes, and spices. Agriculture plays a role in the economy, though constrained by the small amount of cultivable land, and most staple foods must be imported. In the lagoons and the open sea fish are plentiful. Bonito and tuna are leading exports, fishing being the second leading growth sector of the economy. Manufacturing, consisting mainly of garment production, boat building, and handicrafts, accounts for 15 percent of gross domestic product. Since the 1980s tourism has been the leading growth sector, and now accounts for more than 60 percent of foreign exchange receipts. At present more than 90 percent of tax revenue comes from import duties and tourism-related taxes.

not meet demand. The main industries on the peninsula are rubber and palm oil processing and manufacturing, light industry, electronics, tin mining, smelting, logging, and timber processing. The main activities on Sabah and Sarawak are logging, petroleum production, and the processing of agricultural products. Malaysia exports more tropical timber than any other country, and the tribal people of Sarawak have been campaigning against the scale of logging on their land. The Asian economic downturn in 1998 saw a depreciation of the Malaysian currency and a marked slowing of the economy.

Rice paddies in east Malaysia (top). Street vendor with customers in Malaysia (above). One of the many palm-fringed beaches in the Maldives (right).

Mongolia

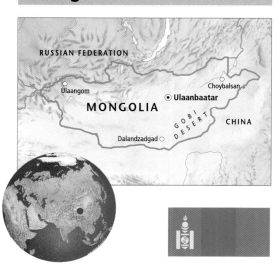

Fact File

OFFICIAL NAME Mongolia

FORM OF GOVERNMENT Republic with single legislative body (State Great Hural)

CAPITAL Ulaanbaatar

AREA 1,565,000 sq km (604,247 sq miles)

TIME ZONE GMT + 8 hours

POPULATION 2,617,379

PROJECTED POPULATION 2005 2,834,466

POPULATION DENSITY 1.7 per sq km (4.4 per sq mile)

LIFE EXPECTANCY 61.8

INFANT MORTALITY (PER 1,000) 64.6

OFFICIAL LANGUAGE Khalka Mongol

OTHER LANGUAGES Turkic, Russian, Chinese

LITERACY RATE 82.2%

RELIGIONS Predominantly Tibetan Buddhist with small Muslim minority

ETHNIC GROUPS Mongol 90%, Kazak 4%, Chinese 2%, Russian 2%, other 2%

CURRENCY Tugrik

ECONOMY Mainly agriculture with some industry

GNP PER CAPITA US$310

CLIMATE Cold and arid

HIGHEST POINT Tavan Bogd Uul 4,374 m (14,350 ft)

MAP REFERENCE Pages 300–01

The world's largest and most thinly populated landlocked country, Mongolia has a reputation for isolation. Its deserts, severe climate, and widely scattered population of nomadic pastoralists have tended to shut it off from modern life. Historically, however, it had its hour of glory. In the thirteenth century the Mongol tribes were united under Ghengis Khan (1162–1227), who then established the largest empire yet known, extending from eastern Europe to the Pacific and into northern India. The Mongol Empire collapsed in 1368, after which Mongolia (also known as Outer Mongolia to distinguish it from Inner Mongolia, one of China's Autonomous Regions) fell under Chinese control. Following the Russian Civil War (1918–22) the Chinese were expelled. Today, after 70 years within the Soviet system, the country is trying to remake itself in a more democratic mold.

Mongolia divides into two regions. In the northwest lie the Mongolian Altai Mountains (Mongol Altayn Nuruu), along with the Hangayn and Hentiyn Ranges. Here, high mountains alternate with river valleys and lakes. Pastures support large herds of cattle and sheep, and wheat is cultivated. At the highest levels of the Altai in the northwest boreal forests cover the slopes. The second region is the southern half of the country. This is semidesert steppe changing further south to salt-pans, shallow depressions, and the arid stony wastes of the Gobi Desert.

While more people today live in towns than in the country, Mongolia remains a land of nomadic pastoralists. Herds of goats, sheep, yaks, camels, and horses still provide the base of the traditional economy, and Mongolia has the highest number of livestock per capita in the world. Cattle raising accounts for more than two-thirds of all production. Under the Soviets textiles and food processing were developed, and with aid from the USSR and Comecon mineral deposits such as copper, molybdenum, and coking coal were developed. Mongolia is the world's third biggest producer of fluorspar.

New laws have been passed regulating mining, banking, foreign investment, tourism, and economic planning. Mongolia continues to attract foreign aid, but suffers from the loss of Russian financial support. So far, foreign funds have not been found for the development of Mongolia's considerable oil and gas reserves.

Myanmar (Burma)

Better known for the name of its Nobel Prize winning opposition leader Aung San Suu Kyi than for that of its prime minister, Myanmar is struggling to overcome 50 years of ethnic strife, one-party socialist government, and military rule. With an ancient literary tradition and style of script going back to the Mon civilization (third century BC), Myanmar was at various times ruled by the eleventh century Tibeto-Burman Dynasty of Anarutha the Great, by the Mongols under Khublai Khan (1287), and by the British, who incorporated the country into its Indian Empire in 1886.

After the country won independence in 1948, General Ne Win's Burmese Socialist Program Party abolished all private enterprise and private trade, nationalized industry, and placed the country under military control. Soon one of the region's richest countries had become an impoverished backwater. For decades, much of the government's energy and 35 percent of its budget has gone into trying to suppress ethnic insurgent movements led by Karens, Shans, Kachins, Mons, and others. To fund their resistance these groups grew opium poppies, a traditional crop, which has led to the country becoming the world's largest opium producer.

On the Bay of Bengal between Bangladesh and Thailand, Myanmar consists of central lowlands, where 75 percent of the people live, enclosed by mountains to the north, bordering China, and west, bordering India, and the Shan Plateau to the east forming a frontier with Laos. The western mountains run southwest along the Indian border and form a series of forested ridges, ending in the Arakan Yoma Range (Pegu Yoma). From the mountains in the north the Irawaddy River flows south 2,100 km (1,300 miles), passing the old city of Mandalay and the capital of Yangon (Rangoon) on its way to the Andaman Sea. While the coast has a wet climate, the inner region, sheltered from the monsoon, has an annual rainfall of less than 1,000 mm (40 in). Here, in narrow valleys, small-scale irrigation supports such crops as rice, sugarcane, cotton, and jute.

Myanmar is rich in natural resources, having fertile soils and good fisheries, along with teak, gems, and natural gas and oil. Recently there has been some liberalization of the economy, notably of small scale enterprise. Twenty-five percent, however, remains under state control, the key industries—in energy, heavy industry, and foreign trade—being 20 military-run enterprises. A recent boom in trade with China has filled the north with Chinese goods and visitors. Economic weaknesses include a shortage of skilled labor, and of trained managers and technicians. Price controls mean that the economy is permeated by the black market. Published estimates of Myanmar's foreign trade are therefore greatly understated.

Fact File

OFFICIAL NAME Union of Myanmar (Burma)

FORM OF GOVERNMENT Military regime; legislative body (People's Assembly) never convened since military takeover in 1988

CAPITAL Yangon (Rangoon)

AREA 678,500 sq km (261,969 sq miles)

TIME ZONE GMT + 6.5 hours

POPULATION 48,081,302

PROJECTED POPULATION 2005 52,697,795

POPULATION DENSITY 70.9 per sq km (183.6 per sq mile)

LIFE EXPECTANCY 54.7

INFANT MORTALITY (PER 1,000) 76.3

OFFICIAL LANGUAGE Burmese

OTHER LANGUAGES Indigenous languages, English

LITERACY RATE 82.7%

RELIGIONS Buddhist 89%, Christian 4% (Baptist 3%, Roman Catholic 1%), Muslim 4%, other 3%

ETHNIC GROUPS Burman 68%, Shan 9%, Karen 7%, Rakhine 4%, Chinese 3%, Mon 2%, other 7%

CURRENCY Kyat

ECONOMY Agriculture 64%, services 27%, industry 9%

GNP PER CAPITA Est. < US$765

CLIMATE Tropical monsoon; dry zone around Mandalay; moderate temperature on Shan Plateau

HIGHEST POINT Hkakabo Razi 5,881 m (19,294 ft)

MAP REFERENCE Pages 202, 205

Buddhist temple ruins at Pagan in Myanmar (bottom left).
A Mongolian musician playing a horsehair fiddle (top left).
Mt Everest and surrounding peaks in Nepal (top right).

Nepal

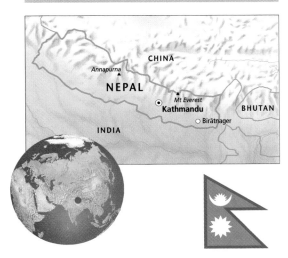

The birthplace of the Buddha c. 568 BC, Nepal is a small landlocked kingdom on the southern slopes of the Himalayas. It is surrounded by India to the west, south, and east, and has a border with China (Tibet) to the north. Tourists coming to trek in the mountains and climb the peaks contribute to national income, but Nepal remains one of the world's poorest countries. Historically, it was influenced both by the Buddhist/Mongol culture of Tibet and by the Hindu/Indian culture of the subcontinent. The present royal family established its rule in 1769. During British colonial rule in India a British resident was installed to provide "guidance" in foreign affairs. In 1959 the country's first elections were held (the Nepali Congress party winning), but in 1960 the king suspended the constitution, and no further elections were held until 1992. In the late 1990s a parliamentary impasse existed: neither the Nepali Congress nor the United Marxist-Leninist (UML) parties had clear majorities enabling them to govern in their own right.

The mountainous heart of Nepal, consisting of the towering Himalayas (including the highest and third-highest peaks in the world, Mt Everest and Kanchenjunga) and the lower Siwalik Range to the south, forms three-quarters of the country. Three main river systems cut the Himalayas, the Karnali (feeding the Ganges), the Gandak, and the Kosi. Kathmandu stands among fruit trees and rice fields typical of Nepal's densely populated uplands. Further south, on the Terai/Ganges Plain, farming settlements grow rice, wheat,

maize, sugarcane, and jute which are the country's economic maintstay.

Some 90 percent of Nepalis live by subsistence farming, and many do not live well: more than 40 percent of Nepal's citizens are undernourished. Most industry is concerned with the processing of jute, sugarcane, tobacco, and grain. Recently textile and carpet production has expanded and now provides 85 percent of foreign exchange earnings. The country has limitless hydropower resources. Electricity could be sold to Indian industry south of the border, and various schemes have been proposed, but environmental considerations weigh against them. Restructuring is needed. International aid funds 62 percent of Nepal's development budget and 34 percent of total budgetary expenditure.

Fact File

OFFICIAL NAME Kingdom of Nepal

FORM OF GOVERNMENT Constitutional monarchy with two legislative bodies (National Council and House of Representatives)

CAPITAL Kathmandu

AREA 140,800 sq km (54,363 sq miles)

TIME ZONE GMT + 5.5 hours

POPULATION 24,302,653

PROJECTED POPULATION 2005 28,172,635

POPULATION DENSITY 172.6 per sq km (447 per sq mile)

LIFE EXPECTANCY 58.4

INFANT MORTALITY (PER 1,000) 73.6

OFFICIAL LANGUAGE Nepali

OTHER LANGUAGES Indigenous languages

LITERACY RATE 27%

RELIGIONS Hindu 90%, Buddhist 5%, Muslim 3%, other 2%

ETHNIC GROUPS Newar, Indian, Tibetan, Gurung and many smaller minorities

CURRENCY Nepalese rupee

ECONOMY Agriculture 93%, services 6%, industry 1%

GNP PER CAPITA US$200

CLIMATE Subtropical in south, with wet season July to October; cold and snowy in north, wetter in east

HIGHEST POINT Mt Everest 8,848 m (29,028 ft)

MAP REFERENCE Pages 218–19

North Korea

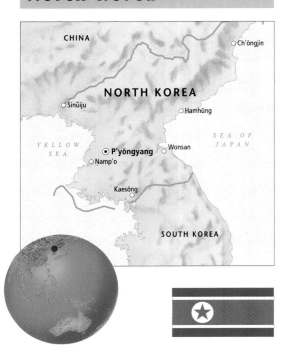

Fact File

OFFICIAL NAME Democratic People's Republic of Korea

FORM OF GOVERNMENT Communist state with single legislative body (Supreme People's Assembly)

CAPITAL P'yongyang

AREA 120,540 sq km (46,540 sq miles)

TIME ZONE GMT + 9 hours

POPULATION 22,337,878

PROJECTED POPULATION 2005 23,348,444

POPULATION DENSITY 185.3 per sq km (480 per sq mile)

LIFE EXPECTANCY 67.5

INFANT MORTALITY (PER 1,000) 35.0

OFFICIAL LANGUAGE Korean

LITERACY RATE 95%

RELIGIONS Buddhist and Confucian 51%, traditional beliefs 45%, Christian 4%

ETHNIC GROUPS Korean 100%

CURRENCY Won

ECONOMY Services and industry 64%, agriculture 36%

GNP PER CAPITA Est. US$7,940

CLIMATE Temperate, with cold, snowy winters and warm, wet summers

HIGHEST POINT Mt Paektu 2,744 m (9,003 ft)

MAP REFERENCE Page 208

North Korea occupies the northern half of the Korean Peninsula. It is separated from South Korea along the ceasefire line that was established at the end of the Korean War (1950–53), roughly along the 38th parallel. After a period as an independent kingdom in the tenth century AD, control of Korea was disputed for hundreds of years between China and Japan, the latter seizing it as a colony in 1910. Following the Second World War it became a separate communist state and after the Korean War it developed into a rigidly closed totalitarian state system. The 50-year-long personal rule of Kim Il Sung ("Great Leader") passed by hereditary succession to his son Kim Jong Il ("Dear Leader")

in 1994. The people of North Korea are classed by the state into three quasi-castes: loyal, wavering, and hostile. Membership of a caste determines whether an individual receives either education or employment. Citizens are subject to arbitrary arrest and execution for criticizing the Korean leaders or listening to foreign broadcasts. Unceasing political indoctrination takes place through the media, the workplace, the military, mass spectacles, and cultural events.

Mountains and rugged hills occupy most of the Korean Peninsula, and dominate its northern half. In the northeast the volcanic peak of Mt Paektu is surrounded by the Kaema Plateau. High forested mountains, cut by river gorges, lie along the border with Manchuria, northeast China. Other mountain chains extend north to south along the east coast. The Yalu River valley in the northwest marks the Korean–Chinese border, while to the southwest the fertile Chaeryŏng and Pyongyang plains are the main areas for agricultural activity. The principal crop is rice, followed by millet and other grains. Fruit and vegetables are grown, and also oilseed rape, flax, and cotton.

The North Korean economy is run according to the Stalinist model. More than 90 percent of operations are controlled by the state, agriculture is totally collectivized, and state-owned industry produces 95 percent of all manufactured goods. Despite over 50 years of complete control by the state, the country is still not self-sufficient in food. The industrial sector produces military weapons, chemicals, minerals (including coal, magnesite, iron ore, graphite, copper, zinc, lead, and precious metals), along with a number of food products and textiles.

During the late 1990s the economy was in crisis: power supplies were unreliable and food shortages were causing famine in the countryside. Flooding in 1995 damaged harvests and led North Korea to seek foreign aid for the first time in decades; aid donors were muted in their response, demanding proof that aid had been properly distributed. North Korea continues to fall farther and farther behind South Korean development and living standards.

The Korean War, 1950–53

Occupied by Japan from 1910 until the Second World War, Korea found itself in 1945 divided between a Soviet-controlled north and an American-controlled south, with a frontier along the 38th parallel. This de facto division of the peninsula was formalized in 1948. In June 1950 heavily armed troops and tanks from the communist People's Republic of North Korea invaded the south, precipitating three years of bitter conflict.

Authorised by a UN resolution, American and South Korean troops, supported by contingents from Britain, Canada, France, and other allies, then fought to reclaim southern territory under the UN flag. Their success soon had the North Koreans in retreat, and American seaborne landings put allied troops far behind the North Korean lines. A crisis then arose when the allied commander, General Douglas MacArthur, neared

Oman

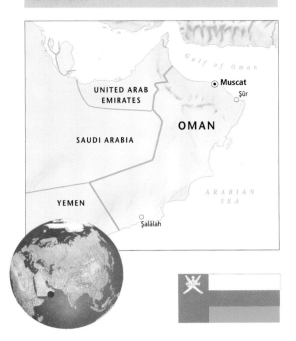

the border of China. Hundreds of thousands of Chinese "volunteers" poured across the Yalu River into North Korea, and drove the allies far into the south once more. A counter-offensive in 1951 pushed the North Koreans and Chinese troops back to the vicinity of the 38th parallel, where an armistice took place in 1953.

After almost 40 years of tension and a series of minor military clashes a non-aggression pact was negotiated between North and South Korea in 1991. While the war resulted in North Korea becoming a rigid Stalinist state, it also ensured decades of US economic and military protection for South Korea.

For some the war is still not over: in October 1998 a 72-year-old South Korean soldier, who escaped from the north after 45 years as a prisoner-of-war, reported that 30 others like him were still being held in North Korean camps.

Oman is the second largest country in the Arabian Peninsula. Standing on the peninsula's eastern corner, it looks across the Arabian Sea toward Baluchistan and India—in fact Baluchis form a small but significant part of the population. A small, separate, and highly strategic piece of Oman's territory is the tip of the Musandam Peninsula, commanding the entrance to the Strait of Hormuz. The Omani capital of Muscat was a trading center for hundreds of years, dhows sailing to India in one direction and down the African coast to Zanzibar in the other. Zanzibar itself was an Omani conquest, and in the 1960s, when it became part of Tanzania, many Arab Zanzibaris came to Oman. From 1798 Oman had strong ties with the British, and it became a British protectorate. Full independence came in 1971. Sultan Qabus Ibn Sa'id rules his country as an absolute monarch, advised by a *majlis alshura* ("consultative council"), but in the late 1990s the country was moving toward constitutional government. In the late 1960s Oman faced a leftist rebellion in the western province of Dhofur, encouraged and supported by the People's Republic of Yemen across the border. This was defeated in 1975. Since then, with the country enjoying the prosperity of its oil and natural gas (huge additional reserves were discovered in 1991), peace has reigned.

In the north the limestone Hajar Mountains overlook the fertile coastal plain of al-Batinah. Most of Oman's population lives along the alluvial al-Batinah strip, where date gardens stretch for more than 250 km (155 miles). The Jabal Akhdar ridge is the highest part of the Hajar Range, rising to 3,107 m (10,193 ft). Soils in the upland region are poor: herders use the area for running camels, sheep, and goats. Wadis cutting the Jabal Akhdar ridge, underground canals, and wells provide a certain amount of irrigation. North of the Zufār (Dhofar) uplands in the southwest the desert meets the sandy wastes of the Saudi Arabian Ar Rub' al Khāli (or "Empty Quarter").

Rural Omanis live by subsistence agriculture, growing dates, limes, bananas, alfalfa, and vegetables. Pastoralists keep camels, cattle, sheep, and goats. The smaller urban population, however,

including a considerable number of guest workers, depends on imported food. The national economy as a whole is dominated by the oil industry: petroleum accounts for nearly 90 percent of export earnings, about 75 percent of government revenues, and roughly 40 percent of gross domestic product. Oman has proved oil reserves of 4 billion barrels, which are equal to 20 year's supply at the present rate of extraction.

Fact File

OFFICIAL NAME	Sultanate of Oman
FORM OF GOVERNMENT	Monarchy with advisory Consultative Council
CAPITAL	Muscat
AREA	212,460 sq km (82,031 sq miles)
TIME ZONE	GMT + 4 hours
POPULATION	2,446,645
PROJECTED POPULATION 2005	2,999,546
POPULATION DENSITY	11.5 per sq km (29.8 per sq mile)
LIFE EXPECTANCY	71.3
INFANT MORTALITY (PER 1,000)	24.7
OFFICIAL LANGUAGE	Arabic
OTHER LANGUAGES	English, Baluchu, Urdu
LITERACY RATE	35%
RELIGIONS	Ibadhi Muslim 75%, Sunni Muslim, Shi'a Muslim and Hindu 25%
ETHNIC GROUPS	Mainly Arab with Baluchi, Indian, Pakistani, Sri Lankan, Bangladeshi, African minorities
CURRENCY	Omani rial
ECONOMY	Agriculture 50%, services 28%, industry 22%
GNP PER CAPITA	US$4,820
CLIMATE	Mainly hot and arid; light rains in south June to September
HIGHEST POINT	Jabal Ash Shām 3,019 m (10,199 ft)
MAP REFERENCE	Pages 220–21

The Gubra Bowl in Oman (top left). A village in the Oman mountains, surrounded by terraced cultivation (below).

Pakistan

Fact File

OFFICIAL NAME Islamic Republic of Pakistan

FORM OF GOVERNMENT Republic with two legislative bodies (Senate and National Assembly)

CAPITAL Islāmābād

AREA 803,940 sq km (310,401 sq miles)

TIME ZONE GMT + 5 hours

POPULATION 138,123,359

PROJECTED POPULATION 2005 156,135,833

POPULATION DENSITY 171.8 per sq km (445 per sq mile)

LIFE EXPECTANCY 59.4

INFANT MORTALITY (PER 1,000) 91.9

OFFICIAL LANGUAGES Urdu, English

OTHER LANGUAGES Punjabi, Sindhi, Urdu, Pashto, Baluchi, Brahvi

LITERACY RATE 37.1%

RELIGIONS Muslim 97% (Sunni 77%, Shi'a 20%), other (Christian, Hindu) 3%

ETHNIC GROUPS Punjabi 60%, Sindhi 14%, Pashtun (Pathan) 9%, other (Baloch and Mohajir) 17%

CURRENCY Pakistani rupee

ECONOMY Agriculture 50%, services 38%, industry 12%

GNP PER CAPITA US$460

CLIMATE Mainly arid; temperate in northwest, cold and snowy in mountains

HIGHEST POINT K2 8,611 m (28,251 ft)

MAP REFERENCE Page 221

Pakistan occupies the valley of the Indus and its tributaries in the northwest of the Indian subcontinent. Its most sensitive political frontiers are with India to the east and Afghanistan to the west. It has shorter borders with Iran and China.

Forming a part of India until 1947, Pakistan shares a history of early civilizations, migrations, and invasions—farmers in the Indus Valley were already using elaborate irrigation works by the second millennium BC. At the time of partition in 1947, Pakistan was two widely separated territories (West and East Pakistan). A dispute over Kashmir has poisoned relations with India since that time.

In 1971 East Pakistan achieved independence as Bangladesh. In that year the populist leader Ali Bhutto assumed power in Pakistan, and in 1973 announced a program of "Islamic socialism" under which banks, insurance companies, heavy industry, and even education were nationalized. Since 1977, when he was overthrown by General Zia ul-Haq (and subsequently executed), military and civilian rule have alternated, accompanied by varying degrees of violence and disorder.

Although 97 percent of Pakistan's population is Muslim, there is a wide range of ethnic groupings, languages, and conflicts. The main linguistic separation is between Iranian languages such as Baluchi and Pashto, and the Indo-Aryan languages of Punjabi, Sindhi, and Urdu. Each of Pakistan's minorities has its own particular concerns. In the northwest of the country the Pathans want to join their kinsmen over the Afghan frontier. The Urdu-speaking Mohajirs migrated in their millions from India at the time of partition and make up the majority of the population in Karachi and Hydera-bad. They resent Punjabi domination and the rule of the old land-owning elite.

The whole of Pakistan is drained by the Indus River. Rising in the Great Highlands of the north it flows southwest, joined by tributaries such as the Jhelum, Chenab, Beas, Ravi, and Sutlej, and forms a fertile and densely populated floodplain in the east of the country before spilling into the Arabian Sea. The waters of this basin feed into one of the largest irrigation systems in the world, the total area being 13 million hectares (32 million acres). Two constructions, one at Tarbela on the Indus, and the other at Mangla on the Jhelum, are among the world's biggest earth- and rock-filled dams. West of the Indus Delta is an ascending landscape of alternating ridges and arid basins, some containing salt marshes like the Hamun-i-Mashkel. In the extreme northwest are the Great Highlands, with the Khyber Pass on the frontier with Afghan-istan to the west and the spectacular peaks of the Karakoram and Pamirs to the east. Along with Nanga Parbat, these include the second highest mountain in the world—K2, Mt Godwin Austen (8,611 m; 28,251 ft) on the border of Tibet.

Irrigation agriculture combined with the new plant varieties that were introduced as part of

the "green revolution" during the 1970s produces abundant cotton, wheat, rice, and sugarcane. Fruit and vegetables are also grown widely, while opium poppies and cannabis are illegally cultivated to supply the international drug trade. Despite the fact that approximately half the population work on the land, agriculture now accounts for less than a quarter of the national income.

Karachi is a considerable manufacturing center for the production of textiles, as is Lahore. Other industries produce a wide variety of petroleum products, construction materials, foodstuffs, and paper products. The country has large reserves of unused minerals: copper, bauxite, phosphates, and manganese. However, Pakistan also faces a range of problems. The country's economy is dependent on the highly competitive textile sector, there is a chronic trade deficit and debt burden, and much of the nation's revenue goes into funding massive defense spending on items such as nuclear weaponry and the army.

Philippines

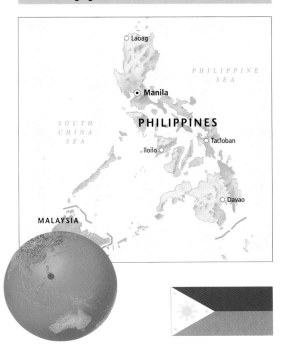

Fact File

OFFICIAL NAME Republic of the Philippines

FORM OF GOVERNMENT Republic with two legislative bodies (Senate and House of Representatives)

CAPITAL Manila

AREA 300,000 sq km (115,830 sq miles)

TIME ZONE GMT + 8 hours

POPULATION 79,345,812

PROJECTED POPULATION 2005 89,055,628

POPULATION DENSITY 264.5 per sq km (685 per sq mile)

LIFE EXPECTANCY 66.6

INFANT MORTALITY (PER 1,000) 33.9

OFFICIAL LANGUAGES Filipino, English

OTHER LANGUAGES About 87 indigenous languages

LITERACY RATE 94.4%

RELIGIONS Roman Catholic 83%, Protestant 9%, Muslim 5%, Buddhist and other 3%

ETHNIC GROUPS Malay 95.5%, Chinese 1.5%, other 3%

CURRENCY Philippine peso

ECONOMY Services 48%, agriculture 42%, industry 10%

GNP PER CAPITA US$1,050

CLIMATE Tropical, with wet season June to November

HIGHEST POINT Mt Apo 2,954 m (9,692 ft)

MAP REFERENCE Page 204

The islands of the Philippines present a combination that is unique in Asia. The people are Malayo-Polynesian; the majority of the population is Roman Catholic; English is the only common language in a country that has 87 native tongues; nearly four centuries of Spanish colonialism have left a flavor of Latin America; and 100 years of US influence (following the Spanish–American War in 1898) mean that the Philippines is also somewhat Americanized.

Long ago, and before the Spaniard explorer Ferdinand Magellan arrived from across the Pacific on his round-the-world voyage in 1521, Islam had reached the southern island of Mindanao. It is still the religion of a substantial minority in that part of the country. The Spanish then imposed whatever unity the archipelago can be said to have (there are 7,107 islands), building haciendas and sugar plantations on its main islands. Administered by the USA from 1898, the Philippines was occupied by the Japanese during the Second World War, was governed by the corrupt and authoritarian Marcos regime from 1965 to 1986, and faced a wide range of insurgencies during the last half of the twentieth century. The first insurgents were communist; more recently they have been members of the Islamic Moro National Liberation Front.

There are three main island groupings within the archipelago of the Philippines: the Luzon group, the Visayan group, and the Mindanao and Sulu Islands. Luzon to the north and Mindanao to the south are the two biggest islands and together they constitute two-thirds of the country's total land area.

Common to all the main islands is a ruggedly mountainous and volcanic topography with narrow coastal belts, a north–south alignment of upland ridges, and rivers that drain toward the north. Lying to the north of Manila Bay, and stretching to the shores of the Lingayen Gulf, is Luzon's heavily populated central plain. This is an important rice-producing area. Beyond hills to the northeast lies the fertile valley of the Cagayan River. Irrigated rice terraces, constructed by the Igorot people, rise tier upon tier up the mountain slopes of northern Luzon. The peninsulas of southeastern Luzon contain a number of volcanoes. The highest peak in the Philippines, Mt Apo (2,954 m; 9,692 ft), is on Mindanao.

Government investment and a range of tax concessions have been used to try to encourage industrial development. Mixing agriculture and light industry, the Philippine economy has been growing at a steady rate in recent years, without approaching the dynamic performance of other countries in the region.

While rice is the Philippines' main food crop, maize is the staple on the islands of Cebu, Leyte, and Negros, reflecting the country's old connection with Spanish America.

The country is well supplied with mineral resources and nickel, tin, copper, zinc and lead are processed in smelting and refining works. The Philippines is also the world's biggest supplier of refractory chrome, and the second biggest user of geothermal power after the USA. Foreign investment turned sluggish as a consequence of the 1998 regional economic slowdown. Persistent weaknesses in the economy include rudimentary infrastructure, power failures due to inadequate generating capacity, low domestic savings rates, and a foreign debt of US$45 billion.

Villagers on a suspension bridge in northern Pakistan (bottom left). The road between Quetta in Pakistan and the border with Iran (top left). A coral reef in the Philippines (below). The "Chocolate Hills" in Bohol in the Philippines (bottom).

Qatar

Fact File

OFFICIAL NAME State of Qatar

FORM OF GOVERNMENT Monarchy with Advisory Consultative Council

CAPITAL Ad Dawhah (Doha)

AREA 11,000 sq km (4,247 sq miles)

TIME ZONE GMT + 3 hours

POPULATION 723,542

PROJECTED POPULATION 2005 874,179

POPULATION DENSITY 65.8 per sq km (170.4 per sq mile)

LIFE EXPECTANCY 74.2

INFANT MORTALITY (PER 1,000) 17.3

OFFICIAL LANGUAGE Arabic

OTHER LANGUAGE English

LITERACY RATE 78.9%

RELIGIONS Muslim 95%, other 5%

ETHNIC GROUPS Arab 40%, Pakistani 18%, Indian 18%, Iranian 10%, other 14%

CURRENCY Qatari rial

ECONOMY Services 50%, industry (particularly oil production and refining) 48%, agriculture 2%

GNP PER CAPITA US$11,600

CLIMATE Hot and arid; humid in summer

HIGHEST POINT Qurayn Aba al Bawl 103 m (338 ft)

MAP REFERENCE Page 220

Qatar is a small, wealthy emirate in the Persian Gulf. In 1971 it chose not to join the neighboring United Arab Emirates as a member state, but to go it alone. Recently it has continued to act with independence, signing a security pact with the USA in 1995 involving the stationing of 2,000 US troops, while simultaneously challenging the Gulf Cooperation Council's policy on Iraq. The peninsula it occupies, projecting north from the southern shore of the Persian Gulf near Bahrain, consists of flat and semiarid desert. Most of its population are guest workers from the Indian subcontinent, Iran, and north Africa.

Qatar was ruled for centuries by the Khalifah dynasty. A rift in dynastic affairs opened in 1783, war with Bahrain followed in 1867, and then the British intervened to set up a separate emirate under the al-Thani family. Qatar became a full British

protectorate in 1916. At this time it was occupied by nomadic Bedouin wandering the peninsula with their herds of goats and camels. Oil production, which commenced in 1949, changed everything and now almost 90 percent of the people live in the capital city of Doha or its suburbs. The northern parts of Qatar are dotted with abandoned villages.

A bloodless palace coup in 1995 saw the present emir displace his father, a move that was accepted without fuss. The emir of Qatar rules as an absolute monarch, he occupies the office of prime minister and he appoints his own cabinet. He is advised by a partially elected 30-member *majlis al-shura* (consultative council). From time to time there are calls for democratic reforms from prominent citizens.

The Qatar Peninsula is mainly low-lying except for a few hills in the west of the country at Jabal Dukhān (the Dukhan Heights) and some low cliffs in the northeast. Sandy desert, salt flats, and barren plains cut by shallow wadis (creek beds) occupy 95 percent of its land area. There is little rainfall aside from occasional winter showers. As a result of the shortage of fresh water Qatar is dependent on large-scale desalinization facilities. Summers are usually hot and humid; winter nights can be cool and chilly. Drought-resistant plant life is mainly found in the south. However, by tapping ground-water supplies, Qatar is now able to cultivate most of its own vegetables.

Crude oil production and refining is by far the most important industry. Oil accounts for more than 30 percent of gross domestic product, about 75 percent of export earnings, and 70 percent of government revenues. Reserves of 3.3 billion barrels should ensure continued output at present levels for at least another 25 years. Oil has given Qatar a per capita gross domestic product that is comparable to some of the leading western European industrial economies. Long-term goals include the development of offshore wells and economic diversification.

Saudis at a market wearing traditional dress (below). A view of Singapore's central business district (top right).

Saudi Arabia

Fact File

OFFICIAL NAME Kingdom of Saudi Arabia

FORM OF GOVERNMENT Monarchy with advisory Consultative Council

CAPITAL Ar Riyad (Riyadh)

AREA 1,960,582 sq km (756,981 sq miles)

TIME ZONE GMT + 3 hours

POPULATION 21,504,613

PROJECTED POPULATION 2005 26,336,476

POPULATION DENSITY 11 per sq km (28.4 per sq mile)

LIFE EXPECTANCY 70.6

INFANT MORTALITY (PER 1,000) 38.8

OFFICIAL LANGUAGE Arabic

OTHER LANGUAGE English

LITERACY RATE 61.8%

RELIGIONS Sunni Muslim 85%, Shi'a Muslim 15%

ETHNIC GROUPS Arab 90%, mixed African–Asian 10%

CURRENCY Saudi riyal

ECONOMY Agriculture 49%, services 37%, industry 14%

GNP PER CAPITA US$7,040

CLIMATE Mainly hot and arid; some areas rainless for years

HIGHEST POINT Jabal Sawdā 3,133 m (10,279 ft)

MAP REFERENCE Pages 220–21

Saudi Arabia occupies most of the Arabian Peninsula and covers an area about the size of western Europe. With one-quarter of the world's petroleum reserves, it supplies several major industrial nations with oil. Its role as the custodian of Islam's most holy places, Mecca (Makkah) and Medina (Al Madīnah), is equally important. Aloof from international affairs for many years, Saudis steeled themselves to fight Iraq (which they had earlier supported) in 1990–91. The 500,000 western troops who entered the country (considered a profanation of Muslim land) were seen by Saudis as both necessary and unwelcome. The war highlighted tensions in a society which politically is largely feudal (192 people were beheaded in 1995), yet because of its oil cannot escape the modern world.

Mecca was Muhammad's birthplace (c.570) and Medina the place where Islam was born. In the eighteenth century a severe branch of Islam was adopted by the Sa'ud Bedouin —the Wahhabi Movement—and this, with its austere criminal code, was established by the Saudis throughout their lands early this century. During the 1930s most Saudis were still living traditional desert lives, but this changed when oil was found near Riyadh in 1937. The spending for which the royal family was known in the 1960s and 1970s ended with the drop in oil prices of the 1980s. This is now starting to have social effects. People who were content to live under absolute monarchic rule with prodigious benefits may now be questioning the balance of power. Per capita income fell from $17,000 in 1981 to $10,000 in 1995.

Paralleling the Red Sea, a range of mountains extends northwest to southeast, rising to 3,133 m (10,279 ft) at Jabal Sawdā in the southwest, Saudi Arabia's highest peak. The Asir Highlands in this southwestern corner is the only region with reliable rainfall. Benefiting from the monsoon, the slopes are terraced to grow grain and fruit trees. Further east, separated from the mountains by a wide stretch of basaltic lava, is the high central desert plateau of Najd. The eastern border of this region is a vast arc of sandy desert, broadening into the two dune-wastes of Arabia: An Nafūd in the north, and Ar Rub' al Khāli, or "Empty Quarter" to the south—the world's largest expanse of sand. Some Bedouin nomads still live here as traders and herdsmen. Over 95 percent of Saudi Arabia is arid or semiarid desert.

Petroleum accounts for 75 percent of budget revenue, 35 percent of gross domestic product, and 90 percent of export earnings. Saudi Arabia has the largest reserves of petroleum in the world (26 percent of the proven total), is the largest exporter of petroleum, and backs this up with world-class associated industries. For more than a decade, however, expenditures have outstripped income. The government plans to restrain public spending and encourage non-oil exports. As many as 4 million foreign workers are employed. The 2 million pilgrims who come to visit Mecca each year also contribute to national income.

Singapore

A muddy, mangrove-swampy islet nobody wanted in 1819, Singapore is now a leading Asian city-state with one of the highest standards of living in the world. This was achieved without any resources beyond the skills and commitment of its citizens and the economic vision of its leadership. Standing at the southern extremity of the Malay Peninsula, Singapore was established as a free-trading port and settlement early in the nineteenth century by the English colonial administrator Sir Stamford Raffles. Without customs tariffs or other restrictions it drew numbers of Chinese immigrants, and after the opening of the Suez Canal played a leading role in the growing trade in Malaysian rubber and tin.

After the Second World War, during which it was occupied by the Japanese, it reverted to its former status as a British crown colony. In 1963 it became part of Malaysia, but, after two years, tensions between Chinese Singapore and the Malay leadership in Kuala Lumpur led Malaysia to force the island to go it alone. Under Lee Kuan Yew, prime minister for 31 years until 1990, a strategy of high-tech industrialization enabled the economy to grow at a rate of 7 percent a year. However, freedom of speech is constrained,

political debate limited, and both public behavior and private life (chewing gum is forbidden, and vandalism punished by caning) are watched closely.

Singapore Island is largely low-lying, with a hilly center. With limited natural freshwater resources, water is brought from the Malaysian mainland nearby. Reservoirs on high ground hold water for the city's use. Urban development has accelerated deforestation and swamp and land reclamation: 5 percent of the land is forested, and 4 percent is arable. In addition to the main island of Singapore there are 57 smaller islands lying within its territorial waters, many of them in the Strait of Singapore, which opens from the busy seaway of the Strait of Malacca. Between the main island and the Malaysian mainland is the narrow channel of the Johore Strait. A causeway across this strait links Malaysia to Singapore.

While the foundation of its economic growth was the export of manufactured goods, the government has in recent years promoted Singapore as a financial services and banking center, using the latest information technology. In 1995 this sector led economic growth. Singapore is a world leader in biotechnology. Rising labor costs threaten the country's competitiveness today, but its government hopes to offset this by increasing productivity and improving infrastructure. Despite the reduced growth rate accompanying the Asian economic downturn in 1998 there are plans for major infrastructural development: an additional stage for Changi International Airport, extensions to the mass rapid transit system, and a deep-tunnel sewerage project to dispose of wastes. In applied technology, per capita output, investment, and industrial harmony, Singapore possesses many of the attributes of a large modern country.

Fact File

OFFICIAL NAME	Republic of Singapore
FORM OF GOVERNMENT	Republic with single legislative body (Parliament)
CAPITAL	Singapore
AREA	633 sq km (244 sq miles)
TIME ZONE	GMT + 8 hours
POPULATION	3,531,600
PROJECTED POPULATION 2005	3,725,838
POPULATION DENSITY	5,579.1 per sq km (14,449.8 per sq mile)
LIFE EXPECTANCY	78.8
INFANT MORTALITY (PER 1,000)	3.8
OFFICIAL LANGUAGES	Malay, Chinese, Tamil, English
LITERACY RATE	91%
RELIGIONS	Buddhist and Taoist 56%, Muslim 15%, Christian 19%, Hindu 5%, other 5%
ETHNIC GROUPS	Chinese 76.5%, Malay 15%, Indian 6.5%, other 2%
CURRENCY	Singapore dollar
ECONOMY	Services 70%, industry 29%, agriculture 1%
GNP PER CAPITA	US$26,730
CLIMATE	Tropical
HIGHEST POINT	Bukit Timah 162 m (531 ft)
MAP REFERENCE	Page 200

South Korea

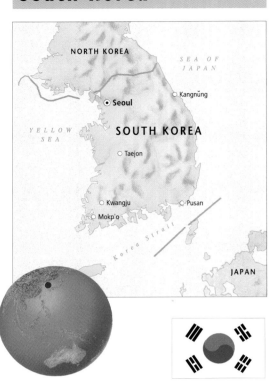

Fact File

OFFICIAL NAME Republic of Korea

FORM OF GOVERNMENT Republic with single legislative body (National Assembly)

CAPITAL Seoul

AREA 98,480 sq km (38,023 sq miles)

TIME ZONE GMT + 9 hours

POPULATION 46,884,800

PROJECTED POPULATION 2005 49,489,750

POPULATION DENSITY 476.1 per sq km (1,223.1 per sq mile)

LIFE EXPECTANCY 74.3

INFANT MORTALITY (PER 1,000) 7.6

OFFICIAL LANGUAGE Korean

OTHER LANGUAGE English

LITERACY RATE 97.9%

RELIGIONS Christianity 21%, Buddhism 24%, Confucianism 1.5%, other 1%, no religion 52.5%

ETHNIC GROUPS Korean 99.9%, Chinese 0.1%

CURRENCY Won

ECONOMY Services 55%, industry 27%, agriculture 18%

GNP PER CAPITA US$9,700

CLIMATE Temperate, with cold winters and hot, wet summers

HIGHEST POINT Halla-san 1,950 m (6,398 ft)

MAP REFERENCE Page 208

South Korea occupies the southern half of the Korean Peninsula. The border between South and North Korea consists of the ceasefire line established at the end of the Korean War (1950–53), roughly corresponding to the original pre-1950 border at the 38th parallel. The kingdom of Korea was dominated by either China or Japan for many centuries and finally annexed by Japan in 1910. After Japan's defeat at the end of the Second World War, Korea was divided between a northern Soviet zone of influence, and a southern zone under US control. These zones soon became separate political entities. In 1950 communist North Korea invaded South Korea, and though the war ended in a stalemate in 1953, bitter hostility between north and south endures to the present day, with covert operations continuing.

In the 40-year period following 1953, both Koreas diverged socially, politically, and economically. South Korea, after a few years under the authoritarian rule of its first president, established constitutional liberalism in the Second Republic of 1960. From then until his assassination in 1979 it was under the elected presidency of General Park Chung Hee, who laid the basis for the economic success of the modern South Korean state with a combination of state planning and free-market incentives.

While questionable practices flourished at the top (two former presidents have been jailed) the country achieved a remarkable record of growth. Only 30 years ago its standard of living was much the same as the poorer countries of Africa. Today its gross domestic product per capita is nine times India's, fourteen times North Korea's, and on a par with some economies of the European Union. Regionally, its technological and scientific prowess is second only to Japan's.

More than 80 percent of South Korea's terrain is mountainous. Along the eastern side of the country the Tabaek-Sanmaek Mountains descend north to southwest. The Han and Naktong Rivers drain from these mountains through low-lying plains—the Han to the northwest, the Naktong to the south. Densely populated and intensively farmed, these plains cover 15 percent of South Korea's total land area. Rice, a staple crop in which the country is almost self-sufficient, is grown on family-owned farms. Other food crops include barley and fruit such as apples, grapes, peaches, nectarines, and plums. Silk and tobacco are produced for the export market. About two-thirds of South Korea is forested. As many as 3,000

Rural scenery in South Korea (below). A broad avenue in Seoul, South Korea (above). The facade of a Hindu temple in Sri Lanka (top right). Tea-pickers on a tea estate in the highlands of Sri Lanka (bottom right).

small islands lie off the west and south coasts, including Cheju which has South Korea's highest peak, the extinct volcano Halla-san at 1,950 m (6,398 ft).

There is little at the high-tech end of modern industry that South Korea does not manufacture and sell. It produces electronic equipment, machinery, ships, and automobiles. Textiles, an early item in its drive for export success, remain significant, along with clothing, food processing, chemicals, and steel. Real gross domestic product grew by an average 10 percent from 1986 to 1991, then tapered off. With the downturn in the Asian economies in 1998 the economy shrank for the first time in years, but the country won IMF praise for acting promptly in order to wipe out billions in bad bank loans and purge companies that were unviable.

Sri Lanka

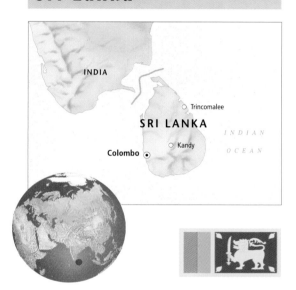

Sri Lanka is a large, scenically dramatic island off India's southeast coast, and was known as Ceylon until 1972. It has a mountainous center, and a string of coral islets called "Adam's Bridge" link it to India in the northwest. Over the last 50 years the country has suffered intermittent strife. For over 1,000 years a minority of Hindu Tamils in the north and a majority of Sinhalese elsewhere have lived side by side. From the sixteenth century successive European nations—the Portuguese, the Dutch, and the British—visited and left their ethnic mark. Britain controlled the whole island from 1815, and brought in large numbers of additional Tamil plantation workers from south India later that century.

When Sri Lanka gained its independence in 1948 the majority Sinhalese stripped 800,000 Tamils of citizenship and the right to vote, and made Sinhala the country's sole official language. From then on there was civil unrest and from 1983 there has been civil war. The Tamil demand for an autonomous northern state has been complicated by separate leftist insurrections by radical Sinhalese seeking to overthrow the government. Sri Lanka has a large number of political parties and movements on the left (including one which is officially Trotskyist)

which have added intransigence to its political life. Civil war and insurgencies have taken at least 50,000 lives.

With high mountains, intermontane plateaus, and steep river gorges, the rugged terrain of the central uplands dominates the island. Much of this higher ground is used for growing tea on large plantations. Falling away to the southwest, the terrain declines toward the sandy coastal lowlands where coconuts are grown (Sri Lanka is the world's fifth-largest producer). Rubber is the third important plantation crop. Overall, 37 percent of the country supports tropical vegetation and open woodland. Though reduced by deforestation, rainforest still covers the wettest areas. The fertile, rice-growing northern plains are bordered to the southeast by the Mahaweli River.

Among Sri Lanka's mineral resources are a variety of precious and semi-precious stones including sapphire, ruby, tourmaline, and topaz. Also mined are graphite, mineral sands, and phosphates. About 43 percent of the workforce is engaged in agriculture, the main subsistence crop being rice—although production falls considerably short of the country's requirements. Fruit,

vegetables, and spices are grown as staples and for export and Sri Lanka is one of the world's main exporters of tea. But today industry, dominated by the manufacture of clothing and expanding in special Export Processing Zones, has overtaken agriculture as the principal source of export earnings. The uncertain economic climate created by civil strife continues to cloud the nation's prospects, deterring tourists and discouraging foreign investment.

Fact File

OFFICIAL NAME Democratic Socialist Republic of Sri Lanka

FORM OF GOVERNMENT Republic with single legislative body (Parliament)

CAPITAL Colombo

AREA 65,610 sq km (25,332 sq miles)

TIME ZONE GMT + 5.5 hours

POPULATION 19,144,875

PROJECTED POPULATION 2005 20,418,172

POPULATION DENSITY 291.8 per sq km (755.8 per sq mile)

LIFE EXPECTANCY 72.7

INFANT MORTALITY (PER 1,000) 16.1

OFFICIAL LANGUAGE Sinhala

OTHER LANGUAGES Tamil, English

LITERACY RATE 90.1%

RELIGIONS Buddhist 69%, Hindu 15%, Christian 8%, Muslim 8%

ETHNIC GROUPS Sinhalese 74%, Tamil 18%, Sri Lankan Moor 7%, other 1%

CURRENCY Sri Lankan rupee

ECONOMY Services 45%, agriculture 43%, industry 12%

GNP PER CAPITA US$700

CLIMATE Tropical; southwest wetter with most rain falling April to June and October to November; northeast drier with most rain falling December to February

HIGHEST POINT Mt Pidurutalagala 2,524 m (8,281 ft)

MAP REFERENCE Page 216–17

Syria

Fact File

OFFICIAL NAME Syrian Arab Republic

FORM OF GOVERNMENT Republic with single legislative body (People's Council)

CAPITAL Damascus (Dimashq)

AREA 185,180 sq km (71,498 sq miles)

TIME ZONE GMT + 2 hours

POPULATION 17,213,871

PROJECTED POPULATION 2005 20,530,413

POPULATION DENSITY 93 per sq km (240.8 per sq mile)

LIFE EXPECTANCY 68.1

INFANT MORTALITY (PER 1,000) 36.4

OFFICIAL LANGUAGE Arabic

OTHER LANGUAGES Kurdish, French, Armenian, Aramaic, Circassian

LITERACY RATE 69.8%

RELIGIONS Sunni Muslim 74%, other Muslim sects 16%, Christian 10%; tiny Jewish communities

ETHNIC GROUPS Arab 90%; Kurdish, Armenian and other 10%

CURRENCY Syrian pound

ECONOMY Services 63%, agriculture 22%, industry 15%

GNP PER CAPITA US$1,120

CLIMATE Temperate, with mild, wet winters and dry, hot summers; arid in interior

HIGHEST POINT Jabal ash Shaykh 2,814 m (9,232 ft)

MAP REFERENCE Pages 200, 225

Syria is in the eastern Mediterranean, with Iraq and Turkey to the east and north and Lebanon, Israel and Jordan to the west and south. Throughout history it has played a key role in the region. Over the years Egyptians, Hittites, Persians, Greeks, and Romans came and went. Converted to Islam when overrun by the Arabs in 634, the Syrians' capital Damascus became a major center during the Umayyad Dynasty. Crusaders seized much of Syria in the twelfth century, but were ousted by the Kurdish general Saladin. Under French control from 1920, Syria became independent in 1946. After various military coups and counter-coups the Ba'ath Party seized power in 1963, and from 1971 party leader Hafez al-Assad has ruled Syria with an iron fist. A member of the minority Alawite religious sect, he has faced resistance from other Muslims, notably the Sunni majority. But in 1992 when the Sunni Moslem Brotherhood rose against Damascus their revolt was crushed, with up to 20,000 deaths. Following the Second Gulf War in 1991 Syria received huge amounts of aid as a result of its unexpected support for the coalition against Iraq.

Syria's Mediterranean coast, well-watered from subterranean sources, is one of the country's most fertile, intensively farmed, and densely populated regions. Inland is the Ghab Depression, a rift valley flanked by two mountain ranges. Here the Orontes ('Āşī) River flows through gorges and wide valleys. To the south, the Heights of Hermon rise above the eastern slopes of the Anti-Lebanon Range (Jabal ash Sharqī). Snowmelt from the range provides water for Damascus. Inland lies the Syrian Desert (Bādiyat ash Shām), crossed by the Euphrates River (Firat Nehri). Oil was discovered along the Euphrates in the 1980s. Power from the Euphrates barrage produces 70 percent of Syria's electricity.

Under the socialist Ba'ath Party most industry is government controlled. The main industries are textiles, food processing, beverages, tobacco, phosphate rock mining, petroleum, and cement. Oil, textiles, cotton, and agricultural produce are the main exports. The country has many weak government-owned firms and low productivity. Oil production has begun to ebb and unemployment is expected to rise as the more than 60 percent of the population that is under 20 years old enters the labor force. Syria's Gulf War aid windfall of $5 billion has been spent.

Krac des Chevaliers in Syria, a French Crusader castle built in the twelfth century (below). A Taiwanese family in Taipei (right). A yurt in the Pamir region of Tajikistan (far right).

Taiwan

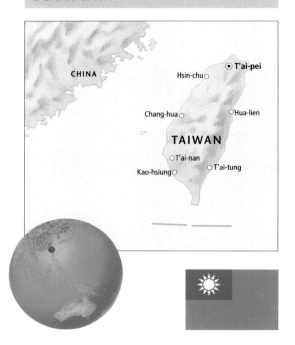

Taiwan is a large island off the coast of China which, with support from the USA, has acted as a de facto independent country for the past 50 years. This is strongly opposed by China, which from the seventeenth century controlled the island and made it a Chinese province in the 1880s. However, Beijing has not had effective control of Taiwan for 100 years. It was ceded to Japan in 1895 (after Japanese victory in the Sino-Japanese War). From 1949 until the present it has been under the Nationalist Kuomintang (KMT), who after being driven from mainland China by the communists in 1949 used Taiwan as their last refuge. Ruling dictatorially over the Taiwanese until 1987, the KMT turned the country into a political, military, and economic fortress.

Seated in the UN as the official representative of China for two decades, Taiwan was displaced in 1971, and still has a marginal status in the international community. Today, after democratic elections, multiple parties are represented in the

National Assembly, and both the president and the prime minister are native-born Taiwanese.

High mountains extending the length of the island occupy the central and eastern parts of Taiwan. The mountains of the Central Range, or Taiwan Shan, are the top of a submerged mountain chain, and rise steeply up from the east coast. Lush vegetation is found through much of the interior—the poor commercial quality of most of the timber having preserved it as forest cover. Rising to altitudes of more than 3,000 m (10,000 ft), the lower slopes support evergreens such as camphor and Chinese cork oak, while further up pine, larch, and cedar dominate. Rice is grown on the well-watered lowlands of the western coastal plain. Other crops include sugarcane, sweet potatoes, tea, bananas, pineapples, and peanuts.

Economically, agriculture is now of less importance than Taiwan's thriving industrial sector. The country as a whole demonstrated an almost unprecedented growth rate of 9 percent annually for three decades until 1996. During this period it was successively the world's biggest producer of television sets, watches, personal computers, and track shoes. Among Taiwan's strengths are its highly educated workforce, many US-trained, with an inside knowledge of the US market. Today the leading exports are electrical machinery, electronic products, textiles, footwear, foodstuffs, and plywood and wood products. With huge dollar reserves, Taiwan has become a major investor in China, Malaysia, and Vietnam. The Asian economic downturn in 1998 has had a steadying effect, but Taiwan is better situated than most to weather the storm. Political relations with China remain cool.

Fact File

OFFICIAL NAME Republic of China

FORM OF GOVERNMENT Republic with two legislative bodies (National Assembly and Legislative Yuan)

CAPITAL T'ai-pei (Taipei)

AREA 35,980 sq km (13,892 sq miles)

TIME ZONE GMT + 8 hours

POPULATION 22,113,250

PROJECTED POPULATION 2005 23,325,314

POPULATION DENSITY 614.6 per sq km (1,591.8 per sq mile)

LIFE EXPECTANCY 77.5

INFANT MORTALITY (PER 1,000) 6.0

OFFICIAL LANGUAGE Mandarin Chinese

OTHER LANGUAGES Taiwanese, Hakka languages

LITERACY RATE Not available

RELIGIONS Buddhist, Confucian, and Taoist 93%; Christian 4.5%; other 2.5%

ETHNIC GROUPS Taiwanese 84%, mainland Chinese 14%, indigenous 2%

CURRENCY New Taiwain dollar

ECONOMY Services 49%, industry 30%, agriculture 21%

GNP PER CAPITA US$10,500

CLIMATE Tropical, with wet season May to September

HIGHEST POINT Yu Shan 3,997 m (13,113 ft)

MAP REFERENCE Page 206

Tajikistan

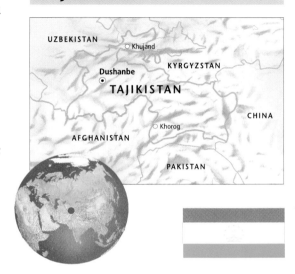

Tajikistan lies between Uzbekistan, Afghanistan, and China on the western slope of the Pamirs. It also shares borders with Kyrgyzstan to the north and Pakistan to the south. The country is an irregular shape because it was carved out of the Soviet Republic of Uzbekistan on Stalin's orders in 1929. This was intended to deal with Tajik resistance to the Soviet regime, but as it left the two Tajik centers of Samarqand and Bukhoro in Uzbekistan, it merely added another grievance. The Tajiks are Persian–Iranian culturally and linguistically, not Turkic–Mongol like many other peoples of Central Asia. Immigration of both Uzbeks and Russians during the Soviet era caused further resentment. Since independence in 1991 ethnic hostility has resulted in a state of near civil war. Tens of thousands have been killed and thousands more have fled to Afghanistan and Kyrgyzstan. Fighting between government and opposition forces goes on, marked by random violence and banditry.

A long finger of territory in the north contains the only fertile agricultural region. This is the western end of the Fergana Valley through which the Syrdar'ya drains northwest toward the Aral Sea. Cotton is the chief crop, though cereals and fruit are also grown. The region has seen the overuse of pesticides on cotton, and the drying up of the distant Aral Sea has been aggravated by water taken for irrigation. Between this valley and one to the south drained by the Vakhsh stand the Turkestan and Gissar Ranges. This substantial physical divide also corresponds to the political divide between the Uzbek communists in the

north and the Islamic secularists in the south. Most of eastern Tajikistan consists of the Pamirs, a part of the Tien Shan Range of western China.

Tajikistan has the second-lowest per capita gross domestic product of any former USSR republic, the fastest growing population, and a low standard of living. Agriculture is the most important sector and cotton the main crop. The country has limited mineral resources, including silver, gold, uranium, and tungsten. Hydropower provides energy for the manufacture of aluminum, cotton textiles and clothing, and for food processing. The economy is weak from years of conflict. Subsidies once provided by the USSR are gone, along with markets—Russia once bought Tajik uranium for its weapons program. Basic subsistence for many people depends on foreign aid. Social instability, plus the continuation in power of Soviet-era politicians and officials, has prevented economic reforms.

Fact File

OFFICIAL NAME Republic of Tajikistan

FORM OF GOVERNMENT Republic with single legislative body (Supreme Assembly)

CAPITAL Dushanbe

AREA 143,100 sq km (55,251 sq miles)

TIME ZONE GMT + 6 hours

POPULATION 6,102,854

PROJECTED POPULATION 2005 6,719,665

POPULATION DENSITY 42.6 per sq km (110.3 per sq mile)

LIFE EXPECTANCY 64.3

INFANT MORTALITY (PER 1,000) 114.8

OFFICIAL LANGUAGE Tajik

OTHER LANGUAGE Russian

LITERACY RATE 96.7%

RELIGIONS Sunni Muslim 80%, Shi'a Muslim 5%, other (including Russian Orthodox) 15%

ETHNIC GROUPS Tajik 65%, Uzbek 25%, Russian 3.5%, other 6.5%

CURRENCY Tajik ruble

ECONOMY Agriculture 43%, services 35%, industry 22%

GNP PER CAPITA US$340

CLIMATE Mild winters and hot summers in valleys and on plains, drier and much colder in mountains

HIGHEST POINT Pik imeni Ismail Samani 7,495 m (24,590 ft)

MAP REFERENCE Page 223

Thailand

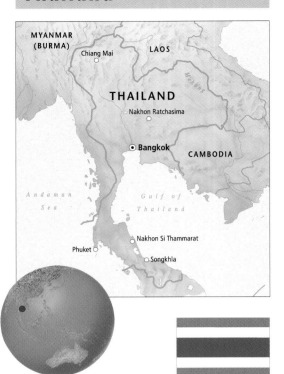

Fact File

OFFICIAL NAME Kingdom of Thailand

FORM OF GOVERNMENT Constitutional monarchy with two legislative bodies (Senate and House of Representatives)

CAPITAL Bangkok

AREA 514,000 sq km (198,455 sq miles)

TIME ZONE GMT + 7 hours

POPULATION 60,609,046

PROJECTED POPULATION 2005 63,794,047

POPULATION DENSITY 117.9 per sq km (305.4 per sq mile)

LIFE EXPECTANCY 69.2

INFANT MORTALITY (PER 1,000) 29.5

OFFICIAL LANGUAGE Thai

OTHER LANGUAGES Chinese, Malay, English

LITERACY RATE 93.5%

RELIGIONS Buddhist 95%, Muslim 3.8%, Christian 0.5%, Hindu 0.1%, other 0.6%

ETHNIC GROUPS Thai 75%, Chinese 14%, other 11%

CURRENCY Baht

ECONOMY Agriculture 70%, services 24%, industry 6%

GNP PER CAPITA US$2,740

CLIMATE Tropical, with wet season June to October, cool season November to February, hot season March to May

HIGHEST POINT Doi Inthanon 2,590 m (8,497 ft)

MAP REFERENCE Pages 202–03

Lying between Burma, Laos, and Cambodia, Thailand has a system of "semi-democracy" that has somehow preserved it from the misfortunes of its neighbors. Known as Siam until 1939, it was the home of the Buddhist kingdom of Ayutthaya from the fourteenth to the eighteenth century, during which time the monarch came to be regarded as a sort of god-king, and a bureaucratic administration system was developed. The Chakkri Dynasty was founded in 1782 at Bangkok, and in the late

nineteenth century its representatives ushered Siam into the modern age: treaties with the West were signed, slavery abolished, and study abroad encouraged. The king acquiesced in a bloodless coup which set up a constitutional monarchy in 1932. Since then civilian and military governments have alternated, climaxing in the events of 1992, when violent demonstrations against another general taking over the government led the king to intervene, and the constitution was amended. The prime minister now has to be an elected member of parliament. The military, however, still plays an important part in both political and industrial life.

Thailand can be divided into four regions. To the north there are forested mountain ranges which are the southernmost extension of the Himalayas. The rich intermontane valleys of the Rivers Ping, Yom, Wang, and Nan support intensive agriculture and the forests produce teak and other valuable timbers. The forests provide a home for many hill tribes who live by the shifting cultivation of dry rice and opium poppies. In the northeast lies the Khorat Plateau, a region of poor soils sparsely vegetated with savanna woodlands where crops of rice and cassava are grown. The third region is the central plains—Thailand's rice bowl—with vistas of rice fields, canals, rivers, and villages on stilts. The mountainous southern provinces on the Malay Peninsula are dominated by tropical rainforest. The hills produce tin ore and plantation rubber and the picturesque islands off the west coast draw tourists.

Agriculture is still the main employer, although its economic importance is declining. Rice is the principal crop and Thailand is still one of the world's leading exporters. Other crops include sugar, maize, rubber, manioc, pineapples, and seafoods. Mineral resources include tin ore, lead, tungsten, lignite, gypsum, tantalum, fluorite, and gemstones. Thailand is the world's second largest producer of tungsten, and the third largest tin producer. Tourism is the largest single source of foreign exchange, the development of resorts on the coast along the Andaman Sea having been a major success.

The development of urban manufacturing industry, involving the export of high-technology goods, has been the most significant feature of the economy in recent years. This and the development of the service sector have fueled a

growth rate of 9 percent since 1989. Thailand's domestic savings rate of 35 percent is a leading source of capital, but the country has also received substantial investment from overseas. Beginning in 1997, Thailand was the first country in the region to be affected by a range of problems associated with the Asian economic downturn—a falling currency, rising inflation, and unemployment heading toward 2 million.

Turkey

Fact File

OFFICIAL NAME Republic of Turkey

FORM OF GOVERNMENT Republic with single legislative body (Grand National Assembly of Turkey)

CAPITAL Ankara

AREA 780,580 sq km (301,382 sq miles)

TIME ZONE GMT + 2 hours

POPULATION 65,597,383

PROJECTED POPULATION 2005 71,662,725

POPULATION DENSITY 84 per sq km (217.6 per sq mile)

LIFE EXPECTANCY 73.3

INFANT MORTALITY (PER 1,000) 35.8

OFFICIAL LANGUAGE Turkish

OTHER LANGUAGES Kurdish, Arabic

LITERACY RATE 81.6%

RELIGIONS Muslim 99.8% (mostly Sunni), other 0.2%

ETHNIC GROUPS Turkish 80%, Kurdish 20%

CURRENCY Turkish lira

ECONOMY Agriculture 50%, services 35%, industry 15%

GNP PER CAPITA US$2,780

CLIMATE Temperate, with mild, wet winters and hot, dry summers; arid in the interior

HIGHEST POINT Ağri Daği (Mt Ararat) 5,166 m (16,949 ft)

MAP REFERENCE Page 224

Asia Minor, a large mountainous plateau lying between the Black Sea and the Mediterranean, forms the main part of Turkey. A much smaller part, European Turkey or Thrace, lies across the narrow straits of the Bosphorus and the Dardanelles. Early in the twentieth century Turkey's leader Kemal Ataturk (1881–1938) attempted to create a modern Islamic state that was willing and able to be a part of Europe. At the end of the twentieth century, with Islamic fundamentalism a growing internal force and no end in sight to the repression of the Kurds, his legacy is uncertain. Full integration with Europe still seems remote. Two long-running sources of conflict remain unresolved—Cyprus and the Turkish Kurds. Turkey has occupied the Muslim north of Cyprus since 1974, but their claim is unrecognized internationally. The Kurds in southeastern Turkey are demanding an independent homeland. Opposed by the State, this conflict has resulted in an estimated 19,000 deaths so far.

Historically, Asia Minor or Anatolia was the stage on which some famous scenes have been enacted. The legendary city of Troy stood on the shore of the Aegean. Ephesus and its ruins can still be visited today. Astride the Bosphorus, Constantinople (now Istanbul) was the capital of the Byzantine Empire from the fourth century AD until it fell to the Seljuk Turks in 1071. Later, during the height of its expansion in the sixteenth century, the Empire of the Ottoman Turks spread throughout the Middle East and North Africa, carrying Islam through the Balkans to Vienna. From this time the Ottoman Empire steadily declined (becoming known as "the sick man of Europe") until it was finally dismembered at the end of the First World War. The boundaries of the present Turkish state were set in 1923.

European Turkey has fertile rolling plains surrounded by low mountains. The main feature of the Asian provinces is the largely semiarid Central Anatolian Plateau (1,000 to 2,000 m; 3,300 to 6,600 ft) much of which is used for grazing sheep. On its southern flank the three main ranges of the Taurus Mountains lie inland from the Mediterranean coast. In addition to timber, the uplands provide summer grazing for the flocks of the plateau. The Pontic Mountains stretching west to east along the Black Sea boundary of the plateau are more densely wooded, and have fertile plains. A number of other ranges further east culminate in the volcanic cone of Ağri Daği (Mt Ararat) (5,166 m; 16,949 ft). Important minerals found in the thinly populated eastern regions include chrome, copper, oil, and gold. Tobacco and figs are grown in two fertile valleys that lead westward down from the plateau to the Aegean Sea. Cotton is produced on the deltaic plain near the southern city of Adana.

The Turkish economy combines modern industry and commerce with village agriculture and crafts. Though still of importance, agriculture has been overtaken by manufacturing. A busy industrial sector produces textiles, processed foods, steel, petroleum, construction materials, lumber, and paper, while coal, chromite, and copper are mined. Energy for industry comes in part from oil that is imported, but also from domestic coal and from the country's abundant hydroelectric power.

During the 1980s growth averaged more than 7 percent a year. In 1994 an outbreak of triple-digit inflation led to a period during which public debt, money supply, and the current account deficit were simultaneously out of control. Severe austerity measures and structural reforms were required in order to correct the situation. Shifting political coalitions and economic instability present a challenge for Turkey today.

Landscape near Chiang Mai, in Thailand (top). Two hill tribe women from the mountains of northern Thailand (center left). Ruins of a Thai Buddhist temple (below left). Buildings carved from rock in Cappadocia, Turkey (below).

Turkmenistan

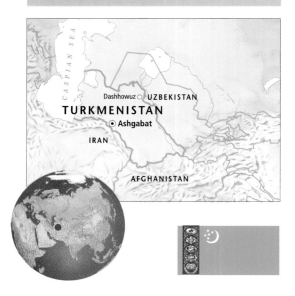

Turkmenistan is in southern Central Asia. From the Caspian Sea it stretches east to Afghanistan, and borders Iran to the south. Kazakhstan and Uzbekistan lie to the north. The Turkmen are probably descended from the same tribes as the Seljuk and Ottoman Turks who conquered what is now Turkey in the eleventh century. Russia annexed Turkmenistan in 1884 and began colonizing it in 1906. In 1924 it became the Turkmen Soviet Socialist Republic. Fierce local resistance to Sovietization continued into the 1930s and there were mass arrests of cultural and religious leaders. Turkmenistan declared its independence in 1991 but little has changed politically. It remains a one-party state and the first secretary of the former Communist Party is now the president, elected with a 99.5 percent share of the vote. The chief difference is that the government can now seek outside capital to develop the country's vast natural gas reserves, and looks to Muslim countries rather than Russia for support.

More than 90 percent of the country is arid, the greater part of it being the Kara Kum Desert. Most of the Kara Kum is made up of the plains of the Krasnovodskoye Plato, but 10 percent consists of huge sand dunes. In the east the Amu Darya River forms part of the Afghanistan border. This river once fed the Aral Sea but from the 1950s much of its water was diverted into the Kara Kum Canal which crosses two-thirds of the country westward to Kizyl-Arvat (Gyzlarbat). This provided irrigation for cotton, but also helped dry up the Aral Sea. To the west of the plateau the land falls to the Caspian shore.

Turkmenistan is poor, despite its natural gas and oil reserves. Half its irrigated land is planted in cotton but industrial development has been limited. Apart from Astrakhan rugs and food processing, industry is largely confined to mining sulfur and salt, and natural gas production. Through 1995 inflation soared, and falling production saw the budget shift from a surplus to a deficit. Since independence in 1991 there have been few changes in economic policy, leading to growing poverty and a shortage of basic foods. Cotton and grain harvests were disastrous in 1996 and desertification remains a serious problem.

Fact File

OFFICIAL NAME	Republic of Turkmenistan
FORM OF GOVERNMENT	Republic with single legislative body (Parliament)
CAPITAL	Ashgabat
AREA	488,100 sq km (188,455 sq miles)
TIME ZONE	GMT + 5 hours
POPULATION	4,366,383
PROJECTED POPULATION 2005	4,791,263
POPULATION DENSITY	9 per sq km (23.3 per sq mile)
LIFE EXPECTANCY	61.1
INFANT MORTALITY (PER 1,000)	73.1
OFFICIAL LANGUAGE	Turkmen
OTHER LANGUAGES	Russian, Uzbek
LITERACY RATE	97.7%
RELIGIONS	Muslim 87%, Eastern Orthodox 11%, other 2%
ETHNIC GROUPS	Turkmen 73.3%, Russian 9.8%, Uzbek 9%, Kazak 2%, other 5.9%
CURRENCY	Manat
ECONOMY	Agriculture 44%, services 36%, industry 20%
GNP PER CAPITA	US$920
CLIMATE	Mainly arid, with cold winters and hot summers
HIGHEST POINT	Ayrybaba 3,139 m (10,298 ft)
MAP REFERENCE	Page 222

United Arab Emirates

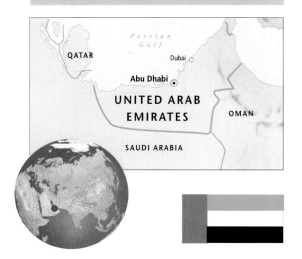

People in the seven small principalities that form the United Arab Emirates lived for centuries as seagoing traders on the shores of the Persian Gulf. When piracy became a nuisance in 1820, Britain entered into truces with the local emirs to end attacks on shipping, and established a protectorate in the region. Soon the principalities were known as the Trucial States. In 1971 they became independent and formed the federation of sheikdoms now known as the United Arab Emirates (UAE). They are situated along the southern coast of the Persian Gulf between the Qatar Peninsula to the west and the Straits of Hormuz, and share borders with Qatar, Saudi Arabia, and Oman.

Abu Dhabi is more than six times the size of all the other states put together, has the biggest population, and is the main oil producer. In the form of federal funds, it contributes to development projects in the poorer states. The port in Dubai is one of the world's largest maritime facilities, and has attracted companies from 58 countries active in the petroleum industry, trading, and financial services. A major economic contribution has been made by expatriates who flocked to the country during the 1970s' oil boom—only 20 percent of UAE citizens are native born. Whether this workforce can now be 'Emiratized' is a concern, as is the growth of Islamic fundamentalism among the young. In world affairs the UAE is a force for moderation in the Arab world. It maintains close links with the UK and USA.

The Gulf coast features saline marshes merging inland with barren desert plains. In the east there is a range of steep mountains. These are an extension of Oman's Hajar Mountains, running northward along the Musandam Peninsula. The sheikhdom of Al-Fujayrah looks out from this peninsula onto the Gulf of Oman, and contains the only highland expanse. Less than 1.2 percent of UAE land is arable, and most vegetation is sparse and scrubby. Virtually all agricultural activity is found in the emirates of Sharjah, Ras al-Khaimana, Ajman, and Fujairah, where oasis date palms grow. Government incentives, however, plus irrigation works, have increased the number of farmers fourfold in recent years. While much food is imported, self-sufficiency in wheat was a target for the year 2000.

Once an impoverished region of small desert sheikhdoms, the UAE has since 1973 been transformed into a modern state with a high

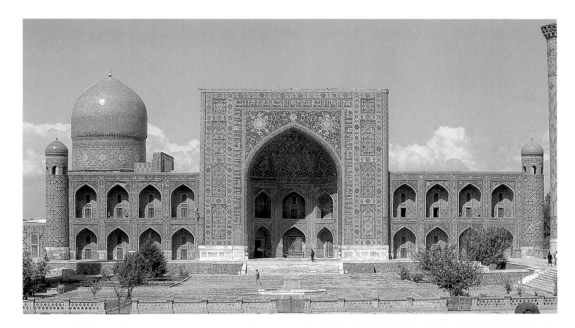

Melon sellers at a market in Turkmenistan (below left).
The Tila Kara Marasa, in Registan Square, Samarqand,
Uzbekistan, built in the seventeenth century (left).

standard of living. Oil and gas production is the largest economic sector, accounting for 89 percent of export revenue. Though in the short term the fortunes of the economy fluctuate with the price of gas and oil, at the present level of production oil reserves should last more than 100 years. Increased privatization is being encouraged by the government, and service industries are being developed. Although the UAE is much stronger economically than most of the Gulf states, a number of weaknesses remain. While the largest solar-powered water-production plant in the Gulf region is at Taweela, industrial development is likely to be limited by the fact that water will always be in short supply. There is a lack of skilled labor. Most raw materials and foodstuffs have to be imported.

Fact File

OFFICIAL NAME United Arab Emirates

FORM OF GOVERNMENT Federation of Emirates with one advisory body (Federal National Council)

CAPITAL Abu Dhabi

AREA 75,581 sq km (29,182 sq miles)

TIME ZONE GMT + 4 hours

POPULATION 2,344,402

PROJECTED POPULATION 2005 2,610,901

POPULATION DENSITY 31 per sq km (80.3 per sq mile)

LIFE EXPECTANCY 75.2

INFANT MORTALITY (PER 1,000) 14.1

OFFICIAL LANGUAGE Arabic

OTHER LANGUAGES English, Farsi (Persian), Hindi, Urdu

LITERACY RATE 78.6%

RELIGIONS Muslim 96% (Shia 16%); Christian, Hindu, other 4%

ETHNIC GROUPS Emiri 19%, other Arab and Iranian 23%, South Asian 50%, other expatriates 8% (only 20% of population are citizens)

CURRENCY Emirian dirham

ECONOMY Services 57%, industry 38%, agriculture 5%

GNP PER CAPITA US$17,400

CLIMATE Mainly arid; cooler in eastern mountains

HIGHEST POINT Jabal Yibir 1,527 m (5,010 ft)

MAP REFERENCE Pages 220–21

Uzbekistan

Uzbekistan stretches from the shrinking Aral Sea to the heights of the western Pamirs. Its main frontiers are with Kazakhstan to the north and Turkmenistan to the south. The Uzbek people are of Turkic origin and seem to have taken their name from the Mongol Öz Beg Khan (AD 1313–40), who may also have converted them to Islam. In the fifteenth century they moved south into their present land. The Muslim cities of Samarqand and Bukhoro are in Uzbekistan, Bukhoro being a major religious center. Muslims unable to visit Mecca can become hajis by visiting Bukhoro seven times instead. In the former USSR the territory was the Uzbek Soviet Socialist Republic, Uzbek leaders suffering much during Stalin's purges. In 1991 Uzbekistan became independent and is today ruled by the old communist elite as a de facto one-party state. The most populous of the Central Asian republics, Uzbekistan also has the greatest variety of ethnic groups. This is often a source of conflict. The Turkish-speaking Uzbeks clash with the Farsi-speaking Tajiks, and the Meskhetian Turks (deported from Georgia to Central Asia by Stalin) clash with the Uzbeks in the Fergana Valley. Hundreds died during fighting between the latter groups in 1989 and 1990.

The middle region of Uzbekistan consists of the desert plains of the Kyzyl Kum (Peski Kyzylkum).

While some of this area supports herders with cattle and sheep, it is today more important for its oil and gas reserves. To the west is the river delta formed where the Syrdar'ya (Oxus) enters the Aral Sea, while the Ustyurt Plateau lies in the extreme northwest. East of the Kyzyl Kum, beyond the capital of Toshkent and the Chatkal Mountains, is a spur jutting into Kyrgyzstan. This contains a large part of the fertile Fergana Basin. Uzbekistan is the world's fourth-largest cotton producer, and the Fergana Valley bears the environmental scars of the fertilizers and pesticides which helped to bring this about.

Although it grows large quantities of cotton, Uzbekistan is unable to produce enough grain for its own needs, importing it from Russia, Kazakhstan, and the USA. A rethinking of the Soviet-style economy has yet to take place.

As well as one of the world's largest gold-mines, at Murantau, Uzbekistan has large deposits of natural gas, petroleum, coal, and uranium. Gas is currently used domestically, but it could become a major export. After 1991 the government tried to strengthen the economy with subsidies and tight price controls. Inflation rose to 1,500 percent at one point and in 1995 food rationing had to be introduced. At present, efforts are being made to tighten monetary policies, expand privatization, and to reduce the state's role in the economy, but so far there have been few serious structural changes.

Fact File

OFFICIAL NAME Republic of Uzbekistan

FORM OF GOVERNMENT Republic with single legislative body (Supreme Assembly)

CAPITAL Toshkent (Tashkent)

AREA 447,400 sq km (172,741 sq miles)

TIME ZONE GMT + 6 hours

POPULATION 24,102,473

PROJECTED POPULATION 2005 26,111,101

POPULATION DENSITY 53.9 per sq km (139.6 per sq mile)

LIFE EXPECTANCY 63.9

INFANT MORTALITY (PER 1,000) 71.6

OFFICIAL LANGUAGE Uzbek

OTHER LANGUAGES Russian, Tajik

LITERACY RATE 97.2%

RELIGIONS Muslim 88% (mostly Sunnis), Eastern Orthodox 9%, other 3%

ETHNIC GROUPS Uzbek 71.5%, Russian 8.3%, Tajik 4.7%, Kazak 4%, Tatar 2.5%, other 9%

CURRENCY Som

ECONOMY Agriculture 43%, services 35%, industry 22%

GNP PER CAPITA US$970

CLIMATE Mainly arid, with cold winters and long, hot summers

HIGHEST POINT Adelunga Toghi 4,299 m (14,105 ft)

MAP REFERENCE Pages 222–23

Indochina

Vietnam

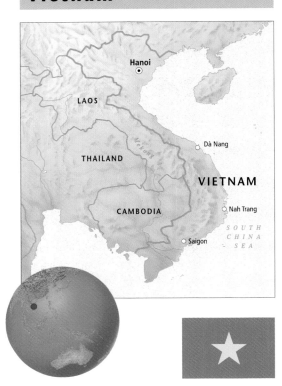

The term Indochina indicates that cultural influences from India and China are intermingled throughout this region. Also once known as French Indochina, it consists of the three states of Vietnam, Laos, and Cambodia, all of which were formerly associated with France in a political group known as the French Union. Despite the fact that the French exercised political control over their countries from the late nineteenth century, the Vietnamese, Cambodian, and Laotian royal houses continued to exercise wide authority. The Japanese occupied Indochina during the Second World War, but interfered little in the existing colonial arrangements; only after 1945 did the military turmoil begin which was to convulse the region.

In 1945, following the withdrawal of the Japanese, the Vietnamese communist nationalist leader Ho Chi Minh proclaimed the Democratic Republic of Vietnam. The returning French attempted to hold their colonial possession together, but soon the protracted guerrilla struggle that became known as the First Indochina War broke out. The forces in the North received support from the Chinese. In 1954 after the siege of Dien Bien Phu, a ceasefire was agreed to by both France and China. This resulted in two independent states: North Vietnam and South Vietnam, which were divided by the 17th parallel.

During the 1960s the attempt of North Vietnamese forces to infiltrate and subvert the southern area led to the Second Indochina War,

also know as the Vietnam War. This period saw increasing United States military involvement in the defense of South Vietnam. The US gave strong support to the South Vietnamese government and in 1961 the US commenced sending military advisers.

The US actively entered the Viernam War in 1964. Fighting continued until the Paris ceasefire of 1973, and Saigon was ultimately captured by the North Vietnmese in 1975.

Between 1954 and 1975 about 1,000,000 North Vietnamese soliders, 200,000 South Vietnamese soldiers and 500,000 civilians were killed. Between 1961 and 1975 about 56,500 US soldiers were killed. In 1976 the Socialist Republic of Vietnam was established.This period also saw the rise and fall of the Khmer Rouge regime in Cambodia, and was followed byaa Vietnamese invasion of Cambodia in 1978. Before withdrawing from Cambodia Vietnam installed in power the Communist Khmer People's Revolutionary Party (now the Cambodian People's Party) whose domination of the political system, reinforced by a violent coup in 1997, is a source of widespread discontent.

Today several boundary disputes exist between the three countries of Indochina. In addition to Vietnam's claims to various islands in the South China Sea, sections of the boundary between Cambodia and Vietnam are in dispute, and the maritime boundary between these countries is not defined. A boundary dispute also exists between Laos and Thailand.

Vietnam is located on the eastern side of the Indochinese Peninsula. A long, narrow strip of country lying between two major river systems, Vietnam bears the scars of one of the longest and most devastating wars of the second half of the twentieth century. Historically, it was for more than a thousand years under Chinese domination, achieving a degree of independence in AD 939. Christian missionary activity began in the seventeenth century and it was a French colony from 1883. During the Second World War a communist-led resistance movement fought the Japanese, and later fought the returning French, defeating them decisively in 1954. The country was divided into two mutually hostile regimes, with a communist government in the north and a

Vietnamese farmers working in the rice fields (below). A fisherman casting his net from a basket boat in Vietnam (top right). Women at a market in Hanoi (above right).

French- and later US-backed government in the south. The north initiated 20 years of insurgency and then full-scale war (the north backed by the USSR, the south by the USA with at one stage 500,000 troops), eventually winning in 1975 and establishing the Socialist Republic of Vietnam.

About 66 percent of Vietnam's land area is dominated by the heavily forested terrain of the Annam Highlands (or Chaîne Annamitique). The crest of this range mostly follows the western border with Laos in the north and Cambodia to the south. At either end of the country are intensively cultivated and densely populated river deltas—the Red River Delta in the north, which is also fed by waters from the valley of the Da, and the Mekong Delta in the south. Both are major rice-growing areas. Rice is the main staple and export crop, Vietnam being the world's third-largest exporter. Other food crops include sweet potato and cassava. On the mountain slopes of the Annam Highlands tea, coffee, and rubber plantations have been established. Most mineral resources are located in the north and include anthracite and lignite. Coal is the main export item and is the principal energy source.

After 10 years during which a typical communist command economy was imposed, along with collectivized agriculture, the government changed direction. In 1986 the more liberal *doi moi* ("renovation") policy was introduced. Investment was welcomed from outside, and during the period 1990 to 1995 real growth averaged more than 8 percent annually. Foreign capital contributed to a boom in commercial construction, and there was strong growth in services and industrial output. Crude oil remains the country's largest single export, now amounting to a quarter of exports overall, slightly more than manufactures. But progress is handicapped by a continuing strong commitment to state direction and bureaucratic controls. Banking reform is needed and administrative and legal barriers delay investment. There is no evidence of a relaxation of the political grip of the Communist Party to match the attempted economic liberalization: in 1991 open anti-communist dissent was made a criminal offence.

Fact File

OFFICIAL NAME Socialist Republic of Vietnam

FORM OF GOVERNMENT Communist state with single legislative body (National Assembly)

CAPITAL Hanoi

AREA 329,560 sq km (127,243 sq miles)

TIME ZONE GMT + 7 hours

POPULATION 77,311,210

PROJECTED POPULATION 2005 83,441,920

POPULATION DENSITY 234.6 per sq km (607.6 per sq mile)

LIFE EXPECTANCY 68.1

INFANT MORTALITY (PER 1,000) 34.8

OFFICIAL LANGUAGE Vietnamese

OTHER LANGUAGES French, Chinese, English, Khmer, indigenous languages

LITERACY RATE 64%

RELIGIONS Buddhist 60%, Roman Catholic 7%, Taoist, Islam and indigenous beliefs 33%

ETHNIC GROUPS Vietnamese 85%–90%, Chinese 3%, other 7–12%

CURRENCY Dong

ECONOMY Agriculture 65%, industry and services 35%

GNP PER CAPITA US$240

CLIMATE Tropical in south, subtropical in north; wet season May to October

HIGHEST POINT Fan Si Pan 3,143 m (10,312 ft)

MAP REFERENCE Page 203

Regional conflicts

1946 Vietnam: Return of French after Second World War. Outbreak of First Indochina War.
1954 Vietnam: Defeat of French at Dien Bien Phu. Division of Vietnam into North supported by USSR and South supported by USA.
1960 Vietnam: Communists in South initiate guerrilla war as Viet Cong.
1961 Vietnam: USA sends "military advisers" to South Vietnam to fight Viet Cong.
1964 US Congress approves war with Vietnam. US bombs Vietnamese sanctuaries in Laos, plus Ho Chi Minh Trail—north–south supply route.
1965 Vietnam: Arrival of first US combat troops. Start of intense US bombing of North which continues until 1968.
1970 Right-wing coup in Cambodia deposes Prince Sihanouk. In exile Sihanouk forms movement backed by communist Khmer Rouge.
1974 Cambodia: Sihanouk and Khmer Rouge capture Phnom Penh. Thousands die as revolutionary programs enforced.
1975 Vietnam: Fall of Saigon. North Vietnamese and Viet Cong take power in South. Laos: Communist Pathet Lao seize power.
1976 Cambodia: Sihanouk resigns—all power held by Pol Pot, leader of the Khmer Rouge.
1978 Vietnam invades Cambodia.
1979 Vietnam captures Phnom Penh. Pol Pot flees, and is held responsible for more than 2 million deaths.
1989 Vietnamese troops leave Cambodia.
1991 Cambodia: Sihanouk again head of state. Flight of Khmer Rouge officials.
1992 Vietnam: Foreign investment permitted; Communist Party monopoly unchanged.
1993 Cambodia: UN-supervised elections. Departure of UN peace mission.
1995 Normalization of US–Vietnam diplomatic relations.
1997 Cambodia: Violent coup restores power to communists under Hun Sen.
1998 Cambodia: Pol Pot dies.

Yemen

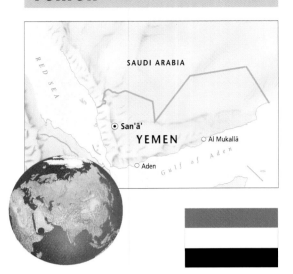

Fact File

OFFICIAL NAME Republic of Yemen

FORM OF GOVERNMENT Republic with single legislative body (House of Representatives)

CAPITAL Şan'ā'

AREA 527,970 sq km (203,849 sq miles)

TIME ZONE GMT + 3 hours

POPULATION 16,942,230

PROJECTED POPULATION 2005 20,806,931

POPULATION DENSITY 32.1 per sq km (83.1 per sq mile)

LIFE EXPECTANCY 60

INFANT MORTALITY (PER 1,000) 69.8

OFFICIAL LANGUAGE Arabic

OTHER LANGUAGE English

LITERACY RATE 41.1%

RELIGIONS Muslim: predominantly Sunni in the south, Shi'ite majority in the north

ETHNIC GROUPS Predominantly Arab; small mixed African–Arab and Indian minorities

CURRENCY Yemeni rial

ECONOMY Agriculture 63%, services 26%, industry 11%

GNP PER CAPITA US$260

CLIMATE Mainly arid; humid in southwest and cooler in western highlands; drier in east

HIGHEST POINT Jabal an-Nabi Shu'ayb 3,760 m (12,336 ft)

MAP REFERENCE Page 220

Dependencies and

British Indian Ocean Territory

Otherwise known as the Chagos Islands, and the location of the major US–UK military base of Diego Garcia, the British Indian Ocean Territory is a group of 2,300 islets located about 1,600 km (1,000 miles) from southern India and 600 km (400 miles) south of the Maldives. The islets are coral atolls and once supported a few people who produced copra for export. The islets were bought for $3 million by Britain from Mauritius but have been uninhabited since the copra plantations were closed and the population relocated to Mauritius in 1973.

Fact File

OFFICIAL NAME British Indian Ocean Territory

FORM OF GOVERNMENT Dependent territory of the United Kingdom

CAPITAL None

AREA 60 sq km (23 sq miles)

TIME ZONE GMT + 5 hours

POPULATION No permanent population

ECONOMY Air Force base

CLIMATE Tropical, moderated by trade winds

MAP REFERENCE Page 104

Yemen occupies the southwestern corner of the Arabian Peninsula. Although its people have been Muslim for centuries it has deeply divided political allegiances and was two separate countries until 1990. North Yemen became independent of the Ottoman Empire in 1918, and in 1962 the Yemen Arab Republic (YAR) was proclaimed. The politics of the YAR tended to be conservative and Islamic. South Yemen came under British influence in 1839 and Aden became a vital port on the sea route to India. In 1967 the British withdrew from the region, and in 1969 the People's Democratic Republic of Yemen was proclaimed—the only Marxist state in the Arab world.

Since independence both north and south were mutually hostile but a turning point came with the Soviet collapse in 1989. Having lost USSR support, South Yemen sought political union with the YAR. In 1990 the two countries became the Republic of Yemen. In 1994 an assassination attempt on a northern politician led to civil war and the south's attempted secession. An uneasy peace prevails.

The narrow Red Sea coastal plain of Tihāma, extending south from Saudi Arabia, is generally barren: here, cotton-growing predominates. From the coast the land rises steeply to a comparatively fertile and well-cultivated interior. Around Şan'ā vines are cultivated and a variety of fruit crops are grown. The mountains overlooking Şan'ā rise to Jabal an-Nabi Shu'ayb, the highest point on the Arabian Peninsula. From these heights a number of rivers drain east toward the Ar Rub' al Khālī (Empty Quarter) where they disappear into the sands. Along the coast of the Gulf of Aden a sandy plain rises inland to the rugged Yemen Plateau, which to the north slopes down to the uninhabited wastes of the Rub al-Khali. In this region 10 percent of the mainly rural population are nomadic.

Despite oil and gas reserves, Yemen is weak economically. In the Gulf War of 1990–91 Yemen supported Iraq. As punishment, Saudi Arabia and Kuwait expelled hundreds of thousands of Yemeni workers. Their remittances ceased and they became a huge burden on the economy. The government then abandoned agricultural subsidies and farmers stopped growing food and export crops. Instead they planted a shrub called qat—a stimulant used by Yemenis that has no export value. High inflation and political conflicts make it difficult to implement long-range economic policies and reforms.

Women herd goats outside a small village near Dhamār in the Central Highlands of Yemen (below). A Yemeni desert town (left). A semi-permanent home on the West Bank, an area still in dispute (top right).

Territories in Asia

Paracel Islands

Fact File

OFFICIAL NAME Paracel Islands

FORM OF GOVERNMENT Disputed territory occupied by China, but claimed by Taiwan and Vietnam

CAPITAL None

AREA Not available

TIME ZONE GMT + 8 hours

POPULATION No permanent population; Chinese garrisons

CLIMATE Tropical. Prone to typhoons

MAP REFERENCE Page 203

Situated in the South China Sea, the Paracel Islands are a collection of coral atolls about one-third of the way from central Vietnam to the northern Philippines. The Chinese have garrisoned the islands and have built port facilities and an airport on Woody Island. They are the center of a regional dispute because oil and natural gas are thought to exist within their territorial waters.

Spratly Islands

The Spratly Islands consist of a collection of reefs, islands, and atolls scattered across a large area of the South China Sea, about two-thirds of the way from southern Vietnam to the southern Philippines. Brunei has made Louisa Reef an exclusive economic zone, but has not publicly claimed the island. The islands are subject to territorial disputes because of their proximity to oil- and gas-producing sedimentary basins.

Fact File

OFFICIAL NAME Spratly Islands

FORM OF GOVERNMENT Disputed territory claimed by China, Taiwan, Vietnam, Malaysia, and the Philippines

CAPITAL None

AREA 5 sq km (1.9 sq miles)

TIME ZONE GMT + 8 hours

POPULATION No permanent population

CLIMATE Tropical. Prone to typhoons

MAP REFERENCE Page 203

Autonomous regions

Gaza Strip

A disputed territory on the Mediterranean with a large permanent exile population of Palestinians, most of whom are descended from those who fled Israel in 1948. Egypt lies to the south and Israel surrounds it to the east and north. As with the West Bank, the Gaza Strip has been in Israeli hands since the Six Days War of 1967. Formally incorporated into Israel in 1973, it has eight Israeli settlements built since 1967. From when Israel assumed control, the Gaza Strip has been the scene of unrest and violence, the town of Gaza witnessing the Palestinian *intifada* ("uprising") in 1987–88. The accord reached between the Palestine Liberation Organization (PLO) and Israel in May 1994 gave self-rule to the Gaza Strip pending "final status" talks to take place in the future. The cycle of violence, involving Palestinian bombings in Israel and Israeli reprisals, makes a resolution of the territory's status difficult to achieve.

Fact File

OFFICIAL NAME Gaza Strip (preferred Palestinian term, Gaza District)

FORM OF GOVERNMENT Disputed by Israel and Palestinian National Authority; interim self-government administered by Palestinian Legislative Council

CAPITAL Gaza

AREA 360 sq km (139 sq miles)

TIME ZONE GMT + 2 hours

POPULATION 1,112,654

LIFE EXPECTANCY 73.4

INFANT MORTALITY (PER 1,000) 22.9

LITERACY RATE Not available

CURRENCY Israeli shekel

ECONOMY Industry 44%, services 36%, agriculture 20%

CLIMATE Temperate. Mild winters; warm, dry summers

MAP REFERENCE Page 225

West Bank

Under a 1947 UN agreement this area on the west bank of the Jordan River was to become Palestinian when the State of Israel was formed. After the 1967 Six Day War Israel had control of a larger area than originally proposed. The building of Israeli settlements since then has been bitterly resented by the more than 95 percent Palestinian Arab population. The area depends on remittances from workers in Israel. Lack of jobs has also led to many working in the Gulf States. But the *intifada* in 1988 reduced the numbers working in Israel, and many West Bank workers were sent home following Palestinian support for Iraq in the Gulf War. Unemployment is about 30 percent. Under a 1993–95 Israeli–PLO declaration certain powers were to be transferred to a Palestinian Legislative Council, but ongoing Palestinian bombings in Israel, Israeli reprisals, and persistent Israeli settlement construction, make a speedy end to strife unlikely.

Fact File

OFFICIAL NAME West Bank

FORM OF GOVERNMENT Disputed by Israel and Palestinian National Authority; interim self-government administered by Palestinian Legislative Council

CAPITAL Jerusalem

AREA 5,860 sq km (2,263 sq miles)

TIME ZONE GMT + 2 hours

POPULATION 1,611,109

LIFE EXPECTANCY 72.8

INFANCY MORTALITY (PER 1,000) 25.2

LITERACY RATE Not available

CURRENCY Israeli shekel, Jordanian dinar

ECONOMY Industry 45%, services 34%, agriculture 21%

CLIMATE Temperate, with cool to mild winters and warm to hot summers

MAP REFERENCE Page 225

Asia and the Middle East: Physical

Asia and the Middle East

2   70°   3   60°   4   50°   5   40°   6   30°

Tropic of Cancer

CHUKCHI SEA

Ostrov
Vrangelya

Chukotskoye Nagor'ye

*VOSTOCHNO-
SIBIRSKOYE
MORE*

Ostrov
Kotel'nyy

*MORE
LAPTEVYKH*

Aleutian Islands

BERING
SEA

Kolymskoye Nagor'ye

Sredinnyy Khrebet

Poluostrov
Kamchatka

Khrebet Cherskogo

Verkhoyanskiy Khrebet

*Sredne-
Siber' (Siberia)
Sibirskoye*

OKHOTSKOYE
MORE

PACIFIC

OCEAN

8

Tunguska

*Vilyuyskoye
Vodokhranilishche*

Ploskogor'ye

Ostrov
Sakhalin

Stanovoy Khrebet

Stanovoye
Nagor'ye

*Zeyskoye
Vodokhranilishche*

Kuril'skiye Ostrova

*Ozero
Baykal
(Lake
Baikal)*

Yablonovyy Khrebet

Xiao Hinggan Ling

Amur

Sikhote-Alin

*Ostrov
Khakan*

Hokkaidō

10°

Da Hinggan Ling

Plateau of
Mongolia

Changbai Shan

SEA OF
JAPAN

Honshū

▲ Fuji-san
3776m

Gobi

Korea
Bay

Korea Strait

Shikoku

Huangtu Gaoyuan

Bo Hai

YELLOW SEA

Kyūshū

9

Huang (Yellow)

Huang

Qin Ling

Tai Hu

EAST CHINA
SEA

Nansei-shotō

Huan Har Shan

Sichuan
Pendi

*Poyang
Hu*

Chang Yang

Dongting
Hu

Wuyi Shan

0°   Equator

Hengduan Shan

Salween

Taiwan

Maddy

Luzon Strait

10

Gulf
of
Tonkin

Hainan

PHILIPPINE
SEA

Luzon

Palau

New
Ireland

Solomon
Islands

Indo-China Peninsula

SOUTH
CHINA
SEA

Mindoro

Samar

Philippines

Panay

Admiralty
Islands

*BISMARCK
SEA*

Bougainville
Island

Tônlé Sap

Mekong

Palawan

Negros

New
Britain

10°

Mindanao

*SULU
SEA*

SOLOMON
SEA

Gulf
of
Thailand

*CELEBES
SEA*

Halmahera

*Andaman
Sea*

G. Kinabalu ▲
4101 m

Maluku (Moluccas)

Jazirah
Doberai

New Guinea

▲ Pk Jaya
5030 m

Natuna
Besar

Borneo

Buru

Seram

Kepulauan
Aru

*Gulf of
Papua*

Malay
Peninsula

Selat Makassar

Sulawesi
(Celebes)

BANDA SEA

Dolak

Torres Strait

Cape
York
Peninsula

Great Barrier Reef

CORAL
SEA

20°

Nias

Sumatera
(Sumatra)

Bangka

Buton

Kepulauan
Tanimbar

ARAFURA SEA

Kepulauan
Mentawai

G. Kerinci ▲
3800 m

Selat Karimata

FLORES SEA

Flores

Timor

*TIMOR
SEA*

Gulf of
Carpentaria

Tropic of Capricorn

12

JAVA SEA

BALI SEA

SAVU SEA

Jawa (Java)

Bali   Sumbawa   Sumba

100°   M   110°   N   120°   P   130°   Q   140°   R   150°   S

Asia and the Middle East: Political

© Random House Australia Pty Ltd

Asia and the Middle East

Tropic of Ca

80° 2 70° 3 60° 4 50° 5 40° 6 30°

St Lawrence I.
(U.S.A.)

Ostrov
Vrangelya

MIDWAY ISLANDS
(U.S.A.)

BERING
SEA

Novosibirskiye
Ostrova

Anadyr'

Aleutian Islands

Magadan

Petropavlovsk-Kamchatskiy

PACIFIC
OCEAN

OKHOTSKOYE
MORE

ERATION

Yakutsk

Ostrov
Sakhalin

Kuril'skiye Ostrova

Ust'-Ilim'sk

8

Bratsk

Ozero
Baykal

Komsomol'sk-na-Amure

Khabarovsk

Yuzhno-Sakhalinsk

WAKE ISLAND
(U.S.A.)

Blagoveshchensk

Asahikawa

Hokkaidō

Chita

Jiamusi

Sapporo

rkutsk Ulan-Ude

Qiqihar Harbin Jixi

Hakodate
Aomori

Mudanjiang

Vladivostok

Akita

MARSHALL
ISLANDS

Ulaanbaatar

Changchun Jilin

Yamagata Fukushima

Honshū

Siping Liaoyuan

Ch'ŏngjin

MONGOLIA

Shenyang Fushun

NORTH
KOREA

Sea of
Japan

Tōkyō Yokohama

10°

Anshan

P'yŏngyang

Kyōto Ōsaka

Zhangjiakou

Dalian

Inch'ŏn Sŏul

Kōbe
Shikoku

MARIANA

Beijing Tangshan

Pusan

Hiroshima

JAPAN

Shizuishan

Shijiazhuang Tianjin

Taegu

Kitakyūshū

Jinchang

Taiyuan Jinan

SOUTH
KOREA

Fukuoka Kumamoto

Wuwei Yuci Xinxiang Xintai

Qingdao

Kyūshū

Xining Zhengzhou Kaifeng

Kagoshima

Lanzhou Luoyang Xuchang

Nantong

9

Xi'an Hefei

Nanjing

Shanghai

NA Wuhan Wuhu

Ningbo

NORTHERN
MARIANA ISLANDS
(U.S.A.)

Nanchong Huangshi

Hangzhou

Chengdu

Nanchang

Wenzhou

Nansei-shotō
(Japan)

Neijiang Chongqing Changsha Fuzhou

Luzhou Hengyang

T'ai-pei

GUAM (U.S.A.)

Zunyi Huaihua Zixing

T'ai-chung

0°

Dali

Guilin Xiamen Chia-i

TAIWAN

Equator

Myitkyinā Liuzhou Guangzhou Shaoguan

Kao-hsiung

Nanning Foshan Dongguan

MICRONESIA

Zhuhai Juilong

Xianggang (Hong Kong)

Mandalay

Hà Nôi Zhanjiang

Luzon PHILIPPINES

YANMAR

Hải Phòng

Baguio

New Ireland

Bougainville

LAOS

Hainan
Dao

Angeles Quezon City

New
Britain

SOLOMON
ISLANDS

10°

Viangchan

Manila Lucena

Đà Nang

SOUTH

Tacloban

PALAU

ngon THAILAND

CHINA

Mindoro

PAPUA NEW GUINEA

Moulmein

VIETNAM

SEA

Bago Cebu

Krung Thep CAMBODIA

Negros

Chon Buri Phnum Pénh

Palawan

Cagayan de Oro

Jayapura

Thanh Phố
Hồ Chí Minh

Mindanao Davao

Zamboanga

CELEBES

New Guinea

Gulf of
Thailand

Kota
Kinabalu

SEA

Halmahera

Bandar Seri
Begawan BRUNEI

Manado

Kota Baharu

11

George Town Kuala

MALAYSIA

Ipoh Terengganu

CORAL SEA ISLANDS (Aust.)

Medan Kuala Lumpur

Seremban

Kalimantan Samarinda

Ambon Seram

Pekanbaru Singapore

Balikpapan

Sulawesi

20°

SINGAPORE Pontianak

Padang Jambi

Banjarmasin

ARAFURA SEA

INDONESIA

Sumatera

Palembang

Ujungpandang

Bandarlampung

Flores

Melville I.

Gulf of
Carpentaria

Semarang Madura

Sumbawa

12

Jakarta Jawa Surabaya

Timor

Bandung Yogyakarta Malang

Bali Lombok
Sumba

AUSTRALIA

0 500 1000 1500 2000 kilometers
0 250 500 750 1000 1250 miles

Scale 1:35,000,000

Projection: Two Point Equidistant

100° M 110° N 120° P 130° Q 140° R 150° S

East Indonesia

E 132° F 136° G 140°

1

4°

Morotai
○ Pangeo
○ Berebere
Jayabula

Tg Gila

2

Tatam
○ Akelamo
○ Dorolemo
○ Watam

HALMAHERA
SEA

PACIFIC

Tel. Buli
Maba
towasi
○ Patani
Weda

OCEAN

Equator 0°

○ P. Waigeo

○ Rabia

Selat Dampier

Warmandi ○

Tg Manundi   P. Supiori

Koor ○   Ambuaki   Kaironi ○   Korido ○
Mega ○   G. Kwoka   ○ Mubrani   Korim ○
             3000 m ▲   Sajam ○   *Manokwari*   P. Biak
Tg Dadi   Sorong ○   Rawas ○ Tg Memori   Biak ○ Tg Wararisbari
                 Germakolo ○   Namber ○
P. Salawati Gasim ○   G. Mebo ▲   Tg D'Urville
                Seget ○   2940 m   ○ Oransbari   Teba ○   *Danau*
○ Atkri   *Ransiki*   P. Numfor   *Rombebai*   Sarmi ○
○ Tamulol   Baru ○   *Selat Yapen*   Pamdai ○   Maffin ○
P. Misool   Inanwatan ○   Robooksibia ○   P. Num   P. Yapen   Serui ○   Betaf ○
CERAM SEA   Tomu ○   P. Rumberpon   Tg Ranbausawa *Tel.*   Kaptiau ○   Demta ○
(MOLUCCAS) Wahai ○   *Tg Sabra*   P. Waar   *Tel.*   *Waropen*   Depapre ○ Jayapura ⊛
                                         Tel. Bintuni *Cenderawasih* G. Dom PEG. VAN REES
            Kokas ○   Babo ○   ▲   1430 m   *Tariku*   Krau ○
Amahai ○   Tanisapata ○ ○ Rufrufua   *IRIAN JAYA*   Wapoga
  Bulao ○   Fakfak ○ ○ Siembra   Kwatisore ○   Nabire ○   G. Angemuk ▲
Haya ○ Bemu ○   Wandai ○   3962 m
P. Seram   *Tg Marsimang* Kaimana ○   *Danau*   Wamena ○   *Batem*
                P. Karas ○   Mirobia ○   *Yamur*   G. Ubia ▲   Pk Jaya ▲
mbon ○   Urung ○   *Tel. Sebakor*   *Danau*   4234 m   5030 m   Pk Trikora ▲
              Tg Tongerai   *Tel.*   *Pantai* Enarotali ○   Tembagapura ○ 4730 m
Kep. Gorong Tg Papisoi   *Kamrau*   Wanapiri ○ Uta ○
                     P. Adi ○ Aiduna ○   Kokenau ○
Kep. Watubela

MALUKU

Kep. Kai   Tg Borang
               P. Kai Besar
P. Kai   Banda Elat   Dobo ○
Kecil   ○ Dosi
          Tg Weduar   *Kep. Aru*
              Tg Ngoni

Kep. Damar

Tg Laru Mat
Kep. Tanimbar   Tg Waarlangier   Tafermaar ○
                       Tg Ngabordamlu

Tepa ○   Watmuri ○
          P. Yamdena
         Batkes ○
Latdalam ○ Saumlaki ○
Kep. Sermata *Kep. Babar* ○ Adaut
                Eliase ○

3

WEST
SEPIK
Vanimo ⊛
○ Leitre   Sissano ○
Ossima ○   ○ Aitape
○ Imonda
Torricelli Mts
○ Amanab

○ Green River   4°

EAST *Sepik*
SEPIK   ○ Kubkain

New *Guinea*
○ Tabubil   Telefomin ○
○ Ningerum
○ Rumginae
○ Kiunga

Amamapare ○   *Peg.*   *Jayawijaya* Pk Yamin ▲
                         Agats ○   4595 m   Pk Mandala ▲
                                        4700 m

Maoke

Lake
Murray

Tanahmerah ○

Tg De Jongs   Mapi ○

P. Dolak   Pembre ○   Kimaan ○
           Kladar ○   Wamal ○   Okaba ○
Tg Vals ○   P. Komoran   Kumbe ○
                                   Merauke ○

Aiambak ○

WESTERN

○ Duru
Goe ○
Serki ○   Buk ○
       Morehead ○
Bula ○   Mari ○

Boigu I.

4

ARAFURA SEA

Torres   Strait

Badu I. ○
Moa I.
Thursday I.
Prince of Wales I.
Bamaga ○

5

C. Van Diemen
Dundas
Strait

Cobourg   C. Cockburn
Pen.
C. Keith   Goulburn Is

Cape Wessel

Wessel
Is

Bathurst I.   *Melville I.*
C. Hotham
Beagle   Gulf   Van Diemen Gulf   *Melville Bay*
Darwin ○   *AUSTRALIA*
                  Howard
                  Island
              ○ Nhulunbuy

6

140°

E 132° F 134 F 136° G 140° H

0   100   200   300   400   kilometers
0   100   200   miles

Scale 1:7,000,000   Projection: Mercator

West Indonesia · Malaysia · Singapore

Nicobar Islands (India)
Little Nicobar
Great Nicobar
Bananga

THAILAND

Ko Lanta
Kantang
Songkhla
Hat Yai
Pattani
Satun
Yala
Narathiwat
Rangae
P. Langkawi
PERLIS
Kangar
Jitra
Kota Baharu
Pasir Puteh
Alor Setar
KEDAH
P. Redang
Sungai Petani
PINANG
Jeli
Macang
Kuala Kerai
Noring
G. Bintang
1862 m
Kuala Terengganu
Butterworth
George Town
P. Pinang
(Penang)
Taiping
Kuala Kangsar
G. Camah
2171 m
KELANTAN
G. Lawit
1519 m
TERENGGANU
Ipoh
Kampar
G. Tahan
2187 m
G. Gagau
1376 m
G. Mandi Angin
1455 m
Kuala Dungun
Bidor
G. Batu Puteh
2131 m
Kuala Lipis
G. Benom 2107 m
Cukai
G. Tapis
1512 m Tg Gelang
Tg Beras Basah
G. Liang East
1933 m
Raub PAHANG
Kuantan
Gambang
Karak
Marah
Pekan

P. We
Sabang
P. Breuh
Banda Aceh
Sigli
Bireuen
Lhokseumawe
Tg Jambuair
Lhoksukon
Lhokkruet
Tangse
G. Geureudong
2855 m
Peureulak
Calang
Langsa
Takengon
G. Lembu
3077 m
U. Tamiang
ACEH
Tel. Aru
G. Abongabong
2985 m
Blangkejeren
G. Bandahara
3012 m
Pangkalanbrandan
Belawan
Tg Raya
G. Leuser
3404 m
Binjai
Medan
SELANGOR
Kuala Selangor
Shah Alam
Kuala Lumpur
KUALA LUMPUR
Seremban
Labuhanhaji
Tapaktuan
Kabanjahe
G. Sibayak
2094 m
Tebingtinggi
Tanjungbalai
Temerloh
NEGERI SEMBILAN
Tg Dewa
Sidikalang
Pematangsiantar
Port Dickson
Tg Tuan
Segamat
Tg Resàng
P. Tioman
Kep. Anambas
P. Simeulue
Sinabang
Danau Toba
P. Samosir
Prapat
Labuhanbilik
Tg Senebui
G. Ledang
1276 m
MELAKA
Labis
Jemaluang
Siborongborong
Balige
Bagansiapiapi
Melaka
G. Belumut
1010 m
JOHOR
Barus
Tarutung
Kotapinang
Muar
Batu Bahat
Ayer Hitam
P. Tuangku
P. Bangkaru
Sibolga
SUMATERA
UTARA
Langgapayung
P. Rupat
P. Bengkalis
Pontian
Kecil
Kota Tinggi
Johor Baharu
Tg Dowi
P. Musala
Padangsidempuan
Dumai
Duri
P. Padang
Singapore
Lahewa
Gunungsitoli
P. Nias
Pasirpengarayan
RIAU
Tebingtinggi
P. Rangsang
P. Rempang
P. Kundur
Tandjungpinang
P. Bintan
Kep. Riau
Natal
Kotanopan
Buatan
Pekanbaru
P. Mendol
P. Galang
Telukdalam
G. Malea
2012 m
Panti
Bangkinang
SINGAPORE
Airbangis
G. Ophir
2912 m
Payakumbuh
Tembilahan
Tg Datuk
P. Lingga
Kep. Lingga
P. Pini
Sasak
Japura
Kelume
P. Sebangka
P. Tanahmasa
Kep. Batu
Danau Maninjau
Bukittinggi
G. Marapi
2891 m
Taluk
Rengat
Seberida
P. Singkep
Equator
P. Tanahbala
Danau Singkarak
Solok
INDRAGIRI
Labu
P. Berhala
Tg Sigep
SUMATERA
Painan
BARAT
Sungaidareh
Dusunmudo
JAMBI
P. Bang
Kagologolo
Padang
Tg Jabung
Belinyu
P. Siberut
Muarasiberut
G. Kerinci
3800 m
Muarabungo
Jambi
Tel. Kampa
Muntok
Tapan
Bangko
Bayunglincir
SUMATERA
SELATAN
Koba
Siberimanua
P. Sipura
Katiet
Sungaipenuh
Surulangun
Ra
Pasapuat
Mukomuko
G. Masurai
2935 m
Sekayu
Pangkalpinang
P. Pagai Utara
Pa
Sungaidareh
P. Pagai
Selatan
Muaraaman
Muarabeliti
Perabumulih
Palembang
Tg Beritarikap
Lais
Dauh
2467 m
Muaraenim
P. Sanding
Ketaun
Kepahiang
Muaradua
Kayuagung
Umbulan
Gayohpecoh
Tg Lu
Bengkulu
G. Dempo
3159 m
Lahat
Pagaralam
Baturaja
Talangbatu
BENGKULU
Tais
G. Patah
2817 m
Martapura
Muaradua
Menggala
Manna
Danau
Ranau
Kotabumi
Gunungsugih
Bintuhan
G. Pesagi
2231 m
Metro
Labuhanmeringg
Krui
LAMPUNG
Kotaagung
Bandarlampung
P. Enggano
Kayaapu
Bakauheni
Me
Tg Batuberagam
Se
Tg Rataø
Balimbing
P. Tabuan
P. Sertung
Krakatau
P. Panaitan
Pandege
Tg Guhakolak
Pelabuhanr
Tel. Pelabuhanra
Genteng

INDIAN

OCEAN

SUMATERA

CHRISTMAS ISLAND
(Aust.)

MALAYSIA

Sembawang
Woodlands
Yishun
Tg Punggol
MALAYSIA
Kranji
Res.
Murai
Res.
P. Seletar
Sarimbun
Res.
Choa
Chu Kang
Bukit
Panjang
Selat Johor
Sungei
Seletar Res.
Tg Punggol
P. Serangoon
Punggol
P. Ubin
Selat
Johor
Serangoon
Harbour
Poyan Res.
Upper
Peirce Res.
Bukit Batok
Ang Mo Kio
Hougang
Pasir Ris
Changi
Jurong
West
Bishan
Serangoon
Tampines
Changi
Airport
Tengeh Res.
Jurong
Town
Lower
Peirce Res.
SINGAPORE
Bukit Timah
162 m
MacRitchie
Res.
Toa
Payoh
Bedok Res.
Jurong
East
Clementi
Bedok
Tuas
Jurong
Industrial
Estate
Pandan Res.
Geylang
Katong
Pasir
Panjang
Tiong
Bahru
Paya Lebar
P. Pesek
P. Pesek
Kechil
P. Merlimau
P. Seraya
Telok
Blangah
Singapore
P. Ayer
Chawan
P. Ayer
Merbau
Tg Berlayar
P. Brani
P. Sakra
Sentosa
Straits of Singapore
Straits of Singapore

0   5   10 kilometers
0   5   miles
Scale 1:297,000

204

SOUTH CHINA SEA

P. Balambangan
P. Banggi
P. Malawali
○ Kudat
Langkon ○
P. Jambongan
Kaningoban
Tuaran ○ G. Kinabalu ▲ 4101 m
Lingkabau
Kota Kinabalu ⊛
SABAH
○ **Sandakan**
Tel. Labuk
LABUAN
Kuala Penyu
Telupid ○
Sukau ○
Tapul Group
Victoria ○ ⊛
G. Trus Madi ▲ 2649 m
Lamag ○
Lahad Datu ○
Tawitawi I.
BRUNEI
Muara
Beaufort ○
Tel. Darvel
Bandar Seri ○ ⊛
Begawan
Brunei Bay
Pinangah ○
Kunak ○
P. Timbun Mata
Sibutu I.
Tg Baram ○
Sapulut ○
Kalabakan ○
Tawau ○
Semporna ○
Sibutu Group
Lutong ○
G. Pagon ▲ 1850 m
P. Sebatik
Miri ●
G. Mulu ▲ 2371 m
G. Harun ▲ 2160 m
P. Mandul
Long Teru ○
MALAYSIA
Tg Payong ○
Batu Niah ○
G. Murud ▲ 2438 m
Longbawan ○
G. Basakan ▲ 1372 m
Sesayap ○
Tarakan ○
SARAWAK
Tangung ○
Mantadau ○
Tg Kidurong ○
Nyurang ○
Bintulu ●
Long Murum ○
Tanjungselor ○
Mukah ○
Tatau ○
G. Bakayan ▲ 1599 m
Tg Batu ○
P. Maratua
Tg Sirik ○
Kejaman ○
Rumah Kulit ○
G. Kemal ▲ 2053 m
Tanjungredeb ○
P. Bruit
BORNEO
Barung ○
Sibu ●
Sarikei ○
Julau ○
Song ○
Kapit ○
Longnawan ○
KALIMANTAN TIMUR
G. Guguang ▲ 2467 m
Tintang ○
Pulai ○
Tg Datu
Sematan ○ Tg Sipang
Saratok ○
G. Lawit ▲ 1767 m
G. Liangpran ▲ 2240 m
Pelawanbesar ○
Tg Mangkalihat
G. Dako ▲ 2304 m
Tel. Datu
Tg Po
Debak ○
G. Kerihun ▲ 1980 m
Tinabogan ○
Tolitoli ○
Paloh ○
Tg Munguresak
Kuching ⊛
Bau ○
Bandar Sri Aman ○
(Simanggang)
G. Menyapa ▲ 2000 m
G. Ogoamas ▲ 2565 m
Sambas ○
G. Niut ▲ 1701 m
Putussibau ○
Sigenti ○
Tinombo ○
Singkawang ●
Danau Luar
Danau Sentarum
Samarinda ⊛
Tg Dampelas
Equator
Tg Gunung
Pemangkat ○
Ngabang ○
Kembangjanggut ○
Tg Manimbaya
Kasimbar ○
Tg Bangkai
Mempawah ○
Sanggau ○
Sintang ○
Longiram ○
Danau Melintang
SULAWESI
TENGAH
Tg Putus
Pontianak ●
KALIMANTAN BARAT
Danau Semayang
Bontang ○
Donggala ○
Tawaeli ○
Toboli ○
Teluk Tomini
P. Padangtikar
G. Saran ▲ 1758 m
Nangapinoh ○
G. Raya ▲ 2278 m
Purukcahu ○
Danau Jempang
Palu ⊛
Parigi ○
P. Maya
Sukadana ○
G. Sebayan ▲ 1377 m
Peg. Schwaner
Kualakurun ○
Benangin ○
Muarapayang ○
G. Lumut ▲ 1233 m
Balikpapan ●
Pakuli ○
Sedoa ○
Kep. Karimata
Telukbatang ○
Sandai ○
Tumbangsamba ○
Tel. Sukadana
KALIMANTAN TENGAH
G. Serempaka ▲ 1380 m
Tel. Adang
Poso ○
Taripa ○
SULAWESI
(CELEBES)
Nangatayap ○
Memala ○
Pendang ○
Kupangnunding ○
Tanahgrogot ○
Mamuju ○
G. Kambuno ▲ 2950 m
Ketapang ○
Danau
Sembulu
Palangkaraya ⊛
Sampit ○
Amuntai ○
Jangeru ○
Majene ○
G. Gandadiwata ▲ 3074 m
Wotu ○
P. Belitung
Kendawangan ○
Sukaraja ○
Pangkalanbuun ○
Kumai ○
Pulangpisau ○
G. Besar ▲ 1892 m
Rantau ○
KALIMANTAN SELATAN
Polewali ○
Rantepao ○
G. Rantekombola ▲ 3455 m
Berikat
Tanjungpandan ○
P. Bawal
Semuda ○
Pagatan ○
Singkang ○
Manggar ○
P. Gelam
Banjarmasin ●
Kotabaru ○
P. Sebuku
Parepare ●
Membalong ○
Dendang ○
Tg Sambar
Tg Keluang
Martapura ○
P. Laut
Siwa ○
Tel. Kumai
Mangganan ○
Kintap ○
Semaras ○
SULAWESI SELATAN
Bone
Tg Puting
Tg Malatayur
Martapura ○
Maros ○
Batakan ○
Watampone ○
Tg Selatan
Tg Layar
Maros ○
Tg Arus

INDONESIA

Ujungpandang
(Makassar)
G. Lompobatang ▲ 2876 m
Sinjai ○
Bira

JAVA SEA

Kep. Masalembu
Selat Selayar
Benteng ○

KARTA RAYA
Kep. Karimunjawa
P. Bawean
P. Selayar
karta
Pamanukan ○
JAWA TENGAH
P. Bawean
Kep. Kangean
P. Tanahjampea
Subang ○
Indramayu ○
Tg Bugel
G. Muria ▲ 1602 m
Tg Benda
Kep. Kangean
P. Kalao
Purwakarta
Cirebon
Keling ○
Jepara ○
Kudus ○
Rembang ○
Tuban ○
Ketapang ○
P. Madura
Cianjur ⊛
Bandung
Pekalongan ●
Blora ○
Bangkalan ○
BALI SEA
Tegal ●
Semarang ⊛
Salatiga ○
Gresik ○
Pamekasan ○
bumi
G. Careme ▲ 3078 m
Wonosobo ○
Surabaya ⊛
Situbondo ○
Garut
G. Slamet ▲ 3418 m
Surakarta (Solo) ⊛
Selat Madura
FLORES SEA
Tasikmalaya **Ciamis**
Purwokerto ○
G. Lawu ▲ 3265 m
Madiun ●
Pasuruan ○
Bali ○
Singaraja ○
G. Rinjani ▲ 3726 m
G. Tambora ▲ 2821 m
Tg Besi
ngbarang
Magelang
Probolinggo ○
G. Tambora
Sumbawa ○
Dompu ○
Bima ○
P. Komodo
Labuhanbajo ○
Reo ○
AWA BARAT
Cilacap ●
Yogyakarta ⊛
Ponorogo ○
G. Liman ▲ 2561 m
Kediri ○
G. Argopuro ▲ 3088 m
Bondowoso ○
Besar
Raba ○
G. Ranakah ▲ 2382 m
Ruteng ○
JAWA (JAVA)
Parangtritis ○
YOGYAKARTA
○ Pacitan
Blitar ○
Kepanjen ○
Malang ●
G. Semeru ▲ 3676 m
Jember ○
G. Raung ▲ 3332 m
Mataram ○
Selong ○
Praya ○
Plampang ○
P. Rinca
Flores
Tg Sasar
JAWA TIMUR
P. Nusa Barung
Banyuwangi ○
G. Agung ▲ 3142 m
Negara ○
Bali
Denpasar ●
Lombok
Sumbawa
Tg Sasar
P. Nusa Penida
NUSA TENGGARA BARAT
Waingapu ○
Waikabubak ○
G. Wanggamet ▲ 1225 m
Sumba
Baing ○

NUSA TENGGARA TIMUR

0   100   200   300   400 kilometers
0   100   200   miles
Scale 1:7,000,000   Projection: Mercator

201

Thailand • Laos • Cambodia • Vietnam

INDIA

WEST BENGAL

KHULNA

BANGLADESH

Calcutta

Diamond Harbour
Port Canning

Hugli-Chunchura
Bhātpāra
Basirhat
Haora
Khulna
Barisāl
Jessore
Mādāripur
Baj
Baj
Patuākhāli

Chāndpur
Feni
Noākhāli
Rangāmati
Chittagong
Dohazar

Belonia
Lunglei
Haka
Bardarban
Ramu
Daletme
Khreum
Paletwa
Kyauktaw
Kyindwe
Saw
Cox's Bāzār

CHITTAGONG
MIZORAM

Kalewa
Kalemyo
Ye-u
Kin-u
Kani
Gangaw
Kan
Siatlai
Pagan

Kanbalu
Shwebo
Sagaing
Monywa
Budalin
Myitha
Myinmu

Namtu
Mong Mit
Na-lang
Namlan
Indaw

Mandalay
Amarapura
Myingyan
Taungtha
Pakokku
Myotha
Yesagyo

Lashio
Kyaukme
Tonglau
Mong Yai
2031 m
2675 m
Maymyo
Ke-hsi Mānsām
Keng Lon

Cangyuan
Shangyun
Munai
Mengzhe

Mohei
Pu'er
Simao
Jinghong
Menghai
Mengla
Bān Bou
Phongsali

YUNNAN
Shan
2865 m
2490 m

SAGAING

Pauksa Taung
1708 m
Minbu
Magwe
Sagu
Mindon
Migyaungye

Mt Popa
1518 m
Chauk
Meiktila
Pyawbwe
Thagaya
Pyinmana
Loi-kaw
Ngwedaung

Samka
Hsi-hseng

Hopong
Taunggyi
Mong Pawn
Keng Tawng
Loi-lem
Mong Pu
Keng Hkam
Namsang
1615 m
Keng

Mong Kung
2491 m
Loi Sang
Lawksawk
Lai-hka
Kunhing
Ta-Kaw

Mong Ping
Loi Pangnao
2607 m
Mae Sai
Mong Hpayak
Louang
Namtha
Viangphoukha

SHAN STATE

MYANMAR
(BURMA)

MANDALAY

MAGWE

Pyè
(Prome)
Taungup
Kamao
Paungde
Kyangin
Zigon
Okpo
Kyeintali
Gwa
Minhla
Letpadan
Yegyi
Lemyethna

Toungoo
Pyu
Nattaung
2623 m
Papun

Mae Sariang
Pang

Doi Chiang Dao
2175 m
Mae Hong Son
Doi Mae Ya
2005 m
Doi Inthanon
2590 m
Chom Thong
Doi Mae Tho
2031 m

Chiang Rai
Fang
Sop Huai
Chiang Kham
Chiang Mai
Lamphun
Lampang

Muang
Pakbeng
Luangphrab

Wiang Pa Pao
Phayao
Wang Nua
Ngao
Nan

Thung Chang
Muang
Xaignabour
Ban Nalè

Phrae
Den Chai
Uttaradit
Sawankhalok
Wang Saphung

Phu Soai Dao
2102 m
Ban Pak Pat

PEGU

PEGU YOMA

TENASSERIM

ARAKAN

Kyaukpyu
Ramree I.
Cheduba I.

Magyichaung
Ywathitke
Sittwe
(Akyab)
Combermere Bay

Sinbyugyun

Nyaunglebin
Pyuntaza
Payagyi
Tha
Taikkyi
Pegu
Danubyu
Henzada

Kyaikto
Tha Song Yang
Thaton
Pa-an
Mae Ramat
Mae Sot

Mae Tubi Res.

Sam Ngao
Tak

Sukhothai
Phitsanulok
Lom Sak

IRRAWADDY

Kangyidaung
Bassein
Myaungmya
Ma-ubin
Bogale
Pyapon

Yangon
(Rangoon)
Syriam

Bilugyun I.
Mudon
Kyaikkami
Kalegauk I.
Manaung

Moulmein
Wagaru
Sedaung Taung
1420 m
Ye

Kamphaeng Phet
Phichit
Khlong Khlung

Phetchabun
Ban Khao Sai

Chaiyaphum

Nakhon Sawan
Nong Bua

YANGON
MON
KAREN

Gulf of Martaban

Heinze Chaung

Khao Yai
1554 m
Uthai Thani
Ban Rai
Chai Nat
Sing Buri
Lop Buri

Khao Kamphaeng
1257 m
Phra Nakhon
Si Ayutthaya

Chumsaeng

Srinakarin Res.

Khok Samrong
Ang Thong
Saraburi

Nakhon Ratchasima
(Khorat)

Pak Th
Cha

THAI

Tavoy (Dawei)
Tavoy Pt
Mali Kyun
(Tavoy I.)
Palaw
Kadan Kyun
(King I.)
Mergui

Myinmoletkat Taung
2072 m
Photharam
Ratchaburi
Samut Songkhram
Phet Buri Res.
Kyaukpya
Cha-am
Hua Hin
Khao Yai
1204 m

Krung Thep
(Bangkok)
Nonthaburi

Phetchaburi

Samut Sakhon
Samut Prakan

Chon Buri
Pattaya

Nakhon Nay
Prachin Bu
Sa Kaeo
Kabin Buri

Khao S
Dao T
1633 m
Rayong
Chanthab
Ko Cha

BILAUKTAUNG RANGE
TENASSERIM RANGE
Khwae Noi
Phet Buri

Bight of Bangkok

Prachuap Khiri Khan
Ban Huai Yang
Theinkun
Lenya
Thap Sakae

Mergui

Archipelago

Investigator Channel

Than Kyun

Pathiu
Chumphon
Ao Sawi
Kra Buri
Ranong
Lang Suan

Ko Tao
Ko Phangan
Ko Samui

Gulf of Thailand

Lenam Bay

Isthmus of Kra
Ko Phra Thong
Takua Pa
Phangnga
Ban Khok Kloi
Ko Phuket
Phuket

Ao Luk
Krabi
Huai Yot
Ko Lanta

Surat Thani
1530 m
Ban Na San
Ron Phibun
Thung Song
Trang
Kantang

Ao Ban Don
Chico

Nakhon Si Thammarat

Songkhla
Hat Yai

P. Langkawi
Satun
Kangar
Alor Setar

Pattani
Yala
Narathiwat
Rangae
Jitra

Tasek Temengor

MALAYSIA

Bay of Bengal

Preparis North Channel

Preparis I.

Preparis South Channel

Coco Channel

Great Coco I.
Little Coco I.
Landfall I.
C. Price
North Andaman
Saddle Peak
738 m
Pahlāgaon
Middle Andaman

Andaman Islands

South Andaman
Port Blair
Rutland I.

Duncan Passage

Nachuge
Little Andaman

Ten Degree Channel

Car Nicobar I.
Kakana

Andaman and Nicobar Islands (India)

ANDAMAN SEA

Tarasa Dwip
Camorta I.
Misha

Sombrero Channel

Nicobar Islands
(India)
Little Nicobar
Great Nicobar
Bananga

INDONESIA
P. We
Sabang

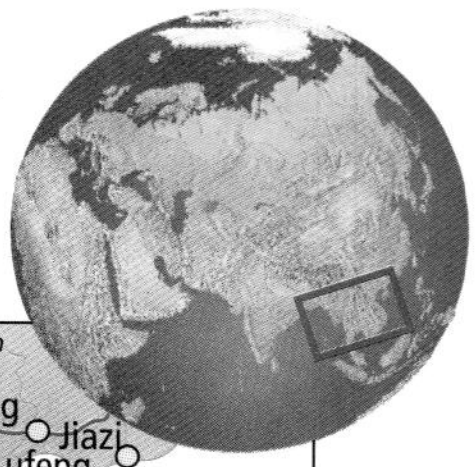

Map

CHINA

GUANGXI ZHUANGZU ZIZHIQU

GUANGDONG

Gejiu · Wenshan · Malipo · Pingguo · Binyang · Wuming · Guiping · Teng Xian · Yunan · Sihui · Guangzhou (Canton) · Boluo · 1336 m
Jingxi · Tiandeng · Litang · Guigang · Rong Xian · Cenxi · Deqing · Zhaoqing · Zhaoqing · Foshan · Dongguan · Huizhou · Haifeng · Jiazi
Hà Giang · 2419 m · Daxin · Fusui · Nanning · Heng Xian · Lingshan · Yulin · Luoding · Yunfu · Zhaoqing · Xinxing · Shunde · Taiping · Huidong · Lufeng
Bắc Quang · Longzhou · Taiping · Qinzhou · Zhanghuang · Bobai · Yangchun · Gaozhou · Nahuo · Taishan · Zhuhai · Macao

Qinzhou · 1312 m · Hepu · Beihai · Lianjiang · Huazhou · Maoming · Zhanjiang

Hà Nôi (Hanoi) · Hải Phòng · Hồng Gai

LAOS · **VIETNAM** · **THAILAND** · **CAMBODIA**

Gulf of Tonkin

HAINAN · Haikou · Hainan Dao

SOUTH CHINA SEA

XISHA QUNDAO (Paracel Island) (Sovereignty disputed)

SPRATLY ISLANDS (Sovereignty disputed)

Thanh Phố Hồ Chí Minh (Saigon)

MALAYSIA · Kota Kinabalu

Scale 1:7,000,000 · Projection: Mercator

Philippines

Asia and the Middle East

A 116° **B** 120° **C** 124° **D**

PHILIPPINE

SEA

PHILIPPINE

SEA

PHILIPPINES

Batan Is
Basco

Babuyan Is

Babuyan Channel

Mayraira Pt
Bangui
Abulog
Palaui I.
C. Engaño
Bacarra
Aparri
Laoag
Gonzaga
Batac
Agbulu
Alcala
Mt Sicapoo
2048 m
Badoc
Tuao
Vigan
Bangued
Tuguegarao
Narvacan
Lubuagan
Palanan Pt
Candon
Ilagan
Cervantes
Bontoc
Cauayan
Santiago
San Fernando
Banaue
Bagabag
Luzon
Bauang
Mt Pulog
2934 m
Bolinao
Baguio
Tarigtig Pt
Cabauyan I.
C. San Ildefonso
Agno
Dagupan
Lingayen
Villasis
Baler Bay
San Carlos
San Jose
Baler
High Peak
2037 m
Tarlac
Iba
Capas
Cabanatuan
Botolan
Angeles
Gapan
Dingalan Bay
Mt Pinatubo
1759 m
San Fernando
Malolos
Olongapo
Quezon
Infanta
Polillo Is
Balanga
City
Bagac
Manila
Lamon
Bay
Calagua Is
Mariveles
Santa Cruz
Muntinglupa
Labo
Daet
Yog Pt
Nasugbu
Calamba
Mt Labo
1544 m
Viga
Catanduanes I.
Calatagan
San Pablo
Calauag
Tinambac
Lagonoy
Virac
Lipa
Lucena
Sipocot
Naga
Pili
Lobo
Batangas
Boac
Santa Cruz
Nabua
Batan I.
Lubang Is
Calapan
Marinduque I.
San Andres
Tabaco
Rapu Rapu I.
Golo I.
San Francisco
Legaspi
C. Calavite
Paluan
Mt Halcon
2587 m
Donsol
Sorsogon
Mamburao
Pinamalayan
Bulan
Matnog
Mindoro
Bongabong
Burias I.
Masbate
Catarman
Mt Capotoan
850 m
Sablayan
Romblon
Sibuyan I.
Ticao I.
Allen
Calintaan
Mt Baco
2488 m
Tablas I.
Mt Guitinguitin
2050 m
Masbate I.
Calbayog
San Jose
Bulalacao
(San Pedro)
Mandaon
Placer
Catbalogan
Taft
Samar
Busuanga
Busuanga I.
Balud
Biliran I.
Borongan
Coron
Ilin I.
Pulanduta Pt
Naval
Llorente
Semirara Is
Nabas
VISAYAN
Carigara
Tacloban
Guiuan
Culion I.
Kalibo
SEA
San Remigio
Nelyan Pt
Pucio Pt
Roxas
Linapacan I.
Culasi
Tibiao
Daanbantayan
Ormoc
Leyte
Homonhon I.
Iloc I.
Sara
Bantayan
Baybay
Gulf
El Nido
Batas I.
Bugasong
Passi
Camotes Is
Sogod
Desolation Pt
Maytiguid I.
Panay
Silay
Cadiz
Danao
Maasin
Oloreto
Taytay
Cuyo Is
San Jose
Iloilo
Dinagat I.
Dumaran I.
Miagao
Bacolod
Mandaue
Hilongos
Boayan I.
Bacao
Anini-y
San
Toledo
Lapu-Lapu
Pintuyan
Siargao I.
Caruray
Roxas
Bago
Carlos
Cebu
Dapa
Uluguan
Bay
Cleopatra Needle
1593 m
Negros
Cebu
Bucas Grande I.
Bacungan
Kabankalan
Bohol
Guindulman
Surigao
Anepahan
Cauayan
Tagbilaran
Cantilan
Long Pt
Puerto Princesa
Sipalay
Dalaguete
Camiguin I.
Diuta Pt
Tandag
Victoria Peak
1709 m
Panagtaran Pt
Hinoba-an
Santander
Mt Hilonghilong
2012 m
Quezon
Aborlan
Santa Catalina
Dumaguete
Siquijor I.
Balingoan
Butuan
Palawan
Rasa I.
Siaton
Camiguin I.
Bayugan
Island Bay
Tolong Bay
Dipolog
Dapitan
Balingasag
Salvacion
Mt Mantalingajan
2073 m
Brooke's Point
Oroquieta
El Salvador
Gingoog
Lianga
Rio Tuba
San Antonio
Bay
Iligan
Cagayan de Oro
Hinatuan
C. Buliluyan
Sindangan
Mt Malindang
2425 m
Lugait
Malaybalay
Sanco Pt
Pandanan I.
Bugsuk I.
Liloy
Ozamiz
Iligan
Bay
Iligan
Bislig
Balabac
Panganuran
Pagadian
Marawi
Valencia
Mindanao
Balabac I.
Siocon
Ipil
Kabasalan
Kalatungan
Mts
2865 m
Kibawe
Monkeyo
Cateel
P. Balambangan
P. Banggi
Sibuco
Tungawan
Margosatubig
Malabang
Tagum
Baganga
P. Malawali
Kudat
Langkon
Olutanga I.
Parang
Midsayap
Mabini
Caraga
Langkon
P. Jambongan
Zamboanga
Sacol I.
Cotabato
Pikit
Mt Apo
2954 m
Davao
Samal I.
Mati
Kanibongan
Isabela
Lamitan
Moro Gulf
Kidapawan
Digos
Lamigan Pt
Tuaran
G. Kinabalu
4101 m
Lingkabau
Sandakan
Maluso
Basilan I.
Linao Pt
Tacurong
Davao
Gulf
C. San Agustin
Kota Kinabalu
SABAH
Telupid
Lamag
Patikul
Jolo I.
1011 m
Lebak
Norala
Koronadal
Malita
Kuala Penyu
Sukau
Jolo
Kiamba
Mt Matutum
2295 m
Beaufort
G. Trus Madi
2649 m
Kinabatangan
Tapul I.
Surallah
Victoria
MALAYSIA
Tapul Group
General Santos
(Dadiangas)
Muara
Brunei
Bay
Pinangah
Tawitawi I.
Siasi
Sulu Archipelago
Glan
Bandar Seri
Begawan
BRUNEI
Tel. Darvel
Sibutu I.
Batulaki
Geme
G. Murud
2438 m
Longbawan
G. Harun
2160 m
Tawau
P. Sebatik
Sibutu Group
Sarangani Is
Kep. Talaud
Beo
G. Basakan
1372 m
Kunak
P. Timbun
Mata
CELEBES
Tahuna
P. Sangihe
Mangaran
Sesayap
Semporna
SEA
INDONESIA
P. Mandul

SOUTH

CHINA

SEA

Palawan Passage

SULU SEA

kilometers 0   100   200   300   400

miles 0   100   200

Scale 1:7,000,000   Projection: Mercator

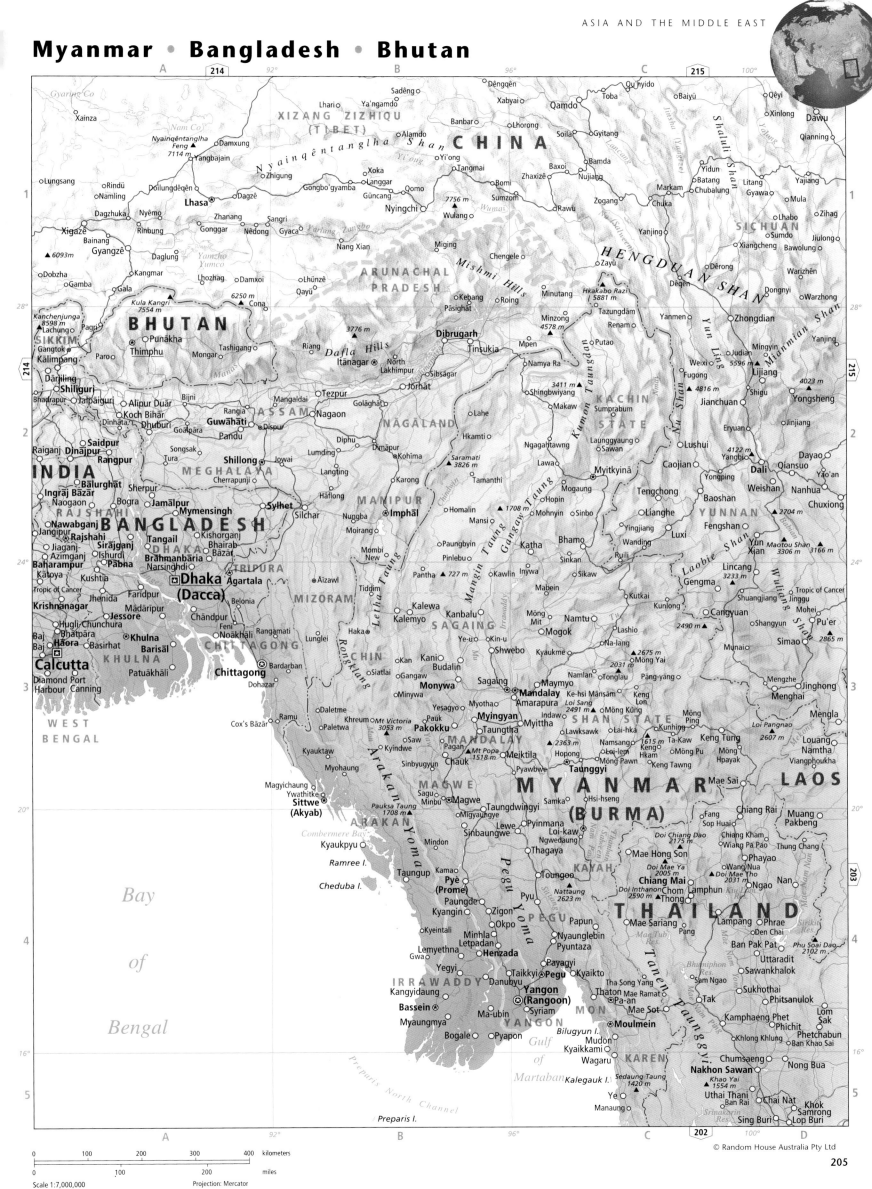

Myanmar • Bangladesh • Bhutan

CHINA

XIZANG ZIZHIQU (TIBET)

Nyainqêntanglha Shan

BHUTAN

Thimphu

SIKKIM

ARUNACHAL PRADESH

Mishmi Hills

HENGDUAN SHAN

SICHUAN

INDIA

ASSAM

MEGHALAYA

NAGALAND

KACHIN STATE

YUNNAN

RAJSHAHI

BANGLADESH

DHAKA

Dhaka (Dacca)

TRIPURA

MANIPUR

Imphal

SAGAING

SHAN STATE

KHULNA

Calcutta

WEST BENGAL

CHITTAGONG

Chittagong

MIZORAM

CHIN

ARAKAN

Arakan Yoma

MANDALAY

Mandalay

MAGWE

MYANMAR (BURMA)

LAOS

Pegu Yoma

KAYAH

THAILAND

PEGU

IRRAWADDY

Yangon (Rangoon)

Bassein

YANGON

MON

Moulmein

KAREN

Tanen Taunggyi

Bay of Bengal

Preparis North Channel

Gulf of Martaban

Scale 1:7,000,000   Projection: Mercator

0   100   200   300   400 kilometers

0   100   200 miles

© Random House Australia Pty Ltd

205

Southeast China

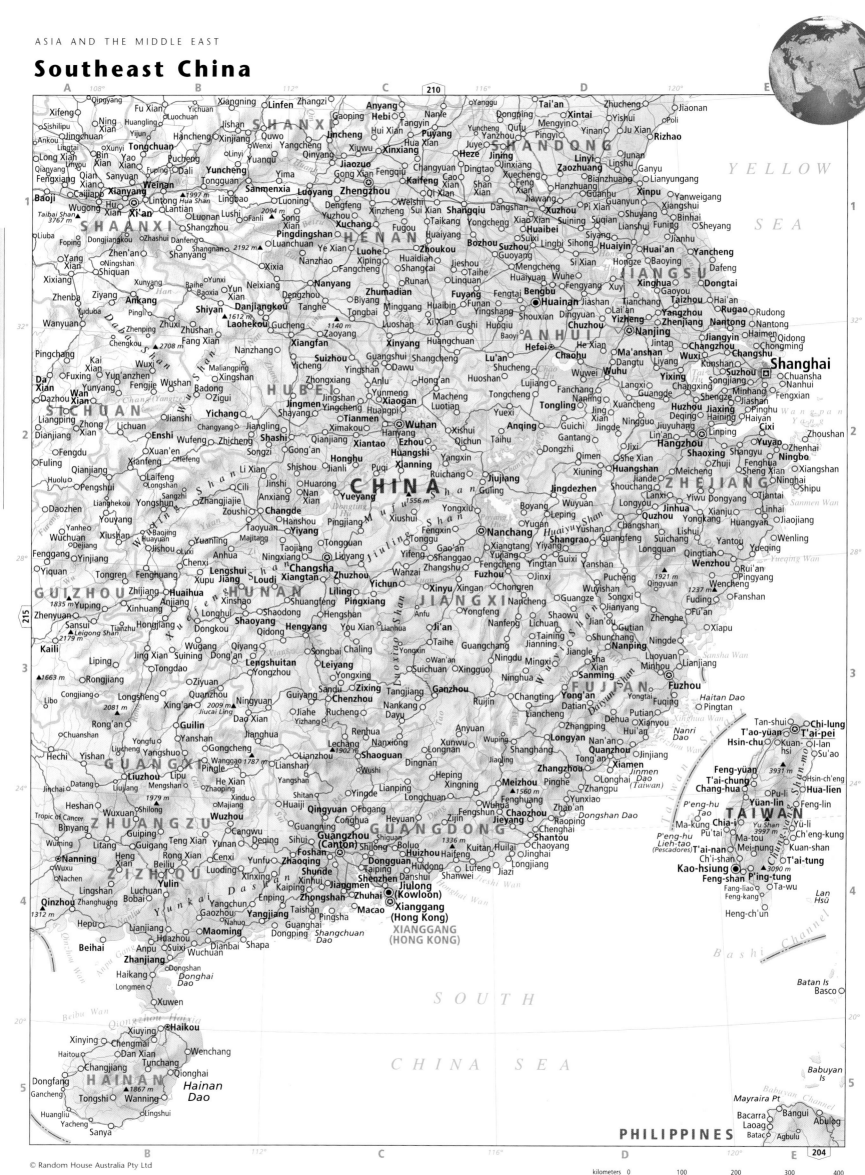

Scale 1:7,000,000   Projection: Equidistant Conic

Xianggang (Hong Kong) and Guangdong, China

206

Hengshi
Fogang
Shuitou
Quingyun Shan
Lantian
Dong
Xinfengjiang Shuiku
Heyuan
Baibu
Huangtang

Longshan
Tangtang
Liuxihe Reservoir
Lütian
Longmen
Pingling

Gaoqiao
Minle
Liangkou
Zuotan

Longtan
Wenquan
Shajing
Longhua
Buqian

Aotou
Beixia
Yonghan
Guzhu
Jiuhe

Qigan
Conghua
Yangcun
Lantang

Huacheng
Shengang
Paitan
Qijing
Xiniuwei
Juzi
Guanyinge

Lianglong
Tropic of Cancer
Tuiguang
Taipingchang
Lapu
Zhengguo
Mazha
Ping'an
Baitang
Taimei
Dalan

Zhuliao
Zhongluotan
Jiufo
Fuhe
Xiaolou
Henghe
Ruhu
Hengli

Taihe
Zhongxin
Zengcheng
Shiguan 1281 m
Luofu Shan
Huzhen
Xiangshui
Andun

Jianggao
Zhucun
Futian
Changning
Longhua
Xinzuotang
Boluo
Hengli

Jiahe
Longyandong
Ningxi
Yayag
Xiancun
Shitan
Tiechang
Masi
GUANGDONG
Huizhou
Xin'an

Shahe
Lianhe
Luogang
Nangang
Xintang
Zhongtang
Shilong
Qishi
Qiaotou
Chengjiang
Duozhu

Guangzhou (Canton)
Shipai
Huangpu
Mayong
Tangxia
Chashan
Hengli
Lilin
Huidong

Dashi
Xinzao
Wangniudun
Dongguan
Baima
Liaobu
Changping
Sima
Zhenlong
Danshui

Shatou
Panyu (Shiqiao)
Shilou
Daojiao
Houjie
Dalang
Huangjiang
CHINA
Xinxu
Renshan

Shawan
Baihao
Jinjuling
Songmushan
Zhangmutou
Qingxi

Yuwotou
Huangge
Taiping
Humen
Beizha
Changan
Gongming
Tangtouxia
Fonggang
Pingdi
Longgang
Aotou
Xiayong
Jilong

Lanhe
Dagang
Songgang
Guanlan
Tiantangwei
Pingshan

Rongqi
Guizhou
Huangpu
Nansha
Wanqingsha
Shajing
Fuyong
Shiyan 591 m
Longhua
Pinghu
Henggang
Kuiyong
Pinghai

Dongfeng
Fusha
Sanjiao
Langwang
Minzhong
Buji
Yantian
Gangkou

Tanbei
Gangkou
Hengmen Dao
Xin'an
Baoan
Nantou
Shenzhen
Shatoujiao (Sha Tau Kok)
Crooked Island
Dashuikeng
Maliaohe
Sanmen Dao

Shaxi
Zhangjiabian
Zhongshan
Shekou
Hau Hoi Wan
Lo Wu
Sheung Shui
Sam A Tsuen
Tap Mun Chau

Dayong
Huancheng
Zhuhai
Nanlang
Cuihengcun
San Tin
Fanling
Hoi Ha
Tai Long

Banfu
Qi'ao Dao
Qi'ao
Yuen Long 573 m
Shek Kong
Tai Po
Sai Kung
Pak Tam Chung

Shenwan
Xiazha
Tangjia
Neilingding Dao
Tuen Mun
Shek Kong 957 m
Tai Mo Shan
Sai Kung
Kau Sai Chau
Basalt Island

Sanxiang
Tanzhou
Qianshan
Lung Kwu Tan
Sham Tseng
Tsuen Wan
Sha Tin
Tai Po Tsai

Doumen
Baijiao
Nanping
Wanzai
Macao
Chek Lap Kok
Ma Wan Chung
Xianggang (Hong Kong)
Jiulong (Kowloon)
Chai Wan
Clear Water Bay

Dai Yue Shan (Lantau Island) 935 m
Tai O
Shek Pik
Niutou Dao
Pui O Wan
Hong Kong Island
Wong Chuk Hang
XIANGGANG (HONG KONG)

Xiaolin
Modao Wan
Guishan Dao
Cheung Chau 351 m
Tong O
Po Toi
Pok Liu Chau (Lamma Island)

Sanzao
Sanzao Dao
Tianxin
Jiu'ao Dao
Wailingding Dao
Zhiwan Dao
Dangan Dao
Dangan Liedao

Gaolan Dao
Wanshan Qundao
Dawanshan Dao
Beijian Dao
Honghai Wan

Zhujiang
Hu Wan
Kou

Luo Fu Shan
Lianhua Shan
Hai'an Shan
Dajiang
Xizhi
Daya Wan

SOUTH CHINA SEA

0 25 50 kilometers
0 20 miles
Scale 1:900,000
Projection: Equidistant Conic

Japan • Korea

A 116° B 120° C 124° 211 D 128° E 132° F

CHINA

**NEI MONGOL ZIZHIQU
(INNER MONGOLIA)**

Dong Ujimqin Qi
Nungnain Sum
Jus Hua
Liuhu
Ulanhot
Lanxi
Anda
Xinglongzhen
Dongxing
Yilan
Shuangyashan
Baoqing
Burlit

Jirin Gol
Xi Ujimqin Qi
Injgan Sum
Horqin Youyi
Zhongqi
Tuquan
Baicheng
Zhenlai
Anguang
Zhaodong
Xiji
Bayan
Mulan
Tonghe
Huanan
Woken
Yanggang
Pozharsko

Holt Sum
Jirh
Jurh
Jarud Qi
Daqin
Zhaozhou
Zhaoyuan
Harbin
Bin
Xian
Fangzheng
Boli
Qitaihe
Mishan
Hulin
Novopokro

Xilin Hot
Xinbo
Yudaokou
Horqin Zouyi Zhongqi
Tongyu
Qian'an
Fuyu
Shuangcheng
Acheng
HEILONGJIANG
Hadagang
Mashan
Jixi
Lesozavodsk

Nart
Dalai Nur
Subrag
Han Sum
Naiman Qi
Zhanyu
Changling
Dehui
Yushu
Shanhetun
Yabuli
Weihe
Yimianpo
Shangzhi
Linkou
Muling
Majiagang
Hulin

Duolun
Linxi
Bairin Zuoqi
Ar Horqin Qi
Horqin Zouyi Zhongqi
Hure Qi
Fanjiatun
Jiuzhan
Changchun
Jilin
Jiaohe
Dunhua
Dashitou
Daxinggou
Tavrichanka
Sergeyevka
Artem
Uglekamensk

Senjitu
Gangoumen
Weichang
Pingzhuang
Harqin Qi
Zhangwu
Shuangliao
Lishu
Siping
Gongzhuling
Xiyang
Huangnihe
Mingyuegou
Shixian
Hunchun
Vladivostok
Livadiya
Nakhodka

Fengning
Chifeng
Naiman Qi
Hartao
Xifeng
Changtu
Liaoyuan
Dongfeng
Panshi
Huadian
Huinan
Baishan
Antu
Helong
Tumen
Slavyanka
Zarubino

HEBEI
Ningcheng
Chaoyang
Beipiao
Fuxin
Xinlitun
Tiefa
Kaiyuan
Qingyuan
Liuhe
Fusong
Shiren Wangou
Musan
Ch'ŏngjin
Nanam
Kyŏngsŏng

Longhua
Lingyuan
Harqin Zuoqi
Qinghemen
Heishan
Liaozhong
Xinmin
Xian
Tieling
Xinbin
Hunjiang
Linjiang
Huchang
Hoeryŏng

Chengde
Ringguan
Nanpiao
Jinxi
Jinzhou
Tianzhuangtai
Fushun
Shenyang
Tonghua
Tiechang
Kanggye
Kapsan
Hyesan

LIAONING
Anshan
Liaoyang
Benxi
Anping
Nanfen
Paoziyan
Ji'an
Manp'o
Samsu
Kilchu

Xingcheng
Haicheng
Gaizhou
Xiuyan
Huanren
Qidaogou
Chinsong-ri
Ch'osan
Kimch'aek
Tanch'ŏn

NORTH KOREA

Yingkou
Qingchengzi
Kuandian
Kanggye
P'ungsan
Iwon

Beijing (Peking)
Langfang
Suizhong
Shanhaiguan
Xiongyuecheng
Gaizhou
Dandong
Sinŭiju
Ch'angsŏng
Hŭich'ŏn
Pukch'ŏng
Sinp'o

Tianjin
Tangshan
Qinhuangdao
Changli
Huatong
Wafangdian
Gushan
Donggou
Zhuanghe
Pikou
Sŏnch'ŏn
Pakch'ŏn
Anju
Hamhŭng
Hŭngnam

Tianjin
Dulu
Jinghai
Dagu
Machang
Jinzhou
Xinjin
Anbo
Chŏngju
P'yŏngsŏng
Kowon
Munch'ŏn
Wonsan

Cangzhou
Yanshan
Huanghua
Zhaojiapu
Lüshun
Dalian
Bo Hai
Korea Bay
Sunan
Kangdong
T'ongch'ŏn
Kosŏng

Wudi
Fuguo
Bohai
Penglai
Longkou
P'yŏngyang
Namp'o
Songnim
Hoeyang
Kosŏng

Binzhou
Huimin
Dongying
Guangrao
Shouguang
Huang Xian
Yantai
Weihai
Kwail
Hwangju
Sariwŏn
Chaeryŏng
Sinch'ŏn
Yanggu
Yangyang

Boxing
Zibo
Qingzhou
Weifang
Laizhou
Qixia
Muping
Wendeng
Rongcheng
Changyŏn
Haeju
Kaesŏng
Kŭmch'ŏn
Hwach'ŏn
Yanggu
Sokch'o

Boshan
Linqu
Pingdu
Laiyang
Rushan
Shidao
Ongjin
Kaesŏng
Uijŏnbu
Hongch'ŏn

SHANDONG
Laiwu
Yiyuan
Jingzhi
Jiaozhou
Jimo
Haiyang
Laixi
Lancun
Sŏul (Seoul)
Inch'ŏn
Hoengsŏng
Samch'ŏk

Xintai
Yishui
Zhucheng
Qingdao
Jiaonan
Anyang
Ich'ŏn
Wonju
Ullŭngdo

Mengyin
Yinan
Ju Xian
Poli
Jiaozhou
Suwon
P'yŏngt'aek
Ch'ungju
Ulchin

Fei Xian
Linyi
Junan
Rizhao
Ch'ŏnan
Yesan
Kongju
Chŏmch'on
Yŏngju
Andong

SOUTH KOREA

Linshu
Bianzhuang
Ganyu
Taech'on
Kongju
Ch'ŏngju
Yŏngdong
Ŭisŏng
P'ohang

Pi Xian
Guanyun
Lianyungang
Taejŏn
Iri
Kimch'ŏn
Kyŏngju
Ulsan

Suqian
Guanyun
Yanweigang
Kunsan
Chŏnju
Kumi
Taegu

Sihong
Shuyang
Xiangshui
Binhai
Kimje
Namwŏn
Masan
Chinhae
Kyŏngju

Huaiyin
Lianshui
Funing
Sheyang
Kwangju
Naju
Chinju
Pusan

Huai'an
Baoying
Kosŏng

Xuyi
Hongze
Yancheng
Mokp'o
Sunch'ŏn
Kosŏng
Yŏsu

JIANGSU
Xinghua
Dafeng
Changhŭng
Posŏng
Haenam

Tianchang
Gaoyou
Dongtai
Hai'an
Chindo

Chuzhou
Yizheng
Taizhou
Rugao
Cheju
Chejudo

Nanjing
Zhenjiang
Jiangyin
Nantong
Rudong
Nantong
Halla-san 1950 m
Sŏgwip'o
Mosŭlp'o

Ma'anshan
Dangtu
Changzhou
Haimen
Qidong

Liyang
Jintan
Wuxi
Qidong
Chongming

Langxi
Yixing
Changshu
Kunshan

Xuancheng
Suzhou
Shengze
Shanghai
Chuansha

Guangde
Huzhou
Jiaxing
Songjiang
Jiashan
Nanhui

Ningguo
Deqing
Linping
Pinghu
Fengxian

Jixi
Jiuyuhang
Linping
Haiyan
Haiyan

Hangzhou
Lin'an
Haining
Shangyu
Cixi
Zhenhai

Meicheng
Shaoxing
Zhuji
Sheng
Yuyao
Zhoushan

Jiande
Shouchang
Xian
Ningbo

ZHEJIANG
Lanxi
Dongyang
Ninghai
Xiangshan

Quzhou
Jinhua
Xianju
Sanmen Wan

Yongkang
Suichang
Linhai

Lishui
Huangyan
Jiaojiang

Longquan
Qingtian
Yantou
Linhai

Wenzhou
Yueqing

Wencheng
Rui'an
Yueqing Wan

Pingyang

Bohai Wan
Laizhou Wan
Bohai Haixia
Huang He (Yellow)
Hongze Hu
Tai Hu
Wangpan Yang

YELLOW SEA

EAST CHINA SEA

SEA OF JAPAN

Oki-shotō
Dōgo
Dōzen
Matsue
Tottori
Izumo
Ōda
Yonago
Kurayoshi
Fukuchiyama
Tsuyama
Kasai

Kōra
Kūre
Chūgoku-sanchi
Miyoshi
Okayama
Himeji
Kakogawa

Hamada
Masuda
Hiroshima
Fukuyama
Kurashiki
Kōbe

Yamaguchi
Hagi
Iwakuni
Imabari
Nihama
Tokushima

Shimonoseki
Ube
Hōfu
Tokuyama
Matsuyama
Shikoku-sanchi

Kitakyūshū
Iizuka
Nōgata
Tagawa
Shikoku
Kōchi

Fukuoka
Karatsu
Hita
Beppu
Usa
Yawatahama
Susaki
Muroto

Imari
Saga
Kurume
Ōita
Saiki
Uwajima
Tosa-wan
Muroto-zaki

Sasebo
Ōmura
Isahaya
Kumamoto
Shiiba
Ashizuri-misaki

Nagasaki
Yatsushiro
Hitoyoshi
Nobeoka
Hyūga

Kyūshū
Amakusa-shotō
Ebino
Miyazaki
Miyakonojō

Koshikijima-rettō
Sendai
Kokubu
Nichinan
Kushima

Makurazaki
Kagoshima
Kanoya
Satamisaki

Ōsumi-shotō

Tokara-rettō

**RUSSIAN FEDERATION
PRIMORSKIY KRAY**

Pogranichnyy
Arsen'yev
Ussuriysk
Anuchino
Kavalero
Lazo

Wanda Shan

JILIN

Paektu-san 2744 m
Changbai Shan

Chang Jiang
Huang He

© Random House Australia Pty Ltd

Asia and the Middle East

RUSSIAN FEDERATION

Bikin'
▲ 1745 m
Svetlaya
Maksimovka
Amgu
Velikaya Kema
Terney
Plastun
Dal'negorsk
Rudnaya Pristan'

Gornozavodsk
Shebunino
Zaliv Aniva
Mys Kril'on
Yuzhnoye
La Perouse Strait
Mys Aniva

Kuril'skiye Ostrova (Kuril Islands)
Proliv Friza
Urup
Kuril'sk
Burevestnik
Iturup
Slavnoye

Administered by Russian Federation, claimed by Japan.

Kunashir
Yuzhno-Kuril'sk
Golovnino
Shikotan

Wakkanai
Rebun-tō
Rishiri-tō
Hamatombetsu
Esashi
Shiretoko-misaki

Hokkaidō
Kitami-sanchi
Nayoro
Shibetsu
Mombetsu
Engaru
Abashiri
Shari

Rumoi
Fukagawa
Asahikawa
Akabira Asahi-dake ▲ 2290 m
Takikawa
Sunagawa
Bibai
Shihoro
Ashibetsu
Ashoro
Kitami
Teshikaga
Shibecha
Nemuro

Kamui-misaki
Ishikari-wan
Otaru
Iwamizawa
Ikeda
Kushiro

Iwanai
Sapporo
Ebetsu
Chitose
Obihiro
2052 m

Oshamambe
Date
Tomakomai
Kamui-dake ▲ 1600 m
Hiroo

Okushiri-tō
Yakumo
Noboribetsu
Muroran
Urakawa
Mori
Erimo

Esashi
Mutsu
Erimo-misaki

1072 m ▲
Hakodate
Ūma
Shiriya-zaki

Matsumae

Rokkasho

Goshogawara
Aomori
Misawa
1584 m ▲
Hirosaki
Towada
Hachinohe
Noshiro
Ōdate
Ninohe
Kuji

Nyūdō-zaki
2038 m ▲
Kuzumaki
Miyako

Akita
Morioka
Hanamaki
Kamaishi
Ōmagari
Yokote
Ofunato

Ogachi
Shinjō
Ichinoseki
Kesennuma

Sakata
Tsuruoka
Furukawa

Murakami
Tendō
Sendai
Ryōtsu
Shibata
Yamagata
Sado-shima
Niigata
Niitsu
Yonezawa
Fukushima

Suzu
Sanjō
Aizu-Wakamatsu
Wajima
Nagaoka
Kashiwazaki
Kōriyama
Nanao
Jōetsu
Sukagawa
Himi
Tōkamachi
Shirakawa
Iwaki
Honshū
Toyama-wan
2454 m ▲
Takaoka
2484 m ▲
Hitachi
Shioya-saki
Kanazawa
Toyama
Suzaka
Nagano
Mito
Komatsu
3190 m
Ueda
Utsunomiya
Kaga
Takayama
Matsumoto
Ashikaga
Tsuchiura
Fukui
Shiojiri
2932 m ▲
Takasaki
Oyama
Sabae
Okaya
Suwa
Kumagaya
Takefu
Ina
Kōfu
Urawa
JAPAN
Tsuruga
Nakatsugawa
Iida
Fuji-san 3776 m
Tōkyō
Sakura
Maizuru
Gifu
Nagoya
Odawara
Chiba
Inubō-zaki
Yokkaichi
Toyota
Atsugi
Kawasaki
Kisarazu
Nagasaki
Toyohashi
Fuji
Yokohama
Nara
Matsusaka
Fujieda
Shizuoka
Tateyama
Osaka
Yaizu
Sagami-wan
Kishiwada
Hamamatsu
Shimoda
Inan
Ise
Shimoda
Owase
Nii-jima
Owase-zaki
Miyake-jima
Kushimoto
Mikura-jima
ono-misaki
Hachijō-jima
Izu-shotō

PACIFIC OCEAN

INSET MAP:

EAST CHINA SEA

Amami-shotō
Ō-shima
Tokuno-shima
Okinoerabu-jima
Okinawa-shotō
Nago
Okinawa
Okinawa-jima
Kume-jima
Naha
Nansei-shotō (Ryukyu Islands)

Yonaguni-jima
Sakishima-shotō
Hirara
Miyako-jima
Ishigaki-jima
Iriomote-jima

Tropic of Cancer

PACIFIC OCEAN

0 100 200 300 400 kilometers
0 100 200 miles
Scale 1:7,000,000
Projection: Equidistant Conic

Northeast China • Mongolia

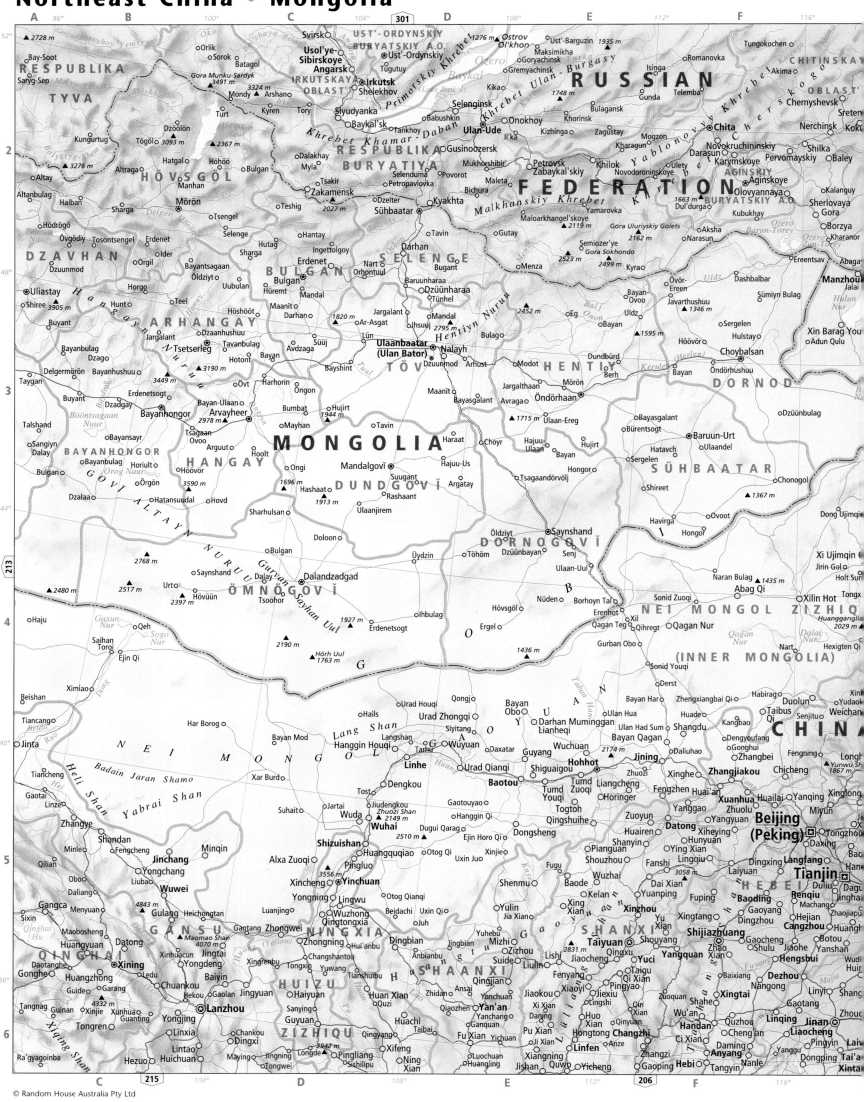

AMURSKAYA

OBLAST'

Mogocha
Chador
Dzhalinda
Magdagachi
301
Stoyba
Lukachek
Ol'ginsk
Yashkino
Ozero
Chukchagirskoye
Sofiysk

Sbega
Gorbitsa
Qiyahe
Mohe
Ershiwuzhan
Tygda
Ust'-Tygda
Norsko
Fevral'sk
Sofiysk
Duki
Ozero
Evoron
Boktor

Yimuhe
Fukeshan
Panguí
Ershizhan
Oupu
Ushumun
Sivaki
Mukhino
Byssa
Ust'-Umal'ta
Chegdomyn
2167 m
Komsomol'sk-na-Amure
Gurskoye
1628 m

Yudi Shan 1054 m
Walagán
1398 m
Tahe
Naodahan
Shimanovsk
Chagoyan
2512 m
Mogdy
Amursk
Vysokogornyy

Kurleya
Qiqian
Mangui
Huzhong
Linhai
Shizhan
Novogeorgiyevka
Svobodnyy
Seryshevo
Belogorsk
KHABAROVSKIY
KRAY
El'ban
1796 m
Sel'gon
Bolon
Innokent'yevka

1298 m
Alongshan
Niu'erhe
Cangshan
1290 m
Bishuio
Qizhan
Zhangdiyingzi
Jiuzhan
Zhanhe
Raychikhinsk
Novobureyskiy
969 m
Talakan
Troitskoye
Ozero
Bolon

Niu'erhe
Huolongmen
Sanzhan
Bogenli
Arkhara
Uril
1081 m
Bira
Birobidzhan
Smidovich
Litovko
Gora Tardoki-Yani 2078 m

Genhe
Keyihe
Orqen
Zizhiqi
Sunwu
Xunhe
Furao
Obluch'ye
YEVREYSKAYA 1013 m
Khabarovsk
Pereyaslavka

Yituliihe
Tulihe
Jiwen
Xinzhangfang
Heihe
Kusite
Chelu
Jiayin
Pompeyevka
AVTONOMNAYA
Leninskoye
Amurzet
Fuyuan
Khor
Xinlincun

Chen
Barag Qi
Yakeshi
Orqohan
Mianduhe
Yiliekede
Nenjiang
Yilaha
Longzhen
Zhanhe
Wuyiling
Hongxing
Youhao
OBLAST'
Luobei
Dong'an
Erlongshan
Vyazemskiy
2004 m

Hadat
Hailar
Onor
Bugt
Nehe
Laha
Tongbei
Cuiluan
Yichun
Jinshantun
Hegang
Fujin
Xifeng
Bikin
1115 m
Svetlaya

Amgalang Bulag
Sugehe
Songling
Zhaor
Bei'an
Kedong
Keshan
Hailun
Suileng
Nancha
Heli
Xincheng
Jixian
Burlit
1745 m
Maksimovka

Barag Zouqi
Huihe
Yirshi
Zalantun
Gannan
Yi'an
Baiquan
Mingshui
HEILONGJIANG
Shenshu
Tieli
Tangyuan
Jiamusi
Shuangyashan
Baoqing
Pozharskoye
Novopokrovka
Amgu

Yudi Shan
Arxan
Bailang
1712 m
Moguqi
Nianzhishan
Qiqihar
Lindian
Wangkui
Qing'an
Yilan
Huanan
Woken
Boli
Dongfanghong
Dal'nerechensk
PRIMORSKIY
Velikaya Kema

Wuchagou
Dashizhai
Solon
Jalaid Qi
Longfeng
Daqing
Qinggang
Suihua
Xinglongzhen
Xiji
Tonghe
Qitaihe
Mishan
Hulin
Lesozavodsk
Terney

Guiler
Ulanhot
Qarsan
Tailai
Anda
Zhaodong
Lanxi
Bayan
Mulan
Fangzheng
Hadagang
Qitaihe
Mishan
Ozero
Khanka
Plastun

Jurho
Liuhuo
Zhenlai
Zhaoyuan
Zhaozhou
Hulan
Bin Xian
Linkou
Máshan
Xingkai Hu
Dal'negorsk

Nungnain Sum
Jus Hua
Baicheng
Anguang
Da'an
Harbin
Acheng
Shangzhi
Weihe
Erdaohezi
Jixi
Rudnaya Pristan'

Bairin Zuoqi
Daiqin Tal
Taonan
Fuyu
Shuangcheng
Lalin
Yimianpo
Yabuli
Mudanjiang
Muling
Suiyang
KRAY

Bairin Youqi
Tuquan
Zhanyu
Qian'an
Sanchahe
Wuchang
Yushu
Shanhetun
Hailin
Muling
Pogranichnyy
Arsen'yev
Kavalerovo
Ol'ga
1855 m

Bairin Qiao
Horqin Youyi Zhongqi
Tongyu
Dongsanjia
Nong'an
Shulan
Kaiyuan
Ning'an
Dongning
Pokrovka
Ussuriysk
Anuchino

Ongniud Qi
Han Sum
Horqin Youyi
Zhongqi
Changling
Dehui
Jiutai
Xinzhan
Bohai
Laoheishan
Tavrichanka
Varfolomeyevka
Artem
Uglekamensk

Chifeng
Naiman Qi
Ar Horqin Qi
Kailu
Jiuzhan
Jilin
Jiaohe
Huangnihe
Daxinggou
Wangqing
Tianqiaoling
Spassk-Dal'niy
Partizansk
Preobrazheniye

Pingzhuang
Harqin Qi
Tongliao
Jargalang
Bamiancheng
Changchun
Fanjiatun
Xiyang
Wanqi
Dunhua
Dashitou
Shixian
1498 m
Senlin Shan
Uglovoye
Vladivostok
Nakhodka

Naiman Qi
Zhongqi
Zhuozi
Lishu
Siping
Guojiadian
JILIN
Panshi
Mingyuegou
Hunchun
Zarubino
Livadiya
Slavyanka

Bairin Youqi
Kangping
Xinglitun
Xinmin
Liaoyuan
Huadian
Baishan
Antu
Yanji
Helong
Hoeryong
Khasan

Kailu
Horqin Zuoyi
Faku
Tiefa
Qingyuan
Dongfeng
Huinan
Jingyu
Fusong
Baihe
Musan
Najin
585 m
Zhangwu
Hartao
Tieling
Meihekou
Liuhe
Shiren
Wangou
Paektu-san 2744 m
Nanam
Kyongsong

Fuxin
Qinghemen
Heishan
Xinbin
Tonghua
Tiechang
Qidaogou
Chinsong-ri
Samjiyon
2540 m
Ch'ongjin

Beipiao
Yi Xian
Fushun
Shenyang
Paoziyan
Huanren
Ji'an
Manp'o
Hesan
Samsu
Kilchu

Chaoyang
Lingyuan
Panshan
Liaoyang
Benxi
Anping
Huanren
Ch'osan
Kanggye
P'ungsan
Kimch'aek

Harqin Zuoyi
Nanpiao
Jinzhou
Anshan
Kuandian
Hyesan
Kapsan
2522 m
Iwon
Tanch'on

Ningcheng
Jinxi
Tianzhuangtai
Haicheng
Xiuyan
Qingchengzi
Kuancheng
1677 m
Xingcheng
Yingkou
Gaizhou
Huanren
Ch'angsong
Huich'on
Pukch'ong

Suizhong
Shanhaiguan
Xiongyuecheng
Huatong
1131 m
Gushan
Fengcheng
Sinuiju
Chongp'yong
Hamhung
Sinp'o

Luan Xian
Qinhuangdao
Wafangdian
Xinjin
Dandong
Donggou
Sonch'on
Changju
Sunan
Kumya
Kowon
Hungnam

Changli
Jinzhou
Pikou
Zhuanghe
Anbo
Ongjin
Anju
P'yongsong
Munch'on
Wonsan

Tangshan
Lushun
Dalian
Korea Bay
NORTH
KOREA
Kosan
T'ongch'on
Kosong

Bohai
Bo Hai
Pikou
Kangdong
Hwangju
Hoeyang
Sokch'o
Yangyang

Bohai Haixia
P'yongyang
Songnim
Sariwon
Kaesong
Ch'unch'on
Kangnung

Dongying
Penglai
Longkou
Huang Xian
Yantai
Namp'o
Chaeryong
Kwail
Sinch'on
Kumch'on
Hwach'on
Samch'ok

Qixia
Muping
Weihai
Changyon
Haeju
Uijongbu
Hongch'on
Hoengsong
Ullungdo

HANDONG
Laizhou
Laiyang
Rongcheng
Shidao
Ongjin
Soul
(Seoul)
Inch'on
Suwon
Wonju
Ulchin
Dogo
Dozen

Zibo
Weifang
Pingdu
Laixi
Haiyang
Anyang
Suwon
Ich'on
Ch'ungju
JAPAN

Jingzhi
Lancun
Jimo
Ch'onan
Yesan
Ch'ongju
Yongju
Andong
Matsue
Tottori
Toyooka

Qingdao
Jiaonan
Jiaozhou
SOUTH
Kongju
Taejon
Iri
Yongdong
Kumi
P'ohang
Yonago
Tsuyama
Himeji

Taech'on
Kunsan
Kimje
Chonju
Kimch'on
Kyongju
Taegu
Ulsan
Kobe

KOREA
Namwon
Hamada
Miyoshi
Okayama
Kakogawa

AMUR
HEILONG
Songhua
SEA OF JAPAN
YELLOW SEA
Bo Hai
Korea Bay

Scale 1:7,000,000

Projection: Equidistant Conic

0 100 200 300 400 kilometers
0 100 200 miles

Northwest China • East Kazakhstan • Mongolia

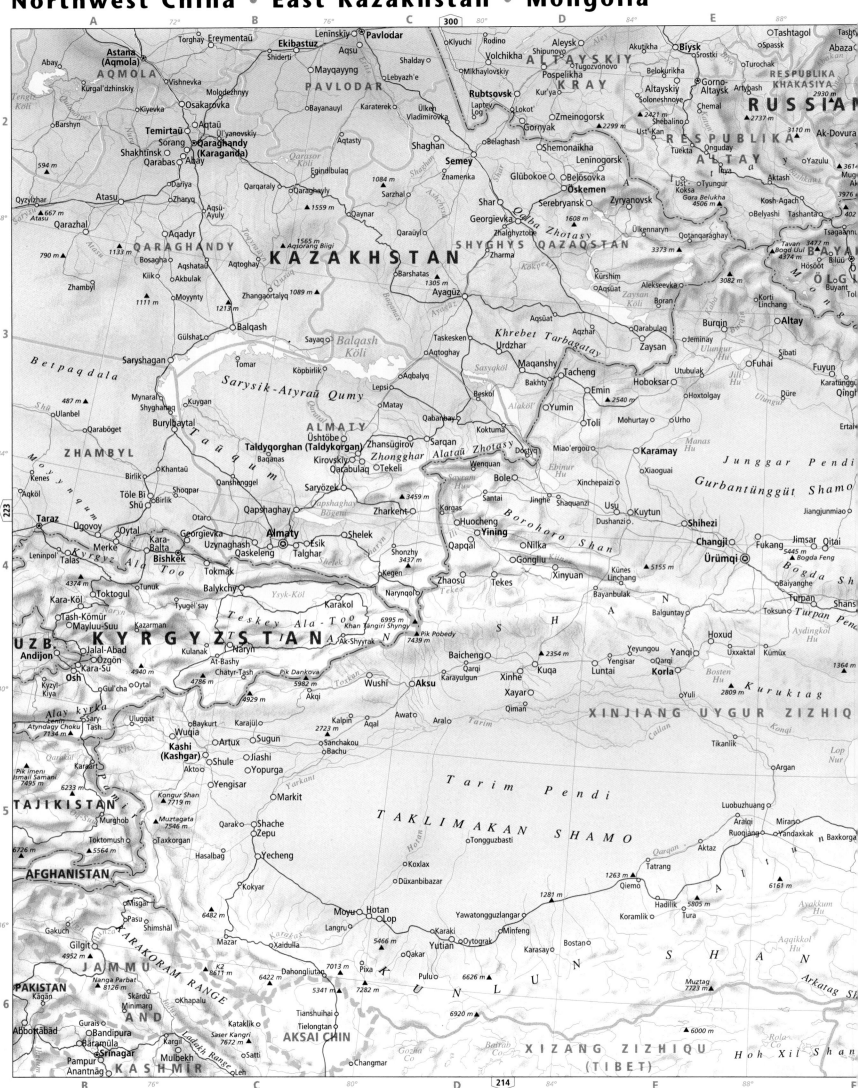

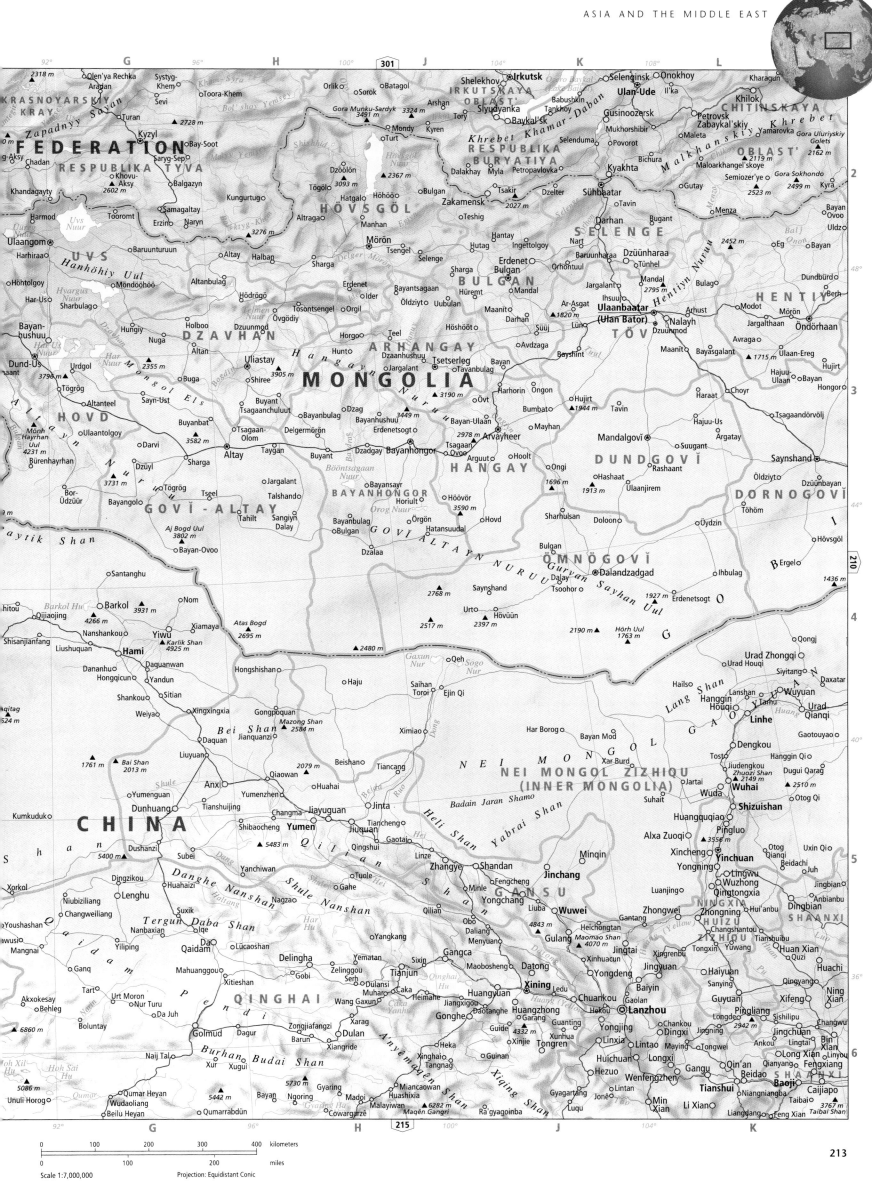

FEDERATION

KRASNOYARSKIY
KRAY

RESPUBLIKA TYVA

IRKUTSKAYA
OBLAST'

RESPUBLIKA
BURYATIYA

SELENGE

CHITINSKAYA

OBLAST'

HÖVSGÖL

HENTIY

UVS

BULGAN

Ulaanbaatar
(Ulan Bator)

TÖV

DZAVHAN

ARHANGAY

MONGOLIA

HOVD

HANGAY

DUNDGOVĬ

DORNOGOVĬ

GOVĬ-ALTAY

BAYANHONGOR

ÖMNÖGOVĬ

GOVĬ ALTAYN NURUU

Gurvan Sayhan Uul

Dalandzadgad

Barkol

Hami

Yumen

NEI MONGOL

NEI MONGOL ZIZHIQU
(INNER MONGOLIA)

Wuhai

Shizuishan

CHINA

Dunhuang

Jiayuguan

Jiuquan

GANSU

Jinchang

Yinchuan

NINGXIA
HUIZU
ZIZHIQU

SHAANXI

Qaidam Pendi

QINGHAI

Xining

Lanzhou

Golmud

Baoji

Scale 1:7,000,000

Projection: Equidistant Conic

0 100 200 300 400 kilometers

0 100 200 miles

213

Southwest China

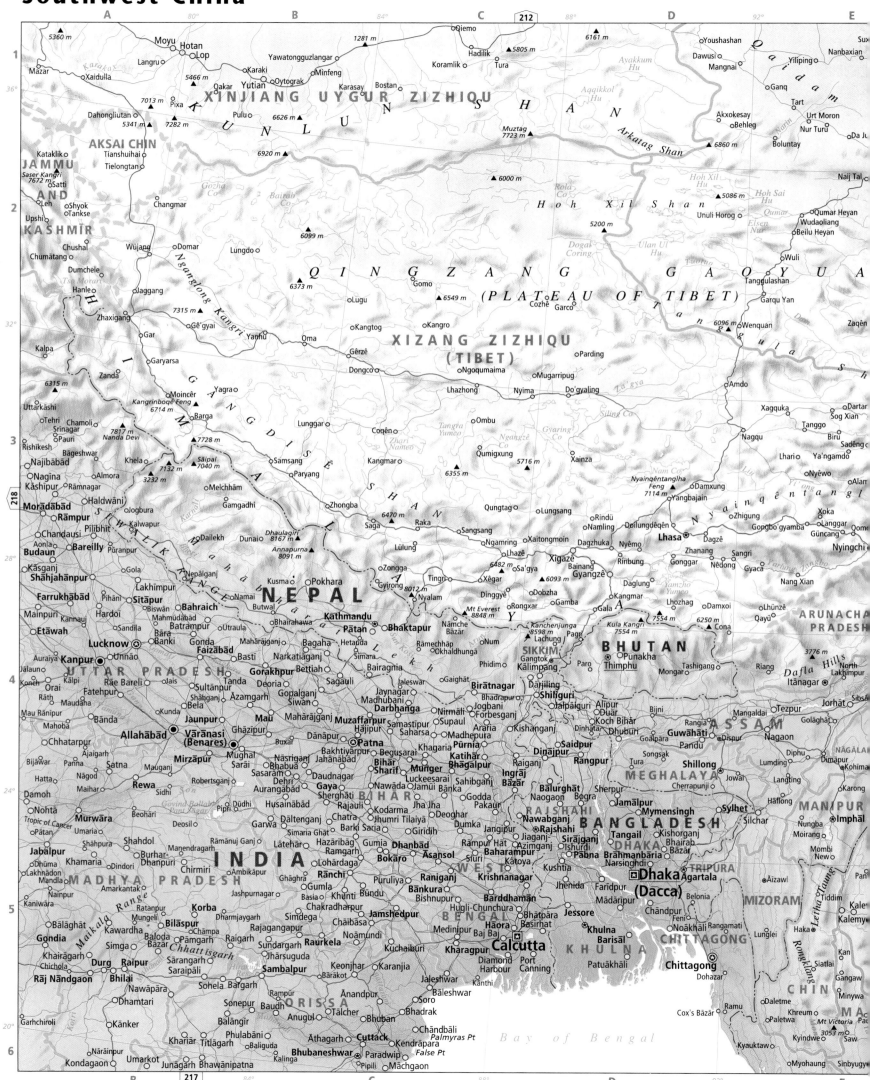

Asia and the Middle East

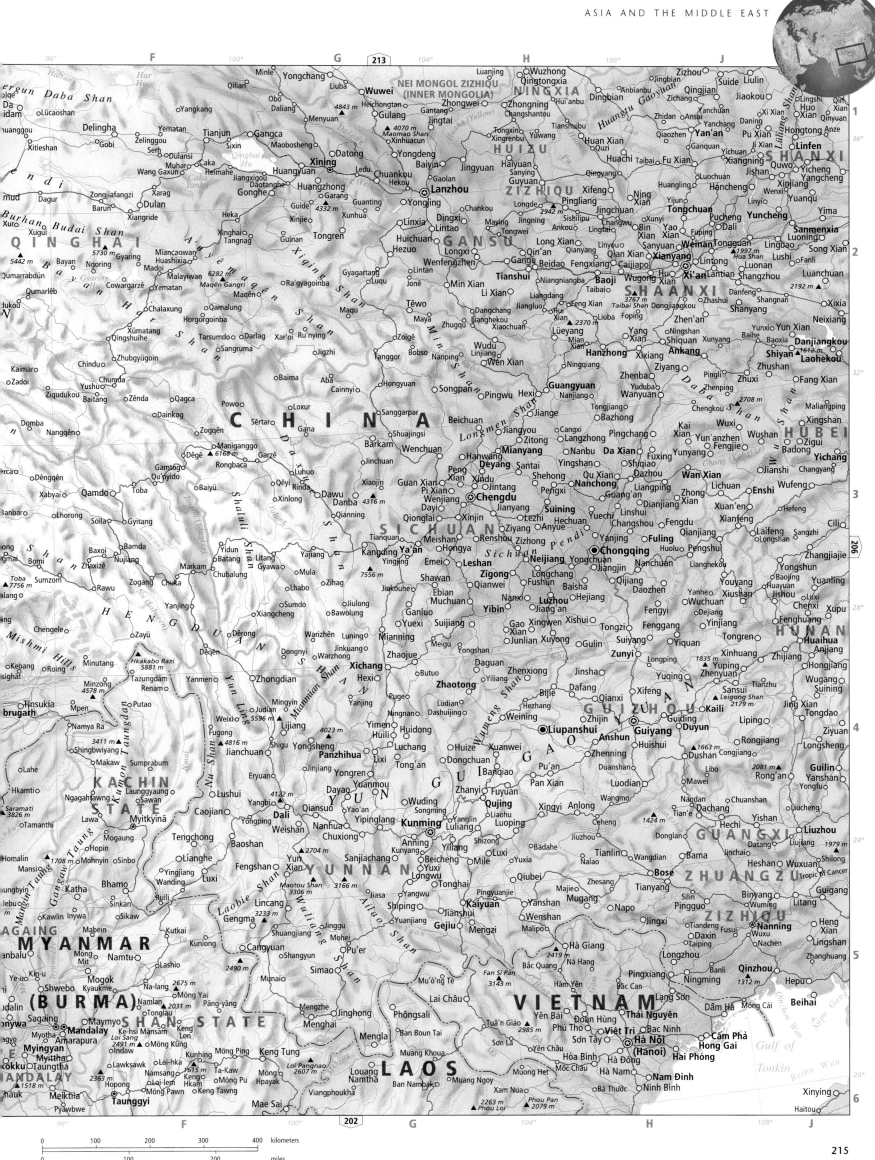

Scale 1:7,000,000   Projection: Equidistant Conic

South India • Sri Lanka

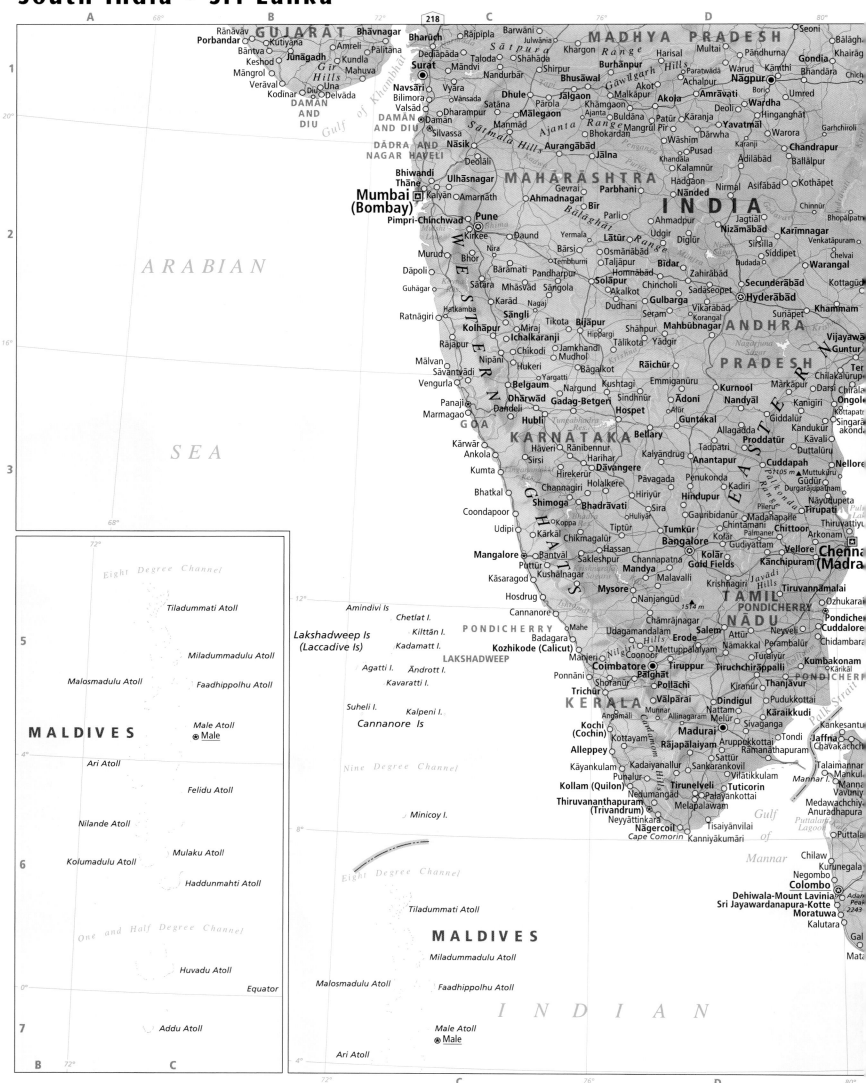

218

GUJARĀT

Rānāvāv · Porbandar · Kutiyāna · Amreli · Bhāvnagar · Bharūch · Rājpīpla · Barwāni
Bāntva · Keshod · Junāgadh · Kundla · Pālitāna · *Sātpura* · Khargon · Harisal · Multai · Pāndhurna
Māngrol · Verāval · Kodīnar · Una · *Gir Hills* · Mahuva · Dediāpāda · Taloda · Shāhāda · Shirpur · Bhusāwal · Burhānpur · Achalpur · Amrāvati · Warud · Kāmthi
Diu · Delvāda · **DAMĀN AND DIU** · Navsāri · Vyāra · Vānsada · Mandvi · Nandurbār · Bhusāwal · Malkāpur · Akola · Amrāvati · Boric · Umred · **Nāgpur**

MADHYA PRADESH
Seoni · Bālāgh · Gondia · Khairāg · Bhandāra · Chich

MAHĀRĀSHTRA
INDIA

Gulf of Khambhāt · **Surat** · Bilimora · Dharampur · Valsād · Silvassa · Daman · **DĀDRA AND NAGAR HAVELI** · Nāsik · Deolāli · Amarnāth
Bhiwandi · **Thāne** · Ulhāsnagar · Kalyān · Amarnāth
Mumbai (Bombay) · Pimpri-Chinchwad · Kirkee · **Pune** · Daund

ARABIAN

Murud · Bhor · Nira · Baramati · Pandharpur · Sāngola · **Solāpur** · Akalkot
Dāpoli · Satāra · Mhāsvad · Karād · Nagaj

SEA

Guhāgar · Ratnāgiri · Hatkamba · Sāngli · Miraj · Tikota · Bijāpur · Tālikota · Yādgir
Rājapur · Kolhāpur · Ichalkaranji · Jamkhandi · Mudhol · Bāgalkot · Rāichūr
Mālvan · Nipāni · Hukeri · Yargatti · Nargund · Kushtagi · Emmigānūru
Sāvantvādi · Belgaum · Bāgalkot · Sindhnūr · Ādoni
Vengurla · **Dhārwād** · Gadag-Betgeri · **Hospet** · Kurnool · Nandyāl
Panaji · Dandeli · **Hubli** · Guntakal
Marmagao · **GOA** · **KARNĀTAKA** · **Bellary** · Proddatūr · Kāvali
Kārwār · Haveri · Rānibennur · Harihar · Kalyāndrug · **Anantapur** · Cuddapah · Duttalūru
Ankola · Sirsi · Tadpatri
Kumta · Hirekerur · Holalkere · **Dāvangere** · Pāvagada · Penukonda · Kadiri · Gūdūr
Bhatkal · Channagiri · Hiriyūr · Sira · **Hindupur** · Gauribidanūr · Madanapalle · Tirupati
Shimoga · Bhadrāvati · Huliyūr · Chintāmani · Pileru · Thiruvattiyu
Coondapoor · Koppa · Tiptūr · **Tumkūr** · Kolar · Palmaner · Chittoor · Arkonam
Udipi · Kārkāl · Chikmagalūr · **Bangalore** · Kolār · Gudiyattam · **Vellore**
Mangalore · Bantvāl · Hassan · Sakleshpur · Channapatna · Gold Fields · Krishnagiri · **Chennai (Madras)**
Puttūr · Kushālnagar · **Mandya** · Malavalli · *Javādi Hills* · Tiruvannāmalai
Kāsaragod · **Mysore** · Nanjangūd · Krishnagiri · **TAMIL** · Ozhukarai
Hosdrug · **PONDICHERRY** · **NĀDU** · Pondicher
Cannanore · Chāmrājnagar · **Salem** · Neyveli · **Cuddalore**
Amindivi Is · Chetlat I. · **PONDICHERRY** · Mahe · Udagamandalam · Attūr · Perambalūr · Chidambaram
Kilttān I. · Badagara · *Nilgiri* · Coonoor · Nāmakkal · Turaiyūr
Lakshadweep Is (Laccadive Is) · Kadamatt I. · **Kozhikode (Calicut)** · Manjeri · **Mettuppālaiyam** · **Kumbakonam**
Agatti I. · Ãndrott I. · **LAKSHADWEEP** · Ponnāni · **Coimbatore** · **Tiruppur** · Tiruchchirāppalli · Kārikāl
Kavaratti I. · Shoranūr · **Palghāt** · Pollāchi · Kirañūr · **Thanjāvur** · **PONDICHERRY**
Suheli I. · Kalpeni I. · **Trichūr** · **Vālpārai** · **Dindigul** · Pudukkottai
Cannanore Is · Angamāli · Munnar · Nattam · Melūr · **Kāraikkudi**
Allinagaram · Sivaganga · Kankesantu
Kochi (Cochin) · Kottayam · **Madurai** · Tondi · **Jaffna**
Kottayam · Aruppukkottai · Rāmanāthapuram · Chavakachch
Alleppey · **Rājapālaiyam** · Sāttur · Talaimannar · Mankul
Kāyankulam · Kadaiyanallur · Sankarankovil · Vilātikkulam · Mannar I. · Manna
Nine Degree Channel · Punalur · Nedumangād · **Tirunelveli** · Palāyankottai · Vavuniy
Kollam (Quilon) · **Tuticorin** · Medawachchiy
Minicoy I. · **Thiruvananthapuram (Trivandrum)** · Melapālawam · Anuradhapura
Neyyāttinkara · Tisaiyānvilai · *Puttalam Lagoon* · Puttala
Nāgercoil · Kanniyākumāri
Cape Comorin · *Gulf of Mannar* · Chilaw · Kurunegala
Negombo · **Colombo**
Dehiwala-Mount Lavinia · Adam Peak 2243
Sri Jayawardanapura-Kotte
Moratuwa · Kalutara · Gal · Mata

Eight Degree Channel
Tiladummati Atoll
Miladummadulu Atoll
Malosmadulu Atoll · Faadhippolhu Atoll
Male Atoll · ⊛ Male
MALDIVES
Ari Atoll
Felidu Atoll
Nilande Atoll
Mulaku Atoll
Kolumadulu Atoll
Haddunmahti Atoll
One and Half Degree Channel
Huvadu Atoll
Equator
Addu Atoll

MALDIVES
Miladummadulu Atoll
Malosmadulu Atoll · Faadhippolhu Atoll
Male Atoll · ⊛ Male
Ari Atoll

INDIAN

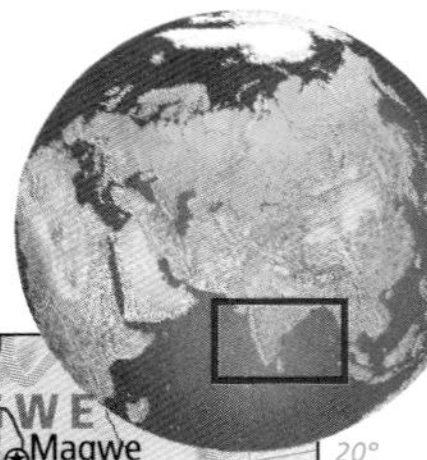

Asia and the Middle East

ORISSA

Kawardha
imga
Pāmgarh
Jhārsuguda
Bārakot
Keonjhar
Soro
Bāleshwar

Baloda
Sārangarh
Saraipāli
Sambalpur
Ānandpur
Bhadrak

Raipur Bāzar
Bargarh
Rampūr
Bhuban
Chāndbāli

Bhilai
Nawāpāra
Sohela
Baudh
Jājapur
Kendrāpara
Palmyras Pt

dgaon
Sonepur
Tālcher
Anugul
Athagarh
False Pt

Dhamtari
Balāngir
Phulabāni
Cuttack
Paradwip

Kānker
Khariār
Titlāgarh
Baliguda
Kalinga
Pipili
Māchgaon

Junāgarh
Bhawānipatna
Khallikot
Bhubaneshwar
Konārak

Kondagaon
Pāppadāhāndi
Āsika
▲1076 m

Sosanpal
Jagdalpur
Jaypur
Brahmapur
Chatrapur

Kirandul
Palkonda
Gunupur

Sukma
Narasannapeta
Sompeta

Mālkāngiri
Vizianagaram
Parlākimidi

Konta
Anakāpalle
Srikākulam

Chinturu
Krishnadevipeta
Waltair

Chodavaram
Vishākhapatnam

Rājahmundry
Tuni

depallegūdem
Kākināda
Yanam
PONDICHERRY

Bhimavaram
Pālakollu

Nivāda
Narasapur

Machilipatnam

Cape Chirāla

Bay

of

Bengal

SRI LANKA

Trincomalee
Mutur
niyai

Batticaloa

andy
idurutalagata
Amparai
24 m
enandyake
Pottuvil

dulla
Wellawaya

Madampe

Hambantota

ondra Head

O C E A N

MYANMAR (BURMA)

Kyauktaw
Sinbyugyun
MAGWE

Myohaung
Sagu
Magwe

Magyichaung
Migyaungye
Taungdwingyi

Ywathitke
Pauksa Taung
1708 m

Sittwe (Akyab)
MYANMAR (BURMA)

Oyster I.
Mindon

ARAKAN
PEGU

Kyaukpyu
Pyè (Prome)

Ramree I.
Taungup
Paungde
Zigon

Cheduba I.
Kyangin

Kyeintali
Okpo
Minhla

Henzada
Letpadan

Gwa
Lemyethna

Yegyi
Danubyu

Kangyidaung
Ma-ubin

IRRAWADDY
Myaungmya

Bassein
Bogale

Combermere Bay

Preparis North Channel

Preparis I.

Preparis South Channel

Great Coco I.

Little Coco I.

Coco Channel

Landfall I.
C. Price

North Andaman
Saddle Peak
738 m ▲

Pahlāgaon

Middle Andaman

South Andaman
Port Blair

Rutland I.

Duncan Passage

ANDAMAN AND NICOBAR ISLANDS

Nachuge
Little Andaman

Andaman Is

Ten Degree Channel

Car Nicobar I.
Kakana

Tarasa Dwip I.
Camorta I.

Misha

Nicobar Is

Sombrero Channel

Little Nicobar

Bananga

Great Nicobar

A n d a m a n   a n d   N i c o b a r   I s l a n d s   (I n d i a)

84°   88°   92°

20°

2

214

16°

3

12°

4

8°

5

4°

6

North India • Pakistan • Nepal

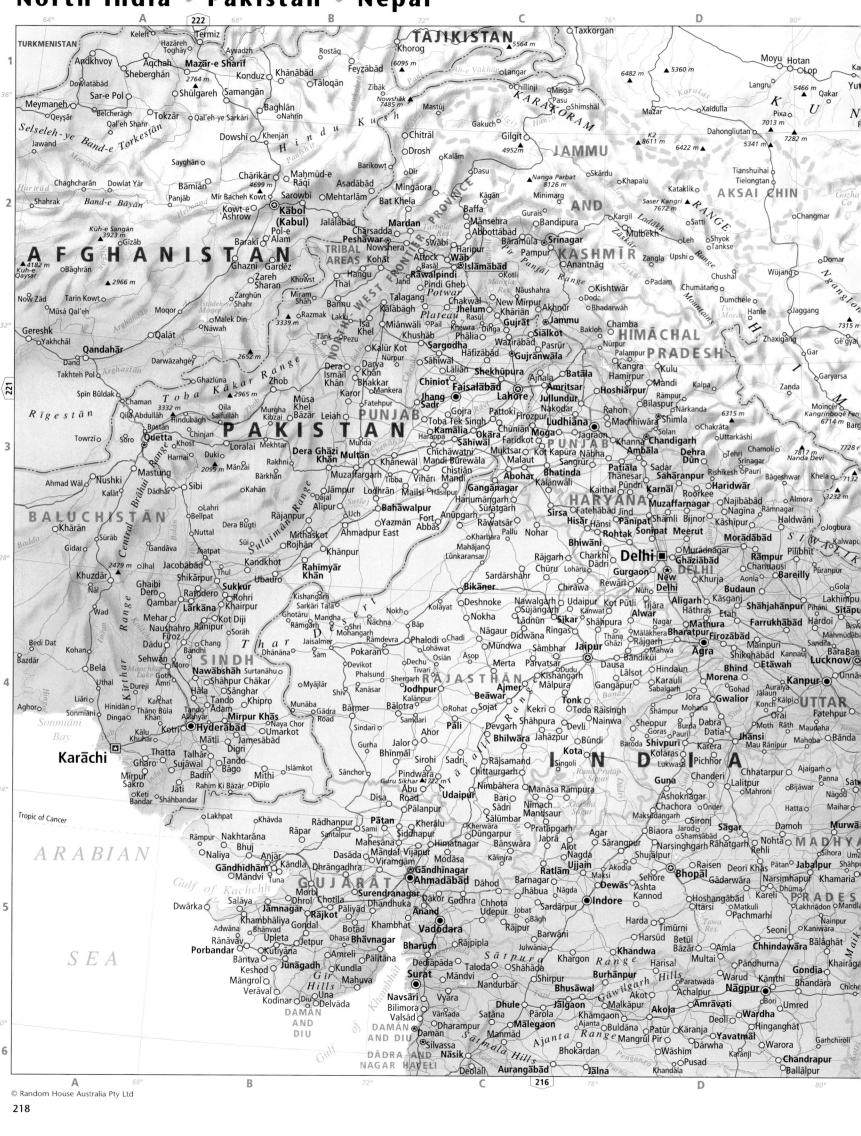

TURKMENISTAN

TAJIKISTAN

Khorog
5564 m
6095 m

KARAKORAM

JAMMU

AFGHANISTAN

Kabol
(Kabul)

NORTH WEST FRONTIER PROVINCE

TRIBAL AREAS

KASHMIR

Nanga Parbat
8126 m

AKSAI CHIN

HIMACHAL PRADESH

PAKISTAN

Islamabad

Rawalpindi

Lahore

PUNJAB

PUNJAB

HARYANA

Delhi

DELHI

New Delhi

BALUCHISTAN

SINDH

THAR

RAJASTHAN

Jaipur

Agra

Lucknow

UTTAR

Kanpur

Karachi

Hyderabad

Sonmiani Bay

Tropic of Cancer

ARABIAN

GUJARAT

Gandhinagar
Ahmadabad

Indore

MADHYA

SEA

Gulf of Kachchh

Vadodara

Bhopal

PRADESH

Surat

Nagpur

DAMAN AND DIU

DADRA AND NAGAR HAVELI

Nasik

Aurangabad

213

215

217

XINJIANG UYGUR
6626 m
ZIZHIQU
6920 m

Yawatongguzlangar
Minfeng
Bostan
Koramlik
Ograk
Karasay
Muztag 7723 m

Aqqikkol Hu
Arkatag Shan

S H A N

Akxokesay
Behleg
Narin
Urt Moron
Nur Turu
Da Juh
Zongjiafangzi
Dulan
Xiangride
Miancaowan
Huashixia
6282 m
Maqên Gangri
Qamalung

6860 m
Boluntay
Golmud
Burhan Budai Shan
Dagur
Barun
5730 m
QINGHAI

Hoh Xil Hu
5086 m
Qumar
Unuli Horog
Elsen Nur
Naij Tal
Xur
Xugui
Bayan
Noring
Gyaring
5442 m
Madoi
Cowargarzê
Yematan
Horgorgoinba
Chalaxung
Zhubgyügoin
Zoggên

6000 m

Hoh Xil Shan
5200 m
Dogai Coring

C H I N A

QINGZANG   GAOYUAN

6549 m

(PLATEAU OF TIBET)

6373 m
6099 m
Lungdo
Gomo
Cozhê
Garco

Wenquan
6096 m

Qumar Heyan
Wudaoliang
Beilu Heyan
Wuli
Tanggulashan
Garqu Yan
Zaqên
Tanggula Shan
Qumarrabdün
Qumarlêb
Qidukou
Zadoi
Ziqudukou
Baitang
Chindu
Chumda
Yushu
Zênda
Dainkog

Domba
Nangqên
Dêgê
Gamtog
Qu'nyido

XIZANG ZIZHIQU
(TIBET)

Yanhu
Oma
Gêrzê
Parding
Ngoqumaima
Mugarripug
Do'gyaling

Amdo
Xagquka
Sog Xian
Tanggo
Biru
Sadêng
Dartang
Sêrca
Dêngqên
Xabyai
Soila
Qamdo
Toba
Gyitang
Bamda

Kangro
Kangtog
Kangmar
Zhabyai

32°

2

3

Dongco
Lhazhong
Nyima
Za'gya

Nagqu
Lhari
Ya'ngamdo
Banbar
Lhorong

ngri
40 m
Melchhām
Gamgadhi

Lunggar
Samsang
Paryang

Ombu
Coqên
Qumigxung
Rindü
Namling
Xainza
Siling Co
Nam Co
Nyêwo
Alamdo
Xoka
Langgar
Qomo
Nyingchi
Zayü
Zagang
Nujiang
5881 m

Tangra Yumco
Ngangze Co

6355 m
5716 m

Nyainqêntanglha Feng 7114 m
Damxung
Yangbajain
N y a i n q ê n t a n g l h a   S h a n
Yi'ong
Gongbo'gyamba
Güncang
7756 m
Rawu
Zhaxizê
Bomi
Sumzom
Wulang

ipal
Zhongba
Kangmar
6470 m
Raka
Sangsang
Ngamring
Lhazê
Saga
Lülung

Xigazê
6482 m
Sa'gya
6093 m
Gyangzê

Zhigung
Doilungdêqên
Nyêmo
Dagzê
Lhasa
Zhanang
Sangri
Gyaca
Nang Xian
Nêdong
Miging
Chengele
Hkakabo Razi
Minutang
Tazungdām
Putao

GANGDISÊ SHAN

Qungtag
Xaitongmoin
Dazhuka
Bainang
Rinbung

Gonggar
Yarlung
Yamzho Yumco

Daglung
Lhozhag
Lhünzê
Qayu
Kebang
Pasighat
Roing
4578 m
Mpen

ARUNACHAL
PRADESH

28°

Dhaulagiri 8167 m
Annapurna 8091 m
Zongka
Gyirong
Tingri
Dinggyê
Dobzha
Gamba
Kula Kangri 7554 m
Damxoi
6250 m
Cona
3776 m
Dibrugarh
Tinsukia
Namya Ra
3411 m

ilekh
Dunai
H I M A L A Y A
Mt Everest 8848 m
8012 m
Nyalam
Rongxar
8598 m
Kanchenjunga
Num
Lachung
Pagri
BHUTAN
Punākha
Tashigang
Mongar
Riang
Dafla Hills
Itānagar
North Lakhimpur
Jorhat
Sibsāgar
Shingbwiyang
Makaw
Ngagahtâwng
Lawa

NEPAL
Kusma
Namai
Pokhara
Namche Bāzār
SIKKIM
Gangtok
Kālimpang
Paro
Thimphu
Tezpur
Golāghāt
Lahe
Hkamti
KACHIN
STATE

RANGE
Bahraich
Nepālganj
Butwal
Mahābhārat
Kathmandu
Bhaktapur
Pātan
Hetauda
Okhaldhungā
Phidim
Dārjiling
Shiliguri
Alipur Duar
Bijni
Rangia
Mangaldai
Dispur
ASSAM
NĀGĀLAND
Diphu
Kohima
Saramati 3826 m
Tamanthi
Myitkyinā
Mogaung
Hopin
Sinbo

4

Bhairawa
Bhairahawa
Bagaha
Simara
Bairagnia
Gaighāt
Rāmechhāp
Jalpaiguri
Koch Bihar
Dhuburi
Dinhata
Goalpara
Pandu
Guwāhāti
Nagaon
Lumding
Langting
Karong
Homalin
Mansi
Mohnyin

Batrampur
Utraula
Gonda
Mahārājganj
Narkatiāganj
Bettiah
Jaynagar
Madhubani
Nirmāli
Supaul
Araria
Kishanganj
Saidpur
Dinājpur
Rangpur
Tura
MEGHALAYA
Cherrapunji
Shillong
Jowai
Hāflong
Silchar
MANIPUR
Imphāl
Nungba
Moirang
Mombi New
SAGAING
Paungbyin
Pinlebu
Pantha
Kawlin
Inywa
Mabein
Sikaw
Sinkan

Gorakhpur
Faizābād
Bastī
Deoria
Gopalganj
Siwān
Muzaffarpur
Samastipur
Saharsa
Khagaria
Pūrnia
Raiganj
Bālurghāt
Naogaon
Bogra
Sherpur
Jamālpur
Mymensingh
24°

RADESH
Shāhganj
Āzamgarh
Mau
Tanda
Jaunpur
Ghāzipur
Dānāpur
Patna
Begusarai
Munger
Bhāgalpur
Sāhibganj
Godda
Bihār Sharīf
Luckeesarai
Jamūi
Bānka
Deoghar
Pakaur
Ingrāj Bāzār
RAJSHAHI
Jamālpur
Tangail
BANGLADESH
Kishorganj
Bhairab
Āīzawl
MIZORAM
Tiddim
Haka
Kalewa
Mawlaik
Kin-u
Kani
Shwebo
Mongmit
Mogok

Bela
Vārānasi (Benares)
Mughal
Bhabua
Buxar
Bakhtiyārpur
Jahānābād
Nāsriganj
Daudnagar
Gayā
Rajauli
Jamūi
Jha
Nawbganj
Sirājganj
Ishurdi
Pābna
Narsinghdi
DHAKA
Brāhmanbāria
Dhaka (Dacca)
Agartala
Sylhet
TRIPURA
Belonia
Feni
Rangamati
Lunglei
Siatlai
CHIN
Kalemyo
Ye-u
Budalin
Kanbalu

Mirzāpur
Robertsganj
Dehri
Aurangābād
Sherghāti
Jhumri Tilaiyā
Giridih
Dumka
Rāmpur Hāt
Siuri
Jiaganj-Azimganj
Rajshahi
Kātoya
Kushtia
Jhenida
Mādāripur
Chāndpur
Feni
Bardarban
Dohazar
Chittagong
Sagaing
Mandalay
Monywa
Amarapura
Yesagyo
Myotha
Myittha
Myingyan
Taungtha
Meiktila
Pyawbwe

ahabad
Kewa
Māuganj
Sīdhi
Dūdhi
Pipri
Garwa
Dāltenganj
Chatra
Barki Saria
Gumia
Hazāribāg
Dhanbād
Bokāro
Sindri
Asansol
Krishnanagar
Barddhaman
Hugli-Chunchura
Jessore
Khulna
Barisāl
Patuākhāli
Cox's Bāzār
Ramu
Daletme
Kalewa

Beohāri
Deosil
Rāmānuj Ganj
Lātehar
Lohārdaga
Rānchi
Purulia
Bānkura
Bishnupur
Bhatpara
Hāora
Baj Baj
Basirhat
Canning
KHULNA
Kyauktaw
Pauk
Chauk
Mt Victoria 3053 m
Khreum
Paletwa
Kyindwe
Saw
1518 m
Mt Popa
Sinbyugyun
Minbu
Magwe
Mandalay

Chirmiri
Burhar-Dhānpuri
Ambikāpur
Jashpurnagar
Gumla
Basia
Chakradharpur
Simdega
Chāibāsa
Noāmundi
Jamshedpur
Medinipur
Kharagpur
Calcutta
Diamond Harbour
Diamond Port
Palmyras Pt
MAGWE

Amarkantak
Manendragarh
Korba
Ratanpur
Dharmjaygarh
Raigarh
Rajagangapur
Sundargarh
Raurkela
Khunti
WEST BENGAL
CHITTAGONG
Sittwe (Akyab)
1708 m
Pauka Taung
Migyaunghla
Sinbaungwe

dori
Mungeli
Bilāspur
Kawardha
Pāmgarh
Sambalpur
Bargarh
Sārangarh
Saraipāli
Bhadrak
Jharsuguda
Kuchaiburi
Karanjia
Jaleshwar
Kānthi
Bāleshwar
Soro
Myohaung
Magyichaung
Wathatok

imga
Raipur
Baloda Bāzār
Sohela
Sonepur
Bilāspur
Bhilai
Nawāpāra
Balāngir
Bhuban
Anugul
Chāndbāli
Kendrāpara
Paradwip
False Pt
Bay of Bengal
Ramree I.
ARAKAN
Cheduba I.
Kyaukpyu
PEGU

dgaon
Dhamtari
Kānker
Khariār
Titlāgarh
Phulabāni
Bhubaneshwar
Āthagarh
Cuttack
Pipili
Māchgaon
Pyè (Prome)
Paungde
Zigon

āinpur
Kondagaon
Umarkot
Junāgarh
Balangu
Bhawānipatna
Khallikot
Konārak
Āsika
1076 m
Puri
Taungup
Kyangin

20°

ORISSA

6

84°   88°   92°

0   100   200   300   400   kilometers
0   100   200   miles

Scale 1:7,000,000   Projection: Equidistant Conic

219

Middle East

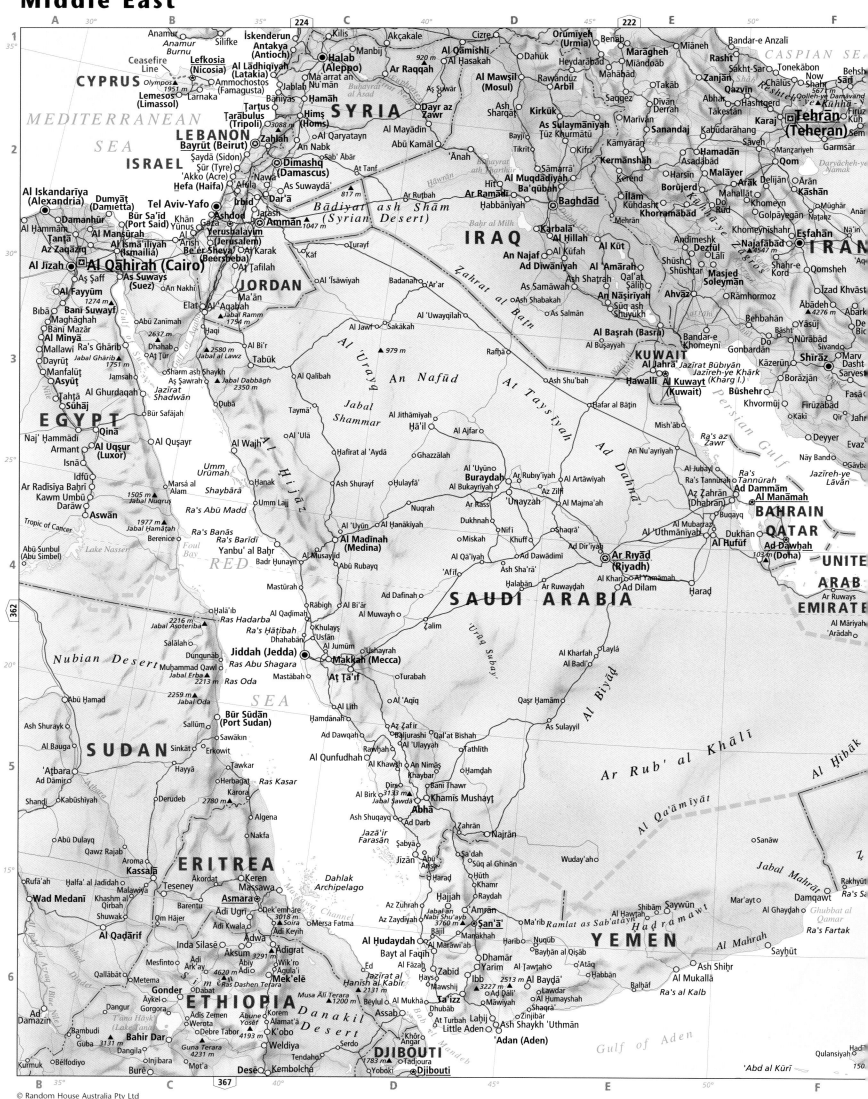

Asia and the Middle East

222

218

216

TURKMENISTAN

Gyzyletrek
Gonbad-e Qābūs
Galand
Mayamey
Dāmghān
Emāmshahr
Bīārjomand
Shāmkūh
Kashmar
 Torūd
Bajestān
Ferdows
Khvor
Shūrāb
Nowghāb
Bayāzīyeh
Posht-e Bādām
Yazd
Sāghand
Kūh-e Nāy Band 2992 m
Nāy Band
Anār
Bāfq
Zarand
dakan
Rāvar
Kermān
Mashīz
Bāghīn
Kūh-e Hazār 4420 m
Sīrjān
Bam
Pārīzo
Beshneh
Darzīn
Shūr-e Gaz
Qatrūyeh
Rafsanjān
Dārāb
Sabzevārān
Kūh-e Bazmān 3489 m
Kahnūj
Kūh-e Taftān 4042 m
yom
Lār
Sa'ādatābād
Bandar-e 'Abbās
Mīnāb
Manūjān
Bazmān
Bastak
Jazīreh-ye Qeshm
Angohrān
Nīkshahr
dar-e
Jazīreh-ye Forūr
reh-ye irrī
Al Khaṣab
Jāsk
Sadīch
Hūmedān
Dubayy (Dubai)
Jabal Yibīr 1527 m
Al Fujayrah
ū Zaby u Dhabi
Shuḥ ar
Al Khābūrah
wānīyah
'Ibrī
Jabal ash Sham 3019 m
Al Hajar
Ibrā'
Nizwā
Masqaṭ (Muscat)
Sūr
Ra's al Ḥadd
Al Kāmil
Kidan
OMAN
Haymā'
Dawwah
Khalūfū
Jazīrat Maṣīrah
wkah
Khalīj Maṣīrah
Jiddat al Ḥarāsīs
Ghubbat Ṣawqirah
Ra's al Madrakah
Ḥadbaram
Jazā'ir Khurīyā Murīyā (Kuria Muria Is)
marīt
Ḥāsik
Ra's Naws
Mirbāṭ
Ṣadh
ālah
Ra's Mirbāṭ
Suquṭrā (Socotra) (Yemen)

Babadurmaz
Dushak
Tejen
Mary
Bayramaly
Jolotan'
Bojnūrd
Esfarāyen
Qūchān
Tashkepri
Sandykgachy
Tagtabazaro
Meymaneh
Mashhad
Neyshābūr
Sabsevār
Asadābād
Torbat-e Ḥeydarīyeh
Ṭayyebāt
Qā'en
Sedeh
Deyhūk
Tabas
Nowghāb
Ghūrīān
Herāt
Kūh-e Sangān 3923 m
Shahrak
Chaghcharān
Qal'eh-ye Now
AFGHANISTAN
Mandelo
Shindand
Anār Darreh
Farāh
2560 m
Delārām
Now Zād
Bāghrān
2488 m
Zābol
Lūṭak
Zaranj
Dasht-e Mārgow
Deh Shū
Rūdbār
Rīgestān
Spīn Būldak
Chaman
Takhteh Pol
Qandahār
Zāhedān
Saindak
2333 m
Dālbandīn
3007 m
Kharān
Sūrāb
Nok Kundi
Khāsh
Kārvāndar
Sarāvān
Esfandak
Bampūr
2093 m
Sarbāz
Rāsk
Bāhū Kalāt
Polāno
Pidarak
Kikki
Chābahār
Jiwani
Gwādar
Pasni
Ormāra
Turbat
Hoshāb
Bazdār

Mazār-e Sharīf
Andkhvoy
Sheberghān
Dowlatābād
Sar-e Pol
Belcherāgh
Sarowbī
Qeyṣār
Bālā Morghāb
Jawand
Tokzār
Dowshī
Kābol (Kabul)
Chārīkār
Bāmīān
Panjāb
Dowlat Yār
Ghaznī
Ghazlūna
Moqor
Tarin Kowt
Qalāt
Darwāzahgēy
Ghorband
Quetta
Nushki
Kalāt
Dādhar
Bellpat
Khuzdār
Jhal
Nāl
Wad
Bela
Uthal
Liāri
Sonmiāni
Sonmiāni Bay
Gharo
Thatta
Badin
Jātī

Konduz
Khānābād
Baghlān
Nahrin
Chārsadda
Peshāwar
Hangu
Gardēz
Barakī
Miram Shāh
Zarghūn Shahr
Nāwah
Razmak
Khost
Harnai
Sibi
Rājanpur
Dera Bugti
Kandhkot
Jacobābād
Shikārpur
Ratodero
Larkāna
Mehar
Kot Diji
Dādu
Moro
Kohan
Nawābshāh
Tando Adam
Hāla
Kotri
Hyderābād
Mirpur Khās
Digri

Ṭāloqān
Khānābād
Nowshāk 7485 m
Mastūj
Gakuch
Gilgit
Chitrāl
Kālam
Drosh
Barīkowt
Mīngāora
Kāgān
Asadābād
Jalālābād
Islāmābād
Rāwalpindi
Pindi Gheb
Talagang
Lakkī
Tānk
Dera Ismaīl Khān
Bhakkar
Khushāb
Mīanwāli
Sargodha
Faisalābād
Gojra
Chiniot
Shekhūpura
Kamālia
Sāhīwal
Multan
Muzaffargarh
Bahāwalpur
Ahmadpur East
Rahīmyār Khān
Khānpur
Sādiqābād
Ghotki
Sukkur
Rohri
Khairpur

K2 8611 m
Skārdu
Kataklik
Saser Kangri 7672 m
Nanga Parbat 8126 m
Gurais
Bāndipura
Srīnagar
Anantnāg
Kargil
Leh
Upshi
Tankse
Chushul
Padam
Hanle
JAMMU AND KASHMIR
Pir Panjāl Range
Zaskar Range
Ladakh Range
Karakoram Range
Kishtwār
Bhadarwah
Doda
Nūrpur
Jammu
Kangra
Kulu
Rāmpur
Shimla
Kalpa
Chandigarh
Dehra Dūn
Ludhiāna
Moga
Khanna
Ambāla
Sahāranpur
Kaithal
Karnāl
Patiāla
Sangrur
Bhatinda
Fatehābād
Hānsi
Hisār
Rohtak
Meerut
Ghāziābād
Delhi New Delhi
Rewari
Nawalgarh
Kot Pūtli
Alwar
Shāhpura
Jhunjhunu
Ringas
Jaipur
Lālsot

Pir Panjāl Range
Wazīrābād
Gujrānwāla
Batāla
Amritsar
Lahore
Gujrāt
Phālia
Hāfizābād
Sialkot
Narowal
Wāh
Mardan
Abbottābād
Mānsehra
Bāramūla
Jhelum
Mirpur

PAKISTAN
Zhob
Leiah
Dera Ghāzi Khān
Hanumāngarh
Sūratgarh
Bīkāner
Nokha
Lūnkaransar
Sardārshahr
Chūru
Sīkar
Dīdwāna
Nāgaur
Deshnoke
Nokh
Bāp
Pokaran
Phalodi
Lohāwat
Mandha
Nāchna
Mūndwa
Merta
Parvatsar
Ajmer
Beāwar
Nasīrābād
Bhīlwāra
Kota
Būndi
Chittaurgarh
Basi
Kālpi
Nimbāhera
Nimach
Manāsa
Pratāp Sāgar
Rāna Pratāp Sāgar
Gāndhi Sāgar

Jaisalmer
Devikot
Osiān
Jodhpur
Bilāra
Sojat
Devli
Nāinwa
Shergarh
Bāp
Mālpura
Sāmbhar
Tonk
Sheopur
Shivpuri

Thar Desert
Bārmer
Sānchor
Bhīnmāl
Gurha
Sindari
Gadra Road
Jalor
Pāli
Gurha
Āhor
Devgarh
Mount Ābu
Ābu Road
Dūngarpur
Bānswāra
Sāgwāra
Udaipur
Nimach
Nāthdwāra
Pindwāra
Sirohi
Guru Sikhar 1722 m

Khāvda
Lakhpat
Nakhtarāna
Naliya
Bhuj
Rāpar
Rādhanpur
Santalpur
Mahesāna
Viramgām
Mūndra
Māndvi
Gāndhīdhām
Morbi
Dhrāngadhra
Dholka
Dākor
Ānand
Gāndhinagar
Ahmadābād
Dhod
Jhābua
Ratlām
Dewās
Indore
Ujjain
Agar
Jaora
Sārangpur

Dwārka
Okha
Salāya
Jāmnagar
Rānāvāv
Porbandar
Bāntva
Mangrol
Verāval
Rājkot
Gondal
Jetpur
Jūnāgadh
Mahuva
Upleta
Bhāynagar
Amreli
Dhāri
Pālitāna
Kodinar
Diu
Delvāda
Surendranagar
Limbdi
Bhāvnagar
Sihor
Talāja
Vadodara
Bhārūch
Rājpipla
Bāgh
Barwāni
Khargon
Bhusāwal
Nandurbar
Dhule
Julwānia

Surat
Navsāri
Bilīmora
Valsād
Daman
Silvāssa
Manmād
Mālegaon
Jalgaon
Bhor
Ajanta
Aurangābād
Sātmala Hills
Nāsik
Deolāli
Ahmadnagar
Gevrai
Bhiwandi
Thāne
Ulhāsnagar
Pune
Murud
Bārāmati
Daund
Bārsi
Bhor
Sātāra
Pandharpur
Dāpoli
Guhāgar
Karād
Hatkamba
Ratnāgiri
Sāngli
Kolhāpur
Miraj
Rājapur
Ichalkaranji
Belgaum
Mālvan
Sāvantvādi
Dāndeli
Panaji
WESTERN GHATS
Marmagao
Kārwār
Ankola
Kumta
Bhatkal

Nagaj

INDIA

Mumbai (Bombay)
Mumbai Harbour

Karachi
Mirpur Sakro

Gulf of Oman
Gwatar Bay
Dashtī
Sonmiāni Bay

ARABIAN

SEA

Gulf of Kachchh
Gulf of Khambhat
Gīr Hills

Laccadive Is

Hindu Kush
Karakoram Range
Sulaimān Range
Kīrthar Range
Central Makrān Range
Siāhān Range
Toba Kākar Range
Dasht-e Kavīr
Dasht-e Lūt
Dasht-e Mārgow
Rīgestān
Thar Desert
Strait of Hormuz

0 100 200 300 400 kilometers
0 100 200 miles
Scale 1:10,000,000   Projection: Equidistant Conic

Kazakhstan • Republics of Central Asia

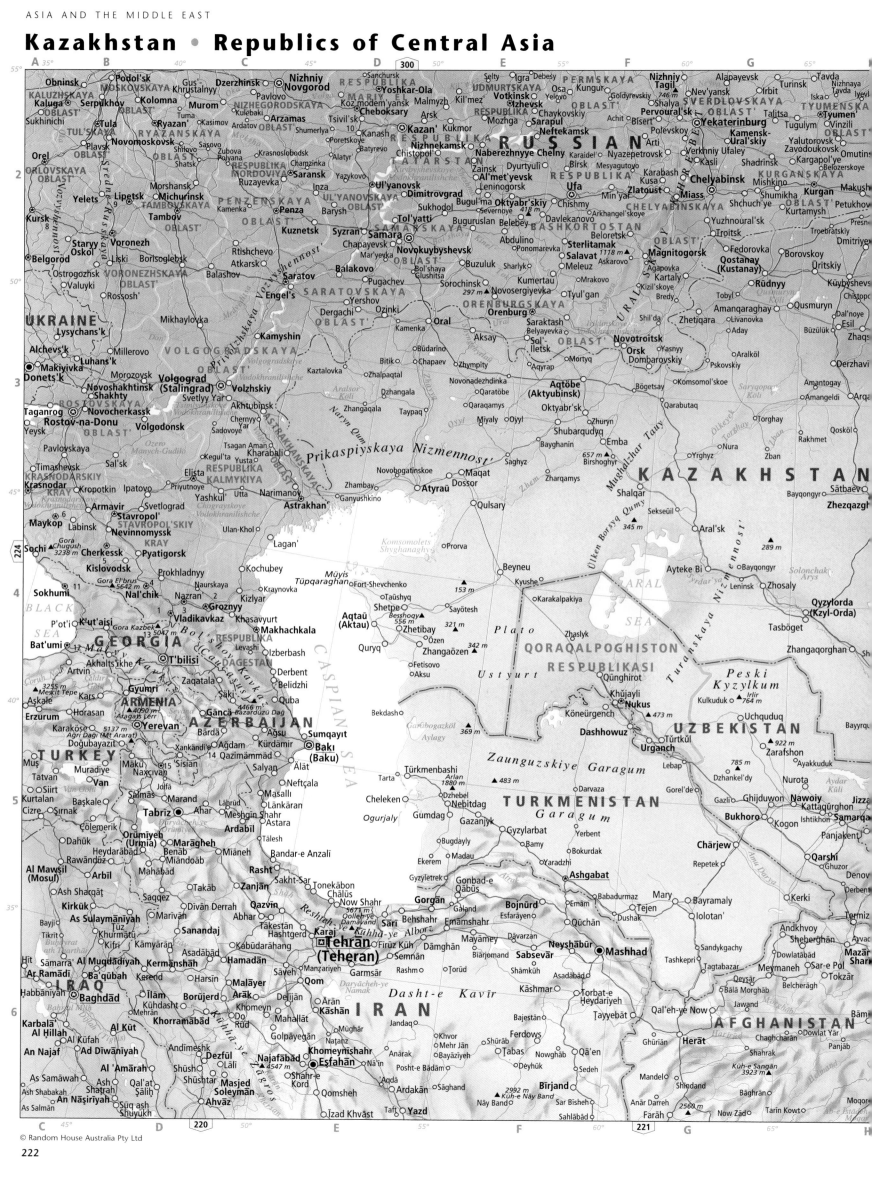

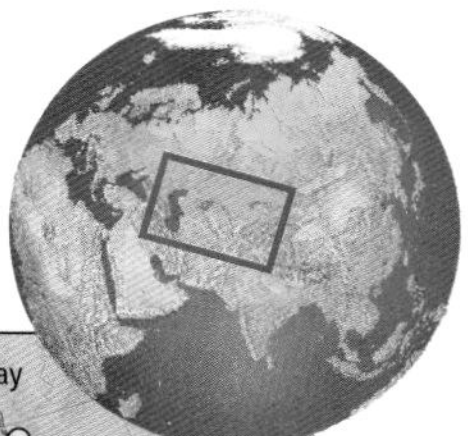

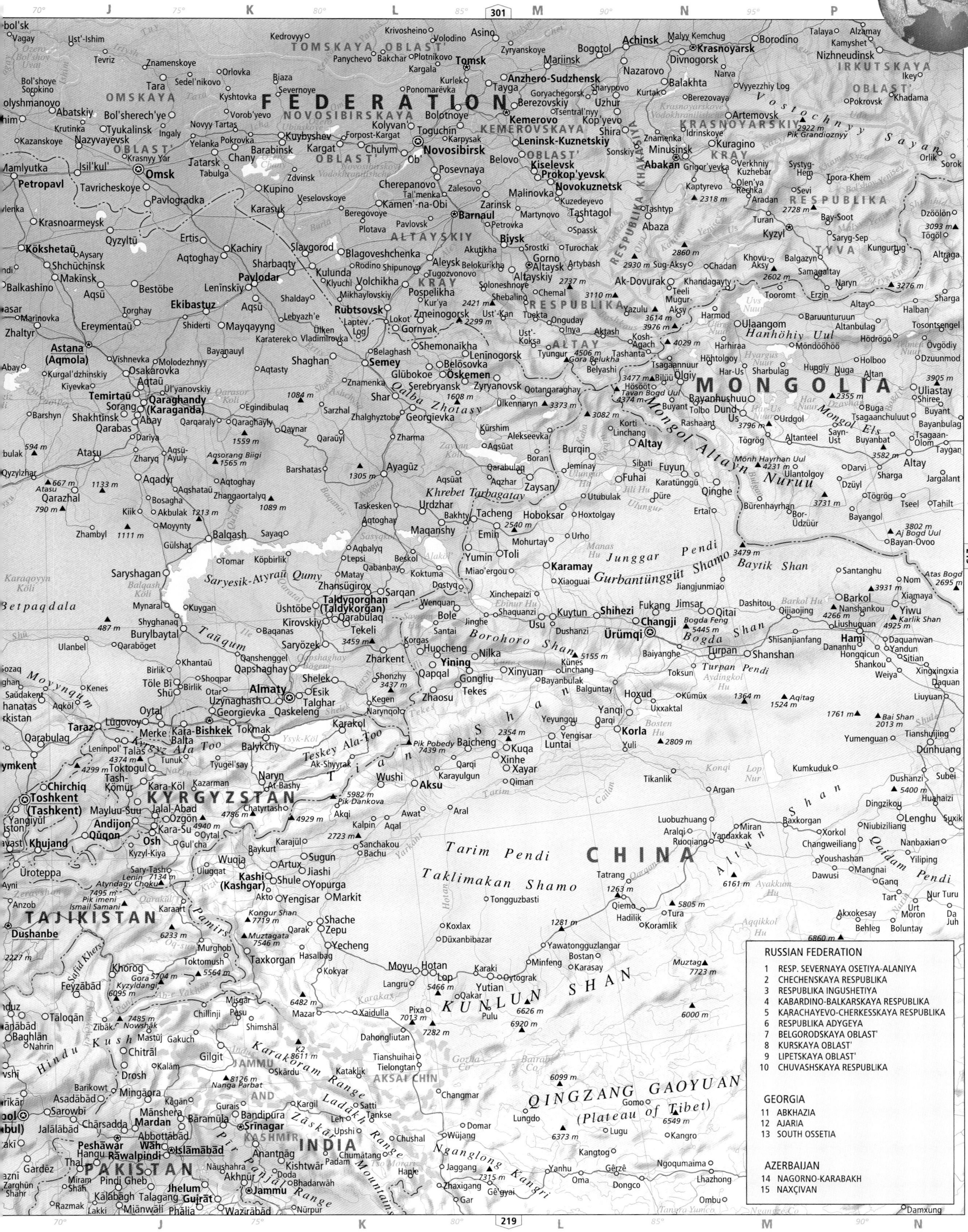

RUSSIAN FEDERATION

NOVOSIBIRSKAYA OBLAST'
OMSKAYA OBLAST'
KEMEROVSKAYA OBLAST'
KRASNOYARSKIY KRAY
IRKUTSKAYA OBLAST'
ALTAYSKIY KRAY
RESPUBLIKA KHAKASIYA
RESPUBLIKA TYVA
RESPUBLIKA ALTAY

MONGOLIA

CHINA

KAZAKHSTAN

KYRGYZSTAN

TAJIKISTAN

PAKISTAN

INDIA

JAMMU AND KASHMIR

AKSAI CHIN

QINGZANG GAOYUAN
(Plateau of Tibet)

Tarim Pendi
Taklimakan Shamo
Kunlun Shan
Tian Shan
Junggar Pendi
Gurbantünggüt Shamo
Turpan Pendi
Hindu Kush
Karakoram Range
Pamirs
Altun Shan
Qaidam Pendi
Nganglong Kangri

Krasnoyarsk
Tomsk
Novosibirsk
Omsk
Barnaul
Biysk
Kemerovo
Novokuznetsk
Abakan
Achinsk
Petropavl
Astana (Aqmola)
Pavlodar
Semey
Öskemen
Karaganda (Qaraghandy)
Ürümqi
Almaty
Bishkek
Tashkent (Toshkent)
Dushanbe
Islāmābād
Srinagar
Kashi (Kashgar)
Hotan
Korla
Hami
Turpan
Changji
Shihezi
Karamay
Altay
Uliastay

0 100 200 300 400 kilometers
0 100 200 miles
Scale 1:10,000,000
Projection: Equidistant Conic

Turkey • East Europe

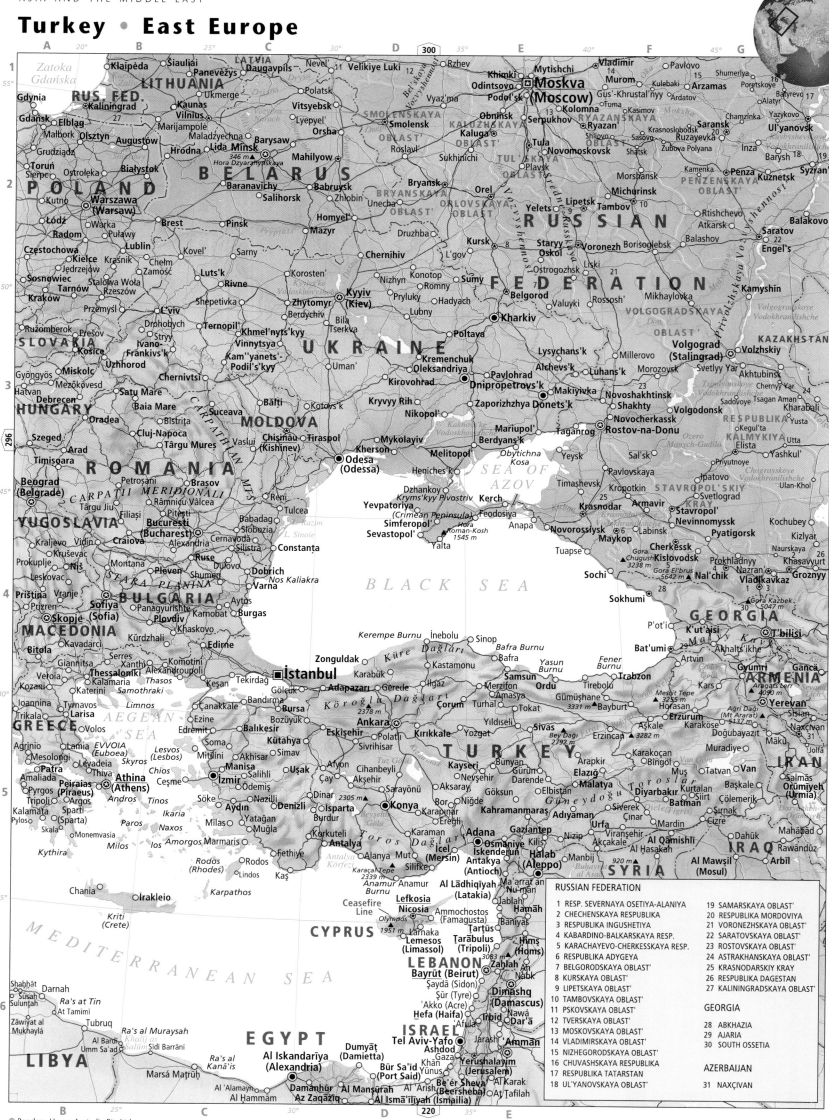

RUSSIAN FEDERATION

1 RESP. SEVERNAYA OSETIYA-ALANIYA	19 SAMARSKAYA OBLAST'
2 CHECHENSKAYA RESPUBLIKA	20 RESPUBLIKA MORDOVIYA
3 RESPUBLIKA INGUSHETIYA	21 VORONEZHSKAYA OBLAST'
4 KABARDINO-BALKARSKAYA RESP.	22 SARATOVSKAYA OBLAST'
5 KARACHAYEVO-CHERKESSKAYA RESP.	23 ROSTOVSKAYA OBLAST'
6 RESPUBLIKA ADYGEYA	24 ASTRAKHANSKAYA OBLAST'
7 BELGORODSKAYA OBLAST'	25 KRASNODARSKIY KRAY
8 KURSKAYA OBLAST'	26 RESPUBLIKA DAGESTAN
9 LIPETSKAYA OBLAST'	27 KALININGRADSKAYA OBLAST'
10 TAMBOVSKAYA OBLAST'	
11 PSKOVSKAYA OBLAST'	**GEORGIA**
12 TVERSKAYA OBLAST'	
13 MOSKOVSKAYA OBLAST'	28 ABKHAZIA
14 VLADIMIRSKAYA OBLAST'	29 AJARIA
15 NIZHEGORODSKAYA OBLAST'	30 SOUTH OSSETIA
16 CHUVASHSKAYA RESPUBLIKA	
17 RESPUBLIKA TATARSTAN	**AZERBAIJAN**
18 UL'YANOVSKAYA OBLAST'	31 NAXÇIVAN

kilometers 0 100 200 300 400
miles 0 100 200
Scale 1:10,000,000   Projection: Equidistant Conic

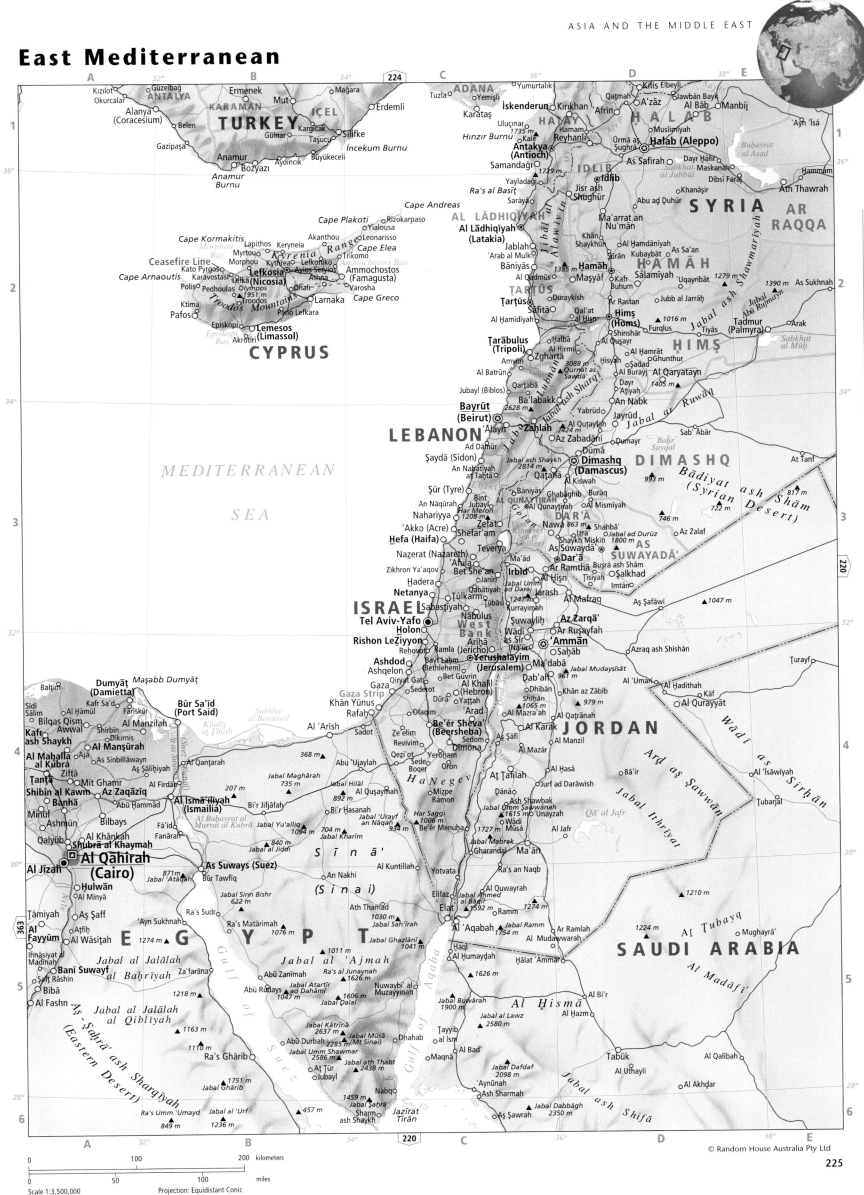

East Mediterranean

TURKEY

Kızılot
Okurcalar
Güzelbağ
ANTALYA
Ermenek
Mut
Mağara
Erdemli
Tuzla
ADANA
Yumurtalık
Yemişli
Qatmah
Kilis Elbeyli
Jawbān Bayk
Al Bāb
Manbij
Alanya
(Coracesium)
Belen
Gülnar
Kargıcak
Taşucu
Silifke
İncekum Burnu
İskenderun
Kırıkhan
Afrin
A'zāz
KARAMAN
İÇEL
HATAY
Ūrmā aş
Şughūr
Muslimīyah
Gazipaşa
Anamur
Bozyazı
Aydıncık
Büyükeceli
Karataş
Uluçınar
1735 m
Hamam
Reyhanlı
HALAB
Halab (Aleppo)
As Safirah
'Ayn 'Īsā
Anamur
Burnu
Hınzır Burnu
Kale
Antakya
(Antioch)
Samandağı
1729 m
IDLIB
Idlib
Abu aḍ Ḍuhūr
Khānāzir
Dayr Ḥāfir
Maskanah
Dibsi Faraj
Ath Thawrah
Hammām
Ra's al Basīṭ
Yayladağı
Jisr ash
Shughūr
SYRIA
AR
RAQQA
Buḩayrat
al Asad

CYPRUS

Cape Andreas
Rizokarpaso
Cape Plakoti
Yialousa
Cape Kormakitis
Lapithos
Keryneia
Leonarisso
Cape Elea
Akanthou
Morphou
Bay
Myrtou
Kyrenia Range
Trikomo
Cape Arnaoutis
Morphou
Kythrea
Lefkoniko
Athna
Ammochostos Bay
Ceasefire Line
Kato Pyrgos
Lefka
Ayios Seryios
Ammochostos
(Famagusta)
Polis
Lefkosia
(Nicosia)
Dhali
Varosha
Pedhoulas
Olympos
1951 m
Troodos
Larnaka
Ktima
Troodos Mountains
Pano Lefkara
Cape Greco
Pafos
Episkopi
Akrotiri
Lemesos
(Limassol)
Episkopi
Bay

AL LĀDHIQĪYAH
Al Lādhiqīyah
(Latakia)
Jablah
'Arab al Mulk
Bāniyās
Al Qadmūs
Maṣyāf
Kafr
Buḩum
Ma'arrat an
Nu'mān
Khān
Shaykhūn
Al Ḥamdānīyah
As Sa'an
1385 m
Hamāh
Ṣalamīyah
'Uqayribāt
1279 m
HAMĀH
1390 m
As Sukhnah
TARṬŪS
Duraykīsh
Ar Rastan
Jubb al Jarrāḥ
Jabal ash Shawmarīyah
Ṭarṭūs
Ṣāfītā
Qal'at
al Ḥisn
Shinshār
Furqluṣ
Tiyās
Tadmur
(Palmyra)
Arak
Al Ḥamīdīyah
Abū
Rujmayn
1016 m
Jabal

Ṭarābulus
(Tripoli)
Ḥalbā
Al Hirmil
Ḥimṣ
(Homs)
Ḩisyah
Ghunthur
Dayr
'Aṭīyah
1405 m
Al Qaryatayn
Sabkhat
al Mūḩ
Zgharta
Amyūn
Al Quṣayr
Al Ḥamrān
Şadad
An Nabk
Jabal ar Ruwāq
Al Batrūn
3088 m
Qurnāt as
Sawdā'
Yabrūd
Jayrūd
At Tanf
Jubayl (Biblos)
Qarṭabā
Ba'labakk
2628 m
HIMṢ

LEBANON

Bayrūt
(Beirut)
'Ālayh
Zaḩlah
Az Zabadānī
Ad Damūr
2424 m
Al Quṭayfah
Dumayr
Sab' Ābār
Bāir
Saygal
Şaydā (Sidon)
Jabal ash Shaykh
2814 m
Dimashq
(Damascus)
DIMASHQ
Bādiyat ash Shām
(Syrian Desert)
An Nabaṭīyah
at Taḩtā
Qaṭanā
Al Kiswah
993 m
817 m
Şūr (Tyre)
Bint
AL QUNAYṬIRAH
Ghabāghib
Burāq
746 m
722 m
An Nāqūrah
Jubayl
Al Qunayṭirah
Al Mismīyah
Az Zalaf
Nahariyya
Har Meron
1208 m
DAR'Ā
Shahbā'
'Akko (Acre)
Zefat
Nawa
863 m
Izra
Jabal ad Durūz
AS
SUWAYDĀ'
Ḥefa (Haifa)
Shefar'am
Teverya
Shaykh Miskīn
1800 m
Az Zalaf
Naẓerat (Nazareth)
Ma'ad
Aş Şuwaydā'
Dar'ā
Buşrā ash Shām
Şalkhad
'Afula
Ar Ramthā
Jabal Umm
ad Daraj
Al Ḥiṣn
Tisīyah
Imtān
Zikhron Ya'aqov
Bet She'an
Janin
Irbid
Jarash
Bet Sheʻan

ISRAEL

Hadera
Qābāṭiyah
1247 m
Tūbās
Kurrayimah
An Mafraq
1047 m
Netanya
Tūlkarm
Nābulus
Suwaylih
Az Zarqā'
Sabasṭiyah
Ar Ruṣayfah
Tel Aviv-Yafo
Holon
West
Bank
Wādi
aş Sir
'Ammān
Azraq ash Shīshān
Rishon LeZiyyon
Ramla
Arīḥā
(Jericho)
Na'ūr
Saḩāb
Turayf
Rehovot
Bayt Laḩm
(Bethlehem)
Yerushalayim
(Jerusalem)
Ma'dabā
Jabal Mudaysīsāt
961 m
Ashdod
Qiryat Gat
Bet Guvrin
Al Khalīl
(Hebron)
Dhībān
Khān az Zābīb
Al 'Umarī
Al Ḥadītha
Ashqelon
Sederot
Dūra
Yaṭṭā
Shīḩān
1065 m
979 m
Al Qurayyāt
Gaza
Gaza Strip
Khān Yūnis
Rafaḩ
Ofaqim
Ar 'Arad
Al Mazra'ah
Ṭafīlah
Dumyāṭ
(Damietta)
Maşabb Dumyāṭ
Be'er Sheva'
(Beersheba)
Al Qaṭrānah
Baltīm
Sīdī
Sālim
Al Ḥāmūl
Kafr Sa'd
Fāriskūr
Al Manzilah
Sabkhat
al Bardawīl
Al 'Arīsh
Sadot
Ze'elim
Dimona
Sedom
Al Karak
JORDAN
Bilqas Qism
Awwal
Shirbin
Dīkirnis
Khalīj
aṭ Ṭīnah
Revivim
Yeroḩam
Oron
Aş Şāfī
Al Manzil
Kafr
ash Shaykh
Al Manşūrah
Ajā
As Sinbillāwayn
Aş Şāliḩiyah
Aṭ Qanṭarah
368 m
Qezi'ot
Sede
Boqer
HaNegev
Al Ḥasā
Bā'ir
Al Maḩalla
al Kubrā
Ṭanṭā
Zifta
Mīt Ghamr
Abū Ḩammād
Al Firdān
207 m
Abū 'Ujaylah
Mizpe
Ramon
Har Saggi
1006 m
Ash Shawbak
Jabal Umm
Şawwānah
1615 m
Aṭ Ṭafīlah
Jurf ad Darāwīsh
Shibīn al Kawm
Banhā
Az Zaqāzīq
Al Ismā'īlīyah
(Ismailia)
892 m
Bi'r Jifjāfah
Jabal Maghārah
735 m
Jabal Hilāl
Bi'r Ḥasanah
Al Quşaymah
Be'er Menuḩa
934 m
1727 m
Jabal Mūsā
Unayzah
Minūf
Ashmūn
Fā'id
Bilbays
Al Buḩayrat
al Murrat al Kubrā
Jabal Yu'alliq
1094 m
704 m
Jabal Kharīm
Wādī
Mūsā
Jabal Mabrak
1210 m
Qalyūb
Al Khānkah
840 m
Jabal al Jiddī
Ma'ān
Shubrā al Khaymah
Al Qāhirah
(Cairo)
As Suways (Suez)
Sīnā'
An Nakhl
Al Kuntillah
Yotvata
Gharandal
Ra's an Naqb
Al Jīzah
Ḥulwān
871 m
Jabal 'Aṭāqah
Būr Tawfīq
(Sinai)
Elifaz
Jabal Aḩmed
al Baḩir
1592 m
Al Quwayrah
Ṭāmiyah
Al Minyā
Ra's Sudr
622 m
Jabal Sinn Bishr
Ath Thamad
1030 m
Jabal Sah'īrah
Elat
Ramm
1274 m
Ar Ramlah
1224 m
Aṭ Ṭubayq
Mughayrā'
Aş Şaff
Aṭfīḩ
1076 m
Ra's Maṭārimah
1041 m
Al 'Aqabah
Jabal Ramm
1754 m
Al Mudawwarah
Al
Fayyūm
Al Wāsiṭah
1274 m
1011 m
Jabal Ghazlānī
Ḩaql
Al Ḥumaydah
Ḩālat 'Ammār
SAUDI ARABIA

EGYPT

Iḩnāsiyat al
Madīnah
Jabal al Jalālah
al Baḩrīyah
Za'farāna
Jabal al 'Ajmah
1626 m
Al Ḥismā
Banī Suwayf
Abū Zanīmah
Abū Rudays
Jabal Atarṭīr
ad Dahāmī
1047 m
1218 m
1606 m
Jabal Dalal
Nuwaybi' al
Muzayyinah
Jabal Buwayrah
1900 m
1626 m
Al Bi'r
Biba
1163 m
Jabal al Jalālah
al Qiblīyah
(Eastern Desert)
1110 m
1751 m
Ra's Ghārib
Jabal Kātrīnā
2637 m
Dhahab
Jabal al Lawz
2580 m
Tabūk
Al Uthaylī
Al Fashn
As-Şaḩrā' ash Sharqīyah
Jabal Ghārib
1236 m
Abū Durbah
Jabal Mūsā
2285 (Mt Sinai)
Jabal Umm Shawmar
2586 m
Ṭayyib
al Ism
Al Bad'
Jabal Dafdaf
2098 m
Ra's Umm 'Umayd
849 m
Aṭ Ṭūr
Jubayl
Jabal ath Thābt
2438 m
Maqnā
'Aynūnah
Jabal Dabbāgh
2350 m
Al Qalībah
1459 m
Jabal Şaḩrā'
457 m
Nabq
Ash Sharmah
Al Akhḍar
Jazīrat
Tīrān
Sharm
ash Shaykh

MEDITERRANEAN
SEA

Gulf of Suez
Gulf of Aqaba

0   100   200 kilometers
0   50   100 miles

Scale 1:3,500,000
Projection: Equidistant Conic

225

Europe and the Russian Federation

Europe and the Russian Federation

Covering 10.5 million sq km (4 million sq miles), Europe is the second smallest continent in the world. It is part of the Eurasian landmass and its conventional separation from Asia is therefore more cultural than physical. The Ural Mountains and Ural River, the Caspian and Red seas, and the Dardanelles Straits separate Europe from Asia and, to the south, the Mediterranean Sea separates it from Africa.

The countries of Europe can be divided into three groups: Western Europe, Eastern Europe (most countries of which came under the influence of the former Soviet Union), and the countries that emerged from the break-up of the former Soviet Union. Each of these groups can be distinguished by the history of its political systems.

Western Europe includes Andorra, Austria, Belgium, Denmark, Finland, France, Germany, Greece, Iceland, Ireland, Italy, Liechtenstein, Luxembourg, Malta, Monaco, the Netherlands, Norway, Portugal, San Marino, Spain, Sweden, Switzerland, the United Kingdom and Vatican City. There are also several dependencies: Guernsey, Jersey, the Isle of Man, and Gibraltar are dependencies of the United Kingdom, the Faeroe Islands of Denmark and Svalbard of Norway.

The nations of Eastern Europe are Poland, Hungary, the Czech Republic, Slovakia, Bulgaria, Romania, Slovenia, Croatia, Bosnia and Herzegovina, Macedonia, Yugoslavia and Albania. Yugoslavia currently consists of Serbia and Montenegro.

When the former Soviet Union broke up, several new nations emerged in Europe and Asia; the European nations consist of the Russian Federation, Ukraine, Belarus, Latvia, Lithuania, Estonia, and Moldova.

During the last 500 years, Europe has exerted a strong influence on the rest of the world through colonialism. Several Western European countries were colonial powers and their languages have become international; European sciences, laws, and arts have spread around the globe. European

A valley (with vineyards) in Switzerland (below), and a beech forest in Germany (right), both in Western Europe.

companies developed commercial agriculture, mining, and manufacturing in their colonies. The colonial powers promoted European migration to the Americas, Australia, and New Zealand—Europeans are now the dominant people there. Many Europeans also migrated to South Africa.

Physical features

The elongated Tertiary Period mountain chain that stretches between the Alps in France and the Carpathians in Romania, rising 3,000 to 4,500 m (10,000 to 15,000 ft), is a prominent feature in Europe. In contrast, there are geologically old and worn-down mountains in Scandinavia and northern Britain. Glacial carving, including sharp-peaked mountains (such as the Matterhorn) and flat-bottomed and steep-sided glacial valleys as in Switzerland, is found in most European mountainous areas. Along the Scandinavian coasts there are fiords, which are glacial valleys drowned by the sea. There are extensive plains in Central and Eastern Europe and France. Europe is well watered by a large number of rivers—the Volga, the Danube, the Rhône, and the Rhine. Many of these rivers are navigable far inland and are interconnected in places by canals.

Climate and vegetation

Although much of Europe can be described as humid temperate, significant climatic differences exist within its borders. The climates of Western Europe are moderated by the Atlantic Ocean, which is warmed by the waters of the Gulf Stream.

In contrast, the winter temperatures in continental Russia are below freezing.

The northernmost parts of Europe are treeless, with very cold winters and mild summers. Further south is the taiga, with broad-leaf deciduous and needle-leaf coniferous trees covering large tracts of land, particularly in Russia.

Cool, humid temperate climates stretch along the coast of the Atlantic Ocean between northern Spain and Norway, including Iceland. This area is characterized by mixed forests, but most of the original trees have been cleared. Some forests, like the Black Forest, have been harmed by acid rain.

Further inland, Central and Eastern Europe experience more extreme temperature ranges. There is a semiarid belt in the south, and forests are found in the wetter and higher areas. The drier regions with less reliable rainfall, such as the Ukraine and southwestern Russia, are characterized by extensive steppes of short grasses.

The southern Mediterranean belt experiences hot, dry summers and cool, wet winters. Forests and scrub cover large areas.

Population

The population of Europe at present (excluding the Russian Federation) totals 701 million. The relatively high standards of living in most European nations are reflected in life expectancies of 68.3 years for males and 77 years for females. Population numbers are stable, with a near zero growth rate. The Russian Federation has 147.2 million people; its life expectancies are 58 years for males and 75 years for females.

There has been significant urbanization in Europe since the nineteenth century, and this accelerated following the Second World War. Currently 74 percent of the population lives in cities and towns (84 percent in northern Europe and 65 percent in southern Europe); the figure for the Russian Federation is 76 percent.

Agriculture

Europe has a well-developed agricultural economy based on a wide range of food and animal products. Farming is more advanced in Western Europe, in terms of technology and organization, than in the former communist countries of Eastern Europe, which experimented with collectivized agriculture for several decades. Farm size varies considerably, but pressure to create larger farm units is changing the agricultural landscape.

Within Europe's cool, humid zone, mixed farming (grain growing and livestock rearing) is widespread. Wheat, barley, and rye are the main grains, and sheep and cattle the main livestock. Dairy farming is important in some of the cool countries such as the Netherlands and Denmark. Apples and pears are significant fruits.

Southern Europe, with its warm, dry summers and mild winters is suited to growing grapes, citrus fruits, and olives. Irrigation is extensively used in parts of the Mediterranean areas; for growing rice, for example.

There is extensive fishing in the Atlantic Ocean and in both the Mediterranean and Black Seas.

Industrialization

Europe was the first part of the world to become industrialized, and through scientific innovation and extensive use of technology, remains one of the world's most developed regions. British and French industries, in particular, benefited from raw materials supplied by their colonies; the colonies in turn provided markets for manufactured goods.

Manufacturing in Europe ranges from the processing of agricultural raw materials, as in the production of wine and olive oil, and the manufacturing of basic industrial items such as steel, petroleum refining, chemicals, fertilizers and cement, to the production of highly sophisticated items like cars, ships, aircraft, and electronic goods.

While European industries largely import the minerals they require, there are some significant mineral deposits in the region—coal (in several places), petroleum (in the North Sea and Eastern Europe), and iron ore (in Ukraine and Russia). The Russian Federation exports natural gas by pipeline to several European countries, and it is also a major producer of gold.

Considerable damage was done to industry and infrastructure during both world wars, particularly the second, but Europe rebuilt. Western Europe prospered, with large-scale restructuring and industrialization, while communist-controlled Eastern Europe lagged behind. These nations are now joining the market economy, but it will take time for them to catch up. Currently some East European nations are economically stagnant and the Russian Federation, facing economic collapse, needs foreign aid to restructure its economy.

Industrialization and urbanization have taken their toll on the environment. Air pollution, acid rain, and river-water pollution are common. Sulfur dioxide levels have been reduced, thanks to international cooperation, but nitrogen oxides emissions remain high. The Mediterranean, Black and Baltic seas have been badly affected by the discharge of waste products.

Languages

Europe has a large number of languages, most of them belonging to the three major Indo-European language family groups: the Latin-based (Romance), the Germanic, and the Slavic.

The Latin-based languages include Spanish, Italian, French, Portuguese, and Romanian. The Germanic languages comprise English, German, Dutch, Danish, Swedish, and Norwegian. Latvian and Lithuanian are distinct Baltic languages. Celtic languages (Irish and Scottish Gaelic and Welsh) are spoken by minorities in the British Isles and also in France (Breton). The main Slavic languages are Russian, Ukrainian, Belarusian, Polish, Czech, Slovak, and Bulgarian, while another group (Serbo-Croatian, Slovene, and Macedonian) is found in the Balkans.

Other languages include Greek, Albanian, and Turkish, which are spoken in parts of the Balkans; Finnish in Scandinavia; and Basque and Catalan in Spain and France.

While most European nations have a dominant language, there are some exceptions. Switzerland has French, German, and Italian-speaking zones, and Belgium is divided into Flemish and French-speaking areas. There are German-speaking areas in Hungary, the Czech Republic, Poland, and France, and there are Russian-speaking minorities in all the former Soviet Union nations.

Boundary disputes and wars

The First and Second World Wars both began as boundary disputes between European countries before engulfing most of the continent. The domination of Eastern Europe by the powerful former Soviet Union resulted in a political, ideological, and military "iron curtain" dividing the continent until the early 1990s. Currently most of Europe's national boundaries are accepted, with some exceptions. The break-up of Yugoslavia resulted in ethnic wars which sought to redraw the existing boundaries; this was notable in the division of Bosnia and Herzegovina. The current division of Cyprus into Greek and Turkish areas is a source of friction between those countries. Spain's claim to British-held Gibraltar is another contested issue, though otherwise these countries remain friendly.

Several language-based separatist movements exist in Europe, some involving armed conflict—in the Basque and Catalan regions of Spain, Corsica (in France), and Kosovo (in Serbia).

St Basil's Church, in Moscow, Russia (below), shows the art that has been so often created in the name of religion. Nikia, in the Aegean Islands (above left), has been inhabited by humans for thousands of years.

Nations

Albania

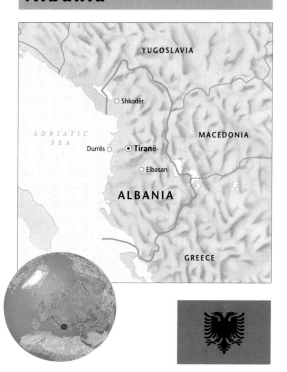

Fact File

OFFICIAL NAME Republic of Albania

FORM OF GOVERNMENT Republic with single legislative body (National Assembly)

CAPITAL Tiranë

AREA 28,750 sq km (11,100 sq miles)

TIME ZONE GMT + 1 hour

POPULATION 3,364,571

PROJECTED POPULATION 2005 3,591,121

POPULATION DENSITY 117 per sq km (303 per sq mile)

LIFE EXPECTANCY 69

INFANT MORTALITY (PER 1,000) 42.9

OFFICIAL LANGUAGE Albanian

OTHER LANGUAGE Greek

LITERACY RATE 85%

RELIGIONS Muslim 70%, Albanian Orthodox 20%, Roman Catholic 10%

ETHNIC GROUPS Albanian 95%, Greek 3%, other 2%

CURRENCY Lek

ECONOMY Agriculture 55%, industry 27%, services 18%

GNP PER CAPITA US$670

CLIMATE Mild temperate with cold, wet winters and warm, dry summers; colder in mountains

HIGHEST POINT Maja e Korabit 2,753 m (9,032 ft)

MAP REFERENCE Pages 296–97

Albania shares borders with Greece to the south-east and Macedonia to the east. Yugoslavia wraps around the northern part of the country. At its western edge it has a coastline 362 km (225 miles) long along the Adriatic Sea. For 500 years until 1912, when it became independent, Albania was part of the Ottoman Empire, and a large majority of the population is Muslim. In 1939 Albania was invaded by Italy. After the Second World War the country came into the Soviet sphere of influence. From 1946 until 1992 Albania was part of the Soviet bloc,

although it often adopted policies independent of, and sometimes at odds with, the Moscow line. When the European communist system unraveled in the early 1990s Albania, in 1992, was the last country in Europe to abandon a communist regime.

Except for a narrow strip of plains along its coastline, Albania is hilly and mountainous. Most Albanian people eke out an existence through farming on the plains, which contain the only cultivable land. Even here, much of the country is marshy and difficult to access. Corn, wheat, barley, and fruits are among the main crops. Little is exported because transport methods are primitive. In most areas people use horse- or mule-drawn vehicles. Mountains cover seven-tenths of the country. In the north are the Albanian Alps, and there are highlands in the center and south. Numerous rivers, notably the Drin in the north, and the Vijose in the south, flow to the coast from the highlands. Albania has significant reserves of natural resources such as petroleum, iron, and other mineral ores, plus natural gas, but most remain undeveloped.

The mountainous landscape makes land access difficult, and marshes restrict access to much of the coast. Rail links are few and there are no railway lines to neighboring countries. This has contributed to Albania's relative cultural and linguistic distinctness. Despite its conversion to free market ideals, Albania has failed to emerge from the cycle of poverty, continuing food shortages, and violence, fed to a large extent by the flood of refugees from the troubles in former Yugoslavia.

Andorra

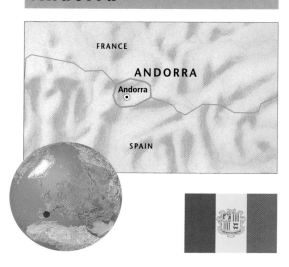

The tiny landlocked principality of Andorra sits high in the Pyrenees, between France and Spain. From 1278 Andorra's government was shared between France and Spain. For 300 years it was jointly administered by the Bishop of Urgel in Spain and the Count of Foix in France. In the sixteenth century sovereignty passed to the French king and, after the French Revolution of 1789, to the French head of state. Today the Bishop of Urgel and the French president are official chiefs of state. Since 1993, however, when the first democratic elections were held, authority has been vested in a 28-member General Council of the Valleys. France and Spain are responsible for defence, and both have a representative on the General Council.

Andorra is mountainous with spectacular peaks. The country is snow-covered for six months in

winter, but summers are warm and dry. Two south-flowing branches of the River Valira—the Valira del Nord and the Valira d'Orient—flow through a series of valleys and gorges between ranges. They join in the center of the country and flow as one stream into Spain. The Valira is a major source of hydroelectric power.

About one in five in the population are citizens of Andorra: the rest are foreign residents, mainly French and Spanish. Almost two-thirds of the population live in the capital and the cities of Les Escaldes and Encamp. Tourism is the mainstay of the economy, and every year there are more than 12 million visitors, mainly skiers. Goods are duty-free in Andorra. This acts as a magnet to tourists and is vital to the economy, as is the sale of hydroelectricity to neighboring Catalonia. Banking services are significant, but there is little secondary industry, apart from cigarette and cigar making. As well as tobacco, some fruit, vegetables, and other crops are grown on the tiny amount of land that can be cultivated. Many of the village-dwellers are small farmers. Their sheep, cattle, and goats graze in the upland meadows during summer.

Fact File

OFFICIAL NAME Principality of Andorra

FORM OF GOVERNMENT Co-principality with single legislative body (General Council of the Valleys)

CAPITAL Andorra la Vella

AREA 450 sq km (174 sq miles)

TIME ZONE GMT + 1 hour

POPULATION 65,939

PROJECTED POPULATION 2005 79,608

POPULATION DENSITY 146.5 per sq km (375.6 per sq mile)

LIFE EXPECTANCY 83.5

INFANT MORTALITY (PER 1,000) 4.1

OFFICIAL LANGUAGE Catalan

OTHER LANGUAGES French, Spanish

LITERACY RATE 99%

RELIGIONS Roman Catholic

ETHNIC GROUPS Spanish 61%, Andorran 30%, French 6%, other 3%

CURRENCY French franc, Spanish peseta

ECONOMY Tourism, financial services, tobacco production

GNP PER CAPITA Est. > US$9,386

CLIMATE Temperate; snowy winter, warm summers

HIGHEST POINT Coma Pedrosa 2,946 m (9,665 ft)

MAP REFERENCE Page 293

Austria

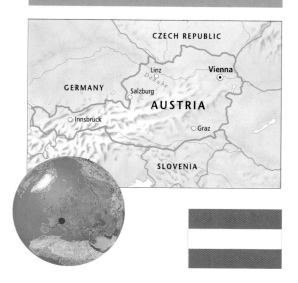

The present borders of this landlocked central European country date back to the Treaty of Versailles of 1919, which presided over the dismantling of the Austro-Hungarian Empire. Germany lies directly to the north of Austria's narrow western boundary, Switzerland and Liechtenstein to its west, and Italy to its south. At its wider eastern end Slovenia lies to the south, Hungary and Slovakia to the east, and the Czech Republic to the north.

Austria's history for most of the last millennium is bound up with the fortunes of the Hapsburg family who ruled it, and at times much of the rest of Europe, from 1278 until the First World War. Roman conquest of most of present-day Austria was followed in the fourth and fifth centuries AD by invasions by Germanic and Celtic tribes and by the Franks under Charlemagne during the eighth century. The land fell to the King of Bohemia in 1252, only to be wrested from him by Rudolf of Hapsburg 26 years later. Rudolf named himself Archduke and declared the title hereditary.

From then until the sixteenth century the Hapsburg Empire expanded until it dominated much of Europe, including Spain (as well as its American colonies), part of Italy, the Netherlands, and Burgundy. During the sixteenth century Hungary and Bohemia came under Hapsburg rule and a Turkish siege of Vienna was repulsed. Catholic Austria's forced capitulation to German Protestantism at the end of the Thirty Years War saw Austria take second place to France as the leading European power. However, it remained a significant force with dominion over much of Europe, despite its loss of control over Spain in the early eighteenth century, a debilitating War of Succession between 1740 and 1748, and defeat by Prussian forces in 1763.

Napoleon's victory at the Battle of Austerlitz was a low point for Austria, but on Napoleon's defeat in 1814 Austria emerged as leader of a new German Confederation. Following the Austro-Prussian War of 1866, Austria and Hungary were combined under Hapsburg rule to form the Austro-Hungarian Empire. Austrian annexation of Bosnia and Herzegovina in 1908 created the circumstances which culminated in the assassination of the heir to the Austro-Hungarian throne in

The fourteenth-century citadel of Gjirokastër in Albania (top left). Winter in the town of Zel am Zeere in Austria (right).

Sarajevo in 1914 and the outbreak of the First World War. When the empire ended after the war, the Hapsburgs were expelled and Austria became a republic bounded by its present borders.

Annexed by Nazi Germany in 1938, Austria was part of the Third Reich until occupied by Allied forces in 1945. The Allies did not withdraw until 1955, when Austria was recognized internationally as an independent, democratic, and permanently neutral state. Today Austria is governed by a bicameral parliament elected for four-year terms. The president, whose role is essentially ceremonial, is directly elected for a six-year term.

Physical features and land use

Almost two-thirds of Austria consists of the Alps, which sweep west to east across the country in a succession of ranges almost as far as Vienna. Much of the alpine area is characterized by snowfields, glaciers, and snowy peaks. About one-third of the country's population lives in the valleys between the ranges. To the north of the Alps, the lower, heavily forested mountains of the Bohemian Massif, which cover about one-tenth of the land area, extend across the borders of the Czech Republic and Slovakia. Lowland areas lie along the eastern end of the Alps, extending into Hungary, and in the Danube Valley in the north. Most of Austria's main transport routes traverse this northern "corridor," which links Germany with Vienna and countries farther east. Almost all the arable land is in the northeast, and is divided between pasture and croplands. Root crops, such as potatoes and cereals, are the principal crops. There are also extensive vineyards which supply a significant wine industry. The main livestock are cattle and pigs.

Industry, commerce, and culture

Austria is not rich in mineral resources, although it has some reserves of oil, iron ore, brown coal, and magnesite—a major resource in chemical industries. It imports most of the raw materials it needs for the manufacturing industries that form the backbone of its economy. More than 70 percent of electricity is generated hydroelectrically. Iron and steel making are the principal heavy industries and are large export earners. Aluminum, chemicals, and food processing are also significant.

Tourism, based largely on the many alpine ski resorts, but also on the cultural attractions of such cities as Vienna and Salzburg, contributes greatly to the country's economic well-being. There are about 18 million visitors each year.

Austrians are generally conservative in their social attitudes and financial habits. They are savers rather than spenders or investors and the country has a high proportion of its wealth in savings deposits. Much of the country's industry, including iron and steel, and energy production is nationalized and there is a well-developed system of state social services. Most Austrians enjoy a comfortable lifestyle, exceptions being the many refugees from the former Yugoslav republics who have been entering the country during the 1990s.

Fact File

OFFICIAL NAME Republic of Austria

FORM OF GOVERNMENT Federal republic with two legislative bodies (Federal Council and National Council)

CAPITAL Vienna

AREA 83,850 sq km (32,374 sq miles)

TIME ZONE GMT + 1 hour

POPULATION 8,139,299

PROJECTED POPULATION 2005 8,194,253

POPULATION DENSITY 97.1 per sq km (251.4 per sq mile)

LIFE EXPECTANCY 77.5

INFANT MORTALITY (PER 1,000) 5.1

OFFICIAL LANGUAGE German

LITERACY RATE 99%

RELIGIONS Roman Catholic 85%, Protestant 6%, other 9%

ETHNIC GROUPS German 99.4%, Croatian 0.3%, Slovene 0.2%, other 0.1%

CURRENCY Schilling

ECONOMY Services 64%, industry 28%, agriculture 8%

GNP PER CAPITA US$26,890

CLIMATE Temperate with cold winters and mild to warm summers; colder in mountains

HIGHEST POINT Grossglockner 3,797 m (12,457 ft)

MAP REFERENCE Page 294

Belarus

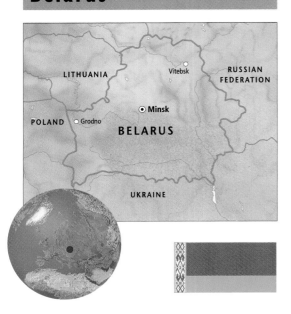

Fact File

OFFICIAL NAME Republic of Belarus

FORM OF GOVERNMENT Republic with single legislative body (Supreme Soviet)

CAPITAL Minsk

AREA 207,600 sq km (80,154 sq miles)

TIME ZONE GMT + 3 hours

POPULATION 10,401,784

PROJECTED POPULATION 2005 10,380,321

POPULATION DENSITY 50.1 per sq km (129.8 per sq mile)

LIFE EXPECTANCY 68.1

INFANT MORTALITY (PER 1,000) 14.4

OFFICIAL LANGUAGE Belarusian

OTHER LANGUAGE Russian

LITERACY RATE 97.9%

RELIGIONS Eastern Orthodox 60%, other (including Roman Catholic and small Muslim and Jewish communities) 40%

ETHNIC GROUPS Belarusian 78%, Russian 13%, Polish 4%, Ukrainian 3%, other 2%

CURRENCY Belarusian rouble

ECONOMY Industry 40%, services 39%, agriculture 21%

GNP PER CAPITA US$2,070

CLIMATE Temperate, with cold winters and mild, wet summers

HIGHEST POINT Mt Dzyarzhynskaya 346 m (1,135 ft)

MAP REFERENCE Pages 287, 299, 300

Until 1991, when it declared its independence of the disintegrating Soviet Union, Belarus was known as the Byelorussian (which means "White Russian") Soviet Socialist Republic. Throughout its extensive and troubled history, Belarus has been dominated, invaded, and sometimes devastated by a succession of foreign powers. Initally settled by Slavic tribes in the sixth century, the country came under the control of Kiev in the ninth century. Three centuries later it was conquered by invading armies from neighboring Lithuania and in the sixteenth century, with the merging of Lithuania and Poland, Polish influences were also dominant. During the course of the eighteenth century the region came under Russian control and even today Belarus is economically dependent on its huge eastern neighbor.

Belarus was ravaged in the First and Second World Wars. The German invasion of 1941 saw the deaths of 1.3 million people and the virtual annihilation of the country's Jewish population. Many of Belarus's buildings were reduced to rubble and its capital, Minsk, was razed. Further devastation, in the form of nuclear contamination, occurred in 1986 after the Chernobyl disaster in Ukraine, its neighbor to the south. Much of the farming land in the southern part of Belarus remains contaminated by fallout from the accident and is unsafe for cultivation.

The country is generally low-lying, the landscape varying from sandy hills in the north to swampy areas in the south, many of which have been drained and their rich soils cultivated. There are about 11,000 lakes and the country is traversed by numerous rivers which complement the extensive road and railway networks as a major means of transporation. Forests and woodland cover about 30 percent of the country and almost half the land area is devoted to agriculture, the main crops being barley, rye, potatoes, sugar beet, and flax. There are large numbers of livestock, and dairy and pig farming are important industries.

Belarus is relatively poor in natural resources although it has significant reserves of peat and rock salt and small reserves of coal. It is deeply in debt to the Russian Federation and relies on Russia for the electricity needed to power its industries, which include vast petrochemical plants and truck manufacturing.

Strikes and industrial and political unrest have been a significant feature of Belarusian life during its short period as an independent nation, sometimes aggravated by the inability of the government to pay many of its workers. A contro-versial treaty that was signed with Russia in 1996 resulted in a substantial merging of aspects of the economy with that of its large neighbor. This was seen by many as a sign of a progressive whittling away of the country's independence.

Belgium

This small, densely populated country has a 60 km (40 mile) coastline on the North Sea and is bounded by France to the south, Luxembourg at its southeastern corner, Germany to the east, and the Netherlands to the north. Its name derives from the Belgae, the Gallic race that occupied the area when invading Roman armies arrived in the first century BC. Over more than 2,000 years the region has been dominated by a succession of foreign powers, which explains Belgium's linguistic diversity. From the eighteenth century, Belgium was ruled by Austria, France, then the Netherlands. In 1830 the Belgians declared their independence and installed Leopold I, a relative of the English Queen Victoria, as their king. Today the country is a parliamentary democracy with a monarch as head of state.

Belgium's population is divided into two main groups. The larger group, the Flemings, lives mostly in the north of the country and speaks Dutch. The south is inhabited by the French-speaking Walloons. There is also a German-speaking community to the east of the city of Liège.

Brussels, the capital, is officially bilingual. It is the headquarters of the European Union and the North Atlantic Treaty Organization.

Inland of the beaches and sand dunes along the North Sea lies a narrow strip of drained, reclaimed marshland, interspersed with dikes and traversed by canals. This region gives way to a central, fertile low-lying plain that rises to a low plateau north of the Meuse–Sambre river system. South of these rivers lie Belgium's uplands. In this rugged, sparsely populated area there are a number of mountain ranges, the most extensive of which is the Ardennes. This heavily wooded high plateau of sandstone and shale is punctuated by flat-topped peaks and cut by deep chasms and valleys. Forestry is the main industry in this southern region, where oak and beech trees predominate. Coal-mining, once important around the city of Charleroi, is now declining.

Belgium's agriculture is centered on its rich northern plain, where crops are secondary to livestock rearing. Although about half the land area has been cleared for agriculture, its contribution to the economy is not significant.

Sugar beet, potatoes, wheat, and barley are the main crops and livestock consists largely of pigs and cattle.

Belgium is a heavily industrialized country and its population is highly urbanized. Except for coal, it is poor in natural resources and relies heavily on imported raw materials to fuel its industries. Almost all the industrial centers are in the Flemish area, in the north of the country. Antwerp, Europe's third-largest port and the most populous city in Belgium, is the center of numerous heavy industries, including petroleum refining, plastics, petrochemical, and heavy machinery manufacture. The manufacture of textiles is particularly associated with the cities of Ghent and Bruges. Iron and steel making, food processing, and glass manufacture are other important industries. Many of the major industrial centers are connected by a network of canals, along which barges transport cargo. One of the most celebrated of these is the Albert Canal, which links Liège with Antwerp.

While heavy industry has contributed significantly to Belgium's export earnings, it has had a decidedly negative impact on the environment. The Meuse River, which is a major source of drinking water, has been severely polluted by industrial wastes and fertilizers. The acid rain that falls on Belgium and its neighboring countries has been attributed largely to the air pollution that is caused by Belgian industry.

Fact File

OFFICIAL NAME	Kingdom of Belgium
FORM OF GOVERNMENT	Federal constitutional monarchy with two legislative bodies (Senate and Chamber of Deputies)
CAPITAL	Brussels
AREA	30,510 sq km (11,780 sq miles)
TIME ZONE	GMT + 1 hour
POPULATION	10,182,034
PROJECTED POPULATION 2005	10,164,106
POPULATION DENSITY	333.7 per sq km (864.3 per sq mile)
LIFE EXPECTANCY	77.5
INFANT MORTALITY (PER 1,000)	6.2
OFFICIAL LANGUAGES	French, Dutch, German
LITERACY RATE	99%
RELIGIONS	Roman Catholic 75%, Protestant or other 25%
ETHNIC GROUPS	Fleming 55%, Walloon 33%, mixed or other 12%
CURRENCY	Belgian franc
ECONOMY	Services 77%, industry 20%, agriculture 3%
GNP PER CAPITA	US$24,710
CLIMATE	Temperate, with mild, wet winters and cool summers
HIGHEST POINT	Mt Botrange 694 m (2,277 ft)
MAP REFERENCE	Pages 288, 291

Buildings in Antwerp, Belgium (bottom left). A winter view of the Svislach River in Minsk, Belarus (top left). The historic city of Bruges in Belgium (left). Cows grazing in the Belgian countryside (bottom right).

Bosnia and Herzegovina

The federation of Bosnia and Herzegovina has a mere 20 km (12 miles) of coast at its southern tip on the Adriatic. It borders Croatia to the north and west and to the east it shares a border with what remains of the former Yugoslavia. Serbs first settled in Bosnia in the seventh century AD. In the twelfth century the country came under Hungarian control, and Ottoman Turks conquered it two centuries later. It was ceded to the Austro-Hungarian Empire in 1908, and in 1918 became part of the Kingdom of Serbs, Croats, and Slovenes, which was later renamed Yugoslavia.

The republic was formed in 1994 when, after several years of fighting, sparked by the breaking up of Yugoslavia in 1991, Bosnian Croats and Muslims agreed to joint control of the region. Fighting went on for a further 18 months as Bosnian Serbs, backed by Serbia, sought to have a portion of the country incorporated into Serbia. The war came to an end uneasily in 1995 when Serbia abandoned its claims on Bosnian territory. Now named Bosnia and Herzegovina, the country is divided for purposes of administration almost equally between the Muslim–Croat Federation and the Bosnian Serbs.

Much of the land is mountainous and the south consists largely of a harsh limestone plateau. About a quarter of the land, especially in the mountains, is covered in forests of pine and beech. Before the economy collapsed, forestry products were a major source of earnings. Most agriculture is centered in the fertile valley of the Sava River, which forms the border with Croatia. Crops include grapes, other fruit, and cereals. Sheep-raising is also significant. Most farms are small and, with the disruption caused by warfare, tend to be inefficient.

Bosnia-Herzegovina imports food and relies heavily on United Nations aid. Years of warfare have brought industry virtually to a standstill. Health and education services have also been severely disrupted.

Fact File

OFFICIAL NAME	Republic of Bosnia and Herzegovina
FORM OF GOVERNMENT	Federal republic with two legislative bodies (Chamber of Municipalities and Chamber of Citizens)
CAPITAL	Sarajevo
AREA	51,233 sq km (19,781 sq miles)
TIME ZONE	GMT + 1 hour
POPULATION	3,482,495
PROJECTED POPULATION 2005	3,758,243
POPULATION DENSITY	68 per sq km (176.1 per sq mile)
LIFE EXPECTANCY	67
INFANT MORTALITY (PER 1,000)	24.5
OFFICIAL LANGUAGES	Serbian, Croatian
LITERACY RATE	82%
RELIGIONS	Muslim 40%, Orthodox 31%, Catholic 15%, Protestant 4%, other 10%
ETHNIC GROUPS	Serb 40%, Bosnian Muslim 38%, Croat 22%
CURRENCY	Dinar
ECONOMY	Not available; war has disrupted employment
GNP PER CAPITA	Est. < US$765
CLIMATE	Cold winters and warm summers; cooler in the north and southern mountains
HIGHEST POINT	Mt Maglic 2,386 m (7,828 ft)
MAP REFERENCE	Pages 294, 296

Bulgaria

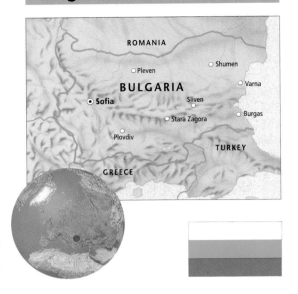

Bulgaria is situated on the east of the Balkan Peninsula with a coastline along the Black Sea. To the west it shares borders with Yugoslavia as well as Macedonia. Turkey lies to its southeast, and Greece to its southwest. In the north the River Danube forms most of the border between Bulgaria and Romania.

Modern Bulgarians are descendants of the Bulgars, who arrived from north of the Danube in the late seventh century AD and established dominance over the Slavic races that had settled the area over the previous two centuries. The Christian religion, which is still dominant in the country, was established in the ninth century. A century of Byzantine domination in the eleventh and twelfth centuries was followed by a period of independence. In 1396 Turkish armies invaded and Bulgaria was then dominated for five centuries by the Turks until Russian intervention ended Ottoman rule in 1878. Full independence, however, did not come until 1908, when Prince Ferdinand of Saxe-Coburg, the elected ruler of Bulgaria, assumed the title of Tsar.

Bulgaria sided with the losing sides in both the First and Second World Wars, and as a result its boundaries changed several times as territories were ceded to it or confiscated. Its present boundaries were established by a 1947 treaty. From then until the fall of the Soviet Union in the early 1990s, Bulgaria remained one of the most loyal of Soviet satellites. A new constitution came into force in 1991 and the following year the first free elections were held.

The country's landscape is defined by three ranges of mountains and two extensive expanses of lowland. The Danube Valley is the country's richest agricultural area, producing significant yields of wheat, maize, and other cereal crops. The Balkan Mountains, running east–west across much of central Bulgaria, reach heights of up to 2,000 m (6,500 ft). They divide the Danube Valley from the southern lowlands, where, in the fertile valleys around the Maritsa River, tobacco and grapes are among the principal crops. The vineyards in this region produce some of southern Europe's finest wines. In the south-west the Rhodopi Massif,

Dubrovnik old town in Croatia (left). One of the many churches in Sofia, Bulgaria (top right).

which contains the country's loftiest peak, forms the mountainous border with Greece.

More than 10 million tourists, attracted to its Black Sea coastline, come to Bulgaria each year and contribute significantly to its economy. Most of the country's export earnings stem from its machinery and other manufacturing industries. While there have been tentative moves towards the establishment of a free market economy, high inflation, foreign debt, and worker unrest have contributed to a short-term economic outlook that is far from robust.

Fact File

OFFICIAL NAME Republic of Bulgaria

FORM OF GOVERNMENT Republic with single legislative body (National Assembly)

CAPITAL Sofia

AREA 110,910 sq km (42,822 sq miles)

TIME ZONE GMT + 1 hour

POPULATION 8,194,772

PROJECTED POPULATION 2005 8,034,301

POPULATION DENSITY 73.9 per sq km (191.4 per sq mile)

LIFE EXPECTANCY 72.3

INFANT MORTALITY (PER 1,000) 12.4

OFFICIAL LANGUAGE Bulgarian

OTHER LANGUAGES Turkish, Romany

LITERACY RATE 93%

RELIGIONS Bulgarian Orthodox 85%, Muslim 13%, Jewish 0.8%, Roman Catholic 0.5%, Uniate Catholic 0.2%; Protestant, Gregorian–Armenian and other 0.5%

ETHNIC GROUPS Bulgarian 85.3%, Turkish 8.5%, Gypsy 2.6%, Macedonian 2.5%, Armenian 0.3%, Russian 0.2%, other 0.6%

CURRENCY Lev

ECONOMY Services 45%, industry 38%, agriculture 17%

GNP PER CAPITA US$1,330

CLIMATE Temperate, with cold, wet winters and hot, dry summers

HIGHEST POINT Mt Musala 2,925 m (9,596 ft)

MAP REFERENCE Pages 296–97

Croatia

Croatia wraps around the northern and western extremities of Bosnia and Herzegovina, allowing its neighbor a tiny 20 km (12 mile) toehold south of its almost 600 km (375 mile) stretch of coastline on the Adriatic Sea. It also shares borders with Slovenia to the northwest, Hungary to the northeast, and Yugoslavia to the east. The state of Croatia emerged in the ninth century AD, peopled by Slavic immigrants from present-day Ukraine. In 1091 it was invaded by Hungary with which it remained united until 1526 when most of the country came under the rule of the Ottoman Turks. In 1699 the Turks were driven out by the Austrian Hapsburgs. Once again, Croatia came under Hungarian rule, but with its own monarchy. In 1867 Croatia became part of the Austro-Hungarian Empire. In 1918 it declared its independence and joined with its neighboring states to form the Kingdom of Serbs, Croats, and Slovenes—the precursor of the state of Yugoslavia. Serbian domination of the new country provoked agitation by Croation separatists, and this led, in 1939, to Croatia's being declared a self-governing

region within Yugoslavia. During the Second World War, the invading Axis powers proclaimed Croatia an independent state and installed a Fascist government intent on eliminating Serbs, Jews, and all political oppostion. At the war's end, Croatia once again became a republic in the re-formed state of Yugoslavia. In 1991, after a referendum, Croatia declared its independence and was then plunged into civil war as Croatian Serbs, supported by the Yugoslav army, sought to incorporate Croatia into a "Greater Serbia." The war ended officially in 1992, but hostilities between Serbs and Croats continued until 1995.

Along Croatia's spectacular Dalmatian coast are scattered about 600 small rocky islands, many of them former alpine peaks, isolated by rises in sea level. Further inland in the north, the Pannonian Plain, traversed by the Drava, Danube, and Sava Rivers, is a fertile region, centered around Zagreb, which is the hub of the country's agricultural production. A little more than one-fifth of the land is devoted to agriculture and about one-fifth of the population is directly involved in agricultural production. Cereal crops, fruit, and tobacco are widely grown and sheep are raised. Timber is a significant resource, and reserves of minerals, coal and iron are mined.

Civil and other regional wars in the 1990s have seriously impeded Croatia's transition to a market economy and cut industrial production. The tourist industry, once of great economic significance, has, since the early 1990s, largely ceased to exist. Much of the historic city of Dubrovnik on the southern Adriatic coast, once a major tourist center, was destroyed by shelling but it is being restored.

Fact File

OFFICIAL NAME Republic of Croatia

FORM OF GOVERNMENT Republic with two legislative bodies (House of Districts and House of Assembly)

CAPITAL Zagreb

AREA 56,538 sq km (21,829 sq miles)

TIME ZONE GMT + 1 hour

POPULATION 4,676,865

PROJECTED POPULATION 2005 4,670,552

POPULATION DENSITY 82.7 per sq km (214.2 per sq mile)

LIFE EXPECTANCY 74

INFANT MORTALITY (PER 1,000) 7.8

OFFICIAL LANGUAGE Croatian

OTHER LANGUAGES Serbian, Italian, Hungarian, Czech, German

LITERACY RATE 97%

RELIGIONS Catholic 76.5%, Orthodox 11.1%, Slavic Muslim 1.2%, Protestant 0.4%, others 10.8%

ETHNIC GROUPS Croat 78%, Serb 12%, Muslim 0.9%, Hungarian 0.5%, Slovene 0.5%, others 8.1%

CURRENCY Kuna

ECONOMY Services 56%, industry 23%, agriculture 21%

GNP PER CAPITA US$3,250

CLIMATE Temperate; cold winters and warm summers inland, cooler and more temperate along coast

HIGHEST POINT Dinara 1,830 m (6,004 ft)

MAP REFERENCE Pages 294, 296

Czech Republic

Fact File

OFFICIAL NAME Czech Republic

FORM OF GOVERNMENT Republic with two legislative bodies (Senate and Chamber of Deputies)

CAPITAL Prague

AREA 78,703 sq km (30,387 sq miles)

TIME ZONE GMT + 1 hour

POPULATION 10,280,513

PROJECTED POPULATION 2005 10,394,294

POPULATION DENSITY 130.6 per sq km (338.3 per sq mile)

LIFE EXPECTANCY 74.4

INFANT MORTALITY (PER 1,000) 6.7

OFFICIAL LANGUAGE Czech

OTHER LANGUAGE Slovak

LITERACY RATE 99%

RELIGIONS Roman Catholic 39.2%, Protestant 4.6%, Orthodox 3%, non-denominational 39.1%, other 13.4%

ETHNIC GROUPS Czech 94.4%, Slovak 3%, Polish 0.6%, German 0.5%, Gypsy 0.3%, Hungarian 0.2%, other 1%

CURRENCY Koruna

ECONOMY Industry 47%, services 45%, agriculture 8%

GNP PER CAPITA US$3,870

CLIMATE Temperate, with cold winters and mild, wet summers

HIGHEST POINT Mt Snezka 1,602 m (5,256 ft)

MAP REFERENCE Pages 288–89

A landlocked country in central Europe, the Czech Republic was until 1993 linked politically to Slovakia, its neighbor to the southeast, from which it is separated by the Carpathian Mountains. The Czech Republic consists mainly of the ancient provinces of Bohemia in the west and Moravia in the east. Part of the province of Silesia is also within the Czech Republic, but most of it now forms a portion of Poland.

Czechoslovakia came into existence in 1918, with the collapse of the Austro-Hungarian Empire at the close of the First World War. The Czechs and the Slovaks had been under one rule since 1471, and since 1526, except for a brief revolt in 1618, had been under Austrian domination. Germany occupied Czech territory in 1939, establishing a protectorate of Bohemia–Moravia and setting up a separate state in Slovakia. In 1948 the communists came to power, and the country, once again united, came under Soviet influence. Nationalist fervor was never far below the surface and in 1968 caused a movement for democracy. The "Prague Spring," led by Alexander Dubcek, was put down by an invasion of Soviet forces. In 1989 a popular movement led to a transition to a democratic state. Tensions between Czechs and the minority Slovaks led to a peaceful separation of the two states on 1 January 1993.

Bohemia consists largely of gentle hills and plateaus. Low ranges of mountains surround the province to the north, west, and south and the central plateau is traversed by the Elbe and Vltava rivers, which merge and flow into Germany. Most of the country's agriculture is centered on this river system, and much of its produce, which includes wheat, barley, and potatoes, is transported along these waterways.

Bohemia and Moravia are separated by a plateau known as the Moravian Heights. While Moravia is hillier than Bohemia, the center of the province, around Brno, consists of an extensive low plain. Winters are colder and rainfall is heavier in Moravia than in Bohemia.

Although not richly endowed with natural resources, reserves of black coal and iron ore have aided the development of iron and steelmaking as the country's major industries. Other important industries include clothing and car manufacture. Bohemian glass is famous and much sought after worldwide. Industrial production, however, has fallen in the 1990s as the country moves toward a free market economy. Tourism has made up for some of this fall-off.

Czech conflict

The country formerly known as Czechoslovakia was at the center of successive conflicts in the twentieth century. It contains a volatile mixture of ethnic and political differences, and in the past fell victim to both German and Soviet totalitarian regimes. Hitler used the disaffection of the German minority in the Sudetenland as an excuse for invading Czechoslovakia in 1938. An insecure period of democracy after 1945 (marred by the expulsion of the still-resident German population) was followed by a communist takeover under Soviet auspices in 1948. In 1968 an effort to democratize the system led by Alexander Dubcek was crushed by Soviet tanks in August of that year. Along with other parts of East Europe it won independence from communist control in 1989, and now seeks EU member-ship—but these developments have been accompanied by the rise of ethnic separatism, and claims by one-time German citizens for restitution of property seized at the time of their expulsion after the Second World War. On 1 January 1993 the free-marketeering Czechs separated from the more statist Slovaks, and separate republics, reflecting different political traditions—the Czech "western," the Slovak "eastern"—came into existence. Under the presidency of the well-known playwright and (former) anti-communist dissident Vaclav Havel, a wholesale dismantling of state economic controls and structures then took place. However, the government which undertook these extensive reforms collapsed amid scandal and economic chaos at the end of 1997.

Denmark

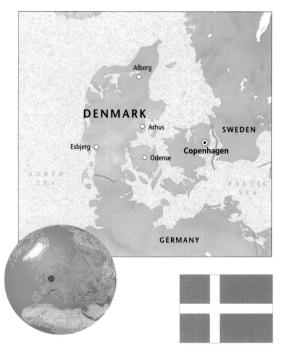

Fact File

OFFICIAL NAME	Kingdom of Denmark
FORM OF GOVERNMENT	Constitutional monarchy with one legislative body (Parliament)
CAPITAL	Copenhagen
AREA	43,070 sq km (16,629 sq miles)
TIME ZONE	GMT + 1 hour
POPULATION	5,356,845
PROJECTED POPULATION 2005	5,432,898
POPULATION DENSITY	124.4 per sq km (322.2 per sq mile)
LIFE EXPECTANCY	76.5
INFANT MORTALITY (PER 1,000)	5.1
OFFICIAL LANGUAGE	Danish
OTHER LANGUAGES	Faroese, Greenlandic, German
LITERACY RATE	99%
RELIGIONS	Evangelical Lutheran 91%, other Protestant and Roman Catholic 2%, other 7%
ETHNIC GROUPS	Scandinavian, Eskimo, Faroese, German
CURRENCY	Danish krone
ECONOMY	Services 75%, industry 20%, agriculture 5%
GNP PER CAPITA	US$29,890
CLIMATE	Temperate, with cold, wet winters and mild summers
HIGHEST POINT	Yding Skovhoj 173 m (568 ft)
MAP REFERENCE	Page 286

The Bohemian city of Český Krumlov in the Czech Republic (left). Cafés along the harbor in Copenhagen, Denmark (above). A model display at the tourist attraction Legoland, at Billund in Denmark (right). The city of Strambeck in the hills of Moravia, the Czech Republic (below left).

Denmark is both the smallest and the most southerly of the Scandinavian countries. Most of its land area consists of the Jutland Peninsula, which pushes northward from the northwestern tip of Germany. The North Sea washes Denmark's western coast, the Skagerrak Strait lies to the north separating it from the southern coast of Norway, and the Kattegat Strait separates it from the southwestern tip of Sweden. The Baltic Sea is to the east and here, stretching almost as far as the southwestern tip of Sweden, is an archipelago of more than 400 islands. The largest of these islands is Sjaelland, on which is situated the Danish capital, Copenhagen.

Like the inhabitants of Sweden and Norway, modern Danes are descended from Viking invaders who from the fifth century AD moved northward into Scandinavia and then outward to other parts of western and eastern Europe. For much of its history, Denmark was the dominant country in Scandinavia. At the end of the fourteenth century, Norway and Sweden, as well as Iceland, were united under the Danish crown. The Swedes elected their own monarch 50 years later, but Norway continued to be part of Denmark for more than 400 years—until 1815, when the Congress of Vienna awarded it to Sweden in retaliation for Denmark having supported Napoleon Bonaparte. Despite its neutrality, Denmark was invaded by Germany during 1940. Liberated by British forces in 1945, Denmark joined the NATO alliance following the war, and is now a member of the European Union. Denmark is a constitutional monarchy, with an hereditary monarch. Its single-house parliament, which is headed by a prime minister, is elected every four years.

Almost the whole of Denmark is low-lying and its surface is covered in many places by rocky glacial debris, most prominently in the undulating mass of moraine that runs down the center of the Jutland Peninsula. This divides the peninsula into two distinct regions. To the west is a sandy landscape with extensive dunes and lagoons along the North Sea coast. To the east lies a loam plain, which extends across the islands of the archipelago, as far as the Baltic coast. This fertile region supports significant crops of barley, wheat, and sugar beet and a thriving livestock and dairying industry. Fishing, which is still a leading Danish industry, is based for the most part on the extensive, shallow lagoons that lie along the western coastline of Jutland.

As well as constituting a significant proportion of the country's exports, Denmark's agricultural and fishing produce also provide the raw materials for food processsing industries, which are a major source of employment. Other significant industries, for which Denmark imports most of the raw materials are iron and metal working, machinery manufacturing, and furniture making. Despite having a relatively high unemployment rate during much of the 1990s, Denmark is a prosperous country and Danes generally enjoy a high standard of living. An extensive social security system means that serious poverty is comparatively rare throughout the country.

OVERSEAS TERRITORIES

Faeroe Islands
Greenland

Estonia

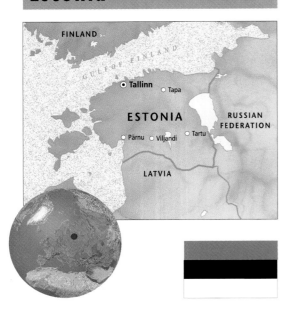

I t has been claimed that Estonia's flag, consisting of a blue, a black, and a white horizontal bar, represents the country's blue skies, black soils, and snowy winters. This, the smallest and least populous of the three Baltic countries, contains within its borders more than 1,500 lakes and its land area includes more than 800 islands in the Baltic Sea and the Gulf of Finland. The largest of the lakes, Lake Peipus, is in the far east of the country and forms most of its border with Russia.

Russia has been the dominant power in Estonia's recent history and the large ethnic Russian minority bears witness to this. From the thirteenth until the eighteenth century the Estonians were ruled by outsiders, first the Germans and then the Swedes. In 1721 Russia assumed control and ruled the country for almost 200 years. Occupied by Germany during the First World War, Estonia declared its independence in 1918. This was achieved in 1920 when, after an armed struggle, Russia formally recognized the small country. It was a short-lived victory, however. During the Second World War Estonia was overrun first by the Russians and then by the Germans. In 1944 it was returned to the Soviets and remained part of the USSR until it once again declared itself independent in August 1991, following Lithuania's example of the previous year.

Most of Estonia is low-lying and flat or gently undulating. Large areas of land are barren and stony, a legacy of the glaciers that once covered much of the landscape. There are extensive woodlands which supply the raw materials for the country's important timber and woodworking industries. Engineering and textile manufacture are also significant. Despite its black soils, little of the land is arable and the main agricultural industries are dairying and livestock raising, especially pig farming. Mineral resources are meager, though extensive deposits of shale are used in the production of gas and chemical products.

Compared with other former Soviet republics, the people of Estonia enjoy a high standard of living. The economy, after declining for some years following independence, has improved steadily as increasing trade with Western countries has shielded Estonia from some of the effects of the declining Russian economy.

Fact File

OFFICIAL NAME	Republic of Estonia
FORM OF GOVERNMENT	Republic with single legislative body (Parliament)
CAPITAL	Tallinn
AREA	45,100 sq km (17,413 sq miles)
TIME ZONE	GMT + 3 hours
POPULATION	1,408,523
PROJECTED POPULATION 2005	1,357,949
POPULATION DENSITY	32.6 per sq km (84.5 per sq mile)
LIFE EXPECTANCY	68.7
INFANT MORTALITY (PER 1,000)	13.8
OFFICIAL LANGUAGE	Estonian
OTHER LANGUAGES	Latvian, Lithuanian, Russian
LITERACY RATE	99%
RELIGIONS	Evangelical Lutheran 96%; Eastern Orthodox and Baptist 4%
ETHNIC GROUPS	Estonian 61.5%, Russian 30.3%, Ukrainian 3.2%, Belarusian 1.8%, Finnish 1.1%, other 2.1%
CURRENCY	Kroon
ECONOMY	Industry 42%, services 38%, agriculture 20%
GNP PER CAPITA	US$2,860
CLIMATE	Cool temperate; cold winters and mild summers
HIGHEST POINT	Mt Munamagi 318 m (1,043 ft)
MAP REFERENCE	Page 287

The Baltic States

The nations of Estonia, Latvia, and Lithuania, on the eastern edge of the Baltic Sea, are collectively known as the Baltic States. Similar in their physical environments and sharing a common history of almost uninterrupted Russian domination since the eighteenth century until they achieved independence in 1991, the three countries have quite distinct ethnic and linguistic identities, as well as diverse earlier histories.

The ethnic composition of Estonia and Latvia reflects the long period of Russian rule, with native Estonians and Latvians comprising under two-thirds of their respective populations, the rest being made up mainly of ethnic Russians and immigrants from other former Soviet countries. Lithuania is more ethnically homogeneous. In all three countries, however, more than nine out of ten people claim the native language as their own. Latvian and Lithuanian are both Indo-European languages, but Estonian is more closely related to Finnish. The strong German influence on both Estonian and Latvian culture is manifested in the dominance of the Lutheran religion in those countries, while the predominance of Catholics in Lithuania stems from that country's past links with Poland. In the fifteenth century Lithuania was a major European power, whose territories took in parts of Belarus and Ukraine and stretched from the Baltic to the Black Seas. In the sixteenth century it merged with Poland and the countries remained united for more than 200 years. Estonia and Latvia, on the other hand, were never great powers, enduring about 1,000 years of foreign domination before gaining their independence.

Near the end of the First World War in 1918, the Baltic States became independent, but in 1940 they were incorporated into the Soviet Union and occupied by Soviet troops, a move that was sanctioned by the Germans but never recognized by the United States, even following the war.

A deliberate policy of Russification took place during the 1950s. This resulted in massive immigration, often of manual workers, from Russia and the forced emigration of many highly qualified native Baltic peoples to other parts of the Soviet Union. Despite this, nationalistic aspirations in the region remained undiminished and after an attempted coup against Soviet leader Mikhail Gorbachev, in 1991, the Baltic States declared and were granted their independence. Soon after, all three were admitted as members of the United Nations.

Finland

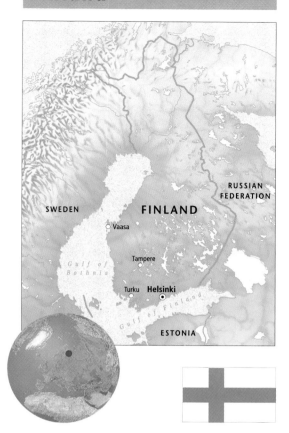

Except for a small section of Norway which cuts it off from the Arctic Ocean, Finland is the most northerly country in continental Europe. As well as its northern boundary with Norway, Finland borders northern Sweden to the west and the Russian Federation in the east. In the south, the Gulf of Finland, the easternmost part of the Baltic Sea, separates it from Estonia, and on the west the Gulf of Bothnia, a northern inlet of the Baltic, sits between it and southern Sweden.

Modern Finland has its roots in a seventh century AD invasion by tribes from the Volga. They displaced the Lapps, Asiatic people who had lived in the area for centuries, and drove them north. Only about 2,500 Lapps, or Sami, who have their own culture and language, now survive in the north, tending reindeer herds. Viking incursions

followed and in the twelfth century Swedes invaded Finland, bringing Christianity. Finland remained under Swedish control for the next 650 years, until 1809, when the Russians took over. Swedish influence is still evident in the country's significant Swedish-speaking minority, and the fact that some towns have both Finnish and Swedish names. A relatively benign Russian rule allowed considerable freedoms and encouraged a resurgence of the Finnish language, which had largely fallen into disuse. A more oppressive regime towards the end of the century fanned Finnish nationalism, and at the time of the Russian Revolution, in 1917, the country seized its independence.

Finland's harsh climate and the ruggedness of its northern regions means that most of its people live in the more moderate south. Much of the land consists of flat expanses of granite rock, the legacy of extensive glaciation. Remnants of an ancient mountain range, rising in places to more than 1,000 m (3,300 ft), exist in Lapland, the northern part of the country. There are more than 60,000 substantial lakes throughout Finland, mainly in the south, and tens of thousands of smaller ones. Forests,

The medieval rooftops of Tallinn, the capital of Estonia, which is the country's main port (below). A square in Tallinn (left). Sleds pulled by reindeer are a traditional but still widely used form of winter transport in Finland (top).

mainly of pine, birch, and spruce cover more than half the land area, contributing to the country's heavy reliance on timber-related industries, including wood processing, pulp, and papermaking.

Less than one-tenth of Finland's land is arable and agricultural production, which includes cereals, potatoes and sugar beet, is confined to the summer months, when the country is not snowbound.

In the 1980s living standards in Finland rose markedly, rivaling those of Sweden, although they fell back in the recession of the early 1990s. The country has an effective government-sponsored health system and the population is one of the most literate and highly educated in the world.

Fact File

OFFICIAL NAME Republic of Finland

FORM OF GOVERNMENT Republic with single legislative body (Parliament)

CAPITAL Helsinki

AREA 337,030 sq km (130,127 sq miles)

TIME ZONE GMT + 1 hour

POPULATION 5,158,372

PROJECTED POPULATION 2005 5,178,305

POPULATION DENSITY 15.3 per sq km (39.6 per sq mile)

LIFE EXPECTANCY 77.3

INFANT MORTALITY (PER 1,000) 3.8

OFFICIAL LANGUAGES Finnish, Swedish

OTHER LANGUAGES Russian, Lapp

LITERACY RATE 99%

RELIGIONS Evangelical Lutheran 89%, Greek Orthodox 1%, none 9%, other 1%

ETHNIC GROUPS Finnish 93.6%, Swedish 6.2%, others (including Lapp, Gypsy, Tatar) 0.2%

CURRENCY Markka

ECONOMY Services 60%, industry 34%, agriculture 6%

GNP PER CAPITA US$20,580

CLIMATE Mainly cold temperate, but polar in arctic regions

HIGHEST POINT Haltiatunturi 1,328 m (4,357 ft)

MAP REFERENCE Pages 284–85, 287

France

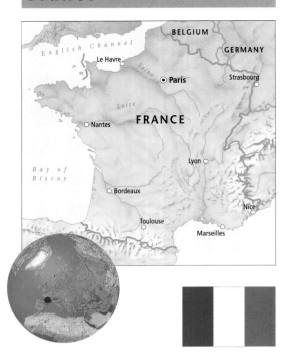

Fact File

OFFICIAL NAME French Republic

FORM OF GOVERNMENT Republic with two legislative bodies (Senate and National Assembly)

CAPITAL Paris

AREA 547,030 sq km (211,208 sq miles)

TIME ZONE GMT + 1 hour

POPULATION 58,978,172

PROJECTED POPULATION 2005 59,624,720

POPULATION DENSITY 107.8 per sq km (279.2 per sq mile)

LIFE EXPECTANCY 78.6

INFANT MORTALITY (PER 1,000) 5.6

OFFICIAL LANGUAGE French

OTHER LANGUAGES Provençal, Breton, Alsatian, Corsican, Catalan, Basque, Flemish, German, Arabic

LITERACY RATE 99%

RELIGIONS Roman Catholic 90%, Protestant 2%, Jewish 1%, Muslim 1%, unaffiliated 6%

ETHNIC GROUPS French 95%; others, including Algerian, Portuguese, Moroccan, Italian, Spanish 5%

CURRENCY French franc

ECONOMY Services 73%, industry 20%, agriculture 7%

GNP PER CAPITA US$24,990

CLIMATE Temperate, with cool winters and mild summers; warmer on the Mediterranean coast

HIGHEST POINT Mont Blanc 4,807 m (15,771 ft)

MAP REFERENCE Pages 290–91

Situated at the west of continental Europe, France has three long stretches of coastline. To the north the English Channel separates it from the southern coast of England (the Channel Tunnel now links the two), to the west it faces the Bay of Biscay, and its southern shores are on the Mediterranean Sea. To the northeast and east, it shares borders with Belgium, Luxembourg, Germany, Switzerland, and Italy, and in the far southwest the Pyrenees Mountains separate it from Spain. Southeast of the mainland, in the Mediterranean, is the French island of Corsica.

History

A political entity roughly equivalent to the area of present-day France was first established in AD 843, when the Treaty of Verdun divided the enormous Frankish Empire, which had reached its high point under Charlemagne, between Charlemagne's three grandsons. These divisions corresponded approximately to what are now France, Germany, and Italy. Charles the Bald thus became king of Francia Occidentalis. His Carolingian Dynasty lasted only until 987, when territorial fighting between feudal lords led to the election of Hugh Capet, who controlled the region around Paris, as king. The Capetian Dynasty lasted for almost 350 years, during which time it consolidated its power and extended its territory. When, in 1328, the crown passed to Philip VI, the first of the Valois rulers, France was a great European power, although much of its present territory was in the hands of the English, who also laid claim to sovereignty over all of France. In 1338 there began a series of wars, which later became known as the Hundred Years War, and which, despite a major French defeat at Agincourt in 1415, led to the expulsion of the English from nearly all of France by the middle of the fifteenth century.

In the second half of the sixteenth century, France was wracked by religious wars between Catholics and Protestants (Huguenots). These finally ended in 1598 with the accession of the first Bourbon king, the Protestant-turned-Catholic Henry of Navarre. Under the Bourbons, and especially under the 72-year reign of Louis XIV that ended in 1715, the monarchy reigned supreme and France acquired colonies in places as far afield as India, North America, and the Caribbean. Under royal patronage, French literature, art, and music flourished and the royal court was the most opulent in Europe. During the eighteenth century, weak leadership and a series of debilitating wars led to the popular unrest that culminated in the French Revolution of 1789, which overthrew the monarchy but soon collapsed into a period of anarchy and savagery. The rise of Napoleon Bonaparte restored some stability, but his foreign military exploits led to his ultimate defeat at the Battle of Waterloo, in Belgium, in 1815.

Napoleon's defeat ushered in a period of political instability that saw first the restoration of the monarchy, which was twice overthrown in revolutions (1830 and 1848), then the installation of Napoleon's nephew, Louis-Napoleon, first as president of a republic and then as the Emperor Napoleon III. The defeat of France in the Franco-Prussian War of 1870–71 led to a new republic and a period of relative stability in which France acquired new colonies in Africa and Indochina.

During the twentieth century France suffered grievously in both world wars. In the trench warfare of the First World War, almost a million and a half French lives were lost and the northwest of the country was devastated. In the Second World War northern France was occupied by German forces and the south was administered from Vichy by a pro-Nazi collaborationist government.

Political instability continued after the Second World War, as France unsuccessfully waged a war against insurgents in Indochina and as unrest in French-controlled Algeria threatened to bring down the government. In 1957 France's Second World War hero, Charles de Gaulle, was invited to assume power, under a constitution that greatly increased the powers of the president. This constitution has since undergone a number of revisions, the latest being in 1976. The French president, who controls defense and finance, is elected by universal suffrage for a seven-year term. There are two houses of parliament, elected at three- and five-year intervals.

Physical features and land use

Much of France is low-lying with almost two-thirds of its land at an elevation of less than 250 m (800 ft). These lowland regions stretch, interspersed with a number of hilly areas, from

Timeline

15,000–10,000 BP Cave paintings at sites such as Lascaux and Pech Merle depicting bulls, mammoths, horses, and humans	**59–50 BC** Roman legions led by Julius Caesar occupy the entire area of Gaul (France)	**AD 987** Hugh Capet becomes the first of the Capetian kings to rule all France	**1337–1453** France and England fight the Hundred Years war; despite English victories at Crécy and Agincourt the French triumph	**1562–98** Wars of religion between Catholics and Huguenots (Protestants)	**1789** The storming of the Bastille by the Paris mob marks the start of the French Revolution	**1799** Napoleon Bonaparte siezes power; first as consul and later as Emperor of France

35,000 BP Neanderthal people living in caves, sometimes burying dead using decorated grave slabs	**30,000–20,000 BP** Cro-Magnon population in the southwest spreads out to northern and eastern regions	**600 BC** Greek merchants establish Massilia (later Marseilles) as a port on the Mediterranean coast	**400 BC** Franks and Visigoths move east into Gaul, defeating the Romans	**1309–77** The Papacy moves from Rome to Avignon in southern France	**1643** Religious persecution causes 200,000 Huguenots to flee, resulting in economic decline	**1792** First French Republic established; Louis XVI executed (1793)	**1814–15** Napoleon exiled to St Helena after losing Battle of Waterloo; monarchy restored under Louis XVIII

France's southern Alps (bottom). A cheese shop in Paris (above). La Roque Gageac on the Dordogne River (right).

the Belgian and German borders, across the north to the rugged Breton Peninsula in the west, and inland to the Pyrenees in the southwest. Further east, along the Mediterranean coast and hemmed in by mountains, is the low-lying region of western Provence in the Rhône Delta. Except for the far northeast, which forms part of the Flanders Plain, most of these lowland areas comprise the basins of France's four main rivers and their tributaries. In the north, the Seine flows northwest, through Paris and the surrounding Île-de-France, to the English Channel; France's longest river, the Loire, flows north through the central region, then westward to the Atlantic Ocean; further south the Garonne, which rises in the Pyrenees, drains much of southwest France on its way to the Atlantic near Bordeaux; and in the east, the Rhône, rising in Switzerland, flows west to Lyon where, fed by the Saône from the north, it courses due south to the Mediterranean.

In the center and south of the country, a vast central plateau, the Massif Central, covers almost a sixth of the total land area. Much of its landscape is rugged, characterized by granite outcrops, extinct volcanic peaks, and deep gorges. At its highest point, it reaches almost 1,900 m (6,000 ft). East of the Massif Central, separated from it by the Rhône Valley, are the Alps, which form the border with Italy and which, in the southeast corner of the country, extend to the coast. North of the Alps, the Jura, characterized by high limestone cliffs, separate France from Switzerland and further north, the heavily forested Vosges Mountains fringe the Rhine Valley near the German border. In the far southwest, the Pyrenees, which rival the Alps in rugged splendor, but which are less accessible, stand between France and Spain.

Industry, commerce, and agriculture

Second only to the USA as an exporter of agricultural produce, France produces a wide range of food, although most farms are relatively small. Over half the land area, mainly in the low-lying regions, is cultivated, the most abundant crops being wheat, maize, barley, and sugar beet. Vast areas, especially in the Burgundy and Champagne regions in the central north, around Bordeaux in the southwest and the Rhone Valley in the south, are devoted to viticulture. France is Europe's second largest wine producer.

After Germany, France is the largest industrial power in Europe, and until recently many of its industries were state-owned. Paris, Lille, Nantes, and Strasbourg in the north, Lyon and Grenoble in the center, and Marseilles and Toulouse in the south are among the major manufacturing centers.

The main industries include steelmaking, car, aircraft, and weapons manufacture, oil refining, machine making, textiles, and chemicals. Mineral resources are not abundant, though there are reserves of iron ore, zinc, and uranium. Most of France's electricity is generated by state-owned nuclear plants.

On average, the French enjoy one of the highest standards of living in the world, but there are considerable disparities between rich and poor, with considerable wealth concentrated in an area around Paris and parts of southern France. The state heavily subsidizes health services, which are particularly stressed by a high level of smoking and alcohol-related disease.

REGIONS

Alsace • Aquitaine • Auvergne • Basse-Normandie • Bourgogne • Bretagne • Centre • Champagne-Ardenne • Corse • Franche-Comté • Haute-Normandie • Île-de-France • Languedoc-Roussillon • Limousin • Lorraine • Midi-Pyrénées • Nord-Pas-de-Calais • Pays de la Loire • Picardie • Poitou-Charentes • Provence-Alpes-Côte d'Azur • Rhônes-Alpes

OVERSEAS TERRITORIES

French Guiana • French Polynesia • French Southern and Arctic Lands • Guadeloupe • Martinique • Mayotte • New Caledonia • Réunion • St Pierre and Miquelon • Wallis and Futuna Islands

1848 Riots in Paris, with street fighting between the army and mobs of hungry, unemployed workers

1870–1 France loses Franco-Prussian War; Alsace and Lorraine ceded to Germany

1889 The Eiffel Tower, an iron structure designed by Gustave Eiffel for the Exhibition of the same year, built in Paris

1918 First World War ends with Treaty of Versailles under which Alsace and Lorraine are returned to France by Germany

1914 First World War starts: Allies create the Western Front in north France to stop German advance; deadlock lasts 3¹/₂ years—1,357,800 French casualties

1939 Start of Second World War and subsequent German invasion of France leads to occupation of Paris (1940)

1944 Allied troops reach Paris; General de Gaulle returns from exile in England to form a provisional government

1957 France joins other European nations in forming the European Common Market by signing the Treaty of Rome

1960 Rapid rise in immigration from ex-colonial territories in North Africa and the Caribbean brings concern over jobs

1960 France begins nuclear weapons testing program

1968 Student protests lead to a general strike over educational policies and political dissatisfaction; General de Gaulle resigns

1994 Railway tunnel under Channel to England in operation; idea first proposed in 1802 by Mathieu to Napoleon I

1995 Jacques Chirac becomes President; France accepts EC lifting of passport control

Europe and the Russian Federation

Germany

Fact File

OFFICIAL NAME Federal Republic of Germany

FORM OF GOVERNMENT Federal republic with two legislative bodies (Federal Council and Federal Assembly)

CAPITAL Berlin

AREA 356,910 sq km (137,803 sq miles)

TIME ZONE GMT + 1 hour

POPULATION 82,087,361

PROJECTED POPULATION 2005 81,860,165

POPULATION DENSITY 230 per sq km (595.7 per sq mile)

LIFE EXPECTANCY 77.2

INFANT MORTALITY (PER 1,000) 5.1

OFFICIAL LANGUAGE German

OTHER LANGUAGES Turkish, Italian, Greek, Dutch, Spanish, English

LITERACY RATE 99%

RELIGIONS Protestant 45%, Roman Catholic 37%, unaffiliated or other 18%

ETHNIC GROUPS German 95.1%, Turkish 2.3%, Italian 0.7%, Greek 0.4%, Polish 0.4%, other 1.1%

CURRENCY Mark

ECONOMY Services 53%, industry 41%, agriculture 6%

GNP PER CAPITA US$27,510

CLIMATE Temperate, with cool, wet winters (colder in east and south) and mild summers

HIGHEST POINT Zugspitze 2,962 m (9,718 ft)

MAP REFERENCE Pages 288–89

andlocked, except for two stretches of coast along the North and Baltic Seas, Germany has land borders with nine countries. Poland is located to the east; the Czech Republic to the southeast; Austria and Switzerland to the south; France to the southwest; and Luxembourg, Belgium and the Netherlands to the west. Germany's coastlines are separated by the Jutland Peninsula, at the southern end of which Germany borders Denmark.

History

The area now occupied by Germany was roughly defined in the tenth century AD when Duke Conrad became king of the German-speaking eastern part of the Frankish Empire that had been established several centuries earlier. Under the Saxon King Otto I (AD 936–973), Germany's territory was extended. In 1273, however, the accession of the Austrian Rudolf of Hapsburg to the throne ushered in a long period of Austrian domination. The rise of Protestantism under Martin Luther during the sixteenth century flamed nationalist as well as religious passions and fuelled a peasants' revolt in 1524 that was savagely suppressed. More than a century of religious wars followed, climaxing in the Thirty Years War of 1618–48 in which, amid wholesale devastation, German states achieved the right to religious, if not political, autonomy.

Austria was weakened by the long years of war and this encouraged individual German states, such as Saxony, Hanover, and Prussia/Brandenburg to increase their power. Under the leadership of Frederick the Great during the eighteenth century, Prussia developed into a major European power, gaining control of much of present-day Poland. At the end of the eighteenth century, Napoleon's armies overran both Austria and Prussia, but after Napoleon's defeat in 1815 Prussia became the dominant force in a German Confederation. This confederation, however, was still nominally under Austrian control. In 1866, under the leadership of Bismarck, the Prussians defeated the Austrian Hapsburgs, driving them out of Germany. Prussian victory in the Franco-Prussian War of 1870–71 consolidated Prussia as the leading European power and brought northern and southern Germany together to form a unified German Empire (Reich).

Germany's expansionist ambitions and its aggressive arms build-up during the last years of the nineteenth century led to international tensions that finally erupted in the First World War. Germany was to emerge from the war defeated and with its emperor, Kaiser Wilhelm, in exile. In 1919, the Weimar Republic, with a president and legislature elected by universal suffrage, was established. However, popular resentment was fanned by the loss of German territory and the harsh regime of reparations that were imposed by the Treaty of Versailles. This resentment was exacerbated by soaring inflation in the 1920s and the onset of depression at the end of the decade. In 1933 Adolf Hitler was elected chancellor as head of the National Socialist (Nazi) Party, promising to return the country to its former influence and power. He instituted a ruthlessly oppressive regime which persecuted Germany's Jewish population, and eventually plunged Europe into the Second World War when he invaded Poland in September 1939.

At the end of the war a defeated and devastated Germany was divided into two principal zones, the western half administered by Britain, France, and the United States, and the eastern part under Soviet control. In 1949 this resulted in the creation of two separate states: the Federal Republic of Germany in the west, under a democratically elected government; and the Democratic Republic of Germany under a central, Soviet-dominated communist government in the east. Thus divided, the two Germanies became a focal point for Cold War tensions in Europe over the next 40 years. Control of the city of Berlin, in East German territory, was divided between the two countries. East Berlin was sealed off when communist authorities constructed a wall between the two parts of the city.

As the Soviet Union faltered in the late 1980s, waves of unrest in East Germany led to the collapse of its government and the reunification of the whole country in October 1990, with Berlin as its capital. In December, elections covering the entire country were held. Germany's political system is based on the 1949 West German constitution, which stipulates a parliament elected by universal suffrage for a four-year term with a president, elected by the parliament for a five-year term, as titular head of state.

Timeline

AD 10 The Romans, who rule much of what becomes Germany, forced back to Rhine by the Germani, led by Arminius	**1241** The Hanseatic League, a union of northern towns, prospers through trade—rest of country divided and poor	**1618–48** The Thirty Years War between Catholics and Protestants causes social and economic problems	**1862–71** Otto von Bismarck becomes the first Chancellor of a united Germany		**1933** Adolf Hitler becomes Chancellor of Germany and supresses opposition, declaring Nazi Party the only legal party

35,000 BP Neanderthals, early humans named for the Neander Gorge near Düsseldorf, disappear from the fossil record	**AD 55** Caesar bridges the Rhine; Romans maintain a fleet on the river, developing it as a trade route and protective barrier	**AD 800–14** Charlemagne, Holy Roman Emperor, sets up court at Aachen and briefly unifies the Germanic tribes	**1517** Luther's Protestant Reformation leads to a Peasants' Revolt in 1524	**1740–86** Frederick the Great of Prussia controls all Germany, giving his own state priority over other German states	**1914–18** First World War: Germany joins Austria–Hungary and declares war on France and Russia but is defeated by Allies	**1919** Formation of democratic Weimar Republic after German Emperor flees to Holland; republic lasts until late 1920s

Physical features and land use

The southern part of the country is generally mountainous and heavily forested. In the southwestern region, east of the Rhine, which forms the border with France, is the vast expanse of rugged wooded peaks that constitute the Black Forest, an extension of Switzerland's Jura Mountains. Further east the thickly wooded Bavarian Plateau rises out of the Danube Valley, leading to the spectacular peaks of the Alps along the border between Austria and Germany in the far southeast.

The central part of Germany is also a highland area, part of a chain of mountains and hills that extends from France as far east as the Carpathians. These, too, are heavily wooded, particularly in the more mountainous regions. The valleys are often fertile and undulating and extensively planted with crops and vines. The highest and most rugged peaks are found in the Harz Mountains in the north of these central uplands. In the northern part of the central uplands, where the country slopes toward the northern plain, there are areas of fertile soil that support crops such as wheat, barley, and sugar beet.

Northern Germany is an extensive lowland plain that covers about one-third of the country's area. Part of the North European Plain that stretches eastward into Russia, it is a region of fertile pasture and croplands, sandy heaths and stretches of marshland. A network of northward-flowing rivers, most notably the Elbe and its tributaries, drains this northern plain.

About one-third of German land is cultivated. Cereal crops are widely grown, as are hops for the German beers that are famous throughout the world. Vineyards are most widespread in the valleys of the Rhine and Mosel rivers. Cattle and pigs are the principal livestock and are concentrated mainly on the northern plain.

Industry, commerce, and culture

Manufacturing industry, centered largely in the Ruhr Valley but also in such cities as Frankfurt, Stuttgart, Munich, and Berlin, is the main strength of the German economy. Coal is the only mineral resource of which Germany has large reserves, although its importance has declined in recent decades as oil has replaced it as an industrial fuel.

Iron and steel production support well-developed machine manufacturing and other metal industries. Cement, chemical, automobile, and electronic industries are also significant.

Unification has resulted in the juxtaposition of one of the world's most developed and efficient industrial economies with one that was mostly uncompetitive and outmoded in its methods and equipment. As a result, Germany has suffered considerable economic and social disruption as the more affluent western part of the country has had to subsidize attempts to improve conditions in the east. There is still a noticeable discrepancy between standards of living in east and west, and wages in the east are considerably lower. The move to a market economy in the former East Germany, with its emphasis on greater efficiency, has created high levels of unemployment. Under the former communist regime unemployment was virtually non-existent.

The Alps in southern Germany (below left). Neuschwanstein Castle in Bavaria, built by King Ludwig II toward the end of the nineteenth century (below).

STATES

Baden-Württemberg • Bavaria • Berlin
Brandenburg • Bremen • Hamburg
Hesse • Lower Saxony
Mecklenburg-West Pomerania
North Rhine-Westphalia
Rhineland-Palatinate • Saarland
Saxony • Saxony-Anhalt
Schleswig-Holstein • Thuringia (Thüringen)

1939 Hitler annexes Austria, invades Poland; Britain, France declare war on Germany; Second World War ends 1945

1945 Germany partitioned into East and West, with the East run as a communist state by Russia and Berlin divided in two

1948 Russia withdraws from ruling council of occupying powers and blockades West Berlin; Allies airlift food and supplies to West Berlin

1949 The Federal Republic of West Germany is created

1950–55 With aid of development funds from US Marshall Plan, Germany's economic expansion becomes an "economic miracle"

1961 East Germany builds Berlin Wall to prevent East German citizens escaping to the more prosperous West Germany

1973 Federal Republic of Germany and German Democratic Republic achieve full UN membership

1989 Berlin Wall is demolished; full reunification with East Germany proposed by Chancellor Kohl

1990 East and West Germany sign a treaty formalizing unification of the separate states

1991 The Bundestag (German Parliament) reinstates Berlin as capital of Germany, replacing Bonn, the West German capital

1993 United Germany holds first free national elections since 1933

1992 Main-Donau Canal links Main (a Rhine tributary) and Danube Rivers

1992–93 Neo-Nazi groups riot against immigration, claiming it to be the cause of unemployment among Germans

1995 Germany lifts passport regulations with six EU nations

Greece

Fact File

OFFICIAL NAME Hellenic Republic

FORM OF GOVERNMENT Republic with single legislative body (Chamber of Deputies)

CAPITAL Athens

AREA 131,940 sq km (50,942 sq miles)

TIME ZONE GMT + 1 hour

POPULATION 10,707,135

PROJECTED POPULATION 2005 10,921,262

POPULATION DENSITY 81.2 per sq km (210.3 per sq mile)

LIFE EXPECTANCY 78.4

INFANT MORTALITY (PER 1,000) 7.1

OFFICIAL LANGUAGE Greek

OTHER LANGUAGES English, French

LITERACY RATE 96.7%

RELIGIONS Greek Orthodox 98%, Muslim 1.3%, other 0.7%

ETHNIC GROUPS Greek 98%, other 2%

CURRENCY Drachma

ECONOMY Services 56%, agriculture 25%, industry 19%

GNP PER CAPITA US$8,210

CLIMATE Temperate, with mild, wet winters and hot, dry summers

HIGHEST POINT Mt Olympus 2,917 m (9,570 ft)

MAP REFERENCE Page 287

Mainland Greece occupies the southernmost part of the Balkan Peninsula. The western shores of this peninsula are washed by the Ionian Sea, while on the east the Aegean Sea lies between it and Turkey. In the north, Greece shares borders with Albania, and to the northeast, with Macedonia and Bulgaria. In its far northeast corner there is a short border with Turkey. Dotted all over the Aegean Sea, and also in the Ionian Sea, are more than 1,500 Greek islands, only about one-tenth of which are inhabited. South of the mainland, in the Mediterranean Sea, is the large island of Crete.

It was in Crete that seeds of Greek civilization were sown. Here, for more than 2,000 years from about 3500 BC, grew and flourished the Minoan civilization, which, in about the sixteenth century BC spread to Mycenae, in the Peloponnese Peninsula. In the fifth century BC, Athens emerged as the center of Greek culture. It developed rich traditions in literature, theater, philosophy and politics which established the values on which most modern Western civilizations are based. In the fourth century BC, under Alexander the Great, a vast Greek Empire spread across Asia as far as India and southward as far as Alexandria. Subsumed into the Roman Empire by the beginning of the second century BC, Greece eventually came under Byzantine rule, where it remained until the fall of Constantinople in AD 1204. Modern Greece dates back to 1832, when the country emerged from almost 400 years of Turkish domination and established a monarchy.

In 1941, Greece was overrun, in the face of fierce resistance, by German and Italian troops. It was liberated during 1944 by British and Greek forces, but almost immediately the country was plunged into civil war as monarchists and communists fought for supremacy. This destructive and debilitating struggle finally ended in 1949 with a victory by the monarchists. However, a military coup in 1967 resulted in the monarchy being expelled and a republic being established under an oppressive dictatorship. This regime fell in 1974 after an abortive attempt to invade Cyprus. In 1975, civilian government was restored and Greece became a democratic republic with a president elected for a five-year term, and a single-chamber parliament headed by a prime minister elected every four years.

Most of mainland Greece is mountainous, being dominated by the Pindos Mountains, an extension of the Dinaric Alps, that extend southeastward throughout the peninsula from the Albanian border. The mountains that form Crete and the island of Rhodes, near the southwestern tip of Turkey, were once part of the same range. In the northeast the Rhodope Mountains form a natural

border with Bulgaria. The only extensive low-lying areas are the northern plain, which extends from the Maritsa River on the Turkish border, across the northern Aegean region to the Greek province of Macedonia, and the plain of Thessaly in the central eastern mainland. Much of the Greek landscape, including that of many of the islands, is sparsely vegetated and has a rugged, rocky grandeur that, together with its warm climate, its beaches, and its rich historic heritage, attracts more than 10 million foreign visitors every year.

Despite its generally poor soils, Greece is heavily dependent on agriculture, which still employs about one-quarter of the workforce, largely on relatively small and inefficient farms. Wheat, olives, tobacco, and citrus and other fruits are among the main crops, and olives, particularly, are a major export item. Sheep and pigs are the principal livestock and are widely raised on the mainland and on Crete. Greece is almost self-sufficient in food production.

Not well endowed with mineral resources, Greece needs to import most of the raw materials for its industries, the majority of which are centered on Athens, though the area around Salonica in the northeast is also heavily industrialized. Food processing, based on local agricultural production, is important, as are textile manufacture and chemical processing. The tourist industry has helped the development of many local small-scale enterprises in such areas as ceramics, crafts, and textiles.

Hungary

A landlocked, central European country, Hungary shares borders with Yugoslavia to the south, Croatia and Slovenia to the southwest, Austria to the west, Slovakia to the north, Ukraine to the northeast and Romania to the southeast. Modern Hungary had its beginnings in the eighth century AD, when the area was settled by the Magyars, nomadic tribes from the central Volga. Their kingdom thrived and expanded. In the sixteenth century the Turks seized the central part of Hungary and the northern and western sections of the country accepted Austrian Hapsburg rule rather than submit to Turkish domination. In 1699 the Turks were driven out and the entire country came under Hapsburg rule. Continuing unrest and the defeat of Austria by the Prussians in 1866 culminated in the establishment of Austria–Hungary as a dual monarchy in 1867. The defeat of Austria–Hungary in 1918 was followed by the establishment of the Hungarian nation, but with two-thirds of its former territory and almost 60 percent of its former population ceded to surrounding states. In the Second World War Hungary sided with Germany against the Soviet Union and was finally occupied by Soviet forces as they pushed southward in 1945. In 1948 communists, with Soviet support, again seized control, beginning 42 years of Soviet domination. A popular anti-communist uprising in 1956 was brutally suppressed by the Soviet Union. As the Soviet Union began to collapse a new constitution in 1989 set the scene for Hungary's first multi-party elections in 1990.

Hungary is drained by two southward-flowing rivers, the Danube and the Tisza. These two rivers traverse the Great Hungarian Plain, which occupies most of the eastern part of the country and more than half the total land area. West of the Danube a line of hills and mountains runs northeast from Lake Balaton, which covers an area of 370 sq km (140 sq miles), to the Slovakian border, where it joins the Carpathian Mountains. Northwest of these hills the Little Hungarian Plain extends to the westward-flowing Danube, which here

The dome of a church on the island of Thíra, in Greece (bottom left). The city of Athens, Greece (top left). Looking across the Danube in Budapest, Hungary (right).

separates Hungary from Slovakia. While most of the low-lying areas have long been cleared of trees, some of the forested areas still survive in the hills and mountains.

Most of the two plains areas are fertile agricultural country, although there are dry sandy expanses, as well as marshlands that are home to a rich variety of waterbirds. More than 70 percent of Hungary's agricultural land is devoted to crops, the most important of which are maize, wheat, sugar beet, and sunflowers. Of the rest, more than four-fifths are meadows and pasturelands and the rest are orchards and vineyards. Pigs and poultry are the most extensively farmed livestock.

Except for natural gas, bauxite, and lignite—a low quality coal that provides much of the country's energy—Hungary is poorly endowed with mineral resources. It imports most of the raw materials for its now largely privatized industries, among which iron and steel production, and the manufacture of fertilizers, pharmaceuticals, and cement are prominent. Most of these industries are located in the north and are centered mainly around the capital, Budapest, and Miskolc, which is the second-largest city and is situated in the far northeast. Aluminum, using local bauxite, is manufactured north of Lake Balaton.

Hungarians enjoy a reasonable standard of living by the standards of former communist countries, though it still compares unfavorably with that in most Western countries. Pollution of air, soil, and water is a major problem and almost half the population lives in seriously affected areas.

Fact File

OFFICIAL NAME	Republic of Hungary
FORM OF GOVERNMENT	Republic with single legislative body (National Assembly)
CAPITAL	Budapest
AREA	93,030 sq km (35,919 sq miles)
TIME ZONE	GMT + 1 hour
POPULATION	10,186,372
PROJECTED POPULATION 2005	10,084,830
POPULATION DENSITY	109.5 per sq km (283.6 per sq mile)
LIFE EXPECTANCY	71.2
INFANT MORTALITY (PER 1,000)	9.5
OFFICIAL LANGUAGE	Hungarian
OTHER LANGUAGE	Romany
LITERACY RATE	99%
RELIGIONS	Roman Catholic 67.5%, Calvinist 20%, Lutheran 5%, other 7.5%
ETHNIC GROUPS	Hungarian 89.9%, Gypsy 4%, German 2.6%, Serb 2%, Slovak 0.8%, Romanian 0.7%
CURRENCY	Forint
ECONOMY	Services 48%, industry 31%, agriculture 21%
GNP PER CAPITA	US$4,120
CLIMATE	Temperate; cold, wet winters and warm summers
HIGHEST POINT	Mt Kekes 1,014 m (3,327 ft)
MAP REFERENCE	Pages 289, 294, 296

Iceland

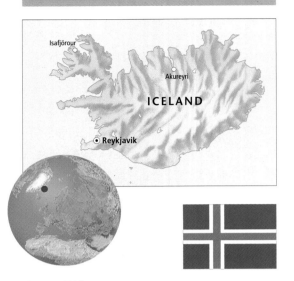

Fact File

OFFICIAL NAME Republic of Iceland

FORM OF GOVERNMENT Republic with single legislative body (Parliament)

CAPITAL Reykjavík

AREA 103,000 sq km (39,768 sq miles)

TIME ZONE GMT

POPULATION 272,512

PROJECTED POPULATION 2005 281,653

POPULATION DENSITY 2.7 per sq km (6.9 per sq mile)

LIFE EXPECTANCY 79

INFANT MORTALITY (PER 1,000) 5.2

OFFICIAL LANGUAGE Icelandic

LITERACY RATE 99%

RELIGIONS Evangelical Lutheran 96%; other Protestant and Roman Catholic 3%; none 1%

ETHNIC GROUPS Icelandic 97%; others including Danish, American, British, Norwegian, German 3%

CURRENCY Króna

ECONOMY Services 61%, industry 35%, agriculture 4%

GNP PER CAPITA US$24,950

CLIMATE Cool temperate, with cool, windy winters and mild, wet summers

HIGHEST POINT Hvannadalshnukur 2,119 m (6,952 ft)

MAP REFERENCE Page 284

True to its name, the island of Iceland, in the north Atlantic Ocean, has one-tenth of its total area covered in icefields and glaciers. The human occupation of this island, which lies just south of the Arctic Circle, dates back to the late ninth century AD when Norwegian Vikings settled there. In the thirteenth century the Icelanders submitted to Norwegian rule and a century and a half later, when the Norwegian and Danish monarchies were combined, they came under Danish control. In 1918 Iceland was granted its independence, but still owed allegiance to the Danish monarch. In 1944, as the result of a referendum, Iceland chose to become a republic. In 1972, because of its economic dependence on the surrounding seas, Iceland, without consultation with other nations,

more than quadrupled the extent of its territorial waters from 12 to 50 nautical miles. Three years later it extended them to 200 nautical miles, a provocative move that brought condemnation, particularly from Britain, and gave rise to serious aggression at sea between Icelandic and British fishing vessels. Britain was later granted some degree of access to the disputed waters.

In addition to icefields and glaciers, Iceland's spectacularly rugged and volcanic landscape includes hot springs, sulphur beds, geysers, lava fields, deep rocky canyons, and plummeting waterfalls. There are numerous small freshwater lakes and 200 volcanoes, many of which are active. Earth tremors, and occasionally larger quakes, are a frequent feature.

The interior of the island consists mainly of an elevated plateau of basalt, interspersed with occasional high peaks. There are small areas of forest and very little arable land. In the north, however, there are extensive grasslands where a small number of sheep, cattle, and horses can graze. More than 90 percent of the population lives in towns and cities around the coast, mainly in the southwest corner near Reykjavík.

Deep-sea fishing is the backbone of Iceland's economy, with fish and associated products constituting more than two-thirds of the country's exports. Apart from fish processing, aluminum smelting from imported bauxite and cement manufacture are growing industries. All of Iceland's domestic and industrial electricity needs are met by locally generated power from hydroelectric or geothermal plants. About one in four Icelanders is employed in manufacturing and processing industries. Iceland attracts about 150,000 tourists a year, more than half its permanent population, making tourism an important income-earner.

The people of Iceland enjoy a very high standard of living. Their economy is robust but is susceptible to variations in international fish prices. The country's free health-care system has contributed to a life expectancy that is among the highest in the world.

Crofts and a patchwork of fields on one of the Aran Islands in Ireland (below). A cobbled shopping street in Dublin, Ireland (top right). A unionist mural in Belfast, Northern Ireland (bottom right).

Ireland

Situated in the northern Atlantic Ocean and separated from the British mainland to the east by the Irish Sea, the Republic of Ireland covers more than three-quarters of the island of Ireland. The northeast corner comprises the six counties that form Northern Ireland, which is part of the United Kingdom. In the fourth century BC, Gaelic-speaking invaders conquered the island and established a Celtic civilization. Tradition has it that St Patrick brought Christianity to Ireland in AD 432, and to this day Catholicism remains the dominant religion. From the eighth century AD Viking raiders attacked the coasts and settled some coastal regions, but they were finally repulsed in 1014. During the twelfth century, the pope, Adrian IV, ceded the entire island to the English crown, but another five centuries were to pass before local opposition was finally subjugated.

From 1846 to 1851 disease destroyed the Irish staple crop, potatoes, leading to famine and more than a million deaths. Roughly half the population emigrated at this time, mainly to the USA.

Although the Irish were granted a degree of autonomy in the eighteenth century, opposition to British rule festered throughout the nineteenth century, leading to the unsuccessful Easter rebellion of 1916 and the eventual granting of home rule to most of the island, as the Irish Free State, in 1921. In 1949 the Republic of Ireland was declared and formal ties with the British crown were severed. Today Ireland is a parliamentary democracy, with a popularly elected president as head of state and two houses of parliament.

Most of the landscape consists of a low-lying limestone plain, with undulating hills and areas of fertile soils. Small lakes and peat bogs abound throughout the countryside. Mountain ranges run along much of the coast, creating, especially in the southwest, some of Europe's most spectacular coastal scenery. The most significant ranges are the Wicklow Mountains in the southeast and Macgillicuddy's Reeks in the far southwest. The Shannon, the country's longest river, rises in the Iron Mountains not far from the Northern Ireland border. It drains the central plain and flows through a number of Ireland's largest lakes.

Traditionally an agricultural country, Ireland now relies mainly on manufacturing and processing industries for its present, relatively healthy, economic strength. The country joined the European Community in 1973. Four in ten members of the population live in urban areas. Clothing, pharmaceuticals, and the manufacture of heavy machinery contribute largely to Ireland's export earnings and tourism is also significant. More than 3 million people visit Ireland every year. About one in eight workers is still involved in agriculture, mainly in livestock raising and dairying, but also in cultivating crops such as potatoes, barley, and wheat. The country has reserves of natural gas, oil and peat.

Fact File

OFFICIAL NAME	Ireland
FORM OF GOVERNMENT	Republic with two legislative bodies (Senate and House of Representatives)
CAPITAL	Dublin
AREA	70,280 sq km (27,135 sq miles)
TIME ZONE	GMT
POPULATION	3,632,944
PROJECTED POPULATION 2005	3,727,595
POPULATION DENSITY	51.7 per sq km (133.9 per sq mile)
LIFE EXPECTANCY	76.4
INFANT MORTALITY (PER 1,000)	5.9
OFFICIAL LANGUAGES	Irish Gaelic, English
LITERACY RATE	99%
RELIGIONS	Roman Catholic 93%, Anglican 3%, other 4%
ETHNIC GROUPS	Celtic 94%, English minority
CURRENCY	Irish pound
ECONOMY	Industry 54%, services 36%, agriculture 10%
GNP PER CAPITA	US$14,710
CLIMATE	Temperate, with cool, wet winters and mild summers; wetter in the west
HIGHEST POINT	Carrauntoohil 1,041 m (3,415 ft)
MAP REFERENCE	Pages 303, 309

The Troubles in Northern Ireland

Ever since Britain's granting of independence to the Irish Free State in 1921, Northern Ireland has been a troubled province, a place where terrorism and sectarian strife have been the norm. The arrangements for the government of Northern Ireland created bitter resentment among its minority Catholic population. Northern Ireland was granted self-government, with its own parliament in Belfast, but maintaining strong links with the British government in London. The government ruled blatantly in favor of the Protestant majority, excluding Catholics from positions of authority or influence. Catholics moved in great numbers from the country to Belfast and other cities in order to find work, almost invariably in menial jobs in shipbuilding, textile, and other industries.

The Irish Republican Army (IRA), which had used guerrilla tactics against the British during Ireland's struggle for independence, became a threat to the stability of Northern Ireland, carrying out sporadic attacks on Protestant targets. When, in 1949, the Irish Free State, as Ireland was then called, left the British Commonwealth and became the Republic of Ireland, battle lines became marked. The IRA began to campaign aggressively for Northern Ireland to be absorbed into the republic and the breaking of ties with Britain, but for the next two decades it made little progress in the face of Northern Ireland's largely apathetic Catholic population.

However, as discrimination, especially in housing and employment, continued in Northern Ireland, Catholics grew increasingly militant, and in the late 1960s waged a widespread campaign for increased civil rights. Their demonstrations provoked counter-demonstrations by militant Protestants and a 30-year period of violent sectarian clashes was launched. The situation was aggravated by the arrival of British troops, ostensibly to maintain the peace. They were soon perceived by Catholics to be acting in the interests of the Protestants, especially after 1972, when they opened fire on Catholic demonstrators in Londonderry, killing 13 of them. In March 1972, in the wake of this incident, the British

government suspended the parliament in Belfast and instituted direct rule for the province from London, a move that antagonized people on both sides of the struggle.

The desire of one section of the IRA to abandon violence led to a split in 1969. A wing of the IRA—the Provisionals, or Provos—consisting mainly of younger members, remained committed to terrorism and during the 1970s and 1980s carried out repeated bombings, murders, and kidnappings of both civilians and British army personnel, not only in Ireland, but also on the British mainland. Protestants in Northern Ireland responded in kind. From the early 1970s until the mid-1990s more than 3,000 people died in the conflict, and many more were wounded. The most prominent victim was Earl Mountbatten, who was assassinated in the Irish Republic in 1979. Northern Ireland towns and cities were divided into Catholic and Protestant zones, and an atmosphere of fear and distrust prevailed.

Any possibility of a negotiated peace was thwarted by the determination of successive British governments not to recognize or to have discussions with the IRA. This situation changed in 1994, when the Provisional IRA suspended its terrorist campaign and talks, at first in secret, but later open, were held in London. The talks broke down in 1996 when the Provisional IRA revoked its cease-fire and continued its attacks. However, over the following years, new overtures were made and new talks, brokered with the help of the USA, have brought hopes for a lasting peace.

Italy

Fact file

OFFICIAL NAME Italian Republic

FORM OF GOVERNMENT Republic with two legislative bodies (Senate and Chamber of Deputies)

CAPITAL Rome

AREA 301,230 sq km (116,305 sq miles)

TIME ZONE GMT + 1 hour

POPULATION 56,735,130

PROJECTED POPULATION 2005 56,253,452

POPULATION DENSITY 188.3 per sq km (487.7 per sq mile)

LIFE EXPECTANCY 78.5

INFANT MORTALITY (PER 1,000) 6.3

OFFICIAL LANGUAGE Italian

OTHER LANGUAGES German, French, Greek, Albanian

LITERACY RATE 98.1%

RELIGIONS Roman Catholic 98%, other 2%

ETHNIC GROUPS Italian, 94%; German–Italian, French–Italian, Slovene–Italian and Albanian–Italian communities 6%

CURRENCY Lira

ECONOMY Services 71%, industry 20%, agriculture 9%

GNP PER CAPITA US$19,020

CLIMATE Temperate; north has cool, wet winters and warm, dry summers; south has mild winters and hot, dry summers

HIGHEST POINT Mont Blanc 4,807 m (15,771 ft)

MAP REFERENCE Pages 294–95

Situated in southern central Europe, the Italian mainland consists of a long peninsula that juts out into the Mediterranean Sea. Shaped roughly like a long, high-heeled boot, this land mass is bordered to the north by Switzerland and Austria, to the west by France, and to the east by Slovenia. At the southwestern tip of the peninsula, the narrow Strait of Messina separates the toe of the boot from the large Italian island of Sicily, while further west in the Mediterranean, separated from the mainland by the Tyrrhenian Sea and sitting just south of the French island of Corsica, is the island of Sardinia, also part of Italy. About 70 other small islands, scattered mainly around the coasts of Sicily and Sardinia and off the western coast of the mainland, make up the rest of present-day Italy. The peninsula's eastern coastline is washed by the waters of the Adriatic Sea, across which lies the coast of Croatia.

History

Italy's capital, Rome, situated in central western Italy, was for 800 years, from about 400 BC, the hub of the mighty Roman Empire. At the height of their powers in the first and second centuries AD the Romans controlled the whole of the Italian Peninsula and vast swathes of Europe. Their empire stretched as far as Britain in the north, the Iberian Peninsula in the west, into Egypt in North Africa and eastward as far as the Persian Gulf. Italy became Christianized after the conversion of the Roman Emperor Constantine in AD 313. The sacking of Rome by the Visigoths in AD 410 precipitated a series of subsequent invasions which resulted, over the centuries, in the fragmentation of Italy into a number of states ruled by different powers. For some time all of Italy came under the control of the eastern Roman Empire, based in Constantinople. The Franks, under Charlemagne, gained control of much of northern Italy at the end of the eighth century AD, and in the eleventh century the Normans invaded Sicily, which led to the creation of a kingdom based around the southern city of Naples.

In the later Middle Ages there emerged, in central and northern Italy, a number of powerful city-states, the most notable being Florence, Venice, Pisa and Genoa. From the fourteenth century, these states, especially Florence, promoted a great cultural revival which saw a blossoming of artistic, musical, literary, and scientific activity. This revival, which gradually spread through most of Europe, is now known as the Renaissance.

France, Spain, and Austria vied for domination of different parts of Italy between the fifteenth and the eighteenth centuries. Most of Italy fell to Napoleon's armies in 1796–97, but after Napoleon's downfall in 1815 Italy was again fragmented, with Austria the dominant power in the north. A series of uprisings during the 1820s and 1830s gave rise

to the movement known as the Risorgimento (resurrection), which eventually led to the total unification of Italy and the installation of Victor Emmanuel II, the King of Sardinia, as King of Italy in 1861. During the next half-century Italy acquired a number of overseas territories, including Eritrea, part of Somalia, and some Greek islands.

Although officially allied to Germany, Italy at first remained neutral in the First World War and later joined the Allied side. In 1919 Benito Mussolini, a former socialist, founded the Fascist Party as a bulwark against communism. In 1922 he seized power, setting up a dictatorship. Embarking on a policy of foreign conquest, Italy invaded Ethiopia in 1935. Fascist Italy joined the side of Nazi Germany in the Second World War but in 1943 it was invaded by Allied troops and subsequently declared war on its former German ally. Dismissed from the Italian government, Mussolini was installed by Germany as head of a puppet government in northern Italy but he was captured and executed by partisans in 1945.

After the war, Italy was stripped of its foreign territories. A referendum in 1946 resulted in the abolition of the monarchy and the establishment of a democratic republic. Since then, government in Italy has been wracked by instability as changing allegiances and coalitions have created a succession of short-lived governments. In 1993 a referendum approved a plan to simplify Italy's complex electoral system. Since 1994 three-quarters of the members of Italy's two houses of parliament have been elected by a simple majority of votes, while the rest are elected by proportional representation. The president, whose duties are largely ceremonial, is elected for a seven-year term. Both houses are elected for a maximum of five years.

Timeline

900 BC Etruscan civilization founded between Arno and Tiber Rivers by people arriving from the east; lasts till c.200 BC	
6th century BC Under rule of Etruscan kings Rome grows from village to wealthy city	
568 BC Langobardi (Lombards) seize much of northern Italy from Roman Empire	
AD 79 Mt Vesuvius near Naples erupts, buries city of Pompeii in lava and ash, and Herculaneum under mud	
476 Germanic leader Odoacer defeats last Roman Emperor; ends dominance of western sector of Roman Empire	
800 Pope Leo III crowns Charlemagne Emperor of the Romans	
962 Otto the Great crowned Emperor of the Holy Roman Empire	
1000 Rise of city states such as Florence, Venice, Genoa, and Pisa which have strong commercial and cultural identities	
c.1300 Renaissance begins. Interest flourishes in arts, sciences, and literature as well as philosophy, politics, and religion	
1345 Black Death, bubonic plague, kills more than one-quarter of the population	
1519 King Charles I of Spain becomes Holy Roman Emperor. Siezes much of Italy including Rome and Milan from France	
1663 Volcano Mt Etna erupts destroying much of the town of Catania, northeast Sicily	
1796 Napoleon Bonaparte invades north Italy, setting up independent republics. Interest in Italian independence grows	

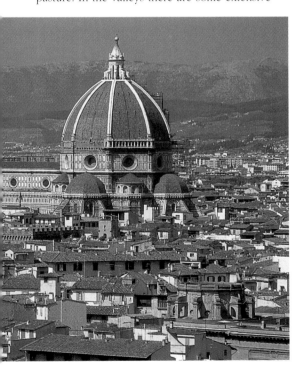

The rooftops of Florence, including the cathedral, seen from Piazzale Michelangelo (below). Fishing boats in the harbor of Camogli in Liguria, northern Italy (above). One of the many palaces on the Grand Canal in Venice (right).

Physical features and land use

Most of Italy is mountainous, with a central range, the Appenines, sweeping down the length of the peninsula and extending into Sicily, where the volcanic, and still active, peak of Mount Etna soars to a height of 3,323 m (10,902 ft) above sea level. Further north, near Naples, the active Mount Vesuvius offers evidence of the volcanic origins of Italy's mountains. The Appenines, which are rich in limestone, reach heights of almost 3,000 m (10,000 ft) in the Gran Sasso Range, east of Rome. The slopes of the Appenines are covered with thin soils, which in some places provide reasonable pasture. In the valleys there are some extensive stretches of arable land. At the far northwestern tip of the Italian peninsula the Appenines merge with the Alps, which are generally higher than the Appenines and which arch right across the north of Italy, forming natural boundaries with the countries of Switzerland, Austria, and France. In the southern extremities of the Alps are a series of large, spectacular lakes, which include the much visited Lago Maggiore, Lago di Como, and Lago di Garda. These lakes and the rivers that feed into them are the source of the hydroelectricity which supplies about half the electricity needs of industrialized northern Italy.

In the northeast of the country, enclosed by the Alps to the north and the west and the Appenines to the south, and stretching in the east as far as the Adriatic coast, is the country's largest lowland region, known as the Plain of Lombardy. Drained by the River Po, which flows from west to east across the widest part of the country, this area is the most fertile, as well as the most heavily industrialized and populous part of Italy. About two-fifths of Italy's crops are grown here. Agriculture is also extensive on the coastal plains on each side of the Appenines. Farms are mainly small. Crops include potatoes, wheat, maize, olives, and other vegetables as well as a wide range of citrus and stone fruits. Italy produces more wine than any other country and there are extensive vine-yards, most particularly in the Chianti region in Tuscany. Sheep, pigs, and cattle are the principal livestock.

Industry, commerce, and culture

Apart from marble in the south, for which it is famous, and some oil deposits in Sicily, Italy is not well endowed with mineral resources and imports most of the energy needed by its highly developed industrial sector. This is concentrated overwhelmingly in the north of the country—although Naples, Bari, and Taranto in the south and Rome in the center have a certain amount of heavy industry—and is based around such cities as Milan, Turin, and Genoa. The building of cars, aircraft, and other transport equipment are major industries, as are tool, textile, clothing, and chemical manufacture.

Italy's manufacturing sector, which was heavily subsidized by the state, developed largely in the half-century since the Second World War, before which the economy was based predominantly on agriculture. It now employs about a fifth of the country's workforce. Tourism is an important source of income, with about 30 million people visiting Italy every year.

There is a great divide in Italy between the high living standards of the industrialized, affluent north and the much lower living standards of the largely undeveloped south, especially in Calabria in the far south. In the south unemployment is chronically high, investment is hard to attract, poverty is widespread, and crime for many people offers the best means of survival.

REGIONS

Abruzzi • Basilicata • Calabria
Campania • Emilia-Romagna
Friuli-Venezia Giulia • Lazio • Liguria
Lombardy • Marche • Molise
Piedmont • Puglia • Sardinia
Sicily • Trentino-Alto Adige • Tuscany
Umbria • Valle d'Aosta • Veneto

1814 Napoleon defeated by European powers; under Congress of Vienna most of Italy returns to Austrian rule	**1861** King Victor Emmanuel announces Kingdom of Italy. To include entire peninsula except Rome, Venice, and San Marino	**1908** Earthquake in Messina, Sicily, kills 120,000 people	**1922** Mussolini becomes leader and the Fascist movement grows	**1940** Italy's forces defeated in Eritrea, Ethiopia, and Greece; Mussolini overthrown, but reinstalled by Germans; Allies retake Italy (1943)	**1960s** Rapid postwar industrialization brings prosperity to northern cities but the south remains largely agricultural and poor	**1980** Earthquake in southern Italy kills more than 4,500 and leaves 400,000 homeless
1858 French troops help Kingdom of Sardinia to push back Austrian troops, regaining most of northern Italy	**1860** Garibaldi's redshirts regain contol of Sicily; eventually they take all southern Italy, including Naples	**1915** Italy joins Allies in First World War	**1939** Start of Second World War; Italy enters on Germany's side nine months later, soon after the fall of France, in June 1940	**1943** Allies invade Italy; Italian prime minister signs armistice with Allies; Italy declares war on Germany	**1946** First free elections held since 1930s after Humbert III takes up the Italian throne; Italians vote to establish a Republic	

Latvia

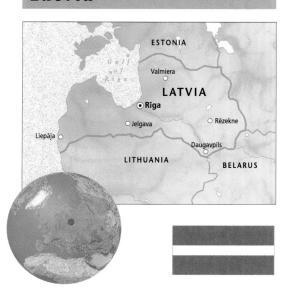

The rooftops of a town in Latvia (right). More than two-thirds of the Latvian population are urbanized.

Fact File

OFFICIAL NAME Republic of Latvia

FORM OF GOVERNMENT Republic with single legislative body (Parliament)

CAPITAL Riga

AREA 64,100 sq km (24,749 sq miles)

TIME ZONE GMT + 3 hours

POPULATION 2,353,874

PROJECTED POPULATION 2005 2,221,761

POPULATION DENSITY 36.7 per sq km (95.1 per sq mile)

LIFE EXPECTANCY 67.3

INFANT MORTALITY (PER 1,000) 17.2

OFFICIAL LANGUAGE Lettish

OTHER LANGUAGES Lithuanian, Russian

LITERACY RATE 99%

RELIGIONS Mainly Lutheran with Russian Orthodox and Roman Catholic minorities

ETHNIC GROUPS Latvian 51.8%, Russian 33.8%, Belarusian 4.5%, Ukrainian 3.4%, Polish 2.3%, other 4.2%

CURRENCY Lats

ECONOMY Services 43%, industry 41%, agriculture 16%

GNP PER CAPITA US$2,270

CLIMATE Temperate. Cold, wet winters and mild summers

HIGHEST POINT Gaizinkalns 312 m (1,024 ft)

MAP REFERENCE Page 287

Latvia lies between its sister Baltic republics of Estonia, to the north, and Lithuania, to the south, its coastline along the Baltic Sea indented by the Gulf of Riga. To the east and southeast respectively it shares borders with the Russian Federation and Belarus. Like Estonia and Lithuania, Latvia has for most of its history been controlled by foreign powers. For more than 1,000 years, its inhabitants, the Letts, have been ruled successively by Germans, Poles, Swedes, and finally Russians. In 1991 Latvia declared its independence from the Soviet Union. It is now a multi-party parliamentary democracy with an elected president as its head of state. Since independence, the Communist Party of Latvia has been banned.

The country is mostly flat with hillier land in the east. There are large areas of bogs and swamps and about 40 percent of the land is woodland or forest, in which oak and pine predominate. Small farms account for most agriculture, which is mainly dairy farming and cattle raising. Some grain and vegetable crops are also grown. Forestry and fishing, which were important in earlier times, have enjoyed a resurgence in recent years.

Latvia is the most heavily industrialized of the Baltic republics. It has few mineral resources and imports the raw materials needed for its industries—the manufacture of electrical goods, shipbuilding, and train and vehicle making. It relies on its former ruler for energy supplies and much of the Russian Federation's oil and gas exports pass through the Latvian port of Venspils. Air and water pollution from industrial wastes is a matter of concern.

Latvia's economy was severely affected in 1995 by bank failures and financial scandals and its dependence on Russia limits its development. Latvians have a reasonable standard of living, although discrepancies in wealth are marked.

Liechtenstein

This small central European country sits high in the Alps. To the west the Rhine River forms a border with Switzerland, with which Liechtenstein has political ties and whose currency it shares. Austria lies to the east and south. The country takes its name from the Austrian Liechtenstein family which, in 1699 and 1713, acquired two fiefdoms and formed them into the principality. It later came under French and then German influence. In 1866 it achieved independence, and two years later declared itself permanently neutral, a position it has since maintained. In all subsequent European wars, Liechtenstein has remained unmolested. Its head of state is an hereditary monarch who appoints a government on the recommendation of an elected parliament. Elections are held every four years and there is universal adult suffrage, although women have had the vote only since 1984.

The Rhine is the source of Liechtenstein's agricultural strength. Its floodplain, once marshy, has been drained and reclaimed for agricultural and pastoral use. The capital sits on a plateau overlooking the undulating expanses of the Rhine Valley. The slopes of the Rhatikon alpine range

rise to impressive peaks in the south. From the southern highlands, the Samina River flows northward through the center of the country. Thick forests—of beech, maple, and ash—cover much of the mountain region.

The main agricultural industries are cattle, sheep, and pig raising, and some vegetables and cereal crops are grown. There is little heavy industry but prominent among light industries are textile and ceramic goods and the manufacture of electronic equipment. There are no mineral resources, and Liechtenstein imports all its fuel and raw materials. A major source of revenue is the sale of postage stamps. More than half the country's residents are foreign nationals, largely attracted by the country's low rates of taxation and its banking laws, which ensure great secrecy.

Fact File

OFFICIAL NAME Principality of Liechtenstein

FORM OF GOVERNMENT Constitutional monarchy with single legislative house (Parliament)

CAPITAL Vaduz

AREA 160 sq km (62 sq miles)

TIME ZONE GMT + 1 hour

POPULATION 32,057

PROJECTED POPULATION 2005 33,981

POPULATION DENSITY 200.4 per sq km (519 per sq mile)

LIFE EXPECTANCY 78.1

INFANT MORTALITY (PER 1,000) 5.2

OFFICIAL LANGUAGE German

LITERACY RATE 99%

RELIGIONS Roman Catholic 87.3%, Protestant 8.3%, other 4.4%

ETHNIC GROUPS Alemannic 95%, Italian and other 5%

CURRENCY Swiss franc

ECONOMY Services 50%; industry, trade and building 48%; agriculture, fishing and forestry 2%

GNP PER CAPITA US$33,000

CLIMATE Temperate, with cold, wet winters and mild, humid summers

HIGHEST POINT Grauspitz 2,599 m (8,527 ft)

MAP REFERENCE Page 288

Lithuania

Russia for oil and most of the raw materials needed for its industries. The main forms of agriculture are dairy farming and pig and cattle raising. Continuing dependence on Russia and a high rate of inflation are among factors that make Lithuania the least prosperous of the Baltic states.

Fact File

OFFICIAL NAME	Republic of Lithuania
FORM OF GOVERNMENT	Republic with single legislative body (Parliament)
CAPITAL	Vilnius
AREA	65,200 sq km (25,174 sq miles)
TIME ZONE	GMT + 3 hours
POPULATION	3,584,966
PROJECTED POPULATION 2005	3,526,180
POPULATION DENSITY	55 per sq km (142.4 per sq mile)
LIFE EXPECTANCY	69
INFANT MORTALITY (PER 1,000)	14.7
OFFICIAL LANGUAGE	Lithuanian
OTHER LANGUAGES	Russian, Polish
LITERACY RATE	98.4%
RELIGIONS	Roman Catholic 90%; Russian Orthodox, Muslim and Protestant minorities 10%
ETHNIC GROUPS	Lithuanian 80.1%, Russian 8.6%, Polish 7.7%, Belarusian 1.5%, other 2.1%
CURRENCY	Litas
ECONOMY	Industry 42%, services 40%, agriculture 18%
GNP PER CAPITA	US$1,900
CLIMATE	Temperate. Cold winters and mild summers
HIGHEST POINT	Mt Juozapine 292 m (958 ft)
MAP REFERENCE	Pages 287, 289

Luxembourg

The largest of the Baltic states, Lithuania has borders with Latvia to the north, Belarus to the east and southeast, Poland to the south, and the Russian Federation to the southwest. The Baltic Sea lies to its west. In the thirteenth century, Lithuania was united under a Christian king, in the sixteenth century it merged with Poland, then in 1795 it came under Russian control. Occupied by Germany in the First World War, Lithuania became independent in 1918. It became part of the Soviet Union in 1940 and was then invaded by Germany. When Soviet armies arrived in 1944, over 200,000 people, more than three-quarters of them Jews, had perished. In 1991 the country declared its independence from the Soviet Union. It is now a multi-party democracy with a president as head of state and a prime minister as head of government.

Most of Lithuania consists of a relatively fertile plain with extensive marshlands and forests. Many marshes have been reclaimed for growing cereal and vegetable crops. Sand dunes predominate along the Baltic coast and there is a range of hills dotted with more than 3,000 lakes in the southeast. Numerous rivers traverse the landscape.

Machine manufacturing, petroleum refining, shipbuilding, and food processing are some of Lithuania's key industries, but they have resulted in soil and groundwater contamination. The country has few natural resources and depends on

The Grand Duchy of Luxembourg is one of the smallest countries in Europe. Situated in northern Europe, it shares borders with Belgium to the west and France to the south. Three connecting rivers—the Our, Sûre, and the Moselle —separate it from Germany to the east. Part of the Holy Roman Empire since the tenth century AD, Luxembourg became an independent duchy in 1354, one of hundreds of such states in medieval Europe. It is the only one to survive today as an independent nation. Throughout the intervening centuries, Luxembourg has come under Austrian, Spanish, French, and Dutch rule. In 1830 part of

the duchy was taken over by Belgium when that country split from the Netherlands. Luxembourg separated from the Netherlands in 1890. Germany occupied Luxembourg during both world wars and annexed it in 1942. After the Second World War it became a founder member of NATO and in 1957 joined the European Economic Community. It has been a keen advocate of European cooperation and was the first country, in 1991, to ratify the Maastricht Treaty. Luxembourg is a constitutional monarchy, with the Grand Duke as head of state, and a prime minister as head of an elected 21-member Council of State.

The northern part of Luxembourg is called the Oesling. Covering about one-third of the country's total area, it is part of the densely forested Ardennes mountain range. Numerous river valleys dissect this northern region and deer and wild boar abound. It is a rugged, picturesque area but has poor soils. In contrast, the southern two-thirds, known as the Gutland or Bon Pays (meaning good land), consists of plains and undulating hills covered with rich soils and extensive pastureland.

Iron ore deposits in the south of the country contributed to the development of a thriving iron and steel industry. These deposits are now less abundant and industries such as food processing, chemical manufacturing and tyre making now rival steel in importance. A growing service sector, especially in banking, has become increasingly central to the country's prosperity. The Gutland area is still strongly agricultural. Wheat, barley, potatoes, and grapes are the principal crops and more than 5 million cattle and 6 million pigs are raised. The people of Luxembourg are among the most affluent in Europe. Unemployment is low and salaries, especially among urban workers, are high.

Fact File

OFFICIAL NAME	Grand Duchy of Luxembourg
FORM OF GOVERNMENT	Constitutional monarchy with single legislative body (Chamber of Deputies)
CAPITAL	Luxembourg
AREA	2,586 sq km (998 sq miles)
TIME ZONE	GMT + 1 hour
POPULATION	429,080
PROJECTED POPULATION 2005	445,932
POPULATION DENSITY	165.9 per sq km (429.7 per sq mile)
LIFE EXPECTANCY	77.7
INFANT MORTALITY (PER 1,000)	5.0
OFFICIAL LANGUAGE	Letzeburgish
OTHER LANGUAGES	French, German
LITERACY RATE	99%
RELIGIONS	Roman Catholic 97%, Protestant and Jewish 3%
ETHNIC GROUPS	Luxembourger (French and German) 70%; Portuguese, Belgian and Italian minorities 30%
CURRENCY	Luxembourg franc
ECONOMY	Services 77%, industry 19%, agriculture 4%
GNP PER CAPITA	US$41,210
CLIMATE	Temperate, with cool winters and mild summers
HIGHEST POINT	Burgplatz 559 m (1,834 ft)
MAP REFERENCE	Page 291

Macedonia

This small, landlocked Balkan country in south-eastern Europe is bordered by Yugoslavia to the north, Bulgaria to the east, Greece to the south, and Albania to the west. During the third century BC Macedonia was the heart of the Greek Empire. It later became a Roman province, but from the fourth century AD it was invaded numerous times. In the fourteenth century it came under Ottoman control. As the Ottoman Empire declined in the nineteenth century, Bulgaria, Greece, and Serbia contended for control of Macedonia and by the First World War it had been divided between them. Present-day Macedonia is essentially the region that was in Serbian hands at the end of the First World War. Macedonia was then incorporated into the Kingdom of Serbs, Croats, and Slovenes, which in 1929 became the Republic of Yugoslavia. In 1946 it became an autonomous republic within Yugoslavia. In 1991 Macedonia withdrew from Yugoslavia and it is now a multi-party democracy, governed by a legislative body with 120 elected members and a directly elected president. Tensions with neighbors remain high. Macedonia is also the name of a Greek province, over which Greece claims the former Yugoslav state has territorial ambitions.

Macedonia is largely isolated from its neighbors by mountains. Mountain ranges separate it from Greece in the south and the Korab Mountains in the west lie along the Albanian border. Much of the country is a plateau more than 2,000 m (6,500 ft) above sea level. The River Vadar rises in the northwest. It flows north, almost to the Yugoslavian border, then continues on a southeasterly course through the center of the country and into Greece.

One-quarter of the land is used for agriculture. Crops include cereals, fruits, vegetables, and cotton, and sheep and cattle are raised extensively. The country is self-sufficient in food and, thanks to its coal resources, in energy. Manufacturing industries have suffered since independence, partly because of trade embargoes imposed by Greece. Macedonia is the least developed of the former Yugoslav republics and is suffering a declining standard of living.

Fact File

OFFICIAL NAME	Former Yugoslav Republic of Macedonia
FORM OF GOVERNMENT	Republic with single legislative body (Assembly)
CAPITAL	Skopje
AREA	25,333 sq km (9,781 sq miles)
TIME ZONE	GMT + 1 hour
POPULATION	2,022,604
PROJECTED POPULATION 2005	2,086,849
POPULATION DENSITY	79.8 per sq km (206.8 per sq mile)
LIFE EXPECTANCY	73.1
INFANT MORTALITY (PER 1,000)	18.7
OFFICIAL LANGUAGE	Macedonian
OTHER LANGUAGES	Albanian, Turkish, Serbian, Croatian
LITERACY RATE	94.0%
RELIGIONS	Eastern Orthodox 67%, Muslim 30%, other 3%
ETHNIC GROUPS	Macedonian 65%, Albanian 22%, Turkish 4%, Serb 2%, Gypsy 3%, other 4%
CURRENCY	Denar
ECONOMY	Services and agriculture 60%; manufacturing and mining 40%
GNP PER CAPITA	US$860
CLIMATE	Temperate, with cold winters and hot summers
HIGHEST POINT	Mt Korab 2,753 m (9,032 ft)
MAP REFERENCE	Pages 296–97, 298

Malta

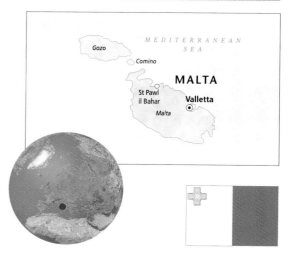

The Republic of Malta consists of an archipelago of three inhabited islands—Malta, Gozo, and Comino—and three tiny uninhabited islands, which are little more than rocky outcrops. They are situated in the center of the Mediterranean Sea 93 km (58 miles) south of Sicily. Malta, the largest and most populous of the islands, contains the capital, Valletta, the country's fifth largest city, picturesquely situated on a promontory between two harbors, and the four larger cities of Birkirkara, Qormi, Hamrun, and Sliema. Successive civilizations have recognized the importance of Malta's position and the advantages of its many harbors. It was occupied successively by the Phoenicians, the Greeks, and the Romans. In the ninth century AD, when it was part of the Byzantine Empire, it was conquered by Arabs but fell two centuries later to Sicily and then, in 1282, to Spain. In 1530 the Spanish king gave Malta to the Knights of St John, a religious order, which built and fortified the town of Valletta and occupied the island of Malta until it was seized by Napoleon in 1798. Britain took the island in 1800 and held it until 1947, when the country was granted self-government as a parliamentary democracy. In 1964, Malta gained full independence. Relations with Britain and other Western nations have often been strained, largely because of Malta's close links with Libya in northern Africa.

The three inhabited islands are mostly flat—although the island of Malta is undulating in places—with spectacular rocky coastlines. There is little natural vegetation and there are no forests or major rivers. Low rainfall, poor drainage, a limestone base and a hot climate all contribute to the paucity of the islands' shallow soils, which, however, support a range of cereal and vegetable crops as well as substantial vineyards.

Apart from limestone for building, Malta has virtually no mineral resources and is heavily dependent on imported materials. It has no natural sources of energy and produces only one-fifth of its population's food needs. Tourism is the mainstay of the economy. Every year about a million visitors, mainly from the United Kingdom, arrive to enjoy its beaches, its historic towns, and its rugged scenery. Ship repairs and clothing and textile manufacture are other significant industries. The average income is low by Western standards and Maltese residents are among the least affluent of Western Europeans.

Europe and the Russian Federation

The town of Ohrid on the shore of Lake Ohrid in southwestern Macedonia (bottom left). One of Malta's megalithic temples, built more than 5,000 years ago (left). The harbor front in Valletta, the capital of Malta (below left).

Fact File

OFFICIAL NAME Republic of Malta

FORM OF GOVERNMENT Republic with single legislative body (House of Representatives)

CAPITAL Valletta

AREA 320 sq km (124 sq miles)

TIME ZONE GMT + 1 hour

POPULATION 381,603

PROJECTED POPULATION 2005 389,772

POPULATION DENSITY 1,192.5 per sq km (3,088.6 per sq mile)

LIFE EXPECTANCY 77.8

INFANT MORTALITY (PER 1,000) 7.4

OFFICIAL LANGUAGES Maltese, English

LITERACY RATE 86%

RELIGIONS Roman Catholic 98%, other 2%

ETHNIC GROUPS Mixed Arab, Sicilian, French, Spanish, Italian and English

CURRENCY Maltese lira

ECONOMY Government 37%, services 30%, manufacturing 27%, construction 4%, agriculture 2%

GNP PER CAPITA US$7,200

CLIMATE Temperate, with mild, wet winters and hot, dry summers

HIGHEST POINT Dingli Cliffs 245 m (804 ft)

MAP REFERENCE Pages 361, 362

Moldova

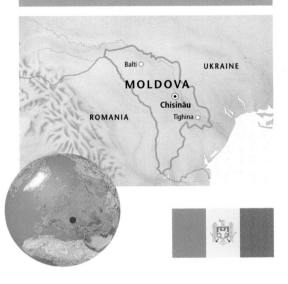

Moldova is a small, landlocked country in southeastern Europe, near the northern shores of the Black Sea. To the west the Prut River separates Moldova from Romania. Otherwise, it is completely enclosed by Ukrainian territory. Bessarabia—the section between the Prut and Dniester rivers—which comprises almost all of present-day Moldova, was under Ottoman rule until 1812, when it passed to Russian control. With the collapse of the Russian Empire after the First World War, Bessarabia merged in 1918 with Romania, with which it is ethnically and linguistically almost identical. The part of Moldova east of the Dniester remained under Russian control. As a result of the Nazi–Soviet Pact of 1940 Romania was forced to cede Bessarabia. Most of it was combined with a narrow strip of the Ukraine east of the Dniester to form the new state of Moldova. The remaining parts were incorporated into Ukraine.

After the Second World War, Moldova became a Soviet republic and systematic attempts were made to suppress all links with Romania. Large numbers of ethnic Romanians were forcibly removed to other countries in the Soviet Union, and Russian and Ukrainian immigration was fostered. Independence came in 1991, as the Soviet Union crumbled, but tensions between the predominantly Russian population in the region lying to the east of the Dniester, who wished to declare a separate republic, and the ethnic

Romanians, who sought closer ties, and even reunification, with Romania, resulted in violent clashes. In 1992, a joint Russian–Moldovan peacekeeping force was instituted to help restore order, although ethnic tensions persist. In 1994 a constitution was adopted, defining the country as a democratic republic.

Most of the countryside of Moldova is low-lying but hilly steppe country. It is eroded by rivers and the landscape is cut by numerous deep valleys and gorges. Thick forests grow on many of the hillsides and most of the country is covered with thick, black, fertile soils. This fertile land, combined with a temperate climate, short winters and high summer rainfall, made Moldova one of the foremost producers of food in the former Soviet Union.

Agriculture remains the main element in the Moldovan economy. Vegetables, sunflower seeds, tobacco, wheat, and maize are the principal crops, as well as grapes, which contribute to a thriving winemaking and exporting industry. Cattle and pig raising are also widespread.

The country has minimal reserves of mineral resources and depends upon Russian imports for all its oil, gas, and coal supplies. Electricity, too, is mainly imported and power shortages occur quite frequently. Industries include machine manufacturing and food processing.

Fact File

OFFICIAL NAME Republic of Moldova

FORM OF GOVERNMENT Republic with single legislative body (Parliament)

CAPITAL Chisinau

AREA 33,700 sq km (13,012 sq miles)

TIME ZONE GMT + 3 hours

POPULATION 4,460,838

PROJECTED POPULATION 2005 4,522,745

POPULATION DENSITY 132.4 per sq km (342.9 per sq mile)

LIFE EXPECTANCY 64.4

INFANT MORTALITY (PER 1,000) 43.5

OFFICIAL LANGUAGE Moldovan

OTHER LANGUAGES Russian, Gagauz (Turkish dialect)

LITERACY RATE 98.9%

RELIGIONS Eastern Orthodox 98.5%, Jewish 1.5%

ETHNIC GROUPS Moldovan/Romanian 64.5%, Ukrainian 13.8%, Russian 13%, Gagauz 3.5%, Jewish 1.5%, Bulgarian 2%, other 1.7%

CURRENCY Leu

ECONOMY Services 46%, agriculture 34%, industry 20%

GNP PER CAPITA US$920

CLIMATE Temperate, with mild winters and warm summers

HIGHEST POINT Mt Balaneshty 430 m (1,411 ft)

MAP REFERENCE Page 296

Monaco

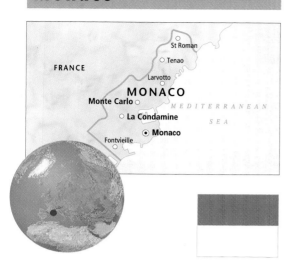

Monaco, the world's smallest independent nation after the Vatican City, sits on the Mediterranean coast in the far southeast corner of France. Except for its coastline, it is completely surrounded by French territory. In the thirteenth century the Genoese built a fortress there and in 1297 members of the Grimaldi family of Genoa established themselves as rulers. Grimaldi princes retained control for almost 500 years, until 1792, when an uprising deposed the reigning prince and declared the state a republic. France annexed Monaco the following year, but in 1815, after the Congress of Vienna, it was placed under the protection of Sardinia. France annexed most of Monaco, including Menton, in 1848. In 1861, the Grimaldis were restored as rulers of less than half their former territory, governing under French protection. In 1911 democratic government was introduced by Prince Albert of Monaco. An 18-member National Council is elected every five years, but the head of government is selected by the monarch from a list drawn up by the French government. The present monarch, Prince Rainier III, is a descendant of the Grimaldis. He achieved fame in 1956 for his much-publicized marriage to the American film actress Grace Kelly.

Occupying the lower slopes of the Maritime Alps, Monaco is hilly and rugged. It is densely populated, mainly by foreign nationals. In the southwest is the industrial district of Fontvieille,

which consists partly of land reclaimed from the sea. Further east is the old town of Monaco-Ville, where the royal palace is situated. La Condamine, the banking, commercial, and fashionable residential center, overlooks a sheltered harbor. Northeast of La Condamine is Monte Carlo, with its casino, luxury hotels, and apartment blocks.

Apart from pharmaceutical, food processing, and other light industries in Fontvieille, Monaco thrives on its attractions as a tourist haven. The major drawcard is the state-run casino, from which the citizens of Monaco are banned. Until 1962, Monaco's status as a tax haven attracted many wealthy French businesses. The people of Monaco still pay no income tax, but foreigners now do, though at quite favorable rates.

Fact File

OFFICIAL NAME	Principality of Monaco
FORM OF GOVERNMENT	Constitutional monarchy with single legislative body (National Council)
CAPITAL	Monaco
AREA	1.9 sq km (0.7 sq miles)
TIME ZONE	GMT + 1 hour
POPULATION	32,149
PROJECTED POPULATION 2005	32,610
POPULATION DENSITY	16,920.5 per sq km (43,824.1 per sq mile)
LIFE EXPECTANCY	78.6
INFANT MORTALITY (PER 1,000)	6.5
OFFICIAL LANGUAGE	French
OTHER LANGUAGES	Italian, English, Monégasque
LITERACY RATE	99%
RELIGIONS	Roman Catholic 95%, other 5%
ETHNIC GROUPS	French 47%, Monégasque 16%, Italian 16%, other 21%
CURRENCY	French franc
ECONOMY	Tourism and services 90%, industry 10%
GNP PER CAPITA	US$18,000
CLIMATE	Temperate, with mild, wet winters and hot, dry summers
HIGHEST POINT	Mt Agel 140 m (459 ft)
MAP REFERENCE	Page 291

Netherlands

Situated in northwestern Europe, with a western and northern coastline on the North Sea, the Netherlands is bordered by Germany to its east and Belgium to its south. About half the area of this low-lying nation is below sea level and the country is saved from inundation only by a series of coastal dikes and sand dunes, heavily planted with marram grass to prevent erosion, and a complex network of canals and waterways, into which excess water is pumped from low-lying areas and then carried to the rivers that flow to the coast. For centuries the Dutch have been engaged in battle with the sea, and have gradually reclaimed huge amounts of land from it. In the last century more than 3,000 sq km (1,000 sq miles) of land were added. The most spectacular reclamation was the Zuiderzee project that began in 1920 and was completed almost 50 years later.

In the first century BC the Germanic peoples of the Low Countries, which include present-day Belgium and Luxembourg, were colonized by Roman armies. From the fifth century AD the region came under the successive control of Frankish, Burgundian, Austrian, and finally, in the fifteenth century, Spanish rulers. In 1568, William of Orange, outraged by Spain's suppression of a

Monaco, looking out over the Mediterranean Sea (left).
Spreading fields of bulbs in the Netherlands (below). Houses and houseboats along one of Amsterdam's canals (top right).

Europe and the Russian Federation

spreading Protestant movement, led a revolt. In 1581 the seven northern provinces of the Low Countries declared their independence as the United Provinces of the Netherlands.

This set the scene for the consolidation and expansion of Dutch power throughout the seventeenth century. Trading posts and colonies were established in the East Indies (now Indonesia), the Caribbean (the Antilles), Africa, and South and North America. This period also saw the emergence of the Netherlands as a great maritime nation and a blossoming of Dutch art, literature, and scientific achievements.

The French, under Napoleon, invaded in 1794. After the defeat of France, the Congress of Vienna united the Netherlands, Belgium, and Luxembourg under a Dutch monarch in 1814. Belgium declared itself independent in 1831 and Luxembourg was granted autonomy in 1848. In 1848 a new constitution was introduced reducing the power of the monarch and investing greater authority in the Estates-General, as the parliament is still called. This laid the groundwork for the later emergence of a parliamentary democracy under a monarch with strictly formalized and limited powers.

The Netherlands remained neutral in the First World War and its neutrality was respected by both sides. In the Second World War it was overrun by Nazi forces in 1940. Its East Indies colonies were invaded by Japan. At the end of the war, the Netherlands began an armed conflict with rebel forces in its East Indies colony. It finally granted them independence, as the Republic of Indonesia, in 1949. Suriname, in South America, became independent in 1975, leaving the Antilles and Aruba as the Netherlands' only overseas territories.

After the Second World War the Netherlands joined the NATO alliance and became a founder member of the European Economic Community, later the European Union. In 1992 the Treaty on European Union, the Maastricht Treaty, was signed in the southern Dutch city of Maastricht.

Physical features and land use
Almost all of the Netherlands is flat and much of the landscape is covered by small farming plots, intensively cultivated and surrounded by ditches or canals. Dotting the landscape are windmills which for centuries have been used to drain the land. These are now largely picturesque as they have been supplanted by motor pumps. Much of this land is dedicated to horticulture, especially the growing of tulips and other bulb plants, often in tandem with vegetable produce.

Cattle farming and dairying, the country's main forms of agriculture, are strongest in the northwest, in the provinces of Nord Holland and Friesland, on either side of the Ijsselmeer, the area of the Zuiderzee project. The Ijsselmeer is an expanse of fresh water, separated by a dike, 32 km (20 miles) long, from the salt water of the Waddenzee. This lies between the northwest coast and a succession of accumulations of sand, which are known as the West Frisian Islands.

Further south, near the coast, is a succession of densely populated urban areas that include Amsterdam and the other major Dutch cities, including Rotterdam, one of the world's largest ports. Just south of this urban conglomeration, the major rivers that flow into the Netherlands—among them the Rhine from Germany and the Schelde and the Meuse from Belgium—share a common delta area. The only relief from flat land is in the far southeast, where a range of hills rises in places to about 100 m (300 ft).

Industry and commerce
Concentrated in the heavily populated urban southwest, manufacturing industry employs about one in five members of the workforce. Food processing, chemical and electrical machinery manufacture, metal and engineering products, and petroleum refining are major industries. Natural gas is the country's principal natural resource, and there are extensive reserves in the north.

Most Dutch people enjoy an affluent lifestyle, although some groups of immigrants on the fringes of the cities live in conspicuous poverty. Social services are well developed and the country has one of the best state-funded health-care systems in the world.

Fact File

OFFICIAL NAME Kingdom of the Netherlands

FORM OF GOVERNMENT Constitutional monarchy with two legislative bodies (First Chamber and Second Chamber)

CAPITAL Amsterdam; The Hague is the seat of government

AREA 37,330 sq km (14,413 sq miles)

TIME ZONE GMT + 1 hour

POPULATION 15,807,641

PROJECTED POPULATION 2005 16,143,653

POPULATION DENSITY 423.5 per sq km (1,096.8 per sq mile)

LIFE EXPECTANCY 78.2

INFANT MORTALITY (PER 1,000) 5.1

OFFICIAL LANGUAGE Dutch

OTHER LANGUAGES Arabic, Turkish, English

LITERACY RATE 99%

RELIGIONS Roman Catholic 34%, Protestant 25%, Muslim 3%, other 2%, unaffiliated 36%

ETHNIC GROUPS Dutch 96%; Moroccan, Turkish, and other 4%

CURRENCY Netherlands guilder

ECONOMY Services 79%, industry 17%, agriculture 4%

GNP PER CAPITA US$24,000

CLIMATE Temperate, with cool winters and mild summers

HIGHEST POINT Mt Vaalserberg 321 m (1,053 ft)

MAP REFERENCE Page 288

OVERSEAS TERRITORIES
Aruba
Netherlands Antilles

Norway

Norway's long, narrow landmass wraps around the western part of Sweden and the north of Finland and shares a land border with the northwest tip of the Russian Federation. Its rugged western coastline is washed by the North Sea in the south and the Norwegian Sea further north. Its northern tip juts into the Arctic Ocean, making it the most northerly part of Europe. To the south the Skagerrak Strait separates it from the northern tip of Denmark. Like the Swedes and Danes, modern Norwegians are descendents of the Vikings, Teutonic peoples who settled the area and who, from the ninth to the eleventh centuries AD, raided and conquered lands to the north, east, and west. In the fourteenth century, Denmark, Sweden, and Norway came under Danish rule. Although Sweden became independent in the sixteenth century, Norwegians remained subject to the Danes. In 1815, at the end of the Napoleonic Wars, in which Denmark sided with France, control of Norway was transferred to the Swedish crown. The modern Norwegian state dates from 1905, when the country declared its independence. Norway remained neutral in the First World War and was not attacked. However, Nazi forces invaded in 1940 and, despite spirited resistance, subdued the country. Norway joined the NATO alliance in 1949, and in the early 1990s attempted to join the European Union, a move that was thwarted when the option was defeated at a referendum. Norway is a parliamentary democracy with a monarch as the titular head of state.

Norway's more than 21,000 km (13,000 miles) of coast is punctuated by deep fiords. Most of the country consists of mountains with deep valleys formed by ancient glaciers. There are also vast areas of high plateaus. More than one-quarter of the land surface is forested, mainly with conifers, and there are many lakes. The population is centered in the lowlands on the southern coasts and in the southeast. Only a tiny proportion of the land area is suitable for cultivation and agriculture is limited mainly to areas around lakes.

Norway has large oil and gas reserves in the North Sea and produces more oil and gas than any other European country. Its electricity, produced mainly from hydroelectric plants, is used largely to power industry. Key industries include pulp and paper manufacture, shipbuilding, and aluminum production. Fishing and fish farming are also major industries and farmed salmon is a major export.

Fact File

OFFICIAL NAME	Kingdom of Norway
FORM OF GOVERNMENT	Constitutional monarchy with single legislative body (Parliament)
CAPITAL	Oslo
AREA	324,220 sq km (125,181 sq miles)
TIME ZONE	GMT + 1 hour
POPULATION	4,438,547
PROJECTED POPULATION 2005	4,523,798
POPULATION DENSITY	13.7 per sq km (35.5 per sq mile)
LIFE EXPECTANCY	78.4
INFANT MORTALITY (PER 1,000)	5.0
OFFICIAL LANGUAGE	Norwegian
OTHER LANGUAGES	Lapp, Finnish
LITERACY RATE	99%
RELIGIONS	Evangelical Lutheran 94%; Baptist, Pentecostalist, Methodist and Roman Catholic 6%
ETHNIC GROUPS	Germanic (Nordic, Alpine, Baltic) 97%, others include Lapp minority 3%
CURRENCY	Norwegian krone
ECONOMY	Services 61%, industry 36%, agriculture 3%
GNP PER CAPITA	US$31,250
CLIMATE	Cold in north and inland, temperate and wet on coast
HIGHEST POINT	Glittertind 2,472 m (8,110 ft)
MAP REFERENCE	Pages 284–85, 286

Houses built along the banks of a small fiord in Norway (right). The Norwegian city of Bergen (center right). High plateau country, dotted with tiny lakes, in Norway (top). The rooftops of Gdansk in northern Poland, a major port and birthplace of the trade union Solidarity (far right).

OVERSEAS TERRITORIES

Bouvet Island
Jan Mayen
Peter Island
Svalbard

Europe and the Russian Federation

Poland

Situated in northern central Europe, Poland has a northern coastline on the Baltic Sea and land borders with seven countries. To the west, the Oder River forms part of the border with Germany, while to the southwest the Sudeten Mountains separate it from the Czech Republic. The Carpathian Mountains form a natural boundary with Slovakia in the south. Ukraine and Belarus lie to the east, Lithuania is to the northeast and a part of the Russian Federation is adjacent to the northern coastline.

In the seventh and eighth centuries AD, Slavic peoples from the south—known as Polanie, or plain-dwellers—occupied most of Poland. In the tenth century their king was converted to Christianity, beginning a Catholic tradition that has survived to the present, despite attempts to suppress it by post-war communist governments. Over the next two centuries, invaders from Prussia divided up the country, which was reunited in the fourteenth century. Poland retained its independence and at times extended its power during the next two centuries, but again came under Prussian and Austrian control in the late eighteenth century. The nation regained its

independence in 1918 with the defeat of Austria–Germany in the First World War. Early in the Second World War, Poland was overrun by Germany and then Russia, which divided the country between them until June 1941, when the Germans took full control. After the war Poland's borders shifted to the west, as part of what was formerly Germany was ceded to Poland, and as the Soviets were given control of substantial territories in the east. Under these arrangements Poland suffered a net loss of both territory and population. From then until 1989 Poland was effectively a vassal state of the Soviet Union.

Growing civil unrest during the 1980s focused on a series of strikes in a range of industries, organized by the trade union Solidarity. In 1989 the besieged government capitulated and allowed Solidarity to contest the government elections, which it won decisively. The first entirely free elections were held in 1991. Poland is now a democratic republic with a directly elected president and a multi-party system.

Except for the mountain ranges in the south and southwest, most of Poland is low-lying, forming part of the North European Plain. The landscape is drained by numerous rivers, the most significant of which is the Vistula, which rises in the Carpathian Mountains and flows through the center of the country, through Warsaw, and to the Baltic Sea near the industrial city of Gdansk. Most of this plain is fertile, covered with rich loess soil which supports a range of cereal and vegetable crops, in which Poland is almost self-sufficient, and livestock, the most important of which are cattle and pigs. In the northeast the country is more undulating, and much of northern Poland is dotted with extensive lakes. Towards the Baltic coast a range of hills, known as the Baltic Heights, slope down to a sandy coastal plain.

Agriculture, which once employed more than half of Poland's workforce, still accounts for just over a quarter of it. The post-war years saw a rapid expansion of heavy industries, which now include shipbuilding, based in Gdansk, and steel and cement manufacture, based around the mining centers in the south. Many industrial activities rely on Poland's rich coal reserves, and coal is used to

generate more than half the country's electricity. Reliance on this form of fuel has resulted in serious air pollution and acid rain. Other mineral resources include natural gas, iron ore, and salt, on which important chemical industries are based.

Poland has been more successful than many former communist states in converting to a privatized economy. While many Poles have prospered from a growing number of entre-preneurial opportunities, however, others have seen their incomes seriously lowered. Unemployment remains comparatively high.

Fact File

OFFICIAL NAME Republic of Poland

FORM OF GOVERNMENT Republic with two legislative bodies (Senate and Parliament or Sejm)

CAPITAL Warsaw

AREA 312,683 sq km (120,727 sq miles)

TIME ZONE GMT + 1 hour

POPULATION 38,608,929

PROJECTED POPULATION 2005 39,257,669

POPULATION DENSITY 123.5 per sq km (319.8 per sq mile)

LIFE EXPECTANCY 73.1

INFANT MORTALITY (PER 1,000) 12.8

OFFICIAL LANGUAGE Polish

LITERACY RATE 99%

RELIGIONS Roman Catholic 95%; others include Eastern Orthodox, Protestant 5%

ETHNIC GROUPS Polish 97.6%, German 1.3%, Ukrainian 0.6%, Belarusian 0.5%

CURRENCY Zloty

ECONOMY Services 40%, industry 32%, agriculture 28%

GNP PER CAPITA US$2,790

CLIMATE Temperate, with cold winters and warm, wet summers

HIGHEST POINT Rysy 2,499 m (8,199 ft)

MAP REFERENCE Page 289

Europe and the Russian Federation

Portugal

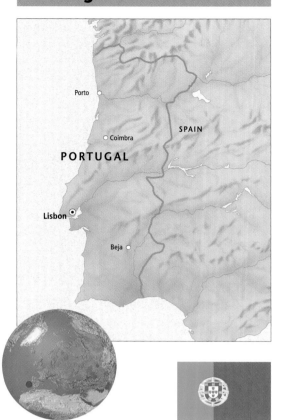

Fact File

OFFICIAL NAME	Portuguese Republic
FORM OF GOVERNMENT	Republic with single legislative body (Assembly of the Republic)
CAPITAL	Lisbon
AREA	92,080 sq km (35,552 sq miles)
TIME ZONE	GMT + 1 hour
POPULATION	9,918,040
PROJECTED POPULATION 2005	9,792,757
POPULATION DENSITY	107.7 per sq km (279 per sq mile)
LIFE EXPECTANCY	75.9
INFANT MORTALITY (PER 1,000)	6.7
OFFICIAL LANGUAGE	Portuguese
LITERACY RATE	89.6%
RELIGIONS	Roman Catholic 97%, Protestant 1%, other 2%
ETHNIC GROUPS	Portuguese 98%, African immigrants from former colonies 2%
CURRENCY	Escudo
ECONOMY	Services 61%, industry 26%, agriculture 13%
GNP PER CAPITA	US$9,740
CLIMATE	Temperate; cool and rainy in north, warm and dry in south
HIGHEST POINT	Ponta de Pico in the Azores 2,351 m (7,713 ft); Serra de Estrela on the mainland, 1,993 m (6,539 ft)
MAP REFERENCE	Page 292

Farm buildings at the foot of Mt Giestoso in Minho Province, Portugal (right). The Transylvanian Alps in Romania (top right). The village of Ponte da Lima, surrounded by terraced fields, in Andrao, Portugal (bottom right).

Situated at the western edge of the Iberian Peninsula, Portugal is shaped somewhat like a long, narrow rectangle. It has a long Atlantic coastline bordering its western edge, and a much shorter one at its southern extremity. Spain surrounds it on the other two sides. From the second century BC until the fifth century AD, Portugal was part of the Roman Empire. As the empire collapsed the territory suffered a series of invasions—by Germanic tribes, Visigoths, and, in the eighth century, by Muslim Moors from northern Africa. The Moors were finally expelled by Christian invaders from Burgundy during the twelfth century and a Burgundian line of monarchs was established. An abortive Castilian attempt to seize the crown in the fourteenth century saw a new dynasty installed under John of Aviz, who reigned as John I. His son, Prince Henry the Navigator, encouraged widespread exploration and the establishment of a vast empire, with colonies in Africa, South America, India, and Southeast Asia. The invasion of Portugal by the Spanish in 1581, even though they were expelled 60 years later, heralded the decline in Portugal's influence. A French invasion in 1807 was reversed three years later when the British expelled the invaders in 1811.

During the nineteenth century widespread poverty and growing resentment at the power of the monarchy culminated in the 1910 revolution, in which the monarchy was overthrown. An army coup in 1926 installed Olivier Salazar as a right-wing dictator. He remained in power until 1968,

but his successor, Marcello Caetano, was overthrown by a left-wing army coup in 1974, which eventually led to democratic elections in 1976. Portugal is now a democratic republic, with a popularly elected president as head of state.

Portugal is divided fairly evenly into its wetter northern and more arid southern regions by the River Tagus. This river flows west into the country from Spain and then takes a southwesterly course toward the Atlantic, entering it at Lisbon. Highland forested areas dominate the north. The highest mountains are in the far north, especially in the east. Here, the landscape is characterized by high plateaus, punctuated by deep gorges and river valleys, which gradually descend to the western coastal plain. In these mountains are thick forests of both conifers and deciduous trees. South of the Douro River the landscape becomes less rugged and the slopes more gentle until they reach the plain around the Tagus. South of the Tagus, the country is mainly flat or undulating. In the Tagus Valley and further south are forests of cork oaks, the bark of which is used to produce wine corks. In the Algarve, in the far south, a range of hills runs across the country from the Spanish border to its southwestern tip.

Portugal has two self-governing regions in the Atlantic: the nine volcanic islands that constitute the Azores and the volcanic archipelago of two inhabited and two groups of uninhabited islets that make up Madeira. In 1987, Portugal signed a treaty to return its last territory, Macau, to China in 1999.

By western European standards Portugal is still a highly rural society, with agriculture and fishing still employing a significant number of the country's workforce. Many farms, especially the smaller ones that predominate in the north, continue to use traditional methods. Cereals and vegetables are widely cultivated, and wine production, especially port wine from the Douro Valley, is the major agricultural activity. Manufacturing is growing in importance, much of it concerned with processing the country's agricultural products. Paper and cork manufacture, and textiles and footwear, are among the significant industries. Tourism, especially in the warm, southern Algarve region, has greatly expanded in recent years, leading to rapid building development and considerable attendant environmental degradation.

Portuguese products

Portugal is famous for two products, cork and port. Before modern plastics were invented, cork had no equal as a strong, lightweight, buoyant, impermeable, and elastic material. It is the bark of the cork oak, found in Portugal, Spain and the Mediterranean. Cork was formerly used for lifebelts and floats on fishing nets, and is only slowly being replaced as a stopper for wine bottles by plastics. Portugal produces more cork than the rest of the world combined.

The bark is first harvested when the tree is about 20 years old, supplies being taken at subsequent 10-year intervals. The cork is removed by making cuts in the bark using an curved knife. The pieces are soaked in water, scraped, washed, and dried.

Port is a dark red, full-bodied fortified wine named after the town of Oporto, from which it has been exported for many years. No one variety of grape is used. The wine's distinctiveness comes from the climate and soil of the mountainous Alto Douro region of north Portugal, and from the methods of cultivation and wine-making used in its production. British capital contributed to the port industry, and the UK was for many years the main destination for the finished product.

Romania

Except for its Black Sea coast, Romania is land-locked—by Ukraine to the north, Moldova to the northeast, Hungary to the west, Yugoslavia to the southwest, and Bulgaria to the south. From the sixth century AD the country was often invaded. From the ninth to the eleventh centuries Magyars occupied part of Transylvania and between the fourteenth and sixteenth centuries Walachia, Moldova, and Transylvania formed part of the Ottoman Empire. At the end of the First World War, Bessarabia—most of present-day Moldova—Transylvania and Bukovina were restored to Romania. Much of this land was lost during the Second World War when Romania, which sided with Nazi Germany, came under Soviet control. During Ceausescu's oppressive regime, beginning in 1967, Romania distanced itself from the Soviets. In 1989 a popular uprising saw Ceausescu arrested and executed. Romania is now ruled by an elected parliament headed by a president.

The Carpathian Mountains curve through the center of the country, dividing the timbered uplands of Transylvania from the Danube Plain. The southern part of the range, the Transylvanian Alps, contains the highest peaks and the most rugged scenery. The fertile eastern plain is crossed by many tributaries of the Danube. To the east, around the Danube Delta, the landscape is marshy and dotted with numerous lakes and lagoons.

There has been a shift toward heavy industries since the 1970s but agriculture is still economically important. Maize, wheat, vegetables, and grapes for wine are the main crops and sheep and pigs the main livestock. Romania is rich in coal, natural gas, iron ore, and petroleum. Most of the raw materials for the country's industries are imported. Prominent industries include chemical and metal processing and machine manufacturing. Lumbering has depleted much of the country's forest and industry has caused widespread pollution. Moves to a market economy have been slow and Romania's standard of living remains relatively low.

Fact File

OFFICIAL NAME	Romania
FORM OF GOVERNMENT	Republic with two legislative bodies (Senate and House of Deputies)
CAPITAL	Bucharest
AREA	237,500 sq km (91,699 sq miles)
TIME ZONE	GMT + 2 hours
POPULATION	22,334,312
PROJECTED POPULATION 2005	22,304,366
POPULATION DENSITY	94 per sq km (243.5 per sq mile)
LIFE EXPECTANCY	70.8
INFANT MORTALITY (PER 1,000)	18.1
OFFICIAL LANGUAGE	Romanian
OTHER LANGUAGES	Hungarian, German
LITERACY RATE	96.9%
RELIGIONS	Romanian Orthodox 87%, Roman Catholic 5%, Protestant 5%, other 3%
ETHNIC GROUPS	Romanian 89.1%, Hungarian 8.9%, other 2%
CURRENCY	Leu
ECONOMY	Industry 38%, services 34%, agriculture 28%
GNP PER CAPITA	US$1,480
CLIMATE	Temperate; cold winters and warm, wet summers; cooler in Carpathian Mountains
HIGHEST POINT	Moldoveanu 2,544 m (8,346 ft)
MAP REFERENCE	Page 296

Russian Federation

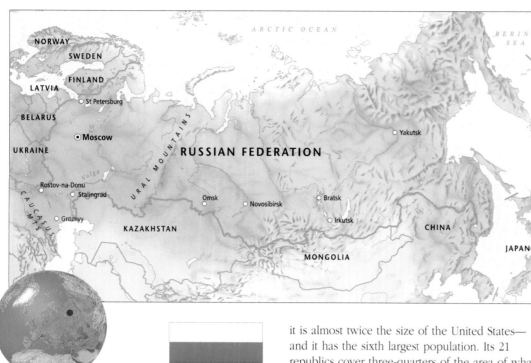

Fact file

OFFICIAL NAME Russian Federation

FORM OF GOVERNMENT Federal republic with two
legislative bodies (Federation Council and
State Duma)

CAPITAL Moscow

AREA 17,075,200 sq km (6,592,735 sq miles)

TIME ZONE GMT + 3–12 hours

POPULATION 146,393,569

PROJECTED POPULATION 2005 144,263,571

POPULATION DENSITY 8.6 per sq km
(22.3 per sq mile)

LIFE EXPECTANCY 65.1

INFANT MORTALITY (PER 1,000) 23.0

OFFICIAL LANGUAGE Russian

OTHER LANGUAGES More than 100 minority languages

LITERACY RATE 98.7%

RELIGIONS Russian Orthodox 27%; Muslim, Jewish,
Roman Catholic and other minorities 73%

ETHNIC GROUPS Russian 81.5%, Tatar 3.8%, Ukrainian
3%, Chuvash 1.2%, Bashkir 0.9%, Belarusian 0.8%,
Moldovan 0.7%, other 8.1%

CURRENCY Ruble

ECONOMY Industry 27%, agriculture 15%, education
and culture 11%, other 47%

GNP PER CAPITA US$2,240

CLIMATE Warm and dry in far south; cold temperate
(long, cold winters and short, mild summers) in most
inland areas; polar in far north

HIGHEST POINT Mt Elbrus 5,633 m (18,481 ft)

MAP REFERENCE Pages 299, 300–01

Sprawling across the easternmost part of
northern Europe and occupying the whole of
northern Asia, the Russian Federation, often called
simply Russia, is the largest country in the world—

it is almost twice the size of the United States—
and it has the sixth largest population. Its 21
republics cover three-quarters of the area of what
was for almost 70 years (until it collapsed in 1991)
the Union of Soviet Socialist Republics.

The Russian Federation has long coastlines
along the Arctic Ocean in the north and along the
Pacific Ocean in the east. Its southeastern coastline
is on the Sea of Japan and north of this the
Kamchatka Peninsula encloses the Sea of Okhotsk.
In its far southwestern corner there is a short
stretch of coast along the Caspian Sea; a little
further north, it briefly borders the Black Sea; and
in the northwest, near St Petersburg, it touches on
the eastern tip of the Gulf of Finland. Its mainland
has borders with 12 other countries. In the far
southeast it borders the northeast tip of North
Korea. In the south it borders China in two places:
to the east and the west of its long border with
Mongolia. The western half of its southern border
is with the former Soviet republic of Kazakhstan.
To the west of the Caspian Sea are Azerbaijan and
Georgia, and north of the Black Sea are Ukraine,
Belarus, Latvia, and Estonia. Northeast of the Gulf
of Finland is a border with Finland and at its very
northwest tip the Russian Federation borders on
a tiny part of Norway. Further west, tucked in
between Lithuania and Poland, and with a coast
on the Baltic Sea, is another small area of Russian
territory, centered on the coastal city of Kaliningrad.

History

Until the sixth century AD, almost all of what is
now Russia was inhabited only by nomadic tribes
of Finnic and Slavic origin. In the sixth century
peoples from what are now Iran and Turkey
settled the part of southwestern Russia between
the Carpathian Mountains and the Volga River,
establishing a capital on the Caspian Sea. They in
turn were overrun by Viking invaders and traders
who spread southward along river routes from the
Baltic Sea. One tradition has it that modern Russia
dates back to the establishment of a dynasty by
the Viking Rurik at Novgorod in AD 862. Soon
after, however, the center of power moved farther
southwest, to Kiev in present-day Ukraine, and a
unified confederation, known as Kievan Rus,

emerged. In the tenth century the leader Vladimir
was converted to Christianity. Over the next two
centuries a Russian culture, based on the traditions
of Orthodox Christianity, developed, but in the
thirteenth century Kievan Rus fell to invaders from
Mongolia and the confederation broke down
into a number of dukedoms, under Mongol
domination. The Muscovite dukes emerged as the
most powerful, mainly through their role as tribute
collectors for the Mongols. Opposition to Mongol
rule gathered strength during the fourteenth
century and in the fifteenth century the Muscovite
Duke Ivan III finally expelled the Mongols. His
grandson, Ivan IV, known as "The Terrible,"
was the first to declare himself "Tsar of all the
Russians." Under his oppressive rule, which lasted
from 1533 to 1584, the power of princes and
landowners (known as "boyars") was broken and
the Muscovite state spread eastward across the
Urals and into what is now Siberia.

After Ivan's death, a series of internal disputes
culminated in Polish invasion in 1609 and, after
the ousting of the Poles in 1612, the emergence
of the first Romanov tsar, Mikhail, in 1613. Under
his grandson, Peter I (known as "The Great"),
who ruled from 1696 to 1725, the country was
renamed "Russia," and a new capital was
established at St Petersburg. Territories along the
Baltic were acquired from Sweden, and western
European ideas, technology, and styles of dress
and other fashions were embraced. During the
eighteenth and nineteenth centuries Russia
extended its borders south and east into Asia.

The defeat of Napoleon's invading armies, in
1812, confirmed Russia's status as a great power,
but the country remained socially and industrially
backward in comparison with Western Europe.

A feudal system, under which peasants were bonded to landlords, remained until 1861, when Tsar Alexander II abolished serfdom. Alexander's political and social reforms earned him powerful enemies and led to his assassination in 1881. The oppressive rule of his successor, Alexander III, spawned the formation of the Marxist Russian Social Democratic Party in 1898, under the leadership of Vladimir Ilich Ulyanov, who called himself Lenin. Civil unrest intensified following Russia's defeat in its war with Japan in 1904–05, forcing Tsar Nicholas II to establish a parliament, known as the Duma, elected by a very limited suffrage, and to institute some civil liberty reforms.

These reforms, however, failed to stem the revolutionary tide, which was further strengthened by the reverses and heavy loss of life in the First World War. In February 1917, rioting and strikes broke out in the capital, St Petersburg, there was a massive defection of Russian troops, and Tsar Nicholas II abdicated, leading to the decisive revolution of October 1917, in which the All-Russian Communist Party emerged as the ruling force, with Lenin as dictatorial leader. Four years of civil war ensued, until the communists fully took control. In December 1922, Russia, with Moscow as capital, became the dominant power in the newly formed Union of Soviet Socialist Republics, having seized Georgia, Armenia, and Azerbaijan and established its ascendancy in Ukraine and central Asia.

Following Lenin's death in 1924, there was a bitter factional struggle for power. By 1929 Josef Stalin was the undisputed leader and remained in power until he died in 1953. Under his regime, agriculture was collectivized, industry expanded, and brutal labor camps were established in Siberia

for those suspected of espousing dissident ideas. Political rivals and enemies, whether real or imagined, were routinely eliminated in a series of ruthless purges. In one purge in 1929–30, hundreds of thousands of peasants who opposed farm collectivization were either murdered or sent away to remote, desolate parts of the country. Farm collectivization led to immense agricultural disruption and resulted in famine in the early 1930s in which many thousands of people died.

Russia, and the rest of the Soviet Union, suffered terribly during the Second World War. At first allied with Germany, the Soviet Union, in 1939 and 1940, seized territory in Poland and Romania, and annexed the Baltic republics of

Estonia, Latvia, and Lithuania. In 1941, Hitler's troops suddenly invaded the Soviet Union, and in the occupation and struggles that ensued in the following four years, an estimated 20 million Soviet citizens were killed.

At the end of the war, the regions that were occupied by Soviet forces—most of Eastern Europe—came under Soviet domination. This gave rise to a 40-year period of international tension as the Soviet Union and the United States assumed the mantles of mutually distrustful, competing superpowers, each building up an arsenal of ever more potentially destructive nuclear weapons. During the premiership of Stalin's successor, Nikita Khrushchev, the Soviet Union and its satellites

St Petersburg, once the capital of Russia, seen from across the misty Neva River (left). Shoppers in Arbat Street, a prosperous part of Moscow (top). Fishing through a hole in the ice, using large nets, in Siberia (above).

Europe and the Russian Federation

Most of Russia's agriculture is concentrated in the south of the plain, as the harsh climates further north are not conducive to the growing of crops or to the raising of livestock. Less than one-tenth of Russia is under cultivation. Cereals are the main crops, although in most years the country produces only about half the grain it requires. The rest has to be imported. Livestock raising, most commonly cattle and dairy farming, is also based mainly in the west.

To the east of the Ural Mountains, the Siberian Plain is largely desolate, treeless, and flat. Central Siberia, to the east of the Yenisey River, is a region of plateaus that range from between 450 and 900 m (1,500 and 3,000 ft) in height and rise in the south to a series of mountain ranges that border Mongolia and China. Lowlands flank these plateaus to the north and east. East of the Lena River the country rises again toward the rugged and mountainous east coast. South of the Bering Sea, the Kamchatka Peninsula and the Kuril Islands form part of the Pacific "Ring of Fire." This is an area of considerable geothermal activity and there are about 30 active volcanoes.

The landscape of northern Russia is mainly arctic tundra—a treeless expanse which remains frozen throughout the year. Tundra vegetation consists of sedges, grasses, mosses, lichens, and ground-hugging plants. Further south, and in the southwest, the landscape varies between tracts of semidesert and expanses of forest, largely conifers, known as the taiga.

A group of Russian women at a festival wearing traditional costume (above left). The gilded domes and turrets of the Catherine Palace in Tsarskoye Selo, today Pushkin (right). A river winding through fertile farming country (below).

entered into a defense treaty, the Warsaw Pact, to oppose the Western NATO alliance. Nuclear war seemed to come close in 1962, when a Soviet attempt to place nuclear weapons on Cuba was met by a United States blockade. Khrushchev's humiliating backdown in this crisis, as well as a serious rift between Russia and communist China, led to his being removed from office the next year and his replacement by Leonid Brezhnev.

The Brezhnev era lasted until 1982 and during this time Soviet–Western relations fluctuated. Periods of relaxation, which became known as "détente," alternated with times of renewed hostility. Despite this, and despite the USSR's invasions of Czechoslovakia in 1968 and Afghanistan in December 1979, genuine agreements about arms reduction were achieved. During the brief premierships of Brezhnev's two immediate successors, East–West relations soured again, but the accession to the leadership of Mikhail Gorbachev in 1985 led to an era of greater trust as well as a less dictatorial and more open style of political leadership, and the first tentative moves toward a loosening of government controls over the economy. The terms *glasnost,* meaning "openness" and *perestroika,* meaning "restructuring" were used widely at this time, in reference to Gorbachev's reforms.

Growing social unrest, deteriorating economic conditions, and a resurgence of nationalism in a number of Soviet republics created immense strains in the Soviet Union. An attempted coup by communist conservatives took place in 1991 but was put down, largely through the heroic opposition of Boris Yeltsin, who emerged as the de facto leader of the country, enjoying widespread popular support.

Against Gorbachev's wishes, the Soviet Union was officially dissolved in December 1991 and replaced by the Commonwealth of Independent States (see box on facing page). Gorbachev then resigned as president and Yeltsin assumed control. Yeltsin's leadership was confirmed in a national referendum that was held in 1993 and, despite a poor economic situation and widespread hardship, as well as serious misgivings about his health, Yeltsin was re-elected president in 1996. In the parliamentary, or Duma, elections, however, conservative nationalists, some of them stridently anti-Western, received widespread support.

A new constitution, adopted in 1993, established a two-chambered Federal Assembly, headed by a prime minister, who is appointed by the president. The president is popularly elected for a five-year term and has considerable independent powers, including the right to dissolve parliament.

Physical features and land use

Stretching all the way from the Arctic Ocean in the north to the border with Kazakhstan in the south, the Ural Mountains separate European Russia in the west from the vast Siberian Plain to the east. European Russia, where most of the population lives and where the bulk of Russian industry and agriculture is located, consists mainly of a huge fertile plain, the East Europe Plain, which has an average elevation of 170 m (550 ft) but rises to a maximum of 400 m (1,300 ft). In the far southwest, the Carpathian Mountains form a natural boundary with Georgia and Azerbaijan, and there are upland areas in the far north near the border with Finland. In the western part of the plain are the Valdai Hills, in which the Volga and Dnieper Rivers have their source.

Timeline						
	300 AD Spread of peoples including Huns, Goths, and Magyars into forests west of the Ural Mountains	**830** Scandinavian merchants establish new base in the Volga region, close to present-day Ryazan	**1237** Russia becomes part of Mongol Empire until late 1400s, extending the empire's boundaries to Arctic, Baltic and Pacific	**1547** Ivan IV, known as "the Terrible," is crowned Tsar and takes the title for all Russia	**1613** Romanovs become the Tsarist family, ruling until the murder of Nicholas II in 1917	**1703** Peter the Great opens Russia to Western ideas. Builds St Petersburg on the Baltic Sea, making it the capital in 1712
20,000 BP Huts made from mammoth bones covered in animal skins in use at Mezhirich in Ukraine region	**4000 BC** Horses domesticated on the steppes, first mainly as draft animals but later (2000 BC) as fast transport in warfare	**770** Germanic traders and soldiers from Baltic move into Volga region previously occupied by Finnic and Slavic groups	**882** Scandinavian groups capture Kiev; Russia takes its name from Kievan Rus, term given by Slavic groups to the Black Sea area	**1318** Mongols appoint Yuri of Moscow Crown Prince; he makes Moscow an important center and later the capital of Russia	**1697** First recorded eruption of Klyuchevskaya volcano in Kamchatka, Siberia	**1725** Catherine the Great becomes Empress. Encourages Western ideas in arts and education. Most Russians impoverished

Industry, commerce, and culture

Russia, and especially Siberia, has abundant mineral resources. These contributed greatly to the country's rapid transformation during the Soviet period from a predominantly agricultural economy to one that was heavily industrialized. These mineral resources underpin the federation's present reliance on heavy industry and provide important mining exports. They include coal, petroleum, natural gas, iron ore, bauxite, copper, lead, zinc, and gold and other precious metals. Steelmaking, the manufacture of agricultural machinery, chemicals, textiles, and food processing are among the principal industries, centered on such large cities to the west of the Urals as Moscow, St Petersburg, Novgorod, and Volgograd, but also in a number of cities in Siberia such as Yekaterinburg and Novosibirsk.

The country's move toward a market economy has been fraught with difficulties and has been accompanied by a marked increase in social and financial inequalities as a new class of rich entrepreneurs has emerged. The majority of Russians live in relative poverty, victims of steeply rising prices and severe shortages of food and other basic consumer items. Corruption and crime have also increased significantly and a number of the leaders of organized crime are among the richest citizens in the nation. These conditions were aggravated by a virtual collapse of the Russian economy in 1998 and continuing political uncertainty based on serious doubts, unallayed by official reassurances, about the capacity of the president, Boris Yeltsin, who suffers chronic ill health. There are strong movements within the country for a return to centralized control of the economy and for a more aggressive nationalistic approach to relations with the West.

Russia has contributed much to literature, music, and the performing arts, especially in the nineteenth century. Writers such as Turgenev prepared the way for other giants of literature like Tolstoy and Dostoyevsky. Among composers, Tchaikovsky and Stravinsky established Russia's place in musical history. The Imperial Russian Ballet was founded in 1735, and Russian ballet has become internationally renowned for its choreography and dancers like Pavlova and Nureyev.

The Commonwealth of Independent States

The Commonwealth of Independent States is a loose confederation of twelve former Soviet republics that was formed after the breakdown of the Soviet Union in 1991. The idea for the formation of the commonwealth was agreed to at a meeting of Russian president Boris Yeltsin and the presidents of Belarus and Ukraine in Minsk, in Belarus, in early December 1991 and was ratified at Alma-Ata in Kazakhstan by 11 of the former Soviet republics on 21 December. Georgia and the three Baltic states of Estonia, Latvia, and Lithuania declined to join, although Georgia has since become a member. Not surprisingly, Russia assumed the status of dominant member of the group, taking control of all former Soviet embassies and consulates and occupying the former Soviet Union's seat on the United Nations Security Council. Minsk was designated as the administrative center of the new commonwealth, which was much more an alliance than a state entity. According to the agreement, the political independence of each state was guaranteed in return for a commitment to certain forms of economic and defence cooperation.

The commonwealth remains a tenuous confederation and there are many areas of dispute between its constituent members. There is a natural suspicion that the Russian Federation seeks to impose its political will on the other members, and this was in no way diminished in 1996 when the Russian parliament, or Duma, passed a non-binding resolution in favor of reinstating the former Soviet Union. Difficult economic conditions throughout the former Soviet Union have led to increasing support, especially in Belarus, for a return to the previous status quo.

1773–74 The Peasants Revolt sweeps across Russia from the Urals to the Volga but is put down by troops	**1890** Migration of large numbers of people from eastern Russia to Siberia and Asia lasts for around 10 years	**1917** Revolution puts Bolsheviks in power after storming of the Winter Palace, at St Petersburg	**1918** Tsar Nicholas II and family are shot, allegedly at the hands of the Bolsheviks; Moscow again capital of Russia	**1928** First Five-Year Plan introduced to further centralize the economy and increase industrial and agricultural production	**1935** Great Purge by Stalin's secret police takes many lives; millions starve in a famine partly caused by farm collectivization	**1956** Bezymianny Volcano in Kamchatka, Siberia, erupts leaving ash 50 cm (20 in) deep 10 km (6 miles) from volcano	**1985** Gorbachev heads Communist Party; pursues policies of *perestroika* ("economic restructuring") and *glasnost* ("openness")

1812 Napoleon's invasion of Russia defeated. Most of the 500,000 French forces die or are captured	**1891** Construction of the Trans-Siberian Railroad from Moscow to Vladivostok begins. Not completed until 1916	**1914** Germany declares war on Russia and for three years Russia sides with Allies	**1918–20** Communists victorious in a civil war with the anti-communist White Russians	**1924** Stalin leader of one of four factions that run party	**1929** Stalin becomes undisputed leader and rules USSR for more than 20 years	**1941** Russia sides with Allies in Second World War after Germany invades USSR and is defeated in the Battle of Stalingrad (1943)	**1986** Chernobyl nuclear reactor in Ukraine explodes; cancers from radiation kill up to 40,000 worldwide

San Marino

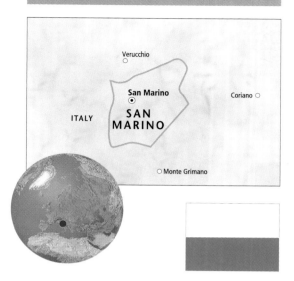

Completely surrounded by Italian territory, most of the tiny state of San Marino sits on the slopes of Mount Titano in the Appenine Mountains, 20 km (12 miles) inland from the city of Rimini on the Adriatic coast of northern Italy. The republic takes its name from St Marinus who, so legend has it, arrived there with a group of followers in the fourth century AD and established a settlement. This makes it arguably the world's oldest surviving republic. Records of its existence can be traced back to the twelfth century. It became one of the many mini-states on the Italian peninsula and was accorded papal recognition in 1631. The Sanmarinesi, as its inhabitants are known, offered refuge to Giuseppe Garibaldi when he passed through in 1849, pursued by his enemies. However, when the newly unified state of Italy was declared in 1861 the Sanmarinesi declined to join. San Marino fought with Italy in the First World War. In the Second World War it began by supporting Fascist Italy but later changed sides and was invaded by Germany. San Marino is a democratic republic with elections held every five years.

This picturesque little country is centered on the fortified medieval town of San Marino, where most of the population lives. On the lower slopes, beneath the rugged limestone peak, are thick forests, expanses of pastureland and a string of ancient villages. Almost one-fifth of the land is used for agriculture. Cereals, olives, and vines are cultivated and sheep and goats are raised. Cheeses and wine are its principal agricultural products.

Since 1862 San Marino has had a friendship and cooperation treaty with Italy. It also shares its currency and enjoys a standard of living roughly equivalent to that of its neighbor. About one in five of Sanmarinesi workers are in the tourism industry, which caters for more than 2 million visitors each year, although many do not stay overnight. Winemaking, textiles, and ceramics are siginificant industries. Even more significant is the sale of the country's distinctive postage stamps, which are sought by collectors and account for up to 10 percent of the country's revenues.

Fact File

OFFICIAL NAME	Republic of San Marino
FORM OF GOVERNMENT	Republic with single legislative body (Great and General Council)
CAPITAL	San Marino
AREA	60 sq km (23 sq miles)
TIME ZONE	GMT + 1 hour
POPULATION	25,061
PROJECTED POPULATION 2005	25,864
POPULATION DENSITY	417.7 per sq km (1,081.81 per sq mile)
LIFE EXPECTANCY	81.5
INFANT MORTALITY (PER 1,000)	5.4
OFFICIAL LANGUAGE	Italian
LITERACY RATE	99%
RELIGIONS	Roman Catholic 95%, other 5%
ETHNIC GROUPS	Sanmarinesi 87.1%, Italian 12.4%, other 0.5%
CURRENCY	Italian lira
ECONOMY	Services 58%, industry 40%, agriculture 2%
GNP PER CAPITA	US$15,000
CLIMATE	Temperate, with mild winters and warm summers
HIGHEST POINT	Monte Titano 739 m (2,425 ft)
MAP REFERENCE	Page 294

Slovakia

This small central European country is bordered by Poland to the north, the Czech Republic to the northwest, Austria to the west, Hungary to the south, and Ukraine to the east. It is the smaller, less populous, and less industrially developed part of the former state of Czechoslovakia, which split peacefully in 1993 to form the two separate nations of Slovakia and the Czech Republic.

Ethnically distinct from their former compatriots, the Slovaks had lived for ten centuries under continuous Hungarian domination when, in 1918, they merged with the Czechs to form a new, independent nation. At the beginning of the Second World War, Czechoslovakia was invaded by Germany and the Germans installed a pro-Fascist government in Slovakia. Soviet troops restored the pre-war status quo in 1945 and communists seized power in 1948, making the country effectively a Soviet satellite. In 1968 Soviet forces invaded to put down an attempt to establish democracy under the leadership of Czechoslovakia's First Secretary, Alexander Dubcek, a Slovak. Twenty-one years later a revival of nationalism and a weakened Soviet Union led to a successful declaration of independence and the establishment of democratic government. Since its separation from the Czech Republic, Slovakia has been

governed by a single-chamber parliament, whose 150 members, or deputies, are elected for a four-year term.

Except for lowland areas in the south and southeast, most of the country is ruggedly mountainous, with extensive forests and tracts of pastureland. In the north of the country the high Carpathian Mountains extend along the Polish border, and further south, the Tatra Mountains, an offshoot of the Carpathians and the Slovakian Ore Mountains, run parallel across the center of the country. Ski resorts in the Tatra Mountains attract large numbers of tourists. The Danube, which forms part of the border with Hungary, flows through an extensive fertile plain. Here, and in the lowland area further to the east, most of Slovakia's agriculture, which employs more than one-tenth of the workforce, is centered. Wheat and potatoes are the principal crops, and sheep, cattle, and pigs are widely raised.

Slovakia is poorly endowed with mineral resources. There are significant deposits of lignite, but most of it is poor in quality. Industries, which employ about one in three workers, are centered mainly around the cities of Bratislava in the southwest and Kosice in the southeast. Significant industries are iron and steelmaking, and car and clothing manufacture. The move from a centrally controlled to a privatized market economy has proceeded fitfully, and the country has suffered economically from the loss of subsidies that it used to receive from the Czech Republic.

Fact File

OFFICIAL NAME Slovak Republic

FORM OF GOVERNMENT Republic with single legislative body (National Parliament)

CAPITAL Bratislava

AREA 48,845 sq km (18,859 sq miles)

TIME ZONE GMT + 1 hour

POPULATION 5,396,193

PROJECTED POPULATION 2005 5,509,202

POPULATION DENSITY 110.5 per sq km (286.2 per sq mile)

LIFE EXPECTANCY 73.5

INFANT MORTALITY (PER 1,000) 9.5

OFFICIAL LANGUAGE Slovak

OTHER LANGUAGE Hungarian

LITERACY RATE 99%

RELIGIONS Roman Catholic 60.3%, Protestant 8.4%, Orthodox 4.1%, other 27.2%

ETHNIC GROUPS Slovak 85.7%, Hungarian 10.7%, others include Gypsy, Czech 3.6%

CURRENCY Koruna

ECONOMY Services 44%, industry 44%, agriculture 12%

GNP PER CAPITA US$2,950

CLIMATE Temperate, with cold winters and warm, wet summers

HIGHEST POINT Gerlachovka 2,655 m (8,711 ft)

MAP REFERENCE Page 289

A crenellated building in San Marino (far left). The city of Trecin in Slovakia (left). Lake Bled in Slovenia (top right).

Slovenia

This former Yugoslav republic shares borders with Italy to the west, Austria to the north, Hungary to the east, and Croatia to the south. The port of Koper on Slovenia's short coastline on the Gulf of Venice is an important transit point for products from Austria and much of central Europe. First settled by Slavic peoples in the sixth century AD, Slovenia became a Hungarian province in the eleventh century. Austria gained control of the region in the sixteenth century, and Slovenia was later absorbed into the Austro-Hungarian Empire. At the end of the First World War it became part of the Kingdom of the Croats, Serbs, and Slovenes, which in 1929 became Yugoslavia. Like the rest of Yugoslavia, it was occupied by Axis powers during the Second World War. In 1991 it became the first Yugoslav republic to declare its independence. This prompted a military response from the Yugoslav army, which, however, withdrew its forces after a 10-day conflict. According to its constitution of 1991, Slovenia is a democratic republic with a directly elected president and prime minister as head of the government.

Slovenia is mountainous, with the highest and most spectacular regions in the Slovenian Alps near the border with Austria in the northwest. Almost half the land is densely forested. There are areas of lowland in the west near the coast and much of the center and east of the country consists of undulating plains. The most fertile region is in the east, where the Drava River flows southward across the Pannonian Plain into Croatia.

Slovenia's tourist industry, based on its alpine scenery and its coastal beaches, remains important, although it has been adversely affected by conflicts in the region. Almost half the workforce is employed in mining and manufacturing industries. Metallurgy and heavy machine manufacture, including trucks and cars, are prominent among these. Textile manufacture is also widespread. The main mineral resource is coal and there are large mercury deposits in the northwest. Dairy farming and pig raising are the main agricultural activities. Slovenia's nuclear power plant, which supplies one-third of the country's electricity, is a cause of some international tension, especially with Austria.

Fact File

OFFICIAL NAME Republic of Slovenia

FORM OF GOVERNMENT Republic with two legislative bodies (National Assembly and National Council)

CAPITAL Ljubljana

AREA 20,256 sq km (7,821 sq miles)

TIME ZONE GMT + 1 hour

POPULATION 1,970,570

PROJECTED POPULATION 2005 1,977,517

POPULATION DENSITY 97.3 per sq km (252 per sq mile)

LIFE EXPECTANCY 75.4

INFANT MORTALITY (PER 1,000) 5.3

OFFICIAL LANGUAGE Slovenian

OTHER LANGUAGES Serbian, Croatian

LITERACY RATE 96%

RELIGIONS Roman Catholic 96%, Muslim 1%, other 3%

ETHNIC GROUPS Slovene 91%, Croatian 3%, Serbian 2%, Muslim 1%, other 3%

CURRENCY Tolar

ECONOMY Services 52%, industry 46%, agriculture 2%

GNP PER CAPITA US$2,950

CLIMATE Temperate, with colder winters and hotter summers inland

HIGHEST POINT Mt Triglav 2,864 m (9,396 ft)

MAP REFERENCE Page 294

Spain

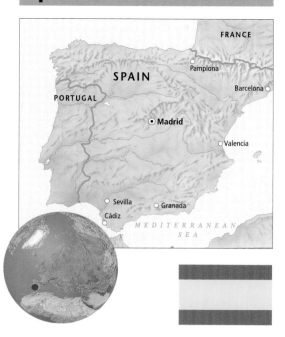

Fact File

OFFICIAL NAME Kingdom of Spain

FORM OF GOVERNMENT Constitutional monarchy with two legislative bodies (Senate and Congress of Deputies)

CAPITAL Madrid

AREA 504,750 sq km (194,884 sq miles)

TIME ZONE GMT + 1 hour

POPULATION 39,167,744

PROJECTED POPULATION 2005 39,334,191

POPULATION DENSITY 77.6 per sq km (201 per sq mile)

LIFE EXPECTANCY 77.7

INFANT MORTALITY (PER 1,000) 6.4

OFFICIAL LANGUAGE Spanish (Castillian)

OTHER LANGUAGES Catalan, Galician, Basque

LITERACY RATE 97.1%

RELIGIONS Roman Catholic 99%, other 1%

ETHNIC GROUPS Ethnically homogenous, but divided into the following cultural/linguistic groups: Spanish 73%, Catalan 17%, Galician 7%, Basque 2%, Gypsy 1%

CURRENCY Peseta

ECONOMY Services 68%, industry 21%, agriculture 11%

GNP PER CAPITA US$13,580

CLIMATE Temperate, with mild, wet winters and hot, dry summers; cooler and wetter in northwest

HIGHEST POINT Mulhacén 3,478 m (11,411 ft)

MAP REFERENCE Pages 292–93

Spain occupies the bulk of the Iberian Peninsula at the southwestern tip of Europe. It shares land borders with Portugal to the west, France to the north, and the tiny principality of Andorra, perched high in the Pyrenees on the border with France. To the west and south, Spain has short stretches of coastline along the Atlantic Ocean and to the north, a long coast on the Bay of Biscay. Its southern tip is separated from Morocco by the narrow Strait of Gibraltar and its southeastern and eastern coastlines are on the western edge of the Mediterranean Sea.

The Iberian Peninsula had already experienced a long history of human habitation when, at the end of the third century BC, the Romans subdued the Celts, Iberians, and Basques who lived there. The region remained a Roman colony until the Visigoths invaded early in the fifth century AD. Over the next three centuries the region became Christianized, but in AD 711 an invasion from Morocco in the south established what would become a flourishing Islamic civilization that lasted for six centuries. In the ninth century Christian invaders from the north gained control of Catalonia in the northeast, thus beginning a process of slow reconquest that would, by the early thirteenth century, see the Moors only retaining control of Granada in the south.

The marriage of Ferdinand II of Aragon and Isabella I of Castile in 1469 brought together the two most powerful states on the peninsula, and in 1492, when the Moors were finally expelled from Granada, Spain became a unified country under Catholic rule. Thus began a century of Spanish exploration and conquest in which Spain

A small farm in the province of Navarra (below). Fertile countryside in Catalonia (right).

acquired colonies in Central and South America, as well as the Philippines in Southeast Asia. The Spanish also conquered a large part of Western Europe, including Portugal, the Netherlands, Austria, and part of Italy.

The beginning of Spain's decline from being a dominant power in the world to a state of secondary importance can be traced to 1588, when Philip II sent his mighty armada of 130 ships in an abortive attempt to invade Protestant England. This defeat by the English spelled the end of Spain's maritime dominance. By 1714 Spain had lost all its European possessions and by 1826 it had been forced to surrender all its American colonies except Cuba and Puerto Rico.

Timeline

10,000 BC Images of bison painted on the walls of a deep cave at Altamira, northern Spain, probably used for ceremonies	**3200 BC** Larger communities develop around southern and southwestern Spain and Portugal, such as Los Millares, Almeria	**1000 BC** Phoenician traders from eastern Mediterranean begin to colonize southern and eastern coasts of Spain	**218 BC** After defeat of Carthaginians in the Second Punic War, Spain slowly becomes part of the Roman Empire	**AD 711** Moors invade from North Africa bringing Muslim religion and building palaces and mosques	**1469** Marriage of Ferdinand of Aragon and Isabella of Castile brings together both kingdoms—almost all of modern Spain	

780,000 BP Stone tools used by hominids in northern Spain; classified as *Homo heidelbergensis*	**280,000 BP** Caves inhabited by *Homo Sapiens* at Atapuerca, Burgos, northern Spain, as well as Torralba and Ambrona	**5500 BC** Sheep and wheat used by early farmers along the western Mediterranean	**3000 BC** Iberian people, including Gauls and Basques, move in from the north to found towns on Iberian Peninsula	**400 BC** Carthaginians of North Africa take over much of Spain	**AD 476** Romans rename peninsula Hispania; lose control to Germanic tribes who occupy whole territory by 573	**962–1212** Christian push back Moors; Moors confined to Granada	**1492** Columbus sails on first voyage in the service of Ferdinand and Isabella; Spanish take last Moorish stronghold, Granada

French revolutionary forces invaded Spain in 1794. They were defeated in 1814 and the Spanish Bourbon monarchy was restored. During the nineteenth and much of the twentieth century Spain has been destabilized by political turmoil and a series of military revolts and wars. Quarrels about the succession to the crown led to the removal of Isabella II from the throne in 1868, the declaration of a republic in 1873, and a military uprising in 1874 that restored the monarchy. In 1898 Spain and the United States fought a war at the end of which a defeated Spain was forced to cede its colonies of Cuba, Puerto Rico, and the Philippines to its adversary.

Spain remained neutral in both world wars, but was wracked by a bitter civil war from 1936 to 1939. Universal adult suffrage was introduced in 1931 and in 1936 the election of a Republican government with socialist leanings prompted an army officer, Francisco Franco, to lead a revolt against the government. With the support of right-wing Spanish forces and of Fascist Italy and Nazi Germany, and after the loss of 750,000 Spanish lives, Franco's forces were eventually victorious and Franco was installed as head of state. His dictatorial regime lasted until his death in 1975. Almost immediately the monarchy was restored and in June 1977 the first parliamentary elections since 1936 were held. In December 1978 a referendum approved a new constitution in which Spain was declared a parliamentary democracy with a monarch as head of state. There are two houses of parliament, both elected by universal adult suffrage for maximum terms of four years.

Physical features and land use

More than half Spain's land area is occupied by a central plateau, the Meseta, which has an average elevation of 700 m (2,300 ft). Much of the Meseta is harsh and barren. It is surrounded by mountain ranges to the north, northeast, south, and southwest, and is traversed by a low mountain range, the Sistema Central. The plateau is drained by three rivers—the Douro to the north of the Sistema Central, and the Tagus and Guadiana to its south—all of these rivers flow westward to the Atlantic.

In the far northeast of the country, between the Sistema Ibérico, a range that fringes the Meseta on the northeast and the Pyrenees to the north, is an extensive lowland area through which the Ebro River, which rises in the Basque country, flows south to the Mediterranean. In the southwest of Spain, beyond the Sierra Morena Range at the Meseta's southwestern edge, the Guadalquivir River drains another extensive low-lying region. In the far southeast is a coastal range, the Sistema Pinibético, which contains the snow-covered peaks of the Sierra Nevada, including the country's highest mountain, Mulhacén.

The Ramblas in Barcelona (above). Storks are among the many bird species found in southern Spain (right).

About one-tenth of Spain is heavily forested. Most of the forests are in the north and northwest, where the weather is wetter and more humid than in the center and south. Beech and oak predominate. Despite the fact that much of the country is arid and covered with low-growing scrub and water is a scarce resource, crops are widely grown. The most productive areas are in the north of the country, especially in the valley of the Ebro. There are significant crops of cereals, vegetables, fruits, and olives.

Spain is one of Europe's main producers of wine and there are 1.5 million hectares (3.7 million acres) of vineyards, mainly in the south and east. About one-fifth of Spain is pastureland, though cattle and dairying are largely confined to the north and pig farming to the southwest. Sheep are widespread on the Meseta, while goats graze in many of the more barren regions.

Industry and commerce

Although Spain has a wide range of mineral resources, it is not rich in any of them and imports the oil and gas needed to fuel its industries. These industries are concentrated towards the north, mainly around the major cities of Madrid and Barcelona. Spain is a major manufacturer of motor vehicles and a number of multinational companies have car manufacturing plants in parts of northern and central Spain. Steelmaking and shipbuilding are among the most significant heavy industries. There are important shipyards at Barcelona, on the Mediterranean coast, La Coruña in the far northwest, and Cadiz in the southwest. Chemical manufacture and fishing are also major industries. Spain has one of the world's largest fishing fleets,

although its activities have been curtailed in recent years by European Union restrictions in response to serious fish stock depletions. About one in ten of Spain's workers are employed in the tourist industry.

While Spain is still a predominantly Catholic country, the influence of the Church has waned in recent years. This is reflected in the fact that Spain has one of the lowest birth-rates in Europe, even though divorce is still relatively rare. Although most Spaniards enjoy a reasonably high standard of living, unemployment during the 1990s has been alarmingly high.

REGIONS

Baleares • Basque Country
Canary Islands • Cantabria
Castilla-La Mancha • Castilla Y León
Catalonia • Ceuta and Melilla
Extremadura • Galicia • La Rioja
Madrid • Murcia • Navarra • Valencia

1516 King Charles I, grandson of Ferdinand and Isabella, is first Hapsburg to rule Spain; becomes Holy Roman Emperor in 1519

1808 French invade Spain; Spanish resistance grows, French expelled in Peninsular War (1814)

1931 King Alfonso XIII flees after elections show preference for a republic; Spain briefly a democracy—deep political divisions

1960s Rapid industrialization, expansion of economy and growth in tourist resort development along Mediterranean

1973 Basque separatists (ETA) assassinate Prime Minister Carrero Blanco in Madrid

1976 Government under Prime Minister Suarez liberalizes politics, permits new parties to participate in elections (1977)

1986 Prime Minister González embarks on more economic development; Spain joins European Community (EC)

1556 Charles's son becomes King Philip II; height of Spanish Empire in Americas, Europe, and Africa

1820 Spanish troops refuse to sail to reconquer American colonies; revolt spreads, crushed with help of French troops

1860 Population begins to decline for almost a century due to emigration

1936–38 Spanish Civil War; victorious Nationalists under Franco enter Madrid in 1939

1970 Population grows following industrialization. More than 1 million immigrants in 10 years, almost half illegal

1975 On the death of Franco, Spain adopts political reform agenda despite accession of Juan Carlos (grandson of Alfonso XIII) as king

1980 The 2.5 million Basque people of northern Spain are granted limited autonomy

1995 Population more than 39 million; Spain lifts passport controls with EC nations

Sweden

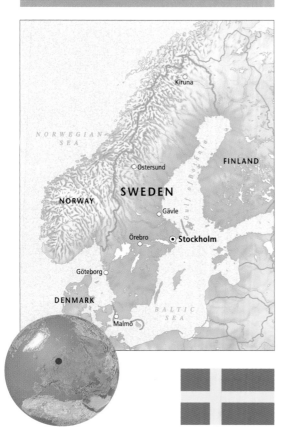

Fact File

OFFICIAL NAME Kingdom of Sweden

FORM OF GOVERNMENT Constitutional monarchy with single legislative body (Parliament, Riksdag)

CAPITAL Stockholm

AREA 449,964 sq km (173,731 sq miles)

TIME ZONE GMT + 1 hour

POPULATION 8,911,296

PROJECTED POPULATION 2005 9,051,287

POPULATION DENSITY 19.8 per sq km (51.3 per sq mile)

LIFE EXPECTANCY 79.3

INFANT MORTALITY (PER 1,000) 3.9

OFFICIAL LANGUAGE Swedish

OTHER LANGUAGES Lapp, Finnish

LITERACY RATE 99%

RELIGIONS Evangelical Lutheran 94%, Roman Catholic 1.5%, Pentecostal 1%, other 3.5%

ETHNIC GROUPS Swedish 91%, others include Lapp, Finnish, Yugoslav, Danish, Norwegian, Greek, Turkish 9%

CURRENCY Swedish krona

ECONOMY Services 69%, industry 28%, agriculture 3%

GNP PER CAPITA US$23,750

CLIMATE Temperate in the south, with cold winters and mild summers; subpolar in the north, with severe winters

HIGHEST POINT Kebnekaise 2,111 m (6,926 ft)

MAP REFERENCE Pages 284–85

A Swedish city in winter (top right). Rows of holiday chalets and small boats in Sweden (right). Early summer foliage in a birch forest (center right).

The fourth largest country in Europe, Sweden shares the Scandinavian Peninsula with Norway, which sits between it and the North Atlantic Ocean. To the northeast Sweden shares a border with Finland, and its eastern coastline is separated from the west coast of Finland by the Gulf of Bothnia. Its southern shores are washed by the Baltic Sea, and south of the land border with Norway the Kattegat Strait divides it from the northern tip of Denmark. Close to Sweden's southeast tip are Gotland and Öland, the largest of many islands dotted around the Swedish coastline.

By the seventh century AD, Teutonic tribes from the south had occupied much of central Sweden, and between the ninth and the eleventh centuries Swedes took part in Viking raids deep into Russia and south to the Black Sea. Over the following five centuries Sweden and Denmark vied for Scandinavian supremacy. Both Sweden and Norway came under the Danish crown in 1397, but 50 years later the Swedes rebelled and elected their own king. The accession to the Swedish throne in 1523 of Gustav I ended Danish claims to all but the south of Sweden. During the next 200 years Sweden became one of the most powerful states in Europe, annexing parts of Estonia, Finland, and Poland, driving the Danes out of southern Sweden, and playing a crucial role in curbing Hapsburg expansion in northern Europe. At the beginning of the eighteenth century, however, a coalition of Russia, Poland, and Denmark forced Sweden to relinquish its Baltic possessions.

At the end of the Napoleonic wars, in 1815, Norway was ceded to Sweden, a union that lasted until 1905. In the mid-nineteenth century the beginnings of parliamentary democracy were introduced in Sweden with the establishment of a two-chamber parliament, although suffrage was limited largely to landowners and industrialists. Universal adult suffrage was introduced in 1919.

Sweden remained neutral in both the First and the Second World Wars. Following the Second World War it tried unsuccessfully to form a military alliance with Denmark and Norway. When these nations joined NATO Sweden did not follow, fearing closer ties with the West might damage its relations with the Soviet Union, and give it an excuse to absorb Finland into the Soviet bloc. Since then, although maintaining a high level of

defence preparedness, it has kept its distance from NATO and maintained its reputation for neutrality, for playing an active role in international affairs, and as a negotiator in international disputes.

During the 1960s and early 1970s, the Social Democrats, who had laid the foundations of a welfare state since 1932, held the majority of seats in the Riksdag and were able to govern alone. They then inaugurated the more radical socialist policies which came to define modern Swedish politics. Welfare services were extended, and "the Swedish Way" was seen by socialists as a model for the rest of Europe. After 1982 Olof Palme's government introduced what it called a middle way between capitalism and communism, with

annual levies on profits and wages which went into "wage-earner funds" used to buy stock in private firms for the benefit of labor. Palme was assassinated in mysterious circumstances in Stockholm in 1986. By then the economic costs of the welfare state were becoming evident. The country had almost zero economic growth, and was becoming less competitive in world markets.

From the late 1970s domestic policy discussion has been less along socialist/capitalist lines and more concerned with ecological issues. Sweden has taken the lead in a number of environmental debates, and has been the venue of influential conferences devoted to such matters as global warming and greenhouse gases. An application for EC membership was lodged in 1992. In 1995 it was admitted to the European Union. Sweden is a constitutional monarchy with a single-chamber parliament that is elected every three years.

Physical features and land use

Northeastern Sweden is a region of low plateaus that drop away to a coastal plain along the Gulf of Bothnia, but rise to the Kjólen Mountains along the Norwegian border. Most of the country's more than 95,000 lakes are in this mountainous region. Shaped by ancient glaciers, many of the lakes are in the upper valleys of the numerous rivers that flow east to the Gulf of Bothnia. They are the source of most of Sweden's hydroelectricity, which is gradually replacing nuclear energy as the main means of power generation. The mountains are heavily forested. Despite extensive land clearing for agriculture in the south, well over half the country remains forested, with spruce, pine and birch among the most prominent trees.

Central Sweden is a lowland area that stretches between Stockholm in the east and the country's second largest city, Göteborg, in the southwest. Four large lakes—the only remnants of a strait that once joined the Baltic to the Kattegat Strait—cover much of this region, the most heavily populated part of the country. The rich soils around these lakes support much of Sweden's agricultural produce, which includes cereals and vegetables and fodder crops for large herds of cattle. Dairy farming is the main form of agriculture, and Sweden is self-sufficient in dairy products.

Scandinavia

Today the term Scandinavia is often understood to refer only to Norway and Sweden, which both occupy the Scandinavian Peninsula, and the more southerly peninsula and islands that make up Denmark. Many people, however, would also include Finland, Iceland, and the Faeroe Islands, which are possessions of Denmark. These countries are also collectively referred to as the Nordic countries, or Norden.

Culturally, geographically, and geologically, the countries of Scandinavia have much in common and the whole region forms a distinctive part of Europe. All of them lie close to the Arctic Circle and share a cold, moist, and often harsh climate, which is mitigated in parts of Scandinavia by the effect of the Gulf Stream. All five countries have a high degree of ethnic and religious homogeneity. Lutheran is the overwhelmingly predominant religion in every part of Scandinavia. The languages of four of the countries are closely related, but Finnish is entirely different and is more closely related to the Estonian language. Historical links are also very strong and during the fifteenth century the countries were united under Danish rule. For five centuries, until 1809, Finland was under Swedish control and Swedish was the language of its ruling classes. For almost a century, until 1905, Norway was ruled by Sweden, and Iceland only gained its independence as late as 1944, after almost five and half centuries of Danish rule and domination.

Greenland has, since the early eighteenth century, been part of Denmark. Situated to the west of Iceland, it is ethnically distinct and geographically closer to North America. Although it was granted home rule in 1979 its inhabitants are still Danish citizens and Denmark still controls Greenland's foreign affairs.

Despite climatic difficulties, Scandinavian economies have traditionally depended heavily on agriculture and fishing. The improvements in agricultural techniques and technologies that flowed from the Industrial Revolution were slow to be implemented in Scandinavia and until late in the nineteenth century the region remained economically stagnant. In recent years, however, there have been significant technological innovations and increasing industrialization and Scandinavians now enjoy some of the highest standards of living in Europe.

South of the lakes is a low, largely infertile plateau and further south, stretching to the tip of the peninsula and across to the island of Gotland, is a rich plain—the most intensively cultivated part of the country. Significant areas of woodland still survive here, dotted between stretches of farming and grazing land.

Although it lacks oil and coal reserves, Sweden is rich in mineral resources, most of which are concentrated in the northeast. These include iron ore, zinc, lead, copper, and silver, and almost one-sixth of the world's known reserves of uranium.

Industry, commerce, and culture

Sweden's vast forests are the basis for timber and paper manufacturing industries that form almost one-fifth of the country's exports. Machines, cars, trucks, aircraft, and chemical and electrical goods and communication equipment are among the chief manufacturing industries, based in the central region and Malmö in the southwest.

Apart from the Saami people (Lapps) in the far north of the country, Sweden is ethnically and culturally quite homogeneous. Despite there being a relatively high rate of unemployment, its citizens enjoy one of the highest standards of living in Europe and an extensive range of government-provided social services. Sweden also boasts one of Europe's highest rates of female participation throughout its workforce.

PROVINCES

Älvsborg • Blekinge • Gävleborg
Göteborg and Bohus • Gotland
Halland • Jämtland • Jönköping
Kalmar • Kopparberg • Kristianstad
Kronoberg • Malmöhus • Norrbotten
Örebro • Östergötland • Skaraborg
Södermanland • Stockholm • Uppsala
Värmland • Västerbotten
Västernorrland • Västmanland

Switzerland

Fact File

OFFICIAL NAME Swiss Confederation

FORM OF GOVERNMENT Federal republic with two legislative bodies (Council of States and National Council)

CAPITAL Bern

AREA 41,290 sq km (15,942 sq miles)

TIME ZONE GMT + 1 hour

POPULATION 7,275,467

PROJECTED POPULATION 2005 7,351,686

POPULATION DENSITY 176.2 per sq km (456.4 per sq mile)

LIFE EXPECTANCY 79

INFANT MORTALITY (PER 1,000) 4.9

OFFICIAL LANGUAGES German, French, Italian

OTHER LANGUAGES Spanish, Romansch

LITERACY RATE 99%

RELIGIONS Roman Catholic 48%, Protestant 44%, other 8%

ETHNIC GROUPS German 65%, French 18%, Italian 10%, Romansch 1%, other 6%

CURRENCY Swiss franc

ECONOMY Services 64%, industry 30%, agriculture 6%

GNP PER CAPITA US$40,630

CLIMATE Temperate, varying with altitude; generally cold winters and warm, wet summers

HIGHEST POINT Dufourspitze 4,634 m (15,203 ft)

MAP REFERENCE Pages 288, 291, 294

A landlocked country in central Europe, Switzerland shares borders with Italy to its south and southeast, France to its west, Germany to its north, and Austria and Liechtenstein to its east. This small nation has enjoyed a generally peaceful independence for more than 450 years, despite the conflicts that have often raged around it. Modern Switzerland dates back to the late thirteenth century when three German districts, or cantons, combined to form a federation. A century later, other cantons had joined the federation, which survived as a unit, despite linguistic differences and often intense and violent conflicts

between Catholics and emerging Protestant groups. Although part of the Holy Roman Empire, and effectively under Hapsburg domination, the Swiss cantons remained neutral during the Thirty Years War of 1618–48, at the end of which they were formally granted independence. In 1798 French revolutionary armies invaded Switzerland and declared it to be a centralized Helvetic Republic, named after Helvetia, the Roman province that had existed there in ancient times. In 1815, after the defeat of Napoleon, the Congress of Vienna declared Switzerland to be independent once more, as well as permanently neutral, and added two more cantons—Valais and the previously separate republic of Geneva.

The country has maintained this military neutrality ever since and its stance has been respected by its neighbors throughout numerous conflicts, including the First and Second World Wars. Religious tensions flared briefly in 1847, when the Catholic cantons seceded. The following year, however, a new constitution, inspired by that of the United States, re-established the former federation and defined Switzerland as a republic with a strong central government but with considerable powers still vested in individual cantons. In 1874 a new constitution was adopted which essentially confirmed this division of power. Switzerland's central government, which controls foreign policy, railway and postal services, and the mint, consists of a an elected bicameral parliament, with a president, elected by the parliament for a one-year term. Women were granted the vote only in 1971.

Physical features and land use

Mountains dominate the Swiss landscape making it Europe's most mountainous country. They cover seven-tenths of the land area. The rest of the country consists of an elevated central plateau on which the majority of the population lives and which is the center of the country's agricultural, industrial, and economic activity. This area is

bordered by a number of large lakes and drained by the River Aare, which rises in Lake Neuchâtel and flows northward into the Rhine, which constitutes Switzerland's border with Germany and part of Austria. Lake Neuchâtel is overlooked by the lightly wooded Jura Mountains, which separate Switzerland from France. More than half of Switzerland is covered by the peaks and glaciers of the Alps, which sweep across the south of the country. The most spectacular sections are in the Pennine Alps along the southwestern frontier with Italy. Both the Rhône and the Rhine rivers rise in this alpine region and drain it in opposite directions, flowing respectively through the two largest lakes in the country, which are Lake Geneva in the far southwest, and Lake Constance in the far northeast.

About one-quarter of Switzerland consists of forests, which are found mainly in the valleys and on the lower slopes. Cypresses and figs are prominent among the tree species. About one-tenth of the land is arable. Crop cultivation is concentrated in the area immediately to the east and southeast of the Jura and in the valleys of the Rhône and Rhine rivers. Wheat, potatoes, and sugar beet are the main crops. The principal agricultural activity, however, is dairy farming, although pig raising is also significant. Switzerland produces less than half its food needs.

Switzerland is not well endowed with mineral resources. Most of the country's electricity is generated by hydropower, but a significant amount is provided by the country's five nuclear power plants. A sixth nuclear plant was planned but was cancelled in the aftermath of the Chernobyl disaster in Ukraine in 1986.

Industry, commerce, and culture

Switzerland has for centuries been a world leader in the production of precision instruments such as clocks and watches. Other industries which are vital to the country's prosperity include heavy engineering, textile manufacture, clothing, chemicals and food processing. Swiss chocolate, sought after the world over because of its high quality, is also a major contributor to the national economy. Tourism, centered mainly on the Alps, attracts more than 12 million visitors annually.

Banking is highly developed and is one of the country's key industries. Switzerland attracts almost half the world's foreign investment capital and is the base of numerous multinational companies.

Although the country is divided geographically among its predominantly German-, Italian- and French-speaking populations, Switzerland is now a unified nation and its people have a strong sense of common purpose. This is attributable in large measure to Switzerland's status as one of the world's most stable and prosperous countries, with a very high per capita income.

Ukraine

Ukraine, formerly part of the USSR, has a southern coastline on the Black Sea and on the almost landlocked Sea of Azov. Surrounding it are seven other countries. From southeast across its northern border to southwest, they are the Russian Federation, Belarus, Poland, Slovakia, Hungary, Romania, and Moldova. The Ukrainian capital, Kiev, has existed since the ninth century AD, when a Viking tribe established a center there. A century later it was a powerful force in eastern Europe. It was overrun by Mongols in the thirteenth century and then came under Polish control. In the seventeenth century the eastern part of Ukraine fell to the Russians, who eventually absorbed the whole of the country into their empire. Despite attempts to establish a separate state after the 1917 Revolution, invading Soviet armies subdued Ukraine in 1920. During the 1930s more than 3 million Ukrainians perished in a famine and another 6 million died in the Nazi occupation during the Second World War. After the war, part of western Ukraine that was under Polish occupation was returned, as was the Crimea, and Ukraine assumed its present boundaries, under Soviet domination.

Ukraine declared its independence in 1991 as the Soviet Union began to break up, although it still retains close ties with Russia. It is now a democratic republic, with a directly elected president as head of state.

Formerly referred to as "the granary of the Soviet Union," most of Ukraine consists of fertile black-soil plains that produce an abundance of wheat and other cereal grains as well as vegetables, fruits, and fodder crops. Much of the country's agricultural output remains affected by the widespread contamination caused by the nuclear accident at Chernobyl, near the Belarus border, in 1986.

There are mountainous areas in the southwest, where the Carpathian Mountains sweep down from Poland, and in the Crimean Peninsula in the far south. The Dnieper River flows through the heart of the country and empties into the Black

The Jungfrau Mountain in Switzerland's Bernese Oberland (left). An alpine vegetable farm in Switzerland (top). Yalta and the crowded promenade on the Sea of Azov, Ukraine (right).

Sea. In its northern plain there are large stretches of marshland and many forest-rimmed lakes. In the south, bordering the Black Sea, much of the landscape is a semiarid, treeless plain.

Coal is Ukraine's most abundant and heavily exploited mineral resource. There are also significant reserves of natural gas, uranium, and oil, though the latter remains largely unexploited. Steel production, machine building, engineering, and chemical processing are the main industries. These industries are centered around the large cities and the coalfields in the east of the country. In the post-Soviet era, the Ukrainian economy has suffered periods of extremely high inflation and growth has been hampered by a largely conservative legislature that has resisted many attempts at reform. There is widespread poverty, exacerbated by a declining health-care system.

Fact File

OFFICIAL NAME Ukraine

FORM OF GOVERNMENT Republic with single legislative body (Supreme Council)

CAPITAL Kiev

AREA 603,700 sq km (233,089 sq miles)

TIME ZONE GMT + 3 hours

POPULATION 49,811,174

PROJECTED POPULATION 2005 48,308,739

POPULATION DENSITY 82.5 per sq km (213.7 per sq mile)

LIFE EXPECTANCY 65.9

INFANT MORTALITY (PER 1,000) 21.7

OFFICIAL LANGUAGE Ukrainian

OTHER LANGUAGES Russian, Romanian, Hungarian, Polish

LITERACY RATE 98.8%

RELIGIONS Predominantly Christian (Ukrainian Orthodox, Ukrainian Autocephalus Orthodox, Roman Catholic); small Protestant, Jewish and Muslim minorities

ETHNIC GROUPS Ukrainian 73%, Russian 22%, other 5%

CURRENCY Hryvna

ECONOMY Services 46%, industry 33%, agriculture 21%

GNP PER CAPITA US$1,630

CLIMATE Temperate, with cold winters and mild summers; warmer on Black Sea coast

HIGHEST POINT Hora Hoverla 2,061 m (6,762 ft)

MAP REFERENCE Pages 289, 298

Europe and the Russian Federation

United Kingdom

Fact File

OFFICIAL NAME United Kingdom of Great Britain and Northern Ireland

FORM OF GOVERNMENT Constitutional monarchy with two legislative houses (House of Lords and House of Commons)

CAPITAL London

AREA 244,820 sq km (94,525 sq miles)

TIME ZONE GMT

POPULATION 57,832,824

PROJECTED POPULATION 2005 58,135,972

POPULATION DENSITY 236.2 per sq km (611.8 per sq mile)

LIFE EXPECTANCY 77.6

INFANT MORTALITY (PER 1,000) 5.8

OFFICIAL LANGUAGE English

OTHER LANGUAGES Welsh, Scots Gaelic; Chinese, Gujarati, Bengali, Punjabi, Urdu, Hindi, Arabic, Turkish, Greek, Spanish, Japanese

LITERACY RATE 99%

RELIGIONS Anglican 63%, Roman Catholic 14%, Presbyterian 4%, Methodist 3%, Muslim 3%, other 13%

ETHNIC GROUPS English 81.5%, Scottish 9.6%, Irish 2.4%, Welsh 1.9%, Northern Irish 1.8%, other 2.8%

CURRENCY Pound sterling

ECONOMY Services 78%, industry 20%, agriculture 2%

GNP PER CAPITA US$18,700

CLIMATE Temperate, with cool winters and mild summers; generally wetter and warmer in the west, and cooler in the north

HIGHEST POINT Ben Nevis 1,343 m (4,406 ft)

MAP REFERENCE Pages 302–03

Lying just north of the westernmost edge of continental Europe, the United Kingdom consists of the large island of Great Britain, the far northeast corner of the island of Ireland, which sits across the Irish Sea to the west, and several hundred small islands scattered around the British coast. The United Kingdom is separated by the English Channel from the north coast of France which, at its nearest point, is no more than 32 km (20 miles) away, and a rail tunnel under the Channel now links England and France. England, in the south and southwest, occupies the greatest part of the island. Scotland is to the north, and Wales in the west juts out into the Irish Sea. The long eastern coast of Great Britain faces the North Sea; its western coastline is on the Atlantic Ocean and the Irish Sea.

History

Thanks partly to the natural protection offered by surrounding waters, but also to its maritime supremacy in certain periods of history and to a degree of good fortune in others, Britain is unique among major European nations in that it has escaped foreign invasion for almost 1,000 years. When William, Duke of Normandy led his successful invasion in 1066, this was the culmination of a long series of incursions that the island kingdom had suffered since the first invasion—the Romans in the first century AD.

Within 60 years of their arrival in Britain in AD 55, the Romans had established control over England and Wales and later introduced Christianity. When they finally withdrew at the beginning of the fifth century, the Britons eventually fell prey to Germanic tribes from Scandinavia and the Low Countries. By the eighth century most of Britain, except the far west and the north, had succumbed and the country was divided into a number of Anglo-Saxon kingdoms.

Viking attacks from Norway and Denmark occurred during the course of the eighth and ninth centuries, with Danish invaders controlling much of north and northeast England by the late ninth century. United under the kings of Wessex by the middle of the tenth century, England again fell to Danish control early in the eleventh century. When Edward the Confessor came to the throne in 1042, he presided over a unified, but fractious, kingdom. On his death in 1066, both his brother-in-law, Harold, and his cousin, William of Normandy, claimed the throne. William was victorious at the Battle of Hastings and was crowned on Christmas Day 1066.

The feudal system of government developed by William gave significant power to the nobles. Under Henry II, the first Plantagenet king, power became more centralized in the crown. This, and increasing civil unrest during the reign of John, led to a revolt by nobles, who in 1215 forced the king to sign the Magna Carta, a document limiting royal power and enshrining basic civil rights. This in turn gave rise to the development of a more consultative style of government, and, by the late thirteenth century, to the establishment of a House of Commons with powers to raise taxes.

Under Edward I (1272–1307) Wales was brought under English control, much of Ireland was subjugated, and a portion of Scotland was conquered. In 1314, however, at the Battle of

Bannockburn, the English were driven out of Scotland. Between 1338 and 1453, in a series of devastating wars, known as the Hundred Years War, England lost all its French territories. This led to a further 30 years of civil war, known as the Wars of the Roses, which culminated in the accession to the throne of Henry VII, the first of the Tudor monarchs, in 1485.

The Tudor dynasty lasted until 1603, and during this time, especially during the reign of Elizabeth I (1558–1603), England became a leading power in the world, enjoying a golden age in which colonies were established in North America, British navigators sailed to remote corners of the globe, and there was a notable flowering of English theatre. During the reign of Elizabeth's father, Henry VIII, Protestantism, in the form of the Church of England, had been established in England.

When Elizabeth died without an heir, James VI of Scotland, the first Stuart king, succeeded her, combining the two kingdoms and reigning as James I of England. Attempts by his son, Charles I, to curb the powers of parliament led to the outbreak of civil war in 1642. With the victory of the parliamentary armies, led by Oliver Cromwell, in 1646, the monarchy was abolished and a commonwealth, virtually a military dictatorship, set up under Cromwell. The Commonwealth did not long survive the death of Cromwell and in 1660 Charles II was installed as king. When, however, his brother, the Catholic James II, attempted to restore Catholic domination, he was ousted and his Protestant daughter, Mary, and her Dutch husband, William of Orange, accepted the crown in 1689. In the same year, parliament enacted legislation barring Catholics from the

throne. In 1690, at the Battle of the Boyne, their armies defeated a Catholic uprising in Ireland. In 1707 an Act of Union, between the Scottish and English parliaments, formally joined the two countries. Scottish rebellions against British rule were finally put down in 1746, when Charles Edward Stuart (Bonnie Prince Charlie) was defeated in the Battle of Culloden.

Under the Hanoverian monarchs, the first of whom, George I, accepted the throne in 1814 as King of Great Britain and Ireland, greater power devolved to the parliament. In 1721, Sir Hugh Walpole became the first prime minister to head a ministry that exercised executive power with the sanction of parliament. The eighteenth century, too, was a period of great expansion of British power that saw the acquisitions of British colonies in India and Canada and the exploration and colonization of Australia. A major setback was the loss of the American colonies in 1776. The military defeat of Irish rebels in 1798 led to an Act of Union that formally joined the two countries in 1801. Defeat of Bonaparte at Waterloo in 1815 confirmed Britain as the world's leading power.

The nineteenth century was a time of further expansion and consolidation of Britain's influence and power. By the end of Queen Victoria's 64-year reign in 1901, Britain's colonies extended throughout much of the world, including large parts of Africa, although by then Australia, New Zealand, and Canada had gained their independence and demands for Irish independence were growing. During the century a number of Reform Bills brought in significant democratic reforms and the Industrial Revolution resulted in increasing industrialization, urban growth, and a slowly rising standard of living.

Three-quarters of a million British soldiers were killed during the First World War, which also left the country considerably weakened economically. This situation was exacerbated by the Great Depression. After a protracted and bitter struggle, Ireland, with the exception of the provinces of Northern Ireland, became independent in 1922 and British troops faced growing unrest in India and in parts of the Middle East. Following the Second World War, in which British cities, especially London, were subjected to sustained German bombardment from the air, Britain endured almost a decade of austerity.

India gained its independence in 1947, and in 1956 Britain suffered a humiliating defeat in its

armed attempt to prevent Egypt's nationalization of the Suez Canal. In 1982, Britain was again at war, this time against Argentina, which attempted to seize the Falkland Islands. In a two-week conflict, Britain repulsed the Argentines with the loss of 255 British lives. In recent years, bitter violence between Catholics and Protestants in Northern Ireland has been a major preoccupation of British governments. Since 1995, however, there have been developments, including the intervention of the United States, that augur well for a peaceful resolution of this conflict.

Britain, as a member of the European Union and a signatory of the Maastricht Treaty, is a significant force in Europe as it moves closer to

The Cuckmere River meanders through pastureland in England (left). The Giant's Causeway, a promontory of hexagonal basalt columns, in County Antrim, Northern Ireland (top). Ebbw Valley British Steel tinplate mill in the town of Ebbw Vale, south Wales (above).

political and economic integration. It is one of the world's most stable multi-party democracies, in spite of ongoing debate about the role and viability of the monarchy and of its unelected, and largely hereditary, upper house of parliament, the House of Lords, which is in the process of reform. Power resides in the House of Commons, which is elected by universal adult suffrage for terms of five years.

Physical features and land use

The United Kingdom has a considerable variety of landscapes, ranging from craggy mountain ranges and tranquil upland lakes in the north, to gently rolling hills and green plains that are characteristic of the south and southeast.

Scotland is the most mountainous part of the country. Mainland Scotland has three main regions:

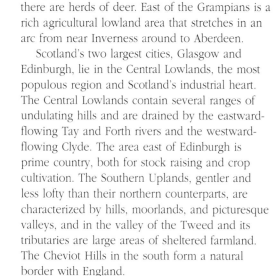

the Highlands in the north, the Southern Uplands near the border with England, and in between the flatter, though often hilly, Central Lowlands. It also has several groups of offshore islands: the Shetlands in the far north, the Orkneys, off the northeastern tip of the mainland, and the Inner and Outer Hebrides off the northwestern coast. The most rugged country is in the north, where two granite ranges, the North West Highlands and the Grampians, dominate the scene. In the northwest the mountains are cut by deep glaciated valleys and the coastline is rocky and deeply indented. South and east of the Great Glen, which contains the famous Loch Ness, are the Grampians, where Britain's highest peaks are found. Here, the country is generally less harsh, and there are stretches of sheep-grazing land and forested slopes where there are herds of deer. East of the Grampians is a rich agricultural lowland area that stretches in an arc from near Inverness around to Aberdeen.

Scotland's two largest cities, Glasgow and Edinburgh, lie in the Central Lowlands, the most populous region and Scotland's industrial heart. The Central Lowlands contain several ranges of undulating hills and are drained by the eastward-flowing Tay and Forth rivers and the westward-flowing Clyde. The area east of Edinburgh is prime country, both for stock raising and crop cultivation. The Southern Uplands, gentler and less lofty than their northern counterparts, are characterized by hills, moorlands, and picturesque valleys, and in the valley of the Tweed and its tributaries are large areas of sheltered farmland. The Cheviot Hills in the south form a natural border with England.

Beginning just south of the Cheviot Hills, and running southward as far as north Derbyshire, are the Pennine Mountains, a predominantly limestone range of hills, plateaus, expanses of moorlands, and soft, green valleys, which are often referred to

CONSTITUENT COUNTRIES

England • London
Scotland • Edinburgh

CONSTITUENT REGION

Northern Ireland • Belfast

PRINCIPALITY

Wales • Cardiff

OVERSEAS TERRITORIES

Anguilla
Bermuda
British Indian Ocean Territory
British Virgin Islands
Cayman Islands
Falkland Islands
Gibraltar
Guernsey
Isle of Man
Jersey
Montserrat
Pitcairn Islands
St Helena
South Georgia and the South Sandwich islands
Turks and Caicos islands

A coastal village in Scotland (top). A tile-hung house in a village in southern England (center). Scotney Castle in Kent, southeastern England (right). Heathland on the rugged Pembrokeshire coast of Wales (top right.)

Timeline

4000 BC Tribes from various parts of Europe arrive; they farm and live in villages, burying their dead in earth mounds	**43 BC–AD 446** Roman occupation of Britain brings wealth, military skills, and Christianity; Hadrian's Wall built AD 120

1066 Norman invasion. William I's Domesday Book assesses Britain's wealth and estimates population about 2 million

1300 Population reaches 5 million after expanding rapidly as a result of more efficient farming methods

1536 Parliament formally makes Wales part of English territory

1664–66 Great Plague kills more than 75,000 of London's population of around 450,000, then spreads to other parts of the country

1801 Act of Union extended to join Ireland to United Kingdom

200,000 BC Hominids living in southeastern Britain use stone tools and hunt animals

12,000 BC Paleolithic hunters carve mammal bones at Cresswell Crags, Derbyshire; one shows a dancing man, others, animal heads

3300 BC Construction of a large stone circle begins: Stonehenge completed 1800 BC

AD 410 Anglo-Saxons settle in south England destroying remains of Roman culture; later, Danish Vikings settle in north and east

1489 Enclosure of common land forces many people off the land, causing rebellions and rural depopulation

1500 Little ice age of cold winters and wet summers (which continues until 1700) causes crop failures across the country

1707 Act of Union between England and Scotland creates United Kingdom of Great Britain

1750 Use of iron grows rapidly; machines for spinning and weaving invented in late 1700s, accelerating Industrial Revolution

as the Dales. West of the Pennines, and separated from it by the valley of the Eden, are the Cumbrian Mountains, a region of craggy peaks with many lakes. This is England's famous Lake District. To the east of the Pennines are the elevated expanses of the North York Moors.

South of the Pennines, beginning around the fertile valleys of the Trent and Avon rivers, the countryside becomes flatter and gently undulating, reaching its lowest point in the marshy fen country north of Cambridge. Numerous ranges of hills provide relief from the generally rolling countryside. The most notable hills are the Cotswolds, in the central southwest, where England's longest river, the Thames, begins its course eastward across the country, passing through London, and out to the North Sea.

Wales, which juts out into the Irish Sea to the west of England, is more mountainous, its center dominated by the Cambrian Mountains, in which the Severn, Britain's second longest river, rises. Mount Snowdon, in Snowdonia, a large national park in northern Wales, rises to 1,085 m (3,559 ft) and is the highest peak in England and Wales.

Northern Ireland is flat for the most part, but to the north of Belfast is the Antrim Plateau, whose basalt cliffs provide some of the country's most arresting coastal scenery.

Industry, commerce, agriculture, and culture

Crop cultivation in Britain is concentrated mainly in the east and southeast of the country. Wheat is the principal crop, though potatoes and fruits are widely cultivated. Pasturelands are more common in the west and southwest, where sheep and cattle raising and dairy farming predominate. Although the United Kingdom exports much of its produce, it still imports about one-third of its food needs.

The United Kingdom has traditionally relied on coal for its energy resources, and there are still adequate reserves. However, the replacement of most coal-fired power stations with gas-powered facilities in recent years has resulted in the near closure of the coalmining industry. The country also has a number of nuclear power stations which are a continuing subject of controversy. Oil and gas reserves in the North Sea are a major source of revenue, and have helped to make the country self-sufficient in energy.

Manufacturing was once the mainstay of the British economy, with a large proportion of heavy industry centered on industrial cities in the Midlands such as Birmingham, Manchester, and Liverpool. Food processing, machinery, and textile manufacture are still among the principal manufacturing industries. Motor vehicle and aircraft manufacture are long-established core industries, although much of the motor vehicle industry is now owned by foreign companies. Most of the

raw materials needed to supply Britain's industries have to be imported from other countries.

Apart from the ethnic and cultural minorities found in Wales and Scotland, Britain's population is relatively homogeneous. Since the 1950s, however, large numbers of immigrants from former British colonies in the Caribbean, Asia (especially India and Pakistan), and Africa have changed the racial composition, most notably in inner-city areas, where the majority of ethnic minorities have congregated. Despite certain tensions, these

immigrants are now generally accepted as an integral, if still relatively disadvantaged, part of British society. Britain's economy is one of the most developed in Western Europe and its people enjoy a high standard of living, although there are considerable variations in levels of affluence. Universal free school education and health systems are maintained by the state, although some social services and the value of pensions, including those for the elderly, have been sharply cut back in recent years.

The European Union

On 1 January 1999 eleven European countries adopted a new and common currency—the euro. This momentous step marked the climax of a movement for closer European integration which had begun in 1957. In March of that year Belgium, France, the Federal Republic of Germany, Italy, Luxembourg, and the Netherlands signed a treaty which proposed the gradual integration of their economies in the European Economic Community (EEC or EC). They planned to gradually eliminate restrictive quotas and import duties between member nations in order to allow the free movement of persons and capital within their common boundaries. It was hoped that the larger market that resulted would promote greater productivity and higher standards of living for all.

The success of the Community led to a number of additional countries seeking membership. Others, however, objected to the surrender of sovereignty that was entailed: at first Britain, along with the Scandinavian nations, Switzerland, Austria, and Portugal, formed their own free-trade area (known as the outer seven) instead. Nor were the policies of the EEC uniformly

successful: the Common Agricultural Policy, for example, led to the overproduction of butter, wine, and sugar in member countries. However, although national referenda on membership and treaty ratification have not been without a degree of controversy, most of the countries in Europe have now decided that the benefits of being a member of the EEC outweigh the costs, and by 1997 all of the following states belonged: Austria, Belgium, Denmark, Finland, France, Germany, Greece, Ireland, Italy, Luxembourg, the Netherlands, Portugal, Spain, Sweden, and the UK.

With the ratification of the Maastricht Treaty, which prepared the way for monetary union and the euro, the EEC and its associated bodies became formally known as the European Union (EU). An important feature of monetary union has been the establishment of an independent European Central Bank (ECB). This bank has as its main goal "price stability," a term meaning inflation of less than 2 percent per year. At present the UK, Denmark, and Sweden have decided not to adopt the euro, while Greece is unable to satisfy the economic criteria for monetary union and the new currency.

1825 World's first public railway opens between Stockton and Darlington, starting a worldwide boom in railway construction

1845–46 Potato crop failure causes Great Famine in Ireland; millions die or emigrate to England, USA, Canada, Australia

1914–18 First World War against Germany causes the loss of more than 900,000 British Empire lives

1930s Unemployment rises to 3 million; some relief provided by economic progress in manufacturing industries

1945 Churchill loses election to Labour Party's Attlee who begins a program of reconstruction, reform, and nationalization

1967 Britain fails to join the EC; membership not achieved until 1973; sterling devalued

1994 Passenger train services through the fixed-link railway tunnel under the English Channel link France and the UK

1837 Queen Victoria crowned. Rule lasts until 1901, coincides with period of great wealth and growth of British Empire

1901 The population of Britain reaches 42 million after rapid population growth in the second half of the nineteenth century

1920 Northern Ireland separates from the rest of Ireland and remains part of the United Kingdom; the Irish Free State (southern Ireland) is set up in 1921

1939–45 Cities across Britain bombed during Second World War—widespread damage and the loss of thousands of lives

1957 Extensive postwar migration from Commonwealth regions such as Pakistan, India, and West Indies

1975 Offshore North Sea oilfields begin operation, boosting the UK economy; Britain becomes self-sufficient in oil

Europe and the Russian Federation

Vatican City

Occupying a hill in the city of Rome on the western bank of the Tiber, and including as well the pope's residence at Castel Gandolfo, southeast of Rome, and ten churches throughout Rome, Vatican City is the world's smallest state, and probably its most homogeneous. Its population is 100 percent Catholic, and it is the home of the pope, the spiritual head of the Roman Catholic Church, and several hundred clergy and Catholic lay people, all employees of the Vatican.

Vatican City is all that remains of the former Papal States, which from the fourteenth to the nineteenth centuries expanded from a palace on the present site to cover an area of almost 45,000 sq km (17,000 sq miles). During the Risorgimento ("resurrection"), which resulted in the unification of Italy in the 1860s, most of this area was absorbed into the new Italian state. From 1870 until 1929, neither the Church nor successive Italian governments recognized each other's sovereignty over the area, which the Church refused to relinquish to the state. In 1929, however, Pope Leo XI and Mussolini concluded an

agreement—the Lateran Treaty—under which the independence of the Vatican City State, and the pope's temporal sovereignty over it, was recognized in return for the Church's recognition of the kingdom of Italy. Under this treaty, Catholicism was also recognized as the state religion of Italy. This provision, along with a number of other privileges enjoyed by the Church in Italy, was removed under a subsequent Church–state agreement, known as a "concordat," signed in 1984. Vatican City, which now has diplomatic relations with more than 100 countries, has the pope as head of state, while responsibility for administration of the area is vested in a Commission of Cardinals. The roles of secretary of state, chief of staff, and foreign minister are filled by senior members of the clergy.

Surrounded by medieval walls, Vatican City contains the huge St Peter's Basilica, built between 1506 and 1626 by a number of architects, including Michelangelo and Bernini. Pilgrims come to visit the basilica in vast numbers throughout the year, but particularly to celebrate Christmas and Easter. Visitors also come to see the richly endowed Vatican Museums, which include the renowned Sistine Chapel (the personal chapel of the popes) in the Vatican Palace. Parklands cover most of Vatican City.

Vatican City has its own radio station, publishes a daily newspaper, and issues its own stamps and coins. It also has an army—the 100-strong Swiss Guard—which is responsible for maintaining security. Vatican state finances depend on voluntary contributions, interest on extensive investments, and on the income derived from millions of tourists.

Fact File

OFFICIAL NAME	Vatican City State (Holy See)
FORM OF GOVERNMENT	Monarchical–sacerdotal state with single legislative body (Pontifical Commission)
CAPITAL	Vatican City
AREA	0.44 sq km (0.16 sq miles)
TIME ZONE	GMT + 1 hour
POPULATION	1,000
PROJECTED POPULATION 2005	Not available
POPULATION DENSITY	2,272.7 per sq km (5,886.3 per sq mile)
LIFE EXPECTANCY	Not available
INFANT MORTALITY (PER 1,000)	Not available
OFFICIAL LANGUAGES	Italian, Latin
LITERACY RATE	Not available
RELIGION	Roman Catholic
ETHNIC GROUPS	Predominantly Italian; some Swiss
CURRENCY	Vatican lira
ECONOMY	Services 100%
GNP PER CAPITA	Not available
CLIMATE	Temperate, with mild winters and hot summers
HIGHEST POINT	Unnamed location 75 m (246 ft)
MAP REFERENCE	Page 295

St Peter's Square in Vatican City, seen from the roof of the basilica (left). An old stone bridge spans a river in Montenegro, Yugoslavia (top right).

Yugoslavia

At its southwestern edge, the "rump" republic of Yugoslavia has a toehold on the Adriatic Sea. Otherwise it is landlocked, sharing borders with seven countries. Moving from the west around to south clockwise, these are Bosnia and Herzegovina, Croatia, Hungary, Romania, Bulgaria, Macedonia, and Albania. Yugoslavia now comprises the republics of Serbia and Montenegro—all that remains of the former federation of Yugoslavia after four of its six constituent republics seceded in the early 1990s. Yugoslavia came into existence in December 1918 as a combination of formerly separate Balkan states, most of which had been under Austro-Hungarian control. Serbia had become independent in 1878, bringing to an end five centuries of almost continuous Ottoman rule. The new country was originally called the Kingdom of Serbs, Croats, and Slovenes, but in 1929 the name Yugoslavia was adopted. During the Second World War Yugoslavia was invaded by Germany and the country was further devastated by civil war. More than a million Yugoslavs perished during this time. At the end of the war, a communist government, led by a Croat, Josip Broz, better known as Marshal Tito, came to power, but remained independent of the Soviet Union. After Tito died in 1980 ethnic tensions began to assert themselves, and in 1991 Croatia and Slovenia seceded, leading to four years of bitter ethnic-based conflict between Serbia and its neighbors. Ethnic conflict still simmers. A constitution adopted in 1992 decreed that democratic elections for the presidency and for two houses of parliament be held every five years.

In 1999, Serbia forced most of the population of the southern province of Kosovo—Muslim Albanians—to leave. Conflict continued between guerrilla forces of the Kosovo Liberation Army (KLO) and Serb forces as a meeting of NATO nations decided to launch air strikes against major administrative and industrial targets in

Serbia. Most of the NATO strikes were aimed at bridges and buildings in the Serb capital of Belgrade, with strikes also affecting the Serb city of Novi Sad and the Kosovo capital of Pristina. Russia, which opposed the NATO air strikes, held talks with Serb President Slobodan Milosevic, as well as US President Clinton, in an attempt to resolve the conflict.

Serbia and Montenegro are largely mountainous. The heavily forested Balkan Mountains, with their rocky peaks, separate Serbia from Bulgaria and Romania and stretch across much of southern and central Serbia and into Bosnia and Herzegovina. Much of Montenegro, in the southwest, is covered by the bare limestone ridges of the Dinaric Alps, which run from Slovenia south into Albania. In the north of the country, and covering most of the province of Vojvodina, is the fertile Pannonian Plain. A number of rivers, including the Sava, the Tisza and the Danube traverse this plain, which extends northwest into Croatia and Hungary.

Agricultural produce is centered on the northern plain, which supports substantial crops of wheat, maize, and vegetables as well as livestock and poultry. Agriculture in Montenegro is based mainly on the raising of sheep and goats. Yugoslavia has considerable reserves of coal and petroleum and is largely self-sufficient in fuel. Most of these resources are in the northern province of Vojvodina and the troubled southern region of Kosovo. Mining and heavy machine manufacture are major contributors to the country's economy, which, however, remains seriously destabilized by years of warfare and the consequent disruption of trade links.

Fact File

OFFICIAL NAME Federal Republic of Yugoslavia

FORM OF GOVERNMENT Federal republic with two legislative bodies (Chamber of Republics and Chamber of Citizens)

CAPITAL Belgrade

AREA 102,350 sq km (39,517 sq miles)

TIME ZONE GMT + 1 hour

POPULATION 10,526,478

PROJECTED POPULATION 2005 10,626,538

POPULATION DENSITY 102.8 per sq km (266.2 per sq mile)

LIFE EXPECTANCY 73.5

INFANT MORTALITY (PER 1,000) 16.5

OFFICIAL LANGUAGE Serbian

OTHER LANGUAGE Albanian

LITERACY RATE 93%

RELIGIONS Eastern Orthodox 65%, Muslim 19%, Roman Catholic 4%, Protestant 1%, other 11%

ETHNIC GROUPS Serbian 63%, Albanian 14%, Montenegrin 6%, Hungarian 4%, other 13%

CURRENCY Yugoslav dinar

ECONOMY Services and agriculture 60%, industry 40%

GNP PER CAPITA US$1,500

CLIMATE Temperate, with cold winters and hot summers

HIGHEST POINT Daravica 2,656 m (8,714 ft)

MAP REFERENCE Page 296

The Balkans

The Balkans is the collective name for the countries that occupy the Balkan Peninsula, the easternmost of the three peninsulas that jut southward into the Mediterranean Sea. It comprises the countries of Greece, Bulgaria, Romania, Moldova, Albania, Macedonia, Yugoslavia, Bosnia and Herzegovina, Croatia, and Slovenia. The word Balkan emerged in the nineteenth century. It was the Turkish name for a mountain range in Bulgaria and at first was applied to the land that lay to the south of this range. At various times since, it has had different meanings. Since the First World War, which was sparked by the assassination of the heir to the Austro-Hungarian Empire in Sarajevo, in Bosnia, the region has often been referred to as "the powder keg of Europe," and has had strong connotations of violence and ethnic conflict. In more recent times that phrase has acquired new significance and the term Balkan is increasingly used to refer specifically to those countries that formerly constituted the state of Yugoslavia.

The present troubles in the Balkans can be traced back to the reawakening of long-dormant nationalist sentiments as the formerly powerful Turkish Empire declined during the nineteenth century. This led to the formation of a number of nation states, some of which were, until the end of the First World War, under Austro-Hungarian domination. Many of these states were formed with scant regard to the ethnic, religious, or linguistic homogeneity of their populations. Thus significant populations of Muslim Albanians were incorporated into predominantly Christian Serbia and Macedonia and large numbers of Serbs, the most widely dispersed of the Balkan peoples, lived in Croatia and Bosnia, which is now called Bosnia and Herzegovina.

The explosive potential of this situation was largely contained after the formation of the federated state of Yugoslavia, in which Serbians were dominant, and during the Second World War, in which all Balkan countries suffered grievously. Ethnic tensions remained suppressed during the regime of the strong communist leader Marshal Tito after the Second World War. During this period, cold war politics dominated Europe, and Yugoslavia adopted relatively liberal socialist policies independently of the Soviet Union. Albania and Romania also pursued their own, albeit more oppressive, socialist agendas, but like Yugoslavia, refused to bow to Soviet domination. Greece remained non-communist, but only after a bitter civil war, which saw the communists finally defeated in 1949.

The death of Tito in 1980 and the later disintegration of communist regimes in Eastern Europe set the scene for the breakdown of Yugoslavia into its component republics. A series of civil wars followed, as Serb minorities in Croatia and Bosnia and Herzegovina fought, with Serbian support, for the extension of Serbian territories. An uneasy truce was brokered in 1995, only after the deployment of United Nations forces. In 1998, simmering resentment by ethnic Albanians in the southern Yugoslav province of Kosovo erupted again into bloody warfare and led to brutal massacres by Yugoslav forces.

Dependencies in Europe

Faeroe Islands

 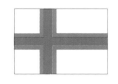

The Faeroes are an archipelago of 22 islands in the north Atlantic Ocean, between Scotland and Iceland, eighteen of which are inhabited. Although they are part of Danish territory, the Faeroes have, since 1948, enjoyed a high degree of autonomy. They have their own parliament, which is elected for four-year terms. In the eleventh century these islands came under Norwegian control, but when, in the fourteenth century, the crowns of Norway and Denmark combined, Denmark became the dominant power. Since 1709 the islands have been administered solely by Denmark.

The Faeroes, formed from volcanic lava, are rocky, with spectacular cliffs along the coasts. Sheep raising has been the economic mainstay, though recently fishing has supplanted it in importance. Despite international criticism, the Faeroese maintain a vigorous whaling industry.

Fact file

OFFICIAL NAME Faeroe Islands

FORM OF GOVERNMENT Self-governing overseas administrative division of Denmark

CAPITAL Torshavn

AREA 1,400 sq km (541 sq miles)

TIME ZONE GMT

POPULATION 41,059

LIFE EXPECTANCY 78.6

INFANT MORTALITY (PER 1,000) 10.3

LITERACY RATE Not available

CURRENCY Danish krone

ECONOMY Mainly fishing; some agriculture, light industry, and services

CLIMATE Mild winters, cool summers; foggy and windy

MAP REFERENCE Page 302

Gibraltar

 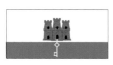

Jutting into the Strait of Gibraltar at the southwest tip of Spain, Gibraltar sits at the entrance to the Mediterranean Sea. Spain's capture of Gibraltar in 1462 ended seven centuries of Moorish rule. Seized by the British and Dutch in 1704, it was ceded to Britain in 1713 and, despite subsequent Spanish attempts to take it back, it has remained in British hands ever since. Spain and Britain still dispute possession of "The Rock," and there is strong support for independence among the inhabitants. Gibraltar has its own elected parliament and is virtually autonomous. Britain maintained a military garrison there until 1991, when it handed over control to the local regiment.

Gibraltar consists of a high rocky mountain, joined to the Spanish mainland by a sandy plain. Tourism, served by an airport on the peninsula, is an important contributor to Gibraltar's economy.

Fact file

OFFICIAL NAME Gibraltar

FORM OF GOVERNMENT Self-governing dependent territory of the United Kingdom

CAPITAL Gibraltar

AREA 6.5 sq km (2.5 sq miles)

TIME ZONE GMT + 1 hour

POPULATION 29,165

LIFE EXPECTANCY 78.7

INFANT MORTALITY (PER 1,000) 8.4

LITERACY RATE Not available

CURRENCY Gibraltar pound

ECONOMY Financial services, tourism, manufacturing, horticulture

CLIMATE Temperate; mild winters and warm summers

MAP REFERENCE Page 292

Guernsey

Guernsey, the second largest of the Channel Islands, lies in the English Channel, 50 km (30 miles) to the west of France. Though it is a British dependency, it is effectively self-governing, and administers all the other Channel Islands bar Jersey. Picturesque scenery, a gentle climate, and the relaxed lifestyle of its inhabitants make tourism an economic mainstay. Market gardening is also important and the island is famed for its distinctive cattle. Immigration is strictly controlled.

Fact File

OFFICIAL NAME Bailiwick of Guernsey

FORM OF GOVERNMENT British crown dependency

CAPITAL St Peter Port

AREA 63 sq km (24 sq miles)

TIME ZONE GMT

POPULATION 65,386

LIFE EXPECTANCY 78.7

INFANT MORTALITY (PER 1,000) 8.4

LITERACY RATE Not available

CURRENCY Guernsey pound

ECONOMY Financial services, tourism, manufacturing, horticulture

CLIMATE Temperate; mild winters and cool summers

MAP REFERENCE Page 304

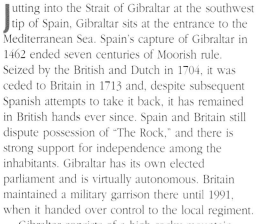

The Isle of Man

The Isle of Man is situated in the Irish Sea between the west coast of England and Northern Ireland, and just south of Galloway in Scotland. At its southern tip is a tiny uninhabited island, the Calf of Man, which is a nature reserve. Two regions of uplands in the center of the main island are divided by a valley extending from Douglas, on the east coast, to Peel, on the west.

The Isle of Man is a dependency of the British crown, but has its own legislature, legal system, and taxation system. Traditionally agriculture and fishing have been the island's main source of income, but it now depends mainly on tourism and financial and business services. Although English is the main language, the local Gaelic language—known as Manx—is still widely spoken and is taught in schools.

Fact File

OFFICIAL NAME Isle of Man

FORM OF GOVERNMENT British crown dependency

CAPITAL Douglas

AREA 588 sq km (227 sq miles)

TIME ZONE GMT

POPULATION 75,686

LIFE EXPECTANCY 77.8

INFANT MORTALITY (PER 1,000) 2.5

LITERACY RATE Not available

CURRENCY Manx pound

ECONOMY Services 72%, industry 22%, transport and communication 6%

CLIMATE Temperate; cool, wet winters and mild summers

MAP REFERENCE Page 306

A seaside town on the Isle of Man (center). A skidoo and sleds on Svalbard (top). St Peter Port, in Guernsey (left).

Jersey

Jersey, the largest and most populous of the Channel Islands, lies in the English Channel, 20 km (12 miles) from the west coast of the Cherbourg Peninsula in northern France. Said to be the sunniest part of the British Isles, it is noted for its superb beaches. These account for the booming tourist industry, which, along with financial services, has in recent years supplanted agriculture as the mainstay of the economy.

Jersey is a dependency of the British crown, but it has its own legislature and a tax regime that is entirely independent and whose low rates attract many foreign businesses. Jersey cattle are among the most important exports and flower cultivation is also a significant income earner.

Fact File

OFFICIAL NAME Bailiwick of Jersey

FORM OF GOVERNMENT British crown dependency

CAPITAL St Helier

AREA 117 sq km (45 sq miles)

TIME ZONE GMT

POPULATION 89,721

LIFE EXPECTANCY 78.8

INFANT MORTALITY (PER 1,000) 2.8

LITERACY RATE Not available

CURRENCY Jersey pound

ECONOMY Financial services, agriculture, tourism

CLIMATE Temperate; mild winters and cool summers

MAP REFERENCE Page 290

The Channel Islands

The Channel Islands lie in the English Channel between 15 and 50 km (10 and 30 miles) off the coast of Normandy in northern France. As well as the two largest islands of Jersey and Guernsey, there are the smaller islands of Sark and Alderney and a number of even smaller islands. In all, the Channel Islands cover an area of only 200 sq km (80 sq miles).

Since the Norman invasion of England in 1066, these islands have been dependencies of the British crown and are the only part of the Duchy of Normandy to have been retained by Britain after 1204. During the Second World War they were the only region of Britain to be occupied by German troops.

Both Jersey and Guernsey have separate legislatures and their own taxation systems, independent of Britain. While English is the most widely spoken language, French is also common and it is the official language of the Jersey legislature. The majority of the place names on Jersey are French.

Svalbard

Situated in the Arctic Ocean about 650 km (400 miles) north of Norway, Svalbard consists of nine bleak, rocky, and icy islands. From Viking times until the sixteenth century, these islands remained unknown. Recently they have served as a base for Arctic explorers. Svalbard's coal reserves have been mined by a number of nations, under Norway's supervision. Now, only Norway and Russia mine the much depleted deposits.

Vegetation on the islands is restricted to mosses, lichens, and a few hardy, low-growing plants.There is an expanding tourist industry. Visitors are attracted mainly by the many migratory birds that come to the islands.

Fact File

OFFICIAL NAME Svalbard

FORM OF GOVERNMENT Territory of Norway

CAPITAL Longyearbyen

AREA 62,049 sq km (23,957 sq miles)

TIME ZONE GMT + 1 hour

POPULATION 2,864 (1996)

LIFE EXPECTANCY Not available

INFANT MORTALITY (PER 1,000) Not available

LITERACY RATE Not available

CURRENCY Norwegian krone

ECONOMY Mainly coal mining, some tourism

CLIMATE Polar, moderated by Gulf Stream ocean current; cold winters and cool summers

MAP REFERENCE Page 300

Especially during the summer, both English and French tourists flock to these islands, and tourism, along with financial services, is now the mainstay of the islands' economies. Tourism on Jersey employs a large number of Portuguese nationals. The residents of the Channel Islands enjoy a high standard of living, maintained in part by strictly enforced residential controls.

Europe and the Russian Federation: Physical

Nordkapp

NORWEGIAN SEA

Arctic Circle

Iceland
Hekla
1491 m ▲
Hvannadalshnúkur
2119 m

Vesterålen
Lofoten
Haltí
1328 m ▲
Kebnekaise ▲
2111 m

Scandinavia

Faeroe
Islands

Shetland
Islands

Rockall

Galdhøpiggen
▲
2469 m

Cape
Wrath

Hebrides

Orkney
Islands

Gulf of Bothnia

Gulf of Finland

ATLANTIC
OCEAN

British
Isles

Ben Nevis
1343 m ▲ Grampian
Mountains

NORTH SEA

Gotland

Gulf of
Riga

Gaizinkalns
311 m ▲

Skagerrak

Öland

BALTIC SEA

Lough
Neagh

IRISH
SEA

Pennines

Jylland

Carrauntoohil
1041 m ▲

Snowdon
1085 m ▲

Mizen
Head

St George's
Channel

Shannon

Severn

Trent

Bornholm

North Eur

CELTIC SEA

Thames

Ostfriesische Inseln

North

Land's End

English Channel

Strait of Dover

Harz

Channel
Islands

Botrange 694 m ▲

Ardennes

Erzgebirge

Sudety

Seine

Marne

Mosel

Taunus

Praděd
1492 m

CARPATHIA

Bay
of
Biscay

Loire

Vosges

Jura

Schwarzwald

Danau

Gerlachovský štit
2655 m

Hora
Hoverla
2061 m

Cabo
Fisterra

Cher

Lac Léman

Bodensee

Inn

Zugspitze
2962 m
▲

Donau

Balaton

Cordillera Cantábrica

Dordogne

Massif
Central

Matterhorn
4478 m ▲
Monte
Rosa
4634 m ▲

A L P S

Großglockner
3797 m
▲

Dolomiti

Triglav
2863 m
▲

Plain of
Hungary

Moldoveanu
2544 m ▲

Duero

Mont Blanc
4807 m ▲

A P

Drava

Sava

CARPAȚII MER

Iberian

Gaonne

PYRENEES

Cévennes

Rhône

LIGURIAN
SEA

Dinara

2522 m ▲

Stara P

Peninsula

Pico de
Aneto
3404 m ▲

Golfe
du Lion

A P P E N N I N O

ADRIATIC SEA

Musala
2925 m ▲

Rodo

Cabo de
São Vicente

Sierra Morena

Júcar

Golfo de
Valencia

Islas Baleares

Menorca

Corse

Strait of Bonifacio

Korab
2764 m ▲

Guadalquivir

Eivissa

Mallorca

Sardegna

TYRRHENIAN
SEA

Golfo di
Taranto

Oros Olympos
2917 m ▲

Pindos

Golfo
de Cádiz

Sierra Nevada
▲ Mulhacén
3481 m

Strait of Gibraltar

M E D I T E R

Strait of Sicily

Monte Etna
3323 m ▲
Sicilia

IONIAN SEA

Ioniol Nisoi

Peloponnisos

ATLAS MOUNTAINS

Jebel
Toubkal
4165 m ▲

Jabal ash Sha'nabi
1544 m ▲

Cap
Bon

Malta

R A N E A N   S E A

Shatt al Jarid

H   J   K   L   M   N

40°   50° 70°   60°   70° 65°   80°   60°

BARENTS SEA

Ostrov
Kolguyev

Cheshskaya Guba

*Z a p a d n o
S i b i r s k a y a
R a v n i n a*

Verkhnetulomskoye
Vodokhranilishche

Kol'skiy
Poluostrov

*BELOYE
MORE*

Ozero
Kovdozero

Timanskiy Kryazh

Ozero
Topozero

Pechora

Pilinen

Ozero
Chany

Onezhskoye
Ozero

Rybinskoye
Vodokhranilishche

*Kamskoye
Vodokhranilishche*

5

50°
80°

Ozero
Il'men'

Chudskoye
Ozero

*Gor'kovskoye
Vodokhranilishche*

Kama

U R A L' S K I Y   K H R E B E T   (U R A L   M O U N T A I N S)

Severnaya Dvina

6

Pskovskoye
Ozero

Suur Munamägi
▲ 318 m

Volga

Kuybyshevskoye
Vodokhranilishche

Vyatka

Ural

Balqash
Köli

45°
70°

Hora Dzyarzhynskaya
▲ 346 m

Sredne-Russkaya Vozvyshennost'

*Privolzhskaya
Vozvyshennost'*

Oka

Volga

Sura

Zhayyq

Mughalzhar Tauy

Syrdar'ya

Esil

*Tengiz
Köli*

7

Prypyats'

Daugava

Volgogradskoye
Vodokhranilishche

Caspian Depression

*ARAL
SEA*

Peski Kyzylkum

40°

Dnister

Tsimlyanskoye
Vodokhranilishche

Amu Darya

Kakhovs'ke
Vodoskhovyshche

Don

Ozero
Manych-Gudilo

Plato Ustyurt

8

MOUNTAINS

SEA OF
AZOV

Kuban'

CASPIAN
SEA

Zaunguzskiye Garagum

Dnieper

Kryms'kyy Pivostriv
(Crimean Pen.)

Gora El'brus
5642 m ▲ BOL'SHOY KAVKAZ

35°

▲ Gora Kazbek
5047 m

▲ Bazardüzü Dag
4466 m

na

BLACK SEA

▲ Aragats Lerr
4090 m

9

Planina

MÁRMARA
DENIZI

Agri Daği
(Mt Ararat)
5137 m ▲

*Van
Gölü*

*Daryācheh-ye
Orūmīyeh*

Reshteh-ye Kūhhā-ye Alborz
(Elburz Mountains)

Dasht-e Kavir

30°

*Qolleh-ye
Damāvand
5671 m* ▲

Dasht-e Lūt

SEA

Kizilirmak

A n a t o l i a

*Tuz
Gölü*

*Iranian
Plateau*

Kyklades

Dodekanisos

Rodos

Toros Dağları
(Taurus Mountains)

Antalya
Körfezi

*Kūhhā-ye Zāgros
(Zagros Mountains)*

Euphrates

Tigris

10

Kriti

Cyprus

Olympos ▲
1951 m

▲ Qurnat as Sawdā'
3088 m

▲ Jabal ash Shaykh
2814 m

*Bādiyat ash Shām
(Syrian Desert)*

Persian Gulf

Strait of Hormuz

G   H   J   K

30°   40°   30°   50°

0 150 300 450 600 750 kilometers
0 150 300 450 miles

Scale 1:15,000,000   Projection: Conic Equidistant

Europe and the Russian Federation: Political

H 40° J 50° 70° K 60° L 70° 65° M 80° 60° N

Arctic Circle

Kirkenes

Nar'yan Mar Inta

Murmansk Pechora Igrim Kolpashevo Anzhero-Sudzhensk

Nizhnevartovsk Tomsk Kemerovo

Monchegorsk Nyagan' Surgut Leninsk-Kuznetskiy

Apatity Novosibirsk

Kandalaksha Mezen' Barnaul Biysk

Ukhta **RUSSIAN FEDERATION** Tatarsk

Severodvinsk Arkhangel'sk Nazyvayevsk Omsk Rubtsovsk

Kem' Ishim

Syktyvkar Serov Tyumen'

Medvezh'yegorsk Kotlas Solikamsk Berezniki Nizhniy Tagil

Petrozavodsk Yekaterinburg Kurgan

Perm' Kamensk-Ural'skiy

Vyatka Pervoural'sk

Votkinsk Chelyabinsk

Sankt-Peterburg Vologda Izhevsk Zlatoust

Kolpino Cherepovets Sarapul

Narva Naberezhnyye

Novgorod Rybinsk Kostroma Cheboksary Chelny Ufa Magnitogorsk

Yaroslavl' Kazan'

Pskov Ivanovo Nizhniy Al'met'yevsk Sterlitamak

Rēzekne Tver' Novgorod Salavat

Velikiye Luki Sergiyev Posad Murom Arzamas Dimitrovgrad Orsk

Moskva Kolomna Ul'yanovsk Samara Orenburg

Vitsyebsk Obninsk Ryazan' Saransk Tol'yatti Novokuybyshevsk

Smolensk Kaluga Penza Syzran' Sol'-Iletsk

Mahilyow Tula Novomoskovsk

Minsk Bryansk Tambov Balakovo

BELARUS Orel Lipetsk Saratov Engel's

Baranavichy Kursk

Homyel' **KAZAKHSTAN**

Mazyr Chernihiv Belgorod Volzhskiy

Zhytomyr Sumy Volograd

Kyyiv Kharkiv **UZBEKISTAN**

Rivne Poltava Luhans'k Astrakhan'

UKRAINE Kremenchuk

Vinnytsya Dniprodzerzhyns'k Donets'k Makiyivka

Chernivtsi Kirovohrad Taganrog Rostov-na-Donu

Kryvyy Rih Zaporizhzhya Mariupol'

Bălți Mykolayiv Melitopol' **TURKMENISTAN**

MOLDOVA Kherson Armavir Stavropol'

Iași Chișinău Krasnodar Cherkessk Groznyy Makhachkala

ANIA Simferopol' Novorossiysk Maykop Nal'chik Vladikavkaz *CASPIAN SEA*

Galați Sevastopol' Sochi

Brașov Brăila **GEORGIA**

București Constanța *BLACK SEA* **AZERBAIJAN**

Ruse Varna **ARMENIA** **AFGHANISTAN**

GARIA Burgas

Stara Zagora

Komotini **IRAN**

TURKEY

Rodos

Irakleio **SYRIA** **IRAQ**

Kriti **CYPRUS**

LEBANON **OMAN**

ISRAEL JORDAN SAUDI ARABIA KUWAIT U.A.E.

0 150 300 450 600 750 kilometers
0 150 300 450 miles
Scale 1:15,000,000 Projection: Conic Equidistant

Europe and the Russian Federation

North Scandinavia • Iceland

GREENLAND SEA

Arctic Circle

Straumnes
Hornbjarg
Rifstangi
Fontur

Suðureyri
Unaðsdalur
Hraun
Siglufjörður
Raufarhöfn
Kópasker
Bakkaflói

Ísafjörður
Mánaðarnes
Ólafsfjörður
Hofsós
Grenivik
Húsavík
Bakkafjörður

Bíldudalur
Vatneyri
Glama 920 m
Hólmavík
Dalvík
Kollumúli

Bjargtangar
Reykhólar
Hvammstangi
Blönduós
Akureyri
Grímsstaðir
Borgarfjörður
Karlfell 1052 m
Seyðisfjörður

Stykkishólmur
Búðardalur
Bergsstaðir
Myri
Herðubreið 1682 m
Egilsstaðir
Fáskrúðsfjörður
Breiðdalsvík

Hellissandur
Búðir
ICELAND
Hofsjökull
Djúpivogur

Borgarnes
Bárðarbunga 2000 m
1248 m
Stokksnes

Faxaflói
Akranes
Sviánúkar 1719 m
Vatnajökull

Reykjavík
Sandgerði
Laki 818 m
Hvannadalshnúkur 2119 m
Höfn
Kálfafellsstaður

Hafnarfjörður
Hekla 1491 m

Hafnir
Hella
Myrdalsjökull

Grindavík
Þorlákshöfn
Hvolsvöllur

Skógar 1450 m
Langholt
Fagurhólsmýri

Dyrhólaey Vík

ATLANTIC OCEAN

TROMS

Vannareid
Nordkvaløy
Årviksand
Seglvik

Rebbenesøy
Vanna
Arnøy

Ringvassøy
Mikkelvik
Skjervøy
Kågen

Tromvik
Skulgam
Oldervik
1337

Hillesøy
Kvaløy
Tromsø
Svensby
Lyngseidet

Bergø
Vikran
Jiekkevarre 1833 m
Skibotn

Andenes
Senja
Gibostad
Finnsnes

Bleik
Gryllefjord
Moen
Nordkjosbotn
Halti 1328 m

Nordmela
Risøyhamn
Sørreisa
Andselv
Øverbygd
Kåhpovuasaa 1144 m

Andøya
Myre
Grytøya
Harstad
Brøstadbotn
Setermoen

Langøya
Sortland
Sjøvegan
Ibestad
Innset 1633 m
Kummavuopio

Hadseløya
Møysalen 1266 m
Dyrøya
Grov
Tennevoll
Fossbakken
Abisko

Melbu
Austvågøy
Lødingen
Kjeldebotn
Narvik
Riksgränsen
Torneträsk

Fiskebøl
Svolvær
Digermulen
Skårberget 1901 m
Storsteinfjellet
Rensjön
Kebnekaise 2111 m
Nikkaluokta

Vestvågøy
Leknes
Kabelvåg
Tranøy
Ballangen
Bjørntoppen 1520 m
Kiruna

Flakstad
Ballstad
Skutvik
Kjøpsvik
Vietas
Esrange

Moskenesøya
Sørvågen
Ålstad
Leiranger
Nordfold
Mørsvik
Tårnvik

Røsvik
Festvåg
Fauske
Riepentjåkka 1551 m
Holmajärvi
Kaitum
Killingi
Skåppavaara

Bodø
Beiarn
Rognan
Sulitjelma
Pårtefjällen 2005 m
Vittja

Inndyr
1404 m
Ruokto
Malmberget
Gällivare
Nilivaara

Ørnes
Glomfjord
Leiråmoen 1754 m
Storjord
Porjus
Leipojärvi
Ulla

Vågaholmen
Ólfjellet
Kvikkjokk
Harsprånget
Hakkas

NORDLAND
Jektvik
Melfjorden
Fierraş 1607 m
Tjåmotis
NORRBOTTEN
Nattavaara

Kilboghamn
Stødi
Randijaure
Kuouka

Tomma
Høgtuvbreen 1291 m
Storforshei
Stenudden
Jokkmokk
Murjek

Nesna
Mo i Rana
Jäckvik
Norra Bergnäs
Tårrajaur
Vuollerim
Vuottas

Dønna
Bjørn
Elsfjord
Laisvall
Sudok
Lakatrå

Alsten
Sandnessjøen
Korgen
Lövnäs
Kåbdalis
Puottaure

Vega
Tjøtta 1158 m
Mosjøen
Norra Storfjället 1765 m
Ammarnäs
Arjeplog
Båtsjaur
Harads
Svartlå

Gladstad
Forvik
Vindelälven
Östansjö
Moskosel
Bredsel
Vidsel

Horn
Anndalsvågen
Västansjö
Marielund
Auktsjaur
Bode

Sømna
Hommelstø
Hattfjelldal
Skansnäs
Avaviken
Arvidsjaur
Lauker
Älvsbyn

Vik
Trofors
Ajaureforsen
Giltjaur
Sorsele
Abborrträsk
Antnä

Leka
Tosbotn
NORWAY
Gränssjö
Slussfors
Kopparnä

Solsem
Terråk
Kroken
Dikanäs
Storuman
Gunnarn
Björkselè
Stavaträsk
Boliden
Piteå

Valøya
Vikna
Rørvik
Klimpfjäll
Långvattnet
Skarvsjö
Norsjö
Kåge

Kongsmoen
1703 m
Stora Blåsjön
Saxnäs
Kristineberg
Jörn
Skelleftè

Otterøy
Høylandet
Namsskogan
1314 m
Risbäck
Vojmån
Pauträsk
Rusele
Bureå

Sør-Flatanger
Namsos
Skorovatn
Björkvattnet
Malå
Lycksele
Åmsele
Burträsk

Osen
Sjøåsen
Grong
Nordli
Gäddede
Sjoutnäset
Norråker
Latikberg
Kalvträsk
Åträsk

Finnvollheia 676 m
Sprova
Snåsa
Hartkjølen 1390 m
Berglia
Fågelberget
Dorotea
Vilhelmina
Kroksjö
Vågsele
Vännäsby
Robertsfors

TRØNDELAG
Malm
Jule
Munsfjället 1187 m
Gärdnäs
Tåsjö
Meselefors
Lillögda
Granön
Botsmark

Lysøysund
Afjord
Steinkjer 1137 m
Valsjöbyn
Tavelsjö
Bygdeå

Frøya
Titran
Brekstad
Verdalsøra
Sösjöfjällen 1247 m
Havsnäs
Åsele
Örträsk
Vindeln
Lövånger

Kvenvær
Hitra
Forsnes
Leksvik
Levanger
Sandvika
Kolåsen
Jänsmässholmen
Röting
Gavsele
Fredrika
Vännäs
Umeå

Dyrnes
Smøla
Aure
Selbekken
Vannvikan
Rönnöfors
Föllinge
Hemling
Nyåker
Holmön

Tømmervåg
Ertvågøy
Kyrksæterøra
Stjørdalshalsen
Flornes
Landön
Hammerdal
Junsele
Näsåker
Björna
Obbola

Kristiansund
Heimdal
Kall
Gorvik
Myckelgensjö
Ångesön

Gossen
Bud
Eide
Nordmøre
Orkanger
Selbu
Kopperå
Åre
Mattmar
Krokom
Lit
Aspeå
Bredbyn
Nordmaling

Midsund
Molde
Skei
Rindal
Meldal
Støren
Kvikne
Stordal
1463 m
Undersåker
Östersund
Skyttmon
Näsåker
Bollstabruk
Husum

Brattvåg
Todal
Reinsfjell 937 m
Östersund
Hammarstrand
Solberg

MØRE OG ROMSDAL
Eidsvåg
1667 m
Rennebu
Berkåk
Ålen
Høglekardalen 1371 m
Myrviken
Brunflo
Stugun
Graninge
Örnsköldsvik

Sykkylven
Stranda
Tresfjord
Marstein
Ulsberg
Innset
Forelshogna 1332 m
Ljungdalen
Persåsen
Hackås
Gällö
Sollefteå
Boteå
Bjästa
Raippaluoto (Vallgrund)
Björkö

Stølen 1578 m
Eidsdal
Pyttegga 1992 m
Oppdal
Tynset
Os
Røros
Sörvika
Funäsdalen
Börtnan
Bräcke
Sörbygden
VÄSTERNORRLAND
Södra Vallgrund

Hellesylt
Geiranger
Snøhetta 2286 m
Kvikne
Glåmos
Tolga
Sörvika
Tännäs
Långå
Svenstavik
Ånge
Ramvik
Ullånger
Vaasa

OPPLAND
Lesjaskog
Dombås
HEDMARK
Folldal
Tynset
Narbuvollen
Hede
Ratan
Överturingen
Fränsta
Liden
Indal
Ljustorp
Härnösand
Maalahti
Petolahti
Korsnäs
Pirttikylä

Otta
Folldal

© Random House Australia Pty Ltd

L 24° M 26° N 28° P 30° Q 32° R 34° S 36° T 38° U 40°

BARENTS SEA

1

70°

Nordkapp
Ingøya · Magerøya · Honningsvåg · Mehamn · Nordkinnhalvøya · Gamvik
Rolvsøya · Havøysund · Kjøllefjord · Berlevåg
Sørøya · Langstrand · Kåfjord · Hopseidet · Skjånes · Bátskapp
Hammerfest · Kvaløya · Repvåg · 578 m · Veidnes · Kalak · 668 m · Båtsfjord · Stangenestind 724 m · Skipskjølen 637 m · Vardø
Seiland 1075 m · Kvalsund · Olderfjord · Ifjord · Rustefjelbma
Saraby · Indre Billefjord · Børselv · Storfjordbotn · Tana · Varangerbotn · Varangerhalvøya
Øksfjord · Nyvoll · Lakselv · Vetsikko · Grasbakken · Nesseby · Vadsø
Alta · 1139 m · Lævvajok · Utsjoki · Jomppala · Bugøyfjord · Bugøynes · Grense Jakobselv · Pummanki
FINNMARK · Skoganvarre · Nuvvus · Outakoski · Neiden · Bjørnevatn · Linakhamari
Rastegai'sa 1067 m · Valjok · 443 m · Svanvik · Nikel' · Pechenga · **Poluostrov Rybachiy**
Masi · Karasjok · Karigasniemi · Nyrud · 637 m · Zapolyarnyy · Port-Vladimir · 299 m
Bidjovagge · Suosjavri · Kaamanen · Gora Kuorpukas · Polyarnyy
Lappoluobbal · Mieron · Inari · Nautsi · Prirechnyy · Gora Kuchin-Tundra 578 m · Severomorsk

2

68°

Aiddejavrre · 632 m · Noarvaš 531 m · Virtaniemi · Talvikyulya · **Murmansk** · Kola · Kil'dinstroy · Rynda · Kharlovka · Vostochnaya Litsa
Palojärvi · Menesjärvi · Ivalo · Raja-Jooseppi · Murmashi · Magnetity · Verkhnetulomskiy
Kaaresuvanto · Enontekiö · Peltovuoma · Viipustunturit 599 m · Lotta · Gora Ionn-N'yugoayv 714 m · Gora Chiltal'd 907 m · Pulozero · Taybola · Varzino · Mys Svyatoy Nos
Palojoensuu · Kuttura · Gora Elgoras 997 m · Olenegorsk · Lovozero · Gora Balkon-Myl'k 340 m · Gremikha
LAPLAND · Saariselkä Sokosti 718 m · Vuotso · Monchegorsk · **MURMANSKAYA** · 375 m
Pallastunturi 807 m · Muonio · Tepasto · Pomovaara 424 m · Lokka · Gora Ebruchorr 1115 m · **OBLAST'** · Kirovsk
Muodoslompolo · Sirkka · Tepsa · Tanhua · Sorsatunturi 629 m · Tulppio · Girvas · Yena · Upoloksha · Apatity · Zasheyek · Krasnoshchel'ye · Kanevka

3

Lainio · Kitkiöjoki · Kittilä · Ylläsjärvi · Petkula · Tuntsa · Kovdor · Polyarnyye Zori · Zasheyek
Kärendöjärvi · Kihlanki · Kaukonen · Sodankylä · Martti · Afrikanda · Kapustnoye · **RUSSIAN**
Kolari · Kurtakko · Vaalajärvi · Aska · Savukoski · Saija · Kandalaksha · Kolvitsa · Arctic Circle
Anttis · Areavaara · Lohiniva · Unari · Pelkosenniemi · Ahvenselkä · Kuolayarvi · Beloye More · Pustaya Guba
Pajala · Sieppijärvi · Meltaus · Gora Rokhmoyva 657 m · Salla · Alakurtti · Zelenoborskiy · Por'ya · Umba
Kainulasjärvi · Aapua · Pello · Konttajärvi · Pyhätunturi 540 m · Kursu · Vuoriyarvi · Zarechensk · Kovda · Kashkarantsy
Jock · Rantajärvi · Kemijärvi · Joutsijärvi · Khetolambina · Keret' · Olenitsa · Varzuga
Övertorneå · Raanujärvi · Vikajärvi · Hautajärvi · Chupa · Sonostrov · Chavan'ga · Tetrino

66°

Ylitornio · Meltosjärvi · Misi · Maaninkavaara · Käylä · Zasheyek · Loukhi · **BELOYE MORE**
Hedenäset · Mellakoski · **FINLAND** · Pirttikoski · Juuma · Gora Nuorunen 577 m · Ozero Tiksheozero · Gridino · **(WHITE SEA)**
Korpikå · Karungi · Arpela · Tervola · Portimo · Pera-Posio · Posio · Ruka · Zasheyek · Sosnovyy · Ambarnyy · Engozero · 300
Morjärv · Övkalix · Koivu · **Rovaniemi** · Ruokojärvi · Kesten'ga · Nil'maguba · Sig · Ostrov Oleniy · Letniy Navolok
Töre · Sangis · Puukkokumpu · Muurola · Mäntyjärvi · Kuusamo · Kärpänkylä · Sofporog · Tungozero · Unduksa · Lopshen'ga
Kalix · Haparanda · Tornio · Keminmaa · Ranua · Kuha · Kuloharju · Kuolio · Tukhkala · Karelaksha · Kuzema · Solovetskiye Ostrova · Letnyaya Zolotitsa

4

64°

Råneå · Seskarö · Kemi · Simo · Yli-Karppä · Oijärvi · Asmunti · Sarajärvi · Rytinki · Tyrävaara · Murtovaara · Voynitsa · Kalevala · Kepa · Yuma · Kreml' · Rabocheostrovsk · **Onezhskiy**
Luleå · Bottenviken · Kuivaniemi · Tannila · Yli-Ii · Livo · Pintamo · Taivalkoski · Hossa · Peranka · Ozero Pyaozero · Shombozero · Kem' · Pushlakhta · Ostrov Myagostrov
Perämeri · Haukipudas · Pudasjärvi · Kipina · Metsäkylä · Juntusranta · Shuyeretskoye · **Poluostrov**
Hailuoto · Pohjois-Ii · Siivikko · Puhos · Näljänkä · Joukokylä · Ozero Verkhneye Kuyto · Belomorsk · Lyamtsa · Una · Nizhmozero
Oulu · Kiiminki · Ketekylä · 384 m · Suomussalmi · Ala-Vuokki · Vokhavolok · Yushkozero · Borovoy · Pushnoy · Virma · Kyanda
Kempele · Ylikiiminki · Juorkuna · Puolanka · Hyrynsalmi · Kuivajärvi · 277 m · Kostomuksha · Sumskiy Posad · Kolezhma · Tamitsa
Keskikylä · Muhos · Sanginkylä · Kotila · Luvozero · Kentozero · **RESPUBLIKA** · Kochkoma · Nadvoitsy · Kusha · Nimen'ga
Raahe · Saloinen · Liminka · Ruukki · **OULUN LÄÄNI** · Kivesjärvi · Moisiovaara · Kimasozero · Ledmozero · Tiksha · Vacha · Virandozero · Vorzogory · Unezhma
Pyhäjoki · Vihanti · Paavola · Rantsila · Säräisniemi · Ristijärvi · Kontiomäki · Rovkuly · Yemel'yanovka · Muyezerskiy · Rugozero · Idel' · Segezha · Polga · **ARKHANGEL'SKAYA**

5

62°

Kalajoki · Merijärvi · Oulainen · Pulkkila · Pippola · Pyhäntä · Hietaperä · Kiekinkoski · Ozero Ondozero · Kryazh Vetrenyy Poyas
Himanka · Alavieska · Ylivieska · Kärsämäki · Nissilä · Sukeva · Kajaani · Kuhmo · Rebolv · Ozero Leksozero · Voloma · Peningat · Popov Porog · Urosozero · Vorozhgora · **OBLAST'**
Kokkola · Kalvia · Rannus · Nivala · Haapajärvi · Pyhäjärvi · Vieremä · Maanselkä · Petäjäkylä · Kimovaara · 398 m · Padany · Segezha · Valday · Ozero Monastyrskoye
Toholampi · Ullava · Reisjärvi · Vuohtomäki · Sonkajärvi · Iisalmi · Valtimo · Hattuselkönen · Nurmes · Tulos 290 m · Sukkozero · Sel'ga · Medvezh'yegorsk · Pindushi · Ogorelyshi · Sergiyevo
Kaustinen · Veteli · Halsua · Kinnula · Pihtipudas · Pielavesi · Lapinlahti · Juuka · Naarva · Sovdozero · Porosozero · Gimoly · 417 m · Yustozero · Povenets · Lobskoye
Kronoby · Kronoby · Perho · Muurasjärvi · Kiuruvesi · Juminen · Koirakoski · Savikylä · Pankakoski · Kitsi · Lendery · Gumarino · Shun'ga · Chelmuzhi
Ytterösse · Evijärvi · Karstula · Saarijärvi · Istunmäki · Keitele · Sääyneinen · Ahmovaara · Koli · Jaakonvaara · Ruolismaa · Lindozero · Girvas · Pyal'ma · Unitsa
Jepua · Alahärmä · Soini · Konginkangas · Vintturi · Tervo · Luikonlahti · Uimaharju · Kontiolahti · Eno · Ilomantsi · Tolvajarvi · Sopokha · Velikaya Guba
Nykarleby · Kauhava · Lapua · Ähtäri · Töysä · Pylkönmäki · Hytola · Talluskylä · Toivala · Kuopio · Tuusniemi · Outokumpu · Liperi · Pyhäselkä · Karvio · Spasskaya Guba · Kondopoga
Seinäjoki · Kurikka · Alavus · Saarijärvi · Vesanto · Suonenjoki · Leppävirta · Joensuu · Kovero · **KARELIYA** · Kurgenitsy

ITÄ-SUOMEN LÄÄNI

LÄNSI-SUOMEN LÄÄNI

Gulf of Bothnia · Pohjanlahti

L 24° M 26° N 287 28° P 30° Q 32° R 34° 299 S 36° T

0 ___ 100 ___ 200 kilometers
0 ___ 50 ___ 100 miles
Scale 1:3,500,000 · Projection: Equidistant Conic

South Scandinavia • Baltic States

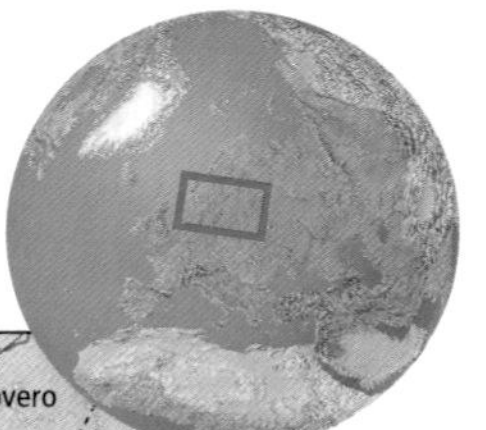

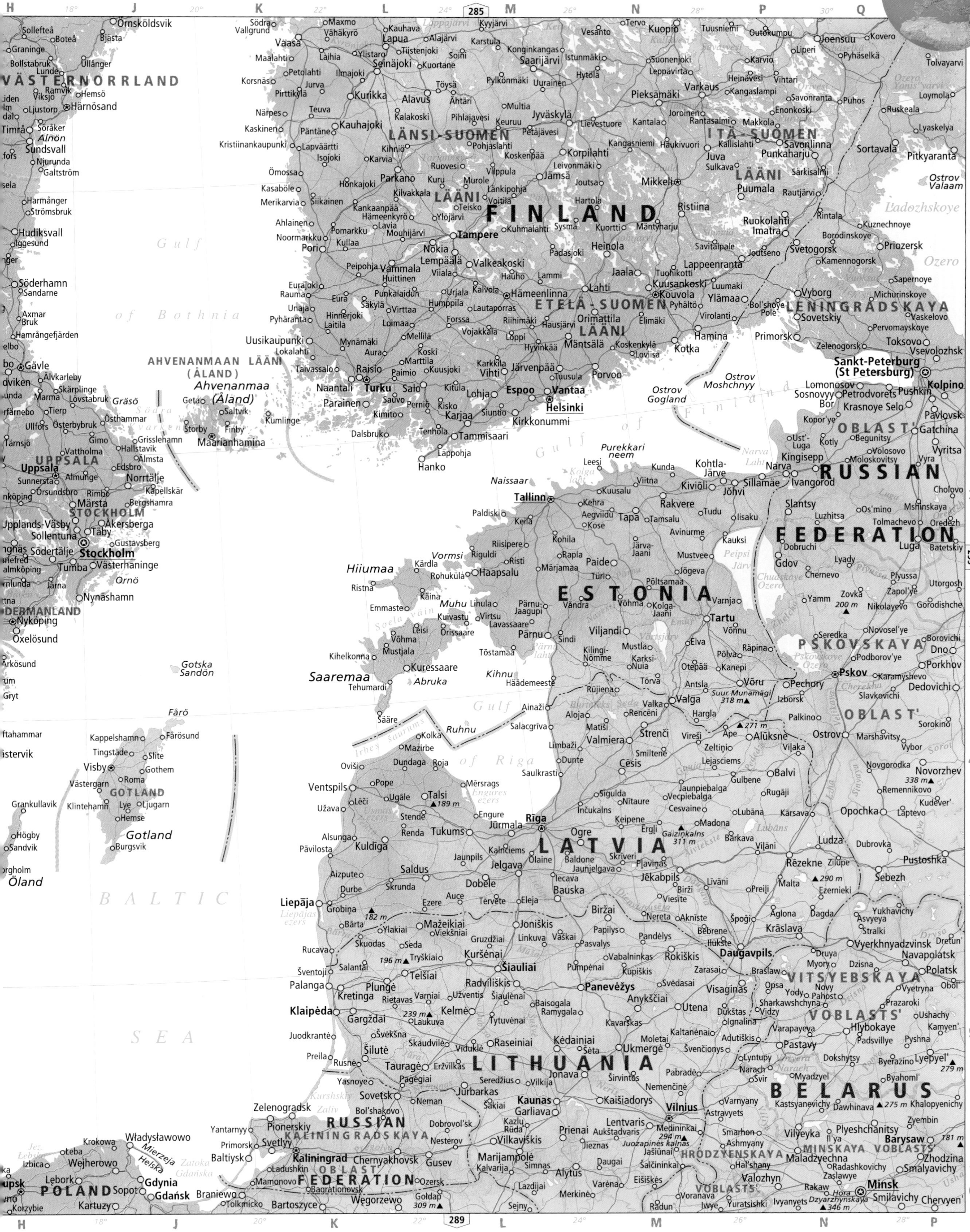

VÄSTERNORRLAND

FINLAND

LÄNSI-SUOMEN

LÄÄNI

ITÄ-SUOMEN

LÄÄNI

ETELÄ-SUOMEN

LÄÄNI

Gulf of Bothnia

AHVENANMAAN LÄÄNI
(ÅLAND)
Ahvenanmaa
(*Åland*)

UPPSALA

STOCKHOLM

Stockholm ⊙

SÖDERMANLAND

Tampere

Turku

Helsinki

Espoo Vantaa

Sankt-Peterburg
(St Petersburg) ⊙

RUSSIAN

FEDERATION

LENINGRADSKAYA

OBLAST'

Gulf of Finland

Tallinn ⊙

Hiiumaa

ESTONIA

Tartu

Pärnu

Saaremaa

Kuressaare

PSKOVSKAYA

OBLAST'

Pskov ⊙

Gulf of Riga

BALTIC

SEA

LATVIA

Riga ⊙
Jūrmala

Ventspils

Liepāja

Daugavpils

Rēzekne

VITSYEBSKAYA

VOBLASTS'

GOTLAND

Gotland

Visby ⊙

Öland

LITHUANIA

Šiauliai

Panevėžys

Kaunas

Vilnius ⊙

Klaipėda

BELARUS

Minsk ⊙

MINSKAYA VOBLASTS'

HRODZYENSKAYA

VOBLASTS'

RUSSIAN

FEDERATION

KALININGRADSKAYA

OBLAST'

Kaliningrad

POLAND

Gdynia Gdańsk

Scale 1:3,500,000
Projection: Equidistant Conic

0   100   200 kilometers

0   50   100 miles

Europe and the Russian Federation

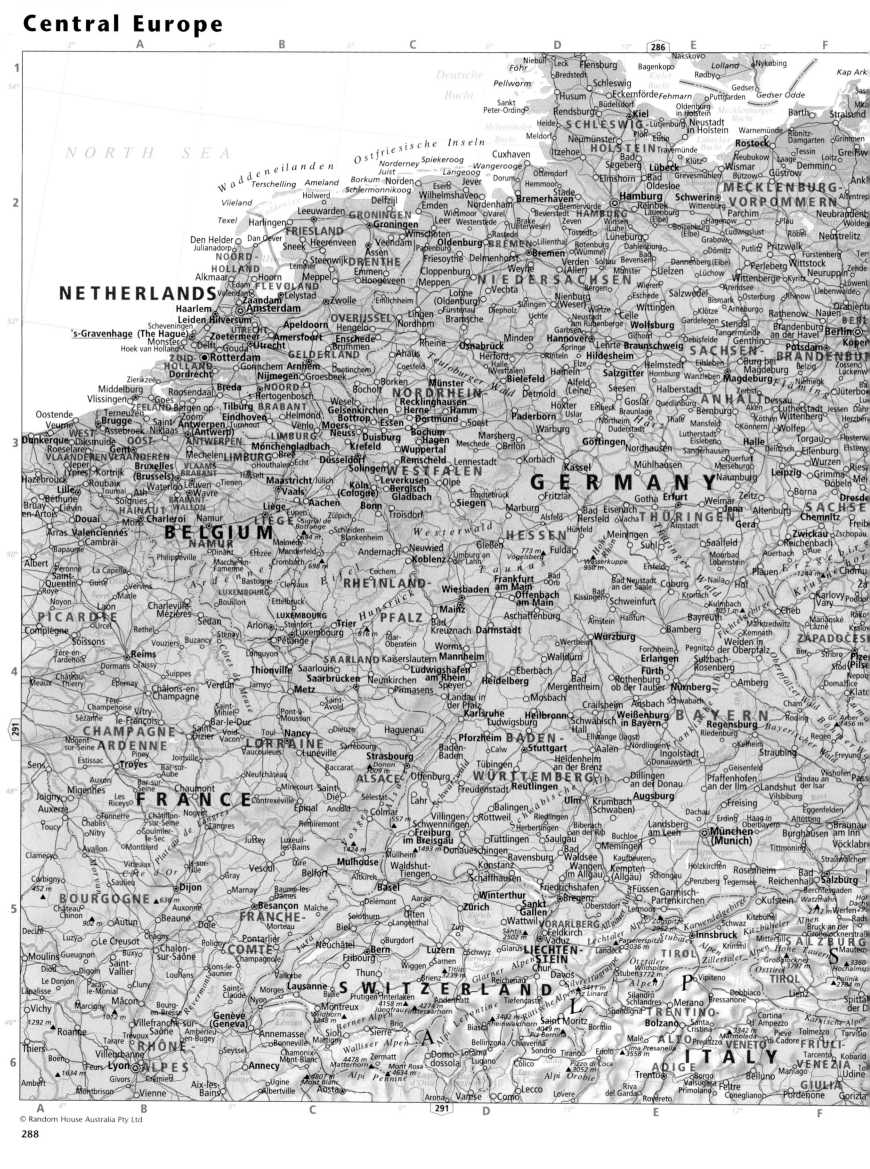

POLAND

Major countries/regions labeled:
BALTIC SEA · RUSSIAN FEDERATION · LITHUANIA · BELARUS · HRODZYENSKAYA VOBLASTS' · BRESTSKAYA VOBLASTS' · UKRAINE · VOLYNS'KA OBLAST' · L'VIVS'KA OBLAST' · IVANO-FRANKIVS'KA OBLAST' · ZAKARPATS'KA OBLAST' · CZECH REPUBLIC · SLOVAKIA · HUNGARY · ROMANIA · AUSTRIA · SLOVENIA · CROATIA

Selected place names:
Kaliningrad, Chernyakhovsk, Gdynia, Gdańsk, Słupsk, Koszalin, Kołobrzeg, Szczecin, Elbląg, Olsztyn, Suwałki, Białystok, Brest, Bydgoszcz, Toruń, Włocławek, Płock, Poznań, Gorzów Wielkopolski, Zielona Góra, Warszawa (Warsaw), Łódź, Kalisz, Wrocław, Legnica, Wałbrzych, Opole, Częstochowa, Radom, Lublin, Kielce, Katowice, Sosnowiec, Gliwice, Bytom, Kraków, Tarnów, Rzeszów, Przemyśl, L'viv, Praha (Prague), Brno, Olomouc, Ostrava, Žilina, Poprad, Prešov, Košice, Uzhhorod, Bratislava, Wien (Vienna), Banská Bystrica, Nitra, Miskolc, Nyíregyháza, Debrecen, Budapest, Győr, Székesfehérvár, Pécs, Szeged, Arad, Oradea, Cluj-Napoca, Satu Mare, Baia Mare, Maribor, Ljubljana, Graz

Scale 1:3,500,000
Projection: Equidistant Conic

0   100   200 kilometers
0   50   100 miles

France • Switzerland

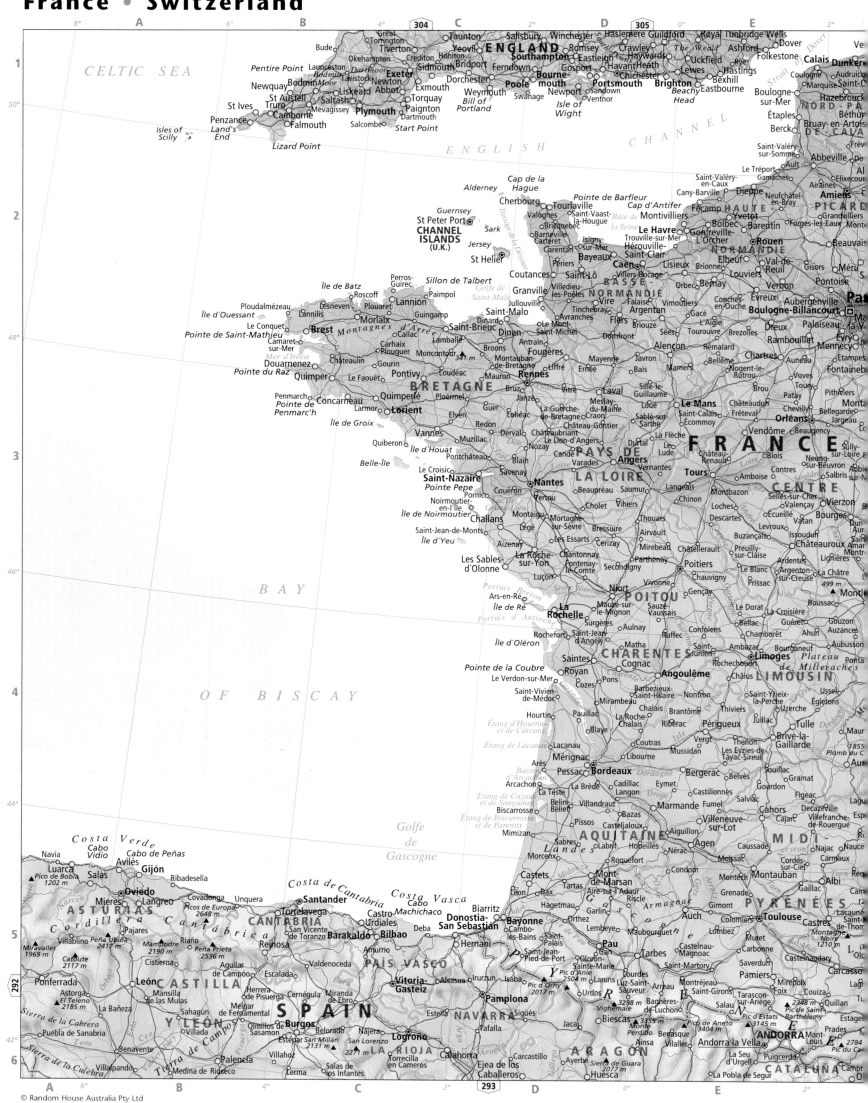

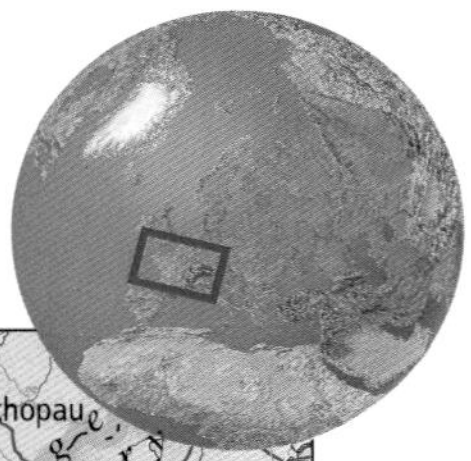

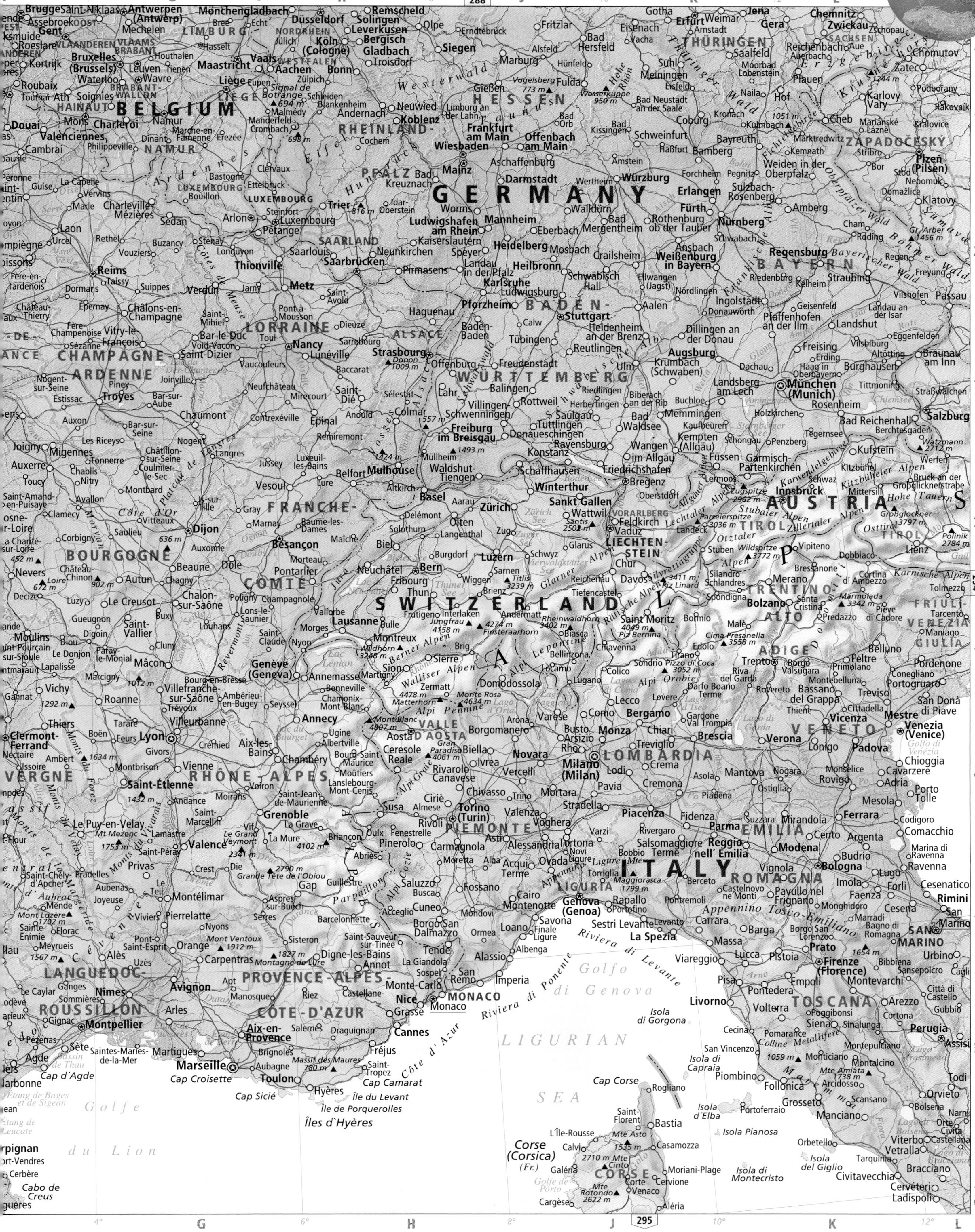

BELGIUM

GERMANY

HESSEN

RHEINLAND-PFALZ

NORDRHEIN-WESTFALEN

LIMBURG

LUXEMBOURG

SAARLAND

THÜRINGEN

SACHSEN

BAYERN

BADEN-WÜRTTEMBERG

LORRAINE

ALSACE

CHAMPAGNE-ARDENNE

BOURGOGNE

FRANCHE-COMTÉ

SWITZERLAND

AUSTRIA

TIROL

VORARLBERG

LIECHTENSTEIN

TRENTINO-ALTO ADIGE

FRIULI-VENEZIA GIULIA

VENETO

LOMBARDIA

PIEMONTE

VALLE D'AOSTA

RHÔNE-ALPES

LIGURIA

EMILIA-ROMAGNA

ITALY

TOSCANA

PROVENCE-ALPES-CÔTE-D'AZUR

LANGUEDOC-ROUSSILLON

MONACO

SAN MARINO

Corse (Corsica) (Fr.)

CORSE

LIGURIAN SEA

Golfo di Genova

Riviera di Ponente

Riviera di Levante

Golfe du Lion

Bruxelles (Brussels), Antwerpen (Antwerp), Mönchengladbach, Düsseldorf, Remscheid, Köln (Cologne), Bonn, Aachen, Koblenz, Frankfurt am Main, Wiesbaden, Mainz, Darmstadt, Mannheim, Heidelberg, Karlsruhe, Stuttgart, Nürnberg, Regensburg, München (Munich), Augsburg, Strasbourg, Nancy, Metz, Reims, Dijon, Bern, Zürich, Basel, Genève (Geneva), Lausanne, Lyon, Grenoble, Torino (Turin), Milano (Milan), Verona, Venezia (Venice), Bologna, Firenze (Florence), Marseille, Nice, Monaco, Cannes, Toulon

Scale 1:3,500,000 Projection: Equidistant Conic

0 — 100 — 200 kilometers

0 — 50 — 100 miles

Europe and the Russian Federation

Spain • Portugal

Europe and the Russian Federation

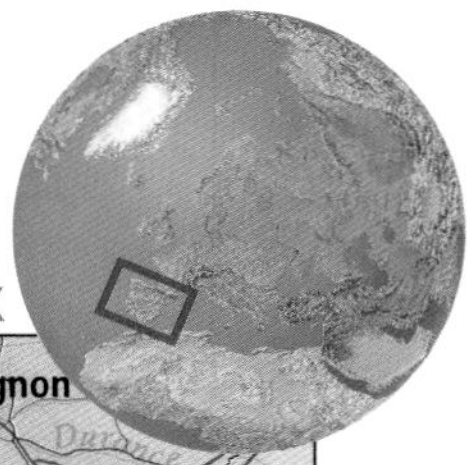

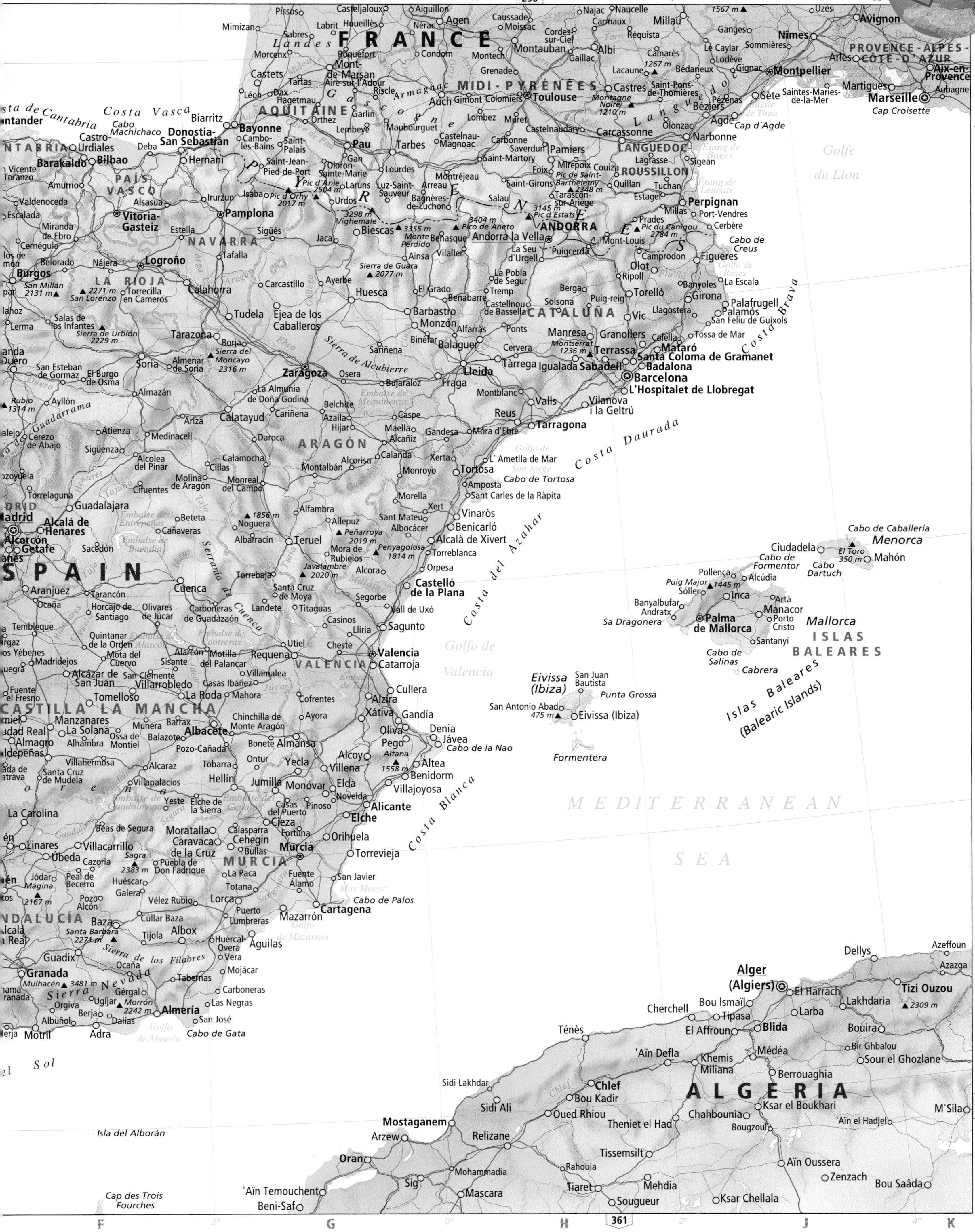

FRANCE

AQUITAINE
MIDI-PYRÉNÉES
LANGUEDOC-ROUSSILLON
PROVENCE-ALPES-CÔTE-D'AZUR

SPAIN
PAÍS VASCO
NAVARRA
LA RIOJA
ARAGÓN
CATALUÑA
CASTILLA-LA MANCHA
VALENCIA
MURCIA
ANDALUCÍA
ANDORRA

Madrid
Zaragoza
Barcelona
Valencia
Murcia
Alicante
Cartagena
Granada
Almería
Bilbao
Pamplona
Logroño
Burgos
Soria
Huesca
Lleida
Tarragona
Castelló de la Plana
Albacete
Cuenca
Guadalajara
Teruel
Calatayud
Toulouse
Bayonne
Pau
Tarbes
Carcassonne
Narbonne
Perpignan
Montpellier
Nîmes
Marseille
Avignon
Aix-en-Provence
Martigues

Palma de Mallorca
Mallorca
Menorca
Mahón
Ciudadela
Eivissa (Ibiza)
Formentera
ISLAS BALEARES (Balearic Islands)

MEDITERRANEAN SEA

Golfe du Lion
Golfo de Valencia
Costa Brava
Costa Daurada
Costa del Azahar
Costa Blanca

ALGERIA
Alger (Algiers)
Oran
Mostaganem
Chlef
Blida
Tizi Ouzou
M'Sila

Pic d'Aneto 3404 m
Mulhacén 3481 m

Scale 1:3,500,000
Projection: Equidistant Conic
0   100   200 kilometers
0   50   100 miles

Italy • Austria

Europe and the Russian Federation

Map labels (south Italy, Sicily, Sardinia, Corsica, Tunisia):

Seas and waters: TYRRHENIAN SEA, IONIAN SEA, MEDITERRANEAN SEA, Malta Channel, Strait of Sicily, Golfo di Taranto, Stretto di Messina

Regions: ABRUZZI, MOLISE, LAZIO, CAMPANIA, PUGLIA, BASILICATA, CALABRIA, Sicilia (Sicily), Sardegna (Sardinia), Corse (Corsica) (Fr.), TUNISIA, ALGERIA, MALTA, VATICAN CITY, Appennino Lucano, Appennino Abruzzese

Cities and places:
Otranto, Tricase, Capo Santa Maria di Leuca, Marina di Leuca, Ugento, Gallipoli, Galatone, Maglie, Lecce, Veglie, Manduria, Squinzano, Brindisi, Martano, Fontana, Francavilla, Massafra, Taranto, Mottola, Laterza, Casamassima, Monopoli, Adelfia, Molfetta, Bari, Barletta, Andria, Canosa, Spinazzola, Altamura, Matera, Pisticci, Scanzano, Rotondella, Policoro, Corigliano Calabro, Rossano, Sibari, Cariati, Cirò Marina, Punta Alice, Crotone, Capo Rizzuto, Catanzaro, Monasterace Marina, Siderno, Locri, Bovalino Marina, Gerace, Bova Marina, Capo Spartivento, Reggio di Calabria, Palmi, Gioia Tauro, Cittanova, Stilo, Serra San Bruno, Vibo Valentia, Pizzo, Capo Vaticano, Nicastro, Amantea, Paola, Cosenza, Acri, Cetraro, Belvedere Marittimo, Laino, Lagonegro, Sapri, Maratea, Policastro, Sala Consilina, Vallo della Lucania, Agropoli, Palinuro, Capaccio, Battipaglia, Salerno, Amalfi, Sorrento, Capri, Isola di Capri, Napoli (Naples), Caserta, Capua, Benevento, Avellino, Torre del Greco, Vesuvio, Sessa Aurunca, Gaeta, Fondi, Terracina, Formia, Latina, Anzio, Aprilia, Velletri, Frosinone, Sora, Avezzano, Sulmona, Isernia, Campobasso, Larino, Termoli, Vasto, Lanciano, L'Aquila, Rieti, Tivoli, Roma (Rome), Civitavecchia, Tarquinia, Viterbo, Bracciano, Lido di Ostia, Cerveteri, Ladispoli, Ostia

Foggia, Lucera, San Severo, Manfredonia, Monte Sant'Angelo, Vieste, Peschici, Lesina, Vasto, Atessa, Agnone

Sardegna: Cagliari, Oristano, Nuoro, Sassari, Olbia, Alghero, Iglesias, Carbonia, Sant'Antioco, Tempio, Ozieri, Macomer, Bosa, Sanluri, Quartu Sant'Elena, Muravera, Capo Carbonara, Capo Teulada

Corse: Ajaccio, Bastia, Bonifacio, Corte, Porto-Vecchio, Propriano, Sartène, Calvi

Islands: Isola di Montecristo, Isola del Giglio, Isola di Ponza, Isola d'Ischia, Isola Ventotene, Isola di Ustica, Isole Eolie o Lipari, Isola Stromboli, Isola Salina, Isola Panarea, Isola Lipari, Isola Filicudi, Isola Alicudi, Isola Vulcano, Isole Egadi, Isola di Pantelleria, Isole Pelagie, Isola di Linosa, Isola di Lampedusa, La Galite (Tunisia), Gozo, Valletta, Isola Tavolara, Isola Asinara, Isole Tremiti, Isola Pianosa, Isola di San Pietro, Isola di Sant'Antioco, Isola Caprera, Isola Maddalena

Sicilia: Palermo, Messina, Catania, Siracusa, Ragusa, Modica, Gela, Agrigento, Caltanissetta, Enna, Trapani, Marsala, Mazara del Vallo, Sciacca, Licata, Cefalù, Milazzo, Patti, Acireale, Taormina, Randazzo, Bronte, Adrano, Paternò, Augusta, Avola, Noto, Pachino, Capo Passero, Vittoria, Comiso, Scicli, Pozzallo, Monte Etna 3323 m, Monti Nebrodi, Madonie Mti, Monti Peloritani, Capo San Vito

Tunisia: Tunis, Sousse, Bizerte, Kairouan, Nabul, Al Hammamat, Mahdia, Al Munastir, Masakin, Zaghwan, Beja, El Kef, Gabes

Algeria: Annaba, Guelma, Souk-Ahras, Tebessa

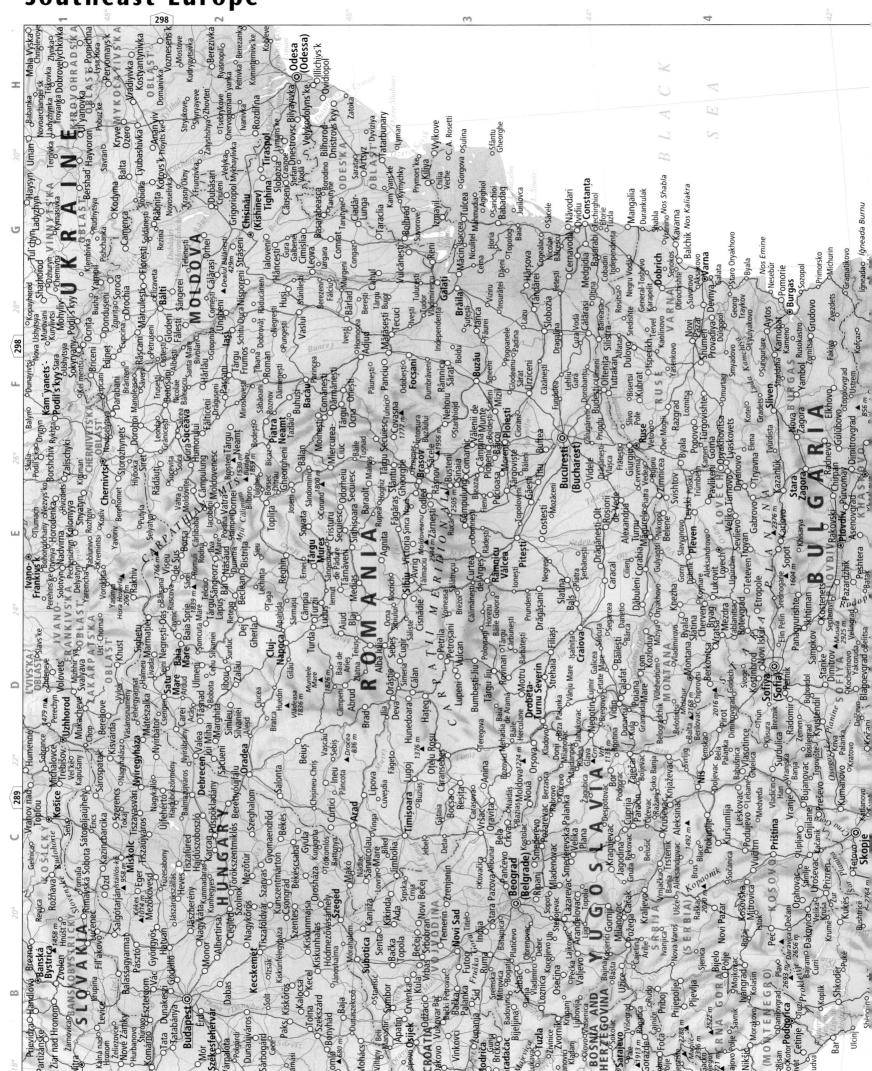

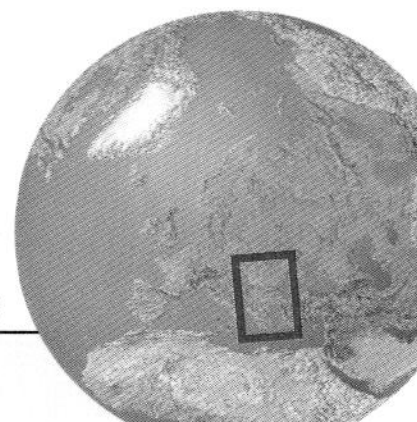

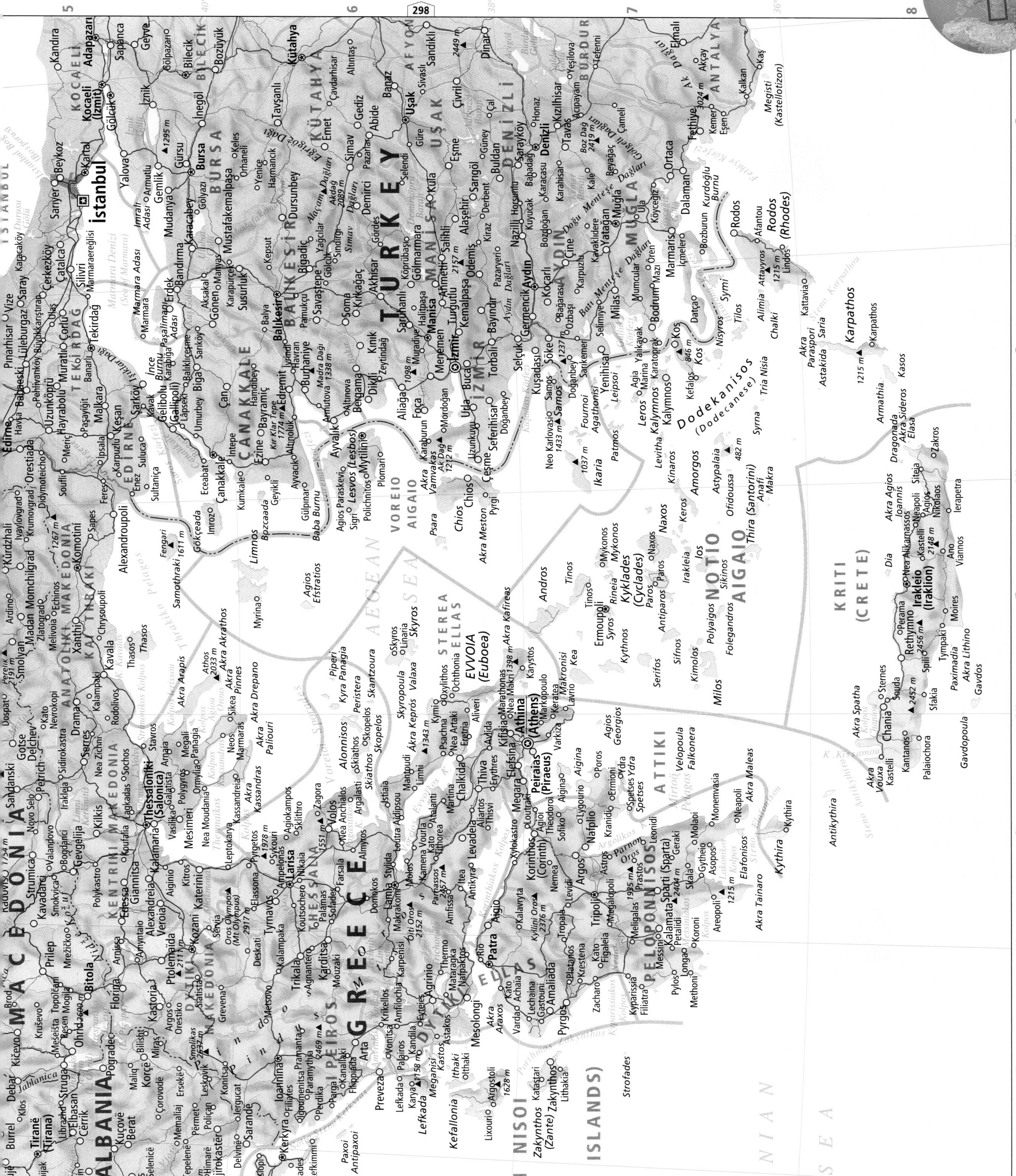

298

TURKEY

GREECE

ALBANIA

MACEDONIA

KRITI (CRETE)

AEGEAN SEA

IONIAN SEA

VOREIO AIGAIO

NOTIO AIGAIO

Dodekanisos (Dodecanese)

Kyklades (Cyclades)

IONIOI NISOI (IONIAN ISLANDS)

Istanbul

Athina (Athens)

Peiraias (Piraeus)

Bursa

İzmir

Denizli

Rodos (Rhodes)

0   100   200 kilometers
0   50   100 miles

Scale 1:3,500,000

Projection: Equidistant Conic

East Europe • Turkey

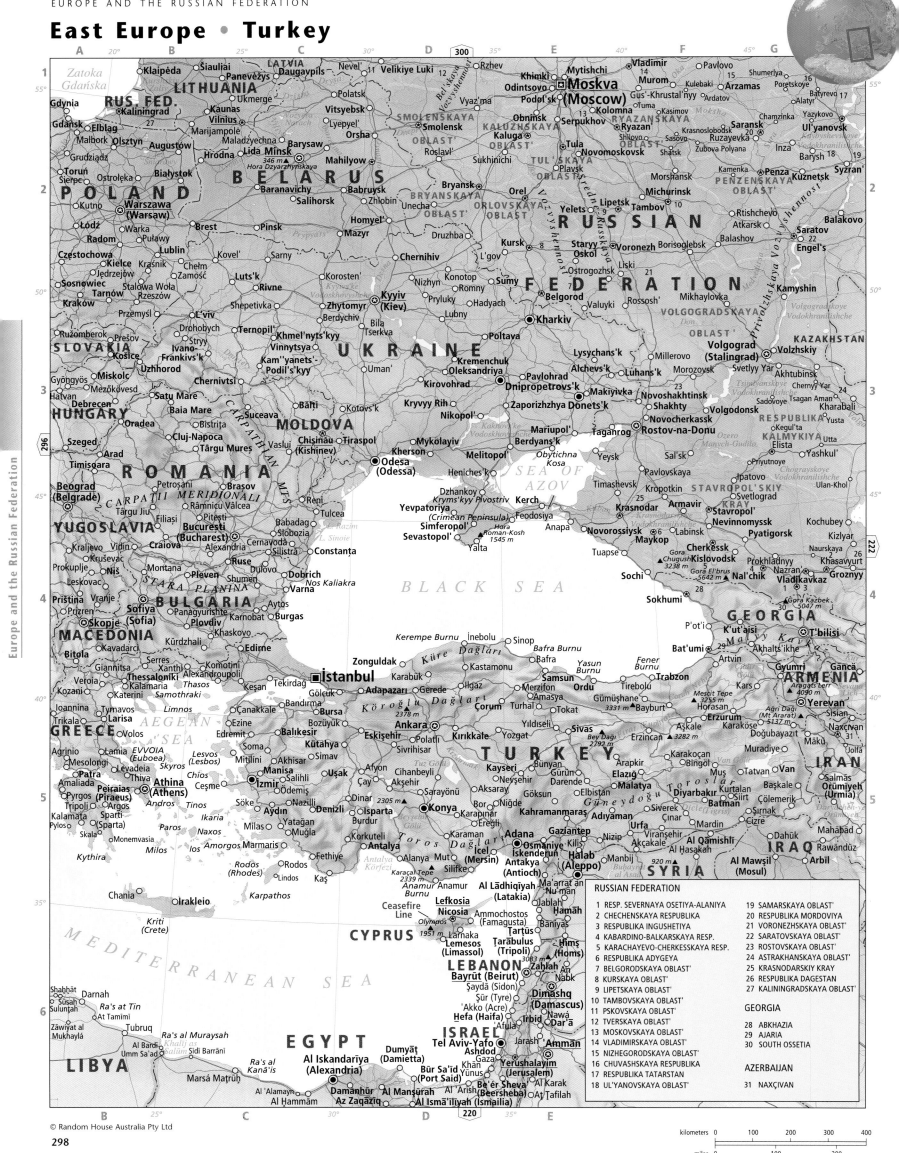

© Random House Australia Pty Ltd

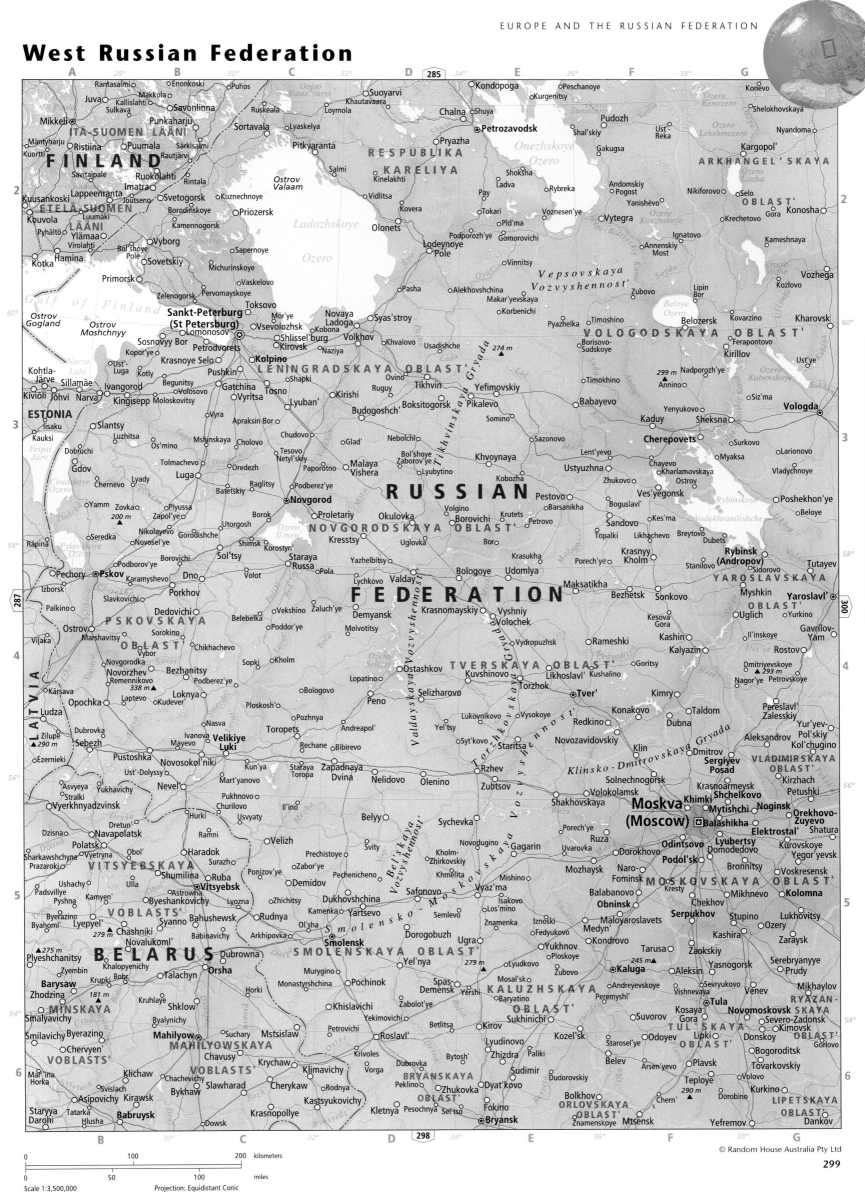

West Russian Federation

FINLAND

ITÄ-SUOMEN LÄÄNI

ETELÄ-SUOMEN LÄÄNI

ESTONIA

LATVIA

BELARUS

MINSKAYA VOBLASTS'

VITSYEBSKAYA VOBLASTS'

MAHILYOWSKAYA VOBLASTS'

RESPUBLIKA KARELIYA

ARKHANGEL'SKAYA OBLAST'

VOLOGODSKAYA OBLAST'

LENINGRADSKAYA OBLAST'

NOVGORODSKAYA OBLAST'

PSKOVSKAYA OBLAST'

RUSSIAN FEDERATION

TVERSKAYA OBLAST'

YAROSLAVSKAYA OBLAST'

SMOLENSKAYA OBLAST'

MOSKOVSKAYA OBLAST'

Moskva (Moscow)

VLADIMIRSKAYA OBLAST'

KALUZHSKAYA OBLAST'

TUL'SKAYA OBLAST'

RYAZAN-SKAYA OBLAST'

BRYANSKAYA OBLAST'

ORLOVSKAYA OBLAST'

LIPETSKAYA OBLAST'

Gulf of Finland

Ladozhskoye Ozero

Onezhskoye Ozero

Sankt-Peterburg (St Petersburg)

Petrozavodsk

Vologda

Cherepovets

Rybinsk (Andropov)

Yaroslavl'

Tver'

Smolensk

Kaluga

Tula

Bryansk

0   100   200 kilometers
0   50   100 miles
Scale 1:3,500,000   Projection: Equidistant Conic

Russian Federation and Surrounding Countries

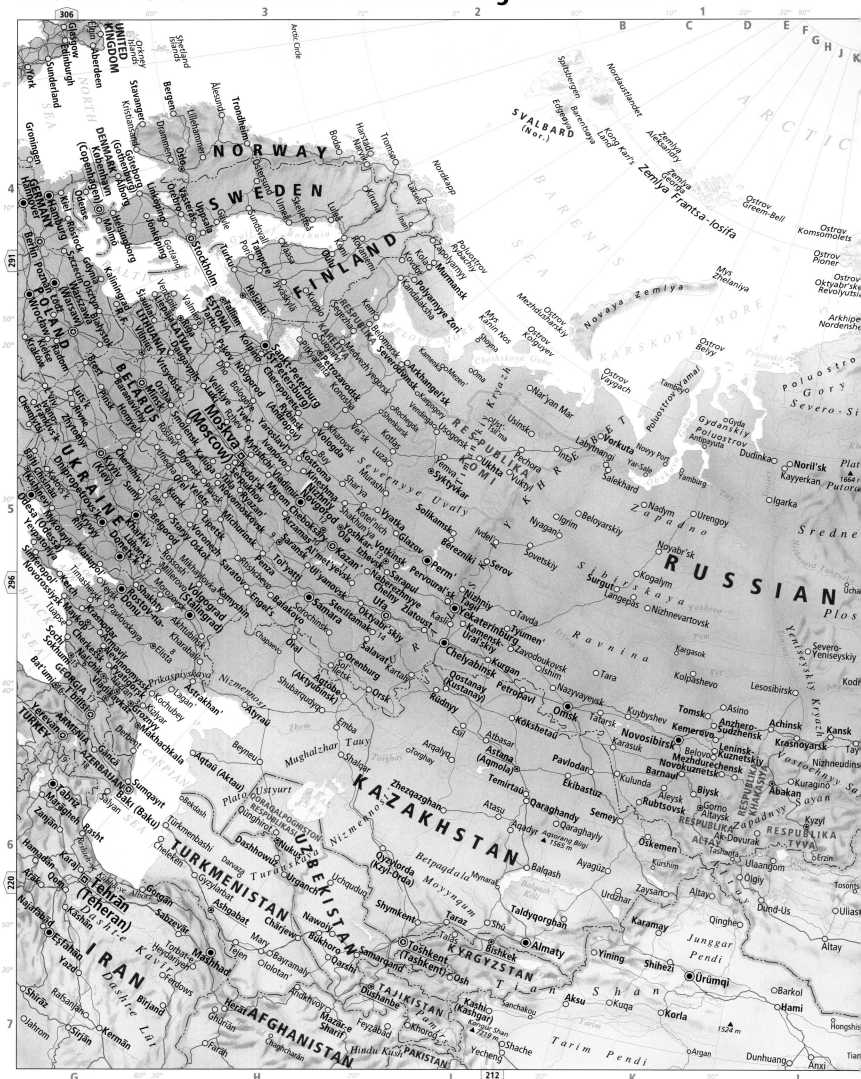

410

RUSSIAN FEDERATION

U.S.A.

Arctic Circle

Wainwrighto
Cape Lisburne
oPoint Hope
oKotlik
Bethel
Dillingham
Toglak
Alaska Peninsula
Seward Peninsula
Nome
Norton Sound
Sammon
Bristol Bay
Cape Newenham
Unimak Island
Nunivak Island

Bering Strait

St Lawrence Island

Ostrov Vrangelya
Ushakovskoye

CHUKCHI SEA

Novosibirskiye Ostrova
Ostrov Faddeyevskiy Ostrov
Novaya Sibir'
Ostrov Kotel'nyy
Lyakhovskiye Ostrova
Ostrov Bol'shoy Lyakhovskiy
Mys Kovalskiy

Ostrova Medvezh'i
Ostrov Ayon
Cherskiy
Bilibino
Pevek
Mys Shelagskiy

VOSTOCHNO-SIBIRSKOYE MORE

Ostrov Bol'shevik
Severnaya
Zemlya
Mys Chelyuskin
Ostrov Bol'shoy Begichev

MORE LAPTEVYKH

Yano-Indigirskaya Nizmennost'
Kolymskaya Nizmennost'

Tiksio
Siktyakh
oZhilinda
Onenek
Deputatskiy
oKhonuu
Verkhoyansk
Gora Pobeda 3147 m

Khrebet Cherskogo

Ust'-Nera ▲2341 m
Omsukchan
Susuman
Sinegor'ye

Khrebet Kular
Khrebet Orulgan ▲2389 m

Gora Volna 1585 m
Magadan
Mys Tolstoy

Chukotskoye Nagor'ye
1355 m Gora Belaya ▲
Ugol'nyye Kopi
Anadyr'
Anadyrskoye Ploskogor'ye
1742 m ▲

Koryakskoye Nagor'ye
Kolymskoye Nagor'ye

Mys Chukotskiy
Poluostrov Chukotskiy
Oul'tin

Ul'tin

Mys Olyutorskiy

BERING SEA

Aleutian Islands
Andreanof Islands
Near Islands
Rat Islands

Komandorskiye Ostrova
Ostrov Beringa
Ostrov Mednyy

RESPUBLIKA SAKHA

FEDERATION

Yakutsk⊛
Mirnyy
Nyurba
Olekminsk
Lensk
Bodaybo
Kirensk
Ust'-Ilim'sk
Ust'-Kut

Sangar
Khandyga
Khrebet Suntar Khayata

Aldan
Dikimdya
Aldanskoye Nagor'ye
Chul'man
Stanovoy Khrebet
Gora Golets Skalistyy ▲2412 m

Neryungri
Tynda
Zeya
Magdagachi
Skovorodino
Shimanovsk ▲1490 m
Belogorsk

Khrebet Dzhugdzhur
Ayan

Okhotsk
Poluostrov Koni

Shantarskiye Ostrova
Mys Yelizavety
Okha

Nikolayevsk-na-Amure
oBerezovyy
Komsomol'sk-na-Amure
Amursk
Chegdomyn

OKHOTSKOYE MORE
(SEA OF OKHOTSK)

Poluostrov Kamchatka
Sredinnyy Khrebet
4750 m Klyuchevskaya Sopka ▲
Ust'-Kamchatsk
Mys Kamchatsk
Ostrov Karaginskiy
Mys Ozernoy

Petropavlovsk-Kamchatskiy
Yelizovo
Kronotskiy Zaliv
Mys Lopatka
Ostrov Paramushir
Ostrov Onekotan
Ostrov Shiashkotan
Ostrov Simushir
Ostrov Urup
Ostrov Iturup

Kuril'skiye Ostrova
(Kuril Islands)
Administered by Russian Federation, claimed by Japan

PACIFIC OCEAN

Ostrov Sakhalin
Nogliki
Poronaysk
Mys Terpeniya
Zaliv Terpeniya

Mys Aniva
Yuzhno-Sakhalinsk

Bratsk
Ust'-Kut
Severobaykal'sk
Zima
Usol'ye-Sibirskoye
Irkutsk
Ulan-Ude
Khilok
Chita
Sherlovaya Gora
Borzya

Stanovoye Nagor'ye
Taksimo
Ozero Baykal (Lake Baikal)
RESPUBLIKA BURYATIYA

Obluch'ye
Blagoveshchensk
Svetlaya
Dal'negorsk
Bikin
Ussuriysk
Vladivostok

Khabarovsk
Sikhote Alin'

Wakkanai
Asahikawa
Otaru
Sapporo
Muroran
Hokkaidō
Kitami

JAPAN

SEA OF JAPAN

MONGOLIA
Ulan Bator (Ulaanbaatar)
Darhan
Erdenet
Choybalsan
Baruun-Urt
Kyra
Uldz
Kerulen (Herlen)
Hulun Nur

Arvayheer
Mandalgovi
Saynshand
Dalandzadgad
Bayan Haro
Erenhot

Manzhouli
Yakeshi
Qiqihar
Anda
Harbin
Mudanjiang
Yichun
Hegang
Jiamusi
Jixi
Nenjiang

Da Hinggan Ling
Xiao Hinggan Ling

Baicheng
Changchun
Jilin
Tongliao
Xi Ujimqin Qi
Duolun
Chifeng
Fushun
Shenyang
Anshan

NORTH KOREA
P'yŏngyang
Sinŭiju
Kanggye
Hŭngnam
Ch'ŏngjin

Zhangjiakou
Beijing (Peking)
Tianjin
Dalian
Hohhot
Datong
Baotou
Linhe

CHINA

Bohai Wan

SOUTH KOREA
Sŏul (Seoul)
Taejŏn
Andong
Haeju

Aomori
Hachinohe
Mōrioka
Akita
Sendai
Niigata
Toyama
Nagoya
Tokyo
Yokohama
Kyoto
Osaka
Matsue
Kōchi
Hiroshima
Shikoku

Honshū

RUSSIAN FEDERATION
1 RESPUBLIKA DAGESTAN
2 RESPUBLIKA INGUSHETIYA
3 CHECHENSKAYA RESPUBLIKA
4 RESP. SEVERNAYA OSETIYA-ALANIYA
5 KABARDINO-BALKARSKAYA RESPUBLIKA
6 KARACHAYEVO-CHERKESSKAYA RESPUBLIKA
7 RESPUBLIKA ADYGEYA
8 RESPUBLIKA KALMYKIYA
9 RESPUBLIKA MORDOVIYA
10 CHUVASHSKAYA RESPUBLIKA
11 RESPUBLIKA TATARSTAN
12 RESPUBLIKA MARIY EL
13 UDMURTSKAYA RESPUBLIKA
14 RESPUBLIKA BASHKORTOSTAN

GEORGIA
15 ABKHAZIA
16 AJARIA
17 SOUTH OSSETIA

AZERBAIJAN
18 NAGORNO-KARABAKH
19 NAXÇIVAN

0   200   400   600   800 kilometers
0   200   400 miles
Scale 1:20,000,000   Projection: Equidistant Conic

Europe and the Russian Federation

The British Isles

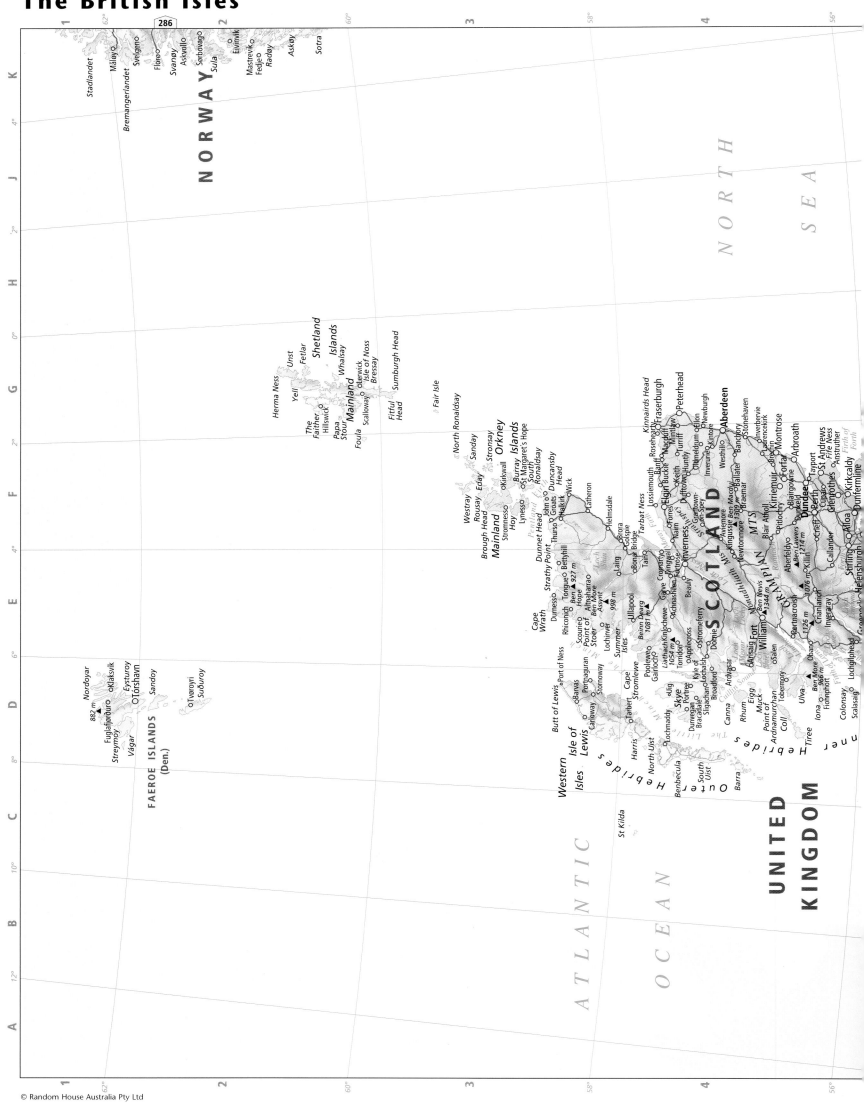

286

NORWAY

Stadlandet
Måløy
Bremangerlandet
Svelgeno
Florø
Svanøy
Askvollo
Sørbøvago
Sula
Eivinvik
Mastrevik
Fedje
Raday
Askøy
Sotra

NORTH SEA

Herma Ness
Unst
Yell
Fetlar
The Faither
Hillswick
Shetland
Papa Stour
Whalsay
Foula
Mainland
Olterwick
Isle of Noss
Scalloway
Bressay
Fitful Head
Sumburgh Head

Fair Isle

North Ronaldsay
Westray
Sanday
Rousay
Eday
Stronsay
Orkney
Brough Head
Kirkwall
Burray
Islands
Mainland
Stromness
Hoy
Lynesso
St Margaret's Hope
South Ronaldsay
Dunnet Head
John o'Groats
Duncansby Head
Strathy Point
Thurso
Halkirk
Wick
Dumesso
Torquoo
Bettyhill
Latheron
Rhiconich
Hope
Altnaharra
Ben 927 m
Scourieo
Point of Stoer
Ben More
998 m
Assynt
Helmsdale
Cape Wrath

Kinnaird's Head
Rosehearty
Fraserburgh
Lossiemouth
Banff
Macduff
Turriff
Peterhead
Elgin Buckie
Keith
Turriff
Newburgh
Forres
Dufftown
Huntly
Ellon
Inverurie
Kintore
Aberdeen
Nairn
Grantown-on-Spey
Oldmeldrum
Westhill
Stonehaven
Cromartyo
Ben Macdhui
1309 m
Banchory
Inverbervie
Kingussie
Braemar
Laurencekirk
Aviemore
GRAMPIAN
Ballater
Montrose
Dingwall
MTS
Arbroath
Tain
Blair Atholl
Forfar
Beauly
Newtonmore
Kirriemuir
Blairgowrie
Inverness
Ben Lawers
Pitlochry
Dundee
1214 m
Forfar
St Andrews
Ben Lawers
Aberfeldyo
Cupar
Fife Ness
SCOTLAND
Ben Nevis
1344 m
Dunkeld
Anstruther
Tarbat Ness
1076 m
Crieff
Perth
Glenrothes
Lochinver
Gairvo
Achnasheen
Fort William
Bertnacroish
965 m
Crianlarich
Kirkcaldy
Lochinver
Kinlochewe
1054 m
Dornie
Strome ferry
Ben More
Callander
Alloa
Dunfermline
Summer Isles
Torridon
Kyle of Lochalsh
Stirling
Ullapool
Appleçross
Salen
Obano
Lochgilphead
Greenock
Helensburgh
Beinn Dearg
1081 m
Poolewe
Broadford
Ulva
Iona
Finnphort
Inveraray
Gairloch
Skye
Dunvegan
Eigg
Ben More
882 m
Uig
Portree
Muck
Mull
Colonsay
Bracadale
Rhum
Point of
Ardnamurchan
Scalasaig
Canna
Coll
Tobermory
Tiree

Port of Ness
Butt of Lewis
Barvas
Portnaguran
Western
Carloway
Isle of
Stornoway
Isles
Lewis
Cape Stronsay
Tarbert
Harris
Lochmaddy
North Uist
Benbecula
South Uist
Outer
Hebrides
Barra

St Kilda

FAEROE ISLANDS
(Den.)
Nordoyar
Klaksvik
Fuglafjørður
882 m
Eysturoy
Streymoy
Tórshavn
Sandoy
Vágar
Tvøroyri
Suðuroy

ATLANTIC

OCEAN

UNITED

KINGDOM

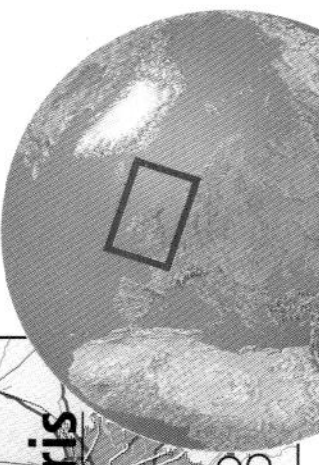

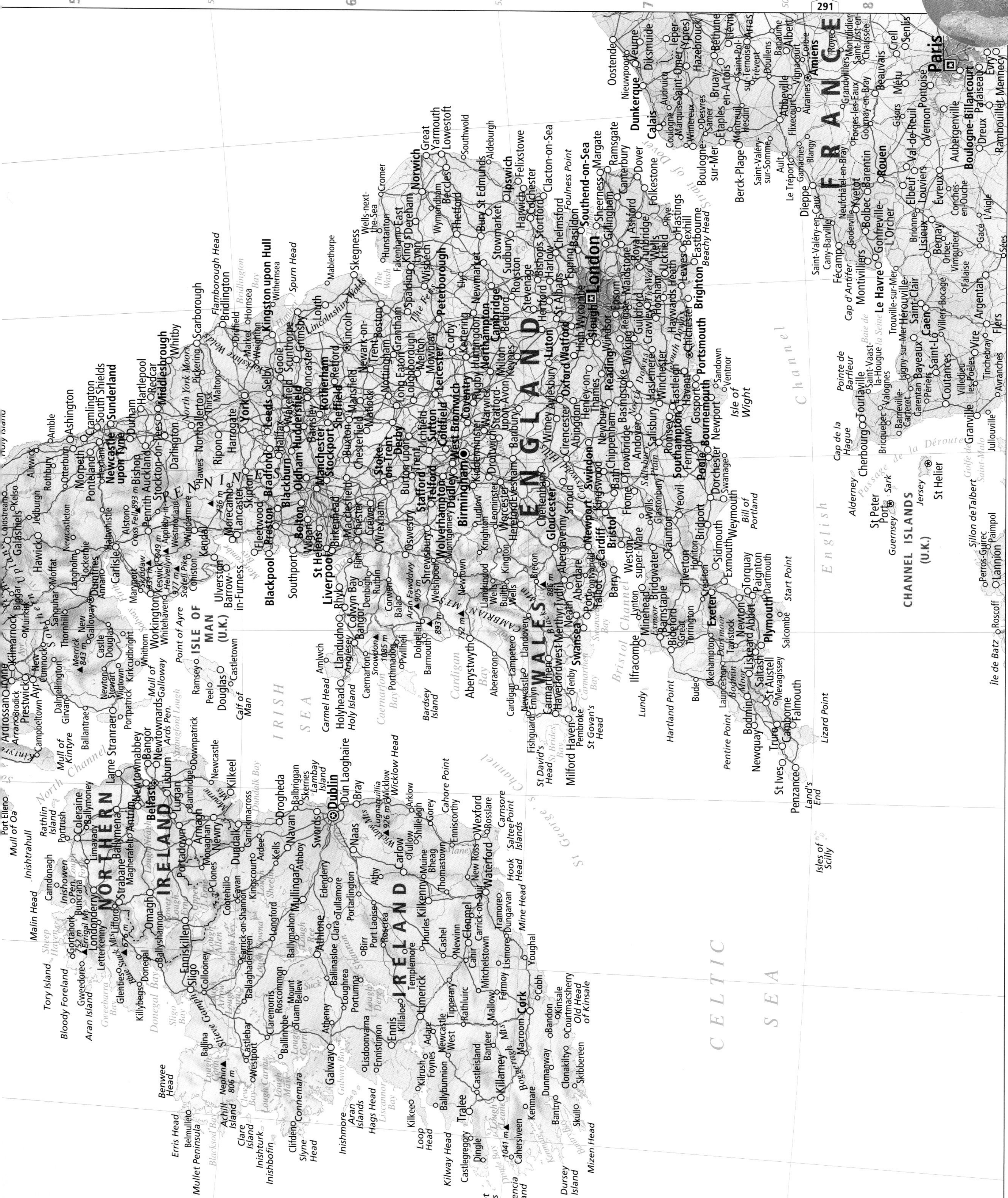

FRANCE

ENGLAND

WALES

IRELAND

NORTHERN IRELAND

SCOTLAND

ISLE OF MAN (U.K.)

CHANNEL ISLANDS (U.K.)

London

Paris

Dublin

IRISH SEA

NORTH CHANNEL

CELTIC SEA

English Channel

Bristol Channel

St George's Channel

Strait of Dover

290

0   100   200   kilometers
0   50   100   miles
Scale 1:3,500,000   Projection: Equidistant Conic

South England • Wales

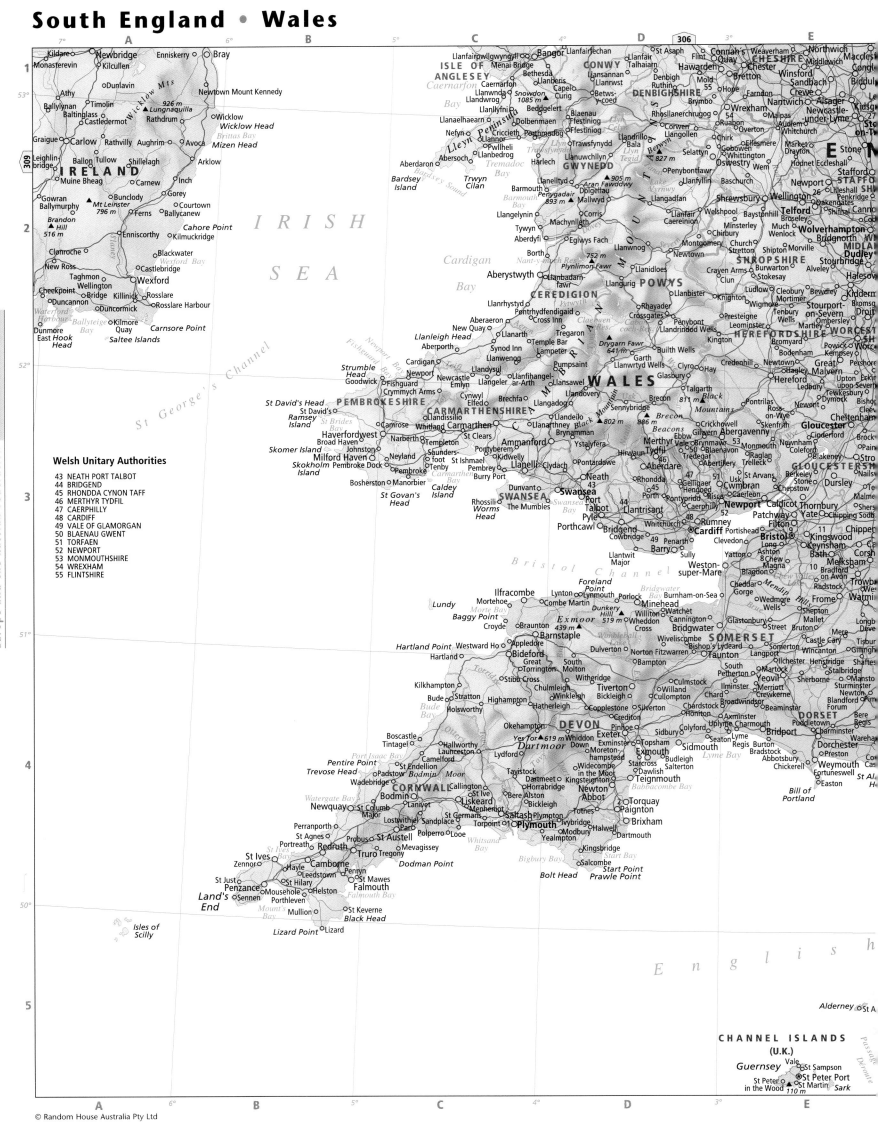

Welsh Unitary Authorities

43 NEATH PORT TALBOT
44 BRIDGEND
45 RHONDDA CYNON TAFF
46 MERTHYR TYDFIL
47 CAERPHILLY
48 CARDIFF
49 VALE OF GLAMORGAN
50 BLAENAU GWENT
51 TORFAEN
52 NEWPORT
53 MONMOUTHSHIRE
54 WREXHAM
55 FLINTSHIRE

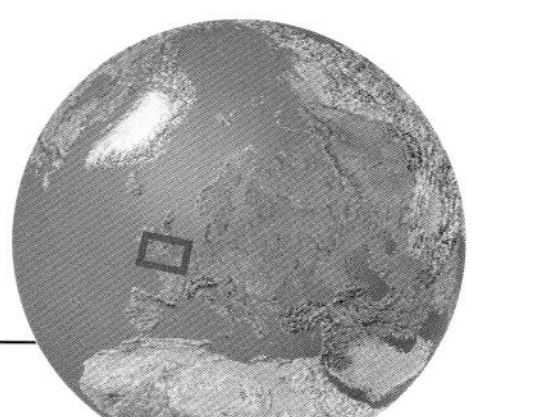

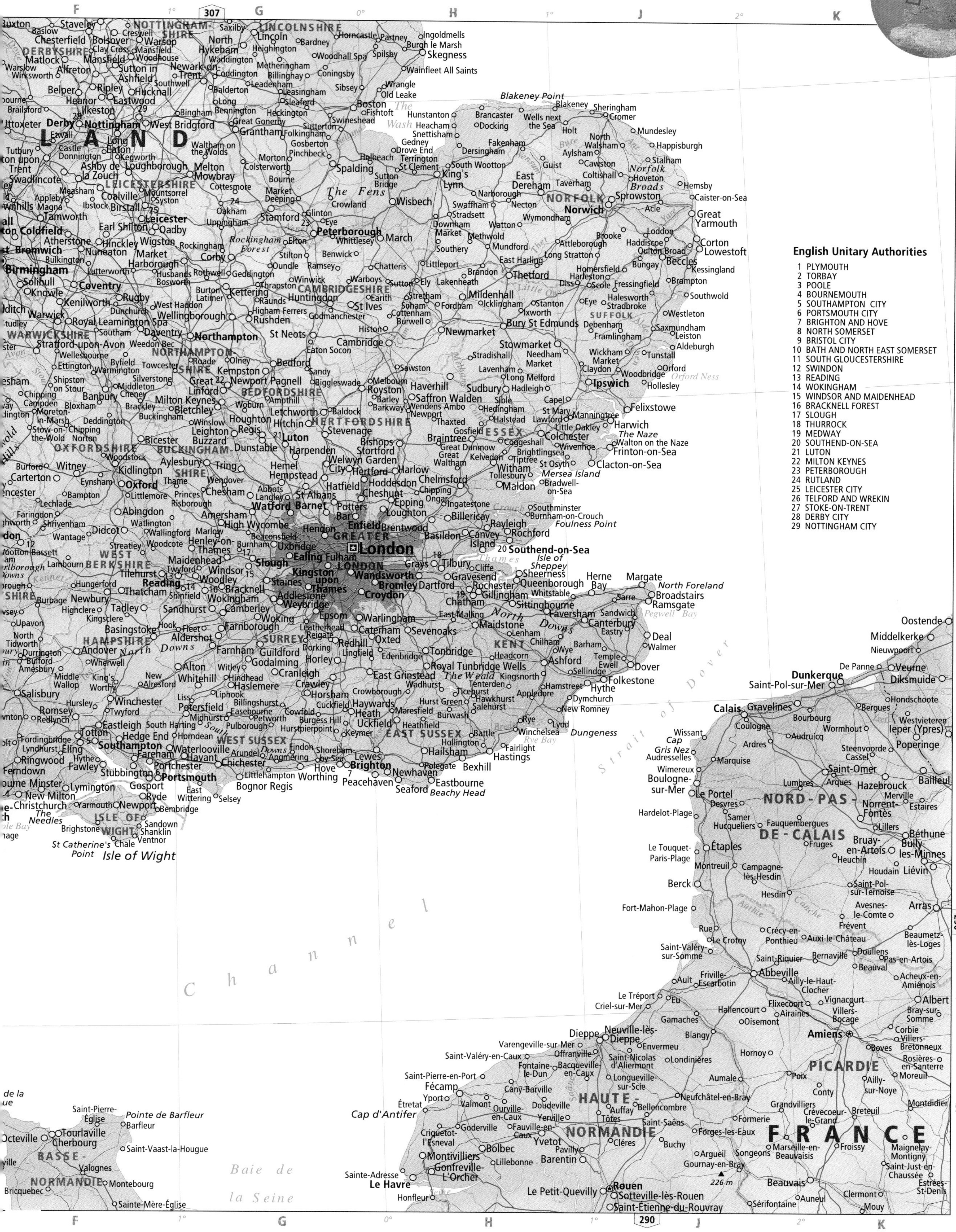

F
G
H
J
K
307
290
LINCOLNSHIRE
NOTTINGHAMSHIRE
DERBYSHIRE
LEICESTERSHIRE
NORFOLK
SUFFOLK
CAMBRIDGESHIRE
NORTHAMPTONSHIRE
BEDFORDSHIRE
HERTFORDSHIRE
ESSEX
OXFORDSHIRE
BUCKINGHAMSHIRE
WARWICKSHIRE
WEST BERKSHIRE
HAMPSHIRE
SURREY
KENT
WEST SUSSEX
EAST SUSSEX
ISLE OF WIGHT
GREATER LONDON
London
NORD-PAS-DE-CALAIS
PICARDIE
HAUTE-NORMANDIE
BASSE-NORMANDIE
FRANCE
The Wash
The Fens
The Weald
North Downs
Strait of Dover
Channel
Baie de la Seine
Isle of Wight
English Unitary Authorities
1 PLYMOUTH
2 TORBAY
3 POOLE
4 BOURNEMOUTH
5 SOUTHAMPTON CITY
6 PORTSMOUTH CITY
7 BRIGHTON AND HOVE
8 NORTH SOMERSET
9 BRISTOL CITY
10 BATH AND NORTH EAST SOMERSET
11 SOUTH GLOUCESTERSHIRE
12 SWINDON
13 READING
14 WOKINGHAM
15 WINDSOR AND MAIDENHEAD
16 BRACKNELL FOREST
17 SLOUGH
18 THURROCK
19 MEDWAY
20 SOUTHEND-ON-SEA
21 LUTON
22 MILTON KEYNES
23 PETERBOROUGH
24 RUTLAND
25 LEICESTER CITY
26 TELFORD AND WREKIN
27 STOKE-ON-TRENT
28 DERBY CITY
29 NOTTINGHAM CITY

0 50 100 kilometers
0 25 50 miles
Scale 1:1,500,000
Projection: Equidistant Conic

North England

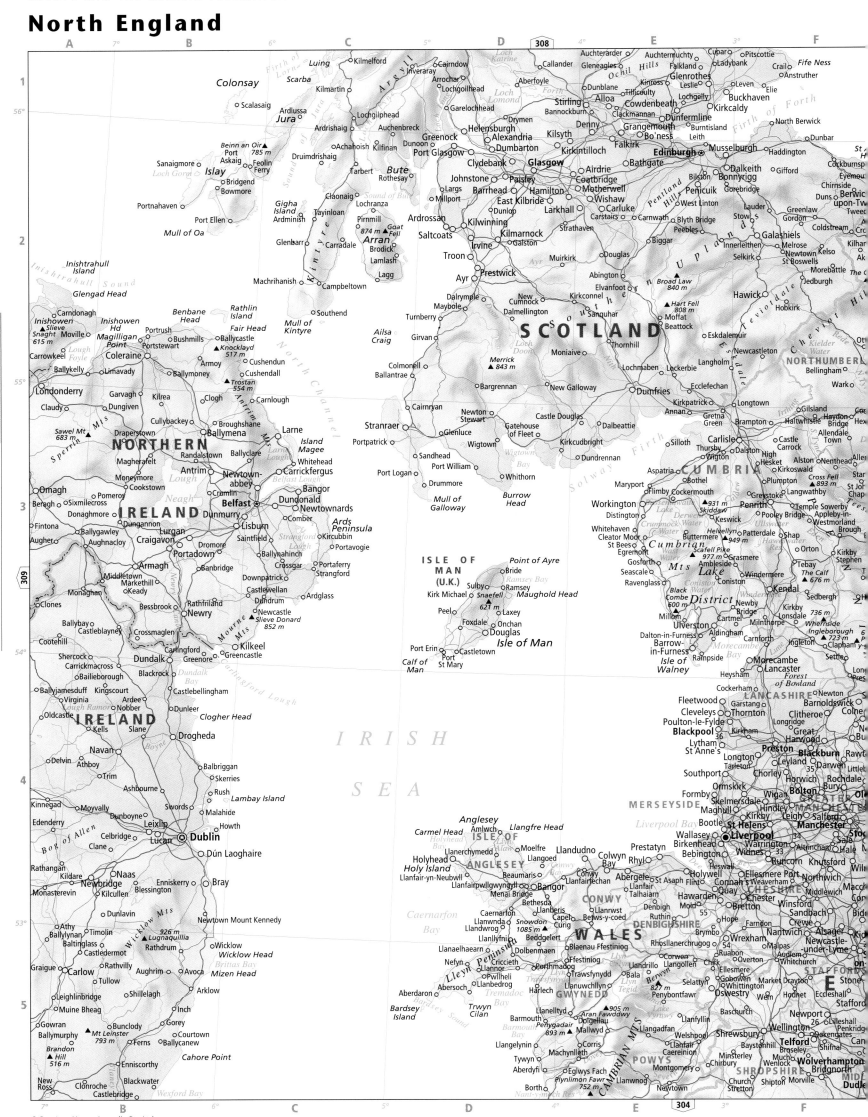

English Unitary Authorities

23 PETERBOROUGH
24 RUTLAND
25 LEICESTER CITY
26 TELFORD AND WREKIN
27 STOKE-ON-TRENT
28 DERBY CITY
29 NOTTINGHAM CITY
30 NORTH EAST LINCOLNSHIRE
31 KINGSTON UPON HULL
32 NORTH LINCOLNSHIRE
33 HALTON
34 WARRINGTON
35 BLACKBURN WITH DARWEN
36 BLACKPOOL
37 YORK CITY
38 DARLINGTON
39 HARTLEPOOL
40 STOCKTON-ON-TEES
41 MIDDLESBROUGH
42 REDCAR AND CLEVELAND

Welsh Unitary Authorities

54 WREXHAM
55 FLINTSHIRE

NORTH SEA

Holy Island
Lindisfarne
Bamburgh
Belford
North Sunderland
Embleton
Boulmer
Lesbury
Warkworth
Amble
Longframlington
Longhorsley
Ashington
Lynemouth
Newbiggin-by-the-sea
Blyth
Cramlington
Ponteland
Whitley Bay
Gosforth
Tynemouth
Newcastle
North Shields
on Tyne
South Shields
Gateshead
TYNE & WEAR
Sunderland
Washington
Chester-le-Street
Houghton-le-Spring
Wolsingham
Durham
Peterlee
Crook
Trimdon
Hartlepool
Ferryhill
Tees Bay
Shildon
Billingham
Bishop
Newton
Middlesbrough
Redcar
Saltburn-by-the-Sea
Aycliffe
Stockton-
Loftus
Darlington
on-Tees
Thornaby
Guisborough
Sandsend
on Tees
Castleton
Whitby
Yarm
Stokesley
Sleights
Scotch Corner
Crathorne
Egton
Robin Hood's Bay
Catterick
Cleveland Hills
North York Moors
NORTH
Northallerton
Rosedale
Hackness
Bedale
Leeming Bar
Abbey
Scalby
Scarborough
Middleham
Thirsk
Kirkbymoorside
Wrelton
Helmsley
Pickering
Seamer
Masham
Filey
Filey Head
YORKSHIRE
Topcliffe
Coxwold
Malton
Yorkshire
Hunmanby
Ripon
Easingwold
North
Bempton
Flamborough
Boroughbridge
Norton
Grimston
Flamborough Head
Ripley
Stillington
Wharram
Langtoft
Bridlington
Fridaythorpe
le Street
Haxby
Wolds
Bridlington Bay
Knaresborough
Skipsea
Harrogate
York
Stamford
EAST RIDING
Otley
Wetherby
Spofforth
Bridge
Pocklington
Brandesburton
OF YORKSHIRE
Boston Spa
Hornsea
Shipley
Tadcaster
Holme upon
Leven
Horsforth
Spalding Moor
Market
Leeds
Selby
Bubwith
Weighton
Beverley
Garforth
South Cave
Bilton
Tunstall
Morley
Castleford
Howden
Anlaby
Kingston
Withernsea
Dewsbury
Snaith
Brough
upon Hull
Pontefract
Knottingley
Goole
Barton-
Patrington
Wakefield
South
Thorne
Winterton
upon-Humber
Darton
Askern
Crowle
Scunthorpe
Immingham
Easington
Barnsley
Bentley
Epworth
Brigg
Grimsby
Spurn Head
Chapeltown
Doncaster
Caistor
Cleethorpes
SOUTH YORKSHIRE
Rossington
Kirton
Tetney
Rotherham
Bawtry
in Lindsey
Maltby
Blyton
Binbrook
Sheffield
Blyth
Gainsborough
Louth
North
Mosborough
Anston
Market
Manby
Somercotes
Dronfield
Retford
Rasen
Maltby
Mablethorpe
Staveley
Creswell
Worksop
Dunholme
le Marsh
Sutton on Sea
Chesterfield
Bolsover
North
Saxilby
Wragby
Alford
Matlock
Clay Cross
Warsop
Hykeham
Lincoln
Horncastle
Partney
Ingoldmells
Mansfield
Waddington
LINCOLNSHIRE
Bardney
Burgh le Marsh
Alfreton
Woodhouse
Heighington
Woodhall Spa
Spilsby
Skegness
Ripley
Sutton
Southwell
Coddington
Metheringham
Wainfleet All Saints
Belper
Hucknall
in Ashfield
Newark-
Billinghay
Coningsby
Heanor
Eastwood
on-Trent
Balderton
Leadenham
Wrangle
Ilkeston
Bingham
Leasingham
Sibsey
Old Leake
Derby
Nottingham
West Bridgford
Bennington
Heckington
Boston
Fishtoft
Long
Grantham
Sutterton
Etwall
Eaton
Waltham on
Swineshead
Kegworth
the Wolds
Great Gonerby
Folkingham
Drove End
Ashby de
Loughborough
Melton
Morton
Pinchbeck
Holbeach
la Zouch
Mowbray
Colsterworth
Spalding
Swadlincote
Measham
LEICESTERSHIRE
Bourne
Sutton
St Clement
South Wootton
Coalville
Mountsorrel
Cottesmore
Market
King's
Ibstock
Birstall
Oakham
Deeping
Lynn
Narborough
Tamworth
Earl
Leicester
Glinton
Crowland
Wisbech
Swaffham
Atherstone
Shilton
Oadby
Uppingham
Stamford
Nuneaton
Hinckley
Wigston
Rockingham
Eye
March
Sutton
Market
Rockingham
Peterborough
Whittlesey
Coldfield
Harborough
Forest
Corby
Benwick
Ramsey
Birmingham
Bulkington
Oundle
CAMBRIDGESHIRE
Littleport
Chatteris

The Wash
The Fens
Rockingham Forest
Nene
Stilton

Blakeney Point
Blakeney
Sheringham
Hunstanton
Brancaster
Wells next
Cromer
Heacham
Docking
the Sea
Holt
Mundesley
Snettisham
Fakenham
Dersingham
North
Happisburgh
Terrington
Walsham
St Clement
Guist
Cawston
Coltishall
Norfolk
Hemsby
Gedney
Taverham
Broads
Hoveton
Caister-on-Sea
East
Sprowston
Great
Dereham
NORFOLK
Acle
Yarmouth
Stradsett
Necton
Wymondham
Norwich
Corton
Downham
Watton
Oulton Broad
Lowestoft
Market
Methwold
Brooke
Loddon
Southery
Mundford
Attleborough
Long
Haddiscoe
Beccles
East Harling
Stratton
Bungay
Kessingland
Homersfield

0   50   100 kilometers
0   25   50 miles

Scale 1:1,500,000   Projection: Equidistant Conic

Scotland

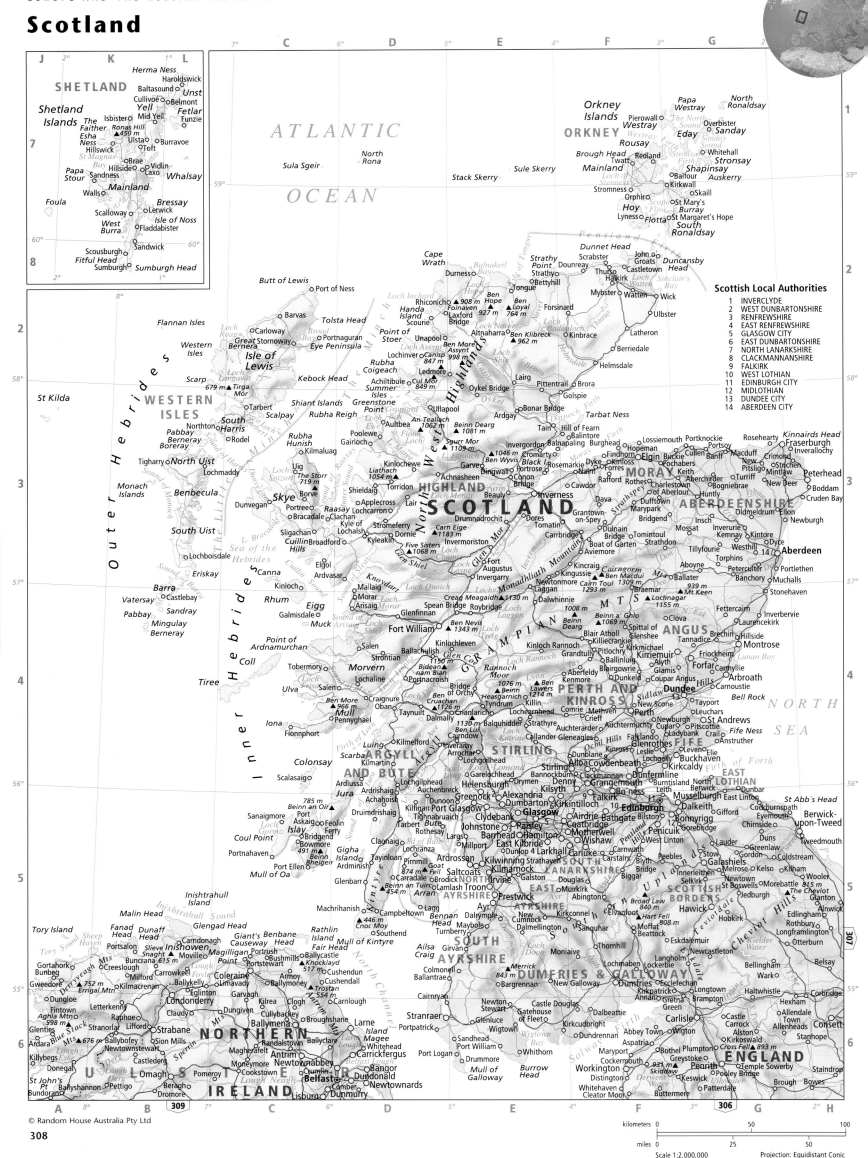

Scottish Local Authorities

1 INVERCLYDE
2 WEST DUNBARTONSHIRE
3 RENFREWSHIRE
4 EAST RENFREWSHIRE
5 GLASGOW CITY
6 EAST DUNBARTONSHIRE
7 NORTH LANARKSHIRE
8 CLACKMANNANSHIRE
9 FALKIRK
10 WEST LOTHIAN
11 EDINBURGH CITY
12 MIDLOTHIAN
13 DUNDEE CITY
14 ABERDEEN CITY

© Random House Australia Pty Ltd

308

kilometers 0   50   100
miles 0   25   50
Scale 1:2,000,000   Projection: Equidistant Conic

Ireland

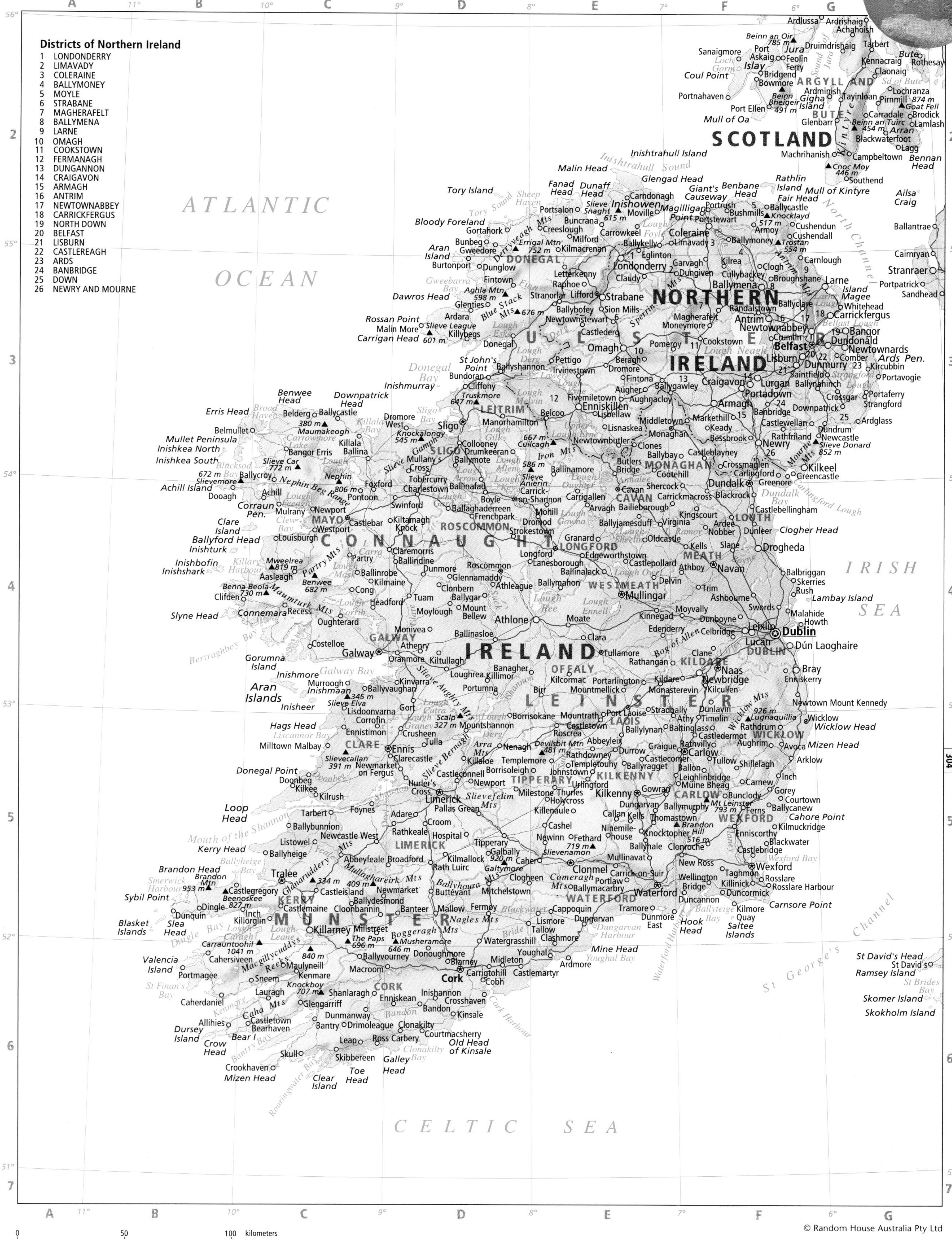

Districts of Northern Ireland

1 LONDONDERRY
2 LIMAVADY
3 COLERAINE
4 BALLYMONEY
5 MOYLE
6 STRABANE
7 MAGHERAFELT
8 BALLYMENA
9 LARNE
10 OMAGH
11 COOKSTOWN
12 FERMANAGH
13 DUNGANNON
14 CRAIGAVON
15 ARMAGH
16 ANTRIM
17 NEWTOWNABBEY
18 CARRICKFERGUS
19 NORTH DOWN
20 BELFAST
21 LISBURN
22 CASTLEREAGH
23 ARDS
24 BANBRIDGE
25 DOWN
26 NEWRY AND MOURNE

ATLANTIC OCEAN

SCOTLAND

ARGYLL AND BUTE

NORTHERN IRELAND

ULSTER

CONNAUGHT

IRELAND

LEINSTER

MUNSTER

IRISH SEA

CELTIC SEA

Mouth of the Shannon

St George's Channel

© Random House Australia Pty Ltd

309

Scale 1:2,000,000
Projection: Equidistant Conic

0 50 100 kilometres
0 25 50 miles

Africa

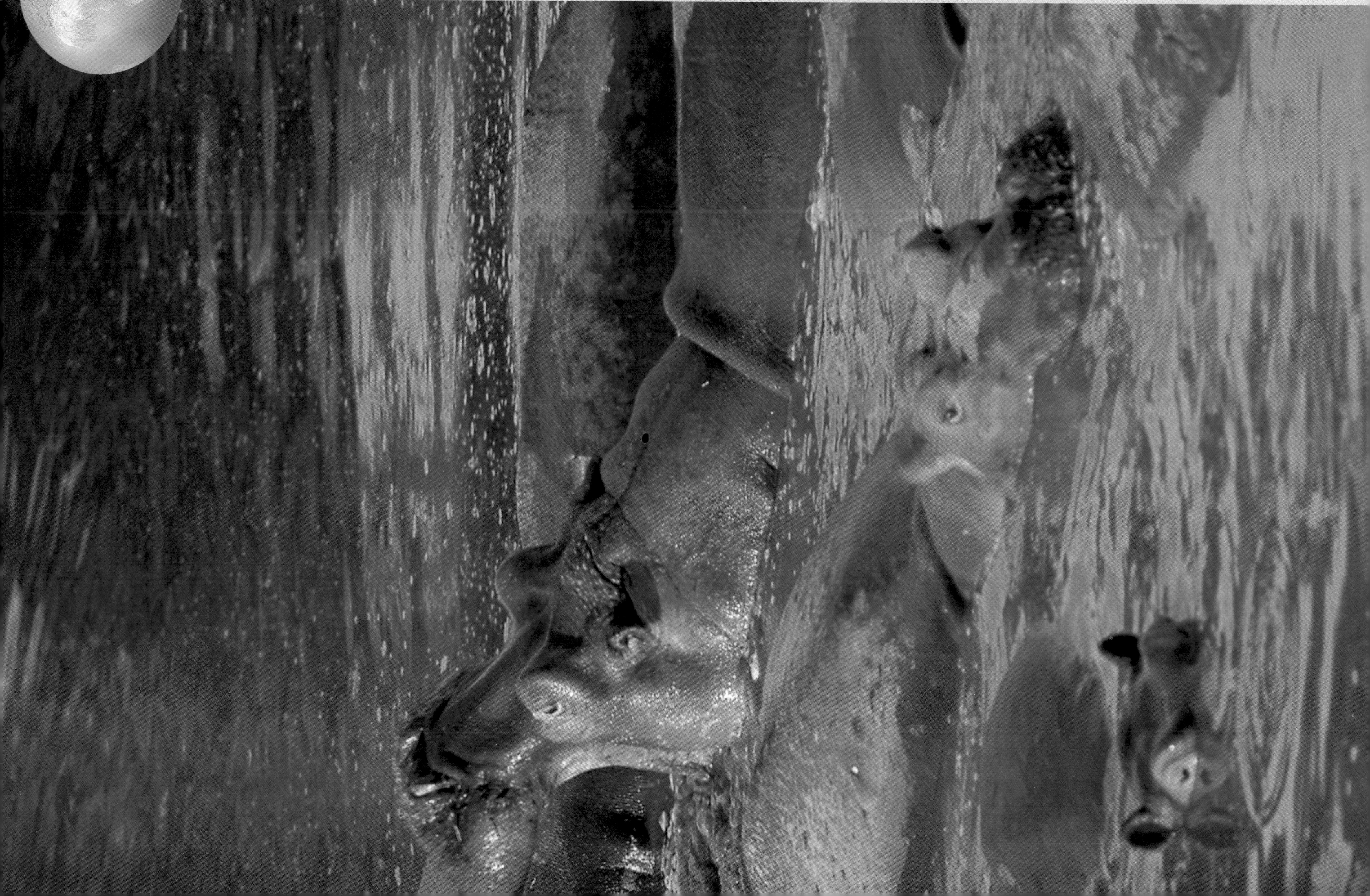

Africa

Africa, the world's second-largest continent, covers 30.3 million sq km (11.6 million sq miles) and is separated from Europe by the Mediterranean Sea and from Asia by the Red Sea and the Suez Canal. It is bounded by the Atlantic Ocean to the west and the Indian Ocean to the east.

Africa can be broadly divided into two, on cultural, and partly climatic, grounds: north Africa, and Africa south of the Sahara. Arid north Africa includes Morocco, Western Sahara, Algeria, Tunisia, Libya, and Egypt, all of which are climatically and culturally akin to the Middle East.

South of these countries a semiarid zone stretches across Mauritania, Mali, Niger, Chad, Sudan, Ethiopia, and Somalia. Humid tropical Africa includes Guinea, Guinea-Bissau, Sierra Leone, Liberia, Côte d'Ivoire, Ghana, Togo, Benin, Nigeria, Cameroon, the Central African Republic, Gabon, Congo, the Democratic Republic of the Congo (formerly Zaire), Uganda, Kenya, Tanzania, Angola, Zambia, Malawi, Zimbabwe, and Mozambique. Southern Africa includes large regions of semiarid and arid land. Namibia is largely desert and there are extensive arid areas in Botswana and South Africa.

Physical features
Africa consists of a number of plateaus, dissected in the east by the Rift Valley. Volcanic eruptions and elongated lakes and valleys are found along this rift. The Atlas Mountains, in the northwest of the continent, are the only geologically recent mountains in Africa.

Africa has several long rivers. The Nile, around 6,693 km (4,160 miles) long, rises in the Kenyan highlands, flows north and disgorges in the Mediterranean. The basins of the Congo (around 4,630 km [2,880 miles] long), the Zambeze (around 2,735 km [1,700 miles] long) and the Niger (around 4,100 km [2,150 miles]) cover vast areas.

Climate and vegetation
Africa is a continent of climatic contrasts. Arid north Africa contains the world's largest hot desert, the Sahara. Drought- and fire-resistant shrubs and grasses are found there. To its north lie narrow zones along the Mediterranean coast, with cool, wet winters and hot, dry summers.

On the southern border of the Sahara lies the Sahel, consisting of thorny woodlands and grasslands with scattered

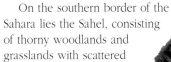

trees. Rainfall is generally low and variable. The area is prone to severe droughts, such as those in the 1980s in Ethiopia and in the 1990s in Somalia. Injudicious cattle herding and grain farming have contributed to desertification.

In central and west Africa, equatorial and tropical conditions prevail, with annual rainfall exceeding 1,270 mm (50 in). Forests and woodlands cover large areas. The forests are layered—shrubs and mosses at lower layers and large tree canopies at higher layers. Each layer possesses abundant and distinct wildlife. East Africa has a monsoon climate, and its forests are less dense. In areas of lesser rainfall (less than 380 mm [15 in]), thorny woodlands and grasslands occur. The forests of Africa harbor chimpanzees and gorillas, and their bird life is profuse.

The vegetation of the semiarid lands of the southernmost part of Africa, notably around the borders of the Kalahari Desert, consists of thorny scrub and grasslands. A greater variety of plants occurs in the wetter coastal and upland areas of the southeast parts of South Africa.

Africa's savannas possess among the richest and most diverse animal populations of the world. Zebras, antelopes, giraffes, elephants, rhinoceros, and wildebeest roam in herds, preyed upon by carnivores such as lions, tigers, leopards, hyenas, jackals, and foxes. Bird life includes ostriches and raptors such as eagles and hawks. Large-scale hunting of wildlife, begun during the colonial era, has had a major impact on Africa's animals. The most notable example has been the quest for ivory—world bans on the trading of ivory have reduced the threat to elephant populations. Other threatened species are white and black rhinoceros, the pygmy hippopotamus, the black wildebeest and some types of zebra.

Islands off the African coast also have their distinct (and distinctive) plant and animal species, notably the lemurs in Madagascar, and the seas are also rich in animal life, including whales, seals, dugongs, and manatees.

Zebras (left) and elephants (top) are among the most well-loved of African animals. These Sudanese people (center) are migrating to Egypt in search of work.

Population
From being the apparent origin of human species, Africa's population has grown to 778.5 million people (1998). The high rate of population increase of 3 percent per annum, between 1985 and 1990, put pressure on resources and food supplies; currently the growth rate has fallen to 2.6 percent. Life expectancies are low in comparison with other continents: 52.3 years for males and 55.3 years for females.

In arid north Africa, populations are concentrated along the Mediterranean. In Egypt, 90 percent of the country's people live along the banks of the Nile River and on its delta. In humid tropical Africa, populations are more dispersed.

A lack of employment in rural areas during the twentieth century has caused a drift to the cities, resulting in fringe urban settlements with poor facilities. In 1995, an estimated 34 percent of Africa's people lived in urban areas.

Agriculture
More than 60 percent of Africa's people depend upon agriculture for their livelihood. Farming is mostly of the subsistence variety—the Hausa people in the west African savannas grow grains and herd animals, the Tuareg people in the Sahara practice pastoralism, for example.

Rice, maize, and wheat are grown in several parts of Africa, either where rainfall is adequate or through the use of irrigation (in Egypt and Nigeria). Fruits and vegetables are also grown; bananas and mangoes in humid tropical areas, date palms in arid areas, and citrus fruits, grapes, and olives in areas with a Mediterranean climate.

Plantation agriculture and large-scale farming were established by Europeans in tropical humid

Africa and southern Africa. The plantations provide some countries with their main export earnings—tea and coffee in Burundi and Rwanda, peanuts in Senegal, and tobacco in Malawi.

Prolonged droughts in several parts of Africa, especially in the semiarid Sahel, have severely affected food production. Agricultural production has also been disrupted by civil wars and wars between neighboring countries.

In the countries of the Gulf of Guinea, tropical forests are logged for valuable timbers, including mahogany, but forest depletion destroys animal habitats and may affect the global climate.

Industrialization

Mineral-rich Africa exports most of the minerals it extracts. Algeria, Libya, and Nigeria are major petroleum producers, and oil is also found in Angola, Benin, Guinea-Bissau, and Egypt; natural gas occurs in Algeria, Libya, and Egypt. A rich metallic ore belt extending from central to southern Africa contains copper, zinc, and lead in the Democratic Republic of the Congo and Zambia, iron ore in South Africa and Zimbabwe, nickel in Botswana and South Africa, and manganese in South Africa. South Africa is a major gold and platinum producer. Diamonds are mined in Namibia, South Africa, the Democratic Republic of the Congo, and Angola. Uranium is found in the Central African Republic.

Several African countries obtain more than half their export earnings from a single commodity: Libya, Nigeria, Gabon, Angola, and Egypt from petroleum; Guinea from bauxite. Even South Africa, with its diversified economy, depends on gold for 40 percent of its export earnings.

Despite the continent's natural resources, there are no developed countries in Africa. A large proportion of African countries have low indicators for nutrition, education, health, and life expectancy. The United Nations designates these as the world's least developed nations. Several countries, such as Somalia and the Sudan, are not self-sufficient in food production and have, during drought and war, needed food aid desperately.

Relatively few African countries have developed significant manufacturing industries. The major exception is South Africa, which now exports machinery and other equipment. During the years of apartheid, however, their racially-based separate development policy created a wide gulf in living standards between the majority black and minority white populations, which will take considerable time to bridge. Egypt and Kenya produce textiles, processed foods, and cement.

Languages

A large number of languages are spoken in Africa, but many, such as Tigre and Chadic in northeast Africa and Berber in north Africa, are restricted to small tribal groups. Zulu is spoken by a large group in South Africa. Arabic is the main language of north Africa and the adjoining countries just south of the Sahara. Some languages are widely used, such as Swahili in east Africa and Hausa in west Africa. Malagasy, spoken in Madagascar, is related to Southeast Asian languages.

This traditionally costumed dancer from Malawi (right) entertains at both funerals and more cheerful festivities.

During the colonial period, several European languages became official languages in various parts of Africa, and French, Portuguese, and English are still spoken over large areas. These languages allow communication between tribal groups which speak different languages.

Boundary disputes and wars

From the sixteenth century onward, Africa was overrun by colonial powers, including France, Britain, Portugal, Spain, and Germany. The colonists made a great impact in the areas of language, law, and education. The current borders of the nations of Africa were determined during colonial times, too, and often cut across tribal areas, separating members of the same ethnic groups while bringing together tribes that were antagonistic: the Somalis found themselves in Somalia, Kenya, and Ethiopia, for instance.

Following decolonization, several tribal conflicts have erupted, such as the genocide of Tutsis by the Hutus in Rwanda in 1994. Nigeria had a lengthy period of insurrection when its southern part seceded to form the short-lived Republic of Biafra. A similar conflict currently rages in southern Sudan. These internal conflicts and military coups have inhibited development in large areas of Africa—currently there are thousands of Rwandan refugees in the eastern part of the Democratic Republic of the Congo; war-torn Somalia has, at present, no effective central government; and Zulu demands for greater autonomy are causing tension in South Africa.

Dependencies & territories

Autonomous communities

Nations

Algeria

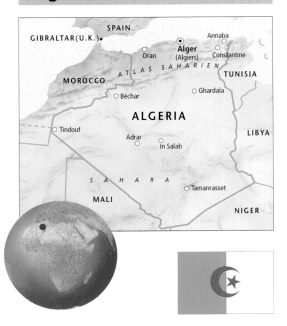

Fact File

OFFICIAL NAME Democratic and Popular Republic of Algeria

FORM OF GOVERNMENT Republic with single legislative body (National People's Assembly), but currently governed by military-backed council

CAPITAL Alger (Algiers)

AREA 2,381,740 sq km (919,590 sq miles)

TIME ZONE GMT

POPULATION 31,133,486

PROJECTED POPULATION 2005 35,118,111

POPULATION DENSITY 13.1 per sq km (33.9 per sq mile)

LIFE EXPECTANCY 69.2

INFANT MORTALITY (PER 1,000) 43.8

OFFICIAL LANGUAGE Arabic

OTHER LANGUAGES French, Berber languages

LITERACY RATE 59.2%

RELIGIONS Sunni Muslim 99%, Christian and Jewish 1%

ETHNIC GROUPS Arab–Berber 99%, European 1%

CURRENCY Algerian dinar

ECONOMY Services 75%, agriculture 14%, industry 11%

GNP PER CAPITA US$1,600

CLIMATE Mild temperate in north, with cool, wet winters and hot, dry summers; arid in south

HIGHEST POINT Mt Tahat 2,918 m (9,573 ft)

MAP REFERENCE Pages 360–61

The largest state in the north of Africa, Algeria was once a province of the Roman Empire known as Numidia, and since early times it has been the home of nomadic Berber peoples. Arabs came to the region during the seventh century, bringing Islam, and in the sixteenth century Algeria was incorporated into the Ottoman Empire. From the sixteenth to the nineteenth centuries Algeria posed a significant threat to all who used the nearby regions of the Mediterranean Sea. The pirates of what was at that time called the Barbary

Coast made a lucrative living by trading in slaves and by attacking passing shipping.

A French colony from 1848, Algeria won its independence in 1962 after eight years of bitter war. Then followed 30 years of peace, but since 1992 the country has been torn by violence once more. In a ruthless civil conflict between the government and an outlawed fundamentalist party, the Islamic Salvation Front (FIS), tens of thousands have died.

More than 90 percent of Algeria's people live on the narrow, fertile, discontinuous coastal strip on the Mediterranean. One-third of the population lives by farming, and it is here that most of the country's arable land is found—only 3 percent of the whole country. Inland, and to the south, are the Maritime Atlas Mountains. Their northern slopes have a relatively reliable rainfall and support a shrinking forest of pines, cedars, and evergreen and cork oaks. A high plateau about 250 km (150 miles) wide lies between the coastal range and the Atlas Saharien Mountains. Beyond these, all the way to the boundaries of Mali and Niger, stretches the sandy, rocky waste of the Sahara Desert, dotted here and there with small oasis settlements.

As much as 85 percent of Algeria's land area is desert. In many parts of the country rain almost never falls and the summer heat is intense. Along the Mediterranean coast, however, while the summers are hot and dry the winters are wet. Wildlife on the inland plateaus includes wild boar and gazelle; in the desert there are small mammals such as the jerboa and the Saharan hare.

Oil and natural gas are the foundation of Algeria's economy and over the years revenue from these sources has encouraged a wide range of industrial development. From the late 1960s, the country's economy was run as a centrally controlled state system along Soviet lines. This began to change following 1989 with the introduction of market mechanisms. The farming region along the northern coast produces wheat, barley, oats, grapes, and olives, and supplies a wide variety of early fruit and vegetables to markets in Europe.

Angola

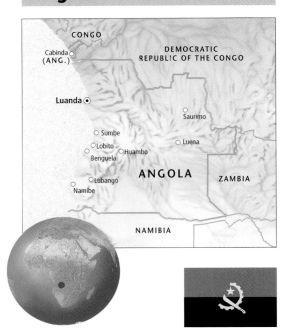

A large country on Africa's southwest coast, Angola is bordered by the states of the Democratic Republic of the Congo to the north, Zambia to the east, and Namibia to the south. The small but resource-rich province of Cabinda lies separated from the rest of Angola to the north of the Congo River. A Portuguese colony since the sixteenth century, Angola was the source of an estimated 3 million slaves who were sent to Brazil and other places across the Atlantic, largely to work on sugar plantations. The country received its independence in 1975 and for the next 20 years was wracked by civil war. The government, having established a Marxist one-party state, was then challenged by the forces of Jonas Savimbi, who was backed by the USA. The truce between the two parties, which came into force in 1994, did not last for long. In the late 1990s violence escalated, verging on civil war.

Angola can be divided into two main regions. There are the relatively narrow coastal plains from which rise an extensive tableland that dominates the rest of the country. Divided roughly east to west across the center, this tableland drains into the Congo Basin to the north, and into the rivers of the Zambeze Basin to the south and east. While the tableland is fairly level in the south, the highlands become mountainous in central and southwestern Angola. In the province of Cabinda there are dense tropical rainforests, and heavy rains can be expected for seven months of the year. Savanna woodland is found on much of the tableland, becoming mainly grassy plains to the south, dotted with acacia and baobab trees. The cold Benguela current that flows north from the southern Atlantic Ocean has a moderating effect on the heat of the coastal region. Toward Namibia on the southern border the coastal strip becomes desert.

Angola is rich in petroleum, gold, and diamonds, and has reserves of iron ore, phosphates, feldspar, bauxite, and uranium. It has large areas of forest, productive fisheries off the Atlantic coast, and extensive areas of arable land. While the country is capable of producing coffee, sisal, and cotton, the years of civil war have resulted in economic disarray and the country's output per capita is one of the lowest in the world. Subsistence agriculture supports up to 90 percent of the people and much of the nation's food has to be imported.

Fact File

OFFICIAL NAME Republic of Angola

FORM OF GOVERNMENT Republic with single legislative body (National Assembly)

CAPITAL Luanda

AREA 1,246,700 sq km (481,351 sq miles)

TIME ZONE GMT + 1 hour

POPULATION 11,177,537

PROJECTED POPULATION 2005 13,104,239

POPULATION DENSITY 9 per sq km (23.3 per sq mile)

LIFE EXPECTANCY 48.4

INFANT MORTALITY (PER 1,000) 129.2

OFFICIAL LANGUAGE Portuguese

OTHER LANGUAGES Bantu, other African languages

LITERACY RATE 42.5%

RELIGIONS Indigenous beliefs 47%, Roman Catholic 38%, Protestant 15%

ETHNIC GROUPS Mainly indigenous, including Ovimbundu 37%, Kimbundu 25%, Bakongo 13%; mixed European–African 2%, European 1%, other 22%

CURRENCY Kwanza

ECONOMY Agriculture 69%, services 21%, industry 10%

GNP PER CAPITA US$410

CLIMATE Mainly tropical with wet season November to April; semiarid in south and along coast

HIGHEST POINT Mt Môco 2,620 m (8,596 ft)

MAP REFERENCE Pages 368, 370

The Algerian town of Ghardaïa lies at the eastern end of the Grand Erg Occidental, on the fringe of the Sahara Desert (top left). Children in a canoe paddle through a village of stilt houses, situated on a river in Benin (right).

Benin

Benin is a small west African country facing the Gulf of Guinea. It was once part of the Kingdom of Benin, famous for the brass portrait heads made for the Oba and his court in the fifteenth century. By 1625 it was known as Abomey (later Dahomey). Slavery and slave-raiding were endemic, and grew when firearms and external slave markets became available. The town of Ouidah became the shipping point for several million slaves, mostly prisoners captured in raids by the Dahomeyans against their enemies. The captives were sent mainly to Brazil, and most Afro-Brazilian religious cults derive from this area. Under French control from 1850, the country became independent in 1960, eventually falling under the control of General Mathieu Kerekou, who changed its name to Benin. In the 1990s there were moves toward multi-party rule.

The Atakora Range (Chaine de l'Akatora) lies in northwestern Benin. To the northeast are the plains of the Niger, part of the boundary with the state of Niger being formed by the Niger River itself. Further south there are plateaus, and then a fertile plain where the Fon and Yoruba people live as subsistence farmers. Still further south, toward the Bight of Benin, lies a sandy strip with many lagoons. In the country's far north small numbers

of Fulani people continue to live as nomads. Also in the north are two wildlife parks—the Parc National de la Pendjan and the Parcs Nationaux du W. du Niger—shared with Burkina Faso and Niger.

Subsistence agriculture, cotton production, and regional trade remain fundamental to Benin's economy. Offshore oilfields promised much when they began producing in 1982, but were soon affected by a fall in petroleum prices. As well as crude oil Benin sells cotton, palm-oil products, cocoa, and peanuts. Goods in transit through the port of Cotonou to Niger are charged a fee, and this is an additional source of revenue. Although a World Bank reform program was adopted in 1991, inefficient state enterprises and an overstaffed civil service are inhibiting economic progress.

Fact File

OFFICIAL NAME Republic of Benin

FORM OF GOVERNMENT Republic with single legislative body (National Assembly)

CAPITAL Porto-Novo

AREA 112,620 sq km (43,483 sq miles)

TIME ZONE GMT + 1 hour

POPULATION 6,305,567

PROJECTED POPULATION 2005 7,662,158

POPULATION DENSITY 56 per sq km (145 per sq mile)

LIFE EXPECTANCY 54.1

INFANT MORTALITY (PER 1,000) 97.8

OFFICIAL LANGUAGE French

OTHER LANGUAGES Indigenous languages

LITERACY RATE 35.5%

RELIGIONS Indigenous beliefs 70%, Muslim 15%, Christian 15%

ETHNIC GROUPS Indigenous 99%, European and other 1%

CURRENCY CFA (Communauté Financière Africaine) franc

ECONOMY Agriculture 70%, services 23%, industry 7%

GNP PER CAPITA US$370

CLIMATE Tropical; hot and humid in south, drier in north

HIGHEST POINT Mt Tanekas 641 m (2,103 ft)

MAP REFERENCE Page 365

Botswana

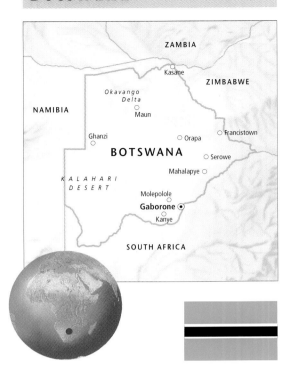

A large, dry, landlocked tableland, Botswana is bordered on the south by South Africa, a country with which it has strong historical and economic links. To the west is Namibia (the border touches on Zambia in the north near Victoria Falls) and to the northeast lies a 600 km (370 mile) frontier with Zimbabwe. Originally peopled by the nomadic San, also known as Bushmen, Botswana's more fertile eastern parts later became settled by Bantu Tswana. In the nineteenth century, after gold had been discovered near the Tati River, the area became the focus of a colonial dispute between the British and the Boers of neighboring Transvaal (now Gauteng) in South Africa. Britain established the British Bechuanaland Protectorate in 1885. This name and status within the British Empire was retained until independence in 1966, when Bechuanaland became Botswana.

Geographically a part of the southern African plateau, more than half of Botswana consists of the Kalahari Desert. Substantial parts of the remainder of the country consist of saltpans and swamps. There is little surface water except in the north and east, in the basins of the Okavango, Chobe, and Limpopo Rivers. Variations in climate and a limited rainfall enable a certain amount of scrub and thornbush to grow in the Kalahari. The dominant vegetation in Botswana is savanna grassland, which provides sufficient grazing for about 100,000 widely scattered Bantu cattle herders to make a living.

At the time of independence, cattle were almost the country's only export, and Botswana was one of the poorest countries in the world. Since that time the economy has been transformed by the development of mining. Both copper and nickel are exported but the main earner has been diamonds, providing as much as 80 percent of export revenue. Tourism is also important, the

A traditional dugout boat on the shore of the Okavango River in Botswana (right). Lions and vultures around a kill in Chobe National Park in northern Botswana (far right). Grass huts are used to store grain in a rural village in Burkina Faso (top right).

17 percent of Botswana's land area that is given over to national parks and game reserves attracting numerous visitors. A large proportion of the population still live as subsistence farmers raising cattle and growing crops such as maize, sorghum, vegetables, and fruit. Difficulties include an unemployment rate of 20 percent, overgrazing, and desertification.

Fact File

OFFICIAL NAME	Republic of Botswana
FORM OF GOVERNMENT	Republic with two legislative bodies (House of Chiefs and National Assembly)
CAPITAL	Gaborone
AREA	600,370 sq km (231,803 sq miles)
TIME ZONE	GMT + 2 hours
POPULATION	1,464,167
PROJECTED POPULATION 2005	1,537,747
POPULATION DENSITY	2.4 per sq km (6.2 per sq mile)
LIFE EXPECTANCY	60
INFANT MORTALITY (PER 1,000)	59.1
OFFICIAL LANGUAGE	English
OTHER LANGUAGES	Setswana and other indigenous languages
LITERACY RATE	68.7%
RELIGIONS	Indigenous beliefs 50%, Christian 50%
ETHNIC GROUPS	Tswana 94%, Khoikhoin 2.5%, Ndebele 1.3%, other 2.2%
CURRENCY	Pula
ECONOMY	Services 51%, mining and agriculture 49%
GNP PER CAPITA	US$3,020
CLIMATE	Semiarid to arid, with warm winters and hot summers
HIGHEST POINT	Tsodilo Hill 1,489 m (4,885 ft)
MAP REFERENCE	Pages 370–71

Burkina Faso

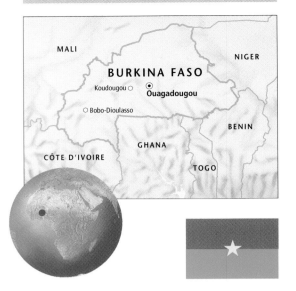

Burkina Faso is a landlocked African country on the southern edge of the Sahara Desert. It is the size of Italy but has difficulty supporting its people. The desertification of the Sahel—the fringe of the Sahara running from Senegal to Chad—has severely affected large areas, though the parched savanna of the north and east still supports a nomadic population of cattle-herding Fulani. French colonial control was established between 1895 and 1897, and independence came in 1960. There have been many military coups in the last 40 years, accompanied by waves of executions, mostly the result of tribal power struggles.

Near the capital city of Ouagadougou live the Mossi, the traditional rulers and the dominant tribal group, who have been in the region since the twelfth century. They grow sorghum and millet for food, and cultivate cash crops such as peanuts, cotton, and sesame seeds.

In the west and south is a sandstone plateau, while in the southwest are the spectacular Banfora Cliffs. The plateau is cut by the watercourses of the Red, White, and Black Volta Rivers (Volta Rouge, Blanche, and Noir), draining toward Ghana. Although these valleys have more farming potential than the arid north, they cannot yet be developed because of the tsetse and simulium flies that flourish near their rivers. At present the diseases carried by these insects prevent settlement.

Burkina Faso has few natural resources. There is manganese in the far northeast, but to develop it a 350 km (220 mile) extension of the Côte d'Ivoire railway from Abidjan is needed. Industries consist of unprofitable state corporations, a legacy of the country's years as a one-party socialist state. About 10 percent of the land area is arable and more than 80 percent of the people work on the land. Drought has caused acute agricultural difficulties and the country depends heavily on foreign aid. Many people have emigrated, their wages, sent back from places such as the Côte d'Ivoire, providing much-needed income for their families. Tourists visit the Parcs Nationaux du W. du Niger, in the east—a reserve shared with Niger and Benin.

Fact File

OFFICIAL NAME Burkina Faso

FORM OF GOVERNMENT Republic with single legislative body (Assembly of People's Deputies)

CAPITAL Ouagadougou

AREA 274,200 sq km (105,869 sq miles)

TIME ZONE GMT

POPULATION 11,575,898

PROJECTED POPULATION 2005 13,565,940

POPULATION DENSITY 40.7 per sq km (105.4 per sq mile)

LIFE EXPECTANCY 45.9

INFANT MORTALITY (PER 1,000) 107.2

OFFICIAL LANGUAGE French

OTHER LANGUAGES Indigenous languages

LITERACY RATE 18.7%

RELIGIONS Muslim 50%, indigenous beliefs 40%, Roman Catholic 8%, Protestant 2%

ETHNIC GROUPS More than 50 indigenous tribes: the largest Mossi 48%, Fulani 10%, Mande 9%; other including Gurunsi, Senufo, Lobi, Bobo 33%

CURRENCY CFA (Communauté Financière Africaine) franc

ECONOMY Agriculture 87%, services 9%, industry 4%

GNP PER CAPITA US$230

CLIMATE Tropical, with warm, dry winters and hot, wet summers

HIGHEST POINT Tena Kourou 749 m (2,457 ft)

MAP REFERENCE Page 364

Burundi

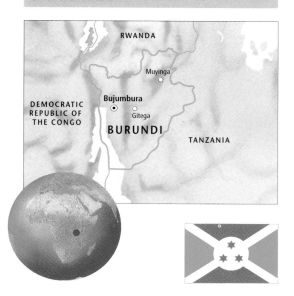

Burundi is a small, landlocked country in central Africa. Some time in the past a tall cattle-herding people known as the Tutsi (or Watussi) moved into Burundi from the north. Originating on the Upper Nile, the Tutsi established themselves as a ruling class over the much more numerous and physically shorter Bantu farmers called Hutu. This deeply divided social order has been the source of periodic outbreaks of violence, hundreds of thousands of people having been massacred by both sides. The region's original inhabitants were the forest-dwelling Twa (or Pygmy), but few remain.

Burundi's topography resembles other lands along the Rift Valley. A narrow strip along the northeastern shore of Lake Tanganyika forms one boundary, which then extends up the valley of the River Ruzizi in the direction of Lake Kivu. From this lowland area an escarpment rises steeply up to the highlands which make up the rest of the country. The mountainous ridge east of Lake Tanganyika forms a watershed between the river systems of the Congo and the Nile. On its eastern slopes the land then falls away into the valley of the Ruvuvu River as it makes its way toward Tanzania and Lake Victoria. Malaria in the lowlands is endemic, a situation the continuing civil disorder makes difficult to change.

About 90 percent of Burundi's people depend on subsistence agriculture, growing corn, sorghum, sweet potatoes, bananas, and manioc. The Tutsi herders produce meat and milk. Export earnings come mainly from coffee, which contributes 81 percent, along with tea, cotton grown in the Ruzizi Valley, and hides. Three factors affect foreign exchange earnings and government revenue: the vagaries of the climate, international coffee prices, and civil unrest. Even when the first two are favorable, the struggle between Tutsi and Hutu which has been a continuing feature of Burundi life since 1993 has virtually brought cash cropping to a halt. Under the direction of the International Monetary Fund the government has tried to diversify exports but continuing discord makes it difficult to implement reforms.

Fact File

OFFICIAL NAME Republic of Burundi

FORM OF GOVERNMENT Republic with single legislative body (National Assembly)

CAPITAL Bujumbura

AREA 27,830 sq km (10,745 sq miles)

TIME ZONE GMT + 2 hours

POPULATION 5,735,937

PROJECTED POPULATION 2005 6,703,652

POPULATION DENSITY 206.1 per sq km (533.8 per sq mile)

LIFE EXPECTANCY 45.4

INFANT MORTALITY (PER 1,000) 99.4

OFFICIAL LANGUAGES Kirundi, French

OTHER LANGUAGES Swahili

LITERACY RATE 34.6%

RELIGIONS Roman Catholic 62%, indigenous beliefs 32%, Protestant 5%, Muslim 1%

ETHNIC GROUPS Hutu 85%, Tutsi 14%, Twa (Pygmy) 1%

CURRENCY Burundi franc

ECONOMY Agriculture 92%, services 6%, industry 2%

GNP PER CAPITA US$160

CLIMATE Tropical, with wet seasons March to May and September to December

HIGHEST POINT Mt Heha 2,760 m (9,055 ft)

MAP REFERENCE Page 369

Africa

Cameroon

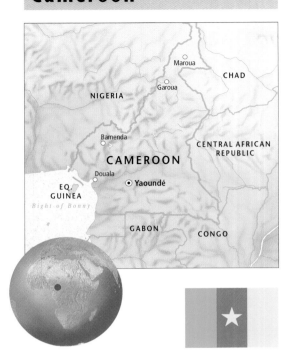

Fact File

OFFICIAL NAME Republic of Cameroon

FORM OF GOVERNMENT Republic with single legislative body (National Assembly)

CAPITAL Yaoundé

AREA 475,440 sq km (183,567 sq miles)

TIME ZONE GMT + 1 hour

POPULATION 15,456,092

PROJECTED POPULATION 2005 18,175,654

POPULATION DENSITY 32.5 per sq km (84.2 per sq mile)

LIFE EXPECTANCY 51.3

INFANT MORTALITY (PER 1,000) 75.7

OFFICIAL LANGUAGES French, English

OTHER LANGUAGES 24 African languages

LITERACY RATE 62.1%

RELIGIONS Indigenous beliefs 51%, Christian 33%, Muslim 16%

ETHNIC GROUPS Cameroon Highlanders 31%, Equatorial Bantu 19%, Kirdi 11%, Fulani 10%, Northwestern Bantu 8%, Eastern Nigritic 7%; other African 13%; non-African 1%

CURRENCY CFA (Communauté Financière Africaine) franc

ECONOMY Agriculture 75%, industry and transport 12%, services 13%

GNP PER CAPITA US$950

CLIMATE Tropical in south and along coast, semiarid in north

HIGHEST POINT Mt Cameroon 4,095 m (13,435 ft)

MAP REFERENCE Page 365

The African state of Cameroon is on the Gulf of Guinea, with Nigeria to the west and Equatorial Guinea and Congo to the south. The Portuguese arrived in 1472, and Cameroon is named after the prawns, *camaràos*, they found here. A German colony from 1884, and later ruled by both British and French, Cameroon became independent in 1960. Although it was a one-party state for 30 years, opposition parties have been allowed since 1991.

One of the more prosperous African countries, Cameroon is home to more than 200 distinct tribes and peoples. There is also a broad distinction between the English- and French-speaking parts of the population. In response to the demands of the former, and the protests and demonstrations they made in 1996, Cameroon applied for entry and was admitted to the British Commonwealth.

The country can be divided into four regions. First, an area of tropical forest, plateau, and coastal plain extends from the southern frontier to the Sanaga River. Most of the population is concentrated in this southern part. Second, north of this river and Lake Mbakaou (M'Bakaou Reservoir), the land rises to the highlands of the Adamaoua Massif. Third is the mountainous western extension of the Adamaoua Massif which includes Mt Cameroon. Occasionally active, this 4,070 m (13,353 ft) volcanic cone is the highest mountain in west Africa. Fourth is the arid savanna north of the Benue (Bénoué River and toward Lake Chad (Lac Tchad). This region of savanna supports elephant, lion, and leopard, and a national park—the Parc National de la Bénoué—has been established there.

Cameroon's prosperity was helped by the oil boom between 1970 and 1985. Since then conditions have been more difficult, with prices falling for coffee, cocoa, and petroleum, the country's major exports. Three-quarters of the population are farmers who, in addition to coffee and cocoa, grow bananas, oilseed, grains, and manioc. Cameroon is self-sufficient in food, but a range of other economic difficulties exists. Serious inflation occurred in 1994. The dismantling of unproductive state industries has been slow to show results, and the swollen ranks of the civil service remain a fiscal burden.

Cape Verde

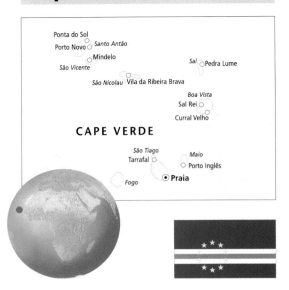

Cape Verde consists of two small groups of islands 560 km (350 miles) off Dakar, on the westernmost part of west Africa. These islands were discovered, uninhabited, by Portuguese navigators in 1456. For several centuries, until 1876, the islands were used by slave-traders as a depot for assembling slaves and provisioning ships. As with other places involved in the slave trade, this activity influenced the composition of the population, with 71 percent being today of Afro-Portuguese background. Portuguese colonial administration came to an end with independence in 1975, but because of limited opportunities on the islands more Cape Verdeans now live abroad than at home. Remittances are an important source of domestic income.

The northern group of islands is called the Barlavento or windward group; the southern is called the Sotavento or leeward group. Volcanic, with slopes weathered into unusual shapes by the wind, the land leads steeply up from the sea to mountainous heights. The active volcano of Mt Cano on the island of Fogo in the southern group is the highest point. The most densely populated areas are the coastal plain of São Tiago in the southern group, and Santa Antão and São Vicente in the northern group. A chronic lack of water makes agriculture difficult, most of the productive farming being done in a small number of irrigated inland valleys. Droughts regularly devastate the crops of maize, beans, and sweet potatoes on which the majority of Cape Verdeans live. The effects of the drought that lasted from 1968 to 1982 were so severe that some 40,000 people emigrated to Portugal.

On the economic front Cape Verde faces a number of severe problems. The natural resource base is limited. The only minerals of any significance are salt and pozzolana, a volcanic rock that is used for making cement. Only two food products are exported—fish and bananas, each representing one-third of total exports. Although almost 70 percent of the population lives in the countryside, the gross national product share of agriculture is only 13 percent, the tuna catch accounting for 4 percent of that figure. About 90 percent of food is imported and Cape Verde is heavily dependent on foreign aid.

Fact File

OFFICIAL NAME Republic of Cape Verde

FORM OF GOVERNMENT Republic with single legislative body (People's National Assembly)

CAPITAL Praia

AREA 4,030 sq km (1,556 sq miles)

TIME ZONE GMT – 1 hour

POPULATION 405,748

PROJECTED POPULATION 2005 438,465

POPULATION DENSITY 100.7 per sq km (260.8 per sq mile)

LIFE EXPECTANCY 71

INFANT MORTALITY (PER 1,000) 45.5

OFFICIAL LANGUAGE Portuguese

OTHER LANGUAGES Crioulo (blend of Portuguese and West African languages)

LITERACY RATE 69.9%

RELIGIONS Roman Catholic and indigenous beliefs, often in combination 98%; Protestant 2%

ETHNIC GROUPS Mixed African–European 71%, African 28%, European 1%

CURRENCY Cape Verdean escudo

ECONOMY Agriculture 66%, services 20%, industry 14%

GNP PER CAPITA US$9,602

CLIMATE Arid, with warm, dry summers

HIGHEST POINT Pico (Mt Cano) 2,829 m (9,281 ft)

MAP REFERENCE Page 360

A small village on Cameroon's arid savanna (left). Falls on the Kotto River in the Central African Republic (top right).

Central African Republic

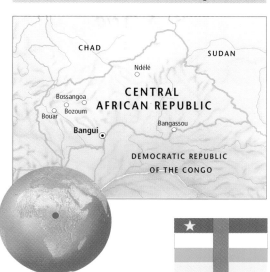

The Central African Republic (CAR) is a land-locked plateau just north of the equator. It is bordered on the west and north by Cameroon and Chad, and on the east and south by Sudan, the Democratic Republic of Congo, and Congo. By the time of European exploration the population of forest-dwelling Pygmies was much reduced, having been largely replaced by Bantu and Azande people. The region was for centuries used as a slave source by African slave-traders from the Sudan. When France took control in 1911 it ended slave-trading. The CAR was run as part of French Equatorial Africa until independence in 1958.

The average elevation of the CAR plateau is between 2,000 and 2,500 m (6,500 and 8,000 ft). These uplands form a watershed dividing the Congo and Nile river basins. North of the high ground of the Massif des Bongos the land drains toward the interior along water courses into swamps in southern Chad. South of this massif numerous rivers feed into the Ubangi. To the west the Massif du Yadé forms a boundary with Cameroon.

In the south and southeast are forests containing hardwoods such as mahogany and ebony. Dense rainforest in this area provides one of the last homes of the lowland gorilla. Much of the rest of the land is savanna. Plantation forestry undertaken by foreign timber interests has in some places added significantly to natural soil erosion.

The CAR economy is based on subsistence agriculture combined with forestry. Food crops include manioc, yams, millet, maize, and bananas. Cotton, coffee, and tobacco are grown for cash. Industries include sawmills, textiles, footwear, and bicycle assembly. About 80 percent of export revenue comes from diamond mining.

The country's economic prospects are constrained by its position, its limited resources, its unskilled workforce, and its poor infrastructure. In addition, tuberculosis, leprosy, and sleeping sickness are widespread. These factors are likely to keep the CAR dependent on foreign aid for some time.

Fact File

OFFICIAL NAME Central African Republic

FORM OF GOVERNMENT Republic with single legislative body (National Assembly)

CAPITAL Bangui

AREA 622,980 sq km (240,533 sq miles)

TIME ZONE GMT + 1 hour

POPULATION 3,444,951

PROJECTED POPULATION 2005 3,904,795

POPULATION DENSITY 5.5 per sq km (14.2 per sq mile)

LIFE EXPECTANCY 47.2

INFANT MORTALITY (PER 1,000) 103.4

OFFICIAL LANGUAGE French

OTHER LANGUAGES Sangho, Arabic, Hunsa, Swahili

LITERACY RATE 57.2%

RELIGIONS Protestant 25%, Roman Catholic 25%, indigenous beliefs 24%, Muslim 15%, other 11%

ETHNIC GROUPS Baya 34%, Banda 27%, Mandjia 21%, Sara 10%, Mboum 4%, M'Baka 4%

CURRENCY CFA (Communauté Financière Africaine) franc

ECONOMY Agriculture 85%, services 12%, industry 3%

GNP PER CAPITA US$340

CLIMATE Tropical, with hot, dry winters and hot, wet summers

HIGHEST POINT Mt Kayagangir 1,420 m (4,659 ft)

MAP REFERENCE Pages 365, 366

Africa

Chad

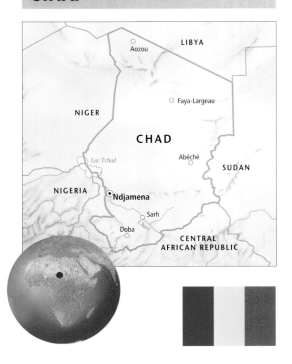

Chad is a landlocked north African country twice the size of France. Much of it is semidesert and thinly populated, and it is one of the poorest and least developed countries in the world. Chad was conquered by the Sudanese warlord Rabah Zobeir late in the nineteenth century, but with 200 distinct ethnic groups in the population a sense of national unity has been slow to emerge. After France established control of the region in 1911 it became for 50 years part of French Equatorial Africa, achieving independence in 1960. Since then there has been almost constant civil war, aggravated by the main ethnic divide—that between the desert-dwelling Muslim Arabs in the north and the non-Muslim African farmers in the south.

The country can be loosely divided into four regions. In the center are broad, arid savanna plains. To the north are deserts with large areas of mobile sand dunes along the southern Sahara. In the northwest are the volcanic mountains of the Tibesti, rising to the 3,415 m (11,204 ft) peak of Emi Koussi. Though surrounded by desert these mountains attract rain, and some farming takes place in the valleys. In the south the valleys of the Chari and Logone Rivers support most of Chad's

agriculture, including cotton-growing. Both these rivers drain into Lake Chad (Lac Tchad). But a series of droughts has reduced them to little more than streams, while the shallow and marshy Lake Chad itself is steadily shrinking as the desert advances.

Chad's economic difficulties have both political and climatic causes. Civil war in the 1980s disrupted agriculture and spread lasting division, while continuing government corruption and its inability to pay its employees have led to resentment in the civil service. Desertification has had an impoverishing effect, especially among pastoral peoples like the Fulbe in the Sahel. While oil production from a field discovered at Doba might provide a significant long-term source of revenue, 80 percent of the population is likely to depend on subsistence farming for some time and the country will continue to rely on foreign aid.

Fact File

OFFICIAL NAME	Republic of Chad
FORM OF GOVERNMENT	Republic with single legislative body (Higher Transitional Council)
CAPITAL	Ndjamena
AREA	1,284,000 sq km (495,752 sq miles)
TIME ZONE	GMT + 1 hour
POPULATION	7,557,436
PROJECTED POPULATION 2005	8,846,000
POPULATION DENSITY	5.9 per sq km (15.3 per sq mile)
LIFE EXPECTANCY	48.6
INFANT MORTALITY (PER 1,000)	115.3
OFFICIAL LANGUAGES	French, Arabic
OTHER LANGUAGES	More than 100 indigenous languages
LITERACY RATE	47%
RELIGIONS	Muslim 50%, Christian 25%, indigenous beliefs 25%
ETHNIC GROUPS	More than 200 indigenous groups: north mainly Arabic, south mainly African
CURRENCY	CFA (Communauté Financière Africaine) franc
ECONOMY	Agriculture 85%, services and industry 15%
GNP PER CAPITA	US$180
CLIMATE	Tropical in south, arid in north
HIGHEST POINT	Emi Koussi 3,415 m (11,204 ft)
MAP REFERENCE	Pages 362, 365, 366

Comoros

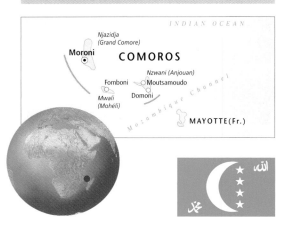

The Comoros are a group of islands in the Mozambique Channel, lying between northern Madagascar and the African coast. Some of the smaller ones are coral islets. The larger islands are volcanic, and three of the four largest constitute the Republic of the Comoros. (Another large island, Mayotte, chose to remain a French dependency.)

For centuries, Indian and Arab traders have sailed across the Indian Ocean and worked their way along the coast of east Africa, visiting the Comoros as they went. The Comoran population reflects this history. There are large groups with African, Arab, Indonesian, and Madagascan backgrounds, and even a minority with Polynesian ancestors. France controlled the islands after declaring them a colony in 1912. They obtained their independence in 1975.

The island of Njazidja (formerly Grande Comore) consists mainly of a rocky lava plateau, rising at its southern end to the active volcano of Kartala. On the coast is the national capital, Moroni. Because of the porous volcanic soils, rain quickly drains away, and despite heavy seasonal falls rainforests are only found on the mountain's upper slopes. On the island of Nzwani (formerly Anjouan) soils are more fertile but clearing of land without proper terracing has led to serious erosion. The island of Mwali (formerly Mohéli) is the smallest of the group. It has dense forests and fertile valleys.

An antelope in Chad (left). A nomadic family in Chad outside their home (top). A village in the Congo highlands (right).

Comoros has few natural resources. Subsistence agriculture is the traditional way of life, the main food crops being cassava, mountain rice, and sweet potato. Nevertheless, the islands are not self-sufficient in food, and rice accounts for 90 percent of all imports. Cattle and goats are kept—the latter are another cause of erosion. There are a few small hydroelectric plants; otherwise, fuel must be imported. Revenue-earning exports are vanilla, cloves, perfume oil, and copra.

The government is trying to diversify exports, privatize industrial enterprises, and reduce the high population growth rate, but its authority has been weakened by chronic political instability and several attempted coups. Foreign aid is likely to be needed for some time.

Fact File

OFFICIAL NAME Federal Islamic Republic of the Comoros

FORM OF GOVERNMENT Federal republic with single legislative body (National Assembly)

CAPITAL Moroni

AREA 2,170 sq km (838 sq miles)

TIME ZONE GMT + 3 hours

POPULATION 562,723

PROJECTED POPULATION 2005 676,257

POPULATION DENSITY 259.3 per sq km (671.5 per sq mile)

LIFE EXPECTANCY 60.9

INFANT MORTALITY (PER 1,000) 81.6

OFFICIAL LANGUAGES Arabic, French

OTHER LANGUAGE Comoran (blend of Swahili and Arabic)

LITERACY RATE 56.7%

RELIGIONS Sunni Muslim 86%, Roman Catholic 14%

ETHNIC GROUPS Mixture of Malagasy, African, Malay and Arab groups

CURRENCY Comoran franc

ECONOMY Agriculture 80%, government 3%, other 17%

GNP PER CAPITA US$470

CLIMATE Tropical, with wet season November to May

HIGHEST POINT Kartala 2,361 m (7,746 ft)

MAP REFERENCE Page 372

Congo

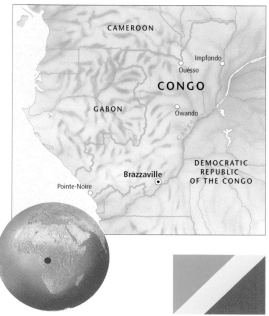

From the Atlantic coast, Congo extends 1,000 km (600 miles) inland to the border of the Central African Republic. Its history is obscure, although the first inhabitants may have been Pygmies. Later it was home to the Kongo peoples who supplied slaves for Portuguese traders. In the nineteenth century it was explored by the French–Italian Pierre Savorgnan de Brazza, who gave his name to the capital city, and whose activities led to the region becoming part of French Equatorial Africa in 1891. Congo has been independent since 1960.

Ten years after independence, Congo declared itself a People's Republic and Africa's first communist state. Since 1991, however, there have been attempts to introduce the principles of legal opposition and multi-party democracy. Road transport within Congo is hampered by tropical rains that make the unpaved roads unuseable but water transport to the interior and the northeast is comparatively easy. Two mighty rivers, the Congo and the Ubangi, provide a commercially navigable highway along virtually the entire eastern frontier.

From a coastal strip on the Atlantic seaboard, the Rivers Kouilou and Niari lead up to the heights of the Massif du Mayombé. This range is crossed by a spectacular French-built railway joining Brazzaville with the port of Pointe-Noire. The Congo below Brazzaville has many cataracts, and the railway was built to carry freight around them. Beyond the massif the land falls away northward to the central plateau, where numerous rivers drain east into the Ubangi and the Congo itself.

Though more than half the Congolese live in towns, subsistence agriculture engages one-third of the workforce, and most of the food produced and consumed is cassava. Rice, maize, and vegetables are also grown, and coffee and cocoa are exported. Some 60 percent of the country is still covered in tropical forest. Timber was once a leading export, but today 90 percent of exports consists of oil. Despite its comparative wealth, the government has mortgaged a large part of its oil earnings for expensive development projects.

Fact File

OFFICIAL NAME People's Republic of the Congo

FORM OF GOVERNMENT Republic with two legislative bodies (Senate and National Assembly)

CAPITAL Brazzaville

AREA 342,000 sq km (132,046 sq miles)

TIME ZONE GMT + 1 hour

POPULATION 2,716,814

PROJECTED POPULATION 2005 3,072,457

POPULATION DENSITY 7.9 per sq km (20.5 per sq mile)

LIFE EXPECTANCY 47.1

INFANT MORTALITY (PER 1,000) 100.6

OFFICIAL LANGUAGE French

OTHER LANGUAGES African languages (particularly Lingala, Kikongo and Monokutuba)

LITERACY RATE 73.9%

RELIGIONS Christian 50%, indigenous 48%, Muslim 2%

ETHNIC GROUPS About 75 different tribes: Kongo 48%, Sangha 20%, Teke 17%; other 15%

CURRENCY CFA (Communauté Financière Africaine) franc

ECONOMY Agriculture 75%, industry and services 25%

GNP PER CAPITA US$680

CLIMATE Tropical, with wet season March to June

HIGHEST POINT Mt Berongou 903 m (2,963 ft)

MAP REFERENCE Page 368

Congo, Democratic Republic of

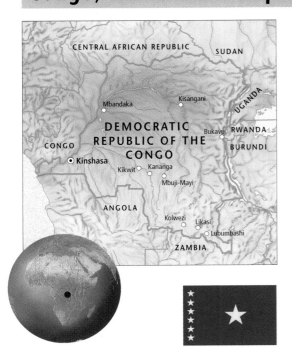

The Democratic Republic of the Congo (DRC) is the centerpiece of central Africa. It is the third largest country on the continent after Algeria and Sudan and has one of the largest navigable rivers in the world. Historically occupied by the Kongo, Luba, Lunda, and Azande peoples, this enormous region fell into the hands of King Leopold of Belgium in 1885, who exploited it as a private domain. After international condemnation of his brutal rule, in 1908 it became a colony of Belgium. The country won its independence in 1960.

Since that time, 35 years of dictatorial mismanagement and corruption as a one-party state under the control of President Mobutu Sese Seko (who died in 1997) have brought the DRC to the point of collapse. The troubles of its neighbors have added to its own. War and disorder in Sudan, Rwanda, Burundi, and Angola have driven hundreds of thousands of refugees across the borders into the DRC. A military occupation of Kinshasa was successful in bringing the Mobutu regime to an end in 1997. The benefits of this transfer of power have yet to be seen.

Geographically the DRC is dominated by a single feature—the immense basin of the Congo River. The eastern rim of this basin is formed by the Mitumba Mountains (Monts Mitumbe) along the Rift Valley, and the volcanic Ruwenzori Range. In the far southeast Lake Mweru feeds into the Congo's main northward-flowing tributary, the Lualaba. Looping north and west in a great horseshoe, the Congo is joined on the borders of the Central African Republic by the Ubangi. After several cascades below Kinshasa, as it descends from the central plateau, the Congo empties into the Atlantic Ocean. The equatorial climate of the main river basin supports one of the world's most extensive rainforests, home to rare animals such as okapi and gorilla. The savanna grasslands of the east and south are home to giraffe, lion, antelope and rhinoceros.

Potentially one of Africa's richest countries, the DRC is currently one of its poorest. Most of its people try to survive the breakdown of civil society by subsistence farming and petty trade.

Cash crops such as coffee, sugar, and palm oil continue to be produced, but a severe lack of infrastructure hampers trade. Meanwhile, hyperinflation, large government deficits, and falling mineral production mean that no end to the nation's economic difficulties is yet in sight.

Fact File

OFFICIAL NAME	Democratic Republic of the Congo
FORM OF GOVERNMENT	Presidential rule
CAPITAL	Kinshasa
AREA	2,345,410 sq km (905,563 sq miles)
TIME ZONE	GMT + 1/2 hour
POPULATION	50,481,305
PROJECTED POPULATION 2005	60,547,672
POPULATION DENSITY	21.5 per sq km (55.7 per sq mile)
LIFE EXPECTANCY	49.4
INFANT MORTALITY (PER 1,000)	99.5
OFFICIAL LANGUAGE	French
OTHER LANGUAGES	Lingala, Kingwana, Kikongo, Tshiluba
LITERACY RATE	76.4%
RELIGIONS	Roman Catholic 50%, Protestant 20%, Kimbanguist 10%, Muslim 10%, other indigenous beliefs 10%
ETHNIC GROUPS	More than 200 indigenous groups, mostly of Bantu origin: Kongo, Luba, Mongo, Mangbetu-Azande 51%; other 48%
CURRENCY	New zaire
ECONOMY	Agriculture 72%, services 15%, industry 13%
GNP PER CAPITA	Not available
CLIMATE	Tropical; wet season north of equator from April to October, wet season south of equator from November to March
HIGHEST POINT	Mt Stanley 5,110 m (16,765 ft)
MAP REFERENCE	Pages 368–69

A traditional village of mud huts with thatched roofs in the Côte d'Ivoire (below). Cloth being woven on hand looms in the Côte d'Ivoire (top right). An aerial view of the city of Djibouti, on the Gulf of Aden (far right).

Côte d'Ivoire

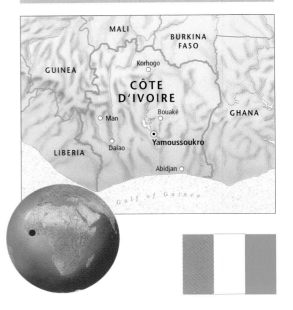

Côte d'Ivoire (Ivory Coast) is a west African country on the Gulf of Guinea. In the eighteenth century it was conquered by Baule people from Ghana. In 1893 it became a French colony, achieving independence in 1960. Since then, while retaining a close association with France, Côte d'Ivoire has been a more liberal and commercially oriented society than the socialist states established elsewhere in Africa in the 1960s. This, combined with political stability, has made it relatively prosperous. Under the 30-year leadership of Félix Houphouet-Boigny (who died in 1993) investment was secure, and most of this period saw sustained economic growth.

A sandy strip of land some 64 km (40 miles) wide runs along the shore of the Atlantic, broken by sandbars and lagoons around Abidjan. Coastal shipping has always had trouble on the west African coast where there is heavy surf and there are no natural harbors. French construction of the Vridi Canal, giving access to Abidjan through the sandbars to the sea, created a valuable deep-water port. From the coast the land rises gently, two rainy seasons and an equatorial climate providing a covering of rainforest further inland. There are three major national parks, with wildlife including elephant and pygmy hippopotamus.

Deforestation is a concern as hardwoods such as mahogany and ebony are felled. Growing in the place of native forest is plantation teak. Farther north the landscape changes to savanna grassland. Highlands are found in the northwest.

Côte d'Ivoire has varied mineral resources—petroleum, diamonds, manganese, bauxite, and copper—and is one of the world's main producers of coffee, cocoa beans, and palm oil. A large percentage of the population is engaged in farming, forestry, and livestock raising. Difficulties arise because of fluctuating coffee and cocoa prices but during the 1990s Côte d'Ivoire prospered, due mainly to the growth of new exports such as pineapples and rubber, trade and banking liberalization, and offshore oil and gas discoveries.

Fact File

OFFICIAL NAME Republic of Côte d'Ivoire

FORM OF GOVERNMENT Republic with single legislative body (National Assembly)

CAPITAL Yamoussoukro

AREA 322,460 sq km (124,502 sq miles)

TIME ZONE GMT

POPULATION 15,818,068

PROJECTED POPULATION 2005 18,303,059

POPULATION DENSITY 49.1 per sq km (127.1 per sq mile)

LIFE EXPECTANCY 46.1

INFANT MORTALITY (PER 1,000) 94.2

OFFICIAL LANGUAGE French

OTHER LANGUAGES Indigenous languages, particularly Dioula

LITERACY RATE 39.4%

RELIGIONS Indigenous beliefs 63%, Muslim 25%, Christian 12%

ETHNIC GROUPS About 60 different indigenous groups: Baule 23%, Bete 18%, Senoufou 15%, other 44%

CURRENCY CFA (Communauté Financière Africaine) franc

ECONOMY Agriculture 70%, services 25%, industry 5%

GNP PER CAPITA US$660

CLIMATE Tropical, but drier in the north

HIGHEST POINT Mt Nimba 1,752 m (5,748 ft)

MAP REFERENCE Page 364

Djibouti

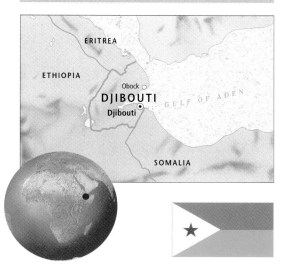

One of the smallest African countries, Djibouti stands at the entrance to the Red Sea from the Gulf of Aden. This strategic location near the world's busiest shipping lanes has resulted in it being used as a base by European nations for a hundred years. After the construction of the Suez Canal, the British and French took an interest in Djibouti as a way of protecting their investment in the Canal route to Europe, the town of Djibouti becoming the capital of French Somaliland in 1892. Although Djibouti won independence in 1977, France continues to play a role in its affairs.

Since 1977 there has been a continuous political struggle between the majority Issa (who are Somali) and the minority Afar (also known as Danakil). Somalia, across the southeastern border, supports the Issa. Eritrea, to the north, supports the Afar, as does Ethiopia. Thus, both Issa and Afar have numerous external allies watching over their interests and inclined to interfere. The port of Djibouti is also the terminus of rail traffic for the vast landlocked hinterland of Ethiopia, a crucial matter for that state.

Djibouti is one of the hottest places on earth, little rain falls, and water is in high demand. A subterranean river named the Ambouli is one essential source. Two-thirds of the population live in the capital city itself. Those who live elsewhere mostly inhabit the relatively fertile coastal strip along the Gulf of Tadjoura (Golfe de Tadjoura),

avoiding the burning interior plateau and its volcanic wastes. Almost 90 percent of the interior terrain is desert, with a vegetation of scrub and desert thorns. Here, nomadic goat and camel herders eke out a living.

Djibouti's economy is that of a free trade zone providing essential services for the region. It has few natural resources (though geothermal energy is being developed, and natural gas has been found), little industry, and agricultural production mainly provides fruit and vegetables for domestic consumption. The services it renders are those of a transit port, of great value to Ethiopia and Somalia, and of an international depot and refueling center. Originally established by the French in the nineteenth century, the port is now being developed as a container facility.

Fact File

OFFICIAL NAME Republic of Djibouti

FORM OF GOVERNMENT Republic with single legislative body (Chamber of Deputies)

CAPITAL Djibouti

AREA 22,000 sq km (8,494 sq miles)

TIME ZONE GMT + 3 hours

POPULATION 447,439

PROJECTED POPULATION 2005 516,114

POPULATION DENSITY 20.3 per sq km (52.6 per sq mile)

LIFE EXPECTANCY 51.5

INFANT MORTALITY (PER 1,000) 100.2

OFFICIAL LANGUAGES Arabic, French

OTHER LANGUAGES Somali, Afar

LITERACY RATE 45%

RELIGIONS Muslim 94%, Christian 6%

ETHNIC GROUPS Somali 60%, Afar 35%, other (including French, Arab, Ethiopian, and Italian) 5%

CURRENCY Djiboutian franc

ECONOMY Services 75%, agriculture 14%, industry 11%

GNP PER CAPITA Not available (est. US$766–3,035)

CLIMATE Semiarid; particularly hot on coast

HIGHEST POINT Mousa Alli (Musa Ālī Terara) 2,063 m (6,767 ft)

MAP REFERENCE Page 367

Egypt

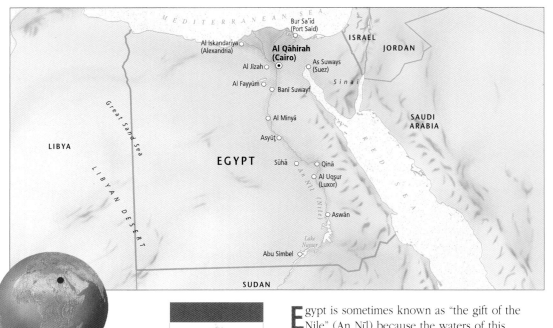

Fact File

OFFICIAL NAME Arab Republic of Egypt

FORM OF GOVERNMENT Republic with two legislative bodies (Advisory Council and People's Assembly)

CAPITAL Al Qāhirah (Cairo)

AREA 1,001,450 sq km (386,660 sq miles)

TIME ZONE GMT + 2 hours

POPULATION 67,273,906

PROJECTED POPULATION 2005 74,635,910

POPULATION DENSITY 67.2 per sq km (174 per sq mile)

LIFE EXPECTANCY 62.4

INFANT MORTALITY (PER 1,000) 67.5

OFFICIAL LANGUAGE Arabic

OTHER LANGUAGES English, French, ethnic languages

LITERACY RATE 50.5%

RELIGIONS Muslim (mostly Sunni) 94%, other (including Coptic Christian) 6%

ETHNIC GROUPS Eastern Hamitic (Egyptian, Bedouin, and Berber) 95%; other (including Greek, Nubian, Armenian, Italian, and French) 5%

CURRENCY Egyptian pound

ECONOMY Services 55%, agriculture 34%, industry 11%

GDP PER CAPITA US$790

CLIMATE Mainly arid, with mild winters and hot, dry summers

HIGHEST POINT Jabal Kātrīnā 2,637 m (8,649 ft)

MAP REFERENCE Pages 362–63

E
gypt is sometimes known as "the gift of the Nile" (An Nīl) because the waters of this famous river have always been the lifeblood of the country. Every year, until the Aswan High Dam was built, the Nile would flood, spreading fertile silt across the floor of the valley. It was in the Nile Valley that Egyptian civilization began, 6,000 years ago, and the country was the first to have a society organized along political lines. The Great Pyramid itself, still one of the largest structures in the world, was built 5,000 years ago. Since then innumerable rulers and conquerors have come and gone—Persians, Greeks, and Romans being followed by the seventh-century conquests of Mahomet's followers and the conversion of the region to Islam. During the nineteenth century, after the construction of the Suez Canal in 1869, Egypt came increasingly under the influence of the French and the British. Britain declared it a protectorate in 1914. It was not until 1953 that Egypt became an independent republic.

Physical features and land use

Egypt is defined by the valley of the Nile and the spreading deserts on either side. The Nile rises at Lake Victoria, further south, and enters the country across the southern border, from Sudan. It first fills huge Lake Nasser, formed by the Aswan High Dam, which was completed in 1965. It then makes an eastward bend near Luxor before flowing steadily north. At Cairo the river fans out into a broad delta before entering the Mediterranean. The area north of Cairo is often known as Lower Egypt and the area south of Cairo as Upper Egypt.

Although the lands of the valley and the delta constitute only 3 percent of Egypt's total land area, this is where 99 percent of the people live and where nearly all agricultural activity takes place. West of the Nile, extending to the Libyan border, lies the Western (or Libyan) Desert. This arid limestone region consists of low valleys and scarps, and in the north contains a large area below sea level called the Qattara Depression. Scattered across the desert are isolated fertile oases where date palms grow. It is hoped to increase the agricultural production of these oases by using deep artesian bores.

Between the Nile and the Red Sea is the Eastern (or Arabian) Desert. Here, grasses, tamarisks, and mimosas grow, providing desert nomads with feed for their sheep, camels, and goats. Between the Gulf of Suez and the border with Israel is the

Timeline

c.2650 BC The first pyramids are built during a 500-year period of peace and prosperity under the Old Kingdom	**1497–1426 BC** King Thutmose III's reign marks height of Empire; buildings include Temple of Amon at Karnak (Al Karnak)	**332 BC** Egypt becomes part of Alexander the Great's empire; he builds the city of Alexandria on the Mediterranean coast	**AD 642** Egypt comes under the control of Muslim Arabs from the regions to the east	**1798** Napoleon conquers Egypt and leaves French troops in control of the country	**1801** British and Ottoman troops expel French occupation forces from Egypt

c.3600 BC Agriculture begins in alluvial soils deposited in the Nile Valley; irrigation used for growing fruit and vegetables	**c.3100 BC** King Menes founds first dynasty to rule nation; civilization begins with uniting of Upper and Lower regions in Nile Valley	**1991 BC** Egypt's power expands—King Amenemhet I and his successors conquer Nubia and trade with Syria and Palestine	**1153 BC** Assassination of Ramses III; Egyptian power declines as a result of corruption and feuding between priests and kings	**31 BC** Rome takes control of Egypt when Mark Antony and Cleopatra's navy is defeated by Octavian's fleet at Battle of Actium	**1517** Ottoman Turks defeat the Mamelukes (Turks, Mongols, and Circassians) and rule for the next 250 years

Statues of the pharaohs from the temple of Abu Simbel, saved from inundation by the Aswan High Dam in 1968 by being cut from the rock and reassembled on a cliff nearby (below left). The Red Sea and the Sinai Desert (right). Cairo and the Nile at dusk (below right). An obelisk, covered with hieroglyphs, among the ruins at Luxor (below).

almost uninhabited triangular limestone plateau of the Sinai Peninsula. Egypt's highest peak, Jabal Kātrīnā, is found in Sinai's mountainous south.

People and culture
While there are significant cultural differences between the 95 percent of the population who are Hamitic, and the Afro-Nubian peoples of the Upper Nile near Sudan, Egypt has a long tradition of ethnic and religious tolerance. In Cairo and Alexandria there have always been sizeable colonies of Greeks and Armenians, and although most Jews have now left for Israel, there is still a small Jewish community in Cairo. The small number of desert Bedouin divide into two main groups. In the southern part of the Eastern Desert live the Arabdah and Bisharin (Hamitic Beja), while Saadi and Murabatin (of Arab and Berber ancestry) are found throughout the Western Desert.

Ancient Egypt's art, architecture, pyramids and tombs are among the treasures of civilization. Evidence from tombs shows that even at the time of the first recorded dynasty, about 4400 BC, furniture inlaid with ivory and ebony was being made, along with alabaster vessels and fine work in copper and gold. In the pyramid-building period between 3700 BC and 2500 BC the Great Pyramid of Cheops was erected, a project thought to have occupied 100,000 men for 20 years. The pyramids were themselves immense tombs,

containing chambers in which dead kings were buried, supplied with all they might need—food, clothing, and furniture—in the afterlife. It is not known when exactly Christianity began in Egypt, but it was very early, around AD 40. The new faith was readily accepted since the hope of a future life coincided with the views of the Egyptians themselves.

Today about 6 percent of the people are Coptic Christians. The Copts claim to have received the gospel directly from St Mark, the first bishop of Alexandria. Their community has always valued education highly, and has contributed many figures to Egyptian public life. Over 90 percent of the population are Muslim, mainly Sunni.

With the rise of Islamic fundamentalism, the most bitter conflict within Egypt is between the modernizing political elite, and the fundamentalist Moslem Brotherhood. The latter is held responsible for terrorist activities. Arabic is the official language, but several other languages are used by ethnic minorities, from Hamito-Sudanic among the Nubians to the Berber-related language of the Siwah tribe east of the Qattara Depression.

Economy and resources
Food crops have been grown in the fertile soils of the Nile floodplain and delta for many thousands of years. But a population of 67 million, increasing by over 1 million per year, is placing considerable pressure on Egypt's agricultural resources. In addition, salination of land below the High Aswan Dam, land lost to growing urbanization, and desertification as a result of wind-blown sand, are all reducing the amount of arable land. Today much of Egypt's food is imported.

In manufacturing, textiles are by far the largest industry, and include spinning, weaving, and the dyeing and printing of cotton, wool, silk, and synthetic-fiber materials. Along with finished textiles, raw cotton remains one of the main exports, only exceeded in value by petroleum. There are plans to restore the Suez Canal's earning capacity by deepening and widening it for modern shipping. Most large-scale industrial plants in Egypt remain state-owned, overstaffed, and over-regulated, in need of both technical improvements and investment. This hampers the country's economic performance and is a challenge to governmental efforts at reform.

1882 British troops occupy Egypt
1922 Britain grants nominal independence
1948–49 Egypt part of Arab League invasion of Israel after Palestine is partitioned into Arab and Jewish nations; Israel repels invasion
1956 President Nasser first nationalizes Suez Canal then closes it. Britain, France, and Israel invade to reopen canal—UN intervenes
1967 Egypt and other Arab nations attack Israel but are defeated in "Six Day War"; Israel occupies the Gaza Strip and Sinai
1981 President Sadat assassinated and succeeded by Hosni Mubarak
1992 Cairo damaged in an earthquake which kills more than 500 people

1869 Suez Canal completed, allowing quicker access to India and the Pacific
1914 Egypt made a protectorate of the United Kingdom
1940–42 German and Italian troops fight battles along the north coast of Egypt and in the Western Desert
1953 Egypt becomes a republic
1960 Construction of the Aswan High Dam on the River Nile begins; it creates Lake Nasser, flooding several ancient sites
1979 President Sadat ends hostilities with Israel and signs an agreement under which Sinai is returned to Egyptian control
1990 Egypt opposes Iraq's invasion of oil-rich Kuwait and sides with US and European allies in the Gulf War

Equatorial Guinea

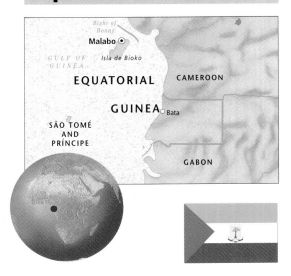

Equatorial Guinea consists of five islands in the Gulf of Guinea, plus the small mainland area of Río Muni that lies between Cameroon and Gabon. The largest of the islands, Bioco, was originally Portuguese, and was known for centuries as the slave depot and trans-shipment base of Fernando Po. The Spanish took over in 1778.

After gaining independence from Spain in 1968 Equatorial Guinea fell into the hands of Francisco Macias Nguema. A member of the Mongomo clan of the Fang tribe, his bloody and despotic rule lasted 11 years, after which he was overthrown and later executed. His nephew, also a Fang, continued to govern in much the same way, observers describing the one-candidate election in 1996 as meaningless. Equatorial Guinea illustrates the problems faced by tribal groups trying to adapt to democratic political arrangements.

The island of Bioco is mountainous and volcanic, with fertile soils. It has long supported cocoa on the lowland, and there are coffee plantations on the higher slopes which rise to Pico Basile. Rugged terrain and waterfalls are found in the southern half of the island. On the thinly populated area of mainland, mangrove swamps along the coast lead inland to dense tropical forests. Here, foreign companies have timber concessions, felling okoume and mahogany.

In addition to timber, the country exports cocoa and coffee. In the years before independence, cocoa plantations on Bioco and the mainland provided Equatorial Guinea with the highest per capita income in west Africa. By the end of the Macias era, however, the state was in political and economic ruins and some 100,000 of the population had fled as refugees to neighboring countries. Most of those who remain in the country today are subsistence farmers growing yams, cassava, and bananas.

Equatorial Guinea has a variety of undeveloped mineral resources: titanium, iron ore, manganese, uranium, and alluvial gold. Recently oil exploration has been successful, and increased production of oil and natural gas is anticipated. Aid programs are currently in limbo, having been cut off because of gross governmental corruption and mismanagement.

Fact File

OFFICIAL NAME	Republic of Equatorial Guinea
FORM OF GOVERNMENT	Republic with single legislative body (House of People's Representatives)
CAPITAL	Malabo
AREA	28,050 sq km (10,830 sq miles)
TIME ZONE	GMT + 1 hour
POPULATION	465,746
PROJECTED POPULATION 2005	542,291
POPULATION DENSITY	16.6 per sq km (43 per sq mile)
LIFE EXPECTANCY	54.4
INFANT MORTALITY (PER 1,000)	91.2
OFFICIAL LANGUAGE	Spanish
OTHER LANGUAGES	Indigenous languages, including Fang, Bubi, Ibo; pidgin English
LITERACY RATE	77.8%
RELIGIONS	Roman Catholic 85%, indigenous beliefs 15%
ETHNIC GROUPS	Fang 80%, Bubi 15%, other 5%
CURRENCY	CFA (Communauté Financière Africaine) franc
ECONOMY	Agriculture 64%, services 24%, industry 12%
GNP PER CAPITA	US$380
CLIMATE	Tropical; wetter on coast
HIGHEST POINT	Pico Basile 3,011 m (9,879 ft)
MAP REFERENCE	Page 365

Eritrea

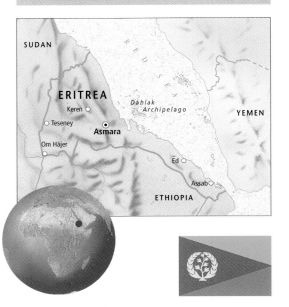

Eritrea was part of the Aksum Kingdom 2,000 years ago. In the fourth century AD Coptic Christianity was brought to the country, and a member of the Coptic Christian community, Issaias Ifawerki, is now its president. Italian influence in the region began in 1882, and despite the depredations of Mussolini between 1935 and 1941, Eritrea's modernization dates from those years. Italy introduced Western education and industry.

Forced to join Ethiopia in 1962, Eritrea began a 30-year war of independence, first against the Emperor and then against Ethiopia's Soviet-armed and financed Mengistu regime. Fighting from trenches dug from rock in the mountains, and in spite of inferior weapons, the Eritrean troops hung on. Victory and separate nationhood were won in 1993. Since that year the country has shown unusual self-reliance and is now rebuilding itself.

Consisting of a hot dry desert strip along the Red Sea shore, Eritrea is dominated by rugged mountains in the north, and in the southeast by the arid coastal plain of the Danakil Desert. In and around this desert live the Afar, camel-keeping nomads. The country is bordered on the north by the Sudan, with whom it has uneasy

Red rooftops in the capital city of Asmara, Eritrea (left). The Eritrean monastery of Abune clings to the hillside at Libanos (top).

relations, and on the south by Djibouti. Before independence, Eritrea provided Ethiopia's only access to the sea, other than through Djibouti. The prospect of being landlocked as a result of Eritrean secession—which is what happened— strengthened Ethiopian resolve during the war.

Poor and war-torn, with its roads and railways destroyed, Eritrea since 1993 has faced the task of reconstruction. Obligatory military service provides labor for public works. During the war trees were cut down by the enemy to deprive Eritrean soldiers of hiding places: these are being replanted by the thousand. In the long term, offshore oil deposits may prove important, but the population currently survives by subsistence farming, growing sorghum, lentils, vegetables, and maize. This is supplemented by food aid on which 75 percent of the people rely.

Fact File

OFFICIAL NAME	State of Eritrea
FORM OF GOVERNMENT	Transitional government with single legislative body (Legislative Assembly)
CAPITAL	Asmara
AREA	121,320 sq km (46,842 sq miles)
TIME ZONE	GMT + 3 hours
POPULATION	3,984,723
PROJECTED POPULATION 2005	4,958,211
POPULATION DENSITY	32.8 per sq km (85 per sq mile)
LIFE EXPECTANCY	51
INFANT MORTALITY (PER 1,000)	76.8
OFFICIAL LANGUAGES	Tigrinya, Arabic
OTHER LANGUAGES	Tigré, other indigenous languages, English
LITERACY RATE	25%
RELIGIONS	Muslim 50%, Christian (Coptic Christian, Roman Catholic, Protestant) 50%
ETHNIC GROUPS	Tigrinya 50%, Tigré and Kunama 40%, Afar 4%, Saho (Red Sea coast dwellers) 3%, other 3%
CURRENCY	Ethiopian birr
ECONOMY	Agriculture 80%, industry and services 20%
GNP PER CAPITA	Est. < US$465
CLIMATE	Hot and arid along coast, cooler and wetter in highlands; wet season June to September
HIGHEST POINT	Soira 3,018 m (9,899 ft)
MAP REFERENCE	Page 367

Causes of famine in Africa

Famine has been a serious problem on the African continent since very early times—there are records of famines in Egypt 6,000 years ago. A good corn harvest in Egypt was essential to the wellbeing of the region as a whole. A bad harvest affected not only Egypt but also the neighbors with whom it traded. Famine usually occurred because of annual variations in the extent of the flooding of the River Nile, and therefore in the yield of grain for food. Such famines were related to inherent difficulties in the kind of intensive floodplain agriculture that has been practiced over the centuries in the Nile Valley.

Prolonged drought and the spread of deserts in marginal areas are other common causes of famine. Hungry people allow their goats to graze on the sparse vegetation that grows on desert fringes, which frequently results in the plants dying and the desert spreading. This can be seen in the vast sub-Saharan region of the Sahel. A third type of famine is largely the result of human actions. Chronic warfare of the kind that has recently plagued the southern Sudan seriously disrupts agricultural production, displacing such large numbers of people that crops are neither planted nor harvested.

Finally, there is the kind of famine that affected Ethiopia under the Marxist Dergue during 1984–85, which was a direct result of government policies. Huge collectivization programs were initiated in the midst of war and cultivators were forcibly taken from their own land to work on state farms—many of those removed were "resettled" as punishment for their suspected hostility to the regime. This seriously affected the morale of the population and food production throughout the country decreased dramatically. A report prepared by the organization Cultural Survival concluded that the principal reasons for food shortages in Ethiopia at that time were the forcible redistribution of land to people unable or unwilling to work it; the confiscation of grain and livestock; forced labor programs and military

recruitment, which resulted in a sharp decline in the labor force available for agricultural work.

In Africa as elsewhere, the United Nations World Food Programme (WFP) is the main agency that is active in famine relief. Helping as many as 53 million people worldwide, it operates in virtually all the sub-Saharan African countries. The WFP's Food for Life Program helps people affected by humanitarian crises, such as that in Rwanda and Burundi in 1994. In April 1994 WFP workers provided food for what amounted to a huge city of refugees on the border of Rwanda and Tanzania, where 250,000 people were gathered without food, water, or shelter.

The WFP Food for Growth Program targets needy schoolchildren, mothers who are breast-feeding, and the elderly. In Ethiopia the WFP Food for Work Program, which pays workers with food for their service on development projects, has contributed to the planting of large numbers of trees; in Somalia the same program has been involved in repairing irrigation canals.

Desert encroaching on an African town (below). Children affected by famine (right).

Ethiopia

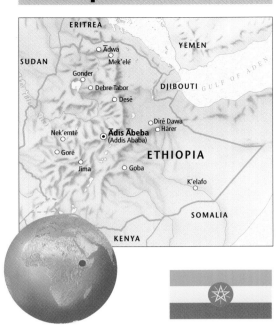

Ethiopia was known as the land of Punt by the Ancient Egyptians. In the fourth century AD it adopted Coptic Christianity, and despite strong Islamic influences since that time, including a Muslim invasion in 1523, many people remain Christian today. Although Mussolini's Italy occupied the country between 1935 and 1941, Ethiopia was never a colony—in fact under Emperor Haile Selassie it had imperial ambitions, and attempted to subjugate both the Somalis and the people of Eritrea. Haile Selassie was deposed in 1974 by a military coup; this triggered a civil war that exacerbated the effects of the famine in 1984. Always poor, Ethiopia is currently destitute—30 years of war and resulting famine are the legacy of the Marxist dictatorship of Mengistu Haile Mariam. His regime ended in 1991, when he was deposed.

The landscape is dominated by a mountainous volcanic plateau divided in two by the Rift Valley. The western highlands, with an average height of 2,700 m (8,800 ft), are the source of the Blue Nile, which spills out in a cataract from Lake Tana to flow south and west, before finally flowing north into Sudan. East of the western highlands is the Danakil Desert, where a depression falls to 116 m (380 ft) below sea level. This is one of the hottest places on earth.

In the highlands, however, the climate is moderate to warm, with frosts at night and occasional falls of snow on the mountains. The eastern highlands below the Rift Valley fall away to the border with Somalia. In the aftermath of Ethiopia's war with its Somali neighbor the southern section of this border is only provisional, and there is a continuing dispute regarding the Ogadēn region.

More than 90 percent of the country's industry concerned with food processing, the manufacture of textiles, and chemical and metal production, is owned and managed by the state. Inefficiencies and overstaffing are widespread. This is the result of the Mengistu regime's effort to establish a centrally controlled Soviet-model economy. Various reform measures have been proposed and the government intends to sell off some state-owned plants, but progress is slow.

Drought in the years 1981 to 1985, combined with an unsuccessful attempt to collectivize agriculture, resulted in a famine in which an estimated 1 million people died. Today, rural production accounts for half of gross domestic product and 80 percent of employment. Repair of war-damaged roads and railways continues. Although Ethiopia still needs food aid there is a growing emphasis on aid in the form of credit for infrastructure development.

Fact File

OFFICIAL NAME	Federal Democratic Republic of Ethiopia
FORM OF GOVERNMENT	Federal republic with two legislative bodies (Federal Council and Council of People's Representatives)
CAPITAL	Ādis Ābeba (Addis Ababa)
AREA	1,127,127 sq km (435,184 sq miles)
TIME ZONE	GMT + 3 hours
POPULATION	59,690,383
PROJECTED POPULATION 2005	67,831,860
POPULATION DENSITY	53 per sq km (137.2 per sq mile)
LIFE EXPECTANCY	40.5
INFANT MORTALITY (PER 1,000)	124.6
OFFICIAL LANGUAGE	Amharic
OTHER LANGUAGES	More than 100 indigenous languages, Arabic, English
LITERACY RATE	34.5%
RELIGIONS	Ethiopian Orthodox 51%, Muslim 35%, animist 12%, other 2%
ETHNIC GROUPS	Oromo 40%, Amhara and Tigrean 32%, Sidamo 9%, Shankella 6%, Somali 6%, Afar 4%, Gurage 2%, other 3%
CURRENCY	Birr
ECONOMY	Agriculture 80%, services 12%, industry 8%
GNP PER CAPITA	US$100
CLIMATE	Tropical on lowlands, uplands more temperate; wet season April to September
HIGHEST POINT	Ras Dashen Terara 4,620 m (15,157 ft)
MAP REFERENCE	Pages 366–67

Gabon

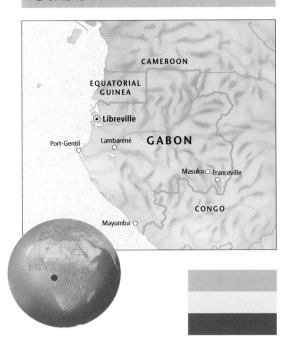

A slave station for the Portuguese after their arrival in 1483, Gabon was administered by France from 1842. After the French navy suppressed the still-continuing local slave trade, it released captives at a place on the coast which it named Libreville (Libertyville). Since Gabon achieved independence in 1966 France has continued to play a role in the country's politics and in its relatively prosperous oil-based economy.

The original inhabitants of this heavily forested equatorial country were probably Pygmy; today the main tribal group is the Fang. However, the 30-year rule of President El Hadj Omar Bongo (a Bateke who converted to Islam under Libyan influence in 1973) depended on a coalition that was designed to exclude the Fang from power. Widespread dissatisfaction with this state of affairs led to the introduction of a multi-party system in 1991. Whether this has allowed other ethnic groups a real voice in Gabonese politics is not yet clear.

Geographically, a coastal plain marked by sandbars and lagoons is interrupted by the estuary

of the Ogooué River. The wooded basin of this large watercourse dominates Gabon, 60 percent of the country's land area being drained by its tributaries. These flow down from the African central plateau and the borders of Equatorial Guinea and Cameroon to the north, and from Congo to the east and south.

Before the development of oil and manganese in the early 1970s, valuable timbers were one of the country's main exports. These included Gabon mahogany, ebony, and walnut. Even today, as much as two-thirds of Gabon's total land area consists of untouched rainforest, but the completion in 1986 of the Trans-Gabon Railway from the port of Owendo to the interior town of Massoukou is likely to lead to further exploitation of timber resources.

Gabon has considerable mineral resources. It has about one-quarter of the world's known reserves of manganese, and is the world's fourth biggest manganese producer. France imports most of its uranium from Gabon. Oil currently accounts for 50 percent of gross domestic product. This figure, when combined with Gabon's small population, gives a distorted picture of the country's per capita earnings, disguising the fact that more than half the country's people still make their living by subsistence farming. A wide gap separates rural people from the urban élite and the country faces economic problems.

Fact File

OFFICIAL NAME Gabonese Republic

FORM OF GOVERNMENT Republic with single legislative body (National Assembly)

CAPITAL Libreville

AREA 267,670 sq km (103,347 sq miles)

TIME ZONE GMT + 1 hour

POPULATION 1,225,853

PROJECTED POPULATION 2005 1,340,781

POPULATION DENSITY 4.6 per sq km (11.9 per sq mile)

LIFE EXPECTANCY 57

INFANT MORTALITY (PER 1,000) 83.1

OFFICIAL LANGUAGE French

OTHER LANGUAGES Indigenous languages (including Fang, Myene, Bateke, Bapounou/Eschira, Bandjabi)

LITERACY RATE 62.6%

RELIGIONS Christian 94%, Muslim 3%, other 3%

ETHNIC GROUPS Mainly Bantu tribes (including Fang, Eshira, Bapounou, Bateke) 92%, foreign Africans and Europeans 8%

CURRENCY CFA (Communauté Financière Africaine) franc

ECONOMY Agriculture 65%, industry and commerce 30%, services 5%

GNP PER CAPITA US$3,490

CLIMATE Tropical, with dry season mid-May to mid-September

HIGHEST POINT Mt Iboundji 1,575 m (5,167 ft)

MAP REFERENCE Page 368

Traders at the goat and donkey market in Lalibela, in northern Ethiopia (left). Fishing boats and fishermen at a beach in Gambia (top right).

Gambia

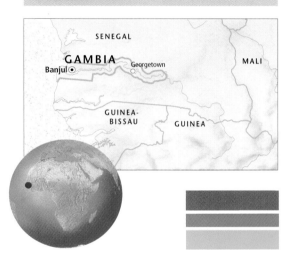

Surrounded on nearly all sides by Senegal, Gambia is Africa's smallest independent state. Once a part of the Mali Empire, it became a British colony in 1816 and has been independent since 1965. Following independence it was governed for almost 30 years by Sir Dawda Jawara and the People's Progressive Party. A military coup displaced him in 1994. The country has been notably stable otherwise, though resentment of the dominant Mandinka exists among minority tribal groups such as the Fula and Wolof.

A subtropical climate and a sunny dry season has enabled Gambia to expand tourism in recent years but the conflict between tourist life and the main religion, Islam, has made this controversial. In 1982 Gambia joined its neighbor, Senegal, in a union named the Senegambian Federation. This proved unsuccessful and was dissolved in 1989.

The Gambia River and its estuary are navigable for some 200 km (125 miles), allowing ships of up to 3,000 tonnes to reach Georgetown. Consisting of a riverine plain running inland 275 km (170 miles) from the estuary, Gambia's countryside is low and undulating, the land beside the river varying from swamp to savanna. Although rice is grown in the swamps and on the river floodplain, not enough is produced to meet domestic needs. Millet, sorghum, and cassava are grown on higher ground. On the

upper river, a dam provides irrigation.

Gambia has unmined deposits of minerals such as ilmenite, rutile, and zircon. The economy has a limited agricultural base, three-quarters of the population growing crops and raising livestock. Peanuts are the main cash crop, providing more than 75 percent of export earnings, and peanut processing is important industrially. Palm kernels are also exported. Because Banjul is the best harbor on the west African coast, much Senegalese produce passes through Gambia, and re-export forms one-third of economic activity.

Fact File

OFFICIAL NAME Republic of the Gambia

FORM OF GOVERNMENT Republic with single legislative body (House of Representatives)

CAPITAL Banjul

AREA 11,300 sq km (4,363 sq miles)

TIME ZONE GMT

POPULATION 1,336,320

PROJECTED POPULATION 2005 1,616,322

POPULATION DENSITY 118.2 per sq km (306.1 per sq mile)

LIFE EXPECTANCY 54.4

INFANT MORTALITY (PER 1,000) 75.3

OFFICIAL LANGUAGE English

OTHER LANGUAGES Indigenous languages (including Madinka, Wolof, Fula), Arabic

LITERACY RATE 37.2%

RELIGIONS Muslim 90%, Christian 9%, indigenous beliefs 1%

ETHNIC GROUPS Indigenous 99% (including Mandinka 42%, Fula 18%, Wolof 16%, Jola 10%, Serahuli 9%), non-Gambian 1%

CURRENCY Dalasi

ECONOMY Agriculture 75%; industry, commerce, and services 19%; government 6%

GNP PER CAPITA US$320

CLIMATE Tropical, with wet season June to November

HIGHEST POINT Unnamed location 53 m (174 ft)

MAP REFERENCE Page 364

Africa

Ghana

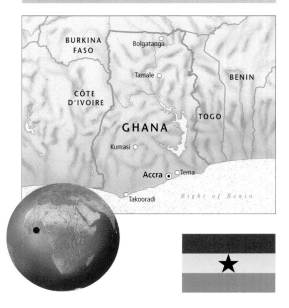

Ghana was once known as the Gold Coast. A well-known source of gold in west Africa for a thousand years, the nation's modern name comes from the Ghana Empire of the eighth to the twelfth centuries. The Ashanti people established themselves in the seventeenth century, selling slaves to Portuguese, British, Dutch and Danish traders. Under British control from 1874, Ghana became the first tropical African colony to win independence in 1956. Soon after this it became a Soviet-style one-party state.

After 1966, Ghana was wracked by military coups for 15 years before Flight-Lieutenant Jerry Rawlings took control in 1981. An election in 1996 returned Rawlings to power once more. Although government pressure is often brought to bear, vigorous political debate takes place in a relatively free media, and despite economic troubles Ghana still has twice the per capita output of the poorer countries in west Africa.

Geographically, the country is formed by the basin of the Volta Rivers. A large area flooded by the Akosombo Dam is now Lake Volta, the world's largest artificial lake. This provides hydroelectric power for smelting alumina into aluminum, and for use in the towns, mines, and industries of the Takoradi-Kumasi-Tema triangle. In the north there is savanna country. In earlier days the southern part of the country was covered by dense tropical forest. Much of this has been cleared for agriculture, especially for growing cocoa, which from 1924 until the present day has usually been the leading export.

Like other west African countries, Ghana has few natural harbors. Its coast consists mainly of mangrove swamps, with lagoons toward the mouth of the River Volta. The rivers are home to crocodile, manatee, and hippopotamus. The wildlife of the northern savanna includes lion, leopard, hyena, and antelope.

Ghana is well endowed with natural resources—gold, timber, industrial diamonds, bauxite, manganese, fish, and rubber. In 1995, largely as a result of increased gold, timber, and cocoa production, overall economic growth was about 5 percent. Although the economy is based on subsistence agriculture, Ghana is not self-sufficient in food. President Rawlings' efforts

to reverse the statist policies of his predecessors continue, but face a number of obstacles. Public sector wage increases, and various peace-keeping missions, both internal and external, have strained the budget and led to inflationary deficit financing. Corruption is a continuing obstacle to growth.

Fact File

OFFICIAL NAME Republic of Ghana

FORM OF GOVERNMENT Republic with single legislative body (Parliament)

CAPITAL Accra

AREA 238,540 sq km (92,100 sq miles)

TIME ZONE GMT

POPULATION 18,887,626

PROJECTED POPULATION 2005 21,128,132

POPULATION DENSITY 79.2 per sq km (205.1 per sq mile)

LIFE EXPECTANCY 57.1

INFANT MORTALITY (PER 1,000) 76.2

OFFICIAL LANGUAGE English

OTHER LANGUAGES Indigenous languages, including Akan, Mole-Dagbani, Ewe

LITERACY RATE 63.4%

RELIGIONS Indigenous beliefs 38%, Muslim 30%, Christian 24%, other 8%

ETHNIC GROUPS Indigenous 99.8% (including Akan 44%, Moshi-Dagomba 16%, Ewe 13%, Ga 8%), European and other 0.2%

CURRENCY Cedi

ECONOMY Agriculture 58%, services 31%, industry 11%

GNP PER CAPITA US$390

CLIMATE Tropical: warm and arid on southeast coast; hot and humid in southwest; hot and arid in north

HIGHEST POINT Mt Afadjato 880 m (2,887 ft)

MAP REFERENCE Page 364

Guinea

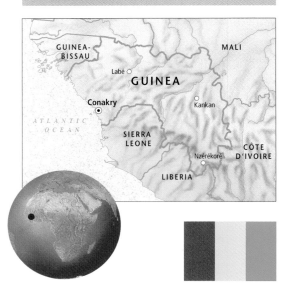

Guinea is on the African Atlantic coast to the north of Sierra Leone and Liberia. A slave-trading center from the fifteenth century, it became the colony of French Guinea in 1890. After achieving independence in 1958 it was for 25 years a one-party Marxist dictatorship under Ahmed Sékou Touré. A member of the Malinke tribe, he centralized and nationalized, attempted to enforce the use of local languages in the place of French, and paid large numbers of state informers to monitor village and family life. Guinea now ranks last or near last on most international social development scales. Women face many disadvantages, including the practice of genital mutilation, which is widespread.

In the past 15 years governmental efforts at reform have led to a number of improvements, and in 1995 Guinea's first multi-party elections took place. The country has had to bear the additional burden of several hundred thousand refugees who have fled from the civil wars in Liberia and Sierra Leone. Many of these people are now returning home.

From mangrove swamps and lagoons along the coast, the land rises through densely forested foothills to the Fouta Djalon Highlands in the east. These highlands—from which the Gambia, Senegal, and Niger Rivers flow north and northeast—form a barrier between the coast and the grassland and savanna woodland of the Upper Niger Plains. Typical wildlife on the savanna includes lion and leopard, while crocodile and hippopotamus are found in the rivers.

The 80 percent of the workforce who live by agriculture are spread fairly evenly through the countryside. Those who live on the wet Atlantic coastal plain, much of which has been cleared for farming, cultivate bananas, palm oil, pineapples, and rice. Cattle are raised by nomadic herders in the interior.

Guinea possesses more than 25 percent of the world's reserves of high-grade bauxite, and three large bauxite mines contribute about 80 percent of the country's export revenue. Since it opened in 1984, the Aredor diamond mine has also been extremely profitable. Good soil and high yields give the country a prospect of self-sufficiency in food but the years of stifling state controls that were imposed by Touré have made market reforms difficult to implement, and infrastructures are few and much in need of modernizing. Corruption and harassment obstruct business growth. Aside from the bauxite industry, there is little foreign investment.

Fact File

OFFICIAL NAME Republic of Guinea

FORM OF GOVERNMENT Republic with single legislative body (People's National Assembly)

CAPITAL Conakry

AREA 245,860 sq km (94,926 sq miles)

TIME ZONE GMT

POPULATION 7,538,953

PROJECTED POPULATION 2005 8,396,806

POPULATION DENSITY 30.7 per sq km (79.5 per sq mile)

LIFE EXPECTANCY 46.5

INFANT MORTALITY (PER 1,000) 126.3

OFFICIAL LANGUAGE French

OTHER LANGUAGES Indigenous languages

LITERACY RATE 34.8%

RELIGIONS Muslim 85%, Christian 8%, indigenous beliefs 7%

ETHNIC GROUPS Peuhl 40%, Malinke 30%, Soussou 20%, smaller tribes 10%

CURRENCY Guinean franc

ECONOMY Agriculture 80%, industry and commerce 11%, services 9%

GNP PER CAPITA US$550

CLIMATE Tropical, with wet season May to November

HIGHEST POINT Mt Nimba 1,752 m (5,748 ft)

MAP REFERENCE Page 364

The large, covered market in Kumasi, central Ghana (far left). A public voodoo ritual in eastern Ghana (left). Children from rural Guinea (top right).

Guinea-Bissau

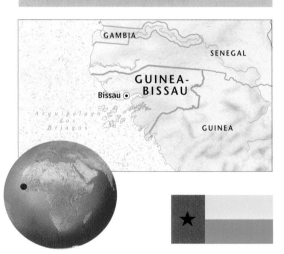

Guinea-Bissau is a small west African state between Guinea and Senegal. A large part of the country consists of mangrove swamps, estuaries, and islands, and it is both poor and underdeveloped. After the French and British used the area as a slave-trading station in the seventeenth and eighteenth centuries, Portugal named it Portuguese Guinea and claimed it as a colony in 1879. Independence, achieved in 1974, came following 12 years of guerrilla war.

One-party rule plus attempted coups and assassinations marked the next 17 years. Moves toward multi-party democracy, designed to allow for ethnic divisons and inequalities, began in 1990. The contrast between the limited opportunities available to the 99 percent of the population which is African, and the privileges of the tiny Afro-Portuguese elite, is a major cause of tension. The existence of the opposition Democratic Front was made legal in 1991. Women face significant disadvantages and female genital mutilation is widespread.

Three main waterways—the Geba, Corubal, and Cacheu Rivers—mark the landscape. These wander across the plains toward broad estuaries and mangrove swamps on the coast. Here, the seasonal rainfall is especially heavy. Rice, the staple food, is grown on the floodplains and in the swamps, as well as on the offshore islands of the Arquipélago dos Bijagós, but not enough is

produced to make the country self-sufficient. An area of upland savanna lies toward the border with Guinea in the southeast.

Mineral resources include phosphates, bauxite, and offshore oil but their development has been hampered by political instability, state controls, and (in the case of oil) disputes with Guinea and Senegal. Agriculture and fishing employ 90 percent of the workforce. Cashew nuts, peanuts, and palm kernels are the main exports. Economic reforms featuring monetary stability and private sector growth have been undertaken but progress is being hampered by the burden of foreign debt and the many cultural and institutional constraints.

Fact File

OFFICIAL NAME Republic of Guinea-Bissau

FORM OF GOVERNMENT Republic with single legislative body (National People's Assembly)

CAPITAL Bissau

AREA 36,120 sq km (13,946 sq miles)

TIME ZONE GMT

POPULATION 1,234,555

PROJECTED POPULATION 2005 1,415,330

POPULATION DENSITY 34.2 per sq km (88.5 per sq mile)

LIFE EXPECTANCY 49.6

INFANT MORTALITY (PER 1,000) 109.5

OFFICIAL LANGUAGE Portuguese

OTHER LANGUAGES Indigenous languages

LITERACY RATE 53.9%

RELIGIONS Indigenous beliefs 65%, Muslim 30%, Christian 5%

ETHNIC GROUPS Indigenous 99% (inclduing Balanta 30%, Fula 20%, Manjaca 14%, Mandinga 13%, Papel 7%), European and mixed 1%

CURRENCY CFA (Communauté Financière Africaine) franc

ECONOMY Agriculture 90%, industry and services 10%

GNP PER CAPITA US$250

CLIMATE Tropical, with wet season June to November

HIGHEST POINT Unnamed location in northeast 300 m (984 ft)

MAP REFERENCE Page 364

Kenya

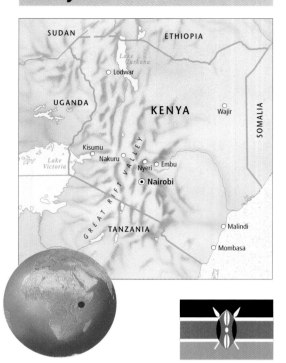

Zebras in the Masai Mara National Reserve in Kenya (above). A Masai woman in traditional dress (top right). A village in the Maluti Mountains foothills in Lesotho (bottom right).

Fact File

OFFICIAL NAME Republic of Kenya

FORM OF GOVERNMENT Republic with single legislative body (National Assembly)

CAPITAL Nairobi

AREA 582,650 sq km (224,961 sq miles)

TIME ZONE GMT + 3 hours

POPULATION 28,808,658

PROJECTED POPULATION 2005 31,156,521

POPULATION DENSITY 49.4 per sq km (128 per sq mile)

LIFE EXPECTANCY 47

INFANT MORTALITY (PER 1,000) 59.1

OFFICIAL LANGUAGES English, Swahili

OTHER LANGUAGES Indigenous languages

LITERACY RATE 77%

RELIGIONS Protestant 38%, Roman Catholic 28%, indigenous beliefs 26%, other 8%

ETHNIC GROUPS Kikuyu 22%, Luhya 14%, Luo 13%, Kalenjin 12%, Kamba 11%, Kisii 6%, Meru 6%, other 16% (including Asian, European, Arab 1%)

CURRENCY Kenya shilling

ECONOMY Agriculture 80%, services 12%, industry 8%

GNP PER CAPITA US$280

CLIMATE Coastal regions tropical, with wet seasons April to May and October to November; inland plateau cooler and drier

HIGHEST POINT Mt Kenya 5,199 m (17,057 ft)

MAP REFERENCE Pages 368–69

Kenya, in east Africa, is where humankind may have originated: remains of humans and pre-humans found in the Olduvai Gorge go back several million years. By the tenth century AD Arabs had settled along the coast, and in the nineteenth century both Britain and Germany became interested in the region. In 1920 Kenya became a British colony, the pleasant climate in the highlands attracting English immigrants who displaced Kikuyu farmers and took their land.

After the Second World War, widespread resentment at this expropriation erupted in the violent Mau Mau rebellion which lasted eight years. Independence came in 1963. Since then, control of the state and its resources has been contested by political parties allied with particular tribes, the domination of the Kikuyu (in recent years under President Daniel Arap Moi) yielding to a trial of multi-party democracy in 1991.

The Kenya Highlands consist of a fertile plateau formed by volcanoes and lava flows. The highlands are divided in two by the Rift Valley, the Eastern Highlands falling away toward the densely populated plain near Lake Victoria, the Western Highlands descending to the valleys of the Tana and Galana Rivers as they cross the Nyika Plain to the north of Mombasa. The populous and fertile coastal belt is fringed by mangrove swamps, coral reefs, and groups of small islands. In the sparsely populated north toward Lake Turkana desert conditions prevail. Kenya's wildlife, consisting of the full range of African fauna, can be seen in the country's several large national parks, and has made it a leading destination for tourists for many years.

By African standards, Kenya has a stable and productive economy. It has a broad and highly successful agricultural base, with cash crops such as coffee and tea. It also has east Africa's largest and most diversified manufacturing sector, producing small-scale consumer goods such as plastics, furniture, batteries, textiles, and soap. But the country also has one of the world's highest rates of population growth: between 1988 and 2000 it is expected to experience an 82 percent increase in population, a figure exceeded only by Haiti.

This continuous increase in the number of its citizens is accompanied by deforestation, lack of drinking water, and infrastructural breakdown. Floods have destroyed roads, bridges, and telecommunications. Crime, including the murder of visitors and ethnic massacres, has caused a steep decline in tourist numbers.

Lesotho

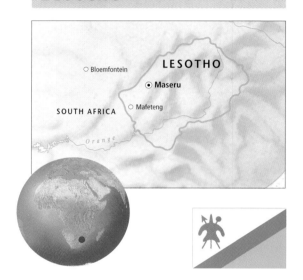

Lesotho is a small landlocked country entirely surrounded by South Africa. Formerly the British Protectorate of Basutoland, it is the only country in the world where all the land is higher than 1,000 m (3,300 ft). About two-thirds of the terrain is mountainous, and at higher altitudes it often snows throughout the winter. As the head of a fragile constitutional monarchy, the king of Lesotho has no executive or legislative powers: traditionally, he could be elected or deposed by a majority vote of the College of Chiefs. Proposals to unite Lesotho with post-apartheid South Africa have been resisted by members of the population who feel an independent state will better defend their cultural heritage.

A high mountainous plateau declining from east to west, Lesotho's highest ridges were formed on basaltic lavas. Treeless, with steep valleys, the wet highlands are soft and boggy in summer and frozen in winter. Numerous river valleys and gorges dissect the plateau, among them the River Orange. To the northwest the border of the country is defined by the Caledon River. This is flanked by a 30 to 65 km (18 to 40 mile) strip of fertile land which supports most of Lesotho's farmers and provides the bulk of its agriculturally useful land. Subsistence crops include maize, sorghum, wheat, and beans. Sheep and goats are kept for wool and mohair on the high plateau.

Lesotho is without important natural resources other than water. Hopes are held for the future of a major hydroelectric facility, the Highlands Water Scheme, which will sell water to South Africa and become a major employer and revenue earner. The scheme will supply all of Lesotho's energy requirements. In scattered hamlets, cottage industry produces woven mohair rugs. Manufacturing based on farm products consists of milling, canning, and the preparation of leather and jute. Roughly 60 percent of Lesotho's male wage earners work across the border in South Africa, mostly as laborers in mines. The wages they send back provide some 45 percent of domestic income.

Fact File

OFFICIAL NAME Kingdom of Lesotho

FORM OF GOVERNMENT Constitutional monarchy with two legislative houses (Senate and National Assembly)

CAPITAL Maseru

AREA 30,350 sq km (11,718 sq miles)

TIME ZONE GMT + 2 hours

POPULATION 2,128,950

PROJECTED POPULATION 2005 2,327,735

POPULATION DENSITY 70.2 per sq km (181.8 per sq mile)

LIFE EXPECTANCY 53

INFANT MORTALITY (PER 1,000) 77.6

OFFICIAL LANGUAGES Sesotho, English

OTHER LANGUAGES Zulu, Afrikaans, French, Xhosa

LITERACY RATE 70.5%

RELIGIONS Christian 80%, indigenous beliefs 20%

ETHNIC GROUPS Sotho 99.7%, European and Asian 0.3%

CURRENCY Loti

ECONOMY Agriculture 75%, services and industry 25%

GNP PER CAPITA US$770

CLIMATE Temperate, with cool, dry winters and hot, wet summers

HIGHEST POINT Thabana-Ntlenyana 3,482 m (11,424 ft)

MAP REFERENCE Page 371

Liberia

Settled by freed slaves after 1822, and a republic since 1847, the west African state of Liberia has always been a socially divided country. The coastal settlements of ex-slaves from America formed an élite with a Christian faith and an American colonial lifestyle. They had little in common with the long-established tribal peoples of the interior. During the long rule of the coastal Americo-Liberian élite the country was politically stable. It also made economic progress, the activities of the Firestone Rubber Company turning Liberia into a major rubber producer.

This ended in 1980 with a coup led by Master Sergeant Samuel Doe (a Krahn). When Doe was ousted by forces led by members of the Gio tribe in 1990, civil war began. Massacres and atrocities have marked succeeding years; famine threatens several regions; some 750,000 refugees have fled the country; organized economic life is at a standstill; and the rule of law has ended.

Liberia has three major geographic regions. Like its neighbors, it has a narrow sandy coastal strip of lagoons and mangrove swamps. Inland from the Atlantic Ocean are rolling hills, covered in tropical rainforest, which rise to a plateau. This ascends to form a mountainous belt along the Guinean border. Most of the plateau region is grassland or forest—forests cover 39 percent of the land area. Only 1 percent of the country is arable.

Until the outbreak of civil war Liberia had been a producer and exporter of iron ore, rubber, timber, and coffee. Industries included rubber processing, food processing, construction materials, furniture making, palm oil processing, and diamond mining. Rice was the main staple, but some food was imported. The catch from coastal fisheries was supplemented by inland fish farms.

By the end of the 1990s war had destroyed much of the Liberian economy, especially the infrastructure in and around Monrovia. The business classes fled, taking with them their capital and expertise. With the collapse of the urban commercial part of the economy, many people have reverted to subsistence farming.

Fact File

OFFICIAL NAME Republic of Liberia

FORM OF GOVERNMENT Republic with single transitional legislative body (Transitional Legislative Assembly)

CAPITAL Monrovia

AREA 111,370 sq km (43,000 sq miles)

TIME ZONE GMT

POPULATION 2,923,725

PROJECTED POPULATION 2005 3,749,894

POPULATION DENSITY 26.3 per sq km (68 per sq mile)

LIFE EXPECTANCY 59.9

INFANT MORTALITY (PER 1,000) 100.6

OFFICIAL LANGUAGE English

OTHER LANGUAGES Indigenous languages

LITERACY RATE 39.5%

RELIGIONS Indigenous beliefs 70%, Muslim 20%, Christian 10%

ETHNIC GROUPS Indigenous tribes 95% (including Kpelle, Bassa, Gio, Kru, Grebo, Mano, Krahn, Gola, Gbandi, Loma, Kissi, Vai, Bella), Americo-Liberian (descendants of repatriated slaves) 5%

CURRENCY Liberian dollar

ECONOMY Agriculture 70%, services 25%, industry 5%

GNP PER CAPITA US$487

CLIMATE Tropical, with wet season May to September

HIGHEST POINT Mt Wuteve 1,380 m (4,528 ft)

MAP REFERENCE Page 364

Libya

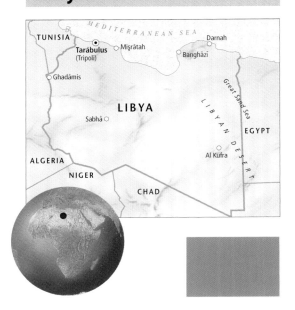

The arid Saharan Plateau takes up 93 percent of Libya's land area. The great expanse of the Sahara gives way to a fertile coastal strip along the Mediterranean, where the majority of the population lives, though only 1 percent of the total land area is arable. Tripoli stands on the Jefra Plain, Libya's most productive farming area. Cereals, especially barley, are a major crop. Sorghum is grown in the Fezzan to the south; wheat, tobacco, and olives are produced in the north; dates and figs are cultivated at a few scattered oases in the desert. Predominantly low-lying, the desert terrain rises southward to Bikubiti in the Tibesti Range on the border with Chad. The country is without lakes or perennial rivers, and artesian wells supply nearly two-thirds of its water requirements.

Oil provides almost all export earnings and about one-third of gross domestic product. Though Libya's per capita gross domestic product is usually Africa's highest, the people suffer from periodic shortages of basic goods and foodstuffs caused by import restrictions and inefficient resource allocation.

The largely state-controlled industrial sector (almost all the oil companies were nationalized in 1973 and the state has a controlling interest in all new ventures) suffers from overstaffing and other constraints. However, oil revenues have enabled important state initiatives to be undertaken: the government has planted millions of trees, and the Great Manmade River Project, being built to bring water from large aquifers under the Sahara to the coastal cities, is one of the world's largest water development projects.

Fact File

OFFICIAL NAME	Socialist People's Libyan Arab Jamahiriya
FORM OF GOVERNMENT	Republic with single legislative body (General People's Congress)
CAPITAL	Tarābulus (Tripoli)
AREA	1,759,540 sq km (679,358 sq miles)
TIME ZONE	GMT + 2 hours
POPULATION	5,903,128
PROJECTED POPULATION 2005	7,315,326
POPULATION DENSITY	3.4 per sq km (8.8 per sq mile)
LIFE EXPECTANCY	65.8
INFANT MORTALITY (PER 1,000)	54.0
OFFICIAL LANGUAGE	Arabic
OTHER LANGUAGES	Italian, English
LITERACY RATE	75.0%
RELIGIONS	Sunni Muslim 97%, other 3%
ETHNIC GROUPS	Berber and Arab 97%; other (including Greek, Maltese, Italian, Egyptian, Pakistani, Turkish, Indian, Tunisian) 3%
CURRENCY	Libyan dinar
ECONOMY	Services 51%, industry 32%, agriculture 17%
GNP PER CAPITA	Not available (c. US$766–3,035)
CLIMATE	Mainly arid; temperate along coast
HIGHEST POINT	Bikubiti 2,285 m (7,497 ft)
MAP REFERENCE	Page 362

First settled by the Greeks, and once part of the empire of Alexander the Great, Libya was ruled by the Romans for 500 years. Tourists visiting the country today are shown the ruins of an impressive 2,000-year-old Roman theater at Leptis Magna. Later, in AD 642, the region was conquered by the Arabs, and later still became part of the Ottoman Empire. It was occupied by Italy in 1911, and the years 1938 to 1939 saw Mussolini bring in 30,000 Italians to farm the Jefra Plain. Libya became independent in 1951. Since 1969, when he seized power, it has been a one-party socialist state ruled dictatorially by Colonel Muammar al Gaddafi.

Madagascar

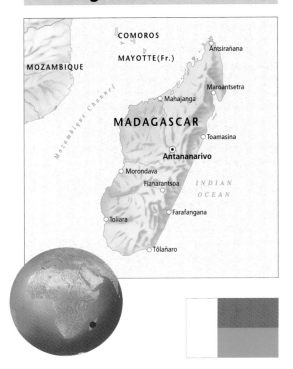

Larger than France, Madagascar is the world's fourth largest island. Located off the southeast coast of Africa, it contrasts sharply with the African mainland in its wildlife, people, culture, language, and history. In the center and the east live the Merina or Hova people who migrated to the island from the islands now known as Indonesia about 2,000 years ago. By the nineteenth century the Merinas, with their capital in Tanarive, ruled much of the country. In 1896 the island became a French colony. It won independence from France in 1960, following a bloody insurrection. From 1975 it was run as a one-party socialist state associated with the Soviet Union. Since 1991, following deepening poverty, riots, and mass demonstrations, there have been attempts to introduce multi-party democracy.

To the east the land drops precipitously to the Indian Ocean through forests dissected by rushing

Antananarivo, the capital of Madagascar (below). A street scene in Toliara, Madagascar (left). Lake Malawi (Lake Nyasa), near Chilumba, looking toward Mozambique (top right).

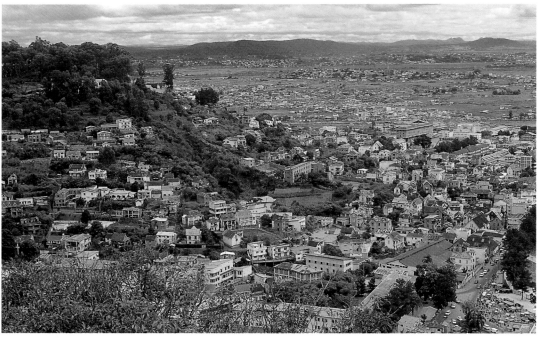

streams. Inland lies the mountainous central plateau, accounting for 60 percent of the island's total area, and rising in several places above 2,500 m (8,200 ft). Various geological eras are represented in the island's rugged topography, which features steep faulting, volcanic outcrops, and deep-cut valleys. On the western slopes of the plateau the land falls away more gently to broad and fertile plains. In the central highlands both the landscape and agriculture have a south Asian character, rice farming being combined with raising cattle and pigs. Land usage is more African in style on the east coast and in the northern highlands, with fallow-farming of food crops such as cassava and maize, and the cultivation of coffee, sugar, and spices for export.

Separated from the African mainland for over 50 million years, Madagascar developed its own distinctive wildlife: three-quarters of the flora and fauna are found nowhere else. The island is known for its 28 species of lemur—dainty, large-eyed primates—and for the tenrec, a small, spiny, insect-eating mammal. Many of the island's 1,000 or so orchid species are endemic, and it is home to half the world's chameleon species.

Among the poorest countries in the world, Madagascar is not self-sufficient in food. The main staples are rice and cassava, but production is failing to keep pace with an annual population growth rate of around 3 percent. Additional problems derive from past government initiatives. When collective farming was introduced in 1975 it resulted in falling production and widespread resentment. Since 1993 corruption and political instability have accompanied economic confusion and a decay in the infrastructure.

Fact File

OFFICIAL NAME Republic of Madagascar

FORM OF GOVERNMENT Republic with two legislative bodies (Senate and National Assembly)

CAPITAL Antananarivo

AREA 587,040 sq km (226,656 sq miles)

TIME ZONE GMT + 3 hours

POPULATION 14,873,387

PROJECTED POPULATION 2005 17,558,869

POPULATION DENSITY 25.3 per sq km (65.5 per sq mile)

LIFE EXPECTANCY 53.2

INFANT MORTALITY (PER 1,000) 89.1

OFFICIAL LANGUAGES Malagasy, French

LITERACY RATE 83%

RELIGIONS Indigenous beliefs 52%, Christian 41%, Muslim 7%

ETHNIC GROUPS Chiefly Malayo-Indonesian inland (including Merina, Betsileo, Betsimisaraka) and mixed African, Arab, Malayo-Indonesian on coasts (including Tsimihety, Sakalava) 99%; other 1%

CURRENCY Malagasy franc

ECONOMY Agriculture 81%, services 13%, industry 6%

GNP PER CAPITA US$230

CLIMATE Tropical in coastal regions; temperate inland (wet season November to April); arid in south

HIGHEST POINT Maromokotro 2,876 m (9,436 ft)

MAP REFERENCE Page 372

Malawi

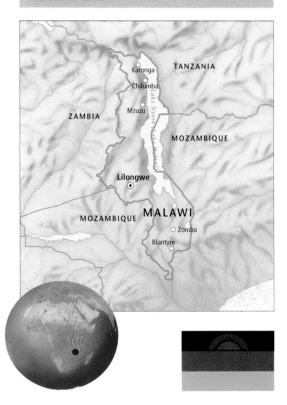

Malawi is a hilly and in places mountainous country at the southern end of Africa's Rift Valley, one-fifth of it consisting of Lake Malawi (Lake Nyasa). The lake contains 500 fish species which support a sizeable fishing industry. Most of the country's people are descended from the Bantu who settled the area centuries ago. Arab slave-trading was suppressed by the incoming British in 1887–89, and in 1907 the country became the British Protectorate of Nyasaland. Independence in 1964 put Dr Hastings Banda in charge and he ruled dictatorially for 30 years. Cumulative difficulties, including drought and crop failures, some 800,000 refugees from Mozambique, and resentment at the apparent assassination of political opponents, led to Dr Banda's removal and Malawi's first multi-party elections in 1994.

At the southern end of Lake Malawi (Lake Nyasa) the Shire River runs through a deep, swampy valley flanked by mountains to the east. Most of the population live in this southern region, growing

maize as the main food crop and cultivating cash crops such as peanuts and sugarcane. The western central plateau rises northward to the Nyika Uplands, where rainfall is highest. In the Shire Highlands to the south, tea and tobacco are grown on large estates. Savanna grassland in the valleys gives way to open woodland, much of which has been cleared for cultivation. Wildlife is largely confined to reserves.

Agriculture provides more than 90 percent of exports. Reserves of bauxite and uranium exist, but not in commercially usable quantities. Hydro-electricity supplies only about 3 percent of total energy use—most needs are met from fuelwood, which is resulting in continued deforestation. The economy depends heavily on foreign aid.

Fact File

OFFICIAL NAME Republic of Malawi

FORM OF GOVERNMENT Republic with single legislative body (National Assembly)

CAPITAL Lilongwe

AREA 118,480 sq km (45,745 sq miles)

TIME ZONE GMT + 2 hours

POPULATION 9,888,601

PROJECTED POPULATION 2005 10,469,217

POPULATION DENSITY 83.4 per sq km (216 per sq mile)

LIFE EXPECTANCY 33.7

INFANT MORTALITY (PER 1,000) 136.9

OFFICIAL LANGUAGES Chichewa, English

OTHER LANGUAGES Indigenous languages

LITERACY RATE 55.8%

RELIGIONS Protestant 55%, Roman Catholic 20%, Muslim 20%, indigenous beliefs 5%

ETHNIC GROUPS Indigenous tribes: Malavi (including Chewa, Nyanja, Tumbuke, Tonga) 58%, Lomwe 18%, Yao 13%, Ngoni 7%; Asian and European 4%

CURRENCY Kwacha

ECONOMY Agriculture 79%, services 16%, industry 5%

GNP PER CAPITA US$170

CLIMATE Tropical, with wet season November to April

HIGHEST POINT Mt Mulanje 3,001 m (9,846 ft)

MAP REFERENCE Page 369

Africa

Mali

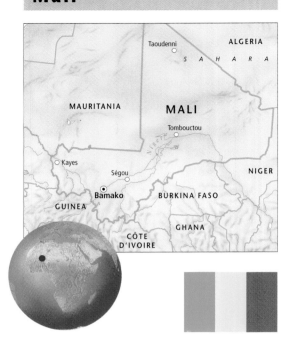

Fact File

OFFICIAL NAME Republic of Mali

FORM OF GOVERNMENT Republic with single legislative body (National Assembly)

CAPITAL Bamako

AREA 1,240,000 sq km (478,764 sq miles)

TIME ZONE GMT

POPULATION 10,429,124

PROJECTED POPULATION 2005 12,536,227

POPULATION DENSITY 8.4 per sq km (21.8 per sq mile)

LIFE EXPECTANCY 47.5

INFANT MORTALITY (PER 1,000) 119.4

OFFICIAL LANGUAGE French

OTHER LANGUAGES Bambara and other indigenous languages

LITERACY RATE 29.3%

RELIGIONS Muslim 90%, indigenous beliefs 9%, Christian 1%

ETHNIC GROUPS Mande 50%, Peul 17%, Voltaic 12%, Songhai 6%, Tuareg and Moor 10%, other 5%

CURRENCY CFA (Communauté Financière Africaine) franc

ECONOMY Agriculture 85%, services 13%, industry 2%

GNP PER CAPITA US$250

CLIMATE Subtropical in south and southwest; arid in north

HIGHEST POINT Hombori Tondo 1,155 m (3,789 ft)

MAP REFERENCE Pages 361, 364–65

Mali is a landlocked west African country, watered by the River Niger in the south and with vast stretches of the Sahara Desert lying to the north. It derives its name from the Malinke or Mandingo people whose empire flourished between the eighth and fourteenth centuries. Later it was a center of trade and Islamic scholarship, based on the city of Timbuktu (now Tombouctou). At the end of the nineteenth century it became a colony of French West Africa, achieving independence in 1960. For the next 30 years the country was ruled by either civilian or military dictators. Demonstrations in 1991 in which about 100 people died were followed by the overthrow of the regime, and free elections were held for the first time in 1992.

There is a major ethnic division between the black African majority in the south, and the minority of Arab Tuareg nomads in the north. Violent Tuareg guerrilla activity in northern Mali ended with a peace pact in 1995.

Mali's flat landscape consists mainly of plains and sandstone plateaus. The need for water is the main concern. The northern and virtually rainless Saharan plains are inhabited almost entirely by Tuareg nomads. The semiarid center—the Sahel—has in recent years suffered from devastating droughts. Such arable land as exists is found in the south, along the Senegal and Niger Rivers, the latter spreading out to form an inland delta before turning southward on its way to the border of Niger. These rivers provide water for stock and for irrigation. Rice is grown on irrigated land; millet, cotton, and peanuts grow elsewhere. Away from the rivers southern Mali is mostly savanna country where mahogany, kapok, and baobab trees grow, these being replaced further north by palms and scrub. Animal life includes lion, antelope, jackal, and hyena.

Some 80 percent of the labor force works in agriculture and fishing—dried fish is exported to Burkina Faso, Côte d'Ivoire, and Ghana. With 65 percent of its land either desert or semidesert, however, and industry limited mainly to a single gold mine, salt production, and small-scale textiles and shoes, Mali is extremely poor. As well as gold there are phosphates, uranium, bauxite, manganese, and copper but development is hampered by poor transport facilities and the fact that the country is landlocked. With expenditures almost double its revenues, Mali is a major recipient of foreign aid.

Mauritania

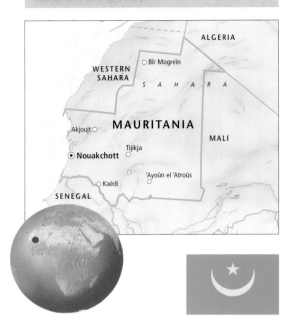

Most of Mauritania consists of the wastes of the western Sahara Desert. Islam in the region dates from the Almoravid Empire of the twelfth century. Later, it was conquered by Arab bidan or "white" Moors (*Maure* in French, meaning Moor), nomads who subjugated and enslaved the black Africans of the south, producing a people of mixed Arab and African descent known as *harratin* or "black" Moors. Deep social tensions between the dominant "white" Moors, the "black" Moors, and the subordinate 30 percent of black African farmers in the south lie at the heart of Mauritanian politics. Slavery in Mauritania was not officially abolished until 1970, and it is estimated that tens of

thousands of *harratin* still live as slaves. France entered the region early in the nineteenth century and established a protectorate in 1903. Independence came in 1960.

Inland from the low-lying coastal plains of the Atlantic seaboard there are low plateaus—a tableland broken by occasional hills and scarps. The Saharan Desert to the north, which forms 47 percent of Mauritania's total land area, rises to the isolated peak of Kediet Ijill. In the southern third of the country there is just enough rain to support Sahelian thornbush and grasses. After rain, cattle herders drive their herds from the Senegal River through these grasslands, in good years the livestock outnumbering the general population five to one. During the 1980s the whole area suffered severely from drought and the nomadic population, which had numbered three-quarters of the national population, fell to less than one-third, many nomads abandoning rural life entirely for the towns.

Farmers near the Senegal River grow millet, sorghum, beans, peanuts, and rice, using the late-summer river floods for irrigation. A hydroelectric project on the river is intended to provide water for the irrigated cultivation of rice, cotton, and sugarcane, but drought has also driven many subsistence farmers from the land. Off the coast, cooled by the Canaries current, lie some of the richest fishing grounds in the world. Although about 100,000 tonnes of fish are landed annually, the potential catch is estimated at about 600,000 tonnes. Exploitation by foreign fishing boats threatens this source of revenue.

Fact File

OFFICIAL NAME	Islamic Republic of Mauritania
FORM OF GOVERNMENT	Republic with two legislative bodies (Senate and National Assembly)
CAPITAL	Nouakchott
AREA	1,030,700 sq km (397,953 sq miles)
TIME ZONE	GMT
POPULATION	2,581,738
PROJECTED POPULATION 2005	3,088,823
POPULATION DENSITY	2.5 per sq km (6.5 per sq mile)
LIFE EXPECTANCY	50.5
INFANT MORTALITY (PER 1,000)	76.5
OFFICIAL LANGUAGES	French, Hasaniya Arabic
OTHER LANGUAGES	Indigenous languages, Arabic
LITERACY RATE	36.9%
RELIGIONS	Muslim 99%, other 1%
ETHNIC GROUPS	"Black" Moors 40%, "White" Moors 30%, African 30%
CURRENCY	Ouguiya
ECONOMY	Agriculture 70%, services 22%, industry 8%
GNP PER CAPITA	US$460
CLIMATE	Mainly arid, with wet season in far south (May to September)
HIGHEST POINT	Kediet Ijill 915 m (3,002 ft)
MAP REFERENCE	Pages 360, 364

The city of Tombouctou, in Mali, following a dust storm (left). Women agricultural workers walking beside a field of sugarcane in Mauritius (top right).

Mauritius

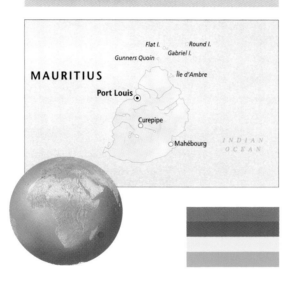

Famous as the home of the now-extinct flightless bird, the dodo, the Republic of Mauritius consists of one large and several smaller islands 800 km (500 miles) east of Madagascar. Mauritius was uninhabited when visited by the Portuguese and the Dutch between the fifteenth and seventeenth centuries. It was first settled by the French, after 1715, who brought African slaves for the sugar plantations. In 1810 it was taken over by the British, who brought in numerous indentured laborers from India. These colonial origins produced two distinct communities, one Afro-French Creole (27 percent), the other English-speaking and Indian (73 percent), who compete for influence and power. Independence within the British Commonwealth was granted in 1968 and Mauritius became a republic in 1992. Despite occasional unrest, the country has a record of political stability and economic growth.

Fringed with coral reefs, the main island rises from coastal plains on its north and east to a plateau surrounded by rugged peaks—the remains of a giant volcano. The climate is tropical, but moderated by rain-bearing winds from the southeast. Sugarcane is grown on 90 percent of the cultivated land, and accounts, with derivatives such as molasses, for 40 percent of export earnings. A by-product of the sugar industry, the cane-waste called bagasse, has been used to fuel power stations. Fast-flowing rivers descending from the plateau are used to produce hydroelectric power.

Industrial diversification (textile and garment manufacture now accounts for 44 percent of export revenue) and the development of a tourist industry (up to half a million visitors per year) have enabled Mauritius to transcend the low income agricultural economy that existed at the time of independence. Since 1968 annual economic growth most years has been about 5 percent, life expectancy has been increasing and the infrastructure has improved.

Fact File

OFFICIAL NAME	Republic of Mauritius
FORM OF GOVERNMENT	Republic with single legislative body (Legislative Assembly)
CAPITAL	Port Louis
AREA	1,860 sq km (718 sq miles)
TIME ZONE	GMT + 4 hours
POPULATION	1,182,212
PROJECTED POPULATION 2005	1,265,011
POPULATION DENSITY	635.6 per sq km (1,646.2 per sq mile)
LIFE EXPECTANCY	71.1
INFANT MORTALITY (PER 1,000)	16.2
OFFICIAL LANGUAGE	English
OTHER LANGUAGES	Creole, French, Hindi, Urdu, Bojpoori, Hakka
LITERACY RATE	82.4%
RELIGIONS	Hindu 52%, Roman Catholic 26%, Protestant 2.3%, Muslim 16.6%, other 3.1%
ETHNIC GROUPS	Indo-Mauritian 68%, Creole 27%, Sino-Mauritian 3%, Franco-Mauritian 2%
CURRENCY	Mauritian rupee
ECONOMY	Services 51%, agriculture 27%, industry 22%
GNP PER CAPITA	US$3,380
CLIMATE	Tropical, moderated by trade winds
HIGHEST POINT	Piton de la Petite Rivière Noire 828 m (2,717 ft)
MAP REFERENCE	Pages 372, 373

Africa

Morocco

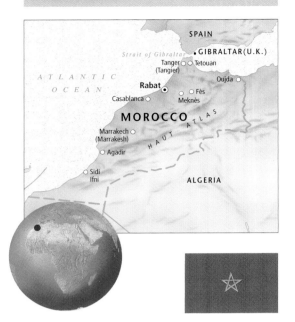

Morocco's earliest inhabitants were the Berbers, who still live in the country today. At one time under Carthaginian rule, and then a part of the Roman Empire, the Berbers were overrun by Arabs in the seventh century AD and converted to Islam. The country's name derives from the Arabic *Maghreb-el-aksa* ("the farthest west"), and because of the protective barrier of the Atlas Mountains, Morocco has always been less a part of the Arab world than the other north African states. Under political pressure from Spain and France during the nineteenth century, Morocco became a French protectorate in 1912. About 35 percent of the people live in the highlands and are Berber-speaking, while the Arab majority live in the lowlands.

Under the rule of King Hassan II since 1961, Morocco has followed generally pro-Western policies. The king's popularity at home owes a good deal to Morocco's disputed territorial claim to the phosphate-rich resources of Western Sahara across the southern border. A costly armed struggle with the Polisario Front guerrilla movement of Western Sahara led to a cease-fire in 1991, by which time 170,000 of the native-born Sahrawis of the region had become refugees in Algeria. Sovereignty is still unresolved.

More than one-third of Morocco is mountainous. Three parallel ranges of the Atlas Mountains run southwest to northeast, where a plateau reaches toward the Algerian border. Most of the people living in the mountains are peasant cultivators and nomadic herders. Modern economic development is found mainly on the Atlantic plains and the plateaus—the fertile Moulouyan, Rharb, Sous, and High (Haut) Atlas plains constituting virtually all of Morocco's cultivable land. In the Rharb and Rif regions extensive areas are covered with cork oak, while on the northern slopes there are forests of evergreen oak and cedar. Wildlife includes Cuvier's gazelle, the Barbary macaque, and the mouflon (a wild sheep), while desert animals such as the fennec fox live in the south.

A gold seller in Morocco (right). Old-style houses in Fès, Morocco (far right). Sand dunes in Namib-Naukluft Park in Namibia (above right).

In 1995 Morocco suffered its worst drought in 30 years. This seriously affected agriculture, which produces about one-third of Morocco's exports and employs about half the workforce. Irrigation is essential over most of the country, the chief crops being barley and wheat, along with citrus fruit, potatoes, and other vegetables. Dates are grown in desert oases. The country's natural resources are still largely undeveloped. It has coal, iron ore, and zinc, along with the world's largest reserves of phosphates. Debt servicing, unemployment, the high rate of population increase, and the unresolved territorial claim to Western Sahara are all long-term problems.

Fact File

OFFICIAL NAME	Kingdom of Morocco
FORM OF GOVERNMENT	Constitutional monarchy with single legislative body (Chamber of Representatives)
CAPITAL	Rabat
AREA	446,550 sq km (172,413 sq miles)
TIME ZONE	GMT + 1 hour
POPULATION	29,661,636
PROJECTED POPULATION 2005	32,923,967
POPULATION DENSITY	66.4 per sq km (172 per sq mile)
LIFE EXPECTANCY	68.9
INFANT MORTALITY (PER 1,000)	11.0
OFFICIAL LANGUAGE	Arabic
OTHER LANGUAGES	Berber languages, French
LITERACY RATE	42.1%
RELIGIONS	Muslim 98.7%, Christian 1.1%, Jewish 0.2%
ETHNIC GROUPS	Arab–Berber 99.1%, other 0.7%, Jewish 0.2%
CURRENCY	Moroccan dirham
ECONOMY	Agriculture 46%, services 30%, industry 24%
GNP PER CAPITA	US$1,110
CLIMATE	Temperate along northern coast, arid in south, cooler in mountains
HIGHEST POINT	Jebel Toubkal 4,165 m (13,665 ft)
MAP REFERENCE	Pages 360–61

Mozambique

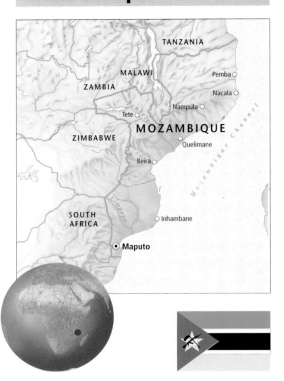

Lying on the southeast coast of Africa facing Madagascar, Mozambique is divided in two by the Zambeze River. This division is also found in its social and political life: people in the north support the Renamo party, while south of the river they support Frelimo. Visited by Vasco da Gama in 1498 and colonized by Portuguese in search of gold, Mozambique remained a slave-trading center until the 1850s.

A long war of liberation against Portugal led to independence in 1975 and brought the Marxist Frelimo to power. Frelimo's one-party regime was then challenged by a guerilla movement, Renamo, supported by South Africa. The ensuing civil war, aggravated by famine, led to nearly 1 million deaths. By 1989 Mozambique was world's poorest country. That year Frelimo renounced Marxism. At multi-party elections in 1994 it won by a narrow majority.

A considerable amount of rain falls in the north: south of the Zambeze conditions are much drier.

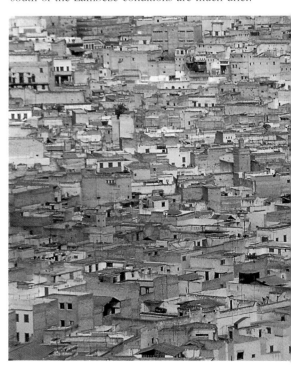

North of Maputo, the only natural harbor, is a wide coastal plain where there are coconut, sugar, and sisal plantations, and smallholders grow maize and peanuts. Inland, the terrain rises to the high veld.

Economically, Mozambique faces a huge task of reconstruction and the government is trying to redistribute to peasants large areas of land that were seized by the state. Agricultural output is only 75 percent of its 1981 level and grain is imported. Industry is operating at less than half capacity. There are substantial agricultural, hydropower and petroleum resources, and deposits of coal, copper and bauxite but these are largely undeveloped.

Fact File

OFFICIAL NAME	Republic of Mozambique
FORM OF GOVERNMENT	Republic with single legislative body (Assembly of the Republic)
CAPITAL	Maputo
AREA	801,590 sq km (309,494 sq miles)
TIME ZONE	GMT + 2 hours
POPULATION	19,124,335
PROJECTED POPULATION 2005	22,155,576
POPULATION DENSITY	23.9 per sq km (61.8 per sq mile)
LIFE EXPECTANCY	45.9
INFANT MORTALITY (PER 1,000)	117.6
OFFICIAL LANGUAGE	Portuguese
OTHER LANGUAGES	Indigenous languages
LITERACY RATE	39.5%
RELIGIONS	Indigenous beliefs 55%, Christian 30%, Muslim 15%
ETHNIC GROUPS	Indigenous tribes (including Shangaan, Chokwe, Manyika, Sena, Makua) 99.7%, other 0.3%
CURRENCY	Metical
ECONOMY	Agriculture 85%, services 8%, industry 7%
GNP PER CAPITA	US$80
CLIMATE	Mainly tropical: wet season December to March
HIGHEST POINT	Monte Binga 2,436 m (7,992 ft)
MAP REFERENCE	Pages 369, 371

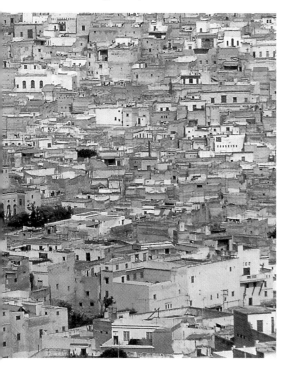

Namibia

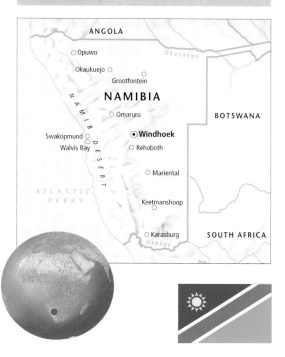

A large, arid country in southwest Africa, Namibia was born of the European scramble for colonies in the nineteenth century. The German connection with the area (formerly South West Africa) began with the arrival of missionaries in the 1840s. Namibia was a German protectorate from 1884; the scene of a brutal German punitive action in 1904 in which the Herero were decimated and scattered; under South African control for many years; and endured 23 years of a bitter anti-colonial war that began in 1966. In 1989 an election gave the guerrilla movement SWAPO (the South West African People's Organization) victory at the polls, and in 1990 came independence.

The virtually uninhabited sand dunes of the Namib Desert fringe the country's south Atlantic coastline. A major escarpment inland separates the desert from a north–south range of mountains which includes the Tsaris Mountains, Aûas Mountains, and Mt Erongo. The interior plateau, which occupies the eastern part of the country, has an average elevation of 1,500 m (5,000 ft) and is covered with the dry scrub grassland typical of the Kalahari Desert. Largely rainless, the coast is often shrouded in fog. Here, welwitschia plants, some of them up to 2,000 years old, live by absorbing moisture from the fog that rolls in from the sea. Namibia's wildlife is typical of southern Africa, with Etosha National Park providing sanctuary for baboon, antelope, elephant, giraffe, zebra, and lion.

Namibia's natural resources include diamonds, copper, uranium (world's fifth largest producer), gold, lead (world's second largest producer), tin, lithium, cadmium, zinc, vanadium, and natural gas, and there are thought to be deposits of oil, coal, and iron ore. Mining accounts for 25 percent of gross domestic product, this sector relying on the expertise of Namibia's small white population. More than half its African peoples depend on agriculture for a livelihood, working poor soils in an unfavorable climate. Livestock farmers produce beef and mutton. About half the country's food is imported, mainly from South Africa.

Fact File

OFFICIAL NAME	Republic of Namibia
FORM OF GOVERNMENT	Republic with two legislative bodies (National Council and National Assembly)
CAPITAL	Windhoek
AREA	825,418 sq km (318,694 sq miles)
TIME ZONE	GMT + 2 hours
POPULATION	1,648,270
PROJECTED POPULATION 2005	1,798,625
POPULATION DENSITY	2 per sq km (5.2 per sq mile)
LIFE EXPECTANCY	41.3
INFANT MORTALITY (PER 1,000)	65.9
OFFICIAL LANGUAGE	English
OTHER LANGUAGES	Afrikaans, German, indigenous languages
LITERACY RATE	40%
RELIGIONS	Christian 85% (Lutheran at least 50%, other Christian denominations 35%), indigenous beliefs 15%
ETHNIC GROUPS	Indigenous tribes 86% (including Ovambo 50%, Kavangos 9%, Herero 7%, Damara 7%), mixed indigenous–European 7.4%, European 6.6%
CURRENCY	Namibian dollar
ECONOMY	Agriculture 60%, industry and commerce 19%, services 8%, government 7%, mining 6%
GNP PER CAPITA	US$2,000
CLIMATE	Mainly arid, with higher rainfall inland
HIGHEST POINT	Brandberg 2,573 m (8,439 ft)
MAP REFERENCE	Page 370

Africa

Niger

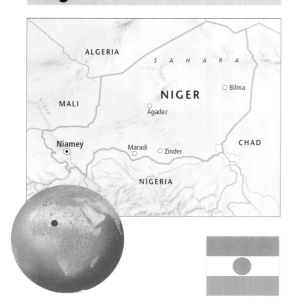

Niger is two-thirds desert, which may seem strange for a country that is named after a great river (the name "Niger" comes from the Tuareg word *n'eghirren*, for flowing water), but the River Niger only cuts across the extreme southwest of this large, landlocked country. Elsewhere, there is an arid landscape of stony basins, drifting sands, and a northern highland that forms part of the mountain chain stretching from Algeria to Chad.

The home of the Sokoto Empire of the Fulani in the nineteenth century, the region became part of French West Africa in 1922, and received independence in 1960. Then followed three decades of dictatorial civilian and military rule. Despite the holding of multi-party elections in 1993, continuing unrest caused by Tuareg rebels in the north and power struggles within the government led to the reimposition of military rule in 1996.

Niger's central geographic feature is the Massif de l'Aïr. In these mountains, which rise out of the Saharan plains to jagged peaks up to 1,900 m (6,230 ft) high, there is sometimes sufficient rain for thorny scrub to grow. Formerly nomads grazed their camels, horses, cattle, and goats in this area, but devastating droughts in 1973 and 1983 destroyed their livelihood. To the east and west of the Massif de l'Aïr are the Saharan Desert plains of Ténéré du Tafassasset and the Western Talk. Sand and sandy soil cover most of the desert plains to the north and east, an area which is virtually rainless and, aside from small numbers of people living at the occasional palm-fringed oasis, uninhabited. Plant life includes kapok and baobab trees. Buffalo, antelope, lion, hippopotamus, and crocodiles are found in Niger but their survival today is more a matter of chance than good management.

With its gross domestic product growth barely matching the growth of its population, Niger is one of the most impoverished countries in Africa. More than 95 percent of its people earn a living from farming and trading. Where the Niger River crosses the country in the far southwest there are fertile arable soils: crops include yams, cassava, and maize, and rice in areas where the river floods. On the drier land toward Lake Chad

(Lac Tchad) millet and sorghum are grown. The drought that has affected extensive areas of the Sahel has reduced Niger from self-sufficiency to being an importer of food. Tin and tungsten are mined, and there are reserves of iron ore, manganese, and molybdenum. During the 1970s, when prices were high, uranium became the main source of revenue, and it continues to be the country's most valuable export. Between 1983 and 1990, however, revenues fell by 50 percent. At present the government of Niger relies on aid for both operating expenses and for public investment.

Fact File

OFFICIAL NAME	Republic of Niger
FORM OF GOVERNMENT	Republic with single legislative body (National Assembly)
CAPITAL	Niamey
AREA	1,267,000 sq km (489,189 sq miles)
TIME ZONE	GMT + 1 hour
POPULATION	9,962,242
PROJECTED POPULATION 2005	11,864,407
POPULATION DENSITY	7.9 per sq km (20.5 per sq mile)
LIFE EXPECTANCY	42
INFANT MORTALITY (PER 1,000)	112.8
OFFICIAL LANGUAGE	French
OTHER LANGUAGES	Hausa, Djerma, Fulani
LITERACY RATE	13.1%
RELIGIONS	Muslim 80%, Christian and indigenous beliefs 20%
ETHNIC GROUPS	Hausa 56%, Djerma 22%, Fula 8.5%, Tuareg 8%, Beri Beri 4.3%, other (including 4,000 French expatriates) 1.2%
CURRENCY	CFA (Communauté Financière Africaine) franc
ECONOMY	Agriculture 87%, services 10%, industry 3%
GNP PER CAPITA	US$220
CLIMATE	Mainly arid; tropical in south, with wet season June to October
HIGHEST POINT	Mt Gréboun 1,994 m (6,540 ft)
MAP REFERENCE	Pages 361, 362, 365

Nigeria

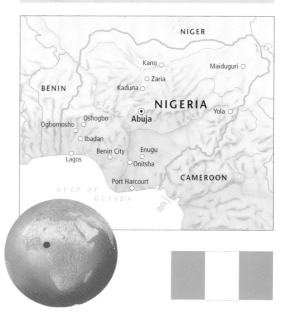

With the continent's largest population, huge oil revenues, and a territory that is four times the size of the United Kingdom, Nigeria is one of Africa's most important nations. It also ranks as one of the most corrupt countries in the world, and a place where tensions between the main tribal groups are close to breaking point.

Such tensions are not new to the region: regional and ethnic conflict go back to the days of Nigeria's ancient city-states. The life of the Yoruba people centered on the city of Ife, while the Hausa kingdom was in the north. The kingdom of Benin, well known for its portrait bronzes of past rulers, was in the west, and a number of communities of Ibo lived in the southeast. Bringing all these peoples together to form a single nation has proved difficult: since independence, in 1960, there has been a series of military dictatorships, and only 10 years of elected government. An unsuccessful attempt to secede by the Ibo in 1967 (who set up an independent state named Biafra) failed in 1970, following a bitter civil war in which thousands of people died. Today, an uneasy peace prevails under military rule.

Africa

Women drawing water from a deep well in Niger (far left). Wooded countryside turned to desert in Niger as a result of drought (left). Donkeys are used to transport produce in a village in Nigeria (below).

Agricultural production has failed to keep pace with population growth, and Nigeria is now a food importer. There are fundamental imbalances in the economy that result in chronic inflation and a steadily depreciating currency. Investors are wary because of political instability and corruption at the highest levels of government. Domestic and international debts prevent an agreement with the IMF on debt relief.

Fact File

OFFICIAL NAME	Federal Republic of Nigeria
FORM OF GOVERNMENT	Military regime
CAPITAL	Abuja
AREA	923,770 sq km (356,668 sq miles)
TIME ZONE	GMT + 1 hour
POPULATION	113,828,587
PROJECTED POPULATION 2005	133,974,486
POPULATION DENSITY	123.2 per sq km (319 per sq mile)
LIFE EXPECTANCY	53.3
INFANT MORTALITY (PER 1,000)	89.5
OFFICIAL LANGUAGES	English
OTHER LANGUAGES	French, Hausa, Yoruba, Ibo, Fulani
LITERACY RATE	55.6%
RELIGIONS	Muslim 50%, Christian 40%, indigenous beliefs 10%
ETHNIC GROUPS	About 250 indigenous groups: the largest of which are Hausa, Fulani, Yoruba, Ibo 68%; Kanuri, Edo, Tiv, Ibidio, Nupe 25%; other 7%
CURRENCY	Naira
ECONOMY	Services 51%, agriculture 45%, industry 4%
GNP PER CAPITA	US$260
CLIMATE	Tropical in south, with wet season April to October; arid in north
HIGHEST POINT	Chappal Waddi 2,419 m (7,936 ft)
MAP REFERENCE	Page 365

Physical features and land use

Nigeria's coast on the west African Gulf of Guinea consists of long, sandy beaches, and mangrove swamps where its rivers flow into the sea. The mouth of the Niger forms an immense delta, threaded with thousands of creeks and lagoons, with Port Harcourt on one of the main channels. Upstream it divides, the Benue (Bénoué) River leading east into Cameroon, the Niger heading northwest toward Benin. These two large rivers provide transport, by boat, for cargo and people. High rainfall on the coast and in the river valleys enables yams, cassava, maize, and vegetables to be grown and on floodland alongside the rivers rice is cultivated.

In the rainy forested belt to the north the hills gradually rise to the semiarid central savanna plateau, and then to the Jos Plateau, reaching 1,780 m (5,840 ft) at Share Hill. Up the Benue (Bénoué) River to the east the land rises to the wooded slopes of the Adamaoua Massif and the Cameroon highlands. From these hill-slope areas come such products as cocoa, rubber, hardwoods, and palm oil. North of the Jos Plateau the savanna becomes dry, in many places degenerating into arid Sahelian scrub, where both herds and herders have difficulty surviving. Around Lake Chad (Lac Tchad) the typical vegetation is hardy acacia and doum palms.

Together, the river systems of the Niger and the Benue (Bénoué) drain 60 percent of Nigeria's total land area. Though much reduced by clearing for cultivation, the Nigerian rainforests still produce mahogany and iriko. Wildlife includes elephant, chimpanzee, and the red river hog.

People and culture

In addition to the Yoruba, Fulani, Hausa, and Ibo, Nigeria has 245 much smaller ethnic groups. Not only are they divided along lines of ethnicity, language, and regional dialect, there is also a major religious division. The north of the country is largely Islamic (the religion of the Hausa and Fulani) while the south is for the most part Christian, combined with indigenous African beliefs. Outbreaks of communal violence in the north sometimes occur as a result of clashes between Islamic fundamentalists and missionary

Christians. Despite widespread Christian proselytizing there is evidence that Islamic influence is gradually growing in the south.

Although 54 percent of the labor force works in agriculture, and many rural people are subsistence farmers, Nigerians have also lived in cities for centuries. This contrasts with many other parts of Africa. Long before European commercial expansion into the region, places such as Benin, Kano, Ibadan, and Ife were administrative and trading centers with sizeable populations. As in other parts of west Africa, women in the non-Islamic Nigerian cultures play a prominent role in commercial life.

Economy and resources

Nigeria is rich in natural resources and these are the basis of its economic strength. They include tin, columbite, iron ore, coal, limestone, lead, zinc, and natural gas. By far the most important, however, is oil: Nigeria is OPEC's fourth largest producer, with oil providing 80 percent of government revenue and 90 percent of export earnings overall. This has led to what many consider over-dependence on a single commodity. In addition it has provided a limitless source of independent wealth for the political elite.

Africa

Rwanda

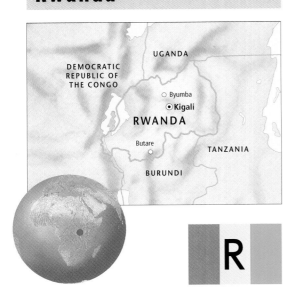

Fact File

OFFICIAL NAME Republic of Rwanda

FORM OF GOVERNMENT Republic with transitional legislative body (National Assembly)

CAPITAL Kigali

AREA 26,340 sq km (10,170 sq miles)

TIME ZONE GMT + 2 hours

POPULATION 8,154,933

PROJECTED POPULATION 2005 9,135,398

POPULATION DENSITY 309.6 per sq km (801.9 per sq mile)

LIFE EXPECTANCY 41.3

INFANT MORTALITY (PER 1,000) 112.9

OFFICIAL LANGUAGES French, Kinyarwanda

OTHER LANGUAGE Kiswahili

LITERACY RATE 59.2%

RELIGIONS Roman Catholic 65%, Protestant 9%, Muslim 1%, indigenous beliefs and other 25%

ETHNIC GROUPS Hutu 80%, Tutsi 19%, Twa (Pygmy) 1%

CURRENCY Rwandan franc

ECONOMY Agriculture 93%, services 5%, industry 2%

GNP PER CAPITA US$180

CLIMATE Tropical, with two wet seasons (October to December and March to May)

HIGHEST POINT Karisimbi 4,507 m (14,783 ft)

MAP REFERENCE Page 369

A small landlocked country in central Africa, Rwanda shares much of its social history with Burundi, across its southern border. In the fifteenth and sixteenth centuries a tall cattle-herding people, named Tutsi, probably from Sudan, came to the region and formed a small feudal aristocracy that dominated the more numerous Hutu farmers who had settled in the area some time before them. Since then, the Hutu people have endured the situation with resentment. In recent times, beginning with a Hutu revolt in 1959 (independence from Belgium coming in 1962), there have been decades of ethnic strife and intermittent violence, with hundreds of thousands of deaths occurring on both sides. This culminated in the massacre of half a million Tutsi (and also some moderate Hutu) by Hutu in 1994, waves of refugees spilling out into the Democratic Republic of Congo, Burundi, Tanzania, and Uganda. An uneasy peace followed.

Rwanda is the most densely populated country in Africa. Almost 30 percent of the land is arable, steep slopes are intensively cultivated, and terracing and contour plowing are used in order to keep erosion to a minimum. Lake Kivu and a part of the southward-flowing Ruzizi River form the western boundary of the country. From here the land rises steeply to the mountains, part of the Rift Valley, which constitute the Nile–Congo divide. To the north are the mountains, and several volcanoes, of the Mufumbiro Range. These include one of the last refuges of the mountain gorilla. From the heights of the eastern rim of the Rift Valley a plateau slopes eastward toward the Tanzanian border, the River Kagera marshes, and a number of lakes.

During peacetime, Rwanda's production of coffee and tea constituted 80 to 90 percent of total exports. Pyrethrum and sugarcane are other cash crops, cassava, maize, bananas, sorghum, and vegetables being crops grown for food. In keeping with their status as one-time nomadic herders, the Tutsi people keep cattle. The Hutu generally keep sheep and goats. Arable land is overused and deforestation and soil erosion are widespread. Natural resources include gold, tin, tungsten, and natural gas, but they are undeveloped because of infrastructure and transport difficulties. Political and ethnic disorders have affected the economy which suffers from infrastructural damage, lack of maintenance, looting, and the widespread destruction of property and crops. Recovery of production to earlier levels will take time.

A crater lake in Volcanoes National Park, Rwanda (below). The endangered mountain gorilla still survives in the highlands of Rwanda (right). Women removing small fish from a fishing net in Senegal (top right).

São Tomé and Príncipe

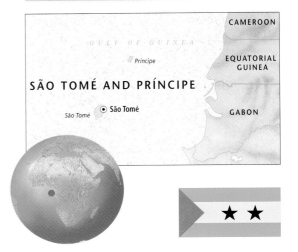

São Tomé and Príncipe are two islands lying off the coast of Gabon in the Gulf of Guinea. They were occupied in the 1520s by the Portuguese, who used slaves as laborers on the sugar plantations. The population now consists mainly of the Afro-Portuguese descendants of these first immigrants, plus contract laborers brought from Mozambique and Cape Verde to work on cocoa plantations in the nineteenth century. Following independence in 1975, a one-party Marxist regime was imposed. For a time the islands were allied to the Soviet bloc and Russian and Cuban military advisors were brought in.

At a referendum in 1990, however, 72 percent of the people voted in favor of democratic government. Now the main concern of the government is to rebuild the country's relationship with Portugal and to secure beneficial working relationships with the EU and the USA.

An extinct volcano, São Tomé is the largest and most populous of the two main islands, some 440 km (273 miles) off the coast of Gabon. Low lying in the northeast and the southwest, it rises to Pico de São Tomé in the volcanic highlands. The island of Príncipe lies about 150 km (100 miles) to the northeast. As well as the two main islands there are also a number of rocky islets—Caroco, Pedras, Tinhosas, and Rôlas. On both São Tomé and Príncipe, streams drain to the sea from mountainous interiors, up to 70 percent of which are densely forested. The climate is hot and humid, moderated to a certain extent by the cold Benguela current that flows up Africa's western shore.

Following independence in 1975 the cocoa plantations which formed the foundation of the country's economy deteriorated as a result of mismanagement aggravated by drought. By 1987 the production of cocoa had fallen to 3,500 tonnes from an annual output of 9,000 tonnes prior to 1975. While there has been some economic recovery in recent years, São Tomé and Príncipe have had serious balance of payments problems. During the 1980s agriculture diversified into palm oil, pepper, and coffee but since then production has faltered. Deforestation and soil erosion are an increasing cause for concern. Today, São Tomé imports 90 percent of its food, all its fuel and most manufactured goods.

Fact File

OFFICIAL NAME Democratic Republic of São Tomé and Príncipe

FORM OF GOVERNMENT Republic with single legislative body (National People's Assembly)

CAPITAL São Tomé

AREA 960 sq km (371 sq miles)

TIME ZONE GMT

POPULATION 154,878

PROJECTED POPULATION 2005 187,394

POPULATION DENSITY 161.3 per sq km (417.8 per sq mile)

LIFE EXPECTANCY 64.7

INFANT MORTALITY (PER 1,000) 52.9

OFFICIAL LANGUAGE Portuguese

OTHER LANGUAGES Various creoles

LITERACY RATE 67%

RELIGIONS Roman Catholic 80%, Protestant and other 20%

ETHNIC GROUPS Predominantly mixed African–Portuguese, with various African minorities

CURRENCY Dobra

ECONOMY Mainly agriculture and fishing

GNP PER CAPITA US$350

CLIMATE Tropical, with wet season October to May

HIGHEST POINT Pico de São Tomé 2,024 m (6,640 ft)

MAP REFERENCE Pages 365, 373

Senegal

Dakar, the capital of Senegal, lies on the westernmost point of west Africa and in the seventeenth and eighteenth centuries it was a major slave-trading base. French colonial control of Senegal was established during the suppression of the slave trade in the nineteenth century. As the administrative center of the huge region of French West Africa, an effective road network was established in Dakar, plus extensive port facilities and a large civil service.

Independence from France came in 1960. Despite being a de facto one-party state for the next 10 years, Senegal avoided military and dictatorial rule, and has recently liberalized its economic and political life. The country's most serious problem is continuing armed revolt in the oil-rich southern province of Casamance, south of Gambia, a region that differs ethnically, economically, and geographically from the north.

Senegal is split by the near-enclave of Gambia and the Gambia River. To the north the land is drier, with sand dunes along the coast. Inland there are plains, savanna, and semidesert, where Fulani cattle-herders eke out an existence. South of Dakar and Cape Vert it is wetter and more fertile, with coastal mangrove swamps and forest inland. Sorghum is grown in the rainier areas of savanna bushland, while south of Gambia rice is cultivated

on the floodplain of the Casamance River—the most fertile part of the country.

Peanuts have long been the foundation of Senegal's economy and are grown on half the cultivated land. Efforts are being made to diversify, and sugarcane, millet, cotton, and rice are now cultivated. Other than the recently developed oil fields in Casamance, with the promise of more offshore, natural resources are few. Though its arrangements are democratic, Senegal's ruling party has been in power since the 1950s, creating a network of patronage through the civil service, the judiciary, and the state-owned industries. Senegal receives a considerable amount of foreign aid.

Fact File

OFFICIAL NAME Republic of Senegal

FORM OF GOVERNMENT Republic with single legislative body (National Assembly)

CAPITAL Dakar

AREA 196,190 sq km (75,749 sq miles)

TIME ZONE GMT

POPULATION 9,051,930

PROJECTED POPULATION 2005 12,235,259

POPULATION DENSITY 51.2 per sq km (132.6 per sq mile)

LIFE EXPECTANCY 57.8

INFANT MORTALITY (PER 1,000) 59.8

OFFICIAL LANGUAGE French

OTHER LANGUAGES Wolof, Pulaar, Diola, Mandingo

LITERACY RATE 32.1%

RELIGIONS Muslim 92%, indigenous beliefs 6%, Christian 2% (mainly Roman Catholic)

ETHNIC GROUPS Wolof 36%, Fulani 17%, Serer 17%, Toucouleur 9%, Diola 9%, Mandingo 9%, European and Lebanese 1%, other 2%

CURRENCY CFA (Communauté Financière Africaine) franc

ECONOMY Agriculture 81%, services 13%, industry 6%

GNP PER CAPITA US$600

CLIMATE Tropical, with wet season June to October

HIGHEST POINT Unnamed location in southeast 581 m (1,906 ft)

MAP REFERENCE Page 364

Seychelles

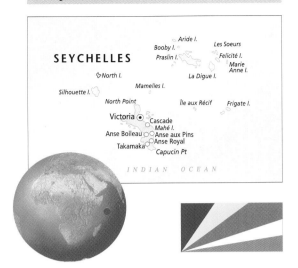

Fact File

OFFICIAL NAME Republic of Seychelles

FORM OF GOVERNMENT Republic with single legislative body (People's Assembly)

CAPITAL Victoria

AREA 455 sq km (176 sq miles)

TIME ZONE GMT + 4 hours

POPULATION 79,164

PROJECTED POPULATION 2005 82,044

POPULATION DENSITY 174 per sq km (450 per sq mile)

LIFE EXPECTANCY 71

INFANT MORTALITY (PER 1,000) 16.5

OFFICIAL LANGUAGES English, French, Creole

LITERACY RATE 88%

RELIGIONS Roman Catholic 90%, Anglican 8%, other 2%

ETHNIC GROUPS Seychellois (mixture of Asian, African, European) 93.8%, Malagasy 3.1%, Chinese 1.6%, British 1.5%

CURRENCY Seychelles rupee

ECONOMY Services 80%, agriculture 10%, industry 10%

GNP PER CAPITA US$6,620

CLIMATE Tropical, with wet season December to May

HIGHEST POINT Morne Seychellois 905 m (2,969 ft)

MAP REFERENCE Pages 372, 373

The Seychelles are a group of 4 large and 36 small granite islands, plus a scattering of about 65 coralline islands, in the Indian Ocean northeast of Madagascar. Some 98 percent of the population live on the four main islands, the great majority on tropical and mountainous Mahé. Uninhabited when occupied by the French in 1742, the Seychelles were ceded to the British at the time of the Napoleonic Wars, and became a crown colony in 1903. After independence in 1976 the islands were ruled for 15 years as a one-party socialist state, North Korean military advisors being hired to guard against attempted coups. The first open elections were held in 1993 and the previous government party won a new term in office.

The granite islands consist of a mountainous central spine—sometimes consisting of bare, eroded rock—surrounded by a flat coastal strip with dense tropical vegetation. In the areas cleared

for farming, vanilla, tobacco, tea, cinnamon and coconuts (for copra) are grown for export, along with food crops such as cassava, sweet potatoes, and bananas. Most food, however, is imported. The outer coralline islands are flat, waterless, and sparsely inhabited, having a total population of only 400. Short droughts periodically occur; though catchments collect some rainwater, there are no natural sources of supply. The Seychelles lie outside the cyclone belt, which is important for an economy depending on tourism.

The island's only natural resources are fish, copra, and cinnamon trees, which in earlier times provided a bare subsistence. Since independence in 1976, however, with the vigorous promotion of the tourist industry, per capita output has increased sevenfold. In recent years foreign investment has been encouraged in order to upgrade hotels and other services. Visitors find many attractions—the unique wildlife includes a rare giant land turtle and the colorful green sea turtle found on the coral reefs. The country's vulnerability in relying so heavily on tourism was shown during the Gulf War, when visitor numbers dropped sharply. The government is moving to reduce over-dependence on this sector by promoting farming, fishing, and small-scale manufacturing, including furniture-making, coconut-fiber rope-making, printing, and the re-export of petroleum products.

Sierra Leone

Sierra Leone's capital, Freetown, was so named when the British government settled freed slaves there in 1787. Once the freed-slave settlers became a ruling class over the Africans already living in the country, deep social divisions opened. Many settlers, and foreign missionaries, were killed in a war with the indigenous Mende in 1898.

Once a British crown colony, and independent from 1961, Sierra Leone's recent history has been marked by military coups, ethnic factionalism, and violence. Since 1992, civil war has raged in the east and the south, thousands of lives have been lost, and thousands of farms have been abandoned in the country's main grain growing areas. Liberian troops have been involved, and Libyan weapons. Child soldiers have been used by both sides.

Unlike most of west Africa, Sierra Leone is mountainous near the sea. These mountains are volcanic, and run southeast of Freetown on the Atlantic forming a thickly wooded peninsula (the Sierra Leone, or Lion Range). The peninsula interrupts a swampy coastal plain, stretching north and south, dominated by mangrove forests. Rolling savanna uplands to the north, known as the Bolilands, were once the scene of government efforts to introduce large-scale mechanized rice cultivation. Rice is also grown in the seasonally flooded riverine grasslands of the southeast, and in the swamps near Port Loko. Inland, to the northeast, the land rises to the Loma Mountains and the Tingi Hills. Rainfall on the coast is extremely high. The soils are heavily leached and weathered.

Subsistence farming dominates the agricultural sector, which employs about two-thirds of the population. Rice is the staple food crop and along with palm oil it is produced throughout Sierra Leone, except in the drier north. There, in the savanna, peanuts and cattle herding predominate. The country has substantial mineral resources, and the mining of diamonds, bauxite, and rutile or titanium ore provides essential hard currency. The economy is currently almost at a standstill because infrastructure has collapsed through neglect and both the mining and agricultural sectors have been disrupted by civil war.

Fact File

OFFICIAL NAME	Republic of Sierra Leone
FORM OF GOVERNMENT	Republic with single legislative body (House of Representatives)
CAPITAL	Freetown
AREA	71,740 sq km (27,699 sq miles)
TIME ZONE	GMT
POPULATION	5,296,651
PROJECTED POPULATION 2005	6,415,757
POPULATION DENSITY	73.8 per sq km (191.1 per sq mile)
LIFE EXPECTANCY	49.1
INFANT MORTALITY (PER 1,000)	126.2
OFFICIAL LANGUAGE	English
OTHER LANGUAGES	Krio, Mende, Temne
LITERACY RATE	30.3%
RELIGIONS	Muslim 60%, indigenous beliefs 30%, Christian 10%
ETHNIC GROUPS	13 indigenous tribes 99%, other 1%
CURRENCY	Leone
ECONOMY	Agriculture 70%, services 17%, industry 13%
GNP PER CAPITA	US$180
CLIMATE	Tropical, with wet season April to November
HIGHEST POINT	Loma Mansa 1,948 m (6,391 ft)
MAP REFERENCE	Page 364

Somalia

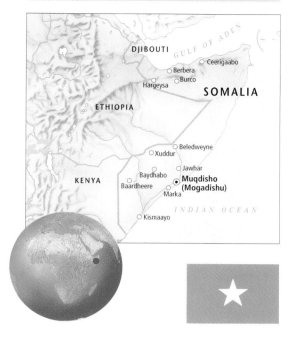

Somalia, a coastal state on the Horn of Africa, is in one respect unlike any other African country. It is the only place where the whole population feels that they are "one people"—Somali—and because of this ethnic homogeneity it has the makings of a nation state. Briefly under the control of Egypt from 1875, the region became a British protectorate in 1885. In 1889 Italy took control of the eastern coast, and from then on the country was divided into British Somaliland in the north and Italian Somaliland in the south and east. It has been independent since 1960.

The history of the people of Somalia since independence has been one of repression (under the Soviet-aligned Siyad Barre), military adventure (the invasion of the Ethiopian Ogaden), and civil war. When in 1992 an estimated 2,000 people a day were dying from war and starvation, the United Nations intervened, but its troops were unable to stop the military and civil unrest and withdrew. Anarchy and banditry now prevail. In the absence of any central authority, and without a functioning government in Muqdisho, the northern area once known as British Somaliland seceded and proclaimed itself an independent state. Centered on the city of Hargeysa, it calls itself the Somaliland Republic. It has not been recognised internationally.

Along the northern shore facing the Gulf of Aden lies the semiarid Guban coastal plain. Behind this is a range of mountains, the Ogo Highlands, running eastward from Ethiopia to the point of the Horn itself. South of the highlands is the Haud Plateau, and beyond this the land slopes down toward the Indian Ocean. Much of Somalia has semidesert thornbush and dry savanna cover. Only in the better watered south is there enough rainfall to support meager forests and grassland. Arable farming takes place between the Rivers Jubba and Shabeelle in the south. The Shabeelle, blocked by dunes, provides water for irrigation. Bananas from this area are a major export, mainly to Italy. Rival clans fight over this important resource; some plantation work is done by women and children in slave-labor conditions guarded by armed militia.

Nomadic pastoralists form much of the population in the north. Searching for grass and water, they wander with their herds across the state boundaries between southern Djibouti, the Ogaden, and northeast Kenya. Livestock accounts for 40 percent of gross domestic product and 65 percent of export earnings. In the south, in addition to the export crop of bananas, food crops of sugar, sorghum, and maize are grown. A small industrial sector is based on the processing of food products, but the prevailing disorder has caused many facilities to be shut down.

Fact File

OFFICIAL NAME	Somali Democratic Republic
FORM OF GOVERNMENT	Republic; no effective central government exists at the present time
CAPITAL	Muqdisho (Mogadishu)
AREA	637,660 sq km (246,200 sq miles)
TIME ZONE	GMT + 3 hours
POPULATION	7,140,643
PROJECTED POPULATION 2005	8,795,258
POPULATION DENSITY	11.2 per sq km (29 per sq mile)
LIFE EXPECTANCY	46.2
INFANT MORTALITY (PER 1,000)	125.8
OFFICIAL LANGUAGE	Somali
OTHER LANGUAGES	Arabic, Italian, English
LITERACY RATE	24%
RELIGIONS	Sunni Muslim with tiny Christian minority
ETHNIC GROUPS	Somali 85%, remainder mainly Bantu with small Arab, Asian, and European minorities 15%
CURRENCY	Somali shilling
ECONOMY	Agriculture 76%, services 16%, industry 8%
GNP PER CAPITA	Est. < US$765
CLIMATE	Mainly hot and arid, with higher rainfall in the south
HIGHEST POINT	Mt Shimbiris 2,416 m (7,927 ft)
MAP REFERENCE	Page 367

The Seychelles nut tree (Coco de Mer) is widespread on those islands (center left). Looking toward Silhouette Island in the Seychelles (top left). A group of Somali villagers (left).

Africa

South Africa

Along the west coast, north of Cape Town, the cold Benguela current inhibits rainfall, producing the desert of the Namib. In the northeast there is dry savanna bushland. On the Mozambique border the best-known of South Africa's eight wildlife reserves, Kruger National Park, contains lions, leopards, giraffes, elephants, and hippopotamuses.

People and culture

First inhabited by San, or Bushmen, southern Africa was in the fifteenth century occupied by a wave of cattle-keeping, grain-growing Bantu peoples from the north—their modern descendants being groups such as the Xhosa and the Zulu. Then in 1652 and 1688 two groups of settlers arrived from Europe—the first Dutch, the second French Huguenot, both firmly Protestant in their faith—and established a colony in the south at Cape Town. They became known as Boers (farmers) and later as Afrikaners (after their language, Afrikaans). The British established themselves on the Cape in 1806. Over the years a population of mixed Afro-European descent emerged who became known as "Cape Coloreds." In the nineteenth century laborers from India were brought in by the British, creating yet another large and distinct ethnic community. There are also a small number of Malays.

After 1948, under the ruling Afrikaners, apartheid (apartness) laws were drafted defining how each community should associate, where each should live, whether they could intermarry, and what work they could do. The entire population was to be organized in a hierarchy of privilege, with whites at the top and blacks at the bottom. Africans were to be confined to a series of internal Black States called "homelands," which were in practice mere labor pools, since the only way people could find

unemployment; high urban crime rates; and the ongoing conflict between Zulu groups and the ruling party, the African National Congress.

Physical features and land use

South Africa has three main geographic regions. First, there is the vast African plateau of the interior. This slopes gradually north and west to form part of the semiarid and sparsely populated Kalahari basin, while to the east it rises to elevations of 2,000 m (6,500 ft). Second, the Great Escarpment, varying in height, structure, and steepness, forms a rim around the entire plateau from the mountains of the Transvaal Drakensberg in the northeast to Namibia in the northwest. Its highest peaks are in the Drakensberg along the Lesotho border. The third region consists of the narrow, fertile strips of land along the peripheral coastal plains.

Agricultural products include maize (a staple for many African farmers); apples, pears, stone fruit, grapes, and wine from Eastern Cape Province; wheat from Western Cape Province; and sugarcane from coastal KwaZulu-Natal. On the grasslands of the plateau large-scale pastoralism produces wool, mohair, skins, and meat. South Africa is geologically ancient—only a few superficial strata are less than 600 million years old. In the 1880s rocks of the Witwatersrand were found to contain gold and diamonds, and since then gold and diamond mining has been the basis of South Africa's national wealth.

O ccupying the southernmost tip of the African continent, South Africa comprises a central plateau or veld, bordered to the south and east by the Drakensberg Mountains and to the north by the countries of Namibia, Botswana, Zimbabwe and Mozambique. The Independent State of Lesotho is contained within South Africa's borders. European settlement in the seventeenth century culminated in white minority rule, and a controversial policy of racial segregation was officially implemented in 1948. After 50 years of deepening crisis and international isolation as a result of its racial policies, South Africa changed course in 1990, held democratic elections in 1994, and under a new government rejoined the international community. Always the economic powerhouse of southern Africa, it is now free from sanctions and able to renew normal trading relations. The abandonment of apartheid, and the freeing of long-term political prisoner (and then president) Nelson Mandela, have had an uplifting effect on national morale and provided a chance for a fresh start. Problems currently facing the nation include discrepancies between the educational level and skills of blacks and whites; vastly different income levels; increasing

<table>
<tr><td>Timeline</td><td>25,000 BP Rock paintings on shelters show ceremonial dancers and animals, like antelope, which were hunted for food</td><td>4–500 AD Bantu people arrive from East Africa to find grazing for sheep and cattle and to plant crops. Displace Khoisan hunter-gatherers</td><td>1100 Different language groups emerge, such as the Xhosa and the Zulu</td><td>1615 British settlement at Table Bay lasts only a few years</td><td>1652 Dutch East India Co. garrison at site of Cape Town supplies Dutch fleet; settlers granted land at Liesbeek River in 1657</td><td>1713 Khoikhoi pastoralists displaced by "trekboer" settlers in search of grazing land; numerous San people die of smallpox</td></tr>
</table>

3 MYA Cave-dwelling Australopithecines in what is now Cape Province and Gauteng, kill animals for meat and eat plants	**120,000 BP** "Modern" humans inhabit cave near Port Elizabeth; they eat shellfish, tortoises, and bird's eggs	**c.2000 BC** Kalahari San (bushmen) inhabit the Kalahari Desert herding animals	**c.1000** Urban centers established; bone and ivory crafts; products traded between groups	**1488** First Portuguese vessels arrive at the Cape of Good Hope	**1657** First slaves brought to the Cape from India, Indonesia, and West Africa as agricultural labor and to act as herders	**1795–1802** British occupy Cape, a vital trade route supply post prior to opening of Suez Canal; more British settlers arrive

employment was by leaving home and traveling to the South African mines. The impracticality, unreality, and injustice of the system aroused widespread international condemnation. The misery it created led to ongoing violent resistance.

Economy and resources

Although both the Bantu and the first Europeans to colonize South Africa were farming people, and agriculture formed the foundation of the economy for hundreds of years, during the nineteenth century gold and diamonds were the attractions that drew a new wave of settlers. Today, gold and precious stones still make up half the country's total exports, and over the last 100 years almost half the world's gold has come from South African mines. Other important minerals include asbestos, nickel, vanadium, and uranium (which can

sometimes be found in old gold mines). In addition, South Africa is the world's largest producer of manganese, platinum, and chromium.

Energy conservation is a vital concern to the country as no petroleum deposits have yet been found. During the long period of South Africa's isolation and of trade boycotts, the state corporation Sasol extracted oil from coal. Though this is a expensive process, extensive deposits of coal make this a feasible supplementary supply. Many white South Africans enjoy a standard of living that is equal to the highest in the world. The challenge for the government in the next century will be to provide the circumstances and conditions in which less privileged social groups can have a share of the wealth. This will not be an easy task: at present there are jobs for less than 5 percent of the 300,000 workers who enter the labor force each year.

Fact File

OFFICIAL NAME Republic of South Africa

FORM OF GOVERNMENT Republic with two legislative bodies (Senate and National Assembly)

CAPITAL Pretoria (administrative); Cape Town (legislative); Bloemfontein (judicial)

AREA 1,219,912 sq km (471,008 sq miles)

TIME ZONE GMT + 2 hours

POPULATION 43,426,386

PROJECTED POPULATION 2005 46,220,919

POPULATION DENSITY 35.6 per sq km (92.2 per sq mile)

LIFE EXPECTANCY 54.8

INFANT MORTALITY (PER 1,000) 52

OFFICIAL LANGUAGES Afrikaans, English, Ndebele, Pedi, Sotho, Swazi, Tsonga, Tswana, Venda, Xhosa, Zulu

OTHER LANGUAGES Indigenous languages, Hindi, Urdu, Gujarati, Tamil

LITERACY RATE 81.4%

RELIGIONS Christian (most Europeans and people of mixed origin and about 60% of Africans) 68%, Hindu (60% of Indians) 2%, Muslim 2%, indigenous beliefs 28%

ETHNIC GROUPS Indigenous 75.2%, European 13.6%, mixed 8.6%, Indian 2.6%

CURRENCY Rand

ECONOMY Services 62%, industry 24%, agriculture 14%

GNP PER CAPITA US$3,160

CLIMATE Mainly semiarid; subtropical on southeast coast

HIGHEST POINT Thabana-Ntlenyana 3,482 m (11,424 ft)

MAP REFERENCE Pages 370–71

High-rise buildings in Pretoria (far left). An elephant browsing in Kruger National Park (below left). The Hexrivier Pass (left). The seaside town of Muizenberg (below).

PROVINCES

Eastern Cape • Free State • Gauteng • KwaZulu-Natal • Mpumalanga • Northern Province • Northern Cape • North West • Western Cape

Africa

c.1800 Zulu nation founded in today's KwaZulu-Natal, forcing Shoshangane clan into Swaziland and Mzilikazi clan into Zimbabwe

1836–38 10,000 Boer settlers unhappy with British rule in Cape set out on Great Trek to seek new land in Natal and Orange River areas

1870 Gold rush in the Kimberley area and discovery of diamonds transform the economic base from agriculture to mining

1899 Gold-mining industry employs 110,000 workers; almost 100,000 are African laborers

1912 The African National Congress (ANC) founded by group of black Africans interested in obtaining political rights

1948 National Party passes law restricting parliamentary representation to whites; "apartheid" official in 1950

1962 Nelson Mandela and other leading members of the ANC are imprisoned

1990 Mandela freed; apartheid abolished (1991); population 37 million (76% black, 13% white, 9% mixed race, 2% Asian)

1860 Laborers from India are imported by Natal farmers to work on farms and plantations

1880–81 British fail to bring Boer republics (Orange Free State, Transvaal) into federation—British defeat in First Boer War

1899–1902 British defeat the Boers (Afrikaners) in Second Boer War

1931 South Africa granted independence by Britain as a member of the Commonwealth

1961 South Africa leaves Commonwealth and becomes a Republic, without asking non-whites

1976 Black African protest over compulsory Afrikaans language lessons results in violence and the loss of 600 lives

1994 Mandela elected president in first non-racial general election—pronounces the new South Africa a "Rainbow Republic"

Sudan

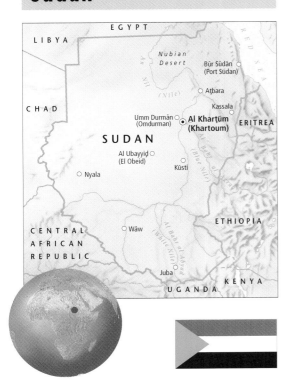

South of Egypt, Sudan is Africa's largest country, and the pathway to the headwaters of the Nile. (An Nīl). It is also one of Africa's most divided countries. Known in Ancient Egypt as Nubia, its northern region came under Islamic Arab control in the fourteenth century, and Egyptian and British rule in the nineteenth. With some 570 distinct ethnic groups and over 100 languages, it has been difficult to form Sudan into a modern state.

Since achieving independence from Egypt and Britain in 1956, Sudan has seen military rule, coups, and civil conflict for all but 10 of the next 40 years. The main cause is the determination of the Muslim north to impose Arab and Islamic values on the varied African, animist, and Christian peoples of the south. Strict sharia (Muslim) law has been proclaimed but is widely ignored. At present the government is conducting a "war of annihilation" against the 1.5 million Nuba people. Over half a million people have died in the past 12 years, the miseries of the ethnic Africans being compounded by famine, displacement, and the enslavement of women and children. One task of relief workers has been to purchase the freedom of slaves.

In northern Sudan the rocky Sahara Desert stretches westward to become a waste of sand dunes, the land rising to 3,071 m (10,075 ft) at the Darfur Massif toward the border with Chad. In the east the Red Sea Mountains rise 2,000 m (6,500 ft) above a narrow coastal plain. Most people live near the south–north flowing Nile (An Nīl), a river that divides into two streams at Khartoum. From here the source of the Blue Nile (Al Bahr al Azraq) can be traced southeast to the Ethiopian border and Lake Tana. The White Nile (Al Bahr al Abyad) runs southwards into the vast marshland of the Sudd (where dense, floating vegetation makes navigation difficult), then further upstream to Uganda and its headwaters in Lake Albert.

Crumbling pyramids in the desert at Meroué in the Sudan (right). A typical kraal (village) in Swaziland (top right). A boy poling a dugout canoe in Tanzania (top, far right).

About two-thirds of Sudan's workforce are farmers. There is a heavy emphasis on growing cotton, at the expense of food crops, as it accounts for 24 percent of export revenue. Food crops include sorghum (the staple) along with millet, wheat, barley, and peanuts. Declining rainfall and huge displacements of the rural population as a result of war have played havoc with production in recent years. The socialist government is resisting reform: in 1990 the IMF declared Sudan noncooperative because of nonpayment of debts. At present aid comes mainly from Iran. Natural resources include copper, chromium ore, zinc, tungsten, mica, silver, and gold. Some gold is mined.

Fact File

OFFICIAL NAME Republic of the Sudan

FORM OF GOVERNMENT Military regime with single transitional legislative body (Provisional National Assembly)

CAPITAL Al Kharṭūm (Khartoum)

AREA 2,505,810 sq km (967,493 sq miles)

TIME ZONE GMT + 2 hours

POPULATION 34,475,690

PROJECTED POPULATION 2005 40,899,171

POPULATION DENSITY 13.8 per sq km (35.7 per sq mile)

LIFE EXPECTANCY 56.4

INFANT MORTALITY (PER 1,000) 70.9

OFFICIAL LANGUAGE Arabic

OTHER LANGUAGES Nubian, Ta Bedawie, English, indigenous languages

LITERACY RATE 44.8%

RELIGIONS Sunni Muslim 70%, indigenous beliefs 25%, Christian 5%

ETHNIC GROUPS African 52%, Arab 39%, Beja 6%, other 3%

CURRENCY Sudanese pound

ECONOMY Agriculture 65%, services 31%, industry 4%

GNP PER CAPITA US$423

CLIMATE North mainly arid; south tropical, with wet season April to October

HIGHEST POINT Mt Kinyeti 3,187 m (10,456 ft)

MAP REFERENCE Pages 362–63, 366–67

Swaziland

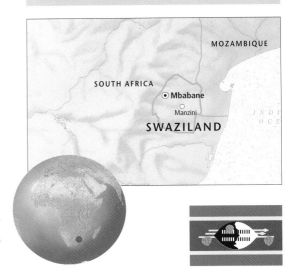

Swaziland is a tiny landlocked kingdom almost surrounded by South Africa. Across its eastern border it is about 130 km (80 miles) from the Indian Ocean and the Mozambique port of Maputo. Enjoying relative stability and prosperity, popular among South African tourists for its wildlife reserves, mountain scenery, and casinos, the kingdom's hereditary Bantu monarchy is now being pressed to modernize and accept constitutional reforms including democracy and political opposition.

The country owes its autonomy to events in the mid-nineteenth century. The Swazi were then facing Zulu expansion, as well as pressure from Boer farmers. They sought and received British protection, and from 1906 Swaziland was administered by the high commissioner for Basutoland (now Lesotho), Bechuanaland (now Botswana), and Swaziland. Full independence came in 1968.

The landscape descends in three steps from west to east. The high veld in the west is mountainous with a temperate climate, and supports grasslands, and plantations of pine and eucalyptus. Mixed farming takes place in the middle veld, the most populous area, where black Swazi subsistence farmers grow maize, sorghum, and peanuts. Cash crops such as sugarcane, citrus fruits, and tobacco are produced by white-run

agribusinesses and by Swazi on resettlement schemes. Livestock are raised on the low veld.

Swaziland's economy is relatively diversified and buoyant: during the 1980s it grew at a rate of 4.5 percent a year. Relaxed investment rules have ensured a supply of development capital, and project aid has been forthcoming from a number of donors. Sugar and forestry products are the main earners of hard currency, and are produced by white residents on large plantations. The country has small deposits of gold and diamonds. Mining was once important, but is now in decline. The high-grade iron ore deposits were depleted by 1978 and health concerns have cut the demand for asbestos. Remittances from workers in South Africa provide up to 20 percent of household income. The main threat to the Swazi way of life comes from land pressure due to high population growth. Family planning is being promoted.

Fact File

OFFICIAL NAME Kingdom of Swaziland

FORM OF GOVERNMENT Monarchy with two legislative bodies (Senate and House of Assembly)

CAPITAL Mbabane

AREA 17,360 sq km (6,703 sq miles)

TIME ZONE GMT + 2 hours

POPULATION 985,335

PROJECTED POPULATION 2005 1,101,082

POPULATION DENSITY 56.8 per sq km (147 per sq mile)

LIFE EXPECTANCY 57.3

INFANT MORTALITY (PER 1,000) 101.9

OFFICIAL LANGUAGES English, Swazi

OTHER LANGUAGES Indigenous languages

LITERACY RATE 75.2%

RELIGIONS Christian 60%, indigenous beliefs 40%

ETHNIC GROUPS Indigenous 97%, European 3%

CURRENCY Lilangeni

ECONOMY Agriculture 60%, industry and services 40%

GNP PER CAPITA US$1,170

CLIMATE Temperate, with wet season November to March

HIGHEST POINT Emlembe Peak 1,862 m (6,109 ft)

MAP REFERENCE Page 371

Tanzania

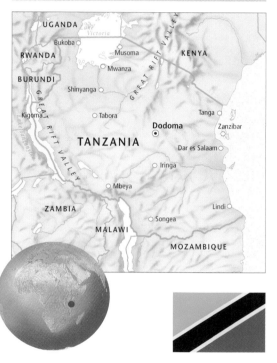

With Africa's highest mountain (Kilimanjaro), and Serengeti National Park, Tanzania is well known to the outside world. It also the home of some of East Africa's most ancient human remains, those found at Olduvai Gorge dating back 2 million years. From the eighth century AD onward, the country's coastal region was subject to Islamic influence from Arab traders who dealt in slaves and ivory. In the nineteenth century both British and German settlers arrived.

Tanzania won independence from England in 1961, becoming a de facto one-party state under Julius Nyerere, whose version of African socialism prevailed until he retired in 1985. Opposition parties were allowed in 1992. An uprising by pro-Tanzanian forces violently incorporated the Muslim island of Zanzibar in 1964: unreconciled Islamic interests on the island represent a potential flashpoint.

From the coast, Tanzania stretches across a plateau averaging about 1,000 m (3,000 ft) to the Rift Valley Lakes of Malawi (Lake Nyasa) and Tanganyika. The eastern Rift Valley, with the alkaline Lake Natron, and Lakes Eyasi and Manyara, divides the Northern Highlands. These are dominated by Mt Kilimanjaro near the Kenyan border. The Southern Highlands overlook Lake Malawi (Lake

Nyasa). Semiarid conditions in the north and tsetse fly in the west–central areas mean that people mainly live on the country's margins. Attempts to farm the savanna woodland have failed.

Though repressive, Nyerere's government achieved relatively high levels of education and welfare, but the economy languished as a result of falling commodity prices abroad and inefficient and corrupt state corporations at home. Over 80 percent of the workforce live off the land, producing cash crops such as coffee, tea, sisal, cotton, and pyrethrum, along with food crops of maize, wheat, cassava, and bananas. Since 1985 there has been some liberalization of the market, along with an effort to boost tourism and a substantial increase in gold production. Reforms have increased private sector growth and investment.

Fact File

OFFICIAL NAME United Republic of Tanzania

FORM OF GOVERNMENT Republic with single legislative body (National Assembly)

CAPITAL Dodoma

AREA 945,090 sq km (364,899 sq miles)

TIME ZONE GMT + 3 hours

POPULATION 31,270,820

PROJECTED POPULATION 2005 35,686,963

POPULATION DENSITY 33.1 per sq km (85.7 per sq mile)

LIFE EXPECTANCY 46.2

INFANT MORTALITY (PER 1,000) 95.3

OFFICIAL LANGUAGES Swahili, English

OTHER LANGUAGES Arabic, indigenous languages

LITERACY RATE 66.8%

RELIGIONS Mainland: Christian 45%, Muslim 35%, indigenous beliefs 20%; Zanzibar: Muslim 99%, other 1%

ETHNIC GROUPS Indigenous 99%, other 1%

CURRENCY Tanzanian shilling

ECONOMY Agriculture 85%, services 10%, industry 5%

GNP PER CAPITA US$120

CLIMATE Mainly tropical; hot and humid along coast, drier inland, cooler in mountains

HIGHEST POINT Mt Kilimanjaro 5,895 m (19,340 ft)

MAP REFERENCE Page 369

Togo

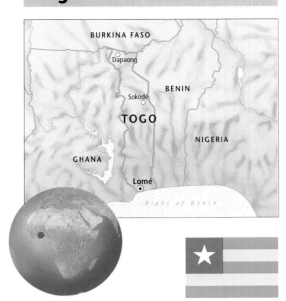

Togo is a small west African country squeezed between Ghana and Benin. It was colonized by Germany in 1884, later becoming French Togoland. It became independent in 1960. A deep social division exists between the Kabye people in the north and the majority Ewe of the south. The Ewe are generally better educated, and live in the more developed part of the country, but have no say in government. This is run by Africa's longest serving president, General Eyadema, a Kabye who has held this position since his coup in 1967. The first multi-party elections took place in 1993.

Most people live on the coast and the adjacent plains. Inland a mountain chain crosses the country north to south. The far northwest is mainly granite tableland. Roads connect the northern savanna with the railhead of Blitta, and the phosphate mining area with its port of Kpeme. The River Oti crosses in the northwest between Burkina Faso and Ghana; the River Mono drains south into the Gulf of Guinea. About a quarter of the land is arable. The most fertile land—28 percent of the country—is forested; here slash-and-burn cultivation occurs.

Togo depends on subsistence agriculture. Food crops include yams, cassava, maize, beans, rice, and sorghum. The main export crops are coffee, cocoa, and cotton, which together generate about 30 percent of earnings. Cattle, sheep, and pigs are

raised in the north. The annual fish catch is about 14,000 tonnes. Togo is normally self-sufficient in food, though drought has recently cut productivity, and the deforestation caused by slash-and-burn agriculture is causing concern. Phosphate mining is the most important industrial activity.

Fact File

OFFICIAL NAME	Republic of Togo
FORM OF GOVERNMENT	Republic with single legislative body (National Assembly)
CAPITAL	Lomé
AREA	56,790 sq km (21,927 sq miles)
TIME ZONE	GMT
POPULATION	5,081,413
PROJECTED POPULATION 2005	6,254,894
POPULATION DENSITY	89.5 per sq km (231.8 per sq mile)
LIFE EXPECTANCY	59.3
INFANT MORTALITY (PER 1,000)	77.6
OFFICIAL LANGUAGE	French
OTHER LANGUAGES	Ewe, Mina, Dagomba, Kabye
LITERACY RATE	50.4%
RELIGIONS	Indigenous beliefs 70%, Christian 20%, Muslim 10%
ETHNIC GROUPS	Indigenous (Ewe, Mina, and Kabye largest of 37 tribes) 99%, European and Syrian–Lebanese 1%
CURRENCY	CFA (Communauté Financière Africaine) franc
ECONOMY	Agriculture 68%, services 28%, industry 4%
GNP PER CAPITA	US$310
CLIMATE	Tropical, with wet seasons Mar to July and Oct to Nov; semiarid in north, with wet season Apr to July
HIGHEST POINT	Pic Baumann 986 m (3,235 ft)
MAP REFERENCE	Page 364

Tunisia

Tunisia has a long history. Located in north Africa, across from Sicily, it was founded by Phoenician sailors 3,000 years ago, became famous as the Carthage of Queen Dido, and fell to the Romans in 146 BC. Arab conquest brought Islam to the region in the seventh century AD.

In modern times control of Tunisia was disputed by Italy, England, and France before it became a French protectorate in 1883. Ruled since independence in 1956 as a de facto one-party state, Tunisia held its first multi-party elections in 1994 (the government claiming 99.9 percent of the vote). Tunisia is a relatively prosperous country, strongly influenced by French and European culture, with a record of modest but steady economic growth. While Islamic fundamentalism is on the rise, women are treated with greater equality in Tunisia than elsewhere in the Arab world.

The eastern end of the Atlas Mountains juts across the border from Algeria in the north. A mountainous plateau called the Dorsale extends northeast, sloping down to the coastal plains. Parallel to the Mediterranean Sea in the extreme northwest, the Kroumirie Mountains, covered with cork oaks, shelter the fertile valley of the Majardah River as it flows down from the Dorsale. Harnessed for hydroelectric power, this enters the sea near Tūnis across broad alluvial lowlands used for growing a wide variety of crops, some extensively irrigated: wheat and barley, olives, sugar beet, citrus fruits, grapes, and vegetables. South of the mountains a dry expanse of plateau-steppe gives way to a series of salt lakes, the largest, Shaṭṭ al Jarīd, extending halfway across the country. The large remaining area to the south is desert.

Tunisia has a diverse economy. Agriculture is the main employer, but in recent years it has declined in importance as an revenue earner relative to mineral and petroleum exports. Most industrial production is based on agricultural and mining products. Real growth averaged 4.2 percent from 1991 to 1995, with moderate inflation. Growth in tourism has been a key factor.

Traditional houses in Togo (left). Workmen taking a break in Tunisia (above left). The Ruwenzoris in western Uganda, Africa's highest range of mountains (right).

Africa

Since the 1960s Tunisia has been a popular destination for European tourists, drawn by winter sunshine, beaches, and Roman remains. In recent times there have been almost 2 million visitors per year, with tourism employing 200,000 people, but the activities of Islamic militants have had a dampening effect.

Fact File

OFFICIAL NAME Republic of Tunisia

FORM OF GOVERNMENT Republic with single legislative body (Chamber of Deputies)

CAPITAL Tūnis

AREA 163,610 sq km (63,170 sq miles)

TIME ZONE GMT + 1 hour

POPULATION 9,513,603

PROJECTED POPULATION 2005 10,302,595

POPULATION DENSITY 58.5 per sq km (151.5 per sq mile)

LIFE EXPECTANCY 73.4

INFANT MORTALITY (PER 1,000) 31.4

OFFICIAL LANGUAGE Arabic

OTHER LANGUAGE French

LITERACY RATE 65.2%

RELIGIONS Muslim 98%, Christian 1%, Jewish 1%

ETHNIC GROUPS Arab–Berber 98%, European 1%, Jewish 1%

CURRENCY Dinar

ECONOMY Agriculture 48%, services 42%, industry 10%

GNP PER CAPITA US$1,820

CLIMATE Temperate in north, with mild, rainy winters and hot, dry summers; desert in south

HIGHEST POINT Jabal ash Sha'nabī 1,544 m (5,065 ft)

MAP REFERENCE Page 361

Uganda

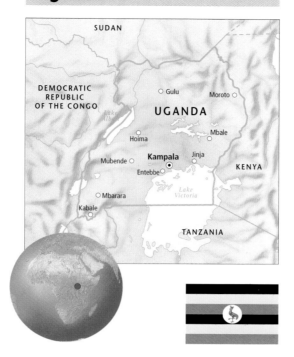

Extending north from Africa's largest body of water, Lake Victoria, the east African state of Uganda is a country of lakes and marshland. With a mild climate and varied resources—from fertile soil to freshwater fish to copper—it was once called "the pearl of Africa." After independence in 1962, however, its people suffered two decades of civil war, military coups, atrocities, and massacres, the worst period being the ten years under Idi Amin. It is estimated that between 1966 and Yoweri Museveni's takeover in 1986 more than half a million Ugandan inhabitants were killed.

The Museveni regime has overseen a return to peace and prosperity. Because the tribal basis of

the old political parties was a cause of conflict, the government banned overt political activity, while inviting participation in a "one-party/no-party" policy of national unity. Multi-party elections in 1994 returned Museveni to power, but this taste of democracy created expectations of greater local autonomy. Some people are demanding the restoration of the region's traditional kingdoms.

Uganda's lake system is the source of the Nile. The pattern of lakes originates in the tilting and faulting of the Rift Valley, with the Ruwenzori Range on the western side of the country and the extinct volcano of Mt Elgon to the east. North of the lakes lies a savanna of trees and grassland, where farmers grow millet and sorghum for food, with cotton and tobacco as cash crops. Certain areas where cattle herding is impossible because of tsetse fly have been designated wildlife parks. Desert nomads live in arid Karamoja still further north. Coffee, tea, and sugarcane are grown in the south, which is the most fertile region and has the highest rainfall. This is the most densely settled part of the country, and is where the industrial center of Jinja is located, not far from Kampala, near the large Owen Falls hydroelectric plant.

Agriculture is the basis of the economy, with coffee the main export. Since 1986 the government has been engaged in raising producer prices for export crops, increasing prices for petroleum products (all oil must be imported), and raising civil service wages. Railways are being rebuilt. With the return of prosperity and public order, Indo-Ugandan entrepreneurs (expelled by the Obote and Amin regimes) are beginning to return from exile. The mining of gold and cobalt in the Ruwenzori region is also expected to resume.

Fact File

OFFICIAL NAME Republic of Uganda

FORM OF GOVERNMENT Republic with single legislative body (National Assembly)

CAPITAL Kampala

AREA 236,040 sq km (91,135 sq miles)

TIME ZONE GMT + 3 hours

POPULATION 21,470,864

PROJECTED POPULATION 2005 24,157,273

POPULATION DENSITY 91 per sq km (235.6 per sq mile)

LIFE EXPECTANCY 38.6

INFANT MORTALITY (PER 1,000) 96.5

OFFICIAL LANGUAGE English

OTHER LANGUAGES Luganda, Swahili, Bantu and Nilotic languages

LITERACY RATE 61.1%

RELIGIONS Roman Catholic 33%, Protestant 33%, indigenous beliefs 18%, Muslim 16%

ETHNIC GROUPS Indigenous tribal groups 99% (mainly Ganda, Teso, Nkole, Nyoro, Soga), other 1%

CURRENCY Ugandan shilling

ECONOMY Agriculture 86%, services 10%, industry 4%

GNP PER CAPITA US$240

CLIMATE Tropical, with two wet seasons March to May and September to November; semiarid in northeast

HIGHEST POINT Mt Stanley 5,110 m (16,765 ft)

MAP REFERENCE Page 366

Zambia

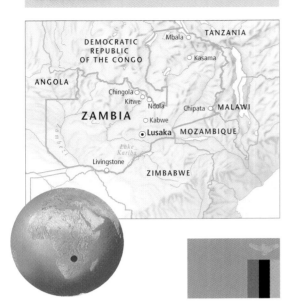

Fact File

OFFICIAL NAME Republic of Zambia

FORM OF GOVERNMENT Republic with single legislative body (National Assembly)

CAPITAL Lusaka

AREA 752,610 sq km (290,583 sq miles)

TIME ZONE GMT + 2 hours

POPULATION 9,663,535

PROJECTED POPULATION 2005 10,972,136

POPULATION DENSITY 12.8 per sq km (33.1 per sq mile)

LIFE EXPECTANCY 37

INFANT MORTALITY (PER 1,000) 91.9

OFFICIAL LANGUAGE English

OTHER LANGUAGES About 70 indigenous languages including Bemba, Kaonda, Lozi, Lunda, Luvale, Nyanja, Tonga

LITERACY RATE 76.6%

RELIGIONS Protestant 84%, Hindu 35%, Roman Catholic 26%, other including Muslim, indigenous beliefs 5%

ETHNIC GROUPS Indigenous 98.7%, European 1.1%, other 0.2%

CURRENCY Kwacha

ECONOMY Agriculture 82%, services 10%, industry 8%

GNP PER CAPITA US$400

CLIMATE Tropical, with three seasons: cool and dry May to August, hot and dry August to November, wet December to April

HIGHEST POINT Mafinga Hills 2,301 m (7,549 ft)

MAP REFERENCE Pages 368–69, 370–71

Zambia is a landlocked country in south-central Africa. It stretches from Victoria Falls in the south to Lake Tanganyika in the north, and is one of the world's major copper producers. Ancestral branches of the Zambian Tonga first entered the area in the eighth century AD, but other African groups now living there are more recent arrivals—the Ngoni and Kololo came as fugitives from Zulu aggression in 1835. Formerly a British colony, and once known as Northern Rhodesia, Zambia became independent in 1964. From that year it was ruled for more than a quarter of a century by President Kaunda, who nationalized commerce and industry and built a one-party socialist state. In 1991, economic decline and political agitation led to Zambia's first free elections. Kaunda was defeated, but recovery from his economic and political legacy may take time.

A wide expanse of high plateau broken by scattered mountains and valleys, Zambia is drained by the Zambeze in the west and south, where the river forms a boundary with Zimbabwe and Namibia. Below Victoria Falls the Zambeze is dammed at the Kariba Gorge to form one of the largest artificial lakes in the world, Lake Kariba. Power from the Lake Kariba hydroelectric station is shared with Zimbabwe. Another major river, the Luangwa, runs southwest from the Malawi border down a broad rift valley to join the Zambeze at the frontier of Mozambique.

Compared with its neighbors, Zambia has a high ratio of urban dwellers who are dependent on the rural sector for food. Commercial farming of maize in the central districts, and other food crops such as sorghum and rice, is proving insufficient to meet their needs. This situation has been aggravated both by drought and the phasing out of agricultural subsidies.

Zambia is dependent on copper production, which accounts for over 80 percent of export earnings. Production is down, however, and so are world copper prices, which is intensifying the

difficulties caused by high inflation and shrinking internal food supplies. In the post-Kaunda years there has been some attempt at privatization and budgetary reform, but this has produced little improvement. In 1995 four of Zambia's 20 banks failed. Most export earnings go toward paying off the 7 billion dollar external debt—itself a product to some extent of bureaucratic misuse of funds.

African wildlife

Nowhere on earth is there anything to equal the variety of African wildlife, much of it still to be seen in a natural setting. There are 90 species of hoofed mammal alone, including a huge variety of antelope, from the giant eland to the swift impala. Africa has the world's fastest animal, the cheetah, and also the world's largest land animal, the African elephant. In the giraffe it has the tallest animal in the world, while Africa's chimpanzees and gorillas represent families of primates closer to *Homo sapiens* than any others.

The future welfare of African wildlife is a major international concern. Today, many animals only survive in the many national parks throughout the continent, the oldest and best-known being Kruger National Park in South Africa. Kenya's parks include the 20,000 sq km (8,000 sq mile) expanse of Tsavo, one of the biggest. Tanzania's Serengeti National Park has unrivaled herds of antelope and the migratory movements of wildebeest amid lions, leopards, and other predators—not to mention crocodiles in the rivers—provide a glimpse of life on the grasslands of east Africa as it has been for thousands of years.

Only one large African mammal is known to have become extinct in historical times: this is an antelope called the blaubok. However, there were so few white rhinoceros at the end of the nineteenth century that they were thought to be extinct. Then a few were discovered in the South African province of Natal, and as a result of careful protection in South African national parks their numbers had grown to 6,375 by 1994. Outside South Africa very few white rhinoceros have survived: there may be no more than 80 in Kenya. A number of other animals are endangered, including the critically endangered mountain gorillas found in the Democratic Republic of the Congo, Uganda, and Rwanda.

In the early twentieth century professional hunters from Europe and America depleted numbers of animals such as lion, rhino, and buffalo. Today, the main threat comes from Africans themselves. Pastoral people kill wildlife because antelope compete for grassland with their cattle. Many mountain gorillas died during the civil wars in Rwanda in the 1990s. Most killing in Kenya and Tanzania is done by poachers seeking decorative skins, ivory, and rhino horn. A 2 kg (4 lb) rhino horn sells for up to US$122,000 in Asia, where in powdered form it is valued as an aphrodisiac. It is estimated that in the last two decades 40,000 rhinos have been killed for their horns.

The management of wild animal populations is not easy. After policies designed to ensure the survival of elephants were followed in Tsavo National Park, herds grew until there are now too many elephants for the land to support. This is damaging the habitat of other native species.

The Round House, one of the Great Ruins in Zimbabwe, built by Bantu peoples (left). Zimbabwean dancers in masks and traditional dress (above). The massive Victoria Falls on the Zambeze River in Zimbabwe (below).

Fact File

OFFICIAL NAME Republic of Zimbabwe

FORM OF GOVERNMENT Republic with single legislative body (Parliament)

CAPITAL Harare

AREA 390,580 sq km (150,803 sq miles)

TIME ZONE GMT + 2 hours

POPULATION 11,163,160

PROJECTED POPULATION 2005 11,703,270

POPULATION DENSITY 28.6 per sq km (74 per sq mile)

LIFE EXPECTANCY 58

INFANT MORTALITY (PER 1,000) 61.2

OFFICIAL LANGUAGE English

OTHER LANGUAGES Shona, Ndebele

LITERACY RATE 84.7%

RELIGIONS Mixed Christian–indigenous beliefs 50%, Christian 25%, indigenous beliefs 24%, Muslim and other 1%

ETHNIC GROUPS Indigenous 98% (Shona 71%, Ndebele 16%, other 11%), European 1%, other 1%

CURRENCY Zimbabwean dollar

ECONOMY Agriculture 65%, services 29%, industry 6%

GNP PER CAPITA US$540

CLIMATE Tropical, moderated by altitude; wet season November to March

HIGHEST POINT Inyangani 2,592 m (8,504 ft)

MAP REFERENCE Page 371

Zimbabwe

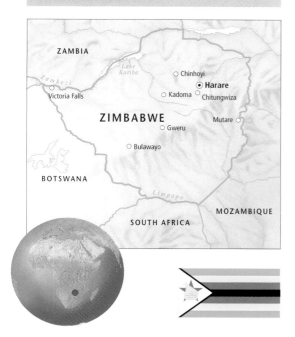

Zimbabwe is a landlocked country south of Zambia. Zimbabwe means "house of the chief" in the Shona language and refers to what are known as the Great Ruins, built by Bantu peoples in the country's south and thought to date from the ninth century AD. The country's two main tribes today, the minority Ndebele (popularly known as Matabele) and the majority Shona, arrived as nineteenth-century fugitives from the warlike expansion of the Zulus under King Shaka.

British settlement began in the 1890s, and there were 280,000 whites in the country in 1965 when their leader, Ian Smith, declared independence from the UK. African guerrilla action to overthrow Smith led to black majority rule in 1980. Since then the government has been led by Robert Mugabe, a Shona. Though he renounced Marxism–Leninism in 1991, and market reforms are on the agenda, during the 1990s Zimbabwe has edged closer to being a de facto one-party state.

Some 25 percent of the country consists of a broad mountainous ridge known as the high veld, which crosses the country southwest to northeast. On the northeastern Mozambique border this climbs to the peak of Inyangani. The rolling plateaus of the middle veld fall gently away north and south of this central upland, reaching the riverine low veld regions near the Limpopo River in the south and the Zambeze in the north. On the northern border the Zambeze plunges over Victoria Falls into a number of gorges. The falls, with Lake Kariba further downriver, along with several national parks, are among Zimbabwe's principal tourist attractions. Almost 40 percent of electricity needs are met by hydroelectric power, much of it from the Kariba Dam facility shared with Zambia.

Zimbabwe's near self-sufficiency in food is a by-product of the trade boycotts and economic isolation imposed on the white minority regime of Ian Smith after 1965. This forced both agriculture and manufacturing to diversify. African farms are still mainly small-scale subsistence operations, growing maize, cassava, and wheat. Large-scale white-owned enterprises produce most of the cash crops such as tobacco, cotton, and sugarcane, and earn much of agriculture's 35 percent share of national export revenue. Zimbabwe's mineral resources include coal, chromium, asbestos, gold, nickel, copper, iron, vanadium, lithium, tin, and platinum. Mining employs only 5 percent of the workforce, but minerals and metals account for about 40 percent of exports.

Dependencies in Africa

Mayotte

Fact File

OFFICIAL NAME Territorial Collectivity of Mayotte

FORM OF GOVERNMENT Territorial collectivity of France

CAPITAL Mamoudzou

AREA 375 sq km (145 sq miles)

TIME ZONE GMT + 3 hours

POPULATION 112,863

LIFE EXPECTANCY 60

INFANT MORTALITY (PER 1,000) 69.1

LITERACY RATE Not available

CURRENCY French franc

ECONOMY Mainly agriculture and fishing

CLIMATE Tropical, with wet season November to May

MAP REFERENCE Page 372

Mayotte is a small island at the northern end of the Mozambique Channel, 34 km (21 miles) long, between Madagascar and the mainland. It is the easternmost of the four large islands of the Comoros group (a group first visited by Europeans ships in the sixteenth century) and was the first to be ceded to France in 1841. When, in the 1974 referendum, the other islands chose to become the Republic of the Comoros, Mayotte decided to become a territorial collectivity of France. Volcanic in origin, Mayotte rises to 660 m (2,165 ft) at its highest point. The people are of African, Arab, and Madagascan descent. Agricultural products include coconuts, cocoa, and spices.

Réunion

Réunion is the largest of the Mascarene Islands which lie southwest of Mauritius and east of Madagascar. A fertile plain surrounds Réunion's rugged and mountainous interior. One of two volcanic peaks, Piton des Neiges rises to 3,069 m (10,069 ft) and is sporadically active. Plentiful rainfall comes with the winter trade winds. On the intensively cultivated lowlands there are large sugarcane plantations which provide 75 percent of exports and are the island's only significant industry. Vanilla, perfume oils, and tea also produce revenue, while vegetables and maize are grown for local consumption. Tourism is growing, but unemployment is high. The population is divided over continued association with France, which uses Réunion as its main military base in the area.

The small, uninhabited islands of Bassas da India, Europa, Glorieuses, Île Juan de Nova, and Tromelin are associated dependencies.

Fact File

OFFICIAL NAME Department of Réunion

FORM OF GOVERNMENT Overseas department of France

CAPITAL Saint-Denis

AREA 2,510 sq km (969 sq miles)

TIME ZONE GMT + 4 hours

POPULATION 717,723

LIFE EXPECTANCY 75.7

INFANT MORTALITY (PER 1,000) 6.9

LITERACY RATE 78.6%

CURRENCY French franc

ECONOMY Services 49%, agriculture 30%, industry 21%

CLIMATE Tropical; cool and dry May to November, hot and rainy November to April

MAP REFERENCE Page 373

St Helena

The island of St Helena lies about 1,950 km (1,200 miles) off the west coast of Africa. Together with Tristan da Cunha and Ascension Island, it is a British crown colony, and is Britain's main dependency in the South Atlantic. The crater rim of an extinct volcano, St Helena is marked by gorges and valleys, has many freshwater springs, and rises to an elevation of 824 m (2,703 ft).

Discovered by the Portuguese in 1502 and first visited by the English in 1588, St Helena was granted to the British East India Company in 1659. It was Napoleon's place of exile from 1815 to 1821. Today, the island's main activities are fishing, livestock raising, and the sale of handicrafts, but it depends on aid from the UK. Tristan da Cunha, 2,000 km (1,243 miles) to the south, has a farming community. Ascension Island, a military base and communications center, has no resident population.

Fact File

OFFICIAL NAME St Helena

FORM OF GOVERNMENT Dependent territory of the United Kingdom

CAPITAL Jamestown

AREA 410 sq km (158 sq miles)

TIME ZONE GMT

POPULATION 7,145

LIFE EXPECTANCY 75.9

INFANT MORTALITY (PER 1,000) 28

LITERACY RATE 97.3%

CURRENCY St Helenian pound

ECONOMY Mainly fishing and agriculture

CLIMATE Tropical, moderated by trade winds

MAP REFERENCE Page 373

Western Sahara

Fact File

OFFICIAL NAME Western Sahara

FORM OF GOVERNMENT Territory disputed by Morocco and Polisario Front independence movement

CAPITAL None

AREA 266,000 sq km (102,703 sq miles)

TIME ZONE GMT

POPULATION 239,333

LIFE EXPECTANCY 49.1

INFANT MORTALITY (PER 1,000) 136.7

CURRENCY Moroccan dirham

ECONOMY Agriculture 50%; fishing 25%, mining 25%

CLIMATE Mainly hot and arid

MAP REFERENCE Page 360

A bay and a small village in Réunion (bottom left). Pico de Teide on the island of Tenerife in the Canary Islands (top). A village with a view of the Atlantic in Madeira (above).

Western Sahara is a former Spanish possession. South of Morocco (and more than half the size of Morocco itself) it consists of the desert country lying between Mauritania and the Atlantic coast. The terrain is largely flat, with large areas of rock and sand, rising to low mountains in the northeast and the south. Possessing the world's largest known deposits of phosphate rock, it is a contested region of uncertain sovereignty, though since 1975 it has been occupied and administered by Morocco. Most of the indigenous people are Sahrawis, a mixture of Berber and Arab. Since 1983 a war has been waged on their behalf by the Polisario Front (Popular Front for the Liberation of the Saguia el Hamra and Rio de Oro) and by 1991 more than 170,000 Sahrawi refugees had fled the country and were living in camps in Algeria. Guerrilla activities continue, despite a United Nations-monitored ceasefire in 1991. Trade and other activities are controlled by the Moroccan government and most food for the urban population must be imported. Western Sahara's standard of living is well below that of Morocco.

Autonomous communities

The municipalities of Ceuta and Melilla on the Moroccan coast, and the Canary Islands, off southern Morocco, are autonomous communities of Spain. The islands of Madeira, to the north of the Canary Islands, constitute an autonomous region of Portugal.

Ceuta and Melilla

In 1912 the Sultan of Morocco signed a treaty with France making Morocco a French protectorate. At the same time the French, recognizing Spanish interests in the region, gave Spain several enclaves along the Moroccan coast. Two of these enclaves remain under Spanish administration—Ceuta and Melilla.

The high promontory of Jebel Musa at Ceuta, on the African side of the Strait of Gibraltar, stands opposite Gibraltar on the northern side. Legend has it that Jebel Musa and the Rock of Gibraltar were the two "Pillars of Hercules", set there by Hercules to commemorate his travels and achievements. Today, Ceuta is a military station and seaport with a population of about 75,000.

Canary Islands

The Canary Islands, grouped off southern Morocco, are an autonomous community of Spain. There are seven large islands and numerous smaller islands, the nearest of which are within 100 km (60 miles) of the African coast. The "inshore" islands of Lanzarote and Fuerteventura are low lying. The more mountainous outer islands of Gran Canaria and Tenerife include the volcanic cone of Pico de Teide (3,718 m; 12,198 ft).

With a subtropical climate and fertile soils, the islands support farming and fruit growing, and such industries as food and fish processing, boat building, and crafts.

Once known as the Fortunate Islands, the Spanish took control of the Canaries in 1479, subjugating the original Guanche and Canario inhabitants. Today, the islands' mild climate makes them a major tourist destination year round. They are divided into two provinces: Las Palmas de Gran Canaria, and Santa Cruz de Tenerife.

Madeira

Madeira is the largest of a group of volcanic islands forming an autonomous region of Portugal. A tourist destination, they are situated 550 km (340 miles) from the coast of Morocco, and 900 km (560 miles) southwest of Lisbon. The two islands of Madeira and Porto Santo are inhabited, unlike the barren islets of the Desertas and Selvagens. Madeira is 55 km (34 miles) long and 19 km (12 miles) wide, has deep ravines and rugged mountains, contains the group's capital, Funchal, and rises to Pico Ruivo (1,862 m; 6,109 ft) in the middle of the island. It was once heavily forested, but settlers cleared the uplands for plantation use. Produce includes wine (madeira), sugar, and bananas.

Africa: Physical

ATLANTIC OCEAN

Scandinavia

NORTH SEA

BALTIC SEA

British Isles

North European Plain

Europe

Channel Is.

Pyrenees

Iberian Peninsula

Golfo de Cádiz

Alps

Appennino

Corse (Corsica)

Sardegna (Sardinia)

Mallorca

TYRRHENIAN SEA

Sicilia (Sicily) ▲ 3323 m Mte Etna

Golfe de Gabès

MEDITER R A N E A N SEA

Plain of Hungary

Stara Planina

AEGEAN SEA

Kythira ▲ 2452 m

Kriti (Crete)

IONIAN SEA

Rodos (Rhodes)

BLACK SEA

CASPIAN SEA

ARAL SEA

▲ 4547 m

▲ 4811 m

▲ 4434 m

▲ 3088 m

Bādiyat ash Shām (Syrian Desert)

▲ 2580 m Jabal al Lawz

2627 m ▲

Gulf of Oman

Persian Gulf

Gulf

Ra's Naws

Zufār

Ghubbat al Qamar

Suquṭrā (Socotra)

Raas Caseyr

Raas Xaafuun

Arabian Peninsula

Ar Ṭawīlah

Ar Rub' al Khālī

▲ 3133 m Jabal Sawdā

▲ 3760 m Jabal an Nabī Shu'ayb

RED SEA

1977 m ▲ Jabal Ḥamāṭah

Lake Nasser

Nubian Desert

2780 m ▲

Tana Hāyk' (Lake Tana) Ras Dashen Terara ▲ 4620 m

Sorā ▲ 3018 m

Shimbiris ▲ 2416 m

Gulf of Aden

Ethiopian Highlands

A f r i c a

Libyan Plateau

Libyan Desert

Jabal Zalṭan

Khalīj Surt

▲ 1200 m Qārat as Sab'ah

▲ 3376 m Targo Emissi

▲ 3088 m

El Ḥ a m r a

Aoukâr

Sahel

S A H A R A

Atlas Saharien ▲ 2326 m

Hoggar ▲ Tahat 2918 m

Plateau du Tademaït

▲ 2022 m Monts Bagzane

Hautes Atlas ▲ 4165 m Jebel Toubkal

Madeira

Islas Canarias (Canary Islands)

La Palma

Hierro

▲ 3718 m Pico de Teide

Gran Canaria

Lanzarote

Râs Nouâdhibou

Cap Vert

Sénégal

Fouta Djalon

Niger

Lac de Kossou

Lake Volta

Cape Palmas

Gulf

Bénoué

Hosséré Vokré ▲ 2049 m

Massif de l'Adamaoua

Cameroon Mtn ▲ 4095 m

▲ 1948 m Loma Mansa

Tropic of Cancer

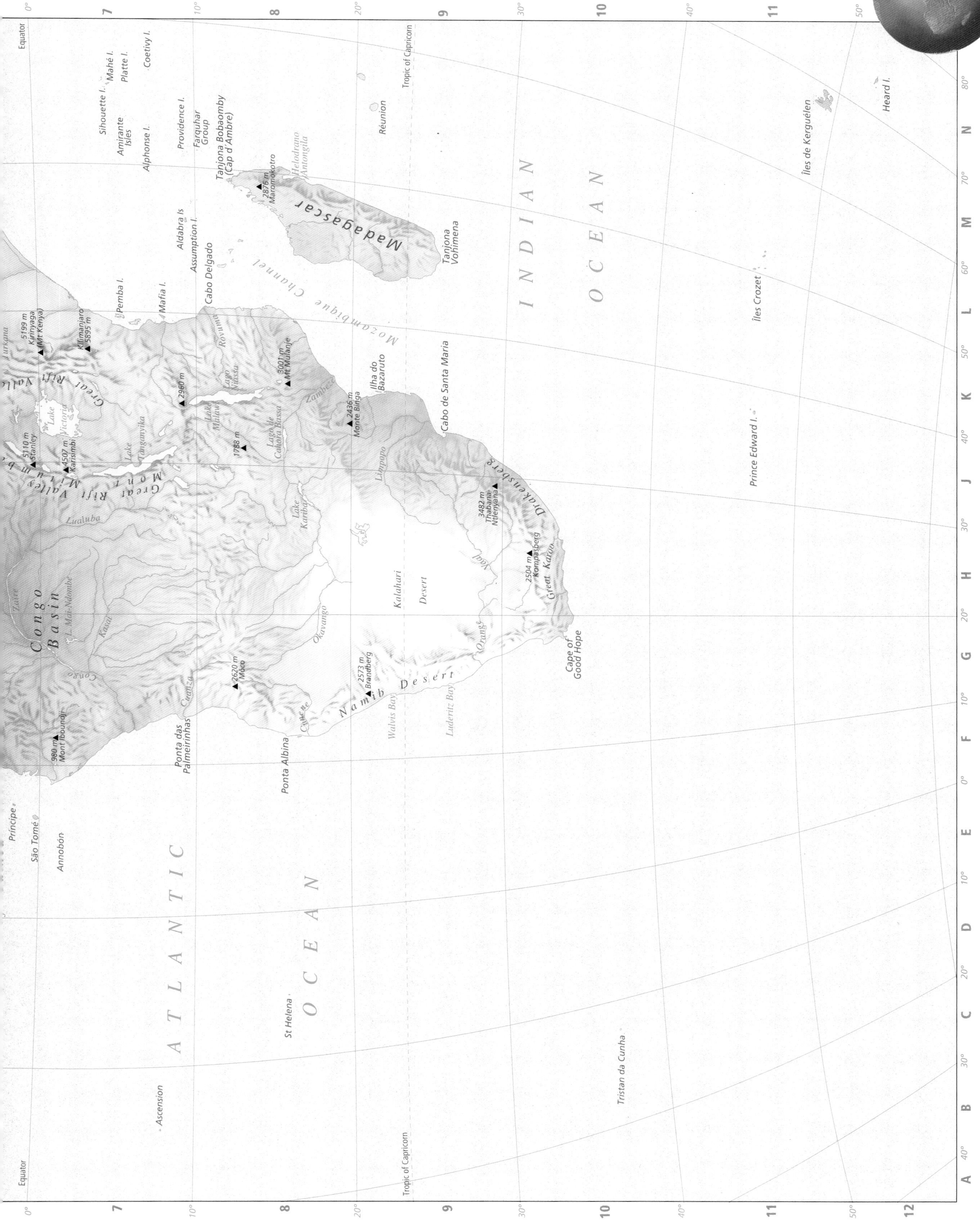

Equator 0°

Sihouette I.
Mahé I.
Platte I.
Coetivy I.

Amirante
Isles
Alphonse I.
Providence I.
Farquhar
Group

Réunion

Tropic of Capricorn

Tanjona Bobaomby
(Cap d'Ambre)
Helodrano
Antongila
2876 m
Maromokotro

Madagascar

Tanjona
Vohimena

Heard I.

Îles de Kerguélen

INDIAN

OCEAN

Îles Crozet

Prince Edward I.

Aldabra Is
Assumption I.
Cabo Delgado
Pemba I.
Mafia I.

Turkana
5199 m
Kirinyaga
(Mt Kenya)
Kilimanjaro
5895 m
Karisimbi
4500 m
5110 m
Stanley
980 m
Mont Iboundji

Lake
Victoria
Lake
Tanganyika
Ruvuma
Lago
Niassa
Lake
Malawi
2960 m
1788 m
3001 m
Mt Mulanje
Lago de
Cahora Bassa
Zambezi
2436 m
Monte Binga
Ilha do
Bazaruto
Cabo de Santa Maria

Mozambique Channel

Great Rift Valley
Mont Mitumba
Great Rift Valley
Lualaba
Zaïre
Congo
Basin
L. Mai-Ndombe
Kasai
Cuango

Lake
Kariba
Limpopo
Kalahari
Desert
Okavango
Vaal
Orange
3482 m
Thabana
Ntlenyana
Drakensberg
2504 m
Kompasberg
Great Karoo
Cape of
Good Hope

2573 m
Brandberg
Namib Desert
Walvis Bay
Lüderitz Bay
Cunene
2620 m
Moco
Cubango

Ponta das
Palmeirinhas
Ponta Albina

ATLANTIC
OCEAN

Príncipe
São Tomé
Annobón
Ascension
St Helena
Tristan da Cunha

Tropic of Capricorn

Equator 0°

0 400 800 1200 kilometers
0 200 400 600 miles
Scale 1:30,000,000   Projection: Azimuthal Equal Area

Africa

357

Africa: Political

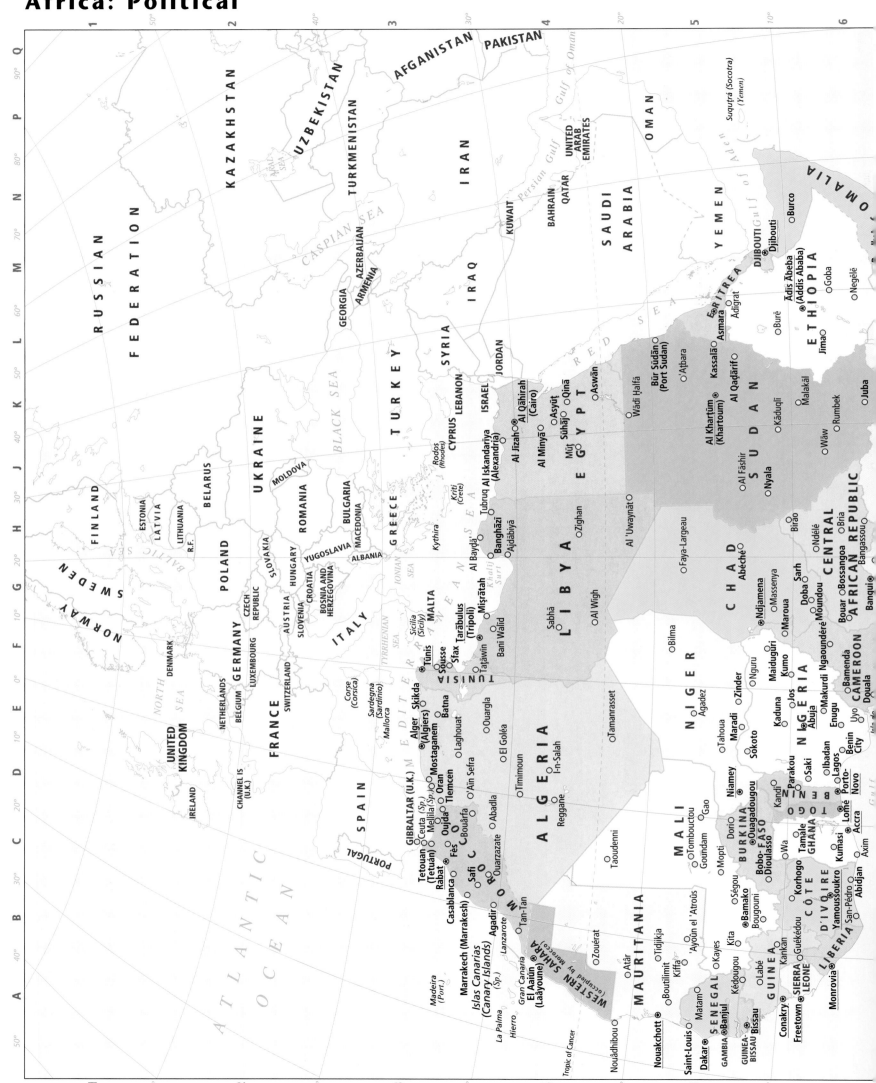

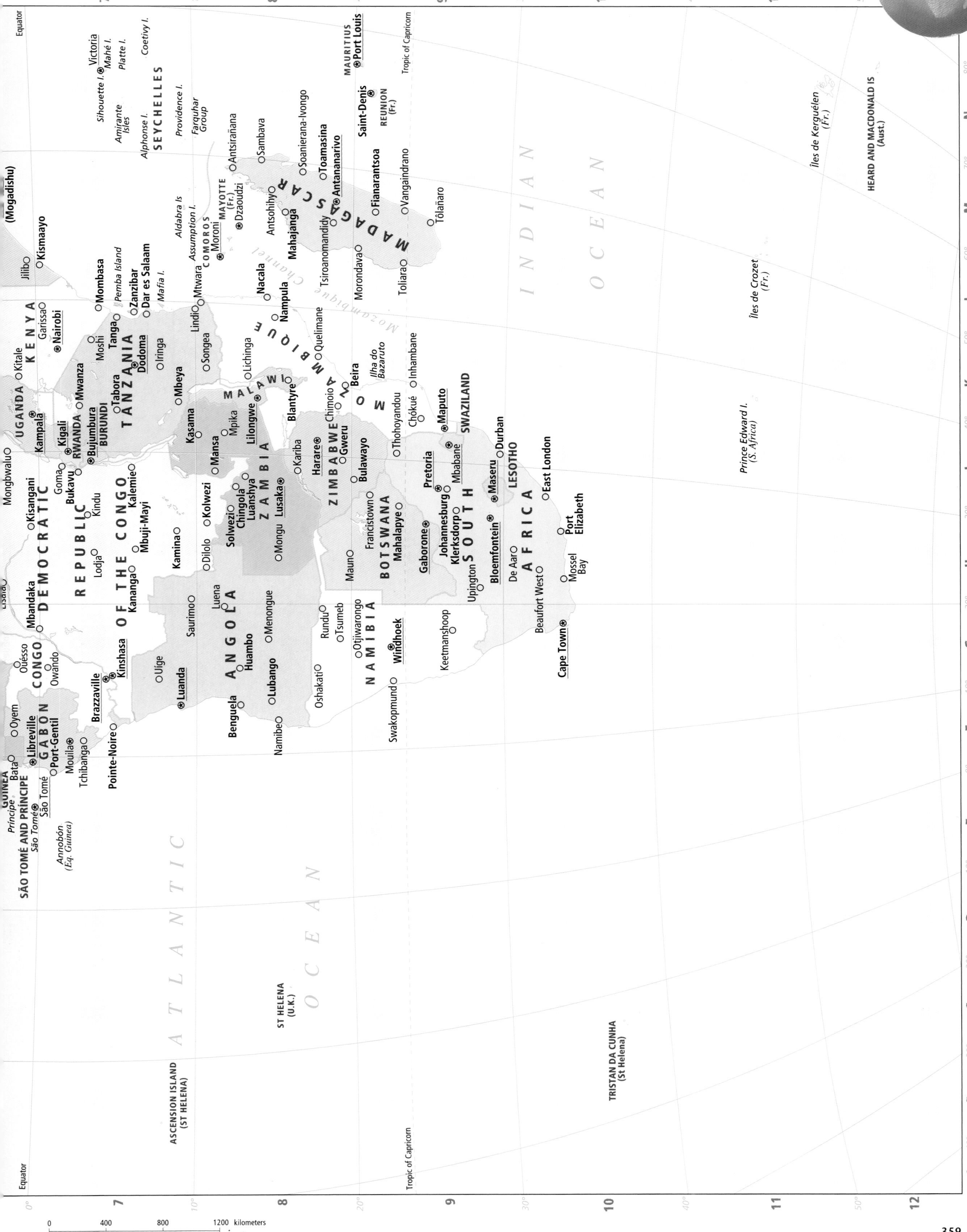

Equator

ATLANTIC OCEAN

INDIAN OCEAN

ASCENSION ISLAND
(ST HELENA)

ST HELENA
(U.K.)

TRISTAN DA CUNHA
(St Helena)

Tropic of Capricorn

SÃO TOMÉ AND PRÍNCIPE
GUINEA
Príncipe
São Tomé
São Tomé
Annobón
(Eq. Guinea)

GABON
Libreville
Port-Gentil
Mouila
Tchibanga
Oyem
Bata

CONGO
Brazzaville
Pointe-Noire
Ouésso
Owando

DEMOCRATIC
REPUBLIC
OF THE CONGO
Kinshasa
Mbandaka
Kisangani
Goma
Bukavu
Kindu
Lodja
Kananga
Mbuji-Mayi
Kamina
Kalemie
Kolwezi

Mongbwalu

ANGOLA
Luanda
Benguela
Huambo
Lubango
Namibe
Uíge
Saurimo
Luena
Menongue

NAMIBIA
Windhoek
Swakopmund
Oshakati
Rundu
Tsumeb
Otjiwarongo
Keetmanshoop

Dilolo
Solwezi

ZAMBIA
Lusaka
Chingola
Luanshya
Mongu
Mansa
Mpika
Kasama
Kariba

BOTSWANA
Gaborone
Francistown
Maun
Mahalapye

SOUTH
AFRICA
Pretoria
Johannesburg
Klerksdorp
Bloemfontein
Upington
De Aar
Beaufort West
Mossel Bay
Cape Town
Port Elizabeth
East London
Durban

LESOTHO
Maseru

SWAZILAND
Mbabane

ZIMBABWE
Harare
Bulawayo
Gweru
Chimoio

MOZAMBIQUE
Maputo
Beira
Quelimane
Nacala
Nampula
Inhambane
Chókué
Thohoyandou
Ilha do Bazaruto

MALAWI
Lilongwe
Blantyre
Lichinga

TANZANIA
Dodoma
Dar es Salaam
Zanzibar
Tanga
Moshi
Mwanza
Tabora
Mbeya
Iringa
Songea
Lindi
Mtwara
Pemba Island
Mafia I.

BURUNDI
Bujumbura

RWANDA
Kigali

UGANDA
Kampala

KENYA
Nairobi
Mombasa
Garissa
Kitale

Mogadishu (Mogadishu)
Kismaayo
Jilib

SEYCHELLES
Victoria
Mahé I.
Silhouette I.
Platte I.
Coetivy I.
Amirante Isles
Providence I.
Farquhar Group
Alphonse I.
Aldabra Is
Assumption I.

COMOROS
Moroni

MAYOTTE
(Fr.)
Dzaoudzi

MADAGASCAR
Antananarivo
Antsirañana
Sambava
Antsohihy
Toamasina
Mahajanga
Fianarantsoa
Morondava
Toliara
Tôlañaro
Vangaindrano
Soanierana-Ivongo
Tsiroanomandidy

MAURITIUS
Port Louis

REUNION
(Fr.)
Saint-Denis

Prince Edward I.
(S. Africa)

Îles de Crozet
(Fr.)

Îles de Kerguélen
(Fr.)

HEARD AND MACDONALD IS
(Aust.)

Mozambique Channel

INDIAN OCEAN

0   400   800   1200 kilometers
0   200   400   600 miles
Scale 1:30,000,000   Projection: Azimuthal Equal Area

Azores
(Port.)

Corvo

Flores

Graciosa
São Jorge
Faial Horta   Terceira
Madalena   Praia da Vitória
Pico   Angra do Heroísmo

São Miguel
Ponta Delgada   Povoação

A T L A N T I C

O C E A N   Santa Maria

PORTUGAL

Coimb
Castelo
Branco
Leiria
Portalegre
Lisboa
(Lisbon)   Beja
Grândola   Serpa
Odemira
Lagos   Huelv
Sagres Faro   Golfo
Cádiz

Kénit
Rabat
Mohammedia Ben
Casablanca   Slima
Berrechid Benahme
Azemmour   Qued Z
El Jadida   Settat
Khouribga
Kasba Tadl
Youssoufia   Beni Mellal
Safi   El Kelaa des Srarhna
Chemaïa
Marrakech (Marrakesh)
Essaouira Ounara
Imi-n-Tanoute   H a u t
Ouarzazate   Je
Cap Rhir   M O R O C C O
Agadir   Taroudannt
Oulad
Teima
Tafraoute   Foum Zguid
Tiznit A n t i   A t l a s
Sidi Ifni Bou Izakarn   Tata   Akka
Guelmim

Madeira
(Port.)

Funchal   Ilhas
Desertas

Ilhas Selvagens
(Port.)

Islas Canarias
(Canary Islands)
(Sp.)   Alegranza
Lanzarote   Graciosa
Santa Cruz   Arrecife
de la Palma   Puerto del Rosario
La Palma   Tenerife **Santa Cruz de Tenerife**
Gomera   Fuerteventura
Pico de Teide
3718 m
Hierro   Gran Canaria **Las Palmas de**
Gran Canaria

Jebel Ouarkziz Hamado
Tisgui-Remz
Tan-Tan

Tarfaya

Tindouf

Cabo Bojador

Hagunia

El Aaiún
(Laâyoune)

Semara

Bu Craa   Tifariti

Aïn Ben Tili   E r

A T L A N T I C   Guelta Zemmur   Bîr Mogreïn

O C E A N   **WESTERN**
SAHARA   Sebkhet Oumm ed **TIRIS**
Droûs Telli **ZEMMOUR**
(occupied by Morocco)   El Hank
Sebkhet Oumm
ed Droûs Guebli   S
Tropic of Cancer   Ad Dakhla   Bir Enzarán   Sebkhet
Punta Durnford El-Aargub   Ti-n-Bessaïs

Ausert   Fdérik
Zouérat
Cabo Barbas   Agüenit

Adrar Souf   Tichla   Zug
Tmeïmîchât   â   Choûm   Ouadane
Sebkhet
Chemchâm   A D R A R
Nouâdhibou   Atâr   Chinguetti
Râs Nouâdhibou   A z e f f a l A d r a r

DAKHLET
NOUÂDHIBOU INCHIRI   Oujeft   **HODH**
Akjoujt   **ECH**
Râs Timiris   **M A U R I T A N I A**   **CHARGU**
Nouâmghâr   **TAGANT**
Sebkha   Tichît
Narhamcha   Tidjikja
Jreïda   A o u k â r
Moudjéria   Oualâta
Nouakchott
T R A R Z A

Cape Verde inset:

Ponta do Sol   Santo Antão
Porto Novo   Mindelo
São Vicente   Pedra Lume Sal
São Nicolau   Vila da Ribeira Brava
Boa Vista
Sal Rei
Curral Velho
CAPE VERDE

São Tiago   Maio
Tarrafal   Porto Inglês
Brava Fogo **Praia**

SPAIN
Fuenlabrada
Plasencia
Mérida
Montes de Toledo
Toledo
Ocaña
Utiel
Ciudad Real
Valdepeñas
Villarrobledo
Albacete
Almansa
Puertollano
afra
Córdoba
Andújar
Linares
Jaén
Granada
Guadix
Hellín
Murcia
Elche
Alicante
Cartagena
evilla
éz de la ontera
Écija
Ubrique
Vélez-Málaga
Málaga
ádiz
Algeciras
Marbella
Adra
Almería
Cabo de Gata
anger
Gibraltar GIBRALTAR (U.K.)
Ceuta (Sp.)
angier
Tetouan (Tetuán)
arache
Al Hoceima
Chefchaouene
Melilla (Sp.)
Cap des Trois Fourches
Nador
ilah
Ksar el Kebir
Souk-el-Arba-du-Rharb
Sidi Kacem
eknes
Azrou
enifra
Boulemane
Midelt
Missour
Moyen Atlas
Sarhro
Er Rachidia
Boudenib
Erfoud
Meridja
agora
u Drâa
Taouz
Hamaguir
Abadla
Taghit
Béchar
Beni-Abbès
Kerzaz
Erg er Raoui
Timmoudi
Ksabi
Tabelbala
Iguidi
El Eglab
Chenachane
egga
Erg Chech
Taoudenni
El Hamada el Haricha
El Khnâchîch

MALI
TOMBOUCTOU
Araouane
Ti-n-Aguelhaj
Bamba
Téméra
Almoustarat
Anéfis
Kidal
KIDAL
Ti-n-Essako
Aguelhok
Timétrine
Tessalit
Boughessa
Ti-n-Zaouâtene
Bordj Mokhtar
GAO
I-n-Tebezas

MEDITERRANEAN SEA
Mallorca
Alcúdia
Menorca
Mahón
Palma de Mallorca
Manacor
Eivissa (Ibiza)
Eivissa
Formentera
Islas Baleares (Balearic Islands) (Sp.)

Alger (Algiers)
Dellys
Cap Sigli
Tipasa
Blida
Ténès
Aïn Defla
Larba
Tizi Ouzou
Akbou
Bejaïa
Jijel
Médéa
Bouira
Berrouaghia
Chlef
Theniet el Had
Sétif
Mila
Bordj Bou Arreridj
El Eulma
Constantine
Souk Ahras
Oum el Bouaghi
Aïn Beida
Ksar el Boukhari
Chahbounia
M'Sila
Barika
Khenchela
Tébessa
Chéria
Al Qaṣrayn
Sidi Ali
Mostaganem
Oran
Mascara
Relizane
Mehdia
Sougueur
Ksar Chellala
Bou Saâda
Sidi Okba
Biskra
Zeribet el Oued
Feriana
Redeyef
Sidi Bel Abbès
Saïda
Aïn Deheb
Frenda
Charef
Djelfa
Sidi Khaled
Ouled Djellal
Gafsa
Al Metlaoui
Tlemcen
Télagh
Aïn Temouchant
Beni-Saf
Ghazaouet
Aflou
Messaad
El Meghaïer
Djamaa
Guemar
El Oued
Al Ḩammah
Qibili
Tawzar
Al Khroub
Guercif
Taza
Fès
Khemisset
Sidi Kacem
Taourirt
Jerada
Sebdou
Oujda
Marhoum
Bougtob
Mecheria
Naama
El Bayadh
Laghouat
Tadjrouna
Tilrhemt
Berriane
Zelfana
El Alia
Touggourt
Ouargla
Hassi Messaoud
Al Burmah
Ghadāmis

TUNISIA
Manzil Bū Ruqaybah
Banzart
Golfe de Tunis
Bājah
Ţabursuq
Bou Salem
Jendouba
Tūnis
Qulaybīyah
Nābul
Zaghwān
Golfe de Hammamet
Sousse
Kairouan
Al Munastīr
Mahdia
Masākin
Al Jamm
Ksour Essaf
Sbeïtla
Sidi Bou Zid
Māḩaris
Sfax
Golfe de Gabès
Qābis
Houmet Essouk
Jazīrat Jarbah
Jarjis
Medenine
Düz
Ra's Ajdir
Zuwārah
Bin Qirdān
Taţāwïn
Ramādah
Az Zāwiyah
Al ʿAzīzīyah
Al Khums
Tarhūnah
Qaṣabāt
Zlīṭan

ITALY
Sardegna (Sardinia)
Iglesias
Cagliari
Sant' Antioco
Isola di Pantelleria (Italy)
Gozo
MALTA
Valletta
Isola di Lampedusa (Italy)
Palermo
Cefalù
Milazzo
Messina
Trapani
Marsala
Caltanissetta
Sicilia (Sicily)
Etna 3323 m
Catania
Agrigento
Gela
Siracusa
Vittória
Ragusa
Modica

Cap de Fer
Skikda
Annaba
El Hadjar
Bou Salem
Aïn M'Lila
Tālah
Sidi Bou Zid
Az Zāwiyah
Tārābulus (Tripoli)
Zuwārah
Mizdah
Jādū
Yafran
Nālūt
Az Zintān
Jabal Nafūsah
Banī Walīd
Adh Dhahībāt
Lorzot
Tiji
Ṣīnāwin
Dirj
Ash Shuwayrif

LIBYA
Al Hamādah al Ḩamrāʾ
ʿUwaynāt Wanin
Birāk
Adīrī
Tamanhint
Sabhā
Awbārī
Ghaddūwah
Tarāghin
Murzuq
Ṣaḩrāʾ Awbārī
Ṣaḩrāʾ Murzuq
Al ʿUwaynāt
Ghāt
Plateau du Manguéni
Madama
Plateau du Djado
Djado
Chirfa
Ténéré du Tafassâsset
Séguédine
Aney
Dirkou
Bilma
Grand Erg de Bilma
DIFFA
ZINDER

ALGERIA
Sahara Atlas
Plateau du Tademaït
Grand Erg Occidental
El Goléa
Hassi Inifel
El Homr
Timimoun
Sbaa
I-n-Belbel
Adrar
Reggane
Sebkha Reggane
Aoulef
Akabli
Foggaret ez Zoua
I-n-Salah
Plaine du Tidikelt
Sebkha Mekerrhane
Sebkha Azzel Matti
Amguid
Arak
Adrar N'Ahnet
Monts du Mouydir
Asedjrad
Tanezrouft
Tefedest
Tassili n'Ajjer
I-n-Eker
Idles
In-Amguel
Abalessa
Silet
Tamanrasset
Hoggar
AHAGGAR
Arak
Tanezrouft Tan-Ahenet
Bordj Mokhtar
Tessalit
Tassili du Hoggar
I-n-Guezzam
Assamakka

Grand Erg Oriental
Hassi Bel Guebbour
Ohanet
Zarzaïtine
Bordj Omar Driss
I-n-Amenas
Edjeleh
El Adeb Larache
Plateau du Tinrhert
Illizi
Tarat
Zaouatallaz
Djanet
Erg Issaouane
Bordj Messouda
Ghadāmis

NIGER
AGADEZ
Iferouâne
Sidaouet
Massif de l'Aïr
Timia
Akrérèb
Aouderas
Arlit
Teguidda-n-Tessoumt
Ingal
Agadez
Falaise de Tiguidit
Fachi
TAHOUA
Tassara
Tassili du Hoggar

Scale 1:9,000,000   Projection: Azimuthal Equal Area
0 100 200 300 400 kilometers
0 100 200 miles

Libya · Egypt · North Sudan · North Chad

295   297

A   10°   B   15°   C   20°   D   25°   E   30

ITALY

Iglesias   **Cagliari**
Sant' Antioco
TYRRHENIAN   SEA
Sibari
Paola   Capo Sta Maria di Leuca
Cosenza   Crotone
1723 m   Capo Rizzuto
Catanzaro
Trapani   **Palermo**   Cefalù   Milazzo   **Messina**
Marsala   **Sicilia**   **Reggio di Calabria**
Mazara del Vallo   Siderno
Agrigento   Mte Etna   **Catania**
3323 m
Gela   Ragusa   **Siracusa**
Vittoria   Modica

Manzil Bū   Banzart
Ruqaybah
Tūnis   Qulaybiyah
Bou Salem   **Carthage**
Jendouba   Nābul
Bājah   Golfe de Tūnis
Tabursuq
Golfe de Hammamet
Tālah   Kairouan
Jabal ash   Masākin
Sha'nabi   **Sousse**
1544 m   Al Qaṣrayn   Al Munastīr
Sbeitla   Mahdia
Feriana   Sidi Bou Zid   Al Jamm   Ksour Essaf
Gafsa   Maharès
Qibilī   **Sfax**
Al Metlaoui
Al Ḥammah   Golfe de Gabès
Dūz   Qābis
TUNISIA   Medenine   Houmet Essouk
Jazīrat Jarbah
Bin   Jarjis
Qirdān   Ra's Ajdīr
Tatāwīn   Zuwārah   **Ṭarābulus (Tripoli)**
Ramādah   Az Zāwiyah   Al Khums
Adh Dhahibāt   Tijī   Al 'Azīzīyah   Al Qaṣābāt   Zlitan
Lorzot   Nālūt   Tarhūnah   **Miṣrātah**
Yafran   Gharyān
Jādū   Az Zintān   Banī Walīd
Sināwin   Jabal Nafūsah   Qaryat al
Mizdah   Qaddāḥiyah   Bu'ayrat al Ḥasūn
Bordj   Surt
Messouda   Dirj   Abū Nujaym   As Sulṭān
Ghadāmis   An Nawfalīyah   As Sidrah
Ash Shuwayrif   As Sulṭān

MALTA   Gozo
Isola di   **Valletta**
Pantelleria   Isola di
(Italy)   Lampedusa
(Italy)

IONIAN   SEA

MEDITERRANEAN   SEA

Ioannina   Trikala   **Larisa**
Karditsa   Volos
GREECE
Lefkada   Mesolongi
Patra
Korinthos   Peiraiás
Athina   (Piraeus)
(Athens)
Pyrgos   Tripoli
Kyparissia   Sparti
Kalamata   Skala
Milos

Kerkyra   (Corfu)
Kefallonia
Zakynthos   (Zante)
Evvoia   (Euboea)
Andros   Tinos
Syros   Samos
Paros   Ikaria
Naxos   Ios   Amorgos
Kythira   Karpathos
Kriti   (Crete)
Chania   Irakleio   (Iraklion)
2452 m
Akra Lithino

Çanakkale   Çan   Susurluk   Bozüyük
Ezine   **Balıkesir**   Dursunbey   **Kütahya**
Edremit   Burhaniye   Bigadiç   Emet
Soma   Kırkağaç   Simav
Lesvos   Akhisar   Simav
Chios   **Manisa**   Alaşehir   Çivril
Menemen   Salihli   Kula
Bornova   Odemiş
Çeşme   Urla   **İzmir**   Turgutlu   Nazilli
Samos   Söke   **Aydın**   Çine   **Denizli**
Milas   Yatağan   Tavas
DODEKANISOS   Muğla   Dalaman
Marmaris   Fethiye   Elma
Kos
Rodos
Rodos   (Rhodes)   Kaş

AEGEAN   SEA

Tūkrah   Al Bayḍā'   Ra's al Hilāl   Darnah
Banghāzī   Shaḥḥāt   Sūsah
Al Marj   Sulunṭah   Ra's at Tīn
Al Abyār   At Tamimī
Qaminis   Sulūq   Zāwiyat Masūs   Tubruq   Ra's al Murayṣah
Sultān   Zāwiyat al Mukhaylā   Al Bardī
Ajdābiyā   Umm Sa'ad   Sidi Barrāni
Khalīj as Salūm   Abu Haggag
Al 'Uqaylah   Marsá al Burayqah   Marsá Maṭrūḥ   Ra's al Kanā'is
Libyan   Plateau   Al 'Alamayn
Al Ḥamm
Qattara   Depression
Al Jaghbūb   Qārah
Siwah
Mabrūk   Marādah   Awjilah   Jālū
Jabal Waddān
671 m   Waddān
Sūknah   Hūn
Zillah
Great   Sand   Sea   Al Bawīṭī
Al Ḥayz
Jabal   Zaltan
Western   Desert
Qaṣr al Farāfirah
Adīrī   Birāk
Tamanhint   Samnū   Al Fuqahā'
Awbārī   **Sabhā**   Qārat as Sab'ah
1200 m
Ghaddūwah   Tmassah
Zawīlah
Murzuq   Tarāghin   Wāw al Kabīr   Tāzirbū
LIBYA
Al Qaṭrūn   Zighan   **EGYPT**
Tajarhī   Al Wīgh   Al Qaṣr
Mūṭ
Ṣaḥrā'   Rabyānah
Sarīr Tibesti   467 m
Al Jawf   Al Khufrah
Ḥaḍabat al   Jilf al Kabīr
Jabal   Arkanū
1435 m
Al 'Uwaynāt   Jabal Al 'Uwaynāt   1893 m
Jabal Kissū   1712 m

ALGERIA
Tropic of Cancer
Djanet
Ṣaḥrā'   Murzuq
Tarat   Al 'Uwaynāt
Ghāt

Zarzaitine
I-n-Amenas
Edjeleh
'Uwaynāt Wanin

Plateau du   Manguéni
Madama   Aozou
Plateau   du Djado   Kamal
Djado   Chirfa   Pic Toussidé
3315 m   Tarso Emissi
3376 m
Bardaï   Yebbi-Souma
Ténéré du   Zouar   Yebbi-Bou
Tafassâsset   Tibesti
AGADEZ
Séguédine
NIGER   Emi Koussi   Gouro
Aney   3415 m
Dirkou
Bilma   Ounianga Kébir
Fachi   **CHAD**   Ounianga Sérir
Grand Erg de Bilma   **BORKOU-ENNEDI-TIBESTI**
Borkou
DIFFA   Faya-Largeau   Dépression du Mourdi
Erg du Djourab   Ennedi
ZINDER   Fada   Basso
1450 m

SHAMĀL DĀRFŪR
SHA

SAHARA

361

366

A   B   15°   C   20°   D   25°   E

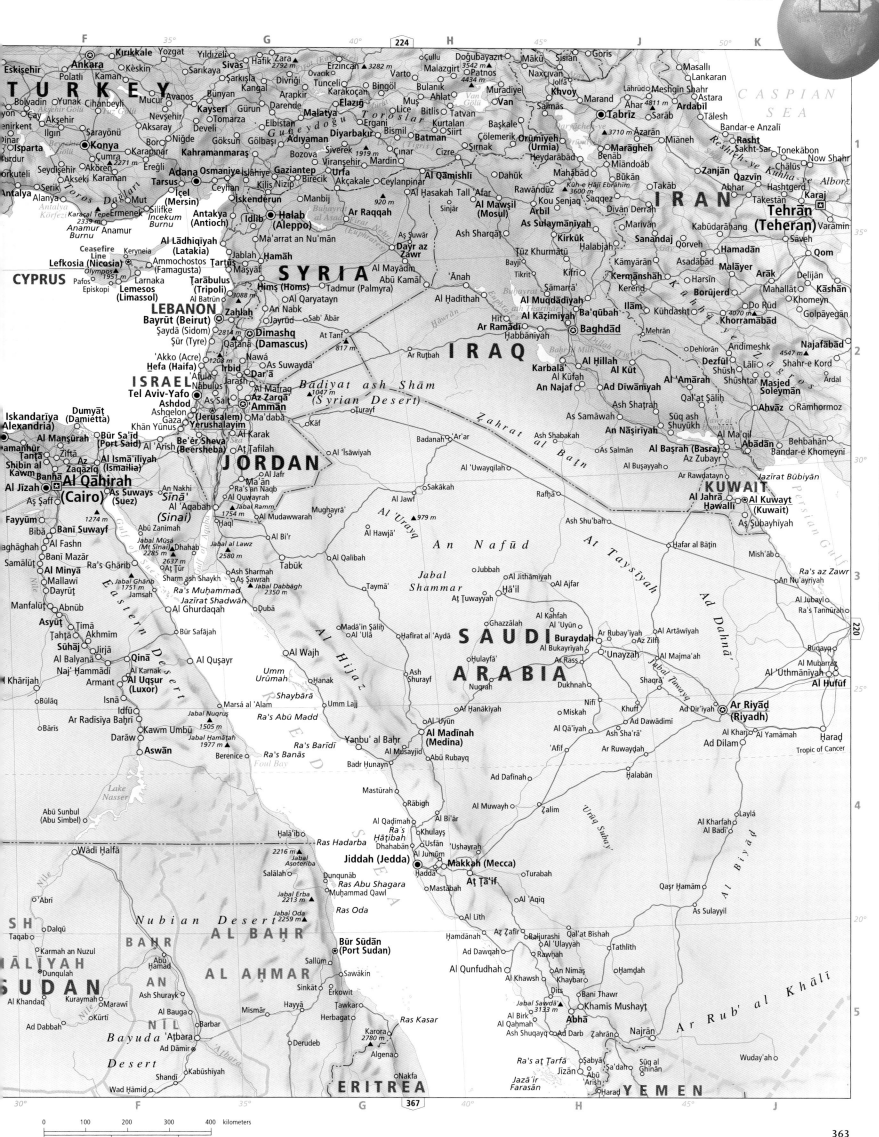

CASPIAN SEA

TURKEY

CYPRUS

Lefkosia (Nicosia)
Lemesos (Limassol)

SYRIA

LEBANON
Bayrūt (Beirut)
Dimashq (Damascus)

ISRAEL
Tel Aviv-Yafo
Yerushalayim (Jerusalem)

JORDAN
Amman

IRAQ
Baghdad

IRAN
Tehrān (Teheran)
Karaj

KUWAIT
Al Kuwayt (Kuwait)

Iskandarīya (Alexandria)
Al Qāhirah (Cairo)

SAUDI ARABIA
Ar Riyāḍ (Riyadh)

Al Uqṣur (Luxor)

Jiddah (Jedda)
Makkah (Mecca)

RED SEA

Būr Sūdān (Port Sudan)

SUDAN

Nubian Desert

AL BAHR AL AHMAR

ERITREA

Khamīs Mushayṭ
Abhā

YEMEN

Ar Rub' al Khālī

West Africa

360

MAURITANIA

Nouakchott

TRARZA
TAGANT
Tidjikja
Tichît
Aoukâr
Araouane
Anéfis
S A
Almoustara

Boutilimit
Moudjéria
TOMBOUCTOU
Al-Moustarah

Magta' Lahjar
BRAKNA
Tiguent
Tâmchekket
HODH ECH
HODH EL
Ti-n-Aguelhaj
Téméra

Mederdra
Aleg
ASSABA
Ouâlâta
CHARGUI
Bourem

Rosso
Guérou
'Ayoûn el 'Atroûs
Néma
Lac
Faguibine

Richard Dagana
Podor
Bogué
Kaédi
GORGAL
Kiffa
Tintâne
Dendâra
Lerneb
Râs el Mâ
Gundam
Diré
Doro
Gossi
Gao

Saint-Louis
Bababé
GHARBI
Touil
Timbedgha
Niafounké
Ansongo

Louga
Keur Momar Sar
Lagbar
Guidimaka
Kobenni
Amourj
Bassikounou
Léré
Ngorkou
Hombori

Kébémer
Koki
Linguère
Ranérou
Ould Yenjé
Kirané
Nara
Goumbou
Boré
Ngouma
Markoy

Mékhé
Dara
GUIDIMAKA
Yélimané
Nioro du Sahel
Nampala
Konna
Douentza
Bankilaré

Pikine
Bambey
Touba
Mbout
Sandaré
Sokolo
MALI
Diafarabé
Djibo
Aribinda
Sebba

Dakar
Thiès
Diourbel
Maghama
Lakamané
Niono
Mourdiah
Ténenkou
Mopti
Bandiagara
Gorom-Gorom
Liptougou

Rufisque
Mbour
Fatick
SENEGAL
Ambidédi
Kayes
Diéma
Dioumara
Massina
Markala
MOPTI
Koro
Bankass
Titao
Dori
Téra

Joal-Fadiout
Kaolack
Kaffrine
KAYES
Goudiri
Ségala
Didiéni
Banamba
Ségou
Tominian
Ouahigouya
Gourcy
Kongoussi
Bogandé

GAMBIA
Farafenni
Koungheul
Koussanar
Mahina
Bafoulabé
Toukoto
Kolokani
KOULIKORO
SÉGOU
San
Yangasso
Tougan
Nouna
Yako
BURKINA

Banjul
Georgetown
Diamounguel
Kidira
Kita
Sébékoro
Kati
Koulikoro
Fana
Bla
Kimparana
Gourcy
Réo
Koudougou
FASO

Brikama
Bignona
Diouloulou
Sédhiou
Pata
Dialakoto
Dialafara
Kokofata
Négala
Dioila
Mpessoba
Koutiala
Dédougou
Mahou
Bondoukui
Ouagadougou

Ziguinchor
Diembéreng
GUINEA-
Maka
Médina Gounas
Saraya
Kédougou
Bamako
Baléya
Ouéléssébougou
Zangasso
Toma
Houndé
Koupéla
Fada N'Gourma

Cacheu
Mansabá
Gabú
Wassadou
Koundara
Niandankoro
Kangaba
Sido
Bougouni
Sikasso
Koundougou
Bobo-Dioulasso
Dano
Léo
Pô
Zabré
Manga
Ouargaye
Arli

Bissau
BISSAU
Bafatá
Xitole
Massif du Tamgué
Mt du Tamgué 1538 m
Dabatou
Kintinian
Kangaba
Kignan
Massigui
Diébougou
Quessa
Tumu
Bolgatanga
Bawku
Dapaong
Natitingou

Arquipélago dos Bijagós
Orango
Bolama
Buba
MOYENNE-GUINÉE
Koumbia
Koundjié
Dinguiraye
Siguiri
Kalana
Garalo
Kolondiéba
Orodara
Toussiana
Gaoua
UPPER WEST
Lawra
Nabolo
Wahabu
Mango
Kanté

Catió
Cacine
GUINÉE-
Boké
Koubia
Tougué
Bissikrima
Kouroussa
Mandiana
Filamana
Manankoro
Kadiolo
Sidéradougou
Banfora
Fian
Wa
Kampti
Savelugu
Gushiago
Yendi
Zabzugu
Bafil

Cap Boffa
Kamsaro
Boké
MARITIM
Labé
HAUTE
Banko
Kankan
GUINÉE
Saladougou
Niangoloko
Kampti
NORTHERN
Gbimbila
Bassar

Cap Verga
Boffa
Fria
Mamou
Dalaba
Mont 1421 m
Kadiondola 1094 m
Béléya
Faranah
Moribaya
Maninian
Mbengué
Ouangolodougou
Boundiali
Varalé
Damóngo
Bimbila
TOGO

Kindia
Mont 1421 m
Dalaba
Yana
Falaba
Komodou
Odienné
Madinani
Séguélon
Korhogo
Ferkessédougou
Téhini
Bole
NORTHERN
Salaga
Kpandae
Blitta

Dubréka
Coyah
NORTHERN
Kabala
Kamaron
Kissidougou
Kérouané
Bako
Morondo
Dianra
Nikaramandougou
Bouna
Kotouba
GHANA
Yeji
Kintampo
Yégue
Kamir

Conakry
Forécariah
Port Loko
Kondembaia
Loma Mansa 1948 m
Beyla
Sinko
Borotou
Katiola
Kakpin
Dabakala
BRONG-AHAFO
Atebubu
Amlamé
Hohoe
Notsé

Freetown
SIERRA
Makeni
Magburaka
Sefadu
Pic de Tibé 1504 m
Touba
Kani
Bouandougou
Mankono
Bondoukou
Tanda
Wenchio
Techiman
Nkoranza
Kpalimé
Tsévié

Lungi
Lunsar
LEONE
Yengema
Guékédou
GUINÉE-
Nzébéla
Gouéké
Séguéla
CÔTE
Daoukro
Dormaa
Berekum
Ejura
Mampong
Agogo
Kpandu
Anécho

WESTERN
Moyamba
EASTERN
Mano
Voinjama
FORESTIÈRE
Lola
Biankouma
Zuénoula
Béoumi
Bouaké
D'IVOIRE
Agnilékrou
Goaso
ASHANTI
EASTERN
Ho

Yawri Bay
Matru
Kenema
Zorzor
Nzérékoré
Nimba 1752 m
Man
Logoualé
Daloa 1002 m
Bouaflé
Dimbokro
Toumodi
Arrah
Abengourou
Kumasi
Konongo
Koforidua
Somanya
Aflao

Sherbro Island
Bandajuma
SOUTHERN
Mano River
Gbatala
Gbarnga
Saglepie
Danané
Duékoué
Bangolo
Sinfra
Qumé
Mbatto
Akoupé
Obuasi
Bibiani
WESTERN
Dunkwa
Asamankese
Nsawam
Ketao
Lom

Pujehun
Zimmi
Haindi
Tototaa
Tapeta
Guiglo
Issia
Gagnoa
Hire
Adzopé
Agboville
CENTRAL
Prestea
Aboso
Foso
Tema
Cape
Anloga

Tubmanburg
Robertsport
Kakata
Toulépleu
Gagnoa
Lakota
Divo
Tiassalé
Bingerville
Tarkwa
Abooso
Winneba
GREATER ACCRA

Monrovia
LIBERIA
Buchanan
Zwedru
Zia Town
Taï
Soubré
Guéyo
Dabou
Bonoua
Axim
Sekondi
Accra
Saint Paul

Harbel
Cess
River Cess
Juazohn
Grabo
Fresco
Abidjan
Grand-Bassam
Takoradi
Cape Coast
Saltpond

Grain Coast
Greenville
Sasstown
Grand Cess
Sassandra
San-Pédro
Cape Three Points
Gold Coast

Harper
Tabou
Cape Palmas
Ivory Coast
Coast

ATLANTIC OCEAN

Equator

KIDAL
Kidal
I-n-Essako
I-n-Tebezas

GAO
Telataï
Tidarméné
Ménaka
Andérámboukane
Tiloa
Bani Bangou
Abala
Ouallam
IILLABÉRI
abéri
Balèyara
othèye
ougou
ande
ndali
Nikki
gou
Parakou
naourou
ntè
Kokoro
clampa
Savè
avalou
Bohicon
bomey
Abeokuta
Sakété-
dah
tonou Porto-
Novo
Lagos

A R A
Assamakka
Iferouâne
▲ Adrar Tamgak 1988 m
Arlit
Massif de l'Aïr
Sidaouet
Timia
▲ Monts Bagzane 2022 m
Akrérèb

AGADEZ
Fachi

A
Teguidda-n-Tessoumt
Tassara
Ingal
Agadez
Falaise de Tiguidit

Tchin-Tabaradene
Abalak
Aderbissinat
Tanout

NIGER
Aney
Dirkou
Bilma

BORKOU-ENNEDI-
TIBESTI
Erg du Djourab
Koro Toro
Nédéley

Borkou
Faya-Largeau

Tilemsès
ZINDER

DIFFA
Termit-Kaboul
Tasker
Ngourti

KANEM
Salal
Ziguéy
Nokou

CHAD
Haraz-Djombo
BATHA
Djédaa
Asnet
Oum-Hadjer
Am Timan

Tiddarméné
Telataï

Tahoua
Bagaroua
Keita
Badéguichéri
Bouza
Dakoro
TAHOUA
Bélbéji
Sabonkafi
MARADI
Mayahi
Tessaoua
Goudoumaria
Maïné-
Soroa
Diffa
Geidam
Ngourti

Niamey
Say
Birnin Gaouré
DOSSO
Loga
Dogondoutchi
Birnin Konni
Gwadabawa
Wurno
Sokoto
Argungu
Isa
Moriki
Namoda

Maradi
Zinder
Daura

Matamey
Magaria
Dungas
Nguru
Gashua
Kukawa
Monguno
Ngala

Nguigmi
LAC
Lac Tchad
Bol
Karal
Fotokol
Kousseri
Ndjamena

Rig-Rig
Nokou
Mao
Mondo
Ngouri
Lioua
Damasak
Massaguet
Massakory
Ngoura
Moyto
Bokoro

Mouzarak
Massaguet
Tourba
Guelfey
Logone Birni
Waza
Bitkine
1613 m
Mongo
Mangalmé

DOSSO
Dosso
Dioundiou
Gaya
KEBBI
Birnin
Kebbi
Bunza
Jega
Dakingari
Kangiwa
Dange
Yabo
Shagari
Gummi
Daki
Takwas
Kwatarkwashi
KATSINA
Katsina
Dutsin-Ma
Dambatta
JIGAWA
Hadejia
Kafin Hausa
Bulangu
Geidam
Damaturu
Gujba
Benisheikh
Magumeri
YOBE
Dikwa
Maiduguri
BORNO
Mora
Logone Birni

Djébrène

GUÉRA
Mongo
Abou Deïa
Kédédéssé
Mousgougou
Bousso
Mogroum
Korbol
Kélo
Guidari
Laï
TANDJILÉ
Bénoy
Goundi
Koumra

Kérou
Malanville
Guéné
Banikoara
Kandi
Gogounou
Ségbana
Singndé
Kalalé
Yashikera
Kaiama
Wawa
New Bussa
NIGER
KWARA
Saki
Kishi
Igboho
Bode-Sadu
Share
Ilorin
Offa
OYO
Iseyin
Oyo
Ogbomosho
Oshogbo
Ede
Iwo
Ikire
Ife
OSUN
Ibadan
Ilesha
Ondo

Kainji
Reservoir
Auna
Tegina
Kontagora
Birnin
Gwari
Kajuru
Zungeru
Minna
Bida
Lafiagi
Patagi
Lapai
Suleja
Abuja
FEDERAL
CAPITAL
TERRITORY
Keffi

Akwanga
Shendam
PLATEAU
Jos
Bukuru
Pankshin
Langtang

BAUCHI
Bauchi
Dindima
Bara
Kumo
Gombe
Gombi
Shani
Biu
Bajoga

ADAMAWA
Numan
Mayo Belwa
Yola
▲ Monts Alantika 1885 m
Jalingo
Gassol
Mutum Biyu
Ganye
TARABA
Beli
Jamtari

Maroua
Kaélé
Guider
Figuil
Pitoa
Bébémi
Garoua
Rey Bouba
▲ 1952 m Monts Numan
Poli
▲ Hosséré Vokré 2049 m
NORD
Mayo Alim

Binder
Léré
Tikem
MAYO-KÉBBI
Pala
Gagal
Fianga
Bongor
Guidari
Guelengdeng
Fianga

Kim
Ngam
Dogoumbo
MOYEN
CHARI
Sarh
Doba
Moundou
LOGONE
OCCIDENTAL
LOGONE
ORIENTAL
Moissala
Goré
Bébéto
Maro
Baïbokoum
Bessao
Madingrin
Koum
Koumogo

Kaga
Bandoro
NANA-
GRÉBIZI
Kendégué
Kabo
Markounda
Ouandago
Dékoa
Bouca
Bossangoa

Kibou
Zuru
Rijau
Birnin-Yauri
Yelwa
Ibeto
Ukata
Kontagora
Rahama
Gubi
Toro

Zaria
Anchau
Darazo
Duku
Gwoza

EXTRÊME-
NORD
Mora
Bogo
Waza

CENTRAL

Kano
KANO
Wudil
Dutse
Azare
Potiskum
Goniri
Buni
Damboa

Gusau
Kaura
Namoda
Zamfara
Funtua
Malumfashi
Ringim
Gaya
Rano
Tudun Wada
Birnin Kudu
Misau
Kari
Faggo
Zalanga

KADUNA
Kaduna
Lère
Kachia
Birnin
Gwari
Kagarko

Birnin
Gwari
Kaduna

Ibadan
Ado-Ekiti
Ila-Orangun
Effon-Alaiye
Akure
ONDO
Ikare
Owo
Idah
Ankpa
OGUN
Ikorodu
Ikeja
LAGOS
Benin City
EDO
Sapele
Boji Boji
ANAMBRA
Onitsha
Awka
Enugu
ENUGU
Abakaliki
CROSS

Slave Coast
Bight
of Benin
Warri
DELTA
Ughelli
Omoku
RIVERS
Nembe
Degema
Port-
Harcourt
Bonny

of Benin
of Guinea

Bight of
Bonny

Príncipe

SÃO TOMÉ
AND PRÍNCIPE

São Tomé
São Tomé

Annobón
(Eq. Guinea)

Kwale
IMO
Mbaidi
Umuahia
Owerri
Aba
Ikot Ekpene
Uyo
AKWA
IBOM
Oron
Eket
Calabar
Ikom
RIVER
Mamfe
Ogoja

Ihiala

Isla
de Bioco
Malabo
Luba
Riaba
▲ Pico Basile 3011 m
Limbe
Buea
▲ Cameroon Mtn. 4095 m
Douala
Edéa
Kribi
Campo
Ma'an
EQUATORIAL
GUINEA
Bata
Mbini
Cogo
Cabo San Juan
Niefang
Ncue
Ebebiyin
Mongomo
Oyem
Evinayong
Acurenam
Nsoko
Médouneu
Mitzic
WOLEU-NTEM
Bitam

Libreville
ESTUAIRE
Ntoum
Kango
Lalara
Ovan
Booué
OGOOUÉ-IVINDO
Makokou

Cap Lopez
Port-Gentil
MOYEN-OGOOUÉ
Lambaréné
Batanga
Bifoun
Ndjolé
Sindara
Fougamou
Mouila
Mandji
NGOUNIÉ
Mimongo
OGOOUÉ-
MARITIME
Omboué
Iguéla
Ndendé
Lébamba
Mbigou
Panao
Bakoumba
Mbinda
Setté Cama
Gamba
Moabi
Tchibanga
NYANGA
Mayumba
Divénié
Kibangou
Mossendjo
Mayoko
Massana-Lewémé

▲ Mont Iboundji 980 m
GABON
Koulamoutou
Lastoursville
Onga
Onga
Ongo
Okondja
Akiéni
LOLO
Moanda
HAUT-
Franceville
Lékoni
OGOOUÉ
Boumango
Zanaga
Mpouya
Mpé
Léfini
PLATEAUX
Djambala
Ngo

Mamfé
Dschang
OUEST
Foumban
Bafoussam
Bangangté
Bafang
Melong
Loum
Nkongsamba
LITTORAL
Yabassi
Mbanga
Kumba
SUD-OUEST

CAMEROON
Bamenda
Kumbo
NORD-
OUEST
Banyo
Tibati
ADAMAOUA
Ngaoundéré
Meiganga

Mont Guimbiri 927 m
Yoko
CENTRE
Nanga
Eboko
Mankim
Bafia
Ntui
Obala
Yaoundé
Mbalmayo
Akonolinga
Monatélé
Bot Makak
SUD
Eséka
Lolodorf
Akom II
Ebolowa
Mvangan
Sangmélima
Djoum
Oveng
Ambam

Banyo
Darlé
Tignère
Massif de l'Adamaoua

Garoua
Boulaï
Batouri
Bertoua
EST
Abong
Mbang
Doumé
Nanga
Eboko

Yokadouma
Moloundou

Bétaré Oya
Kétté
Bélabo
Goyoum

Ndélélé
Gamboula
Boda
Berbérati
Nola
SANGHA-
MBAÉRÉ
Carnot
MAMBÉRÉ-
KADEÏ
Bania
Bambio
Adoumandjali

Bozoum
Bouar
NANA-MAMBÉRÉ
Baoro
Baboua
Bossentélé
Niem
Abba
Bayanga-Didi
OMBELLA-MPOKO
Yaloké
Bossembélé
Damara
Bogangolo

Meiganga
Garoua-
Boulaï
Bouar
AFRICAN
REPUBLIC
Bangui
Bimbo
Mbaïki
LOBAYE
Ngoto
Mbata
Bayanga
Mbata

OUHAM-
PENDÉ
OUHAM
Bossangoa
Bocaranga
Djohong
Babongo

KÉMO
Sibut
Grimari
Dékoa
Marali
KAGA-
Kouango
Pandu

Mbaïki
Libenge
Gemena
Budjala
Bomboma
DEMOCRATIC
REPUBLIC
OF THE
CONGO

Campo
Kribi
Ebolowa
Ambam
Oveng
Minvoul
Nkolabona
Mbalam
Souanké
Sembé
Ngbala
LIKOUALA
Impfondo
Makanza
Bomongo
Basankusu
Losombo
Lulonga
Bolomba
Mbandaka
Ingende
Boteka

Kango
Médouneu
Mitzic
Ovan
Mékambo
SANGHA
Ouésso
Kettea
Epéna
Liouesso
Madjingou
Bélinga
Cogo
Mbomo
Ntokou
Etoumbi
Makoua
CUVETTE
Owando
Boundji
Oyo
Ngabé
Bolobo
Ntandembele
Mushie
BANDUNDU
Kutu

Ewo
Okoyo
Abala
Ollombo
Gambona
Mbinda
Zanaga
Mossendjo

NIARI
LÉKOUMOU
Sibiti
Makabana
Kimba
Moutamba
Vinza
POOL
Loukolela
Loudima
Kinzulu
Yénéganou
Kibangou

Ekouamou
Pikounda
Yengo
Yandja
Nsambi
Selengue
Yumbi
Lukolela
Bikoro
Sungu
Bokatola
Wacka
Boleko
Bolobo
Waka
Inongo
Bolondo
Botemela
Lokolama
Djampie
Tolo
Inono
Nioki
Kiri
Mai-Ndombe

E 5° F 10° 361 G 15° H
E 5° F 10° G 15° H 368 20°

1 2 3 4 5

Africa
366

Sudan · Ethiopia · Somalia

A · 20° · B · 25° · 362 · C · 30° · D · 35°

Borkou
Ouninanga Kébir
Ouninanga Sérir
Dépression du Mourdi
Ennedi
BORKOU-
ENNEDI-
TIBESTI
Faya-Largeau
Erg du Djourab
Fada
Basso 1450 m
ASH SHAMALIYAH
Dunqulah
Keheili
Al Khandaq
Kuraymah
Marawi
Kūrtī
Ash Shuraykh
AL BAHR
AL AHMAR
Barbar
Al Bauga
Mismār
Derudeb

Koro Toro
Nédéley
Oum-Chalouba
Monou
Bakaoré
Iriba
DARFUR
SHAMAL
Malha
Bayuda Desert
Ad Dabbah
Atbara
Ad Dāmir
NIL
Kabūshiyah
Wad Hāmid
Shandī
Qawz Rajab
KASSAL
Arom

Haraz-Djombo
Arada
Biltine
BILTINE
Miski
Jabal Teljo 1954 m
Kutum
SHAMAL KURDUFAN
Hamrat ash Shaykh
Al Wazz
Umm Durmān (Omdurman)
Jabal Harāzah 1127 m
Al Khartūm Bahr (Khartoum North)
Al Khartūm (Khartoum)
KHARTUM
Abū Dulayq
Al Kāmilin
Halfa'a Jadidah
Khashm al Qirbah
Shuwak
Malawi
AL JAZIRAH

BATHA
Haraz-Djombo
Djédaa
Am-Zoer
GHARB DARFUR
Jabal Gurgei 2397 m
Al Junaynah
Abyad
Umm Kaddādah
Sawdiri
Kagmar
Umm Sayyālah
Al Mahqil
Alo Quţaynah
Wad Medanī
As Sūki
Sinjah
Al Qadārif
QADARI
Qala'an Nahl
Al Hawātah
Qallābāt

Abéché
Moura
Adré
Zalingei
Jabal Marrah 3088 m
Al Fāshir
Al Hillah
Wad Bandah
An Nahūd
Khuwayy
Al Ubayyid (El Obeid)
Ar Rahad
Tandaltī
Kūstī
Rabak
Sannār
SINNAR
Rahad
Dinder

Ati
Djébrène
Am-Dam
Goz-Beïda
Mongororo
Garsila
DARFUR
Menawashei
Dibs
JANUB
Muhājiriyah
Ghubaysh
Abū Zabad
Sharafah
GHARB KURDUFAN
Dilling
1413 m
Umm Ruwābah
ABYAD
AN NIL AL AZRAQ
Ad Damāzīn
Ar Ruşayriş
Geiger
3131 Guba
Bambudi

Bitkine 1613 m
Mongo
GUÉRA
Mélfi
Delép
Mangalmé
Zakouma
SALAMAT
Mangueigne
Nyala
Kubbum
'Idd al Ghanam
Ad Du'ayn
Regeb
Buram
Abū Maţāriq
Al Fūlah
Al Lagowa
Al Muglad
Jibāl an Nūbah 1324 m
Kāduqli
KURDUFAN
Talawdī
SUDAN
Kaka
Kurmuk
Bēlfodiyo
Asosa
Mendi
Gara Nasa 2975 m
Tulu Welel 3301 m
Beigi
Dembi
Dolo
Gambēla
Burē

Korbol
Kendégué
Haraze Mangueigne
Boromata
Birao
VAKAGA
Tiroungoulou
Mont Toussoro 1330 m
Radom
As Sumayh
Abyei
Malakāl
Akoke
AN NIL
Nāşir
Kodok
Malūt
Paloich
AALI

Koumra
Kyabé
MOYEN CHARI
Garba
Gordil
Kafia Kingi
Jabal Manda 1227 m
1113 m
Sa'id (Bundas)
GHARB BAHR AL GHAZAL
Raga
SHAMAL BAHR AL GHAZAL
Nyamlell
Uwayl
Gogrial
Wun Rog
Bentiu
Fangak
AL WAHDAH
Mogogh
WARAB
Bir Di
JUNQALI
Pochala
Mizan Teferi
Shewa Gimira
Gech'a

Moissala
Ndélé
Pata
Ouadda
Massif des Bongos
Kaouadja
Daym Zubayr
Warab
Atiedo
Adok
Wun Shwai
Ayod
Wa'th
Duk Fadiat
Duk Faiwil
Akūbū
Tor

BAMINGUI-BANGORAN
Bamingui
HAUTE-KOTTO
Boulouba
Bani
Bria
Bo River
Tonj
Rumbek
AL BUHAYRAT
Akot
Yirol
Bor
Towot
Mui

CENTRAL AFRICAN REPUBLIC
NANA-GRÉBIZI
Ouandago
Yangalia
Pangonda
Ippy
Yalinga
Ira Banda
Djéma
Ouandó
Khogali
Boli
Mvolo
Tali Post
Jerbar
Pibor Post

OUHAM
Kaga Bandoro
Bouca
Dékoa
Bakala
Grimari
Bambari
OUAKA
Bakouma
Fodé
Derbissaka
Ngouyo
Mboki
Obo
Tambura
Bambouti
GHARB AL ISTIWA'IYAH
Maridī
Ibba
Kinyeti 3187 m
Lotuke 2795 m
SHARQ AL ISTIWA'IYAH
Elemi Triangle (Under Kenyan administration)
Todenyan

KÉMO
Sibut
Marali
Bogangolo
Bossembélé
Damara
MPOKO
Bangui
Bimbo
Mbaïki
Mbata
KOTTO
Pandu
Kouango
Alindao
Bianga
Mobaye
Ouango
Kembe
Gambo
BASSE-KOTTO
Mingala
Balifondo
Rafai
Zemio
Doruma
Nzara
Yambio
Bunduqiyah
Juba
Ngangala
Liria
Keyala
Kapoeta
2749 m Morungole
Nagichot
Lokichokio

Bangui
Mongoumba
Bétou
Enyellé
Dongo
Mogalo
Bokode
Libenge
Bari
Bosobolo
Dubulu
Gbadolite
Mobayi-Mbongo
Monga
Bili
Ango
Banda
Gwane
Digba
Gwawele
Aba
Yei
Moyo
Koboko
Nimule
Opari
Arua
RIFT VALLEY

Bogangolo
Damara
Bimbo
Bosembélé
Ombella-Mpoko
Gemena
Budjala
Bongo
Kungu
Abumombazi
Muma
Yandongi
Magbakele
Monveda
Molanda
Aketi
Buta
Isiro
Rungu
Dungu
Faradje
Makoro
Adranga
Aru
Rhino Camp
Gulu
Kitgum
Kotido
Adilang
Moroto 3084 m
Loki
Kāpu

DEMOCRATIC REPUBLIC
Bomongo
Bomba
Businga
Likati
Angu
Leguga
Bambesa
Dili
Poko
Mawa
Niangara
Mungbere
Wamba
Mongbwalu
Fataki
Nioka
Mahagi Port
Apac
Serere
Soroti
Kumi
3068 m
Katakwi
Lira
Nebbi

Dongou
Impfondo
Makanza
Lusengo
Bogbonga
Bomomo
Basankusu
Ekombe
Lisala
Bumba
Lifanga
Busu-Kwanga
Bongandanga
Banalia
Bomili
Nia-Nia
Adusa
Mambasa
Irumu
Kasenye
Bunia
Niri
Aburo 2448 m
Masindi
Hoima
UGANDA
Pallisa
Kapenguria
Kitale
Elgon 4321 m

EQUATEUR
Lulonga
Bolomba
Befale
Samba
Lingomo
Basoko
Yahuma
Isangi
Bengamisa
Banguru
Bafwasende
Mabana
Bundibugyo
Fort Portal
Kyenjojo
Mubende
Kiboga
Luwero
Kamuli
Tororo
Iganga
WESTERN
Eldoret
Kapsabe

Mbandaka
Ingende
Boteka
Bokatola
Bikoro
Embondo
Bokote
Befori
Yalongwa
Yaleko
Opienge
Tabili
Lubero
Butembo
Beni
Ruwenzori Range
Stanleyville 5110 m
Kasese
Masaka
Entebbe
Mpigi
Mukono
Port Bell
Kampala
Jinja
Kakamega
NYANZA
Nakū
Equator
Equator

Wema
Ekuku
Bokungu
Mondombe
Yalokole
Elipa
Oboke
Yumbi
Lowa
Punia
Ubundu
Kirundu
Lutubu
Amamula
Kamande
Bushenyi
Rukungiri
Rakai
Sese Islands
Lake Victoria
2272 m
Homa Bay
Kisumu
Kisii
Kericho

Yandja
Bolia
Inongo
Bolondo
Botembela
Kutu
Djampie
Tolo
Bikoro
Waka
Lokolia
Watsi Kengo
Busanga
Ikela
Lokofe
Yolombo
Kasese
Walikale
Itebero
Goma
Ruhengeri
Karagwe
Bukoba
Muleba
Ukerewe Island
Ukara Island
Nansio
Nyalikungu
MARA
Musoma

BANDUNDU
Nioki
Semendua
Buna
Bagata
Oshwe
Yuki
Lomela
Musadi
KASAI
Lokandu
Kalima
Malela
Kilima
Kindu
Pangi
Shabunda
Kamanyola
Kabare
Bukavu
Cyangugu
Butare
Ngara
Biharamulo
KAGERA
Sengerema
Mwanza
Ngudu

ORIENTAL
Bolaiti
Dekese
Kole
Lodja
Katako-Kombe
Lueki
Kama
Kalole
SUD-KIVU
Uvira
Kayanza
Muyinga
Muramvya
Bujumbura
Mt Heha 2760 m
Kibondo
Lusahunga
MWANZA
Shinyanga

MANIEMA
Lueki
Kampene
RWANDA
Kigali
Gisenyi
Karisimbi 4507 m
Nyiragongo
NORD-KIVU
Masisi
Kisoro
Kabale
Murongo
Bunazi
Kayanga
Kingulube
Nzinguru
Kalole
Kayanza
BURUNDI
Kitega
TANZANIA

SAUDI ARABIA

YEMEN

OMAN

ERITREA

ETHIOPIA

SOMALIA

DJIBOUTI

KENYA

RED SEA

Gulf of Aden

INDIAN OCEAN

Ar Rub' al Khālī

Al Qaʻāmīyāt

Ẕufār

Jabal Mahrāt

Al Mahrah

Ḩaḑramawt

Ramlat as Sabʻatayn

Suquṭrá (Socotra) (Yemen)

'Abd al Kūrī (Yemen)

Danakil Desert

Danakil Depression

Ahmar Mts

Mendebo

Ogaden

WOQOOYI GALBEED

SANAAG

BARI

TOGDHEER

NUGAAL

MUDUG

GALGUDUUD

HIIRAAN

BAKOOL

BAY

GEDO

SHABEELLAHA DHEXE

SHABEELLAHA HOOSE

JUBBADA DHEXE

JUBBADA HOOSE

BANAADIR

EASTERN

NORTH-EASTERN

COAST

CENTRAL

Sawākin
Erkowit
Ṭawkar
Herbagat
Ras Kasar
Karora 2780 m
Algena
Nakfa
Keren
Kelamet
Akordat
Massawa
assalā Teseney
Barentu
Om Häjer
Inda Silasē
Asmara
Dek'emhāre
Ādī Ugrī
Ādi Kwala
Ādi Ark'ay
 Abị Adī
Mesfinto
Debark'
Dabat
Gonder
Azezo
Aykel
Gorgora
Weret
ngila
Bahir Dar
Onjibara
Mot'a
Guna Terara 4231 m
Debre Tabor
Lalibela
Weldiya
Korem
Alamat'ā
Kara K'orē
Desē
Batī
Kembolcha
Debre Werk'
Bichena
Dejen
Debre Mark'os
Talo 4413 m
Dembech'a
Gebre Guracha
Fichē
Shambu
Bako
Hāgere Hiywet
Genet
k'emtē
Ādis Alem
Giyon
Welk'it'ē
Butajira
Ima
Hosa'ina
Jima
Āgaro
Saka
Bedele
Ādis Ābeba (Addis Ababa)
Ak'ak'ī Besek'a
Debre Zeyit
Nazrēt
Asela
Robē
K'ech'a Terara 4190 m
Negēlē
Shashamenē
Awasa
Sodo
Yirga 'Alem
K'olito
Ch'ench'a
Dīla
Gugē 4200 m
Yirga Ch'efē
Ārba Minch
Kibre Mengist
Konso
Gidolē
Negēlē
Āgere Maryam
Filtu
Hargele
Yabēlo
Chumba
Melka Guba
Mega
Gamud 2486 m
Dande
Ch'ew Bahir
leret
Lake Turkana
North Horr
Kulal 2293 m
Marsabit
South Horr
52 m
Maralal
Habaswein
Mado Gashi
Garba Tula
Bura
Laisamis
Nanyuki
Meru
Kirinyaga (Mt Kenya)
Nyeri 5199 m
Embu
ahururu
Naivasha
Muranga
Thika
Nairobi
Machakos
Kitui
Athi River
Garissa
3999 m
Namanga
Makindu
Longido
Kilimanjaro 5895 m
eru 6 m
sha
Moshi
Voi
Kilifi
Malindi
Lamu
Ras Shaka
Ungama Bay
Garsen
Holo
Kaamboni
Buur Gaabo
Kismaayo
Jamaame
Kamsuuma
Baraawe
Makungo
Jilib
Afmadow
Dif
Bu'ale
Saacow
Baardheere
Diinsoor
El Wak
Buna
Bute Helu
Takabba
Wajir
Tarbaj
Kholof Harar
Faafxadhuun
Waajid
Luuq
Garbahaarrey
Mandera
Moyalē
El Lēh
Dolo Odo
Amino
Yeed
Beledweyne
Xarardheere
Ceelbuur
Buulobarde
Mereeg
Muqakoori
Tayeeglow
Xuddur
Baydhabo
Buurhakaba
Wanlaweyn
Afgooye
Awdheegle
Marka
Muqdisho (Mogadishu)
Jawhar
Warshiikh
Mahadday Weyne
Derri
Bud Bud
Maxaas
Dabole
Ted Ceidaar
Dhuusamarreeb
Hobyo
Godinlabe
Sina Dhaqa
Iidaan
Raas Cabaad
Daborow
Beyra
Gaalkacyo
Garacad
Jirriiban
Bacaadweyn
Werder
Geladī
K'orahē
Gedlegubē
K'ebrī Dehar
Denan
Gōdē
El Kerē
Buddi
Godere
K'elafo
Mustahil
Filtu
Domo
Garoowe
Kalis
Eyl
Laascaanood
Sinujiif
Caynabo
Xudun
Garadag
Qardho
Dhuudo
Bandarbeyla
Raas Macbar
Rass Dhuudo
Raas Gabbac
Qooriga Neegro
Hurdiyo
Xaafuun
Raas Xaafuun
Iskushuban
Buraan
Ceerigaabo
Shimbiris 2416 m
Buuraha Cal Madow
Maydh
Xiis
Karin
Lasqoray
Ceel Gaal
Boosaaso
Qandala
Ceel Gaal
Bargaal
Raas Binna
Raas Caseyr
Tooxin
Caluula
Hodda 1400 m
Geesaley
Raas Caluula
Raas Surud
Raas Khansiir
Bullaxaar
Berbera
Mandheera
Boorama
Abdelcader
Lughaye
Jeldesa
Boorama
Hargeysa
Bandar Wanaag
Burco
Oodweyne
Daga Medo
Durukhsi
Awarē
Tukayel
Degeh Bur
Uarandab
Danot
Bircot
El Fud
Deder
Mi'ēso
Jijiga
Hārer
Asbe Teferī
Bedēsa
Ginir
Goba
Batu 4307 m
Megalo
Audo Range
Wabē Gestro
Wabē Shabele
3626 m
4136 m
Dire Dawa
Hargeysa
2010 m
Ayelu Terara
Sela Dingay
Debre Sina
Debre Birhan
Awash
Ras Dashen Terara 4620 m
Amba Alāgē 3446 m
Afrēra Terara 1200 m
Amba Farit 3975 m
Ābuyē Mēda 4000 m
 Mēn
Mek'elē
Agula'i
Ramlū 2131 m
 Ā Terara 2063 m
Musa Ālī Terara
Khōr 'Angar
Ras Bir
Obock
Tadjoura
Djibouti
Dikhil
Yoboki
Ali Sabieh
Sāylac
Ceel Gaal
Serdo
Tendaho
DJIBOUTI
Assab
Bēylul
Ed
Hanīsh al Kabīr
Jazīrat al
Al Fāzah
Al Mukhā
Dhubāb
Bāb al Mandeb
Little Aden
At Turbah
Laḥij
Ta'izz
Ibb
Qa'ṭabah
Jiblah
Mawshij
Hays
Zabīd
Yarīm
Aḑ Ḑāli' 2513 m
3227 m
Māwiyah
Shaqrā
Zinjibār
'Adan (Aden)
Ash Shaykh 'Uthmān
Al Ḩumayshah
Lawdar
Al Bayḑā'
Al Irqah
Balḩāf
Ra's al Kalb
Ash Shiḩr
Al Mukallā
Sayḩūt
Al Ghaydah
Mar'ayt
Damqawt
Ghubbat al Qamar
Rakhyūt
Ra's Sājir
Ra's Mirbāṭ
Mirbāṭ
Ṣalālah
Thamarīt
Hasik
Ra's Naws
Hadbaram
Sanāw
Ash Shiḩr
Atāq
Shabwah
Bayḩān al Qiṣāb
Ḩabbān
Nuqūb
Ḩarīb
Ma'rib
Qulansiyah
Qāḑub
Hadiboh 1503 m
San'ā'
Nabī Shu'ayb 3760 m
Manākhah
Raydah
Amrān
Khamr
Ḩūth
Sa'dah
Sūq al Ghinān
Wuday'ah
Najrān
Zahrān
Ad Darb
Qizān
Ṣabyā
Ra's aṭ Ṭarfā
Jīzān
Harad
Abū 'Arīsh
Al Qunfudhah
Al Khawsh
Khaybar
An Nimāṣ
Ḩamdah
Bani Thawr
Dits
Jabal Sawdā' 3133 m
Abhā
Al Birk
Al Qaḥmah
Ash Shuqayq
Khamīs Mushayṭ
Najrān
Jazā'ir Farasān
Az Zuhrah
Az Zaydīyah
Bājil
Bayt al Faqīh
Dhamār
Al Ḩudaydah
Al Marāwi'ah
Al Ḩawtah
Ḩajjah
Dahlak Archipelago
Massawa Channel
Mersa Fatma
Soira 3018 m
Ādwa
Āksum
Āk sum
Adīgrat
Adī Keyih
Wik'ro
3291 m
Gondar
Nefasit
Genta
K'obo
Weldiya

Central Africa • East Africa

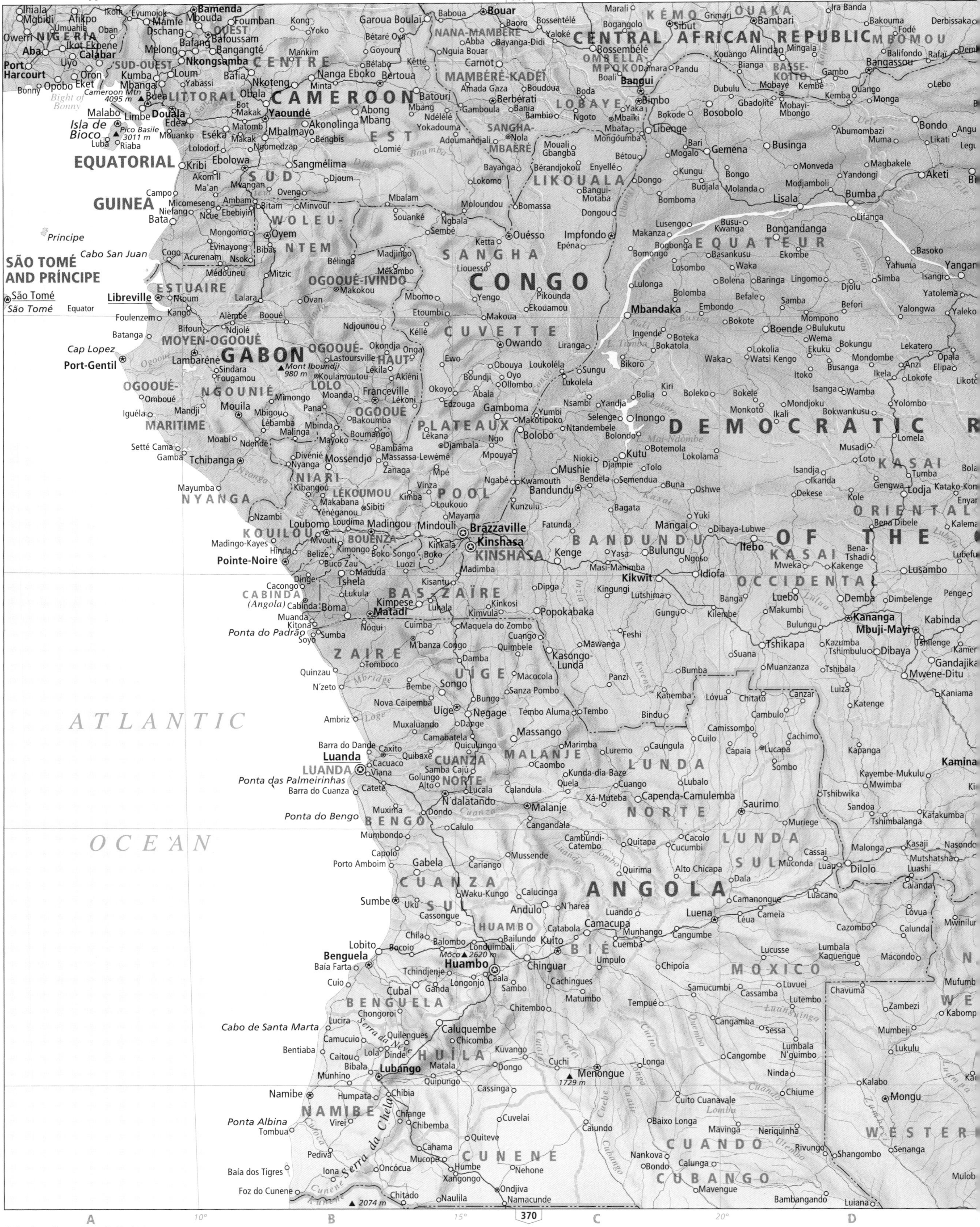

NIGERIA

CAMEROON

EQUATORIAL GUINEA

SÃO TOMÉ AND PRÍNCIPE

Príncipe

São Tomé

Libreville

GABON

Port-Gentil

Cap Lopez

CENTRE

SUD-OUEST

LITTORAL

OUEST

EST

SUD

WOLEU-NTEM

ESTUAIRE

MOYEN-OGOOUÉ

OGOOUÉ-IVINDO

OGOOUÉ-LOLO

NGOUNIÉ

OGOOUÉ-MARITIME

NIARI

NYANGA

LÉKOUMOU

KOUILOU

BOUENZA

POOL

PLATEAUX

CUVETTE

SANGHA

CONGO

LIKOUALA

NANA-MAMBÉRÉ

MAMBÉRÉ-KADÉI

SANGHA-MBAÉRÉ

LOBAYE

OMBELLA-MPOKO

KÉMO

OUAKA

BASSE-KOTTO

MBOMOU

CENTRAL AFRICAN REPUBLIC

Bangui

Brazzaville

Kinshasa

KINSHASA

BAS-ZAIRE

CABINDA (Angola)

Pointe-Noire

ZAIRE

UIGE

CUANZA NORTE

Luanda

LUANDA

CUANZA SUL

BENGUELA

Benguela

Huambo

HUAMBO

BIÉ

MALANJE

BANDUNDU

KASAI OCCIDENTAL

KASAI ORIENTAL

DEMOCRATIC REPUBLIC OF THE CONGO

Kananga

Mbuji-Mayi

Kikwit

Kamina

LUNDA NORTE

LUNDA SUL

MOXICO

ANGOLA

HUILA

Lubango

NAMIBE

Namibe

CUNENE

CUANDO

CUBANGO

WESTERN

ATLANTIC OCEAN

EQUATEUR

Mbandaka

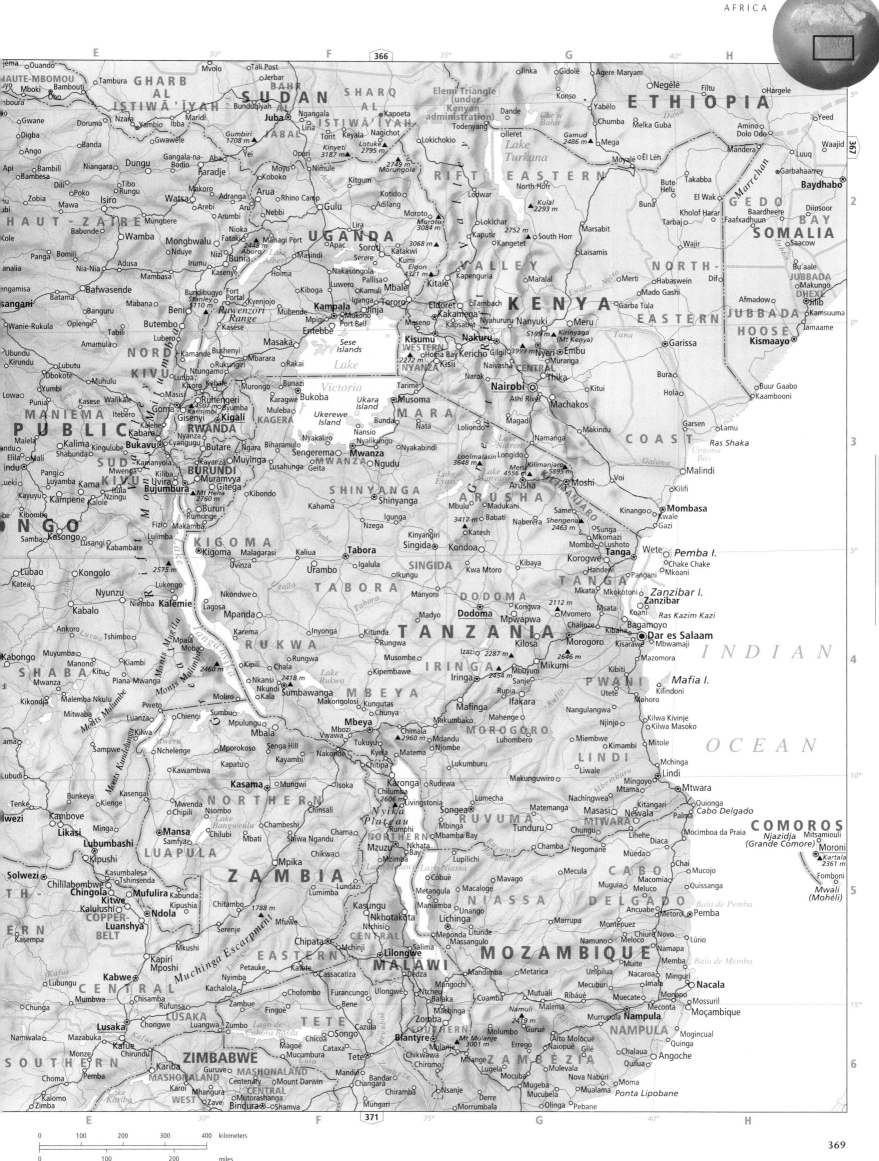

E · 30° · F · 366 · 35° · G · 40° · H

SUDAN

GHARB AL ISTIWĀ'ĪYAH
BAHR AL JABAL
SHARQ AL ISTIWĀ'ĪYAH

Elemi Triangle (under Kenyan administration)

ETHIOPIA

Negēlē   Filtu

Hārgele

RIFT   EASTERN   NORTH-
VALLEY   SOMALIA
                         GEDO   BAY
                                   JUBBADA DHEXE

Baydhabo

UGANDA

Kampala

KENYA

Nairobi ⊙

Kigali RWANDA

BURUNDI
Bujumbura

EASTERN   JUBBADA HOOSE

COAST

Kismaayo

Mombasa

INDIAN

TANZANIA

Dodoma

Dar es Salaam ●

Zanzibar I.

OCEAN

Mafia I.

COMOROS

Njazidja (Grande Comore) Moroni

Mwali (Mohéli)

Lusaka
ZAMBIA

Lilongwe
MALAWI

MOZAMBIQUE

Blantyre

ZIMBABWE

0 100 200 300 400 kilometers
0 100 200 miles
Scale 1:9,000,000   Projection: Azimuthal Equal Area

Southern Africa

Madagascar

A B C D

Mombasa Kilifi

Praslin I.
Silhouette I. La Digue I.
⊛Victoria
Mahé I.

Wete
Pemba I.
Chake Chake

Amirante
Isles

Platte I.

Mafia I.

Alphonse I. Coetivy I.

SEYCHELLES

Aldabra
Is
Assumption I.
Cosmoledo
Group
Astove I.

St Pierre I. Providence I.

Farquhar
Group

Agalega Is
(Mauritius)

TANZANIA
Mtwara
Quionga
Cabo Delgado
Palma
CABO DELGADO
Mocimboa da Praia
Quiaca
Chai Mucojo
Quissanga
Muaguide
Pemba
Baía de Pemba

Njazidja
(Grande Comore)
Mitsamiouli
COMOROS
Moroni ⊛
▲Kartala
2361 m
Fomboni
Mwali
(Mohéli)
Nzwani
(Anjouan)
Moutsamoudou
Domoni
MAYOTTE
(Fr.)
Mamoudzou Dzaoudzi

Îles Glorieuses
(Réunion)
Andranovondronina
Tanjona Bobaomby
(Cap d'Ambre)
Ramena
Ambohitra
1475 m▲
⊛Antsiranana
Bobasakoa
Anivorano Avaratra
Ampisikinana

MOZAMBIQUE

Lúrio
Memba
Minguri
Nacala
Moçapo
Mossuril
Moçambique
NAMPULA
Mogincual
Quinga

Baía de Memba

Nosy Bé
Lohatanjona Angadoka
Ambanja
Marovato
Maromokotro
2876 m▲
Bealanana
Analalava
Lohatanjona Maromony
Antsohihy
Andapa

ANTSIRANANA
Ambilobe
1785 m▲
Ampanefena
Doany
Sambava
Ampahana
Antalaha

Befandriana Avaratra
Mahajanga
Katsepy
Ambalakida
Boriziny
Leanja
Mahalevona
Ampanavoana
Vinanivao
Tanjona Masoala

INDIAN

Tromelin I.
(Réunion)

Tanjona Vilandro
Ambohipaky
Marovoay
Mitsinjo
Soalala
Manarantsandry
Mampikony
Maroantsetra
Mandritsara
Mananara
Avaratra
Helodrano
Antongila

Besalampy
Sitampiky
Madirovalo
Ambato Boeny
1301 m▲

TOAMASINA
Manompana
Soanierana-Ivongo

Île Juan de Nova
(Réunion)
Mahabe
Maevatanana
Tsaratanana
Betrandraka
Andilamena
Andilamena

Tamboharano
Ikahavo
847 m▲
Kandreho
Andriamena
Vavatenina
Fenoarivo Atsinanana

Morafenobe
Beravina
Ambatomainty
Vatoloha
1575 m▲
Ankazobe
Andilanatoby
Amparafaravola
Ambatondrazaka
Didy
Mahavelona
Maintirano
Reharaka

ANTANANARIVO
Antsalova
Ambohidratrimo
Moroserananana
Toamasina
Fanandrana

Masoarivo
Tsiroanomandidy
Miarinarivo
Antananarivo ⊛
Moramanga
Ampasimanolotra

Miandrivazo
Ambatolampy
Anosibe an'Ala
Vatomandry
MADAGASCAR

Belo Tsiribihina
Tanjona Tsiribihina
Tsiribihina
Antsirabe
Ibinty
2254 m▲
Antanambao
Manampotsy
Antanambao
Mahanoro

Morondava
Mahabo
Malaimbandy
Ambato-
finandrahana
2119 m▲
Fandriana
Marolambo

Amborompotsy
2052 m▲
Ambositra
Nosy-Varika

OCEAN

Andranopasy
Mandabe
Manja
Ikalamavony
Ambohimahasoa
Mananjary
Vohitrandriana

Morombe
Beroroha
Fianarantsoa ⊛
Ifanadiana
Ampasimanjeva

Tanjona
Ankaboa
Ambalavao
Zazafotsy
Ikongo
Vohilava
Manakara

TOLIARA
Ankazoabo
1348 m▲
Ihosy
Boby▲
2658 m
Vohipeno
Manombo Atsimo
Mahaboboka
Satrokala
Ranohira
Ivohibe
Vondrozo
Farafangana
Tropic of Capricorn
Toliara
Sakaraha
Andranovory
Betroka
1824 m▲
Lopary
Ranomena
Vangaindrano
Tongobory
Bezaha
Benenitra
Midongy Atsimo
Betioky
Belamoty
Manambondro
Ivakoany
1637 m▲
Manankoliva
Befotaka
Soamanonga
Fotadrevo
Ber014
Berketa
Manantenina
Ejeda
Bekily
Imanombo
Itampolo
Tranoroa
Tranomaro
Androka
Ampanihy
Antanimora Atsimo
Tôlañaro
Beloha
Tsiombe
Amboasary
Ambovombe
Tanjona
Vohimena
Betanty

MAURITIUS
Port Louis ⊛
Curepipe
Mahébourg
Saint-Denis
Saint-
Paul
RÉUNION
(Fr.)
Saint-
Pierre

Mascarene Islands

kilometers 0 100 200 300 400
miles 0 100 200
Scale 1:9,000,000   Projection: Azimuthal Equal Area

Islands around Africa

RÉUNION
(France)
Scale 1:1,500,000

Pte des Galets
Saint-Denis
Sainte-Marie
Sainte-Suzanne
Le Port
La Possession
Bagatelle
Saint-André
Saint-Paul
Pte des Aigrettes
Saint-Gilles-les Bains
Salazie
Bras-Panon
Saint-Benoît
Trois Bassins
Hell-Bourg
2401 m
Le Piton Rouge
Piton des Neiges
3069 m
Sainte-Rose
Saint-Leu
Les Makes
Cilaos
La Plaine des Cafres
Pte Rouge
Les Avirons
Le Riviere
2632 m
Bois-Blanc
Piton de la Fournaise
Saint-Louis
Le Tampon
Saint-Pierre
Takamaka
Pte de la Table
Pte du Parc
Saint-Joseph
Langevin
Saint-Philippe

INDIAN OCEAN

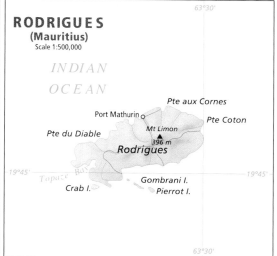

RODRIGUES
(Mauritius)
Scale 1:500,000

INDIAN OCEAN
Pte aux Cornes
Port Mathurin
Pte Coton
Pte du Diable
Mt Limon 396 m
Rodrigues
Topaze Bay
Gombrani I.
Crab I.
Pierrot I.

MAURITIUS
Scale 1:1,500,000

Flat I.
Round I.
Gunners Quoin
C. Malheureux
Pte Butte aux Sables
Cannoniers Pt
Grande Baie
Goodlands
Triolet
Île d'Ambre
Baie du Tombeau
Rivière du Rempart
Pamplemousses
Port Louis
822 m
Centre de Flacq
Beau Bassin
Troud'Eau Dolce
Circonstance
Quartier Militaire
Curepipe
Beau Champ
Tamarin
Quatre Bornes
Mt Lagrave 638 m
Pte Lagrave
Petite Rivière Noire
828 m
Chemin Grenier
Rose Belle
Mahébourg
Pte Sud Ouest
L'Escalier
Benares
Pte Citronniers
Souillac
INDIAN OCEAN

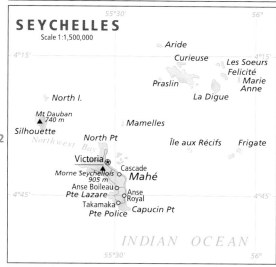

SEYCHELLES
Scale 1:1,500,000

Aride
Curieuse
Les Soeurs
Félicité
Praslin
Marie Anne
La Digue
North I.
Mt Dauban 740 m
Mamelles
Silhouette
North Pt
Île aux Récifs
Frigate
Northwest Bay
Victoria
Cascade
Morne Seychellois 905 m
Mahé
Anse Boileau
Anse Royal
Pte Lazare
Takamaka
Anse
Pte Police
Capucin Pt
INDIAN OCEAN

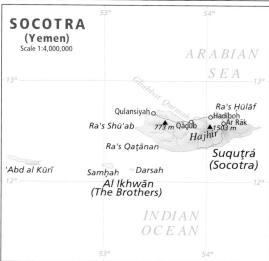

SOCOTRA
(Yemen)
Scale 1:4,000,000

ARABIAN SEA
Ghubbat Qarmah
Ra's Hūlāf
Qulansiyah
Hadiboh
Ar Räk
Ra's Shū'ab
773 m
Qāḍub
1503 m
Hajhir
Ra's Qaṭānan
Suquṭrá (Socotra)
'Abd al Kūrī
Samḥah
Darsah
Al Ikhwān (The Brothers)
INDIAN OCEAN

TRISTAN DA CUNHA
(St Helena)
Scale 1:750,000

Edinburgh
Rookery Pt
Queen Mary's Peak
Anchorstock Pt
2060 m
Sandy Pt
ATLANTIC OCEAN
Tristan da Cunha
Stonyhill Pt
Seal Bay
West Pt
Inaccessible I.
561 m
East Pt
Stoltenhoff I.
Middle I.
Nightingale I.

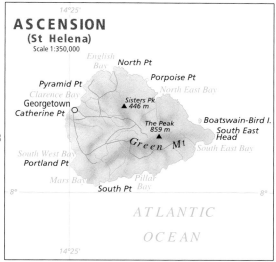

ASCENSION
(St Helena)
Scale 1:350,000

English Bay
North Pt
Porpoise Pt
Pyramid Pt
Clarence Bay
North East Bay
Georgetown
Sisters Pk 446 m
Catherine Pt
The Peak 859 m
Boatswain-Bird I.
South East Head
Green Mt
South West Bay
South East Bay
Portland Pt
Pillar Bay
Mars Bay
South Pt
ATLANTIC OCEAN

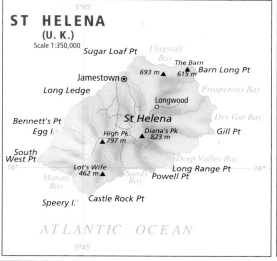

ST HELENA
(U.K.)
Scale 1:350,000

Sugar Loaf Pt
Flagstaff Bay
The Barn
693 m
615 m
Barn Long Pt
Jamestown
Long Ledge
Prosperous Bay
Longwood
Bennett's Pt
St Helena
Dry Gut Bay
Egg I.
High Pk 797 m
Diana's Pk 823 m
Gill Pt
South West Pt
Deep Valley Bay
Long Range Pt
Lot's Wife 462 m
Powell Pt
Manati Bay
Sandy Bay
Speery I.
Castle Rock Pt
ATLANTIC OCEAN

MADEIRA
(Portugal)
Scale 1:2,000,000

Porto Santo
517 m
Ilhéu de Ferro
Porto Santo
Ilhéu de Baixo
Porto Moniz
São Vicente
Santana
Pto do Pargo
Faial
Calheta
1862 m
Pico Ruivo de Santana
Pta de São Lourenço
Ribeira Brava
Machico
Madeira
Câmara de Lobos
Santa Cruz
Funchal
Deserta Grande
Ilhas Desertas
Ilhéu do Bugio
ATLANTIC OCEAN

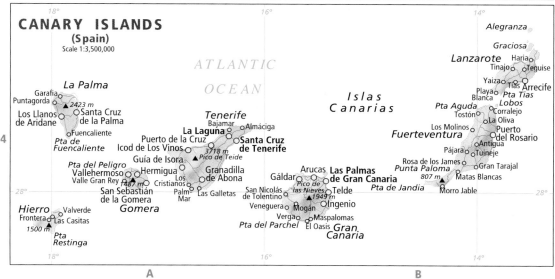

CANARY ISLANDS
(Spain)
Scale 1:3,500,000

ATLANTIC OCEAN
La Palma
Garafia
Puntagorda
2423 m
Santa Cruz de la Palma
Los Llanos de Aridane
Fuencaliente
Alegranza
Graciosa
Lanzarote
Haria
Tinajo
Teguise
Yaiza
Tias
Arrecife
Playa Blanca
Pta Tias
Tenerife
Lobos
Bajamar
Almáciga
Pta Aguda
Corralejo
La Laguna
La Oliva
Puerto de la Cruz
3718 m
Santa Cruz de Tenerife
Los Molinos
Puerto del Rosario
Icod de Los Vinos
Fuerteventura
Pico de Teide
Antigua
Guía de Isora
Islas Canarias
Pájara
Tuineje
Pta del Peligro
Granadilla de Abona
Gran Tarajal
Vallehermoso
Hermigua
Los Cristianos
Rosa de los James
Valle Gran Rey
1487 m
Gáldar
Arucas
Las Palmas de Gran Canaria
Punta Paloma
807 m
San Nicolás de Tolentino
Telde
Pta de Jandia
Matas Blancas
San Sebastián de la Gomera
Pico de las Nieves
Ingenio
Morro Jable
Gomera
Palm Mar
Las Galletas
Venequera
1949 m
Hierro
Frontera
Valverde
Las Casitas
Mogán
Vergao
Maspalomas
1500 m
Pta del Parchel
El Oasis
Gran Canaria
Pta Restinga

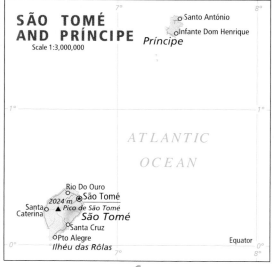

SÃO TOMÉ AND PRÍNCIPE
Scale 1:3,000,000

Santo António
Infante Dom Henrique
Príncipe
ATLANTIC OCEAN
Rio Do Ouro
2024 m
São Tomé
Santa Caterina
Pico de São Tomé
São Tomé
Santa Cruz
Pto Alegre
Ilhéu das Rôlas
Equator

Africa

North and Central America

North America

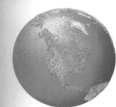

The continent of North America covers an area of 25.3 million sq km (9.3 million sq miles). It is bounded by the Atlantic Ocean to its east and the Pacific Ocean to its west. Broadest toward the north, it tapers at its southern end, where a narrow isthmus connects it to South America.

The North American continent can be conveniently divided into temperate North America and the more tropical Central America. Central America consists of countries on the mainland and islands in the Caribbean Sea.

Infrastructure, provision of services, and quality-of-life indicators of Central American countries contrast markedly with those of Canada and the United States of America. In addition, a large cultural divide separates mainly English-speaking Canada and the USA from their predominantly Spanish-speaking southern neighbors. For these reasons, Central America is introduced separately overleaf.

North America consists of Canada and the United States, plus St Pierre and Miquelon (France), which lie off the east coast of Canada, and Bermuda (UK) which lies off the eastern coast of the USA.

Physical features

In North America there are both old and young mountains. Young folded mountains (the Cordillera) run along the western part of the continent from Alaska to the Central American isthmus and include a number of active volcanoes. This chain arose following the collision of the American and Pacific plates. In the USA, the Cordillera splits into the Rocky Mountains, which form the eastern arm, and the Sierra Nevada and other ranges, which form the western arm. Several peaks in the Rocky Mountains exceed 4,000 m (13,200 ft). The mountain ranges enclose basins

such as the Mojave Desert and Death Valley, and a number of saline lakes. Death Valley lies below sea level at an altitude of –86 m (–282 ft).

The ancient Appalachian Mountains run along the eastern length of the USA; their highest peak, Mt Mitchell, has an altitude of 2,037 m (6,683 ft). An extensive coastal plain lies between this chain and the Atlantic Ocean. Plains and lowlands are found in the continent's interior. Glaciers, which covered much of this area during the ice ages, sculpted the rocky plateaus of Canada and deposited sediments as vast plains that straddle Canada and the USA.

Several important rivers flow through North America: primarily the Missouri, 4,088 km (2,540 miles) long and the Mississippi, 3,766 km (2,340 miles) long. The St Lawrence River links the Great Lakes of Canada and the USA to the Atlantic Ocean. There are several large lakes, of which Lake Superior, which covers 82,100 sq km (31,699 sq miles), is the largest. The Rio Grande flows between the USA and Mexico. The Columbia River drains several states in northwestern USA.

Climate and vegetation

North America contains a broad range of temperate climates from warm temperate along the east coast and Mediterranean in southern California to cooler moist climates in northwest and northeast USA and southern Canada. Most of North America is humid, except for a dry belt across the southwest of the USA, and basins within the Rockies. An extensive tornado zone is found in the continental interior of the USA. Tropical cyclones, known in this region as hurricanes, and mostly originating in the Caribbean Sea, often strike the southeastern parts of the USA.

Extensive forests occur in temperate North America, ranging from the predominantly deciduous forests found in eastern parts of the

USA to the short-tree boreal forests of the subarctic. Tall trees, such as redwoods and firs, are found along the Pacific coastline. Other trees include maple, ash, and oak. Deer, brown and grizzly bears, lynx, and beavers are found in these forests. Boreal forests are home to migrating animals such as deer, elk, caribou, and moose.

In southern California, sclerophyllous shrubs thrive in the mild, wet winters and hot, dry summers. Eucalypt trees are an introduced species in this area and are a fire hazard during summer.

Extensive grasslands cover the interior of the continent. Tall-grass prairies occur where rainfall is over 750 mm (30 in), and short-grass prairies where precipitation is around 370 mm (15 in). Large herds of bison once roamed in these areas, but they were almost eradicated by hunting.

In Alaska and Canada, north of the boreal forest, there is a belt of tundra, where small shrubs, lichens, and grasses grow. Migrating herds of caribou, reindeer and lemmings live in this zone, along with bears, wolves, foxes, and lynx.

Population

North America had a population of 304 million in 1996. High living standards are reflected in the high life expectancies—73.6 years for males and

New York's Statue of Liberty; vast cornfields in Colorado (left). Snow seems out of place on this pine in desert Utah (below). The magma core of an ancient volcano in Wyoming (above).

The crater of Haleakala Volcano, the world's largest dormant volcano, on Maui, Hawaii (above). Much further north, the beginning of the spring thaw in a town in Canada (right). Bermuda (above, right), a tiny island off the USA east coast.

80.3 years for females (1998). The low population growth rate of 0.8 percent also reflects an advanced level of development. Approximately 76 percent of the population is urbanized.

Agriculture, forestry, and fishing

North America is well endowed with water resources, arable land, forests, and fishing areas. These favorable conditions, coupled with scientific farming practices, have enabled the establishment of highly productive agricultural industries. These include grain farming, such as wheat and maize; livestock for meat and dairying; cotton; and intensive farming of fruit and vegetables.

The extensive forests which still remain, following large-scale deforestation in the nineteenth century, are exploited for their valuable timbers. Large areas have been reafforested in order to produce a long-term sustainable industry.

There are fishing grounds off both the Atlantic and Pacific coasts, especially along the east coast where the cold Labrador current flows.

Industrialization

Natural resources, technological innovation, and well-developed infrastructure facilities, including energy supplies, have combined to make North America the world's most important manufacturing region. Continuous innovation in computing, laser technology, optic fibers, and space science have enabled it to withstand strong competition from European and Asian industrial nations.

Manufacturing ranges from chemical industries, metal fabrication, motor cars, aircraft, and high-technology military equipment to books, films, computer software, and recorded music. Tertiary industries, which provide services to a relatively wealthy population, employ millions of people.

North America is well endowed with mineral wealth. Extensive deposits of iron ore and coal have been the cornerstone of the steel industry. However, metals such as chromium and manganese need to be imported. The Cordillera belt contains a large number of metallic ores including copper, zinc, molybdenum, gold, and silver. Nickel and iron ore are extracted from ancient plateau rocks in Canada. Among minerals used for energy supplies, coal, petroleum, and natural gas deposits are widespread. Although a large petroleum producer, the USA also imports large quantities because of heavy consumption.

Languages

English is the dominant language in North America, except in the Canadian province of Québec, where French is the main language. Some surviving Amerindian languages are spoken by minority groups such as the Pueblo Indians of southwestern USA and Amerindians in western Canada. In the southern states of the USA that were once parts of Mexico, such as California, New Mexico and Texas, Spanish is spoken among Hispanics. Considerable Hispanic migration to the USA, particularly from Mexico and Cuba, has made Spanish an increasingly important language in the USA, particularly in parts of the east coast, such as Florida, and in New York.

Boundary disputes and wars

There are no major boundary disputes in the region, nor has the region been directly affected by land war in recent decades. However, continuing illegal immigration from Mexico into the USA remains a source of tension.

Central America

Central America, lying in the tropical zone between North and South America, consists of two distinct parts: a mainland area and a number of islands in the Caribbean Sea.

Mexico, Guatemala, Belize, Honduras, Nicaragua, Costa Rica, El Salvador, and Panama form the mainland. The two largest islands in the Caribbean Sea are Cuba and Hispaniola. The latter is divided into the Dominican Republic and Haiti. There are also several small island nations: Jamaica, Antigua and Barbuda, Dominica, Barbados, Trinidad and Tobago, Grenada, St Kitts and Nevis, St Lucia, St Vincent and the Grenadines, and the Bahamas.

Dependencies include Puerto Rico, the Virgin Islands and Navassa (USA), Aruba and the Netherlands Antilles (Netherlands), Anguilla, Montserrat, the British Virgin Islands, the Cayman Islands and the Turks and Caicos Islands (UK), and Martinique and Guadeloupe (France).

Physical features

Central America is a region of rugged mountains and volcanic peaks that were produced through the collision of several crustal plates. The Central American isthmus was formed by the interaction of the Caribbean and the Cocos plates, while the Caribbean islands were the result of the Caribbean Plate moving against the North American Plate. Further north, in Mexico, the Pacific and North American plates collided.

Volcanic activity is found in several sectors of these ranges, particularly in the area south of Mexico City, which contains volcanoes ranging in height from 3,000 to 4,000 m (10,000 to 14,000 ft). Volcanic eruptions have caused considerable damage through lava flows and ash deposits. Numerous islands in the Caribbean Sea, such as

Nelson's Harbour in Caribbean Antigua (below) contrasts with Mexican scenes, old and new: an ancient pyramid (right) and a woman washing radishes at the market (top).

Martinique, with the famous Mt Pelée active volcano, and Antigua, are volcanic. In contrast, the Bahamas are an example of coral islands.

Climate and vegetation

Central America lies within the tropics but because of its mountainous relief, climatic conditions vary with altitude. Such changes are notable in the narrow isthmus where variations in elevation are reflected in variations in vegetation. Low-lying areas, which are limited in extent, may have a hot, humid tropical climate with rainforest vegetation, while in elevated areas such as in the central Mexican Plateau, the climate approaches temperate conditions. Mountain slopes facing rain-bearing winds are densely vegetated while, in contrast, northeastern Mexico is semiarid.

In areas of high rainfall there are large tropical evergreen forests, which provide cover for a dense undergrowth made up of smaller plants such as ferns and lianas. Animal life is abundant in these areas, but loss of habitat due to deforestation and hunting have caused several animal species to become endangered.

In drier areas, such as in the Yucatán region of Mexico, shrub vegetation dominates in areas previously farmed during the Mayan civilization.

The region lies within a belt which is affected almost every year by hurricanes. In November 1998 a hurricane devastated the countries lying on the isthmus, particularly Honduras and Nicaragua.

Population

The population of the mainland is 130.7 million people while the Caribbean has 36.9 million inhabitants (1998). Life expectancies for the mainland are 68.8 years for males and 74.6 years for females, while in the Caribbean they are 67 years for males and 71.4 years for females. The mainland's annual population growth rate is 1.9 percent annually; that of the Caribbean is 1.1 percent. Urbanization is high—68 percent for the mainland and 62 percent for the Caribbean. Urban population increases, mainly as a result of rural to urban drift, have resulted in overcrowding and slum areas in many places. Mexico City is one of the world's largest cities.

Agriculture, forestry, and fishing

The economies of Central America are mainly agricultural. Maize, wheat, and rice are the principal cereals. The main livestock on the mainland are cattle, particularly where there are stretches of grassland; in the Caribbean, the main livestock are pigs. Extensive cattle ranches provide beef for export to North America.

Tropical plantation products such as sugarcane, coffee, cocoa, and bananas and other fruit are major export commodities, particularly to North America. Sugar is important in Cuba and Jamaica. Bananas are grown in several countries, such as Guatemala, Honduras, and Belize, for export. Coffee is grown in some areas, including Honduras and Nicaragua.

Many of the countries are economically dependent on the USA, which is the principal buyer of their exports. Cuba is the sole exception; since the communist revolution of 1958, Cuba has been selling its sugar to the former Soviet Union (now to Russia). Citrus fruit are also grown in several areas. Coconuts are an important product of the coastal areas around the Caribbean Sea.

Coniferous and broad-leaf forests occur on mountain slopes; these have been exploited for timber and firewood. Tropical forests have been logged for valuable hardwoods such as mahogany. Mexico, Cuba, and Guatemala all have forest industries.

Marine resources are abundant around the Caribbean islands, and for many of these nations fishing is a key activity. Belize, for example, relies on lobster and shrimp fishing.

Industrialization
Several countries have been shifting their economies from agriculture to manufacturing. Mexico is the most industrialized of the Central American countries, producing iron and steel, transport equipment, chemicals, and clothing. Its main export market is the USA. In most countries, manufacturing is either based on locally produced raw materials, such as rum made from sugar and cigars and cigarettes from tobacco in Jamaica, or on other light industry.

Several countries have become tourist destinations, and for some Caribbean countries, with their attractive tropical environments, tourism is a mainstay.

Languages
Central America was carved up by colonial powers, resulting in the presence of four official languages: Spanish, English, French and Dutch. All the mainland countries, except for Belize, where English is important, are Spanish-speaking.

Cuba, Puerto Rico and the Dominican Republic are Spanish-speaking, although English is also spoken in Puerto Rico. There are several English-speaking Caribbean islands, the largest of which is Jamaica; others are Antigua, the Bahamas, and Barbuda. Martinique is French-speaking, and the tiny Antilles islands are Dutch-speaking.

A beautifully symmetrical Volcan Concepción appears in the background of this view of Moyogalpa in Nicaragua (above). A stone carving at Tegucigalpa, Honduras (below, left), and a lush tropical rainforest in Grenada (below, right).

Boundary disputes and wars
There have been no major boundary disputes in Central America, except for the Guatemalan claim to the former British Honduras, which is now the independent country of Belize. However, the region has been beset with a variety of insurgencies, often helped by external sources. The USA has several times intervened in the region, invading Grenada in 1983 and Panama in 1989, supporting right-wing opponents of leftist governments in Guatemala and Nicaragua, and imposing economic sanctions on Cuba. The communist revolution in Cuba, and its policy of exporting revolution, had a considerable effect on the region. Cuba received substantial support from the Soviet Union. A leftist guerilla movement succeeded in taking over Nicaragua in 1979 but its government lost office in the 1990 elections. An Amerindian revolt took place in 1994 in the Chiapas region of Mexico.

Antigua and Barbuda

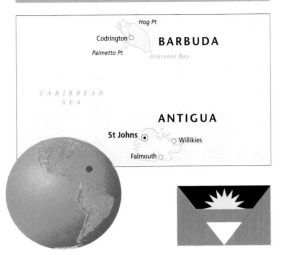

Fact File

OFFICIAL NAME Antigua and Barbuda

FORM OF GOVERNMENT Democracy with two legislative bodies (Senate and House of Representatives)

CAPITAL St Johns

AREA 440 sq km (170 sq miles)

TIME ZONE GMT – 4 hours

POPULATION 64,246

PROJECTED POPULATION 2005 65,285

POPULATION DENSITY 146 per sq km (378.1 per sq mile)

LIFE EXPECTANCY 71.5

INFANT MORTALITY (PER 1,000) 20.7

OFFICIAL LANGUAGE English

OTHER LANGUAGES Indigenous languages

LITERACY RATE 96%

RELIGIONS Protestant 90%, Roman Catholic 10%

ETHNIC GROUPS African 94.5%, other 5.5%

CURRENCY East Caribbean dollar

ECONOMY Services 67%, industry 21%, agriculture 12%

GNP PER CAPITA US$7,290

CLIMATE Tropical, moderated by sea breezes

HIGHEST POINT Boggy Peak 405 m (1,328 ft)

MAP REFERENCE Page 427

Antigua and Barbuda consists of three islands in the eastern Caribbean. In 1493 the largest of the group was visited by Columbus, who named it Antigua. It became a British colony in 1667 and in the eighteenth century flourished under a plantation system using African slaves to produce sugar. Once populated by Arawak and Carib Indians, today the islands are peopled by Afro-Caribbean descendants of the plantation days. They are run by the Antiguan Labour Party and the Bird family, a combination that has held power almost constantly since 1956. Full independence was obtained in 1981.

Antigua rises to 405 m (1,328 ft) at Boggy Peak, a volcanic prominence in the southwest. Unlike the other Leeward Islands, to which it belongs, Antigua was denuded of forest long ago, and lacks both trees and rivers. In contrast, the flat coral-island game reserve of Barbuda, 40 km (25 miles) to the north, is fairly well wooded. Barbuda's one town is Codrington. The third island, Redonda, is an uninhabited islet southwest of Antigua. The tropical climate and palm-fringed beaches make Antigua and Barbuda an attractive tourist location. There is, however, little fresh water, and the region is hurricane-prone, one in 1995 causing much damage.

Since the sugar industry closed in 1971 the islands have relied almost entirely on tourism, with some income from two US military bases on Antigua. The Bird family's hold on power, and allegations of corruption and misuse of funds, plus a high level of external debt, are cause for concern.

Bahamas

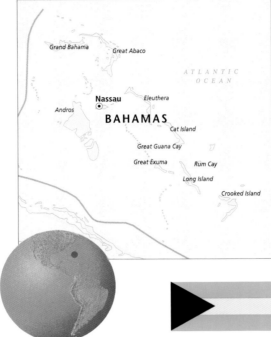

Off the southern tip of Florida in the western Atlantic, the Bahamas consists of 700 islands and about 2,400 cays. Once the home of Arawak Indians, the islands were claimed by Britain in 1690, but have had a checkered history since. A pirates' haven in the seventeenth century, they were held for short periods by the USA and Spain before Britain resumed control in 1783. They have been independent since 1983. The 25-year administration of Lynden Pindling ended in 1992 amid allegations of involvement in narcotics trafficking and money laundering. One of the most prosperous of the Caribbean's island states, the Bahamas has attracted many illegal immigrants from Haiti across the water. This influx has placed severe strain on government services.

All the islands are fragments of a large coralline limestone shelf. Most are only a few meters above sea level. Their coastlines are fringed with lagoons and coral reefs. Water is scarce. There are no rivers and rainfall disappears into the limestone. Much of the big islands are covered with pine forest. On the smaller islands people work mainly in fishing and agriculture. Tourists come in large numbers.

In 1995 there were more than 3,600,000 foreign arrivals. Tourism in turn has given rise to the manufacture of garments, furniture, jewelry, and perfume. All energy resources must be imported. Offshore banking, insurance, and financial services generate income and provide one of the region's highest standards of living. In addition, the Bahamas has a large open-registry fleet.

Fact File

OFFICIAL NAME Commonwealth of the Bahamas

FORM OF GOVERNMENT Constitutional monarchy with two legislative bodies (Senate and House of Assembly)

CAPITAL Nassau

AREA 13,940 sq km (5,382 sq miles)

TIME ZONE GMT – 5 hours

POPULATION 283,705

PROJECTED POPULATION 2005 306,153

POPULATION DENSITY 20.4 per sq km (52.8 per sq mile)

LIFE EXPECTANCY 74.3

INFANT MORTALITY (PER 1,000) 18.4

OFFICIAL LANGUAGE English

OTHER LANGUAGE Creole

LITERACY RATE 98.1%

RELIGIONS Baptist 32%, Anglican 20%, Roman Catholic 19%, Methodist 6%, Church of God 6%, other Protestant 12%, other 5%

ETHNIC GROUPS African 85%, European 15%

CURRENCY Bahamian dollar

ECONOMY Tourism 40%, government 30%, business services 10%, agriculture 5%, industry 4%, other 11%

GNP PER CAPITA US$11,940

CLIMATE Subtropical, with warm summers and mild winters

HIGHEST POINT Mt Alverina 63 m (207 ft)

MAP REFERENCE Page 425

Barbados

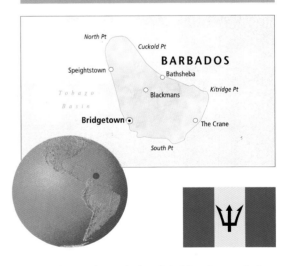

Northeast of Trinidad and 435 km (270 miles) off the coast of Venezuela, Barbados is the most easterly of the Caribbean Windward Islands. It is also one of the most orderly and prosperous. After becoming independent from the UK in 1966, power has alternated between two centrist parties, the Democratic Labour Party and the Barbados Labour Party. Both electoral results and freedom of expression are accepted features of Barbados life. Originally inhabited by Arawak Indians and later settled under the British in the seventeenth century, its population is mainly descended from African slaves brought to work on the sugar plantations. The governor-general of Barbados represents the British sovereign and the country has a strong colonial influence. Its neighbors sometimes refer to it as "little England."

The foundation of the island consists of coral deposits formed around a rocky core, and a fringe of coral reef has produced dazzling white beaches. Inland, the rolling terrain rises to hills in the north and center. About 50 percent of the land area is arable, sugar plantations accounting for 85 percent of the cultivated terrain. Barbados is sunnier and drier than many of its neighbors. There is a shortage of water. Surface water is negligible, though when it rains heavily gullies form natural reservoirs.

A small oil industry provides about one-third of the country's needs. Sugar refining is an important source of employment and revenue but has recently been overtaken by the rapid growth in tourism. Facilities are being upgraded to cope with the surge in visitors. Most arrive from Europe and North America and cruise-ship traffic is increasing. Recently, light industrial manufacture has been developed, much of it component assembly for export. The government has promised to build "a modern, technologically dynamic economy."

Fact File

OFFICIAL NAME Barbados

FORM OF GOVERNMENT Parliamentary democracy with two legislative bodies (Senate and House of Assembly)

CAPITAL Bridgetown

AREA 430 sq km (166 sq miles)

TIME ZONE GMT – 4 hours

POPULATION 259,191

PROJECTED POPULATION 2005 260,535

POPULATION DENSITY 602.8 per sq km (1,561.2 per sq mile)

LIFE EXPECTANCY 75

INFANT MORTALITY (PER 1,000) 16.7

OFFICIAL LANGUAGE English

OTHER LANGUAGE English Creole

LITERACY RATE 97.3%

RELIGIONS Protestant 67% (Anglican 40%, Pentecostal 8%, Methodist 7%, other 12%), Roman Catholic 4%, none 17%, other 12%

ETHNIC GROUPS African 80%, European 4%, other (mixed African–European, East Indian) 16%

CURRENCY Barbadian dollar

ECONOMY Services 76%, industry 18%, agriculture 6%

GNP PER CAPITA US$6,560

CLIMATE Tropical, with wet season June to November

HIGHEST POINT Mt Hillaby 336 m (1,102 ft)

MAP REFERENCE Page 427

Caye Caulker, an island off the coast of Belize that is popular with scuba divers (below). A view of Barbados (top right).

Belize

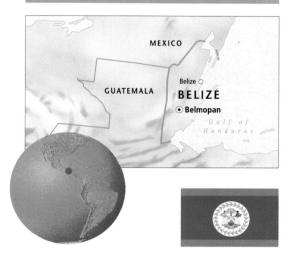

Belize lies on the eastern side of the Yucatan Peninsula. Bordering Mexico to the north and Guatemala to the west and south, it was the last country in the Americas to achieve independence. This came in 1981. Formerly known as British Honduras, its original inhabitants were Maya Indians, with a few Carib Indians along the coast. Though adjacent territory was conquered by the Spanish in the sixteenth century, the first recorded European settlers in the area were British wood-cutters in the seventeenth century. At a later date sugar plantations worked by African slaves were established. When Guatemala became independent in 1821 it laid claim to British Honduras and the sovereignty issue strained relations between the two countries until Guatemala officially recognized Belize as an independent country in 1993.

The northern part of the country is a swampy plain. In the south the Maya Mountains continue from Guatemala in a northeasterly direction, dividing the coastal plain from the interior. Victoria Peak, on a spur of this range, is flanked by tropical forest, grasslands, and farming regions. Rainforests containing jaguar still cover nearly half the country and in the rivers there are crocodile and manatee. The world's second longest coral reef lies offshore. Belize is much affected by hurricanes. After the 1961 hurricane that destroyed Belize City the capital was moved inland to Belmopan.

Agriculture employs more than a quarter of the labor force, and is the mainstay of the economy. The main domestic staples are maize, rice, kidney beans, and sweet potatoes. Belize enjoyed a boom in the years following independence, citrus-fruit processing and tourism helping to reduce the country's earlier dependence on timber, bananas, and sugar. Sugar still accounts for about 30 percent of export earnings. Timber is a less important export than formerly, but the forests still produce valuable rosewood, mahogany, and the gum used for chewing gum, chicle. Fisheries specialize in lobsters and shrimp. Textile manufacturing has also been developed.

Fact File

OFFICIAL NAME Belize

FORM OF GOVERNMENT Constitutional monarchy with two legislative houses (Senate and National Assembly)

CAPITAL Belmopan

AREA 22,960 sq km (8,865 sq miles)

TIME ZONE GMT – 6 hours

POPULATION 235,789

PROJECTED POPULATION 2005 270,561

POPULATION DENSITY 10.3 per sq km (26.7 per sq mile)

LIFE EXPECTANCY 69.2

INFANT MORTALITY (PER 1,000) 31.6

OFFICIAL LANGUAGE English

OTHER LANGUAGES Spanish, Mayan and Garifunan languages, German

LITERACY RATE 70%

RELIGIONS Roman Catholic 62%, Protestant 30%, none 2%, other 6%

ETHNIC GROUPS Mixed indigenous–European 44%, African 30%, Maya 11%, Garifuna 7%, other 8%

CURRENCY Belizean dollar

ECONOMY Services 60%, agriculture 30%, industry 10%

GNP PER CAPITA US$2,630

CLIMATE Tropical, with wet seasons June to July and September to January

HIGHEST POINT Victoria Peak 1,160 m (3,806 ft)

MAP REFERENCE Page 428

Canada

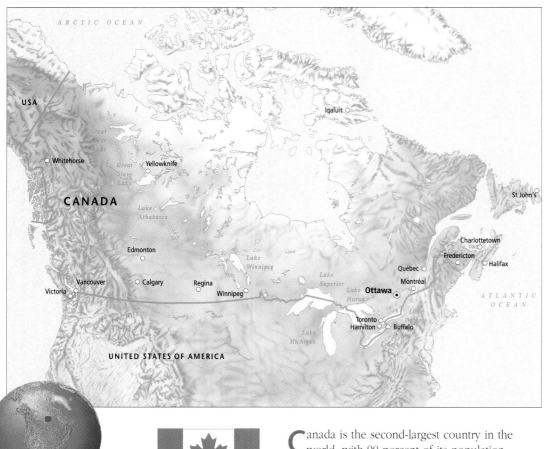

Fact File

OFFICIAL NAME Canada

FORM OF GOVERNMENT Constitutional monarchy with two legislative bodies (Senate and House of Commons)

CAPITAL Ottawa

AREA 9,976,140 sq km (3,851,788 sq miles)

TIME ZONE GMT – 3.5/9 hours

POPULATION 31,006,347

PROJECTED POPULATION 2005 32,855,230

POPULATION DENSITY 3.1 per sq km (8 per sq mile)

LIFE EXPECTANCY 79.4

INFANT MORTALITY (PER 1,000) 5.5

OFFICIAL LANGUAGES English, French

OTHER LANGUAGES Chinese, Italian, German, Polish, Spanish, Portuguese, Punjabi, Ukrainian, Vietnamese, Arabic, indigenous languages

LITERACY RATE 99%

RELIGIONS Roman Catholic 45%, United Church 12%, Anglican 8%, other 35%

ETHNIC GROUPS British 40%, French 27%, other European 20%, indigenous 1.5%, other 11.5%

CURRENCY Canadian dollar

ECONOMY Services 78%, industry 19%, agriculture 3%

GNP PER CAPITA US$19,380

CLIMATE Ranges from cool temperate in south to polar in north; long, cold winters; wetter and more temperate on coasts

HIGHEST POINT Mt Logan 5,950 m (19,521 ft)

MAP REFERENCE Pages 410–11, 412–13, 414–15, 416–17

Canada is the second-largest country in the world, with 90 percent of its population living close to the US border. Its citizens enjoy a standard of living second only to that of the US itself, but the huge scale of Canada's land area, the small, spread out population, and the division between the British and the French have made national unity more difficult to achieve.

Canada was initially populated by Inuit (Eskimo) and First Nation peoples (as indigenous Canadians are called). European settlement began in 1541 after Jacques Cartier's 1534 discovery of the St Lawrence River. Soon, French explorers pushed inland, in search of furs and trade. The French were still in a majority when British victory in a war with France, in 1763, gave Britain control of French settlements in Québec. Following US independence in 1783, however, many British settlers came north, and this marked the start of the long-resented domination of a French minority by a larger English-speaking population. There have been various Francophone initiatives for the secession of Québec in recent years. A 1995 vote in the province failed by 50.6 to 49.4 percent to settle the matter.

Physical features and land use

There is much variety among Canada's geographic regions. In the east lie the Atlantic Provinces of New Brunswick, Nova Scotia, Prince Edward Island, and Newfoundland, as well as Québec.

The geological foundation of the Atlantic Provinces is ancient worn-down mountains, along with sectors of the still older Canadian Shield. Although farming settlements are common, agriculture in this region has always been marginal (with the exception of such places as the Annapolis Valley in Nova Scotia and Prince Edward Island), and is in decline. Pulp and paper is produced from Québec's coniferous forests and the state is also a major producer of hydropower.

West and south lie the most temperate inland parts of Canada, the St Lawrence–Great Lakes lowlands, including the Ontario peninsula. This fertile agricultural region reaches west from southern Québec along Lake Ontario and north from Lake Erie. Rural settlement is more dense here than elsewhere and, given the large urban concentrations of Toronto and Montréal, these lowlands are the most heavily populated part of Canada.

The Canadian, or Laurentian, Shield is an extensive, ancient region floored with some of the world's oldest known rocks. Centered on Hudson Bay, it covers nearly 50 percent of Canadian territory. Except for some low mountains in eastern Québec and Labrador, this is a rolling landscape typified by outcrops of rock and a great amount of surface water in summer. There are hundreds of thousands of water bodies, ranging in size from gigantic to tiny, connected by thousands of rivers and streams. The shield's southern half is covered by boreal forest, whereas the northern half (including the islands of the Canadian Arctic Archipelago) is beyond the tree line and has a cover of rock, ice, and ground-hugging tundra. The Arctic Archipelago Islands range from high mountains in the east to low plains in the west.

West of the Canadian Shield lie the central plains. The southern portion of the "Prairie Provinces"—

Timeline

	1200 BC Ancestors of today's Inuit spread east and north as far as Arctic Circle	1497 John Cabot lands near the mouth of the St Lawrence River and claims land for England	1663 New France made a French colony by Louis XIV; French, English settler rivalry over fur trade; native population c.200,000	1791 British divide Canada into Upper and Lower Canada; French mainly in Lower Canada, along lower St Lawrence
35,000–12,000 BP Humans migrate to North American continent from Asia via land bridge across Bering Strait	5000 BP Communities in east survive by trapping caribou and bears, and fishing; use fur clothing and build wood and skin kayaks	AD 1100 Inuit meet Vikings in Greenland; as a result, more than one-third of Inuit die of such diseases as smallpox and measles	1534 Jacques Cartier sails up St Lawrence River to site of present-day Montréal	1670 Hudson's Bay Company established

Saskatchewan, Manitoba, and Alberta—has a natural vegetation of prairie grasses. The northern part is forested. In the prairies the mechanization of wheat farming long ago reduced the need for rural labor, and population densities are low.

The Canadian Cordillera, reaching from the northern Yukon to southern British Columbia and southwest Alberta, dominates western Canada, and contains a number of national parks including Yoho, Banff, Jasper, and Kootenay. On the Pacific side the Coast Mountains run south through British Columbia, the coastline deeply embayed by fjords. Off the coast lies Vancouver Island, the peak of another mountain range, now cut off by the sea.

People and culture

With its major British and French components, its other Europeans who are largely from eastern and southern Europe, its Asians, and its indigenous First Nations, Métis, and Inuit, Canada is home to many peoples. Most now live in urban settings but this is quite a new development. At Confederation in 1867, when Britain granted home rule, 80 percent of the population was rural, and only Montreal had more than 100,000 people. It was not until after the Second World War that rural and urban populations became about equal in size. The war

years stimulated the economy, industrialization was rapid, people moved into the cities to work in factories, and Canada emerged from the conflict with a powerful industrial base. It was at this time that British influence began to decline and the USA became of increasing economic and cultural importance in Canadian life.

In the past 20 years Canada's ethnic mix has changed significantly, resulting from a move toward a less restrictive immigration policy that welcomes people with money and skills. Under this policy many Asians have come to settle. The government defines Canada as a "community of communities" within which each ethnic group is encouraged to maintain its own culture. While generally welcomed, these liberalization measures have also produced problems. Since the Supreme Court recognized "aboriginal title" First Nations land claims have been or are being negotiated with the governments concerned where prior treaties did not exist, and in some cases demands are being made for revision of existing treaties. Canada's most intractable political problem, however, remains the unsatisfied demand of many Québécois for autonomy.

Economy and resources

Canada's resource base includes nickel (Sudbury, Ontario, usually provides some 20 percent of the western world's supply), while Canada is also a world leader in the output of zinc, potash, uranium, sulphur, asbestos, aluminum and copper. Alberta produces more than 75 percent of the nation's oil, and is an important source of natural gas and coal. Hydroelectric power has led to the expansion of pulp and paper industries. Canada is one of the world's leading exporters of wood products.

Bow Lake in Banff National Park in the Canadian Rockies (left). Ottawa, on the banks of the Ottawa River (top left). Niagara Falls, from the Canadian side (top right).

Agriculture is an important activity, though it only employs around 3 percent of the labor force. Grain, dairying, fruit, and ranching all flourish. In addition to pigs and sheep, Canadian ranches support about 13 million head of cattle. Fruit-growing is found in British Columbia's irrigated southern plateau and the Fraser Delta lands. In addition to wheat other export crops include feed grains, oilseeds, apples, potatoes, and maple syrup.

The country's high taxes, regulatory structures, and low productivity have, however, led to ongoing problems. Starting the 1990s in recession, Canada's real rates of growth have averaged only 1 percent through much of the decade. A traditional commitment to high public service and welfare spending is proving hard to maintain. The current account deficit and national debt have led to the slashing of federal transfers to the provinces in the areas of health, education, and welfare. The continuing debate over Québec's future, and the possibility of a split in the confederation, also damages investor confidence.

PROVINCES

Alberta • Edmonton
British Columbia • Victoria
Manitoba • Winnipeg
New Brunswick • Fredericton
Newfoundland • St. John's
Nova Scotia • Halifax
Ontario • Toronto
Prince Edward Island • Charlottetown
Québec • Québec
Saskatchewan • Regina

TERRITORIES

Northwest Territories • Yellowknife
Nunavut • Iqaluit
Yukon Territory • Whitehorse

1829 Welland Canal links Lakes Erie and Ontario, allowing ships to avoid Niagara Falls

1870 Dominion of Canada acquires the North West Territory

1905 Saskatchewan and Alberta become provinces; Canada's population grows with European immigrants settling western prairies

1930s Depression hits; new national bodies set up including Bank of Canada (1934) and Canadian Wheat Board (1935)

1945–55 Postwar migration from Europe boosts Canada's population by more than 1 million

1959 Completion of St Lawrence Seaway creates waterway from Lake Superior to Atlantic of 3,767 km (2,340 miles)

1960 Demands for French–Canadian rights grow both peacefully and in form of terrorist attacks on public buildings

1988 Canada and USA sign free trade agreement ending wrangling over foreign investment, banking, and agriculture

1867 Britain creates Dominion of Canada, bringing together New Brunswick, Nova Scotia, Ontario, and Québec

1871 British Columbia becomes sixth province; Prince Edward Island later made the seventh (1873)

1898 Yukon Territory added to Canada's official land area

1914 Canada fights alongside Britain and Allies against Germany in First World War

1939–45 More than 1 million Canadian troops aid Allies on European and Pacific fronts in Second World War

1949 Newfoundland becomes tenth province; Canada joins North Atlantic Treaty Organization (NATO)

1982 Constitution Act, signed by Queen Elizabeth II, grants Canada sole power to amend its constitution

1993 Parliament grants Inuit people (numbering around 30,000) self-governing homeland, Nunavut, effective 1 April 1999

Costa Rica

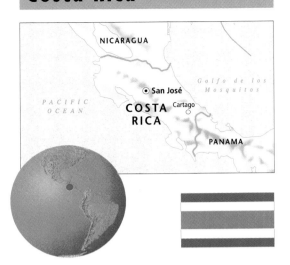

Fact File

OFFICIAL NAME Republic of Costa Rica

FORM OF GOVERNMENT Republic with single legislative body (Legislative Assembly)

CAPITAL San José

AREA 51,100 sq km (19,730 sq miles)

TIME ZONE GMT – 6 hours

POPULATION 3,674,490

PROJECTED POPULATION 2005 4,083,884

POPULATION DENSITY 71.9 per sq km (186.2 per sq mile)

LIFE EXPECTANCY 76

INFANT MORTALITY (PER 1,000) 12.9

OFFICIAL LANGUAGE Spanish

OTHER LANGUAGE English

LITERACY RATE 94.7%

RELIGIONS Roman Catholic 95%, other 5%

ETHNIC GROUPS European and mixed indigenous–European 96%, African 2%, indigenous 1%, Chinese 1%

CURRENCY Costa Rican colón

ECONOMY Services 57%, agriculture 25%, industry 18%

GNP PER CAPITA US$2,610

CLIMATE Tropical, with wet season May to November

HIGHEST POINT Cerro Chirripó 3,819 m (12,530 ft)

MAP REFERENCE Page 428

Costa Rica lies on the Central American isthmus, between Nicaragua and Panama. Its rainforests and wildlife made it popular with tourists in the 1980s, but rising crime has recently reduced tourist interest. Like a number of other Central American countries it was historically influenced by the civilizations of the Maya and Inca, and the earliest human settlements go back 10,000 years. It was named by Christopher Columbus in 1502, *costa rica* meaning "rich coast," and from the 1570s it was a Spanish colony. It gained its independence in 1821 and became a republic in 1848.

Costa Rica is known for its high standards of education, long life expectancy, democratic and stable system of government, high per capita gross domestic product, and a relatively small divide between the rich and the poor. It abolished its national army in 1948. This portrait, however, underestimates the economic role played by US

The Pacuare River running through rainforest in Costa Rica (top). An aerial view of Havana, Cuba (above). The coastal town of Soufrière, Dominica (below right).

aid in recent times. With aid now reduced, Costa Rican governments have had to take austerity measures, and this has led to unrest.

Three ranges form the mountainous skeleton of the country. From the border of Nicaragua the northern Cordillera de Guanacaste descends to meet the Cordillera Central. Between the Cordillera Central and the southern Cordillera de Talamanca lies the temperate Meseta Central, the valley where San José stands. The surrounding area is the main coffee-growing region, coffee production supporting more than 50 percent of the population.

The lowlands on the Caribbean and Pacific coasts are heavily forested and rich in wildlife. While the Pacific side is relatively dry, the Caribbean lowlands receive heavy rain. Both coasts have numerous mangrove swamps and white, sandy beaches. There are several volcanoes on the ranges, some of which are active. Cattle are raised in the dry northwest savanna region of Guanacaste.

Coffee is the country's largest export and along with bananas provides nearly half the country's export earnings. There are large bauxite deposits at Boruca, and aluminum smelting is a major industry. Minerals mined include small quantities of gold, silver, manganese, and mercury. Energy self-sufficiency is being pursued through the development of hydroelectric power.

Cuba

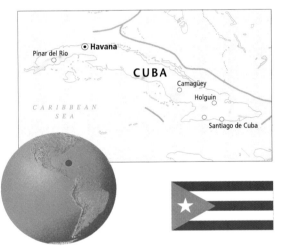

The largest island in the Caribbean, Cuba is the size of all the others combined. Led by Fidel Castro, it is the only communist state in the Americas, and despite internal and external pressures remains politically unchanged after 40 years. Cuba was visited by Columbus in 1492. It was at that time occupied by Arawak and Ciboney Indians. Under Spanish colonial rule sugar plantations worked by African slaves became the foundation of the island's economy—slavery only being abolished, under strong pressure from the Spanish government, in 1878. Gaining independence in 1898 but remaining under American tutelage until 1934, the country was run by a number of corrupt and gangster-ridden regimes until 1958, when Fidel Castro's army captured Havana. In 1976 the de facto monopoly of the Communist Party was formalized, with Castro, supported by his brother, making all decisions. Since the collapse of the Soviet system, on which Cuba had become economically dependent, times have been hard.

Cuba is only 193 km (120 miles) across at its widest point, but it stretches over 1,200 km (745 miles) from the Gulf of Mexico, at its western extremity, to the Windward Passage between Cuba and Haiti in the east. In addition to the main island, the much smaller island of Isla de la

Juventud lies off the southwest coast. Less mountainous than the other islands in the Greater Antilles group, Cuba nevertheless has three distinct ranges—the Oriental (Sierra Maestra), the Central, and the Occidental (Sierra de los Organos). These cover roughly 25 percent of the territory east to west. The remaining 75 percent of Cuba's surface area consists of lowlands and basins. On the more fertile soils sugar plantations, rice fields, coffee plantations, and tobacco fields are found; livestock is run on the central savanna. Cuba's irregular coastline is lined with mangroves, beaches, and coral reefs. Despite deforestation the island still has considerable areas of woodland, ranging from tropical near-jungle to pines growing in upland areas. Cuba has a mostly hot climate and experiences heavy seasonal rainfall and periodic hurricanes.

Sugarcane remains the country's main cash crop, as it has for more than 100 years. Cuba is the world's third-largest sugar producer, and sugar represents almost 50 percent by value of the country's exports. Other crops are tobacco, rice, potatoes, tubers, citrus fruit, and coffee. There are also extensive timber resources, including mahogany and cedar. Cuba has the world's fourth-largest nickel deposits, and production is rising as a result of a joint venture with a Canadian company.

Its situation as one of the world's few remaining communist states has left Cuba isolated and with few trading partners. In addition, because the government has been unwilling to hold multi-party elections, the country has been subject to a severe embargo imposed by the USA. Poor sugar harvests, insufficient funds to pay for fuel, and mounting deficits, have added to the country's difficulties in recent times.

Fact File

OFFICIAL NAME Republic of Cuba

FORM OF GOVERNMENT Communist state with single legislative body (National Assembly of People's Power)

CAPITAL Havana

AREA 110,860 sq km (42,803 sq miles)

TIME ZONE GMT – 5 hours

POPULATION 11,088,829

PROJECTED POPULATION 2005 11,313,934

POPULATION DENSITY 100 per sq km (259 per sq mile)

LIFE EXPECTANCY 75.5

INFANT MORTALITY (PER 1,000) 8.9

OFFICIAL LANGUAGE Spanish

LITERACY RATE 95.4%

RELIGIONS Roman Catholic 40%, Protestant and African Spiritist 10%, non-religious 50%

ETHNIC GROUPS Mixed African–European 51%, European 37%, African 11%, Chinese 1%

CURRENCY Cuban peso

ECONOMY Services 48%, industry 29%, agriculture 23%

GNP PER CAPITA Est. US$766–3,035

CLIMATE Tropical, moderated by trade winds; wet season May to October

HIGHEST POINT Pico Turquino 1,974 m (6,476 ft)

MAP REFERENCE Pages 428–29

Dominica

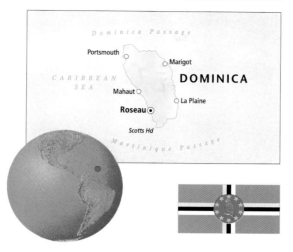

Fought over for years by the English and the French, the Caribbean island of Dominica was mainly occupied by the British after 1759. Locally it is known as the "nature island" because of its extensive forests and wildlife. It is unusual in still having a community of about 3,000 Carib Indians, whose fierce ancestors, protected by the forests in the interior, held off European colonization for 250 years. In the eighteenth century African slaves were brought to the island as labor and their descendants form the majority of the population today. Independence came to Dominica in 1978. Soon after, it was devastated by a series of hurricanes, while two coup attempts complicated its political life. Today, in free elections, power is contested between three parties in a stable democracy.

The most mountainous of the Lesser Antilles, Dominica is a volcanic island with fertile soils and the second largest boiling lake in the world. A high ridge forms the backbone of the island, from which several rivers flow to an indented coastline. There are many vents and hot springs. The rich volcanic soil supports dense tropical vegetation over 41 percent of Dominica's surface; only 9 percent of the land is arable. The climate is warm and humid, with a risk of hurricanes during the rainy season from June to October. During 1995 hurricanes ruined 90 percent of the banana crop.

The wildlife to be seen in the Morne Trois Pitons National Park is an important tourist attraction.

Dominica's only mineral resource is pumice and it has to import all its energy. There is hydro-electric potential in the rivers of the interior. Bananas, citrus fruits, and coconuts are the main cash crops—bananas accounting for 48 percent of exports, and coconut-based soaps 25 percent. Other exports include bay oil and vegetables. The country has to import much of its food and is depending on the development of luxury tourism for economic growth. Ecotourism is increasing, with visitors coming to view rare indigenous birds and volcanic sulphur pools. The lack of an airport able to take jetliners makes the country less accessible than its neighbors for mass-market tourism.

Fact File

OFFICIAL NAME Commonwealth of Dominica

FORM OF GOVERNMENT Parliamentary state with single legislative body (House of Assembly)

CAPITAL Roseau

AREA 750 sq km (290 sq miles)

TIME ZONE GMT – 4 hours

POPULATION 64,881

PROJECTED POPULATION 2005 60,761

POPULATION DENSITY 86.5 per sq km (224 per sq mile)

LIFE EXPECTANCY 78

INFANT MORTALITY (PER 1,000) 8.8

OFFICIAL LANGUAGE English

OTHER LANGUAGE French Creole

LITERACY RATE 94%

RELIGIONS Roman Catholic 77%, Protestant 15%, other 6%, none 2%

ETHNIC GROUPS African 92%, mixed 6%, indigenous 1.5%, European 0.5%

CURRENCY East Caribbean dollar

ECONOMY Services 55%, agriculture 25%, industry 20%

GNP PER CAPITA US$2,990

CLIMATE Tropical, moderated by trade winds

HIGHEST POINT Morne Diablatins 1,447 m (4,747 ft)

MAP REFERENCE Page 427

Dominican Republic

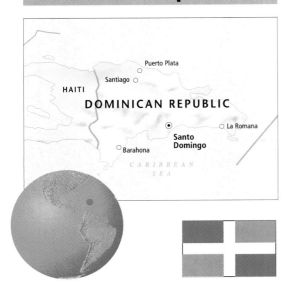

The second largest Caribbean nation in both area and population, the Dominican Republic occupies the eastern two-thirds of the island of Hispaniola. The island was visited by Christopher Columbus in 1492 and in 1496 his brother founded the city of Santo Domingo on its southern coast—the oldest Spanish city in the Americas. It was first colonized by Spain but the development of its sugar industry resulted from a period of French control. The country won independence in 1844 and since that time it has been ruled by a series of dictators with only short intervals of democracy. A bitter civil war in 1965 brought the intervention of the USA, which has kept a watch on Dominican affairs since then. Civil unrest continues.

With a mountainous landscape, including the highest point in the West Indies, Pico Duarte, the Dominican Republic contains three considerable ranges—the Cordillera Septentrional in the north, the massive Cordillera Central, and the southern Sierra de Bahoruco. Between these ranges, and to the east, lie fertile valleys and lowlands. These include the Cibao Valley in the north, the Vega Real, and the coastal plains where sugar plantations are found. Because of the mountainous terrain there are wide variations in temperature and rainfall. Low-lying areas in the south and east support a dry savanna vegetation suitable for livestock raising. The Dominican Republic also has the lowest point in the West Indies—Lake Enriquillo, 44 m (144 ft) below sea level. The lake bisects the mountains in the southwest.

While still heavily dependent on its traditional agricultural base, in recent years the economy has been supplemented by industrial growth (making use of a vast hydroelectric potential), and a large increase in tourism. The Dominican Republic has good beaches, and a hotel capacity of 30,000 rooms, the highest in the Caribbean. Sugar is still the leading agricultural export, followed by coffee, cocoa, tobacco, and fruit. Nickel and gold mining are increasing in economic importance. Subsistence farming provides most of the rural population with its livelihood, the staple crops being rice and corn. State-owned sugar plantations provide another source of employment. Illegal narcotics also play a part in the economy; the country is a transshipment point for drugs bound for the USA.

Fact File

OFFICIAL NAME	Dominican Republic
FORM OF GOVERNMENT	Republic with two legislative bodies (Senate and Chamber of Deputies)
CAPITAL	Santo Domingo
AREA	48,730 sq km (18,815 sq miles)
TIME ZONE	GMT – 4 hours
POPULATION	8,129,734
PROJECTED POPULATION 2005	8,936,667
POPULATION DENSITY	166.8 per sq km (432 per sq mile)
LIFE EXPECTANCY	70.1
INFANT MORTALITY (PER 1,000)	42.5
OFFICIAL LANGUAGE	Spanish
OTHER LANGUAGE	French Creole
LITERACY RATE	81.5%
RELIGIONS	Roman Catholic 95%, other 5%
ETHNIC GROUPS	Mixed African–European 73%, European 16%, African 11%
CURRENCY	Peso
ECONOMY	Agriculture 46%, services 38%, industry 16%
GNP PER CAPITA	US$1,460
CLIMATE	Tropical, with wet season May to November
HIGHEST POINT	Pico Duarte 3,175 m (10,416 ft)
MAP REFERENCE	Page 429

El Salvador

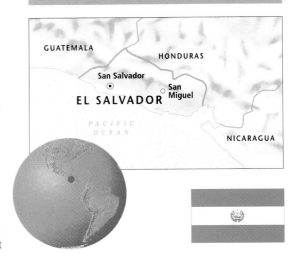

El Salvador is the smallest, most densely populated country in Central America, and the only one without a coast on the Caribbean. It is in a seismic zone and has some 20 volcanoes, several of which are active. Once the home of the Pipil Indians and later a part of the Mexican Empire, the country won full independence in 1841 and established itself as the Republic of El Salvador in 1859. Over 100 years of civil strife and military rule followed.

From the 1880s about 75 percent of the land has been in the hands of 14 families, who farm huge plantations producing coffee, tobacco, and sugar. The potential for conflict between this landed oligarchy and the rural poor has been present since that time and in the 1970s left-wing disillusionment with the electoral process led to the formation of a number of guerrilla groups. Between 1979 and 1991 civil war raged, with the loss of 75,000 lives, and many people emigrated. The political and economic effects of this conflict are still evident.

Behind El Salvador's narrow Pacific coastal plain rises a volcanic range. Inland is a rich and fertile central plain, occupying 25 percent of the country's total land area. The urban and rural population in this area accounts for 60 percent of the country's total, and produces 90 percent of El Salvador's coffee and tobacco, along with most of its sugar and corn. Further inland still, along the frontier with Honduras, are mountain ranges. Once forested and unpopulated, they now draw poor farmers desperate for land.

El Salvador's economy has few strengths other than a large amount of cheap labor. Damage from the civil war is estimated at $2 billion and cotton and sugar cultivation declined significantly during the conflict. Coffee contributes about 90 percent of exports. Foreign aid remains important, much coming from the USA. Manufacturing is based on food and beverage processing, while other industries are textiles, clothing, petroleum products, and cement. The civil war brought tourism to a standstill but peace has resulted in visitors returning to the Pacific beach resorts of El Salvador's Costa del Sol.

El Salvador contains about 20 volcanoes, some still active. Izalco Volcano, El Salvador, seen from lush forest (left). Grenada is volcanic in origin and bisected by a mountain ridge; the coastal capital of St Georges, sheltered by hills (above right).

Fact File

OFFICIAL NAME Republic of El Salvador

FORM OF GOVERNMENT Republic with single legislative body (Legislative Assembly)

CAPITAL San Salvador

AREA 21,040 sq km (8,123 sq miles)

TIME ZONE GMT – 6 hours

POPULATION 5,839,079

PROJECTED POPULATION 2005 6,382,909

POPULATION DENSITY 277.5 per sq km (718.7 per sq mile)

LIFE EXPECTANCY 70

INFANT MORTALITY (PER 1,000) 28.4

OFFICIAL LANGUAGE Spanish

OTHER LANGUAGE Nahua

LITERACY RATE 70.9%

RELIGIONS Roman Catholic 75%, Protestant and other 25%

ETHNIC GROUPS Mixed indigenous–European 94%, indigenous 5%, European 1%

CURRENCY Colón

ECONOMY Services 70%, industry 22%, agriculture 8%

GNP PER CAPITA US$1,610

CLIMATE Tropical, with wet season May to October; cooler in mountains

HIGHEST POINT Cerro El Pittal 2,730 m (8,957 ft)

MAP REFERENCE Page 428

Grenada

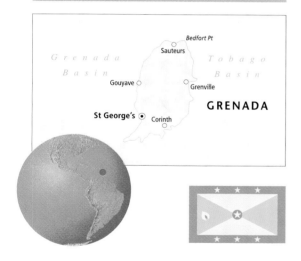

The state of Grenada consists of the island of Grenada, lying off the coast of Venezuela not far from Trinidad, and two small islands of the Southern Grenadines—Carriacou and Petite Martinique. The islands were visited by Columbus in 1498 but the original Carib Indian inhabitants fought off all invaders until French settlers arrived in the 1650s. Grenada then became a typical sugar-producing Caribbean island, with plantations worked by slaves brought from Africa. British since 1762, it has English as an official language, though some Grenadans still speak a French patois. It won independence in 1974 and in 1979 the country became communist after a bloodless coup. When the coup leader was murdered by fellow Marxists in 1983, the USA, with support from a number of other Caribbean countries,

intervened to restore democratic elections. Since then power has been contested, and has alternated between several different political parties. Economic recovery from the events of 1983 has been slow.

The most southerly of the Windward Islands, the main island of Grenada is volcanic in origin and has fertile soils. A forested mountain ridge runs north–south, cut by rivers, and there are a number of lakes, including the Grand Etang at an elevation of 530 m (1,739 ft). The western coastline is precipitous; the southern coastal landscape of beaches is gentler and includes some natural harbors. In recent years the government has become interested in developing ecotourism but protection of key environmental sites remains a concern. Large resort projects have resulted in serious beach erosion.

Grenada is known in the Caribbean as "the spice island," and is the world's leading producer of nutmeg and mace, its main crop. Other exports include cocoa and bananas, but attempts to diversify the economy from an agricultural base have so far been unsuccessful. The farming practised by the rural population is mostly small scale, with the exception of a few cooperatives. The small manufacturing sector is based on food-processing and makes products such as chocolate, sugar, alcoholic beverages, and jam. Garments and furniture are also produced, mainly for export to Trinidad and Tobago. After the political crisis of 1979 to 1983 tourism largely ceased, but it is gradually recovering.

Fact File

OFFICIAL NAME Grenada

FORM OF GOVERNMENT Constitutional monarchy with two legislative houses (Senate and House of Representatives)

CAPITAL St Georges

AREA 340 sq km (131 sq miles)

TIME ZONE GMT – 4 hours

POPULATION 97,008

PROJECTED POPULATION 2005 104,434

POPULATION DENSITY 285.3 per sq km (738.9 per sq mile)

LIFE EXPECTANCY 71.6

INFANT MORTALITY (PER 1,000) 11.1

OFFICIAL LANGUAGE English

OTHER LANGUAGE French patois

LITERACY RATE 98%

RELIGIONS Roman Catholic 64%, Protestant (including Anglican, Seventh Day Adventist, Pentecostal) 27%, other 9%

ETHNIC GROUPS African 84%, mixed 12%, East Indian 3%, European 1%

CURRENCY East Caribbean dollar

ECONOMY Services 65%, agriculture 20%, industry 15%

GNP PER CAPITA US$2,980

CLIMATE Tropical, moderated by trade winds

HIGHEST POINT Mt Saint Catherine 840 m (2,756 ft)

MAP REFERENCE Page 427

Guatemala

Fact File

OFFICIAL NAME Republic of Guatemala

FORM OF GOVERNMENT Republic with single legislative body (Congress of the Republic)

CAPITAL Guatemala

AREA 108,890 sq km (42,042 sq miles)

TIME ZONE GMT – 6 hours

POPULATION 12,335,580

PROJECTED POPULATION 2005 14,423,051

POPULATION DENSITY 113.3 per sq km (293.4 per sq mile)

LIFE EXPECTANCY 66.5

INFANT MORTALITY (PER 1,000) 46.2

OFFICIAL LANGUAGE Spanish

OTHER LANGUAGES Indigenous languages

LITERACY RATE 55.7%

RELIGIONS Roman Catholic 75%, Protestant 25%; some traditional Mayan beliefs

ETHNIC GROUPS Mixed indigenous–European 56%, indigenous 44%

CURRENCY Quetzal

ECONOMY Agriculture 50%, services 38%, industry 12%

GNP PER CAPITA US$1,340

CLIMATE Tropical, but cooler in highlands

HIGHEST POINT Volcan Tajumulco 4,220 m (13,845 ft)

MAP REFERENCE Page 428

Guatemala lies just south of Mexico, and is the most populous of the Central American states. It was once part of the home of the Mayan civilization which reached its peak about AD 300–900. It has numerous volcanoes, including Tajumulco, the highest peak in Central America. In 1523 the region was overrun by Spanish conquistadors. As elsewhere in Central and South America, the newly arrived Spanish established large agricultural estates worked by Amerindian laborers, setting the social and economic pattern for 300 years. After becoming a republic in 1839, Guatemala has had a history of dictatorship, coups d'état, and guerrilla insurgency. Profound social divisions exist between the Amerindian majority, and an elite of mixed Spanish and Amerindian ancestry (called Ladinos) who run the government. Guatemala has had

One of the ruined temples of Tikal, the great Mayan religious center in Guatemala (above). The Sunday market in Chichi, Guatemala (right). An aerial view of Tegucigalpa, the capital of Honduras (far right).

civilian rule since 1985. In 1996 a United Nations mediated accord was signed by President Alvaro Arzu and the members of the URNG guerrilla movement which it is hoped will bring an end to 36 years of armed struggle.

Two large mountain ranges cross the heart of the country. In the north are the older and more eroded Altos Cuchumatanes. To the south the geologically younger Sierra Madre Range includes 33 volcanoes, of which three are still active. Soil enriched with volcanic ash washed down from the Sierra Madre has created a narrow but fertile plain on the Pacific coast. This has been used for agriculture on a commercial scale only since the 1950s, when malaria was first brought under control and access roads were built. Now cattle and cotton are more important than this region's traditional banana crop. On the lower mountain slopes, up to about 1,500 m (5,000 ft), most of the country's highest quality coffee is grown. In the north of Guatemala the highlands fall away to the large, flat, forested Peten Tableland, where many ancient Mayan ruins are found, and to the plains along the Gulf of Honduras.

Guatemala's economy is largely agricultural. Coffee is the main crop and chief export, other exports being sugar, bananas, cardamom, and beef. From the forests, now reduced to about 40 percent of the country's land area, come timber and chicle, the gum used for chewing gum. The country has few mineral or energy reserves, apart from small amounts of petroleum, and until recently guerrilla activity has hindered access to the wells. Industries include sugar refining, furniture, chemicals, metals, rubber, textiles and clothing, and tourism. Tourism, largely comprising visits to the Maya ruins, revived after the military activities of the 1980s, but fell into decline again in 1994 and 1995 following attacks on foreigners. From 1990 the economy has shown mild but consistent growth though, given the extreme disparity of wealth, the government faces many difficulties in implementing its program of modernization and the alleviation of poverty.

Haiti

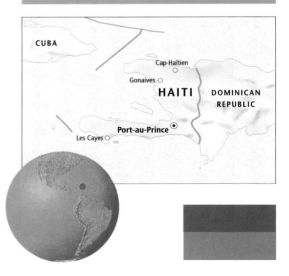

Haiti lies in the Caribbean, east of Cuba. It is the western third of the island of Hispaniola, the Dominican Republic occupying the remainder. Visited by Columbus in 1492, it was used by the Spanish for sugarcane cultivation and was ceded to France in 1697. In the aftermath of the French Revolution it was the scene of a slave rebellion which led to the establishment, in 1804, of the world's first black republic. Since then the country has endured almost two centuries of instability, violence, dictatorship, military rule, and endemic poverty. Today, Haiti is the poorest country in the western hemisphere. Under the brutal regime of the Duvalier family, between 1957 and 1986, it became a police state enforced by a private militia called the Tontons Macoute. Recent years have seen faltering steps toward electoral democracy and modest civil service reforms, but political killings are still occurring under an apparently corrupt and ineffective judicial system.

Two peninsulas enclose the central plain of the Artibonite River, and the bight of the Golfe de la Gonâve beyond. Some 75 percent of Haiti's terrain is mountainous, the Massif du Nord providing the range which forms the northern peninsula, before extending east into the Dominican Republic where it becomes Hispaniola's Cordillera Central. The southern peninsula contains the Massif de la Hotte at its western end, and the Massif de la Selle in the east. The fertile lowland areas are densely populated, the largest of these being the Plaine du Nord. On the plains the major crop is sugarcane, coffee plantations being found on the higher land. The majority of the population is engaged in subsistence farming, growing cassava, bananas, and corn. Haiti's environmental problems are severe: one-third of its soil is seriously eroded, and extensive deforestation has occurred in the course of charcoal production.

Haiti is without strategic resources and, during a period of economic sanctions imposed to put pressure on the government in 1991, it was forced to find clandestine sources of oil. In addition to sugar refining, light industry includes flour and and cement and the manufacture of textiles, shoes, and cooking utensils. The country's location, history, and culture proved attractive to tourists in the 1960s and 1970s, despite the repressive regime, but widespread crime has affected the industry in recent years.

Fact File

OFFICIAL NAME Republic of Haiti

FORM OF GOVERNMENT Republic with two legislative bodies (Senate and Chamber of Deputies)

CAPITAL Port-au-Prince

AREA 27,750 sq km (10,714 sq miles)

TIME ZONE GMT – 5 hours

POPULATION 6,884,264

PROJECTED POPULATION 2005 7,583,777

POPULATION DENSITY 248.1 per sq km (642.6 per sq mile)

LIFE EXPECTANCY 51.7

INFANT MORTALITY (PER 1,000) 97.6

OFFICIAL LANGUAGE French

OTHER LANGUAGE French Creole

LITERACY RATE 44.1%

RELIGIONS Roman Catholic 80% (most of whom also practice Voodoo), Protestant 16% (Baptist 10%, Pentecostal 4%, Adventist 1%, other 1%), other 4%

ETHNIC GROUPS African 95%, mixed African–European 5%

CURRENCY Gourd

ECONOMY Agriculture 50%, services 44%, industry 6%

GNP PER CAPITA US$250

CLIMATE Mainly tropical; semiarid in eastern mountains; wet seasons April to June and August to November

HIGHEST POINT Pic de la Selle 2,680 m (8,792 ft)

MAP REFERENCE Page 429

Honduras

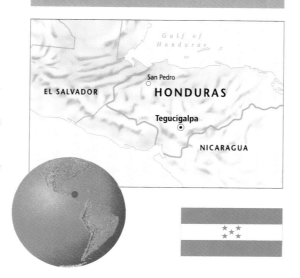

H onduras is the second largest of the Central American countries. Its mountainous mass lies across the isthmus north of Nicaragua, with Guatemala to the west and El Salvador to the southwest. The Caribbean shoreline runs eastward from the Guatemalan border to the flat and almost uninhabited Mosquito Coast. In the west are the historic ruins of Copan, a site of the ancient Maya civilization which ended long before the Spaniards arrived in 1522. Gold first drew the Spanish to Honduras and when they discovered it in the west they founded Tegucigalpa in 1524. The Honduran mountains are highly metalliferous and silver is still an important export. Independent from Spain since 1821, the country has had decades of military rule with only the occasional elected government. The challenge for the present administration is to reduce the role of the military in political and economic life.

At least 75 percent of Honduras is mountainous. From the central highlands several river valleys run northwest to the coast, where the plains along the Caribbean shore broaden toward the east. The lower valleys have been reclaimed and the forests have been replaced by banana plantations. On the Pacific side there is a short stretch of coast in the Gulf of Fonseca. The adjacent lowlands are used for growing cotton. Rainforest in the northeast provides sanctuary for a great variety of wildlife.

The original "banana republic," Honduras was the world's leading exporter during the 1920s and 1930s. Bananas still account for nearly a quarter of all exports but coffee is now the largest earner. The country depends heavily on the USA for trade: 53 percent of its exports and 50 percent of its imports are with the US. Most the workforce are farmers, many of them at a subsistence level: food staples are corn, beans, and rice. Small-scale manufactures include furniture, textiles, footwear, chemicals, and cement. Subject to an International Monetary Fund (IMF) restructuring program in the 1990s, Honduras has faced difficulties, with its already poor people subject to sharp tax rises. In 1998, Hurricane Mitch killed more than 9,000 people in Central America, and devastated crops and left thousands homeless.

Fact File

OFFICIAL NAME Republic of Honduras

FORM OF GOVERNMENT Republic with single legislative body (National Congress)

CAPITAL Tegucigalpa

AREA 112,090 sq km (43,278 sq miles)

TIME ZONE GMT – 6 hours

POPULATION 5,997,327

PROJECTED POPULATION 2005 6,750,160

POPULATION DENSITY 53.5 per sq km (138.6 per sq mile)

LIFE EXPECTANCY 64.7

INFANT MORTALITY (PER 1,000) 40.8

OFFICIAL LANGUAGE Spanish

OTHER LANGUAGES Indigenous languages, English Creole

LITERACY RATE 72%

RELIGIONS Roman Catholic 97%, Protestant 3%

ETHNIC GROUPS Mixed indigenous–European 90%, indigenous 7%, African 2%, European 1%

CURRENCY Lempira

ECONOMY Agriculture 60%, services 24%, industry 16%

GNP PER CAPITA US$600

CLIMATE Tropical on plains, cooler in mountains

HIGHEST POINT Cerro Las Minas 2,849 m (9,347 ft)

MAP REFERENCE Page 428

Jamaica

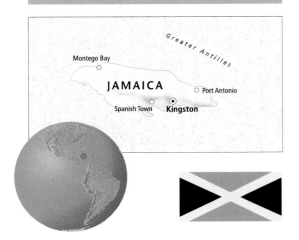

The Caribbean island of Jamaica lies 144 km (98 miles) south of Cuba and southwest of Haiti. Mountainous in the interior, it is the most populous of the English-speaking Caribbean islands. Arawak Indians were its first inhabitants. Columbus visited in 1494 and a slave-based sugar producing plantation society was established by the British after they seized the island in 1655. It won independence from Britain in 1962. An important contributor to world music, Jamaica is the home of reggae, a style originating in Kingston's tough urban environment. Also from Jamaica come the Rastafarians, followers of the one-time Emperor of Ethiopia. In September 1988 Jamaica was devastated by the fiercest hurricane to strike the island this century, causing widespread loss of life and leaving 20 percent of the people homeless.

In the northwest of the island is a limestone area of steep ridges and isolated basins, pitted with sink-holes. This "cockpit country" once gave refuge to escaped slaves. In the east the land rises to become the densely forested Blue Mountains. In the west the River Black is navigable upstream for about 30 km (19 miles). Sugar plantations dominate the densely populated and extensively cultivated lowland coastal fringe. Seasonal rains fall most heavily on the northeastern mountain slopes—still covered in the rainforest once found all over the island. In the rainshadow of the mountains, the southern lowlands support only savanna scrub.

Bauxite has been mined since 1952. Most of it is exported as ore, and about one-fifth as alumina, making Jamaica the world's third-largest producer. This accounts for more than 50 percent of exports. Tourism and bauxite production are Jamaica's two main industries, and comprise almost two-thirds of foreign earnings. Other export industries include printing, textiles and food processing, along with rum distilling and sugar production. In agriculture, sugarcane and bananas are the main cash crops, along with coffee, cocoa, and fruit. In recent years the government has removed most price controls and privatized state enterprises. Unemployment remains high. Jamaica's medium-term prospects depend largely on its ability to attract foreign capital and limit speculation against the Jamaican dollar.

Fact File

OFFICIAL NAME	Jamaica
FORM OF GOVERNMENT	Constitutional monarchy with two legislative bodies (Senate and House of Representatives)
CAPITAL	Kingston
AREA	10,990 sq km (4,243 sq miles)
TIME ZONE	GMT – 5 hours
POPULATION	2,652,443
PROJECTED POPULATION 2005	2,763,836
POPULATION DENSITY	241.4 per sq km (625.2 per sq mile)
LIFE EXPECTANCY	75.6
INFANT MORTALITY (PER 1,000)	13.9
OFFICIAL LANGUAGE	English
OTHER LANGUAGE	Creole
LITERACY RATE	84.4%
RELIGIONS	Protestant (mainly Anglican, Presbyterian–Congregational, Baptist, Methodist) 70%, Roman Catholic 7–8%, other including Rastafari 22–23%
ETHNIC GROUPS	African 76.5%, mixed African–European 15%, East Indian and mixed African–East Indian 3%, European 3%, Chinese and mixed African–Chinese 1%, other 1.5%
CURRENCY	Jamaican dollar
ECONOMY	Services 63%, agriculture 25%, industry 12%
GNP PER CAPITA	US$1,510
CLIMATE	Tropical; cooler inland
HIGHEST POINT	Blue Mountain Peak 2,256 m (7,402 ft)
MAP REFERENCE	Page 429

Mexico

The story of Mexico is the story of Central American civilization itself. For thousands of years people have lived in the central valley, and when the Spanish arrived under Cortés in 1519 the population of the Aztec Empire may have numbered 15 million. The pattern of settlement established by Spain in Mexico, with large estates worked by Indians, was followed in many other Central and South American countries. Although most Mexicans are Roman Catholics, the relation of Church and state has not always been easy, governments often viewing the Church's power as a challenge to their own. Mexico possesses major petroleum resources, is industrializing rapidly, and includes many traditional Indian cultures among its people, from the Tarahumara in the northwest to the Maya of Quintana Roo.

Physical features and land use

The northern and less-populated part of Mexico consists of the basin-and-range country of the Mesa Central. In this region desert scrub is the main plant cover, with grasses, shrubs, and succulents on higher ground. Cattle ranching is notable in this region. The land reaches heights of 2,400 m (7,900 ft) around Mexico City. South of the city three major peaks—Citlaltepetl, Popacatepetl, and Ixtaccihuatl—of the Sierra Volcanica Transversal reach elevations of around 5,500 m (18,000 ft). An active earthquake zone, this is the most densely settled part of the country.

East of the Mesa Central the land falls steeply from the Sierra Madre Oriental to a broad coastal plain on the Gulf of Mexico fringed with swamps, lagoons, and sandbars. Further south is the isthmus of Tehuantepec, a neck of rainforested land dividing the mountains of the Sierra del Sur from the highlands rising toward the Guatemalan

Timeline	2600 BC Beginning of Mayan civilization in Yucatan Peninsula	300 BC Completion of the Great Pyramid of the Sun Temple at Teotihuacán, in the Valley of Mexico
3500 BC Turkeys, corn, beans, and squash are domesticated for food	1200 BC Rise of Olmec civilization on Mexico's Gulf Coast; it lasts until 300 BC	

Port Antonio on the northeast coast of Jamaica (below left).
The Mayan Pyramid of the Magician, Uxmal, Mexico (above).
A market scene in Mexico (right).

border. The Yucatan Peninsula to the east is a limestone plain lying only a little above sea level, marked by natural wells and sinkholes. Petroleum discoveries in the 1970s in Tabasco and Campeche, in the northwest Yucatan, have made Mexico one of the world's biggest oil producers.

The Mesa Central ends just as abruptly on its western frontier, falling from the pine-forested heights of the Sierra Madre Occidental to a narrow coastal strip extending north to the Californian border. In the far northwest is the long narrow, dry, mountain-spined peninsula of Baja California.

Contrasts in altitude and latitude produce wide climatic variations, from the coasts, where temperatures are uniformly high, to the temperate land which prevails over much of the Mesa Central. Above 2,000 m (6,000 ft) lies what is known as the cold land, while on the higher slopes of the snow-capped volcanic cones is the frozen land where temperatures are usually below 10°C (50°F).

People and culture

Most Mexicans are descendants of the Amerindian peoples who lived in the region at the time of the Spanish conquest, and of the Spanish colonists. The Aztecs were one of a number of developed cultures in the region. Their capital, Tenochtitlan, featured monumental architecture in the form of pyramids, and their society was strongly hierarchic, with slaves at the bottom and an emperor at the top. Art, sculpture, and poetry were advanced and they had a form of writing. Aztec religious practices involved the annual sacrifice (and eating) of large numbers of slaves, prisoners, and captives

taken in war. The Maya in Yucatan were another major culture in the region but by the time the Spanish arrived the empire had already collapsed. Only their majestic stone monuments in the jungle remained, with settlements of corn-cultivating Mayan subsistence farmers nearby.

The Spanish brought Christianity and a system of large scale estates using poorly paid (or unpaid) Amerindian labor. Colonial control was exercised by a form of serfdom under which Amerindians paid either tribute or labor in return for conversion to Christianity. This system was abolished in 1829. In 1810 the independence struggle began, in 1822 Mexico declared itself a republic and in 1836 Spain formally recognized the country's independence. A century of political chaos climaxed with the violent Mexican Revolution of 1910 to 1921.

Since 1929 Mexico has been dominated by one party, the PRI, which has ruled until recently in a corporatist and authoritarian fashion. There is widespread dissatisfaction with the political process and with the unsolved 1994 murders of two high-profile reformers within the ruling party. A peasant revolt in Chiapas in 1994 dramatized the problem of rural poverty and the poor understanding of Mexico's urban élite of the world beyond the cities.

Economy and resources

Agriculture occupies around a quarter of the population, many farmers living by growing maize, beans, and squash. The main export crops are coffee, cotton, and sugarcane. Some meat is exported from the north, while fish exports include tuna, anchovies, sardines, and shrimp. About one-fifth of Mexico is forested, producing hardwood and chicle, the base for chewing gum.

Mexico is one of the largest oil exporters outside OPEC, most oil coming from the Gulf of Mexico. Petrochemicals provide most of the country's export earnings and are the chief energy source. Mexico is the world's leading producer of silver. Only about 20 percent of the country's mineral reserves have so far been exploited. There are also sizeable deposits of coal and uranium. Hydroelectricity contributes 34 percent of all power used.

Although the economy is diverse, with food-processing, textiles, forestry, and tourism making a contribution, it has been through a series of crises beginning with devaluation in 1994. Economic activity contracted by 7 percent in 1995 and more than 1 million Mexicans lost their jobs. The health of the banking sector, investor confidence, drug-linked corruption, and the shaky grip of the ruling elite on power are matters of continuing concern.

Fact File

OFFICIAL NAME	United Mexican States
FORM OF GOVERNMENT	Federal republic with two legislative chambers (Senate and Chamber of Deputies)
CAPITAL	Mexico City
AREA	1,972,550 sq km (761,602 sq miles)
TIME ZONE	GMT – 6/8 hours
POPULATION	100,294,036
PROJECTED POPULATION 2005	110,573,561
POPULATION DENSITY	50.8 per sq km (131.6 per sq mile)
LIFE EXPECTANCY	72
INFANT MORTALITY (PER 1,000)	24.6
OFFICIAL LANGUAGE	Spanish
OTHER LANGUAGES	Indigenous languages
LITERACY RATE	89.2%
RELIGIONS	Roman Catholic 93%, Protestant 4%, other 3%
ETHNIC GROUPS	Mixed indigenous–European (mainly Spanish) 60%, indigenous 30%, European 9%, other 1%
CURRENCY	Mexican peso
ECONOMY	Services 57%, agriculture 23%, industry 20%
GNP PER CAPITA	US$3,320
CLIMATE	Tropical in south and on coastal lowlands; cooler and drier in central plateau and mountains
HIGHEST POINT	Vol Citaltepetl (Pico de Orizaba) 5,700 m (18,701 ft)
MAP REFERENCE	Pages 430–31

1000 Rise of Toltec Empire based in Tula, present-day Hidalgo, to the north of the Valley of Mexico; lasts around 200 years	**1325** Aztecs establish their capital of Teotihuacán, a city housing 100,000–300,000 people	**1629** Floods kill 30,000 people in Mexico City; new drainage systems constructed	**1836** Mexico's independence is formally recognized by Spain	**1847–48** US troops capture Mexico City in Mexican–American War until treaty grants large amounts of territory to USA	**1910–20** Mexican revolution; Madero overthrows Diaz government in 1911	**1934** Government begins major land reforms; in 1938 all foreign-owned oil company assets taken over by government	**1985** Two earthquakes occur in south-central Mexico, including Mexico City, killing more than 10,000 people
AD 325 Mayan civilization flourishes during its classic period (which lasts until 925); fine stone buildings with hieroglyphics	**1519** Spanish explorer Cortés expelled by Aztec Emperor Montezuma from Tenochtitlan; Cortés destroys city in 1520	**1521** Spanish rebuild Tenochtitlan and it becomes new Spanish capital, Mexico City	**1810** Hidalgo y Costilla calls for rebellion against Spain; Hidalgo executed in 1811	**1876** Diaz becomes dictator; expands economy by building railways, developing industries, encouraging foreign investment	**1917** New Constitution adopted	**1970s** Massive oil deposits discovered in the Gulf of Mexico	**1997** Paramilitary groups in Acteal massacre 45 Indian villagers

Nicaragua

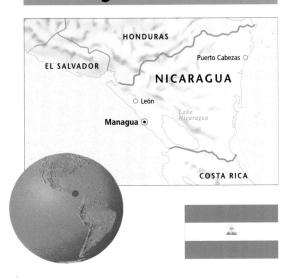

The largest republic in the Central American isthmus, Nicaragua is also the least populated. The western half, including Lake Nicaragua, the largest lake in Central America, was settled by the Spanish in the sixteenth century, and the Caribbean shore was for two centuries the British protectorate of Mosquito Coast (Costa de Miskitos). Becoming independent from Spain in 1821, Nicaragua then experienced much instability. The 45-year right-wing rule of the Somoza family ended in 1979, being overthrown by the Marxist Sandinistas. Their left-wing rule provoked a US-backed insurgency known as the "contras." In free elections held in 1996 a right-of-center party defeated the Sandinistas. In rural areas, however, violence continues.

Nicaragua's broad plain on the Caribbean side leads to a coastal region of lagoons, beaches, and river deltas. Rainfall here is heavy and the tropical wildlife includes crocodile and jaguar. Inland, toward the east, there are mountain ranges broken by basins and fertile valleys. In the west and south a broad depression containing Lakes Managua and Nicaragua runs from the Gulf of Fonseca, on the Pacific Coast, to the mouth of the San Juan del Norte River, on the Caribbean. Before the Panama Canal was built this was an important route across the isthmus. This is a region of cotton growing. Overlooking the lakes are 40 volcanoes, among them the active Momotombo. An earthquake destroyed most of Managua in 1972.

Nicaragua is still reorganizing its economy—at one point under the Sandinistas inflation reached 3,000 percent. Large-scale confiscation of estates took place under the Sandinistas but the peasants to whom land was given have not always been able to live off their allotments, and some land has been resold. Coffee and cotton are the major export crops. Staples grown by the many subsistence farmers include maize, rice, and beans. Mineral production is led by silver and gold, followed by tungsten, lead, and zinc. Falling prices for most of Nicaragua's export commodities, the loss of aid, and the impact of IMF policies reduced the nation's income in 1993 to close to Haiti's—the poorest in the Americas. There is a huge foreign debt. Conditions peculiar to Nicaragua include Sandinista "land reforms" in which luxury properties were seized and given to the movement's leaders and "privatized" state operations that are union-controlled. More than 50 percent of agricultural and industrial firms are state-owned.

Fact File

OFFICIAL NAME	Republic of Nicaragua
FORM OF GOVERNMENT	Republic with single legislative body (National Assembly)
CAPITAL	Managua
AREA	129,494 sq km (49,998 sq miles)
TIME ZONE	GMT – 6 hours
POPULATION	4,717,132
PROJECTED POPULATION 2005	5,521,705
POPULATION DENSITY	36.4 per sq km (94.3 per sq mile)
LIFE EXPECTANCY	67.1
INFANT MORTALITY (PER 1,000)	40.5
OFFICIAL LANGUAGE	Spanish
OTHER LANGUAGES	Indigenous languages, English
LITERACY RATE	65.3%
RELIGIONS	Roman Catholic 95%, Protestant 5%
ETHNIC GROUPS	Mixed indigenous–European 69%, European 17%, African 9%, indigenous 5%
CURRENCY	Córdoba
ECONOMY	Agriculture 47%, services 37%, industry 16%
GNP PER CAPITA	US$380
CLIMATE	Tropical in lowlands, cooler in highlands; wet season May to January
HIGHEST POINT	Pico Mogoton 2,107 m (6,913 ft)
MAP REFERENCE	Page 428

Nicaraguan children outside their thatched home on the island of Omotepe, with the volcano of Concepción in the background (left). A cargo ship heading east through the Gatun locks on the Panama Canal (right). The port of San Juan del Sur on the west coast of Nicaragua (far right).

Panama

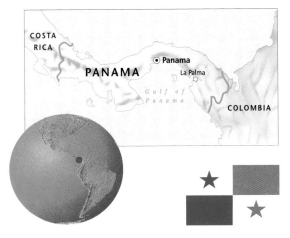

Panama joins two oceans and two continents. With Costa Rica to the west and Colombia to the east, it forms a narrow neck of land connecting Central to South America, while the Panama Canal links the Atlantic Ocean to the Pacific. The first proposal for a canal was made by the Spanish in the early sixteenth century. Later, at the time of the Californian Gold Rush, the USA began to press for action. In 1881 work began on a design prepared by de Lesseps, who was the builder of the Suez Canal, but malaria and yellow fever killed so many workers on the project that it had to be abandoned. Control of these diseases was one of the achievements of the later American builders, who eventually completed the canal in 1914.

Part of Colombia until 1903, Panama has been closely linked with the USA since the construction of the canal gave the latter rights over a 16 km (10 mile) wide Canal Zone. These rights run out in the year 2000. A major upheaval took place in Panama during 1989 when the USA invaded and removed the country's self-proclaimed "maximum leader" General Manuel Noriega in order that he face drug charges in Miami. Electoral democracy was restored in the country, and Noriega was jailed, but the laundering of large amounts of drug money in association with cartels in neighboring Colombia continues to be a problem.

The 3,000 m (9,850 ft) tall mountains of the Serrania de Tabasara (Cordillera Central) run west of the canal along the isthmus, and are separated from the southern Peninsula de Azuera by a long stretch of plain. East of the canal two more ranges of mountains form arcs running parallel to the Pacific and Caribbean coasts. Most of the country, however, including 750 offshore islands, lies below 700 m (2,300 ft) and swelters in tropical heat and high humidity. Rainforests are extensive, and those of the Darien National Park, with their abundant wildlife, are among the wildest areas left in the whole of the Americas. Most Panamanians live within 20 km (12 miles) of the Canal Zone, a quarter of them in the capital itself.

Panama's economy is based on services, and is heavily weighted toward banking, commerce, and tourism. The country has the largest open-registry merchant fleet in the world. Along with the export of bananas (43 percent of total exports) and shrimp (11 percent), plus income derived from the USA's military installation, Panama has the highest standard of living in Central America. However,

the country's commercial debt is also one of the highest in the world in per capita terms, and during the mid-1990s the country experienced an economic slow-down. Despite the presence of a degree of nationalist fervor, with the termination of the US Canal Zone, approximately 75 percent of Panamanians now favor a continuing US presence in the country to help preserve stability.

Fact File

OFFICIAL NAME	Republic of Panama
FORM OF GOVERNMENT	Republic with single legislative body (Legislative Assembly)
CAPITAL	Panama
AREA	78,200 sq km (30,193 sq miles)
TIME ZONE	GMT – 5 hours
POPULATION	2,778,526
PROJECTED POPULATION 2005	3,030,173
POPULATION DENSITY	35.5 per sq km (92 per sq mile)
LIFE EXPECTANCY	74.7
INFANT MORTALITY (PER 1,000)	23.4
OFFICIAL LANGUAGE	Spanish
OTHER LANGUAGE	English
LITERACY RATE	90.5%
RELIGIONS	Roman Catholic 85%, Protestant 15%
ETHNIC GROUPS	Mixed indigenous–European 70%, African 14%, European 10%, indigenous 6%
CURRENCY	Balboa
ECONOMY	Services 60%, agriculture 27%, industry 13%
GNP PER CAPITA	US$2,750
CLIMATE	Tropical, with long wet season May to January
HIGHEST POINT	Volcán Barú 3,475 m (11,401 ft)
MAP REFERENCE	Page 429

St Kitts and Nevis

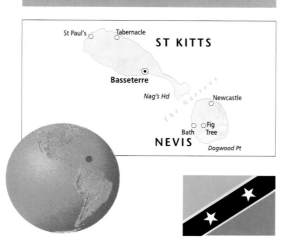

St Kitts and Nevis is a federation of two Caribbean islands in the Leeward Islands group. Each is well-watered and has a mountain of volcanic origin rising to about 1,000 m (3,300 ft). Once inhabited by Carib and Arawak Indians, St Kitts and Nevis were, in 1623 and 1628, the first West Indian islands to be colonized by Britain. Ownership of the islands was disputed with the French until 1783. In 1983 the country became fully independent from Britain.

As on other Caribbean islands, African slaves were imported as labor for sugar and cotton plantations, this ceasing with the abolition of slavery in 1834. Most islanders today are descended from former slaves. The growing and processing of sugarcane remains important, though falling prices have hurt local industry in recent years. The government intends to revitalize this sector. Tourism and export-oriented manufacturing are of growing significance, in addition to manufactured products including machinery, food, electronics, clothing, footwear, and beverages. The main cash crops are sugarcane on St Kitts, cotton and coconuts on

Nevis. Staple foods include rice, yams, vegetables, and bananas, but most food is imported.

Nevis claims it is starved of funds by its partner and is dissatisfied with its place in the federation. In 1996 Nevis announced its intention of seeking independence from St Kitts. Nevis has the constitutional right to secede if two-thirds of the elected legislators approve and two-thirds of voters endorse it through a referendum.

Fact File

OFFICIAL NAME	Federation of St Kitts and Nevis
FORM OF GOVERNMENT	Constitutional monarchy with single legislative body (House of Assembly)
CAPITAL	Basseterre
AREA	269 sq km (104 sq miles)
TIME ZONE	GMT – 4 hours
POPULATION	42,838
PROJECTED POPULATION 2005	46,750
POPULATION DENSITY	159.2 per sq km (412.3 per sq mile)
LIFE EXPECTANCY	67.9
INFANT MORTALITY (PER 1,000)	17.4
OFFICIAL LANGUAGE	English
OTHER LANGUAGE	English Creole
LITERACY RATE	90%
RELIGIONS	Anglican 36%, Methodist 32.5%, Roman Catholic 11%, Pentecostal 5.5%, Baptist 4%, other 11%
ETHNIC GROUPS	African 94.5%, mixed African–European 3%, European 1%, other 1.5%
CURRENCY	East Caribbean dollar
ECONOMY	Services 69%, industry and agriculture 31%
GNP PER CAPITA	US$5,170
CLIMATE	Tropical, moderated by sea breezes
HIGHEST POINT	Mt Misery 1,156 m (3,793 ft)
MAP REFERENCE	Page 427

St Lucia

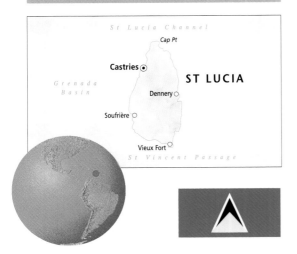

Fact File

OFFICIAL NAME St Lucia

FORM OF GOVERNMENT Constitutional monarchy with two legislative bodies (Senate and House of Assembly)

CAPITAL Castries

AREA 620 sq km (239 sq miles)

TIME ZONE GMT – 4 hours

POPULATION 154,020

PROJECTED POPULATION 2005 164,413

POPULATION DENSITY 248.4 per sq km (643.4 per sq mile)

LIFE EXPECTANCY 71.8

INFANT MORTALITY (PER 1,000) 16.6

OFFICIAL LANGUAGE English

OTHER LANGUAGE French Creole

LITERACY RATE 82%

RELIGIONS Roman Catholic 90%, Protestant 7%, Anglican 3%

ETHNIC GROUPS African 90.5%, mixed 5.5%, East Indian 3%, European 1%

CURRENCY East Caribbean dollar

ECONOMY Services 65%, agriculture 26%, industry 9%

GNP PER CAPITA US$3,370

CLIMATE Tropical, moderated by trade winds; wet season May to August, dry season January to April

HIGHEST POINT Mt Gimie 950 m (3,117 ft)

MAP REFERENCE PAGE 427

An island in the Caribbean, St Lucia is one of the prettiest of the Windward Group of the Lesser Antilles. Tropical beaches and typical Caribbean towns like Soufrière have long drawn tourists to the island, who also come to see its varied plant and animal life. Once inhabited by Arawak and Carib Indians, St Lucia was wrangled over between France and Britain before finally being ceded to Britain in 1814. As elsewhere in the Caribbean, African slaves were imported to work sugar plantations until slavery was abolished in 1834. Most of the population are descended from slaves, though some are from South Asia. Internally self-governing from 1967, St Lucia has been fully independent since 1979.

The main features of the island are its forested mountains stretching north to south, cut by river valleys, and rising to Mt Gimie. In the southwest lies the Qualibou, an area with 18 lava domes and 7 craters. In the west, marking the entrance to Jalousie Plantation harbor, are the spectacular twin Pitons, two peaks rising steeply from the sea to a height of about 800 m (2,625 ft). The climate is tropical, with annual rainfall varying from 1,500 mm (59 in) in the lowlands to 3,500 mm (137 in) in mountainous areas.

While not poor, St Lucia still depends heavily on bananas (60 percent of export income), a crop which is easily ruined by hurricanes and disease. Bananas are also a source of political tension: in recent years the USA has pushed for the abolition of the preferential treatment the EU accords banana imports from the Caribbean. The people of St Lucia have strongly objected to this. Other agricultural exports are coconuts, coconut oil, and cocoa. Clothing is the second largest export, and the free port of Vieux Fort has attracted modern light industry. Grande Cul de Sac Bay in the south is one of the deepest tanker ports in the region and is used for the transshipment of oil.

St Vincent and the Grenadines

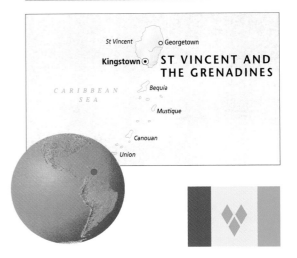

The mountainous, volcanic Caribbean island of St Vincent has 89 percent of the country's total land area and 95 percent of the population, the rest consisting of the islands of the Northern Grenadines—Bequia, Mustique, Canouan, and Union. St Vincent was visited by Columbus in 1498 but the fierce resistance of the Amerindian Caribs meant that settlement was slow. A long dispute with France (the French often being supported by the Caribs) finally led to it becoming a British colony in 1783. As St Vincent and the Grenadines the country became self-governing in 1969 and independent in 1979.

St Vincent is dominated by a north–south spur of densely forested mountains, cut east to west by numerous short, fast-running rivers and streams. In the north, volcanic Mt Soufrière is still very active. It caused serious damage in 1891 and in 1902 it killed 2,000 people. The 1979 eruption, which was followed by a hurricane the next year, devastated agriculture and caused a major setback in tourism.

The Northern Grenadines are coralline islets, extending south of St Vincent toward Grenada, some of them with picturesque names, such as All Awash Island and The Pillories. The tropical climate is moderated by steady trade winds.

Agriculture, led by banana production, is the foundation of the country's economy, most of it small-scale or subsistence farming on the lower mountain slopes or terraces. Other crops exported include arrowroot starch used to make medicines, and paper for computer printers. Tourism is of growing importance, with visitors drawn to the clear, clean waters of Mustique and Bequia. Attempts to develop various industries have so far had little success: unemployment stands at about 35 to 40 percent.

Fact File

OFFICIAL NAME St Vincent and the Grenadines

FORM OF GOVERNMENT Constitutional monarchy with single legislative body (House of Assembly)

CAPITAL Kingstown

AREA 340 sq km (131 sq miles)

TIME ZONE GMT – 4 hours

POPULATION 120,519

PROJECTED POPULATION 2005 125,501

POPULATION DENSITY 354.5 per sq km (918 per sq mile)

LIFE EXPECTANCY 73.8

INFANT MORTALITY (PER 1,000) 15.2

OFFICIAL LANGUAGE English

OTHER LANGUAGE French Creole

LITERACY RATE 82%

RELIGIONS Anglican 42%, Methodist 21%, Roman Catholic 12%, other 25%

ETHNIC GROUPS African 82%, mixed 14%, European, East Indian, indigenous 4%

CURRENCY East Caribbean dollar

ECONOMY Agriculture 50%, services 30%, industry 20%

GNP PER CAPITA US$2,280

CLIMATE Tropical, with wet season May to November

HIGHEST POINT Mt Soufrière 1,234 m (4,048 ft)

MAP REFERENCE Page 427

The spires of the Pitons tower above a small village on the southwest coast of St Lucia (top left). Kingstown Harbor on the island of St Vincent (left). A bay on the north coast of Trinidad (above). A view of one of Tobago's many bays (above right).

Trinidad and Tobago

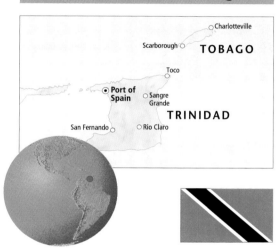

Trinidad is a square-shaped Caribbean island at the south end of the Windward Island chain, only 11 km (7 miles) off the coast of Venezuela. Along with Tobago it is the most prosperous island in the West Indies, oil and asphalt forming the basis of its wealth. It was visited by Columbus in 1498 and then held by the Spanish for three centuries before becoming a British possession after it was seized in 1797. The island's sugar plantations were initially worked by African slaves, and then after the abolition of slavery in 1834 East Indian and Chinese labor was imported. Today, in rural districts, some villages are mainly Afro-Trinidadian, some mainly Asian. Since gaining independence in 1962, Trinidad has been vexed by racial and ethnic complications, notably "Black Power" in 1970 and an attempted coup by black Muslim extremists in 1990. In 1995 the first prime minister from the Asian community was sworn in.

Unlike the Caribbean islands to the north, Trinidad is geologically an extension of South America across the Gulf of Paria. It is traversed by three mountain ranges (northern, central and southern) with El Cerro del Aripo in the Northern Range, and is drained by the Caroni, Ortoire and Oropuche Rivers. The Caroni Swamp is notable for the immense variety of its butterflies. The rest of the island is mostly low-lying, fringed with mangrove swamps.

Tobago Island is a detached piece of the Northern Range, with volcanic uplands, that lies 34 km (21 miles) to the northeast of Trinidad. Tourism is concentrated on Tobago, which is renowned for its wildlife.

The strength of Trinidad's economy is its oil sector, and its large petroleum reserves. But living standards have fallen since the boom years of 1973 to 1982 and the country's prospects depend to a great extent on the success of efforts toward diversification and on economic reforms. The floating of the exchange rate, capital market liberalization, and the partial privatization of such state operations as the main airline are among recent government initiatives.

Fact File

OFFICIAL NAME Republic of Trinidad and Tobago

FORM OF GOVERNMENT Republic with two legislative bodies (Senate and House of Representatives)

CAPITAL Port of Spain

AREA 5,130 sq km (1,981 sq miles)

TIME ZONE GMT – 4 hours

POPULATION 1,102,096

PROJECTED POPULATION 2005 1,032,684

POPULATION DENSITY 214.8 per sq km (556.3 per sq mile)

LIFE EXPECTANCY 70.7

INFANT MORTALITY (PER 1,000) 18.6

OFFICIAL LANGUAGE English

OTHER LANGUAGES Hindi, French, Spanish

LITERACY RATE 97.9%

RELIGIONS Roman Catholic 32%, Hindu 24.5%, Anglican 14.5%, other Protestant 14%, Muslim 6%, other 9%

ETHNIC GROUPS African 43%, East Indian 40%, mixed 14%, European 1%, Chinese 1%, other 1%

CURRENCY Trinidad and Tobago dollar

ECONOMY Services 73%, industry 15%, agriculture 12%

GNP PER CAPITA US$3,770

CLIMATE Tropical, with wet season June to December

HIGHEST POINT El Cerro del Aripo 940 m (3,084 ft)

MAP REFERENCE Page 427

North and Central America

United States of America

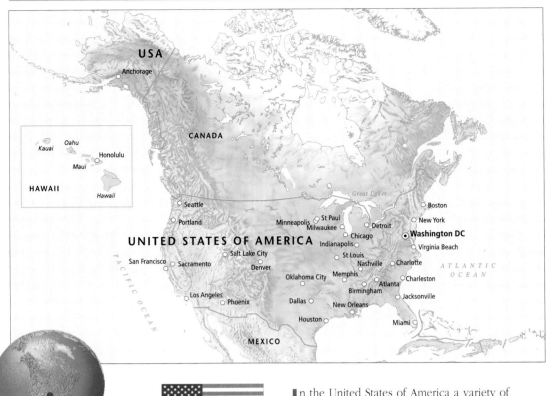

Fact File

OFFICIAL NAME United States of America

FORM OF GOVERNMENT Federal republic with two legislative bodies (Senate and House of Representatives)

CAPITAL Washington DC

AREA 9,372,610 sq km (3,618,765 sq miles)

TIME ZONE GMT – 5/11 hours

POPULATION 272,639,608

PROJECTED POPULATION 2005 286,291,020

POPULATION DENSITY 29.1 per sq km (75.4 per sq mile)

LIFE EXPECTANCY 76.2

INFANT MORTALITY (PER 1,000) 6.3

OFFICIAL LANGUAGE English

OTHER LANGUAGES Spanish, German, French, Italian, Chinese, indigenous languages

LITERACY RATE 99%

RELIGIONS Protestant 56%, Roman Catholic 28%, Jewish 2%, other 4%, none 10%

ETHNIC GROUPS European 83.5%, African 12.5%, Asian 3%, Native American 1%

CURRENCY US dollar

ECONOMY Services 79%, industry 18%, agriculture 3%

GNP PER CAPITA US$26,980

CLIMATE Varied: eastern states are temperate, with warm summers and snowy winters in north and subtropical conditions in south; southwest is arid and semiarid; west coast is temperate but warmer in California and wetter in the Pacific Northwest; Hawaii is mainly tropical; Alaska is mainly polar but cooler and wetter on south coast

HIGHEST POINT Mt McKinley 6,194 m (20,321 ft)

MAP REFERENCE Pages 418–19, 420–21, 422–23, 424–25, 426

In the United States of America a variety of peoples, united by a shared belief in social and economic freedom, have built the most prosperous and powerful nation on earth. Abundant resources, a climate and soils ensuring plentiful food supplies, and an open society rewarding individual energy and initiative, were all advantages from the beginning. In addition, huge oceans on both eastern and western coasts isolated America from the troubles of Europe and Asia, and its relations with Mexico to the south and Canada to the north were generally benign. Starting with these favorable conditions, and guided by the ideals of democracy and freedom, the United States of America—in this respect unique among nations—successfully invented itself according to its own political and social ideals.

The most serious danger to its existence was self-inflicted. From 1861 to 1865 the US was wracked by a civil war in which the implications of universal human liberty were played out in a struggle between slave-owners in the south of the country and slave-liberators in the north, but the nation survived. Later, in the face of widespread domestic opposition, the US entered the First World War in 1917, its military strength leading to Germany's defeat. Even more decisive was its role in the Second World War between 1941 and 1945, in alliance with Great Britain and the Soviet Union, when its industrial power and military might ensured victory over both Germany and Japan. After 1945, challenged for superpower supremacy by the Soviets, it engaged in a protracted trial of strength known as the Cold War. This ended in 1989 with the collapse of the USSR and its communist allies, leaving America stronger politically and economically than ever before.

The economy, already the most powerful, diverse, and technologically advanced in the world, continues to grow. But US prosperity is combined with a variety of problems: drug addiction; crime; long-term unemployment for some sectors of the population; racial tensions; air and water pollution in some areas from automotive and industrial wastes; traffic congestion approaching "gridlock" in major cities; and rising medical costs. All these side-effects appear to be the price of modernity on the American model. It is a price that most other developed countries have been prepared to pay, however, in order to establish high-tech, high-energy industrial societies.

Physical features and land use

Mainland United States can be divided into three major physical regions. The eastern part consists of the range of the Appalachian Mountains and the coastal plain that runs along the Atlantic Ocean. The broad basin of the Mississippi and Missouri Rivers comprises the central section. The western region is composed of mountain ranges, desert landscapes, and the land along the Pacific coast. In addition, there are two outlying sections of the country—Alaska and Hawaii.

In eastern North America the Appalachians, a band of sedimentary mountains and plateaus which are still widely forested, extend from northern Alabama to the Gulf of St Lawrence. They consist of a number of parallel ranges, including the Blue Ridge Mountains in Virginia and the Great Smoky Mountains along the North Carolina–Tennessee border. For a long time these ranges constituted a barrier to inland settlement. In New York State the valley of the Mohawk River divides the mountains of the Appalachians from the Adirondacks, which are a southern extension of the ancient granite mass of the Canadian Shield. Traveling up this valley, from east to west, the early settlers were able to find a way through the range that led on to the land bordering the Great Lakes and the Ohio country beyond.

The original vegetation on these mountains was broadleaf deciduous forest of oak, ash, beech, and maple, grading into yellow birch, hemlock, and pine toward the north. During the eighteenth and nineteenth centuries much of this forest area was cleared for farming, but declining agriculture in New England and the abandonment of farmland has brought widespread regeneration of tree growth. Flying across eastern America, much of the landscape still gives the impression of continuous woodland.

The coastal plain to the southeast through the Carolinas and Georgia is generally low-lying, and includes many areas of swamp. Nearly 1,700 km (more than 1,000 miles) of barrier islands and sandbars run parallel to the shore and are popular seaside resort areas for the inland population, despite being exposed to occasional hurricanes.

To the west of the Appalachian Range lies the enormous continental drainage basin of the Mississippi–Missouri system. This basin is about 2,500 km (1,500 miles) wide, extending south from the Canadian border to the Gulf of Mexico. At its northern limit there are the hills along Lake Superior, a vestige of the Canadian Shield. What are called the Central Lowlands of this drainage basin are bounded on the east by the low plateaus of Kentucky and Tennessee. To the west of the Mississippi lie vast areas planted in wheat, and eventually grasslands, as the Great Plains reach 1,500 km (900 miles) across to the foothills of the Rocky Mountains.

Once the home of such tribes as the Mandan, the Omaha, and the Kansa Indians (settled farmers near the Missouri River), and the nomadic Black-foot, Crow, and Arapaho further west, most of the plains had been taken by incoming ranchers and farmers by the end of the nineteenth century. Former range land was planted in wheat and maize. These crops were hugely productive at first, but overcropping and dry years led to severe soil deterioration in the first decades of the twentieth century. This reached a climax in the disasters of the 1930s, when a large part of the region became a "dustbowl." Although diversification of grain crops, contour plowing, and widespread irrigation have helped to restore agricultural productivity, some areas are still highly sensitive to climatic variation, especially where the original terrain was semidesert. Combined with fluctuations in grain prices, agriculture remains a risky business in a region where much of the land is marginal.

The mountain ranges of the western Cordillera, as it extends south from Canada, are divided by a number of high plateaus and deep valleys. There are two main systems, to the west and the east. The northern and central Rocky Mountains are the eastern arm facing out across the Great Plains, with the Grand Tetons forming spectacular ridges in Wyoming. The southern Rockies of Colorado and New Mexico—the remains of an ancient granite plateau—are also weathered into a series of striking peaks. In Colorado there are more than 1,000 mountains of 3,000 m (10,000 ft) or more. As with the mountains on the east of the continent, the Rockies were a major obstacle for westward-heading settlers. One major route lay through the

A desert landscape in Arches National Park, Utah (left). Fall colors in northern Maine (top). Juneau, in Alaska, lies on the Inside Passage, a marine waterway that runs through the vast Tongass National Forest (above).

Wyoming Basin, a rangeland where bison once grazed, and where yesterday's pioneer trails have become interstate highways.

On the lower slopes of the Rockies grow a mixture of piñon pines and juniper scrub, with ponderosa pine, spruce, and fir at higher altitudes. Wildlife includes elk, deer, moose, mountain sheep, bear, and a variety of smaller animals. National Parks such as Yellowstone and Grand Teton provide an opportunity to see these animals in dramatic natural settings, and draw millions of visitors to the region every year.

High plateaus, rocky ranges, and desert basins extend westward across the states of Utah, Arizona, and Nevada, seamed in many places by vast, abrupt canyons, of which the Grand Canyon of the Colorado River is the most spectacular. On the Pacific side of these plateaus is the western branch of the cordillera. This forms a chain of mountains consisting of the Sierra Nevada in the south and the Cascade Range to the north. Stretching from Washington through Oregon to Lassen Peak in California, the Cascades include several large volcanoes, Mt Saint Helens erupting violently in 1980. The Sierra Nevada faces out over the fertile Central Valley of California, with its fruit and vegetable growing, viticulture, cotton, other crops, and livestock. In the early days long dry summers made farming difficult in the Central Valley. Meltwater from the snows of the Sierra Nevada, much of it diverted in lengthy canals, now provides summer irrigation.

Beyond the Central Valley on its western side rise the comparatively low Coast Ranges, running parallel to the Pacific shore all the way from the Mexican border to Canada. Together, the Coast Ranges, the Cascades, and the Sierra Nevada, all serve to keep precipitation away from the interior plateaus and create its arid landscape. East of the Cascade Range in the Pacific Northwest lies the Columbia Basin. Here, the meltwaters of ancient glaciers have cut deep gorges in the land. In western Washington the most spectacular trees consist of Douglas fir, western hemlock, and Sitka spruce, some almost as tall as the giant redwoods of northern California. The wealth of the US Northwest was originally based on timber from the huge conifers that covered the Cascade Range.

The two non-contiguous parts of the US have very different physical landscapes. The expansive state of Alaska is a mixture of massive glaciated mountains and broad river valleys, with a vegetation cover that varies from dense forest to sparse tundra. For much of the year, large areas of Alaska are covered in snow. The Hawaiian islands mostly consist of the tops of prominent volcanoes which protrude above the sea, with a host of distinctive plants nurtured by the tropical climate.

History and settlement

The first peoples to settle North America probably crossed from Siberia to Alaska during the ice ages between 10,000 and 30,000 years ago. It is thought they became the ancestors of the many Indian tribes living in North America when the first Europeans arrived. Their cultures varied widely, from the Iroquois who lived in bark lodges in the east, to the cliff-dwelling Pueblo peoples of the west, to the salmon-fishing and whale-hunting Northwest Coast Indians of Washington State and British Columbia, who lived in large timber houses. Plains Indians such as the Sioux or the Comanche are sometimes depicted hunting bison on horseback, but this was only possible after horses had been introduced by incoming European settlers from the fifteenth century onward.

The oldest authenticated European settlement in North America was made by Norse Vikings at the northern tip of the island of Newfoundland about AD 1000, but it was occupied for only a short time. The first successful English settlement was at Jamestown, Virginia, in 1607. Not long after this a party of religious dissenters, the so-called Pilgrim Fathers, arrived in 1620 to found the first of the New England colonies at Plymouth. Joined by other migrants later, this became part of the large Massachusetts Bay colony.

A Dutch colony on Manhattan Island (founded in 1624) was captured by the British in 1664, who changed its name from New Amsterdam to New York. The Quaker William Penn founded one of the more successful of the early English colonies in 1682. Part of Pennsylvania later split off to become Delaware; North and South Carolina were established in 1663; Georgia, originally designed as a philanthropic alternative to a debtor's prison, in 1732. The defeat of the French, which ended the Seven Years War in 1763, brought huge territorial accessions to England: all of France's Canadian territories, the land west of the Mississippi River, plus Louisiana and Florida. The settlers throughout these areas became directly subject to the British Crown, and when London sought to recoup the huge expenses of the war (about £101,500,500) by imposing taxes, the cry of "No taxation without representation" was raised in Boston, and resistance to England began. When the American War of Independence broke out in 1776 George Washington commanded the troops, and when it was won and the first elections were held in 1788 he became the inaugural president. In the aftermath, tens of thousands of "loyalists" moved north to Canada.

The British government had forbidden westward expansion beyond the mountains of the Appalachians. After independence, however, this took place with a rush. Indian tribes were quickly dispossessed from the area and exiled, their land taken for farms, and throughout the nineteenth century there was a series of wars in the region to crush resistance. The last armed Indian defiance collapsed with the Ghost Dance Uprising of 1890. But by far the most serious crisis for the new nation was the American Civil War of 1861 to 1865. This was both a clash of ideals (liberty versus servitude) and of ways of life (the industrializing, modern north versus the old agrarian south). Led by the eloquent commonsense of Abraham Lincoln, the northern forces of the Union defeated the southern armies of the Confederacy, but the legacy of bitterness lasted for many decades.

Meanwhile, westward expansion proceeded apace. Pioneers followed trails explored by men such as Lewis and Clark. Railroads spanned the

Timeline

| 35,000–12,000 BP Modern humans *Homo sapiens sapiens* migrate to North America across Bering Strait land bridge and spread south | 13,000 BP Settlements appear from south of Canadian border to Mexico; stone spearpoints in use in New Mexico | 3500 BC Native Americans hunt bison; by 2500 BC squash, goosefoot, and sunflowers (seeds used as winter food) cultivated | 1000 BC The Adena in eastern North America build ceremonial mounds; agriculture established in southwest | 300 BC Hohokam, Mogollon, and Anasazi people inhabit the south and southwest; Anasazi build villages at Chaco, New Mexico | 200 BC Hopewell culture takes over from Adena; Hopewell become first farmers in eastern North America (until AD 500) | AD 700 Start of Pueblo period in southwest; Native Americans of Hopi, Zuni, and other tribes live in villages built mainly of adobe | 790 Vikings explore coasts of Europe and North America for the next 100 years, forming settlements in Greenland and Iceland | 1492 Columbus reaches America while searching for route to Orient; later, French and English establish fur trading posts in Canada | 1539 Hernando de Soto reaches Florida and travels up the Mississippi; following year Coronado explores southwest | 1584 Sir Walter Raleigh claims Virginia for England, but no permanent settlement created until founding of Jamestown in 1607 | 1619 First slaves shipped from West Africa to USA |

continent, coal and iron were discovered and used, and new cities such as Pittsburgh and Chicago grew up in the interior. European migrants pouring in through the ports of Boston, Philadelphia, and New York substantially changed the nation's ethnic composition. Manufacturing cities, which were big markets in their own right, developed along the shores of the Great Lakes, while the mechanized farming of the Midwestern "corn belt" turned it into the granary of much of the Western world.

The history of California differed from that of the rest of the country in many ways, in that it was a part of Spanish conquest rather than of English settlement. The small, semi-nomadic hunting and seed-gathering Indian cultures of the area were little affected by the spread northward of Spanish forts and missions from New Spain (Mexico) in the 1760s. But by the middle of the nineteenth century pressures from land-hungry pioneers moving in from the eastern states were irresistible: by the end of the century the whole of the southwest, including Texas, had been either ceded, purchased, or annexed. Since then the Pacific Coast economy has passed through various stages, from gold-prospecting and lumbering, through agriculture, the expansion of the aircraft industry after the Second World War, to the highest of high-tech today in Silicon Valley south of San Francisco Bay.

Once independence was established by the beginning of the nineteenth century, the US kept Europe at arm's length, and the Monroe Doctrine

Rugged country in Great Basin National Park in Nevada (left). One of California's numerous vineyards (right). The famous Empire State Building in New York City (far right). Undulating farming country in Idaho (below).

warned Europe that the representatives of the old empires—Spanish, Portuguese, and British—were not to intervene in the Americas any more. Isolationism was the other side of this doctrine: the US had no wish to be entangled in Europe's troubles. But as the US developed into a major global power this disengagement was no longer possible. In two world wars in the twentieth century American military intervention was decisive, and with the onset of the Cold War, designed to contain the Soviet Union after 1945, it was prepared to intervene wherever it saw the need. However, subsequent action in Korea from 1950 to 1953, and in Vietnam from 1964 to 1975, both with heavy loss of US lives, has made the nation less enthusiastic about overseas military

commitments and the risks and casualties of policing trouble-spots (Haiti, Somalia, the Persian Gulf) are often unpopular at home. Generally the American mood is inward-looking, more concerned with domestic than with foreign affairs.

People and culture

The US is a prosperous, industrial, capitalistic democracy, in which anyone with training and skills who is prepared to assimilate can usually find a place. It is the most open multicultural society on earth, which is the main reason why there are so many people from other countries wanting to live here. In addition to its huge numbers of legal immigrants (the US still has the highest legal immigration level of any country in

1804 Lewis and Clark explore the Missouri River then cross Rocky Mts and reach the Pacific near mouth of Columbia River	**1848** California gold rush. Within two years 90,000 people from San Francisco, the east, and overseas travel to diggings	**1869** World's first transcontinental railroad is completed when the Union Pacific line and Central Pacific line link up	**1917** USA enters First World War on the side of Allies	**1929** Wall Street Crash ruins many investors and affects industry and farming; millions lose jobs in Depression	**1941** USA joins Allies in Second World War after Japan bombs Pearl Harbor; war ends 1945 after USA drops atomic bombs on Japan	**1992** Hurricane Andrew strikes Florida and Louisiana causing $25 billion damage and the loss of more than 50 lives
1776 USA founded, with American colonies adopting Declaration of Independence. Population 3 million	**1805** The Louisiana Purchase acquires a large area of south from France, almost doubling the land area of the USA	**1861–65** Civil War between southern (Confederate) and northern (Union) states; all slaves freed in Confederate states	**1908** Ford launches Model T, a mass market automobile. It transforms US industry and economy; 15.5 million sold in 19 years	**1920** More Americans now living in industrial cities than on the land; women are given the vote in all elections	**1936** Boulder Dam on Colorado River completed impounding Lake Mead; renamed Hoover Dam (1947)	**1969** Apollo 11 mission opens a new chapter in space exploration by landing three astronauts on Moon

Navajo Indians in Monument Valley, Arizona (left). Chapel of the Alto Vista, on the eastern side of Aruba (top right). Islands of the Great Sound in Bermuda (bottom right).

the world) illegal entry is estimated to bring in up to one million people a year.

The descendants of the original Native American inhabitants are a small but not insignificant element of the population. People arriving from overseas were at first mainly English, and with those of Scots and Irish descent dominated all other arrivals from the other side of the Atlantic until the middle of the nineteenth century. During this period the only other major ethnic group to arrive were African slaves imported to work the plantations in the South. After the Civil War, however, mass immigration was encouraged, and a flood of migrants arrived from Italy, Scandinavia, Germany, the Balkans, and various troubled parts of Eastern Europe, including Russia. Many were Jews fleeing poverty and pogroms. In the 60 years up until 1920, 30 million people arrived, radically changing the ethnic composition of the country. Although there were national concentrations in specific neighborhoods (such as Little Italy in New York) the ideal of assimilation ensured that by the middle of the 20th century most new arrivals, or their children, had come to share the benefits of other citizens. More recently there has been an influx of Japanese, Chinese, Filipinos, Cubans, Vienamese, Koreans, and large numbers of Mexicans and Central Americans. In some places, Puerto Rican, Cuban, and Mexican groups provide a strongly Hispanic cultural orientation.

One group of long-term residents did not enjoy full participation in American life. These were the African–Americans descended from the slaves, who became increasingly concentrated in the cities. Long after the Civil War systematic discrimination barred them from jobs, and from equal access to housing, commercial premises, public facilities, and education—even forcing them to sit at the back of the bus in the old slave states. As a result of agitation and affirmative action, the second half of the twentieth century saw the legal rights of African–Americans secured. What remains, however, are inequalities which law alone seems unable to resolve. In the cities, many African–Americans remain part of an underclass plagued by unemployment, drug addiction, crime, and unstable family life.

Economy and resources

The US economy is the largest among the industrial nations, possessing an invaluable combination of skilled and unskilled labor and natural resources. Internationally, it is the most powerful, diverse, and scientifically advanced. With the early application of research and technology, agriculture developed into a highly mechanized industry for food production and processing, with a distinct zonal pattern across the country. Dairy farming predominates in a broad belt from New England to Minnesota. Further west, where the climate is drier, wheat is grown. The corn (maize) belt, highly productive land which was once prairie and forest, consists of the maize-growing eastern and central states from Ohio to Nebraska. Maize is mainly used for feeding to cattle and pigs. In the warmer southern states where cotton and tobacco were grown—the old "cotton belt"—a variety of other crops are now also cultivated, from vegetables to fruit and peanuts. There has

been a strong tendency for farming to move from small to large-scale operations and from labor-intensive to mechanized. Although agriculture's share of gross domestic product is only 2 percent, the US remains a leading producer of meat, dairy foods, soy beans, maize, oats, wheat, barley, cotton, sugar, and forest products.

Despite 20 years of strong competition from Japan and various other Asian economies, the giant US economy remained resurgent throughout the 1990s. One reason for its success may be the greater flexibility of US capitalist enterprise when compared with either Asia or Western Europe. A labor market responsive to changing demands is another factor, and over the last 20 years there has been a huge shift in employment from manufacturing to services. US unemployment remains today one of the lowest in all the major industrialized states. But the main reason for the health of the economy is probably its dynamic technological inventiveness. In every field, US firms are at or near the frontier of technological advance. This is especially so in computers, medical equipment, and aerospace. The advantages of this onrush of technology are obvious. But there are major social costs as well. What is called a two-tier labor market has evolved in which those at the bottom lack enough skills and education to compete, failing to get pay rises, health insurance cover, and other benefits.

Despite the economy's basic good health, marked by low inflation and low unemployment, debate continues on how a number of its continuing problems should be addressed. These include low rates of saving, inadequate investment in infrastructure, the rising medical costs of an ageing population, large budget and trade deficits, and the stagnation of family income in the lower economic groups.

STATES

Alabama • Montgomery	**Minnesota** • St Paul	**Oregon** • Salem
Alaska • Juneau	**Mississippi** • Jackson	**Pennsylvania** • Harrisburg
Arizona • Phoenix	**Missouri** • Jefferson City	**Rhode Island** • Providence
Arkansas • Little Rock	**Montana** • Helena	**South Carolina** • Columbia
California • Sacramento	**Nebraska** • Lincoln	**South Dakota** • Pierre
Colorado • Denver	**Nevada** • Carson City	**Tennessee** • Nashville
Connecticut • Hartford	**New Hampshire** • Concord	**Texas** • Austin
Delaware • Dover	**New Jersey** • Trenton	**Utah** • Salt Lake City
District of Columbia • Washington DC	**New Mexico** • Santa Fe	**Vermont** • Montpelier
Florida • Tallahassee	**New York** • Albany	**Virginia** • Richmond
Georgia • Atlanta	**North Carolina** • Raleigh	**Washington** • Olympia
Hawaii • Honolulu	**North Dakota** • Bismarck	**West Virginia** • Charleston
Idaho • Boise	**Ohio** • Columbus	**Wisconsin** • Madison
Illinois • Springfield	**Oklahoma** • Oklahoma City	**Wyoming** • Cheyenne
Indiana • Indianapolis		
Iowa • Des Moines		
Kansas • Topeka		
Kentucky • Frankfort		
Louisiana • Baton Rouge		
Maine • Augusta		
Maryland • Annapolis		
Massachusetts • Boston		
Michigan • Lansing		

OVERSEAS TERRITORIES

American Samoa	Navassa Island
Baker and Howland Islands	Northern Mariana Islands
Guam	Palmyra Atoll
Jarvis Island	Puerto Rico
Johnston Atoll	Virgin Islands of the US
Kingman Reef	Wake Island
Midway Islands	

North and Central America

Dependencies and territories

Anguilla

Anguilla's name comes from the Spanish *anguil* meaning "eel." The country is a long, thin, scrub-covered coral atoll in the Caribbean, north of St Kitts and Nevis. First colonized by Britain in 1690, its status as a UK dependent territory was formalized in 1980. While the governor is a crown appointee, a local assembly manages internal matters. Anguilla has few natural resources and depends heavily on tourism, offshore banking, lobster fishing, and overseas remittances. Drawn by a subtropical climate tempered by trade winds, tourists have multiplied in recent years, this reflecting the generally healthy economic conditions in both the USA and the UK. As a result, annual growth has averaged about 7 percent. The offshore finance sector was strengthened by comprehensive legislation enacted in 1994.

Fact File

OFFICIAL NAME	Anguilla
FORM OF GOVERNMENT	Dependent territory of the United Kingdom
CAPITAL	The Valley
AREA	91 sq km (35 sq miles)
TIME ZONE	GMT – 4 hours
POPULATION	11,510
LIFE EXPECTANCY	77.7
INFANT MORTALITY (PER 1,000)	18.7
LITERACY RATE	80%
CURRENCY	East Caribbean dollar
ECONOMY	Services 65%, construction 18%, transportation and utilities 10%, manufacturing 3%, agriculture 4%
CLIMATE	Tropical, moderated by trade winds
MAP REFERENCE	Page 427

Aruba

Aruba is most unusual among the islands of the Caribbean in that it has a 1 percent unemployment rate, numerous unfilled employment vacancies, and a high gross domestic product. A flat, limestone island lying off the Venezuelan coast at the mouth of the Gulf of Venezuela, Aruba is barren on its eastern side and more lush on the west. It was once a part of the Netherlands Antilles, but is now a separate but autonomous part of the Dutch realm. The population is mainly of African, European, and Asian descent.

Closed in 1985, the oil refinery on the island was reopened in 1993. This is a major source of employment and foreign exchange earnings and has greatly spurred economic growth. Tourism is extensive on the western side of the island, known as the Turquoise Coast, and its rapid development has seen an expansion of other activities.

Fact File

OFFICIAL NAME	Aruba
FORM OF GOVERNMENT	Self-governing part of the Kingdom of the Netherlands
CAPITAL	Oranjestad
AREA	193 sq km (74 sq miles)
TIME ZONE	GMT – 4 hours
POPULATION	68,675
LIFE EXPECTANCY	77
INFANT MORTALITY (PER 1,000)	7.8
LITERACY RATE	Not available
CURRENCY	Aruban florin
ECONOMY	Tourism, financial services
CLIMATE	Tropical
MAP REFERENCE	Page 427

Bermuda

Bermuda is an island in the Atlantic Ocean 900 km (560 miles) off the coast of South Carolina, USA. It has one of the highest per capita incomes in the world, its balmy location and lush vegetation drawing tourists and its financial services offering tax-haven advantages. Bermuda also has one of the world's biggest flag-of-convenience fleets. The largest of some 360 low-lying coral islands which have grown atop ancient submarine volcanoes, it was discovered by the Spaniard Juan Bermudez in 1503, was later taken over by the British, and has a tradition of self-government going back to its first parliament in 1620. Its people are mainly descendants of former African slaves or British or Portuguese settlers. A move for full independence was rejected by 73 percent of voters in 1995, partly for fear of scaring away foreign business. With 90 percent of tourists coming from the US, links with that country are strong.

Fact File

OFFICIAL NAME	Bermuda
FORM OF GOVERNMENT	Dependent territory of the United Kingdom
CAPITAL	Hamilton
AREA	50 sq km (19 sq miles)
TIME ZONE	GMT – 4 hours
POPULATION	63,503
LIFE EXPECTANCY	75
INFANT MORTALITY (PER 1,000)	13.2
LITERACY RATE	Not available
CURRENCY	Bermudian dollar
ECONOMY	Clerical 25%, services 29%, laborers 21%, professional and technical 13%, administrative 10%, agriculture 2%
CLIMATE	Subtropical; windy in winter
MAP REFERENCE	Page 476

Greenland

Greenland is nearly 50 times the size of its "mother country," Denmark, yet it has only 1 percent as much population. It is the biggest island in the world and about 85 percent of its land area is covered by an ice-cap with an average depth of 1,500 m (5,000 ft). Though there are a few sandy and clay plains in the ice-free areas of the island, settlement is confined to the rocky coasts.

It was named "Greenland" by the Viking Erik the Red during the tenth century, in the hope that the name would attract other adventurous Norsemen as settlers. The island became a Danish colony in 1721, an integral part of Denmark in 1973, and received full internal self-government in 1981. Most Greenlanders today are of mixed Inuit and Danish descent, and sometimes live uneasily between these two worlds. The social cost of this divide can be heavy; in the towns alcoholism, venereal disease, and suicide are high.

Greenland's economic prospects are some-what limited in that it is now almost completely dependent on fishing and fish processing. These constitute 95 percent of all exports, and there is the added problem of falling catches of shrimp—in recent years the Arctic fishing industry has contracted. Though it has a certain amount of mineral resources, the last lead and zinc mine was closed in 1990. There is some ship building and also potential for the development of adventure tourism. One problem is the large role of the public sector, which accounts for two-thirds of total employment. About half of government revenue comes from Danish government grants.

British Virgin Islands

East of Puerto Rico in the Caribbean, the British Virgin Islands are the most northerly of the Lesser Antilles. There are four low-lying islands—Tortola, Anegada, Virgin Gorda, and Jost Van Dyke—and 36 coral islets and cays. Most are the peaks of a submerged mountain chain, and they share a subtropical climate moderated by trade winds. With the exception of Anegada, which is flat, the landscape is hilly, with sandy beaches and coral reefs around the coasts. Visited by Columbus in 1493, the British Virgin Islands were for 200 years pirate bases used by the English and the Dutch, until Tortola was annexed by the British in 1672. Today, they are a British dependency enjoying a large measure of self-government, and highly dependent on the tourism which produces some 45 percent of national income. International business makes use of offshore services, incorporation fees generating substantial revenues. Livestock raising is agriculturally important. Soil fertility is low and much food must be imported.

Fact File

OFFICIAL NAME British Virgin Islands

FORM OF GOVERNMENT Dependent territory of the United Kingdom

CAPITAL Road Town

AREA 150 sq km (58 sq miles)

TIME ZONE GMT – 4 hours

POPULATION 13,732

LIFE EXPECTANCY 72.9

INFANT MORTALITY (PER 1,000) 18.7

LITERACY RATE 98.2%

CURRENCY US dollar

ECONOMY Tourism, agriculture

CLIMATE Subtropical, moderated by trade winds

MAP REFERENCE Page 427

Cayman Islands

The largest of Britain's dependencies in the Caribbean, the Cayman Islands consist of three low-lying coral islands south of Cuba and 300 km (186 miles) west of Jamaica. Until the 1960s the main occupations were farming and fishing. Today the islands are one of the world's biggest offshore financial centers, offering a confidential tax haven to some 35,000 companies and several hundred banks. Tourism is also a mainstay, accounting for 70 percent of gross domestic product and 75 percent of foreign currency earnings. Tourism is aimed at the luxury end of the market and caters mainly to visitors from North America. The Cayman Islands were uninhabited when first discovered by Europeans. Most residents today are of mixed Afro-European descent, while an immigrant Jamaican labor force makes up about one-fifth of the population.

Fact File

OFFICIAL NAME Cayman Islands

FORM OF GOVERNMENT Dependent territory of the United Kingdom

CAPITAL George Town

AREA 260 sq km (100 sq miles)

TIME ZONE GMT – 5 hours

POPULATION 39,335

LIFE EXPECTANCY 77.1

INFANT MORTALITY (PER 1,000) 8.4

LITERACY RATE Not available

CURRENCY Caymanian dollar

ECONOMY Services 20%, clerical 20%, construction 13%, finance and investment 10%, directors and business managers 10%, other 27%

CLIMATE Tropical, with cool, dry winters and warm, wet summers

MAP REFERENCE Page 429

Fact File

OFFICIAL NAME Greenland

FORM OF GOVERNMENT Self-governing overseas administrative division of Denmark

CAPITAL Nuuk (Godthab)

AREA 2,175,600 sq km (839,999 sq miles)

TIME ZONE GMT – 1/4 hours

POPULATION 59,827

LIFE EXPECTANCY 70.1

INFANT MORTALITY (PER 1,000) 20.1

LITERACY RATE Not available

CURRENCY Danish krone

ECONOMY Fishing

CLIMATE Polar, with bitterly cold winters and cool to cold summers

MAP REFERENCE Page 411

Most of Greenland is covered by a thick ice cap. Ice floes are visible in the water surrounding the town of Narsaruaq (above left). The French Island of Martinique in the eastern Caribbean (above right).

North and Central America

Guadeloupe

Guadeloupe consists of seven Caribbean islands in the Lesser Antilles, to the southeast of Puerto Rico. The biggest is the high, volcanic Basse-Terre (the active volcano of La Soufrière is the highest point in the Lesser Antilles) lying alongside the slightly smaller flat limestone island of Grande-Terre. A narrow sea channel separates the two. Arawak and Carib Indians were the original inhabitants. The first European settlers to arrive were the French, in 1635. Although there has been considerable agitation for independence, no vote in favor of it has succeeded, and the country is still governed by France—on which it is entirely dependent for subsidies and imported food. Tourism is important, most visitors coming from the USA. Sugar production is being phased out; bananas now supply about 50 percent of export earnings and the cultivation of other crops such as aubergines and flowers is being encouraged.

Fact File

OFFICIAL NAME Department of Guadeloupe

FORM OF GOVERNMENT Overseas department of France

CAPITAL Basse-Terre

AREA 1,780 sq km (687 sq miles)

TIME ZONE GMT – 4 hours

POPULATION 420,943

LIFE EXPECTANCY 78

INFANT MORTALITY (PER 1,000) 8.5

LITERACY RATE 90%

CURRENCY French franc

ECONOMY Services 65%, industry 20%, agriculture 15%

CLIMATE Subtropical, moderated by trade winds

MAP REFERENCE Page 427

Jan Mayen

The mountainous island of Jan Mayen lies in the Arctic Ocean about 900 km (560 miles) west of Norway. It is volcanic, with the mighty active Beerenberg volcano rising 2,400 m (7,874 ft) straight out of the surf. From its ice-cap some 15 glaciers descend into the sea. Once an important base for Arctic whaling, Jan Mayen's only resources today are rich fishing grounds. These were the subject of a long dispute with Greenland over fishing rights, and possible oil and gas

deposits. Mediated by the International Court of Justice, the two parties reached a compromise on this issue in 1993. The island's birdlife is spectacular and includes millions of fulmar, petrel, kittiwake, little auk, guillemot, and puffin.

Fact File

OFFICIAL NAME Jan Mayen

FORM OF GOVERNMENT Territory of Norway

CAPITAL None

AREA 373 sq km (144 sq miles)

TIME ZONE GMT – 1 hour

POPULATION No permanent population

ECONOMY Radio and meteorological stations

CLIMATE Polar: cold, windy, and foggy

MAP REFERENCE Page 411

Martinique

Christopher Columbus described Martinique as "the most beautiful country in the world" when he laid eyes on it in 1493. This island in the eastern Caribbean was colonized by France in 1635 and has been French ever since. It consists of three groups of volcanic hills and the intervening lowlands, and is dominated by the dormant volcano Mt Pelée. Mt Pelée is famous for the eruption of 1902, when it killed all the inhabitants of the town of St-Pierre except one prisoner, who was saved by the thickness of his prison cell. The economy is based on sugarcane, bananas, tourism, and light industry, the export of bananas being of growing importance. Most sugarcane is used for making rum. The majority of the workforce is in the service sector and administration, tourism having become more important than agricultural exports as a source of foreign exchange.

Fact File

OFFICIAL NAME Department of Martinique

FORM OF GOVERNMENT Overseas department of France

CAPITAL Fort-de-France

AREA 1,100 sq km (425 sq miles)

TIME ZONE GMT – 4 hours

POPULATION 411,539

LIFE EXPECTANCY 79.3

INFANT MORTALITY (PER 1,000) 6.8

LITERACY RATE 92.8%

CURRENCY French franc

ECONOMY Services 73%, industry 17%, agriculture 10%

CLIMATE Tropical, moderated by trade winds; wet season June to October

MAP REFERENCE Page 427

The colonial legacy

The Caribbean contains many small island states and a significant number of dependencies. This diversity in status is the legacy of centuries of engagement with colonial powers. After Columbus discovered the area at the end of the fifteenth century, Spain took possession of many islands, but Great Britain, France and the Netherlands also claimed, fought over and exploited the Caribbean. From the end of the fifteenth century to the middle of the eighteenth century the indigenous people were nearly wiped out and replaced by a much larger population of Europeans and African slaves, imported to work in the sugar, tobacco and coffee plantations that dominated the local economies. The Caribbean has long served as an important trading route between North and South Americas and to Europe and the East.

The result is a diversity of economic, social and political interests. Some islands have retained their colonial status while others chose independence. The mixture of races (Carib, African and European) and cultures has created national identities marked by different peoples, languages, customs and political systems.

North and Central America

Montserrat

Montserrat is a Caribbean island with seven active volcanoes. In 1995 deep ash from one of them destroyed numerous crops and forced the evacuation of the capital, Plymouth. Montserrat was colonized in 1632 by the British, who at first brought in Irish settlers. (Together with its lush green foliage, this is why it is locally known as "the Emerald Isle.") Later, the island's sugar plantations were worked by African slaves. It has been a self-governing UK dependent territory since 1960. Tourism provides a quarter of the national income, other support coming from the export of electronic components which are assembled on the island, plastic bags, clothing, rum, hot peppers, live plants, and cattle. Data processing facilities and offshore banking are available.

Fact File

OFFICIAL NAME Montserrat

FORM OF GOVERNMENT Dependent territory of the United Kingdom

CAPITAL Plymouth

AREA 100 sq km (39 sq miles)

TIME ZONE GMT – 4 hours

POPULATION 4,000 (after volcanic eruption led to evacuation; formerly 12,853)

LIFE EXPECTANCY 75.6

INFANT MORTALITY (PER 1,000) 12

LITERACY RATE Not available

CURRENCY EC dollar

ECONOMY Tourism, industry, agriculture

CLIMATE Tropical

MAP REFERENCE Page 427

Navassa Island

Navassa Island is an uninhabited rocky outcrop in the Caribbean halfway between Cuba and Haiti. It is strategically located for the USA, since it is 160 km (100 miles) south of the Guantanamo Bay (Bahía de Guantánamo) naval base. The island is administered by the US Coast Guard. The surface is mostly exposed rock but it has dense stands of fig-like trees, cacti, and enough grass to support herds of goats. Its principal resource is guano.

Fact File

OFFICIAL NAME Navassa Island

FORM OF GOVERNMENT Unincorporated territory of the United States

CAPITAL None

AREA 5.2 sq km (2 sq miles)

TIME ZONE GMT – 5 hours

POPULATION No permanent population

CLIMATE Tropical, moderated by sea breezes

MAP REFERENCE Page 429

The oceanfront in old San Juan, Puerto Rico (below). Mud and lava from the 1995 volcanic eruption on Montserrat (bottom). The Virgin Islands of the United States (above right).

Netherlands Antilles

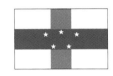

The Netherlands Antilles consist of two very different island groups in two parts of the Caribbean. Curaçao and Bonaire are located off the coast of Venezuela, and while they may once have made money from the well-known orange liqueur, today 98 percent of their income comes from petroleum—either processed for products or for transshipment facilities. The other group, which lies east of the Virgin Islands, consists of the three islands of Saba, St Eustasius, and part of St Maarten. The people are largely of African and European descent, the original inhabitants having been killed in the sixteenth century by Spanish settlers. All told, the islands have a high per capita income and a well-developed infrastructure in comparison with others in the region. Nearly all consumer and capital goods are imported from the USA and Venezuela. Crops grown include aloes, sorghum, peanuts, vegetables, and tropical fruit, but poor soils and limited water make agriculture difficult.

Fact File

OFFICIAL NAME Netherlands Antilles

FORM OF GOVERNMENT Self-governing part of the Kingdom of the Netherlands

CAPITAL Willemstad

AREA 960 sq km (371 sq miles)

TIME ZONE GMT – 4 hours

POPULATION 215,139

LIFE EXPECTANCY 77.4

INFANT MORTALITY (PER 1,000) 8.5

CURRENCY Netherlands Antillean guilder

ECONOMY Tourism, offshore finance

CLIMATE Tropical, moderated by trade winds

MAP REFERENCE Page 427

Puerto Rico

Fact File

OFFICIAL NAME Commonwealth of Puerto Rico

FORM OF GOVERNMENT Commonwealth associated with the United States

CAPITAL San Juan

AREA 9,104 sq km (3,515 sq miles)

TIME ZONE GMT – 4 hours

POPULATION 3,890,353

LIFE EXPECTANCY 75.2

INFANT MORTALITY (PER 1,000) 10.5

LITERACY RATE 87.8%

CURRENCY US dollar

ECONOMY Government 22%, manufacturing 17%, trade 20%, construction 6%, communications and transportation 5%, other 30%

CLIMATE Tropical, moderated by sea breezes

MAP REFERENCE Page 427

Puerto Rico is a large Caribbean island east of the Dominican Republic. Ceded by Spain to the USA in 1898, its citizens enjoy a number of privileges as a result of their American connection (for example, Puerto Ricans have full US citizenship, pay no federal taxes, and have free access to the US). In 1993 the population once more voted to continue their self-governing commonwealth status and forgo becoming either the 51st state of the USA or independent. Mountainous, with a narrow coastal plain, the little flat ground available for agriculture is used for growing sugarcane, coffee, bananas, and tobacco. Today, Puerto Rico's economy is essentially modern and industrialized. Tax relief and cheap labor have brought many businesses to the island and tourism is growing. Industries include petrochemicals, pharmaceuticals (the island produces over 90 percent of all US

tranquillizers), and electronics. The standard of living in Puerto Rico is the highest in Latin America (outside the island tax havens), and is rising.

St Pierre and Miquelon

 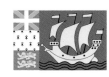

St Pierre and Miquelon are islands in the North Atlantic Ocean, south of Newfoundland. They are cold and wet and have little vegetation. Surrounded by some of the world's richest fishing grounds, the islands were settled by French fishermen in the seventeenth century. Since then the inhabitants have earned a living from fishing and by servicing the foreign trawler fleets that operate off the coast. A dispute between Canada and France over fishing and mineral rights was settled in 1992. Since the French subsidize the islands, and their economy has been declining, the authorities are now trying to diversify by developing port facilities and encouraging tourism.

Fact File

OFFICIAL NAME Territorial collectivity of St Pierre and Miquelon

FORM OF GOVERNMENT Territorial collectivity of France

CAPITAL St-Pierre

AREA 242 sq km (93 sq miles)

TIME ZONE GMT – 4 hours

POPULATION 6,966

LIFE EXPECTANCY 77.1

INFANT MORTALITY (PER 1,000) 8.1

LITERACY RATE 99%

CURRENCY French franc

ECONOMY Mainly fishing and fish processing

CLIMATE Cold, wet, and foggy

MAP REFERENCE Page 417

Turks and Caicos Islands

The Turks and Caicos Islands are a group of 30 islands, 8 of them inhabited, north of Hispaniola. They are composed of low, flat, scrub-covered limestone, with areas of marsh and swamp. There is little land for agriculture, though cassava, maize, citrus fruits, and beans are grown on Caicos by subsistence farmers. Today, the islands' economy is mainly based on tourism, fishing, and offshore

financial services. Nearly all consumer and capital goods are imported. The islands have been British since 1766, and a crown colony since 1973.

Fact File

OFFICIAL NAME Turks and Caicos Islands

FORM OF GOVERNMENT Dependent territory of the United Kingdom

CAPITAL Grand Turk

AREA 430 sq km (166 sq miles)

TIME ZONE GMT – 5 hours

POPULATION 15,192

LIFE EXPECTANCY 75.5

INFANT MORTALITY (PER 1,000) 12.4

LITERACY RATE Not available

CURRENCY US dollar

ECONOMY Fishing, tourism, agriculture

CLIMATE Tropical, moderated by trade winds

MAP REFERENCE Page 429

Virgin Islands of the United States

The US Virgin Islands consist of 68 hilly volcanic islands east of Puerto Rico in the Caribbean. They are on a key shipping lane and were bought from Denmark by the USA in 1917 to protect the approaches to the Panama Canal. They contain, on St Croix, one of the world's largest oil refineries but tourism is still the main economic activity, accounting for over 70 percent of the island's gross domestic product and 70 percent of employment. Manufacturing includes textiles, pharmaceuticals, electronics, and watch assembly. Business and financial services are also of growing importance. Agriculture is limited, most food being imported.

Fact File

OFFICIAL NAME Virgin Islands of the United States

FORM OF GOVERNMENT Unincorporated territory of the United States

CAPITAL Charlotte Amalie

AREA 352 sq km (136 sq miles)

TIME ZONE GMT + 7 hours

POPULATION 119,555

LIFE EXPECTANCY 78.5

INFANT MORTALITY (PER 1,000) 9.4

LITERACY RATE Not available

CURRENCY US dollar

ECONOMY Tourism, light industry, agriculture

CLIMATE Subtropical; wet season May to November

MAP REFERENCE Page 427

North and Central America

North and Central America: Physical

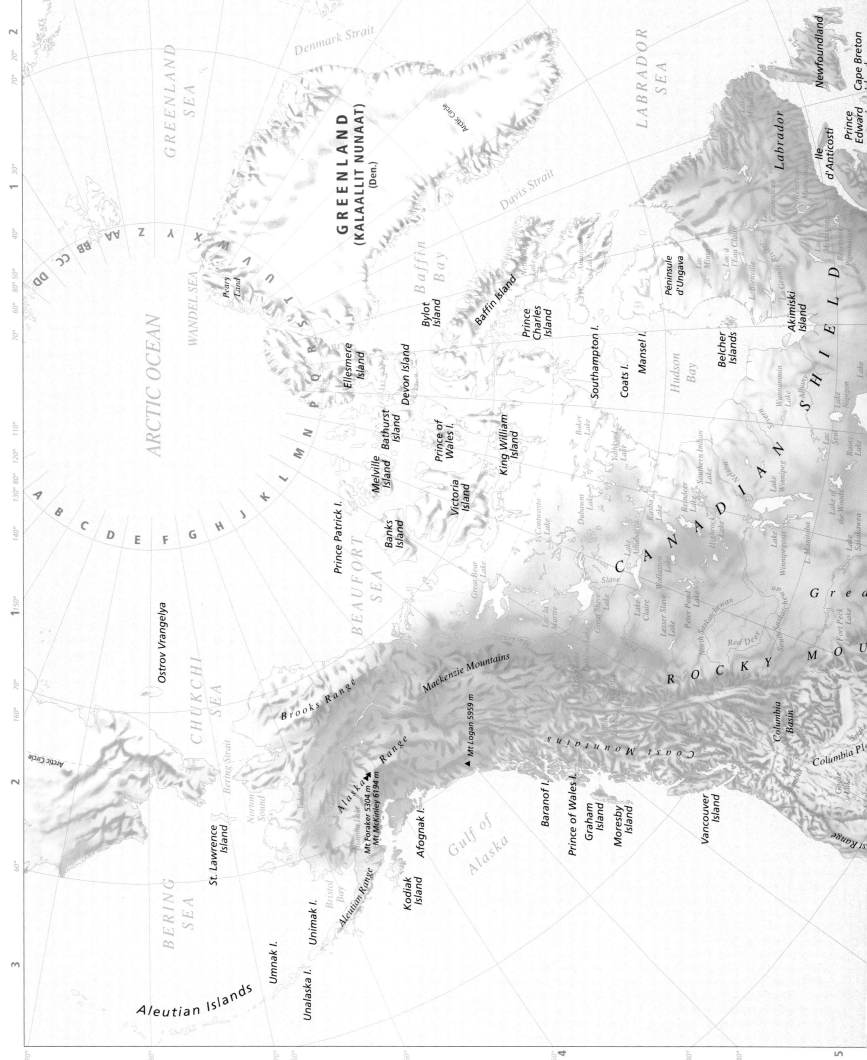

GREENLAND SEA

Denmark Strait

ARCTIC OCEAN

WANDEL SEA

Peary Land

GREENLAND
(KALAALLIT NUNAAT)
(Den.)

Arctic Circle

LABRADOR SEA

Newfoundland

Cape Breton I.

Labrador

Ile d'Anticosti

Prince Edward I.

Davis Strait

Baffin Bay

Baffin Island

Bylot Island

Péninsule d'Ungava

Ellesmere Island

Devon Island

Prince Charles Island

Akimiski Island

Southampton I.

Coats I.

Mansel I.

Belcher Islands

Bathurst Island

Melville Island

Prince of Wales I.

King William I.

Hudson Bay

CANADIAN SHIELD

Banks Island

Victoria Island

Baker Lake

Prince Patrick I.

Dubawnt Lake

Lake Winnipeg

Lake Manitoba

Lake of the Woods

Great Bear Lake

Contwoyto Lake

Reindeer Lake

Southern Indian Lake

Lac la Martre

Slave

Lake Athabasca

Great Slave Lake

Wollaston Lake

Peter Pond Lake

Lesser Slave Lake

Lake Claire

North Saskatchewan

South Saskatchewan

Red Deer

Fort Peck

BEAUFORT SEA

Ostrov Vrangelya

Brooks Range

Mackenzie Mountains

Mt Logan 5959 m

ROCKY MOUNTAINS

Columbia Basin

Great

Columbia Pl

CHUKCHI SEA

Arctic Circle

Alaska Range

Mt Foraker 5304 m
Mt McKinley 6194 m

Coast Mountains

Bering Strait

Norton Sound

BERING SEA

St. Lawrence Island

Bristol Bay

Gulf of Alaska

Baranof I.

Prince of Wales I.

Graham Island

Moresby Island

Vancouver Island

Aleutian Range

Kodiak Island

Afognak I.

Umnak I.

Unalaska I.

Unimak I.

Aleutian Islands

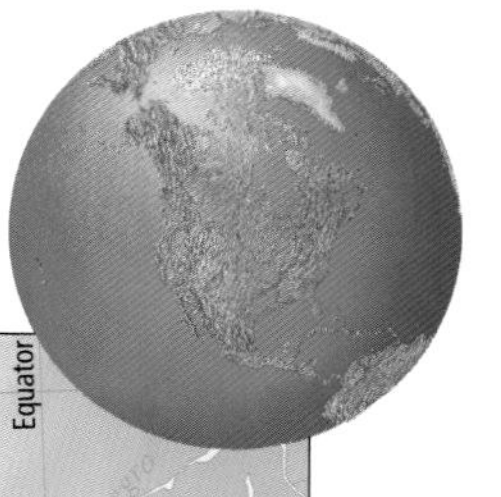

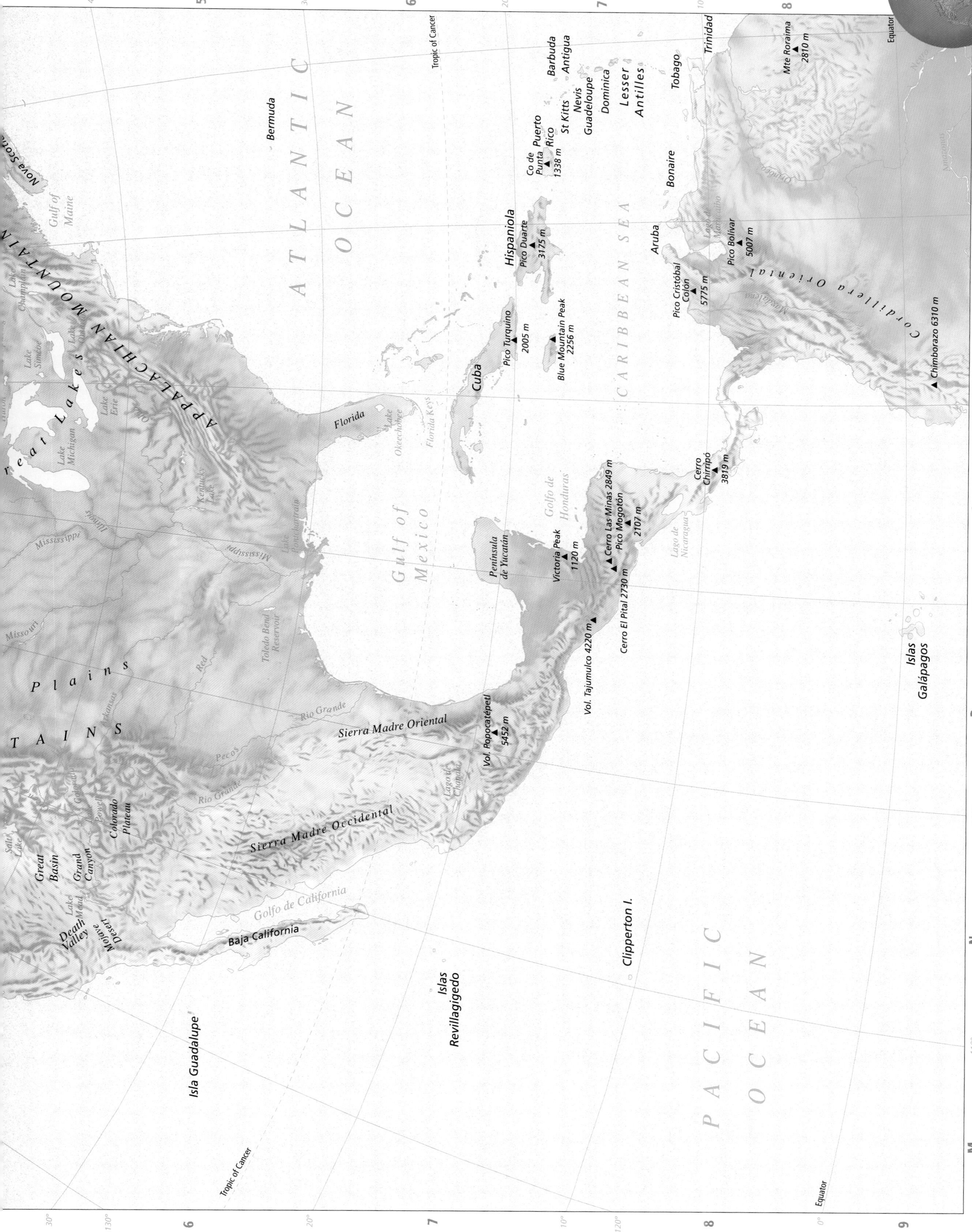

ATLANTIC OCEAN
PACIFIC OCEAN
CARIBBEAN SEA
Gulf of Mexico
Gulf of Maine
Golfo de Honduras
Golfo de California
Nova Scotia
Bermuda
Puerto Rico
Co de Punta 1338 m
Barbuda
Antigua
St Kitts
Nevis
Guadeloupe
Dominica
Lesser Antilles
Tobago
Trinidad
Bonaire
Aruba
Hispaniola
Pico Duarte 3175 m
Cuba
Pico Turquino 2005 m
Blue Mountain Peak 2256 m
Florida
Florida Keys
Lake Okeechobee
Mte Roraima 2810 m
Pico Bolívar 5007 m
Pico Cristóbal Colón 5775 m
Cordillera Oriental
Chimborazo 6310 m
Lago de Maracaibo
Magdalena
Orinoco
Amazonas
Negro
Equator
Tropic of Cancer
APPALACHIAN MOUNTAINS
Great Lakes
Lake Champlain
Lake Ontario
Lake Simcoe
Lake Erie
Lake Huron
Lake Michigan
Kentucky Lake
Illinois
Mississippi
Missouri
Lake Pontchartrain
Toledo Bend Reservoir
Red
Arkansas
Plains
MOUNTAINS
Rio Grande
Pecos
Sierra Madre Oriental
Sierra Madre Occidental
Vol. Popocatépetl 5452 m
Lago de Chapala
Península de Yucatán
Victoria Peak 1120 m
Cerro Las Minas 2849 m
Pico Mogotón 2107 m
Cerro El Pital 2730 m
Vol. Tajumulco 4220 m
Lago de Nicaragua
Cerro Chirripó 3819 m
Islas Galápagos
Clipperton I.
Islas Revillagigedo
Isla Guadalupe
Baja California
Colorado Plateau
Grand Canyon
Lake Powell
Great Basin
Salt Lake
Lake Mead
Death Valley
Mojave Desert
5
6
7
8
9
M
N
P
Q
R
S
10°
20°
30°
40°
70°
80°
90°
100°
110°
120°
130°
0°

0 150 300 450 600 750 kilometers

0 150 300 450 miles

Scale 1:15,000,000 Projection: Conic Equidistant

North and Central America

North and Central America: Political

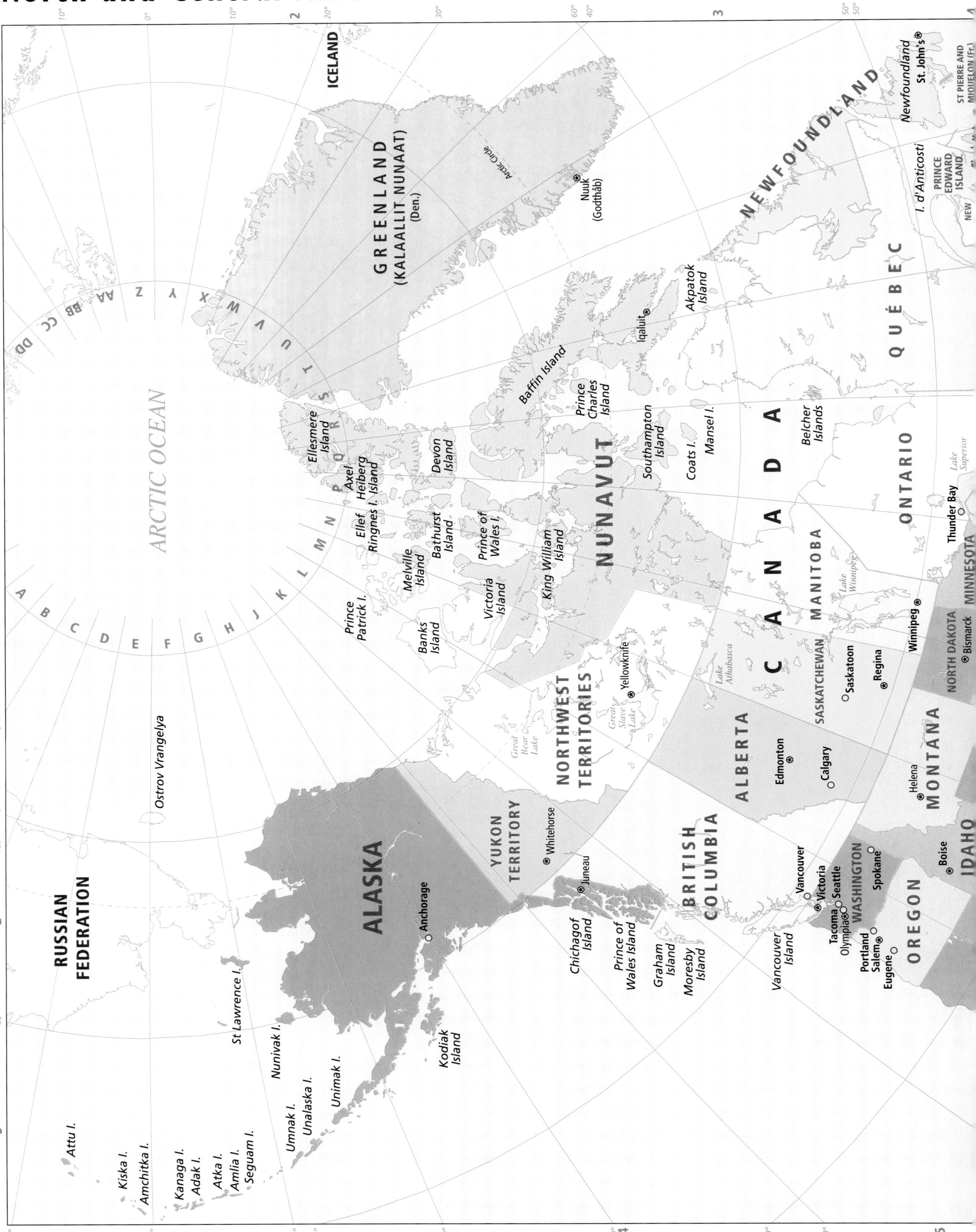

ICELAND

GREENLAND
(KALAALLIT NUNAAT)
(Den.)

Arctic Circle

Nuuk
(Godthåb) ⊛

NEWFOUNDLAND

ST PIERRE AND
MIQUELON (Fr.)
St John's ⊛
Newfoundland

PRINCE
EDWARD
ISLAND
NEW
I. d'Anticosti

ARCTIC OCEAN

QUÉBEC

Baffin Island

Ellesmere
Island

Axel
Heiberg I.

Devon
Island

Prince
Charles
Island

Iqaluit ⊛

Akpatok
Island

Ellef
Ringnes I.

Bathurst
Island

Southampton
Island

Mansel I.

Coats I.

Belcher
Islands

ONTARIO

Lake
Superior

Melville
Island

Prince of
Wales I.

NUNAVUT

CANADA

Prince
Patrick I.

Victoria
Island

King William
Island

Thunder Bay ⊛

Banks
Island

MANITOBA

Lake
Winnipeg

MINNESOTA

Ostrov Vrangelya

NORTHWEST
TERRITORIES

Yellowknife ⊛

SASKATCHEWAN

Saskatoon ○

Winnipeg ⊛

NORTH DAKOTA

Bismarck ⊛

Great
Bear
Lake

Lake
Athabasca

Regina ⊛

Great
Slave
Lake

ALBERTA

Edmonton ⊛

RUSSIAN
FEDERATION

YUKON
TERRITORY

Whitehorse ⊛

Calgary ○

Helena ⊛

MONTANA

ALASKA

BRITISH
COLUMBIA

Juneau ⊛

Anchorage ○

Boise ⊛

IDAHO

Vancouver ○

Spokane ○

St Lawrence I.

Chichagof
Island

Prince of
Wales Island

Graham
Island

Moresby
Island

Vancouver
Island

Victoria ⊛
Seattle ○
Tacoma ○
Olympia ⊛
Portland ○
Salem ⊛
Eugene ○

WASHINGTON

OREGON

Nunivak I.

Umnak I.
Unalaska I.
Unimak I.

Kodiak
Island

Attu I.

Kiska I.
Amchitka I.

Kanaga I.
Adak I.

Atka I.
Amlia I.
Seguam I.

40°

5

30°

6

20°

7

10°

8

Tropic of Cancer

GUYANA

Equator

BRAZIL

NOVA SCOTIA

Halifax

MAINE

Montréal

Ottawa

Lake Ontario

VERMONT

NEW HAMPSHIRE

Augusta

Concord

Montpelier

NEW YORK

MASSACHUSETTS

Boston

Albany

Hartford

Providence

RHODE ISLAND

Buffalo

CONNECTICUT

New York

NEW JERSEY

PENNSYLVANIA

Harrisburg

Trenton

Dover

DELAWARE

Annapolis

Washington D.C.

MARYLAND

Toronto

Hamilton

Detroit

Lake Erie

OHIO

Columbus

W.VIRGINIA

Charleston

Richmond

VIRGINIA

Virginia Beach

MICHIGAN

Milwaukee

Lansing

Chicago

INDIANA

Frankfort

Indianapolis

KENTUCKY

NORTH CAROLINA

Raleigh

Charlotte

WISCONSIN

Madison

ILLINOIS

Springfield

St Louis

Louisville

Nashville

TENNESSEE

Chattanooga

Columbia

SOUTH CAROLINA

Charleston

Savannah

Minneapolis

St.Paul

IOWA

Davenport

MISSOURI

Memphis

Birmingham

Atlanta

GEORGIA

Columbus

ATLANTIC

OCEAN

BERMUDA (U.K.)

Des Moines

Jefferson City

ALABAMA

Montgomery

Tallahassee

Jacksonville

Pierre

NEBRASKA

Lincoln

KANSAS

Topeka

OKLAHOMA

Oklahoma City

ARKANSAS

Little Rock

MISSISSIPPI

Jackson

Mobile

New Orleans

LOUISIANA

Baton Rouge

FLORIDA

Orlando

St Petersburg

Tampa

Fort Lauderdale

Miami

BAHAMAS

Nassau

Tropic of Cancer

WYOMING

Cheyenne

COLORADO

Denver

Pueblo

Amarillo

NEW MEXICO

Santa Fe

Albuquerque

UNITED STATES

OF AMERICA

TEXAS

Lubbock

Fort Worth

Dallas

Shreveport

Austin

Houston

Corpus Christi

Matamoros

La Habana (Havana)

Pinar del Rio

CUBA

Matanzas

Cienfuegos

Bayamo

Santiago de Cuba

CAYMAN ISLANDS (U.K.)

TURKS AND CAICOS ISLANDS (U.K.)

DOMINICAN REPUBLIC

HAITI

Port-au-Prince

Santo Domingo

JAMAICA

Kingston

CARIBBEAN SEA

PUERTO RICO

VIRGIN ISLANDS (U.S.A.)

VIRGIN ISLANDS (U.K.)

ANGUILLA (U.K.)

ST KITTS AND NEVIS

Basseterre

MONTSERRAT (U.K.)

ANTIGUA AND BARBUDA

St Johns

GUADELOUPE (Fr.)

DOMINICA

Roseau

MARTINIQUE (Fr.)

Castries

ST LUCIA

BARBADOS

Bridgetown

ST VINCENT AND THE GRENADINES

GRENADA

St George's

TRINIDAD AND TOBAGO

Port of Spain

VENEZUELA

ARUBA (Neth.)

NETHERLANDS ANTILLES (Neth.)

COLOMBIA

PERU

ECUADOR

SALT LAKE CITY

UTAH

NEVADA

Las Vegas

CALIFORNIA

Modesto

Fresno

Bakersfield

ARIZONA

Phoenix

Mesa

Tucson

San Jose

Oakland

Anaheim

Long Beach

Los Angeles

San Diego

Mexicali

Ensenada

El Paso

Chihuahua

Hermosillo

MEXICO

Nuevo Laredo

Monterrey

San Luis Potosi

Tampico

Léon

Querétaro

Guadalajara

Morelia

México

Cuernavaca

Acapulco

Puebla de Zaragoza

Coatzacoalcos

Tuxtla Gutiérrez

Campeche

Mérida

Veracruz

BELIZE

Belmopan

GUATEMALA

Guatemala

EL SALVADOR

San Salvador

HONDURAS

Tegucigalpa

NICARAGUA

Managua

COSTA RICA

San José

PANAMA

Panamá

Isla de Coiba

Islas Galápagos (Ecu.)

Isla Guadalupe (Mex.)

La Paz

Islas Revillagigedo (Mex.)

PACIFIC

OCEAN

Tropic of Cancer

Equator

| 0 | 150 | 300 | 450 | 600 | 750 | kilometers |
| 0 | 150 | 300 | 450 | miles |

Scale 1:15,000,000   Projection: Conic Equidistant

409

North Canada · Alaska · Greenland

301
418
413

RUSSIAN FEDERATION

Chukotskiy Poluostrov

Koryakskoye Nagor'ye

Mys Navarin

Anadyr
Ugol'nyye Kopi
Iul'tin
Arctic Circle

Ostrov Vrangelya

Ushakovskoye

CHUKCHI SEA

Mys Chukotskiy
St. Lawrence I.
C. Lisburne
Point Hope

BERING SEA

Bering Strait

Anadyrskiy Zaliv

St Matthew I.
St Lawrence I.

Nunivak I.

Scammon Bay
Nome
Kotzebue
Shungnak
Husla

Brooks Range

Wainwright
Pt Barrow
Barrow
Nuiqsuto
Umiat
Sagwon
Deadhorse
Kaktovik
Herschel

BEAUFORT SEA

Borden I.
Mackenzie King I.
Prince Patrick I.

C. Prince Alfred
Melville

Banks Island

Passage Point

Sachso Harbour

Prince Albert Peninsula

Holman

Victoria Island

U. S. A.

ALASKA

Kuskokwim Mountains

Ruby
Tanana
Alakaket

Kotik
Togiako
Dillingham

C. Newenham

Bristol Bay

Kuskokwim Bay
Bethel

Kuskokwim

Mt McKinley 6194 m

Alaska Range

Cantwell
Fairbanks
Delta Junction
Tok

Fort Yukon
Chalkyitsik

Sheenjek

Mt Greenough 2207 m

Old Crow

Aklavik
Inuvik
Fort McPherson
Tsiigehtchic

C. Bathurst

C. Parry

Paulatuk

Wollaston Peninsula

Cambridge Bay

Kugluktuko

Coronation Gulf

Kent Pen.

Alaska Pen.
Aleutian Range

Shelikof Strait
Afognak I.
Kodiak
Kodiak I.

Kenai
Homer
Seward
Palmer
Anchorage
Chugach Mountains
Glennallen
Cordova

Gulf of Alaska

Beaver Creek
Snag
Korden Burwash Landing
Kluane
Haines Junction

Mt Logan 5959 m

Yakutat

Carcross
Skagway

Carmacks
Dawson
Mayo
Pelly Crossing

Ogilvie Mountains

YUKON TERRITORY

Faro
Ross River

Selwyn Mountains

Keele Peak 2972 m

Good Hope
Fort Good Hope

Norman Wells

Colville Lake

Déline

Great Bear Lake

Contwoyto Lake

Bathursto Inlet

NORTHWEST TERRITORIES

Whitehorse
Atlin
Teslin

Juneau
Sitka
Petersburg
Wrangell
Ketchikan

Alexander Archipelago

Watson Lake

Cassiar
Meziah Peak 2164 m
Dease Lake
Telegraph Creek

Toad River
Summit
Fort Nelson

Liard River
Fort Liard

Wrigley

Mackenzie Mountains

Franklin Mountains

Fort Simpson

Kakisa

Edzoo
Rae Lakes

Rae
Yellowknife

Lac la Martre

Great Slave Lake

Fort Providence
Hay River

Lutselk'e

Aylmer Lake

Back

Dubawnt Lake

Thelon

Stewart
Prince Rupert
Graham I.
Moresby I.
Queen Charlotte Is
C. Knox

BRITISH COLUMBIA

Coast Mountains

Cassiar Mountains

Ware
Trutch

Rainbow Lake
High Level

Fort Smith
Fitzgerald
Chipewyan
Fort

Kasba Lake

Black Lake

Stony Rapids

Wollaston Lake

New Hazelton
Hazelton
Terrace
Houston
Kemano
Burns Lake
Smithers

Hudsons Hope
Chetwynd

Fort St John
Dawson Creek

Fort Manning
Fort Vermilion

Carcajou

Birch Mts 843 m

Fort MacKay

Cree Lake

Reindeer Lake

Southendo

Bella Coola
Ootsa Lake
Vanderhoof
Prince George

McLeod Lake

Spirit River
Peace River

Grande Prairie
Hythe

Peace River

Lake Claire

Fort McMurray

Conklin

La Loche

Rivers Inlet
C. Scott
Port Hardy

Mt Waddington 4016 m

Hanceville
Williams Lake
Quesnel
McBride

ALBERTA

ROCKY MOUNTAINS

Columbia

Whitecourt
Hinton
Edson

Assiniboine
Slave Lake
Faust

Atikameg

Athabasca

Westlock

Pierceland
Cold Lake

Churchill Lake

Forto Black

Pukatawa

SASKATCHEWAN

La Ronge

Southendo

Vancouver Island
Kelsey Bay
Campbell River
Tofino
Nanaimo

Cache Creek

Clearwater

Mt Columbia 3747 m

Jasper
Wetaskiwin
Edmonton
Leduc
Vegreville
Vermilion

Lloydminster

Waskesiu
Prince Albert
Biggaro
North Battleford

Victoria
Burnaby
Vancouver

C. Flattery

Mt Olympus 2424 m
Olympia
Tacoma
Seattle

WASHINGTON
U. S. A.

Kamloops
Golden
Didsbury
Banff

Kelowna
Penticton
Cranbrook

Drumheller
Red Deer
Ponoka
Castor
Hanna

Medicine Hat
Cereal

Claresholm
Lethbridge
Cardston
Magrath

Rosetown
Calgary

North Battleford
Unity
Kindersley

Watrouso

Davidson
Wynyard
Yorkton

Melfort
Hudson Bay

Saskatoon

Moose Jaw
Swift Current

Canora
Dauph

Melville
Foxwar

Regina

CANADA

PACIFIC OCEAN

1

2

ARCTIC
OCEAN

LINCOLN SEA
Kap Bridgman
Kap Eiler Rasmussen
WANDEL HAVET
Nord
Hovgaard Ø
Norske Øer
Île de France
Kap Marie Valdemar
Store Koldewey
Shannon Ø
Daneborg

JAN MAYEN (Nor.)

Arctic Circle

10°

1920 m
2103 m
1190 m
Peary Land
Narres Land
Kong Frederik VIII Land
2680 m
Kong Christian X Land
Petermanns Bjerg 2939 m
Mestersvig
Traill Ø
Kong Oscar Fjord
Ittoqqortoormiit
Kangikajik

GREENLAND SEA

Seyðisfjörður
2119 m Höfn
Fagurhólsmýri
ICELAND
Raufarhöfn Akureyri
Blönduós
Stykkishólmur
Reykjavík
Hafnarfjörður
Vík

20°

Alert Pt
Alert
Ellesmere Island
Nares Strait

Kane Basin

2012 m

Meighen I.
Axel
Eureka
Heiberg Island
Graham I.
Amund Ringnes

Queen
Elizabeth
Islands

Norwegian Bay

Bathurst Island

Parry Islands

Smith Sound

Siorapaluk
Qaanaaq (Thule)
Kap Parry
Uummannaq
Grise Fiord
Coburg I.

Kap York
Savissivik
Kap Seddon
Kullorsuaq
Nuussuaq
Upernavik
Tasiusaq

2935 m

Kong Christian IX Land
3147 m
Gunnbjørn Fjeld 3700 m
1920 m
Kap Vedel
Kap Gustav Holm
Sermiligaaq
Ammassalik
Mont Forel 3360 m

Kong Frederik VI Kyst

Timmiarmiut

Kangeq

30°

Jones Sd

Devon Island
Philpots I.
C. Sherard
Resolute
Somerset Island
Crawford
Arctic Bay
Bylot I.
Pond Inlet

Baffin Bay

Illorsuit
Uummannaq
Qeqertarsuaq (Disko)
1234 m
Qeqertarsuatsiaq
Ataa
Qasigiannguit (Christianshåb)
Ilulissat
Kangaatsiaq
Qeqertarsuup Tunua

Kong Frederik VIII Land

Kangerlussuaq

Davis Strait

J.A.D. Jensen Nunatakker 1680 m

40°

50°

60°

Bathurst Island
Prince of Wales Island
Boothia Peninsula

Prince Regent Inlet
Gulf of Boothia

Brodeur Pen.

C. Baffin
C. Adair

Baffin Island

Clyde River
C. Raper
Henry Kater Pen.
Home Bay
Kangeeak Pt

Kangerlussuaq
Sisimiut
2440 m

Maniitsoq
Atammik
Nuuk (Godthåb)
Qeqertarsuatsiaat
Kapisillit

Nunap Isua

Ede Point
King William Island
Gjoa Haven
Pelly Bay
Melville Pen.
Igloolik
Hall Beach

Larsen Sound

Netilling Lake

C. Dyer
Cumberland Pen.
Pangnirtung
C. Mercy

Cumberland Sound

Paamiut
Kangilinnguit
Narsarsuaq
Ivittuut
Qaqortoq
Nanortalik

NUNAVUT

C. Wilson
C. Dominion

Foxe Basin

Amadjuak Lake

Hall Pen.

LABRADOR SEA

ATLANTIC OCEAN

Repulse Bay

Foxe Channel

Iqaluit
Foxe Pen.
Cape Dorset
Salisbury I.
Nottingham I.
Mansel I.

Meta Incognita Pen.
Frobisher Bay
Kimmirut

Resolution I.

C. Dobbs
Southampton Island
Coral Harbour
C. Low
Evans Strait

Baker Lake
Chesterfield Inlet
Rankin Inlet
C. Jones
Whale Cove

Ivujivik
Salluit
Akuliviko
Coats I.

Kangiqsujuaq
Quaqtaq
Killiniq C. Chidley
Akpatok I.

Torngat Mts

Hebron
Okak Is

Baker Lake
Daly Bay

Hudson Strait

Arviat

Yathkyed Lake

Kangirsuk
Péninsule d'Ungava
Puvirnituq
Lac Payne
Ottawa Is
Inukjuak

Ungava Bay
Kangiqsualujjuaq
Kuujjuaq

Nain
Davis Inlet
Hopedale
C. Harrison

NEWFOUNDLAND

Port Hope Simpson
Red Bay
St Anthony

50°

Hudson Bay

Button Bay
C. Churchill
Churchill
C. Tatnam

Seal
Tadoule Lake

Belcher Is
Sanikiluaq

Lac Minto

Lac à l'Eau Claire

Schefferville
Esker
Churchill Falls
Twin Falls
Labrador City
Wabush
Waco
Gagnon
Pitaga

Labrador

Happy Valley-Goose Bay
Cartwright

Hamilton Inlet

Belle Isle

50°

Nelson
York Factory
Gillam
Shamattawa

Kuujjuarapik
Fort Severn
Winisk
Peawanuck
C. Henrietta Maria
Chisasibi

Rés. de La Grande Deux

QUÉBEC

Rés. de Caniapiscau

Laurentian Mts

Natashquan
Sept-Îles
Havre-St-Pierre
Île d'Anticosti

Stephenville
Channel-Port aux Basques
Burgeo

Springdale
Grand Falls-Windsor
La Scie
Wesleyville
Bonavista

St John's
Grand Bank
C. St Mary's

MANITOBA

Wabowden
Norway House
Island Lake
Warren Landing
Deer Lake
Lake Winnipeg

Thompson
Pikangikum
South Bay
Manigotagan
Eriksdale

Summer Beaver
Webequie
Attawapiskat

ONTARIO

Lansdowne House
Pickle Lake
Ogoki
Moosonee
Moose Factory
Albany
Eastmain
Waskaganish
Matagami
Chibougamau
Mistassini

Lac Mistassini
Lac St-Jean

Forestville
Jonquière
Chicoutimi
Dolbeau
Baie-Comeau
Bonaventure
Gaspé

Gulf of St Lawrence

PRINCE EDWARD ISLAND
Charlottetown

NEW BRUNSWICK
Moncton

NOVA SCOTIA

Sydney
Cape Breton I.
Canso

Grand Falls
Rimouski
Bathurst
St Lawrence
St Pierre
ST PIERRE AND MIQUELON (Fr.)

Miquelon

K

L

M

N

90°

80°

70°

60°

0   200   400   600   800 kilometers
0   200   400 miles
Scale 1:15,000,000
Projection: Azimuthal Equal Area

West Canada

A 136° B 134° C 132° D 130° E 410 128° F 126° G 124° H 122° J

YUKON

Whitehorse

Robinson

Carcross

Jakes Corner

Teslin

Johnsons Crossing

TERRITORY

Mt Murray
2162 m

Watson Lake

Fort Liard

Skagway

Mt Hays
2704 m

Atlin

Nakina

Coal River

Liard River

Muncho Lake

Toad River

Fort Nelson

Mt Fairweather
4663 m

Cassiar

Good Hope Lake

Stikine

Plateau

Meszah Peak
2164 m

Dease Lake

King Mtn
2408 m

Mt Roosevelt
2972 m

Summit Lake

Mt Sylvia
2942 m

Prophet River

Trutch

CANADA

Elfin Cove

Hoonah

Hawk Inlet

Juneau

Douglas

Chichagof Island

Admiralty Island

Telegraph Creek

Iskut

Mt Cushing
2469 m

Ware

Sikanni Chief

Sitka Pt

Sitka

Baranof

Kake

Mt Ratz
3136 m

Bob Quinn Lake

Mt Will
2515 m

2896 m
Great Snow Mt

Pink Mountain

ALASKA

Baranof Island

Petersburg

Wrangell

Sustut Peak
2469 m

Wonowon

Rose Prairie

U. S. A.

Prince of Wales Island

Craig

Ketchikan

Stewart

Fort
St John

Taylor

Hudson's Hope

Dawson Creek

Alexander Archipelago

Chetwynd

Pouce Coupe

Hazelton

New Hazelton

Moricetown

2755 m
Seven Sisters Peaks

MacKenzie

C. Knox

Dixon Entrance

Terrace

Smithers

Telkwa

Mcleod Lake

Prince Rupert

Houston

BRITISH COLUMBIA

Forestdale

Masset

Porcher I.

Kitimat

Burns Lake

Fort
St James

Fraser Lake

Engen

Summit Lake

Upper Fraser

Sinclair Mills

Queen Charlotte

Graham Island

Queen Charlotte

Sandspit

Pitt I.

Banks I.

Kemano

Ootsa Lake

Lily Lake

Vanderhoof

Prince George

Giscome

Mt Sir Alexander
3277 m

Dome Creek

Queen Charlotte Mtns

Islands

Red Rock

Hixon

Strathnaver

Crescent Spur

Mt Tea
214

McBride

Lyell I.

Moresby Island

Aristazabel I.

Fawnie Nose
1926 m

Nazko

Wells

Barkerville

Dunst

Kunghit I.

Princess Royal I.

Quesnel

Kersley

Tête
Ca

Bella Coola

Mt Saugstad
2908 m

Marguerite

Soda Creek

Calvert I.

Redstone

Williams Lake

Queen

Charlotte

Sound

Tatla Lake

Hanceville

Springhouse

Lac la Hache

Big Creek

100 Mile House

Clearwater

C. Scott

Port Hardy

Sointula

Mt Waddington
4016 m

Mt Queen Bess
3313 m

Mt Tatlow
3065 m

Dog Creek

Clinton

Vav

Quatsino

Gold Bridge

Pavilion

Cache Creek

Savona

Little
Fort

Port Alice

Kelsey Bay

Brem River

Lillooet

Ashcroft

Kamloops

Mo
Vir

Sayward

Pemberton

Mount Currie

Lytton

Spences Bridge

Merritt

Quilchen

C. Cook

Zeballos

Campbell River

Mt Tinniswood
2606 m

Whistler

PACIFIC

Kyuquot Sound

Gold River

Courtenay

Comox

Powell River

Irvines Landing

Mt Garibaldi
2678 m

Brackendale

Squamish

2385 m

Boston Bar

Yale

Summa
Pen

Nootka I.

Nootka

Vancouver

Britannia Beach

Princeton
Hope

OCEAN

Estevan Point

Flores I.

Tofino

Island

Port Alberni

Nanaimo

Sechelt

Vancouver

Burnaby

Langley

White
Rock

Chilliwack

Abbotsford

Keremeos

Ucluelet

Ladysmith

Blaine

Ferndale

Glacier

Mt Baker
3285 m

Acme

Mazama

Barkley Sound

Duncan

C. Beale

Clo-oose

Sidney

Anacortes

Sedro
Woolley

Rockport

Winthrop

Carlton

Strait of Juan de Fuca

Sooke

Victoria

Oak
Harbor

Hamilton

Oso

Mt Logan
2733 m

WA

Ma

C. Flattery

Neah Bay

Sappho

Joyce

Port
Angeles

Port Renfrew

Sequim

Marysville

Forks

B 134° C 132° D 130° E 128° F 126° G 124° H 122° J 418

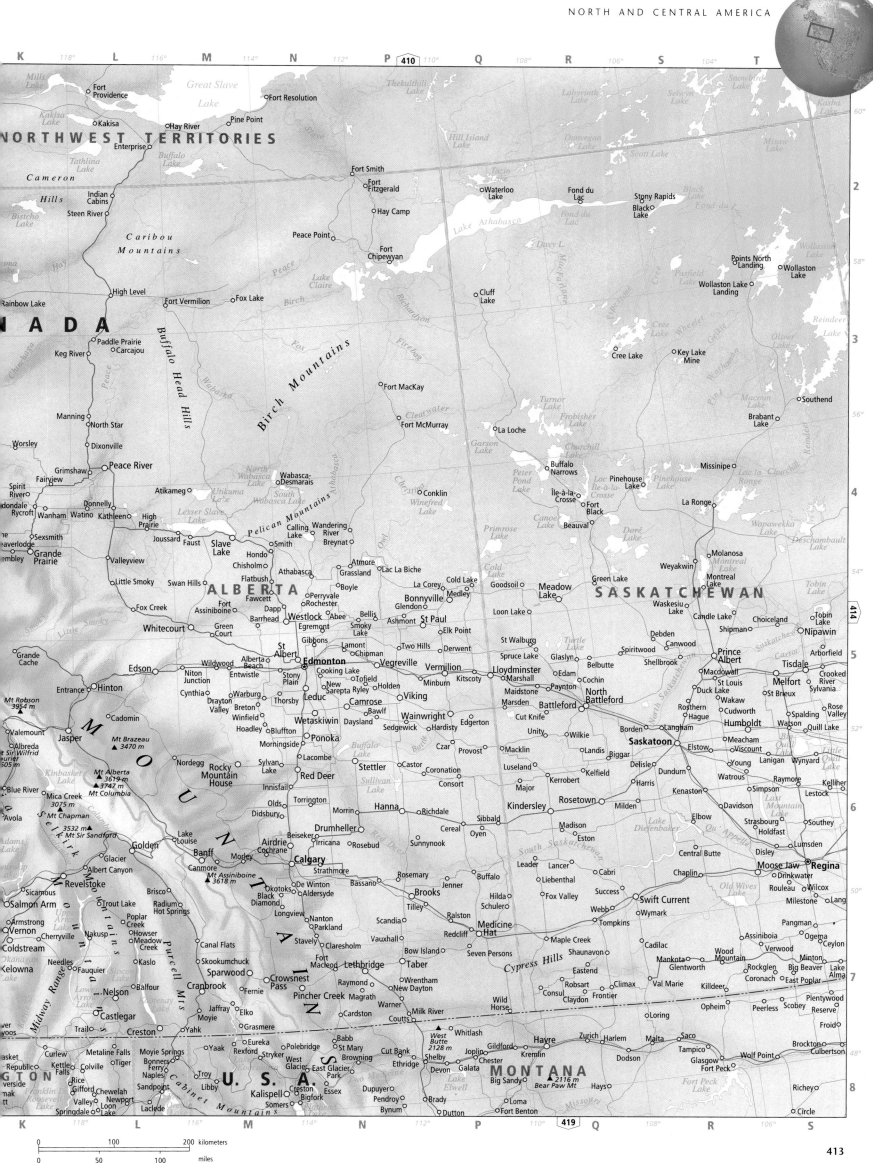

K 118° L 116° M 114° N 112° P 110° Q 108° R 106° S 104° T

Mills Lake
Great Slave Lake
Fort Providence
Kakisa Lake
Kakisa
Hay River
Pine Point
Fort Resolution
Thekulthili Lake
Labyrinth Lake
Selwyn Lake
Snowbird Lake
Kasba Lake

NORTHWEST TERRITORIES
Enterprise
Buffalo Lake
Tathlina Lake
Hill Island Lake
Dunvegan Lake
Scott Lake
Misaw Lake

2

Cameron Hills
Indian Cabins
Steen River
Fort Smith
Fort Fitzgerald
Hay Camp
Waterloo Lake
Fond du Lac
Stony Rapids
Black Lake
Black Lake

Bistcho Lake
uma
Hay
Peace Point
Lake Claire
Fort Chipewyan
Lake Athabasca
Fond du Lac
Davy L.
Cree
Pasfield Lake
Points North Landing
Wollaston Lake
Wollaston Lake Landing

3
NADA
Rainbow Lake
High Level
Fort Vermilion
Fox Lake
Birch
Richardson
Cree Lake
Cluff Lake
Cree Lake
Wheeler
Gethie
Oliver Lake
Reindeer Lake
58°

Chinchaga
Keg River
Paddle Prairie
Carcajou
Buffalo Head Hills
Wabasca
Firebag
Turnor Lake
Frobisher Lake
Cree Lake
Key Lake Mine
Macoun Lake
Southend
56°

Worsley
Manning
North Star
Dixonville
Birch Mountains
Fort MacKay
Clearwater
Fort McMurray
La Loche
Garson Lake
Churchill
Buffalo Narrows
Pinehouse Lake
Missinipe
Luc la Church

Spirit River
Fairview
Grimshaw
Peace River
Atikameg
Wabasca-Desmarais
North Wabasca Lake
Conklin
Winefred Lake
Primrose Lake
Île-à-la-Crosse
Fort Black
Pinehouse Lake
La Ronge
Wapawekka Lake
4

donvale
Rycroft
Donnelly
Wanham
Watino
Kathleen
High Prairie
Lesser Slave Lake
South Wabasca Lake
Utikuma Lake
Calling Lake
Wandering River
Breynat
Cold Lake
Canoe Lake
Beauval
Doré Lake
Deschambault Lake
54°

Sexsmith
Grande Prairie
Joussard
Faust
Slave Lake
Hondo
Chisholm
Smith
Atmore
Grassland
Lac La Biche
La Corey
Cold Lake
Goodsoil
Meadow Lake
Green Lake
SASKATCHEWAN
Molanosa
Weyakwin
Montreal Lake
Tobin Lake

Little Smoky
Swan Hills
ALBERTA
Fawcett
Flatbush
Boyle
Bonnyville
Glendon
Medley
Loon Lake
Turtle Lake
Waskesiu Lake
Montreal Lake
414

Fox Creek
Assiniboine
Dapp
Barrhead
Perryvale
Rochester
Bellis
Ashmont
St Paul
St Walburg
Spruce Lake
Glaslyn
Debden
Canwood
Shipman
Choiceland
Tobin Lake

Whitecourt
Green Court
Westlock
Egremont
Smoky Lake
Elk Point
Derwent
Spiritwood
Belbutte
Shellbrook
Prince Albert
Arborfield
Nipawin
5

Grande Cache
Edson
Wildwood
Alberta Beach
St Albert
Gibbons
Lamont
Chipman
Vegreville
Vermilion
Lloydminster
Marshall
Edam
Cochin
North Battleford
Macdowall
St Louis
Duck Lake
Tisdale
Crooked River
Melfort
Sylvania

Hinton
Niton Junction
Entwistle
Edmonton
Cooking Lake
Tofield
Holden
Minburn
Kitscoty
Maidstone
Marsden
Paynton
Battleford
Rosthern
Wakaw
Cudworth
Spalding
Rose Valley
52°

Mt Robson 3954 m
Entrance
Cynthia
Warburg
Stony Plain
New Sarepta Ryley
Viking
Unity
Wilkie
Borden
Langham
Meacham
Humboldt
Watson
Quill Lake

Cadomin
Drayton Valley
Breton
Leduc
Camrose
Wainwright
Edgerton
Cut Knife
Biggar
Landis
Langham
Viscount
Lanigan
Wynyard

Jasper
Mt Brazeau 3470 m
Winfield
Hoadley
Wetaskiwin
Daysland
Sedgewick
Hardisty
Luseland
Delisle
Saskatoon
Elstow
Young
Watrous
Raymore
Kelliher

Valemount
Mt Alberta 3619 m
Mt Columbia 3747 m
Bluffton
Morningside
Ponoka
Buffalo
Czar
Provost
Macklin
Kerrobert
Kelfield
Dundurn
Simpson
Lestock
6

Blue River
Mica Creek 3075 m
Nordegg
Rocky Mountain House
Sylvan Lake
Lacombe
Stettler
Castor
Coronation
Consort
Major
Harris
Kenaston
Davidson
Strasbourg
Holdfast

Avola
Mt Chapman 3532 m
Mt Sir Sandford
Red Deer
Innisfail
Sullivan Lake
Hanna
Richdale
Cereal
Oyen
Madison
Eston
Elbow
Raymore
Southey

Adams Lake
Golden
Lake Louise
Olds
Torrington
Didsbury
Morrin
Drumheller
Sibbald
Kindersley
Rosetown
Milden
Central Butte
Disley
Lumsden

Revelstoke
Glacier
Banff
Beiseker
Irricana
Rosebud
Sunnynook
Leader
Lancer
Cabri
Chaplin
Moose Jaw
Regina
50°

Sicamous
Salmon Arm
Albert Canyon
Brisco
Morley
Cochrane
Calgary
Strathmore
Rosemary
Buffalo
Liebenthal
Success
Swift Current
Drinkwater
Wilcox

Armstrong
Vernon
Canmore
Mt Assiniboine 3618 m
De Winton
Okotoks
Aldersyde
Bassano
Jenner
Hilda
Schuler
Fox Valley
Webb
Wymark
Milestone
Lang

Coldstream
Kelowna
Radium Hot Springs
Black Diamond
Longview
Brooks
Tilley
Ralston
Maple Creek
Cadillac
Assiniboia
Ogema
Ceylon
Pangman

Needles
Nakusp
Poplar Creek
Howser
Meadow Creek
Canal Flats
Nanton
Parkland
Scandia
Vauxhall
Redcliff
Medicine Hat
Bow Island
Seven Persons
Cypress Hills
Shaunavon
Eastend
Mankota
Wood Mountain
Glentworth
Verwood
Rockglen
Minton
Big Beaver
Alma
7

Cherryville
Fauquier
Kaslo
Skookumchuck
Sparwood
Fort Macleod
Lethbridge
Taber
Consul
Robsart
Climax
Val Marie
Killdeer
Coronach
East Poplar

Nelson
Balfour
Cranbrook
Fernie
Crowsnest Pass
Pincher Creek
Magrath
Raymond
Wrentham
New Dayton
Wild Horse
Claydon
Frontier
Opheim
Peerless
Scobey
Reserve
Plentywood
Froid

Castlegar
Jaffray
Elko
Moyie
Grasmere
Cardston
Milk River
Coutts
Cypress Hills

Trail
Yahk
Creston
Babb
St Mary
Whitlash
West Butte 2128 m
Hayre
Zurich
Harlem
Malta
Saco
Brockton
Culbertson
48°

Curlew
Metaline Falls
Moyie Springs
Bonners Ferry
Yaak
Rexford
Stryker
Polebridge
Cut Bank
Joplin
Gildford
Kremlin
Dodson
Tampico
Wolf Point

Republic
Kettle Falls
Colville
Tiger
Troy
Libby
West Glacier
East Glacier Park
Browning
Ethridge
Shelby
Devon
Galata
Big Sandy
Bear Paw Mt 2116 m
Glasgow
Fort Peck
Richey

GTON
Rice
Gifford
Naples
Sandpoint
Creston
Bigfork
U.S.A.
MONTANA
Fort Peck Lake

Chewelah
Valley
Newport
Loon Lake
Kalispell
Somers
Dupuyer
Pendroy
Brady
Lake Elwell
Big Sandy
Loma
Hays
Circle

Springdale
Laclede
Cabinet Mountains
Essex
Bynum
Dutton
Fort Benton
8

K 118° L 116° M 114° N 112° P 110° Q 108° R 106° S

0   100   200 kilometers
0   50   100 miles
Scale 1:5,000,000   Projection: Albers Equal Area

Central Canada

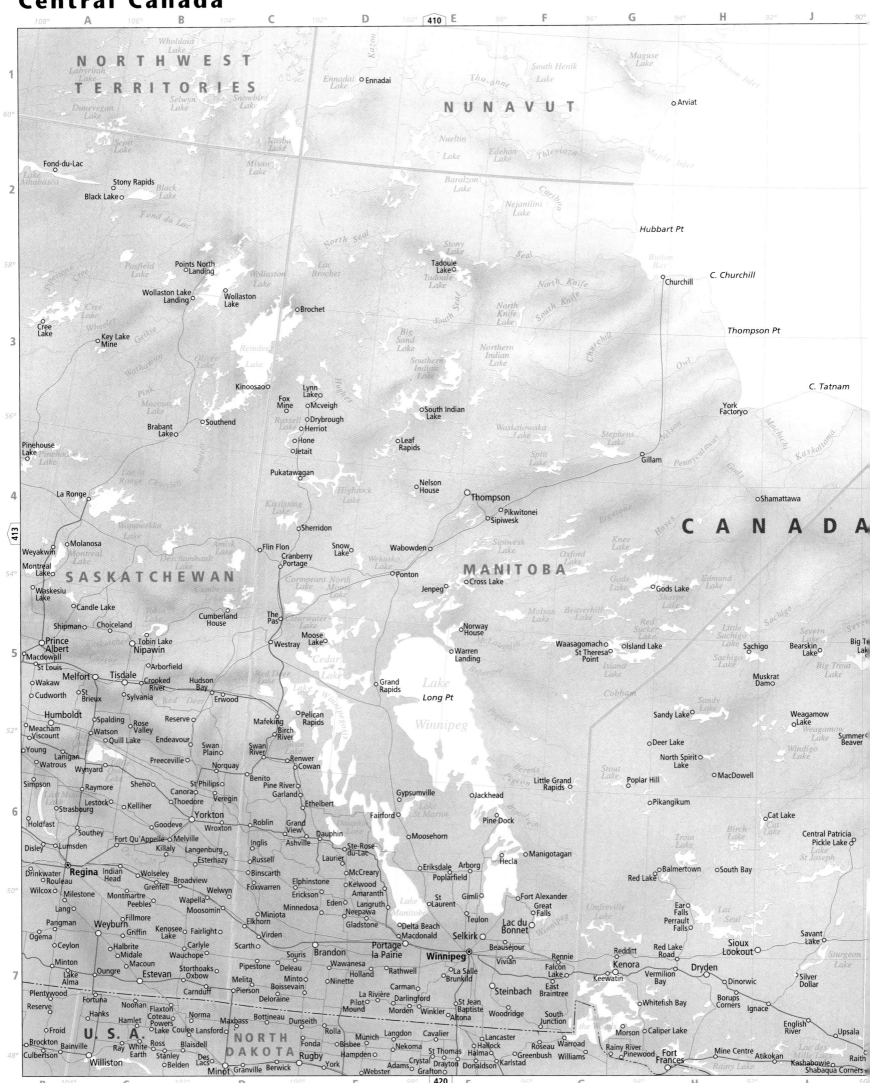

NORTHWEST TERRITORIES

NUNAVUT

CANADA

SASKATCHEWAN

MANITOBA

U.S.A.

NORTH DAKOTA

North and Central America

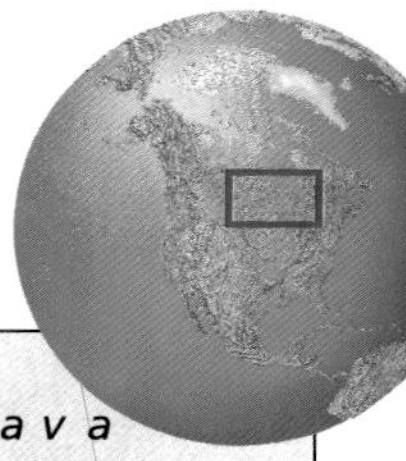

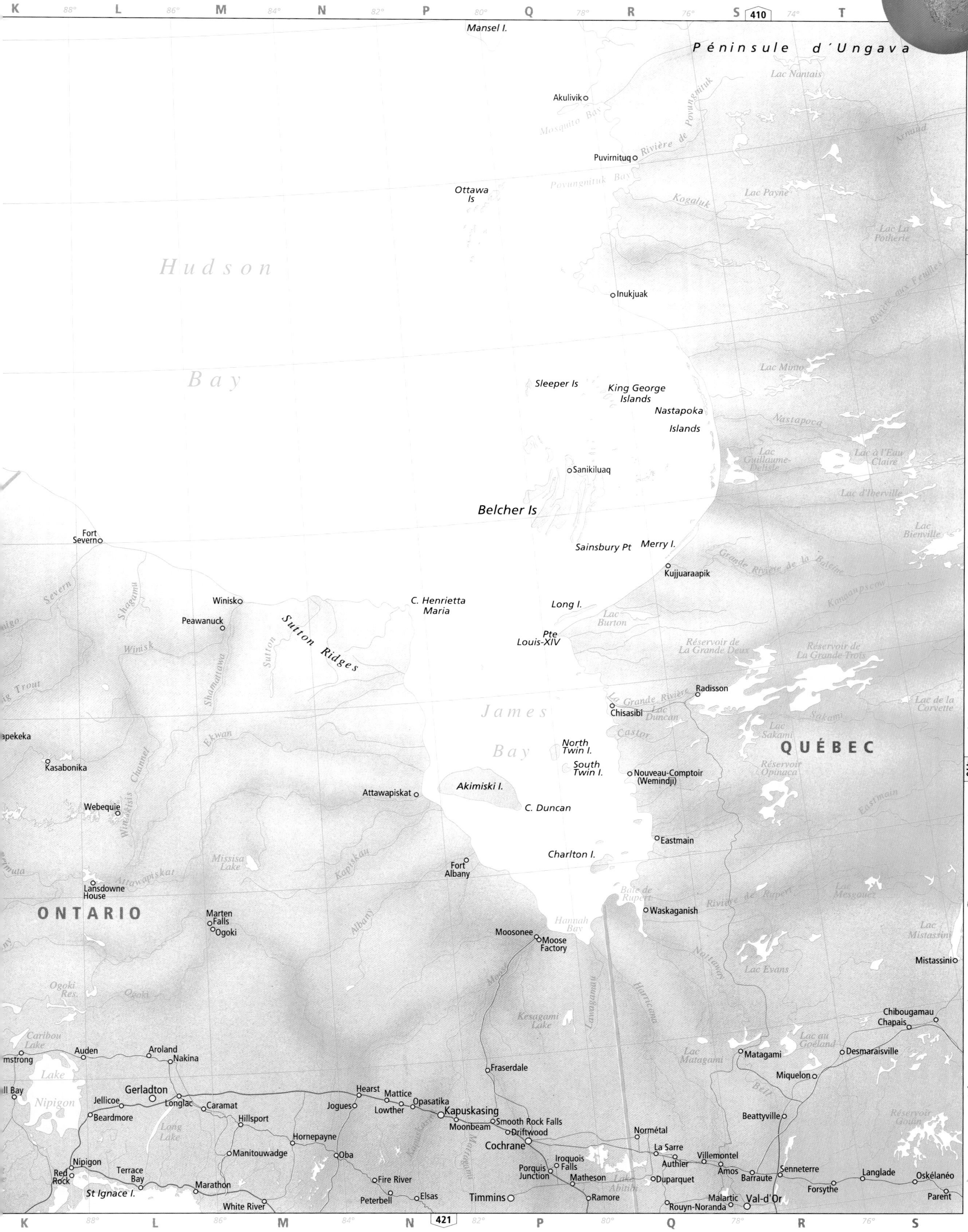

K 88° L 86° M 84° N 82° P 80° Q 78° R 76° S 410 74° T

Mansel I.

Péninsule d'Ungava

Lac Nantais

1

Akulivik

60°

Mosquito Bay

Rivière de Povungnituk

2

Puvirnituq

Arnaud

Povungnituk Bay

Kogaluk

Lac Payne

410

Ottawa Is

58°

Rivière aux Feuilles

Inukjuak

Hudson

Lac Minto

3

Bay

Sleeper Is

King George Islands

Nastapoca

Nastapoka Islands

Lac Guillaume-Delisle

Lac à l'Eau Claire

56°

Sanikiluaq

Lac d'Iberville

Belcher Is

Lac Bienville

Fort Severno

4

Sainsbury Pt   Merry I.

Grande Rivière de la Baleine

Kujjuaraapik

Winisk

Kanaupscow

C. Henrietta Maria

Long I.

54°

Peawanuck

Sutton Ridges

Severn

Shagamu

Winisk

Pte Louis-XIV

Lac Burton

Réservoir de La Grande Deux

Réservoir de La Grande Trois

Big Trout

Shamattawa

Radisson

Lac de la Corvette

apekeka

Ekwan

James

Lac Grande Rivière

Castor

5

Kasabonika

Chisasibi

Lac Duncan

Sakami

QUÉBEC

416

Bay

North Twin I.

Réservoir Opinaca

Webequie

Wunnummin

Attawapiskat

South Twin I.

Nouveau-Comptoir (Wemindji)

Eastmain

Akimiski I.

C. Duncan

Missisa Lake

Kapiskau

Eastmain

Lansdowne House

Fort Albany

Charlton I.

Lac Mesgouez

6

ONTARIO

Marten Falls

Albany

Baie de Rupert

Waskaganish

Rivière de Rupert

Lac Mistassini

Ogoki

Moosonee

Hannah Bay

Moose Factory

Mistassini

Ogoki Res.

Lac Evans

Nottaway

50°

Kesagami Lake

Chibougamau

Caribou Lake

Fraserdale

Harricana

Lac Matagami

Chapais

Lac au Goéland

Armstrong

Auden

Aroland

Nakina

Matagami

Desmaraisville

Lake Nipigon

Gerladton

Hearst

Mattice

Opasatika

Miquelon

7

ll Bay

Jellicoe

Longlac

Caramat

Joques

Lowther

Kapuskasing

Beattyville

Réservoir Gou

Beardmore

Hillsport

Moonbeam

Smooth Rock Falls

Normétal

Long Lake

Hornepayne

Driftwood

La Sarre

Villemontel

Nipigon

Manitouwadge

Oba

Cochrane

Authier

Senneterre

Red Rock

Terrace Bay

Porquis Junction

Iroquois Falls

Amos

Barraute

Langlade

Oskélanéo

St Ignace I.

Marathon

Fire River

Matheson

Duparquet

Forsythe

Parent

White River

Peterbell

Elsas

Timmins

Ramore

Malartic

Val-d'Or

Rouyn-Noranda

K 88° L 86° M 84° N 421 82° P 82° Q 80° R 78° S 76°

North and Central America

East Canada

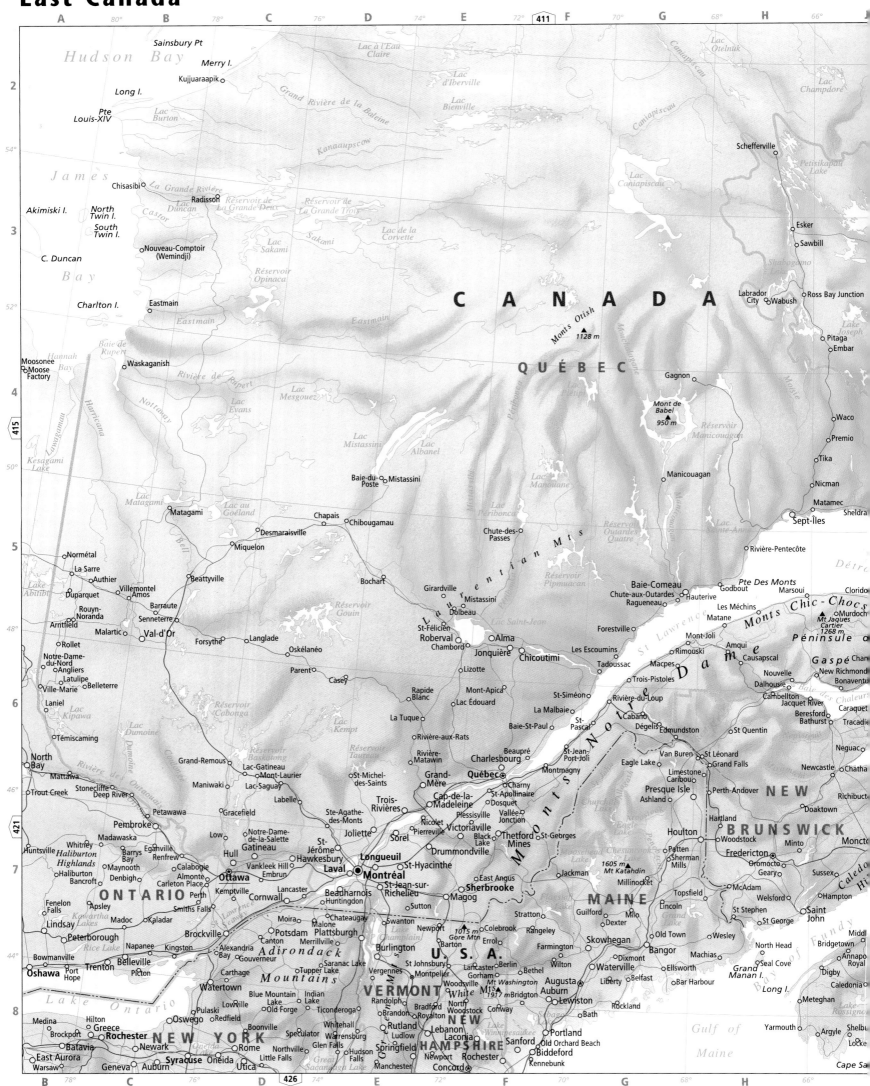

North and Central America

K 64° 62° L 60° M 58° N 56° P 54° Q 52° R 50° S

LABRADOR

SEA

2

54°

Kogaluk

Tunungayualok Island

Mistastin Lake

Davis Inlet

Hopedale

C. Makkovik

C. Harrison
C. Turley

Mt Benedict
829 m

Holton

Kanairiktok

Snegamook Lake

Nipishish Lake

C. Porcupine

Grady Harbour

Groswater Bay

Cartwright

Batteau

3

Labrador

Smallwood Reservoir

Grand Lake

Lake Melville

Happy Valley - Goose Bay

Mealy Mts

Separation Point

Comfort Bight

Square Islands

52°

win alls

Churchill Falls

Churchill

Mecatina

Port Hope Simpson

Table Head

Belle Isle

Strait of Belle Isle

Red Bay

C. Bauld

L'Anse aux Meadows

St Anthony

4

St Augustin

Rivière-St-Paul

Blanc-Sablon

Forteaux

Main Brook

Hare Bay

Brig Bay

Groais I.

Grey Is

St-Augustin

St John I.

Northern

Bell I.

Englee

NEWFOUNDLAND

50°

Mutton Bay

Port aux Choix

Hawkes Bay

Williamsport

Horse Is

Lac Musquaro

Rivière-St-Jean

Baie-Johan Beetz

Daniel's Harbour

Peninsula

C. St John

La Scie

Fogo Fogo I.

pie

Havre-St-Pierre

Natashquan

Kegaska

Pointe-Parent

Gethsémani

Long Range Mts

Baie Verte

Westport

Notre Dame Bay

Musgrave Harbour

Cape Freels

Détroit de Jacques-Cartier

Sally's Cove

Rocky Harbour

Hampden

Grose Morne
806 m

Springdale

White Bay

Gander Bay

Wesleyville

5

Île d' Anticosti

Mt
St Gregory

674 m

Deer Lake

Sandy Lake

Grand Lake

Grand Falls-Windsor

Badger

Gander

Gambo

Bonavista Bay

Bonavista

Chicotte

Pte. de l'Est

Corner Brook

Lewis Hills
815 m

Glover I.

Buchans

Red Indian Lake

Summerville

Honguedo

Cap-des-Rosiers

C. de Gaspé

Barachois

Lourdes

Stephenville

Victoria Lake

Newfoundland

Middle Ridge

Musgravetown

Clarenville

Grates Cove

48°

Miscou I.

Gulf of

St Lawrence

Cape St George

St George's Bay

Cape Anguille

Meelpaeg Lake

St Alban's

Milltown

Goobies

Carbonear

Pouch Cove

Bay Roberts

St John's

oppegan

C. Ray

C. Anguille

Cabot Strait

Rose Blanche

Burgeo

Hermitage Bay

Harbour Breton

Fortune Bay

Placentia Bay

Garnish

Marystown

Placentia

Mount Pearl
Bay Bulls

Avalon

Peninsula

Ferryland

Grand-Entrée

Channel-Port aux Basques

Miquelon

ST PIERRE AND MIQUELON
(Fr.)

Grand Bank

Fortune

St Lawrence

Branch

C. St Mary's

St Mary's Bay

Trepassey

Cape Race

6

46°

Cap aux Meules

Îles de la Madelaine

Havre-Aubert

Cape North

St Pierre

Cape Pine

Miscou I.

North Cape

Tignish

PRINCE EDWARD

ISLAND

erton

Cape North

Ingonish

Chéticamp

Margaree Forks

New Waterford

Glace Bay

touche

Summerside

St Peters

Elmira

East Pt

Inverness

Port Hood

Whycocomagh

Sydney

Main-à-Dieu

ATLANTIC

Charlottetown

Montague

Cape George

Bras d'Or Lake

7

hediac

Cape Tormentine

New Glasgow

Port Hawkesbury

Fourchu

Cape Breton

kville

Amherst

Oxford

Tatamagouche

Stellarton

Monastery

Isle Madam

Arichat

Island

Cobequid Mts

Parrsboro

Truro

Bolyston

Aspen

Canso

olfville

Windsor

Musquodoboit Harbour

Tor Bay

OCEAN

tville

NOVA SCOTIA

Halifax

Dartmouth

Chester

Germany

Sambro

Sheet Harbour

44°

Lunenburg

idgewater

erpool

8

K 64° 62° L 60° M 58° N 56° P 54° Q 52° R

0 100 200 kilometers
0 50 100 miles

Scale 1:5,000,000   Projection: Albers Equal Area

417

North and Central America

Northwest United States

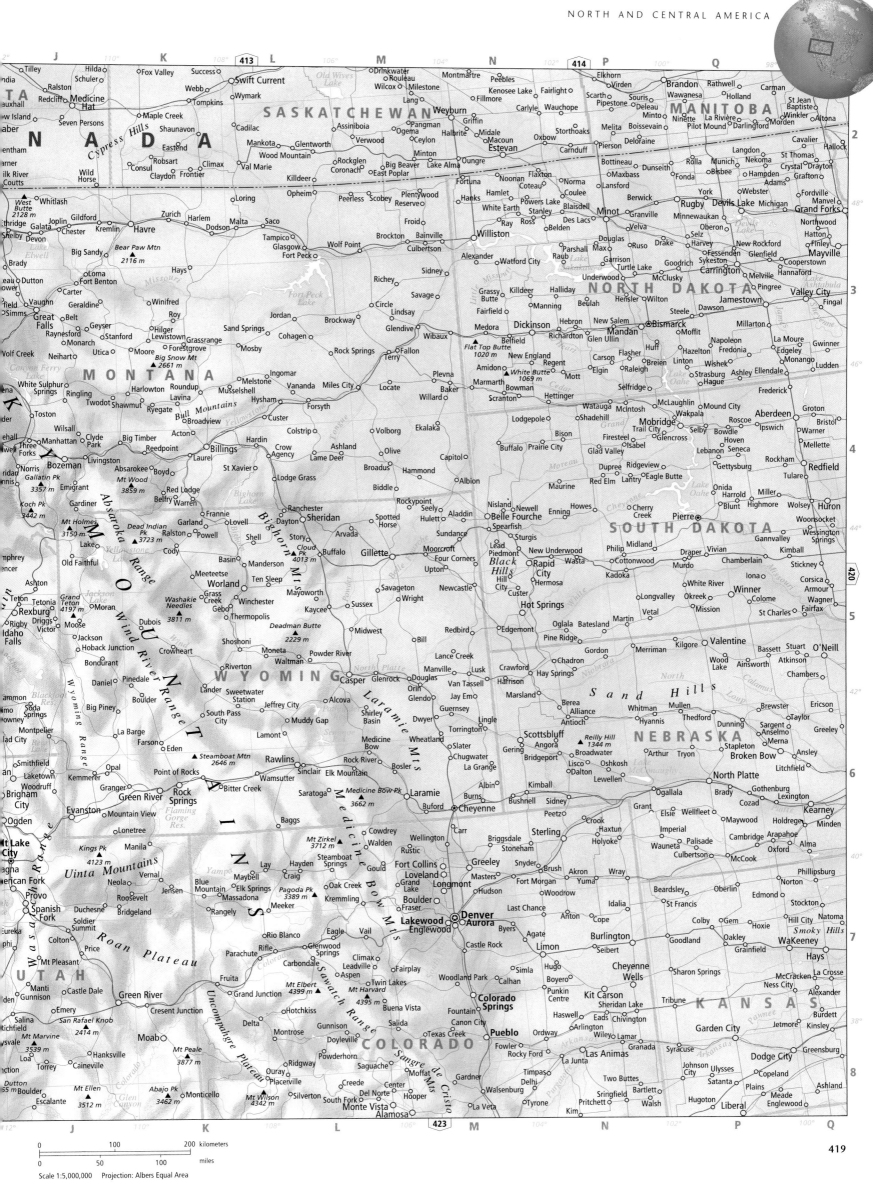

Scale 1:5,000,000 Projection: Albers Equal Area

0   100   200 kilometers
0   50   100 miles

Central United States

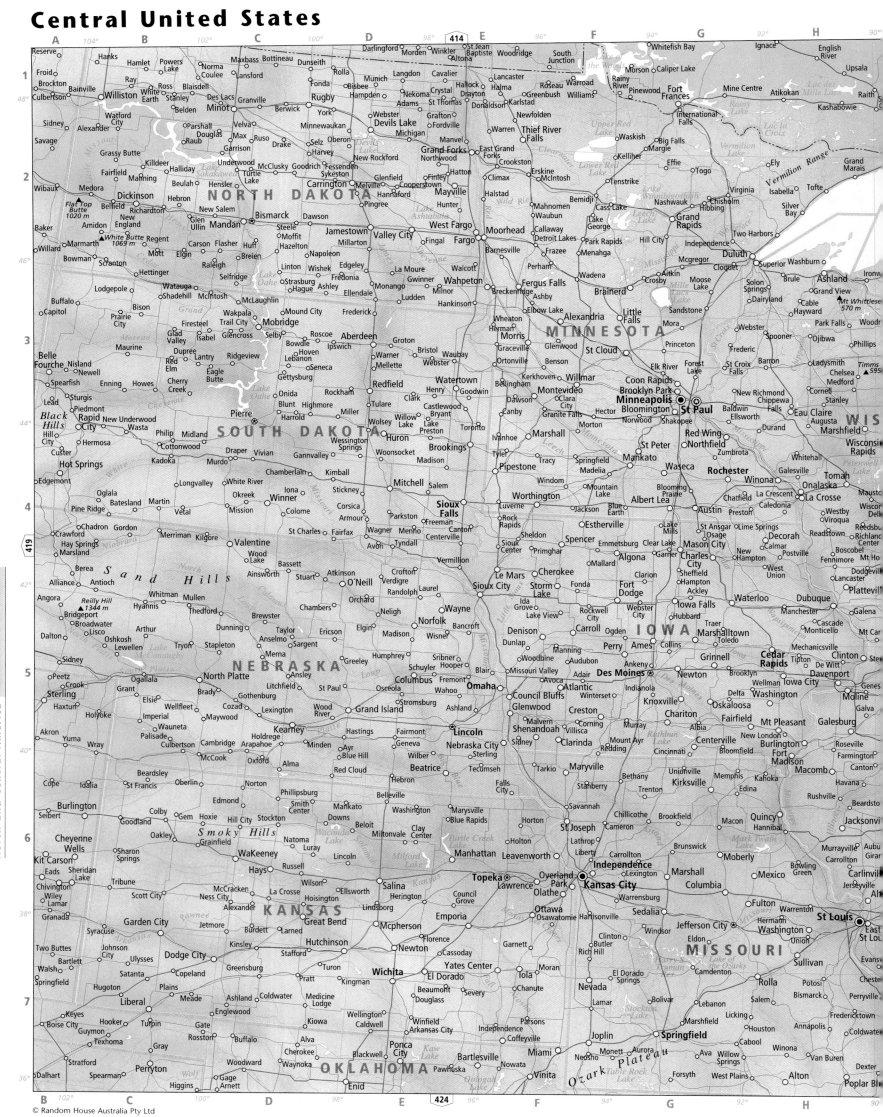

North and Central America

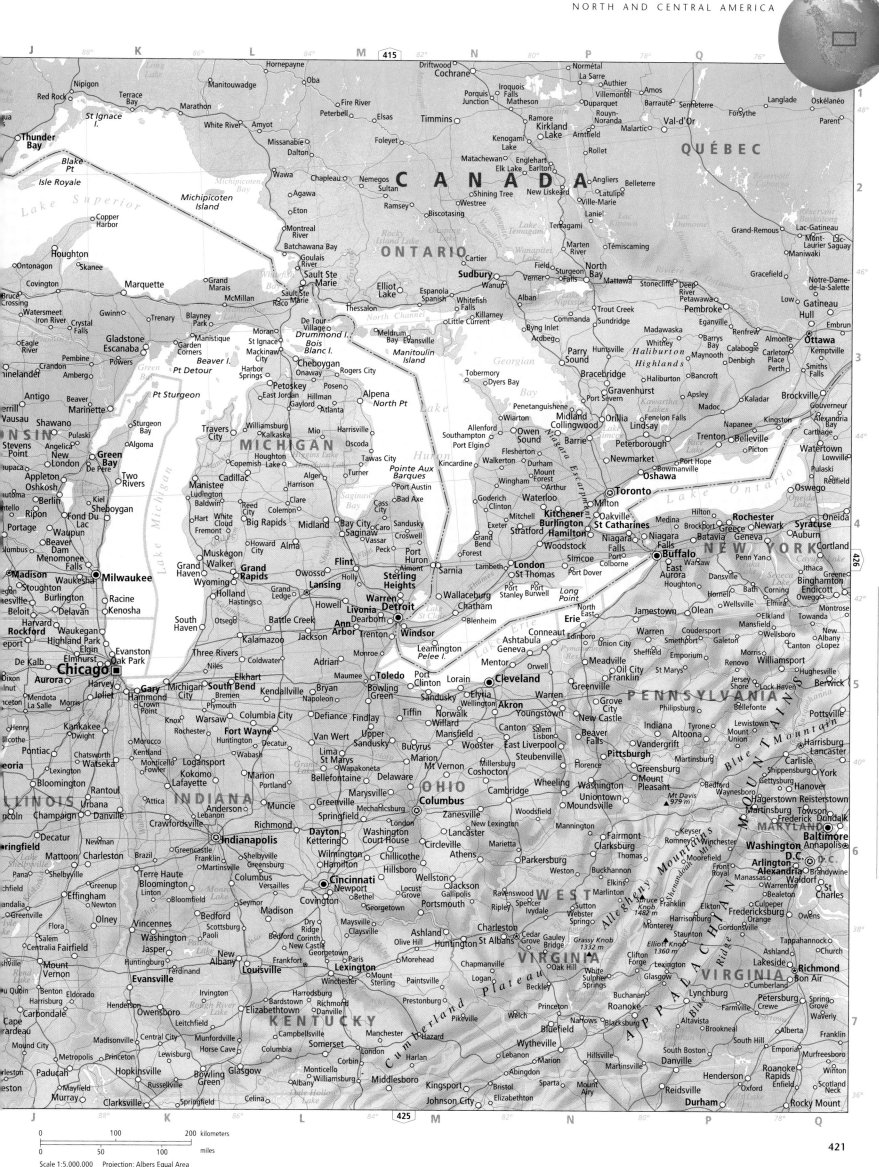

Thunder Bay

QUÉBEC

CANADA

ONTARIO

Lake Superior

Isle Royale

Michipicoten Island

Lake Michigan

MICHIGAN

Lake Huron

Georgian Bay

Manitoulin Island

Toronto

Lake Ontario

NEW YORK

Buffalo

Lake Erie

Erie

Green Bay

Milwaukee

Madison

Rockford

Chicago

Aurora

Gary

Detroit

Windsor

Cleveland

PENNSYLVANIA

Pittsburgh

INDIANA

OHIO

Columbus

Indianapolis

Cincinnati

Dayton

WEST VIRGINIA

Louisville

KENTUCKY

VIRGINIA

Richmond

Baltimore

Washington D.C.

ILLINOIS

MARYLAND

Ottawa

APPALACHIAN MOUNTAINS

Blue Ridge Mountains

Allegheny Mountains

Cumberland Plateau

Mt Davis 979 m

Elliot Knob 1360 m

Spruce Knob 1482 m

Grassy Knob 1332 m

North and Central America

0   100   200 kilometers
0   50   100 miles

Scale 1:5,000,000   Projection: Albers Equal Area

Southwest United States

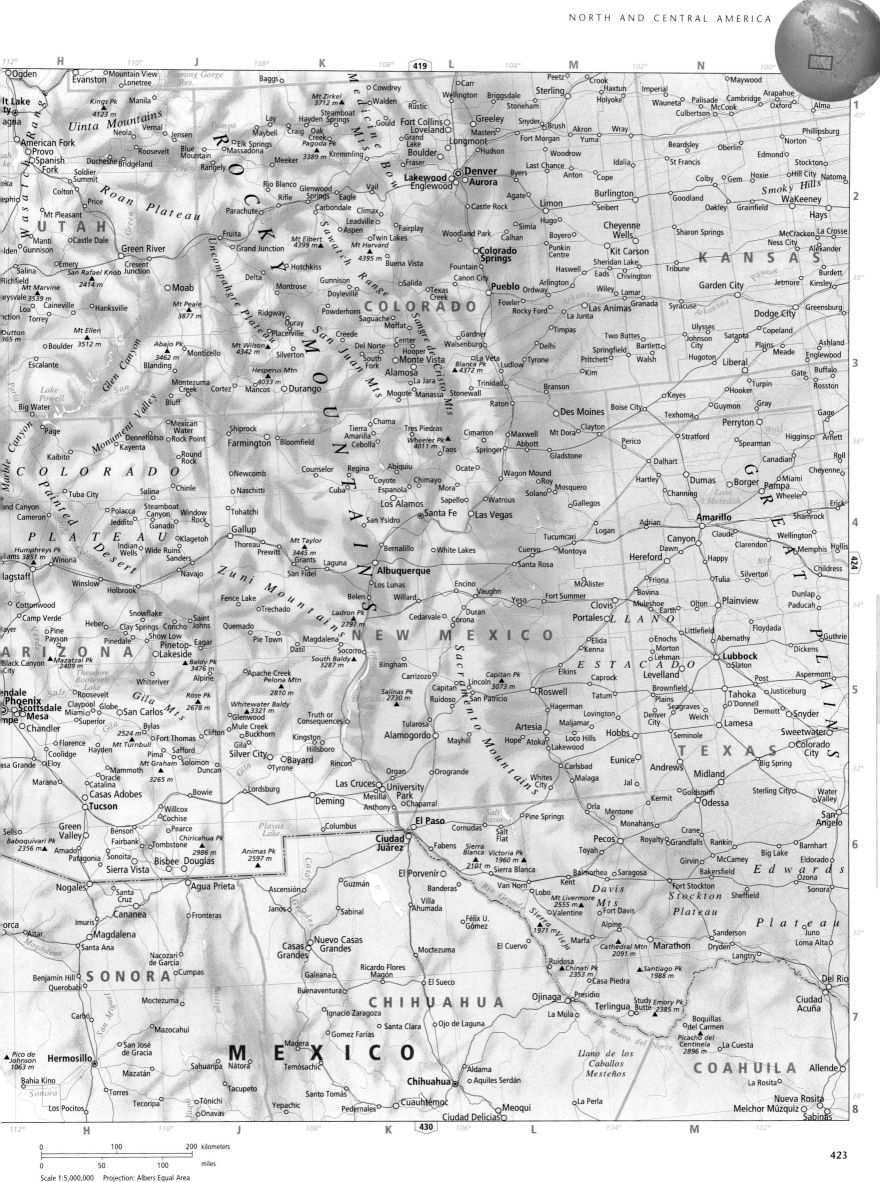

Ogden
Evanston
It Lake
ty
agna
Mountain View
Lonetree
Baggs
419
Cowdrey
Walden
Carr
Wellington
Peetz
Crook
Haxtun
Imperial
Maywood
Arapahoe
Alma
1
Kings Pk
4123 m
Manila
Mt Zirkel
3712 m
Rustic
Briggsdale
Sterling
Holyoke
Wauneta
Palisade
Cambridge
Oxford
40°
Uinta Mountains
Vernal
Lay
Maybell
Hayden
Steamboat
Springs
Gould
Fort Collins
Loveland
Greeley
Stoneham
Brush
Akron
Wray
Beardsley
McCook
Culbertson
Phillipsburg
American Fork
Provo
Spanish
Fork
Neola
Roosevelt
Jensen
Craig
Oak
Creek
Pagoda Pk
3389 m
Grand
Lake
Longmont
Boulder
Fraser
Masters
Snyder
Fort Morgan
Yuma
Woodrow
Idalia
St Francis
Norton
Edmond
Soldier
Summit
Duchesne
Bridgeland
Blue
Mountain
Meeker
Kremmling
Hudson
Denver
Last Chance
Anton
Cope
Colby
Gem
Hoxie
Hill City
Stockton
Natoma
2
Colton
Price
Rangely
Rio Blanco
Glenwood
Springs
Rifle
Eagle
Vail
Lakewood
Englewood
Aurora
Byers
Agate
Castle Rock
Limon
Seibert
Burlington
Goodland
Oakley
Grainfield
WaKeeney
Hays
Smoky Hills

Southeast United States

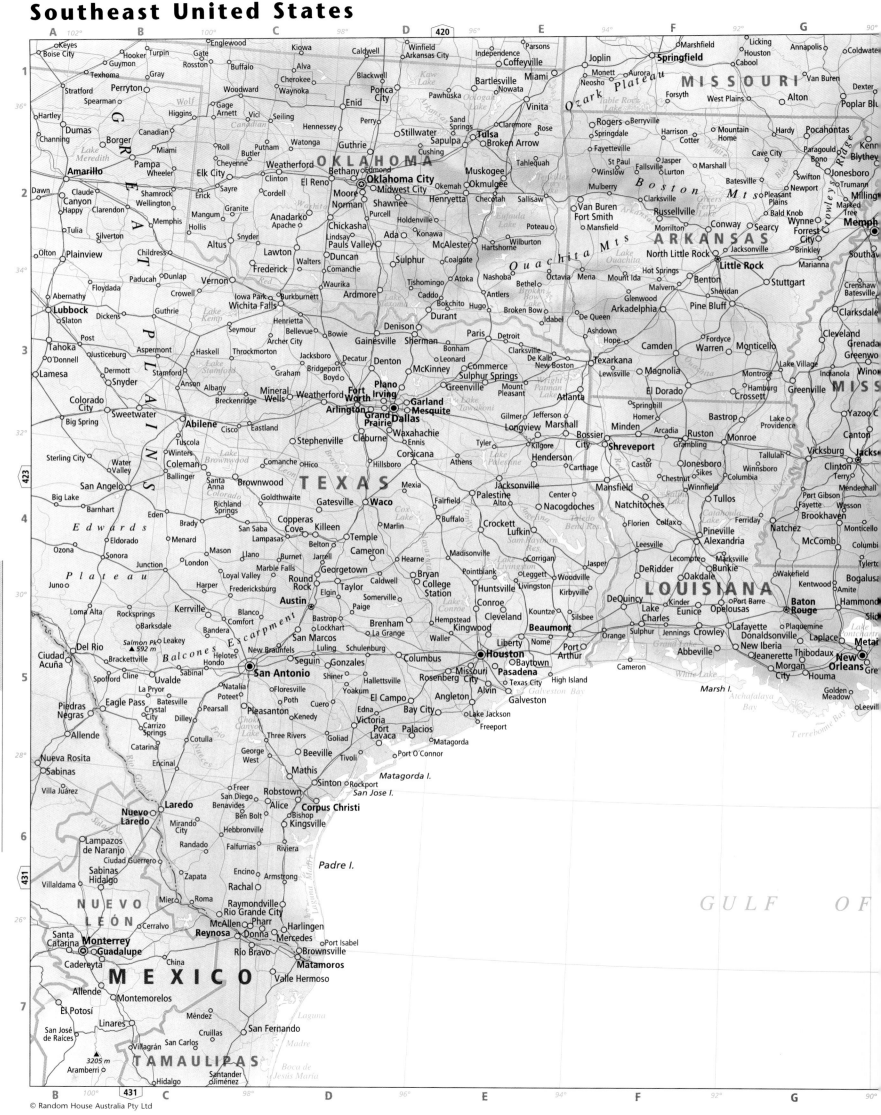

H · 88° · J · 86° · K · 84° · 421 · L · 82° · M · 80° · N · 78°

1

Cape Girardeau · Madisonville · Central City · Munfordville · Campbellsville · Manchester · Hazard · Wytheville · Lebanon · Marion · Hillsville · Martinsville · South Boston · South Hill · Murfreesboro · Winton
Mound City · Metropolis · Lewisburg · Somerset · London · Corbin · Harlan · Abingdon · Bristol · Boone · Mount Airy · North Wilkesboro · Winston-Salem · Durham · Reidsville · Oxford · Henderson · Roanoke Rapids · Scotland Neck
charleston · Paducah · Princeton · Hopkinsville · KENTUCKY · Monticello · Middlesboro · La Follette · Kingsport · Johnson City · Elizabethton · Sparta · High Point · Greensboro · Lexington · Durham
Mayfield · Bowling Green · Glasgow · Albany · Williamsburg · Morristown · Greeneville · North Airy · Statesville · Salisbury · Kannapolis · Concord · Smithfield · Dunn · Goldsboro · Kinston
keston · Murray · Clarksville · Hendersonville · Gallatin · Lebanon · Cookeville · Oak Ridge · Knoxville · Jefferson City · Newport · Asheville · Morganton · Hickory · Statesville · Sanford · NORTH CAROLINA · New Bern

2

Union City · Martin · Dickson · Fairview · Crossville · Harriman · Sweetwater · Mt Mitchell 2037 m · Rutherfordton · Gastonia · Charlotte · Monroe · Fayetteville · Clinton · Garland · Jacksonville
McKenzie · Paris · Nashville · Murfreesboro · Sparta · Maryville · Mt Guyot 2018 m · Bryson City · Hendersonville · Franklin · Inman · Gaffney · Rock Hill · Rockingham · Hamlet · Raeford · Laurinburg · Elizabethtown · Wallace
Dyersburg · TENNESSEE · McMinnville · Manchester · Dayton · Athens · Great Smoky Mts · Murphy · Taylors · Spartanburg · Lancaster · Cheraw · Dillon · Chadbourn · Whiteville · Burgaw · Holly Ridge
Humboldt · Milan · Columbia · Shelbyville · Tullahoma · Red Bank · Cleveland · Murphy · Easley · Greenville · Jonesville · Chester · Great Falls · Kershaw · Bethune · Camden · Marion · Loris · Conway · Southport · Wilmington
Ripley · Brownsville · Lexington · Jackson · Lewisburg · Lawrenceburg · Winchester · Chattanooga · Dalton · La Fayette · Blairsville · Cleveland · Clemson · Anderson · Laurens · Clinton · Newberry · SOUTH · Columbia · Sumter · Lake City · Shallotte · Long Beach
ovington · Henderson · Pulaski · Fayetteville · Stevenson · Calhoun · Ellijay · 1458 m Brasstown Bald · Jasper · Canton · Gainesville · Royston · Abbeville · Saluda · Batesburg · CAROLINA · Manning · Smith I.

3

Holly Springs · Corinth · Booneville · Florence · Sheffield · Scottsboro · Fort Payne · Albertville · Boaz · Gadsden · Cedartown · Marietta · Roswell · Winder · Athens · Elberton · Greenwood · North Augusta · Orangeburg · St Stephen · Myrtle Beach
Oxford · New Albany · Russellville · Decatur · Arab · Cullman · Hayden · Oneonta · Piedmont · Smyrna · Atlanta · Covington · Farmington · Madison · Thomson · Augusta · New Ellenton · Denmark · Bamberg · Moncks Corner · Georgetown
Pontotoc · Tupelo · Hamilton · Winfield · Jasper · Vernon · Pell City · Anniston · East Point · Carrollton · Newnan · Senoia · Monticello · Eatonton · Wrens · Waynesboro · Barnwell · St George · Summerville
SIPPI · Macon · Aberdeen · West Point · Columbus · Starkville · Millport · Fayette · Reform · Leeds · Talladega · Roanoke · Griffin · Forsyth · Milledgeville · Wadley · Swainsboro · Twin City · Sylvania · Allendale · Walterboro · Mount Pleasant · Charleston
sciusko · Louisville · Tuscaloosa · Aliceville · Alabaster · Sylacauga · Alexander City · La Grange · Thomaston · Roberta · Warner Robins · Dublin · Statesboro · Tillman · Hampton · Jacksonboro · Estill
Philadelphia · Eutaw · Greensboro · Woodstock · Centreville · Maplesville · Clanton · Auburn · Opelika · Butler · Fort Valley · Perry · Macon · Hardeeville · Beaufort
arthage · Forest · Demopolis · Linden · Selma · Benton · Prattville · ALABAMA · Phenix City · Cusseta · GEORGIA · Hawkinsville · Eastman · Vidalia · Claxton · Savannah · Hiton Head Island

4

Meridian · Newton · Quitman · Thomasville · Dixons Mills · Camden · Montgomery · Hurtsboro · Columbus · Americus · Rochelle · McRae · Lyons · Glennville · Richmond Hill · Ossabaw I.
Bay · Thomasville · Awin · Union Springs · Glenville · Troy · Eufaula · Dawson · Cordele · Fitzgerald · Baxley · Ludowici · ATLANTIC
Laurel · Waynesboro · Coffeeville · Greenville · Brantley · Luverne · Abbeville · Suttons Corner · Sylvester · Ocilla · Tifton · Douglas · Surrency · Jesup · Riceboro · Darien · St Catherines I. · Sapelo I.
ins · Jackson · Grove Hill · Monroeville · Georgiana · Elba · Headland · Arlington · Albany · Adel · Alapaha · Pearson · Blackshear · Hortense · Waycross · Woodbine · St Simons I. · Brunswick
Hattiesburg · Evergreen · Andalusia · Opp · Enterprise · Blakely · Colquitt · Camilla · Moultrie · Barney · Lakeland · Homerville · Cumberland I.
Beaumont · Frisco City · Dothan · Bainbridge · Thomasville · Valdosta · Fargo · Yulee · Kingsland · Fernandina Beach
Lumberton · Mount Vernon · Atmore · Brewton · De Funiak Springs · Bonifay · Cairo · Quitman · Jasper · Macclenny

5

Wiggins · Bay Minette · Mobile · Milton · Niceville · Freeport · Bloustown · Quincy · Tallahassee · Greenville · Madison · Live Oak · Lake City · Baldwin · Jacksonville · Jacksonville Beach
yune · Ocean Springs · Pensacola · Valparaiso · West Bay · Bristol · Saint Marks · Perry · Mayo · Starke · Green Cove Springs · St Augustine · OCEAN
Gulfport · Biloxi · Pascagoula · Warrington · Fort Walton Beach · Lynn Haven · Panama City · Wewahitchka · Crawfordville · Branford · High Springs · Alachua
Horn I. · Dauphin I. · Gulf Shores · Foley · Marianna · Port St Joe · Carrabelle · Gainesville · Palatka
Chandeleur Is · Chiefland · Williston · Bunnell · Ormond Beach · Daytona Beach
Sulphur · Venice · St Joseph Point · Dog I. · Steinhatchee · Cross City · Ocala · FLORIDA · New Smyrna Beach
East Bay · St George I. · Deadman Bay · Cedar Key · Dunnellon · Leesburg · Eustis · Deltona · Sanford

6

MEXICO · Spring Hill · Brooksville · Floral City · Titusville · Merritt Island · Cape Canaveral · Orlando · Dade City · Kissimmee · Pine Hills · Haines City · Melbourne · Palm Bay
Tampa · Clearwater · Largo · Lakeland · Bartow · Lake Wales · Holopaw · Kenansville · Palm Bay
St Petersburg · Wauchula · Avon Park · Sebring · Yeehaw Junction · Vero Beach
Bradenton · Gardner · Fort Pierce
Sarasota · Myakka City · Arcadia · Brighton · Okeechobee · Stuart · Hobe Sound · Grand Bahama Island
Venice · North Port · Lake Okeechobee · Belle Glade · West Palm Beach · Palm Beach · Freeport
Port Charlotte · La Belle · Clewiston
Knob I. · Fort Myers · Cape Coral · Immokalee · Delray Beach · Boca Raton
Sanibel I. · Sunniland · Plantation

7

Naples · Carol City · Fort Lauderdale · Hollywood · Bimini Islands
Cape Romano · Ochopee · Hialeah · Miami
Coral Gables · South Miami · BAHAMAS
Ten Thousand Is · Cutler Ridge · Homestead
Florida City
Flamingo · Key Largo
Florida Bay · Marathon · Florida Keys · Straits of Florida
Key West

H · 88° · J · 86° · K · 84° · L · 82° · M · 80° · N

0 · 100 · 200 kilometers
0 · 50 · 100 miles

Scale 1:5,000,000 Projection: Albers Equal Area

North and Central America

Northeast United States

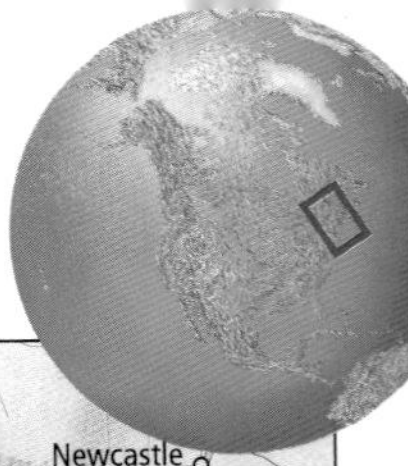

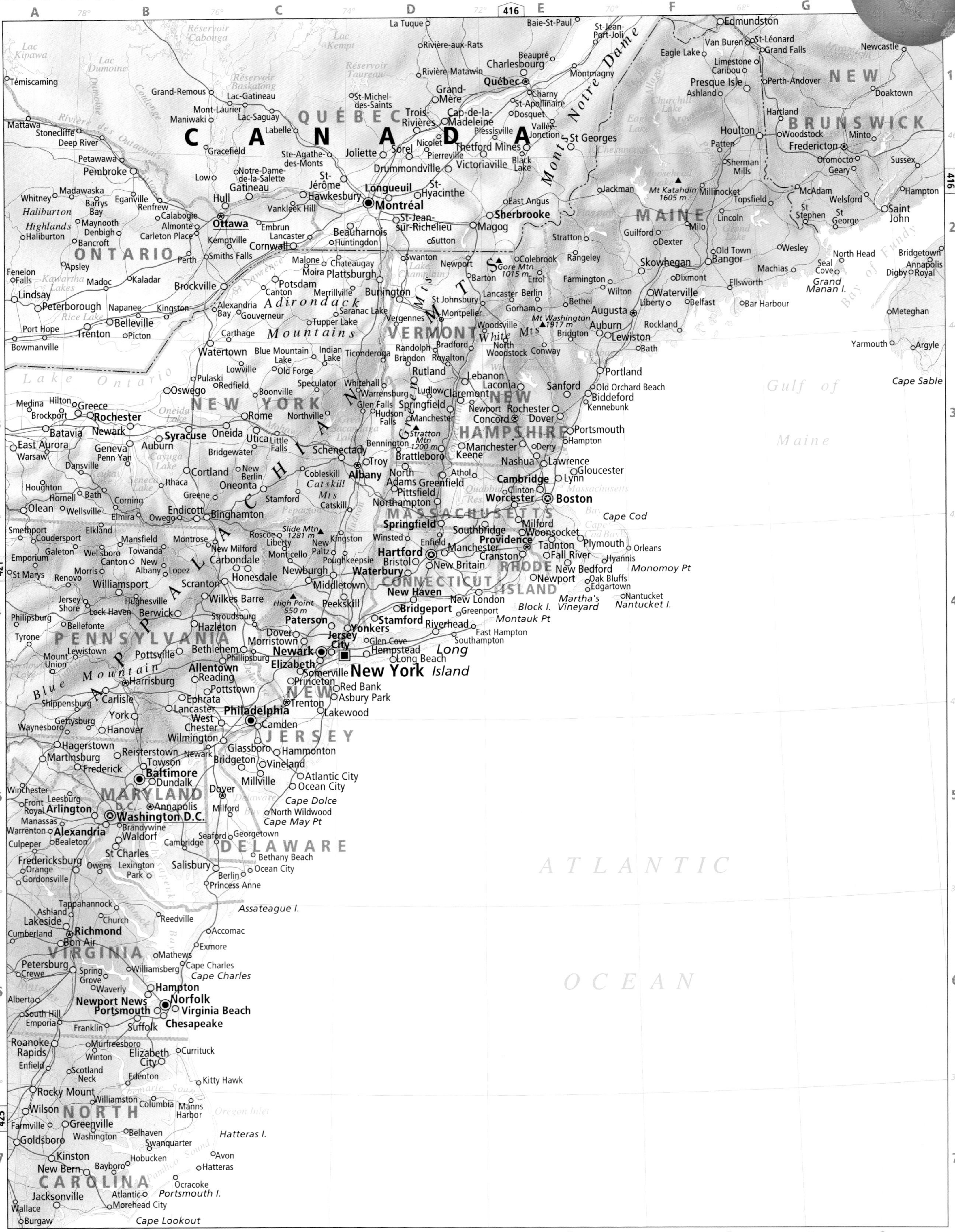

QUÉBEC

CANADA

ONTARIO

NEW BRUNSWICK

MAINE

VERMONT

NEW HAMPSHIRE

NEW YORK

MASSACHUSETTS

RHODE ISLAND

CONNECTICUT

APPALACHIAN

PENNSYLVANIA

NEW JERSEY

MARYLAND

DELAWARE

VIRGINIA

NORTH CAROLINA

ATLANTIC OCEAN

Gulf of Maine

Long Island

Cape Cod

Cape Sable

Bay of Fundy

Québec Montréal Ottawa Boston New York Philadelphia Baltimore Washington D.C. Richmond Norfolk

© Random House Australia Pty Ltd

426

kilometers 0   100   200
miles 0   50   100
Scale 1:5 000 000   Projection: Albers Equal Area

East Caribbean • North Venezuela

A 72° B 68° C 64° D 60°

Tropic of Cancer

ATLANTIC

OCEAN

TURKS AND
CAICOS ISLANDS
(U.K.)

Caicos
Islands
Cockburn
Harbour

Turks Islands
• Grand Turk

LEEWARD ISLANDS

Cabo
Isabela

Cap-
Haïtien
Monte Cristi
Puerto Plata
Cabrera
Santiago
Moca
San Francisco de Macorís
La Vega
Hinche
Bonao
Monte Plata
Bahía de Samaná
HAITI
DOMINICAN
Comendador 3175 m ▲ Pico Duarte
San Juan
Hato Mayor
El Seibo
REPUBLIC
Jimaní
Neiba
San Pedro de Macorís
Cabo
Engaño
Port-au-Prince
Azua
Cristóbal
La Romana
Barahona
San
Santo Domingo
Cabo
Pedernales
Punta
Salinas
Isla Saona

HISPANIOLA

GREATER ANTILLES

VIRGIN
ISLANDS
(U.K.)
Anegada

Aguadilla
Arecibo
San Juan
Carolina
Fajardo
Mayagüez
Cerro de Punta
1338 m
Caguas
San Germán
Ponce
Guayama
PUERTO RICO
(U.S.A.)
Charlotte
Amalie
St Croix
Frederiksted
VIRGIN
ISLANDS
(U.S.A.)

Road
Town

ANGUILLA
(U.K.)
The Valley
Marigot
St Martin (Guad.)
Philipsburg
St Maarten (Neth.)

Saba
St Eustatius
Basseterre
ST KITTS
AND NEVIS
Redonda
Plymouth
MONTSERRAT
(U.K.)

Codrington
Barbuda
ANTIGUA AND
BARBUDA
St John's
Antigua

GUADELOUPE
(Fr.)
Sainte-Rose
Pointe-à-Pitre
Basse-Terre

LESSER ANTILLES

WINDWARD ISLANDS

Dominica Passage
Portsmouth
Morne
Diablotin
1447 m
DOMINICA
Roseau
La Plaine

Martinique Passage
Montagne Pelée
1397 m
Sainte-Marie
Fort-de-France
Le Lamentin
MARTINIQUE
(Fr.)
St Lucia Channel
Castries
ST LUCIA
Micoud
Vieux Fort

St Vincent Passage
Soufrière
1234 m
ST VINCENT AND
THE GRENADINES
Georgetown
Kingstown

BARBADOS
Speightstown
Bridgetown

CARIBBEAN

SEA

The Grenadines

Grenville
GRENADA
St George's

LESSER ANTILLES

ARUBA
(Neth.)
Oranjestad
Curaçao
Bonaire
Pta Gallinas
Puerto Estrella
Península
de Guajira
C. San Román
Pen. de
Paraguaná
Willemstad
Kralendijk
Carrizal
Pueblo Nuevo
NETHERLANDS
ANTILLES
(Neth.)
Los Taques
Punta Fijo
Puerto
Cumarebo
La Orchila
La Blanquilla

Tobago
Charlotteville
Scarborough
Galera Pt
TRINIDAD
AND TOBAGO

Paraguaipoa
Golfo de Venezuela
Coro
Piritu
Jacura
San Juan de los Cayos
Isla de
Margarita
La Asunción
Porlamar
Carúpano
Río Caribe
Pen. de
Paria
Güiria
Arima
Sangre Grande
Port of
Spain
Trinidad
Rio Claro
San Fernando
Galeota Pt

San Rafael
Casigua
Pedregal
Churuguara
La Tortuga
C. Codera
Campo
Maracaibo
Mara
Santa
Rita
Cabimas
Dabajuro
Baragua
de Mauroa
Cerro El Cerrón
1990 m
Carora
San Felipe
Catia
La Mar
Caracas
Petare
Puerto la Cruz
Cumaná
Caripe
Maturín
Mene
Puerto
Cabello
Maracay
Baruta
Los Teques
Barcelona
Caripito
Lagunillas
Barquisimeto
Yaritagua
Valencia
La Victoria
Higuerote
Aragua de
Barcelona
Barranquitas
Mene Grande
El Tocuyo
San Carlos
El Pao
San Juan
de los Morros
San Antonio
de Tamanaco
Anaco
Betijoque
Acarigua
Tinaco
Ortiz
Cantaura
Tucupita
Trujillo
Nueva Florida
Chaguaramas
Valle de
la Pascua
El Chaparro
Barrancas
Boconó
Guanare
Las Mercedes
Zaraza
El Tigre
Valera
Guanarito
El Baúl
Calabozo
Santa María
de Ipire
Pariaguán
San José de Guanipa
El Vigía
Mérida
Barinas
Obispos
San Mauricio
Boca del Pao
Soledad
Ciudad Guayana
San José
de Amacuro
Pico Bolívar
5007 m
Camaguán
Puerto
Ordaz
Morawhanna
Tovar
Pedraza La Vieja
Puerto de Nutrias
Puerto Miranda
San Fernando de Apure
Mapire
Ciudad
Bolívar
El Pao
El Palmar
La Horqueta
Port Kaituma
San Antonio
de Caparo
Achaguas
Cabruta
Parmana
Caicara de Orinoco
Ciudad Piar
El Miamo
Guasipati
Matthews Ridge
VENEZUELA
Palmarito
Mantecal
Maripa
El Toro
Baramanni
Guasdualito
Co Turagua
1839 m
El Callao
Tumeremo
San José
de Las Bocas
San Pedro
Arauquita
Arauca
Elorza
La Urbana
Las Lajitas
Las Trincheras
La Paragua
El Dorado
Tame
1320 m
GUYANA
Puerto Rondón
Cravo Norte
Parguaza
Peter's Mine
COLOMBIA
Puerto Páez
Tumureng
Keweigek
Issano
Puerto Nuevo
Puerto Carreño

0   100   200   300   400 kilometers
0   100   200 miles
Scale 1:7,000,000   Projection: Lambert Conformal Conic

427

North and Central America

Central America • West Caribbean

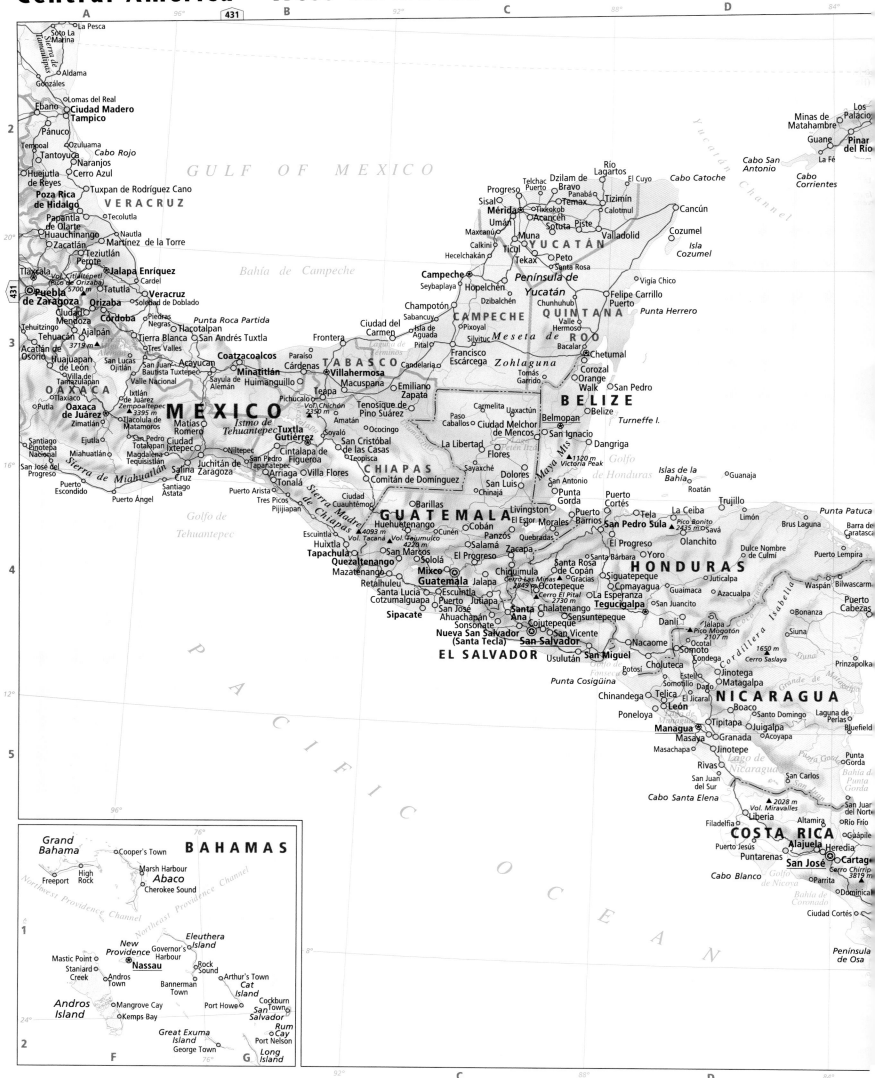

GULF OF MEXICO

VERACRUZ

Bahía de Campeche

YUCATÁN

CAMPECHE

QUINTANA

Península de Yucatán

Meseta de ROO

OAXACA

MEXICO

TABASCO

BELIZE

Istmo de Tehuantepec

Zohlaguna

CHIAPAS

Golfo de Honduras

Islas de la Bahía

Golfo de Tehuantepec

Sierra Madre de Chiapas

GUATEMALA

HONDURAS

PACIFIC

Tegucigalpa

EL SALVADOR

Cordillera Isabelia

NICARAGUA

Managua

Golfo de Fonseca

Lago de Nicaragua

OCEAN

COSTA RICA

San José

Golfo de Nicoya

Península de Osa

BAHAMAS

Grand Bahama

Abaco

Northwest Providence Channel

Northeast Providence Channel

Eleuthera Island

New Providence

Nassau

Andros Island

Cat Island

San Salvador

Great Exuma Island

Long Island

E · · · 80° · · · F · · · 76° · · · G · · · 72° · · · H

Tropic of Cancer

BAHAMAS

Mangrove Cay
Kemps Bay
Andros Island
Port Howe
Cockburn Town
San Salvador
Rum Cay
Port Nelson
Great Exuma Island
George Town
Long Island
Clarence Town
Mortimers
Colonel Hill
Snug Corner
Crooked Island
Acklins Island

TURKS AND CAICOS ISLANDS (U.K.)

Mayaguana Island
Little Inagua Island
Caicos Islands
Northeast Pt
Matthew Town
Great Inagua Island
Grand Turk
Cockburn Harbour
Turks Islands

2

a Habana (Havana)
Guanabacoa
Cárdenas
Marianao
Matanzas
Colón
Artemisa
Güines
Batabanó
Jagüey Grande
Sagua la Grande
Santa Clara
Cienfuegos
Pico San Juan 1156 m
Cabaiguán
Morón
Caibarién
Cayo Romano
Sancti Spíritus
Trinidad
Ciego de Ávila
Esmeralda
Nuevitas
Cayo Sabinal
Cabo Lucrecia
Cayos Vertientes
Cinco Balas
Cayo Grande
Santa Cruz del Sur
Las Tunas
Puerto Padre
Gibara
Banes
Moa
Cayo del Rosario
CUBA
Cayo Largo
Archipiélago de los Canarreos
Camagüey
Guáimaro
Holguín
Cueto
Sagua de Tánamo
Baracoa
Archipiélago de los Jardines de la Reina
Manzanillo
Bayamo
Palma Soriano
Maisí
Golfo de Guacanayabo
Sierra Maestra
Pico Turquino 1974 m
Guantánamo
Santiago de Cuba
Pilón
Cabo Cruz
Cayo del Sur

Île de la Tortue
Monte Cristi
Cabo Isabela
Puerto Plata
Cabrera

20°

GREATER
Cayman Brac
Little Cayman
Grand Cayman
George Town
CAYMAN ISLANDS (U.K.)

Cap-Haïtien
Fort Liberté
Port-de-Paix
Gonaïves
Santiago
Moca
San Francisco de Macorís
Bahía Escocesa
La Vega
Bonao
DOMINICAN
Bahía de Samaná
Monte Plata
El Seibo
Cabo Engaño
Saint-Marc
Hinche
Pico Duarte 3175 m
San Juan
San Pedro de Macorís
Hato Mayor
La Romana
HAITI
Golfe de la Gonâve
Port-au-Prince
Comendador
Jimaní
REPUBLIC
Santo Domingo
Isla Saona
Dame-Marie
Jérémie
Petit Goâve
Neiba
Azua
San Cristóbal
Cayman Trench

Montego Bay
Falmouth
Tiburón
Massif de la Hotte
Les Cayes
Bainet
Pic de la Selle 2680 m
Barahona
Punta Salinas
Jacmel
3
South Negril Pt
Ocho Ríos
NAVASSA ISLAND (U.S.A.)
Port-à-Piment
Pedernales
Savanna-la-Mar
JAMAICA
Port Antonio
Cabo Beata
Mandeville
Blue Mtn Pk 2256 m
Black River
Spanish Town
Kingston
Portland Pt

Jamaica Channel
LESSER ANTILLES
HISPANIOLA

Cayman Trench

C A R I B B E A N

Cayos Miskitos (Nic.)

4

Providencia (Col.)

ARUBA (Neth.)
Oranjestad
Curaçao
Pta Gallinas
Pen. de Paraguaná
Willemstad
Cabo de la Vela
Península de Guajira
Puerto Estrella
C. San Román
12°
San Andrés (Col.)
Carrizal
Uribia
Los Taques
Punto Fijo
Pueblo Nuevo
Puerto Cumarebo
S E A
Ríohacha
Maicao
Coro
Jacura
Carraipía
Paraguaipoa
Golfo de Venezuela
Pedregal
Piritu
Churuguara
Santa Marta
Ciénaga
Barrancas
Tule
Casigua
Dabajuro
Baragua
Barranquilla
Puerto Colombia
Baranoa
P. Cristóbal Colón 5775 m
Villanueva
San Rafael
Santa Rita
Mene de Mauroa
Carora
Yaritagua
Soledad
Sabanalarga
Valledupar
Fundación
Campo Mara
Maracaibo
Rosario
Cerro El Cerrón 1990 m
5
Cartagena
Pivijay
Agustín Codazzi
Cabimas
Barquisimeto
Turbaco
Calamar
Plato
El Difícil
La Jagua de Ibirico
Batranquitas
Machiques
Lagunillas
Mene Grande
El Tocuyo
Arjona
El Carmen de Bolívar
Sierra de Perijá
Lago de Maracaibo
Acarigua
Golfo de Morrosquillo
Tolú
Mompós
El Banco
Betijoque
Trujillo
Boconó
Portobelo
Palenque
El Porvenir
Arch. de San Blás
Golfo del Darién
Sincelejo
Sincé
Magangué
Encontrados
Casigua
San Carlos del Zulia
Valera
Guanare
427
Colón
Ailigandí
Lorica
La Gloria
El Vigía
Mérida
Barinas
Guarito
PANAMA
Golfo del Darién
Puerto Rey
Cereté
Sahagún
Tamalameque
La Fría
Pico Bolívar 5007 m
Obispos
Coclé del Norte
Panama Canal
Lago Gatún
Chimán
Puerto Obaldía
Montería
Sardinata
Tovar
Puerto de Nutrias
Santa Catalina
San Miguelito
San Miguel
Planeta Rica
Ayapel
Simití
Ocaña
Cúcuta
VENEZUELA
Volcán Barú 3475 m
La Chorrera
Panamá
Isla del Rey
Acandí
Turbo
Tierralta
Caucasia
Cáchira
Chinácota
San Antonio de Caparo
Pedraza La Vieja
Boquete
Penonomé
I. San José
Yaviza
Cúcuta
Pamplona
Mantecal
David
La Palma
Garachiné
El Real
Cáceres
San Cristóbal
Palmarito
Tolé
San Francisco
Aguadulce
Zaragoza
Bucaramanga
Cubará
Arauca
Soná
Atalaya
Santiago
Río de Jesús
Chitré
Las Tablas
Chigorodó
Dabeiba
Paramillo 3960 m
Yarumal
Amalfi
Segovia
Barrancabermeja
Floridablanca
Sierra Nevada del Cocuy 5493 m
Araquita
Arauca
Elorza
COLOMBIA
Jaqué
Jurado
Ituango
Antioquia
Anzá
Zapatoca
San Gil
Arauca
Puerto Rondón
Puerto Nuevo
Cupica
Riosucio
Palo de las Letras
Cisneros
Puerto Berrío
Socorro
El Cocuy
Tame
Cravo Norte
Bello
Medellín
Casanare
6

E · · · 80° · · · F · · · 76° · · · G · · · 450 · · · 72° · · · H

0 100 200 300 400 kilometers
0 100 200 miles

Scale 1:7,000,000   Projection: Lambert Conformal Conic

North and Central America

Mexico

423

424

UNITED STATES OF AMERICA

ARKANSAS
MISSISSIPPI
ALABAMA
LOUISIANA
TEXAS

Throckmorton · Jacksboro · Decatur · Denton · McKinney · Commerce · Magnolia · El Dorado · Hamburg · Kosciusko · Eutaw · Centreville · Clanton
Aspermont · Haskell · Graham · Bridgeport · Boyd · Greenville · Sulphur Springs · Atlanta · Bastrop · Monroe · Clinton · Jackson · Newton · Quitman · Butler · Demopolis · Maplesville · Montgomery
Stamford · Breckenridge · Mineral Wells · Plano · Garland · Longview · Jefferson · Marshall · Bossier City · Minden · Ruston · Jonesboro · Vicksburg · Meridian · Linden · Benton · Prattville · Hurtsboro
Snyder · Anson · Weatherford · Fort Worth · Dallas · Mesquite · Tyler · Kilgore · Carthage · Winnsboro · Columbia · Fayette · Selma · Troy
Abilene · Cisco · Stephenville · Cleburne · Ennis · Waxahachie · Athens · Henderson · Sikes · Natchez · Brookhaven · Collins · Laurel · Monroeville · Andalusia · Dothan
Colorado City · Coleman · Comanche · Hillsboro · Corsicana · Jacksonville · Nacogdoches · Alexandria · Pineville · McComb · Hattiesburg · Evergreen · Enterprise · Eufaula
San Angelo · Ballinger · Brownwood · Goldthwaite · Gatesville · Waco · Buffalo · Palestine · Lufkin · Center · Natchitoches · Colfax · Natchez · Beaumont · Mount Vernon · Crestview · De Funiak Springs · Abbeville
Water Valley · Eldorado · Menard · Brady · Lampasas · Belton · Temple · Madisonville · Corrigan · Jasper · Leesville · DeRidder · Bunkie · Tylertown · Lumberton · Wiggins · Milton · Valparaiso · Freeport

EDWARDS PLATEAU

San Antonio · Austin · Houston · Pasadena · Galveston · Corpus Christi

GULF OF MEXICO

LOUISIANA · Baton Rouge · New Orleans · Mobile · Pensacola · Panama City

Chandeleur Is

Tropic of Cancer

MEXICO

TAMAULIPAS · NUEVO LEÓN · Monterrey · Saltillo · Ciudad Victoria · Tampico · Ciudad Madero

SAN LUIS POTOSÍ · San Luis Potosí · Querétaro · Celaya · México · Toluca · Puebla de Zaragoza · Veracruz · Córdoba · Orizaba

GUERRERO · Acapulco · Oaxaca de Juárez · Tuxtla Gutiérrez

Vol. Citlaltepetl (Pico de Orizaba) 5700 m
Vol. Popocatépetl 5452 m

Golfo de Tehuantepec
Istmo de Tehuantepec

Bahía de Campeche

YUCATÁN · Mérida · Progreso · Valladolid · Cancún · Cozumel · Isla Cozumel

Península de Yucatán

CAMPECHE · Campeche · Champotón · Ciudad del Carmen

QUINTANA ROO · Chetumal · Corozal

TABASCO · Villahermosa · Coatzacoalcos · Minatitlán

CHIAPAS · San Cristóbal de las Casas · Comitán de Domínguez

BELIZE · Belmopan · Belize

GUATEMALA · Flores

HONDURAS · San Pedro Sula · La Ceiba · Puerto Cortés · Tela

Golfo de Honduras
Turneffe I.

Scale 1:7,000,000
Projection: Lambert Conformal Conic

0 100 200 300 400 kilometers
0 100 200 miles

South America

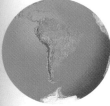

South America has a land area of 17.6 million sq km (6.9 million sq miles). To its east lies the Atlantic Ocean and to its west is the Pacific. South America is triangular in shape, tapering southward.

The countries that make up the continent had their boundaries determined by the colonial powers that engulfed the entire continent from the sixteenth century onwards. Most of the continent was divided between Spain and Portugal. Portugal established the largest South American colony, Brazil, while Spain claimed most of the remaining area. The Spanish colonies were Venezuela, Colombia, Ecuador, Peru, Bolivia, Chile, Argentina, Uruguay, and Paraguay. In the north, three comparatively small countries were created by Britain, France, and the Netherlands: Guyana, French Guiana, and Suriname respectively.

Physical features

The Andes Mountains, which arose when the South American and Pacific plates collided, form an elongated zone along the continent's western margin. The range, which is prone to earthquakes and volcanic eruptions, is narrow in the north, broadens out into a high plateau at 4,000 m (13,000 ft) in the center, where Lake Titicaca is situated, and narrows again toward the south.

The basin of the Amazon River, which is 6,570 km (4,080 miles) long, covers 8 million sq km (3 million sq miles) in equatorial South America. It is bordered to the south by the Mato Grosso Plateau and the highlands of Brazil, and to the north by the Guyana Highlands. Angel Falls, which at 979 m (3,212 ft) is the world's highest waterfall, is in Venezuela.

Climate and vegetation

The continent stretches from the tropics to the sub-polar zones and is climatically diverse. The tropics cover a large area in the north, with the southern part being more temperate.

The broad humid tropical zone is characterized by extensive forests in Brazil, Guyana, and Venezuela, and includes the world's largest remaining rainforest, the Amazon. Vast areas of this zone have been cleared for agriculture—mainly sugarcane plantations, and cattle ranches. Currently, the Amazon forests are under threat from logging and from the spread of agriculture and settlement, and are diminishing in size rapidly. The Amazon is rich in wildlife and contains a large number of plant species unique to the area.

In the north of the continent, where wet and dry seasons alternate, the forest trees are deciduous. In areas where there is little rainfall, shrubs and thorny vegetation prevail. The subtropical and temperate areas in the south of the continent are marked by extensive grasslands, with dispersed trees, as in the pampas of Argentina and in Patagonia. Toward the west lie desert areas, where vegetation is sparse.

In the central Andes, rainfall is concentrated on the eastern slopes, which are forested, though much deforestation has occurred. Along the arid western side, the sparse vegetation is generally thorny shrubs, and animal life is limited. The driest region of all is the Atacama Desert in Chile. There are cool temperate rainforests in southern Chile.

South America has abundant wildlife, including llamas, anteaters, armadillos, and iguanas. The giant anteater and giant armadillo are endangered species. Several unique species inhabit the Galapagos Islands, including the giant tortoise and the marine iguana. The seas off the west coast of temperate South America are rich in marine life due to the nutrient-rich cold waters of the Peru Current.

Population

South America's population is about 335.2 million (1999). Its relatively high living standards are reflected by life expectancies of 65.6 years for males and 72.6 years for females. The current population growth rate is 1.5 percent per year.

The original inhabitants of the continent were Amerindians who, it is believed, migrated from Asia across the Bering Straits. From the seventeenth century, settlers from Portugal and Spain immigrated in considerable numbers, bringing in Africans to work as agricultural labor. In the twentieth century, while migration from Europe was predominant, migrants also came from Asia. People of Italian descent are significant in Argentina, and Japanese people form locally important groups in Brazil and Peru.

The continent is highly urbanized—78 percent of the population lives in urban areas. Within the last 50 years, large numbers of people have moved to cities such as São Paulo (population 18 million), Rio de Janeiro and Buenos Aires (11 million each) and Lima (7 million). The result is urban congestion and the spread of shanty towns amid modern cities.

Agriculture

Several agricultural products, including maize, cashews, peanuts, avocadoes, and cacao, were grown in South America before the coming of the Europeans. Rubber-producing plants also grew there. Agriculture was extensively established when the continent was colonized, with crops including introduced species such as rice, wheat, sugarcane, coffee, bananas, and citrus fruits.

The tropical north of the continent produces sugar, bananas, mangoes, and rubber; wheat and temperate fruits are grown in the temperate south. Introduced animals provide the bulk of livestock; cattle are raised in a range of climate areas, and sheep are raised in the temperate grasslands. Among the indigenous animals reared are llamas and alpacas; alpacas are prized for their wool.

The Moreno Glacier in Argentina (left). A sample of the richness of the diminishing Amazon jungle, on the Ecuadorian side of the Andes (above). Tierra del Fuego, Argentina (previous pages).

Irrigation is important in certain regions, particularly in the west—Ecuador, Peru, and Chile. It is also of significance in Argentina.

Much of the forest areas of South America are logged for their timber. This is particularly the case in the Amazon, and conservationists worldwide are voicing their concern about the rate at which the forest is being lost. Tropical hardwoods are exported.

Illegal cultivation of narcotic drugs, particularly in Colombia, is also a matter of world concern.

Industrialization

South America is endowed with significant mineral deposits, such as tin in Bolivia, iron ore in Brazil, and petroleum in Venezuela. Large quantities of metallic ores are exported, though iron ore is used in Brazil for steel manufacture.

Industrialization has accelerated in South America since the 1950s, as a result of increased electricity generation; much of the continent's hydroelectric potential has been harnessed.

Manufacturing ranges from food processing to metal and chemical industries. Consumer items such as textiles, clothing, and footwear, as well as more expensive items such as motor cars, are manufactured both for the domestic market and for export.

A view of the Lake District in Chile (above), and fishing boats of the minority Uru people, in Peru (left). The blue-footed booby (below), from the Galapagos Islands, and the statue carving site on Easter Island, off Ecuador (below, right).

Languages

The original inhabitants, the Amerindians, belong to various groups and have several languages. Although many no longer speak those languages, in some areas, large numbers still do—Guaraní is widespread in Paraguay, for example. The official languages in South America are now those introduced by the colonial powers: Portuguese in Brazil, Spanish in most other countries, English in Guyana, Dutch in Suriname, and French in Guiana. In Guyana and Suriname, South Asian languages—principally Hindi—are also significant. Government, education, and the media predominantly use introduced European languages.

Boundary disputes and wars

There are currently no major boundary disputes or wars in South America; there was little conflict between the continent's countries during the twentieth century. However, there was considerable civil strife between guerilla groups and governments in several countries—Uruguay, Colombia, and Peru, for example. Armed drug cartels in Colombia also remain a major problem.

In some countries, notably Chile and Argentina, there have been periods of dictatorship during which the military have played a large role in government. During these periods there has been considerable loss of civilian lives.

In 1982 Argentina invaded the United Kingdom-ruled Falkland Islands (Islas Malvinas). After more than 1,000 people lost their lives in the ensuing war, and after international pressure, the islands were returned to United Kingdom rule.

Argentina

government was ousted by a military coup in 1976. A 3-man junta was then installed. Under this government thousands of people "disappeared" in a violent campaign against left-wing elements. Their fate has come back to haunt the present government.

Physical features and land use

There are four main regions. In the north lie the subtropical woodlands and swamps of the Gran Chaco, a zone that spills over the northeastern border into Paraguay. Swampy in parts, dry in others, and covered with thorny scrub, the Chaco is known as "Green Hell." To the west are the wooded slopes and valleys of the Andes; in the far south is the cold, semiarid Patagonian Plateau. It was the temperate region to the west and south of Buenos Aires that made Argentina famous. Here are the plains of the pampas—moist and fertile near the capital, drier but still productive elsewhere. These grasslands, where the gauchos (part Indian, part Spanish cattleherders) once lived and worked, are the basis of Argentina's cattle industry.

The pampas was largely created by gravel and sand brought down by streams from the Andes. A large native clump-grass called pampas grass, with coarse gray blades and silvery plumes, provided stock feed when the Spanish settlers arrived. They brought horses and cattle, and began to fence off the more productive land for ranching and cultivation. While beef raising is still important, much of the fertile parts of the pampas are now used for growing wheat, maize, alfalfa, and flax.

Argentina has many lakes on the slopes of the Andes, and the alpine terrain attracts tourists and skiers from elsewhere in South America. The Andes are widely affected by volcanic activity and there are several active volcanoes along the border with Chile, as well as Aconcagua, the highest mountain

outside the Himalayas. The huge Paraguay–Paraná–Uruguay River system, the second-largest on the continent, drains south from the Chaco and west from the highlands of Uruguay before emptying into the estuary of the River Plate (Río de la Plata). The three cities located here, two of them national capitals (the ports of Buenos Aires and Montevideo), mark the historic importance of this estuary.

People and culture

Hunters and fishermen occupied the Argentine region from 12,000 years ago, and in recent times the Yahgan and Ona people made their home in Tierra del Fuego, despite its bitter climate. In the sixteenth century Spanish settlers began moving into Argentina from Peru, Chile, and Paraguay, and in the nineteenth century a ferocious war cleared the pampas of its remaining Indians.

Today, more than one-third of the population is descended from Italian immigrants. Argentinians are overwhelmingly urban: 88 percent live in towns and cities, with 40 percent in Buenos Aires itself (an urban agglomeration of over 11 million). The European orientation of cultural life is reflected in their art, music, and literature.

With its northern extremity just north of the Tropic of Capricorn, but lying mainly within the temperate zone, Argentina becomes narrower and colder as it tapers south to Tierra del Fuego. The largest Spanish-speaking country of Latin America, it is named for the silver deposits that were sought by early explorers (*Argentina* means "land of silver"). In the nineteenth century Argentina attracted many Spanish and Italian immigrants in search of a better life, and today it contrasts with some of its neighbors in having a population that is mainly middle-class, with cosmopolitan interests, and strongly European in background and culture. Most Argentinians are of Spanish and Italian descent, but there are also people of German, Russian, French, and English background, as well as a Jewish community in Buenos Aires and a Welsh community in Patagonia.

Argentina's politics have been much influenced by the legacy of Colonel Juan Domingo Perón. A major force in Argentine politics from 1946 to 1976, "Perónism" was a mild form of fascism which combined military rule and statist economic policy with progressive labor legislation. After Perón's death in 1974, he was succeeded by his widow. The

Timeline	AD 600 Northwest settled by communities with complex social organizations—some have 10,000 to 20,000 members	1516 Spanish explorer Juan Díaz de Solís, first European to land on what is now Argentine soil; killed by Querandi people	1573 Towns of Córdoba and Mendoza develop on trade routes between Chile and Argentina	1816 Argentina declares independence from Spain	1866 San Roque Dam built on the Primero River providing irrigation and hydroelectric power	1910 Large numbers of European migrants arrive to farm and work on estates in the southern Pampas region	1944 Earthquake kills 5,000 people in San Juan province in the Andes
12,000 BP Small human communities live by hunting and fishing in territory now known as Argentina	**900** Native populations living in Andes in small-scale communities; culture has total population of 250,000–500,000	**1553** Permanent settlements established in northwest by Spanish arriving from Peru in search of gold and silver	**1580** Spanish colonists establish settlement of Buenos Aires on La Plata Estuary	**1830** Argentina lays claim to Islas Malvinas (the Falkland Islands), which are then occupied by Great Britain in 1833	**1876** Exports of meat and grain to Europe grow rapidly following introduction of refrigerated shipping	**1914** First World War followed by export-led boom in agricultural produce; Argentine population reaches 8 million	**1946** Colonel Juan Perón is elected President and later assumes the powers of a dictator

Buenos Aires, Argentina (below left). Autumn colors in Tierra del Fuego, Argentina (left). Llamas grazing on the plains at the foot of Mt Sajama, Bolivia (bottom right).

Economy and resources

Although the rural sector remains important, today industry makes a major contribution to the economy. Roughly one-fifth of the workforce is in manufacturing, mainly in industries producing frozen meat, canned meat, tallow, and leather for export. Wheat and fruit are also major exports. Energy available for industry includes nuclear power, hydroelectric power, and petroleum. There are oilfields in Patagonia and in the Mendoza area near the Andes, directly west of Buenos Aires.

Argentina has varied mineral resources—lead, zinc, tin, copper, silver, and uranium. It has a well-educated workforce and a diversified industrial base. Buenos Aires has a thriving computer industry. Episodes of hyperinflation have shaken investor confidence but increased political stability and reduced inflation in recent years are again attracting overseas investment. Reforms introduced by President Menem have seen a general restructuring, and there are signs that the economy has begun a period of stable and sustained growth.

Fact File

OFFICIAL NAME Argentine Republic

FORM OF GOVERNMENT Federal republic with two legislative bodies (Senate and Chamber of Deputies)

CAPITAL Buenos Aires

AREA 2,766,890 sq km (1,068,296 sq miles)

TIME ZONE GMT – 3 hours

POPULATION 36,737,664

PROJECTED POPULATION 2005 39,625,870

POPULATION DENSITY 13.3 per sq km (34.4 per sq mile)

LIFE EXPECTANCY 74.8

INFANT MORTALITY (PER 1,000) 18.4

OFFICIAL LANGUAGE Spanish

OTHER LANGUAGES English, Italian, German, French

LITERACY RATE 96%

RELIGIONS Roman Catholic 90%, Protestant 2%, Jewish 2%, other 6%

ETHNIC GROUPS European 85%, indigenous, mixed indigenous–European, other 15%

CURRENCY Argentine peso

ECONOMY Services 53%, industry 34%, agriculture 13%

GNP PER CAPITA US$8,030

CLIMATE Mainly temperate; subtropical in northern Chaco, cold and arid in Patagonia; snow on Andes

HIGHEST POINT Aconcagua 6,960 m (22,834 ft)

MAP REFERENCE Pages 458–59, 460

1955 Perón dismissed in military coup; he flees the country with his first wife, Eva	**1982** Argentina invades Falklands after talks with Britain over sovereignty break down—Britain retakes the islands	**1994** Paraguay and Argentina jointly build Corpus Posados Dam on the Pananá River to create hydroelectric power
1973–74 Perón returns, is re-elected, dies; his third wife, "Isabelita", governs until arrested in coup in 1976 in which thousands die	**1990** Full diplomatic relations with Britain are restored	

Bolivia

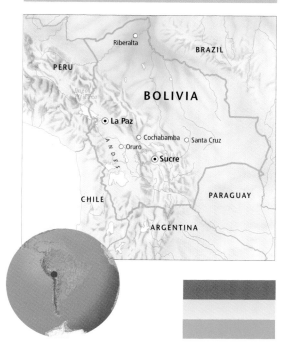

High on the Altiplano, a plateau nearly 3,600 m (12,000 ft) above sea level, La Paz is the world's loftiest capital city. In the sixteenth century, when the Spanish conquistadores arrived in Bolivia, they found silver and the mine they established at Potosi soon became famous. But the silver boom passed, the prices for the minerals and metals that replaced it (mainly tin) have been volatile, and Bolivia is now South America's poorest nation. It is landlocked, and its rugged terrain makes it doubly inaccessible. Notorious for its political instability (192 coups between 1824 and 1981), and for the hyperinflation that rose to 11,700 percent in 1985, it now appears to have a democratic government that is trying to establish economic order.

Quechua and Aymara Indians together form 55 percent of the population. Subsistence farmers, they grow maize, potatoes, and coca on the Altiplano. This cold, treeless region runs 400 km (250 miles) north to south between two major Andean ranges. At its north, Indians still fish in Lake Titicaca from boats made of reeds. In the south are salt flats. The vegetation of the Altiplano is grassland which changes to scrubland at higher elevations. To the

east lies the Oriente, reaching down across the Andean foothills and the plains. It includes the semi-arid Chaco of the southeast, the savanna country of the center, and the plains of the northern forests whose rivers feed into the Amazon Basin.

The hyperinflation of the 1980s damaged the tin industry, causing the country to fall from first producer in the world to fifth. Government efforts reduced inflation to 20 percent by 1988, and to 9.3 percent by 1993. In the mid-1990s the state airline, railroad, and telephone companies were privatized, plus state mining and oil companies. Metals, natural gas, soybeans, and jewelry are officially the main exports but coca grown for cocaine may well be the biggest export earner—Bolivia is the world's second-largest cultivator of coca leaf. This has affected aid arrangements because the main donor, the USA, demands proof of Bolivian efforts to eradicate coca farms.

Fact File

OFFICIAL NAME Republic of Bolivia

FORM OF GOVERNMENT Republic with two legislative bodies (Senate and Chamber of Deputies)

CAPITAL Sucre (official); La Paz (administrative)

AREA 1,098,580 sq km (424,161 sq miles)

TIME ZONE GMT – 4 hours

POPULATION 7,982,850

PROJECTED POPULATION 2005 8,920,665

POPULATION DENSITY 7.3 per sq km (18.8 per sq mile)

LIFE EXPECTANCY 61.4

INFANT MORTALITY (PER 1,000) 62.0

OFFICIAL LANGUAGES Spanish, Quechua, Aymara

LITERACY RATE 82.5%

RELIGIONS Roman Catholic 95%, other 5%

ETHNIC GROUPS Quechua 30%, Aymara 25%, mixed indigenous–European 30%, European 15%

CURRENCY Boliviano

ECONOMY Agriculture 50%, services 36%, industry 14%

GNP PER CAPITA US$800

CLIMATE Tropical north and east; cold, arid west of Andes

HIGHEST POINT Nevado Sajama 6,520 m (21,391 ft)

MAP REFERENCE Page 455

Brazil

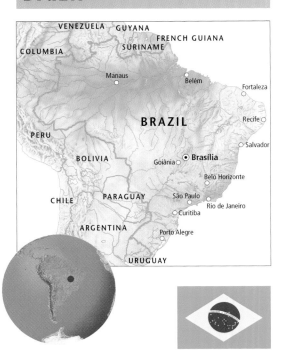

Fact File

OFFICIAL NAME Federative Republic of Brazil

FORM OF GOVERNMENT Federal republic with two legislative bodies (Senate and Chamber of Deputies)

CAPITAL Brasília

AREA 8,511,965 sq km (3,286,470 sq miles)

TIME ZONE GMT – 3/5 hours

POPULATION 171,853,126

PROJECTED POPULATION 2005 182,836,908

POPULATION DENSITY 20.2 per sq km (52.3 per sq mile)

LIFE EXPECTANCY 64.1

INFANT MORTALITY (PER 1,000) 35.4

OFFICIAL LANGUAGE Portuguese

OTHER LANGUAGES Spanish, English, French

LITERACY RATE 82.7%

RELIGIONS Roman Catholic 89%, Protestant 7%, other 4%

ETHNIC GROUPS European 55%, mixed European–African 38%, African 6%, other 1%

CURRENCY Real

ECONOMY Services 55%, agriculture 29%, industry 16%

GNP PER CAPITA US$3,640

CLIMATE Mainly tropical, but temperate in south

HIGHEST POINT Pico da Neblina 3,014 m (9,888 ft)

MAP REFERENCE Pages 450–51, 452–53, 454–55, 456–57

Brazil is the fifth largest country in the world and comprises nearly half of South America. Originally the home of numerous Amerindian tribes, Brazil was ruled by the Portuguese after their arrival in 1500. Political independence of a sort came in 1822, but a form of monarchy, sponsored by Portuguese royalty and featuring a self-styled Emperor of Brazil, existed until the first republic was declared in 1889.

Today, the wellbeing of the Amazon Basin is a cause of international concern, yet for most of Brazil's history this huge region was virtually ignored. In the eyes of the first settlers the most valuable land was the fertile coastal strip from Recife to Rio de Janeiro. In the north of this area they established huge sugarcane plantations, brought 4 million African slaves to do the work, and became so dependent on slavery that it was only abolished in 1888. In the south, around São Paulo (now the world's third largest city), a huge coffee-growing industry became established. Ethnically mixed and rich in resources, Brazil has the potential to play a major role internationally.

Physical features and land use

Brazil has two major and several minor regions. In the north is the vast tropical area—once an inland sea—drained by the Amazon and its more than 1,000 tributaries. Occupying the entire northern half of the country, this river system passes through vast regions of rainforest. A greater variety of plant species grows here than in any other habitat in the world and the forest is home to a phenomenal range of animals and birds. More than 1,000 bird species are found here and as many as 3,000 species of fish swim in the rivers, along with other animals such as caiman (alligator), freshwater dolphin, and the endangered manatee—a large herbivorous mammal.

At present it is estimated that the rainforest is being reduced at a rate of between 1.5 and 4 percent per year as a result of logging, mining, ranching, and the resettlement of Brazil's many landless peasants. In early 1998 forest fires raged through the the northern state of Roraima. Ignited partly by traditional Amerindian slash-and-burn horticulture, partly by settlers clearing land, and aggravated by unusually dry conditions, much devastation was caused.

The second main region, the Brazilian Highlands, lies in the center and south of the country. This is an extensive plateau of hard, ancient rock in which weathering has formed deep river valleys. Much of the interior is covered by savanna woodland, thinning to semi-deciduous scrub in the northeast. There are spectacular waterfalls on the Uruguay River on the southern side of the plateau and on the Paraná River west of the coastal highlands.

The interior of the Nordeste (northeast) region is the most undeveloped and drought-stricken corner of Brazil, and it is from here that large numbers of subsistence farmers who can no

longer make a living have emigrated to the industrial center of São Paulo, looking for work.

The swampy Pantanal, in the southwest, flooded for seven months of the year, is the largest area of wetland in the world and has a striking diversity of wildlife.

People and culture

As in the Caribbean, the sugar industry's demand for slaves strongly influenced the ethnic composition of Brazil. But to a greater extent than in the slave-owning South of the USA, the result has been both economic and social integration. While Brazilian society shows extremes of wealth and poverty, the divisions are drawn along socio-economic rather than ethnic lines. Culturally, Brazil is a mixture of elements. This is particularly reflected in its religious life. Most people are Christian, mainly Roman Catholic. But a variety of African popular cults exist, such as candomblé, which are often mixed with Christianity.

Brazil also has the largest population of Japanese outside Japan. Arriving as poor farmers in the 1920s, 2 million of them now live in São Paulo and are prominent in commercial life. In the upper reaches

Timeline

AD 1500 Portuguese land in Brazil naming it after the *brasa* ("brazilwood" in Portuguese); the native population is about 2 million	**1530** Portuguese settle on Atlantic coast; establish sugarcane plantations, and grow tobacco and cotton for markets in Europe	**1790** Native peoples used as slaves on plantations; slaves also brought from Africa and elsewhere (slavery abolished 1888)	**1822** John's son Pedro declares independence and is Emperor until 1831; his son Pedro II rules 1841–89	**1889** Don Pedro II overthrown and Brazil is proclaimed a republic	**1934** Republic ends; Vargas is President as Depression hits; he becomes dictator (1937) and embarks on major public works	**1942** Brazil joins Allies in Second World War and sends 25,000 troops to fight in Italy

12,000 BP Humans inhabit forests, living in small groups, hunting and fishing in rivers, and eating wild fruit and vegetables	**3500 BC** Amerindian people live in Amazon Basin, growing crops of potatoes and maize, and domesticating guinea pigs and llamas	**1690** Prospectors find gold, diamonds in Minas Gerais and Mato Grosso; thousands of Portuguese settle in these regions	**1808** John, ruler of Portugal, flees to Brazil, names Rio de Janeiro capital of Portuguese Empire; returns to Portugal 1821	**1870** Rubber production soars in Amazon area, attracting migrants from the east and from Europe	**1917** Brazil sides with the Allies in the First World War and declares war on Germany · **1946** New constitution creates democratic system	**1950** Industrialization in southeast results in rural depopulation; by 1960 about 80% of Brazilians are living near Atlantic coast

438

Chile

Chile, the political right under General Pinochet staged a coup and ruled for the next 17 years. During that time, over 2,000 political opponents "disappeared." Economically, the coup's effects were more positive. The regime restored economic liberalism and dismantled state controls. Democracy was restored at a general election in 1989.

After two decades of political turmoil, Chile is now one of the more economically progressive of South America's democracies. It is the world's leading supplier of copper, and high copper prices remain vital to the nation's economic health. Growth in gross domestic product averaged more than 6 percent annually from 1991 to 1995, and in recent years an estimated 1 million Chileans have ceased to be classed as poor.

Fact File

OFFICIAL NAME	Republic of Chile
FORM OF GOVERNMENT	Republic with two legislative bodies (High Assembly and Chamber of Deputies)
CAPITAL	Santiago
AREA	756,950 sq km (292,258 sq miles)
TIME ZONE	GMT – 4 hours
POPULATION	14,839,304
PROJECTED POPULATION 2005	15,716,337
POPULATION DENSITY	19.6 per sq km (50.8 per sq mile)
LIFE EXPECTANCY	75.2
INFANT MORTALITY (PER 1,000)	12.4
OFFICIAL LANGUAGE	Spanish
LITERACY RATE	95%
RELIGIONS	Roman Catholic 89%, Protestant 11%
ETHNIC GROUPS	European and mixed indigenous–European 93%, indigenous 5%, other 2%
CURRENCY	Chilean peso
ECONOMY	Services 63%, agriculture 19%, industry 18%
GNP PER CAPITA	US$4,160
CLIMATE	Arid in north, cold and wet in far south, temperate elsewhere
HIGHEST POINT	Ojos del Salado 6,880 m (22,572 ft)
MAP REFERENCE	Pages 458, 460

Rio de Janeiro, in Brazil (below left). The Igaçu Falls, from the Brazilian side (above). Mountains in the Torres del Paine National Park, Chile (below right).

of the Xingu, Araguaia, and Tocantins Rivers, small groups of Indians such as the Tapirapé survive in forest refuges. Gold prospectors have driven off or killed those Yanomami Indians in Roraima State who have stood in their way.

Economy and resources

Traditional rural activities continue to be important, the rural sector employing 29 percent of the labor force. Brazil is the world's largest producer of coffee and Brazilian livestock numbers are among the world's largest—mainly cattle and pigs—but trends show a steadily falling agricultural contribution to gross domestic product. Industry is increasing in importance, particularly manufacturing, with 90 percent of power coming from hydroelectric schemes. Despite some development of domestic sources, gasoline is still imported. Brazil attempted to substitute ethanol made from sugar for gasoline during the 1980s but falling oil prices made this uneconomical.

With South America's largest gross domestic product, Brazil has the potential to play a leading international role. Yet it must still be considered a developing country as it does not have a fully modern economy. Some difficulties have arisen from heavy state borrowing for unproductive projects; others stem from runaway inflation in the 1980s. Fiscal reforms are difficult to carry through politically—many need constitutional amendments. However, these problems are being addressed (consumer prices rose by 23 percent in 1995 compared with more than 1,000 per cent in 1994) and investor confidence is returning.

1960 Capital moves from Rio de Janeiro to Brasília, a new city built in the highlands of the interior	**1982** Itaipú Dam on Paraná River, one of the world's largest, completed, provides hydroelectric power for growing industries	**1992** Brazil hosts UN summit on global environmental issues, particularly global warming and green-house gas emissions
1973 Trans-Amazon Highway links remote western areas to the rest of the country	**1975** Population reaches 108 million (rising from 53 million in 1950)	**1998** Clearing of rainforest in Roraima attracts international attention—attempts are made to halt the process

Chile lies between the Andes and the sea. It stretches 4,350 km (2,700 miles) along South America's Pacific coast, yet is never more than 180 km (110 miles) wide. In the fifteenth century, the Incas from Peru tried but failed to subjugate its Araucanian Indian population. This was gradually achieved by the Spanish, against strong resistance, after their arrival in the sixteenth century. The Spanish established mining in the north and huge estates in the Central Valley; by the nineteenth century produce was being exported to California, Australia and elsewhere. Today, fruit and vegetables remain important exports, along with wine.

The Atacama Desert (Desierto de Atacama), in the north, has one of the lowest rainfalls in the world. In the nineteenth century it was the world's main source of nitrate for fertilizer, an export which underwrote Chile's early economic development. Santiago and the port of Valparaíso form an urban cluster midway along the length of the country. Santiago lies in a sheltered, temperate valley between a coastal range of mountains to the west and the high Andes in the interior. This fertile 800 km (500 mile) valley is where Chile's main vineyards are located, and where 60 percent of the population live. It is also where most manufacturing industry is located. Volcanoes, active and inactive, mark the length of the Chilean Andes to the east. In the southern third of the country the coastal range disintegrates into a maze of islands, archipelagoes, and fiords.

In 1970 President Allende nationalized the copper industry and other large enterprises, raised wages, and fixed prices. By 1973 inflation had reached 850 percent. Fearing a Cubanization of

Colombia

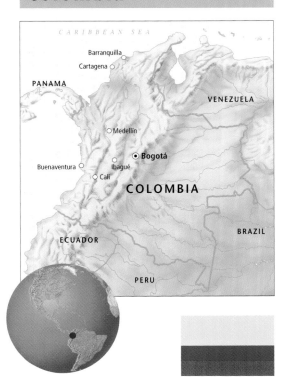

Visited by Christopher Columbus in 1499 and named after him, Colombia straddles the South American continent south of the isthmus of Panama. Once the home of the Chibcha Indians, the country came under Spanish control in 1544, after which it became their chief source of gold. Colombia achieved independence in 1819. From that time on the political and economic fortunes of the country have been contested by the anti-clerical free-trading Liberals and the Conservatives, upholders of protectionism and the Church. While Colombia is notorious for its drug cartels and exports of cocaine, it has a diversified and stable economy that has, for 25 years, shown Latin America's most consistent record of growth.

The country can be divided into three regions. The hot, wet Pacific lowlands run south from the Panamanian border; to the north they merge into drier lowlands along the Caribbean. The cities that face the Caribbean—Barranquilla, Santa Marta, and Cartagena—are tourist resorts. Inland, the parallel Andean ranges running north from the Ecuadorian border define the second region, the high valleys of the Cauca and Magdalena Rivers. This is where most people live. The third region comprises the foothills east of the Andes, where the land falls away into the forested basins of the Amazon (Amazonas) and Orinoco Rivers. This region amounts to almost two-thirds of Colombia's area but only a few cattle ranchers and Indians live here.

With Latin America's largest proven reserves of coal, Colombia is the region's biggest coal exporter. Some 80 percent of the world's emeralds also come from here. Coffee, however, remains the biggest legitimate revenue-earning export. Since 1990 growth in gross domestic product has averaged 4 percent annually, led by expanding construction and financial service industries, and inflows of foreign capital. Nevertheless, earnings from processed cocaine probably exceed all others. Problems include a poverty index of 40 percent, and a continuing political crisis related to allegations of drug connections at high levels.

Fact File

OFFICIAL NAME Republic of Colombia

FORM OF GOVERNMENT Republic with two legislative bodies (Senate and House of Representatives)

CAPITAL Bogotá

AREA 1,138,910 sq km (439,733 sq miles)

TIME ZONE GMT – 5 hours

POPULATION 39,309,422

PROJECTED POPULATION 2005 43,662,177

POPULATION DENSITY 34.5 per sq km (89.4 per sq mile)

LIFE EXPECTANCY 70.5

INFANT MORTALITY (PER 1,000) 24.3

OFFICIAL LANGUAGE Spanish

LITERACY RATE 91.1%

RELIGIONS Roman Catholic 95%; Protestant, Jewish, other 5%

ETHNIC GROUPS Mixed indigenous–European 58%, European 20%, mixed European–African 14%, African 4%, mixed indigenous–African 3%, indigenous 1%

CURRENCY Colombian peso

ECONOMY Services 46%, agriculture 30%, industry 24%

GNP PER CAPITA US$1,910

CLIMATE Tropical along coast and on plains, cool to sometimes cold in highlands

HIGHEST POINT Nevado del Huila 5,750 m (18,865 ft)

MAP REFERENCE Pages 450–51

Riverboats in Puerto Colombia, Colombia (below). Pigs for sale at the market at Otavalo, Ecuador (bottom). The volcano Cotopaxi in Ecuador (above right). A view of one of the Galapagos Islands (bottom right).

Ecuador

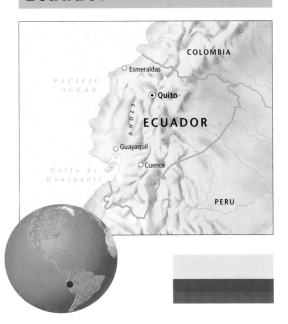

Ecuador is the smallest of the Andean republics, taking its name from the equator which divides it in half. Quito was briefly an Inca city before being conquered by the Spanish in the 1530s. The city is ringed by volcanoes, including Cotopaxi (5,896 m; 19,344 ft), the world's highest active volcano. The groups of Indians that form 25 percent of the population are pressing for recognition as distinct nationalities within the state.

Ecuador's agriculture is based on the coastal plains. Bananas, coffee, and cocoa are the main crops. Most production is on haciendas—huge estates established during the early years of Spanish occupation. Inland, among the Andes, are valleys where livestock is raised. The eastern slopes of the Andes give way to forested upland and the border with Peru. This region is so little known that hostilities between Peru and Ecuador in 1995 arose partly from uncertainty as to where the frontier should be. Petroleum and natural gas from this area are piped over the Andes to the Pacific port of Esmeraldas.

Ecuador grows more bananas than any other country in the world. Until overtaken by petroleum

and natural gas, bananas were its biggest export earner, and access to markets in the USA and the EU is a continuing concern. The highland Indians survive through subsistence farming, growing maize and potatoes. Recent economic reforms have helped control inflation and increased foreign investment. Growth has been uneven, however, because manufacturing is handicapped by a shortage of electricity.

Ecuador owns the Galapagos Islands, home to many unique species of animal, such as the giant tortoise. These islands are a popular ecotourism destination, with visitor numbers limited to 40,000 a year so as to protect the fragile ecosystem.

Fact File

OFFICIAL NAME	Republic of Ecuador
FORM OF GOVERNMENT	Republic with single legislative body (National Congress)
CAPITAL	Quito
AREA	283,560 sq km (109,483 sq miles)
TIME ZONE	GMT – 5 hours
POPULATION	12,562,496
PROJECTED POPULATION 2005	13,837,829
POPULATION DENSITY	44.3 per sq km (114.7 per sq mile)
LIFE EXPECTANCY	72.2
INFANT MORTALITY (PER 1,000)	30.7
OFFICIAL LANGUAGE	Spanish
OTHER LANGUAGES	Indigenous languages, particularly Quechua
LITERACY RATE	89.6%
RELIGIONS	Roman Catholic 95%, other 5%
ETHNIC GROUPS	Indigenous–European 55%, indigenous 25%, Spanish 10%, African 10%
CURRENCY	Sucre
ECONOMY	Services 42%, agriculture 39%, industry 19%
GNP PER CAPITA	US$1,390
CLIMATE	Tropical on coast and plains, cooler in highlands
HIGHEST POINT	Chimborazo 6,310 m (20,702 ft)
MAP REFERENCE	Page 450

Guyana

Guyana means "the land of many waters." In 1616 it was settled by the Dutch, who built dikes, reclaimed coastal land, and planted sugarcane. When the indigenous people refused to work in the sugar plantations, the Dutch, and later the British, imported slaves from Africa and indentured labor from India. The contrast between the communities descended from these two immigrant groups defines Guyanese political life. Beginning in 1953, and sharpened by independence in 1970, a struggle for dominance continues between the Afro-Guyanese and the numerically superior Indo-Guyanese. Some 95 percent of the people live on the coastal strip, and there is concern about flooding because of poor dike maintenance. The savannas, river valleys, and forested plateaus of the interior are largely unpopulated. There are, however, settlements of two neglected minorities in the forests—blacks descended from escaped slaves; and Carib, Warrau, and Arawak Amerindians.

Numerous rivers, including the country's main river, the Essequibo, flow down from the mountains in the west through tropical forests inhabited by a rich assortment of wildlife, including sloth, jaguar, tapir, and capybara. There is diamond dredging in many of the rivers, and in 1995 there was a major cyanide spill at the Omai gold mine near the Essequibo. The effects of mining activities on the wildlife is of major concern to conservationists.

The mining of high-quality bauxite and sugar production accounts for 80 percent of exports. Other resources include gold, diamonds, uranium, manganese, oil, copper, and molybdenum. Under successive governments, state ownership and government controls have stunted development and made adaptation to market fluctuations difficult. The bauxite industry remains a state monopoly. Recent deregulation has, however, shown benefits. Though weak infrastructure hampers tourist development, the spectacular scenery and wildlife of the interior is attracting visitors.

Fact File

OFFICIAL NAME	Cooperative Republic of Guyana
FORM OF GOVERNMENT	Republic with single legislative body (National Assembly)
CAPITAL	Georgetown
AREA	214,970 sq km (83,000 sq miles)
TIME ZONE	GMT – 3 hours
POPULATION	705,156
PROJECTED POPULATION 2005	708,582
POPULATION DENSITY	3.3 per sq km (8.5 per sq mile)
LIFE EXPECTANCY	61.8
INFANT MORTALITY (PER 1,000)	48.6
OFFICIAL LANGUAGE	English
OTHER LANGUAGES	Amerindian languages, Hindi, Urdu
LITERACY RATE	97.9%
RELIGIONS	Protestant 34%, Hindu 34%, Roman Catholic 18%, Muslim 9%, other 5%
ETHNIC GROUPS	East Indian 51%, African and mixed indigenous–African 43%, indigenous 4%, European and Chinese 2%
CURRENCY	Guyana dollar
ECONOMY	Industry 44%, agriculture 34%, services 22%
GNP PER CAPITA	US$590
CLIMATE	Tropical with two rainy seasons (May to mid-August, mid-November to mid-January)
HIGHEST POINT	Mt Roraima 2,810 m (9,219 ft)
MAP REFERENCE	Page 451

South America

441

Paraguay

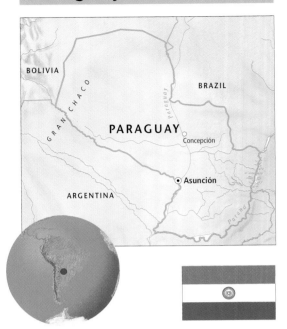

Fact File

OFFICIAL NAME	Republic of Paraguay
FORM OF GOVERNMENT	Republic with two legislative bodies (Senate and Chamber of Deputies)
CAPITAL	Asunción
AREA	406,750 sq km (157,046 sq miles)
TIME ZONE	GMT – 4 hours
POPULATION	5,434,095
PROJECTED POPULATION 2005	6,340,163
POPULATION DENSITY	13.4 per sq km (34.7 per sq mile)
LIFE EXPECTANCY	72.4
INFANT MORTALITY (PER 1,000)	36.4
OFFICIAL LANGUAGE	Spanish
OTHER LANGUAGE	Guaraní
LITERACY RATE	91.9%
RELIGIONS	Roman Catholic 90%; other (including Mennonite, Baptist and Anglican) 10%
ETHNIC GROUPS	Mixed indigenous–European 95%; indigenous, European, Asian, African 5%
CURRENCY	Guaraní
ECONOMY	Agriculture 49%, services 30%, industry 21%
GNP PER CAPITA	US$1,690
CLIMATE	Subtropical; wet in east, semiarid in west
HIGHEST POINT	Cerro San Rafael 850 m (2,789 ft)
MAP REFERENCE	Pages 455, 458–59

A small landlocked country, Paraguay was originally the home of the Guaraní Indians. It was settled by the Spaniards in 1537 who hoped to use the Guaraní as laborers on their big estates. The strong influence of the Jesuits, however, largely prevented the exploitation of the indigenous people by settlers that occurred elsewhere in South America under Spanish Catholic rule, and a socially benign intermix took place. Today, 95 percent of the population are of combined Indian and Spanish descent.

Fully independent since 1813, Paraguay is best known in modern times for the severe regime imposed by General Stroessner between 1954 and

1989. Assuming power after a period of chronic upheaval—six presidents in six years and revolts that had left thousands dead—he brought economic and political stability, and greatly improved the national infrastructure. This was at the price of considerable repression, and the huge hydroelectric projects that were built on the Paraná River incurred sizeable foreign debts.

Across the plains, south of Asunción, the Paraná becomes a highway to the sea. Paraguay has some 3,100 km (1,900 miles) of navigable waterways, the most important being the Paraguay River which bisects the country north to south. To the west of Paraguay are the marshy, insect-infested plains of the Gran Chaco, but as the land rises toward the Bolivian border the Chaco changes to semidesert scrub. East of the river the land rises to a plateau forested with tropical hardwoods.

The economy of Paraguay has long been based on agriculture, and large numbers of people still live by means of subsistence farming. Cattle raising and the production of meat products remain the leading agricultural activity but cash crops such as cotton, soybeans, and timber are of increasing importance as a source of export income. Moreover, Paraguay's excess electricity capacity enables it to export power to Brazil.

The informal sector of the economy is also important. Small enterprises and street vendors flourish by importing and re-exporting consumer goods such as electronic devices, alcoholic beverages, and perfumes. While tourism is poorly developed, day-trippers pour in from Brazil and Argentina to buy these goods.

Peru

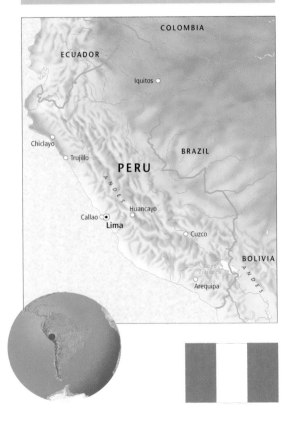

Humans have been living in Peru for about 10,000 years, and by 3,000 years ago Peruvian civilization had emerged, featuring irrigation agriculture, fine pottery, and expertly woven textiles of striking design. The Incas, one of the many tribes that inhabited the highlands of Peru, established a great empire in the thirteenth century that extended from Ecuador south to central Chile. Accomplished engineers, the Incas built an extensive network of roads and bridges, and many fine cities. The most famous of these is Machu Picchu, high above the Urubamba Valley. The Spanish came to Peru in 1532, lured by stories of a "kingdom of gold" and rapidly destroyed Inca civilization.

Recently Peru has experienced serious political trouble. Deep social divisions gave rise in 1980 to

Indians dancing at a festival in Peru (below left). A rural settlement near Cuzco, Peru (top left). A civic building in Paramaribo, Suriname (above).

the movement known as Sendero Luminoso, or Shining Path, a Maoist guerrilla group. By 1990 its activities had resulted in the loss of 23,000 lives— most of them members of its own constituency, the Indians and mixed Spanish–Indians of the Andes—along with damage to the economy in the order of US$20 billion. In recent years the government has been able to bring about greater stability.

Some 40 percent of Peru's population live on its arid coastal plain, which merges in the south with the rainless Atacama Desert of northern

Chile. Numerous rivers crossing the plain from the Andes have made fertile valleys where cotton, rice, and sugarcane are grown. Inland, in the valleys of two high ranges of the Andean Sierra, the western and the eastern Cordilleras, about 50 percent of the people live, most of them Indians practicing subsistence agriculture. East of the Andes the land falls away into the almost uninhabited region of the Amazon Basin. Here, the Ucayali and Marañón Rivers flow through rainforest to Iquitos, the most inland navigable port on the Amazon River.

Peru's economy depends heavily on copper and petroleum exports. Agriculture is limited by the lack of arable land. Fishing for anchovies and sardines has been historically important in the cool Humboldt current offshore, but periodic warming of the ocean from the El Niño effect reduces the catch, as has occurred several times in recent years. In 1992 it fell by 30 percent.

The ruins of Machu Picchu are an incomparable spectacle for tourists, but poor facilities and guerrilla activities have discouraged visitors. Battered by hyperinflation, which reached 7,480 percent in 1990, Peru has recently undergone a series of economic reforms guided by the IMF and the World Bank. By 1995 inflation had been reduced to 11 percent, while growth in gross domestic product for that year was about 7 percent.

Suriname

Formerly known as Dutch Guiana, Suriname is a small country on the northeastern coast of South America. In 1667 two colonial powers exchanged territory: the Dutch gave the British New Amsterdam, which became New York. In return the British gave Suriname to the Dutch. From the Low Countries the new proprietors brought their dike-building skills to reclaim a narrow coastal strip, and soon sugar plantations took the place of marshes and mangrove swamps. At first African slaves were imported to do the work; later labor was brought from India, China, and Java, and these three immigrant groups have determined both the ethnic composition of the country and its political fate.

Since 1954 Suriname has had the status of an equal partner in the "Tripartite Kingdom of the Netherlands." This has benefited those who have

fled the continual military coups and civil disturbance in Suriname, using their Dutch citizenship to enter the Netherlands in large numbers. As was the case in nearby Guyana, escaped African slaves established isolated settlements in the hinterland. Guerrilla uprisings in both 1986 and 1994 have made the descendants of these people an urban political force.

Inland of the cultivated coastal strip lies a zone of sandy savanna, and south of this a vast area of dense forest begins (92 percent of the nation's total land area). Suriname has the world's highest ratio of forested country and it is still virtually untouched as timber is not among the nation's exports. The forests stretch inland to the Guiana Highlands, which are an extension of the Tumucumaque mountain range in northeastern Brazil. Over time, weathered soils have been washed from the uplands down to the alluvial valleys below, providing the foundation of the thriving bauxite industry.

Bauxite accounts for 15 percent of Suriname's gross domestic product and more than 65 percent of export earnings. Other exports include shrimp, fish, rice, bananas, citrus fruits, and coconuts. For most people rice is the staple food, supplemented by tropical fruits and vegetables.

Both ethnic conflict and economic crises have damaged the country's prospects for some years, although the campaign by guerrillas against the urban political elite seems for the present to have faded. Inflation was running at 600 percent in 1994. The resumption of economic aid by the Netherlands has led to a greater confidence in Suriname's economy, but substantial progress is unlikely without major economic reform.

Fact File

OFFICIAL NAME	Republic of Peru
FORM OF GOVERNMENT	Republic with single legislative body (Congress)
CAPITAL	Lima
AREA	1,285,220 sq km (496,223 sq miles)
TIME ZONE	GMT – 5 hours
POPULATION	26,625,121
PROJECTED POPULATION 2005	29,658,649
POPULATION DENSITY	20.7 per sq km (53.7 per sq mile)
LIFE EXPECTANCY	70.4
INFANT MORTALITY (PER 1,000)	41.4
OFFICIAL LANGUAGES	Spanish, Quechua
OTHER LANGUAGE	Aymara
LITERACY RATE	88.3%
RELIGIONS	Roman Catholic 90%; others, including Anglican and Methodist 10%
ETHNIC GROUPS	Indigenous 45%, mixed indigenous–European 37%, European 15%; others (mainly African, Japanese, Chinese) 3%
CURRENCY	Nuevo sol
ECONOMY	Services 53%, agriculture 35%, industry 12%
GNP PER CAPITA	US$2,310
CLIMATE	Tropical in east, arid along coast, cold on high mountains
HIGHEST POINT	Nev. Huascarán 6,768 m (22,204 ft)
MAP REFERENCE	Pages 450, 454–56

Fact File

OFFICIAL NAME	Republic of Suriname
FORM OF GOVERNMENT	Republic with single legislative body (National Assembly)
CAPITAL	Paramaribo
AREA	163,270 sq km (63,038 sq miles)
TIME ZONE	GMT – 3 hours
POPULATION	431,156
PROJECTED POPULATION 2005	445,506
POPULATION DENSITY	2.6 per sq km (6.7 per sq mile)
LIFE EXPECTANCY	70.9
INFANT MORTALITY (PER 1,000)	26.5
OFFICIAL LANGUAGE	Dutch
OTHER LANGUAGES	English, Sranang Tongo (Surinamese), Hindi, Javanese, Chinese
LITERACY RATE	92.7%
RELIGIONS	Hindu 27.4%, Muslim 19.6%, Roman Catholic 22.8%, Protestant 25.2%, indigenous 5%
ETHNIC GROUPS	Hindustani (East Indian) 37%, mixed European–African 31%, Javanese 15%, African 10%, Amerindian 3%, Chinese 2%, European 1%, other 1%
CURRENCY	Suriname guilder
GNP PER CAPITA	US$880
CLIMATE	Tropical: hot and wet year-round
HIGHEST POINT	Julianatop 1,230 m (4,035 ft)
MAP REFERENCE	Page 452

South America

Uruguay

Fact File

OFFICIAL NAME	Eastern Republic of Uruguay
FORM OF GOVERNMENT	Republic with two legislative bodies (Senate and Chamber of Deputies)
CAPITAL	Montevideo
AREA	176,220 sq km (68,038 sq miles)
TIME ZONE	GMT – 3 hours
POPULATION	3,308,583
PROJECTED POPULATION 2005	3,458,798
POPULATION DENSITY	18.8 per sq km (48.7 per sq mile)
LIFE EXPECTANCY	75.8
INFANT MORTALITY (PER 1,000)	13.5
OFFICIAL LANGUAGE	Spanish
LITERACY RATE	97.1%
RELIGIONS	Roman Catholic 66%, Protestant 2%, Jewish 2%, unaffiliated 30%
ETHNIC GROUPS	European 88%, mixed indigenous–European 8%, African 4%
CURRENCY	Uruguayan peso
ECONOMY	Services 67%, industry 18%, agriculture 15%
GNP PER CAPITA	US$5,170
CLIMATE	Temperate, with warm summers and mild winters
HIGHEST POINT	Cerro Catedral 513 m (1,683 ft)
MAP REFERENCE	Page 459

Uruguay, the second-smallest country in South America, lies northeast of Argentina on the estuary of the River Plate (Río de la Plata). Controlled for 150 years alternately by the Portuguese and the Spanish, Uruguay finally gained independence in 1828, after which came 40 years of civil war. When peace was secured, waves of immigrants flocked to Uruguay from Spain and Italy, the cattle industry and meat exports expanded, investment poured in, and the country prospered. It may even have prospered too much: many benefits and welfare provisions were introduced in the days of prosperity which in poorer times have proved difficult to pay for. An urban guerrilla movement known as the Tupamaros paralyzed the cities during the 1960s, provoking a repressive military crackdown and dictatorship. Democracy was restored in 1984.

Most of Uruguay is temperate and mild: it never snows and frosts are rare, though the pampero, a wind coming off the pampas to the south, can be cold and violent. Most of the country is covered with rich grasslands, a continuation of the Argentine pampas, where cattle and sheep are raised. Although 90 percent of Uruguay's land is suitable for cultivation, only some 10 percent is currently used for agriculture, but this is enough to ensure that the country is largely self-sufficient in food. Uruguay's main river is the Negro, flowing east–west across the center of the country. On either side of the Negro the land rises to a plateau that marks the southern limits of the Brazilian Highlands. Water from the uplands feeds down the Negro into a large artificial lake, Lake Rincón del Bonete, which is used for hydroelectric power.

Uruguay's rural economy is based on sheep and cattle raising, and its industries are mainly based on animal products: meat processing, leather, and wool and textile manufacturing. The country is the second largest wool exporter in the world. But Uruguay is not rich in other resources: it has no petroleum or minerals except for agate, amethyst, gold deposits, and small quantities of iron ore. It is entirely dependent on imported oil. The ample supplies of hydroelectricity that are available help to offset this disadvantage, and only governmental regulatory constraints prevent industrial expansion.

Uruguay is at present undergoing a program of modernization, the most prominent issue being the privatization of the extremely large state sector (25 percent of the country's employees are currently civil servants) inherited from its more prosperous past. Tourism is booming, consisting mainly of visitors to Montevideo.

A view of Caracas, the capital of Venezuela (below). The mizzen mast of Great Britain on the harbor foreshore of Stanley in the Falkland Islands (top right).

Venezuela

Venezuela is on the north coast of South America. When the first Spaniards arrived in 1499 they named it "New Venice" because the Indian stilt houses built in the water of Lake Maracaibo reminded them of the Italian city. The famous liberator Simon Bolivar was a Venezuelan general, the military campaign he led resulting in the country becoming independent in 1821. For the next century Venezuela's economy was largely based on agriculture, but in the 1920s it took a new direction with the development of a petroleum industry. In the last 80 years great wealth (unevenly shared) followed by industrialization have produced one of Latin America's most urbanized societies. Out of every 20 Venezuelans, 17 are city-dwellers, and migration from the countryside has left much of the interior depopulated.

Confident that oil revenues would never end, the Venezuelan government expanded the economic role of the state, even buying hotels. Falling oil prices in the early 1980s produced a fiscal crisis, and in 1991 a program of cutbacks and austerity measures triggered street riots in

which hundreds died. Two attempted coups took place during 1992. Since that time there has been a concerted effort to achieve economic diversification and to cut back the state sector.

The hot lowlands surrounding Lake Maracaibo in the far northwest comprise one of the areas of greatest population density. In this region abundant electricity from oil-fired generators provides power for light industry: food processing, pharmaceuticals, electrical equipment, and machinery. A spur of the northern Andes divides the Maracaibo Basin from the drainage system of the Orinoco to the east. Here are the lowland plains of the Llanos, savanna country used for cattle grazing. Much of the Llanos floods during the summer rains, especially in the west, though it is dry for the rest of the year. To the south is the vast granite plateau of the Guiana Highlands, and the highest waterfall in the world—Angel Falls (979 m; 3,212 ft).

Despite fluctuations in oil prices, petroleum continues to provide over 70 percent of Venezuela's export earnings and 45 percent of government revenue. Other minerals exported include iron ore, gold, and diamonds. The main cash crops are coffee, sugarcane, and tobacco; food crops include bananas, sorghum, and maize. Only 5 percent of arable land is cultivated, and agriculture supplies little more than 70 percent of the country's needs. During the 1990s, economic reforms proposed by the IMF have been resisted as "economic totalitarianism" by the populist president, who has responded to economic rationalism by defending exchange controls and other regulatory measures.

Fact File

OFFICIAL NAME Republic of Venezuela

FORM OF GOVERNMENT Federal republic with two legislative bodies (Senate and Chamber of Deputies)

CAPITAL Caracas

AREA 912,050 sq km (352,142 sq miles)

TIME ZONE GMT – 4 hours

POPULATION 23,203,466

PROJECTED POPULATION 2005 25,504,115

POPULATION DENSITY 25.4 per sq km (65.8 per sq mile)

LIFE EXPECTANCY 73

INFANT MORTALITY (PER 1,000) 26.5

OFFICIAL LANGUAGE Spanish

OTHER LANGUAGES Indigenous languages

LITERACY RATE 91%

RELIGIONS Roman Catholic 96%, Protestant 2%, other 2%

ETHNIC GROUPS Mixed indigenous–European 67%, European 21%, African 10%, indigenous 2%

CURRENCY Bolívar

ECONOMY Services 63%, industry 25%, agriculture 12%

GNP PER CAPITA US$3,020

CLIMATE Tropical, with dry season December–April; cooler in highlands

HIGHEST POINT Pico Bolívar 5,007 m (16,427 ft)

MAP REFERENCE Pages 450–51

Dependencies in South America

Falkland Islands

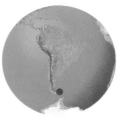

The Falkland Islands are in the South Atlantic. They were named for Lord Falkland, a seventeenth-century British Navy official. Lying 772 km (480 miles) northeast of Cape Horn, they consist of a hilly archipelago where rain falls on average 180 days a year. The area is known for the diversity of the bird life. East Falkland and West Falkland are the two main islands and there are about 200 islets. Most people are employed in sheep farming. Efforts to establish a fishing industry have failed. Sovereignty of the islands is disputed between the United Kingdom and Argentina, which in 1982 invaded, unsuccessfully, in an assertion of its claim. The resulting conflict lasted for 3 months. In 1995 the UK and Argentina launched a joint oil exploration program.

Fact File

OFFICIAL NAME Colony of the Falkland Islands

FORM OF GOVERNMENT Dependent territory of the UK

CAPITAL Stanley

AREA 12,170 sq km (4,699 sq miles)

TIME ZONE GMT – 4 hours

POPULATION 2,607 (1996)

CURRENCY Falkland Islands pound

ECONOMY Agriculture 95%, services and industry 5%

CLIMATE Cold, wet, and windy

MAP REFERENCE Page 460

French Guiana

Located along the northeast coast, French Guiana has a narrow coastal plain and a largely unpopulated, forested hinterland. Brazil lies across its southern and eastern borders. After the French Revolution one of the islands became the French penal colony of Devil's Island (Île du Diable). Now French Guiana is the site of the European Space Agency's rocket base. Sugarcane plantations influenced its development; today, cash crops such as bananas and sugarcane grow on the coast, and the main exports are fish and fish products. It depends on France for its economic viability.

Fact File

OFFICIAL NAME Department of Guiana

FORM OF GOVERNMENT Overseas department of France

CAPITAL Cayenne

AREA 91,000 sq km (35,135 sq miles)

TIME ZONE GMT – 3 hours

POPULATION 167,982

LIFE EXPECTANCY 76.6

INFANT MORTALITY (PER 1,000) 12.9

LITERACY RATE 83%

CURRENCY French franc

ECONOMY Services 61%, industry 21%, agriculture 18%

CLIMATE Tropical with two wet seasons (Dec and June)

MAP REFERENCE Page 452

South Georgia and South Sandwich Islands

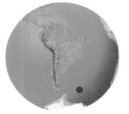

South Georgia is a barren island in the South Atlantic 1,300 km (800 miles) southeast of the Falklands. Annexed by Captain Cook in 1775, the harbor of Grytviken was long used as a whaling base. Until the 1940s it had a population of up to 800 employed in the whaling industry. Its wildlife is now attracting increasing numbers of ecotourists.

The South Sandwich Islands are six uninhabited volcanic cones to the southeast of South Georgia.

Fact File

OFFICIAL NAME South Georgia and the South Sandwich Islands

FORM OF GOVERNMENT Dependent territory of the UK

CAPITAL None; Grytviken is garrison town

AREA 4,066 sq km (1,570 sq miles)

TIME ZONE GMT – 4 hours

POPULATION No permanent population

ECONOMY Military base and biological station only

CLIMATE Cold, wet, and windy

MAP REFERENCE Pages 461, 476

South America: Physical

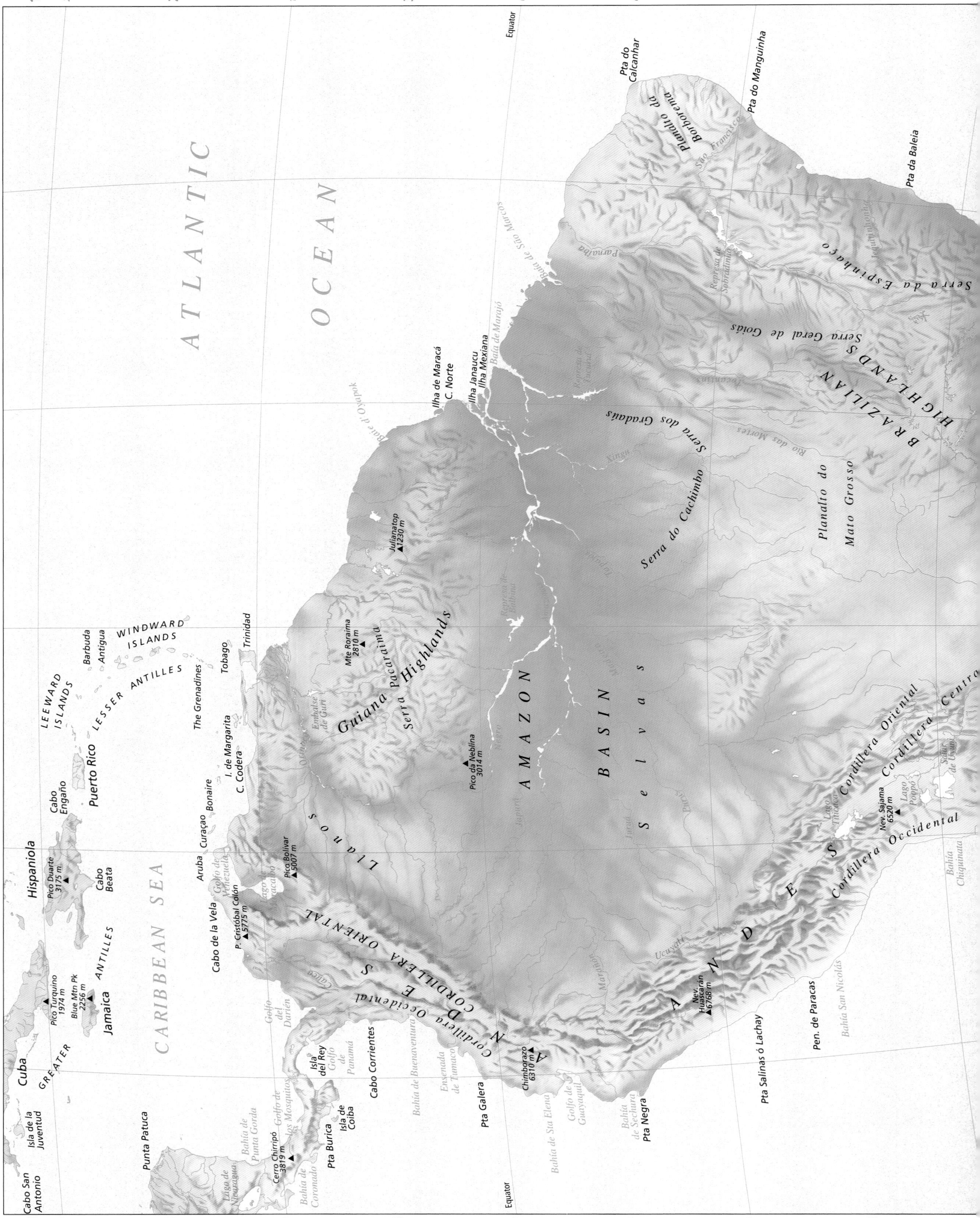

South America

ATLANTIC

OCEAN

CARIBBEAN SEA

Equator

Cabo San Antonio
Isla de la Juventud
Cuba
Punta Patuca
Bahía de Punta Gorda
Golfo de los Mosquitos
Lago de Nicaragua
Cerro Chirripó 3819 m
Bahía de Coronado
Pta Burica
Isla de Coiba
Golfo de Panamá
Pta Galera
Cabo Corrientes
Ensenada de Tumaco
Bahía de Buenaventura
Golfo del Darién
Isla del Rey
Pico Turquino 1974 m
GREATER
Jamaica
Blue Mtn Pk 2256 m
ANTILLES
Hispaniola
Pico Duarte 3175 m
Cabo Beata
Cabo Engaño
Puerto Rico
LEEWARD ISLANDS
Barbuda
Antigua
WINDWARD ISLANDS
LESSER ANTILLES
The Grenadines
Tobago
Trinidad
Aruba
Curaçao
Bonaire
I. de Margarita
C. Codera
Cabo de la Vela
Golfo de Venezuela
Golfo de Maracaibo
P. Cristóbal Colón 5775 m
Pico Bolívar 5007 m
CORDILLERA ORIENTAL
CORDILLERA OCCIDENTAL
Cordillera Occidental
Cauca
Magdalena
Chimborazo 6310 m
Golfo de Guayaquil
Bahía de Sta Elena
Bahía de Sechura
Pta Negra
Pen. de Paracas
Pta Salinas ó Lachay
Bahía San Nicolás
Bahía Chiquinata
A N D E S
Nev. Huáscarán 6768 m
Cordillera Oriental
Cordillera Central
Lago Titicaca
Nev. Sajama 6520 m
Lago Poopó
Salar de Uyuni
Ucayali
Marañón
Huallaga
Napo
Putumayo
Caquetá
Negro
Japurá
Içá
Juruá
Purus
Madeira
AMAZON BASIN
Selvas
Embalse de Guri
Mte Roraima 2810 m
Serra Pacaraima
Guiana Highlands
Pico da Neblina 3014 m
Julianatop 1230 m
Ilha de Maracá
C. Norte
Ilha Janaucu
Ilha Mexiana
Baía de Marajó
Maroni e ó Oyapock
Tapajós
Xingu
Tocantins
Represa de Tucuruí
Represa de Balbina
Rio das Mortes
Serra dos Graduas
Serra do Cachimbo
Planalto do Mato Grosso
Serra Geral de Goiás
BRAZILIAN HIGHLANDS
Planalto da Borborema
Pta do Calcanhar
Pta do Manguinha
Pta da Baleia
Serra da Espinhaço
São Francisco
Baía de São Marcos
Parnaíba
Represa de Sobradinho
Equator

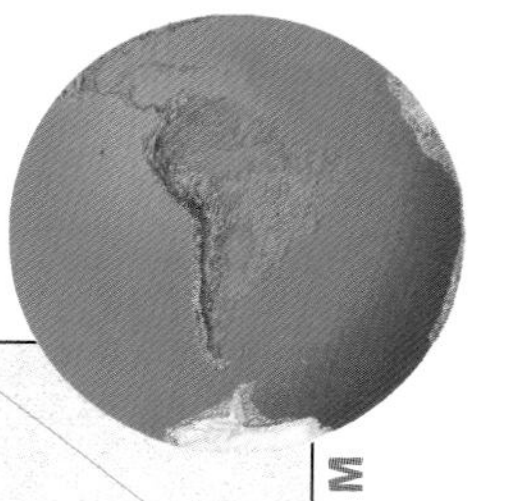

SOUTH ATLANTIC OCEAN

PACIFIC OCEAN

Tropic of Capricorn

I. Grande
I. de São Sebastião
Ilha de Sta Catarina
C. de Sta Marta Grande
Serra Geral

South Georgia

South Orkney Is

South Shetland Is

Antarctic Peninsula

Cuchilla Grande
Uruguay
Paraguay
Represa del Río Negro
Lagoa dos Patos
Lagoa Mirim

Río de la Plata
C. Corrientes

GRAN CHACO

Salado
L. Mar Chiquita
Sierras de Córdoba

PAMPAS

Bahía Blanca
Bahía Anegada
Pta Rasa
Península Valdés
Golfo San Matías

East Falkland
West Falkland

Desierto de Atacama
Vol. Llullaillaco 6723 m
Salar de Arizaro
Co Aconcagua 6960 m
ANDES
Colorado
Golfo de San Jorge
C. Tres Puntas
Pta Medanosa

PATAGONIA

Bahía Camarones
Bahía Grande
Pta Dungeness
Isla Grande de Tierra del Fuego
I. de los Estados

Pta Tetas
I. San Félix   I. San Ambrosio
Bahía Salada
Pta Lengua de Vaca
Pta Curaumilla
Arch. Juan Fernández

Golfo de Arauco
Pta Galera
Canal de Chacao
Isla Grande de Chiloé
Islas Guaitecas
Isla Magdalena
I. Benjamín
Golfo de Penas
I. Patricio Lynch
I. Esmeralda
Isla Wellington
I. Madre de Dios
I. Diego de Almagro
I. Desolación
Bahía Otway
I. Santa Inés
Península Brecknock
I. Londonderry
I. Hoste
Islas Wollaston
Cabo de Hornos (Cape Horn)

0 200 400 600 800 kilometers
0 200 400 miles
Scale 1:21,000,000   Projection: Azimuthal Equal Area

South America

447

South America: Political

South America

ATLANTIC

OCEAN

CARIBBEAN SEA

BRAZIL

VENEZUELA

COLOMBIA

PERU

ECUADOR

BOLIVIA

GUYANA

SURINAME

FRENCH GUIANA (Fr.)

Equator

CUBA

CAYMAN ISLANDS (U.K.)

JAMAICA

HAITI

DOMINICAN REPUBLIC

PUERTO RICO (U.S.A.)

VIRGIN ISLANDS (U.S.A.)

VIRGIN ISLANDS (U.K.)

ANGUILLA (U.K.)

ST KITTS AND NEVIS

ANTIGUA AND BARBUDA

GUADELOUPE (Fr.)

MONTSERRAT (U.K.)

DOMINICA

MARTINIQUE (Fr.)

ST LUCIA

ST VINCENT AND THE GRENADINES

BARBADOS

The Grenadines

GRENADA

TRINIDAD AND TOBAGO

NETHERLANDS ANTILLES (Neth.)

ARUBA (Neth.)

HONDURAS

NICARAGUA

COSTA RICA

PANAMA

Isla del Rey

Golfo de Panamá

Isla de Coiba

B. de Buenaventura

Golfo de Guayaquil

Ilha de Marajó

Baía de Marajó

Ilha Janaucu

Ilha Mexiana

Serra do Mar de São Marcos

I. de Margarita

Tobago

Trinidad

Willemstad

Caracas ⊛

Maracaibo

Cabimas

Coro

Valencia

Barquisimeto

Barinas

San Fernando de Apure

San Cristóbal

Barcelona

Cumaná

Maturín

Ciudad Bolívar

Ciudad Guayana

Tucupita

La Asunción

Port of Spain

Puerto Ayacucho

Puerto Inírida

Normandia

Boa Vista

São Gabriel da Cachoeira

Santa Maria

Óbidos

Parintins

Itaituba

Manaus

Santarém

Altamira

Porto de Moz

Cametá

Belém

Bragança

Castanhal

Abaetetuba

Macapá

Calçoene

St-Laurent du Maroni

Cayenne

Paramaribo ⊛

New Amsterdam

Georgetown ⊛

Linden

Barranquilla

Santa Marta

Cartagena

Valledupar

Sincelejo

Montería

Bucaramanga

Quibdó

Tunja

Manizales

Pereira

Bogotá ⊛

Ibagué

Villavicencio

San José del Guaviare

Armenia

Medellín

Cúcuta

Cali

Popayán

Florencia

Mocoa

Mitú

Pasto

Tulcán

Ibarra

Quito ⊛

Ambato

Riobamba

Cuenca

Machala

Loja

Guayaquil

Sullana

Piura

Talara

Bayóvar

Chiclayo

Trujillo

Chimbote

Moyobamba

Cajamarca

Iquitos

Leticia

Benjamin Constant

Eirunepé

Cruzeiro do Sul

Pucallpa

Yurimaguas

Cerro de Pasco

La Oroya

Huancayo

Ayacucho

Lima ⊛

Callao ⊛

Pisco

Ica

Sicuani

Cuzco

Marcona

Mollendo

Ilo

Tacna

Arica

Iquique

Arequipa

Juliaca

Puerto Maldonado

Riberalta

Guajará-Mirim

Guayaramerín

Brasiléia

Xapuri

Rio Branco

Plácido de Castro

Bôca do Acre

Lábrea

Humaitá

Manicoré

Tefé

Santa Maria

Pimenta Bueno

Ariquemes

Pôrto Velho

Costa Marques

Trinidad

Cáceres

Cuiabá

Rondonópolis

Corumbá

Coxim

Campo Grande

La Paz ⊛

Cochabamba

Oruro

Santa Cruz

Montero

Punata

Huanuni

Sucre ⊛

Potosí

Camiri

Tarija

Rio Branco

Gurupi

Araguaína

São Félix do Xingu

Carolina

Imperatriz

Marabá

Tocantinópolis

Bacabal

Barra do Corda

Santa Maria das Barreiras

Aragarças

Jataí

Itumbiara

Ituiutaba

Presidente Prudente

São José do Rio Prêto

Itaberaí

Campo Grande

São Luís

Caxias

Teresina

Floriano

Picos

Parnaíba

Sobral

Fortaleza

Mossoró

Natal

João Pessoa

Campina Grande

Caruaru

Garanhuns

Recife

Maceió

Alagoinhas

Arapiraca

Aracaju

Salvador

Ilhéus

Itabuna

Canavieiras

Juazeiro do Norte

Paulo Afonso

Juazeiro

Senhor do Bonfim

Barreiras

Bom Jesus da Lapa

São Francisco

Feira de Santana

Jequié

Vitória da Conquista

Grão Mogol

Teófilo Otoni

Governador Valadares

Colatina

Caratinga

Barbacena

Vitória

Montes Claros

Patos de Minas

Belo Horizonte

Uberlândia

Uberaba

Divinópolis

Ribeirão Prêto

Araguari

Anápolis

Goiânia

Brasília ⊛

Gorupi

Tropic of Capricorn

6°
30°
7°
40°
8°
20°
9°
10°

M
L
K
J
H
G
F
E
D
C
B
A

10° 60°
10°
20°
30°
40°
50°
60°
70°
80°
90°
100°
110°

S O U T H

A T L A N T I C

O C E A N

SOUTH GEORGIA AND
SOUTH SANDWICH ISLANDS
(U.K.)

South Sandwich
Islands

South Georgia

South Orkney
Islands (U.K.)

Antarctic Peninsula

South Shetland
Islands (U.K.)

FALKLAND
ISLANDS
(U.K.)

West
Falkland

East
Falkland

Stanley

Cabo Frio
Rio de
Janeiro
Santos
São Paulo
Sorocaba
Itanhaém
Maringá
Ponta
Grossa
Curitiba
Joinville
Itajaí
Chapecó
Lajes
Laguna
Caxias do Sul
Passo
Fundo
Porto Alegre
Foz do Iguaçu
Santa
Maria
Cruz
Alta
Oberá
Rio Grande
Pelotas
Bagé
Rivera
Salto
Treinta-y-Tres
Las Piedras
Montevideo

Concepción
Asunción
San
Lorenzo
Formosa
Posadas
Corrientes
Presidencia Roque
Sáenz Peña
Resistencia
La Banda
Reconquista
Goya
Santiago
del Estero
Uruguaiana
Concordia
URUGUAY
San Nicolas
de los Arroyos
Paraná
Rosario
Zárate
Buenos Aires
La Plata

San Salvador
de Jujuy
Salta
Tafí Viejo
San Miguel
de Tucumán
San Fernando del
Valle de Catamarca
La Rioja
San Francisco
Rafaela
Santa
Fe
Córdoba
Villa María
Venado
Tuerto
Junín
Olavarría
Tandil
Tres Arroyos
Necochea
Mar del Plata
Santa Rosa
Punta Alta
Bahía Blanca
Río Colorado
San Antonio
Oeste
Carmen De Patagones
Viedma
Antofagasta
Copiapó
La Serena
Coquimbo
Ovalle
San Juan
Mendoza
San Luis
Río Cuarto
Mercedes
San Rafael
ARGENTINA
Viña del Mar
Valparaíso
Santiago
San Bernardo
Rancagua
Curicó
Talca
Chillán
Concepción
Talcahuano
Arauco
Los Angeles
Curacautín
Temuco
Valdivia
Osorno
Puerto Montt
Castro
Zapala
Neuquén
San Martín
De Los Andes
San Carlos
de Bariloche
Esquel
Sierra Grande
Rawson
Puerto Madryn
Trelew
Comodoro
Rivadavia
Caleta Olivia
Pico Truncado
Coihaique
Puerto
Natales
Punta Arenas
Río Gallegos
Río Grande
Ushuaia
I. de los
Estados
Islas Wollaston
I. Londonderry
I. Santa
Inés
I. Desolación
I. Diego de Almagro
I. Madre de Dios
Isla Wellington
I. Esmeralda
I. Patricio
Lynch
I. Benjamín
Islas Guaitecas
Isla Magdalena
Isla Grande
de Tierra
del Fuego

Golfo
San Matías
Golfo de
San Jorge
Bahía Grande
Golfo
de Penas
Bahía Blanca
Río de la Plata

Arch. Juan Fernández

I. San Félix
I. San Ambrosio

P A C I F I C

O C E A N

Tropic of Capricorn

6°
90°
30°
7°
40°
8°
9°

6°
90°
30°
7°
40°
8°

110°
100°
90°
80°
70°
60°
50°

South America

South America

0   200   400   600   800   kilometers
0   200   400   miles
Scale 1:21,000,000   Projection: Azimuthal Equal Area

449

Colombia • Venezuela • Ecuador • Guyana • Northwest Brazil

CARIBBEAN SEA

PACIFIC

OCEAN

NICARAGUA

Santo Domingo
Juigalpa
Acoyapa
Bluefields
Laguna de Perlas
Lago de Nicaragua
Punta Gorda
San Carlos
Bahía de Punta Gorda
San Juan del Norte
Vol. Miravalles ▲2028 m
Altamira
Río Frío
Guápiles
Puerto Limón
Puerto Jesús
Alajuela Heredia
Cartago
San José
Cerro Chirripó ▲3819 m
Puntarenas
COSTA RICA
Parrita
Dominical
Ciudad Cortés
B. de Coronado
Península de Osa
Volcán Barú ▲3475 m
La Concepción
Boquete
David
Volcán
Puerto Armuelles
Pta Burica
Santa Catalina
San Francisco
Tolé
Santiago
Soná
Río de Jesús
Atalaya
Golfo de Chiriquí
Isla de Coiba
Isla de Cébaco
Península de Azuero
Pedasí
Pta Mala
Pta Mariato
Tonosí
Las Tablas
Chitré
Parita
Aguadulce
Antón
Penonomé
Coclé
L. Gatún
Panama Canal
PANAMÁ
La Chorrera
San Miguelito
Chimán
Golfo de Panamá

Portobelo
Colón
El Porvenir
Palenque
Arch. de San Blás
Ailigandí
Isla del Rey
I. San José
San Miguel
La Palma
Yaviza
El Real
Garachiné
Jaqué
Puerto Obaldía
Acandí
Riosucio
Chigorodó
Palo de Jás Letras
Cupica
Juradó
Pta Logos
El Valle
Nuquí
Cabo Corrientes
Istmina
Bajo Baudó
Golfo del Darién
Serr. del Darién
Golfo de Urabá
Turbo
Tierralta
Dabeiba
Paramillo ▲3960 m
Ituango
Yarumal
Amalfi
Antioquia
Anzá
Bolívar
Santa Bárbara
Sonsón
Aguadas
Salamina
Pta Charambirá
Buenaventura
B. de Buenaventura
Yumbo
Cali
Palmira
Naya
Pta Coco
Guapi
Co Munchique ▲3012 m
Mosquera
Guapí
Ensenada de Tumaco
Tumaco
Barbacoas
Sotomayor
La Unión
El Divisó
Sandoná
San Lorenzo
Valdez
B. de Ancón de Sardinas
Esmeraldas
Punta Galera
Muisné
Cabo de San Francisco
Rosa Zárate
Santo Domingo de los Colorados
B. de Caráquez
Bahía de Caráquez
B. de Manta
Rocafuerte
Manta
Montecristi
Jipijapa
Pajón
Quevedo
Chone
Portoviejo
Santa Ana
Balzar
Babahoyo
Santa Lucía
Guaranda
Zapotal
Chimborazo ▲6310 m
B. de Sta Elena
Salinas
Santa Elena
Playas
Guayaquil
Durán
Naranjal
Golfo de Guayaquil
Isla Puná
Machala
Zarumilla
Tumbes
Zorritos
Canoas
Máncora
Talara
Lobitos
Pta Pariñas
Negritos
La Huaca
Paita
Catacaos
Castilla
Sullana
Piura
Tambo Grande
Chulucanas
San Ignacio
Las Lomas
Suyo
Macará
Cariamanga
Catacocha
Piñas
Zamora
Loja
Borja

ECUADOR
Otavalo
Cayambe
Ibarra
Volcán Cayambe ▲5790 m
Quito
Vol. Antisana ▲5704 m
Machachi
Vol. Cotopaxi ▲5897 m
Latacunga
Ambato
Puyo
Riobamba
Vol. Sangay ▲5230 m
Guamote
Alausí
Cañar
Azogues
Cuenca
Gualaceo
Girón
Santa Rosa
Saraguro
Macas
Morona

Tulcán
Ipiales
San Gabriel
Nev. de Cumbal ▲4764 m
Túquerres
Pasto
Mocoa
Puerto Asís
Lago Agrio
Cuyabeno
Puerto Francisco de Orellana
Baeza
Tena
Villano
Ayuy
Montalvo
Pantoja
Santa María
Arica
Río Tigre
Andoas
Puerto Tunigrama
Santa Clotilde
Puca Urco
Pebas
Mazán
Francisco de Orellana
Pamar
El Encanto
Arica
Intuto
Santa María de Nanay
Iquitos
Tamshiyacu
Omaguas
Nauta
Brasil
Caballoc
Requena
Palmeiras do Javari
Lagunas
Cahuapanas
Barranca
Orellana
Concordia
PERU

Santo Domingo
Barranquilla
Puerto Colombia
Baranoa
Sabanalarga
Cartagena
Arjona
Turbaco
Calamar
Pivijay
Fundación
Soledad
Ciénaga
Santa Marta
P. Cristóbal Colón ▲5775 m
Barrancas
Villanueva
La Jagua de Ibirico
Valledupar
Codazzi
Augustín
Ríohacha
Carraipía
Uribia
Maicao
Paraguaip
Tulé
San Rafael
Cabo de la Vela
Carrizal
Península de Guaji
Pta Gal
Puerto Estre
Campo
Mara
Maracaibo
R
Cabimas
Ciudad Ojeda
Machiques
Lagunill
San Carlos del Zulia
Encontrados
Casigua
El Vigía
Mé
Lago de Marac
Lage de Marac
El Carmen de Bolívar
Plato
El Difícil
El Banco
Tamalameque
La Gloria
Chiriguaná
Ocaña
Sardinata
La Fría
Pedraza La V
Tovar
San Cristóbal
San Antonio de Caparo
Arauc
Cubará
Tame
El Cocuy
Puerto Rondó
Pamplona
Chinácota
Cúcuta
Golfo de Morrosquillo
Tolú
Sincé
Sincelejo
Lorica
Cereté
Sahagún
Montería
Planeta Rica
Ayapel
Caucasia
Cáceres
Zaragoza
Magangué
Mompós
Sucre
El Banco
Simití
Cáchira
Barrancabermeja
Puerto Berrío
Segovia
Zapatoca
Sierra Nevada del Cocuy ▲5493 m
Barbosa
Paz de Río
Socorro
San Gil
Belén
Vélez
Chiquinquirá
Duitama
Sogamoso
Yopal
Pore
Trinidad
Maní
Ore
San Pe de Arim
Armero
Honda
Líbano
La Dorada
Chocontá
Ubate
Zipaquirá
Facatativá
Soacha
Bogotá
Fusagasugá
Villavicencio
Puerto López
Pasca
Agua de Dios
4560 m
Cerro Nevado
San Martín
Granada
Pavón
Puerto La Concordia
San José del Guaviare
Calamar
Miraflores
Mesa de Yam
Pedro Chi
Macayari
Mesa de Iguaje
Cerro Cumare 720 m
Macujer
Co Maine Hanari 860 m
Araracuara
La Chorrera
Lén
Caquetá
Apaporis
Vaupés

Manizales
Pereira
Cartago
Armenia
Ibagué
Sevilla
Tuluá
Buga
Chaparral
Natagaima
Colombia
Saldaña
Puerto Tejada
Aipe
Baraya
Santander
Nev. de Huila ▲5750 m
Popayán
Volcán Puracé ▲4646 m
La Plata
Garzón
Altamira
Pitalito
La Cruz
Florencia
Tres Esquinas
Santa Rita
Puerto Leguízamo
La Tagua
Hacha
COLOMBIA
Neiva
Campoalegre
Gigante
San Vicente del Caguán
San Martín
Medellín
Itagüí
Envigado
Bello
Quibdó
Andes
Cisneros
Cordillera Occidental
Cordillera Central
Cordillera Oriental
Sierra de la Macarena
Guayabero

Bucaramanga
Floridablanca
Bello

Equator

82° 78° 429 74°
454

BARBADOS

ARUBA (Neth.)
Oranjestad

NETHERLANDS ANTILLES (Neth.)
Curaçao
Bonaire
Willemstad
Kralendijk

Pen. de Paraguaná
C. San Román
Los Taques
Punto Fijo
Pueblo Nuevo
Puerto Cumarebo
Dabajuro
Baragua
auroa
Coro
Piritu
Pedregal
Jacura
Churuguara
San Juan de los Cayos

LESSER ANTILLES
La Orchila
La Blanquilla
La Tortuga

Isla de Margarita
La Asunción
Porlamar
Carúpano

The Grenadines
Grenville
St George's
GRENADA

Tobago
Charlotteville
Scarborough

TRINIDAD AND TOBAGO
Galera Pt
Arima
Sangre Grande
Port of Spain
Trinidad
Río Claro
San Fernando
Galeota Pt

Venezuela
Cerro El Cerron 1990 m
Carora
Trujillo
Boconó
Barquisimeto
Valencia
Maracay
San Felipe
Yaritagua
Maracaibo
Puerto Cabello
Catia La Mar
Caracas
Petare
Baruta
Los Teques
La Victoria
C. Codera
Higuerote
Puerto la Cruz
Cumaná
Caripe
Caripito
Maturín
Golfo de Paria
Güiria
Río Caribe
Pen. de Paria
Bocas del Dragón
Boca de la Serpiente

Grande
Barinas
Obispos
El Tocuyo
San Carlos
Tinaco
El Pao
Acarigua
San Juan de los Morros
Ortiz
San Antonio de Tamanaco
Zaraza
Aragua de Barcelona
Anaco
Cantaura
Barcelona
El Chaparro
El Tigre
San José de Guanipa
Pariaguán
Tucupita
Barrancas

Guanare
Nueva Florida
Calabozo
El Sombrero
Chaguaramas
Valle de la Pascua
Las Mercedes
Santa María de Ipire
El Toro
Waini Pt
San José de Amacuro
Morawhanna
Mabaruma

Puerto de Nutrias
San Mauricio
Boca del Pao
Soledad
Ciudad Guayana
Puerto Ordaz
Upata
El Pao
La Horqueta
Port Kaituma
Baramanni

Palmarito
Camaguán
Puerto Miranda
Parmana
Mapire
Ciudad Bolívar
Ciudad Piar
El Palmar
El Miamo
Guasipati
Matthews Ridge
Charity
Marlborough

Mantecal
Achaguas
San Fernando de Apure
Cabruta
Caicara de Orinoco
Mapire
Orinoco
Embalse de Guri
San Pedro de Las Bocas
El Callao
Tumeremo
Barama
Anna Regina
Suddie
Spring Garden

Elorza
La Urbana
Las Lajitas
Las Trincheras
Co Turagua 1839 m
La Paragua
El Dorado
Cuyuni
Georgetown
Parika
Enmore
Mahaicony

VENEZUELA
GUYANA

Cravo Norte
Meta
▲1320 m
Co Yavi 2285 m
Auyantepui 2585 m
Co Guaiquinima 2100 m
Tumureng
Peter's Mine
Bartica
Fort Wellington
Rosignol
Linden
New Amsterdam

Puerto Páez
Puerto Carreño
Sa de Parguaza
Parguaza
Puerto Páez
Casuarito
Puerto Ayacucho
Samariapo
Sierra Guanay
San Juan
Arabelo
Luepa
Equeipa
La Gran Sabana
Mte Roraima 2810 m
Uacauyén
Arabopó
Pakaraima Mountains
Keweigek
Issano
Kangaruma
Tumatumari
Mahdia
Corriverton
Nieuw Nickerie
Malali
Paradise

Puerto Nuevo
Tomo
Sucuaro
Mituas
Arrecifal
Rejunya
Maihiá
Santa Elena de Uairén
Orinduik
Maipuri Landing
Ituni
Orealla
Kwakwani
Epira
Apoera

San José de Ocuné
Puerto Inírida
San Fernando de Atabapo
San Antonio
Guiana
Meseta del Co Jáua
Ventuari
Co Marahuaca 2579 m
Co Duida 2404 m
Uaicás
Tepequém
Serra Tepequém
Normandia
Annai
Apoteri
Yupukarri
Lethem
Kabalebo stuwmeer

Co Guasacavi 668 m
Co Canapiare 692 m
Tomo
Capibara
Boca Mavaca
La Esmeralda
Serra Parima
Uaricoera
Serra Pacaraima Highlands
Boa Vista
Kanuku Mts
Dadanawa
Aishalton
Isherton
Lucie

Pico Tamacuari 2340 m
San Carlos
Serra de Unturán
Serra Curupira
Mucajaí
Caracaraí
RORAIMA
Kamoa Mts
Biloku
Serra Acaraí
CLAIMED BY SURINAME

Mitú
Iutica
Cucuí
Serra Parima
Serra do Mucajaí
734 m
Serra Iricoumé
502 m

Iauaretê
Taraquá
Içana
Pico da Neblina 3014 m
Pico Padauari 2755 m
Catrimani
Uberlândia
PARÁ
Equator

São Gabriel da Cachoeira
São José
Tapurucuara
Ilha Grande
Boiaçu

Barcelos
BRAZIL

Carvoeiro
Moura
Represa de Balbina
Santa Maria
Faro
Nhamundá

La Pedrera
Vila Bittencourt
Mamori
Maraã
Novo Airão
Balbina
Urucará
Parintins

Santa Clara
Tarapacá
Tonantins
Fonte Boa
Jutaí
Uarini
AMAZONAS
Itapiranga
Silves
Itacoatiara
Urucurituba
Barreirinha

Santo Antônio do Içá
Alvarães
Tefé
Manacapuru
Manaus
Anamã
Ariaú
Maués
Sapucaia

São Paulo de Olivença
Amaturá
Juruá
Badajós
Codajás
Anori
Beruri
Careiro
Autazes
Ilha Tupinambarana
Novo Olinda do Norte

Leticia
Tabatinga
Benjamin Constant
aia do
Coari
Itaboca
Arumã
São Pedro
Axinim
Canumã
Borba
Laranjal
Cantagalo
Vila Nova

Carauari
Jutaí
Lago de Coari
Novo Aripuanã
Lua Nova

Scale 1:7,000,000   Projection: Azimuthal Equal Area

0 100 200 300 400 kilometers
0 100 200 miles

South America

Northeast Brazil • Suriname • French Guiana

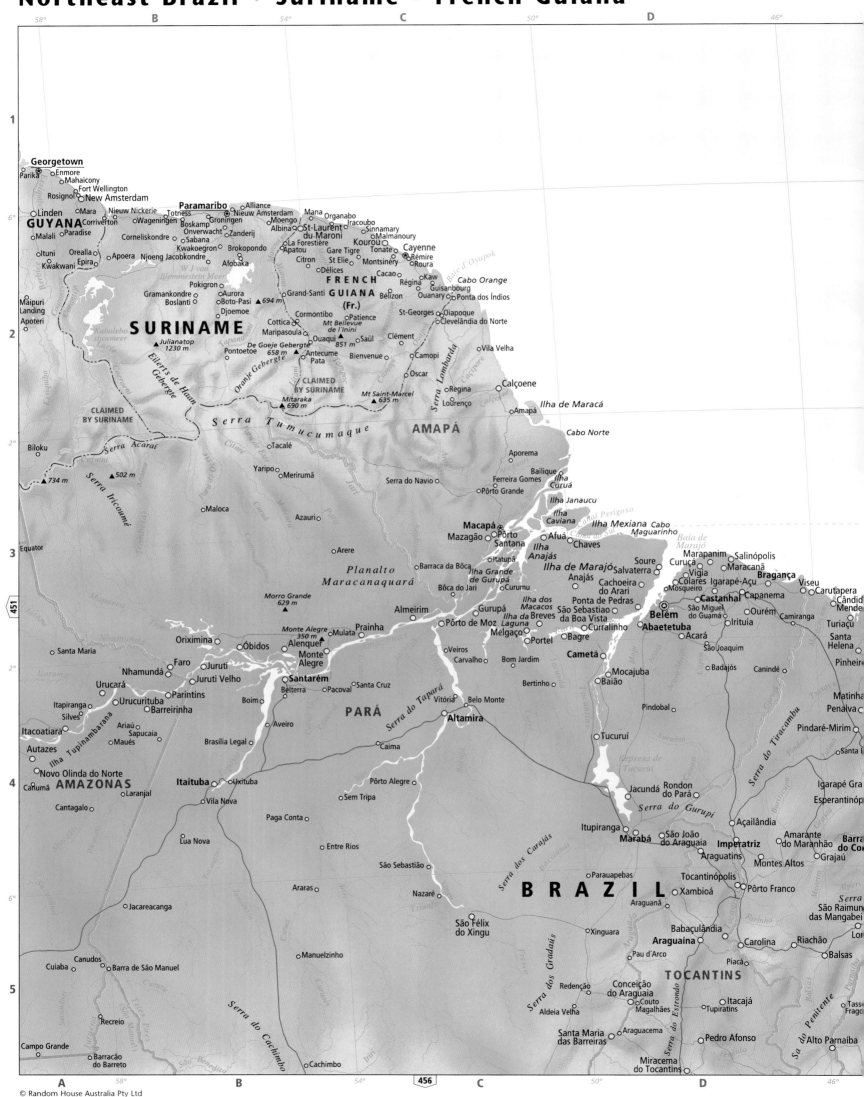

GUYANA

Georgetown
Parika
Enmore
Mahaicony
Fort Wellington
Rosignol
New Amsterdam
Linden
Mara
Nieuw Nickerie
Corriverton
Malali
Paradise
Oltuni
Orealla
Apoera
Njoeng Jacobkondre
Kwakwani
Epira

Maipuri
Landing
Apoteri

Biloku

▲734 m

SURINAME

Paramaribo
Alliance
Nieuw Amsterdam
Mana
Organabo
Totness
Groningen
Moengo
Iracoubo
Boskamp
Albina
St-Laurent
Sinnamary
Wageningen
du Maroni
Malmanoury
Onverwacht
Zanderij
La Forestière
Kourou
Corneliskondre
Brokopondo
Apatou
Gare Tigre
Tonate
Cayenne
Sabana
Kwakoegron
Citron
St Elie
Montsinéry
Rémire
Afobaka
Délices
Cacao
Régina
Roura

Gramankondre
Pokigron
Aurora
Grand-Santi
Belizon
Guisanbourg
Boslanti
Boto-Pasi
▲694 m
FRENCH
Ouanary
Ponta dos Índios
Djoemoe
GUIANA
Patience
St-Georges
(Fr.)
Cormontibo
Oiapoque
Cottica
Mt Bellevue
Clevelândia do Norte
Mariapasoula
de l'Inini
▲Julianatop
De Goeje Gebergte
Ouaqui
Saül
Clément
1230 m
Pontoetoe
658 m
Antecume
Bienvenue
Pata
Camopi
Vila Velha

CLAIMED
Oscar
BY SURINAME
Mt Saint-Marcel
Regina
Mitaraka
▲635 m
Calçoene
CLAIMED
▲690 m
Lourenço
BY SURINAME
Ilha de Maracá
Serra Tumucumaque
AMAPÁ
Amapá
Tacalé
Cabo Norte

Yaripo
Merirumã
Aporema
▲502 m
Serra do Navio
Bailique
Ferreira Gomes
Ilha
Maloca
Pôrto Grande
Curuá
Azauri
Ilha Janaucu
Ilha
Arere
Caviana
Ilha Mexiana
Cabo
Macapá
Maguarinho
Mazagão
Pôrto
Afuá
Ilha Mexiana
Santana
Chaves
Barraca da Bôca
Ilha
Marapanim
Salinópolis
Planalto
Itatupá
Anajás
Curuçá
Vigia
Maracanã
Maracanaquará
Ilha Grande
Ilha de Marajó
Salvaterra
Colares
Igarapé-Açu
Bragança
Bôca do Jari
de Gurupá
Soure
Mosqueiro
Curumu
Anajás
Cachoeira
Castanhal
Capanema
Viseu
Morro Grande
do Arari
Carutapera
629 m
Almeirim
Ilha dos
Ponta de Pedras
Belém
Ourém
Câmid
Monte Alegre
Macacos
São Sebastiao
Abaetetuba
Irituia
Mende
350 m
Mulata
Pôrto de Moz
da Boa Vista
Acará
Camiranga
Oriximina
Prainha
Ilha da Breves
Curralinho
São Joaquim
Turiaçu
Óbidos
Alenquer
Gurupá
Laguna
Santa
Santa Maria
Monte
Veiros
Melgaço
Bagre
São Miguel
Helena
Faro
Alegre
Portel
do Guamá
Pinheiro
Nhamundá
Juruti
Carvalho
Cametá
Badajós
Canindé
Urucará
Juruti Velho
Belterra
Santarém
Bom Jardim
Mocajuba
Pacoval
Santa Cruz
Bertinho
Baião
Matinha
Itapiranga
Urucurituba
Boim
Penalva
Silves
Barreirinha
Vitória
Pindaré-Mirim
Itacoatiara
Ariaú
Aveiro
Belo Monte
PARÁ
Pindobal
Santa
Autazes
Sapucaia
Maués
Brasília Legal
Caima
Altamira
Tucuruí
Novo Olinda do Norte
Canumã
AMAZONAS
Uxituba
Pôrto Alegre
Jacundá
Rondon
Igarapé Gra
Cantagalo
Laranjal
Itaituba
Sem Tripa
do Pará
Esperantinóp
Vila Nova
Açailândia
Lua Nova
Paga Conta
Itupiranga
Amarante
Barra
Entre Rios
São João
Imperatriz
do Maranhão
do Co
Marabá
do Araguaia
Araras
São Sebastião
Araguatins
Montes Altos
Grajaú
Jacareacanga
Nazaré
B R A Z I L
Parauapebas
Tocantinópolis
Pôrto Franco
Serra
São Félix
Xambioá
São Raimun
do Xingu
Xinguara
Araguanã
das Mangabei
Babaçulândia
Lon
Manuelzinho
Pau d'Arco
Araguaína
Carolina
Riachão
Cuiaba
Canudos
Piaçá
Balsas
Barra de São Manuel
TOCANTINS
Redenção
Conceição
Aldeia Velha
do Araguaia
Itacajá
Tasse
Couto
Tupiratins
Frago
Recreio
Magalhães
Santa Maria
Araguacema
Pedro Afonso
Campo Grande
das Barreiras
Barracão
Cachimbo
Miracema
Sa do Penitente
do Barreto
do Tocantins
Alto Parnaíba

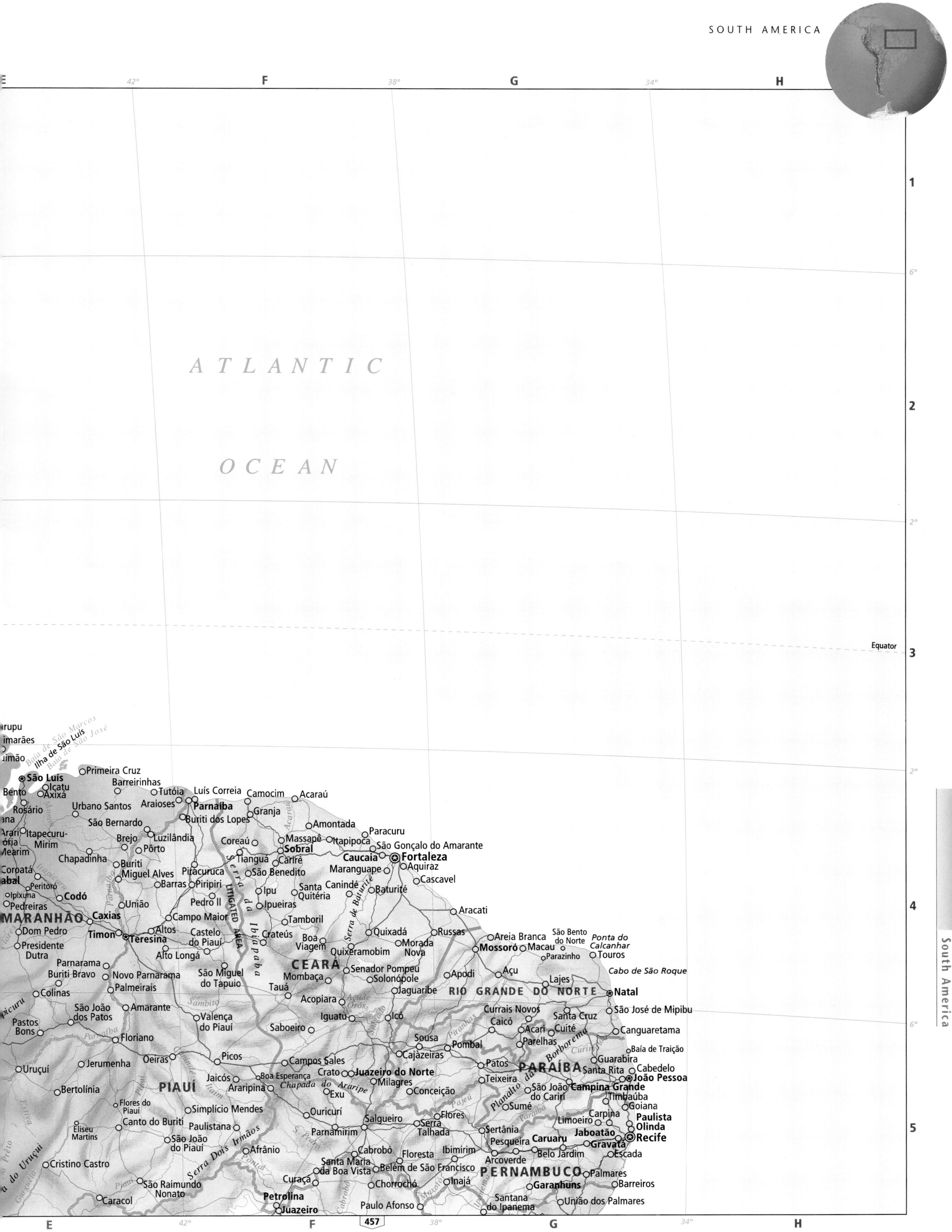

A T L A N T I C

O C E A N

Equator

E   42°   F   38°   G   34°   H

rupu
imarães
uimão
Bento
São Luís
Icatu
Axixá
Primeira Cruz
Barreirinhas
Tutóia
Luís Correia
Camocim
Acaraú
Rosário
ana
Urbano Santos
Araioses
Parnaíba
Granja
Arari
Itapecuru-
ória
Mearim
São Bernardo
Brejo
Luzilândia
Pôrto
Buriti dos Lopes
Amontada
Paracuru
Chapadinha
Coreaú
Massapê
Itapipoca
São Gonçalo do Amarante
Corpatá
abal
Peritoró
Buriti
Miguel Alves
Tianguá
Sobral
Caucaia
Fortaleza
Olpixuna
Codó
Pedreiras
Piracuruca
São Benedito
Maranguape
Aquiraz
Barras
Piripiri
Ipu
Santa
Canindé
Cascavel
União
Pedro II
Ipueiras
Quitéria
Baturité
MARANHÃO
Caxias
Campo Maior
Altos
Tamboril
Quixadá
Russas
Aracati
Dom Pedro
Timon
Teresina
Castelo
do Piauí
Crateús
Boa
Viagem
Quixeramobim
Morada
Nova
Areia Branca
São Bento
do Norte
Ponta do
Calcanhar
Presidente
Dutra
Alto Longá
Mossoró
Macau
Parazinho
Touros
Parnarama
Novo Parnarama
São Miguel
do Tapuio
CEARÁ
Senador Pompeu
Solonópole
Açu
Apodi
Cabo de São Roque
Buriti Bravo
Palmeirais
Tauá
Mombaça
Jaguaribe
RIO GRANDE DO NORTE
Lajes
Colinas
Acopiara
Iguatu
Icó
Currais Novos
Santa Cruz
São José de Mipibu
São João
dos Patos
Amarante
Valença
do Piauí
Saboeiro
Caicó
Acari
Cuité
Canguaretama
Pastos
Bons
Floriano
Sousa
Pombal
Parelhas
Baía de Traição
Uruçuí
Jerumenha
Oeiras
Picos
Campos Sales
Cajàzeiras
Patos
Teixeira
PARAÍBA
Guarabira
Santa Rita
Cabedelo
João Pessoa
Bertolínia
Jaicós
Araripina
Boa Esperança
Crato
Juazeiro do Norte
Milagres
Conceição
São João
do Cariri
Campina Grande
Timbaúba
Flores do
Piauí
Simplício Mendes
Exu
Sumé
Limoeiro
Carpina
Paulista
Eliseu
Martins
Canto do Buriti
Paulistana
São João
do Piauí
Ouricuri
Parnamirim
Salgueiro
Serra
Talhada
Flores
Sertânia
Pesqueira
Caruaru
Jaboatão
Gravatá
Olinda
Recife
Cristino Castro
Afrânio
Cabrobó
Floresta
Ibimirim
Belo Jardim
Escada
São Raimundo
Nonato
Curaçá
Santa Maria
da Boa Vista
Belém de São Francisco
Arcoverde
PERNAMBUCO
Palmares
Caracol
Chorrochó
Inajá
Garanhuns
Barreiros
Petrolina
Juazeiro
Paulo Afonso
Santana
do Ipanema
União dos Palmares

PIAUÍ
Natal

Serra Dois Irmãos
Chapada do Araripe
Serra de Baturité
Serra da Ibiapaba

457

E   42°   F   38°   G   34°   H

0   100   200   300   400   kilometres

0   100   200   miles

Scale 1:7,000,00   Projection: Azimuthal Equal Area

Bolivia • Peru • Southwest Brazil • North Paraguay

A 82° **B** 78° **C** 74° **D**

Máncora
Macará
Cariamanga
Borja
Concordia
Nauta
Brasil
Lobitos
Suyo
Orellana
Barranca
Requena
Palmeiras
Talara
Las Lomas
do Javari
Pta Pariñas
Sullana Tambo Grande
San Ignacio
Cahuapanas
Lagunas
Iberia
Negritos
Chulucanas
La Huaca **Piura**
Huancabamba
Bagua
Moyobamba
Papa Playa
Yurimaguas
Paita
Catacaos
Grande
Jumbilla
Castilla
Jaén
Rioja
Sechura
Chachapoyas
Huimbayoc
Dos de Mayo
Bolognesi
Bahía
Olmos
Tarapoto
Ipixuna
de Sechura
Jayanca
Celendín
Saposoa
Orellana
Bayovar
Ferreñafe
Huambos
Picota
Pta Negra
Lambayeque
Chota
Contamaná
Reventazón
Bambamarca
Bolívar
Juanjuí
Chiclayo
Cajamarca
Cruzeiro
Chepén
Contumazá
Tiruntáno
do Sul
Pacasmayo
Huamachuco
Porto
Tarauacá
Ascope
Chicama
Otuzco
Buldibuyo
Walter
Santiago de Cao
Santiago
El Portugués
Uchiza
Pucallpa
Trujillo
de Chuco
Masisea
Puerto Morin
Sihuas
Huacrachuco
Tournavista
Foz do
Santa Ros
Chao
Corongo
Pomabamba
Monzón
Iparia
Jordão
Espera
Santa
Nev.
Tingo María
P E N
Progresso
Chimbote
Huascarán
Huari
Llata
Nepeña
Caraz ▲ 6768 m
Puerto Portillo
Casma
Huaraz
La Unión **Huánuco** Panao
Puerto Victoria
Bolognesi
Culebras
Cerro
Ambo
Puerto Bermúdez
Huarmey
Cajacay *Yerupaja* ▲ 6634 m
Oxapampa
Unini
Atalaya
Alerta
Cajatambo
Oyón
Cerro de Pasco
Perené
Puerto
Fitzcarrald
Barranca
Sayán
Huayllay
Junín
La Merced Ocopa
Puerto Supe
Huaylas
Tarma
Satipo
Huacho
Pta Salinas ó Lachay
Cantal
La Oroya
Huaral
Yauli
Comas
Ancón
Morococha
Jauja
Huancayo
Callao
Matucana
Pampas
Paucarbamba
Quillabamba
Machupicchu Pillcopa
Lima
San José
Ayna
Quince
Lurín
Yauyos
de Quero
Huancavelica
Calca
Paucartambo
Lanla
Mala
La Mejorada
Huanta
Co Pumasillo
Cuzco
Lircay
San Miguel ▲ 6246 m
Urcos
Macu
San Vicente
Ayacucho
Nev. Auzangate
de Cañete
Imperial
Castrovirreyna
Cangallo
Andahuaylas
Abancay Anta
Acomayo ▲ 6384 m
Chincha Alta
Santiago
Córdova
Pampachiri
Yanaoca
Sicuani
Pisco
de Chocorvos
Antabamba
Santo Tomás
Pen. de Paracas
Ica
Cord. de
Yauri
Ayaviri
Pta Ica
Abra
Huanzo
Cailloma
Puc
Bahía de la
Huashuaccasa
Coracora
Alca
Independencia
Palpa
Puquio
Chumpi
Nev.
Cabanaconde
Nazca
Coropuna
Puerto Caballas
6425 m
Marcona
Cotahuasi
Nev.
Ampato
Imata
San Juan
Iquipi
Chuquibamba *6310 m*
Sumbay
Lomas
Aplao
Nev.
Vol. Misti
Yauca
Chachani ▲ *5822 m*
Chala
Atico
Santa Rita *6075 m* Vitor
Arequipa
de Sihuas
Pta Tinaja
La Joya
Camaná
Cocachacra
Mollendo
Moquegua
Canda
Ilo
Locomb
Pta Coles
Ite
La Yarada
Pta Go

P A C I F I C

O C E A N

Bahía Chiqui

Pta Go

P E R U

CORDILLERA OCCIDENTAL
Cordillera Central
Cordillera Oriental
Cerros de Canchyuaya
Cordillera Azul
Cord. Negra
Cord. Huayhuash
Cordillera Urubamba
Cord. de Carabaya
Gran Pajonal
Cordillera Vilcabamba
Cord. de Chilca

6°
10°
14°
18°

1
2
3
4
5

A 82° **B** 78° **C** 74° **D**

70° E 66° F 451 62° G 58°

AMAZONAS

BRAZIL

PARÁ

Benjamin Constant
Norte
Carauari
Jutaí
São Romão
Eirunepé
Gaviãozinho
Envira
Bôca do Moaco
Pauini
Guajarraã
Vera Cruz
Mamoriá
São Bento
Lábrea
Canutama
Caranapatuba
Humaitá
Tauariá
Tapauá
Constância
dos Baetas
Manicoré
Canumã
Mutum
Castanho
Calama
Axinim
Canumã
Borba
São Pedro
Novo Aripuanã
Itaboca
Arumã
Laranjal
Cantagalo
Vila Nova
Lua Nova
Jacareacanga
Recreio
Cuiaba
Canudos
Barra de São Manuel

Feijó
Manuel Urbano
Pôrto Alegre
Sena Madureira
Floriano
Peixoto
Pôrto Acre
Bom Jardim
Bom
Comércio
Manoa
Abunã
Jaciparaná
Caritianas
ACRE
Agostinho
Rio Branco
Plácido de Castro
Palmares
Canamari
Xapuri
Brasiléia
Iñapari
Cobija
San Miguelito
San Lorenzo
Nuevo Mundo
Humaitá
Guayaramerín
Cachuela
Esperanza
Guajará-Mirim
Riberalta
Ariquemes
São Sebastião
Nova Vida
Jaru
Antuerpia
Pôrto Velho
Campo Grande
Barracão
do Barreto
Aripuanã

PANDO
Puerto
Rico
Sena
Concepción
Tres Mapajos
Santa
Rosa
Asunción
El Perú
Fortaleza
Bolívar
Cavinas
Mayo Mayo
Costa
Marques
Magdalena
Pedras
Negras
Matagua
Puerto Villazón
Piso Firme
Santa Isabel
Puerto Alegre
Presidente Médici
Pimenta Bueno
José Bonifácio
Vilhena
Colorado
do Oeste
Nambiquara
Utiariti
Porto dos Gaúchos
MATO GROSSO
Ponte de Pedra
Alta Floresta

RONDÔNIA

Puerto Maldonado
Astillero
Santo Domingo
Limbani
Sandia
Palomani
5999 m
Anchopaya
Ixiamas
Reyes
Chive
Lucerna
Guarayos
BENI
José Agustín
Palacios
Santa Rosa
Exaltación
San Ramón
Baures
El Carmen
Puerto
Saucedo
La Esperanza
Puerto Frey
El Pensamiento
Perseverancia
Holanda
San Javier
Mato Grosso
Pontes-e-
Lacerda
Pôrto Esperidião
Rio Branco
do Bugres
Araputanga
Nortelândia
Diamantino
Nobres
Rosário
Oeste
Arruda
Chapada dos
Guimarães
Várzea Grande
Nossa Senhora
do Livramento
Cáceres
Poconé
Santo Antônio
do Leverger
Pirizal
Cuiabá
Parecis
Parecis

Santa Ana
Puerto Siles
Chapada

Anánea
Putina
Huancané
Juliaca
Chuma
Mapiri
Apolo
Rurrenabaque
San Borja
Chevejécure
San Ignacio
San Antonio
San Andrés
Loreto
Limoquije
Los Cusis
San Pablo
Ascención
La Unión
Concepción
Santa Rosa
de la Roca
San Ramón
San Miguel
San Ignacio
Las Petas
San Matías
Cambará
Rio Alegre
Pôrto Jofre
Barão de
Joselândia
Melgaço
Promissão

LA PAZ
Escoma
Sorata
Nev. Illampu 6400 m
Achacachi
Huarina
Coroico
Irupana
Tipuani
Santa Ana
Trinidad
San Ignacio
San Lorenzo
Puerto
Márquez
Todos Santos
Puerto Mamoré
La Estrella
El Puente
San Ramón
San Pedro
San Miguel
San Rafael
San José
de Chiquitos
Santo Corazón
Amolar
Paiaguás

Acora
Juli
Yunguyo
Desaguadero
Tiquina
Tiwanacu
La Paz
Viacha
Nev.
Illimani
6460 m
Inquisivi
Cordillera Real
Coroico
Puerto
Grether
Cuatro Ojos
Montero
Warnes
Santa Cruz
Pozo del
Tigre
El Cerro
Roboré
Sa. de Santiago
Puerto
Isabel
Puerto
Suárez
Corumbá
Nhecolândia
Pantanal do
Rio Negro

BOLIVIA
Mazo
Cruz
Pizacoma
Chilliculco
Berenguela
Corocoro
Calacoto
Luribay
Colquiri
Quillacollo
Cochabamba
Cliza
Capinota
Totora
Mizque
Pojo
Comarapa
Terevinto
Pampa Grande
Samaipata
Florida
SANTA CRUZ
Fortín
Suárez Arana
Tucavaca
Puerto
Suárez

COCHABAMBA

Tacora
General
Lagos
Sajama
6520 m
Nev. Sajama
Vol. Guallatiri
6060 m
Putre
Oruro
Machacamarca
Huanuni
Uncia
Andamarca
Corque
Colquechaca
Aiquile
Vallegrande
Quiroga
Masavi
Charagua
Roboré
Mayor Pablo
Lagerenza
Fortín
Galpón
Forte
Coimbra
Bahía Negra
Bodoquena
Miranda

ORURO
Sacaca
Viscarra
Villa
Presto
Ravelo
Sucre
Tarabuco
Villa
Oropeza
Sopachuy
Padilla
Cabezas
Lagunillas
Fortín
Paredes
Fortín Ravelo
General Eugenio
A. Garay
Fortín Coronel
Bogado
Puerto
Mihanovich
Fuerte Olimpo
Puerto
Guaraní
Bonito
Nioaque

Minimiñi
Camiña
Vol. Isluga
5530 m
Sabaya
Huachacalla
Challapata
Huari
Challapata
Pampa
Aullagas
Betanzos
Villar
Vitichi
Vilacaya
Monteagudo
Charagua
Copere
Camiri
Boyuibe
Macharetí
Carandayti
Puesto Estrella
Fortín Madrejón
PARAGUAY
Jardim
Maracaju

TARAPACA
Coscaya
Llica
Salinas de
Garci Mendoza
Rio Mulatos
Chita
Yura
Pulacayo
Cotagaita
Atocha
CHUQUISACA
Villamontes
Sanandita
Fortín Carlos
Antonio López
Fortín Infante Rivarola
Pôrto
Murtinho

CHILE
Caleta Buena
Huara
Pozo Almonte
Pica
Pintados
Lagunas
Collaguasi
Co Caltama
5010 m
Salar
de Uyuni
POTOSÍ
San Cristóbal
Chiguana
Tupiza
San Pablo
Co Bonete
5660 m
Mojo
Villazón
La Quiaca
Padcaya
Yacuiba
Pocitos
Santa
Maria
La Esmeralda
Mariscal Estigarribia
Fortín Hernandarias
Puerto Sastre

Quillagua
Toco
Chuquicamata
Turi
Calama
San Lorenzo
Vol. Ollagüe
5869 m
Ollagüe
Vol. San Pedro
6154 m
Conchi
Villa Martín
Julaca
Atoca
Villa Abecia
Entre Rios
TARIJA
Tarija

**MATO GROSSO
DO SUL**
Aquidauana

455

Southeast Brazil

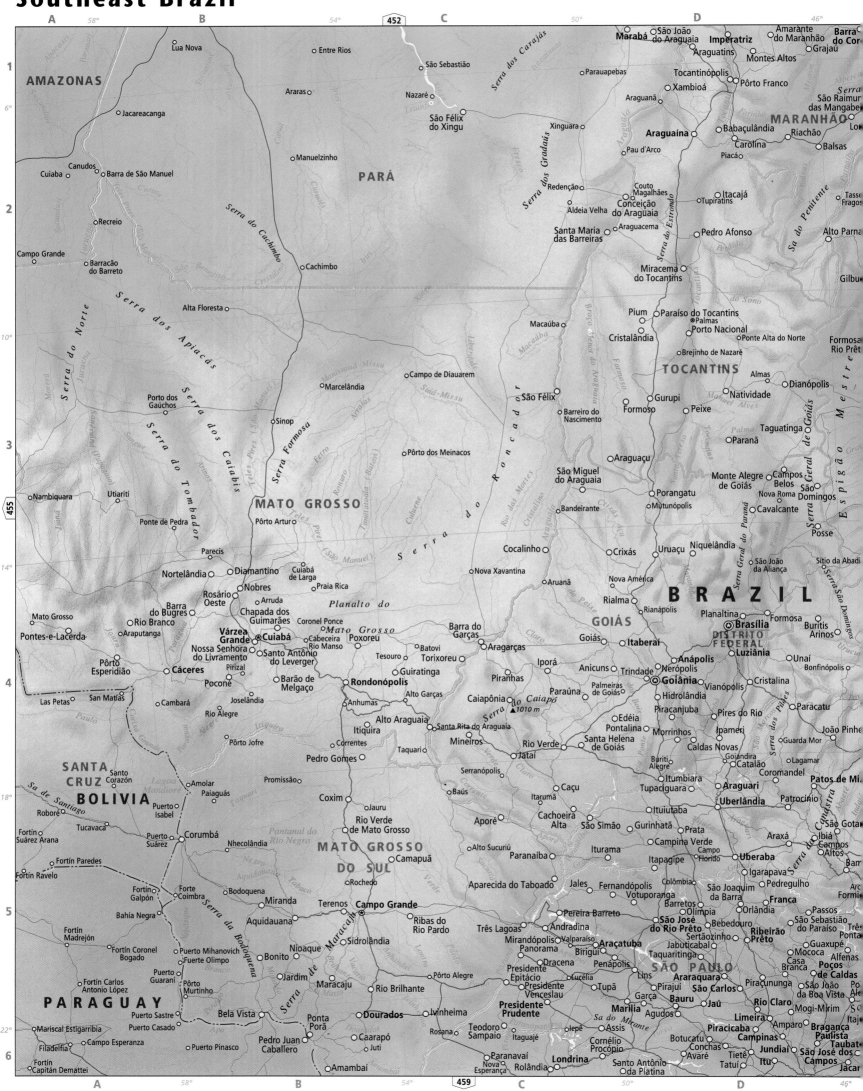

AMAZONAS

Lua Nova
Entre Rios
452
São Sebastião
Araras
Nazaré
Jacareacanga
São Félix
do Xingu
Canudos
Cuiaba
Barra de São Manuel
PARÁ
Manuelzinho
Recreio
Cachimbo
Campo Grande
Barracão
do Barreto
Alta Floresta

Marabá
São João
do Araguaia
Imperatriz
Amarante
do Maranhão
Barra
do Cor
Araguatins
Montes Altos
Grajaú
Parauapebas
Tocantinópolis
Pôrto Franco
Serra
Xambioá
São Raimur
das Mangabe
Araguanã
MARANHÃO
Xinguara
Araguaína
Babaçulândia
Lo
Pau d'Arco
Carolína
Riachão
Couto
Magalhães
Redenção
Piacá
Balsas
Conceição
do Araguaia
Itacajá
Aldeia Velha
Tupiratins
Sa do Peniten
Tasse
Fragos
Santa Maria
das Barreiras
Araguacema
Pedro Afonso
Alto Parna
Miracema
do Tocantins
Gilbu

Serra do Norte
Serra dos Apiacás
Serra do Cachimbo
Pium
Paraíso do Tocantins
Macaúba
Palmas
Formosa
Rio Prêt
Cristalândia
Porto Nacional
Ponte Alta do Norte
Nambiquara
Utiariti
Brejinho de Nazaré
Campo de Diauarem
Marcelândia
TOCANTINS
Almas
Dianópolis
Porto dos
Gaúchos
São Félix
Natividade
Serra dos Caiabis
Serra do Tombador
Sinop
Barreiro do
Nascimento
Gurupi
Manuel Alves
Serra Formosa
Pôrto dos Meinacos
Formoso
Peixe
Taguatinga
Ponte de Pedra
MATO GROSSO
Araguaçu
Paranã
455
Pôrto Artur
São Miguel
do Araguaia
Monte Alegre
de Goiás
Campos
Belos
Serra Geral de Goiás
Parecis
Porangatu
Nova Roma
São
Domingos
Nortelândia
Diamantino
Cuiabá
de Larga
Cocalinho
Crixás
Mutunópolis
Cavalcante
Espigão
Mestre
Nova Xavantina
Bandeirante
Rosário
Oeste
Nobres
Praia Rica
Uruaçu
Niquelândia
Posse
Mato Grosso
Arruda
Planalto do
Aruanã
Nova América
São João
da Aliança
Sitio da Abadi
Rio Branco
Barra
do Bugres
Chapada dos
Guimarães
Mato Grosso
Rialma
Serra São Domingos
Araputanga
Coronel Ponce
BRAZIL
Rianápolis
Pontes-e-Lacerda
Várzea
Grande
Cuiabá
Rio Manso
Barra do
Garças
GOIÁS
Planaltina
Formosa
Pôrto
Esperidião
Nossa Senhora
do Livramento
Santo Antônio
do Leverger
Poxoreu
Goiás
Brasília
Buritis
Unaí
Pirizal
Batovi
Aragarças
Itaberaí
DISTRITO
FEDERAL
Arinos
Cáceres
Pocone
Barão de
Melgaço
Tesouro
Torixoreu
Iporá
Anicuns
Anápolis
Luziânia
Joselândia
Rio Alegre
Guiratinga
Piranhas
Trindade
Nerópolis
Vianópolis
Cristalina
Bonfinópolis
San Matías
Las Petas
Cambará
Alto Garças
Paraúna
Goiânia
Hidrolândia
Pôrto Jofre
Anhumas
Caiapônia
do Caiapó
Palmeiras
de Goiás
Piracanjuba
Pires do Rio
Paracatu
Itiquira
Alto Araguaia
Santa Rita de Araguaia
1010 m
Edéia
Morrinhos
Ipameri
João Pinhe
Correntes
Mineiros
Rio Verde
Santa Helena
de Goiás
Pontalina
Pedro Gomes
Taquari
Jataí
Caldas Novas
Goiandira
Guarda Mor
SANTA
CRUZ
Santo
Corazón
Serranópolis
Buriti
Alegre
Itumbiara
Catalão
Coromandel
Lagamar
Amolar
Promissão
Caçu
BOLIVIA
Paiaguás
Coxim
Baús
Itarumã
Tupaciguara
Araguari
Patos de Mi
Roboré
Puerto
Isabel
Jauru
Aporé
Ituiutaba
Patrocínio
Tucavaca
Rio Verde
de Mato Grosso
Cachoeira
Alta
São Simão
Gurinhatã
Prata
Uberlândia
São Gota
Fortín
Suárez Arana
Puerto
Suárez
Corumbá
Nhecolândia
Alto Sucuriú
Paranaíba
Iturama
Campina Verde
Araxá
Ibiá
Fortín Paredes
Pantanal do
Rio Negro
MATO GROSSO
Camapuã
Itapagipe
Campo
Florido
Campos
Altos
Fortín Ravelo
DO SUL
Rochedo
Uberaba
Fortín
Galpón
Bodoquena
Miranda
Jales
Fernandópolis
Colômbia
Igarapava
Arc
Forte
Coimbra
Aquidauana
Terenos
Campo Grande
Ribas do
Rio Pardo
Aparecida do Taboado
Votuporanga
São Joaquim
da Barra
Pedregulho
Formi
Bahía Negra
Fortín
Madrejón
Três Lagoas
Pereira Barreto
Barretos
Olímpia
Franca
Passos
Fortín Coronel
Bogado
Nioaque
Sidrolândia
Andradina
Orlândia
Puerto Mihanovich
Bonito
Mirandópolis
Valparaíso
São José
do Rio Prêto
Bebedouro
Guaxupé
São Sebastião
do Paraíso
Ponta
Fuerte Olimpo
Panorama
Araçatuba
Sertãozinho
Mococa
Fortín Carlos
Antonio López
Puerto
Guaraní
Pôrto
Murtinho
Jardim
Maracaju
Rio Brilhante
Pôrto Alegre
Presidente
Epitácio
Dracena
Birigui
Penápolis
Jabuticabal
Taquaritinga
Ribeirão
Prêto
Casa
Branca
Poços
de Caldas
Alfenas
PARAGUAY
Lucélia
Tupã
Pirajuí
Araraquara
São Carlos
Piraçununga
São João
da Boa Vista
Mogi-Mirim
S
Mariscal Estigarribia
Bela Vista
Dourados
Ivinheima
Presidente
Venceslau
Lins
SÃO PAULO
Presidente
Prudente
Marília
Garça
Bauru
Jaú
Rio Claro
Amparo
Bragança
Paulista
Taubat
Filadelfia
Puerto Casado
Pedro Juan
Caballero
Caarapó
Juti
Rosana
Teodoro
Sampaio
Itaguajé
Assis
Sa do Mirante
Botucatu
Conchas
Agudos
Piracicaba
Campinas
Jundiaí
São José dos
Jacar
Fortín
Capitán Demattei
Campo Esperanza
Puerto Pinasco
Ponta
Porã
Paranavaí
Nova
Esperança
Rolândia
Lepê
Cornélio
Procópio
Santo Antônio
da Platina
Avaré
Tietê
Tatuí
Itu
São José do
Campos
Amambaí
Londrina

E 42° F 453 38° G 34° H

Parnarama
Buriti Bravo
Novo Parnarama
Palmeirais
São Miguel do Tapuio
Mombaça
Tauá
Senador Pompeu
Solonópole
Apodi
Açu
Lajes
Cabo de São Roque
Natal
Colinas
São João dos Patos
Amarante
Acopiara
Jaguaribe
RIO GRANDE DO NORTE
Pastos Bons
Iguatú
Icó
Currais Novos
Caicó
Santa Cruz
São José de Mipibu
Uruçuí
Floriano
Valença do Piauí
Saboeiro
Sousa
Pombal
Acari
Cuité
Canguaretama
Jerumenha
Oeiras
Picos
CEARÁ
Cajazeiras
Parelhas
PARAÍBA
Baía de Traição
Guarabira
Bertolínia
Flores do Piauí
Jaicós
Campos Sales
Crato
Boa Esperança
Juazeiro do Norte
Milagres
Patos
Teixeira
Conceição
Santa Rita
Cabedelo
João Pessoa
Eliseu Martins
Canto do Buriti
Araripina
Exu
Ouricurí
Salgueiro
Serra Talhada
Sertânia
São João do Carirí
Sumé
Campina Grande
Timbaúba
Goiana
Paulista
PIAUÍ
Simplício Mendes
Paulistana
Afrânio
Parnamirim
Cabrobó Floresta
Ibimirim
Arcoverde
Pesqueira
Belo Jardim
Caruaru
Jaboatão
Gravatá
Olinda
Recife
Cristino Castro
São João do Piauí
São Raimundo Nonato
Santa Maria da Boa Vista
Belém de São Francisco
Chorrochó
Santana do Ipanema
Inajá
PERNAMBUCO
Palmeira dos Indios
Garanhuns
União dos Palmares
Palmares
Barreiros
Escada
Redenção de Gurguéia
Caracol
Remanso
Curaçá
Paulo Afonso
Santana do Ipanema
Atalaia
Rio Largo
Maceió
Curimatá
Pilão Arcado
Sento Sé
Raso da Catarina
Pão de Açúcar
ALAGOAS
Arapiraca
São Miguel dos Campos
Corrente
Buritirama
Uauá
Jeremoabo
SERGIPE
Propriá
Coruripe
Riachão das Neves
Santa Rita de Cássia
Barra
Xique-Xique
Santo Inácio
Juçara
Senhor do Bonfim
Campo Formoso
Queimadas
Monte Santo
Euclides da Cunha
Nossa Senhora das Dores
Simão Dias
Lagarto
Maruim
Laranjeiras
Aracaju
Ponta do Manguinho
gical
Cotegipe
Ibotirama
Copixaba
Irecê
Jacobina
Tucano
Nova Soure
Itabaianinha
Estância
Barreiras
Morpará
Ipupiara
Morro do Chapéu
Conceição do Coité
Serrinha
Inhambupe
Irará
Esplanada
Conde
Palame
São Desidério
Oliveira dos Brejinhos
Palmeiras
Lençóis
Andaraí
BAHIA
Mundo Novo
Riachão do Jacuípe
Ipirá
Feira de Santana
Alagoinhas
Santana
Sitio do Mato
Ibitiara
Itaberaba
Cachoeira
Maragogipe
Santo Amaro
Camaçari
Inhaúmas
Correntina
Bom Jesus da Lapa
Macaúbas
Botuporã
Paramirim
Iramaia
Itaetê
Jurací
Santo Antônio de Jesus
Nazaré
Salvador
Santa Maria da Vitória
Riacho de Santana
Livramento do Brumado
Chapada de Maracás
Gandu
Valença
Côcos
Caetité
Guanambi
Brumado
Ipiaú
Jequié
Camamu
Carinhanha
Palmas de Monte Alto
Caculé
Aracatu
Anagé
Poções
Marau
Montalvânia
Manga
Urandi
Condeúba
Iguaí
Ubaitaba
Itabuna
Januária
Espinosa
Monte Azul
Vitória da Conquista
Itapetinga
Arataca
Ilhéus
São João do Paraíso
Encruzilhada
Una
Rio Pardo de Minas
Porteirinha
Janaúba
Macarani
Salto da Divisa
Canavieiras
Belmonte
São Francisco
Brasília de Minas
Salinas
Pedra Azul
Jacinto
Itapebi
Santa Cruz Cabrália
Pôrto Seguro
Ubaí
Mirabela
Barrocão
Almenara
Jequitinhonha
Coração de Jesus
Miralta
Francisco Sá
Planalto
Itaobim
Caraíva
Mte Pascoal 536 m
Montes Claros
Grão Mogol
Virgem da Lapa
Águas Formosas
Itanhém
Prado
Alcobaça
Bocaiúva
Jequitaí
Caraí
Pavão
Carlos Chagas
Pta da Baleia
Caravelas
Arquipélago dos Abrolhos
Piraporá
Carbonita
Minas Novas
Capelinha
Teofilo Otoni
Nanuque
Mucuri
arzea Palma
Itamarandiba
Itambacuri
Morro d'Anta
Diamantina
Brasil
2033 m
P. de Itambé
Peçanha
Nova Venécia
Conceição da Barra
São Mateus
Corinto
Represa
Três Marias
Curvelo
Sêrro
Guanhães
Tarumirim
Governador Valadares
Conselheiro Pena
ESPÍRITO SANTO
Linhares
lixlândia
Pompeu
Sete Lagoas
Lagoa Santa
MINAS GERAIS
Ipatinga
Coronel Fabriciano
Colatina
Barra do Riacho
tangui
pará
Belo Horizonte
Itabira
Sabará
Caratinga
Ibiraçu
Aracruz
Minas
Contagem
Nova Lima
Itabirito
Manhuaçu
2898 m
Cariacica
Serra
Vitória
Vila Velha
ivinópolis
Ouro Prêto
Conselheiro Lafaiete
Carangola
Muniz Freire
Guarapari
Cachoeira do Itapemirim
Oliveira
Carandaí
Viçosa
Alegre
Itapemirim
Campo Belo
Tombos
Muriaé
Lavras
Barbacena
Ubá
Santos Dumont
Cataguases
Itaperuna
São Fidélis
São João da Barra
arginha
Três
rações
Andrelândia
Juiz de Fora
Leopoldina
Além Paraíba
Três Rios
Campos
Cabo de São Tomé
São Lourenço
Agulhas Negras
Mantiqueira
RIO DE JANEIRO
Nova Friburgo
Macaé
zeiro 2797 m
Volta Redonda
Teresópolis
Petrópolis
Barra Mansa
Nova Iguaçu
Duque de Caxias
São Gonçalo
aratinguetá
Itaguaí
Niterói
Cabo Frio
I. Grande
Rio de Janeiro

ATLANTIC OCEAN

1
6°
2
10°
3
14°
4
18°
5
22°
6

455

BOLIVIA

ARGENTINA

CHILE

PACIFIC

OCEAN

Tropic of Capricorn

POTOSÍ
TARIJA
JUJUY
ANTOFAGASTA
SALTA
TUCUMÁN
CATAMARCA
SANTIAGO DEL ESTERO
ATACAMA
LA RIOJA
CHACO
SANTA FÉ
SAN JUAN
CÓRDOBA
COQUIMBO
VALPARAÍSO
SANTIAGO
MENDOZA
SAN LUIS
LIBERTADOR
MAULE
BÍO BÍO
LA PAMPA
ARAUCANÍA
NEUQUÉN
RÍO NEGRO
BUENOS AIRES

Chíguana · San Cristóbal · Villamontes
Ollagüe · Vol. Ollagüe 5869 m · Tupiza · San Lorenzo · Tarija · Entre Rios · Sanandita
Quillagua · Co Bonete 5660 m · Mojo · Padcaya · Yacuiba · Fortín Infante Rivarola
Tocopilla · Lequena · Vol. San Pedro 6154 m · San Pablo · Villazón · La Quiaca · Pocitos · Santa María · Fortín Hernandarias · Mariscal Estigarri
Toco · Conchi · Turi · Abra Pampa · Bermejo · Tartagal · Fortín Capitán Demattei
María Elena · Chuquicamata · San Ramón de la Nueva Orán · Embarcación · Fortín Capitán Escobar
Pedro de Valdivia · Calama · Humahuaca · Pichanal · Puerto Irigoyen · Fortín Pilcomayo
Michilla · Vol. Licancábur 5930 m · Co Zapaleri 5655 m · Tilcara · La Estrella · Los Blancos · Ingeniero Guillermo N. Juárez
Sierra Gorda · San Pedro de Atacama · Susques · San Salvador de Jujuy · Rivadavia · Las Lomi
Baquedano · Carmen Alto · Toconao · San Pedro · Perico · General Martín Miguel de Güemes · Nueva Pompeya
Mejillones · Co del Rincón 5594 m · Salta · Joaquín V. González · San Camilo
Domeyko · Co Pular 6225 m · San Antonio de los Cobres · Rosario de Lerma · Lumbrera
Augusta Victoria · Paso Socompa · Nev. de Cachi 6720 m · Cachi · Guachipas · Metán · Taco Pozo · Castelli
Escondida · Vol. Llullaillaco 6723 m · Cafayate · Quebracho Coto · Pampa de los Guanacos · Tres Isletas
Salinitas · Vol. Antofalla 6100 m · Antofagasta de la Sierra · Co Galán 6600 m · Trancas · Monte Quemado · Campo Gallo · Aviá Teraí · Presidencia Roque Sáenz Peña
Paposo · Santa María · Tafí Viejo · San Miguel de Tucumán · Patay · Tintina · General Pinedo · San Bernardo · Villa Ángela
Taltal · Altamira · Sa Nevada 6400 m · Bella Vista · Las Cejas · Pozo Hondo · Otumpa · Quimilí · Santa Sylvia
El Salvador · Diego de Almagro · Inca de Oro · Monteros · Aguilares · Termas de Río Hondo · La Banda
Chañaral · Vol. Copiapó 6080 m · Ojos del Salado 6880 m · Concepción · Santiago del Estero · Fernández
Caldera · Algarrobo · Co Bonete 6872 m · Flambalá · Belén · Andalgalá · Las Cañas · Ciudad de Loreto · Añatuya · Colonia Dora · Bandera
Copiapó · Tierra Amarilla · Tinogasta · Copacabana · Aimogasta · Frías · San Antonio · Los Telares · Tostado · Ceres
Castilla · La Guardia · San Fernando del Valle de Catamarca · Villa Mazán · Chumbicha · Recreo · Villa Ojo de Agua · Argentina · Esteban Rams
Totoral · Las Juntas · Jagüé · Sa de Famatina 6250 m · Chilecito · San Martín · Pinto
Carrizal Bajo · Co de Potro 5830 m · Mejicana · Famatina 6375 m · San Francisco del Chañar
Miraflores · Huasco · Vallenar · La Rioja · Patquía · Chamical · Quilino · Deán Funes · San José de la Dormida · San Cristóbal · Morteros · Moisés Ville
Freirina · El Tránsito · Domeyko · Co del Toro 6380 m · Villa Unión · Guandacol · Serrezuela · Cruz del Eje · Río Primero · Jesús María · Río Ceballos · Sunchales · Rafaela
El Tofo · Co Las Tórtolas 6332 m · San Agustín de Valle Fértil · Malanzán · Capilla del Monte · Córdoba · Esperanza
Co de Olivares 6282 m · Rodeo · San José de Jáchal · La Falda · Cosquín · San Francisco · Santa Fé
La Serena · Rivadavia · Andacollo · Chepes · Desiderio Tello · Salsacate · Alta Gracia · Villa del Rosario · San Carlos Centro · Paraná
Coquimbo · SAN JUAN · Tucunuco · Mareyes · Mascasín · Chancaní · Oncativo · Oliva · Las Varillas · San Jorge · Gálvez · Diamante
Ovalle · Punitaqui · Castaño Viejo · Talacasto · Co Champaquí 2880 m · Conlara · Dalmacio Vélez Sarsfield · El Trébol · Rosario
Maitencillo · Ollapel · Barreal · San Juan · Caucete · Quines · Villa Dolores · Villa María · Bell Ville · Las Rosas · Casilda
Combarbalá · Salamanca · Co Mercedario 6770 m · Pampa de la Salinas · Villa Valeria · La Laguna · Marcos Juárez · San Lorenzo · Villa Constitución
Huentelauquén · Co Aconcagua 6960 m · Las Heras · Mendoza · San Antonio · San Luis · Chazón · La Carlota · Arias · Firmat · Alcorta
Los Vilos · La Ligua · San Felipe · Godoy Cruz · Villa Nueva · La Toma · Río Cuarto · Vicuña Mackenna · Venado Tuerto · Pergamino · Colón
VALPARAÍSO · La Calera · Quillota · Co Juncal 6060 m · Luján · Rivadavia · Co del Morro 1727 m · Mercedes · General Levalle · Laboulaye · Rufino · Junín
Viña del Mar · Quilpué · Tupungato 6570 m · Las Catitas · La Paz · Beazley · SAN LUIS · Comandante Salas · Justo Daract · Vedia · Chacabuco
Valparaíso · Santiago · Tunuyán · San Carlos · General Pinto · Lincoln
San Antonio · San Bernardo · Vol. San José 5830 m · Villa Huidobro · General Villegas · Bragado
Melipilla · Paine · Vol. Maipú 5290 m · San Rafael · Media Luna · Buena Esperanza · Nueva Galia · Realicó · Intendente Alvear · Timote · Nueve de Julio
Navidad · Graneros · Rancagua · Monte Comán · General Alvear · Carmensa · Nueva Parera · Meridiano · Rivadavia · Carlos Casa
Rengo · San Rafael · Canalejas · General Pico · Quemú-Quemú · Pehuajó · Corbe
San Fernando · Co Sosneado 5189 m · Victorica · Eduardo Castex · Catriló · Trenque Lauquen · Henderson · San Ca de Boli
Santa Cruz · Vol. Tinguiririca 4300 m · El Sosneado · Santa Isabel · Telén · Salazar · Tres Lomas · Daireaux
Pichilemu · Retén Llico · Curicó · Vol. Descabezado Grande 3830 m · Malargüe · LA PAMPA · Toay · Santa Rosa · Maza · Salliqueló · Guamini
Licantén · Vol. Peteroa 4090 m · Co Nevada 3810 m · Quehué · Rivera · Carhué · General La Madrid
Talca · Vol. Campanario 4020 m · Algarrobo del Aguila · General Acha · Epu-pel · Puán · Pigüé · Coronel Suárez
San Javier · San Clemente · Bardas Blancas · Macachín · Darregueira · Saavedra · Coronel Pringle
Chanco · Linares · Vol. Longaví 3242 m · Co Payún 3680 m · Victoria Telén · Limay Mahuida · Puelén · Bernasconi · Guatraché · Tornquist · Tres Picos 1243 m · Saldungaray
Cauquenes · Parral · Sa Chachahuén 2065 m · Gobernador Duval · Coronel Dorrego · Cabildo
Quirihue · San Carlos · Recinto · Vol. Copahue 2969 m · Sa de Auca Mahuida 2253 m · Bahía Blanca
Chillán · Tomé · Antuco · Chihuido Medio 1494 m · Cuchillo-Có · Villa Iris · Punta Alta
Talcahuano · Concepción · Lota · La Laja · Vol. Tromen 3980 m · Chos Malal · Embalse Cerros Colorados · L. Pellegrini · Médanos · Major Buratovich
Arauco · Antuco · Vol. Domuyo 4709 m · Plaza Huincul · Cipolletti · Pichi Mahuida · Río Colorado · Bahía Blanca
Lebu · Cañete · Los Angeles · Mulchén · Loncopué · Zapala · Cutral-Co · Neuquén · Chelforó · Río Colorado · General Roca · Choele Choel
Angol · Purén · Collipulli · Vol. Llaima 3124 m · Las Lajas · NEUQUÉN · RÍO NEGRO
Traiguén · Victoria · Curacautín · Puerto Saavedra · Carahue · Temuco · Nueva Imperial

460

PARAGUAY

MATO GROSSO DO SUL

BRAZIL

SÃO PAULO

MINAS GERAIS

PARANA

MISIONES

SANTA CATARINA

RIO GRANDE DO SUL

CORRIENTES

URUGUAY

FORMOSA

ENTRE RIOS

AIRES

ATLANTIC OCEAN

Fortín Carlos Antonio López
Puerto Guaraní
Pôrto Murtinho
Jardim
Maracaju
Mirandópolis
Valparaiso
Araçatuba
Bebedouro
São Sebastião do Paraíso
Guaxupé
Alfenas
Varginha
Puerto Sastre
Puerto Casado
Pôrto Alegre
Panorama
Birigüi
Jabuticabal
Sertãozinho
Ribeirão Prêto
Poços de Caldas
Mococa
Três Corações
Campo Esperanza
Bela Vista
Rio Brilhante
Dracena
Presidente Epitácio
Penápolis
Lins
Taquaritinga
Pirassununga
Casa Branca
São João da Boa Vista
Pôrto Murtinho
Ponta Porã
Dourados
Ivinheima
Presidente Venceslau
Tupã
Pirajuí
São Carlos
Araraquara
São João da Boa Vista
Amparo
Pouso Alegre
Itajubá
Cruzeiro
Pedro Juan Caballero
Caarapó
Juti
Rosana
Teodoro Sampaio
Assis
Marília
Garça
Jaú
Bauru
Agudos
Rio Claro
Limeira
Americana
Mogi-Mirim
Piracicaba
Campinas
Guaratinguetá
Bragança Paulista
Taubaté
Horqueta
Coronel Sapucaia
Iguatemi
Nova Esperança
Paranavaí
Rolândia
Londrina
Maringá
Apucarana
Arapongas
Santo Antônio da Platina
Cornélio Procópio
Avaré
Botucatu
Conchas
Tietê
Jundiaí
Amparo
Itu
Itatiba
Jacareí
Concepción
Pozo Colorado
Nueva Germania
San Pedro
Ypé-Jhú
Umuarama
Goio-Erê
Campo Mourão
Venceslau Bras
Tatuí
Sorocaba
São Bernardo do Campo
São Paulo
Santo André
Jacareí
São José dos Campos
Caraguatatuba
Puerto Antequera
San Pedro
Rosario
Iturbe
Itacurubí del Rosario
Puerto Adela
Guaira
Toledo
Telêmaco Borba
Pirai do Sul
Itararé
Capão Bonito
São Vicente
Santos
Guarujá
I. de São Sebastião
Villa Hayes
Asunción
Coronel Oviedo
Hernandarias
Cascavel
Pitanga
Reserva
Castro
Cêrro Azul
Jacupiranga
Iguape
Itanhaém
Peruíbe
San Lorenzo
Caacupé
Paraguarí
Ciudad del Este
Foz do Iguaçu
Laranjeiras do Sul
Prudentópolis
Ponta Grossa
Rio Branco do Sul
Curitiba
I. Comprida
I. do Cardoso
Guaraqueçaba
I. das Peças
Quiindy
Villarrica
Caaguazú
Capanema
Guarapuava
Irati
Palmeira
São José dos Pinhais
Paranaguá
Guaratuba
Co San Rafael 850 m
Eldorado
Mangueirinha
União da Vitória
Rio Negro
Mafra
Joinville
São Francisco do Sul
Paso de Patria
Desmochado
Encarnación
Posadas
El Soberbio
Canoinhas
Jaraguá do Sul
Resistencia
San Luis del Palmar
Corrientes
Candelaria
Oberá
Irai
Xanxerê
Caçador
Barranqueras
Ituzaingó
Leandro N. Alem
Santa Rosa
Chapecó
Joaçaba
Curitibanos
Ibirama
Blumenau
Itajaí
La Sábana
Apóstoles
San Javier
Campo Novo
Palmeira das Missões
Sarandi
Campos Novos
Rio Do Sul
Ituporanga
Pôrto Belo
Goya
Santo Tomé
São Luis Gonzaga
Santo Angelo
Ijui
Carazinho
Erechim
Campo Belo do Sul
Lajes
Bom Retiro
São José
Florianópolis
Ilha de Sta Catarina
Bella Vista
San Roque
São Borja
Cruz Alta
Tapera
Lagoa Vermelha
São Joaquim
Tubarão
Laguna
Esquina
Mercedes
La Cruz
Itaqui
Santiago
Tupanciretã
Soledade
Passo Fundo
Casca
Vacaria
Turvo
Criciúma
Sta Marta Grande
Curuzú Cuatiá
Mariano Loza
São Francisco de Assis
Jaguari
Bom Jesus
Bento Gonçalves
Garibaldi
Caxias do Sul
Araranguá
Uruguaiana
Paso de los Libres
Alegrete
Santa Maria
Cacequi
São Sepé
Santa Cruz do Sul
Lajeado
Montenegro
Novo Hamburgo
São Leopoldo
São Francisco de Paula
Tôrres
La Paz
San José de Feliciano
Monte Caseros
Bella Unión
Tomás Gomensoro
Quarai
Rosário do Sul
São Gabriel
Caçapava do Sul
Canoas
Guaíba
Osorio
Porto Alegre
Palmares do Sul
Concordia
San Salvador
Salto
Artigas
Rivera
Dom Pedrito
Encruzilhada do Sul
Barra do Ribeiro
Bovril
Villaguay
Federación
Colonia Lavalleja
Tacuarembó
Ansina
Minas de Corrales
Lavras do Sul
Santa da Boa Vista
Piratini
Camaquã
São Lourenço do Sul
Mostardas
Maria Grande
Villa Rosario del Tala
San José
Young
Tranqueras
Bagé
Pinheiro Machado
Boqueirão
Canguçu
Paysandú
Guichón
Melo
Pedro Osorio
Concepción del Uruguay
Paso de los Toros
Vergara
Erval
São José do Norte
Gualeguaychú
Gualeguay
Durazno
Treinta-y-Tres
Arroio Grande
Pelotas
Rio Grande
Fray Bentos
Mercedes
Sarandí del Yí
José Pedro Varela
Jaguarão
Trinidad
Sarandí Grande
Lascano
Santa Vitória do Palmar
Dolores
Cardona
Florida
San Nicolás de los Arroyos
Carmelo
San José de Mayo
Minas
Aiguá
Rocha
Baradero
Colonia del Sacramento
Tala
Castillos
Arrecifes
Zárate
Canelones
La Paloma
Campana
Las Piedras
San Carlos
San Fernando
Verónica
Montevideo
Maldonado
Avellaneda
Quilmes
La Plata
Buenos Aires
Lomas de Zamora
Cañuelas
Magdalena
Lobos
Alejandro Korn
San Miguel del Monte
Chascomús
Veinticinco de Mayo
Saladillo
General Belgrano
Pila
Castelli
Dolores
General Guido
General Conesa
General Juan Madariaga
Villa Gesell
Las Flores
Azul
Maipú
Pta Norte del Cabo San Antonio
Pta Sur del Cabo San Antonio
Tandil 500 m
Ayacucho
Coronel Vidal
Benito Juárez
Balcarce
Mar del Plata
C. Corrientes
San Agustin
Lobería
Miramar
Quequén
Necochea
Orense

Lagoa dos Patos
Lagoa Mirim
Rio de la Plata
Bahía Samborombón

Scale 1:7,000,000
Projection: Azimuthal Equal Area

0 100 200 300 400 kilometers
0 100 200 miles

South Chile · South Argentina

458

Grid columns: B 74° | C 70° | D 66° (458) | E 62° | F

Rows: 1 | 2 | 3 | 4 | 5

42° | 46° | 50° | 54°

A 78° | B 74° | C 70° | D 66° | F 62° | G 58°

Region labels
ARAUCANÍA · NEUQUÉN · RÍO NEGRO · LOS LAGOS · ARGENTINA · CHUBUT · AISÉN · SANTA CRUZ · CHILE · PATAGONIA · MAGALLANES · TIERRA DEL FUEGO · BUENOS AIRES

SOUTH ATLANTIC OCEAN

FALKLAND ISLANDS (U.K.) · West Falkland · East Falkland

Place names
Nueva Imperial, Curacautín, Vol. Llaima ▲3124 m, Las Lajas, Cutral-Có, Plaza Huincul, Cipolletti, Gobernador Duval, Bahía Blanca, Coronel Dorrego, Tres Arroyos, Energía, Carahue, Temuco, Zapala, Neuquén, General Roca, Pichi Mahuida, Río Colorado, Médanos, Punta Alta, Oriente, Orense, Puerto Saavedra, Pitrufquén, Villarrica, Vol. Villarrica ▲2840 m, Picún Leufú, Villa Regina, Chelforó, Lamarque, Choele Choel, Major Buratovich, Pucón, Lanco, Vol. Lanín ▲3776 m, Catán Lil, Colonia Josefa, Buenos Aires, Quepe, Villarrica, San José de la Mariquina, Panguipulli, Riñihue, Junín de los Andes, Santa Rosa, General Conesa, Villalonga, Valdivia, Lago Ranco, San Martín De Los Andes, Co Azul ▲2480 m, La Esperanza, Sierra Colorada, Cinco Chañares, Villalonga, Bahía Unión, Pta Galera, Paillaco, Lago Ranco, Río Bueno, Pilcaniyeu, Maquinchao, El Caín, Los Menucos, Valcheta, San Antonio Oeste, Viedma, Bahía Anegada, La Unión, Osorno, Puyehue, Ingeniero Jacobacci, Sierra Grande, Aguada Cecilio, Carmen De Patagones, Pta Rasa, Purranque, Vol. Osorno ▲2652 m, San Carlos de Bariloche, Norquinco, Cona Niyeu, Salado, La Lobería, Pta Bermeja, C. Quedal, Tronador ▲3554 m, Cochamó, Gastre, Sa Huancache, Gan Gan, Telsen, Puerto Lobos, Pta Sierra, Punta Pórfido, Pta Norte, Puerto Varas, Ventisquero 2300 m, El Bolsón, Cholila, Puerto Montt, Maullín, Chacao, Ancud, Calbuco, Chacao, Vol. Huequi ▲1050 m, Esquel, Gualjaina, Puerto Pirámides, Península Valdés, Punta Delgada, Quemchi, Isla Grande de Chiloé, Castro, Minchinmávida 2470 m, Chaitén, Co Cónico ▲2270 m, Tecka, Las Plumas, Puerto Madryn, Pta Ninfas, Quellón, Quellón, Vol. Futaleufú, Corcovado 2300 m, Corcovado, Palena, Paso de Indios, Gaimán, Trelew, Dolavón, Rawson, Pta Castro, C. Quilán, Boca del Guafo, Palena, Mte Melimoyu ▲2400 m, José de San Martín, El Sombrero, Florentino Ameghino, Dos Pozos, I. Guafo, Islas Guaitecas, Isla Magdalena, Nueva Lubecka, Sierra Cuadrada, Meseta de Montemayor, C. Raso, Cabo Raso, I. Benjamín, I. James, Puerto Cisnes, Alto Río Senguer, Facundo, Buen Pasto, Pico de Salamanca, Camarones, Bahía Camarones, Archipiélago I. Melchor, Mte Macá ▲2960 m, Puerto Aisén, Pampa del Castillo, C. Dos Bahías, de los, I. Victoria, Coihaique, Río Mayo, Sarmiento, Bahía Bustamante, Bahía Darwin, Vol. Hudson ▲2500 m, Balmaceda, Bahía Solano, Puerto Visser, Chonos, Bahía Anna Pink, Comodoro Rivadavia, C. Raper, Mte San Valentín ▲4058 m, Perito Moreno, Las Heras, Caleta Olivia, Golfo de San Jorge, Bahía Langara, Península de Taitao, Co Arenales ▲3440 m, Chile Chico, Pampa del Castillo, Pico Truncado, Mazarredo, C. Tres Puntas, Península Tres Montes, L. General Carrera, Cochrane, Bajo Caracoles, Cerro Cojudo Blanco ▲1335 m, Fitz Roy, Cabo Blanco, Golfo de Penas, Mte San Lorenzo ▲3700 m, Meseta el Pedrero, Las Martinetas, Antonio de Biedma, Tortel, Puerto Deseado, Gran Altiplanicie Central, Pta Medanosa, I. Campana, I. Prat, C. Mellizo Sur 3050 m, Gobernador Gregores, Tres Cerros, Florida Negra, Bahía Laura, I. Patricio Lynch, I. Serrano, L. San Martín, El Salado, C. Dañoso, I. Esmeralda, Isla, L. O'Higgins 3380 m, L. Cardiel, Puerto San Julián, Pta Desengaño, Golfo Ladrillero, Pen. Wharton, SANTA CRUZ, Mte Fitz Roy ▲3375 m, L. Viedma, Tres Lagos, Laguna Grande, C. San Francisco de Paula, Golfo Trinidad, Wellington, I. Mornington, Co Murallón ▲3600 m, Chalía, Comandante Luis Piedrabuena, Puerto Santa Cruz, I. Madre de Dios, I. Duque de York, Charles Fuhr, El Calafate, Co Pináculo 2160 m, L. Argentino, Pta León, Bahía Grande, C. Santiago, Bahía Solvación, Puerto Coig, FALKLAND ISLANDS, West Falkland, Pebble I., C. Dolphin, I. Diego de Almagro, Esperanza, Gobernador Mayer, C. Buen Tiempo, Río Gallegos, King George Bay, Queen Charlotte Bay, Mt Adam ▲700 m, Mt Usborne ▲705 m, Stanley, I. Ramírez, I. Contreras, I. Pacheco, MAGALLANES, Mte Burney ▲1750 m, Villa Tehuelche, Río Verde, Gallegos, Bella Vista, Monte Dinero, Pta Dungeness, Weddell I., Port Stephens, Darwin, Goose Green, Lively I., Choiseul Sound, Archipiélago de la Reina Adelaida, I. Manuel Rodríguez, C. Pilar, Península Muñoz Gamero, Isla Riesco, Punta Arenas, Porvenir, Cerro Sombrero, Sierra Balmaceda, Pta de Arenas, Bahía San Sebastián, C. Meredith, Bay of Harbours, East Falkland, I. Desolación, Península de Brunswick, Fuerte Bulnes, Camerón, Isla Grande, San Sebastián, Bahía Onway, Pico Nariz ▲822 m, Río Grande, I. Santa Inés, Clarence, I. Cap Aracena, de Tierra, C. Peñas, TIERRA DEL FUEGO, L. Fagnano, Bahía Thetis, C. San Juan, San Juan de Salvamento, Península Brecknock, Mte Darwin ▲2488 m, del Fuego, Ushuaia, Puerto Harborton, Península Mitre, I. de los Estados, I. Stewart, Puerto Williams, I. Picton, I. Londonderry, I. Hoste, I. Navarino, I. Nueva, I. Lennox, Pen. Rous, Bahía Nassau, Islas Wollaston, Península Hardy, Isla Hermite, Cabo de Hornos (Cape Horn)

Scale
kilometers 0 100 200 300 400
miles 0 100 200
Scale 1:7 000 000
Projection: Azimuthal Equal Area

South America

460

Islands around South America

GALÁPAGOS ISLANDS
(Archipiélago de Colón)
(Ecuador)
Scale 1: 5,000,000

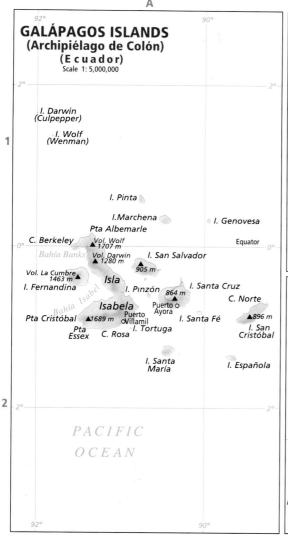

SAN ANDRÉS
(Colombia)
Scale 1: 250,000

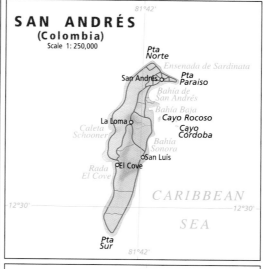

PROVIDENCIA
(Colombia)
Scale 1: 200,000

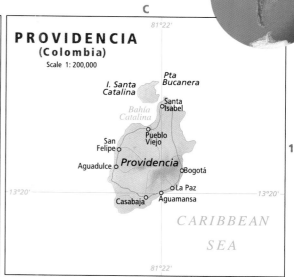

EASTER ISLAND
(Chile)
Scale 1: 350,000

RÓBINSON CRUSOE ISLAND
(Archipiélago Juan Fernández)
(Chile)
Scale 1: 250,000

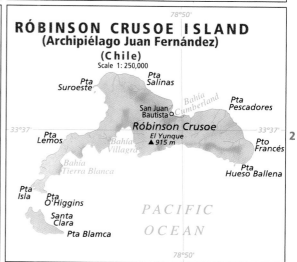

SOUTH GEORGIA
(U.K.)
Scale 1: 3,000,000

ARUBA
(Netherlands)
Scale 1:1,000,000

CURAÇAO
(Netherlands Antilles)
Scale 1:1,000,000

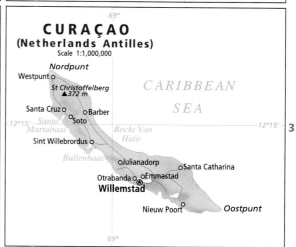

BONAIRE
(Netherlands Antilles)
Scale 1:1,000,000

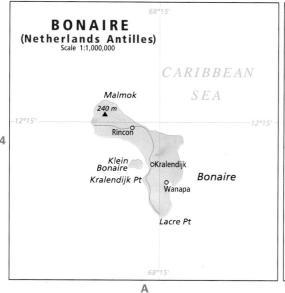

TOBAGO
(Trinidad and Tobago)
Scale 1:1,000,000

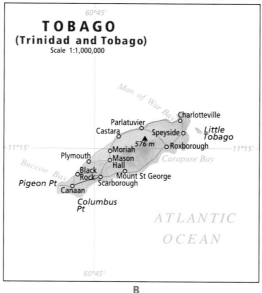

TRINIDAD
(Trinidad and Tobago)
Scale 1: 2,000,000

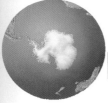

Polar Regions

The polar regions lie between 66° latitude and the North and South poles. The continent of Antarctica, which is 14 million sq km (5.5 million sq miles) in area, is almost completely enclosed within the Antarctic Circle (66°S) and the South Pole. Antarctica is surrounded by the only continuous seas circling Earth, and during winter the seas freeze around it, making the continent appear larger than it actually is. Various nations have laid claim to certain parts of Antarctica, several of which overlap. Most non-claimant countries—and the United Nations—do not recognize these claims.

The region between the Arctic Circle (66°N) and the North Pole includes the Arctic Ocean and the northern fringes of the Eurasian and North American landmasses. The arctic lands are shared by several countries: Canada, the USA, Russia, Finland, Sweden, and Norway.

Physiography

Eastern Antarctica was once part of the ancient supercontinent of Gondwana, while the Western Peninsula is an island chain related to the geologically younger Andean ranges. Floating ice shelves cover the seas around the land areas, giving the appearance of one large ice-covered continent. Volcanic chains, such as the Scotia Arc,

are found in the Antarctic Peninsula, and there are several active volcanoes. The highest point in Antarctica is Vinson Massif (5,140 m; 16,863 ft), while the average elevation of the continent exceeds 2,440 m (8,000 ft).

The Arctic Circle region encompasses the fringes of the North American, European, and Asian continents which surround the Arctic Ocean. The Arctic Ocean was formed when the Eurasian Plate moved towards the Pacific Plate, while the North American and Eurasian plates separated to form the Atlantic Ocean. The Arctic Ocean, reaching depths of 969 m (3,200 ft), is connected to the Atlantic and Pacific oceans by several straits through which its cold waters move southward.

Climate

Very cold climates prevail in the polar regions. Because of Earth's axial tilt, the polar regions receive the Sun's rays obliquely, so although during the summer months there is practically no darkness, there is nevertheless little solar radiation. During the long polar winter "nights," which also last for months, there is no net solar radiation at all to warm the land surface.

Snow reflects a large proportion of solar radiation back to space. This is particularly true of Antarctica, which is covered by extensive ice sheets. Temperatures within the Arctic Circle are higher than those of Antarctica because of the presence of a warming ocean. Within Antarctica, temperatures fall as low as –89.2°C (–128.6°F). In contrast, the lowest recorded temperature on the ice sheet of Greenland is –68°C (–90°F). Temperatures during summer in the Arctic Ocean, when parts of the floating ice melt, are around 0°C (32°F) and during winter, when larger areas are covered by ice, they fall to –34°C (–30°F).

The polar areas are characterized by cold air masses which blow toward warmer, temperate latitudes. In Antarctica, strong, chilly winds blow

over the land surface. Winds blow continuously from west to east (the West Wind Drift) in the seas surrounding Antarctica; the seas are so often stormy that they have prevented explorers reaching the continent until relatively recently.

Winters within the Arctic Circle are windy, cold, and harsh; temperatures in northern Siberia can fall to –50°C (–122°F). During the arctic summer, temperatures in the southern margins average around 10°C (50°F), with some short spells up to 30°C (86°F). In Antarctica, only the northern part of the Antarctic Peninsula becomes warm (up to 15°C; 59°F), the temperatures of the interior remaining below freezing.

Flora and fauna

Marine life thrives in the nutrient-rich waters around Antarctica. Phytoplankton abound, and so do the tiny shrimp-like krill, which form part of an elaborate food chain that includes crustaceans, mollusks, fish, whales, porpoises, dolphins, and seals. Most of the fish are unique to the region. The ozone hole above the South Pole could adversely affect the phytoplakton of the Antarctic seas, which would disturb the food chain.

Around the Arctic lies the treeless tundra, south of which is boreal forest where firs, spruce, and larch grow. Lichens and mosses are common in the tundra; low-growing plants sprout in spring and blossom in summer.

There is marked contrast between the natural life of the Arctic Circle in summer and in winter. During summer there are large quantities of fish and whales in the sea, seals on the ice floes, and foxes, wolves, bears, caribou, and reindeer on land. There are also weasels, hares, and lemmings. Birds migrate to the Arctic during the summer in huge numbers; many birds and animals migrate to warmer lands and waters in winter.

Polar bears (left), and people fishing under the ice (above left) in Arctic Siberia. An iceberg towers over this group of Adélie penguins in Antarctica (top).

Antarctic scenes: a summer night at Cape Bird (above), a Weddell seal (above right), and penguins galore—a crowd scene (below right), an inquisitive-looking Gentoo penguin (below left), and an Emperor penguin group (left).

Natural resources

The world's largest deposits of ice are in Antarctica. A large quantity of fresh water is frozen in these, but this water cannot easily be exploited. Currently there is a concern that global warming could cause the ice sheets to melt, which would raise the levels of the world's oceans. Sea levels have risen in recent times but research indicates that the Antarctic ice sheets have not, to date, diminished in thickness.

As a large part of Antarctica was once part of Gondwana, minerals that occur in other parts of Gondwana, such as coal in Australia, might lie beneath the ice sheets. Likewise, because the Antarctic Peninsula can be considered an extension of the Andes, there is a possibility of metallic ore deposits being found in Antartica, as they have been in the Andes. In addition, the continental shelf around Antarctica could contain petroleum deposits. However, given the current state of technology, mining is not economically feasible in the harsh antarctic conditions.

International agreements which forbid mining and non-peaceful uses of Antarctica have been signed by claimant and non-claimant countries. These aim to ensure the conservation of its environment.

Human habitation

Antarctica is uninhabited, except for several scientific research stations. The nearest human habitations lie on the subantarctic islands of Macquarie, Crozet, South Georgia, and Kerguelen. There is now a small amount of tourism developing in the area, mainly in the Antarctic Peninsula; tourists make short, supervized trips ashore from small cruise vessels. There are also tourist flights over the Antarctic.

In contrast, the Arctic region has been inhabited for thousands of years by indigenous groups such as the Inuit (Eskimo) in Canada, the Saami (Lapps) in Scandinavia, and the Nanets and Yakuts of Russia. Relationships have recently been discovered between these now scattered peoples—there is evidence that some of these indigenous groups migrated from Asia to North America, across the Bering Strait.

As the Arctic is not conducive to agriculture, its inhabitants have to gather food, and their ability to succeed in this is determined primarily by environmental conditions. Saami who live in the traditional way herd reindeer, taking their herds to high ground to graze in summer, then moving to woodlands in low mountain territory in winter. Caribou are hunted by the Nanets and Yakuts in the Russian tundra during spring and summer and in the forests during winter; both animals and people need to migrate with the seasons to survive. In Canada, the Inuit hunt seals along the coast during winter and move inland to hunt caribou during summer.

Polar exploration

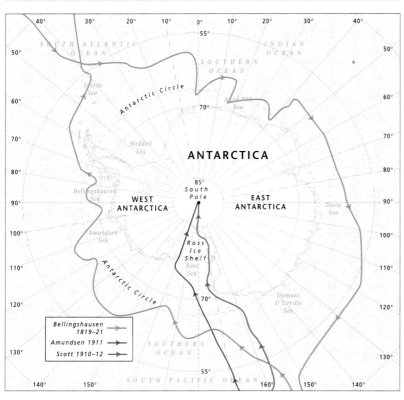

A Russian icebreaker (below right), the Cape Evans hut used by both Shackleton and Scott (top right), and the inside of Scott's discovery hut (top, far right), all in Antarctica. The remains of an ancient hut stand on the shore of the Arctic Ocean (bottom, far right).

The Russian Fabian von Bellingshausen circumnavigated Antarctica in his voyage of 1820–21 (left). In the early twentieth century the epic contest to be the first to reach the South Pole, between Englishman Robert Scott and the Norwegian Roald Amundsen was won by Amundsen when he finally reached the Pole on December 14, 1912. Scott arrived almost a month later on January 17, 1912.

A number of motives have driven men to explore the frozen wildernesses at the uttermost ends of Earth—commerce, national glory, a personal desire for fame, and scientific discovery are just some of them. The long search for a better route from Europe to Asia through polar seas (either to the northwest or the northeast) combined political and commercial interests. The Norsemen had already discovered Iceland, Greenland, and northeast North America between the ninth and the twelfth centuries.

Then, in the sixteenth century, both English and Dutch seafarers began searching for a way through the Arctic to the riches of China and India. Looking for a Northwest Passage, the English mariner Martin Frobisher discovered and entered Hudson Strait in 1576, marched into the interior, and found a bleak landscape of mosses, juniper bushes, and stunted firs.

Davis Strait between Greenland and Baffin Island was explored by John Davis between 1585 and 1587. The Dutch navigator Willem Barents explored the west coast of Novaya Zemlya and Spitsbergen between 1594 and 1597, while he searched for a Northeast Passage around the top of Russia. He perished in the attempt—his possessions, including his flute, were found intact in a wooden hut 300 years later. With this episode, the search for a sailing route to Asia via the northeast came to an end.

In 1607, Henry Hudson navigated and explored the east coast of Greenland, discovering the island of Jan Mayen on his return. In 1610 he was also to discover both the strait and the enormous bay in Canada which now bear his name. After enduring a freezing winter, however, his crew mutinied, and Hudson was killed.

From Hudson's explorations until the nineteenth century, much pioneering navigation in this region was undertaken by agents of the Hudson's Bay Company, whose main interest was to buy furs. Samuel Hearne navigated the Coppermine River,

and Alexander Mackenzie reached the mouth of the river which bears his name. Meanwhile, Russian merchants explored the Siberian coast, and at the direction of Peter the Great, in 1741, the Danish explorer Vitus Bering discovered a strait into the Arctic Ocean between Siberia and Alaska. His grave lies on Bering Island in the Aleutian chain.

Despite disaster, the famous expedition of Sir John Franklin in 1845 found a possible route around the top of North America. Although his party of 129 officers and men disappeared, more was probably learnt about the Arctic Archipelago by the 40 relief expeditions that were sent to find him than had been discovered in all the years previously. Among the leaders of these searches, Sir James Ross (who located the position of the north magnetic pole), Captains Penny, Austin, and Ommaney, and Lieutenants M'Clintock, Collinson, and M'Clure all made valuable contributions to the world's knowledge of the Arctic region.

Following this period, the most famous polar explorer was the Norwegian Fridtjof Nansen. In 1893, believing that a polar current flowed beneath the ice from east to west, he forced his small wooden ship *Fram* into the ice on the eastern side of the Arctic. Three years later it emerged north of Spitsbergen. Previously, in 1888, he had crossed the Greenland ice cap on skis.

The Northwest Passage was first successfully traversed from 1903 to 1906 by the Norwegian explorer Roald Amundsen; the first person to reach the North Pole itself was the American explorer Robert Peary. Accompanied by a few companions, assisted by 50 Inuit, and with sleds pulled by 200 dogs, he reached the Pole on April 6, 1909. His success was in part attributable to his use of dogs—an example the British failed to follow two years later in Antarctica. Peary located the North Pole on the frozen surface of a deep ocean with no land nearby. Soundings showed the depth of water below to be 2,743 m (9,000 ft) within only

8 km (5 miles) of the Pole. Research carried out much later has established a maximum depth for the Arctic Ocean of 5,450 m (17,880 ft).

Finding Antarctica

Unlike the Arctic, Antarctica was unlikely to be a route to anywhere, but the prospect it offered was even more attractive—the possibility of finding a new and humanly habitable continent. The notion of a vast Unknown South Land (Terra Australis Incognita) had been around since the time of the ancient Greeks, and was endorsed by the geographer Ptolemy (c. AD 100–150). It was believed to be a continuation of southern Africa, but Vasco da Gama's voyage round the Cape of Good Hope in 1498 showed this belief to be false. Nor could it be an extension of the South American continent: in 1578 Sir Francis Drake found himself blown by gales to latitude 57°S, far below Cape Horn, where he reported that the Atlantic and Pacific Oceans "meete in a most large and free scope."

The British merchant Anthony de la Roche kept hopes alive when he sheltered at South Georgia in 1675, claiming to have seen "High Land" to the south, but this land was probably just the Clerke Rocks. When Captain James Cook circumnavigated Antarctica in the course of his second voyage (1771–75), it finally became clear that the age-old vision of a humanly habitable Great South Land had been only a dream.

During the nineteenth century a number of men from a range of nations expanded our knowledge of the land at the Antarctic perimeter. There were claims and counter claims to being the first to see the mainland (was it one of the Britons—Bransfield or Smith—in 1820, or the Russian Bellingshausen one year later?), and to being the first to step

466

ashore (was it the American Nathanael Palmer in 1820 or the Norwegian Carsten Borchgrevink long after this in 1895?).

Borchgrevink was in fact the explorer to lead the first expedition to winter on the mainland of Antarctica, in 1899, by which time a number of scientific expeditions were being planned for the region, as well as more ventures to reach the South Pole for its own sake.

These plans led to the epic contest to be first to reach the South Pole, in the years 1910 to 1912, between the Englishman Robert Falcon Scott and the Norwegian Roald Amundsen. It was a clash between amateurism and professionalism, between a Royal Navy man who turned to expeditionary

work to pass the time, and an experienced and hardened polar explorer who had spent 20 years preparing himself for the task.

Scott took ponies and mechanical tractors which had not been tried or tested; Amundsen took dog teams and experienced drivers, unsentimentally killing and eating the sled dogs as he went. Amundsen won the race, reaching the South Pole on December 14, 1911. Scott arrived almost a month later, on January 17, 1912. But the death of the British party during their return—exhausted, frozen, and out of food—plus Scott's moving journal of events, found with his body later, have ensured them an imperishable place in the annals of polar exploration.

Polar research

Since the Second World War, the polar regions have very much become the preserve of scientists—mapping Antarctica and conducting oceanographic, geological, glaciological, and biological research programs. Environmental pollutants and global climate change are issues of particular concern. Today some 800 scientists and support staff from around 16 nations are based in Antarctica year-round. Key programs have included:

1947 US Operation Highjump and Operation Windmill mapped large parts of the Antarctic coastline and interior.

1954 Mawson Base (Australian) was set up. Over 25 years its scientists mapped 3,200 km (2,000 miles) of coastline and 1.3 million sq km (500,000 sq miles) of Antarctic territory.

1957–58 Scientists from 67 nations conducted research programs in both polar regions.

1961 The Antarctic Treaty (signed in 1959) came into force, guaranteeing freedom of access and scientific research in all areas south of 60°S latitude.

1964–74 International Biological Programme contributed to understanding of Arctic ecology.

1986 2,000-m (6,500-ft) ice core recovered at the Russian Vostok Station provided information on climate change from 160,000 years ago.

1990 International Arctic Sciences Committee was set up to coordinate research programs.

1991 Arctic Monitoring and Assessment Program was set up by the eight Arctic rim nations and organizations representing indigenous peoples living in the region.

Antarctica

Fact File

AREA	14,000,000 sq km (5,405,400 sq miles)
POPULATION	No permanent population
ECONOMY	Research stations
CLIMATE	Extremely cold and windy
MAP REFERENCE	Page 470

The fifth largest continent, Antarctica is the coldest and most inhospitable, and differs in important respects from the polar regions of the northern hemisphere. Whereas the Arctic consists of a frozen sea surrounded by land masses, the Antarctic consists of a foundation of continental rock surmounted by a massive ice cap thousands of meters thick, separated from all other major land masses by the wild and stormy waters of the Southern Ocean. Again in contrast to the northern polar region, which was inhabited by hunting peoples within the Arctic Circle, Antarctica had never seen a human being before around 1800. Even today only about 1,000 people, all of them temporary visitors, live there during the long, severe Antarctic winter. Although a number of countries active in the exploration of the continent made territorial claims to parts of it, all such claims were indefinitely deferred after the signing of the Antarctic Treaty in December 1959.

Several factors make the climate uniquely harsh. Although Antarctica receives plenty of sunlight in midsummer, 80 percent of this radiation is reflected back by the permanent cover of snow. Altitude also plays a part: Antarctica has by far the greatest average elevation of any of the continents—2,300 m (7,500 ft)—which helps produce the high winds prevailing over much of the region. Called katabatic (or downflowing) winds, these are gravity-driven, and consist of air pouring down at high speed from the elevated interior toward the coast. At one location the annual mean windspeed recorded was over 70 km/h (44 mph). Although some 90 percent of the world's fresh water is locked up in the ice cap (at places 4,800 m [15,700 ft] thick), Antarctica is also the world's driest continent, the very low temperatures limiting the moisture the air can hold. In fact only 120–150 mm (5–6 in) of water accumulates over the entire continent in the average year. Unique dry valleys, where the rock is exposed and rain has not fallen for about 2 million years, are the driest places in the world. Mummified animal carcases in these valleys have changed little in thousands of years.

The Transantarctic Mountains, which form a boundary between East and West Antarctica, are one of the world's great mountain chains, many peaks exceeding 4,000 m (13,000 ft). Geologically, East Antarctica consists mainly of an ancient continental shield with a history going back 3,000 million years. This was once part of the supercontinent known as Gondwana, from which Africa, South America, India, Australia, and New Zealand broke away. Many Antarctic rocks and fossils match up with those found in other southern continents, showing that the continents were once joined together. Ancient crystalline rocks of the shield are closely similar to those along the east coast of the Indian peninsula and Sri Lanka. Forming the base of the Transantarctic Mountains, and facing West Antarctica, is a belt of folded sediments 500 to 600 million years old.

It is a sedimentary formation dating from about 280 million years ago, however, that is most revealing. Up to 300 m (1,000 ft) thick, it is found in Australia, India, South Africa, and South America, as well as Antarctica. About 80 million years ago a series of earth movements accompanied extensive volcanic activity and it is thought that eruptions between 20 and 15 million years ago may be linked to the formation of the Transantarctic Mountains.

Plant life on the continent today consists almost entirely of mosses, lichens, and algae. Though soil mites and midges are able to survive, not a single land vertebrate can endure the winter. In contrast, life in the ocean is very rich, with a variety of seals and whales. Antarctica has five species of true or "earless" seals, including the predatory leopard seal, and both orcas and blue whales, the latter an ocean giant growing to a length of 30 m (100 ft). There are 43 species of bird, the best-known being the penguins. The Emperor Penguin, which breeds during the months of Antarctic darkness, is the only warm-blooded animal to remain on the continent during the bitter winter months. The most numerous birds are the Antarctic petrels, among which are the albatrosses.

The Antarctic Treaty of 1959 provides the legal framework for the management of Antarctica. This treaty superseded and indefinitely deferred the political partition of the continent among a number of separate nations. At present there are 42 treaty member nations, with 26 consultative nations and 16 acceding. Important Articles of the Treaty include No 1 (that the region is to be used for peaceful purposes only), No 2 (that freedom of scientific investigation and cooperation shall continue), and No 4 (that it does not recognize, dispute, or establish territorial claims, and that no new claims shall be asserted while the Treaty is in force). Agreed-to measures adopted at consultative meetings include several conventions on the conservation of Antarctic flora and fauna.

The French Antarctic research station at Dumont d'Urville, built in 1956 (below). The Gerlache Strait on the western shore of the Antarctic Peninsula; this sheltered spot has allowed some ice to melt, bottom left. New Zealand's Scott base, Antarctica (bottom right).

Dependencies in Antarctica

Bouvet Island

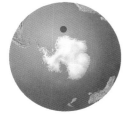

Bouvet Island is named for its discoverer, Jean-Baptiste Charles Bouvet de Lozier, who came across it on 1 January 1739. Imagining that he had found a cape of the fabled Great Southern Land, he had in fact stumbled on the loneliest island on earth—the nearest land, in South Africa, being over 1,600 km (1,000 miles) away. Uninhabited except for occasional visiting meteorologists, it rises 935 m (3,068 ft) out of the Southern Ocean, and is largely covered with snow and ice.

Fact File

OFFICIAL NAME Bouvet Island

FORM OF GOVERNMENT Dependent territory of Norway

CAPITAL None; administered from Oslo

AREA 58 sq km (22 sq miles)

TIME ZONE GMT

POPULATION No permanent population

ECONOMY Meteorological station

CLIMATE Cold and windy

MAP REFERENCE Page 470

French Southern and Antarctic Lands

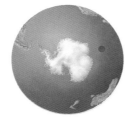

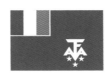

The French Southern and Antarctic Lands include Ile Amsterdam, Ile Saint-Paul, and Crozet and Kerguelen islands in the southern Indian Ocean. Mean annual temperatures range from 4°C to 10°C (39°F to 50°F) and the islands are wet and stormy. The main island of Kerguelen is mountainous (Mt Ross is 1,960 m; 6,430 ft), with an irregular coastline and deep fiords, and there are snowfields in the central area. Vegetation consists of coastal tussock grass and peaty uplands. Breeding colonies of seals and penguins are found in summer.

Fact File

OFFICIAL NAME Territory of the French Southern and Antarctic Lands

FORM OF GOVERNMENT Overseas territory of France

CAPITAL None; administered from Paris

AREA 7,781 sq km (3,004 sq miles)

TIME ZONE GMT + 3.5/5 hours

POPULATION No permanent population

ECONOMY None

CLIMATE Cold and windy

MAP REFERENCE Page 104

Heard and McDonald Islands

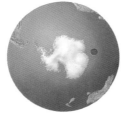

Heard and McDonald islands are two bleak outposts in the Southern Ocean. Heard Island has the distinction of having the highest point in all Australian territory—2,750 m (9,021 ft). Classed as subantarctic islands, their mean annual sea level temperatures are between freezing and 3°C (37°F). They have ice caps, glaciers that descend to sea level, and furious gales. Vegetation consists of tussock grassland and small peaty fields. Seals and penguins breed ashore in summer.

The most inhospitable continent and one of the last regions on Earth to be explored, Antarctica is a long way from everywhere. This sign is at Scott Base, Antarctica (above left). Adélie penguin at Cape Bird, Antarctica (above right).

Fact File

OFFICIAL NAME Territory of Heard and McDonald Islands

FORM OF GOVERNMENT External territory of Australia

CAPITAL None; administered from Canberra

AREA 412 sq km (159 sq miles)

TIME ZONE GMT + 5 hours

POPULATION No permanent population

ECONOMY None

CLIMATE Cold and windy

MAP REFERENCE Page 104

Peter I Island

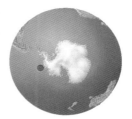

One of the Antarctic maritime islands, Peter I Island lies off the continent near the Venable Ice Shelf. It was named by Thaddeus Bellingshausen in honor of the founder of the Russian Navy. Though slightly moderated by the sea, the climate is basically that of the adjacent continent and the temperature rises above freezing only for short periods in summer. In winter the island is entirely surrounded by pack ice.

Fact File

OFFICIAL NAME Peter I Island

FORM OF GOVERNMENT Dependent territory of Norway

CAPITAL None; administered from Oslo

AREA 180 sq km (70 sq miles)

TIME ZONE GMT – 6 hours

POPULATION No permanent population

ECONOMY None

CLIMATE Cold and windy

MAP REFERENCE Page 470

Polar Regions

Antarctica

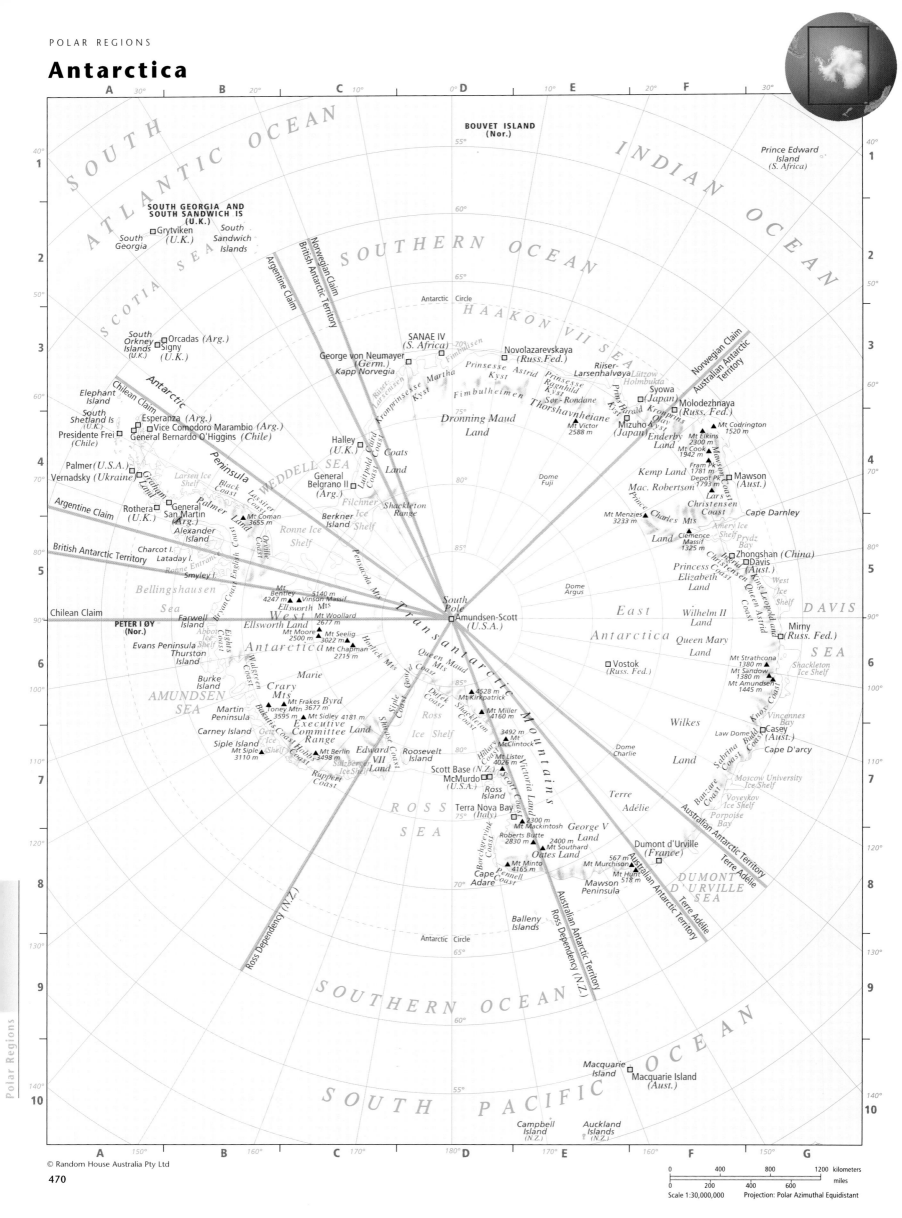

Polar Regions

Scale 1:30,000,000   Projection: Polar Azimuthal Equidistant

The Arctic

Polar Regions

PACIFIC OCEAN

BERING SEA

OKHOTSKOYE MORE (SEA OF OKHOTSK)

Bristol Bay
Alaska Pen.
C. Newenham
Nunivak I.
Kodiak I.
Kodiak
Dillingham
Bethel
Tanunak
St Lawrence I.
Mys Chukotskiy
Mys Olyutorskiy
Klyuchevskaya Sopka 4750 m
Ust'-Kamchatsk
Mys Ozernoy
Ostrov Karaginskiy
Poluostrov Kamchatka
Sredinnyy Khrebet
Ostrov Sakhalin
Nogliki
Okha
Homer
Gulf of Alaska
Iliamna Lake
Kotlik
Norton Sound
Nome
Bering Strait
Chukotskiy Poluostrov
Koryakskoye Nagor'ye
Anadyr'
Ugol'nyye Kopi
Kolymskoye Nagor'ye
Omsukchan
Sinegor'ye
Magadan
Mys Tolstoy
Zaliv Shelikhova
Okhotsk
Ayan
Nikolayevsk-na-Amure
Anchorage
Cordova
U.S.A. ALASKA
Yakutat
Juneau
Skagway
Mt Logan 5959 m
Allakaket
Shungnak
Point Hope
Iul'tin
Gora Belaya 1359 m
1742 m
Anadyrskoye Ploskogor'ye
Gora Volna 1585 m
Susuman
Khrebet Suntar Khayata
Khrebet Dzhugdzhur
Aldan
Amga
Whitehorse
Watson Lake
Ross River
Dawson
Fort Yukon
Wainwright
Bilibino
Cherskiy
Pevek
Arctic Circle
Gora Pobeda 3147 m
Ust'-Nera
2341 m
Khandyga
Khrebet Cherskogo
Prilenskoye Plato
Yakutsk
Lena
Pelly
Ogilvie Mountains
Old Crow
Mt Greenough 2207 m
Kaktovik
Brooks Range
Ushakovskoye
Ostrov Vrangelya
Mys Kovaskiy
Khonuu
Deputatskiy
Sangar
2389 m
Zhigansk
Nyurba
Mirnyy
Fort Simpson
Déline
Fort Good Hope
Tuktoyaktuk
Mackenzie
BEAUFORT SEA
Indigirka
Lyakhovskiye Ostrova
Tiksi
Siktyakh
Yana
Udachnyy
Zhilinda
Lac la Martre
Great Bear Lake
Paulatuk
C. Bathurst
C. Parry
Sachs Harbour
Banks Island
C. Prince Alfred
Novosibirskiye Ostrova
ARCTIC OCEAN
Aylmer Lake
Maud
Kugluktuk
Holman
Prince Patrick I.
85°
Kotuy
Olenek
CANADA
Contwoyto Lake
Victoria Island
Cambridge Bay
Melville I.
Queen Elizabeth Islands
Borden I.
Ellef Ringnes Island
Amund Ringnes I.
Axel Heiberg Island
North Pole
Poluostrov Taymyr
Severnaya Zemlya
Ozero Taymyr
Severo-Sibirskaya Nizmennost'
Khatanga
1664 m
Plato Putorana
King William Island
Prince of Wales Island
Somerset Island
Resolute
Pelly Bay
Brodeur Pen.
Devon Island
Melville Pen.
Repulse Bay
Hall Beach
Arctic Bay
Ellesmere Island 2012m
Eureka
Grise Fiord
Noril'sk
Dudinka
Igarka
Foxe Basin
Prince Charles I.
Pond Inlet
Bylot I.
Kap Parry
Siorapaluk
Qaanaaq (Thule)
Alert
LINCOLN SEA
1920 m
Kap Bridgman
Kap Eiler Rasmussen
Zemlya Frantsa-Iosifa
Mys Zhelaniya
Gydanskiy Poluostrov
Gyda
Antipayuta
Urengoy
Baffin Island
C. Baffin
C. Adair
Uummannaq
Kap York
Savissivik
Knud Rasmussen Land
1190 m
2103 m
Nord
Novaya Zemlya
Ostrov Belyy
Tambey
Yamburg
Poluostrov Yamal
Novyy Port
Yar-Sale
Nadym
Baffin Bay
Home Bay
Iqaluit
Hall Pen.
Cumberland Pen.
Nuussuaq
Kullorsuaq
Tasiusaq
Upernavik
2935 m
GREENLAND
Kong Frederik VIII Land
Île de France
Spitsbergen
Longyearbyen
Nordaustlandet
Barentsøya
Edgeøya
BARENTS SEA
Ostrov Vaygach
Ostrov Kolguyev
Vorkuta
Gorki
Igrim
URALSKIY KHREBET
C. Mercy
C. Dyer
Qeqertarsuaq (Disko)
Illorsuit
1234 m
Uummannaq
Maarmorilik
Qeqertarsuaq
Kangaatsiaq
(KALAALLIT NUNAAT) (Den.)
Kap Marie Valdemar
Store Koldewey
Shannon Ø
Daneborg
SVALBARD (Nor.)
Mys Kanin Nos
Nar'yan Mar
Usinsk
Pechora
Ust'-Tsil'ma
Vuktyl
Sisimiut
2440 m
Kangerlussuaq
Petermanns Bjerg 2939 m
Mesters Vig
Traill Ø
GREENLAND SEA
Nordkapp
Poluostrov Rybachiy
Shoyna
Oma
Mezen'
Ukhta
Yemva
Syktyvkar
Maniitsoq
Atammik
Nuuk (Godthab)
Kapisillit
J.A.D. Jensen Nunatakker 1680 m
3147 m
Kong Christian IX Land
Mont Forel 3360 m
Gunnbjørn Fjeld 3700 m
It토qqortoormiit
1920 m
JAN MAYEN (Nor.)
Lakselv
Nordkapp
Usogorsk
Arkhangel'sk
Severodvinsk
Kotlas
Luza
Vel'sk
Vyatka
Qeqertarsuatsiaat
Paamiut
Ivittuut
Ittoqqortoormiit
Ammassalik
Sermiligaaq
Tromsø
Inari
FINLAND
Murmansk
Polyarnyye Zori
Kandalaksha
Kem'
Medvezh'yegorsk
Petrozavodsk
Onezhskoye Ozero
Yoshkar-Ola
Cheboksary
Narsarsuaq
Qaqortoq
Nanortalik
Timmiarmiut
Nunap Isua
Harstad
Bodø
Kiruna
Luleå
Skellefteå
Oulu
Ladozhskoye Ozero
Vologda
Nizhniy Novgorod
Kostroma
Yaroslavl'
Stykkishólmur
Blönduós
Reykjavik
Seyðisfjörður
Arctic Circle
NORWAY
Vaasa
Tampere
Helsinki
Sankt-Peterburg (St Petersburg)
Novgorod
Moskva (Moscow)
Kaluga
Vi k
2119 m
Höfn
ICELAND
Trondheim
Ålesund
Östersund
Sundsvall
Kuopio
Pori
Turku
Tallinn
Pskov
FAEROE ISLANDS (Den.)
Bergen
Lillehammer
Gävle
Uppsala
Västerås
Stockholm
ESTONIA
Riga
Vitsyebsk
Bryansk
Kursk
Shetland Islands
ATLANTIC OCEAN
Drammen
Oslo
Örebro
Linköping
Liepaja
LATVIA
Cape Wrath
Outer Hebrides
Orkney Islands
Inverness
Fort William
SWEDEN
Stavanger
Jönköping
Göteborg (Gothenburg)
Kristiansand
Helsingborg
Šiauliai
Vilnius
LITHUANIA
Kaliningrad
BELARUS
Chernihiv
Minsk
UKRAINE
Aberdeen
Helsingør
Belgorod
Orsha

© Random House Australia Pty Ltd

kilometers
0 200 400 600 800 1000
miles
0 200 400 600
Scale 1:26,000,000
Projection: Polar Azimuthal Equidistant

The Oceans

The Oceans

Oceans constitute one of Earth's great frontiers. Scientists, environmentalists, governments, industrialists and 'dreamers' all want to understand how oceans function in physical, chemical, ecological and economic terms. The role of oceans in military conflicts and for the security of nations is also still of concern, with many countries spending considerable sums of money on finding ways to exploit oceanic secrets to their advantage.

In stark contrast to all other known planets, oceans constitute approximately 70 percent of Earth. There are five main oceans of the world— the Atlantic, Pacific, Indian, Arctic, and Antarctic (also known as the Southern or South Polar Ocean). The biggest ocean is the Pacific, at about 170 million sq km (66 million sq miles), which occupies almost twice the area of the next biggest, the Atlantic.

Throughout history, these vast oceanic expanses and adjoining seas have challenged humans as to how they should be used. At least some 100,000 years ago, and especially over the last 10,000 years, successful efforts have been made to cross the oceans, allowing human migrations. Trade routes involving various kinds of ships have also developed, growing from local to transoceanic journeys. Today the sea is used, and at times abused, by oceanic craft transporting people and goods to form the connections vital for international commerce.

It is only in the past century or so that humans have really started to make an impact on oceanic environments. These environments have evolved and changed over billions of years. Ecosystems have become established and been modified by changes in atmospheric composition, sea-floor spreading, climatic and current regimes, the discharges of solutes and sediments from rivers, and the development of new life forms. Human interference and exploitation, including the pollution of ocean waters, has quickly altered conditions in many oceanic areas, leading to a decline in fish and mammal stocks, the destruction of habitats and even, potentially, to increased

water temperatures. The challenge for the future will be to use our technological knowledge to protect oceanic environments, while allowing increased use of ocean resources by the world's growing population.

Ocean topography

Oceanographers over the past century have greatly expanded our knowledge of the sea floor. Using first primitive line soundings, then early echo sounders and now sophisticated electronic surveying techniques, it has been possible to build up detailed images of the bottom of the ocean. Submersibles have been used to photograph and document specific features, including remnants of wrecks like the Titanic which lie at great depths.

In recent decades there has been a great acceleration in the exploitation of ocean topography. In particular, the mapping of features such as faults, volcanic ridges and vents, slumps, and canyons, has enabled scientists to reconstruct the history of these features. The theory of plate tectonics has been greatly supported by geological and geophysical studies of the sea floor, especially the identification and interpretation of paleomagnetic strips contained in oceanic basalts. These form as new basalt moves away from mid-ocean spreading centers, and record the magnetic field of the period.

Typically, ocean floors are covered by thin, oozy sediment layers that form abyssal plains separated by ridges, seamounts and plateaus representing past geologic events. Continental margins descend steeply from bordering shelves down steep, often dissented, slopes to plains, the flattest surfaces on Earth. The plain may be as deep as 3,000 to 5,000 m (9840 to 16,400 ft). Beyond these depths there are relatively narrow trenches reaching 10,000 m (32,800 ft) below sea level, such as those found adjacent to the island areas and rising mountain chains of the Pacific.

A broad, rugged and near-continuous mountain range occurs in the centers of the Atlantic, Indian and Southern Pacific Oceans. This is the mid-

oceanic ridge, now very clearly shown on all topographic maps of the ocean floor. Its crest is characterized by a rift valley which is the source area for new basaltic floors. Oceanographers have described deep gashes or fractures cutting the ocean floor at right angles to the crest of the ridge. These eventually become obscured, away from the ridge, by collections of sediment.

Islands and former islands or seamounts in ocean basins are often related to the oceanic ridge and its fractures. Active and dormant volcanoes provide the rocks that form the foundation of these islands. As oceanic basalt moves away from a volcanic "hot spot", the volcano dies and the island surface erodes and gradually subsides (as in the Emperor Seamounts near Hawaii). Corals colonize the shores of such islands in tropical areas, eventually forming atolls–the legacy of a once active volcanic system.

Ocean chemistry

The chemical composition of ocean waters is generally constant. Seawater is a solution containing a complex mixture of dissolved solids or solutes. Its evolution over time since the beginning of the Earth is little understood, but it is clearly linked to the development of a protective ozone layer in the atmosphere, to evolving life forms in shallow and deeper waters, to the gasses emitted by volcanoes or deepwater vents, and to run-off from the land. Many different minerals have accumulated in ocean waters, but about one billion years ago the concentration reached a steady-state position. In other words, dry new inputs were balanced by processes that removed the minerals, the most important of which was the deposition of minerals as sediments on continental shelves, slopes and ocean floors.

The uniformity of ocean chemistry results from continuous mixing—the circulation of waters between oceans and seas—and numerous chemical reactions that take place over a comparatively restricted range of temperatures. Seven dominant elements form the dissolved

The oceans support a vast diversity of marine life: Southern right whales (left) live in the cold Antarctic Ocean, while shoals of Mao Mao (above) prefer warm tropical waters.

solids in H_2O. They are chlorine (as chloride CE-), sodium (as Na+), magnesium (as Mg2+), potassium (as K+) and bromide (as bromide Br-). Gases in a dissolved state, such as carbon dioxide, nitrogen and oxygen, are also present; the availability of oxygen is critical for many life forms. Other minor components of oceanic waters include trace elements, organic particles and suspended matter.

Salinity is a term used to describe dissolved solids by volume in seawater. It is commonly expressed in parts per thousand (ppt), with the average value for oceanic waters being 35 ppt, varying between 34 and 37ppt. Rainfall and ice melt tends to dilute the average value of salinity; evaporation has the opposite effect, especially under the influence of hot, dry, subtropical high pressure systems.

One property of oceans that can vary quite widely is temperature. In polar regions, vast areas of oceans freeze to form sea ice and ice shelves. Seawater freezes at −2°C (28.4°F) at the surface of oceans. At the other end of the scale, tropical waters may have temperatures as high as 30°C (86°F). Ocean waters are typically layered, with marked differences in temperature and salinity between mixed surface waters and deeper zones, where temperatures approach freezing.

Ocean circulation

Differences in temperature and salinity between waters at varying depths, combined with Earth's rotational influence and wind forces, help drive ocean water masses within and between oceanic basins. At depth, the great movements of water are quite slow in comparison with the surface. This results in an upwelling of cold, nutrient-rich currents toward the margins of some continents, such as along the west coast of South America. Surface flows redistribute heat from the tropics to higher latitudes; the Gulf Stream flowing along the east coast of North America towards Europe is a classic example, helping to maintain milder temperatures in countries such as the Republic of Ireland, the United Kingdom and Denmark.

In some parts of oceans, water circulation is somewhat limited. This is the case at the centers of subtropical gyres (circular surface rotations of water), such as the gyre within the North Atlantic

Ocean, where the Sargasso Sea develops salinities up to 30ppt.

During the Quaternary Period it is hypothesized that significant changes in oceanic circulation occurred. The so-called "conveyor belts" of surface and deeper currents moving masses of water between the basins would have been influenced by the spread of ice on and adjacent to continents. Microscopic organisms buried in sediments on the ocean floor have been used to determine in some detail shifts in temperature and salinity conditions over the past 2 million years.

Ocean exploration

The exploration of oceans can be described in three phases. First there was the pioneering period of great sea-going nations looking for new lands to exploit and colonize. From Europe the Vikings led the way, followed by the great voyages of the Portuguese, Spanish, Dutch, British and French. These were later joined by other nations, including Germany, Russia and the USA. From Asia and the Middle East came other maritime travellers, crossing the oceans for trade and also to promulgate religious beliefs.

The second phase consolidated the discoveries of the first and led to the establishment of ports and trading routes. Knowledge increased about hazards to shipping, climatic and current conditions, the best use of the sea for naval purposes, and the social and economic conditions of lands bordering the oceans.

The third phase encompasses the scientific exploration of the past five decades, including the use of satellites, permanent recorders, and surface and submerged survey techniques to greatly expand our knowledge of the oceanic realm. This includes an understanding of perhaps the largest mineral deposit on Earth—manganese nodules. It is estimated that about two billion tonnes of manganese nodules lie on the floor of our oceans.

Deep-sea drilling has proved invaluable in helping us determine the type of materials found on ocean floors and their age and modes of formation. Increasingly, this new knowledge is alerting scientists and decision-makers to our capacity to adversely affect ocean ecosystems.

Exploitation and pollution

The pressure to use large tracts of ocean and coastal waters for fishing and the extraction of minerals, including oil, has led in some cases to over-exploitation of our biggest natural resource, the sea. International conventions on rights to ocean use have become a mechanism to resolve disputes and to prevent the loss of endangered species. That differences of opinion still exist between nations—for instance, over whaling rights—indicate that serious issues remain unresolved. Two issues of global significance need to be considered by all countries of the world— water pollution and the impact of the greenhouse effect on ocean levels.

For a long time oceans have been considered a convenient dumping ground for human and chemical waste. It used to be thought that the oceans were big enough either to dilute the waste or at least to carry it conveniently out of sight. This is no longer the case—pollution by radioactive wastes in areas like the Arctic Ocean has proven that our planet is not big enough to absorb such toxic material. Urban industrial societies need to develop informed strategies for waste disposal before it is too late.

Oceans and the climate

It has been known for some time that oceans moderate the world's climate. Scientists are now able to use computers to model the interaction between oceans and the atmosphere, and are warning governments of potentially serious disturbances to climatic patterns. Phenomena such as El Niño already highlight the variability in ocean–climate patterns and the extreme climatic conditions (floods, droughts, storm surges) that can occur. Ocean warming due to the greenhouse effect also increases the possibility of extreme weather patterns and rising sea levels. These effects are particularly serious for low-lying nations built on coral reefs and coral debris. such as the Maldives.

Oceanic exploration includes the study of rich plant and marine life (top). Oil is a valuable oceanic resource (center). Lighthouses have ensured safe ocean travel for centuries (right).

Indian Ocean

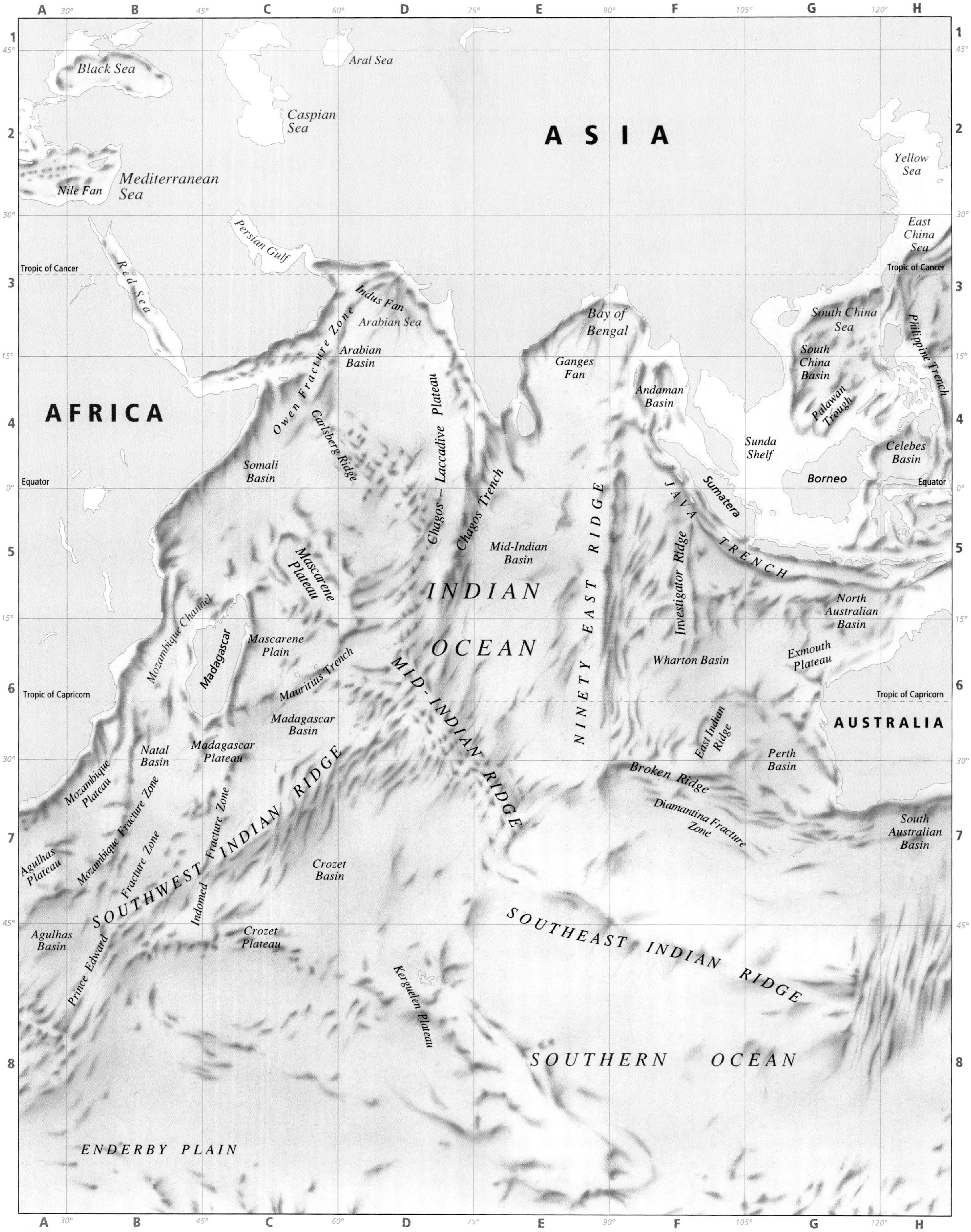
A B C D E F G H
30° 45° 60° 75° 90° 105° 120°
1 2 3 4 5 6 7 8
45° 30° 15° 0° 15° 30° 45°
Black Sea
Aral Sea
Caspian Sea
ASIA
Yellow Sea
Nile Fan
Mediterranean Sea
East China Sea
Persian Gulf
Tropic of Cancer
Red Sea
Indus Fan
Arabian Sea
Bay of Bengal
South China Sea
Philippine Trench
Owen Fracture Zone
Arabian Basin
Ganges Fan
South China Basin
AFRICA
Andaman Basin
Palawan Trough
Carlsberg Ridge
Chagos – Laccadive Plateau
Sunda Shelf
Celebes Basin
Somali Basin
Chagos Trench
Borneo
Equator
Sumatera
JAVA TRENCH
NINETY EAST RIDGE
Mid-Indian Basin
Investigator Ridge
Mascarene Plateau
INDIAN OCEAN
North Australian Basin
Mozambique Channel
Madagascar
Mascarene Plain
Wharton Basin
Exmouth Plateau
Mauritius Trench
MID-INDIAN RIDGE
Tropic of Capricorn
Madagascar Basin
AUSTRALIA
East Indian Ridge
Natal Basin
Madagascar Plateau
Perth Basin
Broken Ridge
Mozambique Plateau
Mozambique Fracture Zone
SOUTHWEST INDIAN RIDGE
Diamantina Fracture Zone
South Australian Basin
Agulhas Plateau
Fracture Zone
Indomed Fracture Zone
Crozet Basin
SOUTHEAST INDIAN RIDGE
Agulhas Basin
Crozet Plateau
Prince Edward
Kerguelen Plateau
SOUTHERN OCEAN
ENDERBY PLAIN

kilometers 0 1000 2000 3000
miles 0 500 1000 1500
Scale 1:60,000,000
Projection: Mercator

Atlantic Ocean

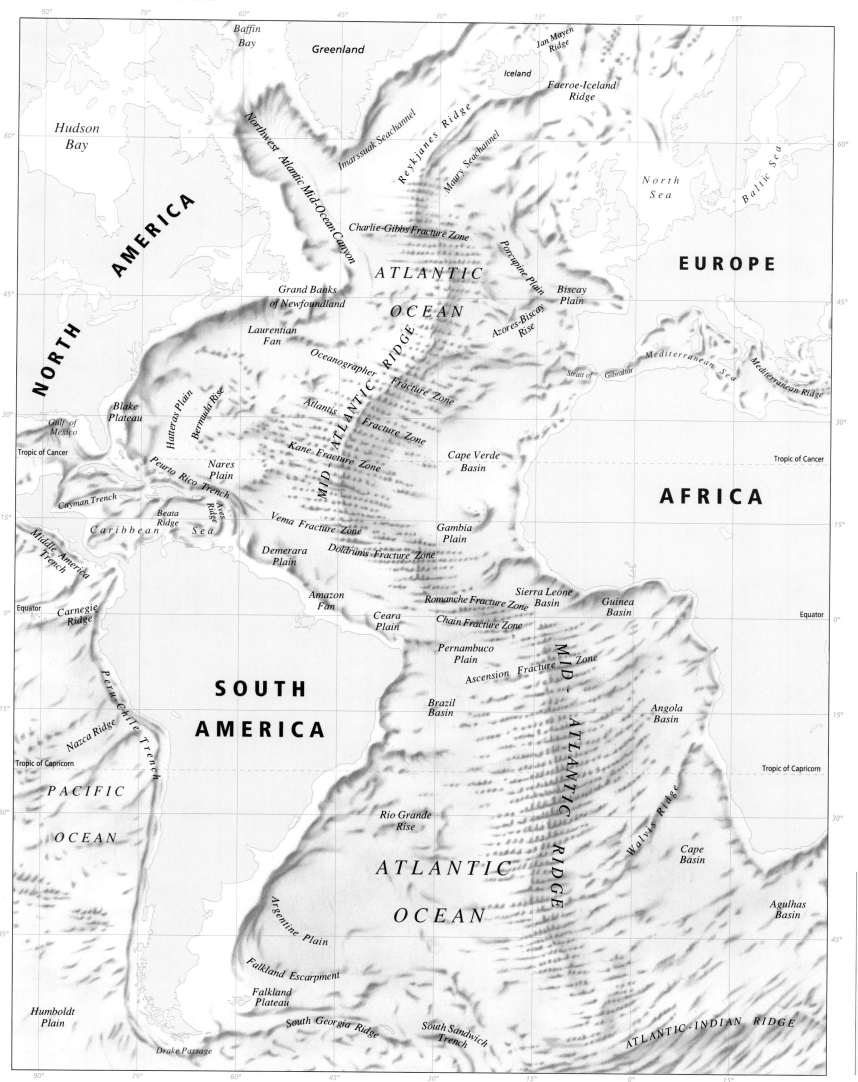

Hudson Bay

Baffin Bay

Greenland

Jan Mayen Ridge

Iceland

Faeroe-Iceland Ridge

NORTH AMERICA

North Sea

Baltic Sea

EUROPE

Northwest Atlantic Mid-Ocean Canyon

Imarssuak Seachannel

Reykjanes Ridge

Maury Seachannel

Charlie-Gibbs Fracture Zone

ATLANTIC OCEAN

Porcupine Plain

Biscay Plain

Azores-Biscay Rise

NORTH

Grand Banks of Newfoundland

Laurentian Fan

Oceanographer Fracture Zone

MID-ATLANTIC RIDGE

Mediterranean Sea

Mediterranean Ridge

Strait of Gibraltar

Blake Plateau

Hatteras Plain

Bermuda Rise

Atlantis Fracture Zone

Gulf of Mexico

Tropic of Cancer

Peurto Rico Trench

Nares Plain

Kane Fracture Zone

Cape Verde Basin

AFRICA

Tropic of Cancer

Cayman Trench

Beata Ridge

Aves Ridge

Caribbean Sea

Vema Fracture Zone

Gambia Plain

Middle America Trench

Demerara Plain

Doldrums Fracture Zone

Amazon Fan

Ceara Plain

Romanche Fracture Zone

Sierra Leone Basin

Guinea Basin

Equator

Carnegie Ridge

Chain Fracture Zone

Equator

Nazca Ridge

Pernambuco Plain

Ascension Fracture Zone

MID-ATLANTIC RIDGE

SOUTH AMERICA

Brazil Basin

Angola Basin

Tropic of Capricorn

Peru-Chile Trench

PACIFIC OCEAN

Tropic of Capricorn

Walvis Ridge

Cape Basin

Rio Grande Rise

ATLANTIC OCEAN

Agulhas Basin

Argentine Plain

Humboldt Plain

Falkland Escarpment

Falkland Plateau

South Georgia Ridge

South Sandwich Trench

ATLANTIC-INDIAN RIDGE

Drake Passage

| 0 | 1000 | 2000 | 3000 | kilometers |

| 0 | 500 | 1000 | 1500 | miles |

Scale 1:60,000,000   Projection: Mercator

© Random House Australia Pty Ltd

The Oceans

Pacific Ocean

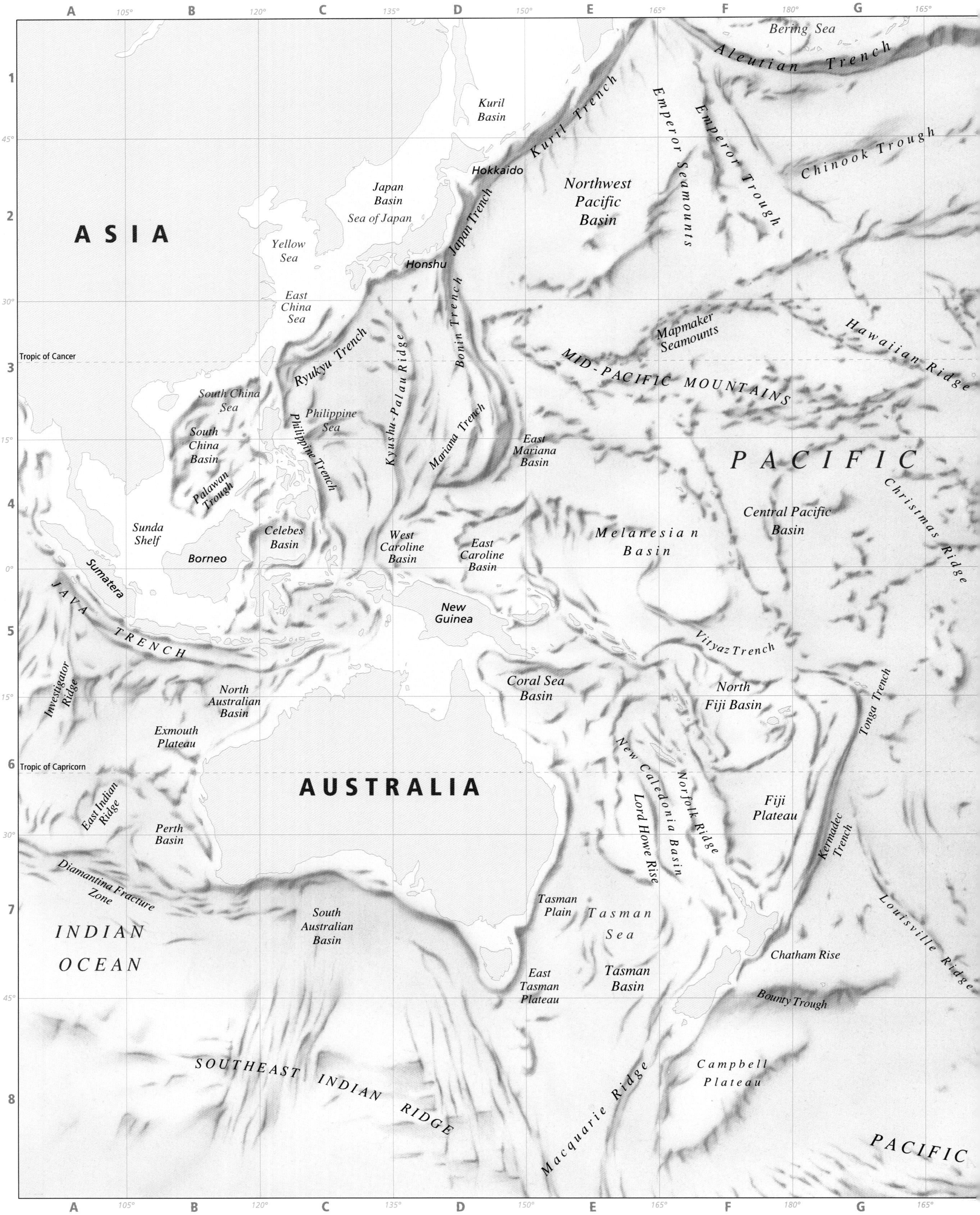

A
105°
B
120°
C
135°
D
150°
E
165°
F
180°
G
165°
1
2
3
4
5
6
7
8
45°
30°
15°
0°
Tropic of Cancer
Tropic of Capricorn
ASIA
Bering Sea
Aleutian Trench
Kuril Trench
Kuril Basin
Emperor Seamounts
Emperor Trough
Chinook Trough
Hokkaido
Japan Basin
Sea of Japan
Northwest Pacific Basin
Japan Trench
Yellow Sea
Honshu
East China Sea
Bonin Trench
Mapmaker Seamounts
Hawaiian Ridge
Ryukyu Trench
Kyushu-Palau Ridge
MID-PACIFIC MOUNTAINS
South China Sea
Philippine Sea
Philippine Trench
Mariana Trench
South China Basin
East Mariana Basin
PACIFIC
Palawan Trough
Christmas Ridge
Central Pacific Basin
Sunda Shelf
Celebes Basin
West Caroline Basin
East Caroline Basin
Melanesian Basin
Borneo
Sumatera
JAVA TRENCH
New Guinea
Vityaz Trench
Investigator Ridge
North Australian Basin
Coral Sea Basin
North Fiji Basin
Tonga Trench
Exmouth Plateau
New Caledonia Basin
Norfolk Ridge
Lord Howe Rise
AUSTRALIA
East Indian Ridge
Fiji Plateau
Perth Basin
Kermadec Trench
Diamantina Fracture Zone
Tasman Plain
Tasman Sea
South Australian Basin
INDIAN OCEAN
Louisville Ridge
Chatham Rise
East Tasman Plateau
Tasman Basin
Bounty Trough
SOUTHEAST INDIAN RIDGE
Macquarie Ridge
Campbell Plateau
PACIFIC

Gulf of Alaska

Tufts Plain

Mendocino Fracture Zone

Pioneer Fracture Zone

Patton Escarpment

NORTH AMERICA

ATLANTIC

OCEAN

Laurentian
Fan

Murray Fracture Ridge

Cedros Trench

Blake
Plateau

Hatteras Plain

Bermuda Rise

Molokai Fracture Zone

Gulf of Mexico

Mexico
Basin

Puerto Rico Trench

Tropic of Cancer

Nares
Plain

Clarion Fracture Zone

Cayman Trench

Beata
Ridge

Aves
Ridge

O C E A N

Middle America Trench

Caribbean Sea

Clipperton Fracture Zone

P A C I F I C   R I S E

Guatemala
Basin

Cocos
Ridge

Panama
Basin

Galapagos Fracture
Zone

Carnegie
Ridge

SOUTH
AMERICA

Marquesas Fracture Zone

Peru
Basin

Galapagos Rise

Easter Fracture Zone

Nazca Ridge

Peru-Chile Trench

Chile
Basin

Tropic of Capricorn

Challenger Fracture Zone

Chile Rise

Southwest
Pacific
Basin

E A S T

Agassiz Fracture
Zone

Southeast
Pacific Basin

Argentine Plain

Menard Fracture Zone

ATLANTIC

OCEAN

Eltanin Fracture Zone

Peru - Chile Trench

Falkland
Plateau

Vointsev Fracture Zone

ANTARCTIC   RIDGE

Humboldt
Plain

Bellingshausen Plain

Drake Passage

The Oceans

0   1000   2000   3000   kilometers

0   500   1000   1500   miles

Scale 1:50,000,000   Projection: Mercator

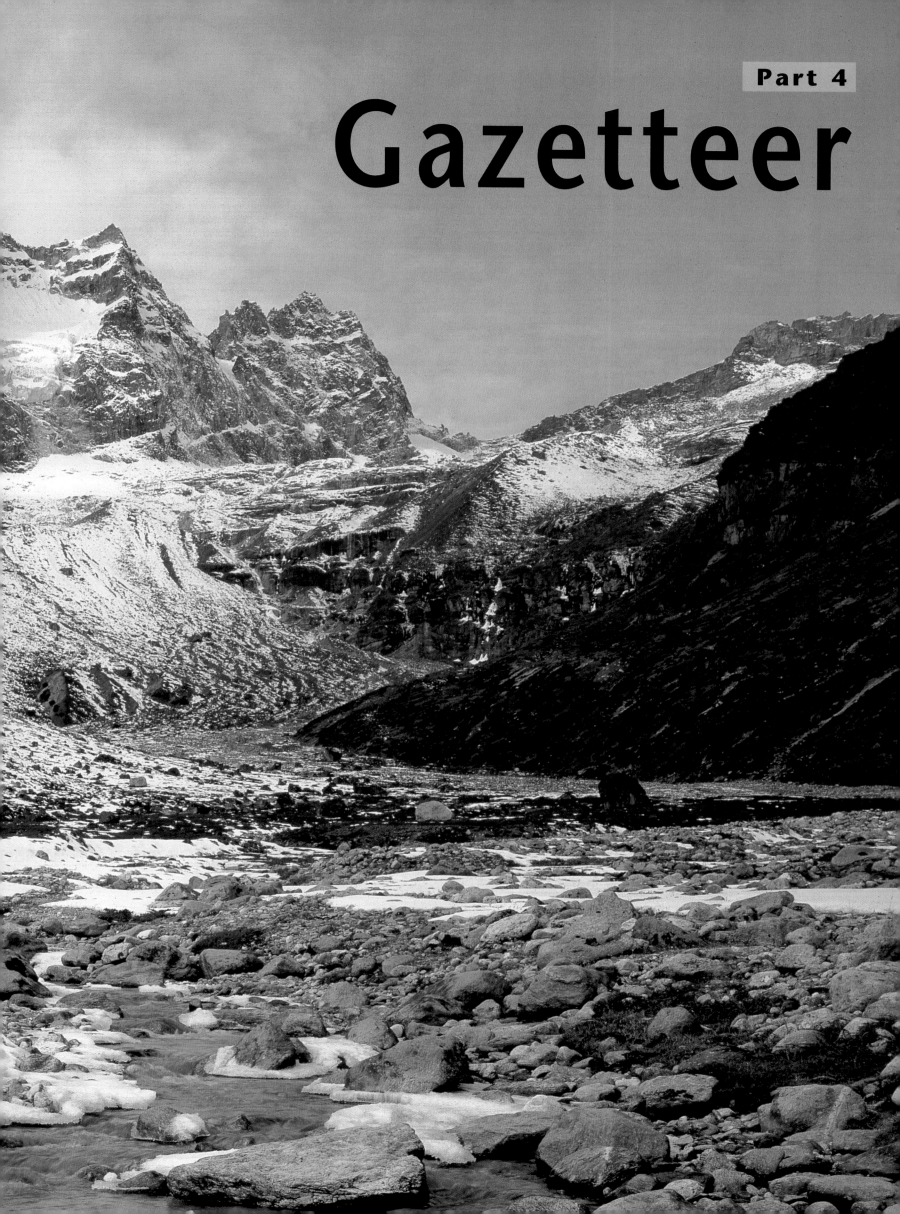

GAZETTEER

Abbreviations Used on Maps

Arch. Archipelago, Archipel, Archipiélago, Arquipélago
Arg. Argentina
Arm. Armenia
Aust. Australia
Azer. Azerbaijan

B. Bay, Baía, Baie, Bahía
B.-H. Bosnia and Herzegovina
Belg. Belgium

C.A.R. Central African Republic
C. Cape, Cabo, Cap, Capo
Co Cerro
Col. Colombia
Cord. Cordillera
Croat. Croatia
Cuch. Cuchillo
Czech Rep. Czech Republic

D.C. District of Columbia
Dem. Rep. of the Congo Democratic Republic of the Congo
Den. Denmark

E. East
Ecu. Ecuador
Emb. Embalse
Eq. Guinea Equatorial Guinea
Est. Estrecho

Fr. France

G. Gora
G. Gulf, Golfe, Golfo, Gulfo
G. Gunung
Germ. Germany

Harb. Harbor
Hung. Hungary

I. Island, Île, Ilha, Isla, Isola
Is Islands, Îles, Ilhas, Islas

Jez. Jezioro

K. Kolpos
Kep. Kepulauan

L. Lake, Lac, Lacul, Lago, Limni, Loch
Liech. Liechtenstein
Lux. Luxembourg

Mace. Macedonia
Mex. Mexico
Mt Mount, Mont
Mte Monte
Mti Monti
Mtn Mountain
Mts Mountains, Monts

N. North
N.Z. New Zealand
Neth. Netherlands
Nev. Nevado
Nor. Norway

P. Pic, Pico
P. Pulau
P.N.G. Papua New Guinea
Peg. Pegunungan
Pen. Peninsula, Péninsula, Péninsule
Pk Peak
Pk Puncak
Port. Portugal
Pt Point
Pta Ponta, Punta
Pte Pointe
Pto Porto, Pôrto, Puerto

R. River
Ra. Range
Rep. Republic
Res. Reservoir
Russ. Fed. Russian Federation

S. San
S. South
S.A. South Africa
Sa Serra
Sd Sound
Serr. Serranía
Slov. Slovenia
Sp. Spain
St Saint
Sta Santa
Ste Sainte
Sto Santo
Switz. Switzerland

Tel. Teluk
Tg Tanjong

U. Ujung
U.A.E. United Arab Emirates
U.K. United Kingdom
U.S., U.S.A. United States of America

Vol. Volcán

W. West

Yug. Yugoslavia

Foreign Geographical Terms

Açude *(Portuguese)* reservoir
Adası *(Turkish)* island
Adrar *(Berber)* mountains
Agios *(Greek)* saint
Akra *(Greek)* cape, point
Alpen *(German)* Alps
Alpi *(Italian)* Alps
Alta *(Spanish)* upper
Altiplanicie *(Spanish)* high plain, plateau
-älven *(Swedish)* river
Ao *(Thai)* bay
Archipel *(French)* archipelago
Archipiélago *(Spanish)* archipelago
Arquipélago *(Portuguese)* archipelago
Avtonomnaya Oblast' *(Russian)* autonomous region
Avtonomnyy Okrug *(Russian)* autonomous area

Bab *(Arabic)* strait
Bælt *(Danish)* strait
Bahía *(Spanish)* bay
Baḩr, Bahr *(Arabic)* lake, river, sea
Baía *(Portuguese)* bay
Baie *(French)* bay
Barajı *(Turkish)* dam
Barragem *(Portuguese)* reservoir
Bassin *(French)* basin
Beinn, Ben *(Gaelic)* mountain
Bjerg *(Danish)* hill, mountain
Bôca *(Portuguese)* river mouth
Boca *(Spanish)* river mouth
Bocht *(Dutch)* bay
Bodden *(German)* bay
Bogazi *(Turkish)* strait
Bögeni *(Kazakh)* reservoir
-bre/en *(Norwegian)* glacier
Bucht *(German)* bay
Bugt, -bugten *(Danish)* bay
Buḩayrat *(Arabic)* lake
Bukit *(Malay)* mountain
-bukten *(Swedish)* bay
Burnu, Burun *(Turkish)* cape, point
Buuraha *(Somali)* hill/s, mountain/s

Cabo *(Portuguese, Spanish)* cape
Canal *(Spanish)* channel
Cap *(French)* cape
Capo *(Italian)* cape
Cerro/s *(Spanish)* hill/s, peak/s
Chaîne *(French)* mountain range
Chapada *(Portuguese)* hills, upland/s
Chhâk *(Cambodian)* bay
Chott *(Arabic)* marsh, salt lake
Cima *(Italian)* mountain
Ciudad *(Spanish)* city
Co *(Tibetan)* lake
Colline *(Italian)* hill/s
Cordillera *(Spanish)* mountain range, mountain chain
Côte *(French)* coast, slope
Cù Lao *(Vietnamese)* island
Cuchilla *(Spanish)* mountain range

Dag/ı *(Turkish)* mountain
Daglar/ı *(Turkish)* mountains
-dake *(Japanese)* peak
Danau *(Indonesian)* lake
Dao *(Chinese)* island
Ðao *(Vietnamese)* island
Daryācheh *(Persian)* lake
Dasht *(Persian)* desert
Denizi *(Turkish)* sea
Desierto *(Spanish)* desert
Détroit *(French)* strait
Djebel *(Arabic)* mountain, mountain range

-elva *(Norwegian)* river
Embalse *(Spanish)* reservoir
Ensenada *(Spanish)* bay
Erg *(Arabic)* sand dunes
Estrecho *(Spanish)* strait
Étang *(French)* lagoon, lake
ezers *(Latvian)* lake

Falaise *(French)* cliff
Feng *(Chinese)* peak
Fjeld *(Danish)* mountain
-fjell *(Norwegian)* mountain
-fjord/en *(Danish, Norwegian, Swedish)* fiord

Gang *(Chinese)* harbor
Gaoyuan *(Chinese)* plateau
Garet *(Arabic)* hill
Gebergte *(Dutch)* mountain chain, mountain range
-gebirge *(German)* mountain range
Ghubbat *(Arabic)* bay
Gjiri *(Albanian)* bay
Golfe *(French)* gulf
Golfo *(Italian, Portuguese)* gulf
Gölü *(Turkish)* lake
Gora *(Russian)* mountain
Góry *(Polish)* mountains
Gross/er *(German)* big
Gryada *(Russian)* ridge
Guba *(Russian)* bay, gulf
Gulfo *(Spanish)* gulf
Gunung *(Indonesian, Malay)* mountain

Haixia *(Chinese)* strait
-halvøya *(Norwegian)* peninsula
Har *(Hebrew)* mountain
Haut, Haute *(French)* high
Hawr *(Arabic)* lake
Hāyk' *(Amharic)* lake
Helodrano *(Malagasy)* bay
Hohe *(German)* height
Hora *(Belorussian, Czech)* mountain
-horn *(German)* peak
Hory *(Czech)* mountains
Hsü *(Chinese)* island, islet
Hu *(Chinese)* lake

Île/s *(French)* island/s
Ilha/s *(Portuguese)* island/s
Ilheu *(Portuguese)* islet
Isla/s *(Spanish)* island/s
Isola, Isole *(Italian)* island/s

Jabal *(Arabic)* mountain, mountain range
Jarv *(Estonian)* lake
-järvi *(Finnish)* lake
Jazīrat, Jaza'īr *(Arabic)* island/s
Jazīreh *(Persian)* island
Jbel *(Arabic)* mountain
Jezioro *(Polish)* lake
-jima *(Japanese)* island
-joki *(Finnish)* river

Kalnas *(Lithuanian)* mountain
Kangri *(Tibetan)* mountain
Kap *(Danish, German)* cape
-kapp *(Norwegian)* cape
Kepi *(Albanian)* cape, point
Kepulauan *(Indonesian)* islands
Khalīj *(Arabic)* bay, gulf
Khao *(Thai)* peak
Khrebet *(Russian)* mountain range
Ko *(Thai)* island
Köli *(Kazakh)* lake
Kolpos *(Greek)* bay
Körfezi *(Turkish)* bay, gulf
Kray *(Russian)* territory
Kryazh *(Russian)* ridge
Kūh/hā *(Persian)* mountain/s
-kŭl *(Tajik)* lake
Kyst *(Danish)* coast
Kyun *(Burmese)* island

Lac *(French)* lake
Lacul *(Romanian)* lake
Lago *(Italian, Portuguese, Spanish)* lake
Lagoa *(Portuguese)* lagoon, lake
Laht *(Estonian)* bay
Lich *(Armenian)* lake
Liedao *(Chinese)* archipelago, islands
Limni *(Greek)* lake
Ling *(Chinese)* mountain range
Loch, Lough *(Gaelic)* lake
Lohatanjona *(Malagasy)* point
Loi *(Burmese)* mountain
Loma *(Spanish)* hill

Mae Nam *(Thai)* river
-man *(Korean)* bay
Mar *(Spanish)* lake, sea
Maşabb *(Arabic)* river mouth
Massif *(French)* mountains, upland
Meer, -meer *(Dutch)* lake, sea
Mesa *(Spanish)* tableland
Meseta *(Spanish)* plateau, tableland
-misaki *(Japanese)* cape, point
Mont/s *(French)* mountain/s
Montagne/s *(French)* mountain/s
Monte *(Italian, Portuguese, Spanish)* mountain
Montes *(Spanish)* mountain
Monti *(Italian)* mountain/s
More *(Russian)* sea
Morne *(French)* mountain
Morro *(Portuguese)* hill
Munţii *(Romanian)* mountains
Mys *(Russian)* cape, point

-nada *(Japanese)* gulf, sea
Nagor'ye *(Russian)* upland
Nevado *(Spanish)* snow-capped mountain
Nieuw *(Dutch)* new
Nisoi *(Greek)* islands
Nizmennost' *(Russian)* lowland
Nord *(French)* north
Norte *(Portuguese, Spanish)* north
Nos *(Bulgarian)* point
Nosy *(Malagasy)* island
Nur, Nuur *(Mongolian)* lake
Nuruu *(Mongolian)* mountain range

Ø, Øer *(Danish)* island/s
-ö, -ön *(Swedish)* island
Oblast' *(Russian)* province
Odde *(Danish)* cape, point
Oros *(Greek)* mountain
Ostrov/a *(Russian)* island/s
Oued *(Arabic)* river, watercourse
-øy, -øya *(Norwegian)* island
Ozero *(Russian)* lake

Pantanal *(Portuguese)* marsh, swamp
Pegunungan *(Indonesian)* island
Pelagos *(Greek)* sea
Pendi *(Chinese)* basin
Pertuis *(French)* strait
Phnum *(Cambodian)* mountain
Phou *(Laotian)* mountain
Pic *(French)* peak
Pico *(Spanish)* peak
Pik *(Russian)* peak
Piton *(French)* peak
Pivostriv *(Ukrainian)* peninsula
Piz, pizzo *(Italian)* peak
Planalto *(Portuguese)* plateau
Planina *(Bulgarian, Macedonian)* mountains
Plato *(Russian)* plateau
Ploskogor'ye *(Russian)* plateau, upland
Pointe *(French)* point
Poluostrov *(Russian)* peninsula
Ponta *(Portuguese)* point
Porthmos *(Greek)* strait
Porto, Pôrto *(Portuguese)* port
Proliv *(Russian)* strait
Puerto *(Spanish)* port
Pulau *(Indonesian, Malay)* island
Puncak *(Indonesian)* mountain
Punta *(Italian, Spanish)* point

Qārat *(Arabic)* hill
Qooriga *(Somali)* bay
Qundao *(Chinese)* archipelago, islands
Qurnat *(Arabic)* peak

Raas *(Somali)* cape, point
Ras, Ra's *(Arabic)* cape, point
Ravnina *(Russian)* plain
Represa *(Portuguese, Spanish)* reservoir
Réservoir *(French)* reservoir
Reshteh *(Persian)* mountain range
Respublika *(Russian)* republic
Respublikasi *(Uzbek)* republic
-retto *(Japanese)* island chain
Rio, Río *(Portuguese, Spanish)* river
Rivière *(French)* river
Rubha *(Gaelic)* cape, point
Rudohorie *(Slovak)* mountains

Sāgar/a *(Hindi)* lake
Şaḩrā' *(Arabic)* desert
-saki *(Japanese)* cape, point
Salar *(Spanish)* salt-flat, salt-pan
Salina/s *(Spanish)* salt-pan/s
Salto/s *(Portuguese, Spanish)* waterfall
-san *(Japanese, Korean)* mountain
San, Santa, Santo *(Spanish)* saint
-sanchi *(Japanese)* mountains
São *(Portuguese)* saint
Sarīr *(Arabic)* desert
Sebkha, Sebkhet *(Arabic)* salt-flat
See, -see *(German)* lake
Selat *(Indonesian)* strait
Serra *(Portuguese)* mountain range
Serranía *(Spanish)* mountain range
Shamo *(Chinese)* desert
Shan *(Chinese)* mountain/s
-shima *(Japanese)* island
-shotō *(Japanese)* islands
Shuiki *(Chinese)* reservoir
Sierra *(Spanish)* mountain range
Slieve *(Gaelic)* mountain
-spitze *(German)* peak
Steno *(Greek)* strait
Štít *(Slovak)* peak
Stretto *(Italian)* strait
Sud *(French)* south
Sul *(Portuguese)* south

Tanjona *(Malagasy)* cape
Tanjong *(Indonesian, Malay)* cape, point
Tao *(Chinese)* island
Tasek *(Malay)* lake
Tassili *(Berber)* plateau
Taungdan *(Burmese)* mountain range
Tekojärvi *(Finnish)* reservoir
Teluk *(Indonesian, Malay)* bay
Ténéré *(Berber)* desert
Tepe *(Turkish)* peak
Terara *(Amharic)* mountain
Tierra *(Spanish)* land
-to *(Japanese)* island

Ujung *(Indonesian)* cape, point
'Urūq *(Arabic)* dunes
Uul *(Mongolian)* mountain/s

väin *(Estonian)* channel, strait
-vatn *(Norwegian)* lake
-vesi *(Finnish)* lake, water
Voblasts' *(Belorussian)* province
Vodokhranilishche *(Russian)* reservoir
Vodoskhovyshche *(Ukrainian)* reservoir
Volcán *(Spanish)* volcano
Vozvyshennost' *(Russian)* plateau, upland
Vozyera *(Belorussian)* lake
Vrchovina *(Czech)* mountains

Wabē *(Amharic)* river, stream
Wādī *(Arabic)* watercourse
-wald *(German)* forest
Wan *(Chinese)* bay
-wan *(Japanese)* bay

Yam *(Hebrew)* lake, sea
Yang *(Chinese)* ocean
Yoma *(Burmese)* mountain range

-zaki *(Japanese)* cape, point
Zaliv *(Russian)* bay
Zangbo *(Tibetan)* river
Zatoka *(Polish)* bay, gulf
-zee *(Dutch)* sea
Zemlya *(Russian)* land
Zizhiqu *(Chinese)* autonomous region

Gazetteer

- The gazetteer contains the names shown on the continental and detailed regional maps at the end of each section.

- In the code given to locate a place, the **bold** number refers to the page on which the map is to be found, and the letter–number combination refers to the grid square formed by the lines of latitude and longitude on the map. Inset maps have their own letter–number combination.

- Where a name appears on more than one map, the gazetteer generally lists the largest scale map on which the name appears.

- Names that have a symbol (town or mountain peak) are given an area reference according to the location of the symbol. Names without a symbol are entered in the gazetteer according to the first letter of the name.

- Words in italics describe features in the gazetteer, e.g. *island*, *point* and *mountain peak*.

- All entries include the country or area in which the name is located.

- Features composed of a description and a proper name, e.g. Cape Hatteras, are positioned alphabetically by the proper name: Hatteras, Cape.

- Where a name contains a subordinate or alternative name in brackets on the map, the bracketed names are entered in the gazetteer with a cross-reference to the first name, eg. Peking *see* Beijing, China, **210** G5.

- Words abbreviated on the map, e.g. C. or I., are spelt out in the gazetteer. If the word is English, the description in italics is not included. For example, if I. (standing for island) is abbreviated on the map and spelt out in the gazetteer, *island* is not added. However, if Island is not in English, e.g. Isla, *island* is added.

- The location (ocean, area of a continent) is included before the area reference when a place is part of a country but not located within the country, e.g. Madeira, Portugal, Atlantic Ocean; and Ceuta, *enclave*, Spain, N.W. Africa.

A

A Cañiza, Spain, **292** C1
A Coruña, Spain, **292** C1
A Estrada, Spain, **292** C1
A Fonsagrada, Spain, **292** D1
A Guardia, Spain, **292** C2
A Gudiña, Spain, **292** D1
Aachen, Germany, **288** C3
Aalen, Germany, **288** E4
A'ali An Nīl, *state*, Sudan, **366** D2
Aapua, Sweden, **285** L3
Aarau, Switzerland, **291** J3
Aare, *river*, Switzerland, **291** J3
Aasleagh, Ireland, **309** C4
Aba, China, **215** G2
Aba, Democratic Republic of the Congo, **366** D4
Aba, Nigeria, **368** A1
Abacaxis, *river*, Brazil, **452** A4
Abaco, *island*, Bahamas, **428** F1
Ābādeh, Iran, **220** F2
Abadla, Algeria, **361** F2
Abaeté, *river*, Brazil, **456** D5
Abaetetuba, Brazil, **452** D3
Abag Qi, China, **210** F4
Abagaytuy, Russian Federation, **210** G2
Abaji, Nigeria, **365** F3
Abajo Peak, *mountain peak*, U.S.A., **423** J3
Abakaliki, Nigeria, **365** F3
Abakan, *river*, Russian Federation, **223** M2
Abakan, Russian Federation, **223** N2
Abala, Congo, **368** C3
Abala, Niger, **365** E2
Abalak, Niger, **365** E3/F1
Abalessa, Algeria, **361** G4
Abancay, Peru, **454** D3
Abarkūh, Iran, **220** F2
Abashiri, Japan, **209** J2
Abatskiy, Russian Federation, **223** J1
Abau, Papua New Guinea, **140** C5
Abay, Aqmola, Kazakhstan, **212** A2
Abay, Qaraghandy, Kazakhstan, **212** B2
Abaza, Russian Federation, **223** N2

Abba, Central African Republic, **368** C1
Abbeville, Alabama, U.S.A., **425** K4
Abbeville, France, **290** E1
Abbeville, Louisiana, U.S.A., **424** F5
Abbeville, South Carolina, U.S.A., **425** L2
Abbeyfeale, Ireland, **309** C5
Abbeyleix, Ireland, **309** E5
Abborrträsk, Sweden, **284** J4
Abbot Ice Shelf, Antarctica, **470** B6
Abbots Langley, England, U.K., **305** G3
Abbotsbury, England, U.K., **304** E4
Abbotsford, Canada, **412** H7
Abbott, U.S.A., **423** L3
Abbottābād, Pakistan, **218** C2
'Abd al Kūrī, *island*, Suquţrá (Socotra), Yemen, **373** B2
Abdelcader, Somalia, **367** F2
Abdulino, Russian Federation, **222** E2
Abéché, Chad, **366** B2
Abee, Canada, **413** N4
Abemama, *island*, Kiribati, **139** F4
Abengourou, Côte d'Ivoire, **364** D3
Åbenrå, Denmark, **286** D5
Abeokuta, Nigeria, **365** E3
Aberaeron, Wales, U.K., **304** C2
Aberchirder, Scotland, U.K., **308** G3
Aberdare, Wales, U.K., **304** D3
Aberdaron, Wales, U.K., **304** C2
Aberdeen, Idaho, U.S.A., **418** H5
Aberdeen, Mississippi, U.S.A., **425** H3
Aberdeen, Scotland, U.K., **308** G3
Aberdeen, South Africa, **370** D5
Aberdeen, South Dakota, U.S.A., **420** D3
Aberdeen, Washington, U.S.A., **418** C3
Aberdeen City, *local authority*, Scotland, U.K., **308** G3
Aberdeenshire, *local authority*, Scotland, U.K., **308** G3
Aberdyfi, Wales, U.K., **304** C2

Aberfeldy, Scotland, U.K., **308** F4
Aberfoyle, Scotland, U.K., **306** D1
Abergavenny, Wales, U.K., **304** E3
Abergele, Wales, U.K., **306** E4
Abernathy, U.S.A., **424** B3
Aberporth, Wales, U.K., **304** C2
Abersoch, Wales, U.K., **304** C2
Abert, Lake, U.S.A., **418** D5
Abertillery, Wales, U.K., **304** D3
Aberystwyth, Wales, U.K., **304** C2
Abhā, Saudi Arabia, **363** H5
Abhar, Iran, **222** D5
Abia, *state*, Nigeria, **365** F3
Abibe, Serranía de, *mountain range*, Colombia, **450** C2
Abide, Turkey, **297** G6
Abidjan, Côte d'Ivoire, **364** D3
Abilene, U.S.A., **424** C3
Abingdon, England, U.K., **305** F3
Abingdon, U.S.A., **421** N7
Abington, Scotland, U.K., **308** F5
Abiquiu, U.S.A., **423** K3
Abisko, Sweden, **284** J2
Abitibi, Lake, Canada, **415** Q7
Ābiy Ādī, Ethiopia, **367** E2
Abkhazia, *autonomous republic*, Georgia, **222** C4
Abnūb, Egypt, **363** F3
Abohar, India, **218** C3
Aboisso, Côte d'Ivoire, **364** D3
Abomey, Benin, **365** E3
Abong Mbang, Cameroon, **368** B2
Abongabong, Gunung, *mountain peak*, Indonesia, **200** B1
Abooso, Ghana, **364** D3
Aborlan, Philippines, **204** B4
Abou Deïa, Chad, **366** A2
Aboyne, Scotland, U.K., **308** G3
Abra Pampa, Argentina, **458** D2
Abra, *river*, Philippines, **204** C2
Abrantes, Portugal, **292** C3
Abrī, Sudan, **363** F4
Abriès, France, **291** H4
Abrolhos, Arquipélago dos, *islands*, Brazil, **457** F4
Abrud, Romania, **296** D2
Abruka, *island*, Estonia, **287** L3
Abruzzi, *autonomous region*, Italy, **295** D4

Absaroka Range, *mountain range*, U.S.A., **419** J4
Absarokee, U.S.A., **419** K4
Abu aḑ Ḑuhūr, Syria, **225** D2
Abū 'Arīsh, Saudi Arabia, **363** H5
Abu Dhabi *see* Abū Ẓaby, United Arab Emirates, **221** F4
Abū Dulayq, Sudan, **366** D1
Abū Durbah, Egypt, **225** B5
Abū Haggag, Egypt, **362** E2
Abū Ḩamad, Sudan, **363** F5
Abū Ḩammād, Egypt, **225** A4
Abū Kamāl, Syria, **363** H2
Abū Madd, Ra's, *point*, Saudi Arabia, **363** G4
Abū Maţāriq, Sudan, **366** C2
Abū Nujaym, Libya, **362** C2
Ābū Road, India, **218** C4
Abū Rubayq, Saudi Arabia, **363** G4
Abū Rudays, Egypt, **225** B5
Abū Rujmayn, Jabal, *mountain range*, Syria, **225** E2
Abu Shagara, Ras, *point*, Sudan, **363** G4
Abū Shanab, Sudan, **366** C2
Abu Simbel *see* Abū Sunbul, Egypt, **363** F4
Abū Sunbul (Abu Simbel), Egypt, **363** F4
Abū Zabad, Sudan, **366** C2
Abū Ẓaby (Abu Dhabi), United Arab Emirates, **221** F4
Abū Zanīmah, Egypt, **225** B5
Abu 'Ujaylah, Egypt, **225** C4
Abuja, Nigeria, **365** F3
Abulog, Philippines, **204** C2
Abumombazi, Democratic Republic of the Congo, **368** D2
Abunã, Brazil, **455** F2
Abunã, *river*, Bolivia/Brazil, **455** E2
Ābune Yosēf, *mountain peak*, Ethiopia, **367** E2
Aburo, *mountain peak*, Democratic Republic of the Congo, **366** D4
Ābuyē Mēda, *mountain peak*, Ethiopia, **367** E2
Åby, Sweden, **286** H3
Abyaḑ, Al Baḩr al (White Nile), *river*, Sudan, **366** D2
Abyaḑ, Sudan, **366** C2
Åbybro, Denmark, **286** D4

Abyei, Sudan, **366** C3
Åbyn, Sweden, **284** K4
Açailândia, Brazil, **452** D4
Acámbaro, Mexico, **431** E5
Acancéh, Mexico, **431** H4
Acandí, Colombia, **450** C2
Acaponeta, Mexico, **430** D4
Acapulco, Mexico, **431** F5
Acará, Brazil, **452** D3
Acará, *river*, Brazil, **452** D4
Acará-Mirim, *river*, Brazil, **452** D4
Acaraí, Serra, *mountain range*, Brazil, **452** B3
Acaraú, Brazil, **453** F4
Acaraú, *river*, Brazil, **453** F4
Acaray, Represa de, *reservoir*, Paraguay, **459** F2
Acari, Brazil, **453** G5
Acarigua, Venezuela, **451** E2
Acâş, Romania, **296** D2
Acatlán de Osorio, Mexico, **431** F5
Acayucan, Mexico, **431** G5
Acceglio, Italy, **294** A3
Accomac, U.S.A., **426** C6
Accra, Ghana, **364** D3
Aceh, *province*, Indonesia, **200** B1
Aceh, *river*, Indonesia, **200** A1
Achacachi, Bolivia, **455** E4
Achaguas, Venezuela, **451** E2
Achahoish, Scotland, U.K., **308** D5
Achalpur, India, **218** D5
Acheng, China, **211** J3
Acheryok, *river*, Russian Federation, **285** U3
Acheux-en-Amiénois, France, **305** K4
Achill, Ireland, **309** C4
Achill Island, Ireland, **309** B4
Achiltibuie, Scotland, U.K., **308** D2
Achinsk, Russian Federation, **300** L4
Achit, Russian Federation, **222** F1
Achnasheen, Scotland, U.K., **308** D3
Achwa, *river*, Uganda, **369** F2
Acigöl, *lake*, Turkey, **297** G7
Acıpayam, Turkey, **297** G7
Acireale, Sicilia, Italy, **295** E7

India, 218 C5
Ajaria, *autonomous republic*, Georgia, 222 C4
Ajaureforsen, Sweden, 284 G4
Ajax, Mount, *mountain peak*, New Zealand, 133 D6
Ajdābiyā, Libya, 362 D2
Ajdovščina, Slovenia, 294 D3
Ajmah, Jabal al, *plateau*, Egypt, 225 B5
Ajmer, India, 218 C4
Ajnala, India, 218 C3
Ajo, U.S.A., 422 G5
Ak Dağ, *mountain peak*, Turkey, 297 F6
Ak Dağlar, *mountain range*, Turkey, 297 G7
Ak-Dovurak, Russian Federation, 223 N2
Ak-Shyyrak, Kyrgyzstan, 223 K4
Akabira, Japan, 209 H2
Akabli, Algeria, 361 G3
Āk'ak'ī Besek'a, Ethiopia, 367 E3
Akalkot, India, 216 D2
Akanthou, Cyprus, 225 B2
Akaroa, New Zealand, 133 D6
Akaroa Harbour, New Zealand, 133 D6
Akatora, Chaine de l', *mountain range*, Benin, 364 E2
Akbou, Algeria, 361 G1
Akbulak, Kazakhstan, 223 J3
Akçakale, Turkey, 224 E5
Akçay, Turkey, 297 G7
Akdağ, *mountain peak*, Turkey, 297 G6
Akelamo, Indonesia, 199 E2
Akeld, England, U.K., 306 F2
Aken, Germany, 288 F3
Åkersberga, Sweden, 287 J3
Akershus, *county*, Norway, 286 E3
Aketi, Democratic Republic of the Congo, 368 D2
Akhalts'ikhe, Georgia, 222 C4
Akhisar, Turkey, 224 C5
Akhmīm, Egypt, 363 F3
Akhnūr, India, 218 C2
Akhtubinsk, Russian Federation, 222 D3
Aki, Japan, 208 F4
Akiaki, *island*, French Polynesia, 137 H2
Akiéni, Gabon, 368 B3
Akima, *river*, Russian Federation, 210 G1
Akima, Russian Federation, 210 F1
Akimiski Island, Canada, 415 P5
Akita, Japan, 209 H3
Akjoujt, Mauritania, 360 D5
Akka, Morocco, 360 E3
Akkajaure, *lake*, Sweden, 284 H3
Akkavare, *mountain peak*, Sweden, 284 H3
'Akko (Acre), Israel, 225 C3
Aklampa, Benin, 365 E3
Aklavik, Canada, 410 F3
Aknīste, Latvia, 287 M4
Akodia, India, 218 D5
Akoke, Sudan, 366 D3
Akola, India, 218 D5
Akom II, Cameroon, 368 B2
Akonolinga, Cameroon, 368 B2
Äkordat, Eritrea, 367 E1
Akören, Turkey, 363 F1
Akot, India, 218 D5
Akot, Sudan, 366 D3
Akoupé, Côte d'Ivoire, 364 D3
Akpatok Island, Canada, 411 N3
Akqi, China, 212 C4
Akra Lithino, Greece, 362 D2
Akranes, Iceland, 284 X7
Akrathos, Akra, *point*, Greece, 297 E5
Åkrehamn, Norway, 286 B3
Akrérèb, Niger, 365 F1
Åkrestrømmen, Norway, 286 E2
Akron, Colorado, U.S.A., 423 M1
Akron, Ohio, U.S.A., 421 N5

Akrotiri, Cyprus, 225 B2
Aksai Chin, *disputed region*, China/India, 218 D2
Aksakal, Turkey, 297 G5
Aksakovo, Bulgaria, 296 F4
Aksaray, Turkey, 224 D5
Aksay, Kazakhstan, 222 E2
Akşehir, Turkey, 224 D5
Akşehir Gölü, *lake*, Turkey, 363 F1
Akseki, Turkey, 363 F1
Aksha, Russian Federation, 210 F2
Aksu, China, 212 D4
Aksu, Kazakhstan, 222 E4
Āksum, Ethiopia, 367 E2
Aktash, Russian Federation, 223 M2
Aktau *see* Aqtaū, W. Kazakhstan, 222 E4
Aktaz, China, 212 E5
Akto, China, 212 D5
Aktyubinsk *see* Aqtöbe, Kazakhstan, 222 F2
Akübū, Sudan, 366 D3
Akulivik, Canada, 415 Q1
Akure, Nigeria, 365 F3
Akureyri, Iceland, 284 Y7
Akutikha, Russian Federation, 223 L2
Akwa Ibon, *state*, Nigeria, 365 F4
Akwanga, Nigeria, 365 F3
Akxokesay, China, 213 F5
Akyab *see* Sittwe, Myanmar, 205 B3
Al Abyār, Libya, 362 D2
Al Ajfar, Saudi Arabia, 363 H3
Al Akhḑar, Saudi Arabia, 225 D5
Al 'Alamayn, Egypt, 362 E2
Al 'Amārah, Iraq, 363 J2
Al 'Aqabah, Jordan, 225 C5
Al 'Aqīq, Saudi Arabia, 363 H4
Al 'Arīsh, Egypt, 225 B4
Al Artāwīyah, Saudi Arabia, 363 J3
Al 'Azīzīyah, Libya, 362 B2
Al Bāb, Syria, 225 D1
Al Bad', Saudi Arabia, 225 C5
Al Badi', Saudi Arabia, 363 J4
Al Baḩr Al Aḩmar, *state*, Sudan, 363 F5
Al Balyanā, Egypt, 363 F3
Al Bardī, Libya, 362 E2
Al Barun, Sudan, 366 D2
Al Başrah (Basra), Iraq, 363 J2
Al Batrūn, Lebanon, 225 C2
Al Bauga, Sudan, 363 F5
Al Bawīṭī, Egypt, 362 E3
Al Baydā', Libya, 362 D2
Al Bayḑā', Yemen, 220 E6
Al Bi'ār, Saudi Arabia, 363 G4
Al Bi'r, Saudi Arabia, 225 D5
Al Birk, Saudi Arabia, 363 H5
Al Biyāḑ, *desert*, Saudi Arabia, 220 E4
Al Buḩayrat, *state*, Sudan, 366 C3
Al Bukayrīyah, Saudi Arabia, 363 H3
Al Burayj, Syria, 225 D2
Al Burmah, Tunisia, 362 A2
Al Buşayyah, Iraq, 363 J2
Al Fāshir, Sudan, 366 C2
Al Fashn, Egypt, 363 F3
Al Fayyūm, Egypt, 363 F3
Al Fāzah, Yemen, 220 D6
Al Firdān, Egypt, 225 B4
Al Fujayrah, United Arab Emirates, 221 G3
Al Fūlah, Sudan, 366 C2
Al Fuqahā', Libya, 362 C3
Al Ghayḑah, Yemen, 220 F5
Al Ghurdaqah, Egypt, 363 F3
Al Ḩadīthah, Iraq, 363 H2
Al Ḩadīthah, Saudi Arabia, 225 D4
Al Ḩamdānīyah, Syria, 225 D2
Al Ḩamīdīyah, Syria, 225 C2
Al Ḩammah, Tunisia, 362 A2
Al Ḩammām, Egypt, 362 E2
Al Ḩammāmāt, Tunisia, 295 C7

Al Ḩamrāt, Syria, 225 D2
Al Ḩāmūl, Egypt, 225 A4
Al Ḩanākīyah, Saudi Arabia, 363 H4
Al Ḩasā, Jordan, 225 C4
Al Ḩasakah, Syria, 363 H1
Al Ḩawātah, Sudan, 366 D2
Al Ḩawjā', Saudi Arabia, 363 G3
Al Ḩawṭah, Yemen, 220 E5
Al Ḩayz, Egypt, 362 E3
Al Ḩazm, Saudi Arabia, 225 D5
Al Ḩibāk, *desert*, Saudi Arabia, 220 F5
Al Hijaz, *desert*, Saudi Arabia, 363 G3
Al Ḩillah, Iraq, 363 H2
Al Ḩillah, Sudan, 366 C2
Al Hirmil, Lebanon, 225 D2
Al Ḩişn, Jordan, 225 C3
Al Hoceima, Morocco, 361 F1
Al Ḩudaydah, Yemen, 220 D6
Al Hufūf, Saudi Arabia, 220 E3
Al Ḩumaydah, Saudi Arabia, 225 C5
Al Ḩumayshah, Yemen, 220 E6
Al Īsāwīyah, Saudi Arabia, 225 D4
Al Iskandarīya (Alexandria), Egypt, 363 E2
Al Ismā'īlīyah (Ismailia), Egypt, 225 B4
Al Jafr, Jordan, 225 D4
Al Jaghbūb, Libya, 362 D3
Al Jahrā', Kuwait, 363 J3
Al Jamm, Tunisia, 362 B1
Al Jawf, Jordan, 225 D4
Al Jawf, Saudi Arabia, 363 G3
Al Jazīrah, *state*, Sudan, 366 D2
Al Jithāmīyah, Saudi Arabia, 363 H3
Al Jīzah, Egypt, 225 A5
Al Jubayl, Saudi Arabia, 220 E3
Al Jumūm, Saudi Arabia, 363 G4
Al Junaynah, Sudan, 366 B2
Al Kahfah, Saudi Arabia, 363 H3
Al Kāmil, Oman, 221 G4
Al Kāmilīn, Sudan, 366 D1
Al Karīb, Tunisia, 295 B7
Al Karak, Jordan, 225 C4
Al Karnak, Egypt, 363 F3
Al Kāẓimīyah, Iraq, 363 H2
Al Khābūrah, Oman, 221 G4
Al Khalil (Hebron), West Bank, 225 C4
Al Khandaq, Sudan, 363 F5
Al Khānkah, Egypt, 225 A4
Al Khārijah, Egypt, 363 F3
Al Kharfah, Saudi Arabia, 363 J4
Al Kharj, Saudi Arabia, 220 E4
Al Khartūm, *state*, Sudan, 366 D1
Al Kharţūm (Khartoum), Sudan, 366 D1
Al Kharţūm Baḩr (Khartoum North), Sudan, 366 D1
Al Khaşab, Oman, 221 G3
Al Khawsh, Saudi Arabia, 363 H5
Al Khufrah, Libya, 362 D4
Al Khums, Libya, 362 B2
Al Kidan, *desert*, Saudi Arabia, 221 F4
Al Kiswah, Syria, 225 D3
Al Kūfah, Iraq, 363 H2
Al Kuntillah, Egypt, 225 C5
Al Kūt, Iraq, 363 J2
Al Kuwayt (Kuwait), Kuwait, 363 J3
Al Lādhiqīyah, *district*, Syria, 225 C2
Al Lādhiqīyah (Latakia), Syria, 225 C2
Al Lagowa, Sudan, 366 C2
Al Lith, Saudi Arabia, 363 H4
Al Madāfi', *plateau*, Saudi Arabia, 225 D5
Al Madīnah (Medina), Saudi Arabia, 363 G4
Al Mafraq, Jordan, 225 D3
Al Maḩalla al Kubrá, Egypt, 225 A4

Al Mahrah, *mountain range*, Yemen, 220 F5
Al Majma'ah, Saudi Arabia, 363 J3
Al Manāmah, Bahrain, 220 F3
Al Manāqil, Sudan, 366 D2
Al Manşūrah, Egypt, 225 A4
Al Manzil, Jordan, 225 D4
Al Manzilah, Egypt, 225 A4
Al Ma'qil, Iraq, 363 J2
Al Marāwi'ah, Yemen, 220 D6
Al Māriyah, Oman, 220 F4
Al Marj, Libya, 362 D2
Al Mawşil (Mosul), Iraq, 363 H1
Al Mayādīn, Syria, 363 H2
Al Mazār, Jordan, 225 C4
Al Mazra'ah, Jordan, 225 C4
Al Metlaoui, Tunisia, 362 A2
Al Minyā, Egypt, 363 F3
Al Mismīyah, Syria, 225 D3
Al Mubarraz, Saudi Arabia, 220 E3
Al Mudawwarah, Jordan, 225 C5
Al Muglad, Sudan, 366 C2
Al Mukallā, Yemen, 220 E6
Al Mukhā, Yemen, 220 D6
Al Munastīr, Tunisia, 362 B1
Al Muqdādīyah, Iraq, 363 H2
Al Musayjid, Saudi Arabia, 363 G4
Al Muwayh, Saudi Arabia, 363 H4
Al Qa'āmīyāt, *physical feature*, Saudi Arabia, 367 G1
Al Qa'āmīyāt, *region*, Saudi Arabia, 220 E5
Al Qaḑārif, *state*, Sudan, 366 E2
Al Qaḑārif, Sudan, 366 E2
Al Qaḑīmah, Saudi Arabia, 363 G4
Al Qāhirah (Cairo), Egypt, 225 A4
Al Qaḩmah, Saudi Arabia, 363 H5
Al Qā'īyah, Saudi Arabia, 363 H4
Al Qalībah, Saudi Arabia, 225 D5
Al Qāmishlī, Syria, 363 H1
Al Qanţarah, Egypt, 225 B4
Al Qaryatayn, Syria, 225 D2
Al Qaşabāt, Libya, 362 B2
Al Qaşr, Egypt, 362 E3
Al Qaşrayn, Tunisia, 362 A1
Al Qaţrānah, Jordan, 225 D4
Al Qaţrūn, Libya, 362 B4
Al Quşaymah, Egypt, 225 C4
Al Quşayr, Egypt, 363 F3
Al Quţaynah, Sudan, 366 D2
Al Quţayfah, Syria, 225 D3
Al Qunayţirah, *district*, Syria, 225 C3
Al Qunayţirah, Syria, 225 C3
Al Qunfudhah, Saudi Arabia, 363 H5
Al Qurayyāt, Saudi Arabia, 225 D4
Al Quwayrah, Jordan, 225 C5
Al Ţawţah, Yemen, 220 E6
Al Ubayyiḑ (El Obeid), Sudan, 366 D2
Al 'Ulā, Saudi Arabia, 363 G3
Al 'Ulayyah, Saudi Arabia, 363 H5
Al 'Umarī, Jordan, 225 D4
Al 'Uqaylah, Libya, 362 C2
Al Uqşur (Luxor), Egypt, 363 F3
Al 'Urayq, *desert*, Saudi Arabia, 363 G3
Al Uthaylī, Saudi Arabia, 225 D5
Al 'Uthmānīyah, Saudi Arabia, 220 E3
Al 'Uwaynāt, E. Libya, 362 D4
Al 'Uwaynāt, W. Libya, 362 B3
Al 'Uwayqilah, Saudi Arabia, 363 H2
Al 'Uyūn, N. Saudi Arabia, 363 H3
Al 'Uyūn, W. Saudi Arabia, 363 G4
Al Wīgh, Libya, 362 B4

Al Waḩdah, *state*, Sudan, 366 C3
Al Wajh, Saudi Arabia, 363 G3
Al Wāsiţah, Egypt, 225 A5
Al Waslātīyah, Tunisia, 295 B8
Al Wazz, Sudan, 366 D2
Al Yamāmah, Saudi Arabia, 220 E4
Ala-Vuokki, Finland, 285 P4
Alabama, *river*, U.S.A., 425 J4
Alabama, *state*, U.S.A., 425 J3
Alabaster, U.S.A., 425 J3
Alaçam Dağları, *mountain range*, Turkey, 297 G6
Alachua, U.S.A., 425 L5
Aladdin, U.S.A., 419 M4
Alaejos, Spain, 292 E2
Alagoas, *state*, Brazil, 457 G2
Alagoinhas, Brazil, 457 F3
Alahärmä, Finland, 285 L5
Alajärvi, Finland, 285 L5
Alajuela, Costa Rica, 428 D5
Alaköl', *lake*, Kazakhstan, 212 D3
Alakurtti, Russian Federation, 285 Q3
Alalau, *river*, Brazil, 451 G4
Alamagan, *island*, Northern Mariana Islands, 138 C3
Ālamaṭ'ā, Ethiopia, 367 E2
Alamdo, China, 214 E3
Alamo, U.S.A., 422 F3
Alamo Lake, U.S.A., 422 G4
Alamogordo, U.S.A., 423 L5
Alamos, Mexico, 430 C3
Alamosa, U.S.A., 423 L3
Åland see Ahvenanmaa, *island*, Finland, 287 J2
Åland see Ahvenanmaan Lääni, *province*, Finland, 287 J2
Alantika, Monts, *mountain range*, Cameroon, 365 G3
Alanya (Coracesium), Turkey, 225 A1
Alapaha, U.S.A., 425 L4
Alapayevsk, Russian Federation, 222 G1
Alarcón, Embalse de, *reservoir*, Spain, 293 F3
Alarcón, Spain, 293 F3
Alaşehir, Turkey, 297 G6
Alaska, Gulf of, U.S.A., 410 E4
Alaska, *state*, U.S.A., 410 D3
Alaska Peninsula, U.S.A., 410 C4
Alaska Range, *mountain range*, U.S.A., 410 D3
Alassio, Italy, 294 B4
Ālāt, Azerbaijan, 222 D5
Alatri, Italy, 295 D5
Alatyr', Russian Federation, 222 D2
Alausí, Ecuador, 450 B5
Alavieska, Finland, 285 M4
Alavus, Finland, 287 L1
'Alawīyīn, Jibāl al, *mountain range*, Syria, 225 D2
Alay kyrka, *mountain range*, Kyrgyzstan/Tajikistan, 212 B5
'Ālayh, Lebanon, 225 C3
Alazeya, *river*, Russian Federation, 301 S2
Alba, Italy, 294 A3
Alba, Mount, *mountain peak*, New Zealand, 133 B7
Alba Iulia, Romania, 296 D3
Albacete, Spain, 293 G3
Ålbæk, Denmark, 286 E4
Alban, Canada, 421 N2
Albanel, Lac, *lake*, Canada, 416 E4
Albania, *country*, Europe, 282 F7
Albany, Australia, 134 D5
Albany, Kentucky, U.S.A., 425 K4
Albany, New York, U.S.A., 426 D3
Albany, New Zealand, 132 E3
Albany, Oregon, U.S.A., 418 C4
Albany, *river*, Canada, 415 N6
Albany, Texas, U.S.A., 424 C3
Albarracín, Spain, 293 G2

Albatross Bay, Australia, **135** J1
Albatross Point, Antipodes Islands, New Zealand, **133** P15
Albatross Point, North Island, New Zealand, **132** E4
Albemarle, Punta, *point*, Islas Galápagos (Galapagos Islands), Ecuador, **461** A1
Albemarle Sound, U.S.A., **426** B6
Albenga, Italy, **294** B3
Alberdi, Paraguay, **459** E3
Alberga, *river*, Australia, **135** H4
Albergaria-a-Velha, Portugal, **292** C2
Albert, France, **290** F1
Albert, Lake, Democratic Republic of The Congo/Uganda, **369** F2
Albert Canyon, Canada, **413** L6
Albert Edward, Mount, *mountain peak*, Papua New Guinea, **140** B5
Albert Lea, U.S.A., **420** G4
Alberta, Mount, *mountain peak*, Canada, **413** L5
Alberta, *province*, Canada, **413** M4
Alberta, U.S.A., **426** B6
Alberta Beach, Canada, **413** M5
Albertirsa, Hungary, **289** J5
Alberton, Canada, **417** J6
Albertville, France, **291** H4
Albertville, U.S.A., **425** J2
Albeşti, Romania, **296** F2
Albi, France, **290** F5
Albia, U.S.A., **420** G5
Albin, U.S.A., **419** M6
Albina, Ponta, *point*, Angola, **368** B6
Albina, Suriname, **452** B2
Albion, U.S.A., **419** M4
Albocácer, Spain, **293** H2
Alborán, Isla del, *island*, Spain, **293** F5
Ålborg, Denmark, **286** D4
Alborz, Reshteh-ye Kūhhā-ye, *mountain range*, Iran, **222** E5
Albox, Spain, **293** F4
Albreda, Canada, **413** K5
Albuñol, Spain, **293** F4
Albuquerque, U.S.A., **423** K4
Alburquerque, Spain, **292** D3
Albury, Australia, **135** K6
Alca, Peru, **454** D4
Alcácer do Sal, Portugal, **292** C3
Alcala, Philippines, **204** C2
Alcalá de Guadaira, Spain, **292** E4
Alcalá de Henares, Spain, **293** F2
Alcalà de Xivert, Spain, **293** H2
Alcalá la Real, Spain, **293** F4
Alcamo, Sicilia, Italy, **295** D7
Alcañices, Spain, **292** D2
Alcañiz, Spain, **293** G2
Alcántara, Embalse de, *reservoir*, Spain, **292** D3
Alcántara, Spain, **292** D3
Alcaracejos, Spain, **292** E3
Alcaraz, Spain, **293** F3
Alcaudete, Spain, **292** E4
Alcázar de San Juan, Spain, **293** F3
Alcester, England, U.K., **305** F2
Alchevs'k, Ukraine, **298** E3
Alcobaça, Brazil, **457** F4
Alcolea del Pinar, Spain, **293** F2
Alcora, Spain, **293** G2
Alcorcón, Spain, **293** F2
Alcorisa, Spain, **293** G2
Alcorta, Argentina, **458** E4
Alcoutim, Portugal, **292** D4
Alcova, U.S.A., **419** L5
Alcoy, Spain, **293** G3
Alcubierre, Sierra de, *mountain range*, Spain, **293** G2
Alcúdia, Spain, **293** J3
Aldabra Islands, Seychelles, **372** B2
Aldama, Chihuahua, Mexico, **430** D2
Aldama, Tamaulipas, Mexico, **431** F4
Aldan, *river*, Russian Federation, **301** Q4
Aldan, Russian Federation, **301** P4
Aldanskoye Nagor'ye, *mountain range*, Russian Federation, **301** P4
Alde, *river*, England, U.K., **305** J2
Aldeburgh, England, U.K., **305** J2
Aldeia Velha, Brazil, **452** C5
Alderholt, England, U.K., **305** F4
Aldermen Islands, The, New Zealand, **132** F3
Alderney, *island*, *Guernsey dependency*, English Channel, **290** C2
Aldershot, England, U.K., **305** G3
Aldersyde, Canada, **413** N6
Aldingham, England, U.K., **306** E3
Aleg, Mauritania, **364** B1
Alegranza, *island*, Islas Canarias, Spain, **373** B4
Alegre, Brazil, **457** F5
Alegre, Monte, *mountain peak*, Brazil, **452** B3
Alegre, *river*, Brazil, **456** B4
Alegrete, Brazil, **459** F3
Alejandro Korn, Argentina, **459** E5
Alekhovshchina, Russian Federation, **299** D2
Aleksandrov, Russian Federation, **299** G4
Aleksandrovac, Yugoslavia, **296** C4
Aleksandrovo, Bulgaria, **296** E4
Aleksandry, Zemlya, *island*, Russian Federation, **300** F1
Alekseevka, Kazakhstan, **212** E2
Aleksin, Russian Federation, **299** F5
Aleksinac, Yugoslavia, **296** C4
Ålem, Sweden, **286** H4
Além Paraíba, Brazil, **457** E5
Alèmbé, Gabon, **368** B3
Ålen, Norway, **284** E5
Alençon, France, **290** E2
Alenquer, Brazil, **452** B3
Alenuihaha Channel, Hawaiian Islands, U.S.A., **422** R9
Aleppo *see* Ḩalab, Syria, **225** D1
Aléria, Corse, France, **295** B4
Alert, Canada, **411** N1
Alert Point, Canada, **411** K1
Alerta, Peru, **454** D3
Alès, France, **291** G4
Aleşd, Romania, **296** D2
Alessandria, Italy, **294** B3
Ålesund, Norway, **286** C1
Aleutian Islands, United States of America, **301** U4
Aleutian Range, *mountain range*, U.S.A., **410** D4
Aleutian Trench, *underwater feature*, Pacific Ocean, **478** F1
Alexander, Kansas, U.S.A., **420** D6
Alexander, North Dakota, U.S.A., **420** B2
Alexander Archipelago, *islands*, U.S.A., **412** B3
Alexander Bay, South Africa, **370** C4
Alexander City, U.S.A., **425** J3
Alexander Island, Antarctica, **470** B5
Alexandra, Cape, South Georgia, **461** A3
Alexandra, New Zealand, **133** B7
Alexandria, Louisiana, U.S.A., **424** F4
Alexandria, Minnesota, U.S.A., **420** F3
Alexandria, Romania, **296** E4
Alexandria, Scotland, U.K., **308** E5
Alexandria *see* Al Iskandarīya, Egypt, **363** E2
Alexandria, Virginia, U.S.A., **426** B5
Alexandreia, Greece, **297** D5
Alexandria Bay, U.S.A., **426** C2
Alexandrina, Lake, Australia, **135** H6
Alexandroupoli, Greece, **297** E5
Alexis, *river*, Canada, **417** N3
Alexishafen, Papua New Guinea, **140** B4
Aley, *river*, Russian Federation, **212** D1
Aleysk, Russian Federation, **212** D1
Alfambra, Spain, **293** G2
Alfarràs, Spain, **293** H2
Alfatar, Bulgaria, **296** F4
Alfeld (Leine), Germany, **288** D3
Alfenas, Brazil, **456** E5
Alford, England, U.K., **307** J4
Alfreton, England, U.K., **305** F1
Ålgård, Norway, **286** B3
Algarrobo, Chile, **458** B3
Algarrobo del Aguila, Argentina, **458** C5
Algarve, *region*, Portugal, **292** C2
Algeciras, Spain, **292** E4
Algena, Eritrea, **220** C5
Alger (Algiers), Algeria, **361** G1
Alger, U.S.A., **421** L3
Algeria, *country*, Africa, **358** E4
Alghero, Sardegna, Italy, **295** B5
Algiers *see* Alger, Algeria, **361** G1
Algoa Bay, South Africa, **371** E5
Algodonales, Spain, **292** E4
Algoma, U.S.A., **421** K3
Algona, U.S.A., **420** F4
Alhama de Granada, Spain, **293** F4
Alhambra, Spain, **293** F3
'Ali Sabieh, Djibouti, **367** F2
Alia, Sicilia, Italy, **295** D7
Aliağa, Turkey, **297** F6
Aliakmonas, Limni, *lake*, Greece, **297** D5
Aliartos, Greece, **297** D6
Alibunar, Yugoslavia, **296** C3
Alicante, Spain, **293** G3
Alice, Punta, *point*, Italy, **295** F6
Alice, U.S.A., **424** C6
Alice Springs, Australia, **134** G3
Aliceville, U.S.A., **425** H3
Alicudi, Isola, *island*, Italy, **295** E6
Aligarh, India, **218** D4
Alimia, *island*, Dodekanisos, Greece, **297** F7
Alindao, Central African Republic, **368** D1
Alingsås, Sweden, **286** F4
Alipur, Pakistan, **218** B3
Alīpur Duar, India, **219** G4
Aliseda, Spain, **292** D3
Aliveri, Greece, **297** E6
Aliwal North, South Africa, **371** E5
Aljezur, Portugal, **292** C4
Aljustrel, Portugal, **292** C4
Alkali Lake, U.S.A., **418** E5
Alkamari, Niger, **365** G2
Alkmaar, Netherlands, **288** B2
Allagadda, India, **216** D3
Allagash, *river*, U.S.A., **416** G6
Allahābād, India, **219** E4
Allakaket, U.S.A., **410** D3
Alldays, South Africa, **371** E3
Allegheny, *river*, U.S.A., **421** P5
Allegheny Mountains, *mountain range*, U.S.A., **421** N6
Allen, Lough, *lake*, Ireland, **309** D3
Allen, Mount, *mountain peak*, New Zealand, **133** A8
Allen, Philippines, **204** D3
Allendale, U.S.A., **425** M3
Allendale Town, England, U.K., **306** F3
Allende, Coahuila, Mexico, **431** E2
Allende, Nuevo Léon, Mexico, **431** E3
Allenford, Canada, **421** N3
Allenheads, England, U.K., **306** F3
Allentown, U.S.A., **426** C4
Alleppey, India, **216** D4
Allepuz, Spain, **293** G2
Aller, *river*, Germany, **288** D2
Allgäuer Alpen, *mountain range*, Austria, **288** E5
Alliance, Suriname, **452** B2
Alliance, U.S.A., **420** B4
Allier, *river*, France, **291** F3
Allihies, Ireland, **309** B6
Allinagaram, India, **216** D4
Allinge-Sandvig, Denmark, **286** G5
Alloa, Scotland, U.K., **308** F4
Alma, Canada, **416** F5
Alma, Georgia, U.S.A., **425** L4
Alma, Michigan, U.S.A., **421** L4
Alma, Nebraska, U.S.A., **420** D5
Almáciga, Islas Canarias, Spain, **373** A4
Almada, Portugal, **292** C3
Almadén, Spain, **292** E3
Almagro, Spain, **293** F3
Almansa, Spain, **293** G3
Almanzor, *mountain peak*, Spain, **292** E2
Almas, Brazil, **456** D3
Almaty, Kazakhstan, **212** C4
Almaty, *province*, Kazakhstan, **212** C3
Almazán, Spain, **293** F2
Almeirim, Brazil, **452** C3
Almeirim, Portugal, **292** C3
Almenar de Soria, Spain, **293** F2
Almenara, Brazil, **457** F4
Almendra, Embalse de, *reservoir*, Spain, **292** D2
Almendralejo, Spain, **292** D3
Almería, Golfo de, *gulf*, Spain, **293** F4
Almería, Spain, **293** F4
Almese, Italy, **294** A3
Al'met'yevsk, Russian Federation, **222** E2
Älmhult, Sweden, **286** G4
Almina, Punta, *point*, Morocco, **292** E5
Almodôvar, Portugal, **292** C4
Almodóvar del Campo, Spain, **292** E3
Almont, U.S.A., **421** M4
Almonte, Canada, **416** C7
Almora, India, **218** D3
Almoustarat, Mali, **364** E1
Älmsta, Sweden, **287** J3
Almunge, Sweden, **287** J3
Almyros, Greece, **297** D6
Alnön, *island*, Sweden, **287** H1
Alnwick, England, U.K., **307** G2
Alofi, *island*, Wallis and Futuna, **139** G6
Alofi, Niue, **132** M13
Alofi Bay, Niue, **132** M13
Aloja, Latvia, **287** M4
Alolya, *river*, Russian Federation, **299** B4
Alongshan, China, **211** H2
Alonnisos, *island*, Voreioi Sporades, Greece, **297** D6
Alor, *island*, Indonesia, **198** D5
Alor, Kepulauan, *islands*, Indonesia, **198** D5
Alor, *mountain peak*, Spain, **292** D3
Alor Setar, Malaysia, **200** C1
Alot, India, **218** C5
Alotau, Papua New Guinea, **140** C5
Alpalhão, Portugal, **292** D3
Alpena, U.S.A., **421** M3
Alpercatas, *river*, Brazil, **452** E5
Alpes, *mountain range*, France, **291** H4
Alpha, Australia, **135** K3
Alphonse Island, Seychelles, **372** C2
Alpine, Arizona, U.S.A., **423** J5
Alpine, Texas, U.S.A., **423** M6
Alps, *mountain range*, Austria/Italy/Switzerland, **280** E6
Alsace, *administrative region*, France, **291** H2
Alsace, *region*, France, **291** H2
Alsager, England, U.K., **304** E1
Alsasua, Spain, **293** F1
Alsfeld, Germany, **288** D3
Ålstad, Norway, **284** G3
Alsten, *island*, Norway, **284** F4
Alsterbo, Sweden, **286** G4
Alston, England, U.K., **306** F3
Alsunga, Latvia, **287** K4
Altınoluk, Turkey, **297** F6
Altınova, Turkey, **297** F6
Altıntaş, Turkey, **297** H6
Alta, Norway, **285** L2
Alta, *river*, Brazil, **459** F3
Alta Floresta, Brazil, **456** B2
Alta Gracia, Argentina, **458** D4
Altaelva, *river*, Norway, **285** L2
Altamah, *river*, U.S.A., **425** L4
Altamira, Brazil, **452** C4
Altamira, Chile, **458** C2
Altamira, Colombia, **450** C3
Altamira, Costa Rica, **428** D5
Altamont, U.S.A., **418** D5
Altamura, Isla de, *island*, Mexico, **430** C3
Altamura, Italy, **295** F5
Altan, Mongolia, **213** G2
Altanbulag, Mongolia, **213** H2
Altanteel, Mongolia, **213** G3
Altar, Mexico, **430** C2
Altata, Mexico, **430** D4
Altavista, U.S.A., **421** P7
Altay, China, **212** F3
Altay, Dzavhan, Mongolia, **213** H2
Altay, Govĭ-Altay, Mongolia, **213** H3
Altay, *mountain range*, Asia, **212** E2
Altay, Respublika, *republic*, Russian Federation, **212** E2
Altay, Russian Federation, **300** K5
Altayskiy, Russian Federation, **212** E2
Altayskiy Kray, *territory*, Russian Federation, **212** D1
Altea, Spain, **293** G3
Alteidet, Norway, **285** L1
Altenburg, Germany, **288** F3
Altentreptow, Germany, **288** F2
Alter do Chão, Portugal, **292** D3
Altevatnet, *lake*, Norway, **284** J2
Altiplano, *plateau*, Bolivia/Peru, **455** E4
Altkirch, France, **291** H3
Altnaharra, Scotland, U.K., **308** E2
Alto, U.S.A., **424** E4
Alto Araguaia, Brazil, **456** C4
Alto Chicapa, Angola, **368** C5
Alto de Pencoso, Sierra de, *mountain range*, Argentina, **458** C4
Alto Garças, Brazil, **456** C4
Alto Longá, Brazil, **453** E4
Alto Molócuè, Mozambique, **369** G6
Alto Parnaíba, Brazil, **452** E5
Alto Purús, *river*, Peru, **454** D3
Alto Río Senguer, Argentina, **460** C2
Alto Sucuriú, Brazil, **456** C5
Alto Vista, *mountain peak*, Aruba, **461** B3
Alton, England, U.K., **305** G3
Alton, Missouri, U.S.A., **420** H7
Alton, Utah, U.S.A., **422** G3
Altona, Canada, **414** F7
Altoona, U.S.A., **421** P5
Altos, Brazil, **453** E4
Altötting, Germany, **288** F4
Altraga, Mongolia, **213** H2
Altrincham, England, U.K., **306** F4

Altun Shan, *mountain range*, China, **212** E5
Alturas, U.S.A., **418** D6
Altus, U.S.A., **424** C2
Alu *see* Shortland, *island*, Solomon Islands, **141** A1
Alūksne, Latvia, **287** N4
Alūr, India, **216** D3
Alva, U.S.A., **420** D7
Älvängen, Sweden, **286** F4
Alvarães, Brazil, **451** F5
Alvdal, Norway, **286** E1
Älvdalen, Sweden, **286** G2
Alveley, England, U.K., **304** E2
Alvesta, Sweden, **286** G4
Ålvik, Norway, **286** C2
Alvin, U.S.A., **424** E5
Älvkarleby, Sweden, **287** H2
Älvsborg, *county*, Sweden, **286** F4
Älvsbyn, Sweden, **284** K4
Alwar, India, **218** D4
Alxa Zuoqi, China, **210** D5
Alyth, Scotland, U.K., **308** F4
Alytus, Lithuania, **287** M5
Alzamay, Russian Federation, **223** P1
Alzira, Spain, **293** G3
Am-Dam, Chad, **366** B2
Am Timan, Chad, **366** B2
Am-Zoer, Chad, **366** B2
Amada Gaza, Central African Republic, **368** C2
Amadeus, Lake, Australia, **134** G3
Amadjuak Lake, Canada, **411** M3
Amado, U.S.A., **423** H6
Amadora, Portugal, **292** C3
Amagasaki, Japan, **209** F4
Amager, *island*, Denmark, **286** F5
Amahai, Indonesia, **199** E3
Amakusa-shotō, *islands*, Japan, **208** E4
Åmål, Sweden, **286** F3
Amalfi, Colombia, **450** C2
Amalfi, Italy, **295** E5
Amaliada, Greece, **297** C7
Amamapare, Indonesia, **199** G4
Amambaí, Brazil, **459** F2
Amambaí, *river*, Brazil, **459** F2
Amambaí, Serra de, *mountain range*, Brazil/Paraguay, **459** F2
Amami-shotō, *islands*, Japan, **209** P8
Amamula, Democratic Republic of the Congo, **369** E3
Amanab, Papua New Guinea, **140** A3
Amangeldi, Kazakhstan, **222** H2
Amanqaraghay, Kazakhstan, **222** G2
Amantea, Italy, **295** F6
Amantogay, Kazakhstan, **222** H2
Amanu, *island*, French Polynesia, **137** G2
Amanzimtoti, South Africa, **371** F5
Amapá, Brazil, **452** C2
Amapá, *state*, Brazil, **452** C3
Amapari, *river*, Brazil, **452** C3
Amarante, Brazil, **453** E5
Amarante do Maranhão, Brazil, **452** D4
Amaranth, Canada, **414** E6
Amarapura, Myanmar, **205** C3
Amargosa Valley, U.S.A., **422** E3
Amarillo, U.S.A., **424** B2
Amarkantak, India, **219** E5
Amarnāth, India, **216** C2
Amaro, Monte, *mountain peak*, Italy, **295** E4
Amasya, Turkey, **224** E4
Amatán, Mexico, **431** G5
Amatlán de Cañas, Mexico, **430** D4
Amatrice, Italy, **294** D4
Amaturá, Brazil, **451** E5

Amazon Basin, South America, **446** F4
Amazon Fan, *underwater feature*, Atlantic Ocean, **477** D5
Amazonas, *river*, Brazil/Peru, **447** G4
Amazonas, *state*, Brazil, **451** F5
Āmba Ālagē, *mountain peak*, Ethiopia, **367** E2
Amba Farit, *mountain peak*, Ethiopia, **367** E2
Ambāla, India, **218** D3
Ambāla Sadar, India, **218** D3
Ambalakida, Madagascar, **372** B4
Ambalavao, Madagascar, **372** B5
Ambam, Cameroon, **368** B2
Ambanja, Madagascar, **372** B3
Ambarnyy, Russian Federation, **285** R4
Ambato, Ecuador, **450** B4
Ambato Boeny, Madagascar, **372** B4
Ambatofinandrahana, Madagascar, **372** B5
Ambatolampy, Madagascar, **372** B4
Ambatomainty, Madagascar, **372** B4
Ambatondrazaka, Madagascar, **372** B4
Ambazac, France, **290** E4
Amberg, Germany, **288** E4
Amberg, U.S.A., **421** K3
Ambérieu-en-Bugey, France, **291** G3
Amberley, New Zealand, **133** D6
Ambert, France, **291** F4
Ambidédi, Mali, **364** B2
Ambikāpur, India, **219** E5
Ambilobe, Madagascar, **372** B3
Amble, England, U.K., **307** G2
Ambleside, England, U.K., **306** F3
Ambo, Peru, **454** C3
Amboasary, Madagascar, **372** B6
Ambohidratrimo, Madagascar, **372** B4
Ambohimahasoa, Madagascar, **372** B5
Ambohipaky, Madagascar, **372** A4
Ambohitra, *mountain peak*, Madagascar, **372** B3
Amboise, France, **290** E3
Ambon, Indonesia, **199** E3
Amborompotsy, Madagascar, **372** B5
Ambositra, Madagascar, **372** B5
Ambovombe, Madagascar, **372** B6
Amboy, U.S.A., **422** F4
Ambre, Cap d' *see* Bobaomby, Tanjona, Madagascar, **372** B3
Ambre, Île d', *island*, Mauritius, **373** C1
Ambriz, Angola, **368** B4
Ambrym, *island*, Vanuatu, **141** A2
Ambuaki, Indonesia, **199** F3
Amchitka Island, Aleutian Islands, U.S.A., **408** E3
Amdo, China, **214** D2
Ameca, Mexico, **430** D4
Ameland, *island*, Netherlands, **288** B2
American Falls, U.S.A., **418** H5
American Falls Reservoir, U.S.A., **418** H5
American Fork, U.S.A., **423** H1
American Samoa, *U.S. territory*, Pacific Ocean, **131** H3
Americana, Brazil, **459** H2
Americus, U.S.A., **425** K3
Amersfoort, Netherlands, **288** B2
Amersham, England, U.K., **305** G3
Amery Ice Shelf, Antarctica, **470** F5

Ames, U.S.A., **420** G4
Amesbury, England, U.K., **305** F3
Amfilochia, Greece, **297** C6
Amfissa, Greece, **297** D6
Amga, *river*, Russian Federation, **301** Q4
Amgalang Bulag, China, **211** G2
Amgu, Russian Federation, **209** G1
Amguid, Algeria, **361** H3
Amgun', *river*, Russian Federation, **211** L2
Amherst, Canada, **417** J7
Amiata, Monte, *mountain peak*, Italy, **294** C4
Amidon, U.S.A., **420** B2
Amiens, France, **290** F2
Amindivi Islands, India, **216** C4
Amino, Ethiopia, **369** H2
Aminuis, Namibia, **370** C3
Amirante Isles, Seychelles, **372** C2
Amisk Lake, Canada, **414** C4
Amite, U.S.A., **424** G4
Amla, India, **218** D5
Amlamé, Togo, **364** E3
Åmli, Norway, **286** D3
Amlia Island, Aleutian Islands, U.S.A., **408** F3
Amlwch, Wales, U.K., **306** D4
'Ammān, Jordan, **225** D4
Ammanford, Wales, U.K., **304** C3
Ammarnäs, Sweden, **284** H4
Ammassalik, Greenland, **411** R3
Ammersee, *lake*, Germany, **288** E4
Ammochostos (Famagusta), Cyprus, **225** B2
Ammochostos Bay, Cyprus, **225** C2
Amnat Charoen, Thailand, **203** E3
Amok, Vanuatu, **141** A2
Amolar, Brazil, **456** B5
Amontada, Brazil, **453** F4
Amorgos, *island*, Kyklades, Greece, **297** E7
Amory, U.S.A., **425** H2
Amos, Canada, **416** B5
Åmot, Norway, **286** D3
Åmot, Sweden, **286** H2
Åmotfors, Sweden, **286** F3
Amourj, Mauritania, **364** C1
Ampahana, Madagascar, **372** C3
Ampanavoana, Madagascar, **372** C4
Ampanefena, Madagascar, **372** B3
Ampanihy, Madagascar, **372** A5
Amparafaravola, Madagascar, **372** B4
Amparai, Sri Lanka, **217** E5
Amparo, Brazil, **459** H2
Ampasimanjeva, Madagascar, **372** B5
Ampasimanolotra, Madagascar, **372** B4
Ampato, Nevado, *mountain peak*, Peru, **454** D4
Ampelonas, Greece, **297** D6
Amper, *river*, Germany, **288** E4
Ampisikinana, Madagascar, **372** B3
Amposta, Spain, **293** H2
Ampthill, England, U.K., **305** G2
Amqui, Canada, **416** H5
'Amrān, Yemen, **220** D5
Amrāvati, India, **218** D5
Amreli, India, **218** B5
Amritsar, India, **218** C3
Åmsele, Sweden, **284** J4
Amstein, Germany, **288** D4
Amsterdam, Île, *island*, French Southern and Antarctic Islands, **104** E12
Amsterdam, Netherlands, **288** B2
Amstetten, Austria, **289** G4
Amu Darya, *river*, Turkmenistan/Uzbekistan, **222**

G5
Amund Ringnes Island, Canada, **411** K2
Amundsen, Mount, *mountain peak*, Antarctica, **470** G5
Amundsen Gulf, Canada, **410** G2
Amundsen-Scott, *U.S. research station*, Antarctica, **470** D5
Amundsen Sea, Antarctica, **470** A6
Amuntai, Indonesia, **201** F3
Amur, *river*, Russian Federation, **195** Q5
Amurang, Teluk, *bay*, Indonesia, **198** C2
Amurrio, Spain, **293** F1
Amursk, Russian Federation, **211** M2
Amurskaya Oblast', *province*, Russian Federation, **211** K1
Amurzet, Russian Federation, **211** K3
Amvrakikos Kolpos, *bay*, Greece, **297** C6
Amyntaio, Greece, **297** C5
Amyot, Canada, **421** L1
Amyūn, Lebanon, **225** C2
An Hai, Vietnam, **203** F3
An Nabatīyah at Taḥtā, Lebanon, **225** C3
An Nabk, Syria, **225** D3
An Nafūd, *desert*, Saudi Arabia, **363** H3
An Nahūd, Sudan, **366** C2
An Najaf, Iraq, **363** H2
An Nakhi, Egypt, **225** B5
An Nāqūrah, Lebanon, **225** C3
An Nāṣirīyah, Iraq, **363** J2
An Nawfalīyah, Libya, **362** B2
An Nil Al Abyaḍ, *state*, Sudan, **366** D2
An Nimāṣ, Saudi Arabia, **363** H5
An Nu'ayrīyah, Saudi Arabia, **220** E3
An Teallach, *mountain peak*, Scotland, U.K., **308** D3
Anaco, Venezuela, **451** F2
Anaconda, U.S.A., **418** H3
Anacortes, U.S.A., **418** C2
Anadarko, U.S.A., **424** C2
Anadyr', Russian Federation, **301** U3
Anadyrskiy Zaliv, *bay*, Russian Federation, **410** A3
Anadyrskoye Ploskogor'ye, *plateau*, Russian Federation, **301** T3
Anafi, *island*, Kyklades, Greece, **297** E7
Anagé, Brazil, **457** F4
'Ānah, Iraq, **363** H2
Anaheim, U.S.A., **422** D5
Anahola, Hawaiian Islands, U.S.A., **422** R9
Anajás, Brazil, **452** D3
Anajás, Ilha, *island*, Brazil, **452** C3
Anakāpalle, India, **217** E2
Analalava, Madagascar, **372** B3
Anamã, Brazil, **451** G5
Anambas, Kepulauan, *islands*, Indonesia, **200** D2
Anambra, *state*, Nigeria, **365** F3
Anamu, *river*, Brazil, **452** B3
Anamur, Turkey, **225** B1
Anamur Burnu, *cape*, Turkey, **363** F1
Anan, Japan, **208** F4
Ānand, India, **218** C5
Ānandpur, India, **219** F5
Ananea, Peru, **455** E4
Anantapur, India, **216** D3
Anantnag, India, **218** C2
Anan'yiv, Ukraine, **296** H2
Anapa, Russian Federation, **298** E4
Anápolis, Brazil, **456** D4
Anār, Iran, **221** G2
Anār Darreh, Afghanistan, **221** H2
Anārak, Iran, **220** F2

Anare Station, Macquarie Island, **134** R11
Anarjokka, *river*, Norway, **285** M2
Ånäset, Sweden, **284** K4
Anatahan, *island*, Northern Mariana Islands, **138** C3
Anatolia, *region*, Turkey, **194** E6
Anatoliki Makedonia Kai Thraki, *administrative region*, Greece, **297** E5
Anatom, *island*, Vanuatu, **141** A3
Anatone, U.S.A., **418** F3
Añatuya, Argentina, **458** D3
Anauá, *river*, Brazil, **451** G4
Anbianbu, China, **210** E5
Anbo, China, **211** H5
Ancasti, Sierra de, *mountain range*, Argentina, **458** D3
Anchau, Nigeria, **365** F2
Anchopaya, Bolivia, **455** E4
Anchorage, U.S.A., **410** E3
Anchorstock Point, Tristan da Cunha, **373** C2
Ancón, Peru, **454** C3
Ancón de Sardinas, Bahía de, *bay*, Ecuador, **450** B4
Ancona, Italy, **294** D4
Ancroft, England, U.K., **306** G2
Ancuabe, Mozambique, **369** G5
Ancud, Chile, **460** C1
Ancud, Golfo de, *gulf*, Chile, **460** C2
Anda, China, **211** J3
Andacollo, Chile, **458** B4
Andahuaylas, Peru, **454** D3
Andalgalá, Argentina, **458** C3
Andalucia, *autonomous community*, Spain, **293** F4
Andalusia, U.S.A., **425** J4
Andaman and Nicobar Islands, India, Indian Ocean, **217** G3
Andaman and Nicobar Islands, *union territory*, India, Indian Ocean, **217** H4
Andaman Basin, *underwater feature*, Indian Ocean, **476** F4
Andaman Islands, Andaman and Nicobar Islands, India, **217** H4
Andaman Sea, Indian Ocean, **202** B3
Andamarca, Bolivia, **455** E5
Andance, France, **291** G4
Andapa, Madagascar, **372** B3
Andaraí, Brazil, **457** F3
Andenes, Norway, **284** H2
Andéramboukane, Mali, **365** E1
Andermatt, Switzerland, **291** J3
Andernach, Germany, **288** C3
Anderson, Indiana, U.S.A., **421** L5
Anderson, *river*, Canada, **410** G3
Anderson, South Carolina, U.S.A., **425** L2
Andes, Colombia, **450** C3
Andes, *mountain range*, South America, **447** E4
Andfjorden, *bay*, Norway, **284** H2
Andhra Pradesh, *state*, India, **216** D2
Andijon, Uzbekistan, **212** B4
Andilamena, Madagascar, **372** B4
Andilanatoby, Madagascar, **372** B4
Andīmeshk, Iran, **220** E2
Andkhvoy, Afghanistan, **218** A1
Andoas, Peru, **450** C5
Andoga, *river*, Russian Federation, **299** F3
Andomskiy Pogost, Russian Federation, **299** F2
Andong, South Korea, **208** E3
Andoom, Australia, **140** A6
Andorra, *country*, Europe, **282** D7
Andorra la Vella, Andorra, **293** H1

Apucarana, Brazil, **459** G2
Apucarana, Serra da, *mountain range*, Brazil, **459** G2
Apurímac, *river*, Peru, **454** D4
Aqaba, Gulf of, Red Sea, **225** C5
Aqadyr, Kazakhstan, **223** J3
Aqal, China, **212** C4
Aqbalyq, Kazakhstan, **212** C3
Āqchah, Afghanistan, **218** A1
'Aqdā, Iran, **220** F2
Aqitag, *mountain peak*, China, **213** F4
Aqköl, Kazakhstan, **223** J4
Aqmola, *province*, Kazakhstan, **212** A2
Aqmola see Astana, Kazakhstan, **223** J2
Aqqikkol Hu, *lake*, China, **212** F5
Aqshataū, Kazakhstan, **212** B3
Aqsorang Biigi, *mountain peak*, Kazakhstan, **212** B2
Aqsū, Aqmola, Kazakhstan, **223** J2
Aqsu, Kazakhstan, **212** C1
Aqsū, Pavlodar, Kazakhstan, **223** K2
Aqsū-Ayuly, Kazakhstan, **212** B2
Aqsūat, Central Shyghys Qazaqstan, Kazakhstan, **212** D3
Aqsūat, E. Shyghys Qazaqstan, Kazakhstan, **212** D2
Aqtasty, Kazakhstan, **223** K2
Aqtaū, E. Kazakhstan, **223** J2
Aqtaū (Aktau), W. Kazakhstan, **222** E4
Aqtöbe (Aktyubinsk), Kazakhstan, **222** F2
Aqtoghay, Pavlodar, Kazakhstan, **223** K2
Aqtoghay, Qaraghandy, Kazakhstan, **212** B2
Aqtoghay, Shyghys Qazaqstan, Kazakhstan, **212** C3
Aquidabán, *river*, Paraguay, **459** F2
Aquidauana, Brazil, **456** B5
Aquidauana, *river*, Brazil, **456** B5
Aquila, Mexico, **430** E5
Aquiles Serdán, Mexico, **430** D2
Aquiraz, Brazil, **453** F4
Aquitaine, *administrative region*, France, **290** D4
Aqyrap, Kazakhstan, **222** F2
Aqzhar, Kazakhstan, **223** L3
Ar-Asgat, Mongolia, **210** D2
Ar Horqin Qi, China, **211** H4
Ar Radīsīya Baḩrī, Egypt, **363** F4
Ar Rahad, Sudan, **366** D2
Ar Rāk, Suquţrá (Socotra), Yemen, **373** B2
Ar Ramādī, Iraq, **363** H2
Ar Ramlah, Jordan, **225** D5
Ar Ramthā, Jordan, **225** D3
Ar Rank, Sudan, **366** D2
Ar Raqqa, *district*, Syria, **225** E2
Ar Raqqah, Syria, **363** G1
Ar Rass, Saudi Arabia, **363** H3
Ar Rastan, Syria, **225** D2
Ar Rawḑatayn, Kuwait, **363** J3
Ar Riyāḑ (Riyadh), Saudi Arabia, **220** E4
Ar Ru'āt, Sudan, **366** D2
Ar Rub' al Khālī, *desert*, Saudi Arabia, **220** E5
Ar Rubay'īyah, Saudi Arabia, **363** H3
Ar Ruşayfah, Jordan, **225** D4
Ar Ruşayriş, Sudan, **366** D2
Ar Ruţbah, Iraq, **363** H2
Ar Ruwaydah, Saudi Arabia, **220** E4
Ar Ruways, Oman, **220** F4
'Arab, Baḩr al, *river*, Sudan, **366** C2
Arab, U.S.A., **425** J2
'Arab al Mulk, Syria, **225** C2
Arabelo, Venezuela, **451** F3

Arabian Basin, *underwater feature*, Indian Ocean, **476** D3
Arabian Peninsula, Asia, **194** F7
Arabian Sea, Indian Ocean, **194** H8
Arabopó, Venezuela, **451** G3
Araçá, *river*, Brazil, **451** F4
Aracaju, Brazil, **457** G3
Aracati, Brazil, **453** G4
Aracatu, Brazil, **457** F4
Araçatuba, Brazil, **456** C5
Aracena, Spain, **292** D4
Aracena, Sierra de, *mountain peak*, Spain, **292** D4
Aracena, Sierra de, *mountain range*, Spain, **292** D4
Aracruz, Brazil, **457** F5
'Arad, Israel, **225** C4
Arad, Romania, **296** C2
Arada, Chad, **366** B2
'Arādah, Oman, **220** F4
Aradan, Russian Federation, **213** G1
Arafura Sea, Australia/ Indonesia, **138** B5
Aragarças, Brazil, **456** C4
Aragats Lerr, *mountain peak*, Armenia, **222** C4
Aragón, *autonomous community*, Spain, **293** G2
Aragón, *river*, Spain, **293** G1
Aragua de Barcelona, Venezuela, **451** F2
Araguacema, Brazil, **456** D2
Araguaçu, Brazil, **456** D3
Araguaia, *river*, Brazil, **456** D2
Araguaína, Brazil, **452** D5
Araguao, Boca, *bay*, Venezuela, **451** G2
Araguari, Brazil, **456** D5
Araguari, *river*, Amapá, Brazil, **452** C3
Araguari, *river*, Minas Gerais, Brazil, **456** D5
Araguatins, Brazil, **452** D4
Araioses, Brazil, **453** E4
Arak, Algeria, **361** G3
Arāk, Iran, **220** E2
Arak, Syria, **225** E2
Arakan, *state*, Myanmar, **205** B4
Arakan Yoma, *mountain range*, Myanmar, **205** B3
Aral, China, **212** D4
Aral Sea, Kazakhstan/ Uzbekistan, **222** F3
Aralköl, Kazakhstan, **222** G2
Aralqi, China, **212** E5
Aral'sk, Kazakhstan, **222** G3
Aralsor Köli, *lake*, Kazakhstan, **222** D3
Aramberri, Mexico, **431** F3
Aramia, *river*, Papua New Guinea, **140** A4
Ārān, Iran, **220** F2
Aran Fawddwy, *mountain peak*, Wales, U.K., **304** D2
Aran Island, Ireland, **309** D2
Aran Islands, Ireland, **309** C4
Aranda de Duero, Spain, **293** F2
Aranđelovac, Yugoslavia, **296** C3
Aranjuez, Spain, **293** F2
Aranos, Namibia, **370** C3
Aranyaprathet, Thailand, **202** D3
Arao, Japan, **208** E4
Araouane, Mali, **361** F5
Arapahoe, U.S.A., **420** D5
Arapey Grande, *river*, Uruguay, **459** F4
Arapiraca, Brazil, **457** G2
Arapis, Akra, *point*, Greece, **297** E5
Arapkir, Turkey, **224** E5
Arapongas, Brazil, **459** G2
Araputanga, Brazil, **455** G4
'Ar'ar, Saudi Arabia, **363** H2
Araracuara, Colombia, **450** D4
Araranguá, Brazil, **459** H3
Araraquara, Brazil, **456** D5
Araras, Brazil, **452** B5

Araras, Serra das, *mountain range*, Brazil, **459** G2
Ararat, Australia, **135** J6
Ararat, Mount see Ağrı Dağı, *mountain peak*, Turkey, **224** F4
Arari, Brazil, **453** E4
Araria, India, **219** F4
Araripe, Chapada do, *mountain range*, Brazil, **453** F5
Araripina, Brazil, **453** F5
Aras, *river*, Armenia/ Azerbaijan/Iran, **363** J1
Arataca, Brazil, **457** F4
Arataua, *mountain peak*, New Zealand, **132** E4
Aratika, *island*, French Polynesia, **137** G2
Aratika, New Zealand, **133** C6
Arauca, Colombia, **451** D2
Arauca, *river*, Venezuela, **451** E2
Araucanía, *administrative region*, Chile, **458** B6
Arauco, Chile, **458** B5
Arauco, Golfo de, *gulf*, Chile, **458** B5
Arauquita, Colombia, **450** D2
Arāvalli Range, *mountain range*, India, **218** C4
Arawa, Papua New Guinea, **140** E2
Araxá, Brazil, **456** D5
Araxos, Akra, *cape*, Greece, **297** C6
Árba Minch', Ethiopia, **367** E3
Arbīl, Iraq, **363** H1
Arboga, Sweden, **286** G3
Arborfield, Canada, **414** C5
Arborg, Canada, **414** F6
Arbrå, Sweden, **286** H2
Arbroath, Scotland, U.K., **308** G4
Arcachon, Bassin d', *inlet*, France, **290** D4
Arcachon, France, **290** D4
Arcadia, Florida, U.S.A., **425** M6
Arcadia, Louisiana, U.S.A., **424** F3
Arcata, U.S.A., **418** B6
Arcelia, Mexico, **431** E5
Arch Cape, U.S.A., **418** C4
Archer City, U.S.A., **424** C3
Arcidosso, Italy, **294** C4
Arco, U.S.A., **418** H5
Arcos, Brazil, **456** E5
Arcos de la Frontera, Spain, **292** E4
Arcoverde, Brazil, **453** G5
Arctic Bay, Canada, **411** L2
Arctic Ocean, **471** C4
Arḑ aş Şawwān, *plain*, Jordan, **225** D4
Ardabīl, Iran, **222** D5
Ardakān, Iran, **221** F2
Ardal, Iran, **363** K2
Ārdalstangen, Norway, **286** C2
Ardara, Ireland, **309** D3
Ardatov, Russian Federation, **298** F1
Ardbeg, Canada, **421** N3
Ardee, Ireland, **309** F4
Ardennes, *region*, Belgium/ France, **288** E6
Ardentes, France, **290** E3
Ardgay, Scotland, U.K., **308** E3
Ardglass, Northern Ireland, U.K., **309** G3
Ardino, Bulgaria, **297** E5
Ardlussa, Scotland, U.K., **308** D4
Ardminish, Scotland, U.K., **308** D5
Ardmore, Ireland, **309** E6
Ardmore, U.S.A., **424** D2
Ardnamurchan, Point of, Scotland, U.K., **308** C4
Ardrishaig, Orkney, Scotland, U.K., **308** D4
Ardrossan, Scotland, U.K., **308** E5

Ards, *district*, Northern Ireland, U.K., **309** G3
Ards Peninsula, Northern Ireland, U.K., **309** G3
Ardud, Romania, **296** D2
Ardvasar, Scotland, U.K., **308** D3
Åre, Sweden, **284** F5
Areavaara, Sweden, **285** L3
Arebi, Democratic Republic of the Congo, **369** E2
Arecibo, Puerto Rico, **427** C2
Areia Branca, Brazil, **453** G4
Arena, Point, U.S.A., **422** A2
Arena, Punta, *point*, Mexico, **430** C4
Arenales, Cerro, *mountain peak*, Chile, **460** C3
Arenas, Punta de, *point*, Argentina, **460** D4
Arenas de San Pedro, Spain, **292** E2
Arendal, Norway, **286** D3
Arendsee, Germany, **288** E2
Areopoli, Greece, **297** D7
Arequipa, Peru, **454** D4
Arere, Brazil, **452** C3
Arès, France, **290** D4
Arévalo, Spain, **292** E2
Arezzo, Italy, **294** C4
Arga, *river*, Spain, **293** G1
Argalasti, Greece, **297** D6
Argan, China, **212** F4
Argan, China, **223** M4
Argatay, Mongolia, **210** D3
Argens, *river*, France, **291** H5
Argenta, Italy, **294** C3
Argentan, France, **290** D2
Argentina, Argentina, **458** D3
Argentina, *country*, South America, **448** F7
Argentine Plain, *underwater feature*, Atlantic Ocean, **477** D8
Argentino, Lago, *lake*, Argentina, **460** C4
Argentino, *river*, Argentina, **460** C4
Argenton-sur-Creuse, France, **290** E3
Argeş, *river*, Romania, **296** E3
Arghandāb, *river*, Afghanistan, **218** A2
Arghastān, *river*, Afghanistan, **218** A3
Argolikos Kolpos, *bay*, Greece, **297** D7
Argos, Greece, **297** D7
Argos Orestiko, Greece, **297** C5
Argostoli, Ionioi Nisoi, Greece, **297** C6
Argueil, France, **305** J5
Arguello, Point, U.S.A., **422** C4
Argun', *river*, Russian Federation, **211** H1
Argungu, Nigeria, **365** E2
Argus, Dome, *ice dome*, Antarctica, **470** E5
Arguut, Mongolia, **213** J3
Argyle, Canada, **416** J8
Argyle, Lake, Australia, **134** F2
Argyll, *region*, Scotland, U.K., **308** D4
Argyll and Bute, *local authority*, Scotland, U.K., **308** D4
Arhangay, *province*, Mongolia, **213** J3
Århus, Denmark, **286** E4
Arhust, Mongolia, **210** D3
Ari Atoll, Maldives, **216** C5
Aria, *river*, Papua New Guinea, **140** C4
Ariamsvlei, Namibia, **370** C4
Ariano Irpino, Italy, **295** E5
Arias, Argentina, **458** D4
Ariaú, Brazil, **452** B4
Aribinda, Burkina Faso, **364** D2
Arica, Chile, **455** D5
Arica, Colombia, **450** D5
Arica, Peru, **450** C4

Arichat, Canada, **417** L7
Arid, Cape, Australia, **134** E5
Aride, *island*, Seychelles, **373** A2
Ariguani, *river*, Colombia, **450** C1
Arīḩā (Jericho), West Bank, **225** C4
Ariki, New Zealand, **133** D5
Arilje, Yugoslavia, **296** C4
Arima, Trinidad, Trinidad and Tobago, **461** C4
Arimo, U.S.A., **419** H5
Arinos, Brazil, **456** D4
Arinos, *river*, Brazil, **456** B3
Ario de Rosales, Mexico, **430** E5
Aripuanã, Brazil, **455** G2
Aripuanã, *river*, Brazil, **455** G2
Ariquemes, Brazil, **455** F2
Arisaig, Scotland, U.K., **308** D4
Arisaig, Sound of, Scotland, U.K., **308** D4
Aristazabal Island, Canada, **412** D5
Aritzo, Sardegna, Italy, **295** B6
Ariza, Spain, **293** F2
Arizaro, Salar de, *salt-pan*, Argentina, **458** C2
Arizona, *state*, U.S.A., **423** H4
Årjäng, Sweden, **286** F3
Arjeplog, Sweden, **284** H3
Arjona, Colombia, **450** C1
Arkadelphia, U.S.A., **424** F2
Arkanū, Jabal, *mountain peak*, Libya, **362** D4
Arkansas, *river*, U.S.A., **407** M5
Arkansas, *state*, U.S.A., **424** F2
Arkansas City, U.S.A., **420** E7
Arkatag Shan, *mountain range*, China, **212** F5
Arkhangel'sk, Russian Federation, **300** F3
Arkhangel'skaya Oblast', *province*, Russian Federation, **299** G2
Arkhangel'skoye, Russian Federation, **222** F2
Arkhara, Russian Federation, **211** K2
Arkhipovka, Russian Federation, **299** C5
Arklow, Ireland, **309** F5
Arkona, Kap, *cape*, Germany, **288** F1
Arkonam, India, **216** D3
Arkösund, Sweden, **287** H3
Arlan, *mountain peak*, Turkmenistan, **222** E5
Arlee, U.S.A., **418** G3
Arles, France, **291** G5
Arli, Burkina Faso, **364** E2
Arlington, Colorado, U.S.A., **423** M2
Arlington, Georgia, U.S.A., **425** K4
Arlington, Texas, U.S.A., **424** D3
Arlington, Virginia, U.S.A., **426** B5
Arlit, Niger, **361** H5
Arlon, Belgium, **288** B4
Armagh, *district*, Northern Ireland, U.K., **309** F3
Armagh, Northern Ireland, U.K., **309** F3
Armagnac, *region*, France, **290** E5
Armant, Egypt, **363** F3
Armathia, *island*, Greece, **297** F8
Armavir, Russian Federation, **222** C3
Armenia, Colombia, **450** C3
Armenia, *country*, Asia, **196** F5
Armero, Colombia, **450** C3
Armidale, Australia, **135** L5
Armour, U.S.A., **420** D4
Armoy, Northern Ireland, U.K., **309** F2
Armstrong, British Columbia, Canada, **413** K6
Armstrong, Ontario, Canada, **415** K6
Armstrong, U.S.A., **424** D6

D7
Athens, Tennessee, U.S.A., **425** K2
Athens, Texas, U.S.A., **424** E3
Atherstone, England, U.K., **305** F2
Atherton, Australia, **135** K2
Athi River, Kenya, **369** G3
Athina (Athens), Greece, **297** D7
Athleague, Ireland, **309** D4
Athlone, Ireland, **309** E4
Athna, Cyprus, **225** B2
Athol, U.S.A., **426** D3
Athos, *mountain peak*, Greece, **297** E5
Athy, Ireland, **309** F5
Ati, Chad, **366** A2
Atico, Peru, **454** D4
Atiedo, Sudan, **366** C3
Atienza, Spain, **293** F2
Atikameg, Canada, **413** M4
Atikokan, Canada, **420** H1
Atiu, *island*, Cook Islands, **137** F3
Atka Island, Aleutian Islands, U.S.A., **408** F3
Atkarsk, Russian Federation, **222** C2
Atkinson, U.S.A., **420** D4
Atkri, Indonesia, **199** E3
Atlanta, Georgia, U.S.A., **425** K3
Atlanta, Idaho, U.S.A., **418** G5
Atlanta, Michigan, U.S.A., **421** L3
Atlanta, Texas, U.S.A., **424** E3
Atlantic, Iowa, U.S.A., **420** F5
Atlantic, North Carolina, U.S.A., **426** B7
Atlantic City, U.S.A., **426** C5
Atlantic-Indian Ridge, *underwater feature*, Atlantic Ocean, **477** H9
Atlantic Ocean, **477** E8
Atlantis, South Africa, **370** C5
Atlantis Fracture Zone, *tectonic feature*, Atlantic Ocean, **477** D3
Atlas Saharien, *mountain range*, Algeria, **356** F3
Atlin, Canada, **412** C2
Atlin Lake, Canada, **412** C2
Atlixco, Mexico, **431** F5
Atmore, Canada, **413** N4
Atmore, U.S.A., **425** J4
Atnbrua, Norway, **286** E2
Atocha, Bolivia, **455** E5
Atoka, New Mexico, U.S.A., **423** L5
Atoka, Oklahoma, U.S.A., **424** D2
Atori, Solomon Islands, **141** A1
Atouat, Phu, *mountain peak*, Laos/Vietnam, **203** E2
Atoyac de Alvarez, Mexico, **431** E5
Atrak, *river*, Iran/Turkmenistan, **222** F5
Atran, *river*, Sweden, **286** F4
Ätran, Sweden, **286** F4
Atrato, *river*, Colombia, **450** C2
Atsugi, Japan, **209** G4
Attapu, Laos, **203** E3
Attavyros, *mountain peak*, Dodekanisos, Greece, **297** F7
Attawapiskat, Canada, **415** N5
Attawapiskat, *river*, Canada, **415** L5
Attempt Hill, *mountain peak*, New Zealand, **133** D5
Attica, U.S.A., **421** K5
Attiki, *administrative region*, Greece, **297** D7
Attleborough, England, U.K., **305** J2
Attock, Pakistan, **218** C2
Attu Island, Aleutian Islands, U.S.A., **408** A2
Attür, India, **216** D4
Atuel, *river*, Argentina, **458** C5
Åtvidaberg, Sweden, **286** H3
Atyraū, Kazakhstan, **222** E3

Auas Mountains, Namibia, **370** C3
Aubagne, France, **291** G5
Aubenas, France, **291** G4
Aubergenville, France, **290** E2
Aubigney-sur-Nère, France, **290** F3
Aubrac, Monts d', *mountain range*, France, **291** F4
Auburn, Alabama, U.S.A., **425** K3
Auburn, California, U.S.A., **422** C2
Auburn, Illinois, U.S.A., **420** J6
Auburn, Maine, U.S.A., **426** E2
Auburn, New York, U.S.A., **426** B3
Auburn, Washington, U.S.A., **418** C3
Aubusson, France, **290** F4
Auca Mahuida, Sierra de, *mountain peak*, Argentina, **458** C5
Auce, Latvia, **287** L4
Auch, France, **290** E5
Auchenbreck, Scotland, U.K., **308** D5
Auchterarder, Scotland, U.K., **308** F4
Auchtermuchty, Scotland, U.K., **308** F4
Auckland, New Zealand, **132** E3
Auckland Island, Auckland Islands, New Zealand, **132** J10
Auckland Islands, New Zealand, **132** J10
Auden, Canada, **415** K6
Audlem, England, U.K., **304** E2
Audo Range, *mountain range*, Ethiopia, **367** F3
Audresselles, France, **305** J4
Audruicq, France, **290** F1
Audubon, U.S.A., **420** F5
Aue, Germany, **288** F3
Auerbach, Germany, **288** F3
Auffay, France, **305** J5
Augher, Northern Ireland, U.K., **309** E3
Aughnacloy, Northern Ireland, U.K., **309** E3
Aughrim, Ireland, **309** F5
Augsburg, Germany, **288** E4
Augusta, Australia, **134** D5
Augusta, Georgia, U.S.A., **425** L3
Augusta, Golfo di, *gulf*, Sicilia, Italy, **295** E7
Augusta, Maine, U.S.A., **426** F2
Augusta, Sicilia, Italy, **295** E7
Augusta, Wisconsin, U.S.A., **420** H3
Augusta Victoria, Chile, **458** C2
Augustin Codazzi, Colombia, **450** D1
Augustów, Poland, **289** L2
Augustus, Mount, *mountain peak*, Australia, **134** D3
Auki, Solomon Islands, **141** A1
Aukštadvaris, Lithuania, **287** M5
Auktsjaur, Sweden, **284** J4
Auld, Lake, Australia, **134** E3
Auletta, Italy, **295** E5
Aulnay, France, **290** D3
Ault, France, **290** E1
Aultbea, Scotland, U.K., **308** D3
Aumale, France, **305** J5
Auna, Nigeria, **365** E2
Auneau, France, **290** E2
Auneuil, France, **305** K5
Auponhia, Indonesia, **198** D3
Aura, Finland, **287** L2
Auraiya, India, **218** D4
Aurangābād, Bihār, India, **219** F4
Aurangābād, Mahārāshtra, India, **216** C2
Aurdal, Norway, **286** D2
Aure, Norway, **284** D5
Aurillac, France, **290** F4
Aurlandsvangen, Norway, **286** C2
Aurora, Colorado, U.S.A., **423**

L2
Aurora, Illinois, U.S.A., **421** J5
Aurora, Missouri, U.S.A., **420** G7
Aurora, Suriname, **452** B2
Aus, Namibia, **370** C4
Ausert, Western Sahara, **360** D4
Auskerry, *island*, Orkney, Scotland, U.K., **308** G1
Aust-Agder, *county*, Norway, **286** C3
Austin, Lake, Australia, **134** D4
Austin, Minnesota, U.S.A., **420** G4
Austin, Nevada, U.S.A., **422** E2
Austin, Texas, U.S.A., **424** D4
Australes, Îles (Îles Tubuai), *islands*, French Polynesia, **137** F3
Australia, *country*, Oceania, **130** B4
Australian Capital Territory, *territory*, Australia, **135** K6
Austria, *country*, Europe, **282** F6
Austvågøy, *island*, Norway, **284** F2
Autazes, Brazil, **451** G5
Authie, *river*, France, **290** E1
Authier, Canada, **416** B5
Autlán de Navarro, Mexico, **430** D5
Autun, France, **291** G3
Auvergne, *administrative region*, France, **291** F4
Auxerre, France, **291** F3
Auxi-le-Château, France, **305** K4
Auxon, France, **291** F2
Auxonne, France, **291** G3
Auyantepui, *mountain peak*, Venezuela, **451** F3
Auzances, France, **290** F3
Auzangate, Nevado, *mountain peak*, Peru, **454** D3
Ava, U.S.A., **420** G7
Avallon, France, **291** F3
Avalon Peninsula, Canada, **417** Q6
Avalos, *river*, Argentina, **459** E3
Avanos, Turkey, **363** F1
Avaré, Brazil, **459** H2
Avarua, Cook Islands, **137** E3
Avatele, Niue, **132** M13
Avaviken, Sweden, **284** J4
Avdzaga, Mongolia, **213** J3
Aveiro, Brazil, **452** B4
Aveiro, *district*, Portugal, **292** C2
Aveiro, Portugal, **292** C2
Avellaneda, Argentina, **459** E5
Avellino, Italy, **295** E5
Avenal, U.S.A., **422** C3
Avery, U.S.A., **418** G3
Aves Ridge, *underwater feature*, Caribbean Sea, **479** P3
Avesnes-le-Comte, France, **305** K4
Avesta, Sweden, **286** H2
Aveyron, *river*, France, **290** E4
Avezzano, Italy, **295** D4
Aviá Terai, Argentina, **458** E3
Aviemore, Scotland, U.K., **308** F3
Avigliano, Italy, **295** E5
Avignon, France, **291** G5
Ávila, Spain, **292** E2
Avilés, Spain, **292** E1
Avinurme, Estonia, **287** N3
Avión, *mountain peak*, Spain, **292** C1
Avlida, Greece, **297** D6
Avoca, Ireland, **309** F5
Avoca, U.S.A., **420** F5
Avola, Canada, **413** K6
Àvola, Sicilia, Italy, **295** E7
Avon, Montana, U.S.A., **418** H3
Avon, North Carolina, U.S.A., **426** C7
Avon, *river*, England, U.K., **305** F3

Avon, *river*, Midlands, England, U.K., **305** F2
Avon, South Dakota, U.S.A., **420** D4
Avon Park, U.S.A., **425** M6
Avondale, U.S.A., **422** G5
Avradsberg, Sweden, **286** F2
Avraga, Mongolia, **210** E3
Avranches, France, **290** D2
Avrig, Romania, **296** E3
Avu Avu, Solomon Islands, **141** A1
Awakino, New Zealand, **132** E4
Awanui, New Zealand, **132** D2
Awarē, Ethiopia, **367** F3
Awarua, New Zealand, **132** D2
Āwasa, Ethiopia, **367** E3
Awat, China, **212** D4
Awatere, *river*, New Zealand, **133** D5
Awbārī, Libya, **362** B3
Awbārī, Şaḥrā', *desert*, Libya, **362** B3
Awdheegle, Somalia, **367** F4
Awe, Loch, *lake*, Scotland, U.K., **308** D4
Awin, U.S.A., **425** J4
Awjilah, Libya, **362** D3
Awka, Nigeria, **365** F3
Axel Heiberg Island, Canada, **411** K1
Axim, Ghana, **364** D4
Aximin, Brazil, **451** G5
Axixá, Brazil, **453** E4
Axmar Bruk, Sweden, **287** H2
Axminster, England, U.K., **304** E4
Ayacucho, Argentina, **459** E5
Ayacucho, Peru, **454** C3
Ayagüz, Kazakhstan, **212** D3
Ayagüz, *river*, Kazakhstan, **212** C3
Ayakkuduk, Uzbekistan, **222** H4
Ayakkum Hu, *lake*, China, **212** F5
Ayamonte, Spain, **292** D4
Ayan, Russian Federation, **301** Q4
Ayangba, Nigeria, **365** F3
Ayapata, Peru, **455** D3
Ayapel, Colombia, **450** C2
Ayaviri, Peru, **454** D4
Aydar Kŭli, *lake*, Uzbekistan, **222** H4
Aydin, *province*, Turkey, **297** F7
Aydın, Turkey, **297** F7
Aydın Dağları, *mountain range*, Turkey, **297** F6
Aydıncık, Turkey, **225** B1
Aydingkol Hu, *lake*, China, **212** F4
Āyelu Terara, *mountain peak*, Ethiopia, **367** F2
Ayer Chawan, Pulau, *island*, Singapore, **200** J7
Ayer Hitam, Malaysia, **200** C2
Ayer Merbau, Pulau, *island*, Singapore, **200** J7
Ayerbe, Spain, **293** G1
Ayers Rock see Uluru, *mountain peak*, Australia, **128** C4
Ayios Seryios, Cyprus, **225** B2
Āykel, Ethiopia, **367** E2
Aylesbury, England, U.K., **305** G3
Aylesbury, New Zealand, **133** D6
Ayllón, Spain, **293** F2
Aylmer Lake, Canada, **410** J3
Aylsham, England, U.K., **305** J2
'Ayn ad Darāhim, Tunisia, **295** B7
'Ayn 'Īsā, Syria, **225** E1
'Ayn Sukhnah, Egypt, **225** B5
Ayna, Peru, **454** D3
Ayni, Tajikistan, **223** H5
'Aynūnah, Saudi Arabia, **225** C5
Ayod, Sudan, **366** D3
Ayon, Ostrov, *island*, Russian Federation, **301** T2
Ayora, Spain, **293** G3

Ayorou, Niger, **364** E2
'Ayoûn el 'Atroûs, Mauritania, **364** C1
Ayr, Australia, **135** K2
Ayr, *river*, Scotland, U.K., **308** E5
Ayr, Scotland, U.K., **308** E5
Ayr, U.S.A., **420** D5
Ayre, Point of, Isle of Man, **306** D3
Aysary, Kazakhstan, **223** J2
Ayteke Bi, Kazakhstan, **222** G3
Aytos, Bulgaria, **296** F4
Ayuy, Ecuador, **450** C5
Ayvacık, Turkey, **297** F6
Ayvadzh, Tajikistan, **218** B1
Ayvalık, Turkey, **297** F6
Az Zabadānī, Syria, **225** D3
Az̧ Z̧afīr, Saudi Arabia, **363** H5
Az̧ Z̧ahrān (Dhahran), Saudi Arabia, **220** E3
Az Zalaf, Syria, **225** D3
Az Zaqāzīq, Egypt, **225** A4
Az Zarqā', Jordan, **225** D3
Az Zāwiyah, Libya, **362** B2
Az Zaydiyah, Yemen, **220** D5
Az Zilfī, Saudi Arabia, **363** H3
Az Zintān, Libya, **362** B2
Az Zubayr, Iraq, **363** J2
Az Zuhrah, Yemen, **220** D5
Azacualpa, Honduras, **428** D4
Azaila, Spain, **293** G2
Azalea, U.S.A., **418** C5
Āzamgarh, India, **219** E4
Azapa, Chile, **455** D5
Āzarān, Iran, **363** J1
Azare, Nigeria, **365** G2
Azauri, Brazil, **452** B3
A'zāz, Syria, **225** D1
Azazga, Algeria, **293** K4
Azeffâl, *mountain range*, Mauritania/Western Sahara, **360** C4
Azeffoun, Algeria, **293** K4
Azemmour, Morocco, **360** E2
Azerbaijan, *country*, Asia, **196** F6
Āzezo, Ethiopia, **367** E2
Azogues, Ecuador, **450** B5
Azores, *islands*, Portugal, Atlantic Ocean, **360** M6
Azores-Biscay Rise, *underwater feature*, Atlantic Ocean, **477** F3
Azov, Sea of, Russian Federation/Ukraine, **298** E3
Azraq, Al Baḥr al (Blue Nile), *river*, Ethiopia, **366** E2
Azraq, Al Baḥr al (Blue Nile), *river*, Sudan, **220** B6
Azraq ash Shīshān, Jordan, **225** D4
Azrou, Morocco, **361** E2
Azua, Dominican Republic, **429** H3
Azuaga, Spain, **292** E3
Azuero, Península de, Panama, **429** E6
Azul, Argentina, **459** E5
Azul, Cerro, *mountain peak*, Argentina, **460** C1
Azul, Cordillera, *mountain range*, Peru, **454** C2
Azurduy, Bolivia, **455** F5
Azzory, Belarus, **289** M2
Azzel Matti, Sebkha, *salt-pan*, Algeria, **361** G3

B

Ba, Fiji, **141** A4
Ba, *river*, Vietnam, **203** F3
Bá Thước, Vietnam, **215** H5
Baamonde, Spain, **292** D1
Baardheere, Somalia, **369** H2
Baba Burnu, *point*, Turkey, **297** E6
Bababé, Mauritania, **364** B1

Broad Haven, *bay*, Ireland, **309** C3
Broad Haven, Wales, U.K., **304** B3
Broad Law, *mountain peak*, Scotland, U.K., **308** F5
Broadford, Ireland, **309** D5
Broadford, Scotland, U.K., **308** D3
Broadmeadows, New Zealand, **133** E5
Broadstairs, England, U.K., **305** J3
Broadus, U.S.A., **419** M4
Broadview, Canada, **414** C6
Broadview, U.S.A., **419** K3
Broadwater, U.S.A., **420** B5
Broadway, England, U.K., **305** F2
Broadwindsor, England, U.K., **304** E4
Brochet, Canada, **414** D3
Brochet, Lac, *lake*, Canada, **414** D2
Brockport, U.S.A., **426** B3
Brockton, U.S.A., **419** M2
Brockville, Canada, **416** D7
Brockway, U.S.A., **419** M3
Brockworth, England, U.K., **304** E3
Brod, Macedonia, **297** C5
Brodeur Peninsula, Canada, **411** L2
Brodick, Scotland, U.K., **308** D5
Brodnica, Poland, **289** J2
Brogan, U.S.A., **418** F4
Broken Arrow, U.S.A., **424** E1
Broken Bow, Nebraska, U.S.A., **419** Q6
Broken Bow, Oklahoma, U.S.A., **424** E2
Broken Bow Lake, U.S.A., **424** E2
Broken Hill, Australia, **135** J5
Broken Ridge, *underwater feature*, Indian Ocean, **476** F7
Brokopondo, Suriname, **452** B2
Bromley, England, U.K., **305** H3
Brömsebro, Sweden, **286** G4
Bromsgrove, England, U.K., **304** E2
Bromyard, England, U.K., **304** E2
Brønderslev, Denmark, **286** D4
Brong-Ahafo, *administrative region*, Ghana, **364** D3
Bronnitsy, Russian Federation, **299** G5
Bronte, Sicilia, Italy, **295** E7
Brooke, England, U.K., **305** J2
Brooke's Point, Philippines, **204** B4
Brookfield, U.S.A., **420** G6
Brookhaven, U.S.A., **424** G4
Brookings, Oregon, U.S.A., **418** B5
Brookings, South Dakota, U.S.A., **420** E3
Brooklyn, U.S.A., **420** G5
Brooklyn Park, U.S.A., **420** G3
Brookneal, U.S.A., **421** P7
Brooks, Canada, **413** P6
Brooks Range, *mountain range*, U.S.A., **410** C3
Brooksville, U.S.A., **425** L5
Broom, Loch, *inlet*, Scotland, U.K., **308** D3
Broome, Australia, **134** E2
Broome, Mount, *mountain peak*, Australia, **134** F2
Broons, France, **290** C2
Brora, *river*, Scotland, U.K., **308** E2
Brora, Scotland, U.K., **308** F2
Broseley, England, U.K., **304** E2
Brøstadbotn, Norway, **284** H2
Broșteni, Romania, **296** E2
Brothers, The, *see* Ikhwān, Al, Suquṭrá (Socotra), Yemen, **373** B2
Brothers, U.S.A., **418** D5
Brou, France, **290** E2

Brough, Cumbria, England, U.K., **306** F3
Brough, East Riding of Yorkshire, England, U.K., **307** H4
Brough Head, *point*, Orkney, Scotland, U.K., **308** F1
Broughshane, Northern Ireland, U.K., **309** F3
Broughton Island, Snares Islands, New Zealand, **132** H9
Brownfield, U.S.A., **423** M5
Brownhills, England, U.K., **305** F2
Browning, U.S.A., **418** H3
Brownsville, Tennessee, U.S.A., **425** H2
Brownsville, Texas, U.S.A., **424** D7
Brownwood, Lake, U.S.A., **424** C4
Brownwood, U.S.A., **424** C4
Brozas, Spain, **292** D3
Bru, Norway, **286** B2
Bruay-en-Artois, France, **290** F1
Bruce, U.S.A., **425** H2
Bruce Bay, New Zealand, **133** B6
Bruce Crossing, U.S.A., **421** J2
Bruck an der Großglocknerstraße, Austria, **288** F5
Bruck an der Mur, Austria, **289** G5
Brue, *river*, England, U.K., **304** E3
Brugge, Belgium, **288** A3
Bruit, Pulau, *island*, Malaysia, **201** E2
Brukkaros, *mountain peak*, Namibia, **370** C4
Brule, U.S.A., **420** H2
Brumado, Brazil, **457** F4
Brummen, Netherlands, **288** C2
Bruneau, *river*, U.S.A., **418** G5
Brunei, *country*, Asia, **197** N9
Brunei Bay, Brunei, **201** F1
Brunflo, Sweden, **284** G5
Brunkild, Canada, **414** F7
Brunswick, Georgia, U.S.A., **425** M4
Brunswick, Missouri, U.S.A., **420** G6
Brunswick, Península de, Chile, **460** C4
Bruntál, Czech Republic, **289** H4
Brus, Yugoslavia, **296** C4
Brus Laguna, Honduras, **428** D4
Brush, U.S.A., **423** M1
Brussels *see* Bruxelles, Belgium, **288** B3
Brusy, Poland, **289** H2
Bruton, England, U.K., **304** E3
Bruxelles (Brussels), Belgium, **288** B3
Bruz, France, **290** D2
Bryan, Ohio, U.S.A., **421** L5
Bryan, Texas, U.S.A., **424** D4
Bryan Coast, *region*, Antarctica, **470** B5
Bryansk, Russian Federation, **299** E6
Bryanskaya Oblast', *province*, Russian Federation, **299** D6
Bryant, U.S.A., **420** E3
Brymbo, Wales, U.K., **304** D1
Brynamman, Wales, U.K., **304** D3
Brynderwyn, New Zealand, **132** E3
Bryne, Norway, **286** B3
Brynmawr, Wales, U.K., **304** D3
Bryson City, U.S.A., **425** L2
Brza Palanka, Yugoslavia, **296** D3
Brzeg, Poland, **289** H3
Brzeg Dolny, Poland, **289** H3
Brzoza, Poland, **289** J2
Bu Craa, Western Sahara, **360** D3
Bua Yai, Thailand, **202** D3
Bu'aale, Somalia, **369** H2
Buala, Solomon Islands, **141** A1

Buatan, Indonesia, **200** C2
Bu'ayrāt al Ḥasūn, Libya, **362** C2
Buba, Guinea-Bissau, **364** A2
Bubi, *river*, Zimbabwe, **371** F3
Būbiyān, Jazīrat, *island*, Kuwait, **220** E3
Bubwith, England, U.K., **307** H4
Buca, Fiji, **141** A4
Buca, Turkey, **297** F6
Bucanera, Punta, *point*, Providencia, Colombia, **461** C1
Bucaramanga, Colombia, **450** D2
Bucas Grande Island, Philippines, **204** D4
Buccoo Bay, Tobago, Trinidad and Tobago, **461** B4
Buchanan, Liberia, **364** B3
Buchanan, Oregon, U.S.A., **418** E5
Buchanan, Virginia, U.S.A., **421** P7
Buchans, Canada, **417** N5
Buchardo, Argentina, **458** D5
Bucharest *see* Bucureşti, Romania, **296** E3
Buchloe, Germany, **288** E4
Buchy, France, **305** J5
Buckeye, U.S.A., **422** G5
Buckhannon, U.S.A., **421** N6
Buckhaven, Scotland, U.K., **308** F4
Buckhorn, U.S.A., **423** J5
Buckie, Scotland, U.K., **308** G3
Buckingham, England, U.K., **305** F3
Buckinghamshire, *unitary authority*, England, U.K., **305** F3
Buckles Bay, Macquarie Island, **134** R11
Buco Zau, Angola, **368** B3
Bučovice, Czech Republic, **289** H4
Buctouche, Canada, **417** J6
Bucureşti (Bucharest), Romania, **296** E3
Bucyrus, U.S.A., **421** M5
Bud, Norway, **286** C1
Budacu, *mountain peak*, Romania, **296** E2
Budalin, Myanmar, **205** B3
Budapest, Hungary, **289** J5
Búðardalur, Iceland, **284** X7
Būdārīno, Kazakhstan, **222** E2
Budaun, India, **218** D3
Bud Bud, Somalia, **367** G4
Budd Coast, *region*, Antarctica, **470** G7
Buddi, Ethiopia, **367** F3
Buddusò, Sardegna, Italy, **295** B5
Bude, England, U.K., **304** C4
Bude Bay, England, U.K., **304** C4
Büdelsdorf, Germany, **288** D1
Budeşti, Romania, **296** F3
Búðir, Iceland, **284** X7
Budjala, Democratic Republic of the Congo, **368** C2
Budleigh Salterton, England, U.K., **304** D4
Budogoshch', Russian Federation, **299** D3
Budrio, Italy, **294** C3
Budva, Yugoslavia, **296** B4
Buea, Cameroon, **368** A2
Buêch, *river*, France, **291** G4
Buen Pasto, Argentina, **460** D2
Buen Tiempo, Cabo, *cape*, Argentina, **460** D4
Buena Esperanza, Argentina, **458** D5
Buena Vista, U.S.A., **423** K2
Buenaventura, Bahía de, *bay*, Colombia, **450** B3
Buenaventura, Colombia, **450** C3
Buenaventura, Mexico, **430** D2
Buendia, Embalse de, *reservoir*, Spain, **293** F2

Bueno, *river*, Chile, **460** C1
Buenos Aires, Argentina, **459** E5
Buenos Aires, Lago, *lake*, Argentina, **460** C3
Buenos Aires, *province*, Argentina, **458** E5
Búfalo, Mexico, **430** D3
Buffalo, Canada, **413** P6
Buffalo, New York, U.S.A., **421** P4
Buffalo, Oklahoma, U.S.A., **420** D7
Buffalo, South Dakota, U.S.A., **420** B3
Buffalo, Texas, U.S.A., **424** D4
Buffalo, Wyoming, U.S.A., **419** L4
Buffalo Head Hills, Canada, **413** L2
Buffalo Lake, Alberta, Canada, **413** N5
Buffalo Lake, Northwest Territories, Canada, **413** M1
Buffalo Narrows, Canada, **413** Q4
Buford, U.S.A., **419** M6
Buftea, Romania, **296** E3
Bug, *river*, Belarus/Poland/Ukraine, **289** L2
Buga, Colombia, **450** C3
Buga, Mongolia, **213** G3
Bugana, Nigeria, **365** F3
Bugant, Mongolia, **210** D2
Bugasong, Philippines, **204** C4
Bugdayly, Turkmenistan, **222** E5
Bugel, Tanjong, *point*, Indonesia, **201** E4
Bugio, Ilhéu do, *island*, Madeira, Portugal, **373** C3
Bugøyfjord, Norway, **285** P2
Bugøynes, Norway, **285** P2
Bugsuk Island, Philippines, **204** B4
Bugt, China, **211** H2
Bugul'ma, Russian Federation, **222** E2
Buguruslan, Russian Federation, **222** E2
Buhera, Zimbabwe, **371** F2
Buhl, U.S.A., **418** G5
Buhuşi, Romania, **296** F2
Builth Wells, Wales, U.K., **304** D2
Buin, Papua New Guinea, **140** E2
Buitepos, Namibia, **370** C3
Bujanovac, Yugoslavia, **296** C4
Bujaraloz, Spain, **293** G2
Buji, China, **207** C3
Bujoru, Romania, **296** E4
Bujumbura, Burundi, **369** E3
Buk, Papua New Guinea, **140** A5
Buka Island, Papua New Guinea, **140** E8
Bukaan, Indonesia, **198** C2
Bukalo, Namibia, **370** D2
Bukama, Democratic Republic of the Congo, **369** E4
Būkan, Iran, **363** J1
Bukavu, Democratic Republic of the Congo, **369** E3
Bukhoro, Uzbekistan, **222** G5
Bukit Batok, Singapore, **200** J6
Bukit Panjang, Singapore, **200** J6
Bukit Timah, Singapore, **200** J6
Bukittinggi, Indonesia, **200** C3
Bukoba, Tanzania, **369** F3
Bukuru, Nigeria, **365** G3
Bula, Indonesia, **199** E3
Bula, Papua New Guinea, **140** A5
Bulag, Mongolia, **210** E2
Bulagansk, Russian Federation, **210** E1
Bulalacao (San Pedro), Philippines, **204** C3
Bulan, Philippines, **204** C3
Bulangu, Nigeria, **365** G2
Bulanık, Turkey, **363** H1

Būlāq, Egypt, **363** F3
Bulawa, Gunung, *mountain peak*, Indonesia, **198** C2
Bulawayo, Zimbabwe, **371** E3
Buldan, Turkey, **297** G6
Buldāna, India, **218** D5
Buldibuyo, Peru, **454** C2
Bulford, England, U.K., **305** F3
Bulgan, Bayanhongor, Mongolia, **213** H3
Bulgan, Bulgan, Mongolia, **213** J2
Bulgan, Hövsgöl, Mongolia, **213** J2
Bulgan, Ömnögovĭ, Mongolia, **213** J3
Bulgan, *province*, Mongolia, **213** J2
Bulgan, *river*, Mongolia, **213** F3
Bulgaria, *country*, Europe, **282** G7
Buli, Indonesia, **199** E2
Buli, Teluk, *bay*, Indonesia, **199** E2
Buliluyan, Cape, Philippines, **204** B4
Bulkington, England, U.K., **305** F2
Bull Mountains, *mountain range*, U.S.A., **419** K3
Bullas, Spain, **293** G3
Bullaxaar, Somalia, **367** F2
Bulle, Switzerland, **291** H3
Bullenbaai, *bay*, Curaçao, Netherlands Antilles, **461** C3
Buller, *river*, New Zealand, **133** D5
Bullhead City, U.S.A., **422** F4
Bulloo, *river*, Australia, **135** J4
Bulls, New Zealand, **132** E4
Bully-les-Minnes, France, **305** K4
Bulolo, Papua New Guinea, **140** B4
Buluan Lake, Philippines, **204** D5
Bulukutu, Democratic Republic of the Congo, **368** D3
Bulungu, Bandundu, Democratic Republic of the Congo, **368** C3
Bulungu, Kasai Occidental, Democratic Republic of the Congo, **368** D4
Bulupulu, Tanjong, *point*, Indonesia, **198** C3
Bumba, Bandundu, Democratic Republic of the Congo, **368** C4
Bumba, Equateur, Democratic Republic of the Congo, **368** D2
Bumbat, Mongolia, **210** D3
Bumbeşti-Jiu, Romania, **296** D3
Buna, Democratic Republic of the Congo, **368** C3
Buna, Kenya, **369** G2
Bunapas, Papua New Guinea, **140** B4
Bunazi, Tanzania, **369** F3
Bunbeg, Ireland, **309** D2
Bunbury, Australia, **134** D5
Bunclody, Ireland, **309** F5
Buncrana, Ireland, **309** E2
Bunda, Tanzania, **369** F3
Bundaberg, Australia, **135** L3
Būndi, India, **218** C4
Bundibugyo, Uganda, **369** F2
Būndu, India, **219** F5
Bunduqīyah, Sudan, **369** F1
Bungalaut, Selat, *strait*, Indonesia, **200** B3
Bungay, England, U.K., **305** J2
Bungo, Angola, **368** C4
Buni, Nigeria, **365** G2
Bunia, Democratic Republic of the Congo, **369** F2
Bunić, Croatia, **294** E3
Bunkeya, Democratic Republic of the Congo, **369** E5

Carthage, New York, U.S.A., **426** C2
Carthage, Texas, U.S.A., **424** E3
Carthage, Tunisia, **362** B1
Cartier, Canada, **421** N2
Cartier Islet, *island*, Ashmore and Cartier Islands, **134** P9
Cartmel, England, U.K., **306** F3
Cartwright, Canada, **417** N3
Caruaru, Brazil, **453** G5
Carúpano, Venezuela, **451** F1
Caruray, Philippines, **204** B4
Carutapera, Brazil, **452** E3
Carvalho, Brazil, **452** C4
Carvers, U.S.A., **422** E2
Carvoeiro, Brazil, **451** G4
Carvoeiro, Cabo, *cape*, Portugal, **292** C3
Casa Branca, Brazil, **456** D5
Casa Grande, U.S.A., **423** H5
Casa Piedra, U.S.A., **423** L7
Casabaja, Providencia, Colombia, **461** C1
Casablanca, Morocco, **360** E2
Casamance, *river*, Senegal, **364** A2
Casamassima, Italy, **295** F5
Casamozza, Corse, France, **294** B4
Casanare, *river*, Colombia, **451** D2
Casas Adobes, U.S.A., **423** H5
Casas del Puerto, Spain, **293** G3
Casas Grandes, Mexico, **430** D2
Casas Grandes, *river*, Mexico, **430** D2
Casas Ibáñez, Spain, **293** G3
Casca, Brazil, **459** G3
Cascade, Seychelles, **373** A2
Cascade, U.S.A., **420** H4
Cascade Bay, Norfolk Island, **135** T13
Cascade Point, New Zealand, **133** A6
Cascade Range, *mountain range*, U.S.A., **418** C6
Cascais, Portugal, **292** C3
Cascavel, Ceará, Brazil, **453** F4
Cascavel, Parana, Brazil, **459** G2
Caserta, Italy, **295** E5
Casey, *Australian research station*, Antarctica, **470** G7
Casey, Canada, **416** D6
Caseyr, Raas, *point*, Somalia, **367** H2
Cashel, Ireland, **309** E5
Cashel, Zimbabwe, **371** F2
Casigua, N. Venezuela, **450** D2
Casigua, W. Venezuela, **451** D1
Casilda, Argentina, **458** E4
Casino, Australia, **135** L4
Casinos, Spain, **293** G3
Casiquiare, *river*, Venezuela, **451** E3
Casma, Peru, **454** B2
Caspe, Spain, **293** G2
Casper, U.S.A., **419** L5
Caspian Depression *see* Prikaspiyskaya Nizmennost', *lowland*, Kazakhstan/Russian Federation, **222** D3
Caspian Sea, Asia/Europe, **222** E4
Cass City, U.S.A., **421** M4
Cass Lake, U.S.A., **420** F2
Cassacatiza, Mozambique, **369** F5
Cassai, Angola, **368** D5
Cassamba, Angola, **368** D5
Cassel, France, **305** K4
Cassiar, Canada, **412** E2
Cassiar Mountains, *mountain range*, Canada, **412** D2
Cassinga, Angola, **368** C6
Cassino, Italy, **295** D5
Cassley, *river*, Scotland, U.K., **308** E2
Cassoday, U.S.A., **420** E6
Cassongue, Angola, **368** B5
Castanhal, Brazil, **452** D3
Castanho, Brazil, **455** G2
Castaño, *river*, Argentina, **458** C4
Castaño Viejo, Argentina, **458** C4
Castara, Tobago, Trinidad and Tobago, **461** B4
Castelbuono, Sicilia, Italy, **295** E7
Casteljaloux, France, **290** E4
Castellane, France, **291** H5
Castelli, Buenos Aires, Argentina, **459** F5
Castelli, Chaco, Argentina, **458** E2
Castellnou de Bassella, Spain, **293** H1
Castelló de la Plana, Spain, **293** G2
Castelnau-Magnoac, France, **290** E5
Castelnaudary, France, **290** E5
Castelnovo ne'Monti, Italy, **294** C3
Castelo Branco, *district*, Portugal, **292** D2
Castelo Branco, Portugal, **292** D3
Castelo do Piauí, Brazil, **453** F4
Castelvetrano, Sicilia, Italy, **295** D7
Casterton, Australia, **135** J6
Castets, France, **290** D5
Castilla, Chile, **458** B3
Castilla, Peru, **454** B1
Castilla La Mancha, *autonomous community*, Spain, **293** F3
Castilla Y León, *autonomous community*, Spain, **292** E1
Castillo, Pampa del, *plain*, Argentina, **460** D3
Castillonnès, France, **290** E4
Castillos, Uruguay, **459** G5
Castle Carrock, England, U.K., **306** F3
Castle Cary, England, U.K., **304** E3
Castle Dale, U.S.A., **423** H2
Castle Dome Peak, *mountain peak*, U.S.A., **422** F5
Castle Donnington, England, U.K., **305** F2
Castle Douglas, Scotland, U.K., **308** F6
Castle Rock, Colorado, U.S.A., **423** L2
Castle Rock, Washington, U.S.A., **418** C3
Castle Rock Point, St Helena, **373** B3
Castlebar, Ireland, **309** C4
Castlebay, Scotland, U.K., **308** B4
Castlebellingham, Ireland, **309** F4
Castleblayney, Ireland, **309** F3
Castlebridge, Ireland, **309** F5
Castlecomer, Ireland, **309** E5
Castleconnell, Ireland, **309** D5
Castlederg, Northern Ireland, U.K., **309** E3
Castledermot, Ireland, **309** F5
Castleford, England, U.K., **307** G4
Castlegar, Canada, **413** L7
Castlegregory, Ireland, **309** B5
Castleisland, Ireland, **309** C5
Castlemaine, Ireland, **309** C5
Castlemartyr, Ireland, **309** D6
Castlepoint, New Zealand, **133** F5
Castlepollard, Ireland, **309** E4
Castlereagh, *district*, Northern Ireland, U.K., **309** G3
Castleton, England, U.K., **307** H3
Castletown, Ireland, **309** E5
Castletown, Isle of Man, **306** D3
Castletown, Scotland, U.K., **308** F2
Castletown Bearhaven, Ireland, **309** C6
Castlewellan, Northern Ireland, U.K., **309** G3
Castlewood, U.S.A., **420** E3
Castor, Canada, **413** P5
Castor, *river*, Canada, **415** Q5
Castor, U.S.A., **424** F3
Castres, France, **290** F5
Castries, St Lucia, **427** D3
Castro, Brazil, **459** G2
Castro, Chile, **460** C2
Castro, Punta, *point*, Argentina, **460** E2
Castro Marim, Portugal, **292** D4
Castro-Urdiales, Spain, **293** F1
Castro Verde, Portugal, **292** C4
Castrovillari, Italy, **295** F6
Castrovirreyna, Peru, **454** C3
Castuera, Spain, **292** E3
Casuarito, Colombia, **451** E3
Caswell Sound, New Zealand, **133** A7
Cat Island, Bahamas, **428** G1
Cat Lake, Canada, **414** J6
Cat Lake, *lake*, Canada, **414** J6
Catabola, Angola, **368** C5
Catacaos, Peru, **454** B1
Catacocha, Ecuador, **450** B5
Cataguases, Brazil, **457** E5
Catahoula Lake, U.S.A., **424** F4
Catalão, Brazil, **456** D5
Çatalca, Turkey, **297** G5
Catalina, Bahía, *bay*, Providencia, Colombia, **461** C1
Catalina, U.S.A., **423** H5
Cataluña, *autonomous community*, Spain, **293** H2
Catamarca, *province*, Argentina, **458** C3
Catan Lil, Argentina, **460** C1
Catandica, Mozambique, **371** F2
Catanduanes Island, Philippines, **204** D3
Catania, Golfo di, *gulf*, Sicilia, Italy, **295** E7
Catania, Sicilia, Italy, **295** E7
Catanzaro, Italy, **295** F6
Catarina, Raso da, *mountain range*, Brazil, **457** F2
Catarina, U.S.A., **424** C5
Catarman, Philippines, **204** D3
Catarroja, Spain, **293** G3
Catatumbo, *river*, Venezuela, **450** D2
Cataxa, Mozambique, **369** F6
Catbalogan, Philippines, **204** D4
Catedral, Cerro, *mountain peak*, Uruguay, **459** F5
Cateel, Philippines, **204** D5
Caterham, England, U.K., **305** G3
Catete, Angola, **368** B4
Cathedral Mountain, *mountain peak*, U.S.A., **423** M6
Catherine Point, Ascension, **373** A3
Cathlamet, U.S.A., **418** C3
Catia La Mar, Venezuela, **451** E1
Catió, Guinea-Bissau, **364** A2
Catnip Mountain, *mountain peak*, U.S.A., **418** E6
Catoche, Cabo, *cape*, Mexico, **431** J4
Catorce, Mexico, **431** E4
Catoute, *mountain peak*, Spain, **292** D1
Catriel, Argentina, **458** C5
Catriló, Argentina, **458** D5
Catrimani, Brazil, **451** G4
Catrimani, *river*, Brazil, **451** F4
Catskill, U.S.A., **426** D3
Catskill Mountains, *mountain range*, U.S.A., **426** C3
Catterick, England, U.K., **307** G3
Catuane, Mozambique, **371** F4
Cauaxi, *river*, Brazil, **452** D4
Cauayan, Luzon Island, Philippines, **204** C2
Cauayan, Negros Island, Philippines, **204** C4
Cauca, *river*, Colombia, **450** C2
Caucaia, Brazil, **453** F4
Caucasia, Colombia, **450** C2
Caucasus *see* Bol'shoy Kavkaz, *mountain range*, Asia/Europe, **222** D4
Caucete, Argentina, **458** C4
Caungula, Angola, **368** C4
Cauquenes, Chile, **458** B5
Caura, *river*, Venezuela, **451** F2
Caures, *river*, Brazil, **451** F4
Causapscal, Canada, **416** H5
Căușeni, Moldova, **296** G2
Caussade, France, **290** E4
Cautário, *river*, Brazil, **455** F3
Cauto, *river*, Cuba, **429** F2
Cavalcante, Brazil, **456** D3
Cavalier, U.S.A., **420** E1
Cavalla, *river*, Liberia, **364** C3
Cavalli Islands, New Zealand, **132** D2
Cavallo, Île, *island*, Corse, France, **295** B5
Cavally, *river*, Côte d'Ivoire, **364** C3
Cavan, *county*, Ireland, **309** E4
Cavan, Ireland, **309** E4
Cavarzere, Italy, **294** D3
Çavdarhisar, Turkey, **297** G6
Cave, New Zealand, **133** C7
Cave City, U.S.A., **424** G2
Cavern Peak, *mountain peak*, Auckland Islands, New Zealand, **132** J10
Caviana, Ilha, *island*, Brazil, **452** C3
Cavinas, Bolivia, **455** E3
Cavnic, Romania, **296** D2
Cawdor, Scotland, U.K., **308** F3
Cawston, England, U.K., **305** J2
Caxias, Brazil, **453** E4
Caxias do Sul, Brazil, **459** G3
Caxito, Angola, **368** B4
Çay, Turkey, **224** D5
Cayambe, Ecuador, **450** B4
Cayambe, Volcán, *mountain peak*, Ecuador, **450** C4
Cayenne, French Guiana, **452** C2
Cayman Brac, *island*, Cayman Islands, **429** F3
Cayman Islands, *U.K. dependency*, Caribbean Sea, **409** Q7
Cayman Trench, *underwater feature*, Caribbean Sea, **479** N3
Caynabo, Somalia, **367** G3
Cayuga Lake, U.S.A., **426** B3
Cazalla de la Sierra, Spain, **292** E4
Căzănești, Romania, **296** F3
Cazaux et de Sanguinet, Étang de, *lake*, France, **290** D4
Čazma, Croatia, **294** F3
Cazombo, Angola, **368** D5
Cazorla, Spain, **293** F4
Cazula, Mozambique, **369** F6
Cea, *river*, Spain, **292** E1
Ceará, *state*, Brazil, **453** F4
Ceara Plain, *underwater feature*, Atlantic Ocean, **477** E6
Cébaco, Isla de, *island*, Panama, **429** E6
Ceballos, Mexico, **430** D3
Cebolla, U.S.A., **423** K3
Cebollati, *river*, Uruguay, **459** F4
Cebu, *island*, Philippines, **204** C4
Cebu, Philippines, **204** C4
Ceccano, Italy, **295** D5
Cece, Hungary, **289** J5
Cecina, Italy, **294** C4
Cedar, *river*, Iowa, U.S.A., **420** G4
Cedar, *river*, North Dakota, U.S.A., **420** B2
Cedar City, U.S.A., **422** G3
Cedar Grove, U.S.A., **421** N6
Cedar Key, U.S.A., **425** L5
Cedar Lake, Canada, **414** D5
Cedar Rapids, U.S.A., **420** H5
Cedartown, U.S.A., **425** K2
Cedarvale, U.S.A., **423** L4
Cedros, Isla, *island*, Mexico, **430** B2
Cedros Trench, *underwater feature*, Pacific Ocean, **479** L3
Ceduna, Australia, **134** G5
Cedynia, Poland, **289** G2
Cée, Spain, **292** C1
Ceel Gaal, Bari, Somalia, **367** H2
Ceel Gaal, Woqooyi Galbeed, Somalia, **367** F2
Ceelbuur, Somalia, **367** G4
Ceerigaabo, Somalia, **367** G2
Cefalù, Sicilia, Italy, **295** D6
Cega, *river*, Spain, **292** E2
Cegléd, Hungary, **289** J5
Cehegin, Spain, **293** G3
Ceheng, China, **215** H4
Cehu Silvaniei, Romania, **296** D2
Celaya, Mexico, **431** E4
Celbridge, Ireland, **309** F4
Celebes Basin, *underwater feature*, South China Sea, **478** C4
Celebes Sea, Indonesia/Philippines, **198** C2
Celebes *see* Sulawesi, *island*, Indonesia, **198** B3
Celendín, Peru, **454** C2
Celina, U.S.A., **425** K1
Celje, Slovenia, **294** E2
Celle, Germany, **288** E2
Celny, Russian Federation, **211** M2
Celorico da Beira, Portugal, **292** D2
Celyn, Llyn, *lake*, Wales, U.K., **304** D2
Cenajo, Embalse del, *reservoir*, Spain, **293** G3
Cenderawasih, Teluk, *bay*, Indonesia, **199** F3
Centenary, Zimbabwe, **371** F2
Center, Colorado, U.S.A., **423** L3
Center, Texas, U.S.A., **424** E4
Centerville, Iowa, U.S.A., **420** G5
Centerville, South Dakota, U.S.A., **420** E4
Centinela, Picacho del, *mountain peak*, Mexico, **430** E2
Cento, Italy, **294** C3
Central, *administrative region*, Ghana, **364** D3
Central, *administrative region*, Malawi, **369** F5
Central, Cordillera, *mountain range*, Bolivia, **447** F5
Central, Cordillera, *mountain range*, Panama, **429** E5
Central, *district*, Botswana, **370** D3
Central, *province*, Kenya, **369** G3
Central, *province*, Papua New Guinea, **140** B5
Central, *province*, Zambia, **369** E5
Central African Republic, *country*, Africa, **358** G6
Central Brāhui Range, *mountain range*, Pakistan, **218** A3
Central Butte, Canada, **413** R6
Central City, U.S.A., **421** K7
Central Makrān Range, *mountain range*, Pakistan, **221** H3
Central Pacific Basin, *underwater feature*, Pacific Ocean, **478** F4
Central Patricia, Canada, **414** J6
Central Range, *mountain range*, Papua New Guinea, **140** A4
Centralia, Illinois, U.S.A., **421** J6
Centralia, Washington, U.S.A., **418** C3

Chefchaouene, Morocco, **361** E1
Chegdomyn, Russian Federation, **301** Q4
Chegga, Mauritania, **361** E3
Chegutu, Zimbabwe, **371** F2
Chehalis, U.S.A., **418** C3
Cheju, South Korea, **208** D4
Chejudo, *island*, South Korea, **208** D4
Chek Lap Kok, *island*, China, **207** B4
Chekhov, Russian Federation, **299** F5
Chekunda, Russian Federation, **211** L2
Chela, Serra da, *mountain range*, Angola, **368** B6
Chelan, Lake, U.S.A., **418** D2
Cheleken, Turkmenistan, **222** E5
Chelforó, Argentina, **460** D1
Chełm, Poland, **289** L3
Chełmno, Poland, **289** J2
Chelmsford, England, U.K., **305** H3
Chelmuzhi, Russian Federation, **285** S5
Chełmża, Poland, **289** J2
Chelsea, U.S.A., **420** H3
Cheltenham, England, U.K., **304** E3
Cheltenham, New Zealand, **132** E5
Chelu, China, **211** K2
Chelvai, India, **216** E2
Chelyabinsk, Russian Federation, **222** G1
Chelyabinskaya Oblast', *province*, Russian Federation, **222** F2
Chelyuskin, Mys, *cape*, Russian Federation, **301** M2
Chemaïa, Morocco, **360** E2
Chemal, Russian Federation, **223** M2
Chemchâm, Sebkhet, *salt-pan*, Mauritania, **360** D4
Chemin Grenier, Mauritius, **373** C1
Chemnitz, Germany, **288** F3
Chen Barag Qi, China, **211** G2
Chenāb, *river*, Pakistan, **218** B3
Chenachane, Algeria, **361** F3
Ch'ench'a, Ethiopia, **367** E3
Cheney, U.S.A., **418** F3
Ch'eng-kung, Taiwan, **206** E4
Cheng'an, China, **210** F5
Chengde, China, **211** G4
Chengdu, China, **215** H3
Chengele, India, **219** J3
Chenghai, China, **206** D4
Chengjiang, China, **207** C2
Chengkou, China, **206** B2
Chengmai, China, **203** F2
Chennai (Madras), India, **216** E3
Chenxi, China, **206** B3
Chenzhou, China, **206** C3
Chepelare, Bulgaria, **297** E5
Chepén, Peru, **454** B2
Chépénéhé, New Caledonia, **141** A3
Chepes, Argentina, **458** C4
Chepo, Panama, **450** B2
Chepstow, Wales, U.K., **304** E3
Cher, *river*, France, **290** E3
Cheraw, U.S.A., **425** N2
Cherbourg, France, **290** D2
Cherchell, Algeria, **293** J4
Cherekha, *river*, Russian Federation, **299** B4
Cherepanovo, Russian Federation, **223** L2
Cherepovets, Russian Federation, **299** F3
Chéria, Algeria, **361** H1
Cherkessk, Russian Federation, **222** C4
Chern', Russian Federation, **299** F6
Chernevo, Russian Federation, **299** B3
Chernihiv, Ukraine, **298** D2

Chernivets'ka Oblast', *province*, Ukraine, **296** E1
Chernivtsi, Chernivets'ka Oblast', Ukraine, **296** E1
Chernivtsi, Vinnyts'ka Oblast', Ukraine, **296** G1
Chernyakhovsk, Russian Federation, **287** K5
Chernyshevsk, Russian Federation, **210** G1
Chernyy Yar, Russian Federation, **222** D3
Cherokee, Iowa, U.S.A., **420** F4
Cherokee, Oklahoma, U.S.A., **420** D7
Cherokee Sound, Bahamas, **428** F1
Cherrapunji, India, **219** G4
Cherry Creek, U.S.A., **420** C3
Cherryville, Canada, **413** K6
Cherskiy, Russian Federation, **301** T3
Cherskogo, Khrebet, *mountain range*, Russian Federation, **301** Q3
Cherven Bryag, Bulgaria, **296** E4
Chervonohrad, Ukraine, **289** M3
Chervonoznam'yanka, Ukraine, **296** H2
Chervyen', Belarus, **299** B6
Cherykaw, Belarus, **299** C6
Chesapeake, U.S.A., **426** B6
Chesapeake Bay, U.S.A., **426** B5
Chesham, England, U.K., **305** G3
Cheshire, *unitary authority*, England, U.K., **304** E1
Cheshskaya Guba, *bay*, Russian Federation, **300** F3
Cheshunt, England, U.K., **305** G3
Cheste, Spain, **293** G3
Chester, California, U.S.A., **422** C1
Chester, Canada, **417** J7
Chester, England, U.K., **304** E1
Chester, Illinois, U.S.A., **420** J7
Chester, Montana, U.S.A., **419** J2
Chester, South Carolina, U.S.A., **425** M2
Chester-le-Street, England, U.K., **307** G3
Chesterfield, England, U.K., **305** F1
Chesterfield, Îles, *islands*, New Caledonia, **136** A2
Chesterfield Inlet, Canada, **411** K3
Chestnut, U.S.A., **424** F3
Chesuncook Lake, U.S.A., **426** E1
Chet', *river*, Russian Federation, **223** M1
Chetaibi, Algeria, **295** A7
Cheticamp, Canada, **417** L6
Chetlat Island, India, **216** C4
Chetumal, Mexico, **431** H5
Chetwode Island, New Zealand, **133** E5
Chetwynd, Canada, **412** J4
Cheugda, Russian Federation, **211** K2
Cheung Chau, *island*, China, **207** C4
Chevejécure, Bolivia, **455** E4
Chevilly, France, **290** E2
Cheviot, New Zealand, **133** D6
Cheviot, The, *mountain peak*, England, U.K., **306** F2
Cheviot Hills, England, U.K., **306** F2
Che'w Bahir, *lake*, Ethiopia, **369** G2
Chew Magna, England, U.K., **304** E3
Chew Valley Lake, England, U.K., **304** E3
Chewelah, U.S.A., **418** F2
Cheyenne, Oklahoma, U.S.A., **424** C2
Cheyenne, *river*, U.S.A., **419** P4
Cheyenne, Wyoming, U.S.A., **419** M6

Cheyenne Wells, U.S.A., **423** M2
Chhatarpur, India, **218** D4
Chhattīsgarh, *plain*, India, **219** E5
Chhindawāra, India, **218** D5
Chhnăng, *river*, Cambodia, **203** E3
Chhota Udepur, India, **218** C5
Chi-lung, Taiwan, **206** E3
Ch'i-shan, Taiwan, **206** E4
Chia-i, Taiwan, **206** E4
Chiang Dao, Doi, *mountain peak*, Thailand, **202** C2
Chiang Kham, Thailand, **202** D2
Chiang Khan, Thailand, **202** D2
Chiang Mai, Thailand, **202** C2
Chiang Rai, Thailand, **202** C2
Chiange, Angola, **368** B6
Chiapas, *state*, Mexico, **431** G5
Chiari, Italy, **294** B3
Chiautla de Tapia, Mexico, **431** F5
Chiavenna, Italy, **294** B2
Chiba, Japan, **209** H4
Chibemba, Angola, **368** B6
Chibia, Angola, **368** B6
Chibougamau, Canada, **416** D5
Chic-Chocs, Monts, *mountain range*, Canada, **416** H5
Chicago, U.S.A., **421** K5
Chicama, Peru, **454** B2
Chicama, *river*, Peru, **454** B2
Chichagof Island, U.S.A., **412** A3
Chichas, Cordillera de, *mountain range*, Bolivia, **455** E5
Chichāwatni, Pakistan, **218** C3
Chicheng, China, **210** F4
Chichester, England, U.K., **305** G4
Chichi-jima, *island*, Japan, **138** C2
Chichola, India, **218** E5
Chichón, Volcán, *mountain peak*, Mexico, **431** G5
Chickasawhay, *river*, U.S.A., **425** H4
Chickasha, U.S.A., **424** D2
Chickerell, England, U.K., **304** E4
Chiclana de la Frontera, Spain, **292** D4
Chiclayo, Peru, **454** B2
Chico, *river*, Chubut, Argentina, **460** D2
Chico, *river*, Río Negro, Argentina, **460** C2
Chico, *river*, Santa Cruz, Argentina, **460** C3
Chico, *river*, S. Santa Cruz, Argentina, **460** D4
Chico, U.S.A., **422** C2
Chicoa, Mozambique, **369** F6
Chicomba, Angola, **368** B5
Chicotte, Canada, **417** K5
Chicoutimi, Canada, **416** F5
Chicualacuala, Mozambique, **371** F3
Chidambaram, India, **216** D4
Chidenguele, Mozambique, **371** F3
Chidley, Cape, Canada, **411** N3
Chiefland, U.S.A., **425** L5
Chiemsee, *lake*, Germany, **288** F5
Chiengi, Zambia, **369** E4
Chieo Lan Reservoir, Thailand, **202** C4
Chiese, *river*, Italy, **294** C3
Chieti, Italy, **295** E4
Chietla, Mexico, **431** F5
Chifeng, China, **211** G4
Chigorodó, Colombia, **450** C2
Chiguana, Bolivia, **455** E5
Chigubo, Mozambique, **371** F3
Chihuahua, Mexico, **430** D2
Chihuahua, *state*, Mexico, **430** D2
Chihuido Medio, *mountain peak*, Argentina, **458** C6
Chikhachevo, Russian Federation, **299** B4

Chikmagalūr, India, **216** C3
Chikodi, India, **216** C2
Chikoy, *river*, Russian Federation, **210** E2
Chikwa, Zambia, **369** F5
Chikwawa, Malawi, **369** F6
Chila, Angola, **368** B5
Chilakalūrupet, India, **216** E2
Chilapa de Alvarez, Mexico, **431** F5
Chilaw, Sri Lanka, **216** D5
Chilca, Cordillera de, *mountain range*, Peru, **454** D4
Chilcotin, *river*, Canada, **412** G5
Chilcott Island, Coral Sea Islands, **135** K2
Childers, Australia, **135** L4
Childress, U.S.A., **424** B2
Chile, *country*, South America, **449** E7
Chile Basin, *underwater feature*, Pacific Ocean, **479** N6
Chile Chico, Argentina, **460** C3
Chile Rise, *underwater feature*, Pacific Ocean, **479** M7
Chilecito, Argentina, **458** C3
Chilham, England, U.K., **305** H3
Chilia Veche, Romania, **296** G3
Chililabombwe, Zambia, **369** E5
Chilka Lake, India, **219** F6
Chillán, Chile, **458** B5
Chillar, Argentina, **459** E5
Chillicothe, Illinois, U.S.A., **421** J5
Chillicothe, Missouri, U.S.A., **420** G6
Chillicothe, Ohio, U.S.A., **421** M6
Chilliculco, Peru, **455** E4
Chillinji, Pakistan, **218** C1
Chilliwack, Canada, **412** J7
Chilpancingo de los Bravos, Mexico, **431** F5
Chiltal'd, Gora, *mountain peak*, Russian Federation, **285** Q2
Chilubi, Zambia, **369** E5
Chilumba, Malawi, **369** F5
Chimala, Tanzania, **369** F4
Chimán, Panama, **429** F5
Chimanimani, Zimbabwe, **371** F2
Chimayo, U.S.A., **423** L3
Chimborazo, *mountain peak*, Ecuador, **450** B4
Chimbote, Peru, **454** B2
Chiméal, Cambodia, **203** D4
Chimoio, Mozambique, **371** F2
Chin, *state*, Myanmar, **205** B3
China, *country*, Asia, **196** L6
China, Mexico, **431** F3
Chinácota, Colombia, **450** D2
Chinajá, Guatemala, **428** C3
Chinandega, Nicaragua, **428** D4
Chinati Peak, *mountain peak*, U.S.A., **423** L7
Chincha Alta, Peru, **454** C3
Chinchaga, *river*, Canada, **413** K3
Chinchilla, Australia, **135** L4
Chinchilla de Monte Aragón, Spain, **293** G3
Chincholi, India, **216** D2
Chinde, Mozambique, **371** G2
Chindo, *island*, South Korea, **208** D4
Chindu, China, **215** F2
Chindwin, *river*, Myanmar, **205** B2
Chingola, Zambia, **369** E5
Chinguar, Angola, **368** C5
Chinguetti, Mauritania, **360** D4
Chinguil, Chad, **366** A2
Chinhae, South Korea, **208** E4
Chinhoyi, Zimbabwe, **371** F2
Chiniot, Pakistan, **218** C3
Chinipas, Mexico, **430** C3
Chinjan, Pakistan, **218** A3
Chinju, South Korea, **208** E4
Chinle, U.S.A., **423** J3
Chinnūr, India, **216** D2
Chinon, France, **290** E3

Chinook Trough, *underwater feature*, Pacific Ocean, **478** G2
Chinsali, Zambia, **369** F5
Chinsong-ri, North Korea, **208** D2
Chintāmani, India, **216** D3
Chinturu, India, **217** E2
Chioggia, Italy, **294** D3
Chios, Greece, **297** F6
Chios, *island*, Greece, **297** E6
Chipata, Zambia, **369** F5
Chipili, Zambia, **369** E5
Chipinge, Zimbabwe, **371** F3
Chipman, Canada, **413** N5
Chipoia, Angola, **368** C5
Chippenham, England, U.K., **304** E3
Chippewa, *river*, U.S.A., **420** H3
Chippewa Falls, U.S.A., **420** H3
Chipping Campden, England, U.K., **305** F2
Chipping Norton, England, U.K., **305** F3
Chipping Ongar, England, U.K., **305** H3
Chipping Sodbury, England, U.K., **304** E3
Chiprovtsi, Bulgaria, **296** D4
Chiquimula, Guatemala, **428** C4
Chiquinata, Bahía, *bay*, Chile, **454** D5
Chiquinquirá, Colombia, **450** D3
Chirāla, Cape, India, **217** E3
Chirāla, India, **216** E3
Chirāwa, India, **218** C3
Chiradzulu, Malawi, **371** G2
Chiralto, *river*, Mexico, **431** E5
Chiramba, Mozambique, **369** F6
Chirbury, England, U.K., **304** D2
Chirchiq, Uzbekistan, **223** H4
Chiredzi, Zimbabwe, **371** F3
Chirfa, Niger, **362** B4
Chiricahua Peak, *mountain peak*, U.S.A., **423** J6
Chiriguaná, Colombia, **450** D2
Chiriquí, Golfo de, *gulf*, Panama, **429** E6
Chirk, Wales, U.K., **304** D2
Chirmiri, India, **219** E5
Chirnside, Scotland, U.K., **308** G5
Chiromo, Malawi, **369** G6
Chirpan, Bulgaria, **296** E4
Chirripó, Cerro, *mountain peak*, Costa Rica, **428** E5
Chirundu, Zambia, **369** E6
Chisamba, Zambia, **369** E5
Chisasibi, Canada, **415** Q5
Chishmy, Russian Federation, **222** F2
Chisholm, Canada, **413** M4
Chisholm, U.S.A., **420** G2
Chishui, *river*, China, **215** H4
Chişinău (Kishinev), Moldova, **296** G2
Chişineu-Criş, Romania, **296** C2
Chistiān Mandi, Pakistan, **218** C3
Chistopol', Russian Federation, **222** E1
Chīstopol'e, Kazakhstan, **222** H2
Chita, Bolivia, **455** E5
Chita, Russian Federation, **301** N4
Chitado, Angola, **368** B6
Chitambo, Zambia, **369** F5
Chitato, Angola, **368** D4
Chitembo, Angola, **368** C5
Chitinskaya Oblast', *province*, Russian Federation, **210** F1
Chitipa, Malawi, **369** F4
Chitobe, Mozambique, **371** F3
Chitose, Japan, **209** H2
Chitrāl, Pakistan, **218** B2
Chitré, Panama, **429** E6
Chittagong, Bangladesh, **214** D5
Chittagong, *division*, Bangladesh, **214** D5
Chittaurgarh, India, **218** C4

Cleopatra Needle, *mountain peak*, Philippines, **204** B4
Cléres, France, **305** J5
Clermont, Australia, **135** K3
Clermont, France, **305** K5
Clermont-Ferrand, France, **291** F4
Clervaux, Luxembourg, **291** H1
Clevedon, England, U.K., **304** E3
Cleveland, Georgia, U.S.A., **425** L2
Cleveland, Mississippi, U.S.A., **424** G3
Cleveland, Ohio, U.S.A., **421** N5
Cleveland, Tennessee, U.S.A., **425** K2
Cleveland, Texas, U.S.A., **424** E4
Cleveland Hills, England, U.K., **307** G3
Clevelândia, Brazil, **459** G3
Clevelândia do Norte, Brazil, **452** C2
Cleveleys, England, U.K., **306** E4
Clew Bay, Ireland, **309** C4
Clewiston, U.S.A., **425** M6
Clifden, Ireland, **309** B4
Cliffdell, U.S.A., **418** D3
Cliffe, England, U.K., **305** H3
Cliffony, Ireland, **309** D3
Clifford Bay, New Zealand, **133** E5
Clifton, U.S.A., **423** J5
Clifton Forge, U.S.A., **421** P7
Climax, Canada, **413** Q7
Climax, Colorado, U.S.A., **423** K2
Climax, Minnesota, U.S.A., **420** E2
Cline, U.S.A., **424** B5
Clinton, British Columbia, Canada, **412** J6
Clinton, Iowa, U.S.A., **420** H5
Clinton, Massachusetts, U.S.A., **426** E3
Clinton, Mississippi, U.S.A., **424** G3
Clinton, Missouri, U.S.A., **420** G6
Clinton, Montana, U.S.A., **418** H3
Clinton, North Carolina, U.S.A., **425** N2
Clinton, Oklahoma, U.S.A., **424** C2
Clinton, Ontario, Canada, **421** N4
Clinton, South Carolina, U.S.A., **425** M2
Clipperton Fracture Zone, *tectonic feature*, Pacific Ocean, **479** J4
Clitheroe, England, U.K., **306** F4
Cliza, Bolivia, **455** F4
Clo-oose, Canada, **412** G7
Clogh, Northern Ireland, U.K., **309** F3
Clogheen, Ireland, **309** D5
Clogher Head, *point*, Ireland, **309** F4
Clonakilty, Ireland, **309** D6
Clonakilty Bay, Ireland, **309** D6
Clonbern, Ireland, **309** D4
Cloncurry, Australia, **135** J3
Clones, Ireland, **309** E3
Clonmel, Ireland, **309** E5
Clonroche, Ireland, **309** F5
Cloonbannin, Ireland, **309** C5
Cloppenburg, Germany, **288** D2
Cloquet, U.S.A., **420** G2
Cloridorme, Canada, **416** J5
Clorinda, Argentina, **459** F2
Cloud Peak, *mountain peak*, U.S.A., **419** L4
Clova, Scotland, U.K., **308** F4
Cloverdale, U.S.A., **422** B2
Clovis, U.S.A., **423** M4
Cluanie, Loch, *lake*, Scotland, U.K., **308** D3
Cluff Lake, Canada, **413** Q2
Cluj-Napoca, Romania, **296** D2
Clun, England, U.K., **304** D2

Cluny, France, **291** G3
Clutha, *river*, New Zealand, **133** B7
Clydach, Wales, U.K., **304** D3
Clyde, *river*, Scotland, U.K., **308** F5
Clyde Park, U.S.A., **419** J4
Clyde River, Canada, **411** N2
Clydebank, Scotland, U.K., **308** E5
Clydevale, New Zealand, **133** B8
Clyro, Wales, U.K., **304** D2
Cnoc Moy, Scotland, U.K., **308** D5
Coahuila, *state*, Mexico, **430** E3
Coal, *river*, Canada, **412** E1
Coal River, Canada, **412** F2
Coaldale, U.S.A., **422** E2
Coalgate, U.S.A., **424** D2
Coalinga, U.S.A., **422** C3
Coalville, England, U.K., **305** F2
Coari, Brazil, **451** F5
Coari, Lago de, *lake*, Brazil, **451** F5
Coari, *river*, Brazil, **451** F5
Coast, *province*, Kenya, **369** G3
Coast Mountains, *mountain range*, Canada, **412** C2
Coast Range, *mountain range*, U.S.A., **406** L5
Coatbridge, Scotland, U.K., **308** E5
Coats Island, Canada, **411** L3
Coats Land, *region*, Antarctica, **470** C4
Coatzacoalcos, Mexico, **431** G5
Cobadin, Romania, **296** G3
Cobán, Guatemala, **428** C4
Cobar, Australia, **135** K5
Cobequid Mountains, *mountain range*, Canada, **417** J7
Cobh, Ireland, **309** D6
Cobham, *river*, Canada, **414** G5
Cobija, Bolivia, **455** E3
Cobleskill, U.S.A., **426** C3
Cobourg Peninsula, Australia, **134** G1
Cobram, Australia, **135** K6
Cóbuè, Mozambique, **369** F5
Coburg, Germany, **288** E3
Coburg Island, Canada, **411** M2
Coca, Pizzo di, *mountain peak*, Italy, **294** B2
Cocachacra, Peru, **454** D4
Cocalinho, Brazil, **456** C4
Cochabamba, Bolivia, **455** E4
Cochabamba, *department*, Bolivia, **455** E4
Cochamó, Chile, **460** C1
Cochem, Germany, **288** C3
Cochin, Canada, **413** Q5
Cochin *see* Kochi, India, **216** D4
Cochise, U.S.A., **423** J5
Cochrane, Alberta, Canada, **413** M6
Cochrane, Chile, **460** C3
Cochrane, Ontario, Canada, **415** P7
Cockburn, Canal, *channel*, Chile, **460** C5
Cockburn, Cape, Australia, **199** F5
Cockburn Harbour, Turks and Caicos Islands, **429** H2
Cockburn Town, Bahamas, **428** G1
Cockburnspath, Scotland, U.K., **308** G5
Cockerham, England, U.K., **306** F4
Cockermouth, England, U.K., **306** E3
Coclé del Norte, Panama, **429** E5
Coco, Punta, *point*, Colombia, **450** B3
Coco, *river*, Honduras/Nicaragua, **428** D4
Coco Channel, Andaman and Nicobar Islands, India, **217** H3
Cocorná, Colombia, **450** C2
Côcos, Brazil, **457** E4

Cocos Bay, Trinidad, Trinidad and Tobago, **461** C4
Cocos (Keeling) Islands, *Australian territory*, Indian Ocean, **134** Q10
Cocos Ridge, *underwater feature*, Pacific Ocean, **479** N4
Cocula, Mexico, **430** E4
Cod, Cape, U.S.A., **426** E3
Cod Island, Canada, **411** N4
Codajás, Brazil, **451** F5
Coddington, England, U.K., **305** G1
Codera, Cabo, *cape*, Venezuela, **451** E1
Codfish Island, New Zealand, **133** A8
Codigoro, Italy, **294** D3
Codlea, Romania, **296** E3
Codó, Brazil, **453** E4
Codrington, Antigua and Barbuda, **427** D2
Codrington, Mount, *mountain peak*, Antarctica, **470** F4
Codsall, England, U.K., **304** E2
Cody, U.S.A., **419** K4
Coe, Glen, *valley*, Scotland, U.K., **308** D4
Coen, Australia, **135** J1
Coeroeni, *river*, Suriname, **452** B2
Coesfeld, Germany, **288** C3
Coetivy Island, Seychelles, **372** D2
Coeur d'Alene, U.S.A., **418** F3
Coeur d'Alene Lake, U.S.A., **418** F3
Coffee Bay, South Africa, **371** E5
Coffeeville, U.S.A., **425** H4
Coffeyville, U.S.A., **420** F7
Coffs Harbour, Australia, **135** L5
Cofrentes, Spain, **293** G3
Cogealac, Romania, **296** G3
Coggeshall, England, U.K., **305** H3
Cognac, France, **290** D4
Cogo, Equatorial Guinea, **368** A2
Cohagen, U.S.A., **419** L3
Coiba, Isla de, *island*, Panama, **429** E6
Coig, *river*, Argentina, **460** C4
Coigeach, Rubha, *point*, Scotland, U.K., **308** D2
Coihaique, Chile, **460** C2
Coimbatore, India, **216** D4
Coimbra, *district*, Portugal, **292** C2
Coimbra, Portugal, **292** C2
Coin, Spain, **292** E4
Coipasa, Lago de, *lake*, Bolivia, **455** E5
Coipasa, Salar de, *salt-pan*, Bolivia, **455** E5
Cojudo Blanco, Cerro, *mountain peak*, Argentina, **460** D3
Cojutepeque, El Salvador, **428** C4
Colac, Australia, **135** J6
Colac Bay, New Zealand, **133** A8
Colares, Brazil, **452** D3
Colatina, Brazil, **457** F5
Colby, U.S.A., **420** C6
Colchester, England, U.K., **305** J3
Cold Lake, Canada, **413** P4
Cold Lake, *lake*, Canada, **413** Q4
Cold Springs, U.S.A., **422** E2
Coldstream, Canada, **413** K6
Coldwater, Kansas, U.S.A., **420** D7
Coldwater, Michigan, U.S.A., **421** L5
Coldwater, Missouri, U.S.A., **420** H7
Colebrook, U.S.A., **426** E2
Coleford, England, U.K., **304** E3
Coleman, U.S.A., **424** C4
Çölemerik, Turkey, **224** F5

Colemon, U.S.A., **421** L4
Coleraine, *district*, Northern Ireland, U.K., **309** F2
Coleraine, Northern Ireland, U.K., **309** F2
Coleridge, Lake, New Zealand, **133** C6
Coles, Punta, *point*, Peru, **454** D4
Colesberg, South Africa, **370** E5
Colfax, California, U.S.A., **422** C2
Colfax, Louisiana, U.S.A., **424** F4
Colfax, Washington, U.S.A., **418** F3
Colhué Huapi, Lago, *lake*, Argentina, **460** D2
Colico, Italy, **294** B2
Colima, Mexico, **430** E5
Colima, *state*, Mexico, **430** D5
Colinas, Brazil, **453** E5
Coll, *island*, Scotland, U.K., **308** C4
Collaguasi, Chile, **455** E5
College Station, U.S.A., **424** D4
Collie, Australia, **134** D5
Collier Bay, Australia, **134** E2
Collingwood, Canada, **421** N3
Collingwood, New Zealand, **133** D5
Collins, Iowa, U.S.A., **420** G5
Collins, Mississippi, U.S.A., **425** H4
Collipulli, Chile, **458** B5
Collooney, Ireland, **309** D3
Colmar, France, **291** H2
Colmonell, Scotland, U.K., **308** E5
Coln, *river*, England, U.K., **305** F3
Colne, England, U.K., **306** F4
Colne, *river*, England, U.K., **305** H3
Cologne *see* Köln, Germany, **288** C3
Colômbia, Brazil, **456** D5
Colombia, Colombia, **450** C3
Colombia, *country*, South America, **449** E3
Colombo, Sri Lanka, **216** D5
Colome, U.S.A., **420** D4
Colomiers, France, **290** E5
Colón, Buenos Aires, Argentina, **458** E4
Colón, Cuba, **429** E2
Colón, Entre Rios, Argentina, **459** E4
Colón, Panama, **429** F5
Colonel Hill, Bahamas, **429** G2
Colonia del Sacramento, Uruguay, **459** F5
Colonia Dora, Argentina, **458** D3
Colonia Josefa, Argentina, **460** E1
Colonia Lavalleja, Uruguay, **459** F4
Colonia Vicente Guerrero, Mexico, **430** A2
Colonsay, *island*, Scotland, U.K., **308** C4
Colorado, *river*, Argentina, **460** E1
Colorado, *river*, Brazil, **455** F3
Colorado, *river*, Mexico/U.S.A., **407** M5
Colorado, *state*, U.S.A., **423** K2
Colorado City, Colorado, U.S.A., **422** G3
Colorado City, Texas, U.S.A., **424** B3
Colorado Desert, U.S.A., **422** E5
Colorado do Oeste, Brazil, **455** G3
Colorado Plateau, U.S.A., **423** H3
Colorado Springs, U.S.A., **423** L2
Colotlán, Mexico, **430** E4
Colquechaca, Bolivia, **455** E5
Colquiri, Bolivia, **455** E4

Colquitt, U.S.A., **425** K4
Colsterworth, England, U.K., **305** G2
Colstrip, U.S.A., **419** L4
Coltishall, England, U.K., **305** J2
Colton, U.S.A., **423** H2
Columbia, District of, *district*, U.S.A., **421** Q6
Columbia, Kentucky, U.S.A., **421** L7
Columbia, Louisiana, U.S.A., **424** F3
Columbia, Mississippi, U.S.A., **424** H4
Columbia, Missouri, U.S.A., **420** G6
Columbia, Mount, *mountain peak*, Canada, **413** L5
Columbia, North Carolina, U.S.A., **426** B7
Columbia, *river*, Canada/U.S.A., **406** L4
Columbia, South Carolina, U.S.A., **425** M3
Columbia, Tennessee, U.S.A., **425** J2
Columbia Basin, U.S.A., **406** M4
Columbia City, U.S.A., **421** L5
Columbia Falls, U.S.A., **418** G2
Columbia Mountains, *mountain range*, Canada, **412** J5
Columbia Plateau, U.S.A., **418** E4
Columbiana, U.S.A., **425** J3
Columbine, Cape, South Africa, **370** C5
Columbus, Georgia, U.S.A., **425** K3
Columbus, Indiana, U.S.A., **421** L6
Columbus, Iowa, U.S.A., **421** J4
Columbus, Mississippi, U.S.A., **425** H3
Columbus, Nebraska, U.S.A., **420** E5
Columbus, New Mexico, U.S.A., **423** K6
Columbus, Ohio, U.S.A., **421** M6
Columbus, Texas, U.S.A., **424** D5
Columbus Point, Tobago, Trinidad and Tobago, **461** B4
Colville, Cape, New Zealand, **132** E3
Colville, *river*, U.S.A., **410** D3
Colville, U.S.A., **418** F2
Colville Lake, Canada, **410** G3
Colwyn Bay, Wales, U.K., **306** E4
Colyford, England, U.K., **304** D4
Comacchio, Italy, **294** D3
Comallo, *river*, Argentina, **460** C1
Coman, Mount, *mountain peak*, Antarctica, **470** B5
Comanche, Oklahoma, U.S.A., **424** D2
Comanche, Texas, U.S.A., **424** C4
Comandante Salas, Argentina, **458** C4
Comănești, Romania, **296** F2
Comarapa, Bolivia, **455** F4
Comarnic, Romania, **296** E3
Comas, Peru, **454** C3
Comayagua, Honduras, **428** D4
Combarbalá, Chile, **458** B4
Combe Martin, England, U.K., **304** C3
Comber, Northern Ireland, U.K., **309** G3
Combermere Bay, Myanmar, **205** B4
Comendador, Dominican Republic, **429** H3
Comeragh Mountains, *mountain range*, Ireland, **309** E5
Comfort, U.S.A., **424** C5
Comfort Bight, Canada, **417** P3
Comino, Capo, *cape*, Sardegna, Italy, **295** B5

F

Fuxing, China, **215** H3
Fuyang, China, **206** C1
Fuyang, *river*, China, **210** F5
Fuyong, China, **207** B3
Fuyu, Heilongjiang, China, **211** J3
Fuyu, Jilin, China, **211** J3
Fuyuan, Heilongjiang, China, **211** L2
Fuyuan, Yunnan, China, **215** H4
Fuyun, China, **212** F3
Füzesabony, Hungary, **289** K5
Fuzhou, Fujian, China, **206** D3
Fuzhou, Jiangxi, China, **206** D3
Fyn, *island*, Denmark, **286** E5
Fyne, Loch, *inlet*, Scotland, U.K., **308** D5
Fynshav, Denmark, **286** D5
Fyresdal, Norway, **286** D3
Fyresvatn, *lake*, Norway, **286** C3
Fyteies, Greece, **297** C6

G

Gaalkacyo, Somalia, **367** G3
Gabbac, Raas, *point*, Somalia, **367** H3
Gabbs, U.S.A., **422** E2
Gabela, Angola, **368** B5
Gabès, Golfe de, *gulf*, Tunisia, **362** B2
Gabon, *country*, Africa, **359** G7
Gaborone, Botswana, **371** E3
Gabriel y Galán, Embalse de, *reservoir*, Spain, **292** D2
Gabrovo, Bulgaria, **296** E4
Gabú, Guinea-Bissau, **364** B2
Gacé, France, **290** E2
Gacko, Bosnia and Herzegovina, **294** G4
Gadag-Betgeri, India, **216** C3
Gādarwāra, India, **218** D5
Gäddede, Sweden, **284** G4
Gādra Road, India, **218** B4
Gadsden, U.S.A., **425** K2
Găești, Romania, **296** E3
Gaeta, Golfo di, *gulf*, Italy, **295** D5
Gaeta, Italy, **295** D5
Gaferut, *island*, Micronesia, **138** C4
Gaffney, U.S.A., **425** M2
Gafsa, Tunisia, **362** A2
Gagal, Chad, **365** H3
Gagarin, Russian Federation, **299** E5
Gagau, Gunung, *mountain peak*, Malaysia, **200** C1
Gage, U.S.A., **420** D7
Gagnoa, Côte d'Ivoire, **364** C3
Gagnon, Canada, **416** G4
Gahe, China, **213** H5
Gaighāt, Nepal, **219** F4
Gail, *river*, Austria, **288** F5
Gaillac, France, **290** E5
Gaimán, Argentina, **460** E2
Gainesville, Florida, U.S.A., **425** L5
Gainesville, Georgia, U.S.A., **425** L2
Gainesville, Texas, U.S.A., **424** D3
Gainsborough, England, U.K., **307** H4
Gairdner, Lake, Australia, **135** H5
Gairloch, Scotland, U.K., **308** D3
Gaizhou, China, **211** H4
Gaiziņkalns, *mountain peak*, Latvia, **287** M4
Gakarosa, *mountain peak*, South Africa, **370** D4
Gakem, Nigeria, **365** F3
Gakuch, Pakistan, **218** C1
Gakugsa, Russian Federation, **299** F2
Gal, *river*, Sri Lanka, **217** E5
Gala, China, **219** G3

Galán, Cerro, *mountain peak*, Argentina, **458** C3
Galana, *river*, Kenya, **369** G3
Galand, Iran, **222** F5
Galang, Pulau, *island*, Indonesia, **200** D2
Galápagos, Islas, (Galapagos Islands), *islands*, Ecuador, Pacific Ocean, **461** A1
Galapagos Fracture Zone, *tectonic feature*, Pacific Ocean, **479** J5
Galapagos Islands see Galápagos, Islas, *islands*, Ecuador, Pacific Ocean, **461** A1
Galapagos Rise, *underwater feature*, Pacific Ocean, **479** M5
Galashiels, Scotland, U.K., **308** G5
Galata, Bulgaria, **296** F4
Galata, U.S.A., **419** J2
Galați, Romania, **296** G3
Galatista, Greece, **297** D5
Galatone, Italy, **295** G5
Galbally, Ireland, **309** D5
Gáldar, Islas Canarias, Spain, **373** B4
Galdhøpiggen, *mountain peak*, Norway, **286** D2
Galeana, Mexico, **430** D2
Galena, U.S.A., **420** H4
Galeota Point, Trinidad, Trinidad and Tobago, **461** C4
Galera, Punta, *point*, Chile, **460** B1
Galera, Punta, *point*, Ecuador, **450** B4
Galera, Spain, **293** F4
Galera Point, Trinidad, Trinidad and Tobago, **461** C4
Galéria, Corse, France, **295** B4
Galesburg, U.S.A., **420** H5
Galesville, U.S.A., **420** H3
Galeton, U.S.A., **426** B4
Galets, Pointe des, *point*, Réunion, **373** A1
Galguduud, *administrative region*, Somalia, **367** G3
Galicea Mare, Romania, **296** D3
Galicia, *autonomous community*, Spain, **292** D1
Galilee, Sea of see Kinneret, Yam, *lake*, Israel, **225** C3
Gallatin, U.S.A., **425** J1
Gallatin Peak, *mountain peak*, U.S.A., **419** J4
Galle, Sri Lanka, **216** E5
Gállego, *river*, Spain, **293** G1
Gallegos, *river*, Argentina, **460** C4
Gallegos, U.S.A., **423** M4
Galley Head, *point*, Ireland, **309** D6
Gallinas, Punta, *point*, Colombia, **450** D1
Gallipoli, Italy, **295** F5
Gallipoli see Gelibolu, Turkey, **297** F5
Gallipolis, U.S.A., **421** M6
Gällivare, Sweden, **284** K3
Gällö, Sweden, **284** G5
Galloway, Mount, *mountain peak*, New Zealand, **133** P15
Galloway, Mull of, *point*, Scotland, U.K., **308** E6
Gallup, U.S.A., **423** J4
Galmisdale, Scotland, U.K., **308** C4
Galston, Scotland, U.K., **308** E5
Galtström, Sweden, **287** H1
Galtymore, *mountain peak*, Ireland, **309** D5
Galva, U.S.A., **420** H5
Galveston, U.S.A., **424** E5
Galveston Bay, U.S.A., **424** E5
Gálvez, Argentina, **458** E4
Galway, *county*, Ireland, **309** C4
Galway, Ireland, **309** C4
Galway Bay, Ireland, **309** C4

Gâm, *river*, Vietnam, **203** E1
Gamaches, France, **290** E2
Gamba, China, **219** G3
Gamba, Gabon, **368** A3
Gambang, Malaysia, **200** C2
Gambēla, Ethiopia, **366** D3
Gambia, *country*, Africa, **358** D5
Gambia Plain, *underwater feature*, Atlantic Ocean, **477** F5
Gambier, Îles, *islands*, French Polynesia, **137** H3
Gambo, Canada, **417** P5
Gambo, Central African Republic, **368** D2
Gamboma, Congo, **368** C3
Gamboula, Central African Republic, **368** C2
Gamgadhi, Nepal, **219** E3
Gamleby, Sweden, **286** H4
Gammelstaden, Sweden, **285** L4
Gamph, Slieve, *mountain range*, Ireland, **309** C3
Gamtog, China, **215** F3
Gamud, *mountain peak*, Ethiopia, **369** G2
Gamvik, Norway, **285** P1
Gan, France, **290** D5
Gan, *river*, N. China, **211** J2
Gan, *river*, S. China, **206** C3
Gan Gan, Argentina, **460** D2
Gana, China, **215** G2
Ganado, U.S.A., **423** J4
Gäncä, Azerbaijan, **222** D4
Gancheng, China, **203** F2
Ganda, Angola, **368** B5
Gandadiwata, Gunung, *mountain peak*, Indonesia, **198** B3
Gandajika, Democratic Republic of the Congo, **368** D4
Gandak, *river*, India, **219** F4
Gandāva, Pakistan, **218** A3
Gander, Canada, **417** P5
Gander Bay, Canada, **417** P5
Gandesa, Spain, **293** H2
Gāndhī Sāgar, *lake*, India, **218** C4
Gāndhīdhām, India, **218** B5
Gāndhīnagar, India, **218** C5
Gandía, Spain, **293** G3
Gandu, Brazil, **457** F3
Gangānagar, India, **218** C3
Gangāpur, India, **218** D4
Ganga, *river*, India, **219** E4
Gangala-na-Bodio, Democratic Republic of the Congo, **369** E2
Gangara, Niger, **365** F2
Gangaw, Myanmar, **205** B3
Gangaw Taung, *mountain range*, Myanmar, **205** C2
Gangca, China, **213** J5
Gangdisê Shan, *mountain range*, China, **219** E3
Ganges, France, **291** F5
Ganges, Mouths of the, Bangladesh/India, **194** K7
Ganges, *river*, Bangladesh/India, **205** A3
Ganges Fan, *underwater feature*, Indian Ocean, **476** E4
Gangkou, E. Guangdong, China, **207** D3
Gangkou, W. Guangdong, China, **207** A3
Gangoumen, China, **208** B2
Gangtok, India, **219** G4
Gangu, China, **215** H2
Ganluo, China, **215** G3
Gannan, China, **211** H3
Gannat, France, **291** F3
Gannvalley, U.S.A., **420** D3
Ganq, China, **213** G5
Ganquan, China, **210** E5
Gänserndorf, Austria, **289** H4
Gansu, *province*, China, **213** J5
Gantang, Anhui, China, **206** D2
Gantang, Ningxia Huizu Zizhiqu, China, **210** D5
Ganye, Nigeria, **365** G3
Ganyu, China, **206** D1

Ganyushkino, Kazakhstan, **222** D3
Ganzhou, China, **206** C3
Gao, *administrative region*, Mali, **365** E1
Gao, Mali, **364** D1
Gao Xian, China, **215** H3
Gao'an, China, **206** C2
Gaocheng, China, **210** F5
Gaolan, China, **213** J5
Gaolan Dao, *island*, China, **207** A5
Gaoping, China, **206** C1
Gaoqiao, China, **207** A1
Gaotai, China, **213** H5
Gaotang, China, **210** G5
Gaotouyao, China, **210** E4
Gaoua, Burkina Faso, **364** D2
Gaoyang, China, **210** F5
Gaoyou, China, **206** D1
Gaozhou, China, **206** B4
Gap, France, **291** H4
Gapan, Philippines, **204** C3
Gar, China, **218** E2
Gara, Lough, *lake*, Ireland, **309** D4
Gara Nasa, *mountain peak*, Ethiopia, **366** E3
Garabogazköl Aylagy, *bay*, Turkmenistan, **222** E4
Garacad, Somalia, **367** G3
Garachiné, Panama, **429** F5
Garadag, Somalia, **367** G3
Garafia, Islas Canarias, Spain, **373** A4
Garagum, *desert*, Turkmenistan, **222** F5
Garaina, Papua New Guinea, **140** B5
Garalo, Mali, **364** C2
Garang, China, **213** J5
Garanhuns, Brazil, **457** G2
Garba, Central African Republic, **366** B3
Garba Tula, Kenya, **369** G2
Garbahaarrey, Somalia, **369** H2
Garberville, U.S.A., **422** B1
Garbsen, Germany, **288** D2
Garça, Brazil, **459** H2
Garco, China, **214** D2
Garda, Lago di, *lake*, Italy, **294** C3
Garde, Cap de, *cape*, Algeria, **295** A7
Gardelegen, Germany, **288** E2
Garden City, U.S.A., **420** C7
Garden Corners, U.S.A., **421** K3
Gardey, Argentina, **459** E5
Gardēz, Afghanistan, **218** B2
Gardiner, U.S.A., **419** J4
Gärdnäs, Sweden, **284** G4
Gardner, Colorado, U.S.A., **423** L3
Gardner, Florida, U.S.A., **425** M6
Gardner Pinnacles, *islands*, Hawaiian Islands, U.S.A., **139** H2
Gardone Val Trompia, Italy, **294** C3
Gare Tigre, French Guiana, **452** C2
Garelochhead, Scotland, U.K., **308** E4
Garforth, England, U.K., **307** G4
Gargždai, Lithuania, **287** K5
Garhchiroli, India, **218** E5
Garibaldi, Brazil, **459** G3
Garibaldi, Mount, *mountain peak*, Canada, **412** H4
Garies, South Africa, **370** C5
Garissa, Kenya, **369** G3
Garland, Canada, **414** D6
Garland, North Carolina, U.S.A., **425** N2
Garland, Texas, U.S.A., **424** D3
Garland, Wyoming, U.S.A., **419** K4
Garliava, Lithuania, **287** L5
Garlin, France, **290** D5
Garmisch-Partenkirchen, Germany, **288** E5

Garmo, Norway, **286** D2
Garmsār, Iran, **220** F1
Garner, U.S.A., **420** G4
Garnett, U.S.A., **420** F6
Garnish, Canada, **417** P6
Garnpung Lake, Australia, **135** J5
Garonne, *river*, France, **290** D4
Garoowe, Somalia, **367** G3
Garoua, Cameroon, **365** G3
Garoua Boulaï, Cameroon, **368** B1
Garove Island, Papua New Guinea, **140** C4
Garqu Yan, China, **214** E2
Garrison, Montana, U.S.A., **418** H3
Garrison, North Dakota, U.S.A., **420** C2
Garsen, Kenya, **369** H3
Garsila, Sudan, **366** B2
Garson Lake, Canada, **413** Q3
Garstang, England, U.K., **306** F4
Gartempe, *river*, France, **290** E3
Garth, Wales, U.K., **304** D2
Garut, Indonesia, **201** D4
Garut, Tanjong, *point*, Indonesia, **201** D4
Garvagh, Northern Ireland, U.K., **309** F3
Garve, Scotland, U.K., **308** E3
Garwa, India, **219** E4
Garwolin, Poland, **289** K3
Gary, U.S.A., **421** K5
Garyarsa, China, **218** E3
Garzê, China, **215** G3
Garzón, Colombia, **450** C3
Gascogne, *region*, France, **290** D5
Gascoyne, Golfe de, *gulf*, France, **290** C4
Gascoyne, *river*, Australia, **134** D4
Gashua, Nigeria, **365** G2
Gasim, Indonesia, **199** E3
Gasmata, Papua New Guinea, **140** C4
Gaspé, Canada, **417** J5
Gaspé, Cap de, *cape*, Canada, **417** J5
Gaspé, Péninsule de, Canada, **416** H5
Gasquet, U.S.A., **418** C6
Gassol, Nigeria, **365** G3
Gastonia, U.S.A., **425** M2
Gastouni, Greece, **297** C7
Gastre, Argentina, **460** D2
Gata, Cabo de, *cape*, Spain, **293** F4
Gătaia, Romania, **296** C3
Gataivai, Samoa, **141** B1
Gatchina, Russian Federation, **299** C3
Gate, U.S.A., **420** C7
Gatehouse of Fleet, Scotland, U.K., **308** E6
Gateshead, England, U.K., **307** G3
Gatesville, U.S.A., **424** D4
Gatineau, Canada, **416** D7
Gatún, Lago, *reservoir*, Panama, **429** F5
Gau, *island*, Fiji, **141** A4
Gaua see Santa Maria, *island*, Vanuatu, **141** A2
Gauja, *river*, Latvia, **287** N4
Gauley Bridge, U.S.A., **421** N6
Gauribidanūr, India, **216** D3
Gausta, *mountain peak*, Norway, **286** D3
Gāv, *river*, Iran, **220** E1
Gāvbandī, Iran, **220** F3
Gavdopoula, *island*, Greece, **297** D8
Gavdos, *island*, Greece, **297** E8
Gave de Pau, *river*, France, **290** D5
Gaviãozinho, Brazil, **455** E2
Gävle, Sweden, **287** H2
Gävleborg, *county*, Sweden, **286** G2
Gavrilov-Yam, Russian Federation, **299** G4

Glåma, *river*, Norway, **286** E2
Glamis, Scotland, U.K., **308** F4
Glåmos, Norway, **286** E1
Glan, Philippines, **204** D5
Glanaruddery Mountains, Ireland, **309** C5
Glanton, England, U.K., **307** G2
Glarner Alpen, *mountain range*, Switzerland, **291** J3
Glarus, Switzerland, **291** J3
Glasbury, Wales, U.K., **304** D2
Glasgow, Kentucky, U.S.A., **421** L7
Glasgow, Montana, U.S.A., **419** L2
Glasgow, Scotland, U.K., **308** E5
Glasgow, Virginia, U.S.A., **421** P7
Glasgow City, *local authority*, Scotland, U.K., **308** E5
Glaslyn, Canada, **413** Q5
Glass Butte, *mountain peak*, U.S.A., **418** D5
Glassboro, U.S.A., **426** C5
Glastonbury, England, U.K., **304** E3
Glazov, Russian Federation, **300** G4
Gleisdorf, Austria, **289** G5
Glen Canyon, *gorge*, U.S.A., **423** H3
Glen Cove, U.S.A., **426** D4
Glen Falls, U.S.A., **426** D3
Glen Innes, Australia, **135** L4
Glen Ullin, U.S.A., **419** P3
Glenavy, New Zealand, **133** C7
Glenbarr, Scotland, U.K., **308** D5
Glencross, U.S.A., **420** C3
Glendale, Arizona, U.S.A., **423** G5
Glendale, California, U.S.A., **422** D4
Glendambo, Australia, **135** H5
Glendive, U.S.A., **419** M3
Glendo, U.S.A., **419** M5
Glendon, Canada, **413** P4
Gleneagles, Scotland, U.K., **308** F4
Glenelg, *river*, Australia, **135** J6
Glenfield, U.S.A., **420** D2
Glenfinnan, Scotland, U.K., **308** D4
Glengad Head, *point*, Ireland, **309** E2
Glengarriff, Ireland, **309** C6
Glenluce, Scotland, U.K., **308** E6
Glennallen, U.S.A., **410** E3
Glennamaddy, Ireland, **309** D4
Glennville, U.S.A., **425** M4
Glenorchy, New Zealand, **133** B7
Glenrock, U.S.A., **419** M5
Glenrothes, Scotland, U.K., **308** F4
Glenties, Ireland, **309** D3
Glentworth, Canada, **413** R7
Glenville, U.S.A., **425** K3
Glenwood, Arkansas, U.S.A., **424** F2
Glenwood, Iowa, U.S.A., **420** F5
Glenwood, Minnesota, U.S.A., **420** F3
Glenwood, New Mexico, U.S.A., **423** J5
Glenwood Springs, U.S.A., **423** K2
Glide, U.S.A., **418** C5
Glina, Croatia, **294** F3
Glinojeck, Poland, **289** K2
Glinton, England, U.K., **305** G2
Glittertind, *mountain peak*, Norway, **286** D2
Gliwice, Poland, **289** J3
Globe, U.S.A., **423** H5
Glodeanu-Sărat, Romania, **296** F3
Glodeni, Moldova, **296** F2
Głogów, Poland, **289** H3
Glomfjord, Norway, **284** F3
Glommersträsk, Sweden, **284** J4
Glonn, *river*, Germany, **288** E4

Glorieuses, Îles, *islands*, Réunion, **372** B3
Glossop, England, U.K., **307** G4
Gloucester, England, U.K., **304** E3
Gloucester, Papua New Guinea, **140** C4
Gloucester, U.S.A., **426** E3
Gloucestershire, *unitary authority*, England, U.K., **304** E3
Glover Island, Canada, **417** N5
Głubczyce, Poland, **289** H3
Glübokoe, Kazakhstan, **223** L2
Gmünd, Austria, **289** G4
Gmunden, Austria, **289** F5
Gniew, Poland, **289** J2
Gniewkowo, Poland, **289** J2
Gniezno, Poland, **289** H2
Gnjilane, Yugoslavia, **296** C4
Goa, *state*, India, **216** C3
Goālpāra, India, **219** G4
Goaso, Ghana, **364** D3
Goat Fell, *mountain peak*, Scotland, U.K., **308** D5
Goba, Ethiopia, **367** F3
Gobabis, Namibia, **370** C3
Gobernador Duval, Argentina, **460** D1
Gobernador Gregores, Argentina, **460** C4
Gobernador Mayer, Argentina, **460** C4
Gobi, China, **213** H5
Gobi, *desert*, Mongolia, **195** M5
Gobowen, England, U.K., **304** D2
Gochas, Namibia, **370** C3
Godalming, England, U.K., **305** G3
Godavari, *river*, India, **216** D2
Godbout, Canada, **416** H5
Godda, India, **219** F4
Godē, Ethiopia, **367** F3
Godech, Bulgaria, **296** D4
Godere, Ethiopia, **367** F3
Goderich, Canada, **421** N4
Goderville, France, **305** H5
Godhra, India, **218** C5
Godinlabe, Somalia, **367** G3
Godmanchester, England, U.K., **305** G2
Gödöllő, Hungary, **289** J5
Godoy Cruz, Argentina, **458** C4
Gods, *river*, Canada, **414** H3
Gods Lake, Canada, **414** G4
Gods Lake, *lake*, Canada, **414** G4
Godthåb *see* Nuuk, Greenland, **411** P3
Goe, Papua New Guinea, **140** A5
Goéland, Lac au, *lake*, Canada, **416** C5
Goes, Netherlands, **288** A3
Goffs, U.S.A., **422** F4
Gogland, Ostrov, *island*, Russian Federation, **287** N2
Gogounou, Benin, **365** E2
Gogrial, Sudan, **366** C3
Gohad, India, **218** D4
Goiana, Brazil, **453** G5
Goiandira, Brazil, **456** D5
Goiânia, Brazil, **456** D4
Goiás, Brazil, **456** C4
Goiás, *state*, Brazil, **456** C4
Goio-Erê, Brazil, **459** G2
Góis, Portugal, **292** C2
Gojra, Pakistan, **218** C3
Gökçeada, *island*, Turkey, **297** E5
Göksun, Turkey, **224** E5
Gokwe, Zimbabwe, **371** E2
Gol, Norway, **286** D2
Gola, India, **218** E3
Golāghāt, India, **219** H4
Golan, *region*, Syria, **225** C3
Gölbaşı, Turkey, **363** G1
Golbembal, Nigeria, **365** G3
Golconda, U.S.A., **422** E1
Gölcük, Kocaeli, Turkey, **297** G5
Gölcük, Turkey, **297** F6
Gold Beach, U.S.A., **418** B5

Gold Bridge, Canada, **412** H6
Gold Coast, Australia, **135** L4
Gold Coast, *coastal area*, Ghana/Togo, **364** D4
Gold River, Canada, **412** F7
Gołdap, Poland, **289** L1
Golden, Canada, **413** L6
Golden Bay, New Zealand, **132** D5
Golden Meadow, U.S.A., **424** G5
Goldendale, U.S.A., **418** D4
Goldfield, U.S.A., **422** E3
Goldsboro, U.S.A., **425** N2
Goldsmith, U.S.A., **423** M6
Goldthwaite, U.S.A., **424** C4
Goldyrevskiy, Russian Federation, **222** F1
Goleniów, Poland, **289** G2
Goleta, U.S.A., **422** D4
Golets Skalistyy, Gora, *mountain peak*, Russian Federation, **301** Q4
Golfo Aranci, Sardegna, Italy, **295** B5
Gölgeli Dağları, *mountain range*, Turkey, **297** G7
Goliad, U.S.A., **424** D5
Gölmarmara, Turkey, **297** F6
Golmud, China, **213** G5
Golnik, Slovenia, **294** E2
Golo, *river*, Corse, France, **294** B4
Golo Island, Philippines, **204** C3
Golovnino, Russian Federation, **209** J2
Golpāyegān, Iran, **220** F2
Gölpazarı, Turkey, **299** H5
Golspie, Scotland, U.K., **308** F3
Golungo Alto, Angola, **368** B4
Golyam Perelik, *mountain peak*, Bulgaria, **297** E5
Gölyazı, Turkey, **297** G5
Golyshmanovo, Russian Federation, **223** H1
Goma, Democratic Republic of the Congo, **369** E3
Gomati, *river*, India, **219** E4
Gombe, Nigeria, **365** G2
Gombi, Nigeria, **365** G2
Gombrani Island, Rodrigues, **373** B1
Gomera, *island*, Islas Canarias, Spain, **373** A4
Gómez Farías, Mexico, **430** D2
Gómez Palacio, Mexico, **430** E3
Gomo, China, **219** F2
Gomorovichi, Russian Federation, **299** E2
Gonaïves, Haiti, **429** G3
Gonâve, Golfe de la, *gulf*, Haiti, **429** G3
Gonâve, Île de la, *island*, Haiti, **429** G3
Gonbad-e Qābūs, Iran, **222** F5
Gonda, India, **219** E4
Gondal, India, **218** B5
Gonder, Ethiopia, **367** E2
Gondia, India, **218** E5
Gönen, *river*, Turkey, **297** F5
Gönen, Turkey, **297** F5
Gonfreville-L'Orcher, France, **290** E2
Gong Xian, China, **206** C1
Gong'an, China, **206** C2
Gongbo'gyamba, China, **214** E3
Gongcheng, China, **206** B3
Gonggar, China, **214** D3
Gonghe, China, **213** J5
Gonghui, China, **210** F4
Gongliu, China, **223** L4
Gongming, China, **207** B3
Gongpoquan, China, **213** H4
Gongzhuling, China, **211** J4
Goniri, Nigeria, **365** G2
Gonzaga, Philippines, **204** C2
Gonzales, California, U.S.A., **422** C3
Gonzales, Texas, U.S.A., **424** D5
González, Mexico, **431** F4
Goobies, Canada, **417** P6
Good Hope, Cape of, South Africa, **370** C5

Good Hope Lake, Canada, **412** E2
Goodenough Island, Papua New Guinea, **140** C5
Goodeve, Canada, **414** C6
Gooding, U.S.A., **418** G5
Goodland, U.S.A., **420** C6
Goodlands, Mauritius, **373** C1
Goodrich, U.S.A., **420** C2
Goodsoil, Canada, **413** Q4
Goodwick, Wales, U.K., **304** C2
Goodwin, U.S.A., **420** E3
Goole, England, U.K., **307** H4
Goomalling, Australia, **134** D5
Goondiwindi, Australia, **135** L4
Goose Green, Falkland Islands, **460** F4
Goose Lake, U.S.A., **418** D6
Gopalganj, India, **219** F4
Góra, near Płock, Poland, **289** K2
Góra, Poland, **289** H3
Gora, Russian Federation, **299** G2
Gorakhpur, India, **219** E4
Goram, Tanjong, *point*, Indonesia, **198** C4
Goras, India, **218** D4
Goražde, Bosnia and Herzegovina, **294** G4
Gorbitsa, Russian Federation, **211** G1
Gorda, Punta, *point*, Chile, **454** D5
Gördalen, Sweden, **286** F2
Gördes, Turkey, **297** G6
Gordil, Central African Republic, **366** B3
Gordon, Lake, Australia, **135** J7
Gordon, Scotland, U.K., **308** G5
Gordon, U.S.A., **420** B4
Gordondale, Canada, **413** K4
Gordonsville, U.S.A., **426** A5
Goré, Chad, **365** H3
Gorē, Ethiopia, **366** E3
Gore, New Zealand, **133** B8
Gore Mountain, *mountain peak*, U.S.A., **426** E2
Gorebridge, Scotland, U.K., **308** F5
Gorel'de, Turkmenistan, **222** G4
Gorey, Ireland, **309** F5
Gorgal, *administrative region*, Mauritania, **364** B1
Gorge Creek, New Zealand, **133** B7
Gorgona, Isola di, *island*, Italy, **294** B4
Gorgora, Ethiopia, **367** E2
Gorgova, Romania, **296** G3
Gorham, U.S.A., **426** E2
Gorinchem, Netherlands, **288** B3
Goris, Armenia, **363** J1
Goritsy, Russian Federation, **299** F4
Gorizia, Italy, **294** D3
Gorlice, Poland, **289** K4
Görlitz, Germany, **289** G3
Gorlovo, Russian Federation, **299** F4
Gorm, Loch, *lake*, Scotland, U.K., **308** C5
Gorna Oryakhovitsa, Bulgaria, **296** E4
Gornja Dŭbnik, Bulgaria, **296** E4
Gornji Milanovac, Yugoslavia, **296** C3
Gorno Altaysk, Russian Federation, **223** M2
Gornozavodsk, Russian Federation, **209** H1
Gornyak, Russian Federation, **223** L2
Gorodishche, Russian Federation, **299** B3
Gorogoro, Indonesia, **198** D3
Goroka, Papua New Guinea, **140** B4
Gorom-Gorom, Burkina Faso, **364** D2
Gorong, Kepulauan, *islands*, Indonesia, **199** E4

Gorongosa, Mozambique, **371** F2
Gorongosa, Serra da, *mountain range*, Mozambique, **371** F2
Gorontalo, Indonesia, **198** C2
Gort, Ireland, **309** D4
Gortahork, Ireland, **309** D2
Gorumna Island, Ireland, **309** C4
Görvik, Sweden, **284** G5
Goryachegorsk, Russian Federation, **223** M1
Goryachinsk, Russian Federation, **210** E1
Gorzów Wielkopolski, Poland, **289** G2
Gosberton, England, U.K., **305** G2
Gosfield, England, U.K., **305** H3
Gosford, Australia, **135** L5
Gosforth, Cumbria, England, U.K., **306** E3
Gosforth, Tyne and Wear, England, U.K., **307** G2
Goshogawara, Japan, **209** H2
Goslar, Germany, **288** E3
Gospić, Croatia, **294** E3
Gosport, England, U.K., **305** F4
Gossen, *island*, Norway, **286** C1
Gossi, Mali, **364** D1
Gostivar, Macedonia, **296** C5
Gostyń, Poland, **289** H3
Gostynin, Poland, **289** J2
Gota, Ethiopia, **367** F3
Göteborg (Gothenburg), Sweden, **286** E4
Göteborg Och Bohus, *county*, Sweden, **286** E3
Götene, Sweden, **286** F3
Goth Amri, Pakistan, **218** A4
Gotha, Germany, **288** E3
Gothem, Sweden, **287** J4
Gothenburg *see* Göteborg, Sweden, **286** E4
Gothenburg, U.S.A., **420** C5
Gothèye, Niger, **365** E2
Gotland, *county*, Sweden, **287** J4
Gotland, *island*, Sweden, **287** J4
Gotō-rettō, *islands*, Japan, **208** E4
Gotowasi, Indonesia, **199** E2
Gotse Delchev, Bulgaria, **297** D5
Gotska Sandön, *island*, Sweden, **287** J3
Göttingen, Germany, **288** D3
Gouda, Netherlands, **288** B3
Goudiri, Senegal, **364** B2
Goudoumaria, Niger, **365** G2
Gouéké, Guinea, **364** C3
Gouin, Réservoir, Canada, **416** D5
Goulais River, Canada, **421** L2
Goulburn, Australia, **135** K5
Goulburn Islands, Australia, **134** G1
Gould, U.S.A., **423** K1
Gould Coast, *region*, Antarctica, **470** D6
Goulfey, Cameroon, **365** G2
Goumbou, Mali, **364** C2
Goundam, Mali, **364** D1
Goundi, Chad, **365** H3
Gourcy, Burkina Faso, **364** D2
Gourdon, Cape, Papua New Guinea, **140** B4
Gourdon, France, **290** E4
Gouré, Niger, **365** G2
Gourin, France, **290** C2
Gourma-Rharous, Mali, **364** D1
Gournay-en-Bray, France, **305** J5
Gouro, Chad, **362** C5
Gouverneur, U.S.A., **426** C2
Gouzon, France, **290** F3
Governador Valadares, Brazil, **457** F5
Governor's Harbour, Bahamas, **428** F1
Govī-Altay, *province*, Mongolia, **213** G3

Greenville, Illinois, U.S.A., **421** J6
Greenville, Liberia, **364** C3
Greenville, Louisiana, U.S.A., **424** G3
Greenville, North Carolina, U.S.A., **425** P2
Greenville, Ohio, U.S.A., **421** L5
Greenville, Pennsylvania, U.S.A., **421** N5
Greenville, South Carolina, U.S.A., **425** L2
Greenville, Texas, U.S.A., **424** D3
Greenwood, Mississippi, U.S.A., **424** G3
Greenwood, South Carolina, U.S.A., **425** L2
Greers Ferry Lake, U.S.A., **424** F2
Gregório, *river*, Brazil, **454** D2
Gregory, Lake, Australia, **134** F3
Gregory, *river*, Australia, **135** H2
Greifswald, Germany, **288** F1
Greifswalder Bodden, *bay*, Germany, **288** F1
Grein, Austria, **289** G4
Gremć, *physical feature*, Bosnia and Herzegovina, **294** F3
Gremikha, Russian Federation, **285** U2
Gremyachinsk, Russian Federation, **210** E1
Grenå, Denmark, **286** E4
Grenada, *country*, Caribbean Sea, **409** S7
Grenada, U.S.A., **424** H3
Grenade, France, **290** E5
Grenadines, The, *islands*, St Vincent and the Grenadines, **427** D3
Grenfell, Canada, **414** C6
Grenivík, Iceland, **284** Y7
Grenoble, France, **291** G4
Grense Jakobselv, Norway, **285** Q2
Grenville, Cape, Australia, **135** J1
Grenville, Grenada, **427** D3
Gresik, Indonesia, **201** F4
Gretna, U.S.A., **424** G5
Gretna Green, Scotland, U.K., **308** F6
Grevena, Greece, **297** C5
Grevesmühlen, Germany, **288** E2
Grey, *river*, New Zealand, **133** C6
Grey Islands, Canada, **417** P4
Grey Range, *mountain range*, Australia, **135** J4
Greymouth, New Zealand, **133** C6
Greystoke, England, U.K., **306** F3
Greytown, New Zealand, **133** E5
Greytown, South Africa, **371** F4
Gridino, Russian Federation, **285** S4
Griffin, Canada, **414** C7
Griffin, U.S.A., **425** K3
Griffith, Australia, **135** K5
Grigoriopol, Moldova, **296** G2
Grigor'yevka, Russian Federation, **223** N2
Grim, Cape, Australia, **128** D6
Grimari, Central African Republic, **365** J3
Grimma, Germany, **288** F3
Grimmen, Germany, **288** F1
Grimsby, England, U.K., **307** H4
Grimshaw, Canada, **413** L3
Grímsstaðir, Iceland, **284** Y7
Grimstad, Norway, **286** D3
Grindavík, Iceland, **284** X8
Grindsted, Denmark, **286** D5
Grinnell, U.S.A., **420** G5
Grintavec, *mountain peak*, Slovenia, **294** E2
Griquatown, South Africa, **370** D4

Gris Nez, Cap, *cape*, France, **305** J4
Grise Fiord, Canada, **411** L2
Grisslehamn, Sweden, **287** J2
Groais Island, Canada, **417** P4
Grobiņa, Latvia, **287** K4
Grødes, Norway, **286** C2
Grodków, Poland, **289** H3
Groesbeek, Netherlands, **288** B3
Groix, Île de, *island*, France, **290** C3
Grójec, Poland, **289** K3
Grong, Norway, **284** F4
Groningen, Netherlands, **288** C2
Groningen, *province*, Netherlands, **288** C2
Groningen, Suriname, **452** B2
Groote Eylandt, *island*, Australia, **135** H1
Grootfontein, Namibia, **370** C2
Gropniţa, Romania, **296** F2
Grose Morne, *mountain peak*, Canada, **417** N5
Gross Ums, Namibia, **370** C3
Grossa, Punta, *point*, Islas Baleares, Spain, **293** H3
Grosser Arber, *mountain peak*, Germany, **288** F4
Grosseto, Italy, **294** C4
Großglockner, *mountain peak*, Austria, **288** F5
Groswater Bay, Canada, **417** N2
Groton, U.S.A., **420** D3
Grov, Norway, **284** H2
Grove City, U.S.A., **421** N5
Grove Hill, U.S.A., **425** J4
Grover City, U.S.A., **422** C4
Groznyy, Russian Federation, **222** D4
Grua, Norway, **286** E2
Grudovo, Bulgaria, **296** F4
Grudziądz, Poland, **289** J2
Gruinard Bay, Scotland, U.K., **308** D3
Grums, Sweden, **286** F3
Grünau, Namibia, **370** C4
Gruvberget, Sweden, **286** H2
Gruža, Yugoslavia, **296** C4
Gruzdžiai, Lithuania, **287** L4
Gryfice, Poland, **289** G2
Gryllefjord, Norway, **284** H2
Gryt, Sweden, **287** H3
Grytøya, *island*, Norway, **284** H2
Grytviken, South Georgia, **461** A3
Grytviken, *U.K. research station*, Antarctica, **470** A2
Guacanayabo, Golfo de, *gulf*, Cuba, **429** F2
Guachipas, Argentina, **458** D2
Guaçu, *river*, Brazil, **459** F2
Guadajoz, *river*, Spain, **292** E4
Guadalajara, Mexico, **430** E4
Guadalajara, Spain, **293** F2
Guadalcanal, *island*, Solomon Islands, **141** A1
Guadalimar, *river*, Spain, **293** F3
Guadalmena, Embalse de, *reservoir*, Murcia, **293** G3
Guadalmena, *river*, Spain, **293** F3
Guadálmez, *river*, Spain, **292** E3
Guadalope, *river*, Spain, **293** G2
Guadalquivir, *river*, Spain, **292** E4
Guadalupe, Baja California, Mexico, **430** A1
Guadalupe, Isla, *island*, Mexico, **409** M6
Guadalupe, Nuevo Léon, Mexico, **430** E4
Guadalupe, Spain, **292** E3
Guadalupe Aguilera, Mexico, **430** D3
Guadalupe Victoria, Mexico, **430** D3
Guadarrama, Sierra de, *mountain range*, Spain, **293** F2

Guadeloupe, *French department*, Caribbean Sea, **409** S7
Guadeloupe Passage, Caribbean Sea, **427** D2
Guadiana, *river*, Portugal/ Spain, **280** D4
Guadix, Spain, **293** F4
Guafo, Boca del, *river mouth*, Chile, **460** B2
Guafo, Isla, *island*, Chile, **460** B2
Guaíba, Brazil, **459** G4
Guaimaca, Honduras, **428** D4
Guáimaro, Cuba, **429** F2
Guaiquinima, Cerro, *mountain peak*, Venezuela, **451** F3
Guaira, Brazil, **459** F2
Guaitecas, Islas, *islands*, Chile, **460** B2
Guajará-Mirim, Brazil, **455** F3
Guajarraã, Brazil, **455** E2
Guajira, Península de, Colombia, **450** D1
Gualaceo, Ecuador, **450** B5
Gualdo Tadino, Italy, **294** D4
Gualeguay, Argentina, **459** E4
Gualeguay, *river*, Argentina, **459** E4
Gualeguaychú, Argentina, **459** E4
Gualicho, Salina, *salt-pan*, Argentina, **460** E1
Gualjaina, Argentina, **460** C2
Guallatiri, Volcán, *mountain peak*, Chile, **455** E5
Guam, *U.S. territory*, Pacific Ocean, **138** C3
Guamini, Argentina, **458** D5
Guamúchil, Mexico, **430** C3
Guan Xian, China, **215** G3
Guanabacoa, Cuba, **429** E2
Guanaja, Honduras, **428** D3
Guanajuato, Mexico, **431** E4
Guanajuato, *state*, Mexico, **431** E4
Guanambi, Brazil, **457** E4
Guanare, Venezuela, **451** E2
Guanarito, Venezuela, **451** E2
Guanay, Sierra, *mountain range*, Venezuela, **451** E3
Guandacol, Argentina, **458** C3
Guane, Cuba, **428** D2
Guang'an, China, **215** H3
Guangchang, China, **206** D3
Guangde, China, **206** D2
Guangdegong, China, **211** G4
Guangdong, *province*, China, **206** C4
Guangfeng, China, **206** D2
Guanghai, China, **206** C4
Guangning, China, **206** C4
Guangrao, China, **211** G5
Guangshui, China, **206** C2
Guangxi Zhuangzu Zizhiqu, *autonomous region*, China, **206** B3
Guangyuan, China, **215** H2
Guangze, China, **206** D3
Guangzhou (Canton), China, **207** A2
Guanhães, Brazil, **457** E5
Guanhu, China, **206** D1
Guanipa, *river*, Venezuela, **451** F2
Guanlan, China, **207** C3
Guantánamo, Cuba, **429** G2
Guanting, China, **215** G2
Guanyinge, China, **207** D2
Guanyun, China, **206** D1
Guapay, *river see* Grande, *river*, Bolivia, **455** F5
Guapí, Colombia, **450** C3
Guápiles, Costa Rica, **428** E5
Guapo Bay, Trinidad, Trinidad and Tobago, **461** C4
Guaporé, *river*, Bolivia/Brazil, **455** F3
Guara, Sierra de, *mountain peak*, Spain, **293** G1
Guarabira, Brazil, **453** G5
Guaranda, Ecuador, **450** B4
Guarapari, Brazil, **457** F5

Guarapuava, Brazil, **459** G2
Guaraqueçaba, Brazil, **459** H2
Guaratinguetá, Brazil, **457** E6
Guaratuba, Brazil, **459** H2
Guarayos, Bolivia, **455** E3
Guarda, *district*, Portugal, **292** D2
Guarda, Portugal, **292** D2
Guarda Mor, Brazil, **456** D4
Guárico, *river*, Venezuela, **451** E2
Guarita, *river*, Brazil, **459** G3
Guarujá, Brazil, **459** H2
Guasacaví, Cerro, *mountain peak*, Colombia, **451** E3
Guasave, Mexico, **430** C3
Guasdualito, Venezuela, **451** D2
Guasipati, Venezuela, **451** G2
Guatemala, *country*, Central America, **409** P7
Guatemala, Guatemala, **428** C4
Guatemala Basin, *underwater feature*, Pacific Ocean, **479** M4
Guateng, *province*, South Africa, **371** E4
Guatrache, Argentina, **458** D5
Guatuaro Point, Trinidad, Trinidad and Tobago, **461** C4
Guaviare, *river*, Colombia, **451** D3
Guaxupé, Brazil, **456** D5
Guayabero, *river*, Colombia, **450** D3
Guayaguayare, Trinidad, Trinidad and Tobago, **461** C4
Guayama, Puerto Rico, **427** C2
Guayaquil, Ecuador, **450** B5
Guayaquil, Golfo de, *gulf*, Ecuador, **450** B5
Guayaramerin, Bolivia, **455** F3
Guaycurú, *river*, Argentina, **459** E3
Guaymas, Mexico, **430** C3
Guayquiraró, *river*, Argentina, **459** E4
Guba, Ethiopia, **366** E2
Guban, *physical feature*, Somalia, **367** F2
Gubbio, Italy, **294** D4
Guben, Germany, **289** G3
Gubi, Nigeria, **365** F2
Gubin, Poland, **289** G3
Gubio, Nigeria, **365** G2
Gucheng, China, **206** B1
Gudivāda, India, **217** E2
Gudiyattam, India, **216** D3
Güdür, India, **216** D3
Gudvangen, Norway, **286** C2
Guékédou, Guinea, **364** B3
Guélengdeng, Chad, **365** H2
Guelma, Algeria, **361** H1
Guelmim, Morocco, **360** D3
Guelta Zemmur, Western Sahara, **360** D3
Guemar, Algeria, **361** H2
Güémez, Mexico, **431** F4
Guéné, Benin, **365** E2
Guer, France, **290** C3
Guéra, *prefecture*, Chad, **366** A2
Guerara, Algeria, **361** G2
Guercif, Morocco, **361** F2
Guéret, France, **290** E3
Guernsey, *island*, Channel Islands, **290** C2
Guernsey, U.S.A., **419** M5
Guérou, Mauritania, **364** B1
Guerrero, *state*, Mexico, **431** E5
Guerrero Negro, Mexico, **430** B3
Gueugnon, France, **291** G3
Guéyo, Côte d'Ivoire, **364** C3
Gugē, *mountain peak*, Ethiopia, **367** E3
Guguan, *island*, Northern Mariana Islands, **138** C3
Guguang, Gunung, *mountain peak*, Indonesia, **201** G2
Guhāgar, India, **216** C2
Guhakolak, Tanjong, *point*, Indonesia, **200** D4
Gui, *river*, China, **206** B3

Guía de Isora, Islas Canarias, Spain, **373** A4
Guiana Highlands, South America, **447** F3
Guichi, China, **206** D2
Guichón, Uruguay, **459** F4
Guidari, Chad, **365** H3
Guide, China, **215** G2
Guider, Cameroon, **365** G3
Guidimaka, *administrative region*, Mauritania, **364** B1
Guiding, China, **215** H4
Guigang, China, **206** B4
Guiglo, Côte d'Ivoire, **364** C3
Guijuelo, Spain, **292** E2
Guildford, England, U.K., **305** G3
Guiler, China, **211** H3
Guilford, U.S.A., **426** F2
Guilin, China, **206** B3
Guillaume-Delisle, Lac, *lake*, Canada, **415** S3
Guillestre, France, **291** H4
Guimarães, Brazil, **453** E4
Guimarães, Portugal, **292** C2
Guimbiri, Mont, *mountain peak*, Cameroon, **365** G4
Guinan, China, **215** G2
Guindulman, Philippines, **204** D4
Guinea, *country*, Africa, **358** D5
Guinea Basin, *underwater feature*, Atlantic Ocean, **477** G5
Guinea-Bissau, *country*, Africa, **358** D5
Guinée-Forestière, *administrative area*, Guinea, **364** C3
Guinée-Maritime, *administrative region*, Guinea, **364** B2
Güines, Cuba, **429** E2
Guingamp, France, **290** C2
Guinguinéo, Senegal, **364** A2
Guiping, China, **206** B4
Guir, Oued, *river*, Algeria/ Morocco, **361** F2
Guiratinga, Brazil, **456** C4
Güiria, Venezuela, **451** F1
Guisanbourg, French Guiana, **452** C2
Guisborough, England, U.K., **307** G3
Guise, France, **291** F2
Guishan Dao, *island*, China, **207** B4
Guist, England, U.K., **305** H2
Guitinguitin, Mount, *mountain peak*, Philippines, **204** C3
Guitiriz, Spain, **292** D1
Guiuan, Philippines, **204** D4
Guixi, China, **206** D2
Guiyang, Guizhou, China, **215** H4
Guiyang, Hunan, China, **206** C3
Guizhou, China, **207** A3
Guizhou, *province*, China, **215** H4
Gujarāt, *state*, India, **218** B5
Gujrānwāla, Pakistan, **218** C2
Gujrāt, Pakistan, **218** C2
Gulang, China, **213** J5
Gulbarga, India, **216** D2
Gulbene, Latvia, **287** N4
Gul'cha, Kyrgyzstan, **223** J4
Gulf, *province*, Papua New Guinea, **140** B5
Gulf Shores, U.S.A., **425** J4
Gulfport, U.S.A., **425** H4
Gulin, China, **215** H4
Guling, China, **206** C2
Guliston, Uzbekistan, **223** H4
Gull Bay, Canada, **415** K7
Gullspång, Sweden, **286** G3
Güllük Körfezi, *bay*, Turkey, **297** F7
Gülnar, Turkey, **225** B1
Gülpınar, Turkey, **297** F6
Gülshat, Kazakhstan, **223** J3
Gulu, Uganda, **369** F2
Gülübovo, Bulgaria, **296** E4
Gulyantsi, Bulgaria, **296** E4

Hamilton City, U.S.A., **422** C2
Hamilton Inlet, Canada, **417** M3
Hamina, Finland, **287** N2
Hamīrpur, India, **218** D3
Hamlet, North Carolina, U.S.A., **425** N2
Hamlet, North Dakota, U.S.A., **420** B1
Hamm, Germany, **288** C3
Ḩammām, Syria, **225** E2
Hammamet, Golfe de, *gulf*, Tunisia, **362** B1
Ḩammār, Hawr al, *lake*, Iraq, **363** J2
Hammarstrand, Sweden, **284** H5
Hammerdal, Sweden, **284** G5
Hammerfest, Norway, **285** L1
Hammond, Indiana, U.S.A., **421** K5
Hammond, Louisiana, U.S.A., **424** G4
Hammond, Montana, U.S.A., **419** M4
Hammonton, U.S.A., **426** C5
Hampden, Canada, **417** N5
Hampden, New Zealand, **133** C7
Hampden, U.S.A., **420** D1
Hampshire, *unitary authority*, England, U.K., **305** F3
Hampton, Canada, **416** J7
Hampton, Iowa, U.S.A., **420** G4
Hampton, New Hampshire, U.S.A., **426** E3
Hampton, Oregon, U.S.A., **418** D5
Hampton, South Carolina, U.S.A., **425** M3
Hampton, Virginia, U.S.A., **426** B6
Hampton Butte, *mountain peak*, U.S.A., **418** D5
Ḩamrā', Al Ḩamādah al, *plateau*, Libya, **362** B3
Hamrångefjärden, Sweden, **287** H2
Ḩamrat ash Shaykh, Sudan, **366** C2
Hamstreet, England, U.K., **305** H3
Han, *river*, China, **206** B1
Han, *river*, South Korea, **208** D3
Han Pijesak, Bosnia and Herzegovina, **294** G3
Han Sum, China, **211** G3
Hana, Hawaiian Islands, U.S.A., **422** R9
Hanahan, Papua New Guinea, **140** E2
Ḩanak, Saudi Arabia, **363** G3
Hanalei, Hawaiian Islands, U.S.A., **422** R9
Hanamaki, Japan, **209** H3
Hâncești, Moldova, **296** G2
Hanceville, Canada, **412** H6
Hancheng, China, **206** B1
Handa Island, Scotland, U.K., **308** D2
Handan, China, **210** F5
Handeni, Tanzania, **369** G4
Handlová, Slovakia, **289** J4
HaNegev, *desert*, Israel, **225** C4
Hanestad, Norway, **286** E2
Hanford, U.S.A., **422** D3
Hanga-Roa, Isla de Pascua (Easter Island), Chile, **461** B2
Hangay, *province*, Mongolia, **213** J3
Hangayn Nuruu, *mountain range*, Mongolia, **213** H3
Hanggin Houqi, China, **210** D4
Hanggin Qi, China, **210** E5
Hangu, China, **210** G5
Hangu, Pakistan, **218** B2
Hangzhou, China, **206** E2
Hanhöhiy Uul, *mountain range*, Mongolia, **213** G2
Ḩanīsh al Kabīr, Jazīrat al, *island*, Yemen, **220** D6
Hankinson, U.S.A., **420** E2
Hanko, Finland, **287** L3
Hanks, U.S.A., **420** B1
Hanksville, U.S.A., **423** H2
Hanle, India, **218** D2
Hanmer Springs, New Zealand, **133** D6
Hanna, Canada, **413** P6
Hannaford, U.S.A., **420** D2
Hannah Bay, Canada, **415** P6
Hannibal, U.S.A., **420** H6
Hannover, Germany, **288** D2
Hanöbukten, *bay*, Sweden, **286** G5
Hanoi *see* Hà Nôi, Vietnam, **203** E1
Hanover, U.S.A., **426** B5
Hanpan, Cape, Papua New Guinea, **140** E2
Hanshou, China, **206** C2
Hānsi, India, **218** C3
Hanson Bay, Chatham Islands, New Zealand, **133** Q16
Hanstholm, Denmark, **286** D4
Hantay, Mongolia, **213** J2
Hanumāngarh, India, **218** C3
Hanuy, *river*, Mongolia, **213** J2
Hanwang, China, **215** H3
Hanyang, China, **206** C2
Hanzhong, China, **215** H2
Hanzhuang, China, **206** D1
Hao, *island*, French Polynesia, **137** G2
Hāora, India, **219** G5
Haoud el Hamra, Algeria, **361** H2
Hapai, Solomon Islands, **141** A1
Haparanda, Sweden, **285** M4
Happisburgh, England, U.K., **305** J2
Happy, U.S.A., **424** B2
Happy Camp, U.S.A., **418** C6
Happy Valley-Goose Bay, Canada, **417** L3
Ḩaql, Saudi Arabia, **225** C5
Har Borog, China, **213** J4
Har Hu, *lake*, China, **213** H5
Har Nuur, *lake*, Mongolia, **213** G2
Har-Us, Mongolia, **213** F2
Har Us Nuur, *lake*, Mongolia, **213** F2
Haraat, Mongolia, **210** D3
Ḩaraḑ, Saudi Arabia, **220** E4
Ḩaraḑ, Yemen, **220** D5
Haradok, Belarus, **299** B5
Harads, Sweden, **284** K3
Haraiki, *island*, French Polynesia, **137** G2
Harappa, Pakistan, **218** C3
Harare, Zimbabwe, **371** F2
Harata, Mount, *mountain peak*, New Zealand, **133** C6
Haraz-Djombo, Chad, **366** A2
Ḩarāzah, Jabal, *mountain peak*, Sudan, **366** D1
Haraze Mangueigne, Chad, **366** B3
Harbel, Liberia, **364** B3
Harbin, China, **211** J3
Harbor Springs, U.S.A., **421** L3
Harbour Breton, Canada, **417** P6
Harbours, Bay of, Falkland Islands, **460** F4
Harda, India, **218** D5
Hardap, *administrative region*, Namibia, **370** C3
Hardeeville, U.S.A., **425** M3
Hardelot-Plage, France, **305** J4
Hardin, U.S.A., **419** L4
Hardisty, Canada, **413** P5
Hardoī, India, **218** E4
Hardy, Península, Chile, **460** D5
Hardy, U.S.A., **424** G1
Hare Bay, Canada, **417** P4
Hārer, Ethiopia, **367** F3
Hargant, China, **211** G2
Hargele, Ethiopia, **367** F3
Hargeysa, Somalia, **367** F3
Hargla, Estonia, **287** N4
Harhiraa, Mongolia, **213** F2
Harhorin, Mongolia, **213** J3
Hari, *river*, Indonesia, **200** C3
Haria, Islas Canarias, Spain, **373** B4
Ḩarīb, Yemen, **220** E5
Haricha, Hamada el, *plateau*, Mali, **361** F4
Haridwār, India, **218** D3
Harihar, India, **216** C3
Harihari, New Zealand, **133** C6
Harīrūd, *river*, Afghanistan/Iran, **218** A2
Harisal, India, **218** D5
Harkány, Hungary, **289** J6
Harlan, U.S.A., **421** M7
Hârlău, Romania, **296** F2
Harlech, Wales, U.K., **304** C2
Harlem, U.S.A., **413** Q7
Harleston, England, U.K., **305** J2
Harlingen, Netherlands, **288** B2
Harlingen, U.S.A., **424** D6
Harlow, England, U.K., **305** H3
Harlowton, U.S.A., **419** K3
Harmancık, Turkey, **297** G6
Harmånger, Sweden, **287** H2
Harmod, Mongolia, **213** F2
Harnai, Pakistan, **218** A3
Harney Basin, U.S.A., **418** E5
Harney Lake, U.S.A., **418** E5
Härnösand, Sweden, **287** H1
Haroldswick, Scotland, U.K., **308** L7
Harpenden, England, U.K., **305** G3
Harper, Liberia, **364** C4
Harper, Oregon, U.S.A., **418** F5
Harper, Texas, U.S.A., **424** C4
Harqin Qi, China, **211** G4
Harqin Zuoyi, China, **211** G4
Harricana, *river*, Canada, **415** Q6
Harriman, U.S.A., **425** K2
Harris, Canada, **413** R6
Harris, Sound of, Scotland, U.K., **308** B3
Harrisburg, Illinois, U.S.A., **421** J7
Harrisburg, Pennsylvania, U.S.A., **426** B4
Harrismith, South Africa, **371** E4
Harrison, Arkansas, U.S.A., **424** F1
Harrison, Cape, Canada, **417** N2
Harrison, Michigan, U.S.A., **421** L3
Harrison, Nebraska, U.S.A., **419** N5
Harrison Lake, Canada, **412** H7
Harrisonburg, U.S.A., **421** P6
Harrisonville, U.S.A., **420** F6
Harrisville, U.S.A., **421** M3
Harrodsburg, U.S.A., **421** L7
Harrogate, England, U.K., **307** G4
Harrold, U.S.A., **420** D3
Harry S. Truman Reservoir, U.S.A., **420** G6
Harsīn, Iran, **220** E2
Hârșova, Romania, **296** F3
Harsprånget, Sweden, **284** J3
Harstad, Norway, **284** H2
Harsūd, India, **218** D5
Hart, U.S.A., **421** K4
Hart Fell, *mountain peak*, Scotland, U.K., **308** F5
Hartao, China, **211** H4
Hartberg, Austria, **289** G5
Hårteigen, *mountain peak*, Norway, **286** C2
Hartford, U.S.A., **426** D4
Hartkjølen, *mountain peak*, Norway, **284** F4
Hartland, Canada, **416** H6
Hartland, England, U.K., **304** C4
Hartland Point, England, U.K., **304** C3
Hartlepool, England, U.K., **307** G3
Hartlepool, *unitary authority*, England, U.K., **307** G3
Hartley, U.S.A., **423** M4
Hartline, U.S.A., **418** E3
Hartola, Finland, **287** M2
Hartshorne, U.S.A., **424** E2
Harun, Gunung, *mountain peak*, Indonesia, **201** G1
Harvard, California, U.S.A., **422** E4
Harvard, Idaho, U.S.A., **418** F3
Harvard, Illinois, U.S.A., **421** J4
Harvard, Mount, *mountain peak*, U.S.A., **423** K2
Harvey, Illinois, U.S.A., **421** K5
Harvey, North Dakota, U.S.A., **420** D2
Harwich, England, U.K., **305** J3
Haryana, *state*, India, **218** C3
Harz, *mountain range*, Germany, **288** E3
Hasalbag, China, **212** C5
Hashaat, Mongolia, **210** D3
Hashtgerd, Iran, **220** F1
Ḩāsik, Oman, **221** G5
Hāsilpur, Pakistan, **218** C3
Haskell, U.S.A., **424** C3
Haslemere, England, U.K., **305** G3
Haslev, Denmark, **286** E5
Hassan, India, **216** D3
Hassela, Sweden, **287** H1
Hasselborough Bay, Macquarie Island, **134** R11
Hasselt, Belgium, **288** B3
Haßfurt, Germany, **288** E3
Hassi Bel Guebbour, Algeria, **361** H3
Hassi Inifel, Algeria, **361** G3
Hassi Messaoud, Algeria, **361** H2
Hässleholm, Sweden, **286** F4
Hastings, England, U.K., **305** H4
Hastings, Michigan, U.S.A., **421** L4
Hastings, Nebraska, U.S.A., **420** D5
Hastings, New Zealand, **132** F4
Hasvik, Norway, **285** L1
Haswell, U.S.A., **423** M2
Hat Yai, Thailand, **202** D4
Hatansuudal, Mongolia, **213** J3
Hatavch, Mongolia, **210** F3
Hatay, *province*, Turkey, **225** D1
Hațeg, Romania, **296** D3
Hatfield, Hertfordshire, England, U.K., **305** G3
Hatfield, S. Yorkshire, England, U.K., **307** G4
Hatgal, Mongolia, **213** J2
Hatherleigh, England, U.K., **304** C4
Hāthras, India, **218** D4
Ḩāţibah, Ra's, *point*, Saudi Arabia, **363** G4
Hatkamba, India, **216** C2
Hatlestrand, Norway, **286** B2
Hato Mayor, Dominican Republic, **429** H3
Hatpaas, Indonesia, **198** D4
Hatta, India, **218** D4
Hatteras, U.S.A., **426** C7
Hatteras Island, U.S.A., **426** C7
Hatteras Plain, *underwater feature*, Atlantic Ocean, **477** C4
Hattfjelldal, Norway, **284** F4
Hattiesburg, U.S.A., **425** H4
Hatton, U.S.A., **420** E2
Hattuselkonen, Finland, **285** Q5
Hattuvaara, Finland, **285** Q5
Hatuma, New Zealand, **132** F5
Hatvan, Hungary, **289** J5
Hau Hoi Wan, *bay*, China, **207** B3
Haud, *region*, Ethiopia, **367** F3
Haugesund, Norway, **286** B3
Hauho, Finland, **287** M2
Hauhungaroa Range, *mountain range*, New Zealand, **132** E4
Haukeligrend, Norway, **286** C3
Haukipudas, Finland, **285** M4
Haukivesi, *lake*, Finland, **287** N1
Haukivuori, Finland, **287** N1
Haumonia, Argentina, **459** E3
Hauraha, Solomon Islands, **141** A1
Hauraki Gulf, New Zealand, **132** E3
Hausjärvi, Finland, **287** M2
Haut Atlas, *mountain range*, Morocco, **356** E4
Haut-Ogooué, *province*, Gabon, **368** B3
Hautajärvi, Finland, **285** P3
Haute-Guinée, *administrative region*, Guinea, **364** B2
Haute-Kotto, Central African Republic, **366** B3
Haute-Mbomou, *prefecture*, Central African Republic, **366** C3
Haute-Normandie, *administrative region*, France, **290** E2
Haute-Zaïre, *administrative region*, Democratic Republic of the Congo, **369** K2
Hautere *see* Solander Island, New Zealand, **133** A8
Hauterive, Canada, **416** G5
Hauts Plateaux, *plateau*, Algeria, **361** F2
Havana, U.S.A., **420** H5
Havana *see* La Habana, Cuba, **429** E2
Havant, England, U.K., **305** G4
Havel, *river*, Germany, **288** F2
Havelock, New Zealand, **133** D5
Haverfordwest, Wales, U.K., **304** C3
Haverhill, England, U.K., **305** H2
Hāveri, India, **216** C3
Havirga, Mongolia, **210** F3
Havlíčkuv Brod, Czech Republic, **289** G4
Havneby, Denmark, **286** D5
Havøysund, Norway, **285** M1
Havran, Turkey, **297** F6
Havre, U.S.A., **419** K2
Havre-Aubert, Canada, **417** L6
Havre-St-Pierre, Canada, **417** K4
Havsa, Turkey, **297** F5
Havsnäs, Sweden, **284** G4
Hawaii, *island*, Hawaiian Islands, U.S.A., **422** R9
Hawaii, *state*, Hawaiian Islands, U.S.A., **422** R9
Hawaiian Islands, U.S.A., Pacific Ocean, **422** R9
Hawaiian Ridge, *underwater feature*, Pacific Ocean, **478** G3
Ḩawallī, Kuwait, **363** J3
Hawarden, Wales, U.K., **304** D1
Hawea, Lake, New Zealand, **133** B7
Hawera, New Zealand, **132** E4
Hawes, England, U.K., **306** F3
Haweswater Reservoir, *lake*, England, U.K., **306** F3
Hawi, Hawaiian Islands, U.S.A., **422** R9
Hawick, Scotland, U.K., **308** G5
Hawk Inlet, U.S.A., **412** B2
Hawke Bay, New Zealand, **132** F4
Hawkes Bay, Canada, **417** N4
Hawkesbury, Canada, **416** D7
Hawkhurst, England, U.K., **305** H3
Hawkinsville, U.S.A., **425** L3
Hawkswood, New Zealand, **133** D6
Ḩawrān, *river*, Iraq, **363** H2
Hawthorne, U.S.A., **422** D2
Haxby, England, U.K., **307** G3
Haxtun, U.S.A., **423** M1
Hay, Australia, **135** J5
Hay, Mount, *mountain peak*, Canada, **412** A2
Hay, *river*, Canada, **413** K2
Hay, Wales, U.K., **304** D2
Hay Camp, Canada, **413** P2
Hay River, Canada, **413** M1
Hay Springs, U.S.A., **420** B4
Haya, Indonesia, **199** E3
Hayden, Alabama, U.S.A., **425** J3
Hayden, Arizona, U.S.A., **423** H5
Hayden, Colorado, U.S.A., **423** K1
Haydon Bridge, England, U.K., **306** F3

Hinnerjoki, Finland, **287** L2
Hinoba-an, Philippines, **204** C4
Hinton, Canada, **413** L5
Hınzır Burnu, *point*, Turkey, **225** C1
Hippargi, India, **216** D2
Hira, New Zealand, **133** D5
Hirakud Reservoir, India, **219** E5
Hirara, Japan, **209** N8
Hiré, Côte d'Ivoire, **364** C3
Hirekerūr, India, **216** C3
Hiriyūr, India, **216** D3
Hiroo, Japan, **209** H2
Hirosaki, Japan, **209** H2
Hiroshima, Japan, **208** F4
Hirtshals, Denmark, **286** D4
Hiruharama, New Zealand, **132** G3
Hirwaun, Wales, U.K., **304** D3
Hisār, India, **218** C3
Hisarönü Korfezi, *bay*, Turkey, **297** F7
Ḩismā, Al, *plain*, Saudi Arabia, **225** C5
Hispaniola, *island*, Dominican Republic/Haiti, **429** G3
Histon, England, U.K., **305** H2
Ḩisyah, Syria, **225** D2
Hīt, Iraq, **363** H2
Hita, Japan, **208** E4
Hitachi, Japan, **209** H3
Hitchin, England, U.K., **305** G3
Hitoyoshi, Japan, **208** E4
Hitra, *island*, Norway, **284** D5
Hiva Oa, *island*, French Polynesia, **137** H1
Hixon, Canada, **412** H5
Hjälmaren, *lake*, Sweden, **286** G3
Hjellestad, Norway, **286** B2
Hjelmeland, Norway, **286** C3
Hjo, Sweden, **286** G3
Hjørring, Denmark, **286** D4
Hjortkvarn, Sweden, **286** G3
Hkakabo Razi, *mountain peak*, Myanmar, **205** C1
Hkamti, Myanmar, **205** B2
Hlatikulu, Swaziland, **371** F4
Hlohovec, Slovakia, **289** H4
Hlusha, Belarus, **299** B6
Hlyboka, Ukraine, **296** E1
Hlybokaye, Belarus, **287** N5
Hnúšt'a, Slovakia, **289** J4
Ho, Ghana, **364** E3
Hòa Bình, Vietnam, **203** E1
Hoachanas, Namibia, **370** C3
Hoadley, Canada, **413** M5
Hoback Junction, U.S.A., **419** J5
Hobart, Australia, **135** K7
Hobbs, U.S.A., **423** M5
Hobbs Coast, *region*, Antarctica, **470** C7
Hobe Sound, U.S.A., **425** M6
Hobkirk, Scotland, U.K., **308** G5
Hoboksar, China, **212** E3
Hobro, Denmark, **286** D4
Hobucken, U.S.A., **426** B7
Hobyo, Somalia, **367** G3
Hochalmspitze, *mountain peak*, Austria, **288** F5
Hochfeld, Namibia, **370** C3
Hochschwab, *mountain range*, Austria, **289** G5
Hodda, *mountain peak*, Somalia, **367** H2
Hoddesdon, England, U.K., **305** G3
Hodh ech Chargui, *administrative region*, Mauritania, **360** E5
Hodh el Gharbi, *administrative region*, Mauritania, **364** B1
Hódmezővásárhely, Hungary, **289** J5
Hodnet, England, U.K., **304** E2
Hodonín, Czech Republic, **289** H4
Hödrögö, Mongolia, **213** H2
Hoek van Holland, Netherlands, **288** B3
Hoengsŏng, South Korea, **208** D3
Hoeryŏng, North Korea, **208** E2
Hoeyang, North Korea, **208** D3
Hof, Germany, **288** E3
Höfn, Iceland, **284** Z7
Hofsjökull, *ice cap*, Iceland, **284** Y7
Hofsós, Iceland, **284** Y7
Hōfu, Japan, **208** E4
Hog Harbour, Vanuatu, **141** A2
Höganäs, Sweden, **286** F4
Högby, Sweden, **287** H4
Hoggar, *mountain range*, Algeria, **361** G4
Hoggar, Tassili du, *plateau*, Algeria, **361** H4
Hoghiz, Romania, **296** E3
Höglekardalen, Sweden, **284** F5
Högsäter, Sweden, **286** F3
Høgtuvbreen, *mountain peak*, Norway, **284** F3
Hoh Sai Hu, *lake*, China, **214** E2
Hoh Xil Hu, *lake*, China, **214** D2
Hoh Xil Shan, *mountain range*, China, **214** D2
Hohe Rhön, *mountain range*, Germany, **288** D3
Hohe Tauern, *mountain range*, Austria, **288** F5
Hoher Dachstein, *mountain peak*, Austria, **288** F5
Hohhot, China, **210** E4
Hohoe, Ghana, **364** E3
Höhöö, Mongolia, **213** J2
Höhtolgoy, Mongolia, **213** F2
Hội An, Vietnam, **203** F3
Hoi Ha, China, **207** C4
Hoima, Uganda, **369** F2
Hoisington, U.S.A., **420** D6
Hokianga Harbour, New Zealand, **132** D2
Hokitika, New Zealand, **133** C6
Hokkaidō, *island*, Japan, **209** H1
Hokksund, Norway, **286** D3
Hokua, Vanuatu, **141** A2
Hol, Norway, **286** D2
Hola, Kenya, **369** G3
Holalkere, India, **216** D3
Holanda, Bolivia, **455** F4
Holbæk, Denmark, **286** E5
Holbeach, England, U.K., **305** H2
Holboo, Mongolia, **213** G2
Holbrook, Arizona, U.S.A., **423** H4
Holbrook, Idaho, U.S.A., **418** H5
Holden, Canada, **413** N5
Holden, U.S.A., **423** G2
Holdenville, U.S.A., **424** D2
Holderness, *peninsula*, England, U.K., **307** H4
Holdfast, Canada, **413** S6
Holdrege, U.S.A., **420** D5
Holešov, Czech Republic, **289** H4
Holguín, Cuba, **429** F2
Höljes, Sweden, **286** F2
Hollabrunn, Austria, **289** H4
Holland, Canada, **414** E7
Holland, U.S.A., **421** K4
Hollesley, England, U.K., **305** J2
Hollington, England, U.K., **305** H4
Hollis, U.S.A., **424** C2
Hollister, U.S.A., **418** G5
Holly, U.S.A., **421** M4
Holly Ridge, U.S.A., **425** P2
Holly Springs, U.S.A., **425** H2
Hollywood, U.S.A., **425** M6
Holm, Sweden, **287** H1
Holmäjärvi, Sweden, **284** J3
Holman, Canada, **410** H2
Hólmavík, Iceland, **284** X7
Holme upon Spalding Moor, England, U.K., **307** H4
Holmes, Mount, *mountain peak*, U.S.A., **419** J4
Holmfirth, England, U.K., **307** G4
Holmön, Sweden, **284** K5
Holmsund, Sweden, **284** K5
Holoby, Ukraine, **289** M3
Ḫolon, Israel, **225** C3
Holonga, Vava'u Group, Tonga, **141** B3
Holoog, Namibia, **370** C4
Holopaw, U.S.A., **425** M5
Holøydal, Norway, **286** E1
Holstebro, Denmark, **286** D4
Holsted, Denmark, **286** D5
Holsworthy, England, U.K., **304** C4
Holt, England, U.K., **305** J2
Holt Sum, China, **210** G3
Holton, Canada, **417** N2
Holton, U.S.A., **420** F6
Holwerd, Netherlands, **288** B2
Holy Island, England, U.K., **307** G2
Holy Island, Wales, U.K., **306** D4
Holycross, Ireland, **309** E5
Holyhead Bay, Wales, U.K., **306** D4
Holyhead, Wales, U.K., **306** D4
Holyoke, U.S.A., **423** M1
Holywell, Wales, U.K., **306** E4
Holzkirchen, Germany, **288** E5
Homa Bay, Kenya, **369** F3
Homalin, Myanmar, **205** B2
Hombori, Mali, **364** D1
Home Bay, Canada, **411** N3
Home Island, Cocos (Keeling) Islands, **134** Q10
Homer, Alaska, U.S.A., **410** D4
Homer, Louisiana, U.S.A., **424** F3
Homersfield, England, U.K., **305** J2
Homerville, U.S.A., **425** L4
Homestead, U.S.A., **425** M7
Hommelstø, Norway, **284** F4
Homnābād, India, **216** D2
Homocea, Romania, **296** F2
Homoine, Mozambique, **371** G3
Homonhon Island, Philippines, **204** D4
Homs *see* Ḩimş, Syria, **225** D2
Homyel', Belarus, **298** D2
Hòn Diên, Núi, *mountain peak*, Vietnam, **203** F4
Honaz, Turkey, **297** G7
Honda, Colombia, **450** C3
Honda Bay, Philippines, **204** B4
Hondo, Canada, **413** M4
Hondo, U.S.A., **424** C5
Hondschoote, France, **305** K4
Honduras, *country*, Central America, **409** Q7
Honduras, Golfo de, *gulf*, Caribbean Sea, **428** D3
Hone, Canada, **414** D3
Hønefoss, Norway, **286** E2
Honesdale, U.S.A., **426** C4
Honey, Mount, *mountain peak*, Campbell Island, New Zealand, **132** K11
Honey Lake, U.S.A., **422** C1
Honfleur, France, **305** H5
Hông, *river*, Vietnam, **203** E1
Hồng Gai, Vietnam, **203** E1
Hong Kong *see* Xianggang, China, **207** C4
Hong Kong *see* Xianggang, *special administrative region*, China, **207** C4
Hong Kong Island, China, **207** C4
Hong'an, China, **206** C2
Hongch'ŏn, South Korea, **208** D3
Honghai Wan, *bay*, China, **206** C4
Honghu, China, **206** C2
Hongjiang, China, **206** B3
Hongor, Dornogovĭ, Mongolia, **210** E3
Hongor, Sühbaatar, Mongolia, **210** F3
Hongqicun, China, **213** G4
Hongshishan, China, **213** H4
Hongshui, *river*, China, **215** H4
Hongtong, China, **210** E5
Honguedo, Détroit d', *strait*, Canada, **416** J5
Hongxing, China, **211** K2
Hongya, China, **215** G3
Hongyuan, China, **215** G2
Hongze, China, **206** D1
Hongze Hu, *lake*, China, **206** D1
Honiara, Solomon Islands, **141** A1
Honiton, England, U.K., **304** D4
Honkajoki, Finland, **287** L2
Honningsvåg, Norway, **285** N1
Honokaa, Hawaiian Islands, U.S.A., **422** R9
Honolulu, Hawaiian Islands, U.S.A., **422** R9
Honolulu, *island*, Hawaiian Islands, U.S.A., **139** J2
Honshū, *island*, Japan, **209** G3
Hood, Mount, *mountain peak*, U.S.A., **418** D4
Hoogeveen, Netherlands, **288** C2
Hook, England, U.K., **305** F3
Hook Head, *point*, Ireland, **309** F5
Hooker, Mount, *mountain peak*, New Zealand, **133** B6
Hooker, U.S.A., **420** C7
Hoolt, Mongolia, **213** J3
Hoonah, U.S.A., **412** B2
Hooper, Colorado, U.S.A., **423** L3
Hooper, Nebraska, U.S.A., **420** E5
Hooper, Washington, U.S.A., **418** E3
Hoorn, Netherlands, **288** B2
Höövör, Dornod, Mongolia, **210** F2
Höövör, Hangay, Mongolia, **213** J3
Hope, Arkansas, U.S.A., **424** F3
Hope, Ben, *mountain peak*, Scotland, U.K., **308** E2
Hope, Canada, **412** J7
Hope, Lake, Australia, **134** D5
Hope, Loch, *lake*, Scotland, U.K., **308** E2
Hope, New Mexico, U.S.A., **423** L5
Hope, Wales, U.K., **304** D1
Hopedale, Canada, **417** L2
Hopelchén, Mexico, **431** H5
Hopeman, Scotland, U.K., **308** F3
Hopetoun, Australia, **135** J6
Hopetown, South Africa, **370** D4
Hopin, Myanmar, **205** C2
Hopkins, Lake, Australia, **134** F3
Hopkinsville, U.S.A., **421** K7
Hopland, U.S.A., **422** B2
Hopong, Myanmar, **205** C3
Hopongo, Solomon Islands, **141** A1
Hopseidet, Norway, **285** N1
Horasan, Turkey, **224** F5
Hörby, Sweden, **286** F5
Horcajo de Santiago, Spain, **293** F3
Horda, Norway, **286** C3
Hordaland, *county*, Norway, **286** B2
Horezu, Romania, **296** D3
Horgo, Mongolia, **213** H2
Horgorgoinba, China, **215** F2
Hörh Uul, *mountain peak*, Mongolia, **210** D4
Horia, Romania, **296** G3
Horinger, China, **210** E4
Horiult, Mongolia, **213** J3
Horki, Belarus, **299** C5
Horley, England, U.K., **305** G3
Horlick Mountains, *mountain range*, Antarctica, **470** C6
Hormuz, Strait of, Arabian Peninsula/Iran, **221** G3
Horn, Austria, **289** G4
Horn, Cape *see* Hornos, Cabo de, *cape*, Chile, **460** D5
Horn, Norway, **284** F4
Horn Island, U.S.A., **425** H4
Hornavan, *lake*, Sweden, **284** H3
Hornbjarg, *point*, Iceland, **284** X6
Hornburg, Germany, **288** E2
Horncastle, England, U.K., **305** G1
Horndal, Sweden, **286** H2
Horndean, England, U.K., **305** G4
Hörnefors, Sweden, **284** J5
Hornell, U.S.A., **426** B3
Hornepayne, Canada, **415** M7
Hornos, Cabo de (Cape Horn), *cape*, Chile, **460** D5
Hornoy, France, **305** J5
Hornsea, England, U.K., **307** H4
Horodenka, Ukraine, **296** E1
Horokhiv, Ukraine, **289** M3
Horotiu, New Zealand, **132** E3
Horqin Youyi Zhongqi, China, **211** H3
Horqin Zuoyi Houqi, China, **211** H4
Horqin Zouyi Zhongqi, China, **211** H3
Horqueta, Paraguay, **459** F2
Horrabridge, England, U.K., **304** C4
Horred, Sweden, **286** F4
Horsburgh Island (Luar), Cocos (Keeling) Islands, **134** Q10
Horse Cave, U.S.A., **421** L7
Horse Islands, Canada, **417** P4
Horsefly Lake, Canada, **412** J5
Horsens, Denmark, **286** D5
Horseshoe Bend, U.S.A., **418** F5
Horsforth, England, U.K., **307** G4
Horsham, Australia, **135** J6
Horsham, England, U.K., **305** G3
Horslunde, Denmark, **286** E5
Horsunlu, Turkey, **297** G7
Horta, Azores, Portugal, **360** M7
Horten, Norway, **286** E3
Hortense, U.S.A., **425** M4
Horton, *river*, Canada, **410** G3
Horton, U.S.A., **420** F6
Horwich, England, U.K., **306** F4
Hosa'ina, Ethiopia, **367** E3
Hosdrug, India, **216** C3
Hose, Pegunungan, *mountain range*, Malaysia, **201** F2
Hoséré Vokré, *mountain peak*, Cameroon, **365** G3
Hoshāb, Pakistan, **221** H3
Hoshangābād, India, **218** D5
Hoshiārpur, India, **218** C3
Höshööt, Mongolia, **213** J2
Hoskins, Papua New Guinea, **140** C4
Hösööt, Mongolia, **212** F2
Hospet, India, **216** D3
Hospital, Ireland, **309** D5
Hossa, Finland, **285** P4
Hoste, Isla, *island*, Chile, **460** D5
Hot Springs, Arkansas, U.S.A., **424** F2
Hot Springs, South Dakota, U.S.A., **420** B4
Hotagen, *lake*, Sweden, **284** G5
Hotan, China, **212** C5
Hotan, *river*, China, **212** D5
Hotazel, South Africa, **370** D4
Hotchkiss, U.S.A., **423** K2
Hotham, Cape, Australia, **199** E5
Hotham, Mount, *mountain peak*, Australia, **135** K6
Hoting, Sweden, **284** H4
Hotont, Mongolia, **210** C3
Hottentots Bay, Namibia, **370** B4
Houaïlou, New Caledonia, **141** A3
Houat, Île d', *island*, France, **290** C3
Houdain, France, **305** K4
Houeillès, France, **290** E4
Hougang, Singapore, **200** K6
Houghton, Michigan, U.S.A., **421** J2
Houghton, New York, U.S.A., **426** A3
Houghton Lake, U.S.A., **421** L3
Houghton Lake, *lake*, U.S.A., **421** L3

Hyesan, North Korea, **208** E2
Hyrynsalmi, Finland, **285** P4
Hysham, U.S.A., **419** L3
Hythe, Canada, **413** K4
Hythe, Hampshire, England, U.K., **305** F4
Hythe, Kent, England, U.K., **305** J3
Hytölä, Finland, **287** N1
Hyvinkää, Finland, **287** M2

I

I-lan, Taiwan, **206** E3
I-n-Amenas, Algeria, **361** H3
I-n-Amguel, Algeria, **361** H4
I-n-Belbel, Algeria, **361** G3
I-n-Eker, Algeria, **361** H4
I-n-Guezzam, Algeria, **361** H5
I-n-Salah, Algeria, **361** G3
I-n-Tebezas, Mali, **365** E1
Iacobeni, Romania, **296** E2
Iaçu, Brazil, **457** F3
Ialomița, *river*, Romania, **296** F3
Ialoveni, Moldova, **296** G2
Ianca, Romania, **296** F3
Iargara, Moldova, **296** G2
Iași, Romania, **296** F2
Iauaretê, Brazil, **451** E4
Iba, Philippines, **204** B3
Ibadan, Nigeria, **365** E3
Ibagué, Colombia, **450** C3
Ibar, *river*, Yugoslavia, **296** C4
Ibarra, Ecuador, **450** B4
Ibarreta, Argentina, **459** E2
Ibb, Yemen, **220** D6
Ibba, Sudan, **369** E2
Iberá, Esteros del, *marshes*, Argentina, **459** E3
Iberia, Peru, **454** C1
Iberian Peninsula, Portugal/Spain, **280** D7
Iberville, Lac d', *lake*, Canada, **416** E2
Ibestad, Norway, **284** H2
Ibeto, Nigeria, **365** F2
Ibi, Nigeria, **365** F3
Ibiá, Brazil, **456** D5
Ibiapaba, Serra da, *mountain range*, Brazil, **453** F4
Ibicuí, *river*, Brazil, **459** F3
Ibimirim, Brazil, **453** G5
Ibinty, *mountain peak*, Madagascar, **372** C5
Ibiraçu, Brazil, **457** F5
Ibirama, Brazil, **459** H3
Ibirapuita, *river*, Brazil, **459** F4
Ibitiara, Brazil, **457** E3
Ibiza, *mountain peak*, Spain, **292** E2
Ibiza *see* Eivissa, *island*, Islas Baleares, Spain, **293** H3
Ibiza *see* Eivissa, Islas Baleares, Spain, **293** H3
Ibotirama, Brazil, **457** E3
Iboundji, Mont, *mountain peak*, Gabon, **368** B3
Ibrā', Oman, **221** G4
'Ibrī, Oman, **221** G4
Ibstock, England, U.K., **305** F2
Ica, Peru, **454** C4
Ica, Punta, *point*, Peru, **454** C4
Içá, *river*, Brazil, **451** E5
Icacos Point, Trinidad, Trinidad and Tobago, **461** C4
Içana, Brazil, **451** E4
Içana, *river*, Brazil, **451** E4
Icatu, Brazil, **453** E4
Içel, *province*, Turkey, **225** B1
Içel (Mersin), Turkey, **363** F1
Iceland, *country*, Europe, **282** C3
Icha, *river*, Russian Federation, **223** K1
Ichalkaranji, India, **216** C2
Ichilo, *river*, Bolivia, **455** F4
Ichinoseki, Japan, **209** H3
Ich'ŏn, South Korea, **208** D3
Icklingham, England, U.K., **305** H2
İçmeler, Turkey, **297** G7
Icó, Brazil, **453** F5
Icod de Los Vinos, Islas Canarias, Spain, **373** A4
Ida Grove, U.S.A., **420** F4
Idabel, U.S.A., **424** E3
Idaburn, New Zealand, **133** B7
Idah, Nigeria, **365** F3
Idaho, *state*, U.S.A., **418** G4
Idaho Falls, U.S.A., **419** H5
Idalia, U.S.A., **423** M2
Idar-Oberstein, Germany, **288** C4
'Idd al Ghanam, Sudan, **366** B2
Idel', Russian Federation, **285** S4
Ideles, Algeria, **361** H4
Ider, Mongolia, **213** H2
Ider, *river*, Mongolia, **213** H2
Idfū, Egypt, **363** F4
Idiofa, Democratic Republic of the Congo, **368** C4
Idivuoma, Sweden, **285** L2
Idlib, *district*, Syria, **225** D1
Idlib, Syria, **225** D2
Idre, Sweden, **286** F2
Idrija, Slovenia, **294** D3
Idrinskoye, Russian Federation, **223** N2
Iecava, Latvia, **287** M4
Iepê, Brazil, **459** G2
Ieper (Ypres), Belgium, **288** A3
Ierapetra, Kriti, Greece, **297** E8
Ierissou, Kolpos, *bay*, Greece, **297** D5
Iernut, Romania, **296** E2
Ifakara, Tanzania, **369** G4
Ifalik, *island*, Micronesia, **138** C4
Ifanadiana, Madagascar, **372** B5
Ife, Nigeria, **365** E3
Iferouâne, Niger, **361** H5
Ifetesene, *mountain peak*, Algeria, **361** G3
Ifjord, Norway, **285** N1
Igabi, Nigeria, **365** F2
Igal, Hungary, **289** H5
Igalula, Tanzania, **369** F4
Iganga, Uganda, **369** F2
Igarapava, Brazil, **456** D5
Igarapé-Açu, Brazil, **452** D3
Igarapé Grande, Brazil, **453** E4
Igarka, Russian Federation, **300** K3
Igboho, Nigeria, **365** E3
Iggesund, Sweden, **287** H2
Iglesias, Sardegna, Italy, **295** B6
Igloolik, Canada, **411** L3
Ignace, Canada, **414** J7
Ignacio Zaragoza, Mexico, **430** D2
Ignalina, Lithuania, **287** N5
Ignatovo, Russian Federation, **299** F2
İğneada, Turkey, **296** F5
İğneada Burnu, *cape*, Turkey, **296** G5
Igombe, *river*, Tanzania, **369** F3
Igoumenitsa, Greece, **297** C6
Igra, Russian Federation, **222** E1
Igrim, Russian Federation, **300** H3
Iguaçu, *river*, Brazil, **459** G2
Iguaçu, Saltos do, *waterfall*, Argentina/Brazil, **459** F2
Iguaí, Brazil, **457** F4
Iguaje, Mesa de, *plateau*, Colombia, **450** D4
Iguala, Mexico, **431** F5
Igualada, Spain, **293** H2
Iguape, Brazil, **459** H2
Iguatemi, Brazil, **459** F2
Iguatemi, *river*, Brazil, **459** F2
Iguatu, Brazil, **453** F5
Iguéla, Gabon, **368** A3
Iguidi, Erg, *desert*, Algeria/Mauritania, **360** E3
Igunga, Tanzania, **369** F3
Iharaña, Madagascar, **372** B3
Ihbulag, Mongolia, **210** D4
Ihiala, Nigeria, **365** F3
Ihnāsiyat al Madīnah, Egypt, **225** A5
Ihosy, Madagascar, **372** B5
Ihsuuj, Mongolia, **210** D2
Iida, Japan, **209** G4
Iidaan, Somalia, **367** G3
Iijärvi, *lake*, Finland, **285** N2
Iijoki, *river*, Finland, **285** N4
Iisaku, Estonia, **287** N3
Iisalmi, Finland, **285** N5
Ijebu-Ode, Nigeria, **365** E3
Ijill, Kediet, *mountain peak*, Mauritania, **360** D4
Ijsselmeer, *lake*, Netherlands, **288** B2
Ijui, Brazil, **459** G3
Ijuí, *river*, Brazil, **459** F3
Ikahavo, *mountain peak*, Madagascar, **372** B4
Ikalamavony, Madagascar, **372** B5
Ikali, Democratic Republic of the Congo, **368** D3
Ikamatua, New Zealand, **133** C6
Ikanda, Democratic Republic of the Congo, **368** D3
Ikare, Nigeria, **365** F3
Ikaria, *island*, Dodekanisos, Greece, **297** F7
Ikawai, New Zealand, **133** C7
Ikeda, Japan, **209** H2
Ikeja, Nigeria, **365** E3
Ikela, Democratic Republic of the Congo, **368** D3
Ikey, Russian Federation, **223** Q2
Ikhtiman, Bulgaria, **296** D4
Ikhwān, Al (The Brothers), *islands*, Suquṭrá (Socotra), Yemen, **373** B2
Ikire, Nigeria, **365** E3
Ikohahoene, Adrar, *mountain peak*, Algeria, **361** H3
Ikom, Nigeria, **365** F3
Ikongo, Madagascar, **372** B5
Ikorodu, Nigeria, **365** E3
Ikot Ekpene, Nigeria, **368** A1
Ikungu, Tanzania, **369** F4
Ila-Orangun, Nigeria, **365** E3
Ilagan, Philippines, **204** C2
Īlām, Iran, **220** E2
Iława, Poland, **289** J2
Ilchester, England, U.K., **304** E4
Ile, *river*, Kazakhstan, **223** K4
Île-à-la-Crosse, Canada, **413** R4
Île-à-la-Crosse, Lac, *lake*, Canada, **413** R4
Île-de-France, *administrative region*, France, **291** F2
Ilebo, Democratic Republic of the Congo, **368** D3
Ileksa, *river*, Russian Federation, **285** T5
Ileret, Kenya, **369** G2
Ilesha, Nigeria, **365** E3
Ilfracombe, England, U.K., **304** C3
Ilgaz, Turkey, **224** D4
Ilgın, Turkey, **363** F1
Ilha Grande, Brazil, **451** F4
Ilhéus, Brazil, **457** F4
Ili, *river*, China, **212** D4
Ilia, Romania, **296** D3
Iliamna Lake, U.S.A., **410** D3
Ilidža, Bosnia and Herzegovina, **294** G4
Iligan, Philippines, **204** D4
Iligan Bay, Philippines, **204** C4
Ilin Island, Philippines, **204** C3
Il'ino, Russian Federation, **299** C5
Il'inskoye, Russian Federation, **299** G4
Ilirska Bistrica, Slovenia, **294** E3
Il'ka, Russian Federation, **210** E2
Ilkeston, England, U.K., **305** F2
Ilkley, England, U.K., **307** G4
Illampu, Nevado de, *mountain peak*, Bolivia, **455** E4
Illapel, Chile, **458** B4
Iller, *river*, Germany, **288** E4
Illichivs'k, Ukraine, **296** H2
Illimani, Nevado, *mountain peak*, Bolivia, **455** E4
Illinois, *river*, U.S.A., **420** H6
Illinois, *state*, U.S.A., **421** J5
Illizi, Algeria, **361** H3
Illorsuit, Greenland, **411** P2
Illulissat, Greenland, **411** P3
Ilmajoki, Finland, **285** L5
Il'men', Ozero, *lake*, Russian Federation, **299** C3
Ilminster, England, U.K., **304** E4
Ilo, Peru, **454** D4
Iloc Island, Philippines, **204** B4
Iloilo, Philippines, **204** C4
Ilomantsi, Finland, **285** Q5
Ilorin, Nigeria, **365** E3
Iłowa, Poland, **289** G3
Ilūkste, Latvia, **287** N5
Ilva Mare, Romania, **296** E2
Ilwaco, U.S.A., **418** C3
Il'ya, Belarus, **287** N5
Imabari, Japan, **208** F4
Imala, Mozambique, **369** G5
Imandra, Ozero *lake*, Russian Federation, **285** R3
Imanombo, Madagascar, **372** B5
Imari, Japan, **208** E4
Imarssuak Seachannel, *underwater feature*, Atlantic Ocean, **477** E2
Imata, Peru, **454** D4
Imataca, Serranía de, *mountain range*, Venezuela, **451** G2
Imatra, Finland, **287** P2
Imbituba, Punta, *point*, Brazil, **459** H3
Imi-n-Tanoute, Morocco, **360** E2
Imlay, U.S.A., **422** D1
Immingham, England, U.K., **307** H4
Immokalee, U.S.A., **425** M6
Imo, *state*, Nigeria, **365** F3
Imola, Italy, **294** C3
Imonda, Papua New Guinea, **140** A3
Imperatriz, Brazil, **452** D4
Imperia, Italy, **294** B4
Imperial, Peru, **454** C3
Imperial, U.S.A., **420** C5
Impfondo, Congo, **368** C2
Imphāl, India, **214** E4
Imralı Adası, *island*, Turkey, **297** G5
Imroz, Turkey, **297** E5
Imtān, Syria, **225** D3
Imuris, Mexico, **430** C2
Imuruan Bay, Philippines, **204** B4
Ina, Japan, **209** G4
Inaccessible Island, Tristan da Cunha, **373** C2
Inajá, Brazil, **453** G5
Inambari, Peru, **455** E3
Inambari, *river*, Peru, **455** D3
Inangahua, New Zealand, **133** C5
Inanwatan, Indonesia, **199** F3
Iñapari, Peru, **455** E3
Inari, Finland, **285** N2
Inarijärvi, *lake*, Finland, **285** N2
Inauini, *river*, Brazil, **455** E2
Inca, Spain, **293** J3
Inca de Oro, Chile, **458** C3
İnce Burnu, *point*, Turkey, **297** F5
İncekum Burnu, *point*, Turkey, **225** C1
Inch, Kerry, Ireland, **309** C5
Inch, Wexford, Ireland, **309** F5
Inchard, Loch, *inlet*, Scotland, U.K., **308** D2
Inchiri, *administrative region*, Mauritania, **360** C5
Inch'ŏn, South Korea, **208** D3
Incudine, Monte, *mountain peak*, Corse, France, **295** B5
Inčukalns, Latvia, **287** M4
Inda Silasē, Ethiopia, **367** E2
Indaiá, *river*, Brazil, **456** E5
Indal, Sweden, **287** H1
Indalsälven, *river*, Sweden, **284** G5
Indaw, Myanmar, **205** C3
Indé, Mexico, **430** D3
Independența, near Galati, Romania, **296** F3
Independența, Romania, **296** G4
Independence, Kansas, U.S.A., **420** F7
Independence, Minnesota, U.S.A., **420** G2
Independence, Missouri, U.S.A., **420** F6
Independence Mountains, *mountain range*, U.S.A., **422** E1
Independencia, Bahía de la, *bay*, Peru, **454** C4
India, Bassas da, *islands*, Réunion, **371** G3
India, *country*, Asia, **196** J8
Indian Cabins, Canada, **413** L2
Indian Head, Canada, **414** C6
Indian Lake, U.S.A., **426** C3
Indian Ocean, **476** C6
Indian Springs, U.S.A., **422** F3
Indian Wells, U.S.A., **423** H4
Indiana, *state*, U.S.A., **421** K5
Indiana, U.S.A., **421** P5
Indianapolis, U.S.A., **421** K6
Indianola, Iowa, U.S.A., **420** G5
Indianola, Mississippi, U.S.A., **424** G3
Indigirka, *river*, Russian Federation, **301** R3
Inđija, Yugoslavia, **296** C3
Indio, U.S.A., **422** E5
Indo-China Peninsula, Asia, **195** L8
Indo-Gangetic Plain, India/Pakistan, **194** J7
Indomed Fracture Zone, *tectonic feature*, Indian Ocean, **476** B7
Indonesia, *country*, Asia, **197** N10
Indore, India, **218** C5
Indragiri, *river*, Indonesia, **200** C3
Indramayu, Indonesia, **201** E4
Indravati, *river*, India, **216** E2
Indre Arna, Norway, **286** B2
Indre Billefjord, Norway, **285** M1
Indre, *river*, France, **290** E3
Indura, Belarus, **289** L2
Indus, *river*, Asia, **218** A4
Indus Fan, *underwater feature*, Indian Ocean, **476** D3
İnebolu, Turkey, **224** D4
İnegöl, Turkey, **297** G5
Ineu, Romania, **296** C2
Infanta, Philippines, **204** C3
Infante Dom Henrique, São Tomé and Príncipe, **373** C4
Infiernillo, Presa del, *dam*, Mexico, **430** E5
Ingal, Niger, **365** F1
Ingaly, Russian Federation, **223** J1
Ingatestone, England, U.K., **305** H3
Ingende, Democratic Republic of the Congo, **368** C3
Ingeniero Guillermo N. Juárez, Argentina, **458** E2
Ingeniero Jacobacci, Argentina, **460** D1
Ingenio, Islas Canarias, Spain, **373** B4
Ingettolgoy, Mongolia, **210** D2
Ingham, Australia, **135** K2
Ingleborough, *mountain peak*, England, U.K., **306** F3
Ingleton, England, U.K., **306** F3
Inglewood, U.S.A., **422** D5
Inglis, Canada, **414** D6
Ingoda, *river*, Russian Federation, **210** F2
Ingoldmells, England, U.K., **305** H1
Ingolstadt, Germany, **288** E4
Ingomar, U.S.A., **419** L3

Itapagipe, Brazil, **456** D5
Itapebi, Brazil, **457** F4
Itapecuru-Mirim, Brazil, **453** E4
Itapemirim, Brazil, **457** F5
Itaperuna, Brazil, **457** F5
Itapetinga, Brazil, **457** F4
Itapetininga, Brazil, **459** H2
Itapeva, Brazil, **459** H2
Itapicuru, *river*, Bahia, Brazil, **457** F3
Itapicuru, *river*, Maranhão, Brazil, **453** E4
Itapicuru, Serra do, *mountain range*, Brazil, **452** E5
Itapipoca, Brazil, **453** F4
Itapiranga, Brazil, **451** G5
Itaqui, Brazil, **459** F3
Itararé, Brazil, **459** H2
Itararé, *river*, Brazil, **459** H2
Itārsi, India, **218** D5
Itarumã, Brazil, **456** C5
Itatupã, Brazil, **452** C3
Ite, Peru, **454** D4
Itea, Greece, **297** D6
Itebero, Democratic Republic of the Congo, **369** E3
Ithaca, U.S.A., **426** B3
Ithaki, Ionioi Nisoi, Greece, **297** C6
Ithaki, *island*, Ionioi Nisoi, Greece, **297** C6
Ithrīyat, Jabal, *mountain range*, Jordan, **225** D4
Itimbiri, *river*, Democratic Republic of the Congo, **368** D2
Itinga, Brazil, **457** F4
Itiquira, Brazil, **456** B4
Itiquira, *river*, Brazil, **456** B4
Itoko, Democratic Republic of the Congo, **368** D3
Ittiri, Sardegna, Italy, **295** B5
Ittoqqortoormiit, Greenland, **411** S2
Itu, Brazil, **459** H2
Ituango, Colombia, **450** C2
Ituí, *river*, Brazil, **454** D1
Ituiutaba, Brazil, **456** D5
Itula, Democratic Republic of the Congo, **369** E3
Itumbiara, Brazil, **456** D5
Ituni, Guyana, **451** G3
Itupiranga, Brazil, **452** D4
Ituporanga, Brazil, **459** H3
Iturama, Brazil, **456** C5
Iturbe, Paraguay, **459** F3
Iturup, *island*, Kuril'skiye Ostrova, Russian Federation, **209** J1
Iturup, Ostrov, *island*, Russian Federation, **301** R5
Ituxi, *river*, Brazil, **455** E2
Ituzaingó, Argentina, **459** F3
Itzehoe, Germany, **288** D2
Iul'tin, Russian Federation, **301** V3
Iutica, Brazil, **451** E4
Iva, Samoa, **141** B1
Ivai, *river*, Brazil, **459** G2
Ivakoany, *mountain peak*, Madagascar, **372** B5
Ivalo, Finland, **285** N2
Ivalojoki, *river*, Finland, **285** N2
Ivanec, Croatia, **294** F2
Ivangorod, Russian Federation, **299** B3
Ivangrad, Yugoslavia, **296** B4
Ivanhoe, Australia, **135** J5
Ivanhoe, U.S.A., **420** E3
Ivanić Grad, Croatia, **294** F3
Ivanivka, Ukraine, **296** H2
Ivanjica, Yugoslavia, **296** C4
Ivanjska, Bosnia and Herzegovina, **294** F3
Ivankovtsy, Russian Federation, **211** L2
Ivano-Frankivs'k, Ukraine, **298** B3
Ivano-Frankivs'ka Oblast', *province*, Ukraine, **296** D1
Ivanova, Russian Federation, **299** C4
Ivanovka, Russian Federation,

211 G2
Ivanovo, Russian Federation, **300** F4
Ivatsevichy, Belarus, **289** M2
Ivaylovgrad, Bulgaria, **297** F5
Ivdel', Russian Federation, **300** H3
Iveşti, near Bârlad, Romania, **296** F2
Iveşti, Romania, **296** F3
Ivindo, *river*, Gabon, **368** B3
Ivinheima, Brazil, **459** G2
Ivinheima, *river*, Brazil, **456** C6
Ivittuut, Greenland, **411** Q3
Ivohibe, Madagascar, **372** B5
Ivory Coast, *coastal area*, Côte d'Ivoire, **364** C4
Ivrea, Italy, **294** A3
İvrindi, Turkey, **297** F6
Ivujivik, Canada, **411** M3
Ivybridge, England, U.K., **304** D4
Ivydale, U.S.A., **421** N6
Iwaki, Japan, **209** H3
Iwakuni, Japan, **208** F4
Iwamizawa, Japan, **209** H2
Iwanai, Japan, **209** H2
Iwo, Nigeria, **365** E5
Iwon, North Korea, **208** E2
Iwye, Belarus, **289** M2
Ixiamas, Bolivia, **455** E3
Ixmiquilpan, Mexico, **431** F4
Ixtlán de Juárez, Mexico, **431** F5
Ixtlán del Río, Mexico, **430** D4
Ixworth, England, U.K., **305** H2
Iyevlevo, Russian Federation, **222** H1
Iza, *river*, Romania, **296** E2
Īzad Khvāst, Iran, **220** F2
Izazi, Tanzania, **369** G4
Izberbash, Russian Federation, **222** D4
Izbica, Poland, **289** H1
Izborsk, Russian Federation, **299** A4
Izhevsk, Russian Federation, **222** E1
Izhma, *river*, Russian Federation, **281** K3
Izmayil, Ukraine, **296** G3
İzmir, *province*, Turkey, **297** F6
İzmir, Turkey, **297** F6
İzmit *see* Kocaeli, Turkey, **297** G5
Iznájar, Embalse de, *reservoir*, Spain, **292** E4
İznik, Turkey, **297** G5
İznik Gölü, *lake*, Turkey, **297** G5
Iznoski, Russian Federation, **299** E5
Izra', Syria, **225** D3
Izsák, Hungary, **289** J5
Izu-Shotō, *islands*, Japan, **209** G4
Izuhara, Japan, **208** E4
Izumi, Japan, **208** E4
Izumo, Japan, **208** F4

J

J.A.D. Jensen Nunatakker, *mountain peak*, Greenland, **411** Q3
Jaakonvaara, Finland, **285** Q5
Jaala, Finland, **287** N2
Jabalpur, India, **218** D5
Jabbūl, Sabkhat al, *lake*, Syria, **225** D1
Jabiru, Australia, **134** G1
Jablah, Syria, **225** C2
Jablanica, Bosnia and Herzegovina, **294** F4
Jablanica, *mountain range*, Albania/Macedonia, **297** C5
Jabłonowo-Pomorskie, Poland, **289** J2

Jaboatão, Brazil, **453** G5
Jabukovac, Yugoslavia, **296** D3
Jabung, Tanjong, *point*, Indonesia, **200** D3
Jaca, Spain, **293** G1
Jacaré, *river*, Brazil, **457** F3
Jacareacanga, Brazil, **452** B5
Jacareí, Brazil, **459** J2
Jáchal, *river*, Argentina, **458** C4
Jacinto, Brazil, **457** F4
Jaciparaná, Brazil, **455** F2
Jaciparaná, *river*, Brazil, **455** F2
Jack Creek, U.S.A., **418** F6
Jackhead, Canada, **414** F6
Jackman, U.S.A., **426** E2
Jacksboro, U.S.A., **424** C3
Jackson, Alabama, U.S.A., **425** J4
Jackson, California, U.S.A., **422** C2
Jackson, Cape, New Zealand, **133** E5
Jackson, Michigan, U.S.A., **421** L4
Jackson, Minnesota, U.S.A., **420** F4
Jackson, Mississippi, U.S.A., **424** G3
Jackson, Montana, U.S.A., **418** H4
Jackson, Ohio, U.S.A., **421** M6
Jackson, Tennessee, U.S.A., **425** H2
Jackson, Wyoming, U.S.A., **419** J5
Jackson Bay, New Zealand, **133** B6
Jackson Lake, U.S.A., **419** J5
Jacksonboro, U.S.A., **425** M3
Jacksons, New Zealand, **133** C6
Jacksonville, Arkansas, U.S.A., **424** F2
Jacksonville, Florida, U.S.A., **425** M4
Jacksonville, Illinois, U.S.A., **420** H6
Jacksonville, North Carolina, U.S.A., **425** P2
Jacksonville, Texas, U.S.A., **424** E4
Jacksonville Beach, U.S.A., **425** M4
Jäckvik, Sweden, **284** H3
Jacmel, Haiti, **429** G3
Jaco, Mexico, **430** E3
Jacobābād, Pakistan, **218** B3
Jacobina, Brazil, **457** F3
Jacquemart Island, Auckland Islands, New Zealand, **132** K11
Jacques-Cartier, Détroit de, *strait*, Canada, **417** J4
Jacquet River, Canada, **416** H6
Jacui, *river*, Brazil, **459** G3
Jacuípe, *river*, Brazil, **457** F3
Jacundá, Brazil, **452** D4
Jacundá, *river*, Brazil, **452** C4
Jacupiranga, Brazil, **459** H2
Jacura, Venezuela, **451** E1
Jadū, Libya, **362** B2
Jaén, Peru, **454** B1
Jaén, Spain, **293** F4
Jaffa, Cape, Australia, **135** H6
Jaffna, Sri Lanka, **216** E4
Jaffray, Canada, **413** M7
Jafr, Qā' al, *salt-pan*, Jordan, **225** D4
Jagdalpur, India, **217** E2
Jagdaqi, China, **211** J2
Jagersfontein, South Africa, **370** E4
Jaggang, China, **214** A2
Jagodina, Yugoslavia, **296** C4
Jagraon, India, **218** C3
Jagtiāl, India, **216** D2
Jaguarão, Brazil, **459** G4
Jaguarão, *river*, Brazil, **459** G4
Jaguari, Brazil, **459** F3
Jaguari, *river*, Brazil, **459** F3
Jaguaribe, Brazil, **453** F4

Jaguaruna, Brazil, **459** H3
Jagüé, Argentina, **458** C3
Jagüey Grande, Cuba, **429** E2
Jahānābād, India, **219** F4
Jahāzpur, India, **218** C4
Jahrom, Iran, **220** F3
Jaicós, Brazil, **453** F5
Jaipur, India, **218** C4
Jais, India, **219** E4
Jaisalmer, India, **218** B4
Jājapur, India, **219** F5
Jajce, Bosnia and Herzegovina, **294** F3
Jakarta, Indonesia, **201** D4
Jakarta Raya, *autonomous district*, Indonesia, **200** D4
Jakes Corner, Canada, **412** C1
Jakrupica, *mountain range*, Macedonia, **297** C5
Jal, U.S.A., **423** M5
Jalai Nur, China, **210** G2
Jalaid Qi, China, **211** H3
Jalal-Abad, Kyrgyzstan, **212** B4
Jalālah al Baḥrīyah, Jabal al, *mountain range*, Egypt, **225** A5
Jalālah al Qiblīyah, Jabal al, *mountain range*, Egypt, **225** A5
Jalālābād, Afghanistan, **218** B2
Jalapa Enríquez, Mexico, **431** F5
Jalapa, Guatemala, **428** C4
Jalapa, Nicaragua, **428** D4
Jālaun, India, **218** D4
Jales, Brazil, **456** C5
Jaleshwar, India, **219** F5
Jaleswar, Nepal, **219** F4
Jālgaon, India, **218** C5
Jalingo, Nigeria, **365** G3
Jalisco, *state*, Mexico, **430** D4
Jālna, India, **218** C6
Jalor, India, **218** C4
Jalostotitlán, Mexico, **430** E4
Jalpāiguri, India, **219** G4
Jalpa, Mexico, **430** E4
Jalpan, Mexico, **431** F4
Jālū, Libya, **362** D3
Jaluit, *island*, Marshall Islands, **139** F4
Jamaame, Somalia, **369** H3
Jamaica, *country*, Caribbean Sea, **409** R7
Jamaica Channel, Haiti/Jamaica, **429** G3
Jamālpur, Bangladesh, **214** D4
Jamanota, *mountain peak*, Aruba, **461** B3
Jamanxin, *river*, Brazil, **452** B5
Jamari, *river*, Brazil, **455** F2
Jambi, Indonesia, **200** C3
Jambi, *province*, Indonesia, **200** C3
Jambongan, Pulau, *island*, Malaysia, **201** G1
Jambuair, Tanjong, *point*, Indonesia, **200** B1
James, Isla, *island*, Chile, **460** B2
James, *river*, U.S.A., **420** D2
James Bay, Canada, **415** P5
Jamesābād, Pakistan, **218** B4
Jamestown, New York, U.S.A., **421** P4
Jamestown, North Dakota, U.S.A., **420** D2
Jamestown, St Helena, **373** B3
Jamkhandi, India, **216** C2
Jammerbugten, *bay*, Denmark, **286** D4
Jammu, India, **218** C2
Jammu and Kashmīr, *state*, India, **218** C2
Jāmnagar, India, **218** B5
Jāmpur, Pakistan, **218** B3
Jämsä, Finland, **287** M2
Jamsah, Egypt, **363** F3
Jamshedpur, India, **219** F5
Jamtari, Nigeria, **365** G3
Jämtland, *county*, Sweden, **284** F5
Jamūi, India, **219** F4

Jaguaruna, Brazil, **459** H3
Jan Mayen, *Norwegian dependency*, Greenland Sea, **471** D8
Jan Mayen Ridge, *underwater feature*, Atlantic Ocean, **477** G1
Janāb Kurdufān, *state*, Sudan, **366** D2
Janaúba, Brazil, **457** E4
Janaucu, Ilha, *island*, Brazil, **452** C3
Jand, Pakistan, **218** B2
Jandaq, Iran, **221** F2
Jandia, Punta de, *point*, Islas Canarias, Spain, **373** B4
Jane Peak, *mountain peak*, New Zealand, **133** B7
Janesville, U.S.A., **421** J4
Jangeru, Indonesia, **201** G3
Jangipur, India, **219** F4
Janīn, West Bank, **225** C3
Janja, Bosnia and Herzegovina, **296** B3
Janjina, Croatia, **294** F4
Janos, Mexico, **430** C2
Jánoshalma, Hungary, **289** J5
Jánosháza, Hungary, **289** H5
Janów Lubelski, Poland, **289** L3
Janów Podlaski, Poland, **289** L2
Jänsmässholmen, Sweden, **284** F5
Januária, Brazil, **457** E4
Janūb Dārfūr, *state*, Sudan, **366** B2
Janzé, France, **290** D3
Jaorā, India, **218** C5
Japan, *country*, Asia, **197** Q6
Japan Basin, *underwater feature*, Sea of Japan, **478** C2
Japan Trench, *underwater feature*, Pacific Ocean, **478** D2
Japurá, Brazil, **451** E4
Japura, Indonesia, **200** C3
Japurá, *river*, Brazil, **451** F5
Jaqué, Panama, **429** F6
Jaques Cartier, Mont, *mountain peak*, Canada, **416** J5
Jaraguá do Sul, Brazil, **459** H3
Jaraicejo, Spain, **292** E3
Jarama, *river*, Spain, **293** F2
Jarandilla de la Vera, Spain, **292** E2
Jarash, Jordan, **225** C3
Jarauçu, *river*, Brazil, **452** C4
Jarbah, Jazīrat, *island*, Tunisia, **361** J2
Jardim, Brazil, **456** B5
Jardines de la Reina, Archipélago de los, *islands*, Cuba, **429** F2
Jargalang, China, **211** H4
Jargalant, Arhangay, Mongolia, **213** J3
Jargalant, Govĭ-Altay, Mongolia, **213** H3
Jargalant, Töv, Mongolia, **210** D2
Jargalthaan, Mongolia, **210** E3
Jargeau, France, **290** F3
Jari, *river*, Brazil, **452** C3
Jarīd, Shaṭṭ al, *lake*, Tunisia, **361** H2
Jarjīs, Tunisia, **362** B2
Järna, Kopparberg, Sweden, **286** G2
Järna, Stockholm, Sweden, **287** H3
Jarny, France, **291** G2
Jarocin, Poland, **289** H3
Jarod, India, **218** D5
Jarosław, Poland, **289** L4
Jarrāhi, *river*, Iran, **220** E2
Jarrell, U.S.A., **424** D4
Jartai, China, **210** D5
Jaru, Brazil, **455** F3
Jarud Qi, China, **211** H3
Järva-Jaani, Estonia, **287** M3
Järvenpää, Finland, **287** M2
Jarvis Island, *U.S. territory*, Pacific Ocean, **131** J2
Järvsö, Sweden, **286** H2
Jashpurnagar, India, **219** F5

Kushtagi, India, **216** D3
Kushtia, Bangladesh, **219** G5
Kusite, China, **211** K2
Kuskokwim, *river*, U.S.A., **410** D3
Kuskokwim Bay, U.S.A., **410** C4
Kuskokwim Mountains, *mountain range*, U.S.A., **410** D3
Kusma, Nepal, **219** E3
Kustanay *see* Qostanay, Kazakhstan, **222** G2
Kūsti, Sudan, **366** D2
Kut, Ko, *island*, Thailand, **202** D4
Kūtahya, *province*, Turkey, **297** G6
Kūtahya, Turkey, **224** C5
K'ut'aisi, Georgia, **222** C4
Kutarere, New Zealand, **132** F4
Kutina, Croatia, **294** F3
Kutiyāna, India, **218** B5
Kutkai, Myanmar, **205** C3
Kutkai, Myanmar, **205** C3
Kutno, Poland, **289** J2
Kuttura, Finland, **285** N2
Kutu, Democratic Republic of the Congo, **368** C3
Kutum, Sudan, **366** B2
Kúty, Slovakia, **289** H4
Kuujjuaq, Canada, **411** N4
Kuusalu, Estonia, **287** M3
Kuusamo, Finland, **285** P4
Kuusankoski, Finland, **287** N2
Kuusjoki, Finland, **287** L2
Kuvango, Angola, **368** C5
Kuvshinovo, Russian Federation, **299** E4
Kuwait, *country*, Asia, **196** F7
Kuwait *see* Al Kuwayt, Kuwait, **363** J3
Kuwalan, *river*, Indonesia, **201** E3
Kuyal'nyts'kyy Lyman, *lake*, Ukraine, **296** H2
Kuybyshev, Russian Federation, **223** K1
Kūybyshevskïy, Kazakhstan, **222** H2
Kuybyshevskoye Vodokhranilishche, *reservoir*, Russian Federation, **298** G2
Kuye, *river*, China, **210** E5
Kuygan, Kazakhstan, **223** J3
Kuytun, China, **212** E3
Kuyucak, Turkey, **297** G7
Kuyuwini, *river*, Guyana, **451** G3
Kuzedeyevo, Russian Federation, **223** M2
Kuzema, *river*, Russian Federation, **285** R4
Kuzema, Russian Federation, **285** S4
Kuznechnoye, Russian Federation, **299** B2
Kuznetsk, Russian Federation, **298** G2
Kuzomen', Russian Federation, **285** T3
Kuzreka, Russian Federation, **285** S3
Kuzumaki, Japan, **209** H2
Kvænangen, *bay*, Norway, **284** K1
Kvænangsbotn, Norway, **285** L2
Kværndrup, Denmark, **286** E5
Kvaløy, *island*, Norway, **284** J2
Kvaløya, *island*, Norway, **285** L1
Kvalsund, Norway, **285** L1
Kvarner, *gulf*, Croatia, **294** E3
Kvarnerič, *bay*, Croatia, **294** E3
Kvenvær, Norway, **284** D5
Kvikne, Norway, **286** E1
Kvinesdal, Norway, **286** C3
Kwa Mashu, South Africa, **371** F4
Kwa Mtoro, Tanzania, **369** G4
Kwa Nobuhle, South Africa, **370** E5
Kwail, North Korea, **208** D3
Kwajalein, *island*, Marshall Islands, **138** E4

Kwakoegron, Suriname, **452** B2
Kwakwani, Guyana, **451** G3
Kwale, Kenya, **369** G3
Kwale, Nigeria, **365** F3
Kwamouth, Democratic Republic of the Congo, **368** C3
Kwangju, South Korea, **208** D4
Kwara, *state*, Nigeria, **365** E3
Kwatarkwashi, Nigeria, **365** F2
Kwatisore, Indonesia, **199** F3
Kwazulu-Natal, *province*, South Africa, **371** F4
Kwekwe, Zimbabwe, **371** E2
Kweneng, *district*, Botswana, **370** D3
Kwenge, *river*, Democratic Republic of the Congo, **368** C4
Kwidzyn, Poland, **289** J2
Kwikila, Papua New Guinea, **140** B5
Kwinana, Australia, **134** D5
Kwoka, Gunung, *mountain peak*, Indonesia, **199** F3
Kyabé, Chad, **366** A3
Kyaikkami, Myanmar, **202** C2
Kyaikto, Myanmar, **205** C4
Kyakhta, Russian Federation, **210** D2
Kyancutta, Australia, **135** H5
Kyanda, Russian Federation, **285** U4
Kyangin, Myanmar, **205** B4
Kyaukme, Myanmar, **205** C3
Kyaukpyu, Myanmar, **205** B4
Kyauktaw, Myanmar, **205** B3
Kyeintali, Myanmar, **205** B4
Kyela, Tanzania, **369** F4
Kyenjojo, Uganda, **369** F2
Kyindwe, Myanmar, **205** B3
Kyklades (Cyclades), *islands*, Greece, **297** E7
Kyle of Lochalsh, Scotland, U.K., **308** D3
Kyleakin, Scotland, U.K., **308** D3
Kyll, *river*, Germany, **288** C3
Kyllini Oros, *mountain peak*, Greece, **297** D7
Kylmälä, Finland, **285** N4
Kymi, Greece, **297** E6
Kyŏnggi-man, *bay*, South Korea, **208** D3
Kyŏngju, South Korea, **208** E4
Kyŏngsŏng, North Korea, **208** E2
Kyōto, Japan, **209** F4
Kyparissia, Greece, **297** C7
Kyparissiakos Kolpos, *bay*, Greece, **297** C7
Kyra, Russian Federation, **210** E2
Kyra Panagia, *island*, Greece, **297** E6
Kyren, Russian Federation, **213** J2
Kyrenia Range, *mountain range*, Cyprus, **225** B2
Kyrgyz Ala Too, *mountain range*, Kazakhstan/Kyrgyzstan, **212** B4
Kyrgyzstan, *country*, Asia, **196** J5
Kyritz, Germany, **288** F2
Kyrksæterøra, Norway, **284** D5
Kyrnasivka, Ukraine, **296** G1
Kyrnychky, Ukraine, **296** G3
Kyrönjoki, *river*, Finland, **285** L5
Kyshtovka, Russian Federation, **223** K1
Kythira, Greece, **297** D7
Kythira, *island*, Greece, **297** D7
Kythnos, *island*, Kyklades, Greece, **297** E7
Kythrea, Cyprus, **225** B2
Kyuquot Sound, Canada, **412** F7
Kyushe, Kazakhstan, **222** F3
Kyūshū, *island*, Japan, **208** F4
Kyushu-Palau Ridge, *underwater feature*, Pacific Ocean, **478** D3
Kyustendil, Bulgaria, **296** D4
Kyyiv (Kiev), Ukraine, **298** D2

Kyyivs'ke, Vodoskhovyshche, *reservoir*, Ukraine, **298** C2
Kyyjärvi, Finland, **285** M5
Kyzyl, Russian Federation, **223** N2
Kyzyl-Kiya, Kyrgyzstan, **223** J4
Kzyl-Orda *see* Qyzylorda, Kazakhstan, **222** H4
Kyzyldangi, Gora, *mountain peak*, Tajikistan, **223** J5
Kyzylkum, Peski, *desert*, Kazakhstan/Uzbekistan, **222** G4

L

La Almunia de Doña Godina, Spain, **293** G2
La Asunción, Venezuela, **451** F1
La Banda, Argentina, **458** D3
La Bañeza, Spain, **292** E1
La Barge, U.S.A., **419** J5
La Belle, U.S.A., **425** M6
La Blanquilla, *island*, Venezuela, **451** F1
La Boquilla del Conchos, Mexico, **430** D3
La Brea, Trinidad, Trinidad and Tobago, **461** C4
La Brède, France, **290** D4
La Calera, Chile, **458** B4
La Capelle, France, **291** F2
La Carlota, Argentina, **458** D4
La Carolina, Spain, **293** F3
La Ceiba, Honduras, **428** D4
La Charité-sur-Loire, France, **291** F3
La Châtre, France, **290** E3
La Chorrera, Colombia, **450** D4
La Chorrera, Panama, **429** F5
La Ciudad, Mexico, **430** D4
La Cocha, Argentina, **458** D3
La Concepción, Panama, **429** E5
La Corey, Canada, **413** P4
La Crescent, U.S.A., **420** H4
La Croisière, France, **290** E3
La Crosse, Kansas, U.S.A., **420** D6
La Crosse, Wisconsin, U.S.A., **420** H4
La Cruz, Argentina, **459** F3
La Cruz, Colombia, **450** C4
La Cruz, Mexico, **430** D4
La Cumbre, Volcán, *mountain peak*, Islas Galápagos (Galapagos Islands), Ecuador, **461** A2
La Dorada, Colombia, **450** C3
La Escala, Spain, **293** J1
La Esmeralda, Paraguay, **458** D2
La Esmeralda, Venezuela, **451** F3
La Esperanza, Argentina, **460** D1
La Esperanza, Bolivia, **455** F4
La Esperanza, Honduras, **428** C4
La Estrella, Argentina, **458** D2
La Estrella, Bolivia, **455** F4
La Falda, Argentina, **458** D4
La Fayette, U.S.A., **425** K2
La Fé, Isla de la Juventud, Cuba, **429** E2
La Fé, W. Cuba, **428** D2
La Flèche, France, **290** D3
La Foa, New Caledonia, **141** A3
La Forestière, French Guiana, **452** B2
La Fría, Venezuela, **450** D2
La Galite, *island*, Tunisia, **295** B7
La Giandola, France, **291** H5
La Gloria, Colombia, **450** D2
La Goulette, Tunisia, **295** C7
La Grande, U.S.A., **418** E4
La Grande Deux, Réservoir de, Canada, **416** C3
La Grande Rivière, *river*, Canada, **415** Q5

La Grande Trois, Réservoir de, Canada, **416** D3
La Grange, Georgia, U.S.A., **425** K3
La Grange, Texas, U.S.A., **424** D5
La Grange, Wyoming, U.S.A., **419** M6
La Grave, France, **291** H4
La Guardia, Chile, **458** C3
La Guerche-de-Bretagne, France, **290** D3
La Habana (Havana), Cuba, **429** E2
La Horqueta, Venezuela, **451** G2
La Huaca, Peru, **454** B1
La Jagua de Ibirico, Colombia, **450** D2
La Jara, U.S.A., **423** L3
La Joya, Mexico, **430** D3
La Joya, Peru, **454** D4
La Junta, U.S.A., **423** M3
La Laguna, Argentina, **458** D4
La Laguna, Islas Canarias, Spain, **373** A4
La Laja, Chile, **458** B5
La Libertad, Guatemala, **428** C3
La Ligua, Chile, **458** B4
La Linea de la Concepción, Spain, **292** E4
La Loberia, Argentina, **460** E1
La Loche, Canada, **413** Q3
La Loma, San Andrés, Colombia, **461** B1
La Maddalena, Sardegna, Italy, **295** B5
La Malbaie, Canada, **416** F6
La Martre, Canada, **411** N5
La Mejorada, Peru, **454** C3
La Merced, Peru, **454** C3
La Moure, U.S.A., **420** D2
La Mula, Mexico, **430** D2
La Mure, France, **291** G4
La Nava de Ricomalillo, Spain, **292** E3
La Negra, Chile, **458** B2
La Noria, Mexico, **430** D4
La Oliva, Islas Canarias, Spain, **373** B4
La Orchila, *island*, Venezuela, **451** E1
La Oroya, Peru, **454** C3
La Paca, Spain, **293** G4
La Palma, *island*, Islas Canarias, Spain, **373** A4
La Palma, Panama, **429** F5
La Paloma, Uruguay, **459** F5
La Pampa, *province*, Argentina, **458** D5
La Paragua, Venezuela, **451** F2
La Paz, Bahía de, *bay*, Mexico, **430** C3
La Paz, Bolivia, **455** E4
La Paz, *department*, Bolivia, **455** E4
La Paz, Entre Rios, Argentina, **459** F4
La Paz, Mendoza, Argentina, **458** C4
La Paz, Mexico, **430** C3
La Paz, Providencia, Colombia, **461** C1
La Pedrera, Colombia, **451** E4
La Perla, Mexico, **430** D2
La Perouse Strait, Japan/Russian Federation, **209** H1
La Pesca, Mexico, **431** F4
La Piedad Cavadas, Mexico, **430** E4
La Pine, U.S.A., **418** D5
La Plaine, Dominica, **427** D3
La Plaine des Cafres, Réunion, **373** A1
La Plata, Argentina, **459** F5
La Plata, Colombia, **450** C3
La Pobla de Segur, Spain, **293** H1
La Possession, Réunion, **373** A1
La Potherie, Lac, *lake*, Canada, **415** T2
La Pryor, U.S.A., **424** C5
La Push, U.S.A., **418** B3
La Quiaca, Argentina, **458** D2

La Rioja, Argentina, **458** C3
La Rioja, *autonomous community*, Spain, **293** F1
La Rioja, *province*, Argentina, **458** C3
La Rivière, Canada, **414** E7
La Roca de la Sierra, Spain, **292** D3
La Roche, New Caledonia, **141** A3
La Roche-Chalais, France, **290** D4
La Roche-sur-Yon, France, **290** D3
La Rochelle, France, **290** D3
La Roda, Spain, **293** F3
La Romana, Dominican Republic, **429** H3
La Ronge, Canada, **413** S4
La Rosita, Mexico, **430** E2
La Sábana, Argentina, **459** E3
La Salle, Canada, **414** F7
La Salle, U.S.A., **421** J5
La Sarre, Canada, **416** B5
La Scie, Canada, **417** P5
La Serena, Chile, **458** B3
La Seu d'Urgell, Spain, **293** H1
La Solana, Spain, **293** F3
La Spezia, Italy, **294** B3
La Tagua, Colombia, **450** C4
La Teste, France, **290** D4
La Toma, Argentina, **458** D4
La Tortuga, *island*, Venezuela, **451** F1
La Troya, *river*, Argentina, **458** C3
La Tuque, Canada, **416** E6
La Unión, Bolivia, **455** G4
La Unión, Chile, **460** C1
La Unión, Colombia, **450** C4
La Unión, Mexico, **430** E5
La Unión, Peru, **454** C2
La Urbana, Venezuela, **451** E2
La Vega, Haiti, **429** H3
La Ventana, Mexico, **431** E4
La Vibora, Mexico, **430** E3
La Victoria, Venezuela, **451** E1
La Yarada, Peru, **454** D5
Laage, Germany, **288** F2
Laascaanood, Somalia, **367** G3
Laâyoune *see* El Aaiún, Western Sahara, **360** D3
Labasa, Fiji, **141** A4
Labé, Guinea, **364** B2
Labe (Elbe), *river*, Czech Republic, **289** G3
Labelle, Canada, **416** D6
Labin, Croatia, **294** E3
Labinsk, Russian Federation, **222** C4
Labis, Malaysia, **200** C2
Labo, Mount, *mountain peak*, Philippines, **204** C3
Labo, Philippines, **204** C3
Laboulaye, Argentina, **458** D5
Labrador, *region*, Canada, **411** N4
Labrador City, Canada, **416** H3
Labrador Sea, Canada/Greenland, **411** P4
Lábrea, Brazil, **455** F2
Labrit, France, **290** D4
Labu, Indonesia, **200** D3
Labuan, *federal territory*, Malaysia, **201** F1
Labuha, Indonesia, **198** D3
Labuhanbajo, Indonesia, **198** B5
Labuhanbilik, Indonesia, **200** C2
Labuhanhaji, Indonesia, **200** B2
Labuhanmeringgai, Indonesia, **200** D4
Labuk, Teluk, *bay*, Malaysia, **201** L1
Labyrinth Lake, Canada, **414** A1
Labytnangi, Russian Federation, **300** H3
Laç, Albania, **297** B5
Lac, *prefecture*, Chad, **365** G2
Lac du Bonnet, Canada, **414** F6
Lac-Édouard, Canada, **416** E6
Lac-Gatineau, Canada, **416** D6

Macusani, Peru, **454** D4
Macuspana, Mexico, **431** G5
Mcveigh, Canada, **414** D3
Ma'dabā, Jordan, **225** C4
Madadeni, South Africa, **371** F4
Madagascar, *country*, Indian Ocean, **359** K9
Madagascar Basin, *underwater feature*, Indian Ocean, **476** C6
Madagascar Plateau, *underwater feature*, Indian Ocean, **476** B6
Madā'in Şāliḥ, Saudi Arabia, **363** G3
Madalena, Azores, Portugal, **360** M7
Madam, Isle, *island*, Canada, **417** L7
Madama, Niger, **362** B4
Madampe, Sri Lanka, **217** E5
Madan, Bulgaria, **297** E5
Madanapalle, India, **216** D3
Madang, Papua New Guinea, **140** B4
Madang, *province*, Papua New Guinea, **140** B4
Madaoua, Niger, **365** F2
Mādārīpur, Bangladesh, **214** D5
Madau, Turkmenistan, **222** E5
Madawaska, Canada, **416** B7
Maddalena, Isola, *island*, Sardegna, Italy, **295** B5
Madeira, *island*, Portugal, Atlantic Ocean, **373** C3
Madeira, *river*, Brazil, **451** G5
Madeleine, Îles de la, *islands*, Canada, **417** L6
Madelia, U.S.A., **420** F3
Madeline, U.S.A., **418** D6
Madera, Mexico, **430** C2
Madera, U.S.A., **422** C3
Madhepura, India, **219** F4
Madhubani, India, **219** F4
Madhya Pradesh, *state*, India, **218** D5
Madidi, *river*, Bolivia, **455** E3
Madimba, Democratic Republic of the Congo, **368** C3
Madinani, Côte d'Ivoire, **364** C3
Madingo-Kayes, Congo, **368** B3
Madingou, Congo, **368** B3
Madingrin, Cameroon, **365** G3
Madirovalo, Madagascar, **372** B4
Madison, Canada, **413** Q6
Madison, Florida, U.S.A., **425** L4
Madison, Georgia, U.S.A., **425** L3
Madison, Indiana, U.S.A., **421** L6
Madison, Iowa, U.S.A., **421** J4
Madison, Nebraska, U.S.A., **420** E5
Madison, *river*, U.S.A., **419** J4
Madison, South Dakota, U.S.A., **420** E3
Madisonville, Kentucky, U.S.A., **421** K7
Madisonville, Texas, U.S.A., **424** E4
Madiun, Indonesia, **201** E4
Madjingo, Gabon, **368** B2
Mado Gashi, Kenya, **369** G2
Madoc, Canada, **416** C7
Madoi, China, **215** F2
Madona, Latvia, **287** N4
Madonie, *mountain range*, Sicilia, Italy, **295** D7
Madra Daği, *mountain peak*, Turkey, **297** F6
Madrakah, Ra's al, *cape*, Oman, **221** G5
Madras *see* Chennai, India, **216** E3
Madras, U.S.A., **418** D4
Madre, Laguna, *lagoon*, Mexico, **431** F3
Madre, Sierra, *mountain range*, Philippines, **204** C2
Madre de Chiapas, Sierra, *mountain range*, Mexico, **431** G5

Madre de Dios, Isla, *island*, Chile, **460** B4
Madre de Dios, *river*, Bolivia/Peru, **455** D3
Madre Del Sur, Sierra, *mountain range*, Mexico, **431** E5
Madre Occidental, Sierra, *mountain range*, Mexico, **430** C2
Madre Oriental, Sierra, *mountain range*, Mexico, **431** E3
Madrid, *autonomous community*, Spain, **293** F2
Madrid, Spain, **293** F2
Madridejos, Spain, **293** F3
Maduda, Democratic Republic of the Congo, **368** B3
Madukani, Tanzania, **369** G3
Madura, Australia, **134** F5
Madura, Pulau, *island*, Indonesia, **201** F4
Madura, Selat, *strait*, Indonesia, **201** F4
Madurai, India, **216** D4
Madyo, Tanzania, **369** F4
Mae Hong Son, Thailand, **202** C2
Mae Ramat, Thailand, **202** C2
Mae Sai, Myanmar, **215** F5
Mae Sai, Thailand, **205** C3
Mae Sariang, Thailand, **202** C2
Mae Sot, Thailand, **202** C2
Mae Tho, Doi, *mountain peak*, Thailand, **202** C2
Mae Tub Reservoir, Thailand, **202** C2
Mae Ya, Doi, *mountain peak*, Thailand, **202** C2
Mæl, Norway, **286** D3
Maella, Spain, **293** H2
Maestra, Sierra, *mountain range*, Cuba, **429** F3
Maevatanana, Madagascar, **372** B4
Maewo, *island*, Vanuatu, **141** A2
Mafeking, Canada, **414** D5
Mafeteng, Lesotho, **371** E4
Maffin, Indonesia, **199** G3
Mafia Island, Tanzania, **369** G4
Mafikeng, South Africa, **371** E4
Mafinga, Tanzania, **369** G4
Mafra, Brazil, **459** H3
Magadan, Russian Federation, **301** S4
Magadi, Kenya, **369** G3
Magallanes, *administrative region*, Chile, **460** C4
Magallanes, Estrecho de, *strait*, Chile, **460** C4
Magangué, Colombia, **450** C2
Mağara, Turkey, **225** B1
Magaria, Niger, **365** F2
Magat, *river*, Philippines, **204** C2
Magbakele, Democratic Republic of the Congo, **368** D2
Magburaka, Sierra Leone, **364** B3
Magdagachi, Russian Federation, **211** J1
Magdalena, Argentina, **459** F5
Magdalena, Bolivia, **455** F3
Magdalena, Isla, *island*, Chile, **460** C2
Magdalena, Mexico, **430** C2
Magdalena, *river*, Colombia, **450** D2
Magdalena, *river*, Mexico, **430** C2
Magdalena, U.S.A., **423** K4
Magdalena Tequisistlán, Mexico, **431** G5
Magdeburg, Germany, **288** E2
Magdelaine Cays, *islands*, Coral Sea Islands, **135** L2
Magee Island, Northern Ireland, U.K., **309** G3
Magelang, Indonesia, **201** E4
Magerøya, *island*, Norway, **285** M1

Maggiorasca, Monte, *mountain peak*, Italy, **294** B3
Maggiore, Lago, *lake*, Italy, **294** B3
Maggiore, Monte, *mountain peak*, Italy, **295** E5
Maghāghah, Egypt, **363** F3
Maghama, Mauritania, **364** B1
Maghārah, Jabal, *mountain peak*, Egypt, **225** B4
Magherafelt, *district*, Northern Ireland, U.K., **309** F3
Magherafelt, Northern Ireland, U.K., **309** F3
Maghull, England, U.K., **306** F4
Magilligan Point, Northern Ireland, U.K., **309** F2
Mágina, *mountain peak*, Spain, **293** F3
Maglić, *mountain peak*, Bosnia and Herzegovina, **294** G4
Maglie, Italy, **295** G5
Magma Point, Papua New Guinea, **140** C4
Magna, U.S.A., **423** G1
Magnetic Island, Australia, **135** K2
Magnetity, Russian Federation, **285** R2
Magnitogorsk, Russian Federation, **222** F2
Magnolia, U.S.A., **424** F3
Mago, *island*, Fiji, **141** A4
Màgoé, Mozambique, **369** F6
Magog, Canada, **416** E7
Magpie, Canada, **417** J4
Magpie, Lac, *lake*, Canada, **417** J4
Magrath, Canada, **413** N7
Magta' Lahjar, Mauritania, **364** B1
Maguarinho, Cabo, *cape*, Brazil, **452** D3
Magude, Mozambique, **371** F4
Magumeri, Nigeria, **365** G2
Maguse Lake, Canada, **414** G1
Magwe, *division*, Myanmar, **205** B3
Magwe, Myanmar, **205** B3
Magyichaung, Myanmar, **205** B3
Maha Sarakham, Thailand, **203** D2
Mahābād, Iran, **222** D5
Mahabe, Madagascar, **372** B4
Mahābhārat Lekh, *mountain range*, Nepal, **219** E3
Mahabo, Madagascar, **372** A5
Mahaboboka, Madagascar, **372** A5
Mahadday Weyne, Somalia, **367** G4
Mahagi Port, Democratic Republic of the Congo, **369** F2
Mahaicony, Guyana, **452** B1
Mahājan, India, **218** C3
Mahajanga, Madagascar, **372** B4
Mahajanga, *province*, Madagascar, **372** B4
Mahakam, *river*, Indonesia, **201** F2
Mahalapye, Botswana, **371** E3
Mahalevona, Madagascar, **372** B4
Mahallāt, Iran, **220** F2
Mahānadi, *river*, India, **219** F5
Mahanoro, Madagascar, **372** B4
Mahārājganj, Bihār, India, **219** F4
Mahārājganj, Uttar Pradesh, India, **219** E4
Mahārāshtra, *state*, India, **216** C2
Maharès, Tunisia, **361** J2
Mahavelona, Madagascar, **372** B4
Maḥbūb, Sudan, **366** C2
Maḥbūbnagar, India, **216** D2
Mahdia, Guyana, **451** G3
Mahdia, Tunisia, **362** B1
Mahe, India, **216** C4

Mahé, *island*, Seychelles, **373** A2
Mahébourg, Mauritius, **373** C1
Mahenge, Tanzania, **369** G4
Maheno, New Zealand, **133** C7
Mahesāna, India, **218** C5
Mahi, *river*, India, **218** C5
Mahia, New Zealand, **132** F4
Mahia Peninsula, New Zealand, **132** F4
Mahilyow, Belarus, **299** C6
Mahilyowskaya Voblasts', *province*, Belarus, **299** C6
Mahina, Mali, **364** B2
Maḥmūd-e Rāqī, Afghanistan, **218** B2
Mahmūdābād, India, **218** E4
Mahmudia, Romania, **296** G3
Mahnomen, U.S.A., **420** F2
Mahoba, India, **218** D4
Mahoenui, New Zealand, **132** E4
Mahón, Islas Baleares, Spain, **293** K3
Mahora, Spain, **293** G3
Mahou, Mali, **364** B2
Mahrāt, Jabal, *mountain range*, Yemen, **220** F5
Mahroni, India, **218** D4
Mahuanggou, China, **213** G5
Mahuva, India, **218** B5
Mahwa, India, **218** D4
Mai-Ndombe, Lac, *lake*, Democratic Republic of the Congo, **368** C3
Maiao, *island*, French Polynesia, **137** F2
Maicao, Colombia, **450** D1
Maîche, France, **291** H3
Maicuru, *river*, Brazil, **452** B3
Maidenhead, England, U.K., **305** G3
Maidi, Indonesia, **198** D2
Maidstone, Canada, **413** Q5
Maidstone, England, U.K., **305** H3
Maiduguri, Nigeria, **365** G2
Maignelay-Montigny, France, **305** K5
Maigualida, Sierra, *mountain range*, Venezuela, **451** F3
Maihar, India, **218** E4
Maihiá, Venezuela, **451** F3
Maikala Range, *mountain range*, India, **218** E5
Mailsi, Pakistan, **218** C3
Main, *river*, Germany, **288** D4
Main-a-Dieu, Canada, **417** M6
Main Brook, Canada, **417** N4
Maine, Gulf of, U.S.A., **426** F2
Maine, *state*, U.S.A., **426** F2
Maine Hanari, Cerro, *mountain peak*, Colombia, **450** D4
Maïné-Soroa, Niger, **365** G2
Mainit, Lake, Philippines, **204** D4
Mainland, *island*, Orkney, Scotland, U.K., **308** F1
Mainland, *island*, Shetland, Scotland, U.K., **308** K7
Mainpuri, India, **218** D4
Maintirano, Madagascar, **372** A4
Mainz, Germany, **288** D4
Maio, *island*, Cape Verde, **360** Q8
Maipú, Argentina, **459** F5
Maipú, Volcán, *mountain peak*, Argentina/Chile, **458** C5
Maipuri Landing, Guyana, **451** G3
Maisí, Cuba, **429** G2
Maitencillo, Chile, **458** B4
Maitengwe, Botswana, **371** E3
Maitland, New South Wales, Australia, **135** L5
Maitland, South Australia, Australia, **135** H5
Maizuru, Japan, **209** F4
Maja e Korbit *see* Korab, *mountain peak*, Albania/Macedonia, **296** C5
Majardah, Monts de la, *mountain range*, Algeria, **295** A7

Majardah, *river*, Tunisia, **362** A1
Majāz al Bāb, Tunisia, **295** B7
Majdanpek, Yugoslavia, **296** C3
Majene, Indonesia, **198** B3
Majevica, *mountain range*, Bosnia and Herzegovina, **294** G3
Majī, Ethiopia, **366** E3
Majia, *river*, China, **210** G5
Majiagang, China, **211** L3
Majiang, China, **206** B4
Majie, China, **215** H5
Majitang, China, **206** B2
Major, Canada, **413** Q6
Major, Puig, *mountain peak*, Islas Baleares, Spain, **293** J3
Major Buratovich, Argentina, **460** E1
Major Lake, Macquarie Island, **134** R11
Majuro, *island*, Marshall Islands, **139** F4
Makīnsk, Kazakhstan, **223** J2
Maka, Senegal, **364** B2
Maka, Solomon Islands, **141** A1
Makabana, Congo, **368** B3
Makaha, Hawaiian Islands, U.S.A., **422** R9
Makak, Cameroon, **368** B2
Makale, Indonesia, **198** B3
Makamba, Burundi, **369** E3
Makanza, Democratic Republic of the Congo, **368** C2
Makapu Point, Niue, **132** M13
Makaraka, New Zealand, **132** F4
Makarakomburu, Mount, *mountain peak*, Solomon Islands, **141** A1
Makarska, Croatia, **294** F4
Makar'yevskaya, Russian Federation, **299** E2
Makasar Selat, *strait*, Indonesia, **198** B3
Makassar *see* Ujungpandang, Indonesia, **198** B4
Makatea, *island*, French Polynesia, **137** G2
Makaw, Myanmar, **205** C2
Makefu, Niue, **132** M13
Makeni, Sierra Leone, **364** B3
Makhachkala, Russian Federation, **222** D4
Makikihi, New Zealand, **133** C7
Makindu, Kenya, **369** G3
Makira, *island*, Solomon Islands, **141** A1
Makiyivka, Ukraine, **298** E3
Makkah (Mecca), Saudi Arabia, **363** G4
Makkola, Finland, **287** P2
Makkovik, Cape, Canada, **417** M2
Makó, Hungary, **289** K5
Makokou, Gabon, **368** B2
Makongolosi, Tanzania, **369** F4
Makoro, Democratic Republic of the Congo, **369** E2
Makotipoko, Congo, **368** C3
Makoua, Congo, **368** C3
Maków Mazowiecki, Poland, **289** K2
Makra, *island*, Kyklades, Greece, **297** E7
Makrakomi, Greece, **297** D6
Makrany, Belarus, **289** M3
Makronisi, *island*, Kyklades, Greece, **297** E7
Maksatikha, Russian Federation, **299** E4
Maksi, India, **218** D5
Maksimikha, Russian Federation, **210** E1
Maksimovka, Russian Federation, **209** G1
Maksudangarh, India, **218** D4
Makthar, Tunisia, **295** B8
Mākū, Iran, **222** C5
Makumbako, Tanzania, **369** F4
Makumbi, Democratic Republic of the Congo, **368** D4
Makungo, Somalia, **369** H2

Makunguwiro, Tanzania, **369** G5
Makurazaki, Japan, **208** E5
Makurdi, Nigeria, **365** F3
Makushino, Russian Federation, **222** H1
Mala, Peru, **454** C3
Mala, Punta, *point*, Panama, **429** F6
Mala, *river*, Peru, **454** C3
Malå, Sweden, **284** J4
Mala Kapela, *mountain range*, Croatia, **294** E3
Mala Vyska, Ukraine, **296** H1
Malabang, Philippines, **204** D5
Malabar, Mount, *mountain peak*, Lord Howe Island, Australia, **135** U14
Malabo, Equatorial Guinea, **368** A2
Malacca, Strait of, Indonesia/ Malaysia, **200** B1
Malacky, Slovakia, **289** H4
Malad City, U.S.A., **419** H5
Maladzyechna, Belarus, **287** N5
Málaga, Spain, **292** E4
Malaga, U.S.A., **423** L5
Malagarasi, Tanzania, **369** F4
Malahide, Ireland, **309** F4
Malaimbandy, Madagascar, **372** B5
Malaita, *island*, Solomon Islands, **141** A1
Malakāl, Sudan, **366** D3
Mālākhera, India, **218** D4
Malakula, *island*, Vanuatu, **141** A2
Malalamai, Papua New Guinea, **140** B4
Malali, Guyana, **451** G3
Malam, Papua New Guinea, **140** A5
Malån, *river*, Sweden, **284** J4
Malang, Indonesia, **201** F4
Malanje, Angola, **368** C4
Malanje, *province*, Angola, **368** C4
Malanville, Benin, **365** E2
Malanzán, Argentina, **458** C4
Mälaren, *lake*, Sweden, **287** H3
Malargüe, Argentina, **458** C5
Malartic, Canada, **416** B5
Malaryta, Belarus, **289** M3
Malaso, *river*, Indonesia, **198** B3
Malatayur, Tanjong, *point*, Indonesia, **201** F3
Malatya, Turkey, **224** E5
Malaut, India, **218** C3
Malavalli, India, **216** D3
Malawali, Pulau, *island*, Malaysia, **201** G1
Malawi, *country*, Africa, **359** J8
Malawi, Lake, Malawi, **369** F5
Malawiya, Sudan, **366** E1
Malay Peninsula, Malaysia/ Thailand, **195** M9
Malaya Vishera, Russian Federation, **299** D3
Malaybalay, Philippines, **204** D4
Malāyer, Iran, **220** E2
Malayiwan, China, **215** F2
Malaysia, *country*, Asia, **197** N9
Malazgirt, Turkey, **363** H1
Malbork, Poland, **289** J1
Malden Island, Kiribati, **139** J5
Maldives, *country*, Asia, **196** J9
Maldon, England, U.K., **305** H3
Maldonado, Uruguay, **459** F5
Malè, Italy, **294** C2
Male, Maldives, **216** C5
Male Atoll, Maldives, **216** C5
Malé Karpaty, *mountain range*, Slovakia, **289** H4
Malea, Gunung, *mountain peak*, Indonesia, **200** B2
Maleas, Akra, *point*, Greece, **297** D7
Mālegaon, India, **218** C5
Malek Dīn, Afghanistan, **218** B2
Malela, Democratic Republic of

the Congo, **369** E3
Malema, Mozambique, **369** G5
Malemba Nkulu, Democratic Republic of the Congo, **369** E4
Malen'ga, Russian Federation, **285** T5
Mälerås, Sweden, **286** G4
Maleta, Russian Federation, **210** E2
Malgomaj, *lake*, Sweden, **284** G4
Malha, Sudan, **366** C1
Malheur Lake, U.S.A., **418** E5
Malheureux, Cap, *cape*, Mauritius, **373** C1
Mali, *country*, Africa, **358** E5
Mali, Democratic Republic of the Congo, **369** E3
Mali, Guinea, **364** B2
Mali Kanal, *canal*, Yugoslavia, **296** B3
Mali Kyun (Tavoy Island), *island*, Myanmar, **202** C3
Maliangping, China, **206** B2
Maliaohe, China, **207** D3
Mālilla, Sweden, **286** G4
Malimba, Monts, *mountain range*, Democratic Republic of the Congo, **369** E4
Malin Head, *point*, Ireland, **309** E2
Malin More, Ireland, **309** D3
Malindang, Mount, *mountain peak*, Philippines, **204** C4
Malindi, Kenya, **369** H3
Malinga, Gabon, **368** B3
Malingsbo, Sweden, **286** G3
Malinoa, *island*, Tonga, **141** B4
Malinovka, Russian Federation, **223** M2
Malipo, China, **215** H5
Maliq, Albania, **297** C5
Malita, Philippines, **204** D5
Maljamar, U.S.A., **423** M5
Mālkāngiri, India, **217** E2
Malkāpur, India, **218** D5
Malkara, Turkey, **297** F3
Malkhanskiy Khrebet, *mountain range*, Russian Federation, **210** D2
Mallaig, Scotland, U.K., **308** D3
Mallard, U.S.A., **420** F4
Mallawī, Egypt, **363** F3
Mallorca, *island*, Islas Baleares, Spain, **293** J3
Mallow, Ireland, **309** D5
Mallwyd, Wales, U.K., **304** D2
Malm, Norway, **284** E4
Malmal, Papua New Guinea, **140** C4
Malmanoury, French Guiana, **452** C2
Malmberget, Sweden, **284** K3
Malmédy, Belgium, **288** C3
Malmesbury, England, U.K., **304** E3
Malmesbury, South Africa, **370** C5
Malmköping, Sweden, **287** H3
Malmö, Sweden, **286** F5
Malmöhus, *county*, Sweden, **286** F5
Malmok, *point*, Bonaire, **461** A4
Malmyzh, Russian Federation, **222** E1
Malnaş, Romania, **296** E2
Maloarkhangel'skoye, Russian Federation, **210** E2
Maloca, Brazil, **452** B3
Maloelap, *island*, Marshall Islands, **139** F4
Malolos, Philippines, **204** C3
Malone, U.S.A., **426** C2
Malonga, Democratic Republic of the Congo, **368** D5
Malosmadulu Atoll, Maldives, **216** C5
Malott, U.S.A., **418** E2
Måløy, Norway, **286** B2
Maloyaroslavets, Russian Federation, **299** F5
Malpas, England, U.K., **304** E1

Malpica, Spain, **292** C1
Mālpura, India, **218** C4
Malta, *country*, Europe, **282** F8
Malta, Idaho, U.S.A., **418** H5
Malta, Latvia, **287** N4
Malta, Montana, U.S.A., **419** L2
Malta Channel, Italy/Malta, **295** E7
Maltahöhe, Namibia, **370** C3
Maltby, England, U.K., **307** G4
Maltby le Marsh, England, U.K., **307** J4
Malton, England, U.K., **307** H3
Malua, Samoa, **141** B1
Maluku (Moluccas), *islands*, Indonesia, **198** D3
Maluku, *province*, Indonesia, **199** E4
Malumfashi, Nigeria, **365** F2
Malung, Sweden, **286** F2
Maluso, Philippines, **204** C5
Malūṭ, Sudan, **366** D2
Malvan, India, **216** C2
Malvern, Arkansas, U.S.A., **424** F2
Malvern, Iowa, U.S.A., **420** F5
Malvern, Worcestershire, U.K., see p... *(unclear)*
Malyy Kavkaz, *mountain range*, Asia, **222** C4
Malyy Kemchug, Russian Federation, **223** N1
Malyy Yenisey, *river*, Russian Federation, **213** H2
Mambasa, Democratic Republic of the Congo, **369** E2
Mamberamo, *river*, Indonesia, **199** G3
Mambéré-Kadéï, *prefecture*, Central African Republic, **368** C2
Mamburao, Philippines, **204** C3
Mamelles, *island*, Seychelles, **373** A2
Mamelodi, South Africa, **371** E4
Mamers, France, **290** E2
Mamfe, Cameroon, **368** A1
Mamiña, Chile, **455** E5
Mamlyutka, Kazakhstan, **223** H1
Mammoth, U.S.A., **423** H5
Mamonovo, Russian Federation, **287** J5
Mamoré, *river*, Bolivia/Brazil, **455** F3
Mamori, Brazil, **451** E4
Mamoriá, Brazil, **455** E2
Mamou, Guinea, **364** B2
Mamoudzou, Mayotte, **372** B3
Mampikony, Madagascar, **372** B4
Mampodre, *mountain peak*, Spain, **292** E1
Mampong, Ghana, **364** D3
Mamry, Jezioro, *lake*, Poland, **289** K1
Mamuju, Indonesia, **198** B3
Man, Côte d'Ivoire, **364** C3
Man, Isle of, *U.K. dependency*, Europe, **306** D3
Man of War Bay, Tobago, Trinidad and Tobago, **461** B4
Mana, French Guiana, **452** C2
Mana, Hawaiian Islands, U.S.A., **422** R9
Mana, *river*, French Guiana, **452** C2
Manacapuru, Brazil, **451** G5
Manacor, Islas Baleares, Spain, **293** J3
Manado, Indonesia, **198** D2
Managua, Lago de, *lake*, Nicaragua, **428** D4
Managua, Nicaragua, **428** D4
Manakara, Madagascar, **372** B5
Manakau, *mountain peak*, New Zealand, **133** D6
Manākhah, Yemen, **220** D5
Manam Island, Papua New Guinea, **140** B4
Manambondro, Madagascar, **372** B5
Mananara Avaratra, Madagascar, **372** B4

Mananjary, Madagascar, **372** B5
Manankoliva, Madagascar, **372** B5
Manankoro, Mali, **364** C2
Manantenina, Madagascar, **372** B5
Manapouri, Lake, New Zealand, **133** A7
Manapouri, New Zealand, **133** A7
Manarantsandry, Madagascar, **372** B4
Manas, *river*, Bhutan/India, **205** A2
Manas Hu, *lake*, China, **212** E3
Manāsa, India, **218** C4
Manassa, U.S.A., **423** L3
Manassas, U.S.A., **426** B5
Manati Bay, St Helena, **373** B3
Manatuto, Indonesia, **198** D5
Manaung, Myanmar, **202** C3
Manaus, Brazil, **451** G5
Manbij, Syria, **225** E1
Manby, England, U.K., **307** J4
Manchester, Connecticut, U.S.A., **426** D4
Manchester, England, U.K., **306** F4
Manchester, Iowa, U.S.A., **420** H4
Manchester, Missouri, U.S.A., **421** M7
Manchester, New Hampshire, U.S.A., **426** E3
Manchester, Tennessee, U.S.A., **425** J2
Manchester, Vermont, U.S.A., **426** F3
Manchhar Lake, Pakistan, **218** A4
Manciano, Italy, **294** C4
Máncora, Peru, **454** B1
Mancos, U.S.A., **423** J3
Mand, *river*, Iran, **220** F3
Manda, Jabal, *mountain peak*, Sudan, **366** B3
Mandabe, Madagascar, **372** A5
Mandal, Bulgan, Mongolia, **213** J2
Māndal, India, **218** B5
Mandal, Töv, Mongolia, **210** D2
Mandala, Puncak, *mountain peak*, Indonesia, **199** H4
Mandalay, *division*, Myanmar, **205** B3
Mandalay, Myanmar, **205** C3
Mandalgovï, Mongolia, **210** D3
Mandan, U.S.A., **420** C2
Mandaon, Philippines, **204** C3
Mandar, Teluk, *bay*, Indonesia, **198** B3
Mandaue, Philippines, **204** C4
Mandeb, Bab el, *strait*, Red Sea, **367** F2
Mandel, Afghanistan, **221** H2
Mandera, Kenya, **369** H2
Manderfeld, Belgium, **288** C3
Manderson, U.S.A., **419** L4
Mandeville, Jamaica, **429** F3
Mandha, India, **218** B4
Mandheera, Somalia, **367** F3
Mandi, India, **218** D3
Mandi Angin, Gunung, *mountain peak*, Malaysia, **200** C1
Mandi Būrewāla, Pakistan, **218** C3
Mandiana, Guinea, **364** C2
Mandié, Mozambique, **369** F6
Mandimba, Mozambique, **369** G5
Mandioré, Lagoa, *lake*, Bolivia/ Brazil, **456** B5
Mandji, Gabon, **368** B3
Mandla, India, **218** E5
Mandø, *island*, Denmark, **286** D5
Mandritsara, Madagascar, **372** B4
Mandsaur, India, **218** C4
Mandul, Pulau, *island*, Indonesia, **201** G2

Mandurah, Australia, **134** D5
Manduria, Italy, **295** F5
Māndvi, E. Gujarāt, India, **218** C5
Māndvi, W. Gujarāt, India, **218** B5
Mandya, India, **216** D3
Manendragarh, India, **219** E5
Manfalūṭ, Egypt, **363** F3
Manfredonia, Golfo di, *gulf*, Italy, **295** F5
Manfredonia, Italy, **295** E5
Manga, Brazil, **457** E4
Manga, Burkina Faso, **364** D2
Manga, Papua New Guinea, **140** D4
Mangai, Democratic Republic of the Congo, **368** C3
Mangai, Papua New Guinea, **140** C3
Mangaia, *island*, Cook Islands, **137** F3
Mangakino, New Zealand, **132** E4
Mangakura, New Zealand, **132** E3
Mangaldai, India, **219** H4
Mangalia, Romania, **296** G4
Mangalmé, Chad, **366** A2
Mangalore, India, **216** C3
Mangamuka, New Zealand, **132** D2
Mangaran, Indonesia, **198** D2
Mangatupoto, New Zealand, **132** E4
Mangaung, South Africa, **371** E4
Mangaweka, *mountain peak*, New Zealand, **132** F4
Mangaweka, New Zealand, **132** E4
Mangawhai, New Zealand, **132** E3
Mangere Island, Chatham Islands, New Zealand, **133** Q16
Manggar, Indonesia, **201** E3
Manggautu, Solomon Islands, **141** A1
Manggo, Solomon Islands, **141** A1
Mangin Taung, *mountain range*, Myanmar, **205** B3
Mangkalihat, Tanjong, *point*, Indonesia, **201** G2
Mangla Reservoir, Pakistan, **218** C2
Mangnai, China, **213** F5
Mango, Togo, **364** E2
Mangochi, Malawi, **369** G5
Mangoky, *river*, Madagascar, **372** A5
Mangole, Pulau, *island*, Indonesia, **198** D3
Mangonui, New Zealand, **132** D2
Māngrol, India, **218** B5
Mangrove Cay, Bahamas, **428** F1
Mangrūl Pīr, India, **218** D5
Mangueigne, Chad, **366** B2
Mangueirinha, Brazil, **459** G2
Manguéni, Plateau du, *plateau*, Niger, **362** B4
Mangui, China, **211** H1
Manguinho, Ponta do, *point*, Brazil, **457** F2
Mangum, U.S.A., **424** C2
Manhan, Mongolia, **213** J2
Manhattan, Kansas, U.S.A., **420** E6
Manhattan, Nevada, U.S.A., **422** E2
Manhattan, Wyoming, U.S.A., **419** J4
Manhuaçu, Brazil, **457** E5
Manhuaçu, *river*, Brazil, **457** F5
Maní, Colombia, **450** D3
Mania, *river*, Madagascar, **372** B4
Maniago, Italy, **294** D2
Maniamba, Mozambique, **369** F5
Manica, *province*,

Montevarchi, Italy, **294** C4
Montevideo, Uruguay, **459** F5
Montevideo, U.S.A., **420** F3
Montezuma Creek, U.S.A., **423** J3
Montgomery, U.S.A., **425** J3
Montgomery, Wales, U.K., **304** D2
Monti, Sardegna, Italy, **295** B5
Monticello, Arkansas, U.S.A., **424** G3
Monticello, Georgia, U.S.A., **425** L3
Monticello, Indiana, U.S.A., **421** K5
Monticello, Iowa, U.S.A., **420** H4
Monticello, Kentucky, U.S.A., **421** L7
Monticello, Mississippi, U.S.A., **424** G4
Monticello, New York, U.S.A., **426** C4
Monticello, Utah, U.S.A., **423** J3
Monticiano, Italy, **294** C4
Montijo, Golfo de, *gulf*, Panama, **429** E6
Montivilliers, France, **290** E2
Montluçon, France, **290** F3
Montmagny, Canada, **416** F6
Montmarault, France, **291** F3
Montmartre, Canada, **414** C6
Monto, Australia, **135** K4
Montoro, Spain, **292** E3
Montoya, U.S.A., **423** L4
Montpelier, Idaho, U.S.A., **419** J5
Montpelier, Vermont, U.S.A., **426** D2
Montpellier, France, **291** F5
Montréal, Canada, **416** E7
Montreal Lake, Canada, **413** S4
Montreal Lake, *lake*, Canada, **413** S4
Montreal River, Canada, **421** L2
Montréjeau, France, **290** E5
Montreuil, France, **305** J4
Montreux, Switzerland, **291** H3
Montrose, Arkansas, U.S.A., **424** G3
Montrose, Colorado, U.S.A., **423** K2
Montrose, Pennsylvania, U.S.A., **426** C4
Montrose, Scotland, U.K., **308** G4
Montserrat, *mountain peak*, Spain, **293** H2
Montserrat, *U.K. dependency*, Caribbean Sea, **409** S7
Montsinéry, French Guiana, **452** C2
Monument Valley, U.S.A., **423** H3
Monveda, Democratic Republic of the Congo, **368** D2
Monywa, Myanmar, **205** B3
Monza, Italy, **294** B3
Monze, Zambia, **369** E6
Monzón, Peru, **454** C2
Monzón, Spain, **293** H2
Mookane, Botswana, **371** E3
Moonbeam, Canada, **415** N7
Moora, Australia, **134** D5
Moorbad Lobenstein, Germany, **288** E3
Moorcroft, U.S.A., **419** M4
Moore, Idaho, U.S.A., **418** H5
Moore, Lake, Australia, **134** D5
Moore, Montana, U.S.A., **419** K3
Moore, Mount, *mountain peak*, Antarctica, **470** C6
Moore, Oklahoma, U.S.A., **424** D2
Moorea, *island*, French Polynesia, **137** F2
Moorefield, U.S.A., **421** P6
Moorhead, U.S.A., **420** E2
Moose, *river*, Canada, **415** P6
Moose, U.S.A., **419** J5
Moose Factory, Canada, **415** P6
Moose Jaw, Canada, **413** S6

Moose Lake, Canada, **414** D5
Moose Lake, U.S.A., **420** G2
Moosehead Lake, U.S.A., **426** F2
Moosehorn, Canada, **414** E6
Moosomin, Canada, **414** D6
Moosonee, Canada, **415** P6
Mopeia, Mozambique, **371** G2
Mopti, *administrative region*, Mali, **364** D2
Mopti, Mali, **364** D2
Moqor, Afghanistan, **218** A2
Moquegua, Peru, **454** D4
Mor, Glen, *valley*, Scotland, U.K., **308** E3
Mór, Hungary, **289** J5
Mora, Cameroon, **365** G2
Mora, Minnesota, U.S.A., **420** G3
Mora, New Mexico, U.S.A., **423** L4
Mora, Portugal, **292** C3
Mora, Spain, **293** F3
Mora, Sweden, **286** G2
Mora de Rubielos, Spain, **293** G2
Móra d'Ebre, Spain, **293** H2
Morada Nova, Brazil, **453** F4
Morādābād, India, **218** D3
Morafenobe, Madagascar, **372** A4
Morąg, Poland, **289** J2
Mórahalom, Hungary, **296** B2
Morakovo, Yugoslavia, **296** B4
Moraleda, Canal, *channel*, Chile, **460** C2
Moraleja, Spain, **292** D2
Morales, Guatemala, **428** C4
Moramanga, Madagascar, **372** B4
Moran, Kansas, U.S.A., **420** F7
Moran, Michigan, U.S.A., **421** L3
Moran, Wyoming, U.S.A., **419** J5
Morane, *island*, French Polynesia, **137** H3
Morar, Loch, *lake*, Scotland, U.K., **308** D4
Morar, Scotland, U.K., **308** D4
Morari, Tso, *lake*, India, **218** D2
Moratalla, Spain, **293** G3
Moratuwa, Sri Lanka, **216** D5
Morava, *river*, Austria/Czech Republic/Slovakia, **289** H4
Moravské Budějovice, Czech Republic, **289** G4
Morawhanna, Guyana, **451** G2
Moray, *local authority*, Scotland, U.K., **308** F3
Moray Firth, *river mouth*, Scotland, U.K., **308** F3
Morbi, India, **218** B5
Morcenx, France, **290** D4
Morden, Canada, **414** E7
Mordoğan, Turkey, **297** F6
Mordoviya, Respublika, *republic*, Russian Federation, **222** C2
More, Ben, *mountain peak*, Scotland, U.K., **308** C4
More Assynt, Ben, Scotland, U.K., **308** D4
Møre og Romsdal, *county*, Norway, **286** C1
Moreau, *river*, U.S.A., **420** B3
Morebattle, Scotland, U.K., **308** G5
Morecambe, England, U.K., **306** F3
Morecambe Bay, England, U.K., **306** E3
Moree, Australia, **135** K4
Morehead, Papua New Guinea, **140** A5
Morehead, U.S.A., **421** M6
Morehead City, U.S.A., **426** B7
Morelia, Mexico, **431** E5
Morella, Spain, **293** G2
Morelos, *state*, Mexico, **431** F5
Morena, India, **218** D4
Morena, Sierra, *mountain range*, Spain, **292** D3

Moreni, Romania, **296** E3
Morerú, *river*, Brazil, **455** G3
Moresby Island, Canada, **412** C5
Moreton-in-Marsh, England, U.K., **305** F3
Moreton Island, Australia, **135** L4
Moretonhampstead, England, U.K., **304** D4
Moretta, Italy, **294** A3
Moreuil, France, **305** K5
Morgan City, U.S.A., **424** G5
Morgan Hill, U.S.A., **422** C3
Morgan Island, Heard and McDonald Islands, **134** S12
Morganton, U.S.A., **425** L2
Morges, Switzerland, **291** H3
Morghāb, *river*, Afghanistan, **218** A2
Mori, Japan, **209** H2
Moriah, Tobago, Trinidad and Tobago, **461** B4
Moriani-Plage, Corse, France, **295** B4
Moribaya, Guinea, **364** C3
Moricetown, Canada, **412** F4
Morichal, Colombia, **451** D3
Moriki, Nigeria, **365** F2
Morioka, Japan, **209** H3
Morjärv, Sweden, **285** L3
Morlaix, France, **290** C2
Morley, Canada, **413** M6
Morley, England, U.K., **307** G4
Morningside, Canada, **413** N5
Mornington, Isla, *island*, Chile, **460** B3
Mornington Island, Australia, **135** H2
Moro, Pakistan, **218** A4
Moro, U.S.A., **418** D4
Moro Gulf, Philippines, **204** C5
Morobe, Papua New Guinea, **140** B4
Morobe, *province*, Papua New Guinea, **140** B4
Morocco, *country*, Africa, **358** E4
Morocco, U.S.A., **421** K5
Morococha, Peru, **454** C3
Morogoro, *administrative region*, Tanzania, **369** G4
Morogoro, Tanzania, **369** G4
Morokweng, South Africa, **370** D4
Moroleón, Mexico, **431** E4
Morombe, Madagascar, **372** A5
Morón, Cuba, **429** F2
Mörön, Hentiy, Mongolia, **210** E3
Mörön, Hövsgöl, Mongolia, **213** J2
Morón de la Frontera, Spain, **292** E4
Morona, Ecuador, **450** C5
Morondava, Madagascar, **372** A5
Morondo, Côte d'Ivoire, **364** C3
Moroni, Comoros, **372** A3
Morotai, Pulau, *island*, Indonesia, **199** E2
Moroto, *mountain peak*, Uganda, **369** F2
Moroto, Uganda, **369** F2
Morozovsk, Russian Federation, **298** F3
Morpará, Brazil, **457** E3
Morpeth, England, U.K., **307** G2
Morphou, Cyprus, **225** B2
Morphou Bay, Cyprus, **225** B2
Morrilton, U.S.A., **424** F2
Morrin, Canada, **413** N6
Morrinhos, Brazil, **456** D5
Morrinsville, New Zealand, **132** E3
Morris, Illinois, U.S.A., **421** J5
Morris, Minnesota, U.S.A., **420** F3
Morris, Pennsylvania, U.S.A., **426** B4
Morristown, New Jersey, U.S.A., **426** C4
Morristown, Tennessee, U.S.A., **425** L1

Morro, Sierra del, *mountain peak*, Argentina, **458** D4
Morro Bay, U.S.A., **422** C4
Morro d'Anta, Brazil, **457** F5
Morro do Chapéu, Brazil, **457** F3
Morro Jable, Islas Canarias, Spain, **373** B4*
Morrón, *mountain peak*, Spain, **293** F4
Morrosquillo, Golfo de, *gulf*, Colombia, **450** C2
Morrumbala, Mozambique, **371** G2
Morrumbene, Mozambique, **371** G3
Morshansk, Russian Federation, **298** F2
Morshyn, Ukraine, **289** L4
Morson, Canada, **414** G7
Mørsvik, Norway, **284** G3
Mortagne-sur-sèvre, France, **290** D3
Mortara, Italy, **294** B3
Morte Bay, England, U.K., **304** C3
Morteau, France, **291** H3
Mortehoe, England, U.K., **304** C3
Morteros, Argentina, **458** D4
Mortes, Rio das, *river*, Brazil, **456** C3
Mortimers, Bahamas, **429** G2
Mortlock Islands, Micronesia, **138** D4
Morton, England, U.K., **305** G2
Morton, Minnesota, U.S.A., **420** F3
Morton, Texas, U.S.A., **423** M5
Morton, Washington, U.S.A., **418** C3
Mortyq, Kazakhstan, **222** F2
Moruga, Trinidad, Trinidad and Tobago, **461** C4
Morungole, *mountain peak*, Uganda, **369** F2
Morvan, *region*, France, **291** F3
Morvern, *region*, Scotland, U.K., **308** D4
Morville, England, U.K., **304** E2
Morwell, Australia, **135** K6
Mor'ye, Russian Federation, **299** C2
Mosal'sk, Russian Federation, **299** E5
Mosbach, Germany, **288** D4
Mosborough, England, U.K., **307** G4
Mosby, U.S.A., **419** L3
Moscow *see* Moskva, Russian Federation, **299** F4
Moscow, U.S.A., **418** F3
Moscow University Ice Shelf, Antarctica, **470** F7
Mosel, *river*, Germany, **288** C4
Moselle, *river*, France, **291** H2
Moses Lake, *lake*, U.S.A., **418** E3
Moses Lake, U.S.A., **418** E3
Mosetse, Botswana, **371** E3
Moshchnyy, Ostrov, *island*, Russian Federation, **287** N2
Moshi, Tanzania, **369** G3
Mosina, Poland, **289** H2
Mosjøen, Norway, **284** F4
Moskenesøya, *island*, Norway, **284** E3
Moskosel, Sweden, **284** J4
Moskovskaya Oblast', *province*, Russian Federation, **299** F5
Moskva, *river*, Russian Federation, **299** F5
Moskva (Moscow), Russian Federation, **299** F4
Mosonmagyaróvár, Hungary, **289** H5
Mosqueiro, Brazil, **452** D3
Mosquera, Colombia, **450** B3
Mosquero, U.S.A., **423** M4
Mosquito Bay, Canada, **415** Q1
Mosquitos, Golfo de los, *gulf*, Panama, **429** E5
Moss, Norway, **286** E3

Mossat, Scotland, U.K., **308** G3
Mossburn, New Zealand, **133** B7
Mossel Bay, South Africa, **370** D5
Mossendjo, Congo, **368** B3
Mossman, Australia, **135** K2
Mossoró, Brazil, **453** G4
Mossuril, Mozambique, **369** H5
Mostaganem, Algeria, **361** G1
Mostar, Bosnia and Herzegovina, **294** F4
Mostardas, Brazil, **459** G4
Mostove, Ukraine, **296** H2
Mostys'ka, Ukraine, **289** L4
Mosul *see* Al Mawşil, Iraq, **363** H1
Mosûlp'o, South Korea, **208** D4
Møsvatn, *lake*, Norway, **286** C3
Mot'a, Ethiopia, **367** E2
Mota del Cuervo, Spain, **293** F3
Motala, Sweden, **286** G3
Moth, India, **218** D4
Motherwell, Scotland, U.K., **308** F5
Motilla del Palancar, Spain, **293** G3
Motiti Island, New Zealand, **132** F3
Motokwe, Botswana, **370** D3
Motovskiy Zaliv, *bay*, Russian Federation, **285** R2
Motril, Spain, **293** F4
Motru, Romania, **296** D3
Mott, U.S.A., **420** B2
Mottola, Italy, **295** F5
Motu, *river*, New Zealand, **132** F4
Motu Iti, *island*, Isla de Pascua (Easter Island), Chile, **461** B2
Motu Nui, *island*, Isla de Pascua (Easter Island), Chile, **461** B2
Motu One, *island*, French Polynesia, **137** F2
Motu Tautara, *island*, Isla de Pascua (Easter Island), Chile, **461** B2
Motueka, New Zealand, **133** D5
Motunau Beach, New Zealand, **133** D6
Motunui, New Zealand, **132** E4
Motupena Point, Papua New Guinea, **140** E2
Mou, New Caledonia, **141** A3
Mouali Gbangba, Congo, **368** C2
Mouanko, Cameroon, **368** A2
Mouchalagane, *river*, Canada, **416** G3
Moudjéria, Mauritania, **360** D5
Mouhijärvi, Finland, **287** L2
Mouila, Gabon, **368** B3
Moulins, France, **291** F3
Moulmein, Myanmar, **202** C2
Moultrie, Lake, U.S.A., **425** M3
Moultrie, U.S.A., **425** L4
Mound City, Illinois, U.S.A., **421** J7
Mound City, South Dakota, U.S.A., **420** C3
Moundou, Chad, **365** H3
Moundsville, U.S.A., **421** N6
Moŭng Roessei, Cambodia, **203** D3
Mount Airy, U.S.A., **421** N7
Mount Ayr, U.S.A., **420** F5
Mount Barker, Australia, **134** D5
Mount Bellew, Ireland, **309** D4
Mount Caramel Junction, U.S.A., **422** G3
Mount Carroll, U.S.A., **420** J4
Mount Cook, New Zealand, **133** C6
Mount Currie, Canada, **412** H6
Mount Darwin, Zimbabwe, **371** F2
Mount Dora, U.S.A., **423** M3
Mount Forest, Canada, **421** N4
Mount Gambier, Australia, **135** J6

Neapoli, Peloponnisos, Greece, **297** D7
Near Islands, U.S.A., **301** U4
Neath, *river*, Wales, U.K., **304** D3
Neath, Wales, U.K., **304** D3
Neath Port Talbot, *unitary authority*, Wales, U.K., **304** D3
Nebbi, Uganda, **369** F2
Nebbou, Burkina Faso, **364** D2
Nebe, Indonesia, **198** C5
Nebitdag, Turkmenistan, **222** E5
Neblina, Pico da, *mountain peak*, Brazil, **451** E4
Nebolchi, Russian Federation, **299** D3
Nebraska, *state*, U.S.A., **420** D5
Nebraska City, U.S.A., **420** F5
Nebrodi, Monti, *mountain range*, Sicilia, Italy, **295** E7
Nechi, *river*, Colombia, **450** C2
Necker, *island*, Hawaiian Islands, U.S.A., **139** H2
Necochea, Argentina, **459** E6
Necton, England, U.K., **305** H2
Nedas, *river*, Greece, **297** C7
Nédéley, Chad, **366** A1
Nêdong, China, **214** D3
Nedstrand, Norway, **286** B3
Nedumangād, India, **216** D4
Needham Market, England, U.K., **305** J2
Needles, Canada, **413** K7
Needles, The, *point*, England, U.K., **305** F4
Needles, U.S.A., **422** F4
Neegro, Qooriga, *bay*, Somalia, **367** G3
Neepawa, Canada, **414** E6
Neftçala, Azerbaijan, **222** D5
Neftekamsk, Russian Federation, **222** E1
Nefyn, Wales, U.K., **304** C2
Negēlē, Ethiopia, **367** E3
Negage, Angola, **368** C4
Négala, Mali, **364** C2
Negara, Indonesia, **201** F5
Negeri Sembilan, *state*, Malaysia, **200** C2
Negomane, Mozambique, **369** G5
Negombo, Sri Lanka, **216** D5
Negotin, Yugoslavia, **296** D3
Negra, Cordillera, *mountain range*, Peru, **454** B2
Negra, Punta, *point*, Peru, **454** B1
Negreşti, Romania, **296** F2
Negreşti-Oaş, Romania, **296** D2
Negreni, Romania, **296** E3
Negritos, Peru, **454** B1
Negro, *river*, Amazonas, Brazil, **451** G5
Negro, *river*, Bolivia, **455** F4
Negro, *river*, Choco, Argentina, **459** E3
Negro, *river*, Mato Grosso do Sul, Brazil, **456** B5
Negro, *river*, Paraguay, **459** E2
Negro, *river*, Río Negro, Argentina, **460** D1
Negro, *river*, Uruguay, **459** F4
Negros, *island*, Philippines, **204** C4
Negru Vodă, Romania, **296** G4
Neguac, Canada, **416** J6
Nehbandān, Iran, **221** H2
Nehe, China, **211** J2
Nehoiu, Romania, **296** F3
Nehone, Angola, **368** C6
Nei Mongol Gaoyuan, *plateau*, China, **213** J4
Nei Mongol Zizhiqu (Inner Mongolia), *autonomous region*, China, **210** F4
Neiafu, Vava'u Group, Tonga, **141** B3
Neiba, Dominican Republic, **429** H3
Neiden, Norway, **285** P2
Neidersachsen, *state*, Germany, **288** D2

Neiges, Piton des, *mountain peak*, Réunion, **373** A1
Neihart, U.S.A., **419** J3
Neijiang, China, **215** H3
Neilingding Dao, *island*, China, **207** B4
Neiße, *river*, Germany, **289** G3
Neiva, Colombia, **450** C3
Neixiang, China, **206** B1
Nejanilini Lake, Canada, **414** F2
Nek'emtē, Ethiopia, **367** E3
Nekomo, U.S.A., **420** D1
Neksø, Denmark, **286** G5
Nelidovo, Russian Federation, **299** D4
Neligh, U.S.A., **420** D4
Nellore, India, **216** E3
Nelson, Canada, **413** L7
Nelson, Cape, Papua New Guinea, **140** C5
Nelson, England, U.K., **306** F4
Nelson, Estrecho, *strait*, Chile, **460** B4
Nelson, New Zealand, **133** D5
Nelson, *river*, Canada, **414** G3
Nelson House, Canada, **414** E4
Nelspruit, South Africa, **371** F4
Nelyan Point, Philippines, **204** B4
Néma, Mauritania, **364** C1
Neman, Russian Federation, **287** L5
Nembe, Nigeria, **365** F4
Nembrala, Indonesia, **198** C5
Nemea, Greece, **297** D7
Nemegos, Canada, **421** M2
Nemenčinė, Lithuania, **287** M5
Nemor, *river*, China, **211** J2
Nemunas, *river*, Lithuania, **287** L5
Nemuro, Japan, **209** J2
Nemyriv, Ukraine, **289** L3
Nen, *river*, China, **211** J2
Nenagh, Ireland, **309** D5
Nendo, *island*, Solomon Islands, **138** E6
Nene, *river*, England, U.K., **305** G2
Nenjiang, China, **211** J2
Nenthead, England, U.K., **306** F3
Neo Karlovasi, Dodekanisos, Greece, **297** F7
Neola, U.S.A., **423** H1
Neos Marmaras, Greece, **297** D5
Neosho, *river*, U.S.A., **420** F7
Neosho, U.S.A., **420** F7
Nepālganj, Nepal, **219** E3
Nepal, *country*, Asia, **196** K7
Nepean Island, Norfolk Island, **135** T13
Nepeña, Peru, **454** B2
Nephi, U.S.A., **423** H2
Nephin, *mountain peak*, Ireland, **309** C3
Nephin Beg Range, *mountain range*, Ireland, **309** C3
Nepisiguit, *river*, Canada, **416** H6
Nepomuk, Czech Republic, **288** F4
Nérac, France, **290** E4
Nerang, Australia, **135** L4
Nerchinsk, Russian Federation, **210** G1
Nereta, Latvia, **287** M4
Nereto, Italy, **294** D4
Neriquinha, Angola, **368** D6
Neris, *river*, Lithuania, **287** M5
Nerja, Spain, **293** F4
Nerl', *river*, Russian Federation, **299** F4
Nerópolis, Brazil, **456** D4
Neryungri, Russian Federation, **301** P4
Nesbyen, Norway, **286** D2
Nesebūr, Bulgaria, **296** F4
Nesflaten, Norway, **286** C3
Nesjøen, *lake*, Norway, **284** E5
Nesna, Norway, **284** F3
Ness, Loch, *lake*, Scotland, U.K., **308** E3

Ness City, U.S.A., **420** D6
Nesseby, Norway, **285** P1
Nesterov, Russian Federation, **287** L5
Netanya, Israel, **225** C3
Netherlands, *country*, Europe, **282** E5
Netherlands Antilles, *Netherlands autonomous region*, Caribbean Sea, **448** F2
Neto, *river*, Italy, **295** F6
Nettilling Lake, Canada, **411** M3
Neubrandenburg, Germany, **288** F2
Neubuków, Germany, **288** E1
Neuchâtel, Lac de, *lake*, Switzerland, **291** H3
Neuchâtel, Switzerland, **291** H3
Neuenhagen bei Berlin, Germany, **289** F2
Neufchâteau, France, **291** G2
Neufchâtel-en-Bray, France, **290** E2
Neumünster, Germany, **288** D1
Neung-sur-Beuvron, France, **290** E3
Neunkirchen, Germany, **288** C4
Neuquén, Argentina, **460** D1
Neuquén, *province*, Argentina, **460** C1
Neuquén, *river*, Argentina, **458** C5
Neuruppin, Germany, **288** F2
Neusiedler See, *lake*, Austria, **289** H5
Neuss, Germany, **288** C3
Neustadt am Rübenberge, Germany, **288** D2
Neustadt in Holstein, Germany, **288** E1
Neustrelitz, Germany, **288** F2
Neuville-lès-Dieppe, France, **305** J5
Neuwied, Germany, **288** C3
Nevşehir, Turkey, **363** F1
Neva, *river*, Russian Federation, **299** C3
Nevada, Cerro, *mountain peak*, Argentina, **458** C5
Nevada, Sierra, *mountain peak*, Argentina, **458** C3
Nevada, Sierra, *mountain range*, Spain, **293** F4
Nevada, Sierra, *mountain range*, U.S.A., **422** C2
Nevada, *state*, U.S.A., **422** E2
Nevada, U.S.A., **420** F7
Nevada del Cocuy, Sierra, *mountain peak*, Colombia, **450** D2
Nevado, Cerro, *mountain peak*, Colombia, **450** C3
Nevado, Sierra del, *mountain range*, Argentina, **458** C5
Neve, Serra da, *mountain range*, Angola, **368** B5
Nevel', Russian Federation, **299** B4
Nevers, France, **291** F3
Nevesinje, Bosnia and Herzegovina, **294** G4
Nevinnomyssk, Russian Federation, **222** C4
Nevis, Ben, *mountain peak*, Scotland, U.K., **308** E4
Nev'yansk, Russian Federation, **222** G1
New Albany, Indiana, U.S.A., **421** L6
New Albany, Mississippi, U.S.A., **425** H2
New Albany, Pennsylvania, U.S.A., **426** B4
New Alresford, England, U.K., **305** F3
New Amsterdam, Guyana, **451** H2
New Bedford, U.S.A., **426** E4
New Berlin, U.S.A., **426** C3
New Bern, U.S.A., **426** B7
New Boston, U.S.A., **424** E3

New Braunfels, U.S.A., **424** C5
New Britain, *island*, Papua New Guinea, **140** C4
New Britain, U.S.A., **426** D4
New Brunswick, *province*, Canada, **416** H6
New Bussa, Nigeria, **365** E3
New Caledonia, *French territory*, Pacific Ocean, **130** E3
New Caledonia Basin, *underwater feature*, Pacific Ocean, **478** E6
New Castle, Kentucky, U.S.A., **421** L6
New Castle, Pennsylvania, U.S.A., **421** N5
New Cumnock, Scotland, U.K., **308** E5
New Dayton, Canada, **413** N7
New Deer, Scotland, U.K., **308** G3
New Delhi, India, **218** D3
New Ellenton, U.S.A., **425** M3
New England, U.S.A., **420** B2
New Galloway, Scotland, U.K., **308** E5
New Georgia, *island*, Solomon Islands, **141** A1
New Georgia Group, *islands*, Solomon Islands, **141** A1
New Georgia Sound (The Slot), *channel*, Solomon Islands, **141** A1
New Germany, Canada, **417** J7
New Glasgow, Canada, **417** K7
New Grant, Trinidad, Trinidad and Tobago, **461** C4
New Guinea, *island*, Indonesia/Papua New Guinea, **140** A4
New Hampshire, *state*, U.S.A., **426** E3
New Hampton, U.S.A., **420** G4
New Hanover, *island*, Papua New Guinea, **140** C3
New Haven, U.S.A., **426** D4
New Hazelton, Canada, **412** F4
New Iberia, U.S.A., **424** G5
New Ireland, *island*, Papua New Guinea, **140** D3
New Ireland, *province*, Papua New Guinea, **140** D3
New Jersey, *state*, U.S.A., **426** C5
New Lexington, U.S.A., **421** M6
New Liskeard, Canada, **421** P2
New London, Connecticut, U.S.A., **426** D4
New London, Iowa, U.S.A., **420** H5
New London, Wisconsin, U.S.A., **421** J3
New Meadows, U.S.A., **418** F4
New Mexico, *state*, U.S.A., **423** K4
New Milford, U.S.A., **426** C4
New Milton, England, U.K., **305** F4
New Mirpur, India, **218** C2
New Orleans, U.S.A., **424** G5
New Paltz, U.S.A., **426** C4
New Pitsligo, Scotland, U.K., **308** G3
New Plymouth, New Zealand, **132** E4
New Providence, *island*, Bahamas, **428** F1
New Quay, Wales, U.K., **304** C2
New Richmond, Canada, **416** J5
New Richmond, U.S.A., **420** G3
New Rockford, U.S.A., **420** D2
New Romney, England, U.K., **305** H4
New Ross, Ireland, **309** F5
New Salem, U.S.A., **420** C2
New Sarepta, Canada, **413** N5
New Scone, Scotland, U.K., **308** F4
New Smyrna Beach, U.S.A., **425** M5
New South Wales, *state*, Australia, **135** J5
New Underwood, U.S.A., **420** B3

New Waterford, Canada, **417** L6
New York, *state*, U.S.A., **426** B3
New York, U.S.A., **426** D4
New Zealand, *country*, Pacific Ocean, **131** F6
Newala, Tanzania, **369** G5
Newark, Delaware, U.S.A., **426** C5
Newark, New Jersey, U.S.A., **426** C4
Newark, New York, U.S.A., **426** B3
Newark-on-Trent, England, U.K., **305** G1
Newberg, U.S.A., **418** C4
Newberry, U.S.A., **425** M2
Newbiggin-by-the-sea, England, U.K., **307** G2
Newbridge, Ireland, **309** F4
Newburgh, Scotland, U.K., **308** F4
Newburgh, U.S.A., **426** C4
Newbury, England, U.K., **305** F3
Newby Bridge, England, U.K., **306** F3
Newcastle, Australia, **135** L5
Newcastle, Canada, **416** J6
Newcastle, Northern Ireland, U.K., **309** G3
Newcastle, South Africa, **371** E4
Newcastle, U.S.A., **419** M5
Newcastle Emlyn, Wales, U.K., **304** C2
Newcastle-under-Lyme, England, U.K., **304** E1
Newcastle upon Tyne, England, U.K., **307** G3
Newcastle West, Ireland, **309** C5
Newcastleton, Scotland, U.K., **308** G5
Newcomb, U.S.A., **423** J3
Newell, U.S.A., **420** B3
Newenham, Cape, U.S.A., **410** C4
Newent, England, U.K., **304** E3
Newfolden, U.S.A., **420** E1
Newfoundland, *island*, Canada, **417** N5
Newfoundland, *province*, Canada, **411** N4
Newham, England, U.K., **307** G2
Newhaven, England, U.K., **305** H4
Newington, South Africa, **371** F3
Newinn, Ireland, **309** E5
Newman, Australia, **134** D3
Newman, U.S.A., **421** K6
Newmarket, Canada, **421** P3
Newmarket, England, U.K., **305** H2
Newmarket, Ireland, **309** C5
Newmarket on Fergus, Ireland, **309** D5
Newnan, U.S.A., **425** K3
Newnham, England, U.K., **304** E3
Newport, Arkansas, U.S.A., **424** G2
Newport, Essex, England, U.K., **305** H3
Newport, Isle of Wight, England, U.K., **305** F4
Newport, Kentucky, U.S.A., **421** L6
Newport, Mayo, Ireland, **309** C4
Newport, New Hampshire, U.S.A., **426** D3
Newport, Newport, Wales, U.K., **304** E3
Newport, Oregon, U.S.A., **418** B4
Newport, Pembrokeshire, Wales, U.K., **304** C2
Newport, Rhode Island, U.S.A., **426** E4
Newport, Shropshire, England, U.K., **304** E2
Newport, Tennessee, U.S.A., **425** L2
Newport, Tipperary, Ireland, **309** D5

Nok Kundi, Pakistan, **221** H3
Nokh, India, **218** C4
Nokha, India, **218** C4
Nokia, Finland, **287** L2
Nokou, Chad, **365** G2
Nokuku, Vanuatu, **141** A2
Nola, Central African Republic, **368** C2
Nom, China, **213** G4
Nome, Alaska, U.S.A., **410** C3
Nome, Texas, U.S.A., **424** E4
Nong Bua, Thailand, **202** D3
Nong Bua Lamphu, Thailand, **203** D2
Nong Khai, Thailand, **203** D2
Nong'an, China, **211** J3
Nonoava, Mexico, **430** D3
Nonouti, *island*, Kiribati, **139** F5
Nonthaburi, Thailand, **202** D3
Nontron, France, **290** E4
Noonan, U.S.A., **419** N2
Noondie, Lake, Australia, **134** D4
Noord, Aruba, **461** B3
Noord-Brabant, *province*, Netherlands, **288** B3
Noord-Holland, *province*, Netherlands, **288** B2
Noormarkku, Finland, **287** K2
Noosa Heads, Australia, **135** L4
Nootka, Canada, **412** F7
Nootka Island, Canada, **412** F7
Nóqui, Angola, **368** B4
Nora, *river*, Russian Federation, **211** K1
Nora, Sweden, **286** G3
Norala, Philippines, **204** D5
Norcia, Italy, **294** D4
Nord, Greenland, **411** T1
Nord, *province*, Cameroon, **365** G3
Nord-Kivu, *administrative region*, Democratic Republic of the Congo, **369** E3
Nord-Ouest, *province*, Cameroon, **365** G3
Nord-Pas-de-Calais, *administrative region*, France, **290** E1
Nørd-Trøndelag, *county*, Norway, **284** E4
Nordaustlandet, *island*, Svalbard, **300** C1
Nordberg, Norway, **286** D2
Nordegg, Canada, **413** L5
Norden, Germany, **288** C2
Nordenham, Germany, **288** D2
Nordenshel'da, Arkhipelag, *islands*, Russian Federation, **300** L2
Norderney, *island*, Germany, **288** C2
Nordfjordeid, Norway, **286** C2
Nordfold, Norway, **284** G3
Nordhausen, Germany, **288** E3
Nordhorn, Germany, **288** C2
Nordkapp, *cape*, Norway, **285** M1
Nordkinnhalvøya, *peninsula*, Norway, **285** P1
Nordkjosbotn, Norway, **284** J2
Nordkvaløy, *island*, Norway, **284** J1
Nordland, *county*, Norway, **284** F3
Nordli, Norway, **284** F4
Nördlingen, Germany, **288** E4
Nordmaling, Sweden, **284** J5
Nordmela, Norway, **284** G2
Nordmøre, *island*, Norway, **284** C5
Nordøyane, *island*, Norway, **286** B1
Nordoyar, *islands*, Faeroe Islands, **302** D1
Nordpunt, *point*, Curaçao, Netherlands Antilles, **461** C3
Nordrhein-Westfalen, *state*, Germany, **288** C3
Nore, Norway, **286** D2
Noresund, Norway, **286** D2
Norfolk, Nebraska, U.S.A., **420** E4

Norfolk, *unitary authority*, England, U.K., **305** H2
Norfolk, Virginia, U.S.A., **426** B6
Norfolk Broads, *region*, England, U.K., **305** J2
Norfolk Island, *Australian territory*, Pacific Ocean, **135** T13
Norfolk Ridge, *underwater feature*, Pacific Ocean, **478** F6
Noril'sk, Russian Federation, **300** K3
Noring, Gunung, *mountain peak*, Malaysia, **200** C1
Norma, U.S.A., **420** C1
Norman, Lake, U.S.A., **425** M2
Norman, *river*, Australia, **135** J2
Norman, U.S.A., **424** D2
Norman Inlet, *bay*, Auckland Islands, New Zealand, **132** J10
Norman Wells, Canada, **410** G3
Normanby Island, Papua New Guinea, **140** C5
Normandia, Brazil, **451** G3
Normanton, Australia, **135** J2
Normétal, Canada, **416** B5
Norquay, Canada, **414** C6
Ñorquinco, Argentina, **460** C1
Norr-dellen, *lake*, Sweden, **286** H2
Norra Bergnäs, Sweden, **284** J3
Norra Storfjället, *mountain peak*, Sweden, **284** G4
Norråker, Sweden, **284** G4
Norrbotten, *county*, Sweden, **284** J3
Nørre Nebel, Denmark, **286** D5
Norrent-Fontès, France, **305** K4
Nørresundby, Denmark, **286** D4
Norris, U.S.A., **419** J4
Norrköping, Sweden, **286** H3
Norrtälje, Sweden, **287** J3
Norseman, Australia, **134** E5
Norsjø, *lake*, Norway, **286** D3
Norsjö, Sweden, **284** J4
Norsk, Russian Federation, **211** K1
Norske Øer, *islands*, Greenland, **411** T2
Norte, Cabo, *cape*, Brazil, **452** D3
Norte, Cabo, *cape*, Isla de Pascua (Easter Island), Chile, **461** B2
Norte, Cabo, *cape*, Islas Galápagos (Galapagos Islands), Ecuador, **461** A2
Norte, Canal do, *channel*, Brazil, **452** D2
Norte, Punta, *point*, Argentina, **460** E1
Norte, Punta, *point*, San Andrés, Colombia, **461** B1
Norte, Serra do, *mountain range*, Brazil, **455** G3
Norte del Cabo San Antonio, Punta, *point*, Argentina, **459** F5
Nortelândia, Brazil, **456** B4
North, Cape, Canada, **417** L6
North, U.S.A., **425** M3
North Adams, U.S.A., **426** D3
North Andaman, *island*, Andaman and Nicobar Islands, India, **217** H3
North Augusta, U.S.A., **425** M3
North Australian Basin, *underwater feature*, Indian Ocean, **476** G5
North Ayrshire, *local authority*, Scotland, U.K., **308** E5
North Battleford, Canada, **413** Q5
North Bay, Canada, **421** P2
North Bend, U.S.A., **418** B5
North Berwick, Scotland, U.K., **308** G4
North Cape, Antipodes Islands, New Zealand, **133** P15
North Cape, Canada, **417** K6
North Cape, New Zealand, **132** D2

North Carolina, *state*, U.S.A., **425** M2
North Channel, Canada, **421** M2
North Channel, Northern Ireland, U.K., **308** D5
North Dakota, *state*, U.S.A., **420** C2
North Down, *district*, Northern Ireland, U.K., **309** G3
North Downs, *region*, England, U.K., **305** H3
North East, *district*, Botswana, **371** E3
North East, U.S.A., **421** P4
North East Bay, Ascension, **373** A3
North East Harbour, Campbell Island, New Zealand, **132** K11
North East Island, Snares Islands, New Zealand, **132** H9
North East Lincolnshire, *unitary authority*, England, U.K., **307** H4
North East Point, Christmas Island, **134** N8
North-Eastern, *province*, Kenya, **369** G2
North Esk, *river*, Scotland, U.K., **308** G4
North European Plain, Europe, **280** F5
North Fiji Basin, *underwater feature*, Pacific Ocean, **478** F5
North Foreland, *cape*, England, U.K., **305** J3
North Fork, Idaho, U.S.A., **418** H4
North Fork, Nevada, U.S.A., **418** G6
North Grimston, England, U.K., **307** H3
North Head, Canada, **426** G2
North Head, *point*, Lord Howe Island, Australia, **135** U14
North Head, *point*, Macquarie Island, **134** R11
North Head, *point*, New Zealand, **132** D3
North Head, U.S.A., **416** H7
North Horr, Kenya, **369** G2
North Hykeham, England, U.K., **305** G1
North Island, New Zealand, **132** D3
North Island, Seychelles, **373** A2
North Keeling Island, Cocos (Keeling) Islands, **134** Q10
North Knife, *river*, Canada, **414** F2
North Knife Lake, Canada, **414** F2
North Korea, *country*, Asia, **197** P5
North Lakhimpur, India, **219** H4
North Lanarkshire, *local authority*, Scotland, U.K., **308** F5
North Lincolnshire, *unitary authority*, England, U.K., **307** H4
North Little Rock, U.S.A., **424** F2
North Loup, *river*, U.S.A., **420** C4
North Moose Lake, Canada, **414** D4
North Platte, *river*, U.S.A., **419** L5
North Platte, U.S.A., **420** C5
North Point, Ascension, **373** A3
North Point, Seychelles, **373** A2
North Point, U.S.A., **421** M3
North Port, U.S.A., **425** L6
North Powder, U.S.A., **418** F4
North Promontory, *point*, Snares Islands, New Zealand, **132** H9
North Rona, *island*, Scotland, U.K., **308** D1
North Ronaldsay, *island*, Orkney, Scotland, U.K., **308** G1
North Saskatchewan, *river*,

Canada, **413** R5
North Sea, Europe, **280** E4
North Seal, *river*, Canada, **414** D2
North Shields, England, U.K., **307** G3
North Solomons, *province*, Papua New Guinea, **140** E2
North Somercotes, England, U.K., **307** J4
North Somerset, *unitary authority*, England, U.K., **304** E3
North Sound, The, Orkney, Scotland, U.K., **308** G1
North Spirit Lake, Canada, **414** H5
North Star, Canada, **413** L3
North Stradbroke Island, Australia, **135** L4
North Sunderland, England, U.K., **307** G2
North Taranaki Bight, *bay*, New Zealand, **132** D4
North Tidworth, England, U.K., **305** F3
North Twin Island, Canada, **415** Q5
North Tyne, *river*, England, U.K., **306** F2
North Uist, *island*, Scotland, U.K., **308** B3
North Wabasca Lake, Canada, **413** M3
North Walsham, England, U.K., **305** J2
North West, *province*, South Africa, **370** D4
North West Cape, Auckland Islands, New Zealand, **132** J10
North West Cape, Australia, **134** C3
North-West Frontier Province, *province*, Pakistan, **218** B2
North West Highlands, *mountain range*, Scotland, U.K., **308** D3
North West Point, Christmas Island, **134** N8
North-Western, *province*, Zambia, **368** D5
North Wildwood, U.S.A., **426** C5
North Woodstock, U.S.A., **426** E2
North York Moors, *moorland*, England, U.K., **307** H3
North Yorkshire, *unitary authority*, England, U.K., **307** G3
Northallerton, England, U.K., **307** G3
Northam, Australia, **134** D5
Northampton, Australia, **134** C4
Northampton, England, U.K., **305** G2
Northampton, U.S.A., **426** D3
Northamptonshire, *unitary authority*, England, U.K., **305** F2
Northeast Point, Bahamas, **429** G2
Northeast Providence Channel, Bahamas, **428** F1
Northeim, Germany, **288** D3
Northern, *administrative region*, Ghana, **364** D3
Northern, *administrative region*, Malawi, **369** F5
Northern, *province*, Sierra Leone, **364** B3
Northern, *province*, Zambia, **369** F5
Northern Cape, *province*, South Africa, **370** C4
Northern Cook Islands, Cook Islands, **139** H5
Northern Indian Lake, Canada, **414** F3
Northern Ireland, *administrative division*, U.K., **309** E3
Northern Mariana Islands, *U.S. territory*, Pacific Ocean, **138** C3

Northern Peninsula, Canada, **417** N4
Northern (Oro), *province*, Papua New Guinea, **140** C5
Northern Province, *province*, South Africa, **371** E3
Northern Range, *mountain range*, Trinidad, Trinidad and Tobago, **461** C4
Northern Territory, *territory*, Australia, **134** G2
Northfield, U.S.A., **420** G3
Northton, Scotland, U.K., **308** B3
Northville, U.S.A., **416** D8
Northwest Atlantic Mid-Ocean Canyon, *underwater feature*, Atlantic Ocean, **477** D2
Northwest Bay, Seychelles, **373** A2
Northwest Pacific Basin, *underwater feature*, Pacific Ocean, **478** E2
Northwest Providence Channel, Bahamas, **428** F1
Northwest Territories, *territory*, Canada, **410** G3
Northwich, England, U.K., **306** F4
Northwood, U.S.A., **420** E2
Norton, England, U.K., **307** H3
Norton, U.S.A., **420** D6
Norton Fitzwarren, England, U.K., **304** D3
Norton Sound, U.S.A., **410** C3
Norwalk, U.S.A., **421** M5
Norway, *country*, Europe, **282** E3
Norway House, Canada, **414** F5
Norwegian Bay, Canada, **411** K2
Norwegian Sea, Atlantic Ocean, **280** D2
Norwich, England, U.K., **305** J2
Norwood, U.S.A., **420** G3
Noshiro, Japan, **209** H2
Noşratābād, Iran, **221** G3
Noss, Isle of, *island*, Scotland, U.K., **308** K7
Nossa Senhora das Dores, Brazil, **457** G3
Nossa Senhora do Livramento, Brazil, **456** B4
Nossebro, Sweden, **286** F3
Nossombougou, Mali, **364** C2
Nosy Bé, *island*, Madagascar, **372** B3
Nosy-Varika, Madagascar, **372** B5
Nota, *river*, Russian Federation, **285** P3
Notch Peak, *mountain peak*, U.S.A., **422** G2
Notio Aigaio, *administrative region*, Greece, **297** E7
Notio Steno Kerkyras, *channel*, Greece, **297** C6
Notodden, Norway, **286** D3
Notre Dame, Monts, *mountain range*, Canada, **416** F7
Notre Dame Bay, Canada, **417** P5
Notre-Dame-de-la-Salette, Canada, **426** C2
Notre-Dame-du-Nord, Canada, **416** B6
Notsé, Togo, **364** E3
Nottaway, *river*, Canada, **416** B4
Nottingham, England, U.K., **305** F2
Nottingham City, *unitary authority*, England, U.K., **305** F2
Nottingham Island, Canada, **411** M3
Nottinghamshire, *unitary authority*, England, U.K., **305** F1
Nottoway, *river*, U.S.A., **426** A6
Nouâdhibou, Mauritania, **360** C4
Nouâdhibou, Râs, *cape*, Western Sahara, **360** C4

Obispos, Venezuela, **451** D2
Obluch'ye, Russian Federation, **211** K2
Obninsk, Russian Federation, **299** F5
Obo, Central African Republic, **369** E1
Obo, China, **213** J5
Obock, Djibouti, **367** F2
Obokote, Democratic Republic of the Congo, **369** E3
Obol', Belarus, **299** B5
Obol', *river*, Belarus, **299** B5
Oborniki, Poland, **289** H2
Obouya, Congo, **368** C3
Obrenovac, Yugoslavia, **296** C3
O'Brien, U.S.A., **418** C5
Obrochishte, Bulgaria, **296** F4
Obrovac, Croatia, **294** E3
Obskaya Guba, *gulf*, Russian Federation, **300** J3
Obuasi, Ghana, **364** D3
Obytichna Kosa, *physical feature*, Ukraine, **298** E3
Ocala, U.S.A., **425** L5
Ocaña, Andalucía, Spain, **293** F4
Ocaña, Castilla la Mancha, Spain, **293** F3
Ocaña, Colombia, **450** D2
Ocate, U.S.A., **423** L3
Occidental, Cordillera, *mountain range*, Chile/Peru, **447** E5
Occidental, Cordillera, *mountain range*, Colombia, **447** E3
Ocean *see* Banaba, *island*, Kiribati, **139** F5
Ocean Beach, New Zealand, **132** E2
Ocean City, Maryland, U.S.A., **426** C5
Ocean City, New Jersey, U.S.A., **426** C5
Ocean Springs, U.S.A., **425** H4
Oceanographer Fracture Zone, *tectonic feature*, Atlantic Ocean, **477** D3
Oceanside, U.S.A., **422** E5
Ochil Hills, Scotland, U.K., **308** F4
Ocho Rios, Jamaica, **429** F3
Ochopee, U.S.A., **425** M7
Ochthonia, Greece, **297** E6
Ocilla, U.S.A., **425** L4
Ockelbo, Sweden, **287** H2
Ocmulgee, *river*, U.S.A., **425** L3
Ocna Sibiului, Romania, **296** E3
Ocniţa, Moldova, **296** F1
Ococingo, Mexico, **431** G5
Oconee, Lake, U.S.A., **425** L3
Ocotal, Nicaragua, **428** D4
Ocotepeque, Honduras, **428** C4
Ocotillo Wells, U.S.A., **422** E5
Ocotlán, Mexico, **430** E4
Ocracoke, U.S.A., **426** C7
Ocreza, *river*, Portugal, **292** D3
Octavia, U.S.A., **424** E2
Octeville, France, **305** F5
Oda, Ghana, **364** D3
Oda, Jabal, *mountain peak*, Sudan, **363** G4
Ōda, Japan, **208** F4
Oda, Ras, *point*, Egypt, **363** G4
ūdáðahraun, *lava field*, Iceland, **284** Y7
Ōdate, Japan, **209** H2
Odawara, Japan, **209** G4
Odda, Norway, **286** C2
Odeceixe, Portugal, **292** C4
Odemira, Portugal, **292** C4
Ödemiş, Turkey, **224** C5
Ödèngk, Cambodia, **203** E4
Odensbacken, Sweden, **286** G3
Odense, Denmark, **286** E5
Oder *see* Odra, *river*, Germany/Poland, **280** F5
Oderhäff, *lake*, Germany, **289** G2
Odesa (Odessa), Ukraine, **298** D3
Ödeshög, Sweden, **286** G3

Odes'ka Oblast', *province*, Ukraine, **296** G2
Odessa *see* Odesa, Ukraine, **298** D3
Odessa, U.S.A., **423** M6
Odienné, Côte d'Ivoire, **364** C3
Odintsovo, Russian Federation, **299** F5
Odobeşti, Romania, **296** F3
O'Donnell, U.S.A., **424** B3
Odorheiu Secuiesc, Romania, **296** E2
Odoyev, Russian Federation, **299** F6
Odra (Oder), *river*, Germany/Poland, **280** F5
Odrzywół, Poland, **289** K3
Odžaci, Yugoslavia, **296** B3
Odžak, Bosnia and Herzegovina, **294** G3
Oebisfelde, Germany, **288** E2
Oeiras, Brazil, **453** E5
Oeno Island, Pitcairn Islands, **137** H3
Ofaqim, Israel, **225** C4
Offa, Nigeria, **365** E3
Offaly, *county*, Ireland, **309** E4
Offenbach am Main, Germany, **288** D3
Offenburg, Germany, **288** C4
Offranville, France, **305** J5
Ofidoussa, *island*, Kyklades, Greece, **297** E7
Ofu, *island*, American Samoa, **141** B2
Ofu, *island*, Vava'u Group, Tonga, **141** B3
Ōfunato, Japan, **209** H3
Ogachi, Japan, **209** H3
Ogaden, *region*, Ethiopia, **367** F3
Ogallala, U.S.A., **420** C5
Ogan, *river*, Indonesia, **200** D3
Ogasawara-shotō, *islands*, Japan, **138** B2
Ogbomosho, Nigeria, **365** E3
Ogden, U.S.A., **420** F4
Ogeechee, *river*, U.S.A., **425** L3
Ogema, Canada, **419** M2
Ogilvie Mountains, *mountain range*, Canada, **410** F3
Oglala, U.S.A., **420** B4
Ognon, *river*, France, **291** G3
Ogoamas, Gunung, *mountain peak*, Indonesia, **198** C2
Ogoja, Nigeria, **365** F3
Ogoki, Canada, **415** M6
Ogoki, *river*, Canada, **415** L6
Ogoki Reservoir, Canada, **415** K6
Ogooué, *river*, Gabon, **368** A3
Ogooué-Ivindo, *province*, Gabon, **368** B2
Ogooué-Lolo, *province*, Gabon, **368** B3
Ogooué-Maritime, *province*, Gabon, **368** A3
Ogorelyshi, Russian Federation, **285** S5
Ogre, Latvia, **287** M4
Ogulin, Croatia, **294** E3
Ogun, *state*, Nigeria, **365** E3
Ogurjaly, *island*, Turkmenistan, **222** E5
Ohakune, New Zealand, **132** E4
Ohanet, Algeria, **361** H3
Ohangwena, *administrative region*, Namibia, **370** C2
Ohau, Lake, New Zealand, **133** B7
Ohau, New Zealand, **132** E5
Ohaupo, New Zealand, **132** E3
O'Higgins, Cabo, *cape*, Isla de Pascua (Easter Island), Chile, **461** B2
O'Higgins, Lago, *lake*, Chile, **460** B3
O'Higgins, Punta, *point*, Róbinson Crusoe Island, Archipiélago Juan Fernández, Chile, **461** C2
Ohio, *river*, U.S.A., **407** Q5
Ohio, *state*, U.S.A., **421** M5

'Ohonua, Tongatapu Group, Tonga, **141** B4
Ohře, *river*, Czech Republic, **289** F3
Ohrid, Lake *see* Ohridsko Jezero, *lake*, Macedonia, **297** C5
Ohrid, Macedonia, **297** C5
Ohridsko Jezero (Lake Ohrid), *lake*, Macedonia, **297** C5
Ohura, New Zealand, **132** E4
Oiapoque, Brazil, **452** C2
Oijärvi, Finland, **285** N4
Oil City, U.S.A., **421** P5
Oir, Beinn an, *mountain peak*, Scotland, U.K., **308** C5
Oise, *river*, France, **291** F2
Oisemont, France, **305** J5
Ōita, Japan, **208** E4
Oiti Oros, *mountain peak*, Greece, **297** D6
Öje, Sweden, **286** F2
Ojibwa, U.S.A., **420** H3
Ojinaga, Mexico, **430** D2
Ojo de Laguna, Mexico, **430** D2
Ojos del Salado, *mountain peak*, Argentina/Chile, **458** C3
Öjung, Sweden, **286** G2
Ok Tedi, Papua New Guinea, **140** A4
Oka, *river*, Russian Federation, **299** F5
Okaba, Indonesia, **199** G5
Okahandja, Namibia, **370** C3
Okaihau, New Zealand, **132** D2
Okak Islands, Canada, **411** N4
Okakarara, Namibia, **370** C3
Okanagan Lake, Canada, **418** E2
Okaputa, Namibia, **370** C3
Okāra, Pakistan, **218** C3
Okarito Lagoon, *bay*, New Zealand, **133** B6
Okaukuejo, Namibia, **370** C2
Okavango, *administrative region*, Namibia, **370** C2
Okavango, *river*, Southern Africa, **357** G8
Okavango Delta, Botswana, **370** D2
Okawa Point, Chatham Islands, New Zealand, **133** Q16
Okaya, Japan, **209** G3
Okayama, Japan, **208** F4
Okazize, Namibia, **370** C3
Okeechobee, Lake, U.S.A., **425** M6
Okeechobee, U.S.A., **425** M6
Okehampton, England, U.K., **304** C4
Okemah, U.S.A., **424** D2
Okha, Russian Federation, **301** R4
Okhaldhungā, Nepal, **219** F4
Okhotsk, Russian Federation, **301** R4
Okhotsk, Sea of *see* Okhotskoye More, *sea*, Russian Federation, **301** R4
Okhotskoye More (Sea of Okhotsk), *sea*, Russian Federation, **301** R4
Okhtan-Yarvi, Ozero, *lake*, Russian Federation, **285** Q4
Oki-shotō, *islands*, Japan, **208** F3
Okinawa, Japan, **209** N8
Okinawa-jima, *island*, Japan, **209** P8
Okinawa-shotō, *islands*, Japan, **209** N8
Okino-Tori-shima, *island*, Japan, **138** B2
Okinoerabu-jima, *island*, Japan, **209** P8
Okiore, New Zealand, **132** F4
Oklahoma, *state*, U.S.A., **424** C2
Oklahoma City, U.S.A., **424** D2
Okmulgee, U.S.A., **424** E2
Okondja, Gabon, **368** B3
Okotoks, Canada, **413** M6
Okoyo, Congo, **368** C3

Okpo, Myanmar, **205** B4
Okreek, U.S.A., **420** C4
Oksbøl, Denmark, **286** D5
Øksfjord, Norway, **285** L1
Oktyabr'sk, Kazakhstan, **222** F3
Oktyabr'skiy, Russian Federation, **222** E2
Oktyabr'skoy Revolyutsii, Ostrov, *island*, Russian Federation, **300** L2
Okučani, Croatia, **294** F3
Okulovka, Russian Federation, **299** D3
Okurcalar, Turkey, **225** A1
Okushiri-tō, *island*, Japan, **209** G2
Okuta, Nigeria, **365** E3
Ola, U.S.A., **418** F4
ūlafsfjörður, Iceland, **284** Y6
Olaine, Latvia, **287** L4
Olal, Vanuatu, **141** A2
Olanchito, Honduras, **428** D4
Öland, *island*, Sweden, **287** H4
Olanga, *river*, Finland/Russian Federation, **285** Q3
Olathe, U.S.A., **420** F6
Olavarría, Argentina, **459** E5
Olbia, Sardegna, Italy, **295** B5
Old Crow, Canada, **410** F3
Old Faithful, U.S.A., **419** J4
Old Forge, U.S.A., **426** C3
Old Head of Kinsale, *point*, Ireland, **309** D6
Old Leake, England, U.K., **305** H1
Old Orchard Beach, U.S.A., **426** E3
Old Town, U.S.A., **426** F2
Old Wives Lake, Canada, **413** R6
Oldcastle, Ireland, **309** E4
Oldenburg in Holstein, Germany, **288** E1
Olderfjord, Norway, **285** M1
Oldervik, Norway, **284** J2
Oldham, England, U.K., **306** F4
Oldmeldrum, Scotland, U.K., **308** G3
Olds, Canada, **413** M6
Öldziyt, Arhangay, Mongolia, **213** J2
Öldziyt, Dorngovĭ, Mongolia, **210** E3
Olean, U.S.A., **426** A3
Olecko, Poland, **289** L1
Olekminsk, Russian Federation, **301** P3
Oleksandriya, Ukraine, **298** D3
Olenegorsk, Russian Federation, **285** R2
Olenek, *river*, Russian Federation, **301** N3
Olenino, Russian Federation, **299** D4
Olenitsa, Russian Federation, **285** S3
Oleniy, Ostrov, *island*, Russian Federation, **285** S4
Olen'ya Rechka, Russian Federation, **213** G1
Oléron, Île d', *island*, France, **290** D4
Oles'ko, Ukraine, **289** M4
Oleśnica, Poland, **289** H3
Olesno, Poland, **289** J3
Ølfjellet, *mountain peak*, Norway, **284** G3
Olga, Mount *see* Katajtuta, *mountain peak*, Australia, **134** G4
Ol'ga, Russian Federation, **211** L4
Ol'ginsk, Russian Federation, **211** L1
Ölgiy, Mongolia, **212** F2
Ølgod, Denmark, **286** D5
Olhava, Finland, **285** M4
Olib, *island*, Croatia, **294** E3
Olímpia, Brazil, **456** D5
Olinalá, Mexico, **431** F5
Olinda, Brazil, **453** G5
Olinga, Mozambique, **369** G6
Olingskog, Sweden, **286** G2
Oliva, Argentina, **458** D4

Oliva, Cordillera de, *mountain range*, Argentina/Chile, **458** C3
Oliva, Spain, **293** G3
Olivares, Cerro de, *mountain peak*, Argentina/Chile, **458** C4
Olivares de Júcar, Spain, **293** F3
Olive, U.S.A., **419** M4
Olive Hill, U.S.A., **421** M6
Oliveira, Brazil, **457** E5
Oliveira dos Brejinhos, Brazil, **457** E3
Olivenza, Spain, **292** D3
Oliver, Canada, **413** K7
Oliver Lake, Canada, **414** C3
Ölkeyek, *river*, Kazakhstan, **222** G3
Ol'khon, Ostrov, *island*, Russian Federation, **210** D1
Olkusz, Poland, **289** J3
Ollagüe, Chile, **455** E5
Ollagüe, Volcán, *mountain peak*, Bolivia/Chile, **455** E5
Ollita, Cordillera de, *mountain range*, Argentina/Chile, **458** B4
Ollombo, Congo, **368** C3
Olmedo, Spain, **292** E2
Olmillos de Sasamon, Spain, **293** F1
Olmos, Peru, **454** B1
Olney, England, U.K., **305** G2
Olney, U.S.A., **421** J6
Olofström, Sweden, **286** G4
Olomane, *river*, Canada, **417** L4
Olomouc, Czech Republic, **289** H4
Olonets, Russian Federation, **299** D2
Olongapo, Philippines, **204** C3
Olonzac, France, **290** F5
Oloron-Sainte-Marie, France, **290** D5
Olosega, *island*, American Samoa, **141** B2
Olot, Spain, **293** J1
Olovo, Bosnia and Herzegovina, **294** G3
Olovyannaya, Russian Federation, **210** F2
Olpe, Germany, **288** C3
Ol'sha, Russian Federation, **299** C5
Olsztyn, Poland, **289** K2
Olsztynek, Poland, **289** K2
Olt, *river*, Romania, **296** E3
Olten, Switzerland, **291** H3
Olteniţa, Romania, **296** F3
Oltina, Romania, **296** F3
Olton, U.S.A., **424** A2
Olutlanga Island, Philippines, **204** C5
Olympia, U.S.A., **418** C3
Olympic Mountains, *mountain range*, U.S.A., **418** C3
Olympos, *mountain peak*, Cyprus, **225** B2
Olympos, Oros (Mount Olympus), *mountain peak*, Greece, **280** G7
Olympus, Mount, *mountain peak*, U.S.A., **418** C3
Olympus, Mount *see* Olympos Oros, *mountain peak*, Greece, **280** G7
Olyutorskiy, Mys, *cape*, Russian Federation, **301** U4
Om', *river*, Russian Federation, **223** L2
Om Häjer, Eritrea, **367** E2
Oma, China, **219** E2
Ōma, Japan, **209** H2
Oma, Russian Federation, **300** F3
Ōmagari, Japan, **209** H3
Omagh, *district*, Northern Ireland, U.K., **309** E3
Omagh, Northern Ireland, U.K., **309** E3
Omaguas, Peru, **450** D5
Omaha, U.S.A., **420** F5
Omaheke, *administrative region*, Namibia, **370** C3

Paradise, California, U.S.A., **422** C2
Paradise, Guyana, **451** H3
Paradise, Montana, U.S.A., **418** G3
Paradise Valley, U.S.A., **418** F6
Paradwip, India, **219** F5
Paragould, U.S.A., **424** G1
Paraguá, *river*, Bolivia, **455** G4
Paragua, *river*, Venezuela, **451** F3
Paraguaçu, *river*, Brazil, **457** F3
Paraguai, *river*, Brazil, **456** B4
Paraguaipoa, Venezuela, **450** D1
Paraguaná, Peninsula de, Venezuela, **451** E1
Paraguarí, Paraguay, **459** F2
Paraguay, *country*, South America, **449** F6
Paraguay, *river*, South America, **447** G6
Paraiba, *river*, Paraíba, Brazil, **457** G2
Paraíba, *river*, Rio de Janeiro, Brazil, **457** E5
Paraíba, *state*, Brazil, **457** G2
Parainen, Finland, **287** L2
Paraíso, Mexico, **431** G5
Paraiso, Punta, *point*, San Andrés, Colombia, **461** B1
Paraíso do Tocantins, Brazil, **456** D3
Parakou, Benin, **365** E3
Paramaribo, Suriname, **452** B2
Paramillo, *mountain peak*, Colombia, **450** C2
Paramirim, Brazil, **457** E3
Paramirim, *river*, Brazil, **457** E3
Paramushir, Ostrov, *island*, Russian Federation, **301** S4
Paramythia, Greece, **297** C6
Paraná, Argentina, **458** E4
Paranã, Brazil, **456** D3
Paranã, *river*, Brazil, **456** D4
Paraná, *river*, South America, **447** G6
Parana, *state*, Brazil, **459** G2
Paranaguá, Brazil, **459** H2
Paranaíba, Brazil, **456** C5
Paranaíba, *river*, Brazil, **456** C5
Paranapanema, *river*, Brazil, **459** G2
Paranapiacaba, Serra, *mountain range*, Brazil, **459** H2
Paranavaí, Brazil, **459** G2
Parang, Philippines, **204** D5
Parangtritis, Indonesia, **201** E5
Parapara Peak, *mountain peak*, New Zealand, **133** D5
Paraso, Solomon Islands, **141** A1
Paraspori, Akra, *point*, Dodekanisos, Greece, **297** F8
Paratwādā, India, **218** D5
Parauapebas, Brazil, **452** D5
Parauari, *river*, Brazil, **452** A4
Paraúna, Brazil, **456** C4
Paray-le-Monial, France, **291** G3
Parazinho, Brazil, **453** G4
Parbhani, India, **216** D2
Parbig, *river*, Russian Federation, **223** L1
Parc, Pointe du, *point*, Réunion, **373** A1
Parchel, Punta del, *point*, Islas Canarias, Spain, **373** A4
Parchim, Germany, **288** E2
Parczew, Poland, **289** L3
Parding, China, **214** D2
Pardo, *river*, Bahia, Brazil, **457** F4
Pardo, *river*, Mato Grosso do Sul, Brazil, **456** C5
Pardo, *river*, São Paulo, Brazil, **456** D5
Pardoo Roadhouse, Australia, **134** D3
Pardubice, Czech Republic, **289** G3
Parecis, Brazil, **456** B4
Parecis, Chapada dos, *mountain range*, Brazil, **455** F3
Parelhas, Brazil, **453** G5
Parent, Canada, **416** D6
Pareora, New Zealand, **133** C7
Parepare, Indonesia, **198** B3
Parera, Argentina, **458** D5
Parga, Greece, **297** C6
Pargo, Ponta do, *point*, Madeira, Portugal, **373** C3
Parguaza, Sierra de, *mountain range*, Venezuela, **451** E2
Parguaza, Venezuela, **451** E2
Paria, Golfo de, *gulf*, Trinidad and Tobago, Venezuela, **427** D4
Paria, Península de, Venezuela, **451** F1
Paria, U.S.A., **423** H3
Pariaguán, Venezuela, **451** F2
Parigi, Indonesia, **198** C3
Parika, Guyana, **451** G2
Parima, *river*, Brazil, **451** F3
Parima, Serra, *mountain range*, Brazil, **451** F3
Pariñas, Punta, *point*, Peru, **454** B1
Parincea, Romania, **296** F2
Parintins, Brazil, **452** B4
Paris, France, **290** F2
Paris, Kentucky, U.S.A., **421** L6
Paris, Tennessee, U.S.A., **425** H1
Paris, Texas, U.S.A., **424** E3
Parita, Panama, **450** B2
Pārīz, Iran, **221** G3
Park Falls, U.S.A., **420** H3
Park Rapids, U.S.A., **420** F2
Park Valley, U.S.A., **418** H6
Parkano, Finland, **287** L1
Parker, U.S.A., **422** F4
Parkersburg, U.S.A., **421** N6
Parkes, Australia, **135** K5
Parkland, Canada, **413** N6
Parkston, U.S.A., **420** E4
Parlākimidi, India, **217** F2
Parlatuvier, Tobago, Trinidad and Tobago, **461** B4
Parli, India, **216** D2
Parma, Italy, **294** C3
Parmana, Venezuela, **451** F2
Parnaíba, Brazil, **453** F4
Parnaíba, *river*, Brazil, **453** E4
Parnamirim, Brazil, **453** F5
Parnarama, Brazil, **453** E4
Parnassos, *mountain peak*, Greece, **297** D6
Parnon Oros, *mountain range*, Greece, **297** D7
Pärnu, Estonia, **287** M3
Pärnu, *river*, Estonia, **287** M3
Pärnu-Jaagupi, Estonia, **287** M3
Pärnu laht, *bay*, Estonia, **287** M3
Paro, Bhutan, **219** G4
Pārola, India, **218** C5
Paroo, *river*, Australia, **135** J4
Paros, *island*, Kyklades, Greece, **297** E7
Paros, Kyklades, Greece, **297** E7
Parowan, U.S.A., **422** G3
Parpaillon, *mountain range*, France, **291** H4
Parral, Chile, **458** B5
Parras de la Fuente, Mexico, **430** E3
Parrita, Costa Rica, **428** D5
Parrsboro, Canada, **417** J7
Parry, Cape, Canada, **410** G2
Parry, Kap, *cape*, Greenland, **411** M2
Parry Bay, Canada, **411** L3
Parry Islands, Canada, **410** J2
Parry Sound, Canada, **421** N3
Parseierspitze, *mountain peak*, Austria, **288** E5
Parsęta, *river*, Poland, **289** H2
Parshall, U.S.A., **420** B2
Parsons, U.S.A., **420** F7
Partanna, Sicilia, Italy, **295** D7
Pårtefjällen, *mountain peak*, Sweden, **284** H3
Parthenay, France, **290** D3
Partizansk, Russian Federation, **211** L4
Partizánske, Slovakia, **289** J4
Partney, England, U.K., **305** H1
Partry, Ireland, **309** C4
Partry Mountains, *mountain range*, Ireland, **309** C4
Paru, *river*, Brazil, **452** C3
Paru de Este, *river*, Brazil, **452** B3
Paru de Oeste, *river*, Brazil, **452** B3
Parvatsar, India, **218** C4
Paryang, China, **219** E3
Pas-en-Artois, France, **305** K4
Pasadena, California, U.S.A., **422** D4
Pasadena, Texas, U.S.A., **424** E5
Paşalimanı Adası, *island*, Turkey, **297** F5
Pasapuat, Indonesia, **200** C3
Paşayiğit, Turkey, **297** F5
Pascagoula, U.S.A., **425** H4
Paşcani, Romania, **296** F2
Pasco, U.S.A., **418** E3
Pascoal, Monte, *mountain peak*, Brazil, **457** F4
Pascua, Isla de (Easter Island), *island*, Chile, Pacific Ocean, **461** B2
Pasewalk, Germany, **289** G2
Pasfield Lake, Canada, **414** B2
Pasha, *river*, Russian Federation, **299** D2
Pasha, Russian Federation, **299** D2
Pāsighāt, India, **219** H3
Pasir Panjang, Singapore, **200** J7
Pasir Puteh, Malaysia, **200** C1
Pasir Ris, Singapore, **200** K6
Pasirpengarayan, Indonesia, **200** C2
Påskallavik, Sweden, **286** H4
Pasłęk, Poland, **289** J1
Pasley, Cape, Australia, **128** B5
Pasni, Pakistan, **221** H3
Paso Caballos, Guatemala, **428** C3
Paso de Indios, Argentina, **460** D2
Paso de los Libres, Argentina, **459** F3
Paso de los Toros, Uruguay, **459** F4
Paso de Patria, Paraguay, **459** E3
Paso Socompa, Chile, **458** C2
Pasrūr, Pakistan, **218** C2
Passage Point, Canada, **410** H2
Passau, Germany, **288** F4
Passero, Capo, *cape*, Sicilia, Italy, **295** E7
Passi, Philippines, **204** C4
Passo Fundo, Brazil, **459** G3
Passos, Brazil, **456** D5
Pastavy, Belarus, **287** N5
Pastaza, *river*, Peru, **450** C5
Pasto, Colombia, **450** C4
Pastos Bons, Brazil, **453** E5
Pasu, India, **212** B5
Pasu, Pakistan, **218** C1
Pasuruan, Indonesia, **201** F4
Pasvalys, Lithuania, **287** M4
Pasvikelva, *river*, Norway, **285** P2
Pásztó, Hungary, **289** J5
Pata, Central African Republic, **366** B3
Pata, Senegal, **364** B2
Patagonia, U.S.A., **423** H6
Patah, Gunung, *mountain peak*, Indonesia, **200** C4
Patamea, Samoa, **141** B1
Pātan, Gujarat, India, **218** C5
Pātan, Madhya Pradesh, India, **218** D5
Pātan, Nepal, **219** F4
Patani, Indonesia, **199** E2
Patay, Argentina, **458** D3
Patay, France, **290** E2
Patchway, England, U.K., **304** E3
Patea, New Zealand, **132** E4
Patea, *river*, New Zealand, **132** E4
Pategi, Nigeria, **365** F3
Pateley Bridge, England, U.K., **307** G3
Paterno, Sicilia, Italy, **295** E7
Paterson, U.S.A., **426** C4
Pathfinder Reservoir, U.S.A., **419** L5
Pathiu, Thailand, **202** C4
Patía, *river*, Colombia, **450** B4
Patiāla, India, **218** D3
Patience, French Guiana, **452** C2
Patikul, Philippines, **204** C5
Patmos, *island*, Dodekanisos, Greece, **297** F7
Patna, India, **219** F4
Patnos, Turkey, **363** H1
Patoka Lake, U.S.A., **421** K6
Patos, Albania, **297** B5
Patos, Brazil, **453** G5
Patos, Lagoa dos, *lagoon*, Brazil, **459** G4
Patos de Minas, Brazil, **456** D5
Patquía, Argentina, **458** C4
Patra, Greece, **297** C6
Patricio Lynch, Isla, *island*, Chile, **460** B3
Patrington, England, U.K., **307** H4
Patrocínio, Brazil, **456** D5
Pattani, Thailand, **202** D5
Pattaya, Thailand, **202** D3
Patten, U.S.A., **426** F1
Patterdale, England, U.K., **306** F3
Patti, Sicilia, Italy, **295** E6
Pattisson, Cape, Chatham Islands, New Zealand, **133** Q16
Pattoki, Pakistan, **218** C3
Patton Escarpment, *underwater feature*, Pacific Ocean, **479** K2
Patuākhāli, Bangladesh, **214** D5
Patuca, Punta, *point*, Honduras, **428** D4
Patuca, *river*, Honduras, **428** D4
Patūr, India, **218** D5
Patzcuaro, Mexico, **430** E5
Pau, France, **290** D5
Paucarbamba, Peru, **454** C3
Paucartambo, Peru, **454** D3
Pauillac, France, **290** D4
Pauini, Brazil, **455** E2
Pauini, *river*, Brazil, **455** E2
Pauk, Myanmar, **205** B3
Pauksa Taung, *mountain peak*, Myanmar, **205** B4
Paulatuk, Canada, **410** G3
Paulden, U.S.A., **422** G4
Paulista, Brazil, **453** G5
Paulistana, Brazil, **457** F2
Paulo Afonso, Brazil, **457** F2
Paulo, *river*, Bolivia, **455** G4
Pauls Valley, U.S.A., **424** D2
Păunești, Romania, **296** F2
Paungbyin, Myanmar, **205** B2
Paungde, Myanmar, **205** B4
Paup, Papua New Guinea, **140** A3
Paurī, India, **218** D4
Pauri, India, **218** D3
Pauto, *river*, Colombia, **450** D3
Pauträsk, Sweden, **284** H4
Pāvagada, India, **216** D3
Pavão, Brazil, **457** F4
Pavia, Italy, **294** B3
Pavilion, Canada, **412** J6
Pavilly, France, **305** H5
Pāvilosta, Latvia, **287** K4
Pavlikeni, Bulgaria, **296** E4
Pavlodar, Kazakhstan, **223** K2
Pavlodar, *province*, Kazakhstan, **212** C2
Pavlogradka, Russian Federation, **223** J2
Pavlohrad, Ukraine, **298** E3
Pavlovac, Croatia, **294** F3
Pavlovo, Russian Federation, **298** F1
Pavlovsk, Russian Federation, **223** L2
Pavlovskaya, Russian Federation, **298** E3
Pavón, Colombia, **450** D3
Pavullo nel Frignano, Italy, **294** C3
Pawan, *river*, Indonesia, **201** E3
Pawhuska, U.S.A., **420** E7
Pawnee, *river*, U.S.A., **420** C6
Paximadia, *island*, Greece, **297** E8
Paxoi, *island*, Ionioi Nisoi, Greece, **297** B6
Pay, Russian Federation, **299** E2
Paya Lebar, Singapore, **200** K6
Payagyi, Myanmar, **205** C4
Payakumbuh, Indonesia, **200** C3
Payne, Lac, *lake*, Canada, **415** S2
Paynes Creek, U.S.A., **422** C1
Paynton, Canada, **413** Q5
Payong, Tanjong, *point*, Malaysia, **201** F2
Pays de la Loire, *administrative region*, France, **290** D3
Paysandú, Uruguay, **459** E4
Payson, U.S.A., **423** H4
Payún, Cerro, *mountain peak*, Argentina, **458** C5
Payung, Indonesia, **200** D3
Paz de Ariporo, Colombia, **450** D3
Paz de Río, Colombia, **450** D2
Pazardzhik, Bulgaria, **296** E4
Pazarlar, Turkey, **297** G6
Pazaryeri, Turkey, **297** G6
Pazin, Croatia, **294** D3
Pea, Tongatapu Group, Tonga, **141** B4
Peace, *river*, Canada, **413** L3
Peace Point, Canada, **413** N2
Peace River, Canada, **413** L3
Peacehaven, England, U.K., **305** G4
Peach Springs, U.S.A., **422** G4
Peak, The, *mountain peak*, Ascension, **373** A3
Peal de Becerro, Spain, **293** F4
Peale, Mount, *mountain peak*, U.S.A., **423** J2
Pearce, U.S.A., **423** J6
Pearl, *river*, U.S.A., **424** G4
Pearl *see* Zhu, *river*, China, **207** B2
Pearl City, Hawaiian Islands, U.S.A., **422** R9
Pearl Harbor, Hawaiian Islands, U.S.A., **422** R9
Pearsall, U.S.A., **424** C5
Pearson, U.S.A., **425** L4
Peary Channel, Canada, **411** J2
Peary Land, *region*, Greenland, **411** R1
Peawanuck, Canada, **415** M4
Pebane, Mozambique, **369** G6
Pebas, Peru, **450** D5
Pebble Island, Falkland Islands, **460** F4
Peć, Yugoslavia, **296** C4
Peçanha, Brazil, **457** E5
Peças, Ilha das, *island*, Brazil, **459** H2
Pechenga, *river*, Russian Federation, **285** Q2
Pechenga, Russian Federation, **285** Q2
Pechenicheno, Russian Federation, **299** D5
Pechenizhyn, Ukraine, **296** E1
Pechora, *river*, Russian Federation, **300** G3
Pechora, Russian Federation, **300** G3
Pechory, Russian Federation, **299** A4
Peck, U.S.A., **421** M4
Pecka, Yugoslavia, **296** B3
Pecos, *river*, U.S.A., **423** L4
Pecos, U.S.A., **423** M6

Pécs, Hungary, **289** J5
Pedasí, Panama, **429** E6
Pedder, Lake, Australia, **135** J7
Pededze, *river*, Estonia/Latvia, **287** N4
Pedernales, Dominican Republic, **429** H3
Pedernales, Mexico, **430** D2
Pedhoulas, Cyprus, **225** B2
Pediva, Angola, **368** B6
Pedra Azul, Brazil, **457** F4
Pedra Lume, Cape Verde, **360** Q8
Pedras Negras, Brazil, **455** F3
Pedraza La Vieja, Venezuela, **450** D2
Pedregal, Venezuela, **451** D1
Pedregulho, Brazil, **456** D5
Pedreiras, Brazil, **453** E4
Pedrero, Meseta el, *plateau*, Argentina, **460** D3
Pedriceña, Mexico, **430** E3
Pedro Afonso, Brazil, **456** D2
Pedro Chico, Colombia, **450** D4
Pedro de Valdivia, Chile, **458** C2
Pedro Gomes, Brazil, **456** B4
Pedro Juan Caballero, Paraguay, **459** F2
Pedro Osorio, Brazil, **459** G4
Pedro II, Brazil, **453** F4
Peebles, Canada, **414** C6
Peebles, Scotland, U.K., **308** F5
Peekskill, U.S.A., **426** D4
Peel, Isle of Man, **306** D3
Peel, *river*, Canada, **410** F3
Peel Sound, Canada, **411** K2
Peene, *river*, Germany, **288** F2
Peenemünde, Germany, **289** G1
Peerless, U.S.A., **413** S7
Peetz, U.S.A., **423** M1
Pegasus Bay, New Zealand, **133** D6
Pegnitz, Germany, **288** E4
Pego, Spain, **293** G3
Pegu, *division*, Myanmar, **205** C4
Pegu, Myanmar, **205** C4
Pegu Yoma, *mountain range*, Myanmar, **205** B4
Pegwell Bay, England, U.K., **305** J3
Pehlivanköy, Turkey, **297** F5
Pehuajó, Argentina, **458** E5
Peipohja, Finland, **287** L2
Peipsi Järv, *lake*, Estonia, **287** N3
Peiraias (Piraeus), Greece, **297** D7
Peitz, Germany, **289** G3
Peixe, Brazil, **456** D3
Peixe, do, *river*, Brazil, **456** C4
Peixe, *river*, Brazil, **456** C6
Pejirá, Sierra de, *mountain range*, Venezuela, **450** D2
Pekalongan, Indonesia, **201** E4
Pekan, Malaysia, **200** C2
Pekanbaru, Indonesia, **200** C2
Peking *see* Beijing, China, **210** G5
Peklino, Russian Federation, **299** D6
Peksha, *river*, Russian Federation, **299** G4
Pelabuhanratu, Indonesia, **200** D4
Pelabuhanratu, Teluk, *bay*, Indonesia, **200** D4
Pelagie, Isole, *islands*, Sicilia, Italy, **295** D8
Pelawanbesar, Indonesia, **201** G2
Pelée, Montagne, *mountain peak*, Martinique, **427** D3
Pelee Island, Canada, **421** M5
Peleng, Pulau, *island*, Indonesia, **198** C3
Peleng, Selat, *strait*, Indonesia, **198** C3
Pelhřimov, Czech Republic, **289** G4
Pelican Mountains, *mountain range*, Canada, **413** M4

Pelican Rapids, Canada, **414** D5
Peligro, Punta del, *point*, Islas Canarias, Spain, **373** A4
Pelkosenniemi, Finland, **285** N3
Pell City, U.S.A., **425** J3
Pellegrini, Lago, *lake*, Argentina, **460** D1
Pello, Finland, **285** M3
Pellworm, *island*, Germany, **288** D1
Pelly, *river*, Canada, **410** F3
Pelly Bay, Canada, **411** L3
Pelly Crossing, Canada, **410** F3
Pelona Mountain, *mountain peak*, U.S.A., **423** J5
Peloponnisos, *administrative region*, Greece, **297** C7
Peloritani, Monti, *mountain range*, Sicilia, Italy, **295** E7
Pelotas, Brazil, **459** G4
Peltovuoma, Finland, **285** M2
Pemali, Tanjong, *point*, Indonesia, **198** C4
Pemangkat, Indonesia, **201** E2
Pematangsiantar, Indonesia, **200** B2
Pemba, Baía de, *bay*, Mozambique, **369** H5
Pemba, Mozambique, **369** H5
Pemba Island, Tanzania, **369** G4
Pemberton, Canada, **412** H6
Pembine, U.S.A., **421** K3
Pembrey, Indonesia, **199** G4
Pembrey, Wales, U.K., **304** C3
Pembroke, Canada, **416** C7
Pembroke, Wales, U.K., **304** C3
Pembroke Dock, Wales, U.K., **304** C3
Pembrokeshire, *unitary authority*, Wales, U.K., **304** B3
Pen-y-ghent, *mountain peak*, England, U.K., **306** F3
Peña de Francia, *mountain peak*, Spain, **292** D2
Peña Nevada, Cerro, *mountain peak*, Mexico, **431** F4
Penafiel, Portugal, **292** C2
Peñafiel, Spain, **292** E2
Penal, Trinidad, Trinidad and Tobago, **461** C4
Penalva, Brazil, **452** E4
Penamacor, Portugal, **292** D2
Penang *see* Pinang, Pulau, *island*, Malaysia, **200** B1
Penanjung, Teluk, *bay*, Indonesia, **201** E4
Penápolis, Brazil, **456** C5
Peñaranda de Bracamonte, Spain, **292** E2
Peñarroya, *mountain peak*, Spain, **293** G2
Penarth, Wales, U.K., **304** D3
Peñas, Cabo, *cape*, Argentina, **460** D4
Peñas, Cabo de, *cape*, Spain, **292** E1
Penas, Golfo de, *gulf*, Chile, **460** B3
Peñas, Punta, *point*, Venezuela, **461** C4
Pend Oreille Lake, U.S.A., **418** F2
Pendang, Indonesia, **201** F3
Pendleton, U.S.A., **418** E4
Pendroy, U.S.A., **418** H2
Peneda, *mountain peak*, Portugal, **292** C2
Penetanguishene, Canada, **421** P3
P'eng-hu Lieh-tao (Pescadores), *island*, Taiwan, **206** D4
P'eng-hu Tao, *island*, Taiwan, **206** D4
Peng Xian, China, **215** G3
Penganga, *river*, India, **218** D5
Penge, Democratic Republic of the Congo, **368** D4
Penglai, China, **211** H5
Pengshui, China, **206** B2
Pengxi, China, **215** H3
Peniche, Portugal, **292** C3
Penicuik, Scotland, U.K., **308** F5

Peninga, Russian Federation, **285** R5
Penitente, Serra do, *mountain range*, Brazil, **456** D2
Penkridge, England, U.K., **304** E2
Penmarch, France, **290** B3
Penmarc'h, Pointe de, *point*, France, **290** B3
Penn Yan, U.S.A., **426** B3
Pennell Coast, *region*, Antarctica, **470** D8
Pennine, Alpi, *mountain range*, Italy, **294** A3
Pennines, *mountain range*, England, U.K., **306** F3
Pennsylvania, *state*, U.S.A., **426** B4
Pennycutaway, *river*, Canada, **414** H3
Pennyghael, Scotland, U.K., **308** C4
Peno, Russian Federation, **299** D4
Penobscot, *river*, U.S.A., **426** F1
Penong, Australia, **134** G5
Penonomé, Panama, **429** E5
Penrhyn *see* Tongareva, *island*, Cook Islands, **139** J5
Penrith, England, U.K., **306** F3
Penryn, England, U.K., **304** B4
Pensacola, U.S.A., **425** J4
Pensacola Mountains, *mountain range*, Antarctica, **470** C5
Pentecost, *island*, Vanuatu, **141** A2
Penticton, Canada, **413** K7
Pentire Point, England, U.K., **304** B4
Pentland Firth, *strait*, Orkney, Scotland, U.K., **308** F2
Pentland Hills, Scotland, U.K., **308** F5
Penukonda, India, **216** D3
Penybont, Wales, U.K., **304** D2
Penybontfawr, Wales, U.K., **304** D2
Penygadair, *mountain peak*, Wales, U.K., **304** D2
Penza, Russian Federation, **298** G2
Penzance, England, U.K., **304** B4
Penzberg, Germany, **288** E5
Penzenskaya Oblast', *province*, Russian Federation, **298** F2
Peoria, U.S.A., **421** J5
Pepacton Reservoir, U.S.A., **426** C3
Pepe, Pointe, *point*, France, **290** C3
Pepeekeo, Hawaiian Islands, U.S.A., **422** R10
Pepepe, New Zealand, **132** E3
Peperi-Guaçu, *river*, Argentina/Brazil, **459** G3
Pëqin, Albania, **297** B5
Pér, Hungary, **289** H5
Perä-Posio, Finland, **285** N3
Perabumilih, Indonesia, **200** D3
Perak, *river*, Malaysia, **200** C1
Perak, *state*, Malaysia, **200** C1
Perama, Kriti, Greece, **297** E8
Perambalūr, India, **216** D4
Peranka, Finland, **285** P4
Percé, Canada, **417** J5
Percival Lakes, Australia, **134** F3
Perdida, *river*, Brazil, **456** D2
Perdido, Monte, *mountain peak*, Spain, **293** H1
Perdido, *river*, Argentina, **460** D2
Perdido, *river*, Brazil, **456** B5
Perdika, Greece, **297** C6
Perechyn, Ukraine, **289** L4
Pereira, Colombia, **450** C3
Pereira Barreto, Brazil, **456** C5

Peremyshl', Russian Federation, **299** F5
Perené, Peru, **454** C3
Pereslavl' Zalesskiy, Russian Federation, **299** G4
Pereyaslavka, Russian Federation, **211** L3
Perez, U.S.A., **418** D6
Pergamino, Argentina, **458** E4
Pergola, Italy, **294** D4
Perham, U.S.A., **420** F2
Perho, Finland, **285** M5
Perhonjoki, *river*, Finland, **285** L5
Péribonca, Lac, *lake*, Canada, **416** F4
Péribonca, *river*, Canada, **416** F4
Perico, Argentina, **458** D2
Perico, U.S.A., **423** M3
Pericos, Mexico, **430** D3
Périers, France, **290** D2
Perigoso, Canal, *channel*, Brazil, **452** D3
Périgueux, France, **290** E4
Peristera, *island*, Greece, **297** E6
Perito Moreno, Argentina, **460** C3
Peritoró, Brazil, **453** E4
Perleberg, Germany, **288** E2
Perlis, *state*, Malaysia, **200** B1
Perm', Russian Federation, **300** G4
Perma, U.S.A., **418** G3
Përmet, Albania, **297** C5
Permskaya Oblast', *province*, Russian Federation, **222** F1
Pernambuco, *state*, Brazil, **457** G2
Pernambuco Plain, *underwater feature*, Atlantic Ocean, **477** F6
Pernik, Bulgaria, **296** D4
Perniö, Finland, **287** L2
Péronne, France, **291** F2
Perote, Mexico, **431** F5
Perpignan, France, **291** F5
Perranporth, England, U.K., **304** B4
Perrault Falls, Canada, **414** H6
Perros-Guirec, France, **290** C2
Perry, Florida, U.S.A., **425** L4
Perry, Georgia, U.S.A., **425** L3
Perry, Iowa, U.S.A., **420** F5
Perry, Oklahoma, U.S.A., **424** D1
Perryton, U.S.A., **420** C7
Perryvale, Canada, **413** N4
Perryville, U.S.A., **420** J7
Persåsen, Sweden, **286** G1
Perseverance Harbour, Campbell Island, New Zealand, **132** K11
Perseverancia, Bolivia, **455** F4
Pershore, England, U.K., **304** E2
Persian Gulf, Asia, **220** E3
Pertandangan, Tanjong, *point*, Indonesia, **200** C2
Perth, Australia, **134** D5
Perth, Canada, **416** C7
Perth, Scotland, U.K., **308** F4
Perth and Kinross, *local authority*, Scotland, U.K., **308** F4
Perth-Andover, Canada, **416** H6
Perth Basin, *underwater feature*, Indian Ocean, **476** G6
Pertusato, Cap, *cape*, Corse, France, **295** B5
Peru, *country*, South America, **449** E4
Peru Basin, *underwater feature*, Pacific Ocean, **479** M5
Peru-Chile Trench, *underwater feature*, Pacific Ocean, **479** N5
Perugia, Italy, **294** D4
Perugorria, Argentina, **459** E3
Peruíbe, Brazil, **459** H2
Perušić, Croatia, **294** E3

Pervomays´k, Ukraine, **296** H1
Pervomayskiy, Russian Federation, **210** F2
Pervomayskoye, Russian Federation, **299** B2
Pervoural'sk, Russian Federation, **222** F1
Pesagi, Gunung, *mountain peak*, Indonesia, **200** D4
Pesaro, Italy, **294** D4
Pescadores, Punta, *point*, Róbinson Crusoe Island, Archipiélago Juan Fernández, Chile, **461** C2
Pescadores *see* P'eng-hu Lieh-tao, *island*, Taiwan, **206** D4
Pescara, Italy, **295** E4
Peschanoye, Russian Federation, **285** S5
Peschici, Italy, **295** F5
Pesek, Pulau, *island*, Singapore, **200** J7
Pesek Kechil, Pulau, *island*, Singapore, **200** J7
Peshāwar, Pakistan, **218** B2
Peshkopi, Albania, **297** C5
Peshtera, Bulgaria, **296** E4
Pesochnya, Russian Federation, **299** D6
Pesqueira, Brazil, **453** G5
Pessac, France, **290** D4
Pestovo, Russian Federation, **299** E3
Petacalco, Bahía de, *bay*, Mexico, **430** E5
Petäiskylä, Finland, **285** P5
Petäjävesi, Finland, **287** M1
Petalidi, Greece, **297** C7
Petaluma, U.S.A., **422** B2
Pétange, Luxembourg, **291** G2
Petare, Venezuela, **451** E1
Petatlan, Mexico, **431** E5
Petauke, Zambia, **369** F5
Petawawa, Canada, **416** C7
Petén Itzá, Lago, *lake*, Guatemala, **428** C3
Petenwell Lake, U.S.A., **420** H3
Peter I Øy, *Norwegian dependency*, Antarctica, **470** A6
Peter Pond Lake, Canada, **413** Q4
Peterbell, Canada, **415** N7
Peterborough, Australia, **135** H5
Peterborough, Canada, **416** B7
Peterborough, England, U.K., **305** G2
Peterborough, *unitary authority*, England, U.K., **305** G2
Peterculter, Scotland, U.K., **308** G3
Peterlee, England, U.K., **307** G3
Petermanns Bjerg, *mountain peak*, Greenland, **411** S2
Peteroa, Volcán, *mountain peak*, Chile, **458** B5
Peter's Mine, Guyana, **451** G2
Petersburg, U.S.A., **426** B6
Petersfield, England, U.K., **305** G3
Petisikapau Lake, Canada, **416** H2
Petit Goâve, Haiti, **429** G3
Petite Rivière Noire, Piton de la, *mountain peak*, Mauritius, **373** C1
Petitot, *river*, Canada, **412** J2
Petkula, Finland, **285** N3
Peto, Mexico, **431** H4
Petolahti, Finland, **287** K1
Petoskey, U.S.A., **421** L3
Petre Bay, Chatham Islands, New Zealand, **133** Q16
Petrich, Bulgaria, **297** D5
Petrila, Romania, **296** D3
Petrivka, Ukraine, **296** H2
Petrodvorets, Russian Federation, **299** B3
Petrolina, Brazil, **457** F2
Petropavl, Kazakhstan, **223** H2
Petropavlovka, Russian Federation, **210** D2

Petropavlovsk-Kamchatskiy, Russian Federation, **301** S4
Petrópolis, Brazil, **457** E6
Petroșani, Romania, **296** D3
Petrovichi, Russian Federation, **299** D6
Petrovka, Russian Federation, **223** L2
Petrovo, Russian Federation, **299** E3
Petrovsk Zabaykal'skiy, Russian Federation, **210** E2
Petrovskoye, Russian Federation, **299** G4
Petrozavodsk, Russian Federation, **299** E2
Petrușeni, Moldova, **296** F2
Pettigo, Northern Ireland, U.K., **309** E3
Petukhovo, Russian Federation, **222** H1
Petushki, Russian Federation, **299** G5
Petworth, England, U.K., **305** G4
Peureulak, Indonesia, **200** B1
Pevek, Russian Federation, **301** U3
Pewsey, England, U.K., **305** F3
Pézenas, France, **291** F5
Pezinok, Slovakia, **289** H4
Pezu, Pakistan, **218** B2
Pfaffenhofen an der Ilm, Germany, **288** E4
Pforzheim, Germany, **288** D4
Phalaborwa, South Africa, **371** F3
Phalia, Pakistan, **218** C2
Phalodi, India, **218** C4
Phalsund, India, **218** B4
Phan Rang, Vietnam, **203** F4
Phan Thiết, Vietnam, **203** F4
Phang Khon, Thailand, **203** D2
Phangan, Ko, *island*, Thailand, **202** D4
Phangnga, Thailand, **202** C4
Pharr, U.S.A., **424** C6
Phayao, Thailand, **202** C2
Phenix City, U.S.A., **425** K3
Phet Buri Reservoir, Thailand, **202** C3
Phetchabun, Thailand, **202** D2
Phetchaburi, Thailand, **202** C3
Phiamay, Phou, *mountain peak*, Laos, **203** E3
Phichit, Thailand, **202** D2
Phidim, Nepal, **219** F4
Philadelphia, Mississippi, U.S.A., **425** H3
Philadelphia, Pennsylvania, U.S.A., **426** C4
Philip, U.S.A., **420** C3
Philip Island, Norfolk Island, **135** T13
Philippeville, Belgium, **288** B3
Philippine Sea, Philippines, **204** D2
Philippine Trench, *underwater feature*, Pacific Ocean, **478** C3
Philippines, *country*, Asia, **197** P8
Philipsburg, Montana, U.S.A., **418** H3
Philipsburg, Pennsylvania, U.S.A., **421** P5
Philipsburg, St Maarten, Netherlands Antilles, **427** D2
Philipstown, South Africa, **370** D5
Phillip Island, Australia, **135** J6
Phillips, U.S.A., **420** H3
Phillipsburg, Kansas, U.S.A., **420** D6
Phillipsburg, Pennsylvania, U.S.A., **426** C4
Philomath, U.S.A., **418** C4
Philpots Island, Canada, **411** M2
Phimai, Thailand, **203** D3
Phitsanulok, Thailand, **202** D2
Phnom Penh *see* Phnum Pénh, Cambodia, **203** E4

Phnum Pénh (Phnom Penh), Cambodia, **203** E4
Phoenix *see* Rawaki, *island*, Kiribati, **139** G5
Phoenix, U.S.A., **423** G5
Phoenix Islands, Kiribati, **139** G5
Phon, Thailand, **203** D3
Phôngsali, Laos, **202** D1
Photharam, Thailand, **202** C3
Phra Nakhon Si Ayutthaya, Thailand, **202** D3
Phra Thong, Ko, *island*, Thailand, **202** C4
Phrae, Thailand, **202** D2
Phsar Réam, Cambodia, **203** D4
Phú Nhơn, Vietnam, **203** F3
Phú Quô'c, Đao, *island*, Vietnam, **203** D4
Phú Thọ, Vietnam, **203** E1
Phuket, Ko, *island*, Thailand, **202** C4
Phuket, Thailand, **202** C5
Phulabāni, India, **219** F5
Phumĭ Banam, Cambodia, **203** E4
Phumĭ Bântéay Chhmar, Cambodia, **203** D3
Phumĭ Chrăng Khpós, Cambodia, **203** D4
Phumĭ Krêk, Cambodia, **203** E4
Phumĭ Mlu Prey, Cambodia, **203** E3
Phumĭ Moŭng, Cambodia, **203** D3
Phumĭ Phsa Rôméas, Cambodia, **203** E3
Phumĭ Prâmaôy, Cambodia, **203** D3
Phumĭ Prêk Preăh, Cambodia, **203** E3
Phumĭ Prey Chruk, Cambodia, **203** D3
Phumĭ Sâmraông, E. Cambodia, **203** E3
Phumĭ Sâmraông, W. Cambodia, **203** D3
Phumĭ Véal Rénh, Cambodia, **203** D4
Phuthaditjhaba, South Africa, **371** E4
Pi Xian, Jiangsu, China, **206** D1
Pi Xian, Sichuan, China, **215** G3
Piacá, Brazil, **452** D5
Piacenza, Italy, **294** B3
Piadena, Italy, **294** C3
Piana-Mwanga, Democratic Republic of the Congo, **369** E4
Pianguan, China, **210** E5
Pianosa, Isola, Adriatic Sea, *island*, Italy, **295** E4
Pianosa, Isola, Tyrrhenian Sea, *island*, Italy, **294** C4
Piaski, Poland, **289** L3
Piatra, near Bals, Romania, **296** E3
Piatra, Romania, **296** E4
Piatra Neamț, Romania, **296** F2
Piauí, *river*, Brazil, **457** E2
Piauí, *state*, Brazil, **453** E5
Piave, *river*, Italy, **294** D2
Piazza Armerina, Sicilia, Italy, **295** E7
Pibor Post, Sudan, **366** D3
Pica, Chile, **455** E5
Picardie, *administrative region*, France, **290** E2
Picayune, U.S.A., **425** H4
Picentini, Monti, *mountain peak*, Italy, **295** E5
Picháchic, Mexico, **430** D2
Pichanal, Argentina, **458** D2
Pichhor, India, **218** D4
Pichi Mahuida, Argentina, **460** E1
Pichilemu, Chile, **458** B5
Pichilingue, Mexico, **430** C3
Pichucalo, Mexico, **431** G5
Pickering, England, U.K., **307** H3
Pickle Lake, Canada, **414** J6
Pico, *island*, Azores, Portugal, **360** M7

Pico de Salamanca, Argentina, **460** D2
Pico Truncado, Argentina, **460** D3
Picos, Brazil, **453** F5
Picota, Peru, **454** C2
Picton, Canada, **416** C8
Picton, Isla, *island*, Chile, **460** D5
Picton, New Zealand, **133** D5
Picton, U.S.A., **426** B2
Picún Leufú, Argentina, **460** D1
Picún Leufú, *river*, Argentina, **460** C1
Pidārak, Pakistan, **221** H3
Pidi, Democratic Republic of the Congo, **369** E4
Pidurutalagata, *mountain peak*, Sri Lanka, **217** E5
Pie Town, U.S.A., **423** J4
Piedmont, Alabama, U.S.A., **425** K3
Piedmont, South Dakota, U.S.A., **420** B3
Piedrabuena, Spain, **292** E3
Piedrahita, Spain, **292** E2
Piedras, de las, *river*, Peru, **454** D3
Piedras Negras, Coahuila, Mexico, **431** E2
Piedras Negras, Veracruz, Mexico, **431** F5
Pieksämäki, Finland, **287** N1
Pielavesi, Finland, **285** N5
Pielinen, *lake*, Finland, **285** P5
Piemonte, *autonomous region*, Italy, **294** A3
Pieniężno, Poland, **289** K1
Pierce, U.S.A., **418** G3
Pierceland, Canada, **410** J4
Pierowall, Orkney, Scotland, U.K., **308** F1
Pierre, U.S.A., **420** C3
Pierrelatte, France, **291** G4
Pierreville, Canada, **416** E6
Pierrot Island, Rodrigues, **373** B1
Pierson, Canada, **414** D7
Piet Retief, South Africa, **371** F4
Pietarsaari, Finland, **285** L5
Pietermaritzburg, South Africa, **371** F4
Pietersburg, South Africa, **371** E3
Pieve di Cadore, Italy, **294** D2
Pigeon, *river*, Canada, **414** F5
Pigeon Point, Tobago, Trinidad and Tobago, **461** B4
Pigüé, Argentina, **458** D5
Pihāni, India, **218** E4
Pihlajavesi, Finland, **287** M1
Pihtipudas, Finland, **285** M5
Piippola, Finland, **285** N4
Pijijiapan, Mexico, **431** G6
Pikalevo, Russian Federation, **299** E3
Pikangikum, Canada, **414** H6
Piketberg, South Africa, **370** C5
Pikeville, U.S.A., **421** M7
Pikine, Senegal, **364** A2
Pikit, Philippines, **204** D5
Pikou, China, **211** H5
Pikounda, Congo, **368** C2
Pikwitonei, Canada, **414** F4
Pila, Argentina, **459** E5
Piła, Poland, **289** H2
Pilagá, *river*, Argentina, **459** E2
Pilão Arcado, Brazil, **457** E2
Pilar, Argentina, **459** E5
Pilar, Cabo, *cape*, Chile, **460** B4
Pilar, Paraguay, **459** E3
Pilaya, *river*, Bolivia, **455** F5
Pilbara, *region*, Australia, **134** D3
Pilcaniyeu, Argentina, **460** C1
Pilcomayo, *river*, Argentina/ Bolivia/Paraguay, **455** F5
Pīleru, India, **216** D3
Pili, Philippines, **204** C3
Pīlibhīt, India, **218** D3
Pilica, *river*, Poland, **289** K3
Pillar Bay, Ascension, **373** A3
Pillcopata, Peru, **454** D3

Pilões, Serra dos, *mountain range*, Brazil, **456** D4
Pilón, Cuba, **429** F3
Pilot Mound, Canada, **414** E7
Pilot Rock, U.S.A., **418** E4
Pilsen *see* Plzeň, Czech Republic, **288** F4
Pilzno, Poland, **289** K4
Pima, U.S.A., **423** J5
Pimenta Bueno, Brazil, **455** G3
Pimperne, England, U.K., **304** E4
Pimpri-Chinchwad, India, **216** C2
Pináculo, Cerro, *mountain peak*, Argentina, **460** C4
Pinamalayan, Philippines, **204** C3
Pinang (Penang), Pulau, *island*, Malaysia, **200** B1
Pinang, *state*, Malaysia, **200** B1
Pinangah, Malaysia, **201** G1
Pinar del Río, Cuba, **428** E2
Pınarhisar, Turkey, **297** F5
Piñas, Ecuador, **450** B5
Pinatubo, Mount, *mountain peak*, Philippines, **204** C3
Pinchbeck, England, U.K., **305** G2
Pincher Creek, Canada, **413** N7
Pindaré, *river*, Brazil, **452** D4
Pindaré-Mirim, Brazil, **452** E4
Pindi Gheb, Pakistan, **218** C2
Pindobal, Brazil, **452** D4
Pindos Oros (Pindus Mountains), *mountain range*, Albania, **297** C5
Pindushi, Russian Federation, **285** S5
Pindwāra, India, **218** C4
Pine, Cape, Canada, **417** Q6
Pine, U.S.A., **423** H4
Pine Bluff, U.S.A., **424** F2
Pine Creek, Australia, **134** G1
Pine Dock, Canada, **414** F6
Pine Hills, U.S.A., **425** M5
Pine Point, Canada, **413** M1
Pine Ridge, U.S.A., **420** B4
Pine River, Canada, **414** D6
Pine Springs, U.S.A., **423** L6
Pinedale, Arizona, U.S.A., **423** H4
Pinedale, Wyoming, U.S.A., **419** K5
Pinehouse Lake, Canada, **413** R4
Pinehouse Lake, *lake*, Canada, **413** R4
Pineimuta, *river*, Canada, **415** K5
Pineios, *river*, Greece, **297** D6
Pinerolo, Italy, **294** A3
Pines, Isle of *see* Pins, Île des, *island*, New Caledonia, **141** A3
Pinetop-Lakeside, U.S.A., **423** J4
Pineville, U.S.A., **424** F4
Pinewood, Canada, **414** G7
Piney, France, **291** G2
Ping, Mae Nam, *river*, Thailand, **202** C2
P'ing-tung, Taiwan, **206** E4
Ping'an, China, **207** C2
Pingchang, China, **215** H3
Pingdi, China, **207** C3
Pingdingshan, China, **206** C1
Pingdu, China, **211** G5
Pingelap, *island*, Micronesia, **138** E4
Pingguo, China, **215** H5
Pinghai, China, **207** D3
Pinghe, China, **206** D3
Pinghu, Guangdong, China, **207** C3
Pinghu, Zhejiang, China, **206** E2
Pingjiang, China, **206** C2
Pingle, China, **206** B3
Pingli, China, **206** B1
Pingliang, China, **215** H2
Pingling, China, **207** C1
Pingluo, China, **210** D5
Pingquan, China, **211** G4

Pingree, U.S.A., **420** D2
Pingsha, China, **206** C4
Pingshan, China, **207** C3
Pingtan, Fujian, China, **206** D3
Pingtan, Guangdong, China, **207** D2
Pingwu, China, **215** H2
Pingxiang, Guangxi Zhuangzu Zizhiqu, China, **215** H5
Pingxiang, Jiangxi, China, **206** C3
Pingxiang, Vietnam, **203** E1
Pingyang, China, **206** E3
Pingyao, China, **210** F5
Pingyi, China, **206** D1
Pingyin, China, **210** G5
Pingyuanjie, China, **215** G5
Pingzhuang, China, **211** G4
Pinheiro, Brazil, **452** E4
Pinheiro Machado, Brazil, **459** G4
Pinhel, Portugal, **292** D2
Pinhoe, England, U.K., **304** D4
Pini, Pulau, *island*, Indonesia, **200** B2
Pinjarra, Australia, **134** D5
Pink, *river*, Canada, **414** B3
Pink Mountain, Canada, **412** H3
Pinlebu, Myanmar, **205** B2
Pinnacle, *mountain peak*, New Zealand, **133** D5
Pinnes, Akra, *point*, Greece, **297** E5
Pinoso, Spain, **293** G3
Pins, Île des (Isle of Pines), *island*, New Caledonia, **141** A3
Pinsk, Belarus, **298** C2
Pinta, Isla, *island*, Islas Galápagos (Galapagos Islands), Ecuador, **461** A1
Pintados, Chile, **455** E5
Pintamo, Finland, **285** N4
Pintatu, Indonesia, **198** D2
Pinto, Argentina, **458** D3
Pintuyan, Philippines, **204** D4
Pinzón, Isla, *island*, Islas Galápagos (Galapagos Islands), Ecuador, **461** A2
Piombino, Italy, **294** C4
Pioneer Fracture Zone, *tectonic feature*, Pacific Ocean, **479** H2
Pioner, Ostrov, *island*, Russian Federation, **300** K2
Pionerskiy, Russian Federation, **287** K5
Piopio, New Zealand, **132** E4
Piotrków Trybunalski, Poland, **289** J3
Piperi, *island*, Greece, **297** E6
Pipestone, Canada, **414** D7
Pipestone, *river*, Canada, **413** R3
Pipestone, U.S.A., **420** E3
Pipili, India, **219** F5
Pipiriki, New Zealand, **132** E4
Pipmuacan, Réservoir, Canada, **416** F5
Pipri, India, **219** E4
Piquiri, *river*, Brazil, **459** G2
Pīr Panjāl Range, *mountain range*, India, **218** C2
Piracanjuba, Brazil, **456** D4
Piracicaba, Brazil, **459** H2
Piracicaba, *river*, Brazil, **459** H2
Piraçununga, Brazil, **456** D5
Piracuruca, Brazil, **453** F4
Piraeus *see* Peiraias, Greece, **297** D7
Piraí do Sul, Brazil, **459** H2
Pirajuí, Brazil, **456** D5
Pirané, Argentina, **459** E2
Piranhas, Brazil, **456** C4
Piranhas, *river*, Brazil, **453** G5
Pirapó, *river*, Brazil, **459** G2
Pirapora, Brazil, **457** E4
Piratini, Brazil, **459** G4
Piratini, *river*, Brazil, **459** G4
Piray, *river*, Bolivia, **455** F4
Piray Guazu, *river*, Argentina, **459** F3
Pires do Rio, Brazil, **456** D4

Rāichūr, India, **216** D2
Raiganj, India, **219** G4
Raigarh, India, **219** E5
Rainbow Lake, Canada, **413** K2
Rainer, Mount, *mountain peak*, U.S.A., **418** D3
Rainier, U.S.A., **418** C3
Rainy Lake, Canada/U.S.A., **420** G1
Rainy River, Canada, **414** G7
Raippaluoto (Vallgrund), *island*, Finland, **284** K5
Raipur, India, **219** E5
Raisen, India, **218** D5
Raisio, Finland, **287** L2
Raith, Canada, **414** K7
Raivavae, *island*, French Polynesia, **137** G3
Rāj-Nāndgaon, India, **219** E5
Raja-Jooseppi, Finland, **285** P2
Rajagangapur, India, **219** F5
Rājahmundry, India, **217** E2
Rajala, Finland, **285** N3
Rajang, *river*, Malaysia, **201** F2
Rājanpur, Pakistan, **218** B3
Rājapālaiyam, India, **216** D4
Rājapur, India, **216** C2
Rājasthān, *state*, India, **218** C4
Rajauli, India, **219** F4
Rājgarh, E. Central Rājasthān, India, **218** D4
Rājgarh, N. Rājasthān, India, **218** C3
Rājkot, India, **218** B5
Rājpīpla, India, **218** C5
Rājpur, India, **218** D5
Rājsamand, India, **218** C4
Rajshahi, Bangladesh, **214** D4
Rajshahi, *division*, Bangladesh, **214** D4
Raka, China, **214** C3
Rakahanga, *island*, Cook Islands, **139** H5
Rakai, Uganda, **369** F3
Rakaia, New Zealand, **133** D6
Rakaw, Belarus, **287** N6
Rakhiv, Ukraine, **296** E1
Rakhmet, Kazakhstan, **222** H3
Rakhni, Pakistan, **218** B3
Rakhyūt, Oman, **220** F5
Rakiraki, Fiji, **141** A4
Rakkestad, Norway, **286** E3
Rakovník, Czech Republic, **288** F4
Rakovski, Bulgaria, **296** E4
Rakvere, Estonia, **287** N3
Raleigh, North Carolina, U.S.A., **425** N2
Raleigh, North Dakota, U.S.A., **420** C2
Ralston, Canada, **413** P6
Ralston, U.S.A., **419** K4
Ramādah, Tunisia, **362** B2
Ramalho, Serra do, *mountain range*, Brazil, **457** E4
Rāmanāthapuram, India, **216** D4
Rāmānuj Ganj, India, **219** E5
Rambouillet, France, **290** E2
Rāmdevra, India, **218** B4
Rāmechhāp, Nepal, **219** F4
Ramena, Madagascar, **372** B3
Rameshki, Russian Federation, **299** F4
Ramgarh, Bihār, India, **219** F5
Rāmgarh, Rājasthān, India, **218** B4
Rāmhormoz, Iran, **363** J2
Ramírez, Isla, *island*, Chile, **460** B4
Ramla, Israel, **225** C4
Ramlu, *mountain peak*, Eritrea/Ethiopia, **367** F2
Ramm, Jabal, *mountain peak*, Jordan, **225** C5
Ramm, Jordan, **225** C5
Rāmnagar, India, **218** D3
Ramnäs, Sweden, **286** H3
Ramni, Belarus, **299** C5
Râmnicu Sărat, Romania, **296** F3
Râmnicu Vâlcea, Romania, **296** E3
Ramor, Lough, *lake*, Ireland, **309** F4
Ramore, Canada, **415** P7
Ramotswa, Botswana, **371** E3
Rāmpur, Gujarat, India, **218** B5
Rāmpur, Himāchal Pradesh, India, **218** D3
Rampūr, Orissa, India, **217** F1
Rāmpur, Uttar Pradesh, India, **218** D3
Rāmpur Hāt, India, **219** F4
Rāmpura, India, **218** C4
Rampside, England, U.K., **306** E3
Ramree Island, Myanmar, **205** B4
Ramsele, Sweden, **284** H5
Ramsey, Canada, **421** M2
Ramsey, England, U.K., **305** G2
Ramsey, Isle of Man, **306** D3
Ramsey Bay, Isle of Man, **306** D3
Ramsey Island, Wales, U.K., **304** B3
Ramsgate, England, U.K., **305** J3
Ramsjö, Sweden, **286** G1
Ramu, Bangladesh, **214** E5
Ramu, *river*, Papua New Guinea, **140** B4
Ramundberget, Sweden, **284** F5
Ramvik, Sweden, **287** H1
Ramygala, Lithuania, **287** M5
Rana Pratap Sāgar, *lake*, India, **218** C4
Ranakah, Gunung, *mountain peak*, Indonesia, **198** C5
Ranau, Danau, *lake*, Indonesia, **200** C4
Rānāvāv, India, **218** B5
Ranbausawa, Tanjong, *point*, Indonesia, **199** F3
Rancagua, Chile, **458** B5
Ranchester, U.S.A., **419** L4
Rānchī, India, **219** F5
Rancho Cordova, U.S.A., **422** C2
Ranco, Lago, *lake*, Chile, **460** C1
Randado, U.S.A., **424** C6
Randalstown, Northern Ireland, U.K., **309** F3
Randazzo, Sicilia, Italy, **295** E7
Rånddalen, Sweden, **286** F1
Randers, Denmark, **286** E4
Randijaure, *lake*, Sweden, **284** J3
Randolph, Nebraska, U.S.A., **420** E4
Randolph, Vermont, U.S.A., **426** D3
Råneå, Sweden, **285** L4
Ranérou, Senegal, **364** B1
Ranfurly, New Zealand, **133** C7
Rangae, Thailand, **202** D5
Rangamati, Bangladesh, **214** E5
Rangatira Island, Chatham Islands, New Zealand, **133** Q16
Rangaunu Bay, New Zealand, **132** D2
Rangeley, U.S.A., **426** E2
Rangely, U.S.A., **423** J1
Rangia, India, **219** G4
Rangipo, New Zealand, **132** E4
Rangiriri, New Zealand, **132** E3
Rangiroa, *island*, French Polynesia, **137** G2
Rangitaiki, *river*, New Zealand, **132** F4
Rangitata, New Zealand, **133** C7
Rangiuru, New Zealand, **132** F3
Rangoon *see* Yangon, Myanmar, **205** C4
Rangpur, Bangladesh, **214** D4
Rangsang, Pulau, *island*, Indonesia, **200** C2
Rānibennur, India, **216** C3
Raniganj, India, **219** F5
Rānīpur, Pakistan, **218** B4
Rankin, U.S.A., **423** N6
Rankin Inlet, Canada, **411** K3
Rannoch, Loch, *lake*, Scotland, U.K., **308** E4
Rannoch Moor, *moorland*, Scotland, U.K., **308** E4
Rano, Nigeria, **365** F2
Ranobe, *river*, Madagascar, **372** A4
Ranohira, Madagascar, **372** B5
Ranomena, Madagascar, **372** B5
Ranong, Thailand, **202** C4
Ransarn, *lake*, Sweden, **284** G4
Ransiki, Indonesia, **199** F3
Rantajärvi, Sweden, **285** L3
Rantasalmi, Finland, **287** P1
Rantau, Indonesia, **201** F3
Rantekombola, Gunung, *mountain peak*, Indonesia, **198** C3
Rantepao, Indonesia, **198** B3
Rantoul, U.S.A., **421** J5
Rantsila, Finland, **285** M4
Ranua, Finland, **285** N4
Raoping, China, **206** D4
Raoui, Erg er, *desert*, Algeria, **361** F3
Raoul Island, Kermadec Islands, New Zealand, **132** L12
Rapa, *island*, French Polynesia, **137** G3
Rāpar, India, **218** B5
Rapahoe, New Zealand, **133** C6
Rapallo, Italy, **294** B3
Rapel, *river*, Chile, **458** B4
Raper, Cabo, *cape*, Chile, **460** B3
Raper, Cape, Canada, **411** N3
Raphoe, Ireland, **309** E3
Rapid City, U.S.A., **420** B3
Rapide Blanc, Canada, **416** E6
Räpina, Estonia, **287** N3
Rapla, Estonia, **287** M3
Rappahannock, *river*, U.S.A., **426** B5
Rapu Rapu Island, Philippines, **204** D3
Raroia, *island*, French Polynesia, **137** G2
Rarotonga, *island*, Cook Islands, **137** F3
Ra's Ajdīr, Tunisia, **362** B2
Ra's an Naqb, Jordan, **225** C5
Ra's at Tin, Libya, **224** B6
Ras Dashen Terara, *mountain peak*, Ethiopia, **367** E2
Râs el Mâ, Mali, **364** D1
Ra's Ghārib, Egypt, **363** F3
Ra's Matārimah, Egypt, **225** B5
Ra's Sudr, Egypt, **225** B5
Ra's Tannūrah, Saudi Arabia, **220** E3
Raša, Croatia, **294** E3
Rasa, Punta, *point*, Argentina, **460** E1
Rasa Island, Philippines, **204** B4
Râşcani, Moldova, **296** F2
Raseiniai, Lithuania, **287** L5
Rashād, Sudan, **366** D2
Rashaant, Bayan-Ölgiy, Mongolia, **213** F3
Rashaant, Dundgovĭ, Mongolia, **210** D3
Rashm, Iran, **221** F1
Rasht, Iran, **222** D5
Rasi Salai, Thailand, **203** E3
Rāsk, Iran, **221** H3
Raška, Yugoslavia, **296** C4
Råsken, *river*, Norway, **286** C2
Râşnov, Romania, **296** E3
Raso, Cabo, *cape*, Argentina, **460** E2
Rastede, Germany, **288** D2
Rastegai'sa, *mountain peak*, Norway, **285** N2
Råstojaure, *lake*, Sweden, **284** K2
Rasu, Monte, *mountain peak*, Sardegna, Italy, **295** B5
Rasūl, Pakistan, **218** C2
Rat Islands, United States of America, **301** U4
Rata, New Zealand, **132** E5
Rata, Tanjong, *point*, Indonesia, **200** D4
Rätan, Sweden, **286** G1
Ratanpur, India, **219** E5
Ratchaburi, Thailand, **202** C3
Rāth, India, **218** D4
Rath Luirc, Ireland, **309** D5
Rathangan, Ireland, **309** E4
Rathbun Lake, U.S.A., **420** G5
Rathdowney, Ireland, **309** E5
Rathdrum, Ireland, **309** F5
Rathenow, Germany, **288** F2
Rathfriland, Northern Ireland, U.K., **309** F3
Rathkeale, Ireland, **309** D5
Rathlin Island, Northern Ireland, U.K., **309** F2
Rathvilly, Ireland, **309** F5
Rathwell, Canada, **414** E7
Rätische Alpen, *mountain range*, Switzerland, **291** J3
Ratlām, India, **218** C5
Ratnāgiri, India, **216** C2
Ratne, Ukraine, **289** M3
Ratodero, Pakistan, **218** B4
Raton, U.S.A., **423** L3
Rättvik, Sweden, **286** G2
Ratz, Mount, *mountain peak*, Canada, **412** C3
Raub, Malaysia, **200** C2
Raub, U.S.A., **420** B2
Rauch, Argentina, **459** E5
Raufarhöfn, Iceland, **284** Z6
Raukumara Range, *mountain range*, New Zealand, **132** F4
Rauland, Norway, **286** D3
Rauma, Finland, **287** K2
Rauma, *river*, Norway, **286** D1
Raunds, England, U.K., **305** G2
Raung, Gunung, *mountain peak*, Indonesia, **201** F5
Raurkela, India, **219** F5
Răut, *river*, Moldova, **296** G2
Rautavaara, Finland, **285** P5
Rautjärvi, Finland, **287** P2
Rava-Rus'ka, Ukraine, **289** L3
Ravalli, U.S.A., **418** G3
Rāvar, Iran, **221** G2
Ravelo, Bolivia, **455** F5
Ravendale, U.S.A., **422** C1
Ravenglass, England, U.K., **306** E3
Ravenna, Italy, **294** D3
Ravensburg, Germany, **288** D5
Ravenshoe, Australia, **135** K2
Ravensthorpe, Australia, **134** E5
Ravenswood, U.S.A., **421** N6
Rāvi, *river*, India/Pakistan, **218** C3
Rawa Mazowiecka, Poland, **289** K3
Rawaki (Phoenix), *island*, Kiribati, **139** G5
Rāwalpindi, Pakistan, **218** C2
Rawāndūz, Iraq, **363** H1
Rawarra, *river*, Indonesia, **199** F3
Rawas, Indonesia, **199** F3
Rāwatsār, India, **218** C3
Rawḩah, Saudi Arabia, **363** H5
Rawicz, Poland, **289** H3
Rawlins, U.S.A., **419** L6
Rawson, Argentina, **460** E2
Rawtenstall, England, U.K., **306** F4
Rawu, China, **215** F3
Ray, Cape, Canada, **417** M6
Ray, U.S.A., **420** B1
Raya, Gunung, *mountain peak*, Indonesia, **201** F3
Raya, Tanjong, *point*, Aceh, Indonesia, **200** B2
Raya, Tanjong, *point*, Sumatera Selatan, Indonesia, **200** D3
Raychikhinsk, Russian Federation, **211** K2
Raydah, Yemen, **220** D5
Rayleigh, England, U.K., **305** H3
Raymond, Canada, **413** N7
Raymond, U.S.A., **418** C3
Raymondville, U.S.A., **424** D6
Raymore, Canada, **414** B6
Raynesford, U.S.A., **419** J3
Rayong, Thailand, **202** D3
Raystown Lake, U.S.A., **426** A4
Raz, Pointe du, *point*, France, **290** B3
Ražanj, Yugoslavia, **296** C4
Razelm, Lacul, *lake*, Romania, **296** G3
Razgrad, Bulgaria, **296** F4
Razim, Lacul, *lagoon*, Romania, **298** C4
Razlog, Bulgaria, **296** D5
Razmak, Pakistan, **218** B2
Ré, Île de, *island*, France, **290** D3
Reading, England, U.K., **305** G3
Reading, U.S.A., **426** C4
Reading, *unitary authority*, England, U.K., **305** G3
Readstown, U.S.A., **420** H4
Real, Cordillera, *mountain range*, Bolivia, **455** E4
Realicó, Argentina, **458** D5
Reao, *island*, French Polynesia, **137** H2
Rebbenesøy, *island*, Norway, **284** H1
Rebecca, Lake, Australia, **134** E5
Reboly, Russian Federation, **285** Q5
Rebordelo, Portugal, **292** D2
Rebun-tō, *island*, Japan, **209** H1
Recess, Ireland, **309** C4
Rechane, Russian Federation, **299** C4
Recherche, Archipelago of, *islands*, Australia, **134** E5
Recife, Brazil, **453** G5
Recife, Cape, South Africa, **371** E5
Récifs, Île aux, *island*, Seychelles, **373** A2
Recinto, Chile, **458** B5
Recklinghausen, Germany, **288** C3
Reconquista, Argentina, **459** E3
Recreio, Brazil, **455** G2
Recreo, Argentina, **458** D3
Red, *river*, Minnesota, U.S.A., **420** E2
Red, *river*, Oklahoma, U.S.A., **424** C2
Red Bank, New Jersey, U.S.A., **426** C4
Red Bank, Tennessee, U.S.A., **425** K2
Red Bay, Canada, **417** N4
Red Bluff, U.S.A., **422** B1
Red Cloud, U.S.A., **420** D5
Red Deer, Canada, **413** N5
Red Deer, *river*, Alberta, Canada, **413** N6
Red Deer, *river*, Saskatchewan, Canada, **414** C5
Red Deer Lake, Canada, **414** D5
Red Elm, U.S.A., **420** C3
Red Indian Lake, Canada, **417** N5
Red Lake, Canada, **414** H6
Red Lake Road, Canada, **414** H7
Red Lodge, U.S.A., **419** K4
Red Rock, British Columbia, Canada, **412** H5
Red Rock, Ontario, Canada, **421** J1
Red Sea, Africa/Asia, **220** C4
Red Sucker Lake, Canada, **414** G4
Red Wing, U.S.A., **420** G3
Redang, Pulau, *island*, Malaysia, **200** C1
Redbird, U.S.A., **419** M5
Redcar, England, U.K., **307** G3
Redcar and Cleveland, *unitary authority*, England, U.K., **307** G3
Redcliff, Canada, **413** P6
Redcliff, Zimbabwe, **371** E2
Redding, California, U.S.A., **422** B1
Redding, Iowa, U.S.A., **420** F5
Redditch, England, U.K., **305** F2
Redditt, Canada, **414** G7
Rede, *river*, England, U.K., **306** F2

Riobamba, Ecuador, **450** B4
Ríohacha, Colombia, **450** D1
Rioja, Peru, **454** C2
Riom, France, **291** F4
Ríosucio, Colombia, **450** C2
Ripanj, Yugoslavia, **296** C3
Ripley, England, U.K., **307** G3
Ripley, Tennessee, U.S.A., **425** H2
Ripley, West Virginia, U.S.A., **421** N6
Ripoll, Spain, **293** J1
Ripon, England, U.K., **307** G3
Ripon, U.S.A., **421** J4
Risan, Yugoslavia, **296** B4
Risbäck, Sweden, **284** G4
Risca, Wales, U.K., **304** D3
Riscle, France, **290** D5
Rishīkesh, India, **218** D3
Rishiri-tō, *island*, Japan, **209** H1
Rishon LeẒiyyon, Israel, **225** C4
Risør, Norway, **286** D3
Risøyhamn, Norway, **284** G2
Rissa, Norway, **284** E5
Risti, Estonia, **287** M3
Ristiina, Finland, **287** N2
Ristijärvi, Finland, **285** P4
Ristna, Estonia, **287** L3
Ritter, Mount, *mountain peak*, U.S.A., **422** D3
Ritzville, U.S.A., **418** E3
Riva del Garda, Italy, **294** C3
Rivadavia, Buenos Aires, Argentina, **458** D5
Rivadavia, Chile, **458** B3
Rivadavia, Mendoza, Argentina, **458** C4
Rivadavia, Salta, Argentina, **458** D2
Rivarolo Canavese, Italy, **294** A3
Rivas, Nicaragua, **428** D5
River Cess, Liberia, **364** C3
Rivera, Argentina, **458** D5
Rivera, Uruguay, **459** F4
Rivergaro, Italy, **294** B3
Riverhead, U.S.A., **426** D4
Rivers, *state*, Nigeria, **365** F4
Rivers Inlet, Canada, **410** G4
Riversdale, North Island, New Zealand, **133** F5
Riversdale, South Island, New Zealand, **133** B7
Riverside, California, U.S.A., **422** E5
Riverside, Washington, U.S.A., **418** E2
Riverton, New Zealand, **133** B8
Riverton, U.S.A., **419** K5
Riviera, U.S.A., **424** D6
Rivière-aux-Rats, Canada, **416** E6
Rivière-du-Loup, Canada, **416** G6
Rivière du Rempart, Mauritius, **373** C1
Rivière-Matawin, Canada, **416** E6
Rivière-Pentecôte, Canada, **416** H5
Rivière-St-Jean, Canada, **417** J4
Rivière-St-Paul, Canada, **417** N4
Rivne, Ukraine, **298** C2
Rivoli, Italy, **294** A3
Rivùngo, Angola, **368** D6
Riyadh *see* Ar Riyāḑ, Saudi Arabia, **220** E4
Rizhao, China, **206** D1
Rizokarpaso, Cyprus, **225** C2
Rizzuto, Capo, *cape*, Italy, **295** F6
Rjukan, Norway, **286** D3
Roa, Punta, *point*, Isla de Pascua (Easter Island), Chile, **461** B2
Road Town, U.K. Virgin Islands, **427** C2
Roade, England, U.K., **305** G2
Roag, Loch, *inlet*, Scotland, U.K., **308** B2
Roan Plateau, U.S.A., **423** H2
Roanne, France, **291** G3
Roanoke, Alabama, U.S.A., **425** K3
Roanoke, Virginia, U.S.A., **421** P7
Roanoke Rapids, U.S.A., **426** B6
Roaringwater Bay, Ireland, **309** C6
Roatán, Honduras, **428** D3
Robbins Island, Australia, **135** K7
Robē, Ethiopia, **367** E3
Röbel, Germany, **288** F2
Roberta, U.S.A., **425** K3
Roberts Butte, *mountain peak*, Antarctica, **470** E8
Roberts Creek Mountain, *mountain peak*, U.S.A., **422** E1
Robertsfors, Sweden, **284** K4
Robertsganj, India, **219** E4
Robertsport, Liberia, **364** B3
Roberval, Canada, **416** E5
Robin Hood's Bay, England, U.K., **307** H3
Robinson, Canada, **412** B1
Róbinson Crusoe, *island*, Archipiélago Juan Fernández, Chile, Pacific Ocean, **461** C2
Robinvale, Australia, **135** J5
Roblin, Canada, **414** D6
Robooksibia, Indonesia, **199** F3
Roboré, Bolivia, **455** G5
Robsart, Canada, **413** Q7
Robson, Mount, *mountain peak*, Canada, **413** K5
Robstown, U.S.A., **424** D6
Roca Partida, Punta, *point*, Mexico, **431** G5
Rocafuerte, Ecuador, **450** B4
Rocha, Uruguay, **459** F5
Rochdale, England, U.K., **306** F4
Rochechouart, France, **290** E4
Rochedo, Brazil, **456** B5
Rochefort, France, **290** D4
Rochegda, Russian Federation, **300** F3
Rochelle, U.S.A., **425** L4
Rochester, Canada, **413** N4
Rochester, England, U.K., **305** H3
Rochester, Indiana, U.S.A., **421** K5
Rochester, Minnesota, U.S.A., **420** G3
Rochester, New Hampshire, U.S.A., **426** E3
Rochester, New York, U.S.A., **426** B3
Rochford, England, U.K., **305** H3
Rock Hill, U.S.A., **425** M2
Rock Point, U.S.A., **423** J3
Rock Rapids, U.S.A., **420** E4
Rock River, U.S.A., **419** M6
Rock Sound, Bahamas, **428** G1
Rock Springs, Montana, U.S.A., **419** L3
Rock Springs, Wyoming, U.S.A., **419** K6
Rockall, *island*, U.K., **282** C4
Rockford, U.S.A., **421** J4
Rockglen, Canada, **413** S7
Rockham, U.S.A., **420** D3
Rockhampton, Australia, **135** L3
Rockingham, Australia, **134** D5
Rockingham, England, U.K., **305** G2
Rockingham, U.S.A., **425** N2
Rockingham Forest, England, U.K., **305** G2
Rockland, Idaho, U.S.A., **418** H5
Rockland, Maine, U.S.A., **426** F2
Rockport, Texas, U.S.A., **424** D5
Rockport, Washington, U.S.A., **418** D2
Rocksprings, U.S.A., **424** B5
Rockwell City, U.S.A., **420** F4
Rocky Ford, U.S.A., **423** M2
Rocky Harbour, Canada, **417** N5
Rocky Island Lake, Canada, **421** M2
Rocky Mount, U.S.A., **426** B7
Rocky Mountain House, Canada, **413** M5
Rocky Mountains, *mountain range*, Canada/U.S.A., **406** M3
Rocky Point, Namibia, **370** B2
Rockypoint, U.S.A., **419** M4
Rocoso, Cayo, *island*, San Andrés, Colombia, **461** B1
Rødby, Denmark, **286** E5
Rødding, Denmark, **286** D5
Rodel, Scotland, U.K., **308** C3
Roden, *river*, England, U.K., **304** E2
Rodeo, Argentina, **458** C4
Rodeo, Mexico, **430** D3
Rodez, France, **290** F4
Roding, Germany, **288** F4
Rodino, Russian Federation, **223** L2
Rodna, Romania, **296** E2
Rodnya, Belarus, **299** D6
Rodolivos, Greece, **297** D5
Rodonit, Kepi i, *cape*, Albania, **297** B5
Rodopi Planina, *mountain range*, Bulgaria, **296** E4
Rodos, Greece, **297** G7
Rodos (Rhodes), *island*, Dodekanisos, Greece, **297** G7
Rodrigues, *island*, Mauritius, **373** B1
Rødvig, Denmark, **286** F5
Roebourne, Australia, **134** D3
Roebuck Bay, Australia, **134** E2
Roeselare, Belgium, **288** A3
Rogaguado, Lago, *lake*, Bolivia, **455** E3
Rogaland, *county*, Norway, **286** B3
Rogatica, Bosnia and Herzegovina, **294** G4
Rogen, *lake*, Sweden, **286** F1
Rogers, U.S.A., **424** E1
Rogers City, U.S.A., **421** M3
Rogerson, U.S.A., **418** G5
Roggewain, Cabo, *cape*, Isla de Pascua (Easter Island), Chile, **461** B2
Rogliano, Corse, France, **294** B4
Rogliano, Italy, **295** F6
Rognan, Norway, **284** G3
Rogne, Norway, **286** D2
Rohat, India, **218** C4
Rohatyn, Ukraine, **289** M4
Rohri, Pakistan, **218** B4
Rohtak, India, **218** D3
Rohuküla, Estonia, **287** L3
Roi Et, Thailand, **203** D2
Roing, India, **219** H3
Roja, Latvia, **287** L4
Rojas, Argentina, **458** E5
Rojhān, Pakistan, **218** B3
Rojo, Cabo, *cape*, Mexico, **431** F4
Rokan, *river*, Indonesia, **200** C2
Rokhmoyva, Gora, *mountain peak*, Russian Federation, **285** P3
Rokiškis, Lithuania, **287** M5
Rokkasho, Japan, **209** H2
Rola Co, *lake*, China, **214** D2
Rolândia, Brazil, **459** G2
Rôlas, Ilhéu das, *island*, São Tomé and Príncipe, **373** C4
Røldal, Norway, **286** C3
Roll, U.S.A., **424** C2
Rolla, Missouri, U.S.A., **420** H7
Rolla, North Dakota, U.S.A., **420** D1
Rollag, Norway, **286** D2
Rolleston, Mount, *mountain peak*, New Zealand, **133** C6
Rollet, Canada, **416** B6
Rolvsøya, *island*, Norway, **285** L1
Roma, Australia, **135** K4
Roma, Lesotho, **371** E4
Roma (Rome), Italy, **295** D5
Roma, Sweden, **287** J4
Roma, U.S.A., **424** C6
Romaine, *river*, Canada, **417** K4
Roman, Romania, **296** F2
Roman-Kosh, Hora, *mountain peak*, Ukraine, **298** D4
Romanche Fracture Zone, *tectonic feature*, Atlantic Ocean, **477** E5
Romania, *country*, Europe, **282** G6
Romano, Cape, U.S.A., **425** L7
Romano, Cayo, *island*, Cuba, **429** F2
Romanovka, Russian Federation, **210** F1
Rombebai, Danau, *lake*, Indonesia, **199** G3
Romblon, Philippines, **204** C3
Rome, Alabama, U.S.A., **425** J4
Rome, New York, U.S.A., **426** C3
Rome, Oregon, U.S.A., **418** F5
Rome *see* Roma, Italy, **295** D5
Romney, U.S.A., **421** P6
Romny, Russian Federation, **211** K2
Romny, Ukraine, **298** D2
Rømø, *island*, Denmark, **286** D5
Rompin, *river*, Malaysia, **200** C2
Romsey, England, U.K., **305** F3
Romuli, Romania, **296** E2
Ron Phibun, Thailand, **202** C4
Ronan, U.S.A., **418** G3
Ronas Hill, Shetland, Scotland, U.K., **308** K7
Roncador, Serra do, *mountain range*, Brazil, **456** C4
Ronda, Serrania de, *mountain range*, Spain, **292** E4
Ronda, Spain, **292** E4
Rønde, Denmark, **286** E4
Rondon do Pará, Brazil, **452** D4
Rondônia, *state*, Brazil, **455** F3
Rondonópolis, Brazil, **456** B4
Rondslottet, *mountain peak*, Norway, **286** D2
Rông, Kaôh, *island*, Cambodia, **202** D4
Rong, *river*, China, **206** B3
Rong Xian, China, **206** B4
Rong'an, China, **206** B3
Rongbaca, China, **215** F3
Rongcheng, China, **211** H5
Ronge, Lac la, *lake*, Canada, **413** S4
Rongelap, *island*, Marshall Islands, **138** E3
Rongjiang, China, **206** B3
Rongklang, *mountain range*, Myanmar, **205** B3
Rongqi, China, **207** A3
Rongxar, China, **214** C3
Rønne, Denmark, **286** G5
Ronne Entrance, *strait*, Antarctica, **470** B5
Ronne Ice Shelf, Antarctica, **470** C5
Ronneby, Sweden, **286** G4
Rønnede, Denmark, **286** F5
Rönnöfors, Sweden, **284** F5
Ronuro, *river*, Brazil, **456** B3
Rookery Point, Tristan da Cunha, **373** C2
Roorkee, India, **218** D3
Roosendaal, Netherlands, **288** B3
Roosevelt, Arizona, U.S.A., **423** H5
Roosevelt, Mount, *mountain peak*, Canada, **412** G2
Roosevelt, Utah, U.S.A., **423** J1
Roosevelt Island, Antarctica, **470** D7
Ropeid, Norway, **286** C3
Roper, *river*, Australia, **134** G1
Roper Bar, Australia, **135** G1
Ropi, *mountain peak*, Finland, **284** K2
Roquefort, France, **290** D4
Roraima, Monte, *mountain peak*, Guyana, **451** G3
Roraima, *state*, Brazil, **451** G4
Røros, Norway, **286** E1
Rørvik, Norway, **284** E4
Ros', Belarus, **289** M2
Rosa, Cabo, *cape*, Islas Galápagos (Galapagos Islands), Ecuador, **461** A2
Rosa, Monte, *mountain peak*, Italy, **294** A3
Rosa, Punta, *point*, Mexico, **430** C3
Rosa de los James, Islas Canarias, Spain, **373** B4
Rosa Zárate, Ecuador, **450** B4
Rosal de la Frontera, Spain, **292** D4
Rosalia, Punta, *point*, Isla de Pascua (Easter Island), Chile, **461** B2
Rosalia, U.S.A., **418** F3
Rosana, Brazil, **459** G2
Rosantos, Punta, *point*, Mexico, **430** C3
Rosario, Argentina, **458** E4
Rosário, Brazil, **453** E4
Rosario, Cayo del, *island*, Cuba, **429** E2
Rosario, Paraguay, **459** F2
Rosario, Sinaloa, Mexico, **430** D4
Rosario, Sonora, Mexico, **430** C3
Rosario, Venezuela, **450** D1
Rosario de la Frontera, Argentina, **458** D2
Rosario de Lerma, Argentina, **458** D2
Rosario del Tala, Argentina, **459** E4
Rosário do Sul, Brazil, **459** F4
Rosário Oeste, Brazil, **456** B4
Rosarito, Baja California, Mexico, **430** B2
Rosarito, Baja California Sur, Mexico, **430** C3
Roscoe, New York, U.S.A., **426** C4
Roscoe, South Dakota, U.S.A., **420** D3
Roscoff, France, **290** C2
Roscommon, *county*, Ireland, **309** D4
Roscommon, Ireland, **309** D4
Roscrea, Ireland, **309** E5
Rose, *island*, American Samoa, **139** H6
Rose, U.S.A., **424** E1
Rose Belle, Mauritius, **373** C1
Rose Blanche, Canada, **417** M6
Rose Peak, *mountain peak*, U.S.A., **423** J5
Rose Prairie, Canada, **412** J3
Rose Valley, Canada, **414** C5
Roseau, Dominica, **427** D3
Roseau, U.S.A., **420** F1
Rosebud, Canada, **413** N6
Roseburg, U.S.A., **418** C5
Rosedale Abbey, England, U.K., **307** H3
Rosehearty, Scotland, U.K., **308** G3
Rosemarkie, Scotland, U.K., **308** E3
Rosemary, Canada, **413** N6
Rosenberg, U.S.A., **424** E5
Rosendal, Norway, **286** C3
Rosenheim, Germany, **288** F5
Roses, Golfo de, *gulf*, Spain, **293** J1
Roseto degli Abruzzi, Italy, **294** D4
Rosetown, Canada, **413** Q6
Roseville, U.S.A., **420** H5
Rosh Pinah, Namibia, **370** C4
Rosières-en-Santerre, France, **305** K5
Rosignol, Guyana, **451** H2
Roșiorii de Vede, Romania, **296** E3
Rositsa, Bulgaria, **296** F4
Roskilde, Denmark, **286** F5
Roslavl', Russian Federation, **299** D6
Ross, Mount, *mountain peak*, New Zealand, **133** E5
Ross, New Zealand, **133** C6
Ross, Point, Norfolk Island, **135** T13
Ross, U.S.A., **420** B1

Ross Bay Junction, Canada, **416** H3
Ross Carbery, Ireland, **309** C6
Ross Hill, *mountain peak*, Christmas Island, **134** N8
Ross Ice Shelf, Antarctica, **470** D6
Ross Island, Antarctica, **470** D7
Ross-on-Wye, England, U.K., **304** E3
Ross River, Canada, **410** F3
Ross Sea, Antarctica, **470** C7
Rossan Point, Ireland, **309** C3
Rossano, Italy, **295** F6
Rossel Island, Papua New Guinea, **140** D5
Rossignol, Lake, Canada, **416** J7
Rossington, England, U.K., **307** G4
Rosslare, Ireland, **309** F5
Rosslare Harbour, Ireland, **309** F5
Rosso, Mauritania, **364** A1
Rossosh', Russian Federation, **298** E4
Rosston, U.S.A., **420** D7
Røssvatnet, *lake*, Norway, **284** F4
Rostāq, Afganistan, **218** B1
Rosthern, Canada, **413** R5
Rostock, Germany, **288** F1
Rostov, Russian Federation, **299** G4
Rostov-na-Donu, Russian Federation, **222** B3
Rostovskaya Oblast', *province*, Russian Federation, **222** B3
Røsvik, Norway, **284** G3
Roswell, Georgia, U.S.A., **425** K2
Roswell, New Mexico, U.S.A., **423** L5
Rota, *island*, Northern Mariana Islands, **138** C3
Rotenburg (Wümme), Germany, **288** D2
Rothbury, England, U.K., **307** G2
Rothbury Forest, England, U.K., **307** G2
Rothenburg ob der Tauber, Germany, **288** E4
Rothera, *U.K. research station*, Antarctica, **470** A4
Rotherham, England, U.K., **307** G4
Rothes, Scotland, U.K., **308** F3
Rothesay, Scotland, U.K., **308** D5
Rothwell, England, U.K., **305** G2
Roti, *island*, Indonesia, **198** C5
Roti, Selat, *strait*, Indonesia, **198** C5
Rotokohu, New Zealand, **133** C5
Rotomanu, New Zealand, **133** C6
Rotondella, Italy, **295** F5
Rotondo, Monte, *mountain peak*, Corse, France, **295** B4
Rotorua, Lake, New Zealand, **132** F3
Rotorua, New Zealand, **132** F4
Rott, *river*, Germany, **288** F4
Rotterdam, Netherlands, **288** B3
Rottweil, Germany, **288** D4
Rotuma, *island*, Fiji, **139** F6
Roubaix, France, **291** F1
Rouen, France, **290** E2
Rouge, Le Piton, *mountain peak*, Réunion, **373** A1
Rouge, Pointe, *point*, Réunion, **373** A1
Rough River Lake, U.S.A., **421** K7
Rouleau, Canada, **413** S6
Round Island, Mauritius, **373** C1
Round Mountain, *mountain peak*, Australia, **135** L5
Round Mountain, U.S.A., **422** C1
Round Rock, Arizona, U.S.A., **423** J3

Round Rock, Texas, U.S.A., **424** D4
Roundup, U.S.A., **419** K3
Roura, French Guiana, **452** C2
Rous, Península, Chile, **460** D5
Rousay, *island*, Orkney, Scotland, U.K., **308** F1
Rouyn-Noranda, Canada, **416** B5
Rovaniemi, Finland, **285** M3
Rovereto, Italy, **294** C3
Roverud, Norway, **286** F2
Rovigo, Italy, **294** C3
Rovinari, Romania, **296** D3
Rovinj, Croatia, **294** D3
Rovkuly, Russian Federation, **285** Q4
Rovuma, *river*, Mozambique/ Tanzania, **369** G5
Roxas, Palawan Island, Philippines, **204** B4
Roxas, Panay Island, Philippines, **204** C4
Roxborough, Tobago, Trinidad and Tobago, **461** B4
Roxby Downs, Australia, **135** H5
Roy, Montana, U.S.A., **419** K3
Roy, New Mexico, U.S.A., **423** L4
Royal Leamington Spa, England, U.K., **305** F2
Royal Tunbridge Wells, England, U.K., **305** H3
Royale, Isle, *island*, U.S.A., **421** J2
Royalton, U.S.A., **426** D3
Royalty, U.S.A., **423** M6
Royan, France, **290** D4
Roybridge, Scotland, U.K., **308** E4
Roye, France, **291** F2
Royston, England, U.K., **305** G2
Royston, U.S.A., **425** L2
Rožaj, Yugoslavia, **296** C4
Różan, Poland, **289** K2
Rozdil'na, Ukraine, **296** H2
Rozhniv, Ukraine, **296** E1
Rožňava, Slovakia, **289** K4
Roznov, Romania, **296** F2
Rrëshen, Albania, **296** B5
Rtishchevo, Russian Federation, **222** C2
Ružomberok, Slovakia, **289** J4
Ruabon, Wales, U.K., **304** D2
Ruacana, Namibia, **370** B2
Ruahine, New Zealand, **132** E4
Ruahine Range, *mountain range*, New Zealand, **132** F5
Ruakaka, New Zealand, **132** E2
Ruapehu, Mount, *mountain peak*, New Zealand, **129** G5
Ruapuke Island, New Zealand, **133** B8
Ruatahuna, New Zealand, **132** F4
Ruawai, New Zealand, **132** E3
Ruba, Belarus, **299** C5
Rubi, Democratic Republic of the Congo, **369** E2
Rubio, *mountain peak*, Spain, **293** F2
Rubtsovsk, Russian Federation, **223** L2
Ruby, U.S.A., **410** D3
Ruby Mountains, *mountain range*, U.S.A., **422** F1
Rucăr, Romania, **296** E3
Rucava, Latvia, **287** K4
Rucheng, China, **206** C3
Rūdbār, Afghanistan, **221** H2
Rudewa, Tanzania, **369** F5
Rudkøbing, Denmark, **286** E5
Rudky, Ukraine, **289** L4
Rudna Glava, Yugoslavia, **296** D3
Rudnaya Pristan', Russian Federation, **209** F1
Rudnya, Russian Federation, **299** C5
Rudnytsya, Ukraine, **296** G1
Rūdnyy, Kazakhstan, **222** G2
Rudo, Bosnia and Herzegovina, **296** B4

Rudong, China, **206** E1
Rue, France, **305** J4
Rufā'ah, Sudan, **366** D2
Ruffec, France, **290** E3
Rufiji, *river*, Tanzania, **369** G4
Rufino, Argentina, **458** D5
Rufisque, Senegal, **364** A2
Rufrufua, Indonesia, **199** F3
Rufunsa, Zambia, **369** E6
Rugāji, Latvia, **287** N4
Rugao, China, **206** E1
Rugby, England, U.K., **305** F2
Rugby, U.S.A., **420** D1
Rugeley, England, U.K., **305** F2
Rugozero, Russian Federation, **285** R4
Ruguy, Russian Federation, **299** D3
Ruhengeri, Rwanda, **369** E3
Ruhnu, *island*, Estonia, **287** L4
Ruhu, China, **207** C2
Rui'an, China, **206** E3
Ruichang, China, **206** C2
Ruidosa, U.S.A., **423** L7
Ruidoso, U.S.A., **423** L5
Ruijin, China, **206** D3
Ruili, China, **215** F4
Ruivo de Santana, Pico, *mountain peak*, Madeira, Portugal, **373** C3
Ruiz, Mexico, **430** D4
Ruiz, Nevado del, *mountain peak*, Colombia, **450** C3
Rūjiena, Latvia, **287** M4
Ruka, Finland, **285** P2
Rukki, river, Democratic Republic of the Congo, **368** C3
Rukungiri, Uganda, **369** E3
Rukwa, *administrative region*, Tanzania, **369** F4
Rukwa, Lake, Tanzania, **369** F4
Rum Cay, *island*, Bahamas, **428** G2
Ruma, Yugoslavia, **296** B3
Rumah Kulit, Malaysia, **201** F2
Rumbek, Sudan, **366** C3
Rumberpon, Pulau, *island*, Indonesia, **199** F3
Rumginae, Papua New Guinea, **140** A4
Rumney, Wales, U.K., **304** D3
Rumoi, Japan, **209** H2
Rumonge, Burundi, **369** E3
Rumphi, Malawi, **369** F5
Runan, China, **206** C1
Runaway, Cape, New Zealand, **132** F3
Runcorn, England, U.K., **306** F4
Rundu, Namibia, **370** C2
Rungu, Democratic Republic of the Congo, **369** E2
Rungwa, Tanzania, **369** F4
Ru'nying, China, **215** G2
Ruo, *river*, China, **213** H4
Ruokolahti, Finland, **287** P2
Ruokto, Sweden, **284** J3
Ruoqiang, China, **212** F5
Ruovesi, Finland, **287** M1
Rupanco, Lago, *lake*, Chile, **460** C1
Rupat, Pulau, *island*, Indonesia, **200** C2
Rupea, Romania, **296** E2
Rupert, Baie de, *bay*, Canada, **415** Q6
Rupert, Rivière de, *river*, Canada, **416** C4
Rupia, Tanzania, **369** G4
Ruppert Coast, *region*, Antarctica, **470** C7
Rupununi, *river*, Guyana, **451** G3
Rurrenabaque, Bolivia, **455** E4
Rurutu, *island*, French Polynesia, **137** F3
Rusape, Zimbabwe, **371** F2
Ruscova, Romania, **296** E2
Ruse, *administrative region*, Bulgaria, **296** F4
Ruse, Bulgaria, **296** F4
Rusele, Sweden, **284** J4
Rush, Ireland, **309** F4

Rushan, China, **211** H5
Rushden, England, U.K., **305** G2
Rushville, U.S.A., **420** H5
Ruskeala, Russian Federation, **299** C2
Ruskträsk, Sweden, **284** J4
Rusnė, Lithuania, **287** K5
Ruso, U.S.A., **420** C2
Rusokastro, Bulgaria, **296** F4
Russas, Brazil, **453** G4
Russell, Canada, **414** D6
Russell, U.S.A., **420** D6
Russell Islands, Solomon Islands, **141** A1
Russell Lake, Canada, **414** D3
Russellville, Alabama, U.S.A., **425** J2
Russellville, Arkansas, U.S.A., **424** F2
Russellville, Kentucky, U.S.A., **421** K7
Russian Federation, *country*, Asia/Europe, **196** J3
Rustefjelbma, Norway, **285** P1
Rustenburg, South Africa, **371** E4
Rustic, U.S.A., **423** L1
Ruston, U.S.A., **424** F3
Ruten, *mountain peak*, Norway, **286** D2
Ruteng, Indonesia, **198** C5
Ruth, U.S.A., **422** F2
Rutherfordton, U.S.A., **425** M2
Ruthin, Wales, U.K., **304** D1
Rutland, U.S.A., **426** D3
Rutland, *unitary authority*, England, U.K., **305** G2
Rutland, Andaman and Nicobar Islands, India, **217** H4
Ruukki, Finland, **285** M4
Ruvuma, *administrative region*, Tanzania, **369** G5
Ruwāq, Jabal ar, *mountain range*, Syria, **225** D3
Ruwenzori Range, *mountain range*, Uganda, **369** F2
Ruza, *river*, Russian Federation, **299** E5
Ruza, Russian Federation, **299** F5
Ruzayevka, Russian Federation, **222** C2
Ruzhany, Belarus, **289** M2
Ruzizi, *river*, Burundi/Rwanda/ Democratic Republic of the Congo, **369** E3
Rwanda, *country*, Africa, **359** J7
Ry, Denmark, **286** D4
Ryall, Mount, *mountain peak*, New Zealand, **133** C6
Ryanzanskaya Oblast', *province*, Russian Federation, **222** C2
Ryasnopil', Ukraine, **296** H2
Ryazan', Russian Federation, **298** E2
Ryazanskaya Oblast', *province*, Russian Federation, **298** E2
Rybachiy, Poluostrov, *peninsula*, Russian Federation, **285** R2
Rybinsk (Andropov), Russian Federation, **299** G3
Rybinskoye Vodokhranilishche, *reservoir*, Russian Federation, **299** G3
Rybnik, Poland, **289** J3
Rybreka, Russian Federation, **299** D2
Rychwał, Poland, **289** J2
Rycroft, Canada, **413** K4
Ryd, Sweden, **286** G4
Ryde, England, U.K., **305** F4
Rye, Australia, **135** J6
Rye, England, U.K., **305** H4
Rye, *river*, England, U.K., **307** G3
Rye Bay, England, U.K., **305** H4
Ryegate, U.S.A., **419** K3
Rykhta, Ukraine, **296** F1
Ryki, Poland, **289** K3
Ryley, Canada, **413** N5
Rynda, *river*, Russian

Federation, **285** T2
Rynda, Russian Federation, **285** T2
Ryōtsu, Japan, **209** G3
Rypin, Poland, **289** J2
Rysy, *mountain peak*, Slovakia, **289** J4
Rytinki, Finland, **285** N4
Ryukyu Islands *see* Nansei-shotō, *islands*, Japan, **209** N8
Ryukyu Trench, *underwater feature*, Pacific Ocean, **478** C3
Rzeczenica, Poland, **289** H2
Rzepin, Poland, **289** G2
Rzeszów, Poland, **289** L3
Rzhev, Russian Federation, **299** E4

S

's-Gravenhage (The Hague), Netherlands, **288** B2
's-Hertogenbosch, Netherlands, **288** B3
Sa Đéc, Vietnam, **203** E4
Sa Dragonera, *island*, Islas Baleares, Spain, **293** J3
Sa Kaeo, Thailand, **202** D3
Saacow, Somalia, **369** H2
Sa'ādatābād, Iran, **221** G3
Saale, *river*, Germany, **288** E3
Saalfeld, Germany, **288** E3
Saâne, *river*, France, **305** H5
Saarbrücken, Germany, **288** C4
Sääre, Estonia, **287** L4
Saaremaa, *island*, Estonia, **287** K3
Saarijärvi, Finland, **287** M1
Saariselkä, Finland, **285** N2
Saarland, *state*, Germany, **288** C4
Saarlouis, Germany, **288** C4
Saasaai, Samoa, **141** B1
Saavedra, Argentina, **458** D5
Sab' Ābār, Syria, **225** D3
Saba, *island*, Netherlands Antilles, **427** D2
Šabac, Yugoslavia, **296** B3
Sabadell, Spain, **293** J2
Sabae, Japan, **209** G4
Sab'ah, Qārat as, *mountain peak*, Libya, **362** C3
Sabah, *state*, Malaysia, **201** G1
Sabalgarh, India, **218** D4
Sabana, La Gran, *grassland*, Venezuela, **451** F3
Sabana, Surinam, **452** B2
Sabanalarga, Colombia, **450** C1
Sabang, Indonesia, **200** A1
Săbăoani, Romania, **296** F2
Sabará, Brazil, **457** E5
Sabaştīyah, West Bank, **225** C3
Sab'atayn, Ramlat as, *desert*, Yemen, **220** E5
Sabaya, Bolivia, **455** E5
Sabhā, Libya, **362** B3
Sabinal, Cayo, *island*, Cuba, **429** F2
Sabinal, Mexico, **430** D2
Sabinal, U.S.A., **424** C6
Sabinas, Mexico, **431** E3
Sabinas Hidalgo, Mexico, **431** E3
Sabini, Monti, *mountain range*, Italy, **295** D4
Sablayan, Philippines, **204** C3
Sable, Cape, Canada, **416** J8
Sablé-sur-Sarthe, France, **290** D3
Saboeiro, Brazil, **453** F5
Sabonkafi, Niger, **365** F2
Sabra, Tanjong, *point*, Indonesia, **199** E3
Sabres, France, **290** D4
Sabrina Coast, *region*, Antarctica, **470** F7
Sabsevār, Iran, **222** F5
Şabyā, Saudi Arabia, **363** H5

St Simons Island, U.S.A., **425** M4
St Stephen, Canada, **416** H7
St Stephen, U.S.A., **425** N3
St Theresa Point, Canada, **414** G5
St Thomas, Canada, **421** N4
St Thomas, U.S.A., **420** E1
Saint-Tropez, France, **291** H5
Saint-Vaast-la-Hougue, France, **290** D2
Saint-Valéry-en-Caux, France, **290** E2
Saint-Valéry-sur-Somme, France, **290** E1
Saint-Vallier, France, **291** G3
St Vincent, Gulf, Australia, **135** H5
St Vincent and the Grenadines, *country*, Caribbean Sea, **409** S7
St Vincent Passage, Caribbean Sea, **427** D3
Saint-Vivien-de-Médoc, France, **290** D4
St Walburg, Canada, **413** Q5
St Xavier, U.S.A., **419** L4
Saint-Yrieix-la-Perche, France, **290** E4
Sainte-Adresse, France, **305** H5
Sainte-Anne, Lac, *lake*, Canada, **416** H4
Ste-Agathe-des-Monts, Canada, **416** D6
Sainte-Énimie, France, **291** F4
Sainte-Marie, Martinique, **427** D3
Sainte-Marie, Réunion, **373** A1
Sainte-Mère-Église, France, **305** F5
Sainte-Rose, Guadeloupe, **427** D2
Sainte-Rose, Réunion, **373** A1
Ste-Rose-du-Lac, Canada, **414** E6
Sainte-Suzanne, Réunion, **373** A1
Saintes, France, **290** D4
Saintes-Maries-de-la-Mer, France, **291** G5
Saintfield, Northern Ireland, U.K., **309** G3
Sāipal, *mountain peak*, Nepal, **219** E3
Saipan, *island*, Northern Mariana Islands, **138** C3
Saipan, Northern Mariana Islands, **138** C3
Sajam, Indonesia, **199** F3
Sajama, Bolivia, **455** E5
Sajama, Nevado, *mountain peak*, Bolivia, **455** E5
Sājir, Ra's, *cape*, Oman, **220** F5
Sājūr, *river*, Syria/Turkey, **225** D1
Saka, Ethiopia, **367** E3
Sakākah, Saudi Arabia, **363** H3
Sakakawea, Lake, U.S.A., **420** C2
Sakami, Lac, *lake*, Canada, **416** C3
Sakami, *river*, Canada, **416** D3
Sakaraha, Madagascar, **372** A5
Sakassou, Côte d'Ivoire, **364** C3
Sakata, Japan, **209** G3
Saketa, Indonesia, **198** D3
Sakété, Benin, **365** E3
Sakha, Respublika, *republic*, Russian Federation, **301** P3
Sakhalin, Ostrov, *island*, Russian Federation, **301** R4
Sakht-Sar, Iran, **222** E5
Şäki, Azerbaijan, **222** D4
Saki, Nigeria, **365** E3
Šakiai, Lithuania, **287** L5
Sakishima-shotō, *islands*, Japan, **209** M8
Sakleshpur, India, **216** C3
Sakmara, *river*, Russian Federation, **222** F2
Sakon Nakhon, Thailand, **203** E2
Sakra, Pulau, *island*, Singapore, **200** J7
Sakrivier, South Africa, **370** D5
Sakura, Japan, **209** H4
Säkylä, Finland, **287** L2
Sal, *island*, Cape Verde, **360** Q8
Sal Rei, Cape Verde, **360** Q8
Šal'a, Slovakia, **289** H4
Sala, Sweden, **286** H3
Sala y Gómez, *Chilean dependency*, Pacific Ocean, **105** P11
Salacgrīva, Latvia, **287** M4
Salada, Bahía, *bay*, Chile, **458** B3
Saladas, Argentina, **459** E3
Saladillo, Argentina, **459** E5
Saladillo, *river*, Córdoba, Argentina, **458** D4
Saladillo, *river*, Santa Fé, Argentina, **459** E4
Saladillo, *river*, Santiago del Estero, Argentina, **458** D3
Salado, *river*, Buenos Aires, Argentina, **459** E5
Salado, *river*, Formosa, Argentina, **459** E2
Salado, *river*, Mexico, **431** E3
Salado, *river*, Rio Nego, Argentina, **460** E1
Salado, *river*, Santiago del Estero, Argentina, **458** D3
Saladougou, Guinea, **364** C2
Salaga, Ghana, **364** D3
Sala'ilua, Samoa, **141** B1
Salal, Chad, **365** H2
Şalālah, Oman, **221** F5
Salālah, Sudan, **363** G4
Salamá, Guatemala, **428** C4
Salamanca, Chile, **458** B4
Salamanca, Mexico, **431** E4
Salamanca, Spain, **292** E2
Salamat, *prefecture*, Chad, **366** B2
Salamaua, Papua New Guinea, **140** B4
Salamina, Colombia, **450** C3
Salamīyah, Syria, **225** D2
Salamo, Papua New Guinea, **140** C5
Salani, Samoa, **141** B1
Salantai, Lithuania, **287** K4
Salas, Spain, **292** D1
Salas de los Infantes, Spain, **293** F1
Salatiga, Indonesia, **201** E4
Sălătrucu, Romania, **296** E3
Salau, France, **290** E5
Salavat, Russian Federation, **222** F2
Salawati, Pulau, *island*, Indonesia, **199** E3
Salāya, India, **218** B5
Salazar, Argentina, **458** D5
Salazie, Réunion, **373** A1
Salbris, France, **290** F3
Salcea, Romania, **296** F2
Šalčininkai, Lithuania, **287** M5
Salcombe, England, U.K., **304** D4
Sălcuţa, Romania, **296** D3
Salda Gölü, *lake*, Turkey, **297** G7
Saldaña, Colombia, **450** C3
Saldanha, South Africa, **370** C5
Saldungaray, Argentina, **458** E6
Saldus, Latvia, **287** L4
Sale, Australia, **135** K6
Sale, England, U.K., **306** F4
Salehurst, England, U.K., **305** H4
Salekhard, Russian Federation, **300** H3
Salelologa, Samoa, **141** B1
Salem, Illinois, U.S.A., **421** J6
Salem, India, **216** D4
Salem, Missouri, U.S.A., **420** H7
Salem, Ohio, U.S.A., **421** N5
Salem, Oregon, U.S.A., **418** C4
Salem, South Dakota, U.S.A., **420** E4
Salemi, Sicilia, Italy, **295** D7
Salen, Scotland, U.K., **308** D4
Sälen, Sweden, **286** F2
Salernes, France, **291** H5
Salerno, Golfo di, *gulf*, Italy, **295** E5
Salerno, Italy, **295** E5
Salford, England, U.K., **306** F4
Salgado, *river*, Brazil, **453** F5
Salgótarján, Hungary, **289** J4
Salgueiro, Brazil, **453** F5
Salibea, Trinidad, Trinidad and Tobago, **461** C4
Salida, U.S.A., **423** L2
Salihli, Turkey, **297** G6
Salihorsk, Belarus, **298** C2
Salima, Malawi, **369** F5
Salina, Arizona, U.S.A., **423** J3
Salina, Isola, *island*, Italy, **295** E6
Salina, Kansas, U.S.A., **420** E6
Salina, Utah, U.S.A., **423** H2
Salina Cruz, Mexico, **431** G5
Salinas, Brazil, **457** E4
Salinas, Cabo de, *cape*, Islas Baleares, Spain, **293** J3
Salinas, Ecuador, **450** B5
Salinas, Pampa de la, *plain*, Argentina, **458** C4
Salinas, Punta, *point*, Dominican Republic, **429** H3
Salinas, Punta, *point*, Róbinson Crusoe Island, Archipiélago Juan Fernández, Chile, **461** C2
Salinas, U.S.A., **422** C3
Salinas de Garci Mendoza, Bolivia, **455** E5
Salinas de Hidalgo, Mexico, **430** E4
Salinas ó Lachay, Punta, *point*, Peru, **454** B3
Salinas Peak, *mountain peak*, U.S.A., **423** K5
Saline Bay, Trinidad, Trinidad and Tobago, **461** C4
Saline Lake, U.S.A., **424** F4
Salinitas, Chile, **458** B2
Salinópolis, Brazil, **452** D3
Salisbury, England, U.K., **305** F3
Salisbury, Maryland, U.S.A., **426** C5
Salisbury, North Carolina, U.S.A., **425** M2
Salisbury Island, Canada, **411** M3
Salisbury Plain, England, U.K., **305** E3
Săliște, Romania, **296** D3
Salitre, *river*, Brazil, **457** F3
Şalkhad, Syria, **225** D3
Salla, Finland, **285** P3
Salliqueló, Argentina, **458** D5
Sallisaw, U.S.A., **424** E2
Salluit, Canada, **411** M3
Sallūm, Sudan, **363** G5
Sally's Cove, Canada, **417** N5
Salmās, Iran, **224** F5
Salmi, Russian Federation, **299** C2
Salmi, Sweden, **284** K2
Salmon, *river*, U.S.A., **418** F4
Salmon, U.S.A., **418** H4
Salmon Arm, Canada, **413** K6
Salmon Peak, *mountain peak*, U.S.A., **424** B5
Salmon River Mountains, *mountain range*, U.S.A., **418** F4
Salo, Finland, **287** L2
Saloinen, Finland, **285** M4
Salonica *see* Thessaloniki, Greece, **297** D5
Salonta, Romania, **296** C2
Salor, *river*, Spain, **292** D3
Salsacate, Argentina, **458** D4
Sal'sk, Russian Federation, **298** F3
Salso, *river*, Sicilia, Italy, **295** D7
Salsomaggiore Terme, Italy, **294** B3
Salt, *river*, U.S.A., **423** H5
Salt Basin, U.S.A., **423** L6
Salt Flat, U.S.A., **423** L6
Salt Lake City, U.S.A., **423** H1
Salta, Argentina, **458** D2
Salta, *province*, Argentina, **458** D2
Saltash, England, U.K., **304** C4
Saltburn-by-the-Sea, England, U.K., **307** H3
Saltcoats, Scotland, U.K., **308** E5
Saltee Islands, Ireland, **309** F5
Saltillo, Mexico, **431** E3
Salto, Argentina, **459** E5
Salto, *river*, Italy, **295** D4
Salto, Uruguay, **459** F4
Salto da Divisa, Brazil, **457** F4
Salto del Guairá, Paraguay, **459** F2
Salto Santiago, Represa de, *reservoir*, Brazil, **459** G2
Salton Sea, *lake*, U.S.A., **422** E5
Saltpond, Ghana, **364** D3
Saltvik, Finland, **287** K2
Saluafata, Samoa, **141** B1
Saluda, U.S.A., **425** M3
Salūm, Khalīj as, *gulf*, Egypt/Libya, **362** E2
Sālūmbar, India, **218** C4
Saluzzo, Italy, **294** A3
Salvacion, Philippines, **204** D4
Salvador, Brazil, **457** F3
Salvaterra, Brazil, **452** D3
Salvatierra, Mexico, **431** E4
Salviac, France, **290** E4
Salween, *river*, Asia, **195** L7; *see also* Nu, *river*, China, **215** F3; Thanlwin, *river*, Myanmar, **205** C4
Salyan, Azerbaijan, **222** D5
Salzburg, Austria, **288** F5
Salzburg, *state*, Austria, **288** F5
Salzgitter, Germany, **288** E2
Salzkammergut, *region*, Austria, **289** F5
Salzwedel, Germany, **288** E2
Sām, India, **218** B4
Sam A Tsuen, China, **207** C3
Sam Rayburn Reservoir, U.S.A., **424** E4
Sầm Sơn, Vietnam, **203** E2
Samagaltay, Russian Federation, **223** N2
Samaipata, Bolivia, **455** F5
Samal Island, Philippines, **204** D5
Samalaeulu, Samoa, **141** B1
Samālūţ, Egypt, **363** F3
Samaná, Bahía de, *bay*, Dominican Republic, **429** H3
Samandaği, Turkey, **225** C1
Samangān, Afghanistan, **218** B2
Samar, *island*, Philippines, **204** D4
Samara, Russian Federation, **222** E2
Samarai, Papua New Guinea, **140** C5
Samariapo, Venezuela, **451** E3
Samarinda, Indonesia, **201** G3
Samarqand, Uzbekistan, **222** H5
Sāmarrā', Iraq, **363** H2
Samarskaya Oblast', *province*, Russian Federation, **222** D2
Samasodu, Solomon Islands, **141** A1
Samastīpur, India, **219** F4
Samataitai, Samoa, **141** B1
Samatau, Samoa, **141** B1
Samba, Democratic Republic of the Congo, **369** E3
Samba Cajú, Angola, **368** C4
Sambaliung, Pegunungan, *mountain range*, Indonesia, **201** G2
Sambalpur, India, **219** F5
Sambar, Tanjong, *point*, Indonesia, **201** E3
Sambas, Indonesia, **201** E2
Sambau, Indonesia, **200** D3
Sambava, Madagascar, **372** C3
Sāmbhar, India, **218** C4
Sambir, Ukraine, **289** L4
Sambito, *river*, Brazil, **453** F5
Sambo, Angola, **368** C5
Samborombón, Bahía, *bay*, Argentina, **459** F5
Sambre, *river*, France, **291** F1
Sambro, Canada, **417** K7
Samch'ŏk, South Korea, **208** E3
Samdari, India, **218** C4
Same, Tanzania, **369** G3
Samer, France, **305** J4
Samfya, Zambia, **369** E5
Samḩah, *island*, Suquṭrá (Socotra), Yemen, **373** B2
Sami, India, **218** B5
Samia, Tanjong, *point*, Indonesia, **198** C2
Samijiyŏn, North Korea, **211** K4
Samka, Myanmar, **205** C3
Samnū, Libya, **362** B3
Samoa, *country*, Pacific Ocean, **131** H3
Samobor, Croatia, **294** E3
Şamokov, Bulgaria, **296** D4
Šamorín, Slovakia, **289** H4
Samos, Dodekanisos, Greece, **297** F7
Samos, *island*, Dodekanisos, Greece, **297** F7
Samosir, Pulau, *island*, Indonesia, **200** B2
Samothraki, *island*, Greece, **297** E5
Sampit, Indonesia, **201** F3
Sampit, *river*, Indonesia, **201** F3
Sampit, Teluk, *bay*, Indonesia, **201** F3
Sampun, Papua New Guinea, **140** D4
Sampwe, Democratic Republic of the Congo, **369** E4
Samsang, China, **214** B3
Samsø Bælt, *strait*, Denmark, **286** E5
Samsu, North Korea, **208** E2
Samsun, Turkey, **224** E4
Samucumbi, Angola, **368** C5
Samui, Ko, *island*, Thailand, **202** D4
Samut Prakan, Thailand, **202** D3
Samut Sakhon, Thailand, **202** D3
Samut Songkhram, Thailand, **202** D3
San, Mali, **364** D2
San, *river*, Cambodia, **203** E3
San Agustín, Argentina, **459** E5
San Agustín de Valle Fértil, Argentina, **458** C4
San Ambrosio, Isla, *island*, Chile, **449** E6
San Andreas, U.S.A., **422** C2
San Andrés, Bahía de, *bay*, San Andrés, Colombia, **461** B1
San Andrés, Bolivia, **455** F4
San Andrés, *island*, Colombia, Caribbean Sea, **461** B1
San Andres, Philippines, **204** C3
San Andrés, San Andrés, Colombia, **461** B1
San Andrés Tuxtla, Mexico, **431** G5
San Angelo, U.S.A., **424** B4
San Antonio, Belize, **428** C3
San Antonio, Bolivia, **455** F4
San Antonio, Cabo, *cape*, Cuba, **428** D2
San Antonio, Catamarca, Argentina, **458** D3
San Antonio, Chile, **458** B4
San Antonio, Mount, *mountain peak*, U.S.A., **422** E4
San Antonio, San Luis, Argentina, **458** C4
San Antonio, U.S.A., **424** C5
San Antonio, Venezuela, **451** E3
San Antonio Abad, Islas Baleares, Spain, **293** H3
San Antonio Bay, Philippines, **204** B4
San Antonio de Caparo, Venezuela, **450** D2
San Antonio de los Cobres, Argentina, **458** C2
San Antonio de Tamanaco, Venezuela, **451** E2

GEOGRAPHICA

underwater feature, Atlantic Ocean, **477** D9
South Gloucestershire, *unitary authority*, England, U.K., **304** E3
South Harris, *island*, Scotland, U.K., **308** B3
South Harting, England, U.K., **305** G4
South Haven, U.S.A., **421** K4
South Henik Lake, Canada, **414** F1
South Hill, U.S.A., **426** A6
South Horr, Kenya, **369** G2
South Indian Lake, Canada, **414** E3
South Island (Atas), Cocos (Keeling) Islands, **134** Q10
South Island, New Zealand, **133** D6
South Junction, Canada, **414** G7
South Keeling Islands, Cocos (Keeling) Islands, **134** Q10
South Knife, *river*, Canada, **414** F2
South Korea, *country*, Asia, **197** P6
South Lake Tahoe, U.S.A., **422** C2
South Lanarkshire, *local authority*, Scotland, U.K., **308** E5
South Miami, U.S.A., **425** M7
South Molton, England, U.K., **304** D3
South Nahanni, *river*, Canada, **410** G3
South Negril Point, Jamaica, **429** F3
South Orkney Islands, Antarctica, **470** A3
South Ossetia, *former autonomous republic*, Georgia, **222** C4
South Pacific Ocean, **129** J5
South Pass City, U.S.A., **419** K5
South Petherton, England, U.K., **304** E4
South Platte, *river*, U.S.A., **420** C5
South Platte, U.S.A., **419** M7
South Point, Ascension, **373** A3
South Point, Christmas Island, **134** N8
South Promontory, *point*, Snares Islands, New Zealand, **132** H9
South Ronaldsay, *island*, Orkney, Scotland, U.K., **308** G2
South Sandwich Islands, South Georgia and South Sandwich Islands, **449** K9
South Sandwich Trench, *underwater feature*, Atlantic Ocean, **477** E9
South Saskatchewan, *river*, Canada, **413** Q6
South Seal, *river*, Canada, **414** E2
South Shetland Islands, Antarctica, **470** A4
South Shields, England, U.K., **307** G3
South Taranaki Bight, *gulf*, New Zealand, **132** D4
South Twin Island, Canada, **415** Q5
South Tyne, *river*, England, U.K., **306** F3
South Uist, *island*, Scotland, U.K., **308** B3
South Wabasca Lake, Canada, **413** N4
South West Bay, Ascension, **373** A3
South West Cape, Auckland Islands, New Zealand, **132** J10
South West Point, Macquarie Island, **134** R11
South West Point, St Helena, **373** B3
South Wootton, England, U.K.,

305 H2
South Yorkshire, *unitary authority*, England, U.K., **307** G4
Southam, England, U.K., **305** F2
Southampton, Canada, **421** N3
Southampton, England, U.K., **305** F4
Southampton, U.S.A., **426** D4
Southampton City, *unitary authority*, England, U.K., **305** F4
Southampton Island, Canada, **411** L3
Southard, Mount, *mountain peak*, Antarctica, **470** E8
Southaven, U.S.A., **424** H2
Southbridge, U.S.A., **426** E3
Southeast Indian Ridge, *underwater feature*, Indian Ocean, **476** E7
Southeast Pacific Basin, *underwater feature*, Pacific Ocean, **479** M7
Southend, Canada, **414** C3
Southend, Scotland, U.K., **308** D5
Southend-on-Sea, England, U.K., **305** H3
Southend-on-Sea, *unitary authority*, England, U.K., **305** H3
Southern, *administrative region*, Malawi, **369** F6
Southern, *district*, Botswana, **370** D3
Southern, *province*, Sierra Leone, **364** B3
Southern, *province*, Zambia, **369** E6
Southern Alps, *mountain range*, New Zealand, **129** F6
Southern Cook Islands, Cook Islands, **137** F2
Southern Cross, Australia, **128** A6
Southern Highlands, *province*, Papua New Guinea, **140** A4
Southern Indian Lake, Canada, **414** E3
Southern Ocean, **104** D14
Southern Uplands, *mountain range*, Scotland, U.K., **308** E5
Southery, England, U.K., **305** H2
Southey, Canada, **414** B6
Southminster, England, U.K., **305** H3
Southport, Australia, **135** K7
Southport, England, U.K., **306** E4
Southport, U.S.A., **425** N3
Southwell, England, U.K., **305** G1
Southwest Indian Ridge, *underwater feature*, Indian Ocean, **476** E7
Southwest Pacific Basin, *underwater feature*, Pacific Ocean, **479** H7
Southwest Point, Papua New Guinea, **140** B3
Southwold, England, U.K., **305** J2
Sovata, Romania, **296** E2
Sovdozero, Russian Federation, **285** R5
Sovetsk, Russian Federation, **287** K5
Sovetskiy, Russian Federation, **299** B2
Sowa Pan, *lake*, Botswana, **371** E3
Soweto, South Africa, **371** E4
Soyaló, Mexico, **431** G5
Soyda, *river*, Russian Federation, **299** F2
Soyo, Angola, **368** B4
Sozaq, Kazakhstan, **223** H4
Sozh, *river*, Belarus, **299** C6
Sozopol, Bulgaria, **296** F4
Spain, *country*, Europe, **282** D8
Spalding, Canada, **414** B5
Spalding, England, U.K., **305** G2

Spanish, Canada, **421** M2
Spanish Fork, U.S.A., **423** H1
Spanish Peak, *mountain peak*, U.S.A., **418** E4
Spanish Town, Jamaica, **429** F3
Sparks, U.S.A., **422** D2
Sparta, U.S.A., **425** K2
Sparta *see* Sparti, Greece, **297** D7
Spartanburg, U.S.A., **425** M2
Spartel, Cap, *cape*, Morocco, **292** D5
Sparti (Sparta), Greece, **297** D7
Spartivento, Capo, *cape*, Italy, **295** F7
Spas-Demensk, Russian Federation, **299** D5
Spassk, Russian Federation, **223** M2
Spasskaya Guba, Russian Federation, **285** R5
Spassk-Dal'niy, Russian Federation, **211** L3
Spatha, Akra, *point*, Kriti, Greece, **297** D8
Spean Bridge, Scotland, U.K., **308** E4
Spearfish, U.S.A., **420** B3
Spearman, U.S.A., **420** C7
Speculator, U.S.A., **426** C3
Speery Island, St Helena, **373** B3
Speightstown, Barbados, **427** E3
Spencer, Idaho, U.S.A., **419** H4
Spencer, Iowa, U.S.A., **420** F4
Spencer, West Virginia, U.S.A., **421** N6
Spencer Gulf, Australia, **135** H6
Spencerville, New Zealand, **133** D6
Spences Bridge, Canada, **412** J6
Spennymoor, England, U.K., **307** G3
Sperrin Mountains, *mountain range*, Northern Ireland, U.K., **309** E3
Spetses, Greece, **297** D7
Spetses, *island*, Greece, **297** D7
Speyer, Germany, **288** D4
Speyside, Tobago, Trinidad and Tobago, **461** B4
Spiekeroog, *island*, Germany, **288** C2
Spili, Kriti, Greece, **297** E8
Spilsby, England, U.K., **305** H1
Spin Būldak, Afghanistan, **218** A3
Spinazzola, Italy, **295** F5
Spirit River, Canada, **413** K4
Spirits Bay, New Zealand, **132** D2
Spiritwood, Canada, **413** R5
Spit Point, Heard and McDonald Islands, **134** S12
Spitsbergen, *island*, Svalbard, **300** C2
Spittal an der Drau, Austria, **288** F5
Spittal of Glenshee, Scotland, U.K., **308** F4
Split, Croatia, **294** F4
Split Lake, Canada, **414** F3
Spofford, U.S.A., **424** B5
Spofforth, England, U.K., **307** G4
Špoģi, Latvia, **287** N4
Spokane, U.S.A., **418** F3
Spoleto, Italy, **294** D4
Spondinga, Italy, **294** C2
Spooner, U.S.A., **420** H3
Spotted Horse, U.S.A., **419** M4
Sprague, U.S.A., **418** F3
Spratly Islands, *sovereignty disputed*, South China Sea, **203** G4
Spreča, *river*, Bosnia and Herzegovina, **294** G3
Spring Garden, Guyana, **451** G2
Spring Grove, U.S.A., **426** B6
Spring Hill, U.S.A., **425** L5
Springbok, South Africa, **370** C4

Springdale, Arkansas, U.S.A., **424** E1
Springdale, Canada, **417** N5
Springdale, Washington, U.S.A., **418** F2
Springe, Germany, **288** D2
Springer, U.S.A., **423** L3
Springfield, Colorado, U.S.A., **423** M3
Springfield, Illinois, U.S.A., **421** J6
Springfield, Massachusetts, U.S.A., **426** D3
Springfield, Minnesota, U.S.A., **420** F3
Springfield, Missouri, U.S.A., **420** G7
Springfield, Ohio, U.S.A., **421** M6
Springfield, Oregon, U.S.A., **418** C4
Springfield, Tennessee, U.S.A., **425** J1
Springfield, Vermont, U.S.A., **426** D3
Springfontein, South Africa, **371** E5
Springhill, U.S.A., **424** F3
Springhouse, Canada, **412** H6
Springs Junction, New Zealand, **133** D6
Springsure, Australia, **135** K3
Sprova, Norway, **284** E4
Sprowston, England, U.K., **305** J2
Spruce Knob, *mountain peak*, U.S.A., **421** P6
Spruce Lake, Canada, **413** Q5
Spruce Mountain, *mountain peak*, U.S.A., **422** F1
Spurn Head, *point*, England, U.K., **307** J4
Spyglass Point, New Zealand, **133** D6
Squamish, Canada, **412** H7
Square Islands, Canada, **417** P3
Squillace, Golfo di, *gulf*, Italy, **295** F6
Squinzano, Italy, **295** G5
Srbija (Serbia) *republic*, Yugoslavia, **296** C4
Srbobran, Yugoslavia, **296** B3
Srê Âmbêl, Cambodia, **203** D4
Sredinnyy Khrebet, *mountain range*, Russian Federation, **301** T4
Sredishte, Bulgaria, **296** F4
Sredne-Russkaya Vozvyshennost', *mountain range*, Russian Federation, **298** E2
Sredne-Sibirskoye Ploskogor'ye, *mountain range*, Russian Federation, **300** L3
Sredneye Kuyto, Ozero, *lake*, Russian Federation, **285** Q4
Srednogarie, Bulgaria, **296** E4
Śrem, Poland, **289** H2
Sremska Mitrovica, Yugoslavia, **296** B3
Srêpôk, *river*, Cambodia, **203** E3
Sretensk, Russian Federation, **210** G1
Sri Jayawardanapura-Kotte, Sri Lanka, **216** D5
Sri Lanka, *country*, Asia, **196** K9
Sribner, U.S.A., **420** E5
Srikakulam, India, **217** E2
Srinagar, Jammu and Kashmir, India, **218** C2
Srinagar, Uttar Pradesh, India, **218** D3
Srinakarin Reservoir, Thailand, **202** C3
Srostki, Russian Federation, **223** M2
Srpska Crnja, Yugoslavia, **296** C3
Stack Skerry, *island*, Scotland, U.K., **308** E1
Stade, Germany, **288** D2

Stadlandet, *cape*, Norway, **286** B1
Stafford, England, U.K., **304** E2
Stafford, U.S.A., **420** D7
Staffordshire, *unitary authority*, England, U.K., **304** E2
Staindrop, England, U.K., **307** G3
Staines, England, U.K., **305** G3
Stainz, Austria, **289** G5
Stalbridge, England, U.K., **304** E4
Stalham, England, U.K., **305** J2
Stalingrad *see* Volgograd, Russian Federation, **298** F3
Stalowa Wola, Poland, **289** L3
Stamford, Connecticut, U.S.A., **426** D4
Stamford, England, U.K., **305** G2
Stamford, Lake, U.S.A., **424** C3
Stamford, New York, U.S.A., **426** C3
Stamford, Texas, U.S.A., **424** C3
Stamford Bridge, England, U.K., **307** H4
Stamfordham, England, U.K., **307** G2
Stampriet, Namibia, **370** C3
Stanberry, U.S.A., **420** F5
Standerton, South Africa, **371** E4
Stanford, U.S.A., **419** J3
Stange, Norway, **286** E2
Stangenestind, *mountain peak*, Norway, **285** P1
Stanger, South Africa, **371** F4
Stanhope, England, U.K., **306** F3
Staniard Creek, Bahamas, **428** F1
Stănileşti, Romania, **296** G2
Stanilovo, Russian Federation, **299** F3
Stanišić, Yugoslavia, **296** B3
Stanke Dimitrov, Bulgaria, **296** D4
Stanley, England, U.K., **307** G3
Stanley, Falkland Islands, **460** G4
Stanley, Idaho, U.S.A., **418** G4
Stanley, Iowa, U.S.A., **420** H3
Stanley, *mountain peak*, Democratic Republic of the Congo, **369** G4
Stanley, North Dakota, U.S.A., **420** B1
Stanovoy Khrebet, *mountain range*, Russian Federation, **301** P4
Stanovoye Nagor'ye, *mountain range*, Russian Federation, **301** N4
Stanthorpe, Australia, **135** L4
Stanton, England, U.K., **305** H2
Stantsiya Sumerichi, Russian Federation, **285** S5
Stapleton, U.S.A., **420** C5
Stará Ľubovňa, Slovakia, **289** K4
Stara Pazova, Yugoslavia, **296** C3
Stara Planina, *mountain range*, Bulgaria, **296** D4
Stara Ushytsya, Ukraine, **296** F1
Stara Vyzhivka, Ukraine, **289** M3
Stara Zagora, Bulgaria, **296** E4
Starachowice, Poland, **289** K3
Staraya Russa, Russian Federation, **299** C3
Staraya Toropa, Russian Federation, **299** C4
Starbuck Island, Kiribati, **139** J5
Starchiojd, Romania, **296** F3
Starcross, England, U.K., **304** D4
Stargard-Szczeciński, Poland, **289** G2
Staritsa, Russian Federation, **299** E4

Starke, U.S.A., **425** L5
Starkville, U.S.A., **425** H3
Starnberger See, *lake*, Germany, **288** E5
Staro Oryakhovo, Bulgaria, **296** F4
Starosel'ye, Russian Federation, **299** F6
Start Bay, England, U.K., **304** D4
Start Point, England, U.K., **304** D4
Startup, U.S.A., **418** D3
Staryy Oskol, Russian Federation, **298** E2
Staryy Sambir, Ukraine, **289** L4
Staryya Darohi, Belarus, **299** B6
Staszów, Poland, **289** K3
Statesboro, U.S.A., **425** M3
Statesville, U.S.A., **425** M2
Staunton, U.S.A., **421** P6
Stavanger, Norway, **286** B3
Stavaträsk, Sweden, **284** K4
Staveley, England, U.K., **305** F1
Staveley, New Zealand, **133** C6
Stavely, Canada, **413** N6
Stavropol', Russian Federation, **298** F3
Stavropol'skiy Kray, *territory*, Russian Federation, **298** F3
Stavros, Greece, **297** D5
Stawell, Australia, **135** J6
Stawiski, Poland, **289** L2
Stawiszyn, Poland, **289** J3
Steamboat, U.S.A., **418** C5
Steamboat Canyon, U.S.A., **423** J4
Steamboat Mountain, *mountain peak*, U.S.A., **419** K6
Steamboat Springs, U.S.A., **423** K1
Steele, U.S.A., **420** C2
Steels Point, Norfolk Island, **135** T13
Steen River, Canada, **413** L2
Steens Mountain, *mountain range*, U.S.A., **418** E5
Steenvoorde, France, **305** K4
Steenwijk, Netherlands, **288** C2
Steep Point, Australia, **134** C4
Ştefan Vodă, Moldova, **296** G2
Stefansson Island, Canada, **410** J2
Steffen, Cerro, *mountain peak*, Argentina, **460** C2
Stege, Denmark, **286** F5
Steiermark, *state*, Austria, **289** G5
Steinbach, Canada, **414** F7
Steine, Norway, **284** G2
Steinfort, Luxembourg, **291** G2
Steinhatchee, U.S.A., **425** L5
Steinhausen, Namibia, **370** C3
Steinkjer, Norway, **284** E5
Steinkopf, South Africa, **370** C4
Stellarton, Canada, **417** K7
Stellenbosch, South Africa, **370** C5
Stenay, France, **291** G2
Stendal, Germany, **288** E2
Stende, Latvia, **287** L4
Steneby, Sweden, **286** F3
Stenness, Loch of, *lake*, Orkney, Scotland, U.K., **308** F1
Stenstorp, Sweden, **286** F3
Stenudden, Sweden, **284** H3
Stenungsund, Sweden, **286** E3
Stephens, Cape, New Zealand, **133** D5
Stephens Lake, Canada, **414** G3
Stephenville, Canada, **417** M5
Stephenville, U.S.A., **424** C3
Stepojevac, Yugoslavia, **296** C3
Sterea Ellas, *administrative region*, Greece, **297** E6
Sterling, Colorado, U.S.A., **423** M1
Sterling, Illinois, U.S.A., **420** J5
Sterling, Nebraska, U.S.A., **420** E5
Sterling City, U.S.A., **424** B4
Sterling Heights, U.S.A., **421** M4
Sterlitamak, Russian Federation, **222** F2
Sternes, Kriti, Greece, **297** E8
Stettler, Canada, **413** N5
Steubenville, U.S.A., **421** N5
Stevenage, England, U.K., **305** G3
Stevens Point, U.S.A., **421** J3
Stevenson, Mount, *mountain peak*, New Zealand, **133** C6
Stevenson, U.S.A., **425** K2
Stewart, Canada, **412** E4
Stewart, Isla, *island*, Chile, **460** C5
Stewart Island, New Zealand, **133** B8
Stewarts Point, U.S.A., **422** B2
Steyr, Austria, **289** G4
Stibb Cross, England, U.K., **304** C4
Stickney, U.S.A., **420** D4
Stikine, *river*, Canada, **412** D3
Stikine Plateau, Canada, **412** D2
Stillington, England, U.K., **307** G3
Stillwater, Nevada, U.S.A., **422** D2
Stillwater, New Zealand, **133** C6
Stillwater, Oklahoma, U.S.A., **424** D1
Stillwater Range, *mountain range*, U.S.A., **422** D2
Stilo, Italy, **295** F6
Stilton, England, U.K., **305** G2
Štimlje, Yugoslavia, **296** C4
Stintino, Sardegna, Italy, **295** B5
Štip, Macedonia, **297** D5
Stirling, *local authority*, Scotland, U.K., **308** E4
Stirling, Scotland, U.K., **308** F4
Stjernøya, *island*, Norway, **285** L1
Stjørdalshalsen, Norway, **284** E5
Stockerau, Austria, **289** H4
Stockholm, *county*, Sweden, **287** H3
Stockholm, Sweden, **287** J3
Stockport, England, U.K., **306** F4
Stockton, California, U.S.A., **422** C3
Stockton, Kansas, U.S.A., **420** D6
Stockton Lake, U.S.A., **420** G7
Stockton Plateau, U.S.A., **423** M6
Stockton-on-Tees, England, U.K., **307** G3
Stockton-on-Tees, *unitary authority*, England, U.K., **307** G3
Stoczek Łukowski, Poland, **289** K3
Stod, Czech Republic, **288** F4
Stöde, Sweden, **286** H1
Stødi, Norway, **284** G3
Stœng Trêng, Cambodia, **203** E3
Stoer, Point of, Scotland, U.K., **308** D2
Stoke-on-Trent, England, U.K., **304** E1
Stoke-on-Trent, *unitary authority*, England, U.K., **304** E1
Stokes, Bahía, *bay*, Chile, **460** C5
Stokes, Mount, *mountain peak*, New Zealand, **133** E5
Stokesay, England, U.K., **304** E2
Stokesley, England, U.K., **307** G3
Stokksnes, *point*, Iceland, **284** Z7
Stolac, Bosnia and Herzegovina, **294** G4
Stoltenhoff Island, Tristan da Cunha, **373** C2
Ston, Croatia, **294** F4
Stone, Gloucestershire, England, U.K., **304** E3
Stone, Staffordshire, England, U.K., **304** E2
Stonecliffe, Canada, **416** C6
Stoneham, U.S.A., **423** M1
Stonehaven, Scotland, U.K., **308** G4
Stonewall, U.S.A., **423** L3
Stony Lake, Canada, **414** E2
Stony Plain, Canada, **413** M5
Stony Rapids, Canada, **413** S2
Stonyhill Point, Tristan da Cunha, **373** C2
Stör, *river*, Germany, **288** D2
Storå, Sweden, **286** G3
Stora Blåsjön, Sweden, **284** G4
Stora Lulevatten, *lake*, Sweden, **284** J3
Stora Sjöfallet, *lake*, Sweden, **284** H3
Storavan, *lake*, Sweden, **284** J4
Storby, Finland, **287** J2
Stord, *island*, Norway, **286** B3
Stordal, Norway, **284** E5
Store Bælt, *strait*, Denmark, **286** E5
Store Koldewey, *island*, Greenland, **411** T2
Store Sølnkletten, *mountain peak*, Norway, **286** E2
Støren, Norway, **284** E5
Storfjordbotn, Norway, **285** N1
Storfors, Sweden, **286** G3
Storforshei, Norway, **284** G3
Storjord, Norway, **284** G3
Storkow, Germany, **289** F2
Storlien, Sweden, **284** F5
Storm Lake, U.S.A., **420** F4
Stornoway, Scotland, U.K., **308** C2
Storozhynets', Ukraine, **296** E1
Storr, The, *mountain peak*, Scotland, U.K., **308** C3
Storsätern, Sweden, **286** F1
Storsjön, *lake*, near Ljungdalen, Sweden, **284** F5
Storsjön, *lake*, by Östersund, Sweden, **284** G5
Storsteinfjellet, *mountain peak*, Norway, **284** H2
Storthoaks, Canada, **414** D7
Storuman, *lake*, Sweden, **284** H4
Storuman, Sweden, **284** H4
Storvätteshågna, *mountain peak*, Sweden, **286** F1
Storvik, Sweden, **286** H2
Story, U.S.A., **419** L4
Stoughton, U.S.A., **421** J4
Stour, *river*, England, U.K., **305** F2
Stourbridge, England, U.K., **304** E2
Stourport-on-Severn, England, U.K., **304** E2
Stout Lake, Canada, **414** G5
Støvring, Denmark, **286** D4
Stow, Scotland, U.K., **308** G5
Stowmarket, England, U.K., **305** H2
Stow-on-the-Wold, England, U.K., **305** F3
Stoyba, Russian Federation, **211** K1
Strabane, *district*, Northern Ireland, U.K., **309** E3
Strabane, Northern Ireland, U.K., **309** E3
Stradbally, Ireland, **309** E4
Stradbroke, England, U.K., **305** J2
Stradella, Italy, **294** B3
Stradishall, England, U.K., **305** H2
Stradsett, England, U.K., **305** H2
Strahan, Australia, **135** K7
Strakonice, Czech Republic, **289** F4
Straldzha, Bulgaria, **296** F4
Stralki, Belarus, **287** P5
Stralsund, Germany, **288** F1
Strand, South Africa, **370** C5
Stranda, Norway, **286** C1
Strangford, Northern Ireland, U.K., **309** G3
Strangford Lough, *inlet*, Northern Ireland, U.K., **309** G3
Strängnäs, Sweden, **287** H3
Stranorlar, Ireland, **309** E3
Stranraer, Scotland, U.K., **308** D6
Strasbourg, Canada, **413** S6
Strasbourg, France, **291** H2
Strasburg, U.S.A., **420** C2
Strășeni, Moldova, **296** G2
Straßwalchen, Austria, **288** F5
Stratford, Canada, **421** N4
Stratford, New Zealand, **132** E4
Stratford, U.S.A., **423** M3
Stratford-upon-Avon, England, U.K., **305** F2
Strathaven, Scotland, U.K., **308** E5
Strathcona, Mount, *mountain peak*, Antarctica, **470** G5
Strathdon, Scotland, U.K., **308** F3
Strathmore, Canada, **413** N6
Strathnaver, Canada, **412** H5
Strathspey, *valley*, Scotland, U.K., **308** F3
Strathy, Scotland, U.K., **308** E2
Strathy Point, Scotland, U.K., **308** E2
Strathyre, Scotland, U.K., **308** E4
Stratton, England, U.K., **304** C4
Stratton, U.S.A., **426** E2
Stratton Mountain, *mountain peak*, U.S.A., **426** D3
Straubing, Germany, **288** F4
Straumen, Norway, **284** E5
Straumnes, *point*, Iceland, **284** W6
Strawberry, U.S.A., **422** C2
Streaky Bay, Australia, **134** G5
Streatley, England, U.K., **305** F3
Středočeský, *administrative region*, Czech Republic, **289** G4
Street, England, U.K., **304** E3
Strehaia, Romania, **296** D3
Strel'na, *river*, Russian Federation, **285** T3
Strel'na, Russian Federation, **285** U3
Strenči, Latvia, **287** M4
Stretham, England, U.K., **305** H2
Strevell, U.S.A., **418** H5
Streymoy, *island*, Faeroe Islands, **302** D1
Střibo, Czech Republic, **291** L4
Stříbro, Czech Republic, **288** F4
Strichen, Scotland, U.K., **308** G3
Strickland, *river*, Papua New Guinea, **140** A4
Strimonikos Kolpos, *bay*, Greece, **297** D5
Stroeder, Argentina, **460** E1
Strofades, *island*, Ionioi Nisoi, Greece, **297** C7
Strokestown, Ireland, **309** D4
Stromboli, Isola, *island*, Italy, **295** E6
Stromeferry, Scotland, U.K., **308** D3
Stromness, Orkney, Scotland, U.K., **308** F2
Strömsbruk, Sweden, **287** H2
Stromsburg, U.S.A., **420** E5
Strömsnäsbruk, Sweden, **286** F4
Strömstad, Sweden, **286** E3
Strömsund, Sweden, **284** G5
Strong, Mount, *mountain peak*, Papua New Guinea, **140** B4
Stronsay, *island*, Orkney, Scotland, U.K., **308** G1
Stronsay Firth, *channel*, Orkney, Scotland, U.K., **308** G1
Strontian, Scotland, U.K., **308** D4
Stroud, England, U.K., **304** E3
Stroudsburg, U.S.A., **426** C4
Struer, Denmark, **286** D4
Struga, Macedonia, **297** C5
Strumble Head, *point*, Wales, U.K., **304** B2
Strumica, Macedonia, **297** D5
Stryker, U.S.A., **418** G2
Stryukove, Ukraine, **296** H2
Stryy, Ukraine, **289** L4
Strzegom, Poland, **289** H3
Strzelce Opolskie, Poland, **289** J3
Strzelecki Desert, Australia, **135** H4
Strzelin, Poland, **289** H3
Strzelno, Poland, **289** J2
Stuart, Florida, U.S.A., **425** M6
Stuart, Nebraska, U.S.A., **420** D4
Stubaier Alpen, *mountain range*, Austria, **288** E5
Stubbington, England, U.K., **305** F4
Stuben, Austria, **288** E5
Studley, England, U.K., **305** F2
Study Butte, U.S.A., **423** M7
Stugudal, Norway, **284** E5
Stugun, Sweden, **284** G5
Stupino, Russian Federation, **299** G5
Sturgeon, Point, U.S.A., **421** K3
Sturgeon Bay, U.S.A., **421** K3
Sturgeon Falls, Canada, **421** P2
Sturgeon Lake, Canada, **414** J6
Sturgis, U.S.A., **420** B3
Sturminster Newton, England, U.K., **304** E4
Štúrovo, Slovakia, **289** J5
Sturt, *river*, Australia, **134** F2
Stutterheim, South Africa, **371** E5
Stuttgart, Germany, **288** D4
Stuttgart, U.S.A., **424** G2
Stykkishólmur, Iceland, **284** X7
Stylida, Greece, **297** D6
Suaçuí Grande, *river*, Brazil, **457** E5
Suai, Indonesia, **198** D5
Suana, Democratic Republic of the Congo, **368** D4
Su'ao, Taiwan, **206** E3
Subang, Indonesia, **201** D4
Subay', 'Urūq, *desert*, Saudi Arabia, **363** H4
Subei, China, **213** G5
Subi, Pulau, *island*, Indonesia, **201** E2
Subi Besar, Pulau, *island*, Indonesia, **201** E2
Subiaco, Italy, **295** D5
Subotica, Yugoslavia, **296** B2
Subrag, China, **211** G3
Success, Canada, **413** Q6
Suceava, Romania, **296** F2
Sučevići, Croatia, **294** F3
Sucevița, Romania, **296** E2
Suchary, Belarus, **299** C6
Suchorze, Poland, **289** H1
Suchowola, Poland, **289** L2
Suck, *river*, Ireland, **309** D4
Sucre, Bolivia, **455** F5
Sucre, Colombia, **450** C2
Sucuaro, Colombia, **451** E3
Sucunduri, *river*, Brazil, **455** G1
Sucuriú, *river*, Brazil, **456** C5
Sud, *province*, Cameroon, **365** G4
Sud-Kivu, *administrative region*, Democratic Republic of the Congo, **369** E3
Sud Ouest, Pointe, *point*, Mauritius, **373** C1
Sud-Ouest, *province*, Cameroon, **368** A2
Suda, *river*, Russian Federation, **299** F3
Sudan, *country*, Africa, **358** H5
Sudbury, Canada, **421** N2
Sudbury, England, U.K., **305** H2
Suddie, Guyana, **451** G2
Sudety, *mountain range*, Czech Republic/Poland, **289** G3
Sudimir, Russian Federation, **299** E6
Sudok, Sweden, **284** K3
Suðureyri, Iceland, **284** X6

Ulan-Ude, Russian Federation, **210** D2
Ulan Ul Hu, *lake*, China, **214** D2
Ulanbel, Kazakhstan, **223** J4
Ulanhot, China, **211** H3
Ulantolgoy, Mongolia, **223** N3
Ulaş, Turkey, **297** F5
Ulawa, *island*, Solomon Islands, **141** A1
Ulawun, Mount, *mountain peak*, Papua New Guinea, **140** C4
Ulbanep, Mount, *mountain peak*, Papua New Guinea, **140** A3
Ulbster, Scotland, U.K., **308** F2
Ulchin, South Korea, **208** E3
Ulcinj, Yugoslavia, **296** B5
Uldz, Mongolia, **210** E2
Uldz, *river*, Mongolia, **210** F2
Ulety, Russian Federation, **210** F2
Ulfborg, Denmark, **286** D4
Ulhāsnagar, India, **216** C2
Uliastay, Mongolia, **213** H3
Ulithi, *island*, Micronesia, **138** B3
Ülken Borsyq Qumy, *desert*, Kazakhstan, **222** F3
Ülken Vladīmīrovka, Kazakhstan, **212** C2
Ülkennaryn, Kazakhstan, **212** E2
Ulla, Belarus, **299** B5
Ulla, *river*, Spain, **292** C1
Ullånger, Sweden, **287** J1
Ullapool, Scotland, U.K., **308** D3
Ullared, Sweden, **286** F4
Ullatti, Sweden, **284** K3
Ullava, Finland, **285** L5
Ullfors, Sweden, **287** H2
Ullswater, *lake*, England, U.K., **306** F3
Ullŭngdo, *island*, South Korea, **208** E3
Ulm, Germany, **288** D4
Ul'ma, *river*, Russian Federation, **211** K2
Ulmeni, near Baia Mare, Romania, **296** D2
Ulmeni, Romania, **296** F3
Ulog, Bosnia and Herzegovina, **294** G4
Ulongwé, Mozambique, **369** F5
Ulricehamn, Sweden, **286** F4
Ulsan, South Korea, **208** E4
Ulsberg, Norway, **286** D1
Ulsta, Shetland, Scotland, U.K., **308** K7
Ulu, Indonesia, **198** D2
Ulubat Gölü, *lake*, Turkey, **297** G5
Uluçınar, Turkey, **225** C1
Ulugan Bay, Philippines, **204** B4
Uluqqat, China, **212** B5
Ulundi, South Africa, **371** F4
Ulungur, *river*, China, **212** E3
Ulungur Hu, *lake*, China, **212** E3
Uluriyskiy Golets, Gora, *mountain peak*, Russian Federation, **210** E2
Uluru (Ayers Rock), *mountain peak*, Australia, **128** C4
Ulva, *island*, Scotland, U.K., **308** C4
Ulverston, England, U.K., **306** E3
Ulvik, Norway, **286** C2
Ul'yanovka, Ukraine, **296** H1
Ul'yanovsk, Russian Federation, **222** D2
Ul'yanovskaya Oblast', *province*, Russian Federation, **222** D2
Ŭl'yanovskţy, Kazakhstan, **212** B2
Ulysses, U.S.A., **420** C7
Umag, Croatia, **294** D3
Umán, Mexico, **431** H4
Uman', Ukraine, **298** D3
Umaria, India, **218** E5
Umarkot, India, **219** E6
Umarkot, Pakistan, **218** B4

Umba, *river*, Russian Federation, **285** S3
Umba, Russian Federation, **285** S3
Umboi Island, Papua New Guinea, **140** B4
Umbozero, Ozero, *lake*, Russian Federation, **285** S3
Umbria, *autonomous state*, Italy, **294** D4
Umbukul, Papua New Guinea, **140** C3
Umbulan Gayohpecoh, Indonesia, **200** D3
Umeå, Sweden, **284** K5
Umeälven, *river*, Sweden, **284** J4
Umfreville Lake, Canada, **414** G6
Umiat, U.S.A., **410** D3
Umlazi, South Africa, **371** F4
Umm ad Daraj, Jabal, *mountain peak*, Jordan, **225** C3
Umm Bel, Sudan, **366** C2
Umm Durmān (Omdurman), Sudan, **366** D1
Umm Kaddādah, Sudan, **366** C2
Umm Lajj, Saudi Arabia, **363** G3
Umm Ruwābah, Sudan, **366** D2
Umm Sa'ad, Libya, **362** E2
Umm Şawwānah, Jabal, *mountain peak*, Jordan, **225** C4
Umm Sayyālah, Sudan, **366** D2
Umm Shawmar, Jabal, *mountain peak*, Egypt, **225** B5
Umm 'Umayd, Ra's, *mountain peak*, Egypt, **225** B6
Umm Urūmah, *island*, Saudi Arabia, **363** G3
Umnak Island, Aleutian Islands, U.S.A., **408** G3
Umpilua, Mozambique, **369** G5
Umpulo, Angola, **368** C5
Umred, India, **218** D5
Umtata, South Africa, **371** E5
Umuahia, Nigeria, **368** A1
Umuarama, Brazil, **459** G2
Umuna, *island*, Vava'u Group, Tonga, **141** B3
Umurbey, Turkey, **297** F5
Umzinto, South Africa, **371** F5
Una, Brazil, **457** F4
Una, India, **218** B5
Una, Mount, *mountain peak*, New Zealand, **133** D6
Una, *river*, Bosnia and Herzegovina, **294** F3
Una, Russian Federation, **285** U4
Unaðsdalur, Iceland, **284** X6
Unaí, Brazil, **456** D4
Unaja, Finland, **287** K2
Unalaska Island, Aleutian Islands, U.S.A., **408** G3
Unango, Mozambique, **369** G5
Unapool, Scotland, U.K., **308** D2
Unari, Finland, **285** M3
Unari, *lake*, Finland, **285** M3
'Unayzah, Jordan, **225** C4
'Unayzah, Saudi Arabia, **363** H3
Uncia, Bolivia, **455** E5
Uncompahgre Plateau, U.S.A., **423** J2
Undersåker, Sweden, **284** F5
Underwood, U.S.A., **420** C2
Unduksa, Russian Federation, **285** S4
Unea Island, Papua New Guinea, **140** C4
Unecha, Russian Federation, **298** D2
Unezhma, Russian Federation, **285** T5
Ungana Bay, Kenya, **369** H3
Ungava, Péninsule d', *peninsula*, Canada, **411** M3
Ungheni, Moldova, **296** F2
União, Brazil, **453** E4
União da Vitória, Brazil, **459** G3
União dos Palmares, Brazil, **457** G2

Unichowo, Poland, **289** H1
Unije, *island*, Croatia, **294** E3
Unini, Peru, **454** C3
Unini, *river*, Brazil, **451** F4
Unión, Bahía, *bay*, Argentina, **460** E1
Union, Missouri, U.S.A., **420** H6
Union, Oregon, U.S.A., **418** F4
Unión, Paraguay, **459** F2
Union City, Pennsylvania, U.S.A., **421** P5
Union City, Tennessee, U.S.A., **425** H1
Union Creek, U.S.A., **418** C5
Union Springs, U.S.A., **425** K3
Uniontown, U.S.A., **421** P6
Unionville, U.S.A., **420** G5
United Arab Emirates, *country*, Asia, **196** G7
United Kingdom, *country*, Europe, **282** C4
United States of America, *country*, North America, **409** M5
Unitsa, Russian Federation, **285** S5
Unity, Canada, **413** Q5
Unity, U.S.A., **418** E4
University Park, U.S.A., **423** K5
Unnão, India, **218** E4
Unpongkor, Vanuatu, **141** A3
Unquera, Spain, **292** E1
Unst, *island*, Shetland, Scotland, U.K., **308** L7
Unturán, Sierra de, *mountain range*, Venezuela, **451** F3
Unuli Horog, China, **214** D2
Upata, Venezuela, **451** F2
Upavon, England, U.K., **305** F3
Upernavik, Greenland, **411** P2
Upía, *river*, Colombia, **450** D3
Upington, South Africa, **370** D4
Upleta, India, **218** B5
Uplyme, England, U.K., **304** E4
Upoloksha, Russian Federation, **285** Q3
Upolu, *island*, Samoa, **141** B1
Upper Arrow Lake, Canada, **413** K6
Upper East, *administrative region*, Ghana, **364** D2
Upper Fraser, Canada, **412** H4
Upper Hutt, New Zealand, **133** E5
Upper Klamath Lake, U.S.A., **418** D5
Upper Lough Erne, *lake*, Northern Ireland, U.K., **309** E3
Upper Peirce Reservoir, Singapore, **200** J6
Upper Red Lake, U.S.A., **420** F1
Upper Sandusky, U.S.A., **421** M5
Upper West, *administrative region*, Ghana, **364** D2
Uppingham, England, U.K., **305** G2
Upplands-Väsby, Sweden, **287** H3
Uppsala, *county*, Sweden, **287** H3
Uppsala, Sweden, **287** H3
Upsala, Canada, **414** J7
Upshi, India, **218** D2
Upton, U.S.A., **419** M4
Upton upon Severn, England, U.K., **304** E2
'Uqayribāt, Syria, **225** D2
Urabá, Golfo de, *gulf*, Colombia, **450** C2
Urad Houqi, China, **210** D4
Urad Qianqi, China, **210** E4
Urad Zhongqi, China, **210** E4
Urakawa, Japan, **209** H2
Ural, *river*, Russian Federation, **222** E2
Ural Mountains *see* Ural'skiy Khrebet, *mountain range*, Russian Federation, **194** G4
Ural'skiy Khrebet (Ural Mountains), *mountain range*, Russian Federation, **194** G4
Urambo, Tanzania, **369** F4

Urandi, Brazil, **457** E4
Uraricoera, Brazil, **451** G3
Uraricoera, *river*, Brazil, **451** F3
Urawa, Japan, **209** G4
'Urayf an Nāqah, Jabal, *mountain peak*, Egypt, **225** C4
Urbana, U.S.A., **421** J5
Urbano Santos, Brazil, **453** E4
Urbino, Italy, **294** D4
Urbión, Sierra de, *mountain peak*, Spain, **293** F1
Urçay, France, **290** F3
Urcel, France, **291** F2
Urcos, Peru, **454** D3
Urdgol, Mongolia, **213** G3
Urdos, France, **290** D5
Urdzhar, Kazakhstan, **223** L3
Ure, *river*, England, U.K., **307** G3
Urengoy, Russian Federation, **300** J3
'Urf, Jabal al, *mountain peak*, Egypt, **225** B6
Urfa, Turkey, **224** E5
Urganch, Uzbekistan, **222** G4
Urho, China, **212** E3
Uriah, Mount, *mountain peak*, New Zealand, **133** C6
Uribia, Colombia, **450** D1
Urie, *river*, Scotland, U.K., **308** G3
Uril, Russian Federation, **211** K2
Ürttskţy, Kazakhstan, **222** H2
Urjala, Finland, **287** L2
Urla, Turkey, **297** F6
Urlingford, Ireland, **309** E5
Ürmä aş Şughrá, Syria, **225** D1
Urmi, *river*, Russian Federation, **211** L2
Urmia *see* Orūmīyeh, Iran, **363** H1
Uromi, Nigeria, **365** F3
Uroševac, Yugoslavia, **296** C4
Urosozero, Russian Federation, **285** S5
Ŭroteppa, Tajikistan, **223** H5
Urov, *river*, Russian Federation, **211** H1
Urt, Mongolia, **213** J4
Urt Moron, China, **213** G5
Uruáchic, Mexico, **430** C3
Uruaçu, Brazil, **456** D4
Uruapan, Mexico, **430** E5
Uruará, *river*, Brazil, **452** C3
Urubamba, Cordillera, *mountain range*, Peru, **454** D3
Urubamba, *river*, Peru, **454** D3
Urubu, *river*, Brazil, **451** G5
Urucará, Brazil, **451** H5
Uruçuí, Brazil, **453** E5
Uruçui, Serra do, *mountain range*, Brazil, **453** E5
Uruçui Prêto, *river*, Brazil, **453** E5
Urucuia, *river*, Brazil, **456** E4
Urucurituba, Brazil, **451** H5
Uruguai, *river*, Brazil, **459** G3
Uruguaiana, Brazil, **459** F3
Uruguay, *country*, South America, **449** G7
Uruguay, *river*, South America, **447** G6
Ürümqi, China, **212** E4
Urung, Indonesia, **199** E3
Urup, *island*, Kuril'skiye Ostrova, Russian Federation, **209** K1
Urup, Ostrov, *island*, Russian Federation, **301** S5
Uryumkan, *river*, Russian Federation, **211** G2
Urziceni, Romania, **296** F3
Us, *river*, Russian Federation, **213** G2
Usa, Japan, **208** E4
Usa, *river*, Russian Federation, **300** G3
Usadishche, Russian Federation, **299** D3
Uşak, *province*, Turkey, **297** G6
Uşak, Turkey, **297** G6
Usakos, Namibia, **370** C3

Usborne, Mount, *mountain peak*, Falkland Islands, **460** F4
Ušće, Yugoslavia, **296** C4
Usedom, Germany, **289** F2
'Usfān, Saudi Arabia, **363** G4
Usha, *river*, Belarus, **299** B6
Ushachy, Belarus, **299** B5
Ushakovskoye, Russian Federation, **301** V2
'Ushayrah, Saudi Arabia, **363** H4
Üshtöbe, Kazakhstan, **223** K3
Ushuaia, Argentina, **460** D5
Ushumun, Russian Federation, **211** J1
Usino, Papua New Guinea, **140** B4
Usinsk, Russian Federation, **300** G3
Usk, *river*, Wales, U.K., **304** D3
Usk, Wales, U.K., **304** E3
Uslar, Germany, **288** D3
Usmas ezers, *lake*, Latvia, **287** K4
Usogorsk, Russian Federation, **300** F3
Usol'ye-Sibirskoye, Russian Federation, **301** M4
Ussel, France, **290** F4
Ussuriysk, Russian Federation, **211** K4
Ust'-Barguzin, Russian Federation, **210** E1
Ust'-Chorna, Ukraine, **296** D1
Ust'-Dolyssy, Russian Federation, **299** B4
Ust'-Ilim'sk, Russian Federation, **301** M4
Ust-Ishim, Russian Federation, **223** J1
Ust'-Kamchatsk, Russian Federation, **301** T4
Ust'-Kan, Russian Federation, **212** E2
Ust'-Koksa, Russian Federation, **212** E2
Ust'-Kut, Russian Federation, **301** M4
Ust'-Luga, Russian Federation, **299** B3
Ust'-Nera, Russian Federation, **301** R3
Ust'-Ordynskiy Buryatskiy Avtonomnyy Okrug, *autonomous area*, Russian Federation, **210** D1
Ust'-Ordynskiy, Russian Federation, **210** D1
Ust'-Reka, Russian Federation, **299** F2
Ust'-Tsil'ma, Russian Federation, **300** G3
Ust'-Tygda, Russian Federation, **211** J1
Ust'-Umal'ta, Russian Federation, **211** L2
Ust'-Undurga, Russian Federation, **211** G1
Ústí nad Labem, Czech Republic, **289** G3
Ustica, Isola di, *island*, Sicilia, Italy, **295** D6
Ustka, Poland, **289** H1
Ustrem, Bulgaria, **296** F4
Ustronie Morskie, Poland, **289** G1
Ustrzyki Dolne, Poland, **289** L4
Ust'ye, *river*, Russian Federation, **299** G4
Ust'ye, Russian Federation, **299** G3
Ustyurt, Plato, *plateau*, Kazakhstan/Uzbekistan, **222** F4
Ustyuzhna, Russian Federation, **299** F3
Usu, China, **212** E3
Usulután, El Salvador, **428** C4
Usumacinta, Mexico, **431** H5
Usvyaty, Russian Federation, **299** C5
Uta, Indonesia, **199** G4

Vosburg, South Africa, **370** D5
Vosges, *mountain range,* France, **291** H3
Voskresensk, Russian Federation, **299** G5
Voss, Norway, **286** C2
Vostochnaya Litsa, Russian Federation, **285** T2
Vostochno-Sibirskoye More, *sea,* Russian Federation, **301** S2
Vostochnyy Sayan, *mountain range,* Russian Federation, **223** N2
Vostok, *island,* Kiribati, **139** J6
Vostok, *Russian Federation research station,* Antarctica, **470** E6
Votkinsk, Russian Federation, **222** E1
Votuporanga, Brazil, **456** D5
Vouxa, Akra, *point,* Kriti, Greece, **297** D8
Vouziers, France, **291** G2
Voves, France, **290** E2
Voxna, Sweden, **286** G2
Voyeykov Ice Shelf, Antarctica, **470** F7
Voynitsa, Russian Federation, **285** Q4
Vozhe, Ozero, *lake,* Russian Federation, **299** G2
Vozhega, Russian Federation, **299** H2
Voznesens´k, Ukraine, **296** H2
Voznesen'ye, Russian Federation, **299** E2
Vrå, Sweden, **286** F4
Vrådal, Norway, **286** D3
Vradiyivka, Ukraine, **296** H2
Vrangelya, Ostrov, *island,* Russian Federation, **301** U2
Vranica, *mountain peak,* Bosnia and Herzegovina, **294** F4
Vranino, Bulgaria, **296** G4
Vranje, Yugoslavia, **296** C4
Vranjska Banja, Yugoslavia, **296** D4
Vranov nad Topľou, Slovakia, **289** K4
Vratsa, Bulgaria, **296** D4
Vrbas, *river,* Bosnia and Herzegovina, **294** F3
Vrbas, Yugoslavia, **296** B3
Vrbovec, Croatia, **294** F3
Vrbovsko, Croatia, **294** E3
Vredenburg, South Africa, **370** C5
Vredendal, South Africa, **370** C5
Vrgorac, Croatia, **294** F4
Vrhnika, Slovenia, **294** E2
Vrigstad, Sweden, **286** G4
Vrnjačka Banja, Yugoslavia, **296** C4
Vršac, Yugoslavia, **296** C3
Vrtoče, Bosnia and Herzegovina, **294** F3
Vryburg, South Africa, **370** D4
Vryheid, South Africa, **371** F4
Vsetín, Czech Republic, **289** J4
Vsevolozhsk, Russian Federation, **299** E4
Vučitrn, Yugoslavia, **296** C4
Vukovar, Croatia, **294** G3
Vuktyl, Russian Federation, **300** G3
Vulcan, Romania, **296** D3
Vulcăneşti, Moldova, **296** G3
Vulcano, Isola, *island,* Italy, **295** E6
Vŭlchedrŭm, Bulgaria, **296** D4
Vulture, Monte, *mountain peak,* Italy, **295** E5
Vũng Tsu, Vietnam, **203** E4
Vunindawa, Fiji, **141** A4
Vunisea, Fiji, **141** A4
Vuohijarvi, *lake,* Finland, **287** N2
Vuohtomäki, Finland, **285** N5
Vuokatti, Finland, **285** P4
Vuoksa, Ozero, *lake,* Russian Federation, **299** B2
Vuolijoki, Finland, **285** N4

Vuollerim, Sweden, **284** K3
Vuolvojaure, *lake,* Sweden, **284** J3
Vuoriyarvi, Russian Federation, **285** Q3
Vuotso, Finland, **285** N2
Vuottas, Sweden, **284** K3
Vuva, *river,* Russian Federation, **285** Q2
Vwawa, Tanzania, **369** F4
Vyalozero, Ozero, *lake,* Russian Federation, **285** S3
Vyāra, India, **218** C5
Vyatka, Russian Federation, **300** F4
Vyazemskiy, Russian Federation, **211** L3
Vyaz'ma, Russian Federation, **299** E5
Vybor, Russian Federation, **299** B4
Vyborg, Russian Federation, **299** B2
Vychegda, *river,* Russian Federation, **281** J3
Východočeský, *administrative region,* Czech Republic, **289** G3
Vydropuzhsk, Russian Federation, **299** E4
Vyerkhnyadzvinsk, Belarus, **287** N5
Vyetryna, Belarus, **299** B5
Vygozero, Ozero, *lake,* Russian Federation, **285** S5
Vykhcha, *river,* Russian Federation, **285** T3
Vylkove, Romania, **296** G3
Vylok, Ukraine, **296** D1
Vym', *river,* Russian Federation, **281** K3
Vyra, Russian Federation, **299** B3
Vyritsa, Russian Federation, **299** C3
Vyrnwy, Lake, Wales, U.K., **304** D2
Vyshniy Volochek, Russian Federation, **299** E4
Vyškov, Czech Republic, **289** H4
Vysokaye, Belarus, **289** L2
Vysokogornyy, Russian Federation, **211** M2
Vysokoye, Russian Federation, **299** E4
Vytegra, Russian Federation, **299** F2
Vyyezzhiy Log, Russian Federation, **223** N2

W

W J van Blommestein Meer, *lake,* Suriname, **452** B2
Wa, Ghana, **364** D3
Waajid, Somalia, **369** H2
Waal, *river,* Netherlands, **288** B3
Waar, Pulau, *island,* Indonesia, **199** F3
Waarlangier, Tanjong, *point,* Indonesia, **199** F4
Waasagomach, Canada, **414** G5
Wabag, Papua New Guinea, **140** A4
Wabasca-Desmarais, Canada, **413** N4
Wabash, *river,* U.S.A., **421** K6
Wabash, U.S.A., **421** L5
Wabaska, *river,* Canada, **413** M3
Wabowden, Canada, **414** E4
Wabush, Canada, **416** H3
Waccamaw, Lake, U.S.A., **425** N2
Waccasassa Bay, U.S.A., **425** L5
Waco, Canada, **416** J4
Waco, U.S.A., **424** D4
Waconda Lake, U.S.A., **420** D6
Wad, Pakistan, **218** A4

Wad an Nail, Sudan, **366** D2
Wad Bandah, Sudan, **366** C2
Wad Ḥāmid, Sudan, **363** F5
Wad Medanī, Sudan, **366** D2
Waddān, Jabal, *mountain peak,* Libya, **362** C3
Waddān, Libya, **362** C3
Waddeneilanden, *islands,* Netherlands, **288** B2
Waddenzee, *bay,* Netherlands, **288** B2
Waddington, England, U.K., **305** G1
Waddington, New Zealand, **133** D6
Waddlington, Mount, *mountain peak,* Canada, **412** G6
Wadebridge, England, U.K., **304** C4
Wadena, U.S.A., **420** F2
Wadhurst, England, U.K., **305** H3
Wādī as Sīr, Jordan, **225** C4
Wādī Ḥalfā, Sudan, **363** F4
Wādī Mūsá, Jordan, **225** C4
Wadley, U.S.A., **425** L3
Wadowice, Poland, **289** J4
Wafangdian, China, **211** H5
Wagaru, Myanmar, **202** C3
Wagga Wagga, Australia, **135** K6
Wagin, Australia, **134** D5
Wagner, U.S.A., **420** D4
Wagon Mound, U.S.A., **423** L3
Wagontire, U.S.A., **418** E5
Wągrowiec, Poland, **289** H2
Wāh, Pakistan, **218** C2
Wah Wah Mountains, *mountain range,* U.S.A., **422** G2
Wahabu, Ghana, **364** D2
Wahai, Indonesia, **199** E3
Wahala, Togo, **364** E3
Waharoa, New Zealand, **132** E3
Wahiawa, Hawaiian Islands, U.S.A., **422** R9
Wahoo, U.S.A., **420** E5
Wahpeton, U.S.A., **420** E2
Waialua, Hawaiian Islands, U.S.A., **422** R9
Waianae, Hawaiian Islands, U.S.A., **422** R9
Waiau, New Zealand, **133** D6
Waiau, *river,* N. South Island, New Zealand, **133** D6
Waiau, *river,* S. South Island, New Zealand, **133** A7
Waigeo, Pulau, *island,* Indonesia, **199** E2
Waiharara, New Zealand, **132** D2
Waihau Bay, New Zealand, **132** G4
Waiheke Island, New Zealand, **132** E3
Waihi, New Zealand, **132** E3
Waihirere, New Zealand, **132** F4
Waihola, New Zealand, **133** C8
Waiinu Beach, New Zealand, **132** E4
Waikabubak, Indonesia, **198** B5
Waikanae, New Zealand, **133** E5
Waikari, New Zealand, **133** D6
Waikato, *river,* New Zealand, **132** E3
Waikouaiti, New Zealand, **133** C7
Wailea, Hawaiian Islands, U.S.A., **422** R9
Wailingding Dao, *island,* China, **207** A4
Wailuku, Hawaiian Islands, U.S.A., **422** R9
Waimate, New Zealand, **133** C7
Waimea, Hawaiian Islands, U.S.A., **422** R9
Wainfleet All Saints, England, U.K., **305** H1
Waingapu, Indonesia, **198** C5
Waini, *river,* Guyana, **451** G2
Waini Point, *point,* Guyana, **451** G2

Wainuioru, New Zealand, **133** E5
Wainwright, Canada, **413** P5
Wainwright, U.S.A., **410** C2
Waiohau, New Zealand, **132** F4
Waiotama, New Zealand, **132** E2
Waiotapu, New Zealand, **132** F4
Waiouru, New Zealand, **132** E4
Waipahi, New Zealand, **133** B8
Waipara, New Zealand, **133** D6
Waipawa, New Zealand, **132** F4
Waipiro Bay, New Zealand, **132** G4
Waipu, New Zealand, **132** E2
Wairarapa, Lake, New Zealand, **133** E5
Wairau, *river,* New Zealand, **133** D5
Wairau Valley, New Zealand, **133** D5
Wairoa, New Zealand, **132** F4
Wairoa, *river,* New Zealand, **132** F4
Waitahanui, New Zealand, **132** F4
Waitakaruru, New Zealand, **132** E3
Waitakere, New Zealand, **132** E3
Waitaki, *river,* New Zealand, **133** C7
Waitangi, Chatham Islands, New Zealand, **133** Q16
Waitara, *river,* New Zealand, **132** E4
Waitati, New Zealand, **133** C7
Waite, Mount, *mountain peak,* Macquarie Island, **134** R11
Waitotara, New Zealand, **132** E4
Waitsburg, U.S.A., **418** E3
Waiuku, New Zealand, **132** E3
Waiwera, New Zealand, **132** E3
Waiyevo, Fiji, **141** A4
Wajima, Japan, **209** G3
Wajir, Kenya, **369** H2
Waka, Central Equateur, Democratic Republic of the Congo, **368** D2
Waka, S. Equateur, Democratic Republic of the Congo, **368** D3
Waka, Tanjong, *point,* Indonesia, **198** D3
Wakatipu, Lake, New Zealand, **133** B7
Wakaw, Canada, **413** S5
Wakayama, Japan, **208** F4
Wake Island, *U.S. territory,* Pacific Ocean, **138** E2
WaKeeney, U.S.A., **420** D6
Wakefield, England, U.K., **307** G4
Wakefield, U.S.A., **424** G4
Wakkanai, Japan, **209** H1
Wakpala, U.S.A., **420** C3
Waku-Kungo, Angola, **368** C5
Wakunai, Papua New Guinea, **140** E2
Walagan, China, **211** J1
Walanae, *river,* Indonesia, **198** C4
Wałbrzych, Poland, **289** H3
Walcott, U.S.A., **420** E2
Walden, U.S.A., **423** K1
Waldorf, U.S.A., **426** B5
Waldport, U.S.A., **418** B4
Waldshut-Tiengen, Germany, **288** D5
Walea, Selat, *strait,* Indonesia, **198** C3
Wales, *administrative division,* U.K., **304** D2
Walgett, Australia, **135** K4
Walgreen Coast, *region,* Antarctica, **470** B6
Walikale, Democratic Republic of the Congo, **369** E3
Walker, U.S.A., **421** L4
Walker Lake, U.S.A., **422** D2
Walkerton, Canada, **421** N3

Walla Walla, U.S.A., **418** E3
Wallace, Idaho, U.S.A., **418** G3
Wallace, North Carolina, U.S.A., **425** P2
Wallaceburg, Canada, **421** M4
Wallaroo, Australia, **135** H5
Wallasey, England, U.K., **306** E4
Walldürn, Germany, **288** D4
Waller, U.S.A., **424** E5
Wallingford, England, U.K., **305** F3
Wallingford, New Zealand, **132** F5
Wallis (Uvea), *island,* Wallis and Futuna, **139** G6
Wallis and Futuna, *French territory,* Pacific Ocean, **131** G3
Walliser Alpen, *mountain range,* Switzerland, **291** H3
Walls, Shetland, Scotland, U.K., **308** K7
Walmer, England, U.K., **305** J3
Walnut, U.S.A., **421** J5
Walpole, Australia, **134** D5
Walpole, *island,* New Caledonia, **141** A3
Walsall, England, U.K., **305** E2
Walsenburg, U.S.A., **423** L3
Walsh, U.S.A., **423** M3
Waltair, India, **217** E2
Walter F. George Reservoir, U.S.A., **425** K4
Walterboro, U.S.A., **425** M3
Walters, U.S.A., **424** C2
Waltham on the Wolds, England, U.K., **305** G2
Waltman, U.S.A., **419** L5
Walton on the Naze, England, U.K., **305** J3
Walvis Bay, Namibia, **370** B3
Walvis Ridge, *underwater feature,* Atlantic Ocean, **477** G8
Wamal, Indonesia, **199** G5
Wamba, Equateur, Democratic Republic of the Congo, **368** D3
Wamba, Haute-Zaire, Democratic Republic of the Congo, **369** E2
Wamena, Indonesia, **199** G3
Wamsutter, U.S.A., **419** L6
Wan Xian, China, **206** B2
Wanaka, Lake, New Zealand, **133** B7
Wanaka, New Zealand, **133** B7
Wan'an, China, **206** C3
Wanapa, Bonaire, Netherlands Antilles, **461** A4
Wanapiri, Indonesia, **199** F4
Wanapitei Lake, Canada, **421** N2
Wanapitei, *river,* Canada, **421** N2
Wanda Shan, *mountain range,* China, **211** K3
Wandai, Indonesia, **199** G3
Wandel Sea, Greenland, **411** T1
Wandering River, Canada, **413** N4
Wanding, China, **215** F4
Wandsworth, England, U.K., **305** G3
Wang, Mae Nam, *river,* Thailand, **202** C2
Wang Gaxun, China, **213** H5
Wang Nua, Thailand, **202** C2
Wang Saphung, Thailand, **202** D2
Wanganui, New Zealand, **132** E4
Wangaratta, Australia, **135** K6
Wangdian, China, **215** H4
Wangen im Allgäu, Germany, **288** D5
Wangerooge, *island,* Germany, **288** D2
Wanggamet, Gunung, *mountain peak,* Indonesia, **198** C5
Wanggao, China, **206** B3
Wanggar, *river,* Indonesia, **199** F3
Wangkui, China, **211** J3

Y

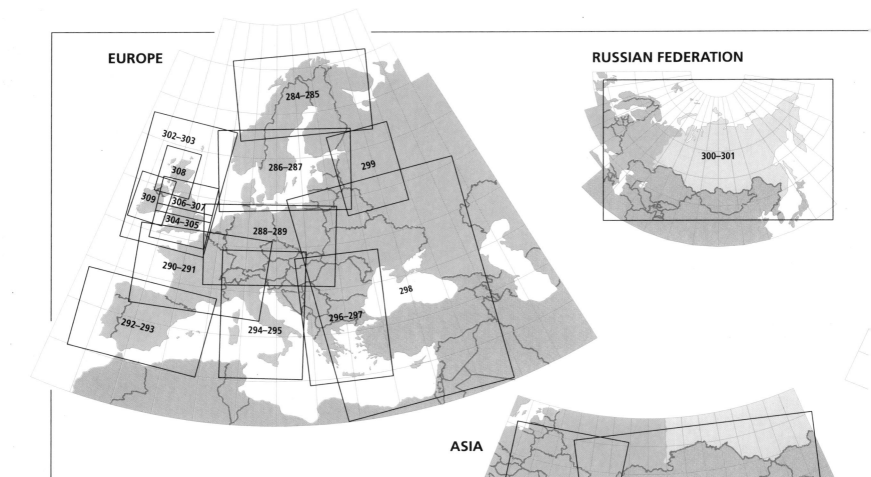

EUROPE

284–285
302–303
308
286–287
299
309
306–307
304–305
288–289
290–291
298
292–293
294–295
296–297

RUSSIAN FEDERATION

300–301

ASIA

222–223
224
225
218–219
220–221
216–217

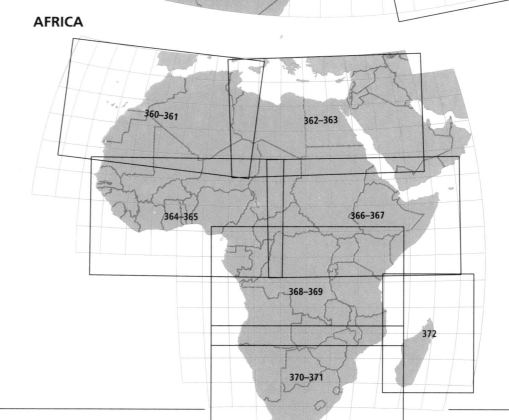

AFRICA

360–361
362–363
364–365
366–367
368–369
372
370–371

Key to Map Pages